A HANDBOOK FOR TRAVELLERS IN INDIA BURMA AND CEYLON

A HANDBOOK FOR TRAVELLERS IN INDIA BURMA AND CEYLON

INCLUDING THE PROVINCES OF BENGAL, BOMBAY, AND MADRAS, THE PUNJAB, NORTH-WEST PROVINCES, ... ETC., THE NATIVE STATES ASSAM AND CASHMERE

By

JOHN MURRAY

GYAN

ISBN : 978-81-212-1592-3(HB)

First Published, 1901

Published, 2018

Published by

Gyan Publishing House
5, Ansari Road
Daryaganj, New Delhi-110002
Phone: 011-47034999, 9811692060
www.gyanbooks.com
E-mail: books@gyanbooks.com

Printed at: G. Print Process, Delhi.

PREFACE TO THE FIFTH EDITION

THE complete revision of a Handbook is perhaps a suitable occasion for an entirely new preface to it, and for the brief record of the birth and growth of the work revised.

The Handbook of India was originally published by Mr John Murray in three separate volumes, for the Bombay, Madras, and Bengal Presidencies. The first two of these parts appeared in 1859, the Bengal volume not till 1882. A fourth volume, dealing with the Panjab and North-West India, was added to them in 1883. They were all prepared by the late Captain E. B. Eastwick, M.P., who made long visits to India, in the fifties, sixties, and seventies, in order to collect the material for them on the spot. When it is recollected how incomplete the railway communications between the different parts of India then were, that the *Imperial Gazetteer*, edited by Sir W. W. Hunter, had not yet appeared, and that up to the time very few volumes of District Gazetteers had been issued, it will readily be conceded that Captain Eastwick's task was a difficult and laborious one, and that allowance might be fairly claimed for any short-comings in the volumes compiled by him.

These volumes were revised and brought up to date on several occasions, and in 1892 the Handbook was issued in a single volume of 500 pages, as compared with 1459 pages in the four separate volumes. On this occasion the work was largely rewritten and thoroughly revised, much assistance in the task being received by the publisher from Dr Burgess, C.I.E., LL.D., Dr Bradshaw, LL.D., Mr H. Beauchamp, Major Spratt, R.E., Mr R. Clarke, B.C.S., Mr T. Westlake, Mr G. Marsden, and Mr E. B. Smith.

The description of Ceylon, with the exception of the account of Colombo, was written by Sir Arthur Gordon, G.C.M.G. (now Lord Stanmore), and the proofs of the whole Handbook were passed by Professor Forrest, C.I.E., then Keeper of the Records of the Government of India in Calcutta. A second edition of the consolidated

Handbook was published in 1894, and a third in 1898, the revision on the latter occasion being undertaken by Mr Norwood Young, and valuable assistance being received from Mr H. Beauchamp, Mr G. Marsden, Mr R. E. Acklom, Surgeon Lieut.-Col. Joubert, Mr Playford Reynolds, and Mr Basil Lang. The account of Ceylon was revised by Lord Stanmore. Much additional information was added to the Introduction regarding the people of India and the religions, architecture and arts of the country ; and maps of the rainfall, temperature, and local products of the country were included for the first time. To a brief special account of the Mutiny of 1857 was added a map showing the distribution of the army in India at that crisis, the faultiness of this being mainly responsible for the serious proportions which that outbreak ultimately assumed. A fourth edition in 1901 was brought up to date by Dr Burgess, C.I.E., LL.D.

The present edition has once again undergone a thorough revision. The arrangement of the book has been largely recast in accordance with recent railway developments, and the account of nearly all the principal places in India has been rewritten on the topographical plan, which is usually found to be the most convenient by travellers using a guide-book on the spot. A special brief sketch has been added of the Mohammedan and Hindu Rulers of India ; that of the Sikhs has been enlarged, while a new one on the Mahrattas has been included ; and brief notices have been inserted of the form of administration of the Indian Government, of famine and plague, of the working of the railway, postal, and telegraph departments, and of the Christian Religion. The section on irrigation has also been greatly extended. All this has been again necessitated, to quote the words of the first edition of the consolidated Handbook, by the fact that "time and events have effected great changes, not only in the country itself, but also in the facilities for reaching it from all parts of the world, and for travelling throughout the peninsula. The public, moreover, are yearly becoming better aware of the glorious field which in India is opened up for the enjoyment of travel and sport, and of the inexhaustible opportunities afforded them for the study of an engrossing history, an interesting nationality, and an unrivalled art, as displayed not only in architectural monuments, but also in native industries and handicrafts."

The present volume extends to 640 pages, as compared with 574 pages in the fourth, and 500 pages in the first edition.

New maps have been made for this edition, of Benares, Colombo, Anuradhapura, and General Wheeler's entrenchment at Cawnpore : while better maps have been substituted in the case of Gwalior, Lucknow, the Fort and the environs of Delhi, Vijayanagar (Hampi) and Bangalore. All maps have been brought up to date.

The spelling followed is that of the Indian Postal Guide, which has the authority of the administrations of the various provinces. It is to be regretted that the older Railways are not required to follow strictly this authority. If not altogether satisfactory, yet the spelling of names in India is now at last free from the hopeless confusion of twenty or twenty-five years ago, and it is hoped that all variations of spelling have been eliminated from the present edition. No attempt has been made to indicate tours in India, as these must depend so much upon the tastes and interests of individuals. The list of routes on pages xiii-xv will, it is believed, enable travellers readily to form for themselves any tours they may wish to make ; and all further details can be obtained from the Railway Guides of India, or from Messrs Thomas Cook & Son, who have branch offices at Bombay, Calcutta, Rangoon, and Colombo.

With the exception of those in Baluchistan and Sindh, nearly all the places described in the Handbook have been visited by the present editor, and all the principal ones on several occasions. He desires to acknowledge the information sent him for the Handbook by many friends in India, and the facilities accorded him by Mr C. Tawney, C.I.E., and Mr F. Thomas, the late and present Librarians of the India Office, for consulting publications of the Government of India. Mr C. G. Ryan, of St Clair, Talawakelle, has been kind enough to revise the Ceylon part.

As was noted in the third edition of the consolidated Handbook, "it is impossible to ensure perfection in any guide-book, however carefully prepared. The publisher therefore hopes that where inaccuracies are found the indulgent traveller will kindly point them out to him, with a view to their correction on the first opportunity. Any such acceptable communications may be addressed to Mr Murray, 50 Albemarle Street, London, W."

To this the present editor would venture to add—

Nota leges quædam, sed lima rasa recenti :
Pars nova major erit : lector utrique fave.

H. C. FANSHAWE, C.S.I.,
Late Chief Secretary to the Panjab Government
and Commissioner of Delhi.

September 1904.

The present (seventh) edition is mainly a reprint of the fifth ; but all information and plans have been brought up to date, and some new information has been included. The plans of the Madura Temple, the palace at Mandalay, and the fort at Lahore were added to the sixth edition, and that of Hyderabad has been added to the present edition. The sections on Burma and Ceylon have been specially revised with the assistance of Mr G. E. Marindin and Mr C. G. Ryan.

Mr Murray desires to acknowledge the valuable aid received from many visitors to India, and to express his gratification at the very kindly recognition accorded by them to the usefulness and completeness of the Handbook. The Editor is again under obligations to many friends and brother officers in India for much information furnished by them.

H. C. FANSHAWE.

September 1909.

PREFACE TO THE EIGHTH EDITION

THE eighth edition of the Handbook is fortunate in making its appearance at the time of the proposed visit of His Majesty the King Emperor, and of Queen Mary, to India, and of the Coronation Durbar which will be held at Delhi in December. The volume, which has now been before the public for over fifty years, has been again revised throughout, and many of the maps and plans have been redrawn in addition to having been brought up to date. The general map of India, illustrating the railway systems of the country, has been specially prepared for this edition. Mr Murray and the Editor once more desire to record their best thanks to many friends and travellers who have so kindly assisted them with information for the present revision.

H. C. FANSHAWE.

September 1911.

CONTENTS

PAGE

LIST OF MAPS AND PLANS xi

LIST OF ROUTES THROUGH INDIA, BURMA, AND CEYLON . . xiii-xv

INTRODUCTORY INFORMATION—

(1.) GENERAL HINTS—

English Language xvii
Season for Visit to India xvii
Expenses xviii
Clothing xviii
Bedding xx
Travelling Servants xxi
Indian Railways xxi
Hotels, Dak Bungalows, and Rest-Houses xxiii
Food xxiv
Health xxv
Sport xxv
Hints for Camping xxvi
Books xxvii

(2.) VOYAGE FROM ENGLAND TO GIBRALTAR, MARSEILLES, MALTA, PORT SAID, THROUGH THE SUEZ CANAL, AND RED SEA TO ADEN AND BOMBAY xxix

(3.) GENERAL INFORMATION, STATISTICAL, ETHNOLOGICAL, HISTORICAL, ARCHÆOLOGICAL, AND MATERIAL—

The People of India xlvii
The Mohammedans xlviii
Mohammedan Festivals xlix
Mohammedan Rule in India l
Some Mohammedan Dates affecting India lii
List of Sovereigns who reigned at Delhi from 1193 to 1857 A.D. liii
The Hindus liv
Hindu Gods lv
The *Mahabharata* and *Ramayana* . . . . . lvii, lviii
Hindu Festivals lx
Hindu Rule in India lxi
The Buddhists lxii

PAGE

(3.) GENERAL INFORMATION, ETC.—*continued.*

Jains lxiv
Buddhist Festivals lxv
Some Early Hindu and Buddhist Dates lxv
The Sikhs lxvi
Gurus of the Sikhs lxvii
The Mahrattas lxviii
The Parsis lxx
Parsi Months lxx
The Parsi Festivals lxxi
Architecture lxxi
The Preservation of Ancient Monuments . . . lxxvi
Arts lxxviii
Irrigation lxxxiii
Famine lxxxv
The Material Condition of the People of India . . . lxxxv
Plague lxxxvi
The Countess of Dufferin's Fund Association . . . lxxxvi
The Indian Administration lxxxvii
Area and Population of British India and Native States (Census of 1901) . . . . lxxxix-xc
Distribution of Population according to Religion (Census of 1901) xci

Christian Population—
Distribution according to Race and Denomination . . xcii
Territorial Distribution according to Race . . . xcii

Details of the Working of Certain Imperial Departments—
Post Office xciii
Telegraphs xciii
Railways xciii
Financial Details xciv

Native Christians xciv
The Mutiny of 1857 xcv
Remarkable Events connecting India with Europe . civ
Glossary of the Principal Native Terms used in this Book . cxii

LIST OF MAPS AND PLANS

		PAGE
Agra, and Environs	*To face*	170
,, the Fort	,,	174
,, Moti Masjid		175
,, Taj Mahal	*To face*	172
,, Fatehpur Sikri		181
Ahmedabad	*To face*	124
Ajmer, the Arhai-din-ka-jhompra Mosque		138
Allahabad	*To face*	32
Anuradhapura	,,	494
Attock	,,	246
Badami, No 3 Cave	,,	370
Bangalore	,,	389
Benares	,,	44
Bijapur	,,	362
,, Gol Gumbaz		364
,, Section of Domes, Jama Masjid	*To face*	364
Bombay	,,	5
,, including Malabar Hill and Colaba	,,	16
,, and Environs	,,	18
Buddha, Figures of. Plate 2	*To follow Plate* 1, *after*	liv.
Calcutta	,,	56
Caste Marks. *Plate* 2	*To follow Plate* 1, *after*	liv.
Cawnpore	*To face*	301
,, General Wheeler's Entrenchment	,,	302
Ceylon	,,	471
Colombo	,,	472
Darjeeling	*To face*	315
Delhi	,,	186
,, Palace in Fort		196
,, Map of country round	*To face*	202
,, Humayun's Tomb		205
,, Mosque Kuwat-ul-Islam and the Kutab Minar		209
Ellora, the Mahawara Dherwara Cave		75
,, the Kailasa Temple		75
Girnar Mountain	*To face*	155
,, Temple of Nemnath		154
,, Temple of Tejahpala and Vastupala		156
Gwalior, the Fort	*To face*	108
Hindu Gods, some common forms of . Plates 1 and 2	,,	liv.

PAGE

Hyderabad . . . . *To face* 373
India, Average Rainfall, (2) during the wet and dry seasons . ,, xx
,, Average temperature, (2) during the hot and cold seasons ,, xvii
,, General Map, showing the Railway Systems . . . *In Pocket*
,, Geological Features of . . . . *To face* xxiv
,, Vegetable Products . . . . ,, xxviii
Jaunpur, West half of Jama Masjid 277
Karachi . . . . *To face* 266
Karli Cave 339
Kashmir and N.W. Frontier . . . . *To face* 250
Lahore . . . . ,, 229
,, the Fort . . . . ,, 234
Lucknow . . . . ,, 284
,, the Residency . . . . ,, 286
Madras . . . . ,, 402
Madura, Plan of Temple and Tirumala's Choultry . . . . ,, 433
Mandalay . . . . ,, 457
,, the Palace . . . . ,, 457
Matheran . . . . ,, 337
Murree . . . . ,, 244
Mussoorie . . . . ,, 281
Mutiny, showing distribution of troops on May 1, 1857 . . ,, xcix
Naini Tal . . . . ,, 282
North-West Frontier and Kashmir . . . . ,, 250
Ootacamund . . . . ,, 413
Pagan, Burma, the Ananda Temple 463
,, ,, the Thapinyu Temple 464
Pattadakal Temple . . . . *To face* 371
Poona and Kirkee . . . . ,, 342
Quetta and Baluchistan 271
Puri, Jagannath, Temple of 330
Railways, *see* India, General Map
Rangoon . . . . *To face* 450
Sanchi, Plan of Great Buddhist Tope 99
,, Section of Great Buddhist Tope 99
Simla . . . . *To face* 218
Somnath Temple 159
,, Verawal and Patan 158
Srinagar . . . . *To face* 253
Trivalur, Bird's-eye View of Temple 426
Vijayanagar (Hampi) . . . . *To face* 381

LIST OF ROUTES

[The names of places are printed in black only in those Routes where the *places* themselves are described.]

ROUTE.		PAGE
1	**Bombay** and the **Environs** .	1
2	Bombay to Calcutta by **Kalyan, Nasik, Manmar, Jalgaon** (Caves of Ajanta), **Bhusawal, Khandwa, Itarsi, Jubbulpore, Katni, Manikpur, Allahabad, Mughal-sarai** (Benares), **Patna, Mokamah, Lakhisarai,** and **Asansol,** with journeys to **Pachmarhi,** the **Marble Rocks, Buddh Gya,** and **Parasnath** .	23
3	**Caves of Ajanta** . . .	39
4	**Benares**	43
5	**Calcutta City** and **Environs**	53
6	**Manmar** to **Daulatabad, The Caves of Ellora, Aurangabad, Jalna,** and **Secunderabad**	71
7	Bhusawal to Calcutta (**Howrah**), by **Akola, Wardha** (expedition to **Warora,** and **Chanda**), **Nagpur, Kampti, Raipur, Bilaspur,** and **Sini,** and from Sini to (*a*) **Purulia** and **Asansol,** and (*b*) **Kharagpur** . .	82
8	Khandwa to Ajmer by **Mhow, Indore, Neemuch, Chitorgarh,** and **Nasirabad,** with expeditions by road to **Unkarji** and **Mandu,** and by rail to **Udaipur** . .	87
9	Itarsi Junction to **Jhansi,** by **Bhopal, Sanchi,** and **Bina** (line to **Saugor** and to **Bárán** and **Kotah**) and from Jhansi to (*a*) **Kalpi** and Cawnpore; (*b*) **Datia, Gwalior, Dholpur,** and Agra; (*c*) **Orchha, Barwa Saugor, Banda** and Manikpur, with excursions to **Nowgong** and **Khajurahu**	97
10	Bombay to Delhi by **Bassein, Surat, Broach, Miyagam, Baroda,** and thence (1) by broad gauge direct to Delhi (863 m.) by **Rutlam, Nagda, Kotah, Bharatpur,** and **Muttra.** (2) to **Ahmedabad** and thence by metre gauge to Delhi (849 m.) by **Mehsana, Palanpur, Abu Road, Marwar** Junction, **Ajmer, Phalera** Junction, **Jaipur, Bandikui** Junction, **Alwar** and **Rewari,** with excursions by road to **Mount Abu,** and by rail to (*a*) **Dabhoi,** (*b*) **Luni** Junction (branch line to Hyderabad Sindh), **Jodhpur, Bikaner,** and **Phalera** Junction, and (*c*) **Hissar, Bhatinda,** and **Ferozepore**	115
11	**From** Ahmedabad through **Kathiawar** by **Viramgam, Kharaghoda, Wadhwan, Bhaunagar, Junagarh, Girnar, Somnath, Porbandar, Rajkot,** and back to **Ahmedabad,** with expedition by road to **Palitana**	148
12	(*a*) Bandikui Junction to **Bharatpur, Achnera Station,** and Agra, (*b*) **Achnera Station** to **Muttra, Brindaban,** and **Hathras Road,** and by road to **Mahaban, Govardhan,** and **Dig,** and (*c*) Agra to **Delhi** direct route through **Muttra**	162
13	**Agra** and **Fatehpur-Sikri** .	170
14	**Delhi**	186
15	(*a*) Delhi to **Kasauli** (171 m.), and **Simla** (219 m.) by **Panipat, Thanesar, Umballa** and **Kalka** (162 m.). (*b*) Delhi to **Lahore** by **Ghaziabad** Junction, **Meerut, Sardhana, Saharanpur, Umballa, Sirhind, Ludhiana, Jullundur, Amritsar** and **Lahore Cantonment** (349 m.) . .	214

ROUTE. PAGE

16 Lahore to **Peshawar** by **Gujranwala, Wazirabad** Junction, **Gujrat, Lala Musa** Junction, **Jhelum, Rohtas, Manikyala, Rawal Pindi, Golra, Attock,** and **Nowshera,** with expeditions by rail from Wazirabad to **Sialkot** and **Jammu,** from Lala Musa to **W. Panjab,** from Golra to **Khushalgarh** and **Kohat,** and from Nowshera to **Hoti Mardan** and the **Malakand** . . 239

17 Kashmir and some of the routes into that country . 250

18 Lahore to **Karachi** by **Mooltan, Sher Shah** Junction, **Bahawalpur, Samasatta, Rohri, Khairpur, Hyderabad** and **Kotri,** with expedition by road from Jungshahi to **Thatta,** and from Rohri to **Sukkur, Ruk** Junction, **Larkana, Sehwan** and Kotri by the right bank of the Indus . 259

19 Ruk Junction to **Chaman** on the frontier of **Afghanistan** by **Shikarpur, Jacobabad, Sibi** Junction and **Quetta,** returning by the **Harnai** route . . 269

20 (*a*) Saharanpur by the Oudh and Rohilkand Railway to Mughal Sarai through **Lhaksar** Junction, **Moradabad, Bareilly** Junction, Lucknow, and thence to Benares by (1) **Fyzabad** and **Jaunpur,** and (2) **Rae Bareli.** (*b*) **Lhaksar** Junction to **Hardwar, Dehra Dun,** and the hill stations of **Mussooree Landour** and **Chakrata.** (*c*) Bareilly Junction to **Naini Tal, Almora,** and **Ranikhet** . . . 273

21 Lucknow 283

22 Delhi to Allahabad by **Ghaziabad, Aligarh, Hathras** Junction, **Tundla** Junction, **Etawah** and **Cawnpore,** and Cawnpore to Lucknow . . . 298

23 (*a*) Calcutta by the East India Railway loop line to **Lakhisarai** and **Mokamah** by **Nalhati** Junction **Azimganj, Tinpahar** Junction (**Rajmahal,** visit to **Malda** for **Gaur** and **Panduah**), **Bhagalpur** and **Jamalpur** for **Monghyr.** (*b*) Mokamah to **Tirhut.** (*c*) Calcutta to **Plassey** and **Murshidabad** by Eastern Bengal Railway and on to Malda. (*d*) Calcutta by Eastern Bengal Railway to **Darjeeling** by **Damukdia, Silliguri** and **Kurseong** . 306

23*a* **Eastern Bengal** and **Assam.** (*a*) Calcutta to **Dacca** *viâ* **Goalundo** and **Naraingañj.** (*b*) Calcutta to **Goalundo** and **Chandpur** to (1) **Chittagong,** and (2) **Assam** . . . 317

24 Calcutta to Madras by **Balasore, Cuttack, Bhuvaneshwar** (visit to **Udyagiri Caves**), **Puri** (visit to **Black Pagoda**), **Ganjam, Vizianagram, Waltair** for **Vizagapatam, Bezwada** and **Nellore**—Bengal Nagpur Railway from **Howrah** to **Waltair,** and Madras and S. Mahratta Railway, N.E. section, from **Waltair** to **Madras** . . 322

25 Bombay to Madras by Kalyan Junction, the **Bore Ghat, Karli, Hotgi** Junction, **Poona, Sholapur, Gulbarga, Wadi** Junction, **Raichur, Guntakal** Junction, **Renigunta** Junction, **Arkonam** Junction, with excursions by road to **Matheran,** the **Caves of Karli** and **Bhaja,** and by rail to **Ahmednagar** and **Tirupati** 336

26 Poona to Goa, by **Wathar, Satara, Miraj, Belgaum Londa,** and **Mormugão,** with excursion by road to

ROUTE.		PAGE
	Mahabaleshwar, and rail to **Kolhapur**	352
27	**Hotgi Junction** to **Bijapur**, **Gadag**, **Hubli**, **Dharwar**, and Londa, with excursion to **caves and temples of Badami**	362
28	**Wadi Junction** to **Hyderabad**, **Secunderabad**, **Warangal**, and Bezwada, with expedition to **Bidar**	374
29	**Gadag Junction** to **Hospet** (for **Hampi** and **Vijayanagar**), **Bellary**, and **Guntakal** Junction, and from **Guntakal** Junction to (*a*) **Nandyal**, **Guntur**, and **Bezwada** (expedition by road to **Kurnool**) and (*b*) **Dharmavaram** and Bangalore	379*b*
30	**Hubli Junction** to **Harihar**, **Birur** (for **Shimoga** and the **Gairsoppa Falls**), **Banavar** (for expedition to the temples at **Hallabid** and **Belur**, also to the hill of **Indrabetta**, near **Shravana Belgola**), **Arsikere**, **Tumkar**, and **Bangalore**	383
31	Bangalore to (*a*) **Falls of the Cauvery**, **Seringapatam** and **Mysore**, and (*b*) **Bowringpet** (for **Kolar Gold Fields**), **Jalarpat** Junction, **Vellore**, **Arcot**, **Arkonam** Junction, **Conjeeveram**, and Chingleput	390
32	**Madras City** and **Environs**	401
33	Madras to **Salem**, **Erode**, **Podanur** for the **Nilgiris**, **Olavakkot**, **Shoranur** (for **Cochin**), **Calicut**, **Tellicherry**, **Cannanore**, and **Mangalore**, 552 m. by the S.W. line of the Madras and S. Mahratta Railway	409
34	Madras by South Indian State Railway to **Chingleput**, **Porto Novo**, **Chidambaram**, **Kumbakonam**, **Tanjore**, **Trichinopoly**, **Dindigal**, **Madura**, **Tinnevelly**, **Quilon** and **Tuticorin**, for **Colombo**, with excursions by road to **Gingee**, **Kodaikanal**, **Kuttallam** and **Cape Comorim** and **Trivandrum**, and by rail to **Pondicherry**, **Negapatam**, and **Ramesvaram**	419
35	Madras to **Mahabalipuram**, or the **Seven Pagodas**, by canal or rail and road	436

BURMA

	Introductory remarks, General Description, History, Climate, etc.	441
	Rangoon	449
1	To **Mandalay**, **Bhamo**, **and the first defile returning to** Rangoon *viâ* **Prome**	455
2	From **Rangoon** to **Moulmein**, **with possible extension to Tavoy and Mergui**	466
3	Rangoon to **Kyaukpyu and Akyab**	469
4	From Rangoon to **Bassein and back**	470
5	**Up the Chindwin** to **Kindat**	470

CEYLON

	Introductory Remarks, History, **Colombo**	471
1	Colombo to **Kandy**	475
2	Colombo to **Nuwara Eliya**, **Badulla, and Batticaloa**	479
3	Colombo to **Ratnapura and Bandarawella**	484
4	Colombo to **Ratnapura** *viâ* **Panadura and Nambapane**	486
5	Colombo to **Galle**, **Matara**, **Hambantotta, and Tissamaharama**	487
6	Colombo to **Trincomalee by Negombo, Puttalam, and Anuradhapura**	490
6a	Colombo to **Kankesanturai** *viâ* **Polgahawela, Kurunegala, Anuradhapura and Jaffna**	491
7	Kandy to **Jaffna by Anuradhapura**	492
8	Kandy to **Trincomalee (with excursion to Polonnaruwa)**	498
9	**Sporting Tours**	500

INDIA—*TEMPERATURE*

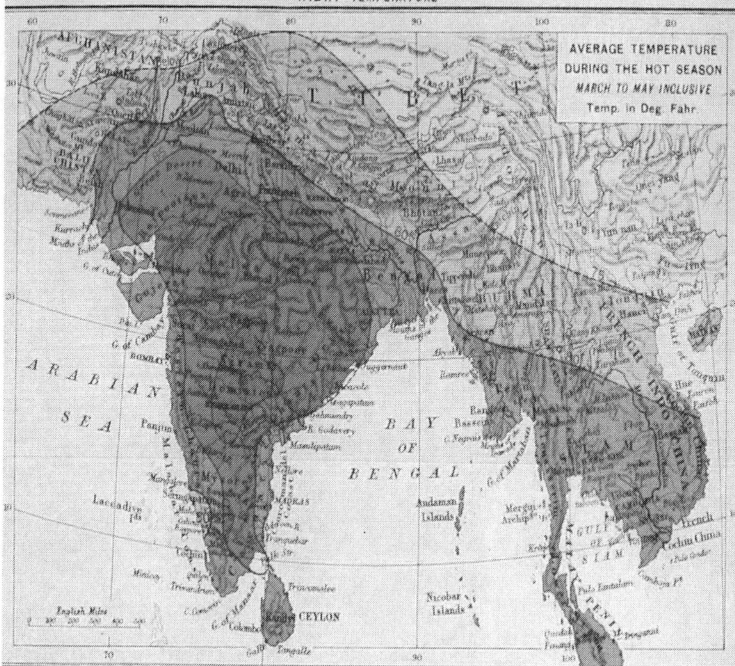

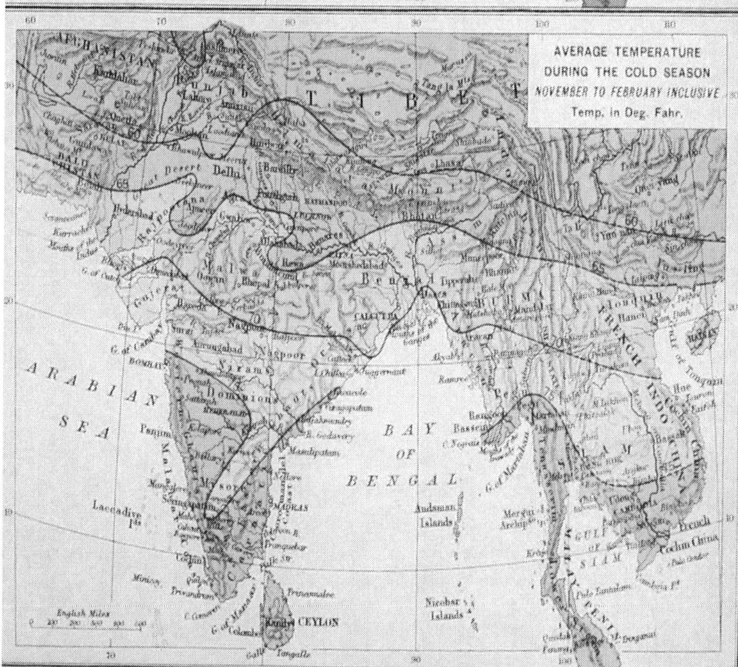

INTRODUCTORY INFORMATION

(1) GENERAL HINTS

English Language

A TRIP to India is no longer a formidable journey, or one that requires very special preparation. Among the difficulties which have disappeared of late years is that of the language. English is now spoken at all hotels and railway stations, and in all post and telegraph offices; and the leading shops in all large places have good articles for ordinary requirements, with attendants who speak English. The same facilities usually exist in those native shops for the sale of works of Indian art and manufacture which travellers are likely to visit; and local guides with a knowledge of English more or less imperfect are available at all important centres. Visitors will also find that a great many of the educated Indians whom they will meet are able to hold simple conversations in English, and that many speak the language exceedingly well; while the courteous request of a gentleman is sure to meet with a willing response.

Season for Visit to India

The season for a pleasant visit to the plains of India lies between 15th November and the end of March. In the Panjab these dates can be slightly extended; but then the heat may be found trying in the Red Sea and at the ports of arrival and departure. Up to 15th October and after 10th April the weather at the ports may be almost as trying as any in the year, much more so than in July, August, and September, when constant rain cools the atmosphere. Owing to the large numbers of officers of the Indian Service who return to India in the autumn, and of annual visitors to the country for "the cold season," the best accommodation on the larger and faster steamers, and especially on the P. & O. boats, is usually booked months ahead—outwards between 15th October and 1st December, and homewards for March and April; and this fact must be borne in mind by intending travellers to India. For further hints regarding the voyage, see p. xxix. It may be added here that a good and strong deck chair is essential to comfort on board ship.

EXPENSES

The rates of fare charged by the principal lines of steamers to India are exceedingly high—about £3 per day, but owing to the depreciation of the rupee the traveller will find India a fairly cheap country, the ordinary hotel charges outside the Presidency towns, and apart from special occasions, being 6 to 8 rupees[1] (8s.-11s.) a day for board and lodging, with usually a small additional charge for a hot bath. It is customary also to give a small gratuity to the water-carrier (*bhisti*) and the sweeper. As walking in the heat of the day is better avoided even in the cold weather, carriages have to be generally used in order to visit the objects of interest. The charge for a day varies from 5 to 7 rupees. Taxi-cabs and motors can now be hired at some of the principal places. All hotel and carriage charges tend to rise slowly. At private houses it is usual to give a present to the headservant on behalf of all the attendants. This need not exceed 5 rupees for a visit of a week or ten days. The railway charges are moderate, being usually 1½ annas, or 1½d., per mile for 1st class, half that sum for 2nd class, and less for journeys over 300 miles. As elsewhere in the world, the traveller will have to constantly supply himself with a sufficiency of small change—2, 4, and 8 anna pieces.

MOTORING

The use of motor-cars is becoming very general in India, and the roads in all large places and the main roads connecting these will ordinarily be found good. A small book on motoring in India by Watney & Lloyd has been published in England, and the Local Governments in India have published, or are publishing, Motor Routebooks.

CLOTHING

Not very long ago it was thought essential to have a special outfit prepared for a journey to India. This is scarcely the case now.

For the Voyage a few warm clothes for the northern part and thin ones for the Red Sea and Arabian Sea are required; otherwise ordinary English summer clothing will suffice. As regards the lighter clothes, a man will find it convenient to have a very thin suit of tweed or grey flannel for day, and a thin dress jacket for dinner.

A lady cannot do better than provide herself with thin skirts of

[1] The value of the rupee is arbitrarily fixed by Government at 1s. 4d. English sovereigns are accepted at all government offices, at hotels, and railway stations at an exchange value of Rs. 15.

tussore silk or some such material, and thin silk or other blouses. Shoes with india-rubber soles are the best for the deck.

As the amount of luggage which can be taken into the traveller's cabin is necessarily limited, a careful arrangement beforehand of articles needed for different parts of the voyage is of considerable importance for comfort. The cabin luggage must contain sufficient underlinen and linen for the whole voyage. The arrangements for obtaining luggage on the voyage are extremely insufficient, and nearly always extremely inconvenient; this is a direction in which the steamship companies need to do much to meet the reasonable requirements of passengers.

For a winter tour in the plains of North and Central India generally and in Upper Burma, a traveller requires similar clothing to that which he would wear in the late spring or autumn in England, but in addition he must take warm winter wraps. A man should have a light overcoat in which he can ride, and a warm long ulster for night travelling or the early morning. A lady, besides a warm jacket and shawl, should have a loose warm cloak to wear in long drives before the sun rises or after it sets, or to sleep in on railway journeys if it is very cold. Visitors to India must remember that while the mid-day is always warm, sometimes very hot, the evening dews may be so heavy as to absolutely *wet* the outer garment, and the nights and mornings are often very sharp, so that the secret of dressing is to begin the day in things that can be thrown off as the heat increases, and can be resumed as the cold returns. In some places in North India in the winter months the temperature will fall between 40°-50° within the two hours on either side of sunset, and the risks of serious chills in consequence of such sudden changes are very great, if due care is not taken to meet them. Real winter clothing will be necessary if it is intended to visit any **hill-station.** Flannel or woollen underclothing and sleeping garments, and a flannel "Kamarband" (a belt of flannel 8 in. to 12 in. wide worn round the waist), are strongly recommended for wear at all times.

Throughout the **south**[1] **of the peninsula,** and at times even in Bombay and Calcutta, much thinner clothing is required. Cool linen suits for men, and very thin dresses for ladies as also khâki riding and shooting suits, can be got cheaper and better in India than in England, and a native tailor will make a very satisfactory suit from an English pattern.

Linen and underclothing for at least three weeks should be taken —with less, the traveller may be inconvenienced on arrival, or even detained until his board-ship clothes are washed. The Indian

[1] This may be taken as applying to all places south of Hyderabad, excluding the higher plateau of Mysore.

washermen, though not as bad as they used to be, still destroy things rather rapidly. A lady will find a light dust-cloak a great convenience for railway travelling.

The hospitality of India involves a considerable amount of dining out, and therefore a lady, unless she intends to eschew society, should be provided with several evening dresses. If it is intended to join friends in camp, or make any long expeditions by road, riding-breeches for men, and riding-habits for ladies should not be forgotten.

A good sun-hat is an essential. The *Tarai hat* (two soft felt hats fitting one over the other) will generally suffice for the cool months, but even in them the mid-day sun in India is dangerous, and it is therefore advisable to wear a cork or felt helmet, which is lighter and better ventilated, and affords more protection from the sun than the Tarai, and is indispensable in real hot weather. Many London hatters have a large choice of sun-hats and helmets for ladies as well as men ; and travellers should be careful to wear such head protection whenever they are exposed to the sun during the voyage. A white cover to the umbrella is also desirable, especially for a lady ; a straw or other light hat will be found convenient for the cool hours of the morning and evening. Much larger hats, which can be best obtained in India, should be worn for shooting expeditions extending over the whole day.

A traveller in **Ceylon** will seldom require any but the lightest of clothing, except in the mountains, where the temperature becomes proportionately cooler as he ascends. At Kandy a light overcoat, and at Nuwara Eliya warm wraps and underclothing, are necessary.

For further hints, Dr Harford's *Hints on Outfit in Tropical Countries* (Royal Geographical Society) may be consulted.

Bedding

Every traveller who contemplates a tour must, on arrival in India, provide himself with some bedding, to be taken with him everywhere, even when on a visit to friends, and which should always be with him in the railway carriage, if he is going to spend a night in the train. Except at the best hotels, there is either no bedding or there is the chance of its being dirty. The minimum equipment is a pillow and two cotton-wadded quilts (*Razais*), one to sleep on, and one which should be larger, as a coverlet ; or a good *razai* and a couple of warm blankets, or still better, an eider-down. The ready-made *razais* are usually thin, but they can be got to order of any thickness. To these should be added a pillow-case, cheap calico sheets, and a light blanket. A canvas or waterproof cover to wrap the bedding in must not be omitted, or the first time it is carried any distance by a coolie

INDIA—*RAINFALL*

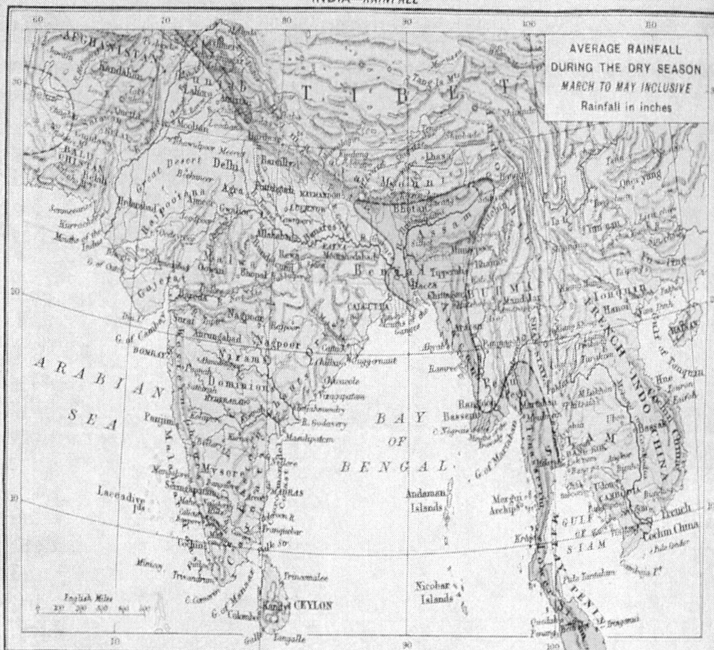

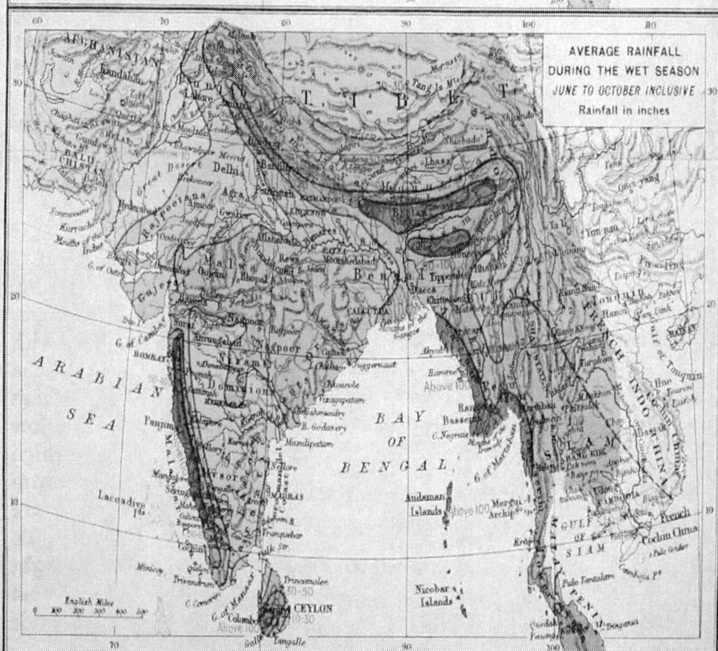

London. John Murray, Albemarle Street.

or taken into camp it may be dirtied. A waterproof sheet is a useful addition to the bedding, but cannot be called an absolute necessity for an ordinary tour. Without such a modest supply of covering as is here indicated, a traveller may at any time have to spend a night in very severe cold, especially if travelling by railway, as the windows and doors of the carriages seldom fit well enough to keep this out. Two or three towels, for use on railway journeys, should also be added to the above outfit.

Travelling Servants

A native travelling servant, who can speak English, is highly desirable, but should not be engaged without a good personal character, or the recommendation of a trustworthy Agent. Such a servant is almost necessary to wait on his master at hotels, where, without him, he would be but poorly served ; and will be found very useful in a hundred different ways when travelling by rail or otherwise, and as an interpreter when dealing with natives. Having ascertained beforehand from his Agents or friends the fair wages which such a servant ought to be paid (these vary from Rs.25-35 per mensem), the master should come to a definite arrangement with him before engaging him ; and it is usually advisable to have an agreement with him in writing. If the servant proves satisfactory, it is the custom to make him a present on parting with him. If the traveller has friends "up country," it may be well to write beforehand and ask them to engage a servant, and send him to meet his master at the port of arrival. "Up-country" servants are often cheaper and more reliable than those to be met with on the coast, but their knowledge of English is not generally very good. Ladies may travel with an accredited man servant without hesitation, and will find him far more useful than an *áyáh* in almost all respects. The services of a good *áyáh* are more difficult to secure than those of a *bearer* servant, and naturally are more expensive. The best *áyáhs* with a knowledge of English come from Madras. During the first two or three days of his service, it should be carefully explained to the travelling servant exactly what he is expected to do, and it will usually be found that he will thereafter do this satisfactorily. It may be added that such servants should be quietly kept in their proper places.

Indian Railways

The *Indian A.B.C. Guide*, the *Indian Railway Travellers' Guide*, and Newman's *Indian Bradshaw*, with maps, railway routes in India, and general information of steamer routes, are the best. For railway purposes the hours are counted up to 24, as in Italy: thus 20.12 is 8.12 P.M., and so on. Railway time throughout India is now Standard time, which is 5½ hours in advance of Greenwich time.

The difference with regard to the local times in India is as follows:—

Standard time	in advance of	Madras	1	min.
,,	,,	Bombay	39	,,
,,	,,	Allahabad	2	,,
,,	,,	Delhi	22	,,
,,	,,	Karachi	61	,,
,,	,,	Lahore	37	,,
,,	behind	Calcutta	24	,,
,,	,,	Chittagong	37	,,

Standard time in Burma is 6½ hours in advance of Greenwich, or 5 minutes in advance of Rangoon time.

At many of the larger towns there are two stations or more. Where there are both the traveller should, as a rule, book, not to the "City," but to the "Cantonment" station; but before booking he should note which station is mentioned in the *Handbook*. The Railway Companies in India do much for the comfort of 1st and 2nd class travellers, but might do more, *e.g.* by supplying electric fans in the carriages, and seeing more closely to the management of the refreshment rooms. Every 1st and 2nd class compartment is provided with a lavatory, and the seats, which are unusually deep, are so arranged as to form couches at night, but bedding and pillows are not furnished. At all terminal stations, and at various large roadside stations, berths in the carriages can be booked beforehand. It will generally be found convenient to send one's servant ahead to the station with the luggage, so that he may book it; if tickets have not been taken beforehand, a slip with the destination of the traveller written on it should be given to him to obviate mistakes. The payment of coolies (porters—usually 2-4 annas) is best left to one's servant.

There are refreshment rooms at frequent intervals, and some of them are well managed and supplied; travellers intending to make use of them should signify their intention to the guard of the train beforehand, and he will telegraph (free of charge) to the station indicated; in Madras tickets for meals are purchased at the same time as the railway ticket. Restaurant cars now run on most of the express mail trains. The failure of the manager of any refreshment room to provide a proper meal or food when ordered beforehand, should never be overlooked, but should be invariably reported to the

Traffic Superintendent of the line. In extreme cases payment of the full price demanded for the meal should be refused.

The Station-masters are particularly civil and obliging, and will arrange for ponies, conveyances, or accommodation at out-of-the-way stations, if notice is given them beforehand; they will also receive letters addressed to their care, which is often a convenience to travellers. For some obscure reason the guards of trains render none of the services expected of them in Europe, and are generally conspicuous by their absence in the large stations.

Travellers must be careful to see that their heavy luggage is secured by locks and is booked to proceed by the same route as themselves ; all small articles in the carriages should be carefully placed out of the reach of possible thieves in the night, especially if the windows are kept open on account of the heat. At every station which the ordinary traveller is likely to visit, conveyances of some sort await the arrival of the trains.

It is a matter for regret that 3rd class passengers are not always considerately treated by the railway staff. Travellers in India will render a public service by bringing instances of such treatment to notice. The comfort of such passengers has been too much overlooked in the past.

Hotels, Dak Bungalows, and Rest-Houses

Outside the Presidency towns, and a few exceptional places, such as Lucknow, Delhi, and Bangalore, there are hardly any hotels in India really up to the European standard of excellence. At all the chief places fairly large airy rooms will be found in the hotels, but the traveller will hardly be well waited upon unless he brings a servant with him. As they are often crowded in the tourist season, he should give notice beforehand of his intended arrival. Some of the clubs admit recommended visitors as honorary members, and a club which has sleeping accommodation is generally more comfortable than a hotel; but it is seldom that such accommodation is available in the cold weather, unless it is arranged for by a friend beforehand. All property should be kept carefully locked in hotels, as there are usually many strange servants in them, and the verandahs of most are frequented by hawkers and other outsiders.

At the dak bungalows (travellers' rest-houses established by Government in all important places) the keeper in charge will provide meals, but it is usually well to give notice of one's intended arrival. The bedrooms in these bungalows have an adjoining bath-room, and are usually sufficiently if roughly provided with furniture and lights. They cannot be retained beforehand—the first comer having the preference, and after occupying a room for twenty-four hours, the traveller must give place, if required, to the next comer. In S. India the name Travellers' Rest-House is generally used. There is a fixed fee for the occupation of the rooms, and usually for each of the simple meals to be supplied. In some cases the servant in charge, usually called the *Khánsáma*, has been in the service of English officers, and will prove to be a good cook. In small and out-of-the-way places it is best to confine his efforts to a curry or *pilau*, which he is sure to prepare well; and when visiting such places it is well to take with one small supplies, such as tinned soups and vegetables, tea and sugar, biscuits and the like, and one's own whisky or wine.

In certain places which deserve to be visited by many travellers such as Ajanta (Fardapur), Vijayanagar (Kamalapur), and Mandu, there is either only very poor and insufficient accommodation or no accommodation at all, and the Governments concerned might well see to this. Higher fees might be reasonably charged for accommodation specially provided at places seldom visited by travellers.

The Rest-House of Ceylon is more like an hotel than the Dak Bungalow in India, in that it is more frequently furnished with bedding and linen, and food is generally provided.

Food

As a rule, the food supplied in hotels and railway refreshment rooms in India is not very good. Outside the really large places and cantonments, the meat, with exception of bullock hump, is often lean and tough, the fowls are skinny, and the eggs ridiculously small. The sea fish at the sea-ports is excellent, and the river fish supplied at table elsewhere is generally fresh; but it does not always agree with persons new to the country, and not even in the case of the *mahsir* does it always commend itself as palatable to them. Game is generally abundant at private tables in the cold weather—quail (early and late in the season), snipe, teal, duck, partridge, and sandgrouse—but hotel-keepers too often neglect to include this in their *menu*. Where there is a good supply of fruit in the market, its proper provision at the hotel table should be insisted upon. Bread is fairly good, but this cannot be said of the butter, and milk is not free from danger. Aerated water should be drunk in preference to plain water, even in private houses; and the water in hotels and refreshment rooms should be absolutely avoided. If the traveller leaves the beaten track, he should have a tiffin (luncheon) basket, containing knives, forks, and other simple fittings and supplies; and, as a matter of fact, whenever any long journey is undertaken, it is

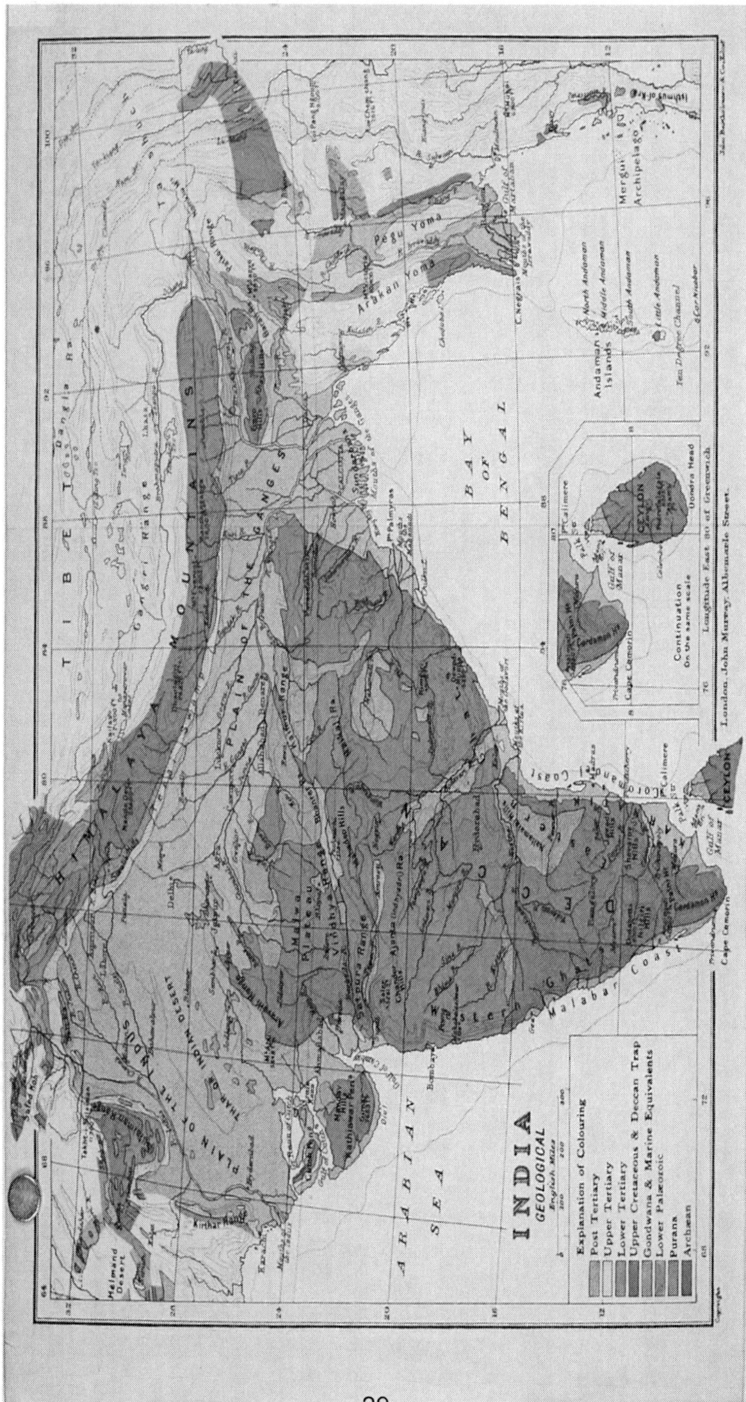
INDIA
GEOLOGICAL
English Miles
Explanation of Colouring
Post Tertiary
Upper Tertiary
Lower Tertiary
Upper Cretaceous & Deccan Trap
Gondwana & Marine Equivalents
Lower Palæozoic
Purana
Archæan
TIBET
HIMALAYA MOUNTAINS
PLAIN OF THE GANGES
PLAIN OF THE INDUS
INDIAN DESERT
ARABIAN SEA
BAY OF BENGAL
Malabar Coast
Coromandel Coast
Pegu Yoma
Arakan Yoma
Andaman Islands
Mergui Archipelago
CEYLON
Continuation
On the same scale
Longitude East 80 of Greenwich
London. John Murray, Albemarle Street.

well to be always provided with such a basket of potted meats, soups or bovril, biscuits, jam, tea and sugar, some spirit, and soda-water, which is good and cheap in India, as this renders one immune against the accident of detention, or of failure to obtain an eatable meal at a railway refreshment room. Added to the above, an Etna will be found a great convenience.

Health

It is of great importance to avoid chills in the East, and underclothing should always be changed after the body has been overheated. The necessity of using warm clothing until the morning has ceased to be cold, and after the sun has set, or even slightly before the sun sets, has been insisted on above. Excessive bodily exertion and consequent fatigue should be avoided by all who are no longer young, and such persons, if unacquainted with the conditions of sub-tropical life, will do well to consult some medical man experienced in them before undertaking a tour in India. Slight indisposition must not be trifled with in India, even though it would be thought nothing of elsewhere; immediate avoidance of all fatigue is necessary upon the occurrence of any indisposition, and only light food should be taken until it passes away. In cases of fever, or of any ailment with the treatment of which the traveller is not practically acquainted, no time should be lost in seeking the services of a qualified medical man. Such an officer will be found in the Civil Surgeon of all places of any size; private practitioners are usually to be found only in the Presidency towns. The ordinary fee for attendance is Rs.16 or a guinea, but Rs.10 per visit are usually charged where a number of visits are made.

Sport

No attempt can be made here to give definite advice to sportsmen, but sporting localities have been incidentally indicated in the routes. A number of useful books on sport in India will be found among the publications of Messrs Thacker, Spink & Co.[1] The equipment for these pursuits varies from day to day, and each man must best know his own wants. Firearms are subject to a heavy duty when brought into the country, see p. 5. Large-game shooting is expensive and takes time; it should not be attempted except in company with a really good *shikari* and with the assistance of persons of local authority, as otherwise it would probably involve a mere waste of time and useless trial of patience.

[1] Mr F. G. Aflalo's *Sportsman's Manual of India* (Horace Marshall & Son), recently published, fills a long-felt want.

Small-game shooting, *i.e.* wild-fowl, hare, etc., with an occasional shot at an antelope, is an easier matter, and will afford excellent sport. It can be got from November till February, often at very small cost, by spending a night or two at some wayside railway station or near some remote spot. In this case also the advice of the "man who knows" will be of the greatest assistance. Near cantonments the ground is always too much shot over to afford good sport.

Hints for Camping

Travellers who leave the beaten track with the intention of shooting, or for the purpose of visiting remote or ruined cities, should take a small tent or two with them. Transport, in the shape of camels, carts, baggage-ponies, or bearers, can be got in any station, and in the larger places riding ponies and light native carts or perhaps even European traps for driving can be obtained. Those who intend to go into camp (as the Anglo-Indian term runs) will probably be experienced in organising such expeditions, or will have friends who will make arrangements for them, and, in any case, a courteous request for assistance made by calling upon the principal English or native officer of the place is sure to meet with courteous consideration ; but perhaps the following suggestions of requirements may prove of some use in the case of a solitary traveller who does not mind a certain amount of roughing. In Kashmir, camp equipment as below can be hired of the Agents there—elsewhere it would have to be purchased, and would cost probably about Rs.200-250.

Tent (Cabul tent, 80 lbs. complete) for self, and if cold or likely to be wet, a *pal* tent for servants—a few iron tent pegs (wooden ones for soft ground), and a mallet. Camp-bed with side poles of one piece, table, chairs, and carpet. India-rubber flat bath, and a board to stand on, or one's tubbing can be done by pouring native pots of water over head (fresh native pots can be obtained at any village), a screen (*kandt*) to use as a bath-room, a washing basin (*chilamchi*) and stand, hooks to strap on tent-pole for hanging clothes on, etc. Aluminium cooking-pots, and fry-pan, an iron dish or two, a few knives, forks, and spoons, aluminium plates, cups, and saucers, and mustard, pepper, and salt pots. Servants required in camp are—a boy to wait, a cook, a water-carrier (*bhisti*), and grooms for horses. All food for oneself, except milk and fresh meat, must be taken with one. Food for servants, milk, and meat (goat or sheep or chickens), can be got in any but the poorest villages. For bedding and clothes take blankets, sheets (luxury), an Indian shooting suit, rough boots and gaiters, a light flannel suit or two, a large sun-hat for shooting in, and a second sun-hat and a cap for wear in one's camp. A mosquito-net and poles for it will be needed if mosquitoes are likely to give trouble at night.

If white ants are about boxes and carpets should be shifted every morning. Persons not accustomed to camping out should always have straw put on the ground under the tent carpet.

For arms—the plainer the better—1 central fire D.B. hammer 12-bore gun, 1 C.F.D.B. express rifle, 500 bore. Empty 12-bore cartridges, Curtis and Harvey's No. 6 powder, and shot of all kinds can be purchased in any ordinary station.

For medicine, plenty of quinine in 3- or 5-grain "tabloids" or pills (to be taken before or after food whenever a chill or feverishness is felt), a bottle or so of chlorodyne, and two boxes of Cockle's pills. If not needed by oneself, the pills may be useful to give to servants or villagers.

Books

Readers who desire to obtain the latest and most accurate information on all subjects connected with India cannot do better than consult the first four volumes of the new edition of the *Imperial Gazetteer of India*, 1907—Descriptive, Historical, Economic, and Administrative, each of which can be bought separately for 6s. A full bibliography will be found under each section in these volumes.

A few books are specially mentioned here.

Sir A. Lyall, *Rise and Expansion of the British Dominion in India* (Murray).

" " *Asiatic Studies* (Murray).

Sir W. W. Hunter, *Brief History of the Indian Peoples* (Clarendon Press).

" " *Indian Empire* (Trubner).

Ruler of India, series, Oxford.

Sir C. P. Ilbert, *Government of India.*

Sir John Strachey, *India* (1903).

General Sir G. Chesney, *Indian Polity*; Sir Monier Williams, *Indian Wisdom, Buddhism*; Professor T. W. Rhys Davis, *Buddhist India*; Professor Stanley Lane Poole *Mediæval India under Mohammedan Rule*; Abul Fazl, *Ain-i-Akbari*, by Mr Blochmann and Col. Jarrett; Mr W. Irvine's *Storia do Mogor*; Mr V. E. Smith, *Early History of India*; Sir T. H. Holdich, *India*, in the series of the "Regions of the World"; T. Morrison, *Imperial Rule in India.*

James Fergusson, *History of Indian and Eastern Architecture* (Revised edition by Dr Burgess and R. Phené Spiers, 1910.) (Murray)—Sir H. H. Risley's *People of India.*

Sir G. Birdwood, *Industrial Arts of India.*

Sir G. Watt, *Commercial Products of India.*

E. B. Havell, *Indian Sculpture and Painting* and *Ideals of Indian Art.*

Maindron, *L'Art Indien.*

W. Crooke, *Things Indian.*

Sir H. Yule and Dr A. C. Burnell, *Hobson-Jobson* (Murray).

Mr T. R. E. Holmes, *History of the Indian Mutiny;* Dr Fitchett's *Tale of the Great Mutiny;* G. W. Forrest, *History of the Indian Mutiny* and *Interesting Cities of India; Bernier's Travels* (Constable). *Tavernier's Travels*, edited by Dr V. Ball; *Col. Sleeman's Rambles and Diaries* (MacMillan); *Bishop Heber's Diaries.*

Meadows Taylor, *Confessions of a Thug.*

A. H. H. Murray, *The Highroad of Empire.*

Rousselet, *India of the Rajas;* W. S. Caine, *Picturesque India;* Miss Scidmore, *Winter India;* Dr Kurt Boeck, *Durch Indien; Picturesque Glimpses of India*, with some 500 fine photos of Messrs Combridge, Bombay.

F. G. Aflalo, *The Sportsman's Book for India.*

Rudyard Kipling, *The Jungle Book.*

T. Lockwood Kipling, *Beast and Man in India.*

Sanderson, *Thirteen Years among the Wild Beasts in India.*

Col. Kinloch, *Large Game Shooting in Thibet and the Himalayas.*

The *Ras Mala* of Mr Forbes, and the *Rajasthan* of Colonel Tod contain more information of Guzerat, Kathiawar and Rajputana than any books ever published on any part of India, but are not light reading. Simple guides to the languages are *Hindustani, Persian, and Tamil Self-Taught* (Marlborough's Self-Taught Series), and *How to speak Hindustani*, by E. Rogers, 1s. (Allen & Co.). Constable's *Hand Atlas of India* contains a number of excellent maps relating to the country, and the Atlas Volume of the *Imperial Gazetteer* (15s.) is very good. Many of the railways have published Guides with capital illustrations, which are well worth buying as mementos of a visit to India.

Modern writers on Kashmir are Dr Neve (*Tourist's Guide,—Picturesque Kashmir*), Lieutenant-Colonel T. Duke, Sir W. R. Lawrence, Dr W. T. Elmslie, and Mr Drew. Route maps have been published by Mr John Collett and Captain Montgomerie.

For books on *Burma*, see p. 447, and on *Ceylon*, p. 472.

Army and Civil Lists, a useful Postal Guide, and the Directory of the Province (Thackers; *Times of India;* Asylum Press), will be found in all Clubs, and at most large hotels.

Those who desire specially detailed information regarding any place in India should turn to the Provincial Gazetteer, in which a separate volume exists for each district. Mr Baden Powell's *Manual* contains a full account of the various systems of land revenue in force in the country.

INDIA—*VEGETABLE PRODUCTS*

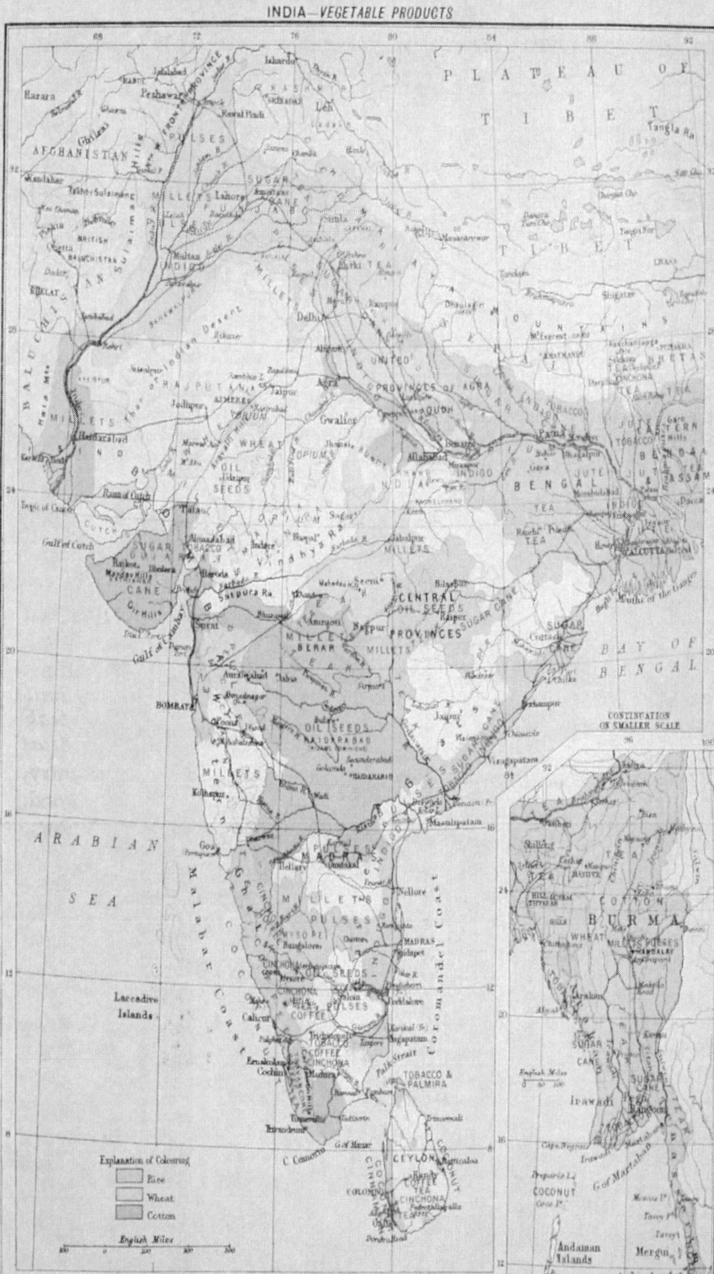

London, John Murray, Albemarle Street.

(2) VOYAGE FROM ENGLAND TO GIBRALTAR, MARSEILLES, MALTA, PORT SAID, THROUGH THE SUEZ CANAL AND RED SEA TO ADEN AND BOMBAY.

The principal steamer lines running to India are the P. & O.[1] Mail (weekly) to Bombay, the Bibby, Ellerman (City and Hall) and Anchor Lines from England, the Messageries Maritimes from Marseilles, and the Austrian Lloyd and Rubattino from Trieste and Genoa; while boats of the Orient Pacific and of the Nord Deutscher Lloyd Lines run twice a month to Colombo, only 38 hours from Madras. For a table of comparative rates of steamer fares see p. 503.

The comfort of the voyage depends much on the choice of the ship, and the cabin. The largest ships, as having less motion and more room on deck, are usually preferable to smaller ones. In going through the Red Sea to India the outer cabins on the port side are the best. On the return voyage the starboard cabins are better, but the difference is not material. The P. & O. charge £1 for each electric fan in the cabins, the messageries 12s.

On going on board, it is well to arrange for one's seat at table as soon as possible, as after the first dinner at sea, when seats have been assigned, it is difficult to make a change. They are usually allotted by the chief steward.

It is usual to give 10s. as a fee to the cabin steward, and 10s. to the one who waits on one at table. Passengers are entitled to gratuitous medical attendance by the ship's surgeon; but all who require his services for more than very simple methods will doubtless be disposed to offer an honorarium in return for these.

The timings of the P. & O. mail steamers are at present as follows:—

	DAYS AFTER LEAVING London	Marseilles	Brindisi
Gibraltar . . .	4	...	...
Marseilles . . .	6	23 hours by special train from London. Every Thursday at 11 A.M.	...
Brindisi	...	...	2 days by special train from London, every Friday, 9 P.M.
Port Said . . .	11	4	2¼
Aden	16	9	6½
Bombay	20¾	13¾	11¼

[1] P. & O. Offices: 122 Leadenball Street, E.C., Northumberland Avenue, W.C., London. Orient. S. N. Co.: 3 Fenchurch Avenue, Cockspur Street, W. Offices of Thos. Cook & Son (General Passage Agents): Ludgate Circus, E.C., Piccadilly, W., and branches.

The time occupied from London by the P. & O. intermediate steamers running to Calcutta, China, and Japan, is:—

Malta,	8 days.	Aden,	18 days.	Calcutta,	32 days.
Port Said,	12 ,,	Colombo,	26 ,,	Hongkong,	39 ,,

The Messageries boats sail from Marseilles, where also the P. & O. and the Orient Line Steamers (from London) touch, and the Nord Deutscher from Southampton. The last and the Orient Pacific call at Naples also. The P. & O. mail steamers start from the Tilbury Dock, and the intermediate steamers from the Royal Albert Docks, London. In the winter months these outward steamers are nearly always in advance of their scheduled time after leaving Port Said.

Travelling by sea from England, through the Bay of Biscay, results in a saving of a few pounds as compared with the expense of the overland route *viâ* Marseilles, although it adds a few days to the voyage; but good sailors will probably prefer the greater quiet of sea life to the scurry of a long overland journey. The first place sighted is generally **Cape La Hague** or **Hogue,** on the W. coast of the Cotentin in France, off which, on the 19th of May 1692, Admiral Russell, afterwards Earl of Orford, defeated De Tourville, and sunk or burned sixteen French men-of-war. Then **Cape Finisterre** (*finis terræ*), a promontory on the W. coast of Galicia in Spain, and in N. lat. 42° 54′, and W. long. 9° 20′, will probably be seen, off which Anson defeated the French fleet in 1747. The next land sighted will be, perhaps, **Cape Roca,** near Lisbon, and then **Cape St Vincent** in N. lat. 37° 3′, W. long. 8° 59′, at the S.W. corner of the Portuguese province Algarve, off which Sir G. Rodney, on the 16th January 1780, defeated the Spanish fleet, and Sir J. Jervis won his earldom on the 14th of February 1797, and Nelson the Order of the Bath, after taking the *S. Josef* and the *S. Nicholas* of 112 guns each. This cape has a fort upon it, and the white cliffs, 150 feet high, are honey-combed by the waves, which break with great violence upon them. From the last three capes steamers are signalled to Lloyd's. Just before entering the Straits of Gibraltar, **Cape Trafalgar** will also probably be seen in N. lat. 36° 9′, W. long. 6° 1′, immortalised by Nelson's victory of the 21st of October 1805. **Tarifa** is next passed, and **Gibraltar** then comes in sight. The table of distances below is from the pocket-book, 3rd edition, of the Peninsular and Oriental Steam Navigation Company. This little book, costing only 2s. 6d., can be highly recommended.

TABLE OF DISTANCES BETWEEN THE VARIOUS PORTS ACCORDING TO THE ROUTES TAKEN BY THE STEAMERS OF THE PENINSULAR AND ORIENTAL STEAM NAVIGATION COMPANY.

	London (*if via Plymouth add* 50)											
	295	Plymouth										
	1309	1054	Gibraltar									
	2003	1748	694	Marseilles								
	2290	2035	981	—	Malta							
	—	—	—	—	—	Brindisi						
Via Malta	*Via Marseilles*											
3225	3511	3256	2202	1508	935	930	Port Said					
3268	3554	3299	2245	1551	978	973	43	Ismailia				
4620	4906	4651	3597	2903	2330	2325	1395	1352	Aden			
6284	6570	6315	5261	4567	3994	3989	3059	3016	1664	Bombay		
6713	6999	6744	5690	4996	4423	4418	3488	3445	2093	875	Colombo	
7973	8259	8004	6950	6256	5683	5678	4748	4705	3353	2135	1260	Calcutta

GIBRALTAR.—As the steamers rarely stop for more than a few hours, passengers will not find time for anything beyond a walk in the town and lower fortifications. The place is a good one to buy tobacco, as there is no duty and it is cheap. There are steamers from Gibraltar three times a week to Tangier, and a number of times daily to Algeciras, the terminus of the Spanish railway.

Gibraltar was reckoned as one of the Pillars of Hercules, the African pillar being Abyla, near Ceuta. It was taken from the Visigoths in 711 A.D. by Tarik Ibn Zayad, after whom it was called Jabal al Tarik = Gibraltar, and retaken 1309, but not finally wrested from the Moors till 1503. In 1704 it was taken by the English, and sustained several sharp sieges by the French and Spaniards between that date and 1779. In the latter year commenced the memorable siege which lasted four years, and ended by the repulse of the combined fleets of France and Spain by the garrison under General Elliott, Lord Heathfield. Since that time it has remained an uncontested possession of the English.

Rounding Point Carnero, the spacious, but exposed bay, 6 m. wide and 10 m. deep, is entered, and a fine view is obtained of the vast rocky promontory, which on the N. face rises in a perpendicular precipice 1200 ft. high, and ascends in the centre to 1408 ft. It is 3 m. in length, and from ½ m. to ¾ m. in breadth; and is joined to the mainland by a low sandy isthmus, 1½ m. in length. On all sides but the W. it is steep and rugged, but on that side there is a general slope of from 200 to 300 ft. from the rock down to the sea.

The approach from the W. reveals three high points; N. is the **Rock Gun,** or **Wolf's Crag,** 1337 ft.; in the centre the **Upper Signal Station,** or **El Hacho,** 1255 ft. high; and S. is **O'Hara's Tower,** 1408 ft. Here the rock descends to **Windmill Hill Flats,** a level plateau ½ m. long, which ends in a still lower plateau from 100 to 50 ft. above the sea, called **Europa Flats.** The new mole, landing-place, and dockyard, occupy the west side from opposite O'Hara's Tower to the Signal Station, and the town lies above them from opposite the latter point to the Rock Gun Peak. The population of the place amounts to 27,000, and the garrison to between 5000 and 6000. The hotels are situated in West Port Street, which, with its continuations, forms the main thoroughfare of the place from the **Land Port** to the **South Port Gate.**

Passports are exacted on landing from all but British subjects, and sketching is strictly prohibited. The hour of evening gun-fire varies according to the time of year; a few minutes later all gates are shut till sunrise, though up to a later fixed hour entrance is permitted with certain police formalities.

The Main Street may be followed as far as the **Alameda,** outside the South Port; this was the parade-ground until 1814, when Sir George Don made a lovely garden of it. A column brought from the ruins of Lepida is surmounted by a bust of the Duke of Wellington, and there is also a bust of General Elliott, the hero of the great siege. Half-way down the street is the **Exchange,** with the **Club House** to the W. The English **Cathedral** Church of the Holy Trinity, built in the Moorish style in 1832, stands near these, and the Governor's residence further on, which once belonged to Franciscan friars, is still called "The Convent." On the left, outside the South Port Gate, is a small cemetery, in which many who died of wounds received at the Battle of Trafalgar are buried; and further south, below the Alameda, is the dockyard. An upper and a lower road lead from here to the Windmill Hill and Europa Flats. Beyond these, on the E. shore, is the summer residence of the Governor, called "The Cottage," built by General Fox.

Those remaining several days can explore the Heights and fortifications of Gibraltar, for which a special order from the Military Authorities is necessary. From the Rock Gun there is a fine view of the Ronda Mountains and the Sierra Nevada; the **Moorish Castle** (746 A.D.) is on the way to it, and under a massive tower, called the Torre de Omenaga, are some well-constructed tanks. Beyond are the wonderful galleries in the north face excavated by convict labour. From the **Signal House** is a noble view, which includes the Atlas Mountains, Ceuta, and Barbary, ending with the Bay of Tangiers. Between the Rock Gun and O'Hara's Tower live a few monkeys, which are jealously protected. S. of the Signal Station, and 1100 ft. above the sea, is the celebrated St Michael's **Cave**, which can be visited by special permission only; an entrance scarcely 6 ft. wide leads into a hall 200 ft. long and 60 ft. high, supported by stalactite pillars like Gothic arches. Beyond are smaller caves, which have been traversed to a distance of 288 ft. In Windmill Hill are the four Genista caves, where many bones of men and animals have been discovered.

Beyond the Land Port Gate is a causeway leading into Spain, with the sea on the left, and the "Inundation," a sheet of water so called, on the right. Beyond these is the North Front, where are the cemetery, the cricket-ground, and the race-course. The eastern beach, called "Ramsgate and Margate," is the general afternoon resort. Across the isthmus is a line of English sentries, then the Neutral Ground, and then the Spanish sentries. Behind the Spanish lines is the town of La Linea de la Conception, with a population of 30,000.

MARSEILLES (826 m. from London by railway).—Passengers to India, joining a P. & O. steamer at Marseilles, and travelling by the P. & O. express (1st class tickets £6, 14s. + £2, 15s.), leave London at 11 A.M. on Thursday in each week, and Calais at 2.55 P.M., and reach Marseilles at 9.45 A.M. Friday, the special train proceeding alongside of the steamer. This is berthed at mole C., at the western end of the new Basin National, and some 2½ m. distant from the ordinary railway station. The Grand Hotel Terminus at this is a convenient place to stay at for one night, or the Grand Hotel de Louvre near the old harbour. Passengers arriving by steamer, who have some hours to spare, should, if possible, drive up the main street or Cannabiere to the Museum, with a Picture Gallery and Zoological Gardens, and then from the middle of the former by the Rue de Rome and the Prado to the coast east of the city, and along that back to the Port by the Via Corniche, finally visiting the lofty situated church of Notre Dame de la Garde for the sake of the splendid view. The same round can be made by the electric tramways.

[**BRINDISI** (1450 m. from London by railway).—Details of this route to Port Said should be obtained from the P. & O. Company, or Messrs Cook.]

MALTA.—On the way from Gibraltar to Malta, by steamers which do not proceed to Marseilles, **Algiers** may possibly be seen, its white buildings stretching like a triangle with its base on the sea, and the apex on higher ground. **Cape Fez**, and the promontory of the **Seven Capes**, jagged, irregular headlands, are passed on the starboard side, also **Cape Bon**, the most northern point of Africa, and the **Island of Pantellaria**, the ancient Cossyra, between Cape Bon and Sicily. It is 8 m. long, volcanic, and rises to a height of more than 2000 ft. There is a town of the same name near the seashore, on the western slope, where there is much cultivation. It is used by the Italians as a penal settlement, and is rather smaller than Gozo.

The Maltese group of islands consists of **Gozo**, **Comino**, and **Malta**, and stretches from N.W. to S.E., the total distance from San Dimitri, the most W. point of Gozo, to Ras Benhisa, the most S. part of Malta, being about 25 m. From the nearest point of Gozo to Sicily is 55 m., and Africa is 187 m. distant from Malta. Malta lies in N. lat. 35° 53′ 49″, E. long. 14° 30′ 28″. It is 17 m. long and 8 m. broad. Its area, together with that of Gozo, is 116 sq. m., and the population of the three islands is about 150,000, the numbers of the garrison being about 10,000. It consists of calcareous rock, the highest point being 590 ft. above the sea-level. Towards the S. it ends in precipitous cliffs. It has a barren appearance, but there are many fertile gardens and fields, enclosed in high walls, where fine oranges, grapes, and figs, and other crops, returning from thirty- to sixty-fold, are grown. The Maltese language is a mixture of Arabic and Italian, but most of the townspeople have sufficient knowledge of Italian to transact business in that tongue. The port of Malta is situated somewhat to the E. of the centre of the northern shore of the island. It consists of two fine harbours, separated by the narrow promontory called **Mount Xiberras**, or Sciberras. The western or quarantine harbour, protected by **Fort Tigne** on the W., is called **Marsamuschetto**; the other is **Valetta**, or the great harbour, and in it the men-of-war are moored. The entrance to the great harbour is protected on the W. by **Fort St Elmo** at the end of Sciberras, and on the E. by **Fort Ricasoli**, both very formidable. At Fort St Elmo is one of the finest lighthouses in the Mediterranean. The great harbour runs away into numerous creeks and inlets, in which are the dockyard, victualling-yard, and arsenal, all of which could be swept by the guns of **St Angelo**, which is a fort behind St Elmo; on the E. side here is the town called Citta Vittoriosa. The mail steamers are moored in the quarantine harbour; the charge for landing is one shilling per head. On landing, a long flight of steps is ascended to the **Strada San Marco**, which leads to the principal street, **Strada Reale**, ½ m. long, in the town of Valetta, so-called from Jean de la Valette, Grand Master of the Knights of St John of Jerusalem, who built it after the Turkish armament sent against Malta by Sultan Suleiman II. had been repulsed. The foundation stone was laid on the 28th of March 1566, and the whole town, designed by one architect, Girolamo Cassar, was completed in May 1571.

Left of the Strada Reale is **St John's Cathedral**, a remarkable church, both historically and architecturally, designed by Cassar. The floor is paved with slabs bearing the arms of scores of knights who have been interred in this church. In the first chapel on the right, the altar-piece represents the beheading of John the Baptist, and is by M. Angelo Caravaggio. In the next chapel, which belonged to the Portuguese, are the monuments of Manoel Pinto and Grand Master Manoel de Vilhena, the latter of bronze. The third, or Spanish chapel, has the monuments of Grand Masters Perellos and N. Cotoner, and two others. The fourth chapel belonged to the Provençals. The fifth chapel is sacred to the Virgin, and here are kept the town keys taken from the Turks. On the left of the entrance is a bronze monument of Grand Master Marc Antonio Sondadario. The first chapel on the left is the sacristy. The second chapel belonged to the Austrians, the third to Italians, containing pictures, ascribed to Caravaggio, of St Jerome and Mary Magdalene. The fourth is the French chapel, and the fifth the Bavarian, and hence a staircase descends to the crypt, where are the sarcophagi of the first Grand Master who ruled in Malta, L'Isle Adam, and of de La Valette and others.

The **Governor's Palace**, formerly the Grand Master's, close to the Strada Reale, is a noble range of building, containing marble-paved corridors and staircase, and many portraits, and armed figures carrying the shields of all the Governors from the first Grand Master to the present day. The armoury is full of interesting relics, including the original deed granted to the Knights of St John of Jerusalem by Pope Pascal II. in 1126, and the deed when they left Rhodes in 1522. **The Library**, close to the Palace, contains 40,000 volumes, and some Phœnician and Roman antiquities. The highest **battery** commands a fine view of both harbours and of the fortifications. There are several statues of Grand Masters and Governors in the walk on the ramparts. The **Opera House**, the **Bourse**, the **Courts of Justice**, once the Auberge d'Auvergne, and the Union Club, once the Auberge de Province, and the statues of L'Isle Adam and de La Valette, are in the Strada Reale. The Auberge d'Italie, to the east of the south end of this street, is the Royal Engineer's office, and the Auberge de Castille, near it, has become the Headquarters of the Artillery; the Auberge de France, in the Strada Mezzodi, is now the house of the Comptroller of Military Stores, and the Auberge d'Aragon the residence of the General of the Garrison. The Auberge d'Allemagne was removed in order to erect St Paul's Church on its site. The Anglo-Bavarian Auberge is the Headquarters of the regiment stationed at St Elmo. In front of the Auberge de Castille are the Piazza Regina and Upper Barracca, affording splendid views of the great harbour. **The Military Hospital** has the largest room in Europe, 480 ft. long, erected in 1628 by Grand Master Vasconcelos. Below the Military Hospital is the Civil **Hospital for Incurables,** founded by Caterina Scappi in 1646.

A mile beyond the Porta Real and the station of the little railway to Civita Vecchia is the Governor's country palace of **St Antonio,** with a lovely garden. About ½ m. further to the S.W. is **Citta Vecchia,** which stands on a ridge from 200 to 300 ft. high, affording a view over nearly the whole island. There is a fine church here, St Paul's, and near it are some curious catacombs. **St Paul's Bay** lies at the N.W. extremity of the island; there is a statue of bronze erected on an islet at its mouth. The Carthaginian or Phœnician ruins at **Hagiar Chem,** properly Hajar Kaim, "upright stone," near the village of Casal Crendi, can be visited on the way to it. These ruins, excavated in 1839, consist of walls of large stonés fixed upright in the ground, forming small enclosures, connected with one another by passages, and all contained within one large enclosure. The building is thought to have been a temple of Baal and Astarte. The main entrance is on the S.S.E., and a passage leads from it into a court, on the left of which is an altar, with the semblance of a plant rudely sculptured on it. Similar remains are found in other parts of Malta and in Gozo.

Malta is said to have been occupied by the Phœnicians in 1500 B.C., and by the Greeks in 750 B.C. The Carthaginians got possession of it in 500 B.C., and the Romans took it towards the close of the second Punic War. The Goths and Vandals invaded it in 420 A.D. In 520 A.D. Belisarius made it a province of the Byzantine Empire, the Moslems conquered it in 730 A.D., and Count Roger, the Norman, captured it in 1100 A.D. It then passed to Louis IX., to the Count of Anjou, and to the Kings of Castile, and then to Charles V., who gave it, in 1530, to the Knights Hospitallers of St John of Jerusalem. On 18th May 1565, the Turks attacked St Elmo, St Angelo, and Sanglea, but the siege was raised on the 8th of September (see Major Whitworth Porter's *History of the Knights of Malta*, Longmans, 1858). The Knights had their own mint, fleet, and army, and accredited ambassadors to foreign Courts. In the archives are letters from Henry VIII., Charles II., and Anne, addressed to them as princes. On the 7th of September 1792 the French Directory commanded the Order to be annulled, and seized all its French possessions. On the 7th of June 1798, Bonaparte arrived with a fleet of 18 ships of the line, 18 frigates, and 600 transports, and Malta was surrendered. A tree of liberty was planted before the Palace, the decorations of the Knights were burned, and the churches, palaces, and charitable houses at Valetta and Citta Vecchia were pillaged.

On the 2nd of September 1798, a general revolt took place, and Nelson blockaded Valetta; and on the 5th of September 1800 their commander, General Vaubois, surrendered.

Egypt, Port Said, and the Suez Canal.—The land about Port Said is so low, that the approach to the harbour would be difficult were it not for a lighthouse 160 ft. high, built of concrete, which stands on the sea-shore to the right of the harbour close to the W. mole, and shows an electric light flashing every 20 seconds, and visible 20 m. off. The harbour is formed by two breakwaters, 1500 yards apart, built of concrete, the western 2726 yards long, the eastern 1962 yards long. The depth of water at the entrance is 30 ft. Since the works were begun, the sea has receded ½ m., and a bank has formed to the N.W. of the entrance, having only 4 to 5 fathoms water on it, caused by a current which sets along the shore, and meeting the sea rolling in from the N., is forced back, and deposits its silt. Near the S. end of the west jetty is a bold statue of Mons. Ferdinand de Lesseps, with the motto "Aperire terram gentibus." **Port Said** town is modern, and since 1890 it has been much improved, and is now a very important coaling-station. The population is about 25,000. Opposite the anchorage on the Marina is the French pilots' office, where the draught, breadth, length, and tonnage of each ship entering the canal is noted. In it there is a wooden plan of the canal, along which wooden pegs, with flags, are placed, showing the exact position of every vessel passing through this great highway. Further south is the fine hospital building. Trains leave for Ismailia, Suez, and Cairo twice daily. The line, being of the narrow gauge, carriages have to be changed at Ismailia. The principal hotels are the Eastern Exchange, Continental, and Metropole. Messrs Cook and the Anglo-American Nile Company and the principal Agents in India have representatives at Port Said.

The **Canal**,[1] opened in 1870, is in round numbers 100 m. in length, and as far as Ismailia, that is for about 42 m., it runs due N. and S. It then bends to the E. for about 35 m., and is again almost straight for the last 20 m.

The following are the dimensions of the canal, which are being constantly increased:—

Width at water-line	240 ft.
"	360 "
" at base	90 "
Depth	30 "
At depth of 24 ft.	114 "

[1] For a detailed history of the canal, see *Handbook of Egypt*, John Murray.

Every few miles there is a gare, or station, and a siding with signal posts, by which the traffic is regulated according to the block system. Every year the navigation is rendered easier by the construction of additional sidings, and traffic at night by electric light; the average duration of transit is now 17 hours. Vessels must not move faster than 6 m. an hour except in the Lakes.

The number of ships which passed through the canal in 1910 was 4533, with a net tonnage of 16,600,000; of this 63 per cent. sailed under the British, and 14 per cent. under the German flag. The dues paid on ships are 7½ fr. per ton for laden passenger and cargo steamers, and 10 fr. for each passenger; and the gross income now earned is 120,000,000 fr. (£4,750,000). Since the latest improvements were made, the average size of the vessels using the canal has increased from 1500 to 3000 tons. The number of passengers carried annually through the canal is nearly 235,000, of whom rather over one-third are classed as military. The capital of the Company is, in round numbers, £13,000,000. The cost of construction was £16,000,000, the difference between the two sums having been paid by the Khedive. Work commenced in 1859, and was completed in 1869, under the direction of M. Ferdinand de Lesseps. The canal route saves nearly half the length of that by the Cape of Good Hope from the principal ports of Europe to Bombay, and one quarter of the same to China.

On the W. of the canal, as far as **Al Kantarah** (the Bridge), that is for about one-fourth of the way, there is a broad expanse of water, called **Lake Manzalah**, and for the rest of the distance to the W., and the whole distance to the E., a sandy desert, on which foxes, jackals, hyenas, wander at night. 20 m. from Port Said, the old Pelusiac branch of the Nile is crossed, and 8 m. to the E. are the ruins of the ancient city of Pelusium. At **Al Kantarah,** 27 m. from Suez, the canal intersects the caravan-track between Egypt and Syria, and is crossed by a flying bridge. 10 m. to the W. is **Tel Dafanah,** the site of Daphne, the Taphnes of Judith, i. 9. At 2 m. S. of Al Kantarah the canal enters the **Lake Ballah,** and after 12 m. reaches the promontory **Al Fardanah,** which it cuts through. Thence, after 4½ m., it reaches **Al Gisr,** the highest ground in the isthmus, 65 ft. above sea-level. There was a great camp here when the works were in progress; and a staircase of 100 steps led down to the canal. Beyond this, near the entrance to **Lake Timsah,** just half-way between Port Said and Suez, a small channel joins the maritime canal and the Fresh-Water Canal. The difference of level is 17 ft., which is overcome by two locks. A steam-launch comes to meet steamers in the lake, and land passengers for

ISMAILIA, population 4000, which once had much of the importance and traffic that formerly belonged to Suez, as the mails and passengers for Egypt were landed here—Hotel Vittoria, Hotel des Voyageurs; but is likely to decline owing to the opening of the railway to Port Said. From the landing-place a broad road lined with trees traverses the town from E. to W. In the W. quarter are the station, the landing-quays of the Fresh-Water Canal, and large blocks of warehouses, and beyond them the Arab Village. In the E. part are the houses of the *employés*, the residence of the Khedive, which was used as a military hospital during the English occupation of Ismailia in 1882, and the works by which water is pumped from the Fresh-Water Canal to Port Said.

The course of the canal through **Lake Timsah**, or Bahr al Timsah, "the Lake of the Crocodile," to which the Red Sea is believed to have formerly extended, is about 2½ m., and is marked by buoys. After 4 m. the canal reaches the higher ground of Tussum, where the level of the desert is 20 ft. above the sea, and here the first working encampment in the S. half of the isthmus was formed in 1859. Three m. to the S. is **Serapeum**, where the level is from 15 to 25 ft. above the sea, so called from some remains of a temple of Serapis, lying 4 m. to the W. A mile and a half from this the canal enters the **Bitter Lakes**, where the course is again buoyed. These lakes are the ancient Gulf of Heræopolis, and some authorities hold that the passage of the Israelites was through this. At the N. and S. ends of the principal lake is an iron lighthouse, 65 ft. high, on a solid masonry base. After 86 m. from Port Said the deep cutting of Shaluf is reached, in which is a band of sandstone, with layers of limestone and conglomerate, in which fossil remains of the shark, hippopotamus, tortoise, and whale, have been found. From this to the Suez mouth of the canal is 12½ m.

All the way from Ismailia the banks are fringed with vegetation, and the plain on either side is dotted with bushes. There is a little fishing in the canal for those who like the amusement, and at Suez there is a great variety of fish.

SUEZ.—The chief historical interest of Suez is derived from its having been long supposed to be the spot near which the Israelites crossed the Red Sea under the guidance of Moses, and where the Egyptian army was drowned, but modern criticism tends to place the scene farther N. In the early years of the 18th century Suez was little better than a small fishing-village, galvanised now and then into commercial life by the passage of caravans going to and fro between Asia and Egypt. But in 1837, owing to the exertions of Lieutenant Waghorn, the route through Egypt was adopted for the transit of the Indian mail, and a few years after the P. & O. Company began running a line of steamers regularly between India and Suez. This was followed in 1857 by the completion of a railway line from Cairo (since removed), and Suez soon began to increase in size and importance. It suffered, however, from the want of fresh water, until the completion (1863) of the Fresh-Water Canal to Suez brought an abundance of Nile water to the town; and the various works in connection with the Suez Canal, the new quays, the docks, etc., raised the population to 15,000. With the completion of the canal, the activity of the town decreased, and since the transfer of the mails from it, the place has been almost deserted, and the fine quays and warehouses are unused, as steamers now usually anchor in the Roads. There is a railway line to Ismailia and so to Cairo and Port Said.

The **Old Town** itself offers few points of interest. To the N. of the town are the storehouses of the P. & O. Company, the lock which terminates the Fresh-Water Canal and the *English Hospital*, and, on the heights above, is the chalet of the Khedive, from which there is a magnificent view; in the foreground is the town, the harbour, the roadstead, and the mouth of the Suez Canal; to the right the range of **Gebel Attakah**, a most striking and beautiful object, with its black-violet heights hemming in the Red Sea; away to the left, though considerably farther S., are the rosy peaks of the Mount Sinai range; and between the two, the deep blue of the gulf.

EXCURSION TO WELLS OF MOSES.—By those landing for Egypt at Suez, a pleasant excursion may be made to the **Wells** or **Fountains of Moses, Ain Musa.** It will occupy, according to the route taken and the time spent at the place, from half a day to a day. The shortest way is to take a sailing-boat, or one of the small steamers that ply between the town and the harbour, as far as the jetty, which has been built out into the sea to communicate with the new Quarantine lately established on the shore of the gulf for the reception of the pilgrims on their return from Mecca. From this point to Ain Musa the distance is not much over a mile; if donkeys are required between the jetty and the Wells, they must be sent from Suez. The other plan is to cross over in a boat to the old Quarantine jetty, about half a mile from the town, either taking donkeys in the boat or sending them on previously, and then to cross the Suez Canal by the ferry used for the passage of caravans between Arabia and Egypt, and ride along the desert to the Wells. Or the boat may be taken down to the entrance to the canal, and then up it a short way to the usual starting-point for the Wells. Either of these routes will take from three to four hours. The sums to be paid for boats and donkeys had better be strictly agreed upon beforehand. Visitors who intend spending the day at Ain Musa should take food with them. This excursion may be combined with a visit to the docks, by landing there on returning.

The "Wells" are a sort of oasis, formed by a collection of springs, surrounded with tamarisk bushes and palm-trees. Since it has become, as Dean Stanley calls it, "the Richmond of Suez"—a regular picnicking place for the inhabitants of that town—some Arabs and Europeans have regularly settled in it, and there are now a few houses, and gardens with fruit-trees and vegetables. The water from the springs has a brackish taste. Most of them are simply holes dug in the soil, which is here composed of earth, sand, and clay: but one is built up of massive masonry of great age. Though not mentioned in the Bible, its position has always caused it to be associated with the passage of the Red Sea by the Israelites, and tradition has fixed upon it as the spot where Moses and Miriam and the Children of Israel sang their song of triumph.

THE RED SEA.—A fresh breeze from the N. generally prevails for two-thirds of the voyage down the Red Sea, and is, during the winter months, succeeded by an equally strong wind from the S. for the rest of the way. During the summer, the wind from the N. blows throughout the sea, but is light in the southern half, and the heat is great. The **Sinaitic Range** is the first remarkable land viewed to the E., but Sinai itself, 37 geographical m. distant, can be seen only for a few minutes.

The Red Sea extends from the head of the Gulf of Suez to the Strait of Bab-el-Mandeb, about 1300 m., and its greatest width is about 200 m. At Ras Mohammed it is split by the peninsula of Sinai into two parts; one, the Gulf of Suez, about 150 m. long, and from 10 to 18 wide, and the other, the Gulf of Akabah, about 100 m. long, and from 5 to 10 wide.

Wherever seen from the sea the shores of the Red Sea present an appearance of absolute sterility. A broad sandy plain slopes inappreciably to the foot of the mountains, which are in most parts a considerable distance inland. The ordinary mail-steamer's track, however, lies down the centre of the sea, and little more than the summits of the distant bare and arid mountains will be seen.

Throughout the Red Sea enormous coral reefs run along the coasts in broken lines parallel to the shores, but not connected with them. They usually rise out of deep water to within a few feet of the surface. A navigable channel, from 2 to 3 m. wide, extends between them and the E. coast, and a narrower one on the W. coast. The whole sea is in course of upheaval. The former seaport of Adulis, in Annesley Bay, near Massowa, is now 4 m. inland.

The tides are very uncertain. At Suez, where they are most regular, they rise from 7 ft. at spring to 4 ft. at neap tides.

During the hottest months, July to September, the prevalence of northerly winds drives the water out of the Red Sea. The S.W. monsoon is then blowing in the Indian Ocean, and the general level of the Red Sea is from 2 to 3 ft. lower than during the cooler months, when the N.E. monsoon forces water into the Gulf of Aden and thence through the Strait of Bab-el-Mandeb.

After leaving Suez the **lighthouses** seen are Zafarana and Ras Gharib, both on the W. coast before Tor is reached. Then follows the light on Ashrafi, just inside the mouth of the Gulf of Suez, and that on Shadwar, just south of it. The light on *The Brothers* is nearly due E. of Kosseir. The Daedalus Reef, small and dangerous, lies in mid-channel in latitude 25°, and was a source of dread before the light was erected. The last light is on Perim Island in the Bab-el-Mandeb.

Below Kosseir (lat. 26°)—the ancient Leucos Limen (White Harbour) and the port of Upper Egypt—and Ras Benas (lat. 24°), near which was the port of Berenice, **SUAKIN**, 900 m. south of Suez, in latitude 19, is the first town of importance on the Egyptian coast. It was the scene of the two English expeditions of 1884, 1885, neither of which led to any result, and in 1896 was again held for the Khedive of Egypt by our troops, which caused a diversion of Osman Digna's forces, thus enabling the Khedive's troops, under Sir Herbert Kitchener, the more easily to reconquer the North Soudan. The principal tribes in the vicinity are the Hadendowa and Amarar.

About 120 m. north of Suakin, on the Arabian coast, is **Jiddah,** the seaport of Mecca (Makka), 60 m. E. The population, including surrounding villages, is about 40,000. English and other steamers call here frequently. The anchorage is 3½ m. from the shore. The town is square in shape, enclosed by a wall with towers at intervals, and on the sea-face by two forts. There is a good street parallel to the sea. The population is most fanatical, and Europeans landing must behave in all respects cautiously. There are three entrances to the town on the sea side, but the central one at the jetty is the only one in ordinary use. The gate on the S. side of the town is seldom opened, that on the N. is free to all, but the E. or Mecca gate, which formerly was strictly reserved for Mohammedans, should be approached with caution. The only sight of the town is the so-called Tomb of Eve, which lies to the north. This is a small mosque in the centre of two long low walls 140 ft. in length, which are supposed to enclose the grave. The antiquity of the tradition is unknown. Jiddah was bombarded by the British in 1858 in retribution for a massacre of the Consul and other British subjects by the population. Over 20,000 pilgrims proceed on the Haj every year from India.

HODEIDA, also on the east coast 200 m. N. of the Straits of Bab-el-Mandeb, in lat. 14° 40′ N., has a population of about 33,000. The anchorage is 3½ m. from the shore. European steamers call weekly or oftener. **Mocha,** which this place has supplanted as a commercial port, is 100 m. S. Hodeida has well-built houses and an amply-supplied market, and its mosques with fine domes and minarets give it a handsome appearance.

The island of **Perim** occupies the narrowest part of the Strait of Bab-el-Mandeb ("the Gate of Tears"). It is distant 1½ m. from the Arabian coast, and 9 to 10 m. from the African. The average width is 1¼ m., the greatest length 3½ m. The formation is purely volcanic, and consists of long low hills surrounding a capacious harbour about 1½ m. long, ½ m. in breadth, with a depth of from 4 to 6 fathoms in the best anchorages. The highest point of the island is 245 ft. above sea-level. All endeavours to find water have failed, and but little is procurable from the mainland near. There are water tanks that used to be supplied from Aden, but a condensing apparatus is found the most convenient means of supply. The British are the only nation who have ever permanently occupied Perim. Albuquerque landed upon it in 1513, and erected a high cross on an eminence, and called it the island of *Vera Cruz*, by which name it is shown on old Admiralty charts. Afterwards it was occupied by pirates who in vain dug for water. In 1799 the East India Company took possession of it, and sent a force from Bombay to hold it and prevent the French then in Egypt from passing on to India, where it was feared they would join Tipu Sultan. The lighthouse on the highest point was completed in 1861, and since then two others have been built on the shore. The garrison furnished from Aden occupies a small block-house for the protection of the lighthouse and coaling-stations. Steamers usually pass to the E. of the island near the Government boat harbour. The western side of the large inner harbour has been assigned to the Perim Coal Company, who have expended £120,000 in making the place one of the most perfect coaling and salvage stations in the East. The powerful salvage steamers are always ready to render assistance to vessels in distress.

ADEN, lat. 12° 46′, long. E. 44° 58′, situated on the E. promontory of a bay 8 m. long and 4 m. deep, was long held by the Turks, who captured the port from the Arabs. Marco Polo, the Venetian, visited Aden on his return from his travels in China. He records: "And it is a fact that when the Soldan of Babylon went against the city of Acre" (in A.D. 1291) "this Soldan of Aden sent to his assistance 30,000 horsemen and 40,000 camels, to the great help of the Saracens and the grievous injury of the Christians. He did this a great deal more for the hate he bears the Christians than for any love he bears the Soldan." This was the Mameluke Sultan of Egypt, Malik Ashraf Khalil. On the 18th February 1513, Albuquerque sailed from India with twenty ships for the conquest of Aden. In the assault on the fortress their ladders broke, and although the Portuguese took "a bulwark which guarded the port with thirty-nine great pieces of cannon," they were obliged to withdraw after a four days' siege. The first English vessel visited Aden in 1619.

Aden was taken from the Arabs by the British on the 16th of January 1839.[1] It was attacked by the Abdalis and Fadhlis on the 11th of November in that year, but they were repulsed with the loss of 200 killed and wounded. The united Arab tribes made a second attack on the 22nd of May 1840, but failed after losing many men. On the 5th of July 1840, a third attack took place, but the assailants, Abdalis and Fadhlis, were driven back and lost 300 men. In January 1846 Saiyad Ismail, after preaching a *jihad*, or religious war, in Mecca, attacked this place, but was easily repulsed. In 1858, 'Ali bin Muhsin, Sultan of the Abdalis, gave so much trouble that Brigadier Coghlan, Commandant at Aden, was compelled to march against him, when the Arabs were routed with a loss of from thirty to forty men, and with no casualties on our side. In December 1865, the Sultan of the Fadhli tract, which has a seaboard of 100 m. extending from the boundary of the Abdalis, attempted to blockade Aden on the land side, but was utterly routed by Lieutenant-Colonel Woolcombe, C.B., at Bir Said, 15 m. from the Barrier Gate. A force under Brigadier-General Raines, C.B., then marched through the Abgar districts, which are the lowlands of this tribe, and destroyed several fortified villages. Subsequently, in January 1866, an expedition went from Aden by sea to Shugrah, the chief port of the Fadhlis, 65 m. from Aden, and destroyed the forts there. Since 1867 this tribe, which numbers 6700 fighting men, have adhered to their engagements. The Abdalis inhabit a district 33 m. long and 8 broad to the N.N.W. of Aden, and number about 8000 souls. Their territory is called Lahej, and the capital is Al-Hautah, 21 m. from the Barrier Gate.

It is under contemplation to construct two short railways from Aden to Sahej and Nobat Dakim, and to Shekh Othman and D'thala.

Aden is hot, but healthy. The promontory is about 5 m. long and 3 m. broad, and the highest point on it, the Rock, rises 1700 ft. above the sea. The lighthouse on Ras Marshag, the S.E. point, has a fixed light visible 20 m. off. The town has a population of 46,000, but its trade is slowly decaying. A visit to the bazaar, if the stay of the steamer will allow of this, will show wild Arabs from the interior of Arabian Yemen, Turks, Egyptians, hideous Swahelis from the coast of East Africa, untamed shock-headed Somalis,

[1] Aden was the first addition to the Empire in the reign of the late Queen.

Jews of various sects, inhabitants of India, Parsis, British soldiers, Bombay Mahrattas, and Jack-tars. The Crater used in former days to be the fortress of Aden. Now modern science has converted "Steamer Point" into a seemingly impregnable position, the peninsula which the "Point" forms to the whole Crater being cut off by a fortified line which runs from N. to S. just to the eastward of the coal wharfs. The Port is visited yearly by 1650 steamers, with a tonnage of 3,000,000 tons: the value of the sea trade is very large, over £6,000,000; the income of the Port Trust is 4½ lakhs, and of the Municipality 2 lakhs.

Inside the Light Ship the water shallows to 4 fathoms, and a large steamer stirs up the mud with the keel and action of the screw. As soon as the vessel stops, scores of canoes, with one or two Somali boys in each, paddle off and surround the steamer, shouting, "Have a dive—have a dive," and "Good boy—good boy," all together, with a very strong accent on the first syllable, and dive for small coins flung to them. Owing to a number of fatalities from sharks, this is prohibited in the S.W. monsoon months.

Steamers seldom stop nowadays for more than a few hours at Aden. Notice is always posted on board as to the desirability or not of landing. Transhipment takes place each alternate week in the case of the P. & O. mail steamers to the local Aden-Bombay Express mail steamer *Salsette* (6000 tons).

It takes from twelve to twenty minutes to land at the Post-Office Pier, which is broad and sheltered. To the left of it are the hotels and shops. At a short distance N. of the hotels is a condenser belonging to a private proprietor. There are three such condensers belonging to Government, and several the property of private companies, and by these and an aqueduct from Sheikh Othman, 7 m. beyond the Barrier Gate, Aden is supplied with water. Condensed water costs about Rs.2 per 100 gallons.

The **tanks** under the Peak are worth a visit, but the distance to them is about 5 m. Their restoration was undertaken in 1856, and they are capable of holding 8,000,000 gallons of water. The ravines which intersect the plateau of the crater converge into one valley, and a very moderate fall of rain suffices to send a considerable torrent down it. This water is partly retained in the tanks which were made to receive it, and which are so constructed that the overflow of the upper tank falls into a lower, and so on in succession. As the annual rainfall at Aden does not exceed 6 or 7 in., Malik al Mansur, King of Yaman, at the close of the 15th century built an aqueduct to bring the water of the Bir Hamid into Aden (see Playfair's *History of Yaman*).

The **Salt Pans** on the way to Sheikh Othman are curious. The sea-water is pumped into shallow pans cut out of the earth, and allowed to evaporate, and the salt which remains is collected. It belongs to an Italian company, who pay royalty on every ton of salt procured. The Keith-Falconer Medical Mission at Sheikh Othman, as well as Steamer Point, was established by the Hon. Ion Keith-Falconer, Arabic Professor, Cambridge, who died there. His tomb, of fine Carrara marble, is in the military cemetery of Aden. The Mission under the care of the doctors of the Free Church of Scotland, is most popular. At Steamer Point there are three churches for the troops, Anglican, Scottish, and Roman. In the Crater there are two churches.

After leaving Aden the only land usually approached by steamers bound for India is the **Island of Socotra,** which is about 150 m. E. of Cape Guardafui, the E. point of the African continent. The island is 71 m. long, and 22 broad. Most of the surface is a table-land about 800 ft. above sea-level. The capital is Tamarida or Hadibu, on the N. coast. The population is only 4000, or 4 to the square mile. It is politically a British possession subordinate to Aden, but administered in its internal affairs by its own chiefs.

Four days after passing Socotra, the mainland will be sighted behind Bombay, which lies 6° N. of Aden in lat. 18° 58′ above the Equator, and long. 72° 48′ E. of Greenwich.

(3) GENERAL INFORMATION, STATISTICAL, ETHNOLOGICAL, HISTORICAL, ARCHÆOLOGICAL, AND MATERIAL.

THE PEOPLE OF INDIA

THE census of 1911 gave the population of British India and Burma as follows :—

	Area in Square Miles.	Population.
British	1,087,404	231,624,807
Feudatory	679,393	62,736,249
	1,766,797	294,361,056

Of this total of 294,000,000 about 160,000 are British born, of whom one-half are soldiers. The army of British India comprises:

British Troops	76,000
Native	162,000
	238,000

In addition, there are Native Reserves, 35,000; Imperial Service Troops furnished by Native States, 21,000; and European and Anglo-Indian Volunteers, 37,000, making altogether 93,000 additional men trained by British officers. The Native States have also semi-trained troops to the number of 90,000, which are not included in this list.

The original races in India consisted of the Aborigines, or non-Aryans, and the pure Aryans, or twice-born castes. The bulk of the population now consists of Hindus, a blend of Aryans and non-Aryans, and the great majority of the Mohammedans are sprung from converts of the same stock.

The census of 1901 gave, in round numbers, the following religious statistics :—

Brahmanic	207,146,000	Sikh	2,200,000
Animist (non-Aryan) .	8,711,000	Jain	1,334,000
Mohammedan . . .	62,458,000	Zoroastrian . . .	94,000
Buddhist	9,477,000	Jews	18,000
Christian	2,923,000		

THE MOHAMMEDANS

Mohammed (Muhammad, "the praised") was born at Mecca (Makka) in 570 A.D., his father being a poor merchant who died soon after the birth of his son. When twenty-five years old he became manager or agent to a rich widow, named Khadija, who, although fifteen years his senior, offered him marriage. By her he had two sons who died young, and four daughters, of whom the best known is Fatima. At the age of forty he received the first divine communication in the solitude of the mountain Hira, near Mecca, where the angel Gabriel appeared, and commanded him to preach the new religion. The Meccans persecuted him; his wife and uncle died; and he became poverty-stricken. On 26th June 622 he fled to Medina, where he was accepted as a prophet. From here he made war upon the Meccans, and finally succeeded in capturing Mecca, and was recognised there. He died on the 8th June 632 in Medina, and is buried there.[1]

The chief tenet of the Mohammedan religion is Islam, which means resignation, submission to the will of God. In its dogmatical form it is Imam (faith), in its practical Din (religion). The fundamental principle is, "There is no God but God; and Mohammed is God's prophet." ("Lá illáha illá 'lláh Muhammadun Rasulu 'lláh.") There are four great duties. 1. Daily prayers. (These should take place five times a day—at sunset, nightfall, daybreak, noon, and afternoon.) 2. The giving of alms. 3. The fast of Ramazan. 4. A pilgrimage to Mecca. In the Koran (much of which was dictated by Mohammed), a holy war or *jihad* is enjoined as a religious duty; but the Mohammedan subjects of a Government under which the practices of the Mohammedan religion are freely permitted, are bound to obey that Government. The Mohammedans believe in resurrection, heaven, and hell. In heaven are all manner of sensuous delights. In hell all who deny the unity of God will be tortured eternally. There is a separate heaven for women if they find their way there. Mohammed enjoined care in ablution of the hands, mouth, and nose, before eating or praying. The Koran forbids the drinking of wine or the eating of the flesh of swine. Usury, and games of chance are prohibited, and the laws against idolatry are very stringent. Every man may have four wives, besides concubine slaves, but he must not look upon the face of any other woman except a near relative. Hope and fear, reward and punishment, with a belief in predestination, form the system of faith. It is contrary to

1 Interesting works on the Mohammedan religion are those of Sir William Muir, K.C.S.I., the *Life of Mohammed*, by Mr Justice Amir Ali, and the *Dictionary of Islam*, by the Rev. Mr Hughes, the last of which is a storehouse of information. Sale's *Translation of the Koran* is still the best for the general reader.

the religion of Mohammed to make any figure or representation of anything living. There are two main Mohammedan sects. According to the Sunnis the first four Khalifahs (Khalifah = representative) after Mohammed are Abubakr, Omar, Othman, and Ali in that order. The Shias consider that Ali was the first, excluding the other three.

Eras.—The Mohammedan era of the Hijrah takes its name from the "departure" of Mohammed from Mecca, but commences with the later date of Friday, the 16th of July 622 A.D., ordered by the Khalifah Omar to be used as their era by Mohammedans. Their year consists of twelve lunar months, as follows :—

Muharram . . .	30 days	Rajab	30 days
Safar	29 ,,	Sh'aban . . .	29 ,,
Rabi ul awal . .	30 ,,	Ramazan . . .	30 ,,
Rabi us-sani . .	29 ,,	Shawwal . . .	29 ,,
Jumada ul awal . .	30 ,,	Zilkadah . . .	30 ,,
Jumada us-sani . .	29 ,,	Zil Hijjah . . .	29 ,,

= 354 days.

Their year, therefore, is 11 days short of the solar year, and their New Year's Day is every year 11 days earlier than in the preceding year. In every 30 years the month Zil Hijjah is made to consist 11 times of 30 days instead of 29, which accounts for the 9 hours in the lunar year, which is thus 354 days, 9 hours. To bring the Hijrah year into accordance with the Christian year, express the former in years and decimals of a year, multiply by ·970225, add 621·54, and the total will correspond exactly to the Christian year. Or to effect the same correspondence roughly, deduct 3 per cent. from the Hijrah year, add 621·54, and the result will be the period of the Christian year when the Mohammedan year begins. The current Mohammedan year, 1329 Hijrah, commenced on the 2nd January 1911, and the following four years Hijrah will commence on the 22nd December 1911, 11th December 1912, 30th November 1913, and 1333 Hijrah on 19th November 1914.

The Tarikh Ilahi or Era of Akbar and the Fasli or Harvest Era.

These eras begin from the commencement of Akbar's reign on Friday the 5th of Rabi us-sani, 963 A.H. = 19th of February 1556 A.D.

MOHAMMEDAN FESTIVALS

Bakar (Bull) *'Id*, or *Id-i-Kurban* (sacrifice), held on the 10th of Zil Hijjah in memory of Abraham's offering of Ishmael, which is the version of the Koran. Camels, cows, sheep, goats, kids, or lambs are sacrificed.

Muharram (The Holiest[1]), a fast in remembrance of the death of Hasan and Husain, the sons of 'Ali by Fatima, the daughter of

[1] The name is derived from the corresponding old Arabic month in which it was unholy to wage war.

d

Mohammed. Hasan was poisoned by the Khalif Yezid in 49 A.H. and Husain was murdered at Karbala on the 10th of Muharram, 61 A.H.=9th October 680 A.D. The fast begins on the 1st of Muharram and lasts ten days. Moslems of the Shi'ah persuasion assemble in the T'aziyah Khana, or house of mourning. On the night of the 7th an image of Burak, the animal (vehicle) on which Mohammed ascended to heaven, is carried in procession, and on the 10th Tabuts[1] or Taziyas (biers). These are thrown into the sea, or other water, and in the absence of water are buried in the earth. The mourners move in a circle, beating their breasts with cries of "Ya! Hasan! Ya Husain!" or "Ya Ali!" At this time fanatical spirit is apt to run high, and serious disturbances sometimes take place (see Hobson-Jobson in the *Glossary of Anglo-Indian Words and Phrases*).

Akhir-i-Chahar Shambah, held on the last Wednesday of Safar, when Mohammed recovered a little in his last illness and bathed for the last time. It is proper to write out seven blessings, wash off the ink and drink it, as also to bathe and repeat prayers.

Bari Wafát (The Great Death), held on the 13th of Rabi ul awal in memory of Mohammed's death, 11 A.H.

Shab-i-barát (Night of Record), held on the 16th of Sh'aban, when, according to Mohammedan tradition, men's actions for next year are recorded. The Koran ought to be read all night, and the next day a fast should be observed.

Ramazan[2]*-ki-Rozah*, the month-long fast of the Mohammedans. The night of the 27th is called Lailat-ul-Kadar, "night of power," because the Koran came down from heaven on that night.

'Idu 'l-fitar, the festival when the fast of the Ramazan is broken. The evening is spent in rejoicings.

MOHAMMEDAN RULE IN INDIA

THE first connection of the Mohammedans with India in the 7th and 8th centuries was naturally by the old sea route from the continent of Asia, and from the seat of power of the Khalifate at Baghdad. When this power grew weak, first the Seljuk kingdom broke away from it on the E. and then the kingdoms of Ghazni and Ghor in the Afghan mountains split off in turn from that. Early in the 11th century the N. of India, as far as Benares, Guzerat and Kathiawar, was subjected to repeated invasions by the famous Mahmud of Ghazni; and at the close of the 12th century the Prince of Ghor and

[1] The shape of this is intended to simulate the tomb of Ali at Karbala.

[2] The name is derived from ramaz, burning, this month being the middle summer month in the first Mohammedan year.

his lieutenants effected the permanent conquest and occupation of that part of the country. For three hundred years the Slave dynasty and the other dynasties, chiefly Pathan, which succeeded it, ruled at Delhi and extended their authority to Bengal, and Guzerat, and even to the Deccan; but the repeated invasions of the Mughals on the N., and probably the failure of robust recruits from the Afghan mountains, led to the gradual weakening of the central power, which was finally shaken to its very foundations by the invasion of Timur at end of the 14th century (p. 207); and when a century later Babar and his Mughals conquered India, the Imperial authority had been reduced to very narrow limits. Meanwhile, one Mohammedan dynasty, an off-shoot of the Imperial line, had been established at Gaur, in Bengal (p. 308), at an early date, and another, known as the Bahmani, rather later at Gulbarga in the Deccan (p. 348), when the power of Delhi recoiled from there, and at the close of the 14th century, Mohammedan Governors had also become independent in Guzerat (p. 123), and Malwa (p. 89), and at Jaunpur (p. 276): and thus though, when Babar became Emperor, the Delhi power was being threatened by the revived Hindu forces of Rajputana, N. India generally was under Mohammedan rule at that time. It was then, too, that the Mohammedan kingdoms of Ahmednager, Bijapur, and Golconda (pp. 346, 363, and 378) were founded on the fall of the Bahmani dynasty; and when these kingdoms crushed the only great Hindu power in S. India, that of Vijayanagar (p. 380) at the battle of Talikot in 1565 A.D., about the time, be it remembered, when Spain attained its greatest power, it looked as if Mohammedan sway would be permanently extended to Cape Comorin.

These kingdoms, however, exhausted their energies in internal and internecine quarrels; and when, after subduing the other states of India the Mughal Emperors turned to them, they fell one by one, but in their fall, and through the consequences of it, dragged down the victor to ruin also. While it lasted, the Mughal dynasty was distinguished by extraordinary outward splendour, which extorted the title of the Great Mughal (o grayo Mogor) from the Europeans who witnessed it; and no dynasty, perhaps, since the world began, ever produced six so great princes, take them all in all, as Babar, Humayun, Akbar, Jahangir, Shah Jahan, and Aurangzeb, whose united reigns covered a period of two hundred years. But as its splendour was unparalleled, so was the suddenness and completeness of the fall of the dynasty; and within sixty years of the death of Aurangzeb, the Mahrattas were temporarily masters of Delhi, which was simply rent to death by the invasions of the Persian Nadir Shah and the Afghan Ahmad Shah in 1739 and 1756. It is almost impossible to realise that these invasions, which can be paralleled only by those of Attila and Timur, took place at a time when Europe was entering on the modern phase in which we still live, and N. America was about to become a great separate power.

Between these two dates the kingdoms of Oudh and Hyderabad had become independent of the central Delhi Power; and if the Great Governors of the Panjab did not become so also, this was due simply to their position between the invaders and the capital, and to the presence of the Sikhs in the Province. Neither of the new Mohammedan kingdoms, however, possessed any real vital power; and both of them, and Bengal would have inevitably fallen a prey to the Mahrattas, after their extraordinary recovery from the carnage of Panipat in 1761, but for the intervention of British power. As it was when Delhi was taken from the Mahrattas in 1803, they practically dominated India from the Panjab to Hyderabad and Mysore, and from Guzerat to Orissa. The resumption of Oudh on account of the reckless misgovernment of its rulers, and the conquests of the Mysore dynasty of Hyder Ali and Tipu Sultan, and of the Amirs of Sindh, have left Hyderabad the sole remaining Mohammedan power of first-class importance in India, to which can be added as instances of Mohammedan States of recent origin—Khairpur in Sindh (p. 263), Junagarh in Kathiawar (p. 152), Bahawalpur in the Panjab (p. 261), and Rampur in Rohilkund.

Some Mohammedan Dates affecting India

	A.D.
Birth of Mohammed	570
His departure from Mecca to Medina. The Hijrah era	622
His death	632
Arab invasions of Sindh	637-828
Mahmud of Ghazni defeats the Rajputs at Peshawar	1001
Mahmud captures Somnath in Guzerat, and carries off the temple gates to Ghazni	1025-7
The Tajiks of Ghor capture Ghazni	1152
Mohammed bin Sam, known as Shahabuddin, Ghori, invades the Panjab, and his lieutenant, Kutab-ud-din takes Delhi after the battle of Thanesar, and Kanauj the next year	1193-94
Kutab-ud-din (originally a Turki slave) proclaims himself sovereign of India at Delhi	1206
Altamsh extends the empire of the Slave dynasty	1229
Ala-ud-din conquers Southern India; defeats several Mughal invasions from Central Asia	1295-1315
Mohammed Tughlak seeks to establish a southern capital at Deogiri	1330-40
Timur, or Tamerlane, sacks Delhi	1398
Babar the Mughal, sixth in descent from Timur, defeats the Pathan (Lodi) Sultans of Delhi at the battle of Panipat	1524
Babar defeats the Rajputs at Fatehpur Sikri, near Agra	1527
Akbar defeats the Pathans at Panipat	1556
Akbar conquers the Rajputs, annexes Bengal, Guzerat, Sindh, Kashmir, and Kandahar	1561-94

	A.D.
Death of Akbar at Agra	1605
Reign of Jahangir	1605-27
Reign of Shah Jahan	1627-58
Reign of Aurangzeb	1658-1707
Commencement of the struggle between the Mughal Emperor and the Mahrattas	1688
Aurangzeb captures Sambhaji, the son of the Mahratta chief Sivaji, and puts him to death	1689
Death of Aurangzeb; decline of the Mughal power	1707
Rajputana lost to the Mughals	1715
Defeat and persecution of the Sikhs. The Mughals put their leader Banda to death with cruel tortures	1716
Kabul severed from the Mughals	1738
Nadir Shah, King of Persia, sacks Delhi	1739
The Mahrattas obtain Malwa; Oudh becomes independent of Delhi	1743
Hyderabad becomes independent	1748
The Mahrattas obtain Southern Orissa, and tribute from Bengal	1751
Invasion of the Afghan Ahmad Shah Durani, and cession of Panjab to him	1751-2
Ahmad Shah Durani sacks Delhi	1756
The Mahrattas capture Delhi	1759
Defeat of the Mahrattas by the Afghans at the battle of Panipat	1761
General Lake captures Delhi	1803

List of Sovereigns who reigned at Delhi from 1193 to 1837 A.D.

The Ghori (Tajik), Turki and Pathan Kings of Hindustan who reigned at Delhi.

	A.H.	A.D.
Muhammad bin Sam, Ghori	589	1193
Kutab-ud-din, *1st Dynasty* of Slave (Turki) Kings	602	1206
Aram Shah	607	1210
Shams-ud-din Altamsh	607	1211
Rukn-ud-u-din Firoz	633	1236
Sultan Raziyah	634	1236
Balban	664	1266
Kaikubad	686	1289
Jelal-ud-din Firoz Shah Khilji, *2nd Dynasty*, Pathan	689	1290
Ala-ud-din Muhammad	695	1296
Shahab-ud-din 'Umar	715	1316
Kutab-ud-din Mubarak	716	1316
Nasir-ud-din Khusru	720	1321
Ghias-ud-din Tughlak *3rd Dynasty*, Pathan	720	1321
Muhammad bin Tughlak	725	1325
Firoz Shah Tughlak	752	1351
Muhammad Shah	793	1391
Khizr Khan Saiyad, *4th Dynasty*, Saiyad	817	1414
Mubarak Shah II.	824	1421
Muhammad Shah	837	1434
'Alam Shah	849	1445
Bahlol Lodi, *5th Dynasty*, Pathan	855	1451
Sikandar Lodi	894	1489
Ibrahim Lodi	923	1517

The Mughal Emperors of Hindustan

	A.H.	A.D.
Babar	899	1494
Humayun [1]	937	1531
Akbar	963	1556
Jahangir	1014	1605
Shah Jahan	1037	1628
Aurangzeb	1068	1658
Bahadur Shah	1118	1707
Jahandar Shah	1124	1713
Farrukhsiyar	1124	1713
Muhammad Shah	1131	1719
'Ahmad Shah	1162	1748
Alamgir II.	1168	1754
Shah Alam	1173	1759
Akbar II.	1221	1806
Bahadur Shah	1252	1837-1857

THE HINDUS

THE first form of the Hindu religion was Vedism, the worship of Nature, as represented in the songs and prayers collectively called Veda, and in which the chief gods were the triad Indra (rain), Agni (fire), and Surya (sun). Then followed Brahmanism, from *brih*, to expand, which introduced the idea of a universal spirit, or essence, which permeated everything, men, gods, and the visible world being merely its manifestations. Prose works, called Brahmanas, were added to the Vedas, to explain the sacrifices, and the duties of the Brahmans, or priests. The oldest of these may have been written about 1000-1200 B.C. The code of Manu, which is believed to have originated several centuries before the Christian era, lays down the rules of domestic conduct and ceremony. It divides Hindus into four castes.[2] First, the Brahmans; second, the warriors, called Kshattriyas or Rajputs, literally "of the royal stock"; and third, the agriculturists and traders, called Vaisyas. All these being of Aryan descent, were honoured by the name of the Twice-born castes. Fourth, were the Sudras, or conquered non-Aryan tribes, who had become serfs. They were not allowed to be present at the great national sacrifices, or at the feasts, and they were given the severest toil in the fields, and the dirty work of the village community. The priests asserted that they, the Brahmans, came from the mouth of Brahma; the Rajputs or Kshattriyas from his arms; the Vaisyas from his thighs; and the Sudras from his feet. Caste was originally a

[1] This reign includes the Pathan Interregnum of Sher Shah (1540-45) Salim Shah, and other Sur Kings up to 1555.

[2] Much interesting information regarding the early Hindu peoples of India will be found in Mr R. C. Dutt's *Ancient India*, Mr V. E. Smith's *Early History of India*, and vol. ii. of the *Imperial Gazetteer* (1908).

PLATE 1.

Some Common Forms of Hindu Gods.

[*To face* p. liv.

PLATE 2.

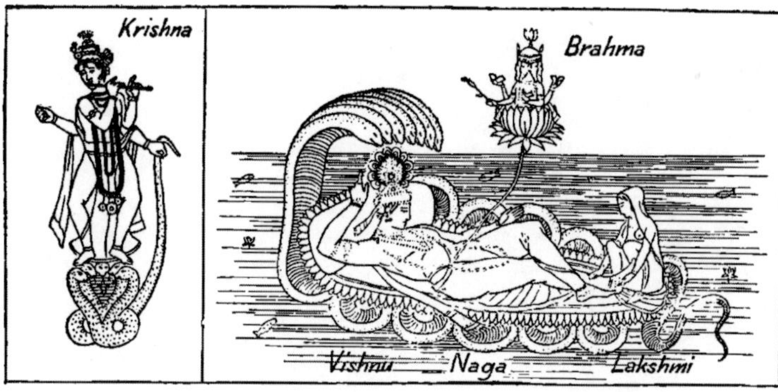

Caste Marks.

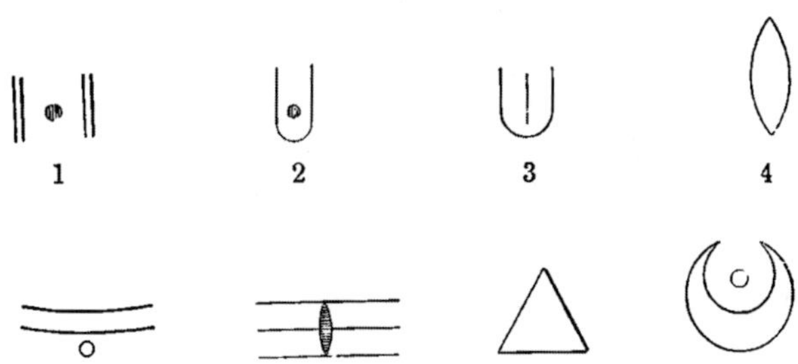

1, 2, 3, and 4, *Followers of Vishnu.*
5, 6, 7, and 8, *Followers of Siva.*

Buddha

To follow Plate 1 *after* p. liv.

distinction between priest, soldier, artizan, and menial. Each trade in time came to have a separate caste; and the priests insisted on the rules of caste as a means of securing their own special supremacy.

The modern Hindu religion is a development of Brahmanism. There is one impersonal and spiritual Being[1] which pervades everything—one God, called Brahma. His three personal manifestations are as *Brahma*, the Creator; *Vishnu*, the Preserver; and *Shiva*, the Destroyer and Reproducer. *Brahma*, the Creator, is generally represented with four heads and four arms, in which he holds a portion of the Veda, a spoon for lustral observations, a rosary, and a vessel of lustral water (see Plate 1). *Saraswati*, the wife of Brahma, rides on a peacock, and has a musical instrument, the "vina," in her arms (see Plate 1). She is the goddess of music, speech, the arts, and literature. The sin of lying is readily expiated by an offering to her.

Vishnu holds a quoit in one hand, a conch shell in another, and sometimes a mace or club in another, and a lotus flower in a fourth (see Plate 1). A common picture shows him with his wife, Lakhshmi, sitting on Shesh, the snake (eternity), with Brahma on a lotus springing from his navel (see Plate 2). He is said to have come down to the earth nine times, and is expected a tenth time. These nine incarnations (*avatara*) were in the form of—(1) a fish; (2) a tortoise; (3) a boar (Varaha); (4) a man lion (Narsingh); (5) a dwarf (Vamana); (6) Parasu rama; (7) *Rama*, the hero of the epic poem, the *Ramayana*; (8) *Krishna;* and (9) Buddha.

Rama carries a bow and arrows (see Plate 1). He is revered throughout India as the model of a son, a brother, and a husband. When friends meet it is common for them to salute each other by uttering Rama's name twice. No name is more commonly given to children, or more commonly invoked at funerals and in the hour of death. His ally, *Hanuman* (p. lviii.) is represented under a monkey form smeared with vermilion (see Plate 1). He is worshipped as the model of a faithful devoted servant.

Krishna's biography is given in the epic of the *Mahabharata*. Although himself a powerful chief, he was brought up among peasants, and is peculiarly the god of the lower classes. As a boy he killed the serpent Kali by trampling upon his head. He lifted the mountain-ridge of Govardhan (p. 167) on his finger to shelter the herdsmen's wives from the wrath of Indra, the Vedic rain-god. He had countless wives and sons, and is painted blue, and stands on a snake, with his

1 "Principio coelum ac terras, camposque liquentes,
Lucentemque globum Lunae, Titaniaque astra
Spiritus intus alit, totamque infusa per artus
Mens agitat molem et magno se corpore miscet."
Virgil, Aen., VI. 726.

left hand holding its body, and a lotus in his right (see Plate 2). Sometimes he is playing the flute.

The adoption of Buddha as one of the incarnations was a compromise with Buddhism. On the last occasion Vishnu will descend as an armed warrior on a winged white horse, and will dissolve the universe at the close of the fourth or Kali age, of 432,000 years, when the world has become wholly depraved.

Devotion to Vishnu in his human incarnations of Rama and Krishna (who were real men) is the most popular form of the Hindu religion in India. His descents upon earth were for the delivery of men from the three-fold miseries of life, viz. (1) from lust, anger, avarice, and their evil consequences; (2) from beasts, snakes, and wicked men; (3) from demons. Vishnu has power to elevate his worshippers to eternal bliss in his own heaven.

Vishnu's wife *Lakhshmi*, the goddess of wealth and beauty, sprang from the froth of the ocean when churned by gods and demons (see Plate 1). An image of her is often to be found in the houses of shop-keepers.

Shiva is also called Mahadeva, the great god, and his wife who is known by several names and in several characters as Parvati, the goddess of beauty (see Plate 1), Durga or Kali, the terrible (see Plate 1), etc., is also called Devi, *the* goddess (see Plate 1). The commonest of these is *Kali*,[1] who requires to be propitiated by sacrifices. Shiva holds in his four hands, a trident, an antelope, a noose for binding his enemies, and a kind of drum, and wears a tiger's skin about the loins. He is a less human and more mystical god than Vishnu, and is worshipped in the form of a symbol, the *lingam*, or a bull (*Nandi*, the Joyous). As destroyer Shiva haunts cemeteries and burning-grounds, but his terrible qualities are now more especially associated with his wife Kali. He is the impersonation of the reproductive power of nature,[2] the word Shiva meaning "blessed" or "auspicious." He is also the typical ascetic and self-mortifier; and as a learned philosopher he is the chief god of the priests.

Shiva has two sons Ganesh, or Ganpati, and Kartikkeya. *Ganesh* has a fat body and an elephant's head (see Plate 1). He is a great favourite, being worshipped for good luck or success, and as a bringer of success he is invoked at the beginning of every Indian book, *Kartikkeya* has six heads and twelve arms, and is the god of war, the leader of the hosts of good demons (see Plate 1). In the south of India he is called Skanda or Subrahmanya.

[1] In S. India Durga in this form is generally known as Bhawáni (vulg. Bowáni).

[2] Probably two-thirds of the Hindus worship Shiva under this aspect embodied in the lingam.

The Hindu theory of metempsychosis, or transmigration of souls, arises from the belief that evil proceeds from antecedent evil, and that the penalty must be suffered in succeeding existences. According to Hindu belief there are eighty-four lakhs of different species of animals through which the soul of a man is liable to pass, and the Hindu's object is to get rid of the series of perpetual transmigrations, so that he may live in the same heaven with the personal god. To this end he makes offerings to the image of a god, Krishna, Ganesh, or Kali being the most generally selected; he abstains from killing any animal; he gives money to the priests; and does penances which sometimes extend to severe bodily torture. His religion amounts to little more than the fear of demons, of the loss of caste, and of the priests. Demons have to be propitiated, the caste rules strictly kept, and the priests presented with gifts. Great care has to be taken not to eat food cooked by a man of inferior caste; food cooked in water must not be eaten together by people of different castes, and the castes are entirely separated with regard to marriage and trades. A sacred thread of cotton is worn by the higher castes. Washing in any holy river, particularly the Ganges, and more especially at Allahabad, Benares, Hardwar, and other exceptionally sacred spots, is of great efficacy in cleansing the soul of impurities. Most of these observances, and the worshipping of idols are rejected by the Arya Samaj,[1] a reformed body founded by Swami Dyanand (1827-1853), which is attracting many of the educated Hindus in N. India. The Arya Samaj accepts the inspiration of the Vedas only; the chief Brahmo Samajists, mainly confined to Bengal (p. 65), reject them as inspired scriptures.

Travellers should remember that all who are not Hindus are outcasts, contact with whom may cause the loss of caste to a Hindu. They should not touch any cooking or water-holding utensil belonging to a Hindu, nor disturb Hindus when at their meals; and they should not seek to approach any holy place if objection is made. The most sacred of all animals is the cow; crocodiles and other animals at holy places, and trees, plants, stones, rivers, and tanks are also sacred. The eagle (Garuda) is the attendant of Vishnu, the bull of Shiva, the goose of Brahma, the elephant of Indra, the tiger of Durga, the buffalo of Rama, the rat of Ganesh, the ram of Agni, the peacock of Kartikkeya, and the parrot of Kama (the god of love).

As many references to the *Mahabharata* and *Ramayana* occur in the *Handbook*, a brief account of these two famous epics is given here.

The *Mahabharata* of Vyasa composed about 500 A.D. but recording events which may be referred to about 1000 B.C., celebrates

[1] The number of Arya Samajists at the late census was 90,000, of Brahmo Samajists only 3,000.

the battle between the Pandava (Pandu) and Kaurava (Kuru) princes. The former, five in number, and named Yudisthara, Bhima, and Arjan, sons of one mother, and Vakula and Sahadeva, sons of another, were the offspring of Pandu, ruler of Hastinapur, an ancient city on the Ganges, 60 m. N.W. of Delhi, who ceded the kingdom to his elder, but blind brother, Dhrita-rashtra. The latter were the sons of Dhrita-rashtra, and compelled him to send their cousins into exile, during which the marriage of Draupadi took place, and most of the adventures which led to their names being attached to so many places all over India. At the end of their exile the Pandavas received the southern portion of the Hastinapur kingdom, and settled at Indraprastha, now Indrapat (p. 204). Having lost this share of their inheritance through gambling with their cousins, the Pandavas again went into exile for twelve years, after which they returned with an army and claimed five "pats" or small towns of their former kingdom (Indrapat, Tilpat, Sonepat, Bhagpat, and Panipat). Over this claim the great battle ensued, in which, after eighteen days, nearly all the Kauravas were finally killed, largely through treacherous acts on the part of the Pandavas. The account of the funeral ceremonies of the slain is famous and almost Homeric. The five brothers then resumed their residence at Indrapat, and Yudisthara celebrated the Aswamedh, or horse sacrifice of imperial rule on the bank of the Jumna. Finally, the brethren and their wives retired to the Himalayas, and sought to reach Mount Meru; but only the elder brother won through to there, and he declined to enter when admittance was refused to his sole remaining companion, a faithful dog.

The *Ramayaña*, ascribed to Valmiki, and also probably composed about the 5th century B.C., relates the adventures of Rama, elder son of a king of Oudh, who was postponed in the succession to the son of a younger wife, and banished by his father. Rama accordingly proceeded into exile with his wife Sita, to the abode of the hermit Valmiki; and, though the younger brother proved loyal to him on his father's death, he refused to return to Oudh until the term of his banishment had expired. Before this Sita was carried off from their forest abode by Ravana, king of Ceylon, inspired by his sister, whose love Rama had rejected. She was rescued from Ceylon by Rama with the help of Hanuman, the monkey general, and proved her chastity by the ordeal of fire; but (according to a later addition) was banished by her husband, and remained sixteen years in exile with Valmiki, after which she was finally reconciled to Rama. Rama is commonly known in India as Ram Chandra; his brother Lakhshman constantly appears in the local legends which relate to him

The Kali-Yug, or Hindu Era

According to the Hindus, the world is now in its fourth Yug, or Age, the Kali-Yug, which commenced from the Equinox in 18th Feb. 3102 B.C., and will last 432,000 years. The three preceding ages were the Satya, the Treta, and the Dwapara. The Satya, or Age of Truth, lasted 1,728,000 years; the Treta (from *tra*, "to preserve") lasted 1,296,000; and the Dwapara (from *dwa*, "two," and *par*, "after") 864,000 years.

The Era of Vikramaditya, Samwat or Samvat

This era commenced from the first year of the legendary King Vikramaditya, fabled to have reigned at Ujjain 57 B.C. It is in ordinary use in N. India. The present Bikramajit year, as it is usually called, is 1967-8, and begins on 23rd October 1911.

The Shaka Era or Era of Shalivahana

Shalivahana [having a sháli (lion) for his vehicle *vahana*], was a king who reigned in the S. of India. The Shaka era dates from his birth 78 A.D. This is the era in general use in S. India. The present year of it, 1834, commenced on 9th March 1911.

The Hindu year has six seasons or *ritus: Vasanta*, "spring"; *grishma*, "the hot season"; *varsha*, "the rains"; *sharada*, "the autumn" (from *shri*, "to wither"); *hemanta*, "the winter"; *shishira*, "the cool season."

Table of the Seasons and Months in Sanskrit, Hindi, and English.

	NAMES OF MONTHS.		
	SANSKRIT.	HINDI.	ENGLISH.
1. VASANTA .	Chaitra (Aries).	Chait.[1]	April.
	Vaishakha.	Baisakh.	May.
2. GRISHMA .	Iyeshtha (Gemini).	Jeth.	June.
	A'shadha.	Asarh.	July.
3. VARSHA .	Sravana (Leo).	Sawan.	August.
	Bhadra (Virgo).	Bhadon.	September.
4. SHARADA .	Ashwina.	Asoj.	October.
	Kartika.	Kartik.	November.
5. HEMANTA .	Margasirsha.	Aghan.	December.
	Pausha.	Pus.	January.
6. SHISHIRA .	Magha.	Magh.	February.
	Phalguna (Pisces).	Phagun.	March.

[1] The Indian months begin about the 15th of the English month; thus Pús is the latter half of January and the first half of February, and so with all the other months.

HINDU FESTIVALS

Makar Sankranti.—On the 1st of the month Magh (about 12th January) the sun enters the sign Capricorn or Makar. From this day till the arrival of the sun at the N. point of the zodiac the period is called Uttarayana, and from that time till he returns to Makar is Dakshinayana, the former period being lucky and the latter unlucky. At this festival the Hindus bathe, and rub themselves with sesamum oil. They also invite Brahmans, and give them pots full of sesamum seed. They wear new clothes with ornaments, and distribute sesamum seed mixed with sugar.

Vasant Panchami is on the 5th day of the light half of Magh, and is a festival in honour of Vasanta or Spring.

Shivarat, the night of Shiva, is held about the middle or end of February, when Shiva is worshipped with flowers during the whole night.

Holi.—A festival in honour of Krishna, held fifteen days before the moon is at its full, in the month Phagun, celebrated with the squirting or throwing of red or yellow powder over every one. It is a kind of carnival, and all sorts of licence are indulged in.

Ashadhi Ekadashi, the 11th of the month Asarh, sacred to Vishnu, when that deity reposes for four months.

Nag Panchami, held on the 5th of Sawan, when the serpent Kali is said to have been killed by Krishna. Ceremonies are performed to avert the bite of snakes.

Janam Ashtami, held on the 8th of the dark half of Sawan, when Krishna is said to have been born at Gokul (p. 166). Rice may not be eaten on this day, but fruits and other grains. At night Hindus bathe and worship an image of Krishna, adorning it with *tulsi* or *basil.*

Ganesh Chaturthi, held on the 4th of Bhadon, in honour of Ganesh, a clay image of the god being worshipped and Brahmans entertained. The Hindus are prohibited from looking at the moon on this day, and if by accident they should see it, they get themselves abused by their neighbours to remove the curse.

Dasahara (*Dashaha*, or ten days, commonly Dusserah), held on the 10th of Asoj, in honour of Durga, or Devi, the wife of Shiva, whom on this day slew the buffalo-headed demon Maheshasur. On this day Rama marched against Ravana, and for this reason the Marathas chose it for their expeditions. Branches of the *Butea frondosa* are offered at the temples. This is an auspicious day for sending children to school. The nine preceding days are called Navaratra, when Brahmans are paid to recite hymns to Durga. The Durga Puja holiday is the principal holiday of the year in Bengal.

Diwali, "feast of lamps," from *diwa*, "a lamp," and *avali*, "a row," held on the new moon of Kartik, in honour of Kali or Bhawani, and more particularly of Lakhshmi, the goddess of prosperity, when merchants and bankers count their wealth and worship it. It is said that Vishnu killed a giant on that day, and the women went to meet him with lighted lamps. In memory of this, lighted lamps are displayed from all houses, and are set afloat in rivers and in the sea, and auguries are drawn from them according as they shine on or are extinguished.

Kartik Ekadashi, held on the 11th of Kartik, in honour of Vishnu, who is said then to rise from a slumber of four months.

HINDU RULE IN INDIA

The settlement in N. India of the Aryans, whose creed slowly developed into what is now known as Hinduism, took place gradually between 2000-800 B.C. The main colonies up to the time of the Mohammedan invasions were located along the valleys of the Panjab and of the Jumna and Ganges ; and though some were pushed further S. into the peninsular, the people and the rulers of that part of the country remained mainly aboriginal, and were gradually absorbed inside the Hindu pale. Of both the stocks which combine to make the mass of the Indian people there were many Ruling Houses, most of which from the time of Buddha and Alexander are known to us from one source or another, but hardly one of which has left any substantial memorials, if the Buddhist relics of antiquity and a few old Hindu temples be excepted. Indeed it is one of the curious facts of the East that while the people are so immutable, the dynasties are extraordinarily ephemeral. The mention of only a few of the chief who ruled in the fifteen hundred years previous to the Mohammedan invasions would include the Nandas and Guptas of the Ganges Valley, the Scythian Kanishka and his successors at Peshawar (p. 245), Vikramaditya and Salivahana in Malwa (p. 91), the Anhilvara and Valabhi kings of Patan and Kathiawar (pp. 131 and 151), the Chalukyas, who held sway from Guzerat to Mysore (p. 24), the various rulers of Orissa (p. 323), the Telanga kings who governed on the Godaveri (p.379*b*), and the great Andhra, Chola, and Chera kingdoms of the S. situated on the Kistna, at Tanjore and in the extreme point of the peninsular. Not only all these, but all the Hindu Kingdoms which were in existence in 1000 B.C., have passed away ; and now, in the 20th century, the oldest Hindu Ruling Houses of India, those of Rajputana, can trace the origin of their present States only from the time of the Mohammedan conquest, while the beautiful capitals of these States are nearly all of a much later period, Jodhpur and Udaipur dating from the middle of the 15th and 16th centuries, and Jaipur from the 18th. Owing partly to the protection afforded by the desert country which surrounded them, and partly to their strong feudal organisation, the Rajput States maintained a really independent position during the first three centuries of Mohammedan Rule, and were able to secure one of subordinate independence under the Mughal Emperors, while the other Hindu Kingdoms of India were being gradually conquered, and the minor Mohammedan States absorbed; and just when this process must have seemed to the ruling race to be complete, the harsh and ruthless treatment of the Rajputs and Mahrattas by the Emperor Aurangzeb evoked an outbreak of Hindu feeling which proved the principal cause of the downfall of the Mughal Empire. The older fashioned chivalrous temperament of the Rajputs was, however, no match for the vigour and hardihood of the younger nation; and when British interference practically checked an Imperial Mahratta domination in India, it also saved the Rajput States from destruction. Of the other great Hindu Ruling Houses of India now existing, Mysore was restored by the British Power at the end of the 18th century (p. 388), while the State of Jammu and Kashmir was created only sixty years ago. The Sikh Ruling States (see p. 223), which date from the middle of the 18th century, owe their present existence to British protection against Maharaja Ranjit Singh, and the great Mahratta States (p. lxix.) are of but slightly longer pedigree than these. The older States of Travancore and Cochin, protected for so long by their remote position, would inevitably have fallen to the Mysore Mohammedan dynasty had that survived, or to the Mahrattas, but for the advent of the British power. As would be expected, the old-world Hindu customs, apart from mere religious observances, have survived to a greater extent in Rajputana than in any other part of India; and the traveller who, by means of a special introduction to the Resident or Political Agent, has the opportunity of properly observing them for a short time at one of the more remote Rajput capitals, will find his interest amply rewarded.

THE BUDDHISTS

Gautama, afterwards called Buddha (the Enlightened), was born in the 6th century B.C. His father was a prince of the Sakya tribe, and of a Rajput clan located in the N. of the present Gorakhpur District. On one occasion Gautama met a man bowed with age; then a man stricken with disease; then a corpse; and finally an ascetic walking in a calm and dignified manner. Much troubled by the spectacle of human suffering, he decided to leave his happy home, his loved wife, and the child which had just been born to him; and cutting off his long hair and exchanging his princely raiment for the rags of a passer-by, he departed from his palace as a homeless beggar. This is called the Great Renunciation. He studied under two Brahman hermits in the Patna district, who taught him to mortify the body. For six years he inflicted severe austerities upon himself; but no peace of mind or divine enlightenment came. He thereupon gave up penance and sat in meditation under a tree (the Pipal), at Buddh Gaya (p. 37), where he was tempted by Mara, the personification of carnal desire, to return to the world, but he resisted, and thus became the Enlightened. He died at a great age about 508 B.C.; part of his ashes have been recently discovered at Pipráwá (p. 313), and Peshawar (p. 247).

Buddha taught that all life is suffering; that suffering arises from indulging desires, especially the desire for continuity of life; and that the only hope of relief lies in the suppression of desire and the extinction of existence. A man's object should be to become enlightened by meditation and introspection, so as to earn a cessation of the cycle of lives through which he would otherwise be destined to pass, and thus finally to reach *Nirvana*, which puts an end to all re-birth. In this task he must depend upon himself alone, and not upon any spiritual aid or guidance. All men are capable of attaining Nirvana, without distinction of caste, and neither sacrifices nor bodily mortifications are of any avail. The creed is a pessimist and atheist one to which, however, excellent moral rules have been attached. Buddhism gave some encouragement to education; it inculcated universal benevolence and compassion; and stimulated exertion by declaring that a man's future depended, not upon sacrifices and self-torture, but upon his own acts. It is "the embodiment of the eternal verity that as a man sows he will reap; associated with the personal duties of mastery over self and kindness to all men; and quickened into a popular religion by the example of a noble and beautiful life" (Sir W. W. Hunter). The real spread of the Buddhist religion dates from the reign of Asoka (272-231 B.C.), who ruled over all India north of a line drawn west from Nellore, and whose work will be found at the Sanchi Tope (p. 98), and Buddh Gaya (p. 37), and whose famous rock edicts, inscribed under his title of Priyadarsi, exist still at Girnar (p. 155), at Dhauli, near Bhuvaneshvar (p. 328), and at Shahbazgarhi, close to Hoti Mardan (p. 246); monolithic columns, lats, erected by him with a portion of the edicts, will be seen at Allahabad (p. 32), and Delhi (p. 203-4). These edicts, deciphered by the genius of Henry Prinsep, embody for the most part the moral rules of Buddhism: they forbid the shedding of blood; inculcate obedience to parents, charity, and rules of conduct; refer to the appointment of censors of morals and missionaries, and the creation of hospitals, roads, and wells; and conclude with prayers for the spread of Buddhism. As well remarked by Professor

Petersen, the creed of Asoka might be summed up in the beautiful lines of the *Ancient Mariner*—

> "He prayeth best who loveth best
> All things, both great and small;
> For the dear God, who loveth us,
> He made and loveth all."

The edicts are of great interest as mentioning the Chola, Pandya, and Kerala kingdoms of the South; and the Yavan (Greek) kings, Turmayaparni (Ptolemy), Antiyochena (Antiochus), Maka (Magus), and Alikasandare. The full number of general edicts is fourteen, but there are also additional ones at Dhauli and Shahbazgarhi. Those specially interested in the subject will find the edicts in vol. i. of the *Corpus Inscriptionum Indicarum.* Buddhism, which became divided into two great sects, the Hinayana and Mahayana,[1] never ousted Brahmanism from India, but the two systems existed together from about B.C. 500 to A.D. 800, when the former disappeared from the open country of the peninsula, but maintained itself in the Himalayas, and in Burma, and Ceylon. Ordinary travellers are likely to come across Buddhists only in the latter places, and at Darjeeling, and to the north of Kashmir. Besides the books named on p. xxvii, the works on Buddhism by Bishop Bigandet, Bishop Coplestone, Dr Waddell and Professor Rhys Davids' *Buddhist India* (Story of Nation series), may be consulted. The best account of the Buddhist religion as it actually affects the lives of the Burmese, will be found in Sir G. Scott's book, *The Burman: His Life and Notions.*

Buddha is generally represented in one of three attitudes; he sits cross-legged, either with his hands in contact in an attitude of profound meditation, or with one hand pointing to the earth, or with both hands raised in the preaching posture. His ears sometimes reach to his shoulders (see Plate 2).

THE JAINS

The small sect of Jains (=conquerors [of vice]) still survives in India. Their founder was Mahavira, a contemporary of Gautama. They are divided into two schools, the Digambara (sky clad or naked) and Swetambara (white clad). The Jains consider bodily penance to be necessary to salvation; and believe that even inorganic matter has a soul, and that a man's soul may pass into a stone. They carry the Buddhist's concern for animal life to an extreme. The figures of their Saints or Tirthankars are naked. The chief of these were the first Adinath, and the last three Nemnath, Parasnath, and Mahavira. Each is known by a symbol, see p. 112. They will be met principally in Ahmedabad and elsewhere in the Bombay Presidency. For their temples consult p. lxxiii.

[1] The names mean the Lesser and Greater Vehicle—the latter sect arose 500 years after Buddha and prevailed in S. India.

BUDDHIST FESTIVALS

The New Year Festival corresponds to the Makar-Sankranti of the Hindus (see p. lx.), but in Burma it often takes place as late as April. At a given moment, which is ascertained by the astrologers of Mandalay, a cannon is fired off, announcing the descent of the King of the Naths (genii) upon earth. Then begin the Saturnalia.

The last birth of Gautama is celebrated at the end of April by the worship of his images, followed by processions. In Ceylon the coming of the Buddha to the island is celebrated by a festival in March or April, when the pilgrims visit either his footprint on Adam's Peak, or the sacred Bo-tree at Anuradhapura.

SOME EARLY HINDU AND BUDDHIST DATES.

	B.C.
The Vedas and hymns . . . . (probably between)	1500-1000
The *Mahabharata*, an epic poem of the heroic age in Northern India; and the *Ramayana*, an epic poem relating to the Aryan advance into South India. Both about	500
The code of Manu laying down the laws and ceremonies for Brahmans, of uncertain age, but perhaps dating from . . .	600-200
Birth of Gautama Buddha (the Enlightened) . . . (probably)	558
Death of Buddha: First Great Council of Buddhists . (probably)	487
Second Great Buddhist Council	378
Alexander the Great crosses the Indus near Attock; defeats Porus at the passage of the Jhelum (Hydaspes); captures Mooltan, where he is severely wounded; and then retires to Persia *viâ* the Indus and Baluchistan, leaving Greek garrisons behind him .	322-298
Chandra Gupta Mauriya (Sandra Cottus), conquers the Gangetic valley	316
Chandra Gupta receives the Greek ambassador, Megasthenes .	306
Asoka, grandson of Chandra Gupta, is converted to Buddhism .	257
Asoka convenes the third Buddhist Council at Patna, and disseminates the principles of the faith	244
The era of Samwat dates from Vikramaditya, of Ujjain, fabled to have withstood the Scythians. The drama of *Sakuntala or the Lost Ring*	57
Indo-Bactrian Kings	100 B.C.-300 A.D.
	A.D.
The Northern, Hinayana, form of Buddhism becomes one of the State religions of China	65
The era of Saka dates from Salivahana	78
The fourth and last Buddhist Council held under King Kanishka (about)	140
Gupta Dynasty, Invasion of the White Huns	320-450
Pilgrimage of the Chinese Traveller, Fa Hiang, to Buddhist shrines in India	406-11
Similar Pilgrimage of the Chinese Traveller Hiouen Thsang . .	629-45
Sankaracharya, the great apostle of Saivism in S. India, c. . .	750
The Vishnuite doctrines embodied in the Vishnu Purana . .	1045
Sect of Lingayats founded	1150
Kabir preaches his doctrine	1400
Birth of Nanak Shah, a Hindu reformer, who preaches the abolition of caste and establishes the Sikh religion	1469

THE SIKHS

THE Sikhs[1] are a reformed sect of Hindus who follow a teacher named Nanak Shah, born near Lahore in 1469. The word Sikh means a "disciple" of the Guru or teacher. Except in denouncing idolatry and in welcoming all ranks without distinction of caste, Nanak's philosophy was very similar to that of the worshippers of Vishnu. Guru Govind finally abolished caste, established the Sikh religion on a political and military basis, stimulated the worship of the Granth, or holy book, which is now the principal object of the Sikh devotions, and definitely established the Khálsa (=select, and so elect), as the Sikh brotherhood is called. (See p. 226.)

In the middle of the 18th century the Sikhs, who had been gradually rising into power, struggled with the Afghans for supremacy in the Panjab and finally won it. In 1716 their last Guru, Banda, had been tortured to death by the Mughals; but in 1763 they avenged his fate by destroying Sirhind utterly. The next year, in 1764, they fought a long and doubtful battle with the Afghan Ahmad Shah Durani in the vicinity of Amritsar, and on his retirement they took Lahore, which soon became the centre of their power, Amritsar being the religious centre. The government was at first in the hands of a number of confederacies, or *misls*, which were gradually absorbed by Ranjit Singh of the Sukarchakia Misl, who finally became Maharaja and the head of the Sikhs. Ranjit Singh died in 1839, and his son Kharak Singh and his grandson Nao Nehal Singh died in November the next year, the latter from injuries received from the fall of a gateway as he was returning from the funeral of his father. After an interval Maharaja Sher Singh became ruler of Lahore and was murdered in September 1843 by the Sindhanwallia Sirdars, who also killed the Prime Minister, Raja Dhian Singh, of Jammu; and upon this Dhalip Singh, a putative son of Maharaja Ranjit Singh, succeeded. His mother Rani Jindan attempted to rule through Hira Singh, son of Dhian Singh, Jowahir Singh, her brother, and Lal Singh, her lover, but the first two of these were murdered, and the real power in the state rested with the army and with Raja Gulab Singh of Jammu. To relieve themselves of their embarrassments with the former the Rani and her counsellors encouraged a war with the British, against whom various causes of complaint were alleged, and finally, the army breaking away from all control, crossed the Sutlej at Hari ki, early in December 1845, and invaded the Ferozepore territory. Upon this followed the first Sikh war, which was ended by the battle of Sobraon on 10th February 1846 (p. 147), the Jullundur Doab being annexed to the British possessions, and Kashmir being

[1] Pronounce like "seeks."

transferred to Gulab Singh, now Maharaja, upon payment by him of the war indemnity. The administration of the rest of the Panjab was placed under a council of regency on behalf of the minor Maharaja Dhalip Singh, subject to the advice of the Resident in Lahore, first Sir Henry Lawrence and then Sir Fred. Currie. Matters were progressing as well as could be expected when the incident of Multan (p. 260) occurred in May 1848, upon which the Sikh soldiery and people rose in defence of their national cause. Serious operations against them were not taken till December, when, after unsatisfactory skirmishes at Ramnagar and Sadulapur (22nd November and 3rd December 1848), the battle of Chillianwalla was fought on 13th January 1849 (p. 242), and the victory of Gujrat (p. 241) was won on 21st February. Since then the Sikhs have been among the most loyal subjects of the Indian Empire, of which they proved the main support in 1857, and provide some of the best recruits of the Indian army.

The following is a chronological table of the Sikh Gurus. Guru Govind refused to name a successor. He said .—"He who wishes to behold the Guru, let him search the Granth."

Gurus of the Sikhs

		A.D.
1.	Nanak, founder of the Sikh sect, born 1469, died	1539
2.	Angad	1552
3.	Amar Das	1552
4.	Ram Das, builder of the original lake-temple at Amritsar	1574
5.	Arjan Mal, compiler of the *Adi Granth*	1581
6.	Har Govind, first war-like leader	1606
7.	Har Rai, his grandson	1644
8.	Har Krishna, died at Delhi	1661
9.	Tegh Bahadur, put to death by Aurangzeb in 1676	1664
10.	Govind Singh remodelled the Sikh Government	1675
11	Banda, put to death by Bahadar Shah	1708

The twelve principal Misls, each under a Sirdar or chief, were—

1. Bhangi, called from their fondness for bhang, the extract of hemp.
2. Nishani, standard-bearers.
3. Shahid or Nihang, martyrs and zealots.
4. Ramgarhia from Ramgarh, at Amritsar.
5. Nakaia, from the tract of country near Lahore so called.
6. Alhuwalia from the village in which Jassa, head of the Misl, lived.
7. Ghaneia or Khaneia.
8. Faizulapuria or Singhpuria.
9. Sukarchakia.
10. Dalahwala.
11. Krora Singhia or Panjgarhia.
12. Phulkia.

The Sikhs are known now either as Malwai, which comprises those S. and E. of the Sutlej, and Beas, or Manjha, lying N. and W. of these, and principally in the Bari Doab between the Beas and Sutlej and the Ravi. They are represented among the Ruling Chiefs of India, by the three Phulkian houses of which the Maharaja of Pattiala and the Rajas of Jind and Nabha are the heads, and by the Rajas of Kapurthalla and Faridkot, the first three and the last in the Malwai country and the fourth in the Jullundur Doab. The present ruling family of the Jammu and Kashmir State, which is Dogra Rajput by descent, is no longer Sikh by religion. It should be remembered that a Sikh is not born of that religion, but is baptized into it when of adult age, and that in consequence some of the sons of Sikhs fall back into the Hindu religion by simply not taking the *pahal*, as the initiatory rite, usually performed at the Amritsar temple, is called.

THE MAHRATTAS (properly MARÁTHAS)

ANOTHER remarkable people in India who deserve brief notice are the Mahrattas, who derive their name from the country of Maharashtra which they occupied in the early Aryan days. They had been noted as a fighting race in the armies of Ahmednagar and Bijapur before they came prominently to notice as the opponents of the Mughals in the person of their famous leader Shivaji (1627-1680), who set the example of ravaging distant territories by his raid on Surat in 1664 (p. 117). His son Sambhaji was captured, blinded, and executed by the Emperor Aurangzeb ; and his grandson Shahu, who was brought up by one of the daughters of that Emperor, proved when released to have none of the hardy Mahratta qualities, and abandoned all power to his minister, a Konkan Brahmin of the name of Balaji Vishvanath (who became the first Peshwa), and sank to the rank of Raja of Satara. This house came to an end in 1848, but the Kolhapur chief still represents the family of Shivaji, though not in direct descent from that great leader. The first Peshwa marched to Delhi in 1718, and in 1720 obtained the right of "chauth," the famous Mahratta demand of one-fourth of the revenues of every country which they could dominate, over the Deccan. The second Peshwa Baji Rao (1721-1740) seized Malwa, which was ceded to the Mahrattas under his successor Balaji Baji Rao (1740-1761), under whom Janoji, son of Raghoji Bhonsla, the chief of Nagpur, and then the leading Mahratta feudatory, invaded Behar and Bengal, and obtained a cession of Orissa, and of the chauth of Bengal from the Murshidabad Viceroy, Ali Vardi Khan. During his life, which is believed to have been terminated by grief at the crushing defeat of the Mahrattas at Panipat by Ahmad Shah, Durani, the Gaekwar and the Holkar and Sindhia chiefs came to the front; and his son Madhu Rao (1761-1772) was rather the head of five separate branches of the Mahratta people than of the people as a whole. The Gaekwars extended their power through Guzerat and the north of Bombay, and Sindhia and Holkar established themselves in Malwa, and gradually extended their authority over Rajputana and the Ganges Doab, with the capitals of Agra and Delhi. The titular emperor of India, Shah Alam, placed himself in the hands of the Mahrattas in 1771, and remained under the control of Sindhia till 1803. The sixth Peshwa Madhu Rao Narayan (1774-1795), who succeeded as an infant, was practically superseded by his minister Nana Farnavis: it was the war of succession between him and his uncle Raghoba which led to the first interference by the British in Mahratta affairs, and the first Mahratta war in 1779-1781. The last Peshwa Baji Rao II. nominally ruled from 1795 to 1818. The Mahratta princes forced him into war with the English, and in the campaigns which ensued in 1803-1804 Sindhia and the Bhonsla chief were destroyed in the south at Assaye and Argaum, while Sindhia's forces in the north were crushed at Delhi and Laswari, and Jaswant Rao Holkar was defeated at Dig, and finally compelled to submit. The last general Mahratta war took place in 1817-1818, in which the Peshwa was defeated at Khirkee, the Bhonsla chief near Nagpur and Holkar at Mahidpur. The first was deported to Bithur, near Cawnpore, and died there in 1851; his adopted son, the Nana Sahib, stands for ever infamous as the author of the Cawnpore massacre of 27th June 1857. It will be seen from the above brief narrative that when the British commenced to acquire inland territories in India, the Mahrattas were the dominant people of the country, from the Kistna to Delhi and from Guzerat to Orissa; and there can be no doubt but that for British interposition they could have extended their power over Hyderabad and Mysore to the extreme south of India, just as they had already occupied Tanjore, and over Bengal and Behar in the north. Unlike the Sikhs the Mahrattas have lost their warlike qualities, and are now merely a race of sturdy agriculturists; their numbers, according to the last census, were about 3,700,000. The Bhonsla House died out in 1853, on the death of the successor of Apa Sahib (p. 84), who had been deposed. The principal chiefs of the Baroda House have been Damaji Gaekwar, the founder (d. 1721), Damaji II. (1731-1770), Sayaji Rao I., Khande Rao (1857), and Mulhar Rao, who was deposed in 1876. The present chief is His Highness Maharaja Sir Sayaji Rao III., G.C.S.I. Of the Sindhia family the most famous rulers have been the founder Ranoji, Mahadaji Sindhia (d. 1794), his grand-nephew Daulat Rao Sindhia (d. 1827), and (Battles of Panniar and Maharajpur 1843) Jaiaji Rao Sindhia (1857). The present chief is

Colonel Maharaja Sir Madhu Rao Sindhia, G.C.S.I. The principal chiefs of the Holkar House have been the founder, Mulhar Rao, who retreated from Panipat, Ahalaya Bai (1765-1795) (p. 90), Jaswant Rao Holkar, Mulhar Rao Holkar (d. 1833), Baiza Bai, regent, and Tukaji Rao Holkar (1857). The present chief is Maharaja Tukaji Holkar II. The actual Mahratta population in these three States is very small—viz. in Baroda 17,000, in Gwalior 12,000, and in Indore 6000.

THE PARSIS

THE Parsis, formerly inhabitants of Persia, are the modern followers of Zoroaster, and now form a numerous and influential portion of the population of Surat and Bombay.

When the Sassanide Empire was destroyed by the Mohammedans, about 650 A.D., the Zoroastrians were persecuted, and some of them fled (c. 717) to Hindustan, where the Ruler of Guzerat became their protector. They suffered considerably from Mohammedan persecution until the time of the British occupation. The sacred fire, which Zoroaster was said to have brought from heaven, is kept burning in consecrated spots, and temples are built over subterranean fires. The priests tend the fires on the altars, chanting hymns and burning incense. A partially successful attempt was made in 1852 to restore the creed of Zoroaster, which had become corrupted by Hindu practices, to its original purity. In order not to pollute the elements, which they adore, the Parsis neither burn nor bury their dead, but expose their corpses to be devoured by birds (see Towers of Silence,[1] Bombay, p. 16). There has long been a marked desire on the part of the Parsis to adapt themselves to the manners and customs of Europeans. The public and private schools of Bombay are largely attended by their children. They largely follow commercial pursuits, and several of the wealthiest merchants of India belong to this community. Their public spirit and charity are well known.

PARSI MONTHS.

There are twelve months, of thirty days each, to which five days are added at the end. They approximate as below to the English months.

1. Farvardin, September.
2. Ardibihisht, October.
3. Khurdad, November.
4. Tir, December.
5. Amardad, January.
6. Sharivar, February.
7. Mihr, March.
8. Avan, April.
9. Adar, May.
10. Deh, June.
11. Bahman, July.
12. Asfandiyar, August.

[1] The vernacular name of these structures is Dokhma.

The Parsi Festivals

Pateti, New Year's Day. The 1st of Farvardin. The Parsis rise earlier than usual, put on new clothes, and pray at the Fire Temples. They then visit friends and join hands, distribute alms and give clothes to servants and others. This day is celebrated in honour of the accession of Yezdajird to the throne of Persia, 632 A.D.

Farvardin-Jasan, on the 19th of Farvardin, on which ceremonies are performed in honour of the dead, called Frohars, or "protectors." There are eleven other Jasans in honour of various angels.

Khurdad-sal, the birthday of Zoroaster, who is said to have been born 1200 B.C. at the city of Rai or Rhages, near Teheran.

Jamshidi Nauroz, held on the 21st of Mihr. It dates from the time of Jamshid, and the Parsis ought to commence their New Year from it.

Zurtoshte Diso, held on the 11th of Deh in remembrance of the death of Zartasht or Zoroaster, in Bactria.

The Muktad, held on the last ten days of the Zoroastrian year, including the last five days of the last month, and the five intercalary days called the *Gatha Gahambars*. A clean place in the house is adorned with fruits and flowers, and silver or brass vessels filled with water are placed there, and ceremonies are performed in honour of the souls of the dead.

ARCHITECTURE

RELIGION has so great an influence upon architecture that the different styles in India may be most conveniently classified as Buddhist, Jain, Brahman, and Mohammedan.

Buddhist.—Though Gautama taught in the 6th century B.C., his religion made little progress before its adoption by the great Asoka, who reigned from 272 to 231 B.C. The palaces, halls, and temples which may have existed before the time of Asoka, were made of wood, and have perished. There was no stone architecture in India before that date, and all the monuments known to us for five or six centuries after it are Buddhist.

Every sanctified Buddhist locality was marked by the erection of a tope (stupa) commemorating some holy event or containing relics, in which case the tope was called a dagoba. The relics of a dagoba were usually contained in a sort of box or case at the summit of it, called a tee. Older even than the tope was the memorial pillar, called stamba, or lát if it was carved out of one stone: these pillars bore Buddhist emblems, such as lions or wheels, and were afterwards converted, in various parts of India, into pedestals for lamps, or vehicles of the gods, and the like. Rails are found surrounding topes, or enclosing sacred trees, pillars, etc. The Chaityas, assembly halls, or temples, correspond to the churches of the Christian religion: the Viharas are monasteries—see plans at pp. 339 and 75.

The best known topes are those at Sanchi and Sarnath, (pp. 98 and 51). There are also a number of them scattered over the ancient province of Gandara, the capital of which was Peshawar —especially at Manikyala (p. 243). In Ceylon there are topes or dagobas at Anuradhapura and Pollanarua (pp. 494 and 498). The lats, or pillars, stood in front of, or beside, each gateway of every tope, and in front of each chaitya (pp. 338-9). Many of these were erected by Asoka, and two of these are still in existence at Delhi, and a more complete specimen at Allahabad. (The Iron Pillar in the mosque at Old Delhi is not Buddhist, but seems to be dedicated to Vishnu.) The most interesting rails are at Sanchi and Buddh Gaya; the remains of the Bharhut rail are at Calcutta, and of the Amaravati (p. 336) rail in the British and Madras Museums. There are fine examples of torans, or gateways, with the rail at Sanchi.

Our knowledge of the Chaitya chapels or temples, and the Viharas or monasteries, is derived mainly from the rock-cut examples (but see p. 100). This method of working is easier and less expensive than the process of building. For a cave nothing but excavation is required; while for a building the stone has to be quarried, transported—perhaps a long distance—and then carved and erected. According to Mr Fergusson[1] the complete excavation of a temple, both externally as well as internally, would cost only about one-tenth of the expenditure necessary for building; and the Buddhist caves were still cheaper, as the rock was not cut away all round, the interior chamber alone being excavated. Examples of Chaityas are to be found at Karli, Bhaja and Bedsa (pp. 338-40), Behar (p. 36), Nasik, Ellora, Ajanta, and Kanhari (p. 22). They usually consist of a long excavation separated by two rows of columns into a nave, and two narrow side aisles. At the further end of the cave is either a small tope or a figure of Buddha, behind which also the colonnade runs; and in the front wall over the entrance-door is a large horse-shoe window which allows the light to fall directly on the tope or image. A Vihara is usually a large rectangular hall with cells off it round the sides, and a shrine chapel in the back wall. The hall is commonly borne by columns often richly carved, and is approached by a verandah; and in some cases it had a forecourt in front of this. In a few instances these halls consisted of two, and even three, storeys. The most notable specimens are at Udayagiri and Khandagiri

[1] *History of Indian and Eastern Architecture*, i. 348.

(p. 323), Bhaja and Bedsa, Ajanta (p. 40), Nasik, Kanhari, and Ellora, and at Jamalgarhi and Takht-i-bahi, near Peshawar.

Among the most characteristic details of Buddhist sculpture are the patterns representing rails and horse-shoe windows, the figures of Nága devotees over-canopied by cobra hoods, and probably intended to represent aboriginal residents of India, and scenes of worship (by animals as well as by human beings), of topes, sacred trees, and emblems of the Buddhist religion—the wheel, trident, swástika cross, etc., which also recur in the decoration generally.

Jain.—The architecture of the Buddhists proper was succeeded by that of the *Jains*, who were great builders. Unlike the Buddhists they were not great excavators, though some examples of their cave-work exist at Ellora. The characteristic Jain feature is the horizontal archway which avoids the strain from the outward thrust of a true radiating arch. Indeed, with the exception of some specimens of the time of Akbar, no radiating arch exists in any Buddhist, Jain, or Hindu temple in India up to the present day. Another Jain feature is the carved bracket form of capital, which, springing from the pillars at about two-thirds of their height, extends to the architraves, and forms a sort of diagonal strut to support them. The leading idea of the plan of a Jain temple was a number of columns arranged in squares (see p. 156). Their domes, like their arches, were built horizontally, on eight pillars forming an octagon, with four external pillars at the angles to form a square. The lateral pressure of a dome built on the radiating plan by the Roman, Byzantine, or Gothic architects prevents the use of elegant pillars, great cylinders with heavy abutments being necessary. The construction of the Jain domes, being horizontal, allows of more variety than can be given to the vertical ribs of Roman or Gothic models, and has rendered some of the Indian domes the most exquisite specimens of elaborate roofing that can anywhere be seen. The Indian dome allows the use of pendents from the centre, and these have a lightness and elegance never imagined in Gothic art. On the other hand, they are necessarily small, and require large stones, while a dome on the radiating principle can be built of small bricks. The Jains often built their temples in groups, or cities of temples, as at Palitana (p. 149) Parasnath (p. 38), Girnar (p. 155), Mount Abu (p. 132), and Khajurahu (p. 114). Their love of the picturesque led them to construct their cities sometimes on hill-tops, as at Mount Abu, and sometimes in deep and secluded valleys. The two towers of Fame and of Victory at Chitor (p. 93) are also examples of Jain work, and splendidly carved specimens of their characteristic pillars, dating from the 10th-12th centuries, still exist in the great mosques at the Kutab Minar, S. of Delhi, and in Ajmer Ahmedabad and Belgaum (p. 358). Of modern

Jain architecture the most notable specimens are at Sonagir (p. 103) and Muktagiri; the temple of Hathi Singh (A.D. 1848) at Ahmedabad; the temple at Delhi, about one hundred years old; and the temples at Calcutta.

Brahman architecture is divided by Mr Fergusson into the three styles of Dravidian, Chalukyan, and Indo-Aryan. The *Dravidian* or Madras architecture is best seen at Tanjore, Trivalur (p. 424), Sri Rangam, Chidambaram, Rameswaram, Madura, Tinnevelly, Conjeeveram, Coimbatore, and Vijayanagar (p. 380). "There is nothing in Europe that can be compared with these Dravidian temples for grandeur and solemnity, and for parallels to them we must go back to ancient Egypt and Assyria" (Sir G. Birdwood). The oldest of the Dravidian temples date from about the 11th century; but in their present form few can go back as far as the 13th, and most are of even more modern date. Quite the oldest temples in India dating from the 7th-8th centuries, are those at Pattadakal and Aiwalli, near Badami (p. 372). The shrine itself, which is called the Vimana, is always square in plan, surmounted by a pyramidal roof of one or more storeys; a porch or Mantapam covers the door leading to the cell in which the image of the god is placed; the gate pyramids or Gopurams are the principal features in the quadrangular enclosures which, with numerous other buildings, surround the Vimanas. The chief Dravidian rock-cut temples, which, unlike the Buddhist caves, are excavated externally as well as internally, are at Mahabalipuram (p. 436) and Ellora. The palaces exhibit Mohammedan influence, having the Moorish pointed arch. They are to be found at Madura, Tanjore, Vijayanagar and Chandragiri (p. 350).

The *Chalukyan* style was at its best in the province of Mysore during the three centuries A.D. 1000 to 1300, when the Bellalas ruled there. They erected groups of temples at Somnathpur (p. 390), Belur, and Hallabid (p. 386). Other Chalukyan examples are at Warangal and Hanamcondah (p. 379*b*). This style is remarkable for elegance of outline and elaboration of detail. The artistic combination of horizontal with vertical lines, and the play of light and shade, especially in the Hallabid example, far surpass anything in Gothic art. The animal friezes begin, as is usual in India, with elephants in the bottom line, then lions, then horses, and then oxen, above which are pigeons or other birds.

Examples of the *Indo-Aryan*, or Northern style, exist at Bhuvaneshwar (p. 326), the black pagoda at Kanarak, the temple of Jagannath at Puri, all dating from the 11th and 12th centuries, the Garuda pillar at Jajpur (p. 322), Khajurahu, the Teli-Ka-Mandir at Gwalior, the temple of Vriji at Chitor, the golden temple of Bisheshwar at Benares, the red temple at Brindaban, and the modern temple erected by Sindhia's mother at Gwalior. There are rock-cut temples of this style near Badami, and at Ellora.

The finest Indo-Aryan palaces, besides the Man Singh Palace at Gwalior, are at Udaipur, Datia, Orchha (pp. 103 and 113), Amber (p. 142), and Dig (p. 167). The beauty of Hindu architecture is greatly enhanced by the use of picturesque sites, either on hills, in valleys, or where the æsthetic value of water may be utilised. At Rajsamundra, in Udaipur, for example, the *band* or dam of the artificial lake is covered with steps, which are broken by pavilions and kiosks, interspersed with fountains, the whole forming a fairy scene of architectural beauty. Of Modern Indo-Aryan civil architecture the best specimens are the tombs of Sangram Singh and Amar Singh at Udaipur, and of Bakhtawar Singh at Alwar. The latter shows the foliated arch which is so common in Mughal buildings; and it also shows the Bengali curved cornices, whose origin was the bending of bamboos used as a support for the thatch or tiles.

The chief styles of *Mohammedan* architecture are the so-called Pathan and the Mughal. The early Turk conquerors found in the colonnaded courts of the Jain temples nearly all that was required for a mosque. They had only to remove the temple in its centre, and erect a new wall on the west side, adorned with niches—*mihrabs*—pointing towards Mecca, in front of which they added a screen of arches with rich carvings. The best examples are at Delhi and Ajmer. Mr Fergusson considers that the carving of the screen at the Kutab Mosque, Delhi, is, without exception, the most exquisite specimen of its class known to exist anywhere. He also considers that the Kutab Minar "both in design and finish far surpasses any building of its class in the whole world"; and that Giotto's Campanile at Florence, "beautiful though it is, wants that poetry of design and exquisite finish of detail which marks every moulding of the minar." During the Pathan period the mosques usually had neither minarets nor prominent domes.

No examples exist of the *Mughal* style in the reigns of Babar or Humayun. Akbar was, in architecture as in religion, extremely tolerant, and his buildings exhibit marked Hindu features. The chief of them still in existence are the tomb of his father Humayun, near Delhi, the town of Fatehpur-Sikri, the fort at Allahabad, the palace at Lahore, and the red palace in the fort at Agra, which by some authorities, in spite of its Hindu features, is ascribed to Jahangir. The tomb of Anar Kali at Lahore was built by Jahangir, and the tomb of Itimad-ud-daulah at Agra was built during the reign of that Emperor. Shah Jahan, under whom the Mughal power was at its highest, was the greatest of all Indian builders. There is a great contrast between the manly vigour and exuberant originality of

Akbar, and the extreme elegance of his grandson, which rapidly tended to become effeminate. Shah Jahan built the palace and Jama Masjid at Delhi, the inner Fort and palace at Agra, and the famous Taj Mahal, perhaps the most beautiful building in the world. His son Aurangzeb was a religious fanatic, who has left little save the mosque at Lahore, another small one at Benares, and the tomb at Aurangabad. The later examples of Mughal architecture at Lucknow show marked deterioration, which is partly attributable to European influence. Other notable examples of earlier Mohammedan architecture exist at Jaunpur, Gaur, and Panduah (pp. 309-10), Mandu (p. 89), Ahmedabad and Sarkhej in the north, and at Gulburga (p. 348), Bijapur, and Golconda (p. 378) in the south.

As mosques in India always face east they should be seen of a morning.

In other styles should be mentioned the ruins at Martand and other places in Kashmir (p. 251), which bear evidence of classical influence; and the modern Golden Temple of the Sikhs at Amritsar.

The *Burmese* pagoda, with its thin spire, has been evolved from the solid hemispherical dome of the Buddhists. The best examples are at Prome, Pagan, Rangoon, Mandalay, Pegu, and Moulmein. A small example may be seen in the Eden Gardens, Calcutta.

The Preservation of Ancient Monuments

As the striking architectural monuments of India will specially attract the attention of visitors, so the means taken for their preservation in the past will be a subject of frequent remark. Largely under outside pressure, the Indian Government has made various attempts at conservation, but as these have for the most part been carried out through the engineering staff of the Public Works Department, the work of protection has too frequently been seriously injurious to the architectural beauties of the monuments repaired. What has been wanted is the guidance of the trained architect who would strictly confine himself to the work of *conservation*, and eschew everything of the nature of restoration. The Government of India carried on for many years an Archæological Survey, almost wholly dissociated from any conservation of the architectural monuments, and rather connected with the identification of ancient sites, coins, dates and relics of forgotten times, interesting chiefly to the savant. Thirty years ago a change in this respect was begun, and a careful survey of the monumental remains at Jaunpur, Ahmedabad, Fatehpur-Sikri, etc., was commenced; but the surveys were again reduced in 1889, and only one architectural assistant and a few native draughtsmen were retained in Upper India, where, however, the most excellent results have followed the ideal labours at Agra and Fatehpur-Sikri of Mr E. W. Smith, who, unhappily, died of cholera at the end of 1901. Thanks to Lord Curzon's keen interest in the subject, which he treated at length in two speeches to the Asiatic Society of Bengal in 1899 and 1900, the Department has been lately placed on a really broader footing; and has been officered by competent architects who can authoritatively advise Government on questions of conservation under the control of a Director - General, at present Mr J. A. Marshall; and it may be expected that with the new régime the safety of all public monuments will be insured, as well as their survey. It is much to be hoped, however, that the Department will as a rule be less engaged in restoration than is indicated in the reports so far published by Mr Marshall. It may be noticed that already the Salimgarh Pavilion and the space in front of the Diwan-i-'Am in the Agra Fort (pp. 178 and 179), and the principal buildings of the Delhi and Lahore Forts (pp. 197 and 234), have been already rescued from profane military purposes; that the unsightly native quarters round the gates of the Taj enclosure have been removed; that a requisite traveller's rest-house has been built at Fatehpur-Sikri (p. 181); and that minor works of conservation have been carried through at Ahmedabad, Lucknow, Delhi, Mandu, Bijapur (p. 362), and Bhuvaneshwar (p. 326) and Kanárak (p. 332), where excavations of the base of the fallen porch have disclosed a magnificent sculpture, eight great wheels, each 9 ft. 8 in. in diameter, on its sides. The famous caves of Ajanta and Ellora, which are situated within the limits of the Hyderabad State, are in much need of certain measures of conservation, if they are to be preserved for the wonderment of future generations. Travellers in India would render a public service by invariably inviting public attention to all instances of inept and barbarous conservation and restoration of ancient monuments which may come under their notice. In justice, however, to the Indian Government, it should be recorded that but for what it has done, many of the principal monuments of India would be no longer in existence; and that with all its shortcomings in this connection, it has not been guilty of the absolute neglect of the memorials of the past which prevailed throughout India until its advent. It may also be noted here that much has been done in the last twenty years under competent artistic advice to produce suitable buildings of architectural merit in India, especially in Bombay and Madras, by Mr Stephens and Mr Chisholm, by Colonel Sir Samuel S. Jacob in Rajputana, and by the late Mr Lockwood Kipling, C.I.E., and Rai Bahadur Ganga Ram, in the Panjab.

ARTS

Mr Fergusson writes of Indian *sculpture*, that when it "first dawns upon us in the rails at Buddh Gaya and Barhut, 250 to 200 B.C., it is thoroughly original, absolutely without a trace of foreign influence, but quite capable of expressing its ideas. Some animals, such as elephants, deer, and monkeys, are better represented there than in any sculptures known in any part of the world; so, too, are some trees, and the architectural details are cut with an elegance and precision which are very admirable." The highest perfection was attained in the 4th and 5th centuries A.D. Little sculpture of any merit has been produced since that time.

The excellence of Indian art production is to be found in its pottery, metal work, carving, jewellery, weaving, dyeing, and embroidery. In these directions the Indian artisan is remarkable for his patience, accuracy of detail, thoroughness, and artistic sense of both colour and form. The elaboration of ornament in the best Indian metal ware, or carving, the composition of colours in the best Indian carpets, or enamel, and the form of the best Indian pottery, have seldom, if ever, been excelled. Much of the skill of the Indian handicraftsman is due to the hereditary nature of his occupation. The potter, the carpenter, the smith, the weaver, each belongs to a separate caste; a son inevitably follows the trade of his father, and the force of custom, with generally a religious basis, impels him to imitate his father's work. The result is that the form and workmanship of artizan work is almost exactly the same now as it was thousands of years ago, and that the artizan, with great technical and imitative skill, has little creative power. The combined competition and prestige of Europe have created a tendency to imitate European methods. The best work used to be done, at leisure, to the order of the wealthy princes and nobles of an ostentatious native court. Many of these courts have now ceased to exist, while others have declined in purchasing power and in influence. The authority of the trade guilds, and of caste, has been relaxed under the freedom of British rule, and the importation of British goods has materially affected certain crafts. British supremacy, having produced peace, has almost destroyed the armourer's trade; the fancy cheap cotton goods of America and Britain have displaced the muslins of Dacca; aniline dyes, and jail work have nearly killed the old carpet industry. Whether the Schools of Art which the Government has established in India have hastened, or retarded, the process of degeneration is a much-disputed point. Some trades which were dying out have been resuscitated by their efforts, and the mania for imitating European designs is sometimes effectually diverted from the worst to the best examples, and in some cases native crafts have actually been revived. The effective working of these institutions is a task which requires much delicacy of perception as well as firmness of touch, as there is always great risk that a school which contains principally casts from the antique, and details of Italian and Gothic ornament, will affect the purity of indigenous ideals, which is much to be deplored. To restrain rather than to strengthen the tendency to imitate the designs and methods of the dominant race, should be the aim of art education throughout the country.

In the very slight sketch of Indian arts[1] which follows, certain places are mentioned as being noted for particular work; but it should be remembered that the small towns are gradually losing their specialities, the best workmen drifting steadily towards the larger centres. A visit is recommended to the art collections in the Indian Museum at S. Kensington, before the visitor to India leaves England.

Nearly every Indian village has its *potter*, who is kept constantly at work making domestic utensils of baked clay, for in many households no earthen vessels can be used a second time. The forms of the utensils which he makes are of great antiquity and beauty. The best glazed pottery is made in the Panjab, of blue and white, and in Sindh, of turquoise blue, copper green, dark purple, and golden brown, under an exquisitely transparent glaze. The usual ornament is a conventional flower pattern, pricked in from paper and dusted along the pricking. The Madura (Madras) pottery deserves mention for the elegance of its form and richness of its colour. The Bombay School of Art produces imitations of Sindh ware. In the Panjab and Sindh, and especially at Thatta (p. 265) and Hyderabad, there are many good specimens of encaustic tiles on the old Mohammedan mosques and tombs. One of the finest examples is the mosque of Wazir Khan at Lahore.

The Panjab has long been noted for its *gold* and *silver* work, and especially for parcel-gilt sarahis, or water-vessels, of elegant shape and delicate tracery. The gold and silver ware of Kashmir, Cutch, Lucknow, Patna, Bombay, Ahmednagar, Cuttack (p. 323), and Tanjore, is worthy of mention. The hammered repoussé silver work of Cutch is of Dutch origin. The embossed silver work of Madras, with Dravidian figures in high relief, is called Swami ware.

Domestic utensils in *brass* and *copper* are made all over India, the Hindus using the brass, and the Mohammedans the copper. The brass is cleaned by scrubbing with sand or earth and water; the copper periodically receives a lining of tin. The copper bazaar of

[1] Mr N. T. Mukharji's *Art Manufactures of India* (1888) may be consulted for further details.

Bombay is celebrated, and so is the brass ware of Moradabad (p. 273). Benares and Jaipur are famous for cast and sculptured mythological images and emblems. Plates, cups, jewellery, etc., of Kansha (bell metal) are made at Burdwan (p. 39) and Midnapore (p. 322). Other places noted for brass and copper ware are Nagpur, Ahmedabad, Nasik, Poona, Murshidabad, and Tanjore. The Kashmir and Peshawar ware has marked Persian features.

The artizans of India were formerly very skilful in the use of *iron* and *steel.* Mr Fergusson says of the Iron Pillar in the Kutab Mosque at Old Delhi, to which he assigns the date of A.D. 400, that "it opens our eyes to an unsuspected state of affairs to find the Hindus at that age capable of forging a bar of iron larger than any that have been forged even in Europe up to a very late date, and not frequently even now. It is almost equally startling to find that, after an exposure for fourteen centuries, it is unrusted, and the capital and inscription are as clear and as sharp as when the pillar was erected." (See p. 332 also). Sir G. Birdwood[1] says: "The blades of Damascus, which maintained their pre-eminence even after the blades of Toledo became celebrated, were, in fact, of Indian steel." Indian *arms* are characterised by their superb, and sometimes excessive, ornamentation. But the modern work in iron, steel, and arms is not of much importance.

Damascening is the art of encrusting one metal upon another. The best or true damascening is done by cutting the metal deep, and filling it with a thick wire of gold or silver. The more common process is to heat the metal to a blue colour, scratch the design upon it, lay a thin gold or silver wire along the pattern, and then sink it carefully with a copper tool. The art comes from Damascus, hence its name. Damascening in gold is carried on chiefly in Kashmir, Gujrat, and Sialkot (p. 240), and is called "koft"-work. In silver or iron it is called bidri, from Bidar (p. 374), in the Nizam's dominions, where such work is still made, though it is now produced principally in Lucknow. A cheap imitation of koft-work is made with gold leaf.

Enamel is an artificial vitreous mass, ground fine, mixed with gum water, applied with a brush, and fixed by fusion. In the champlevé enamelling of Jaipur—the best in India, perhaps in the world—the colours are placed in depressions hollowed out of the metal, and are made to adhere by fire. The Jaipur artist is renowned for the purity and brilliance of his colours, and the evenness with which they are applied. He is particularly famous for a fiery red, which is unique. For enamel on gold—besides Jaipur—Alwar, Delhi, and Benares may be mentioned; on silver, Mooltan, Hyderabad (Sindh), Karachi, Abbotabad (p. 245), Bhoj Cutch (p. 148), Lahore, Kangra (p. 228), and Kashmir; on copper, the Panjab

[1] *The Industrial Arts of India.*

and Kashmir. A quasi-enamel, the mode of preparation being kept secret, is made of green colour at Pertabghar, and of blue at Rutlam (p. 91). Glass was known in India at the time of the *Mahabharata;* glass bangles and other ornaments are made all over the country.

The splendour of Indian *jewellery* is due to the free use of diamonds, rubies, emeralds, and other gems, some of them mere scales so light that they will float on water. A dazzling variety of rich and brilliant colours is thus produced by means of gems which are valueless except as splashes, points, and sparkles of gorgeousness. Rings for the fingers and toes, nose and ears; bracelets, armlets, anklets, nose studs, necklaces made up of chains of pearls and gems; tires, aigrettes, and other ornaments for the head and forehead; chains and zones of gold and silver for the waist—such are the personal ornaments in daily use amongst men and women, Mohammedans and Hindus. One reason for the great popularity of gold and silver jewellery is that it is portable wealth, easily preserved. The silver filigree work of Cuttack and of Ceylon, generally with the design of a leaf, is remarkable for delicacy and finish. For gold and silver jewellery, Trichinopoly, Vizagapatam (p. 334), and Ahmedabad are noted. The best enamelled jewellery comes from Delhi, Benares, and Hyderabad (Deccan). The old Delhi work in cut and gem-encrusted jade is highly prized. The pietra dura *inlaid work* of Agra was fully developed in the Taj Mahal by Austin de Bordeaux. While Florentine in origin and style, the designs have a thoroughly local character.

The well-known Bombay boxes are a variety of inlaid woodwork called piqué. Indian lacquer, so-called, is really *lac turnery.* In it the surface is obtained by pressing a stick of hard shellac to a rapidly revolving wooden object. The friction develops heat sufficient to make it adhere irregularly. Further friction with an oiled rag polishes the surface. The lac is obtained from the incrustations made by the female of an insect (*coccus lacca*) on the branches of certain trees. The numeral lakh, signifying 100,000, is derived from the enormous number of these insects found on a small area. The chief consumption of lac in Europe is for sealing-wax and varnishes. All over India it is used for walking-sticks, mats, bangles, and toys. Lac-turned wooden and papier-mâché boxes and trays are made in Kashmir, Sindh, Panjab, Rajputana, Bareilly (p. 273), and Kurnool Madras (p. 383). Of small objects, the mock ornaments for the idols, made of paper, should be noted at Ahmedabad and in most parts of India. Artificial flowers, and models of the temples, are made of the pith of the sola plant, whence the "sola topee," or sun-hat of pith.

Skilful *carving* is done at Bombay in blackwood, for doors or

f

furniture in a style derived from the Dutch. At Ahmedabad the blackwood is carved into vases, inkstands, and other small objects. Jackwood also is carved in rectangular forms at Bombay. Sandalwood is carved at Bombay, Surat, Ahmedabad, Kanara (p. 418), Mysore, and Travancore; ebony at Nagina (p. 273) and Bijnur; ivory at Amritsar, Delhi, Benares, and Vizagapatam. Sylhet (p. 320) is noted for its ivory fans, Rutlam for its ivory bracelets, and Vizagapatam for boxes of ivory and stag's horn. Figures of animals, and of the gods, are carved in white marble at Ajmer, Jaipur, and Rajputana generally. Excellent building stone is found in Rajputana, where it is carved for architectural purposes. At Fatehpur-Sikri (Agra) models of the ruins are carved in soapstone. Models in clay of fruit and figures are admirably made at Lucknow, Poona, and Calcutta. In the cities of Guzerat, and wherever the houses are made of wood, their fronts are elaborately carved: this is especially the case in various cities in the Panjab, notably in Lahore.

India was the first of all countries that perfected weaving, sewing not being practised until after the Mohammedan invasion. The Greek name for *cotton* fabrics, sindon, is etymologically the same as India or Sindh. The word chintz is from the Hindu chhint, or variegated, while calico is from the place of its production, Calicut (p. 416). In delicacy of texture, in purity and fastness of colour, in grace of design, Indian cottons may still hold their own against the world—but not in cheapness. The famous Dacca muslin (p. 318), one pound weight of which could be made to cover a fabulous extent, is now superseded by the machine-made goods of Europe and America; and European chintz now takes the place of the palampore (palangposh), a kind of bedcover of printed cotton produced at Masulipatam. In the Panjab the weaver's trade still flourishes, but large quantities of the cheaper cottons are now made in India by machinery. Pure *silk* fabrics, striped, checked, and figured, are made at Lahore, Agra, Benares, Hyderabad, (Deccan), and Tanjore. Gold and silver brocaded silks, called kincobs (kimkhwab),[1] are made at Benares, Murshidabad, and Ahmedabad. The printed silks which are worn by the Parsi ladies of Bombay are a speciality of Surat. Bahawulpur is noted for its damasked silks. Most of the raw silk comes from China. The Mohammedans are forbidden by their religion to wear pure silk, but may wear it mixed with cotton. Gold and silver wire, thread lace, and foil are made all over the country, for trimming shoes and caps, for stamping muslin and chintzes, for embroidery and brocades. With such skill is the silver wire prepared, that two shillings' worth of silver

[1] This word is a hybrid, but is connected with *kin*, Chinese for gold.

can be drawn out to 800 yards. The best *embroidery*, remarkable for its subdued elegance and harmonious combination of brilliant colours, comes from Kashmir, Lahore, and Delhi. The patterns and colours diversify plane surfaces without destroying the impression of flatness. Much tinsel is used, but the result has not a tinselly appearance. The famous Kashmir shawls are made of the fine, flossy, silk-like wool obtained from the neck and underpart of the body of the goat of Ladak. Originally a speciality of Kashmir, they are now made in the Panjab also, especially at Amritsar. They have greatly deteriorated since the introduction of French designs and magenta dyes. The finest of the woollen stuffs is called patu in Kangra and Kashmir. A rough but remarkably durable patu is made from goat's hair. The shawls called Rampur *chadars* are made at Amritsar and Ludhiana (p. 224), of Rampur wool. The intrinsic difference between Eastern and Western decorative art is revealed in Oriental *carpets*, where the angular line is substituted for the flowing, classical "line of beauty." The Oriental carpet is also more artistically dyed, and is decorated according to the true principles of conventional design. As a rule the pile carpets of India and Persia are of floral design, while those of Central Asia, Western Afghanistan, and Baluchistan, are geometric. In Persia and India the source of many of the patterns is the tree of life, shown as a beautiful flowering plant, or as a simple sprig of flowers. The *dari* is a carpet of cotton made chiefly in Bengal and Northern India; but the most common cotton carpet is the shatranji, made throughout India, but especially at Agra. The principal patterns are stripes of blue and white, and red and white. In point of texture and workmanship the rugs from Ellore (p. 335), Tanjore, and Mysore are the best. Costly velvet carpets embroidered with gold are made at Benares, Delhi, and Murshidabad. The carpets of Malabar are now the only pile woollen carpets made of pure Hindu design. Fine carpets are made at Amritsar by the well-known firm of Devi Sahai Chamba Mal. Central Asian carpets are best purchased at Amritsar, Peshawar, and Quetta. For art manufactures in Burma, see p. 442.

IRRIGATION

The history of irrigation in India stretches back into remote antiquity, many of the modern works being founded upon old native works which have been restored and extended. The storage of water in tanks is very common in Southern India. The works are for the most part of native origin, but much has been done by the British in repairing old tanks and constructing new ones in Madras, the Bombay Deccan, and Ajmer. In many places the natives have made artificial lakes with dams, which are often of great architectural beauty. In the more level tracts of the south every declivity is dammed up to gather the rain. Innumerable wells cover the whole country. And it is very usual for the upland cultivator to make his own tiny irrigating stream, carrying it along the brows of mountains, round steep declivities, and across yawning gulfs and deep valleys; his primitive buffaloes,; being formed of stones and clay, the scooped-out trunks of palm trees and hollow bamboos. To lift the water a bucket wheel, worked by men and oxen or buffaloes, is employed, where the water is more than 40 ft. below the surface, and the Persian wheel with a line of earthenware vessels on the ropes which run over it where the water is nearer the surface in N. India. A good part of the Panjab and the whole of Sindh would be scarcely habitable without irrigation; and it is practically indispensable also in the south-east of the Madras Presidency.

The greatest British engineering works in India have been in canal irrigation, the water being drawn directly from a river or other source into either a "perennial" or an intermittent or "inundation" canal. A perennial canal is furnished with permanent headworks and weirs, and is capable of irrigating large tracts throughout the year, independently of rainfall. Canals of this class have now a main line mileage of 10,000 m. and a distributary lineage of 28,000 m., more than half of the first, and two-thirds of the last being in the United Provinces and in the Panjab. The net revenue earned by these works amounts to 7 per cent. on the capital outlay, and the area irrigated by them was no less than 14,500,000 acres. A notable example is the Ganges Canal (p. 273), which has been at work since 1854, has cost Rs.30,000,000, comprises 440 miles of main canal, and 2614 miles of distributaries, and in 1895-96 supplied water to 759,297 acres. In one place it is carried over a river channel 920 feet broad, and thence for nearly 3 miles along an embankment 30 ft. high. The Sirhind Canal from the Sutlej (p. 224), completed in 1882, is even larger, while the great Chenab Canal (p. 241), supports a colony of 532,000 souls, settled on Government waste in the Rechna Doab of the Panjab during the last ten years,. and irrigates an area of 1,750,000 of acres. A similar colony will be established on the Jhelam Canal in the Jach Doab, and probably a third in the Sindh Sagar Doab, which will be irrigated by a monster canal taken out of the Indus at Kalabagh. The area brought under irrigation from waste in the Panjab alone, during the last twenty years, has been 3,500,000 of acres.

Inundation canals are rougher channels without masonry dams or sluices, and are supplied with water by the annual rise of the river from which they are drawn. The principal works of this class are in the Panjab and Sindh on the Sutlej, Chenab and Indus rivers;

and these and other works, classed as minor irrigation works, water 2,500,000 of acres annually, and bring in a net return of 28 lakhs of rupees to Government. The main lines of minor works are 5600 m. long, and the line of distributaries 2560 m.

In years of scanty rainfall the area irrigated by Government works is enormously increased; but in years of almost complete drought the supply of water in the rivers has been known to fall short of the great demands on it, owing to failure of rains in the mountains.

Besides the area irrigated by Government works, it is calculated that something like 18,000,000 acres are irrigated by means of tanks, wells, lakes, and the smaller canal channels. This area is likely to be largely increased in the near future, a Commission which has recently sat on the subject having recommended that forty-four crores of rupees should be spent on irrigation during the next twenty years, largely on works indirectly reproductive, and on private irrigation works.

Famine

The importance of irrigation will be fully realised from the figures of the last three famines from which the country has suffered.

In the first of these, in 1896-97, the areas affected were 194,000 sq. m. in British India and 82,000 sq. m. in the Native States, the population of the two areas being 45,000,000 and 7,000,000, of whom 4,250,000 were on State relief works in June 1896. The second famine in 1899-1900 extended to 175,000 sq. m. (population 25,000,000) and 300,000 sq. m. (population, 30,000,000) in British India and Native States, and no less than 6,500,000 people were in receipt of relief in August 1900. The third of 1907-08 affected an area of 66,000 sq. m. and a population of 30,000,000. The recurrence of famine is accepted as a normal feature in the administration of India, and due provision is made beforehand for providing relief whenever that may be required. A special famine fund is devoted yearly to the protection of those areas which are most liable to these visitations by the construction of irrigation works and railways and the adoption of other measures.

The Material Condition of the People of India

It is impossible to enter in detail upon so wide a subject as this. Full information will be found at pp. 325-355 of the Decennial Material Progress Report for 1892-1902, and in subsequent reports; and a perusal of the facts there recorded will probably convince any open-minded person that the material condition of the people in India has greatly improved in the past, and is still improving, putting altogether aside the advantages of peace and order which now prevail in the country. At the same time, the enormous growth of the population is a matter of serious import. It may be mentioned here that the Salt Tax has been reduced since 1903-04 from Rs.2.8 to Rs.1 per maund of 82 lbs. This rate came into force from 1908; and up to the present date the increase in consumption has been 22 per cent. This varies now from 9 lbs. in Rajputana, the Panjab, and the United Provinces, 12 in Bengal, and 13 in Bombay, to 16 in Burma, and 19 in Madras. Though called a Salt Tax, the burden on salt is really its selling price fixed by Government, all sources of supply, apart from the salt imported by sea, being the property of Government, and worked by the State. The principal natural sources are the Jhelam mines (p. 242) and the Sambhar Lake (p. 136). Details of the cotton duties levied in India and the countervailing duties imposed on imported sugar will be found on p. 191 of the above Report.

Plague

Plague in India made its recent appearance at Bombay in 1896, but it was often widespread during the six centuries of Mohammedan rule. The total number of deaths caused by it in the last fourteen years has been nearly 7,000,000, of which 2,000,000 have taken place in the Panjab. It is not easy to realise the effects of such a loss. But beyond a possible examination at certain railway stations, travellers are not likely to see anything connected with plague. It has been proved beyond doubt that the rat flea is the vehicle of contagion between rats, and that from these the disease spreads to man.

The Countess of Dufferin's Fund Association

As many visitors to India will naturally be interested in the work of the above Association for supplying female medical aid to the women of India, a very brief account of it is given here. The Annual Report of the Fund can be purchased in the Presidency towns of India. Started only in 1895 by the Countess of Dufferin, the Fund has now 52 lady doctors of the first grade and 87 of the second grade, Europeans and natives of India (besides 500 hospital assistants), engaged on its work, which yearly brings aid to more than 2,250,000 women and children. The invested resources of the Fund amount to 32 lakhs of rupees, including a sum of 7 lakhs collected by the late Lady Curzon for Queen Victoria Memorial Scholarships for the training of midwives; and the annual income is about Rs. 250,000 which is largely devoted to training and supplying trained medical practitioners as well as to the maintaining of female hospitals. It is much to be hoped that year by year larger gifts and contributions will place the Fund in a position to greatly extend the operations so successfully begun.

Entirely apart from the Dufferin Fund are various provincial Associations in India for providing trained nurses for serious cases of sickness among Europeans, which are also much deserving of general support. There are 8 of these with an annual income of Rs.70,000. The Countess of Minto has taken special interest in this work.

THE INDIAN ADMINISTRATION

The supreme authority in India, subject to the Secretary of State, is vested in the Viceroy and Governor-General, at present the Right Hon. Lord Hardinge of Penshurst, and his Council of eight Members, viz., the Commander-in-Chief and the Members in charge of the Home, Revenue, Public Works, and Irrigation, Finance, Commerce, Education, and Legislative Departments, at the heads of which, and of the Foreign Department, is a Secretary to the Government of India.

Under the Home Department are included the subjects of Justice, Police, Prisons, Education, Public Health, Local Self-Government, Lunatic Asylums, and the like; Forests and Mines are among the subjects dealt with by the Revenue Department; while Commerce, Excise, and Stamps are subject to the Financial Department. The Postal and Telegraph Departments are also administered under the direct control of the Supreme Government by two Director-Generals.

The Legislative Council of the Governor-General includes the Members of the Executive Council, from which it is entirely distinct, and a number of additional members, official and non-official, the latter for the most part selected.

The great experiment made in 1909 of largely increasing the number of elected members of these councils, and of appointing native members to Executive Councils, will be watched with deep interest by all persons interested in India.

The army is under the control of the Commander-in-Chief, at present General Sir O'Moore Creagh, K.C.B., C.I.E., and under the direct orders of two Lieutenant-Generals, commanding the Southern and Northern Armies with Headquarters at Ootacamand and Meerut. Under them the army is distributed into ten Divisions, including Burma. In addition to the usual headquarters staff of the army there are Inspector-Generals of cavalry and artillery.

At the head of each province is a Governor, Lieutenant-Governor, or Chief Commissioner. The two Governors of Bombay and Madras have hitherto been assisted by a Council of two members, to which an Indian member has now been added, and in these Governments, and those of Lower Bengal, the United Provinces of Agra and Oudh, the Panjab and Burma is a Provincial Legislative Council. In every province the administration is, generally speaking, divided into two branches—the Judicial and the Executive. At the head of the former is a High Court, Chief Court, or Judicial Commissioner, and at the head of the latter usually a Board of Revenue or a Financial Commissioner. This link in the revenue administration is, however, missing in Bombay, as the link of Commissioners is lacking in Madras. Next in the official scale come the Commissioners of Divisions, exercising control over a number of districts which constitute the administrative units of the country. At the head of each district is a Collector or Deputy-Commissioner, who is also District Magistrate, and is responsible for the administration of Criminal Justice, Police, Revenue, and all executive work in his jurisdiction. He is assisted by a number of English and Native Magistrates and Officers at the headquarters of each district,—in some cases by officers in charge of sub-divisions of the district,—and in all cases by Native Magistrates and Sub-Collectors in charge of portions of the districts, known variously as tehsils, talukas, and the like. Much of the petty magisterial work of the country is done by honorary magistrates appointed by Government; while the management of the local concerns of Municipalities and District Boards is mainly in the hands of members of the native community selected or elected. At the headquarters of Government are the heads of the various Departments of Public Works, Police, Education, Forests, Medical Relief and Sanitation, while under the Financial Commissioner or the Board of Revenue is usually a Director of Land Records, responsible for the maintenance of the revenue records of the province, and in the first instance for the settlements of Land Revenue, and a Commissioner of Excise, Registration, and the like.

AREA AND POPULATION OF BRITISH INDIA AND NATIVE STATES: (CENSUS OF 1911).

PROVINCE, STATE, OR AGENCY.	Area in Square Miles.	Towns.	Villages.	Persons. Males.	Persons. Females.	Persons. Total.	Population, Census 1901.	Difference per cent. 1911 and 1901.
PROVINCES.								
1. Ajmere Merwara	2,711	4	740	266,170	235,266	501,436	476,912	+5·1
2. Andamans and Nicobars	3,143	—	63	19,570	6,877	26,447	24,649	+7·3
3. Baluchistan * (*Districts and Administered Territories*)	45,804	6	1,274	251,811	186 205	438,016	401.648	+9·1
4. Bengal	115,819	142	137,489	26,264,748	26,391,713	52,656.461	50,715,794	+3·8
5. Bombay	123,064	202	25,699	10,239,722	9,424,824	19,664,546	18,559,650	+6·0
6. Burma * †	236,738	52	60,395	6,144,301	5,913,604	12,057,905	10,490,624	+14·9
7. Central Provinces and Berar ‡	100,345	102	37,905	6,931,505	6,986,132	13,917,637	11,967,132	+16·3
8. Coorg	1,582	5	479	97,315	77,689	175,004	180,607	−3·1
9. Eastern Bengal and Assam §	106,130	61	91,760	17,392,218	16,586.089	33,978,300	30,510.344	+11·4
10. Madras	141,726	234	54,610	20,386,338	21,015,688	41,402,020	38,229,654	+8·3
11. North-West Frontier Province ‖	16,466	20	3,348	1,184,201	1,014,828	2,199,029	2,046,218	+7·5
12. Punjab	97,209	171	32,663	10,985,638	8,976,520	12,962,165	20,330,337	−1·8
13. United Provinces of Agra and Oudh	107,164	453	105,068	24,628,344	22,565,048	47,193,392	47,691,238	−1·0
Total, British Territory	1,097,901	1,452	551,493	124,791.881	119,380,490	244,172.371	231,624.807	+5·4

* Certain areas were imperfectly enumerated owing to tribal disputes.
† Includes Shan States, Chin Hills, and Karenni.
‡ Berar was amalgamated for administrative purposes with the Central Provinces from 1908.
§ Includes Manipur and Hill Tippera.
‖ The North-West Frontier Province was formed in 1901 out of certain Punjab Districts and certain areas not previously included in India.

AREA AND POPULATION OF BRITISH INDIA AND NATIVE STATES.—*continued.*

Province, State, or Agency.	Area in Square Miles.	Towns.	Villages.	Persons. Males.	Persons. Females.	Persons. Total.	Population Census 1901.	Difference per cent. 1911 and 1901.
STATES AND AGENCIES.								
14. Baluchistan (*Agency Tracts*) *	86,511	—	780	201,868	171,127	372,905	409,098	−8·8
15. Baroda State	8,099	47	3,035	1,055,360	976,087	2,031,453	1,952,692	+4·0
16. Bengal States	82,773	13	21,418	2,270,645	2,265,012	4,535,657	3,881,448	+16·9
17. Bombay States	65,761	129	14,995	3,764,379	3,645,645	7,410,024	6,908,559	+7·3
18. Central India Agency	78,772	80	33,282	4,804,914	4,560,251	9,365,165	8,514,114	+10·0
19. Central Provinces States	29,435	11	11,983	1,053,467	1,063,939	2,117,406	1,631,140	+29·8
20. Hyderabad State	82,698	78	20,011	6,795,209	6,580,260	13,375,469	11,141,142	+20·0
21. Kashmir State	80,900	2	8,946	—	—	—	—	—
22. Madras State	9,969	17	4,997	2,413,263	2,400,381	4,813,644	4,188,086	+14·9
23. Mysore State	29,444	128	16,884	2,934,651	2,872,145	5,806,796	5,539,399	+4·8
24. North-West Frontier Province (*Agencies and Tribal Areas*)	—	—	—	864,868	757,210	1,622,078	79,278	—
25. Punjab State	36,532	57	10,997	2,321,997	1,888,039	4,210,036	4,424,398	−4·8
26. Rajputana Agency	127,541	128	29,901	5,506,213	5,007,898	10,514,111	9,842,410	+6·8
27. United Provinces State	5,097	6	3,576	429,367	402,384	831,751	802,091	+3·7
Total, Native States	675,267	696	177,112	36,427,495	34,401,233	70,828,728	62,736,249	+12·9
Grand Total, India	1,773,168	2,148	728,605	161,219,376	153,781,723	315,001,099	294,361,056	+7·0

* Certain areas were imperfectly enumerated owing to tribal disputes.

DISTRIBUTION OF POPULATION ACCORDING TO RELIGION (CENSUS OF 1901).

Administrations.	Hindus.	Sikhs.	Jains.	Budd-hists.	Parsis.	Moham-medans.	Chris-tians.	Jews.	Animistic.	Minor Religions and Religions not returned.	Total.
PROVINCES.											
Ajmer-Merwara	380,819	264	19,922	—	164	72,031	3,712	—	—	—	476,912
Andamans and Nicobars	9,264	370	61	1,860	2	4,207	486	—	8,198	201	24,649
Baluchistan (Districts, &c.)	21,897	2,947	8	—	166	279,154	4,026	48	—	—	308,246
Bengal	39,245,612	806	5,010	47,263	384	9,027,069	245,869	1,925	2,148,407	222	50,722,067
Bombay	14,200,047	1,122	227,696	547	76,009	3,760,175	208,930	12,928	69,980	2,177	18,559,561
Burma	285,484	6,596	93	9,184,121	245	339,446	147,525	685	399,390	127,039	10,490,624
Central Provinces and Berar	9,964,151	1,926	66,931	169	1,499	503,792	26,470	130	1,426,602	—	11,991,670
Coorg	159,817	—	107	—	41	13,654	3,683	—	3,305	—	180,607
Eastern Bengal and Assam	11,639,491	527	4,258	178,275	7	17,868,452	66,076	15	1,204,305	53	30,961,459
Madras	34,043,097	92	27,431	243	356	2,467,351	1,024,071	45	641,730	20	38,209,436
North-West Frontier Province	134,252	28,091	37	—	46	1,957,777	5,273	4	—	—	2,125,480
Punjab	7,874,413	1,517,019	42,745	4,182	445	10,825,698	65,811	14	—	12	20,330,339
United Provinces	40,757,137	15,319	84,401	783	578	6,731,034	102,469	54	—	2	47,691,782
Total	158,720,481	1,574,579	478,700	9,417,443	79,942	53,849,840	1,904,401	15,848	5,901,867	129,726	232,072,832
STATES AND AGENCIES.											
Baluchistan (Agency Tracts)	16,261	25	—	—	—	486,214	—	—	—	—	502,500
Baroda	1,546,992	38	48,290	—	8,409	165,014	7,691	8	176,250	—	1,952,692
Bengal States	2,949,872	12	374	27,265	1	230,074	3,241	7	537,698	—	3,748,544
Bombay States	5,719,116	451	308,420	—	2,871	840,701	11,157	991	24,915	26	6,908,648
Central India	6,983,348	2,004	112,998	—	1,002	528,833	8,114	24	992,458	—	8,628,781
Central Provinces States	1,573,634	95	877	—	11	12,011	782	—	408,973	—	1,996,383
Hyderabad	9,870,839	4,335	20,345	3	1,463	1,155.750	22,996	13	65,315	83	11,141,142
Kashmir	689,073	25,828	442	35,047	11	2,154,695	422	—	—	60	2,905,578
Madras States	2,978,374	15	6	227	7	265,580	910,409	1,288	32,175	5	4,188,086
Mysore	5,099,177	12	13,682	10	101	289,697	50,059	34	86,627	—	5,539,399
Punjab States	2,470,056	585,877	7,238	2,758	32	1,357,647	780	10	—	—	4,424,398
Rajputana	8,090,269	2,054	342,595	—	339	924,656	2,840	5	360,543	—	9,723,301
United Provinces States	558,727	14	181	—	1	242,688	486	—	—	—	802,097
Total	48,545,738	620,760	855,448	65,310	14,248	8,653,560	1,018,977	2,380	2,684,954	174	62,461,549
Grand Total	207,147,026	2,195,339	1,334,148	9,476,759	94,190	62,458,077	2,923,241	18,228	8,584,148	129,900	294,361,056

CHRISTIAN POPULATION.

Distribution according to Race and Denomination.

Race.	Church of England.*	Presbyterian.	Baptist.	Methodist.	Congregationalist.	Lutheran and Allied Denominations.	Roman Catholic.	Syrian.	Others.	Total.
Europeans	111,764	9,693	2,108	5,998	421	1,400	33,964	6	4,323	169,677
Eurasians	35,781	1,439	2,017	2,420	140	287	45,697	1	1,469	89,251
Natives	305,917	42,799	216,915	68,489	37,313	153,768	1,122,508	571,320	145,284	2,664,313
Total	453,462	53,931	221,040	76,907	37,874	155,455	1,202,169	571,327	151,076	2,923,241

* Including 29,644 who described themselves as Protestants.

Territorial Distribution according to Race.

Race.	British Provinces.	Assam.	Bengal.	Bombay Presidency.	Central Provinces.	Madras.	United Provinces.	N.W.F. Provinces.	Panjab.	Burma.	Other Provinces.
Europeans	153,601	2,099	27,377	31,175	4,832	13,998	28,410	4,698	25,807	9,885	5,320
Eurasians	75,375	275	23,038	6,541	2,186	26,185	5,218	42	2,309	8,449	1,132
Natives	1,675,288	33,595	224,710	171,214	17,791	983,888	68,841	533	37,695	129,191	7,830
Total	1,904,264	35,969	275,125	208,930	24,809	1,024,071	102,469	5,273	65,811	147,525	14,282

Race.	States and Agencies.	Baroda.	Central India Agency.	Hyderabad.	Bombay States.	Mysore.	Madras States.	Other States.
Europeans	16,076	91	3,827	4,347	704	4,753	613	1,741
Eurasians	13,876	57	572	3,292	348	5,721	3,007	879
Natives	989,025	7,543	3,715	15,357	10,105	39,585	906,789	5,931
Total	1,018,977	7,691	8,114	22,996	11,157	50,059	910,409	8,551

Details of the Working of Certain Imperial Departments

The following figures will give some idea of the enormous operations to which the Indian Administration extends.

Post Office

The number of post offices in the country is in round figures 18,400, of letter-boxes 43,000, of village postmen 8500, of total establishment 96,000. The length of railways and roads over which mails are conveyed is 156,000 m., and the mails so conveyed comprise in round numbers.

Letters and Post Cards	767,922,728
Parcels	50,107,799
Newspapers	51,084,486
Packets	6,140,819
Total,	875,255,832

Nearly 6,200,000 of parcels were sent under the Value Payable System. The number of money orders amounts to 24,000,000, and the value to £25,000,000. The amount deposited in the Post Office Savings Banks is £10,000,000 sterling, and the number of depositors well over a million.

Telegraphs

The length of telegraph lines open is 70,000 m. (wires 281,000 m.), and of cables 390 m. The number of offices open, largely in connection with post offices, is 2600, and the number of messages sent 13,000,000 (one million being foreign messages), of a value of £649,000. The Indo-European Telegraph Department which controls the service between India and England through Persia has a land line of 2575 m. and a cable line of 1951 knots, and a revenue of £110,000.

Railways

The number of miles of railway open in 1910 was 32,099, of which number nearly one-third were constructed during the last decade. This mileage is considerably larger than that of France, nearly as large as that of Austro-Hungary, three times larger than that of Italy, and about 6000 m. less than that of the Germanic Empire. 18,000 m. of railway are of the standard gauge (5½ ft.) and 12,600 of the metre gauge (3 ft. 3⅜ in.) or less. 257 m. are included in State lines, 900 in guaranteed Companies, 2900 in assisted Companies, and 3500 in Native States. The number of passengers conveyed in the year was 371,000,000; the average late earnings have been 511,422 lakhs, and the net gain 2¾ millions. The development of Indian railways during the last thirty-five years has been phenomenal. The return on capital outlay is now 5·46 per cent.

The mileage under construction or sanction is 3000 m., the principal works being Itarsi to Nagpur 184 m., Nagpur to Chindwara 93 m., Paphaman to Unas 114 m., Kalabagh to Bannu 83 m., Shari to Younghwe 100 m., and Sujangarh to Hissar, 133 m. The control of Railways and Railway Schemes is now exercised by a Government Railway Board.

FINANCIAL DETAILS

The principal sources of revenue and heads of expenditure are as follows, in pounds sterling:—

REVENUE.	million £	EXPENDITURE.	million £
Land Revenue	£19¾	Direct demands on revenue	£9
Opium	6	Interest	2
Salt	3¼	Post Office, Mint, Telegraphs	2¾
Stamps	4¼	Civil Departments	14¼
Customs	5¾	Other civil charges	5
Excise	6½	Famine Relief and Insurance	1
Other main heads	7	Railways	11
Railways	10	Irrigation	3
Post Office, Mint, Telegraph	3	Other public works	4½
Irrigation	3½	Army	20
Miscellaneous	7¼	Miscellaneous	3
Total,	£76¼	Total,	£75½

The total debt of India is £276,000,000, of which £147,000,000 constitute the Home Debt. Against this are more than counterbalancing assets in the value of railways £224,000,000, irrigation works £31,000,000, cash currency 18 millions, loans repayable 15 millions, etc. The Government cash balance is about £17,000,000.

NATIVE CHRISTIANS

THE spread of Christianity[1] in India is a matter of deep interest, upon which full details will be found in the annual reports of the various Missionary Societies at work in the country, and much valuable information in the Provincial Census Reports of 1901. These show a remarkable increase of Native Christians during the previous decade; but it is noticeable that in many instances this is very much more marked in new than in old fields of missionary work. In the Madras Presidency Native Christians of all denominations now number over 1,000,000, showing an increase of 19 per cent. in the previous decade. The converts are chiefly from the lowest Hindu classes: 643,000 belong to the Roman Catholic Communion. 140,000 to the Anglican, 119,000 to the Baptist, and

[1] St Francis Xavier began mission work in India in 1542. The first Protestant missionaries were the Lutherans at Tranquebar in 1706, the Baptists at Serampore in 1793, and the Anglican Church in 1813.

78,000 to the Lutheran. The districts with the largest Christian populations are Tinnewelly, Kistna, Trichinopoly, Tanjore, S. Arcot, and Nellore. The Syrian Christians (see page 414) number 2000 Jacobites and 700 others. In the Bombay Presidency there are now 216,000 Native Christians, an increase of 29 per cent. in the decade; of these, 107,000 are Roman Catholics, and 36,000 members of the Anglican Communion. A remarkable increase of 23,000 occurred in the Kaira Districts, including 5000 soldiers of the Salvation Army. In Bengal the numbers are slightly greater than in Bombay, half being Roman Catholics, 70,000 Lutherans, 58,000 Anglicans, and 22,000 Baptists. An extraordinary development, from 78,000 in 1881 to 125,000 in 1901, has taken place in the Ranchi District of Chhota Nagpur; next to this District the largest numbers of Native Christians are to be found in the Sonthal Pergannahs. In the United Provinces of Agra and Lucknow there are now 69,000 Native Christians—against 13,000 twenty years ago—chiefly belonging to Methodist Communions: in no one district are there so many as 10,000 converts. In the Panjab the numbers are now 38,000, which include 8000 sweepers; the largest numbers are in the Sialkot District and on the Chenab Colony (p. 241), where their development will be a matter of special interest. In 1881 there were only 4000 Native Christians in this Province. Whatever may be individual opinions regarding the work or results of proselytising in India, the value of the work done in the mission colleges and schools and hospitals is immense, and is becoming very far-reaching in its effects. The Protestant missions with the largest numbers of converts are the C.M.S., American Baptist Union, Methodist Episcopal Church, London Missionary Society, and S.P.G. The number of mission Hospitals and Dispensaries is 300, the number of pupils in mission colleges and schools 425,000; the number of European missionaries at work is 4000, and of Indian missionaries, 37,000.

THE MUTINY OF 1857

As the mutiny of the Bengal Army in 1857 forms perhaps the most important episode in the whole history of British rule in India, and as it is fraught with special memories for all Englishmen, a brief sketch of the principal outlines of it is given here.

From 1764 to 1857 the history of British rule is marked by various mutinies among the native troops or sepoys. Ever since the days of Dupleix and Clive, sepoys, led by European officers, have formed the principal part of European armaments in India, in which the fighting races have ever been willing to serve for the sake of two kinds of reward, pay and prestige. The first serious mutiny, in 1764, was for an increase of pay. It was promptly suppressed by Major Hector Munro, who refused the higher pay, and ordered the twenty-four ringleaders to be blown from guns. There was a more extensive rising in Madras in 1806. It began at Vellore (p. 396), where a number of British officers were murdered, but Colonel Gillespie galloped from Arcot, eight miles off, and recaptured the fort, and killed or dispersed the mutineers. On this occasion the complaint of the sepoys was that orders had been issued forbidding the use of earrings, and caste marks, and beards, and that the new hat had a leather cockade made from skins which were unclean to them. The dethroned Mohammedan princes of Mysore, who lived with numerous attendants in the fortress of Vellore, told the sepoys that the new regulations were intended to deprive them of their caste, and force them to become Christians ; and the report was spread that the British power had been extinguished by Napoleon. The mutinous spirit extended nearly throughout Madras before it was finally quenched. The Home Government declared that the mutinies were due to the fear of being Christianised, to the residence of the princes at Vellore, to the annexations of Lord Wellesley, which had shaken confidence in British moderation and good faith, and to a loss of authority by British officers over their men. The analogy between Vellore in 1806, and Meerut in 1857, is very striking, the chief difference being that the sepoys had greater causes of discontent in 1857, and that at Meerut there was no Gillespie. At the latter date the religion of the sepoys seemed to them to be in greater danger than ever; the capital of India, Delhi, was the home of the dethroned descendant of the Mughals; Lord Dalhousie's annexations had far exceeded those of Lord Wellesley, and seemed likely to be still further pursued; the discipline of native regiments was disturbed by the encouragements held out to their British officers to seek employment on the General Staff; and Russia in the Crimea was supposed to have destroyed British power more effectively even than Napoleon. And yet Vellore had been so completely forgotten, that Sir Henry Lawrence was one of the few prominent Englishmen in India who foresaw the rising, or understood what it would mean. Generally there was on all sides a blind, if touching, faith in the loyalty of the sepoys, which in the case of the Officers of native regiments was only extinguished by sepoy murderers.

The eight years from 1848-56, when Lord Dalhousie was Governor-General, will long be remembered in India. They form a period of large social and material reforms, and are also specially remarkable for British annexations of native territory. After a severe struggle with the warlike Sikhs the Panjab was conquered and annexed in 1849. Lower Burma followed in 1852, and Oudh, without conquest, in 1856. By a doctrine, not generally applied in the past, the territory of native princes who died without an heir of the body, was now treated as lapsed to the British, an adopted heir not being recognised, and under this rule were resumed the principalities of Satara, Jhansi, Nagpur, and others. It was also decided that the stipends which had been paid to those native princes who had been deprived of their territories in former years, should not be continued to their successors. Among others, the Nana Sahib, the adopted heir of the ex-Peishwa of Poona, Baji Rao II., once the head of the Mahrattas, was refused the pension of £80,000 per annum which his father had enjoyed during his life. The descendant of the Mughals, Bahadur Shah, had been informed that his successor would not be allowed to live at Delhi, or to retain the regal title. And when the territory of the loyal king of Oudh was annexed, owing to his persistent misgovernment, the surplus revenues of the State, after payment of a substantial pension to the king, were gathered into the coffers of the British Government. All this looked like a policy of unjust and high-handed aggression. The natives understood annexation after conquest, and the conquered provinces of Panjab and lower Burma remained loyal throughout the Mutiny. But now every native prince feared for his dominion, as the British seemed to be absorbing all such territory, either by conquest, or on the plea of misgovernment, or by the new rule excluding adopted heirs; and this policy seemed to be further evidenced by the resumption of pensions, and the confiscation of the surplus revenue of Oudh. Of the chiefs directly affected the kings of Delhi and Oudh were Mohammedans, who consider themselves the natural rulers of India and likely to profit by the ejection of the British; while the Rani of Jhansi and the Nana Sahib were Mahratta Hindus, and the Mahrattas had practically conquered the Mohammedans when the British intervened in 1803. The leaders of two of the most warlike races in India, and of the two religions, were under the belief that they had met with harsh treatment at the hands of the British; and they determined, if possible, to work on the sepoys, the greater number of whom were Brahmans, and other high caste men from the Oudh country and the Gangetic Doab, and a portion of whom were already in an insubordinate condition.

In 1856 one of the first innovations of the new Governor-General, Lord Canning, was the General Service Enlistment Act, by which all future recruits in Bengal were made liable for service outside the Company's dominions without extra pay. This had always been the rule in the Madras and Bombay armies. But the Bengal sepoy was a man of high caste, and had enjoyed privileges in the past. He was now, he considered, threatened with the loss of caste by being taken over the sea (the dreaded kála páni or "black water")

g

to serve in Burma; and while he held that he alone had conquered India for the Company, he believed that he was now to be used for further conquests without any increase of pay in regions far from his home. The agitators impressed upon his superstitious and credulous mind that the railways and telegraphs which had recently been introduced, were a kind of magic designed to oppose him, and that the new law, made by Lord Canning, which permitted the re-marriage of Hindu widows, and the new zeal for education, were really attacks upon his religion. The sepoys knew also that while the British troops had been reduced by drafts sent to the Crimea, and to Persia, the native army had been increased for the purpose of garrisoning the recently acquired territories, and that the British force was now only 40,000 to 240,000 sepoys. The prestige of England had been shaken by the disasters of the Afghan war; it was believed that the British had been beaten in the Crimea; and an old prophecy was revived which foretold that the Company's reign would end in 1857, one hundred years after the battle of Plassey. At this critical moment, with Mughal and Mahratta, Mohammedan and Hindu, Princes seriously disaffected towards the British, with an army of high caste soldiers alarmed concerning their pay, their privileges, and their religion, and with the British force unduly reduced, there occurred the famous cartridge incident. A new type of rifle having been issued to the sepoys, the unhappy blunder was perpetrated of smearing the cartridge with a composition of the fat of the cow, the sacred animal of the Hindūs. On complaints being made, the British officers declared that no cow's fat had been used for the cartridges issued to the men; but this did not satisfy them, and the Commander-in-Chief himself (General Anson) expressed the opinion that he was not surprised at their alarm at the appearance of the greased cartridges. In these circumstances it was clear that any untoward incident might precipitate a general mutiny.

The first regiment to mutiny was the 34th Native Infantry at Barrackpur, near Calcutta, in February 1857, and this was followed in March by the 19th at Berhampore, in the same neighbourhood. Both these regiments were disbanded, and the 84th (British) was brought over from Burma to Barrackpur. But nothing else was done. "Allahabad and Delhi, the two chief fortresses, arsenals, and strategical positions of the North Western Provinces, were still without the protection of British garrisons, and no steps, such as the collection of supplies and carriage, had been taken anywhere for the prompt movement or mobilisation of British troops" (MacLeod Innes). On the 3rd May the 7th Oudh Irregulars mutinied at Lucknow, and were disarmed by Sir Henry Lawrence. Then on the 10th came the great outbreak at Meerut, 40 miles from Delhi. The

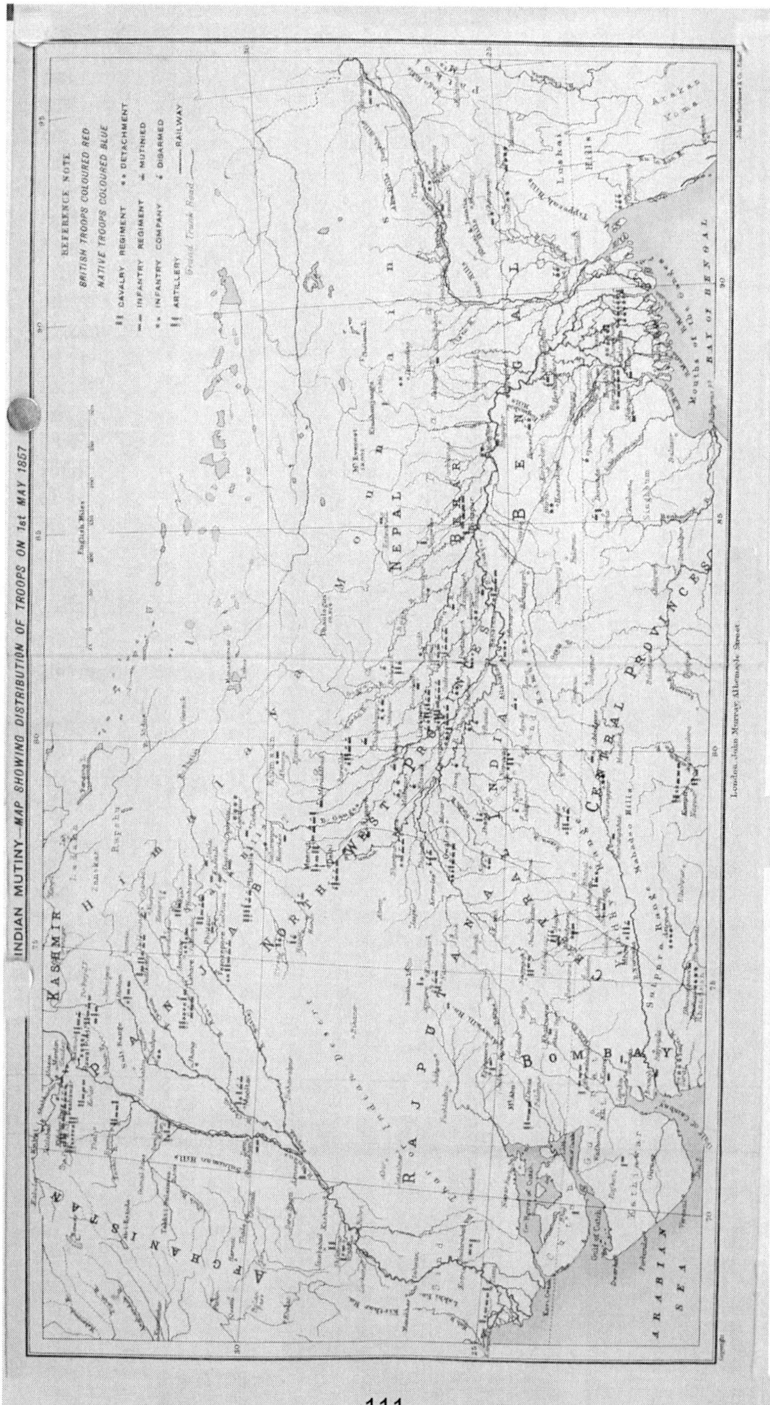
INDIAN MUTINY—MAP SHOWING DISTRIBUTION OF TROOPS ON 1st MAY 1857
REFERENCE NOTE
BRITISH TROOPS COLOURED RED
NATIVE TROOPS COLOURED BLUE
CAVALRY REGIMENT
DETACHMENT
INFANTRY REGIMENT
MUTINIED
INFANTRY COMPANY
DISARMED
ARTILLERY
RAILWAY
Grand Trunk Road
English Miles
KASHMIR
NEPAL
BENGAL
BOMBAY
CENTRAL PROVINCES
ARABIAN SEA
BAY OF BENGAL
London: John Murray, Albemarle Street

sepoys, after murdering some of their officers and other Europeans, and liberating some of their comrades, who had been imprisoned for insubordination, made off for Delhi. On arriving at that place on the 11th they were joined by the three regiments there, when it was seen that no pursuit from Meerut was to be feared; and after the Arsenal had been captured and many officers murdered, and every vestige of British authority destroyed, they declared the King of Delhi Emperor of India, and his sons placed themselves at their head.

Probably this forward move of the Mughal party aroused the jealousy of the other rival conspirators, and for three weeks there was no other mutiny. But when the natives found that days and weeks passed without any punishment being inflicted, they began to think that the British power was really at an end. On the 30th May the 71st Native Infantry mutinied at Lucknow, and from this date there was a general rising. In some cases British officers, women, and children were all murdered; in others the men alone were killed, and in still others they were all spared, and even escorted by the mutineers out of harm's way. As each regiment rose, it made for Delhi, Cawnpore, or Lucknow, which became the centres of the conflict.[1] While Delhi, the historical capital of India, was in the hands of the rebels, at Cawnpore, Sir Hugh Wheeler with a mere handful of soldiers was surrounded by overwhelming numbers from the 6th June, and at Lucknow, a garrison under Sir Henry Lawrence was closely invested from 2nd July.

On the 10th of May there were between Calcutta and Meerut, only three British regiments—the 14th at Dinapore, the 32nd at Lucknow, and a Company's Regt., the 3rd Europeans, at Agra. *Lord Canning*, who was at Calcutta, made energetic efforts to obtain reinforcements. The Madras Fusiliers, under Colonel Neill, arrived at Calcutta on the 23rd May; the 64th and 70th from Persia early in June; and other British troops from Burma, Ceylon, and Singapore, and loyal sepoys from Madras soon followed. A force which was on its way to China was, with the consent of Lord Elgin, diverted to Calcutta; several regiments were despatched from the Cape Colony, and urgent requests for additional troops were sent to England. But the means of transport for those on the spot were sadly insufficient; the railway from Calcutta had been completed only as far as Raniganj, a distance of 120 miles, and there was difficulty in procuring country carriage; and so it happened that the troops from Calcutta were only just in time to secure Benares and Allahabad, and it was not till the 7th July that General Havelock was

[1] A more detailed account of the events at these important places will be found on pp. 189, 301, and 285. The sequence of events throughout India will best be seen by referring to p. cviii. of the Chronology.

able to advance from the last place with an inadequate force of 2000 men. *General Anson*, who was at Simla in May, at once collected the British and Goorkha regiments which were in the hills, and began to move on Delhi; but his progress was slow owing to lack of transport and commissariat, and on the 27th May he died of cholera at Karnal. The attack upon Delhi did not begin until the 8th June, when Sir H. Barnard, with a force amounting to 3800 men, defeated a rebel army of 30,000 men at Badli-ki-sarai, and thus obtained possession of the famous Ridge overlooking the walls of Delhi. General Barnard died of cholera on the 5th July, and was succeeded by General Reed, who resigned on the 17th owing to ill-health, handing over the command to General Archdale Wilson. The mutineers had purposely timed their rising for the beginning of the hot weather, knowing how debilitating active operations are at that period to all Europeans. For some time the British, while affecting to invest Delhi, were themselves closely besieged on the ridge. In the Panjab *Sir John Lawrence* was ably supported by such men as Chamberlain, Nicholson, Edwardes, and Montgomery, and the local mutinies or threats of mutiny at Peshawar, Nowshera, Mooltan, Meean Meer, and Ferozepore were energetically suppressed by disarmament, and the important arsenals at Phillour and Ferozepore were secured. A movable column was formed under the command first of General Chamberlain and afterwards of General Nicholson, to suppress any further risings in the Panjab, and then to march on Delhi, and the value of the courage and decision of the latter can hardly be over-estimated. The Panjab was in a restless condition. With his small force, moving from place to place, disarming or dispersing the mutineers, General Nicholson kept mutiny from spreading. But it was not until the 14th August, three months after the Meerut outbreak, that he was able to join the British force at Delhi. No final move could be made there until on the 6th September the siege guns arrived from Ferozepore. These opened on the walls on the 11th, and prepared the way for the storming of the city on the 14th, and the final capture of Delhi on the 20th. It came not a day too soon. Sir John Lawrence had emptied his province of British troops, sending every possible man to Delhi; and the Sikhs and other Panjabis were becoming uneasy at the idea that the British might not regain their position. If these troops had not stood by us we should have had to begin again the conquest of India.

Meanwhile, the British between Calcutta and Delhi were in sore straits. At Agra the sepoys were disarmed on the 31st May; but although the Maharaja Sindhia of Gwalior was himself loyal, his fine body of disciplined troops only awaited an opportunity to march on Agra. At Cawnpore, Sir H. Wheeler's small garrison capitulated on the 26th June, and were massacred next day, most of the women and children being made prisoners. At Lucknow a small British force was holding out against enormous numbers of the enemy. *General Havelock* advanced to their assistance with 1400 British and 600 Sikh troops, leaving Allahabad on the 7th July. The line between Calcutta and Allahabad was disturbed and communications threatened, and no substantial reinforcements could be sent to him till the middle of September. When he had marched for five days from Allahabad he defeated a large force of mutineers and Mahrattas at Fatehpur, and fought two other successful battles on the 15th of July at Aong and Pandu Naddi. On the evening of that day, being then 22 miles from Cawnpore, he learned that the British women and children of Wheeler's garrison were still alive, and, tired as his men were, he marched them 14 miles that night, defeated the Nana Sahib next day in three separate actions, and rested his weary troops on the outskirts of Cawnpore on the evening of the 16th. The heat was so intense that some of his men died from sunstroke or exhaustion. The captives had, however, been murdered by the orders of the Nana on the 15th, when General Havelock had started on his last desperate effort to save them. On the 17th he occupied Cawnpore. On the 20th, leaving 300 men under General Neill, he began the crossing of the Ganges with 1500 men. On the 29th he defeated the rebels at Unao and Bisirat Ganj, but, finding immense numbers of mutineers still between him and Lucknow, while his own force had been reduced to 850 effectives, he had no alternative but to retire to Cawnpore. On the 4th August he marched out of Cawnpore a second time with 1400 men; on the 5th he again defeated the rebels at Bisirat Ganj, but his losses from disease, as well as battle, had been so great that it was hopeless to proceed further, and he fell back once more, reaching Cawnpore on the 13th. On the 16th he attacked and defeated 4000 sepoys at Bithur. He had now only 1000 effectives. In his front towards Lucknow were some 30,000 rebels; at Farukhabad were probably as many more; he was threatened on both flanks; and had to face on the south the Gwalior contingent, and many other smaller bodies; yet he courageously determined to keep his position at Cawnpore instead of falling back upon Allahabad. The relief of Lucknow was, however, out of the question until reinforcements arrived. These dribbled in during the next month, but there was mischievous delay between Calcutta and Allahabad, some 6000 men, who might have been sent on to Havelock, being detained to suppress local disturbances. On the 15th September Sir James Outram, who had been appointed to command the relieving force, arrived at Cawnpore, but in the most generous and chivalrous manner forebore to supersede General Havelock, and thus left the honour of relieving Lucknow to the man who had already made such able and gallant efforts to that end. At length, on the 19th September, General Havelock crossed the Ganges, with 3000 men. He defeated the rebels at Mangalwar on the 21st, and on the 23rd, 24th, and 25th, gradually fought his way into Lucknow, and finally effected a junction with the garrison late in the evening of the last date with a loss of 700 out of his 3000 men. General Outram then took command of the old and the new garrisons at Lucknow. Delhi having fallen to the British between the 14th and 20th September, many of the mutineers there proceeded to Lucknow, and General Outram found it impossible to fight his way out taking with him the women, children, and sick of the old garrison. He therefore remained on the defensive, closely invested, until the final relief of Lucknow, two months later.

The dangerous period of the mutiny ended with the capture of Delhi and the first relief of Lucknow towards the end of September. From this time the British position was assured by the arrival of reinforcements from England. In front of them came *Sir Colin Campbell*, the newly-appointed Commander-in-Chief in India, who reached Calcutta on the 17th August. His first care was to arrange that regular batches of the reinforcements should be forwarded with all speed. Then he started for the seat of war, and reached Cawnpore early in November. Leaving 1000 men under General Windham at that place, he moved on Lucknow with 5000; reached the Alam Bagh on the 12th November; left a garrison there; marched upon the rebels with 4200 men on the 16th; and effected a junction with Outram's beleaguered force on the 17th, though with a loss of nearly 500 men. The original Lucknow garrison, which had been closely invested since the 2nd July, a period of more than four months, was thus finally relieved. But Sir Colin found the rebels so numerous, and the difficulty of escorting the women, children, and sick safely out of Lucknow so great, that he felt unable to hold Lucknow in addition, and accordingly evacuated it on the 22nd, leaving General Outram at the Alam Bagh with 4000 men to maintain the appearance of British authority. General Havelock died of dysentery on the 24th November. When Sir Colin reached Cawnpore with his precious human freight, he found that General Windham had been defeated by the Mahratta Tantia Topi, and had been gradually forced out of the city of Cawnpore into his entrenchments on the banks of the Ganges. On the 3rd December the families and sick from Lucknow were sent on to Allahabad, and then Sir Colin attacked Tantia Topi and dispersed his army. Beyond clearing the Doab, the country between the Ganges and Jumna, little was done in the next three months except to collect further troops. On the 2nd March Sir Colin joined General Outram at the Alam Bagh with a force which the constant streams from Calcutta had at last raised to 19,000 men with 120 guns. To this was shortly added a brigade under General Franks, and a contingent of Nepalese under Maharaja Jung Bahadur, which brought the army up to a total of 31,000 men and 164 guns. The mutineers in Lucknow numbered 90,000 trained men, and a large force of irregulars, and they had employed their respite in erecting three strong lines of defences around their position. Sir Colin's attack began on the 7th March, and he finally drove off the enemy and captured Lucknow on the 15th.

On the 20th Lord Canning issued the Confiscation Proclamation, by which the estates of all the important chiefs in Oudh were escheated. Most of them, although certainly not loyal, had abstained from active participation in the revolt. They now rose, and were joined by other leaders who believed that they would be similarly treated, and had therefore nothing to lose, but everything to gain by opposing the British. Thus it happened that although the sepoys were dispersed, only small bands of them still remaining in the field, new enemies sprung up who were not subdued until the end of the year 1858, by which time there were 100,000 British troops in India. Of the various British brigades which operated in different parts of the country, the principal was that under *Sir Hugh Rose* (afterwards Lord Strathnairn), in Central India. On the 8th January 1858, General Rose left Mhow with a Bombay force, and marching northwards captured the fortresses of Ratgarh on the 28th, and Garrakota on the 13th February. After several successful battles he arrived before the walls of Jhansi on the 21st March. On the 1st April he totally defeated Tantia Topi, who was marching to the relief of Jhansi with 22,000 men, and stormed and captured Jhansi on the 4th April. The Rani fled with her defeated troops towards Kalpi, where Tantia Topi was collecting another army. General Rose marched out of Jhansi on the 25th April, defeated Tantia Topi on the 6th May, and captured Kalpi on the 23rd. The Rani then fled to Gwalior, where she was joined by the Maharaja's troops, and thus obtained possession of the strong fortress. In spite of the great heat General Rose marched upon Gwalior, and took it on the 20th June, the Rani, dressed as a man, being killed in one of the actions which took place round the fortress. The Mahratta leader was persistently hunted through Central India and Rajputana during the summer and the ensuing cold weather, and covered 3000 miles in his flight before he was betrayed ten months later, on the 7th April 1859, and was tried, and hanged. He had fought against us gallantly for over a year; but he had also given the signal for the massacre on 27th June 1857 at the Sati Chaura Ghat at Cawnpore. Meanwhile the rebellion in Oudh and the North West Provinces had been gradually suppressed, and the Nana had been driven into the Nepal jungle, where he is believed to have died of fever. The prophet who had announced that the Company's rule would end in 1857, a hundred years after the battle of Plassey, was not far out in his reckoning. On the 1st November 1858, at a grand darbar at Allahabad, Lord Canning announced that the Company's possessions in India were transferred to the British Crown.

Since the mutiny there has been a great change in British policy. The British troops, in 1857 one-sixth of the native, are now one half. All the strong fortresses, magazines, and arsenals, are garrisoned by British soldiers ; there are no batteries of native artillery of any importance ; and the modern preparations for transport, commissariat, and mobilisation combined with the railway system, ensure the speedy movement of British troops to any given spot. The high caste sepoy has been to a considerable extent replaced by a less exacting soldier, and the danger of a groundless religious panic thereby lessened. The right of adoption, for which many of the chiefs fought, has been conceded. The policy of annexation in India has been abandoned. The pay of the sepoy has been raised, whether on service in his own country or in foreign districts ; and the British officers of native regiments—still too few in numbers in spite of a wise recent increase—are no longer encouraged to leave their men for the attractions of civil or staff employment. Both races have learned their lesson. The best proof is that whereas formerly sepoy mutinies were of frequent occurrence, no single example has occurred in the space of nearly fifty-four years, to revive memories of the great tragedy of 1857.

REMARKABLE EVENTS CONNECTING INDIA WITH EUROPE

	DATES
Vasco da Gama sails to Calicut round the Cape of Good Hope	1498
The Portuguese Viceroy, Albuquerque, captures Goa	1510
Bassein, Salsette, and Bombay ceded to the Portuguese by the Chief of Guzerat	1534
Thomas Stephens, of New College, Oxford, becomes rector of the Jesuits' College at Salsette	1579
Charter from Queen Elizabeth to "The Governor and Company of Merchants of London trading to the East Indies"	1601
The Dutch East India Company formed	1602
The first French East India Company formed	1604

	DATES
The Dutch occupy Pulicat (40 m. N. of Madras)	1609
The Emperor Jahangir issues a proclamation permitting the English to establish factories at Surat, Ahmedabad, Cambay, and Gogo	1611
The first Danish East India Company formed	1612
Captain Best defeats the Portuguese squadron at Swally, off Surat	1612
Sir Thomas Roe, ambassador to Jahangir, obtains favourable concessions for English trade.	1615
An English factory founded at Armagaon, Madras	1626
An English factory founded at Masulipatam	1622
The English Company allowed to trade in Bengal	1634
Fort St George founded at Madras by Francis Day	1639
Gabriel Broughton, surgeon of the *Hopewell*, obtains from the Emperor Shah Jahan, exclusive privileges of trading in Bengal for the English Company as a reward for his professional services to the Governor of Bengal	1642
The Dutch take Negapatam from the Portuguese	1660
Bombay ceded to England by the Portuguese as part of the Infanta Catherina's dower on her marriage with Charles II.	1661
French settlement established at Pondicherry	1674
A new English Company formed, with a capital of £2,000,000	1698
The old Company buys the site of Calcutta	1700
Death of the Emperor Aurangzeb, and decline of the Mughal power	1707
Through the arbitration of Lord Godolphin the two English Companies are amalgamated	1709
The Austrian Emperor Charles VI. grants a charter to the Ostend Company	1723
England and France at war in Europe	1743
A French fleet under La Bourdonnais captures Madras	1746
A British fleet under Admiral Boscawen besieges Pondicherry, but is repulsed. The treaty of Aix-la-Chapelle restores Madras to the British	1748
Dupleix places nominees of his own on the throne at Hyderabad and Arcot. The British support Muhammad Ali in Arcot. War between the English and French in the Carnatic	1749
Capture and subsequent defence of Arcot by Clive	1751
The French capitulate at Trichinopoly	1752
Clive returns to England	1753
Dupleix superseded. Treaty of peace between the British and French signed at Pondicherry	1754
Clive returns to India	1755
Suraj-ud-daulah, Nawab of Bengal, captures Calcutta. 20th June.—The tragedy of the Black Hole	1756
Recapture of Calcutta by Clive. 23rd June, Battle of Plassey. War with France renewed in the Carnatic	1757
Lally arrives with a French fleet. He takes Arcot. Clive is appointed the first Governor of the Company's settlements in Bengal	1758
Clive defeats the Dutch	1759
Eyre Coote totally defeats Lally at the battle of Wandiwash	1759
Arcot taken by the British.. Clive sails for England	1760
Pondicherry capitulates to the British. Fall of the French power in the Deccan	1760
Pondicherry restored to the French by the treaty of Paris. The first sepoy mutiny is suppressed by Major Hector Munro, who defeats the Nawab-Wazir of Oudh at the decisive battle of Buxar. Dupleix dies in poverty in Paris	1764

DATES

Lord Clive arrives at Calcutta as Governor-General. The revenues of Bengal, Behar, and Orissa granted to the Company by the Emperor Shah Alam II. 1765

The N. Circars (Sirkars) ceded to the British. Clive prohibits the servants of the Company from engaging in private trade or accepting presents, and increases their salaries. Lally is executed at Paris . 1766

Clive leaves India. The Nizam and Haidar Ali attack the British . 1767

The Nizam cedes the Carnatic 1768

Terrible famine in Bengal 1770

Warren Hastings, Governor-General of Bengal. Supreme Court established at Calcutta. The Dutch expelled from Negapatam by the British. The Rohilla chiefs defeated by the British. Salsette and Bassein taken by the Bombay troops. Clive commits suicide in England 1774

The Nawab of Oudh cedes Benares 1775

Chandernagore, Masulipatam, Karikal, and Pondicherry taken from the French 1777

The first Mahratta War begins. General Goddard's celebrated march across India. Convention of Wargaon. Captain Popham captures Gwalior 1779

Haidar Ali takes Arcot. Warren Hastings wounds Sir Philip Francis in a duel 1780

Sir Eyre Coote defeats Haidar Ali at Porto Novo. The British capture the Dutch ports of Pulicat and Sadras 1781

Death of Haidar Ali. The French assist Tipu Sultan, his son . . 1782

The captured French possessions restored to them by the treaty of Versailles 1783

Peace with Tipu Sultan; the conquests on both sides restored. Pitt's Bill establishes a Board of Control. 1784

13th February.—Warren Hastings impeached by the House of Commons, before the House of Lords, for corruption and oppression 1788

Tipu Sultan ravages part of Travancore 1790

Lord Cornwallis leads the British army against Tipu Sultan in person. Takes Bangalore. Is joined by the Nizam and the Peshwa . . 1791

The allies storm the redoubts at Seringapatam. Tipu Sultan yields one-half of his dominions, to be divided between the Nizam, the Peshwa, and the British, and agrees to pay £3,000,000 . . 1792

Regular Civil Courts established in Bengal. The revenue settlement of Lord Cornwallis in Bengal, by which the Zamindars, who had been the revenue agents of the Mughal, were declared to be the land-owners, is made permanent. Pondicherry taken from the French for the third time 1793

23rd April.—Warren Hastings is acquitted after a trial lasting seven years. The Company grant him £4000 a year for life . . . 1795

The Dutch settlements in Ceylon, and the Cape, taken . . . 1796

Seringapatam stormed, and Tipu Sultan slain. His dominions divided between the Nizam and the British 1799

The Nizam gives up his share of Mysore in consideration of British protection 1800

The Nawab of the Carnatic cedes Nellore, North and South Arcot, Trichinopoly, and Tinnevelly. The Nawab-Wazir of Oudh cedes Rohilkund and the Ganges Doab. Ceylon made a Crown Colony 1801

Treaty of Bassein, by which the foreign relations of the Peshwa are supervised by the British 1803

	DATES
Mahratta War. Battle of Assaye, 23rd September; General Wellesley (afterwards the Duke of Wellington) with 4500 men defeats 50,000 Mahrattas under Sindhia and the Raja of Nagpur. Lord Lake defeats the Mahrattas at Aligarh, Delhi, and Laswari, and captures Delhi and Agra. Cession of the Northern districts of what are now the United Provinces. The Mughal king of Delhi becomes the pensioner of the British. Conquest of Cuttack	1803
Monson's advance into Holkar's territory, and disastrous retreat	1804
Capture of Indore. Holkar's attack on Delhi defeated	1804
Lake abandons the siege of Bharatpur. Holkar cedes Bundelkund	1805
Mutiny of sepoys at Vellore suppressed by Colonel Gillespie	1806
Rise of Maharaja Ranjit Singh in the Panjab	1807
War declared against Nepal. Repulse of the British	1814
General Ochterlony defeats the Goorkhas at Malaun	1815
Treaty of Segowlie. Cession of hill stations	1816
Operations against the Pindari bands of freebooters. Mahratta War. Battle of Kirkee: defeat of the Peshwa and capture of Poona. Battle of Sitabaldi: defeat of the Raja of Nagpur. Battle of Mahidpur: defeat of Holkar. Cession of Ajmer by Sindhia	1817
Defence of Korigaum by 800 sepoys, with 10 British officers, against 25,000 Mahrattas. Holkar cedes territory. The dominions of the Peshwa annexed	1818
Burmese War	1824
Capture of Bharatpur, hitherto deemed impregnable. Treaty of Yandaboo; cession by the Burmese of Assam, Arrakan, and Tenasserim	1826
Sati, or widow-burning, declared "culpable homicide" by Lord William Bentinck	1829
Renewal of the Company's charter, on condition that the Company abandons its monopoly of the China trade, and acknowledges the right of Europeans to reside in India and acquire land	1833
Annexation of Coorg	1834
Lord William Bentinck, the first Governor-General of India, leaves India, having abolished sati, suppressed (with the aid of Sir W. Sleeman) Thaggi, reformed the judicial administration, restored the use of the vernacular language in all courts, extended education, effected the revenue settlement of the United Provinces (with the aid of Mr Robert Bird), given the natives a share in the Government, restored the finances, and promoted steam communication *viâ* Suez	1835
Efforts to eradicate female infanticide. The freedom of the Press established. Lord Auckland, Governor-General	1835
Dost Muhammad, Amir of Afghanistan, receives a Russian mission. Lord Auckland declares war	1838
Capture of Kandahar and Ghazni, and occupation of Kabul. Shah Shuja made Amir. Death of Maharaja Ranjit Singh. Capture of Aden	1839
2nd November.—Murder of Sir A. Burnes at Kabul. 23rd December.—Murder of Sir W. Macnaghten	1841
Retreat of British army of 4500 men from Kabul, of whom one only, Dr Brydon, escapes to Jellallabad alive. Lord Ellenborough, Governor-General. Pollock forces the Khaibar and joins Sale's garrison at Jellallabad. Murder of Shah Shuja at Kabul and accession of Akbar Khan. Pollock defeats the Afghans at Tezeen, and re-occupies Kabul. Lady Sale and the Kabul prisoners ransomed. Return of the British army to India	1842
Sir Charles Napier defeats the Sindh armies at Miani and Hyderabad. Annexation of Sindh	1843

DATES

Lord Hardinge, Governor-General 1844

First Sikh War. General Gough fights an indecisive action at Mudki. Assault on the Sikh entrenchment at Ferozeshah 1845

Sir Harry Smith defeats the Sikhs at Aliwal. General Gough fights a desperate battle at Sobraon, which ends in the rout of the Sikh army. Jammu and Kashmir transferred to Maharaja Gulab Singh for £750,000 1846

Lord Dalhousie, Governor-General. Second Sikh War. Unsuccessful siege of Mooltan 1848

Mooltan stormed by General Whish. General Gough fights an indecisive action at Chillianwallah. General Gough defeats the Sikhs at Gujrat; they lay down their arms. Annexation of the Panjab. Annexation of Satara by lapse 1849

Burmese War. Annexation of Pegu 1852

Annexation of Jhansi by lapse 1853

Annexation of Nagpur by lapse. Competitive system for civil appointments approved 1854

7th February.—Annexation of Oudh, owing to persistent misrule. Lord Dalhousie leaves India, having opened the first railway for traffic, formed a department of public works, introduced cheap postage, constructed telegraphs, opened the Ganges Canal, and established an education department with the three universities of Calcutta, Madras, and Bombay. 29th February.—Lord Canning, Governor-General. The General Service Enlistment Act . . . 1856

Jamsetjee Jeejeebhoy, a philanthropic Parsi, made a Baronet. *The Indian Mutiny.* February. Mutinies at Barrackpore and Berhampore. The sepoys refuse to use the new cartridges. 3rd May. Sir Henry Lawrence suppresses a mutiny of the 7th Oudh Irregulars at Lucknow. At Meerut eighty-five sepoys refuse to use even the old cartridges, and (9th May) are imprisoned in irons. 10th May. Rising of the sepoys at Meerut; they release their comrades from jail, burn the cantonment, and make for Delhi. 11th May. The mutineers reach Delhi, murder the Europeans, and proclaim the Mughal king, Bahadur Shah, Ruler of India. 30th May. Mutiny in the cantonment near Lucknow. 4th June. Mutinies at Benares and Allahabad, and slaughter of Europeans. 5th June. Mutiny at Jhansi. Massacre of the Europeans who had surrendered on a promise of their lives. Mutiny at Cawnpore. 6th June. Attack upon Sir Hugh Wheeler in the entrenchment at Cawnpore. 8th June. Battle of Badli-ki-sarai, near Delhi. Defeat of the rebels and occupation of the Ridge. 11th June. Arrival of Colonel Neill with the Madras Fusiliers at Allahabad. 23rd June. This being the anniversary of the Battle of Plassey, the mutineers make a determined assault on the Ridge at Delhi. 26th June. Capitulation of Sir H. Wheeler at Cawnpore on a promise from the Nana Sahib that the lives of all will be spared. 27th June. Massacre of the males of the garrison at Cawnpore by order of the Nana. 2nd July. Investment of the Residency buildings at Lucknow. Sir H. Lawrence mortally wounded by a shell. 7th July. General Havelock advances from Allahabad with 2000 men. 16th July. Murder of the British women and children at Cawnpore by order of the Nana. 17th July. General Havelock retakes Cawnpore. 14th August. Arrival of General Nicholson's column at the Ridge, Delhi. 6th September. Battering train arrives at the Ridge. 14th to 20th September. Delhi stormed with a loss to the British of 1200 men. General Nicholson mortally wounded. 25th September. Generals Havelock and Outram fight their way into

	DATES
Lucknow, and are shut in. Death of General Neill. 17th November. Sir Colin Campbell relieves Lucknow. 22nd November. Lucknow evacuated. 24th November. Death of General Havelock. 27th November. General Windham driven into his entrenchments at Cawnpore by the Gwalior rebels, who plunder the city. 6th December. Sir Colin Campbell defeats the Gwalior rebels	1857
Sir Colin Campbell reconquers Lucknow. Sir Hugh Rose captures Jhansi and Gwalior. Loyalty of Dost Muhammad, Amir of Afghanistan, and Jung Bahadur (of Nepal) throughout the Mutiny. 1st November. The Government of India transferred from the East India Company to the British Crown, represented by a Viceroy. Lord Canning, first Viceroy and Governor-General	1858
The income-tax imposed	1860
Legislative Councils established in the three Presidencies. Creation of the Order of the Star of India	1861
Earl of Elgin, Viceroy	1862-3
Sir John (Lord) Lawrence, Viceroy	1864
Death from famine of a large proportion of the population of Orissa	1866
Samarkand taken by the Russians	1868
Lord Mayo, Viceroy	1869
Assassination of Lord Mayo, while on a visit to the convict settlement in the Andaman Islands. Lord Northbrook, Viceroy	1872
The Russians, under General Kauffmann, take Khiva	1873
Famine in Behar. Government expenditure of £7,000,000	1874
Visit of King Edward to India, 9th November 1875 to 13th March 1876. Lord Lytton, Viceroy	1875-6
Famine in S. India. Government expenditure of £8,000,000. Increase of 5,000,000 deaths. British subscription of half a million sterling	1876-8
1st January.—H.M. the Queen proclaimed Empress of India at Delhi. Creation of the Order of the Indian Empire	1877
Sher Ali, Amir of Afghanistan, receives a Russian mission, but refuses to receive a British one. Three British columns move on Afghanistan. Capture of Ali Masjid. General Roberts storms the Peiwar Kotal. Flight of Sher Ali to Turkestan, and accession of his son, Yakub Khan. Despatch of native troops to Malta	1878
Death of Amir Sher Ali. Treaty of Gandamuk. Sir Louis Cavagnari is received at Kabul as British representative, but murdered in September six weeks later. General Roberts advances from Kurram, carries the heights of Charasiah, takes Sherpur, and enters Kabul. Abdication of Amir Yakub Khan	1879
March of General Sir Donald Stewart from Kandahar to Kabul. Ayub Khan defeats General Burrows at Maiwand. March of General Roberts with 10,000 men to the relief of Kandahar, 313 miles in twenty-one days. General Roberts completely routs Ayub Khan. The British nominate Abdur Rahman as Amir. The British forces return to India. Lord Ripon, Viceroy	1880
Skobeleff defeats the Tekke Turkomans and captures Geok Teppe	1881
Further advance of the Russians Death of Skobeleff. Lord Ripon extends local self-government with some powers of election. Abolition of customs duties on all articles except intoxicants and arms. A contingent of the native army is sent to Egypt	1882
A bill proposing to "invest native magistrates in the interior with powers over European British subjects" gives rise to bitter race feelings. Compromise adopted by which Europeans are entitled to a jury of which one-half at least are of their own race	1883

	DATES
Occupation of Merv and Sarakhs by the Russians. Lord Dufferin, Viceroy	1884
Conflict of a Russian force and Afghans at Panjdeh. The Amir meets Lord Dufferin at Rawal Pindi	1885
King Thebaw, of Mandalay, having made overtures to France and refused to receive a British envoy, is deposed. Annexation of Upper Burma. The National Congress of natives commences its annual meetings. Delimitation of the northern boundary of Afghanistan by an Anglo-Russian Commission	1886
16th February. The Jubilee of Her Majesty the Queen Empress celebrated with great manifestations of native loyalty	1887
Formation of Imperial Service Troops in Native States. Lord Lansdowne, Viceroy	1888
Completion of the Afghan Frontier Railway and Defences. Visit of H.R.H. the Duke of Clarence to India	1889
Murder of British officers at Manipur. Capture and execution of the leaders. Visit of H.I.H. the Cesarewitch, now the Czar of Russia, to India	1891
The Indian Councils Act introduces an elective element into the older Legislative Councils	1892
The Mints closed to the free coinage of silver; the value of the rupee fixed, for Government purposes, at 1s. 4d. Compensation given to officials on account of depreciation of rupee	1893
Lord Elgin, Viceroy. Abolition of Presidential Army commands .	1894
Visit of Sirdar Nasrullah Khan, second son of the Amir, to England. Final delimitation of the Pamir Boundary. Chitral Campaign. Storming of the Malakand Pass, and relief of the British force in Chitral. Re-imposition of import duties	1895
Plague at Bombay. The political boundaries of Afghanistan partly laid down	1896
Burma created a Lieutenant-Governorship. Legislative Councils created in the Panjab and Burma	1897
Plague and Famine. British subscription of more than half a million sterling. Severe earthquake in Bengal and Assam. Rising of tribes on N.W. frontier. Punitive expeditions, the principal against the Afridis in Tirah, lasting till the spring of	1898
Lord Curzon of Kedlestone appointed Viceroy	1899
Famine in the C. Provinces and the Panjab, and in the N. parts of Bombay. Indian troops sent to Pekin under General Sir A. Gaselee	1900
Deep regret in India at the death of Her Majesty the Queen Empress Victoria. Letter of King Edward, dated 26th January, to his Indian subjects. Death of Amir Abdur Rahman and succession of his son Amir Habibullah Khan. Formation of the new province of the N.W. Frontier. Mahsud Wazri blockade	1901
The old province of the N.W. Provinces renamed the United Provinces of Agra and Oudh. Recovery of Indian Finances. Lord Kitchener C.-in-C. in India. Tariff Act to countervail bounties on sugar .	1902
Coronation Durbar of His Majesty, King Edward VII., held at Delhi on 1st January by Lord Curzon, in the presence of T.R.H. the Duke and Duchess of Connaught. Berars attached to C. Provinces. Visit of the Viceroy to the Persian Gulf. Wide spread of plague . .	1903
Viceroyalty of Lord Curzon extended by two years. Expeditionary force sent to Lhasa. Mission to Kabul	1904

	DATES
Constitution of Province of Eastern Bengal and Assam . . .	
Change of Status of military member of Viceroy's Council . . .	
Resignation of Lord Curzon. Lord Minto, Viceroy. 17th November. Visit of King George and Queen Mary to India. 9th November to 19th March 1906. Expedition to Tibet. Severe plague continues .	1905
Death of Lady Curzon. Resignation of the Lieutenant-Governor of Eastern Bengal. Appointment of Lord Kitchener as C.-in-C. continued for two years. Visit of Amir Habibullah Khan to India .	1906
Unrest in Bengal marked by murderous outrages. Act for prevention of seditious meetings. Famine in United Provinces. Continuance of plague	1907-8
Post of military member of the Viceroy's Council abolished . . .	1909
Lord Morley's Indian Councils Bill passed by Parliament. Indian Explosives Act, Newspaper Incitement to Seditious Meetings Act, Act for speedy trial of anarchical offences passed in India . .	
Sir O'Moore Creagh appointed C.-in-C. in India	
Lord Hardinge, Viceroy, 23rd November	1910
Re-enactment of Newspapers Act	1911

GLOSSARY OF THE PRINCIPAL NATIVE TERMS USED IN THIS BOOK.[1]

[A. signifies Arabic; H. Hindûstání or Hindí; K. Kanarese; Mal. Malayálam; M. Mahráṭṭi; My. Malay; P. Persian; S. Sanscrit; Tel. Telugu; Tur. Turkish; T. Tamil.]

AMÍR (Ameer), A. "commander," a title of princes and nobles, as the Amírs of Sindh or of Kabul.
ÁNÁ (Anna), H. the 16th part of a rupee.
ANIKUT, T. weir, dam (*annai kutta*).
ANJUMAN, P. assemblage, society, institute.
BABÛL, A. the Acacia arabica tree, in N. India named the Kíkar.
BAHÁDÛR, P. "brave," "chivalric," a title of honour among Mohammedans.
BAND, H. an embankment or dyke—commonly Bund.
BANDAR, P. a port or harbour.
BÁOLÍ, H. a well with steps, galleries and chambers.
BARAHDARRI, H. (twelve doors) a mansion—also Barahdari.
BÁZÁR, P. a market or market-place; a street of shops.
BEGAM (Begum), Tur. a lady of rank; a queen or princess.
BHÁTÁ (Batta), H. additional allowance to soldiers employed on foreign duty.
BUNGALOW, H. (bangla), a thatched house; the name usually applied to the houses of the English in India, and to the rest-houses for travellers built by Government on the public roads.
CASTE, class; sect; corruption of the Portuguese *casta* or race.
CATAMARAN, T. *kaṭṭu*, "to bind," *maram*, "a tree," a log-raft on which the natives of Madras paddle through the surf.
CHABUTARAH, H. a raised platform, usually of stone or brick; terrace.
CHADAR, H. (Chádar) sheet worn by men and women.
CHAITYA, Tel. a Buddhist chapel or church, p. 340.
CHAURI, H. a fly-whisk; a mark of rank.
CHÁWADI, Tel. a native rest-house for travellers, English corruption *Choultry*.
CHHATRI, H. (Chattar), umbrella; insignia of rank.
CHUNAM, S. an English corruption of H. *chúná*, lime, a plaster or mortar sometimes made of shells of a remarkable whiteness and brilliance.
COMPOUND, an enclosure, probably a corruption of the Malay word *Kampong*.
CRORE (Karor), H. 100 lakhs or 10 millions.
DAGOPA, DAGOBA, S. (*deh*, "the body," *gup*, "to hide,") a circular structure, supposed to contain ashes or relics of Buddha, or some famous Buddhist. Ceylon, Dagoba.
DAK, H. Post. Dak-Bungalow (or Musáfari Bungalow), a rest-house for travellers.
DÁKGHÁRI, H. stage-coach for one or two travellers drawn by ponies.
DARBÁR (Durbar), P. a royal court; an audience or levee; a hall.
DARGAH, place of burial of a Mohammedan saint.
DARWAZAH, P. gateway, door.

[1] Terms relating to religious matters, festivals, etc., which are explained in the Introduction, are generally not included here.

DHARAMSÁLÁ, S. (*dharma*, "justice," "piety," and *shálá*, "a hall"), a place of accommodation for travellers and pilgrims.

DHOLI, H. *Dhooli* (properly dolī), a swinging cot or litter suspended from a pole carried by bearers.

DÍWÁN, P. "a royal court," "a minister," especially the chief financial minister.

DIWAN-I-AM, DIWAN-I-KHAS, P. hall of public and private audience.

DOAB, the country between two rivers.

DWARPÁL, H. a door-keeper, commonly sculptured at sides of doors in Buddhist shrines and Hindu temples.

FAKÍR, P. a religious Mohammedan who has taken a vow of poverty; a poor man.

FARMAN, P. a royal order or grant.

GADDI, H. seat; royal seat; throne of a Hindu Prince.

GANA, H. Buddhist celestial dwarf.

GHÁT (Ghaut), S. *ghaṭṭa*, "a landing-place," "steps on a river-side"; a mountain pass; any narrow passage.

GIRJAH (Port), church.

GOPURAM, H. the gate of a Pagoda.

GUMBAZ, P. a cupola; a dome.

GUSAIN, H. Hindu monk or devotee.

ḤAMMÁL, A. a bearer of a *palkí*; in Bombay, an orderly or house-bearer.

HAMMAM, P. bath.

HARÍM (Haram), P. a sanctuary; ladies' apartments.

HAUZ, A. cistern, tank, reservoir.

ḤAVALDAR, H. an officer in native regiments corresponding to our sergeant.

HUḲḲAH (Hookah), A. a native pipe.

HUZÚR, A. the royal presence; a respectful term applied to high officials.

IDGAH, P. the open enclosure where the Id prayers are offered.

IMAMBARAH, P. a building to which the Shiahs carry the *taziahs* or biers in the *muharram*, often the tomb of the builder.

ISHWAR, S. God, Lord.

JÁGÍR, P. a tenure by which the public revenues of an estate or district were granted to an individual (jagirdar), with powers to collect them, and formerly to administer the general affairs of the estate.

JAM'ADÁR, A. a native officer next to a Ṣúbahdar, and corresponding to our lieutenant.

JHATKA, covered pony cart in S. India.

JHIL, H. pool, lake, swamp.

JOGI, S. a Hindu devotee, as Fakir is a Mohammedan.

JOHAR (Jauhar), H. sacrifice or immolation practised by Rajputs when about to be captured. Scholars will recall the occurrence of such sacrifices at Saguntum and Numantia.

KACHÉRI, H., or **KACHHARÍ**, commonly Cutcherry, a court or office for public business.

KALIMAH, A. (in full, Kalimat-ul-Shahadat, the word of testimony), the Mohammedan profession of faith (*Introduction*, p. xlviii.).

KANKAR, H. nodular limestone, with which roads in N. India are metalled.

KARBALA, A. designation of cemetery or place where *taziahs* are buried, derived from the city on the Euphrates where the Imam Ali is buried.

KHÁN, A. a Mohammedan title of respectability answering to our "Esq."

KIBLAH—see **MIHRAB**.

KILA, KILADAR, P. fort, commandant of fort.

KOTHĪ, H. residence, house, mansion.

KOTWAL, KOTWALI, P. police officer, police station.

KUBBAH, A. a tomb.

h

ḲULÍ (Cooly), T. and Tur. a day labourer; porter at railway stations and elsewhere.

LÁKH (Lac), S. the number 100,000. By customary use "a lakh" means "a lakh *of rupees*."

LAT, H. a stone monolithic pillar.

LINGAM, S. symbol of Shiva as the God of reproduction.

MAIDAN, P. plain, open space, field of battle.

MAKBARAH, P. grave of a saint.

MAMLATDAR, subordinate revenue collector in Bombay.

MAN (Maund), H. a weight, varying in different parts of India. In Bombay it is 25 lbs.; in Bengal, since 1883, 82 lbs.

MANḌAPAM, S. an open pavilion or porch in front of a temple; also Mantapam.

MASJID, A. mosque (place of prostration, *sijdah*). Jáma Masjid, congregational mosque. One prayer in a Jama Masjid is equivalent to 500 elsewhere, and one at Mecca to 100,000 elsewhere.

MASNAD, P. cushion, throne of a Mohammedan prince.

MASULAH, T. a boat sewed together, used for crossing the surf at Madras.

MATH, H. Hindu monastery, of which a Mahant is Abbott.

MELA, H. a fair.

MIHRAB, A. the recess in the wall of a mosque on the side nearest Mecca to which Mohammedans turn at prayer—usually termed Kiblah in India.

MIMBAR, P. the pulpit in a mosque; the preacher stands on the middle step of the three while delivering his sermon (Khutba).

MONSOON, A. a corruption of the A. *mausam*, "a season"; applied now to the periodical rains in India during the S.W. Monsoon, from June to September.

MUNSHÍ (Moonshee), A. a writer; a secretary; a teacher of languages.

NÁIK, S. an officer in native armies corresponding to a corporal; an ancient title.

NANDI, S. bull; vehicle of Shiva, often carved in kneeling attitude facing Shivite temples.

NAUBAT KHÁNA, NAKKAR KHANA, A. the chamber over a gateway, where a band is stationed.

NÁUCH (Nach), S. a dance; an exhibition of dancing-girls.

NÁWÁB, A. this word means *lit.* "deputies," being the plural of *ná'ib*, "a deputy." It is now a title of governors and other high officials.

NIZÁM, A. an arranger; an administrator; a title of the prince whose capital is Hyderábád in the Deccan.

NULLA, H. properly Nala, "water-course," or "depression."

PAGODA, P. an Anglican corruption of the P. word *but-kadah*, "an idol temple" in S. India; also a coin formerly in use = 3½ rupees, called by the natives *hún*, but deriving the former name from its showing a temple on one face.

PALANQUEEN, H. an Anglican corruption of the word *pálkí*, a means of conveyance, of the shape of a long box with sliding sides, in which persons are carried on men's shoulders; but little in use nowadays.

PÁLEGÁR (Polygar), T. Tel. a shareholder; a landed proprietor. A title of persons in the Madras Presidency who correspond to Zamindars in other parts of India.

PÁN, S. the leaf of the betel creeper. Pan-supari is areca nut rolled in betel leaf for chewing.

PEONS, from the Portuguese *peao*, Spanish *peon*, "footman."

PESHWÁ, P. the Brahman prime ministers of the Rájás of Sátárá, who afterwards became the supreme chiefs of the Mahrátta nation.

PHINS, T. the Tuda name for the stone circles on the Nílgiri Hills.

PICE, H. a corruption of the word *paisá*, a copper coin, of which 64 go to a rupee, and 4 to the anna, and which itself contains 3 pie.

PINDÁRI, M. (Pendhara), organised bodies of raiders and robbers.
PÍNJRAPOL, H. animal infirmary.
PIR, P. old, a Mohammedan saint.
RÁJÁ, S. a Hindú king or prince.
RAṆÍ, S. the wife of a Rájá; a queen or princess.
RATH, S. a chariot formerly, now a superior class of cart.
RISÁLAHDÁR, A. a native captain of a troop of horse.
ROZA (Rauza), A. a tomb in an enclosure, originally the garden at Medina adjoining the chamber (hujrah) in which Mohammed was buried.
RYOT, A. an Anglican corruption of the A. word *r'aíyat*, a subject, a peasant.
SADAR, A. top, chief, principal.
ṢADAR 'ADÁLAT, A. formerly the Supreme Court of Justice in India.
ṢÁHIB, A. lord; a title applied to English gentlemen in India.
SAIYAD, A. a descendant from the family of Muhammad.
SAMADH, H. cenotaph of a Hindu.
SANGAM, S. junction of two or more rivers—commonly a sacred place of pilgrimage.
SARÁÍ, P. a rest-house for travellers; a caravanserai.
SARHI, H. (commonly Sari), a sheet worn by Hindu women.
SATÍ (Suttee), S. a chaste wife, especially one burnt with her deceased husband; the burning of such a wife.
SHÁH, P. a king; a title usually applied to the King of Persia.
SHAIKH, A. old respected; a class or rank of Mahommedans.
SHANKH, S. a conch shell, large specimens of which are blown as horns by the Hindús during religious ceremonies.
SHIKÁR; SHIKÁRI, P. game, shooting; native gamekeeper.
SHOLA, T. a patch of jungle; a wooded dell.
SIKRA, S. spire or finial of Hindu temple.
SINHASAN, S. Hindu throne.
SIPÁHÍ H. (Sepoy), a native soldier, one of a *sipáh* or army.
ṢÚBAHDÁR, A. governor of a province; a native infantry officer corresponding to a captain.
TAHSIL, P. a division of Zilla (see below), equivalent to Taluk.
TAHṢÍLDÁR, P. a native sub-collector of revenue, who is also a magistrate.
TAIKHANA, H. underground room for retreat in summer, P. *sardáb*.
TÁJ, P. a crown.
T'ALUK, P. or more properly *ta'allukah*, a tract, or division of a district.
TAPPÁL, H. in Bombay the post; delivery of letters; a relay of horses.
TATTI, M. matting; a mat shade.
TEPPA KULAM, *South India*, a tank surrounded by steps with usually a temple in the centre.
TIFFIN, luncheon, word of hyrid origin.
TIRTH, S. place of Hindu pilgrimage.
TIRTHANKAR, S. Jain saint.
TRIPULIYA, H. a gateway, or approach with three arches.
TULSI, S. Basil plant—sacred to the Hindus.
VAHANA, S. a sacred vehicle of a Hindu god.
VIHÁRA, S. a Buddhist monastery, or an apartment in a monastery or cave.
VIMANAH, S. shrine, and tower over shrine of a Hindu temple.
WÁZIR, A. a prime minister.
ZAMÍNDÁR, P. a landed proprietor, a landlord.
ZANANAH, P. women's quarters—commonly Zenana.
ZIARAT, A. a burial-place, a place of Mohammedan pilgrimage.
ZIL'A (Zillah), A. a province or tract constituting the jurisdiction of a District Magistrate and Collector or Dy-Commissioner.

NOTE.

THE FOLLOWING ABBREVIATIONS ARE USED IN THIS BOOK.

A.H.	Year of Hijrah.
As.	Annas.
B.I.S.N.	British India Steam Navigation Co.
Cants.	Cantonments.
C.M.S.	Church Missionary Society.
D.B.	Dak Bungalow, a rest-house for travellers.
E.	East.
E.I.Company	East India Company.
ft.	Feet.
G.T.Road	Grand Trunk Road.
in.	Inch.
Jn., Junc.	Junction.
m.	Mile.
N.	North.
N.I.	Native Infantry.
p.	Page.
P. & O.	Peninsular and Oriental Steam Navigation Co.
pop.	Population.
R.	Refreshment Room.
R.C.	Roman Catholic.
R.H.	Rest-house.
Rs.	Rupees.
S.	South.
U.P.	United Provinces.
W.	West.
W.J.Canal.	Western Jumna Canal.
yds.	Yards.
B.B.&C.I.	Bombay, Baroda, and Central India Railway.
B.N.W.R.	Bengal and North-Western Railway.
E.B.R.	Eastern Bengal Railway.
E.I.R.	East India Railway.
G.I.P.R.	Great Indian Peninsular Railway.
O.R.R.	Oudh and Rohilkand Railway.
S.I.R.	South Indian Railway.

* This sign in the text appended to a name indicates that further information relating to the subject is to be found in the *Index and Directory* at the end.

I.—BOMBAY AND THE ENVIRONS *

[*For Directory including list of hotels, etc., see Index.*]

CONTENTS

	PAGE
Alfred Sailors' Home	9
Arab Stables	14
Art Museum, Prince of Wales	19
Castle and Arsenal	9
Cemeteries—	
Colaba Cemetery	10
European Cemetery, Sewri	16
Girgaon Cemeteries	16
Hindu Cremation Ground	16
Chamber of Commerce	7
Churches—	
All Saints', Malabar Hill	16
Cathedral	7
Christ Church, Byculla	15
Free Church of Scotland	11
Roman Catholic Cathedral	15
St Andrew's (Scotch Presbyterian)	9
St John's, Colaba	9
St Nicholas'	13
St Peter's, Mazagon	14
Custom House	9
Defences	5
Docks—	
P. & O.	14
Prince's	13
Victoria	13
Merewether	13
Sassoon Graving Dock	9
Dockyard	9
Educational Institutions—	
Alexandra College for Parsi Ladies	11
Anjuman-i-Islam School	11
Cathedral High School for Boys	11
Elphinstone College	10
Elphinstone High School	12
School of Art	12
St Xavier's College	12
Victoria Institute	15
Wilson College	16
Excursions—	
Caves of Kanhari	22
Elephanta	18
Jogeshwar Cave	23
Montpezir Caves	21
Thal and Bore Ghats	23
Tansa Reservoir	23
Vehar Lake	21
Fountains—	
Frere	7
Ruttonsee Mouljee	8
Wellington	9
General Description of Bombay	5
Geographical Position	4
Government Houses, Malabar Point	16
" " Parell	15
Harbour	4
Industrial Arts and Manufactures	14
Institutions (Charitable), Hospitals, etc.—	
Allbless Obstetric Hospital	12
European General Hospital	11
Gokaldas Tejpal Hospital	12
Grant Medical College	15
Jamsetjee Jeejeebhoy Hospital	15
King Edward Memorial Hospital	11
Motlabai Obstetric Hospital	15
Parsi Almshouse	18
Parsi Hospital, Khamballa	16
Pestonji Kama, Hospital for Women and Children	12
Pinjra Pol	14
Sir Jamsetjee Jeejeebhoy's Parsi Benevolent Institution	11
The D. M. Petit Hospital	15
Queen Empress Memorial Orphanage	4
Institutions (Literary and Scientific)—	
Asiatic Society	8
Mechanics' or Sassoon Institute	10
Jama Masjid	15
Landing	5
Lighthouse, Prong	10
" Colaba	10
Markets—	
Cotton Market, Colaba	9
Crawford "	12
Nal "	14
Missions	18
Municipal Buildings	11

A

	PAGE
Museum	15
Native Quarter	14
Observatory at Colaba	9
Princess Street	13
Public Offices—	
Courts of Justice	7
Mint	8
Port Trust	8
Post-Office	7
Presidential Secretariat	7
Public Works' Secretariat	7
Telegraph Office	7
Town Hall	8
University Library and Clock Tower	6
University Hall	6
Reclamations—	
Elphinstone, Sewri	14
Colaba	10
Railway Stations—	
B.B. & C.L., Colaba	9
Church Gate	7
G.I.P.R., Victoria	11
Statues—	
Queen Victoria	7
Prince Albert	15
King Edward (1875)	10
Statues: *continued*—	
King George	9
Lord Reay	7
Sir R. Temple	7
Dr Blaney	11
Lord Cornwallis	8
Marquis of Wellesley	8
Mountstuart Elphinstone	8
Lord Elphinstone	8
Sir Bartle Frere	8
Sir Jamsetjee Jeejeebhoy	8
Mr David Sassoon	11
Suburbs—	
Breach Candy	16
Byculla	15
Malabar Hill	16
Mazagon	13
Parell	15
Tata Hydro Electric Scheme	17
Temples—	
Mombadevi	14
Walkeshwar	16
Mahalakhshmi	16
Towers of Silence	16
Town Hall	8
Victoria Gardens	15

History.—There is little doubt that the W. coast of India had trade relations with the Assyrian, Persian, and Roman empires; but the direct connection of modern Europe with it dates only from 1498, when Vasco da Gama sailed round the Cape of Good Hope to Calicut. Twelve years afterwards Albuquerque conquered Goa, and twenty-four years later again Sultan Bahadur Shah, of Guzerat, ceded Bassein, Salsette, and Bombay to the Portuguese. It was not till 1608 that the English appeared on the scene, or till 1616 that they established a factory at Surat. In 1661 Bombay was ceded to England as part of the dowry of Catherine of Braganza, but the actual possession of it was not transferred till 1665, and three years later it was made over to the East India Company by King Charles II. One of the terms of the transfer was that the English should support the Portuguese in India against the Dutch, who were rapidly supplanting them everywhere. The name of the place was then supposed to be a corruption of Bon Bahia or Fair Bay. In 1672 it was made the seat of the Government of the Company by Gerald Aungier, the real founder of Bombay; and two years later it possessed a castle which mounted 120 pieces of various ordnance, and had a garrison of 300 English, 400 Portuguese, and 500 militia. In 1708 it became the real trading headquarters of the Company on the W. coast, Surat being no longer a safe place; and before 1720 the town, which had grown up outside the castle, contained a population of 50,000, and was enclosed by a wall. At that time it already possessed a mint, and a bank was founded shortly afterwards, and the port flourished considerably from the encouragement given to the China trade. About the middle of the century the town was refortified, and soon came into prominence in connection with the suppression of the Sidi pirates by Admiral Watson and Colonel Clive, a position which was ultimately confirmed by the results of the struggle of the Company with the Mahrattas, who, twenty years before, had taken Bassein and Salsette from the Portuguese. On the Portuguese preparing to recover the latter in 1774, it was seized by the Company, and, with Broach, was retained after the Peace of 1776;[1] and though both were surrendered by the disgraceful Convention of Wargaon, the fulfilment of that was saved by the arrival of

[1] It will interest travellers by the Suez Canal to be reminded that the first English ship from India to Suez reached that port in 1776.

Colonel Goddard with the Bengal troops; and after Bassein had been captured in 1781, the whole of these acquisitions remained with the British by the Treaty of Salbye in the following year. From that time the development of the port and city has proceeded steadily apace, and it is not necessary to follow it in detail. The city was visited by General Wellesley (the Duke of Wellington) in 1804, and to his instance was due the first road practicable for artillery up the Bore Ghat and to Poona; and it seems certain that it must have been visited by Lord Nelson[1] while a midshipman, in 1775, as the *Seahorse*, on which he made his first cruise, was in the Persian Gulf and at Bombay in that year.[2] The framework of the present system of administration of the Presidency and its capital was shaped by Mountstuart Elphinstone in 1820-27. The Chamber of Commerce was established in 1836, the Bishopric in 1837, and the Bombay Bank in 1840; while the University was created in 1857, and the Legislative Council in 1861, and the Municipal Authority, formed in 1872, was converted into a Corporation in 1888. The Port Trust, which now administers an income of £500,000 a year, was created in 1873, and the Bombay City Improvement Trust in 1898. The mail service with England was undertaken by the P. & O. Company in 1855; the G.I.P. Railway had been opened as far as Thana two years previously, and was extended up the Ghats in 1863, and in the same year the Bombay Baroda Railway, which had been opened in 1860, was extended to Ahmedabad. During the American Civil War immense wealth was poured into Bombay in connection with the export of cotton, and over-speculation at this period was followed by a severe financial collapse.

It was at this date that the old fort was at last removed. The castle which guarded the centre of its sea front yet stands, and Fort St George, which stood at the northern end of this front, still gives its name to the European General Hospital. On the S. side the defences followed the line of Rampart Row from the Apollo Gate to the S.W. corner, and then that of Esplanade Road, passing the Church Gate and Hornby Road, to the N.W. corner and the Bazar Gate, whence they turned E. to Fort St George. Outside the W. defences was a fine esplanade, and in the centre of the fort was the green on the site of which Elphinstone Circle now stands. The four most remarkable developments in Bombay during the last half of the 19th century have been (1) the reclamation of land; (2) the construction of docks; (3) the development of cotton mills (the first founded in 1857), of which there are now in Bombay 83, employing 180,000 hands; and (4) the erection of a splendid series of public buildings, many due, as will be seen below, to the munificent charity of private persons. The Corporation consists of seventy-two members, half elected for different wards of the city, twenty elected by the Chamber of Commerce, the University and the Justices of the Peace, and sixteen nominated by Government. Inside the Corporation, which is a deliberative body, is an executive committee termed the Town Council, consisting of twelve members, eight elected by the Corporation and four appointed by Government. The Municipal Commissioner, appointed by Government, exercises supreme executive authority in all Municipal matters. The annual income of the Corporation amounts to 84 lakhs, derived principally from a general tax (29 lakhs), a water tax (16 lakhs), and town duties (12 lakhs). During the same period the value of the trade of

[1] In Lord Nelson's original letter of thanks to the East India Company for the gift of £10,000 voted to him after the Battle of the Nile, a letter dated 3rd July 1797, and written on board the *Fondroyant* at Naples, he says, "Having *in my younger days* served in the East Indies I am no stranger to the munificence of the Honble. Company." This letter may be seen in the Library of the India Office.

[2] See Mr J. Douglas's vols. on Bombay and W. India, 1885. Mr Malabari's *Bombay in the Making* is an interesting work.

the port has increased from 16 crores of rupees to 160 crores, and the number of steamers entering it to nearly 2500, the great majority being ships under the English flag. The principal articles of trade are:—Imports—Cotton piece goods, metals, machinery and railway plant; and exports—cotton, grain, oil seeds, and yarns. The value of the imports is £46,000,000, and of the exports £44,000,000.

After 1896 the export trade received some check from the prevalence of plague, and the consequent imposition of quarantine against Bombay by all foreign ports, but has since recovered. The number of deaths from plague since 1902 has been 100,000. The expenditure on account of plague in Bombay city has been nearly £500,000, in addition to which over £2,000,000 have been spent by the City Improvement Trust in ameliorating conditions favourable to plague. The pest is usually worst in cold weather and spring.

According to the census of 1911, the population of Bombay is 972,900. The population was classified in 1901 as below:—

Hindus	508,000
Mohammedans	156,000
Parsis	46,000
Jains	14,200
Christians	45,000
Jews	5,300

The growth of the population has been somewhat as follows:—latter half of 18th century, 150,000; early in 19th century, 200,000; 1815, 240,000; 1849, 550,000; 1872, 644,000; 1881, 773,000.

It is intended that the Empress Victoria Memorial shall take the shape of an Orphanage in the city.

The principal Governors of Bombay since the early days of Sir John Oxenden and Mr Gerald Aungier, have been Sir John Child (1681-1690), Mr William Hornby (1771-1784), Mr Jonathan Duncan (1795-1811), the Hon. Mountstuart Elphinstone (1819-1827), Sir John Malcolm (1827-1830), Lord Elphinstone (1853-1860), Sir Bartle Frere (1862-1867), and in recent times Sir Richard Temple, Lord Reay, Lord Harris and Lord Northcote. The present Governor is His Excellency Sir George Sydenham Clarke, R.E., G.C.M.G., G.C.I.E.

The Island of Bombay is situated in lat. 18° 53′ 45″, long. 72° 52′. It is one of a group of twelve which were at one time separated from the mainland and from one another by very narrow channels, some of which have now been filled up, the principal being Bassein, Dravi, Salsette, Trombay (in which the hill called the Neat's Tongue, 1000 ft. high, is a conspicuous mark), Bombay, and Elephanta.

Bombay Island is 11½ m. long from the S. extremity of Colaba to Sion Causeway, over which the G.I.P. Railway passes to the island of Salsette, and from 3 to 4 m. broad in that portion which lies to the N. of the Esplanade. It is difficult to estimate its area, but it may be put down as about 22 sq. m.

Climate.—The average temperature of Bombay is 79·2° F. It is neither so hot in summer nor so cold in winter as many places in the interior. The coolest months are from November till March. The S.W. monsoon begins about the second week in June, and the rains continue till the end of September. The average rainfall is 70·30 in.

Bombay Harbour.—As the harbour is approached and entered, the scene is very picturesque. To the W. the shore is crowded with buildings, some of them, as the Colaba Church, the Tower of the University, and that of the Municipal Buildings, very lofty and well proportioned. To the N.

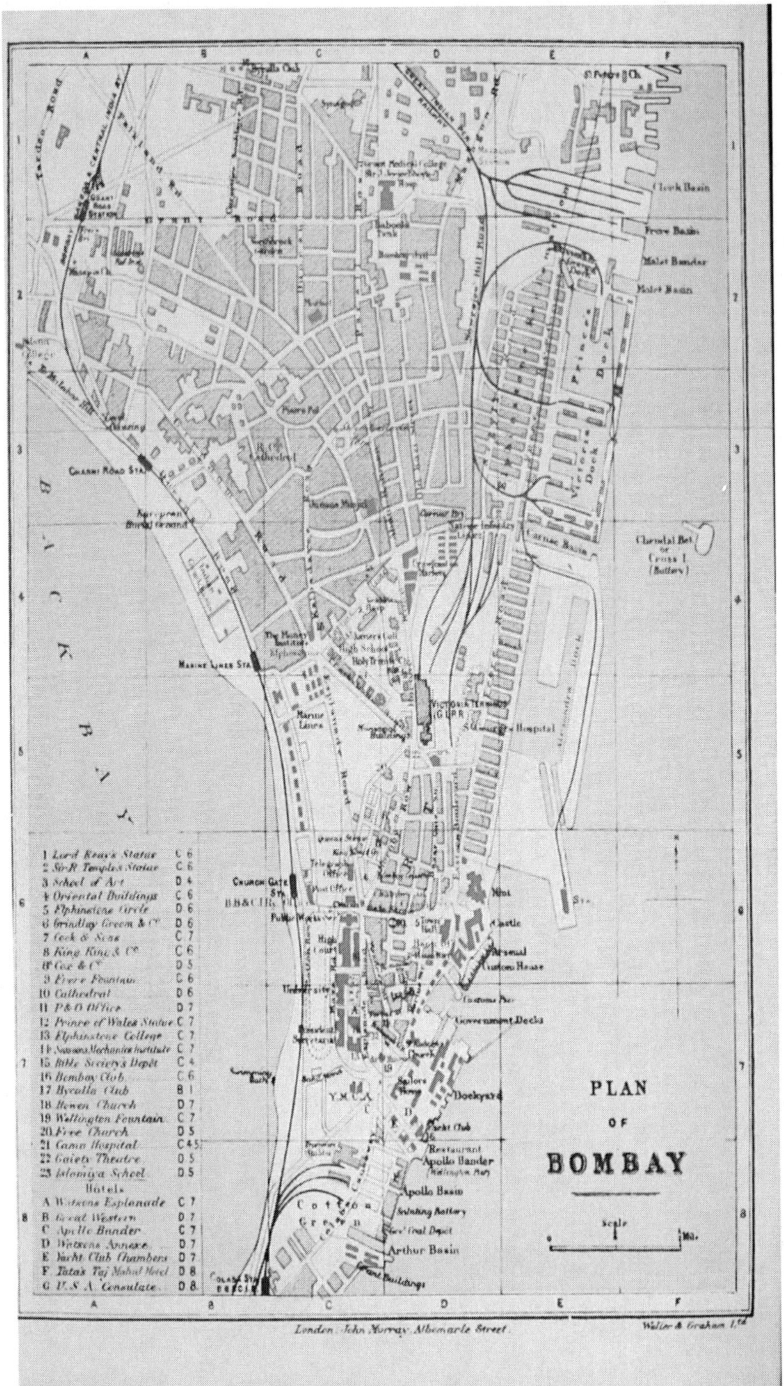
PLAN OF BOMBAY
1 Lord Reay's Statue C 6
2 Sir R. Temple's Statue C 6
3 School of Art D 4
4 Oriental Buildings C 6
5 Elphinstone Circle D 6
6 Grindlay Groom & Co. D 6
7 Cook & Sons C 7
8 King King & Co. C 6
8a Cox & Co. D 5
9 Frere Fountain C 6
10 Cathedral D 6
11 P&O Office D 7
12 Prince of Wales Statue C 7
13 Elphinstone College C 7
14 Sassoons Mechanics Institute C 7
15 Bible Society's Depôt C 4
16 Bombay Club C 6
17 Byculla Club B 1
18 Bowen Church D 7
19 Wellington Fountain C 7
20 Free Church D 5
21 Cama Hospital C 4 5
22 Gaiety Theatre D 5
23 Islamiya School D 5
Hotels
A Watsons Esplanade C 7
B Great Western D 7
C Apollo Bunder C 7
D Watsons Annexe D 7
E Yacht Club Chambers D 7
F Tata's Taj Mahal Hotel D 8
G U.S.A. Consulate D 8
Clerk Basin
Frere Basin
Malet Bunder
Malet Basin
Princes Dock
Victoria Dock
Carnac Basin
Grant Road Station
Charni Road Sta.
Marine Lines Sta.
Church Gate Sta.
Colaba Sta.
Victoria Terminus G.I.P.R.
St. George's Hospital
Cathedral
Government Docks
Dockyard
Yacht Club
Apollo Bunder
Apollo Basin
Arthur Basin
Y.M.C.A.
Cotton Green
University
High Court
Custom House
Sailors Home
Marine Lines
Scale
Mile
London: John Murray, Albemarle Street.
Walker & Graham Ltd.

and E. are numerous islands, and on the mainland hills rising to an altitude of from 1000 to 2000 ft. Pre-eminent amongst these is the remarkable hill of Bawa Malang, otherwise called Mallangarh, on the top of which is an enormous mass of rock with perpendicular sides, crowded with a fort, now in ruins. (See p. 337.)

The main defences of the Harbour remodelled and armed with the newest and heaviest guns, consist of batteries on the islands in the harbour, in addition to which there are three large batteries on the mainland. The South Island fort is called the *Oyster Rock;* that on the *Middle Ground* shoal is in the middle of the anchorage; the third defence is on *Cross Island*, at the N. end of the anchorage, the higher part of which has been cut down and armed with a battery.

Landing.—Passengers are landed at the Ballard Pier in launches. The heavy luggage is sent in advance to the Customs House at the pier, and passengers can take only hand articles with them in the launch. No luggage is now examined on board the steamer. The hotel authorities and various Agents send representatives to meet passengers on landing, and it will be found most convenient to entrust the baggage to one of them, furnishing him with a detailed list of the boxes. Customs forms, to be filled up with the contents of large packages, and with all articles liable to Customs duty, are usually provided on board the steamer. Though the new tariff of 1894 has increased the number of articles dutiable,[1] those which give trouble are firearms only. If these have not been in India before, or have not been in India for a year, a high *ad valorem* duty is levied on them, and they cannot be removed from the Customs House until the duty is paid, or a certificate is given that a full year has not elapsed since the owner left India. The P. & O. steamers, after landing the mail and passengers, proceed about 1 m. N. up the harbour to the Company's docks. Special limited expresses leave Bombay for Calcutta (36 hrs.), Delhi (27½ hrs.), and Madras (26 hrs.), soon after the arrival of the steamer. Places in these trains should be secured in London.

Travellers who have not been in the east before will be struck by the picturesqueness of the scene on landing in Bombay. The quaint native craft at the quay; the crowds of people dressed in the most brilliant and varied costumes; the Hindus of different castes; the Mohammedans, Jews, and Parsis, with a sprinkling from other nationalities; the gaily painted bullock-carts; and other sights of equal novelty, combine to make a lasting impression on the stranger's mind.

General Description of Bombay and its Suburbs.—The road from the Ballard Pier enters the circuit of the old Fort of Bombay just above the ancient Castle. From this point Bazar Gate Street leads N. to the Victoria Station and onwards to the main part of the native city—Marine Street and Apollo Street lead S. to Rampart Row along the S. side of the Fort, and the open space W. of the Apollo Bandar, the landing-place so well known to former generations of visitors to India—and Church Gate Street leads W. to Esplanade Road, which follows the landward line of the former defences, and to the Back Bay on the western side of the Island, beyond which most of the unofficial residences of the more wealthy classes are situated. Between the shore and Esplanade Road, which runs parallel to it, is the splendid range of Public Offices. S. of the open space near which all the principal hotels are situated, extends the promontory of Colaba; and northwards along the course of the Back Bay, Queen's Road leads to

[1] The general duty is 5 per cent. *ad valorem*, but arms are subject to a special duty of Rs. 50 per rifle or gun, Rs. 30 per barrel for these, and Rs. 15 per pistol.

Malabar Hill, which bends round the N.W. side of the bay, and is continued to the N. by Khamballa Hill; from both of these, beautiful views of the Back Bay and of the sea are obtained. E. of the two hills and of the northern part of Queen's Road lies the native city, with the quarters of Byculla and Mazagon along the north side of it. Above Byculla is the principal location of the Bombay mills; in Mazagon are the P. & O. docks, below which, and E. of the main city, lie the Prince's and Victoria Docks. To the S. of the native city and between it and the N.W. side of the Fort, are also a number of fine new buildings, including many places of business, though most of the houses connected with the trade of the port are still situated inside the old Fort.

PUBLIC OFFICES.

The impressive Government buildings already mentioned succeed one another in the following order, from S. to N.: the Government Secretariat, close to Watson's Hotel on the Esplanade, University Hall, Library and Clock Tower, High Court, Public Works' Secretariat, Post-Office and Telegraph Office. There is a building to the N.E. of the Telegraph Office which is used for the accommodation of the *employés* of the telegraph department.

The Presidential Secretariat is 443 ft. long, with two wings 81 ft. long. In the first floor are the Council Hall, 50 ft. long, Committee Rooms, Private Rooms for the Governor and Members of Council, and the Offices of the Revenue Department. The second floor contains the Offices of the Judicial and Military Departments. The style is Venetian Gothic, and the designer was Colonel Wilkins, R.E. The carving is by native artists. The staircase is lighted by the great window, 90 ft. high, over which rises the tower to 170 ft. At the entrance are the arms of Sir B. Frere (who was Governor when the plans were formulated for erecting Public Buildings, and to whom Bombay owes many of its improvements), and Sir S. Fitzgerald.

University Hall.—This fine building, in the French Decorated style of the 15th century, is 104 ft. long, 44 ft. broad, and 63 ft. high to the apex of the groined ceiling, with an apse separated from the Hall by a grand arch, and a gallery, 8 ft. broad, round three sides. The painted glass windows have an excellent effect. The Hall, designed by Sir Gilbert Scott, R.A., is called after Sir Cowasjee Jehangir Readymoney, who contributed Rs. 100,600 towards the cost of erection. It was completed in 1874.

The University Library and Clock Tower form a grand pile, designed by Sir Gilbert Scott in the style of 14th-century Gothic. The Library is a long, low room, adorned with carving, and the Great University or Rajabai Tower on the W. side forms part of it, and is from its height (260 ft.) the most conspicuous building in Bombay. It was built at the expense of Mr Premchand Raichand, in memory of his mother, Rajabai, and cost Rs. 300,000. He also gave Rs. 100,000 for the Library; and these sums, with accumulations, more than sufficed to complete the two buildings. The Tower is divided into six storeys, and is surmounted by an octagonal lantern spire, with figures in niches at the angles. There are twenty-four figures in all upon the tower, representing the castes of W. India. The first floor forms part of the upper room of the Library, and the second contains a study for the Registrar. There is an opening several feet square in the centre of each floor, so that one can look up 115 ft. to the ceiling of the Dial Room. The fourth floor contains the great clock. Under the dials outside are four small galleries, with stone balustrades. From the top of the tower there is a fine view of Bombay. On the E. are the harbour, fringed with islands, Modi Bay, and the Fort: and to the W. are Malabar

Hill and Back Bay; and to the S. Colaba Point.

The Courts of Justice. — This immense building, 562 ft. long, with a tower 175 ft. high, was designed by General J. A. Fuller, R.E.; it is said to have cost £100,000, and was opened in 1879. The style is Early English. The principal entrance is under a large arched porch in the W. façade, on either side of which is an octagon tower 120 ft. high, with pinnacles of white Porbandar stone, and surmounted by statues of Justice and Mercy. The main staircase is on the E. side, and is approached by a noble groined corridor in Porbandar stone, which runs through the building. The offices of the High Court are on the first and third upper floors. The Appellate and Original Courts are on the second floor. The Criminal Court is in the centre of the building, above the main corridor, and has a carved teak gallery for the public running round three sides. The ceiling is of dark polished teak in panels, with a carved centre-piece. The floor is Italian mosaic.

Next to the Courts of Justice, and separated from the Post-Office by a broad road which leads E. to the Fort and W. to the Church Gate Station of the B.B. and C.I. Railway, is the **Public Works' Secretariat,** with a façade 288 ft. long, the central part having six storeys.

The Railway, Irrigation, and other Engineering Departments are accommodated in this office.

On the S. side of the arm of the road leading to the W. are the **Statues** of two recent Governors of Bombay, Sir Richard Temple and Lord Reay. The latter faces the fine office of the B.B. and C.I. Railway, which has a façade 280 ft. long, and a tower 160 ft. high.

The old **General Post-Office** has three floors, and is 242 ft. long, with wings on the N. side. It was designed in the mediæval style by Mr Trubshawe. It now serves as a post-office for the Fort Area only.

The Telegraph Office, in modern Gothic style, has a façade 182 ft. long. The facing of it and of the Post-Office is of coursed rubble stone from Kurla, in Salsette, and the columns are of blue basalt.

North of the Telegraph Office at the junction of the Mayo and Esplanade Roads, which flank the above buildings on either side, is the **Statue of Queen Victoria,** by Noble, which is an object of constant interest to the natives. It is of white marble, and cost Rs. 182,443, of which the large sum of Rs. 165,000 was given by H.H. the late Khande Rao Gaekwar of Baroda. The statue was unveiled by Lord Northbrook in 1872. Her Majesty is represented seated. The Royal Arms are in front of the pedestal, and in the centre of the canopy is the Star of India, and, above, the Rose of England and Lotus of India, with the mottoes "God and my Right," and "Heaven's Light our Guide," inscribed in four languages.

Returning S. from this point to the Frere Fountain, and following Church Gate Street into the area of the Fort, Elphinstone Circle, occupying the site of the old Green, is reached. In Esplanade Road running S. from the fountain, and in Hornby Road running N., and together marking the western limits of the Fort, are the principal shops in Bombay and the principal places of business which travellers are likely to visit. On the N. side of Church Gate Street is the office of the *Bombay Gazette*, and farther back that of the Chamber of Commerce, and on the S. side is the **Cathedral of St Thomas.** This was built as a garrison church in 1718, and was consecrated in 1816 and made a cathedral on the establishment of the See of Bombay in 1833, on which occasion the low belfry was converted into a high tower. It is simple in plan, and a mixture of the classical and Gothic in style. The chancel, added 1865, is a satisfactory specimen of modern Early English. Among the monuments is one by Bacon to Jonathan Duncan, Governor for sixteen years. It represents him receiving the blessings of young Hindus with reference to his successful efforts in suppressing infanticide in certain districts near Benares, and afterwards in Kathiawar, through the zealous and able agency of Colonel Walker.

There are also monuments to Captain G. N. Hardinge, R.N., who died in 1808, in a brilliant engagement when he took the frigate *La Piedmontiare;* to Col. Burr, who commanded at the battle of Kirkee; and to Major Pottinger, who distinguished himself in the defence of Hirat. One of the chalices was the gift of Gerald Aungier in 1675. The fountain in front of the Cathedral was erected by Sir Cowasjee Jehangir Readymoney, at a cost of Rs.7000.

The Elphinstone Circle is surrounded by handsome buildings and at the E. side opens on to the Town Hall; in the middle is a well-kept garden with statues of Lord Cornwallis and the Marquis of Wellesley. From the centre of the S. side on which the Bank of Bengal stands, Bank Street leads to the **Bank of Bombay.**

The **Town Hall,** designed by Col. T. Cowper, was opened in 1835, and cost about £60,000, by far the larger portion being defrayed by the E.I. Company. The building has a colonnade in front, and the façade is 260 ft. long. The pillars in front, and the external character of the edifice, are Doric; the interior is Corinthian.

On the ground floor are: the Medical Board offices, the office of the Military Auditor-General, and some of the weightier curiosities of the Asiatic Society. In the upper storey is the Grand Assembly Room, 100 ft. square, in which public meetings and balls are held; the Assembly Room of the **Bombay Asiatic Society**; and the **Library** of this Society, founded by Sir James Mackintosh, containing about 100,000 volumes. The fine organ was presented by Sir A. Sassoon. The Levee Rooms of the Governor and the Commander-in-Chief, the Council Room, etc., and no longer used for their original purposes. The place of honour in the Grand Assembly Room is occupied by a statue of the distinguished Governor Mountstuart Elphinstone, executed by Chantrey, as are also those of Sir J. Malcolm and Sir C. Forbes. At the head of the staircase, on one side, is a fine statue of Lord Elphinstone, the Governor during the Mutiny, and on the other side is a statue of Sir Bartle Frere, an excellent likeness. Between the circular flights of stairs is the statue of Sir Jamsetjee Jeejeebhoy.

The Council Room contains pictures by Mr Wales, of Baji Rao Peshwa (whose adopted son, Nana Dhundu Pant, will be ever infamous as the author of the massacre at Cawnpore); of Baji Rao's celebrated minister, Nana Farnavis; and of Mahadaji Sindhia. In the Library of the Asiatic Society, instituted in 1804 for the investigation and encouragement of Oriental Arts, Sciences, and Literature, are busts of Sir James Carnac by Chantrey and Sir J. Mackintosh. The Geographical Room contains pictures of Sir A. Burnes, and of Sir J. Malcolm and Captain Ross, the two first Presidents of the Geographical Society; also a very fine collection of maps. These two Societies are now amalgamated.

The **Mint** is close to the Town Hall, but farther back, having a tank in front of it. It is a plain building, with an Ionic portico, designed by Major J. Hawkins, and completed in 1829. Authority was granted to the Company by the Crown to establish a mint so early as 1676. Forty specimens of false coins are exhibited, one of which has been a good coin, but the silver has been scooped out of the centre and lead substituted.

N. of the mint at the E. end of the Ballard Road, which leads to the Ballard Pier (p. 5), are the imposing **Offices of the Port Trust.** At the junction of the W. end of Ballard Road with Frere Road, leading to the N. past St George's General Hospital, is the Ruttonsee Mooljee Fountain.

Immediately behind the Town Hall are the remains of the **Castle** of the Old Fort, now used as an Arsenal. Only the walls facing the harbour remain. There is a flagstaff here from which signals are made to ships, and also a clock tower, where a time signal-ball, connected by an electric wire with the **Observatory** at Colaba, falls at 1 P.M.

In the **Arsenal**, besides the usual warlike materials, harness, tents, and other such necessaries for army equipment, is also an interesting collection of ancient arms and old native weapons of various descriptions.

The **Custom House** is a large, ugly, old building, a little to the S. of the Town Hall. It was a Portuguese barrack in 1665, and then a quarter for civil servants, and became a Custom House in 1802.

The **Dockyard**, originally constructed in 1736, extends hence to the Apollo Gate, with a sea-face of nearly 700 yds., and an area of about 200 acres. It was here that His Majesty King Edward landed on 8th November 1875. There are five graving docks, three of which together make one large dock 648 ft. long, the other two graving docks making a single dock 582 ft. long. There are also four building slips opposite the Apollo Pier, and on the S.E. side of the enclosure. The dockyard is lighted by electricity, so that work can be carried on by night if necessary. Bombay is the only important place near the open sea in India where the rise of the tide is sufficient to permit docks on a large scale. The highest spring tides reach to 17 ft., but the usual height is 14 ft. In the dockyard four generations of a Parsi family of the name of Lowji gained much renown during the 18th century, and built a number of British men-of-war.

From the dockyard Customs House Street leads past the Great Western Hotel, once the High Court building, and St Andrew's Church, built in 1818, to the open space S. of Rampart Row W., marking the southern side of the Old Fort. On the left here is the fine building of the **Royal Alfred Sailors' Home**, with accommodation for 100 inmates. The sculpture in the gable, representing Neptune with nymphs and sea-horses, was executed by Mr Bolton of Cheltenham. His late Highness Khande Rao Gaekwar gave Rs. 200,000 towards the cost of the building to commemorate the Duke of Edinburgh's visit, and the foundation-stone was laid in 1870 by the Duke. Opposite the Home will be the New Prince of Wales Museum of W. India, of which King George laid the foundation-stone on 11th November 1905. It is intended that a statue of His Majesty (the gift of Sir J. David Sassoon) should flank the museum on this side, as that of King Edward (p. 10) flanks the site on the other side.

Beyond this Apollo Bandar Road leads E. from the Wellington Fountain to the Apollo Bandar Pier, officially known as the Wellington Pier, passing between the Esplanade Annexe and the Yacht Club on the left hand, and the Bowen Church, Sirdar's Mansions, and Yacht Club Chambers on the right. The Club has a charming terrace garden on the sea-front. On either side of the head of the Colaba Causeway, running S. from the Fountain, are the Y.M.C. Institute and the Apollo Hotel, and a little further S. is the new Tata Hotel, known as the Taj Hotel, on the sea-shore. The Causeway leads past Cotton Green, the Sassoon Dock (650 ft. long, and the first wet dock made in India), and the B.B. and C.I. Railway terminal station to **Colaba**, formerly a separate island, with **St John's Church**, the European Barracks, the Connaught Hall, and the Observatory. The Church, erected as a memorial of the first Afghan War, and consecrated in 1858, consists of nave and aisles 138 ft. long, with a chancel 50 ft. long, and a tower and spire 198 ft. high, conspicuous for some distance at sea. The effect on entering is good, owing to the length and height of the building, the simplicity of the architecture, and the "dim religious light" diffused through the stained-glass windows. The roof is of teak. The illuminated metal screen, light and elegantly designed, is surmounted by a gilt cross. About ⅛th of the cost of the spire was contributed by Mr Cowasjee Jehangir in 1864, a striking instance of Parsi liberality and of good feeling between Parsis and Europeans.

At the W. end of the N. aisle is a triple window, erected to the memory of General David Barr.

The "memorial marbles" are of alternate colours of white, red, yellow, and blue; and beneath them runs the following inscription, painted on a blue ground:—

> This Church was built in Memory of the Officers whose names are written above, and of the Non-Commissioned Officers and Private Soldiers, too many to be so recorded, who fell, mindful of their duty, by sickness or by the sword, in the Campaigns of Sind and Afghanistan, A.D. 1838-1843.

At the extremity of the promontory is the Old Lighthouse, the European Lunatic Asylum, and a well-kept European Cemetery. The present lighthouse is on Prong Island, ½ m. S. of Colaba Point, with which it is connected by a ridge of rock exposed at low tides; it is 150 ft. high, and the light which flashes every 10 secs. is visible 18 m. off at sea.

It is under consideration to make a great reclamation along the Back Bay from Colaba up to the Marine Lines, providing a large area for a new European residential quarter, a park, cantonment, and Government House.

Returning to the Wellington Fountain, the road along the W. side of the open ground leads past a fine block of buildings consisting of the Elphinstone College, the Sassoon Institute, the Army and Navy Stores, and the Esplanade Hotel. Opposite the last is the equestrian statue of King Edward as Prince of Wales, by Sir Edgar Boehm, presented to the city by Sir A. Sassoon at a cost of £12,500.

It is intended that the memorial of the King Emperor shall take the form of a large general hospital in the northern part of the city, a Convalescent Home, and a Consumptive Sanatorium in the Ghats.

The **Elphinstone College**, removed from Byculla in 1890, now occupies a large building in the mediæval style, which cost 7½ lakhs of rupees. It is called after Sir Cowasjee Jehangir Readymoney, in recognition of his having given 2 lakhs of rupees for the purpose of building the original institution. The Elphinstone Institution was founded as a memorial to the Hon. Mountstuart Elphinstone, the Governor of Bombay. In 1856 it was divided into a High School (see p. 11) and this College for the higher education of natives, who contributed upwards of 2 lakhs to endow professorships in English, and the Arts, Sciences, and Literature of Europe. The sum accumulated to about 4½ lakhs, and Government augments the interest on this by an annual grant-in-aid of Rs.22,000. In 1862 Sir Alexander Grant, Bart., was Principal of the College, and some distinguished scholars have filled Professorships, as, for instance, Mirza Hairat, who translated Malcolm's *History of Persia* into Persian. In the library is a portrait of Elphinstone by Sir T. Lawrence. The **State Record Office** and **Patent Office** occupy the W. wing of the College. Amongst the records are preserved the oldest document relating to the Indian Empire, a letter from Surat, 1630, and the letter of the Duke of Wellington announcing the victory at Assaye.

The **Mechanics' or Sassoon Institute** was founded originally in 1847, but refounded and renamed by David Sassoon and his son Sir Albert in 1870, and cost £15,000. Lectures are delivered and prize medals awarded. Life-members pay Rs.150, and members Rs.6 per quarter. In the entrance hall is a statue of Mr David Sassoon, by Woolner. There is also a good library.

From here Esplanade Road, with the Bombay Club on its W. side beyond the University Gardens, leads to Church Gate Street and Hornby Road. On the W. side of the entrance to the latter are the lofty Oriental Buildings, and a little beyond them on the same side of the road are the fine new Chartered Bank and Standard buildings, while a little back in Outram Road is the Cathedral High School for boys. On the right is the lofty building of the Jamsetjee Jeejeebhoy Institute, founded in 1849 by Sir Jamsetjee Jeejeebhoy, who, with Lady Avabai, his wife, set apart for the purpose 3 lakhs of rupees and 25 shares in the Bank of Bengal, to which the Parsi Panchayat added 35 shares more. The Government of India are the trustees, and pay interest at 6 per cent. on the 3 lakhs, and the capital of the Institution now amounts to 12 lakhs. The income is divided into 400 shares, of which 180 go for the Boys' and Girls' Schools in Bombay, 70 for those in Surat, and 150 for charities for the poor. Further N. rise two great architectural piles, one on either hand —the Terminus Station and Offices of the G.I.P. Railway to the E., and the Municipal Offices on the W. Between them, in front of a triangular garden plot, is a statue of Dr T. Blaney, Coroner of Bombay.

The **Victoria Station** is elaborately ornamented with sculpture and surmounted by a large central dome. The architect was F. W. Stevens, C.I.E.; the style is Italian Gothic, with certain Oriental modifications in the domes. It cost the Railway Company £300,000, and was completed in 1888. It is one of the handsomest buildings in Bombay and finest railway stations in India or any country, with the most excellent and convenient arrangements in every respect. S. of it is the fine large structure of the new **General Post Office** in the Bijapur style of architecture (p. 364). S.E. of the railway station, in a well laid-out garden, is St George's General Hospital for Europeans, with 140 beds: it has a convalescent home at Khandala (Route 25).

The **Municipal Buildings** were also designed by Mr Stevens, and were opened in 1893. The Oriental feeling introduced into the Gothic architecture has a pleasing effect. The tower, 255 feet high, and surmounted by a masonry dome, can be seen from all parts of Bombay. The central gable terminates in a statue 13 ft. high, representing "Urbs prima in Indis." The grand staircase is also crowned by an imposing dome.

Opposite these buildings Waudby Road leads S.W. to the Queen's Statue, passing the Gaiety and Novelty Theatres, the Scotch Free Church, the Masonic Hall, and the Alexandra School for Girls, founded by Mr Maneckjee Cursetjee, to the E. of it, and the open space of the Maidan or General Parade Ground and the Bombay Gymkhana Club on the W.

From the Victoria Railway Station Hornby Road continues N. up to the Crawford Market and the main residential quarters of the native city, passing on the left the new *Times of India* Office, the Islamia School, the Church of the Holy Trinity, and the School of Art; while from the station to the N.W. runs Cruikshank Road in front of the Municipal Offices, and past the Police Courts, the Allbless and Cama Hospitals, and the Elphinstone High School. On Carnac Street, which joins these two roads, and forms the third side of a triangle with them, is the St Xavier College and the Gokaldas Tejpal Native General Hospital.

The **Anjuman-i-Islam School** was erected by the co-operation of Government, which gave the site, valued at Rs.158,000, with a money-grant of Rs.38,000, the Mahommedans themselves subscribing Rs.160,000, of which Rs.50,000 were set apart as an endowment. The building was opened by Lord Harris in 1893, and the erection of it marks an epoch in the history of the Mohammedan community. The building, which is of most pleasing appearance, and has a tower 125 ft. high, was designed by Mr J. Willcocks of the Public Works Dept.

The **Sir Jamsetjee Jeejeebhoy School of Art**, called after that distinguished Parsi gentleman who contributed Rs.100,000 towards it, was first opened for pupils in 1857. In 1877 the present handsome building was erected for it. Excellent drawings and designs are made here, as well as good pottery, arms, artistic work in silver and copper, and decorative carving in wood and stone. The buildings in Western India owe much of their beauty to students of this institution. The latest additions to it are the Sir George Clarke Studios and Technical Laboratories, which include the **Art Pottery Works**, where some beautiful designs purely Indian in form and ornament have been carried out.

The **Gokaldas Tejpal Hospital** for natives can contain 150 patients, and is generally full. The annual number of out-patients is over 13,000. It owes its origin to a gift of £15,000 made by Mr Gokaldas Tejpal, and a similar gift by Mr Rustomjee Jamsetjee Jeejeebhoy.

St Xavier's College, with an octogonal tower, is a Jesuit Institution, which serves the purpose of school as well as college, and grew out of the development of St Mary's Institution and the European R.C. Orphanage. The staff consists of a rector, principal, and 16 professors. Behind it is St Xavier's School. The site for both was given by Government. West of the college at the entrance to Kalbadevi Road is the Money Institute, started in 1838, now a High School under the C.M.S.

The **New Elphinstone High School** is the great public school of Bombay, and retained possession of the original buildings on this site when the *College Department* was separated to form the Elphinstone College. In front of it is a fine flight of steps.

"The object of this school is to furnish a high-class and liberal education up to the standard of the University entrance examination, at fees within the reach of the middle-class people of Bombay and Mufassil. It has classes for the study of English, Marathi, Guzerati, Sanscrit, Latin, and Persian," and contains 28 class-rooms, a hall on the first floor measuring 62 by 35 ft., and a Library. There are 700 scholars in the school under a Principal and 42 masters; there are also coaches in drill and cricket. The building, which is 452 ft. long, was designed by G. T. Molecey. Sir A. Sassoon contributed 1½ lakhs of rupees towards it.

The **Pestonji Kama Hospital**, for *Women* and *Children*, is a Gothic building containing 75 beds. It owes its existence to the gift of Rs.164,000 by Mr Pestonjee Hormusjee Cama, as the Allbless Obstetric Hospital beyond it does to the munificence of Mr Bomanjee Eduljee Allbless. The latter contains 30 beds. Both are under the Dufferin Fund and the sole management of lady doctors, the nursing being done by the Sisters of All Saints, who also nurse in the Jamsetjee Jeejeebhoy and St George's Hospitals. Further E. and adjoining the Municipal Offices, are the lofty buildings of the Esplanade Police Courts, erected in 1884-88.

The **Crawford Market** was founded by Mr Arthur Crawford, C.S., Municipal Commissioner from 1865 to 1871, and cost over 11 lakhs of Rs. It consists of a Central Hall, in which is a drinking-fountain given by Sir Cowasjee Jehangir Readymoney, surmounted by a Clock Tower, 128 ft. high. To the right is a wing, 150 ft. by 100 ft., in which are fruit and flowers, and on the left is another wing, 350 ft. by 100 ft., for wing, tables, etc., etc. The whole is covered with a double iron roof. The ground is paved with flagstones from Caithness. "In that collection of handsome and specious halls . . . fish, flesh, vegetables, flowers, fruit, and general commodities are vended in separate buildings all kept in admirable order and cleanliness, and all opening upon green and shady gardens" (Edwin Arnold). There are many kinds of plantains or bananas; the finest are short, thick, and yellow. The best oranges are those from Nagpur, and the best grapes are from Aurangabad. The mangoes come in in May; the best are grown about Mazagon.[1] The Pummelow, the *Citrus decumana*, is particularly fine in Bombay. The *Fish Market* is at the end of the *Mutton Market*. The turtles come from Karachi in Sind. The oysters are of moderate size and well flavoured. The *Palla* fish, generally about 2 ft. long, the salmon of India, is excellent, but has many troublesome bones. The best fish of all is the pomflet, or pomfret, a flat fish. The *Bombil*, called by the English *Bommelo* and *Bombay duck*, is a glutinous fish, much used when salted and dried. Near the fountain, with its beautiful shrubs, are seats for loungers. On the S. side is the *Poultry Market*, where fowls, ducks, turkeys, snipe, curlew, teal, and occasionally florican may be purchased when in season. The market well deserves a visit early in the morning, though the visitor must expect to find the crowd dense and the hubbub deafening.

A little N.W. of the market, extending to the Back Bay near the Marine Lines Station is Princess Street, named after and on 16th November 1905 declared open by Her Majesty Queen Mary, opening out one of the most congested old quarters of the city. This was the first arterial thoroughfare opened by the City Improvement Trust. Another main one, Sandhurst Road, runs from the Babula Tank to the head of the Back Bay.

N.E. of the market and between the main native city and the sea are the principal commercial docks of Bombay. The **Victoria Dock** occupies the space formerly taken up by the Masjid and Nicol basins. It covers 25 acres, and has an entrance 80 ft. in width. **Prince's Dock**, lying N. of this and connected with it, was commenced during the Prince of Wales's visit in 1875-76. In excavating it the remains of a submerged forest were found at a depth of about 10 ft. About 100 trees from 10 to 20 ft. long were exhumed, the wood being red and very hard. The dock is 1460 ft. + 1600 ft., and extends over 30 acres, and is capable of containing twenty ocean steamers. It is fitted with a tidal observatory. On the N.W. again is the **Merewether Dry Dock**, and adjacent to the docks is a whole street of warehouses and offices, the Church of St Nicholas, and the Seamen's Institute, round which the Harbour Mission centres. South of the Victoria Dock is being constructed the Alexandra Dock, of which the foundation-stone was laid by King George on 13th November 1905, and which will be the largest in India. It will extend S. of the Ballard Pier and enclose an area of 70 acres. The depth of water in it will be 45-49 ft., and the dry dock will be 1000 ft. long, and have an entrance 100 ft. wide. It is expected that the dock will be completed by the end of 1912. The total cost of the works will be 400 lakhs. These recent developments have been carried out under the professional direction of Sir Walter Hughes, C.I.E.

All these docks were excavated on the estate known as the **Elphinstone Reclamation**, which has taken in from the sea 276 acres, and has raised and

[1] It was the failure of supplies of Mazagon mangoes which specially annoyed the Wazir Fazl-ud-din in *Lala Rookh*.

improved 110 acres. This and the **Moody Bay Reclamation** S. of the Victoria Dock have transformed the eastern foreshore of the island from a mud swamp to a busy mercantile quarter worthy of the capital of Western India. A still greater scheme of reclamation is in progress at **Sewri** N. of Mazagon. The largest of all will be that of Colaba (p. 10).

The **Dockyard of the P. & O. Company** lies ¾ m. N. of Prince's Dock, in the suburb of Mazagon. It covers 12 acres, and there are iron sheds for 18,000 tons of coal. The Ritchie Dock is 495 ft. long, and capable of receiving vessels of deep draught. There is a complete engineering establishment at the dock capable of carrying out work of all descriptions.

The Church and School of St Peter are situated close to the P. & O. Dockyard and the Mazagon Bandar, once well known as the point from which passengers by the mail steamers used to embark.

In the **Native City** the streets and bazaars are narrow and tortuous, but generally clean and bright. Some of the houses are remarkably fine as works of art, and display undoubted Portuguese influence. Their fronts are covered with carving, and in some cases they have projecting stories supported upon elaborately sculptured corbels. Here and there are mosques and Hindu temples gaudily painted. The streets teem with life. Sir Edwin Arnold writes of them: "A tide of Asiatic humanity ebbs and flows up and down the Bhendi bazaar, and through the chief mercantile thoroughfares. Nowhere could be seen a play of livelier hues, a busier and brighter city life. Besides the endless crowds of Hindu, Guzerati, and Mahratta people coming and going —some in gay dresses, but most with next to none at all—between rows of grotesquely painted houses and temples, there are to be studied here specimens of every race and nation of the East; Arabs from Muscat, Persians from the Gulf, Afghans from the northern frontier, black, shaggy Beluchis, negroes of Zanzibar, islanders from the Maldives and Laccadives, Malagashes, Malays and Chinese throng and jostle with Parsis in their sloping hats, with Jews, Lascars, fishermen Rajpoots, Fakirs, Europeans, Sepoys and Sahibs."

There are nearly 3000 jewellers of the different Indian nationalities in Bombay who find constant and lucrative employment. One of the most active industries is the manufacture of brass and copper pots and other utensils. "The Copper Bazar, opposite the Mombadevi Tank,[1] is the busiest and noisiest, and one of the most delightful streets."[2] The black wood-carving is famous, as is the sandal-wood and other carving; the term "Bombay Boxes" includes sandal-wood carving as well as inlay work. Tortoise-shell carving is a *specialité*, also lacquered turnery. Gold and silver thread is manufactured and used for lace, and Bombay embroidery is much prized. The Bombay School of Pottery (see above), under the guidance of Mr George Terry, has developed two original varieties of glazed pottery.

In the Bhendi Bazaar also are the **Arab Stables**, well worth a visit in the early morning, not only for the sake of viewing some of the finest horses in the East, but to see the Arabs themselves who bring them to Bombay for sale.

The **Nal Market**, between Parell and Duncan Road, in the N.W. quarter of the city, supplies a large part of Bombay, and is generally immensely crowded.

A little S. of the Bazar is the **Pinjra Pol**, or Native Infirmary for Sick Animals, a curious institution, covering several acres. This place is in the quarter called Bholeshwar, "Lord of the Simple"; and the

[1] Momba itself is a corruption of Maha Amma, Great Mother.

[2] Sir G. Birdwood's *Industrial Arts of India*, which see for further particulars.

temple of the deity so called, a form of Shiva, is within the enclosure.

Near it again, to the S.W., is the Roman Catholic Cathedral, N. S. da Esperanca, and to the S.E. the **Mombadevi Tank** and Temple from which the name of Bombay is believed to be derived. S. of the Tank is the Jama Masjid, and E. of this is the main thoroughfare of the city, Abdul Rahman Street, continued N. by Parell Street. Near the point where the latter crosses Grant Road from the W. is the **Jamsetjee Jeejeebhoy Hospital**, erected in 1845 at the joint expense of that gentleman and the E.I. Company, and having accommodation for 500 patients. In the hall is a bronze statue of Sir Jamsetjee Jeejeebhoy, a copy of one in the Town Hall. Attached to it are a Hospital for Incurables, the Bai Motlabai Obstetric Hospital, and the Dinshaw Maneckjee Petit Hospital for women and children, erected in 1889 and 1890.

Adjoining the Hospital is the **Grant Medical College**, established in 1845, in memory of Sir Robert Grant, Governor of Bombay. Besides the principal and nine professors there are twelve demonstrators and tutors in the College. The Museum is full of curious things. The grounds cover 2 acres, and are made instructive by planting in them all kinds of useful trees and shrubs.

A little to the S.E. of the Hospital are the Babula Tank, the Jail, and an European Workhouse. N. from the Hospital Parell Road leads past Christ Church and the Byculla Station to the Victoria Technical Institute and the Victoria and Albert Museum, and finally to the old Government House. It is now the Plague Research Laboratory. The **Institute** occupies the old building of the Elphinstone College, opposite the Victoria Gardens, built from a gift by Sir Cowasjee Jehangir Readymoney, and given up in 1890. It is under a principal, assisted by eight professors, and is intended to provide a training in Art and Science in their aplication to industrial and other purposes.

The Victoria and Albert Museum is a handsome building, standing in the gardens about 100 yds. back from the road. Until 1857 the collection, which is not an important one, was kept in the Fort Barracks, but on Sir G. Birdwood being appointed curator by Lord Elphinstone, he raised a subscription of a lakh for building this Museum. Sir B. Frere laid the first stone in 1862, and Government completed the building in 1871. The Clock Tower in front of it was erected by Sir Albert Sassoon, who also presented the fine statue of Prince Albert, by Noble. The **Victoria Gardens**, in which the Museum stands, have an area of 34 acres, and are prettily laid out. To the right of the S. entrance to them are the remains of the stone elephant which gave the island of Elephanta its name; and on the E. side of them are a Menagerie and Deer Park. The band plays here twice a week, and over two millions visit the Gardens yearly, one million visiting the Museum.

Parell Road continues from here past the Veterinary College, built on a site given by Sir Dinshaw Maneckjee Petit, to the **Old Government House.** This was a Portuguese place of worship and monastery, confiscated by the English Government on account of the traitorous conduct of the Jesuits in 1720. Governor Hornby was the first who took up his residence there, between 1771-80. To supply the required accommodation Mr Elphinstone built the right and left wings. The public rooms are in the centre facing the W. The drawing-room or ballroom above the dining-room occupies the place of the old Portuguese chapel. On the staircase there is a bust, and in the ballroom a portrait, of the Duke of Wellington. At the end of the ballroom is what is called the Darbar Room. From the S. corridor steps descend to a platform in the garden, where the band plays. The garden of Parell is pretty, and has at its W. extremity a tank, and on its margin a terrace, which rises about 10 ft. above the water and the grounds.

The European Cemetery, at Sewri, E. of Parell, formerly a Botanical Garden, is a sheltered spot under Flagstaff Hill. The garden was turned into a cemetery about 1867.

2 m. N. of the Parell, and beyond the Dadar Railway Station, is a Leper Asylum at Matsonga.

The drive round the Back Bay to **Malabar Hill,** 180 ft. high, by Queen's Road and Malabar Hill Road, is extremely beautiful and interesting. Beyond the Marine Lines Station are an enclosed burning place of the Hindus and a closed Mohammedan and Christian cemetery, and further on is the **Wilson College** (named after Rev. Dr. J. Wilson, F.R.S., Oriental scholar and Scottish missionary), for the education of young men, a fine building which cost a lakh and a half of rupees, and is one of the largest colleges for natives in Western India. The staff consists of a principal and nine professors.

At about 3 m. from the Fort the road begins to ascend a spur of Malabar Hill. Near the top on the left are the entrance gates to the drive through the grounds (private) of **Government House at Malabar Point,** with a pleasant view across Back Bay to the city of Bombay on the farther side. Below, at the extreme point is a battery, which could sweep the sea approach. Not far off to the N. a large ship, the *Diamond,* was wrecked and eighty passengers were drowned. Sir Evan Nepean was the first Governor to reside at Malabar Point. In 1819-20, Mr Elphinstone added a public breakfast-room, and a detached sleeping bungalow on a small scale. In 1828 Sir John Malcolm considerably enlarged the residence at Malabar Point, and constituted it a Government House. Close by is the picturesque temple of **Walkeshwar,** the "Sand Lord," built c. 1000 A.D. Throngs of Hindus will be met coming from it, their foreheads newly coloured with the sectarial mark. Rama, on his way from Ayodhya (Oudh) to Lanka (p. lviii) to recover his bride Sita, carried off by Ravana, halted here for the night. Lakshman provided his brother Rama with a Lingam from Benares every night. This night he failed to arrive in time, and Rama made for himself a Lingam of the sand at the spot. On the arrival of the Portuguese in after ages, this sprang into the sea from horror of the barbarians. There is a small but very picturesque tank here, adorned with flights of steps, surrounded by Brahmans' houses and shrines. When Rama thirsted here, he shot an arrow into the earth, and forthwith appeared the *Vanatirtha,* "Arrow-Tank."

The drive from Malabar Point, and thence along the sea by **Breach Candy,**[1] under the W. side of Khamballa Hill, is one of the most beautiful in the island, especially at evening. On these hills are situated the principal residences of the European community and many wealthy natives, surrounded by small but bright gardens. On Khamballa Hill is the new Bomanji Dinshaw Petit Hospital for Parsis, built at a cost of 15 lakhs, and with a present endowment of 5 lakhs. At the N. end of Breach Candy are the Mahalakhshmi Temple and Tank on the sea. In the centre of Malabar Hill, about 180 ft. above the sea, are the grounds of the Ladies' Gymkhana, and beyond them the Hanging Gardens, affording lovely views of the Back Bay and of the great line of grand buildings rising on the farther side of it, and of the harbour and islands and mountains beyond them. Between the gardens is All Saints' Church, and beyond them and N. of the head of the curve of the bay are the **Five Parsi Towers of Silence.** In order to see them, permission must be obtained from the secretary to the Parsi Panchayat. Sir Jamsetjee Jeejeebhoy, at his own expense, made the road which leads to the Towers on the N. side, and gave 100,000 sq. yds. of land on the N. and E. sides of the Towers. Within the gateway of an outer enclosure

1 Breach Candy means the surf-battered beach (*Twelfth Night,* Act ii. Sc. 1) of the Gap (khind).

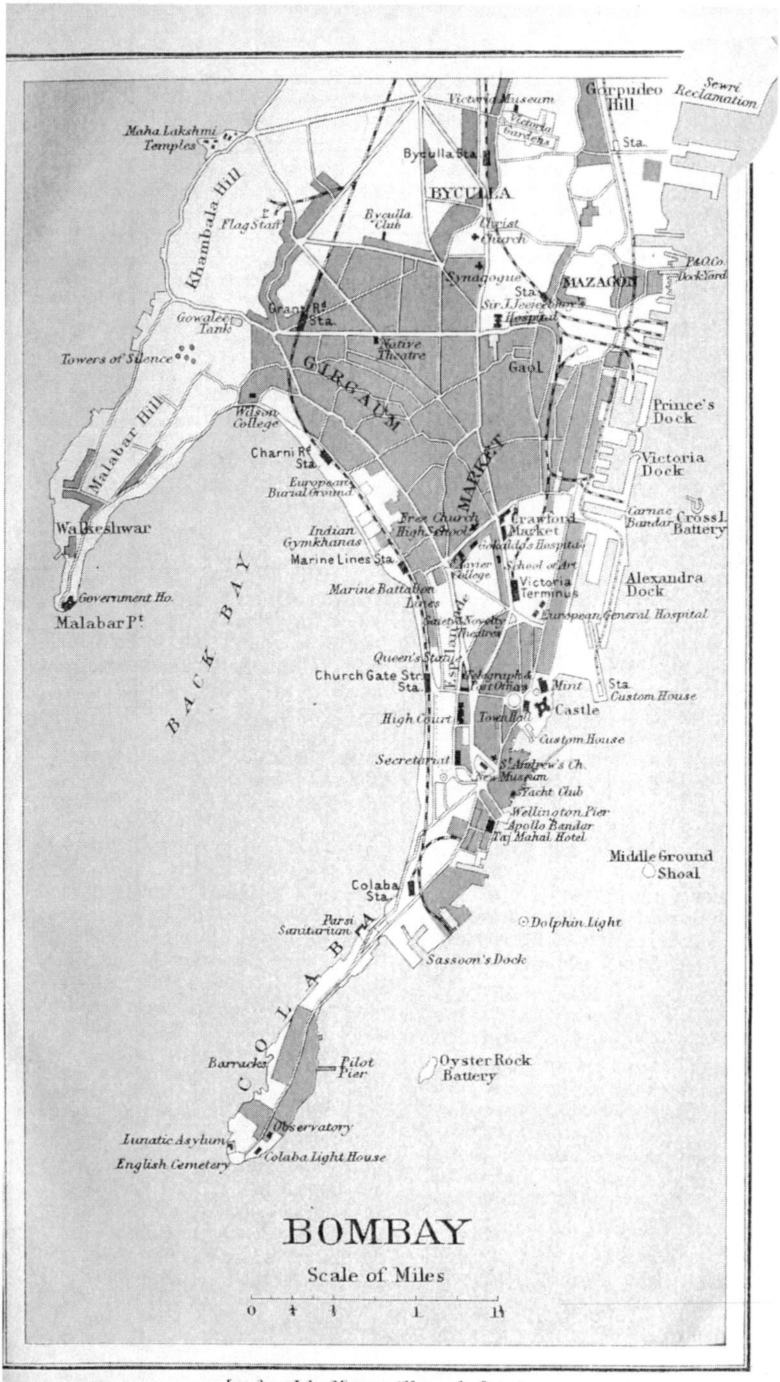

London. John Murray, Albemarle Street.

a flight of eighty steps mounts up to a gateway in an inner wall. From this point the visitor is accompanied by an official of the Panchayat, and turning to the right comes to a stone building, where, during funerals, prayer is offered. At a Parsi funeral the bier is carried up the steps by four Nasr Salars, or "Carriers of the Dead," and followed by two bearded men, and a large number of Parsi mourners in white robes walking two and two in procession. The bearded men who come next the bier are the only persons who enter the Tower. On leaving the Tower, after depositing the corpse on the grating within, they proceed to the purifying place, where they wash and leave the clothes they have worn in a tower built for that express purpose. The general mourners have their clothes linked, in which there is a mystic meaning. There is a model of one of the Towers which was exhibited to the Prince of Wales, and is produced to visitors. They are five in number, cylindrical in shape, and whitewashed. The largest (276 ft. round and 25 ft. high) cost £30,000, while the other four on an average cost £20,000 each. At 8 ft. from the ground is an aperture in the encircling wall about 5½ ft. sq., to which the carriers of the dead ascend by a flight of steps. Inside, the plan of the building resembles a circular gridiron, gradually depressed towards the centre, in which is a well 5 ft. in diameter. Besides the circular wall which encloses this well there are two other circular walls between it and the outside, with footpaths running upon them; the spaces between them are divided into compartments by radiating walls from an imaginary centre. The bodies of adult males are laid in the outer series of compartments thus formed, the women in the middle series, and the children in that nearest the well. They are placed in these grooves quite naked, and in half an hour the flesh is so completely devoured by the numerous vultures that inhabit the trees around that nothing but the skeleton remains. This is left to bleach in sun and wind till it becomes perfectly dry. Then the carriers of the dead, gloved and with tongs, remove the bones from the grooves and cast them into the well. Here they crumble into dust. The dust in the well accumulates so slowly that in forty years it rose only 5 ft. This method of interment originates from the veneration the Parsis pay to the elements. Fire is too highly regarded by them to allow it to be polluted by burning the dead. Water is almost equally respected, and so is earth; hence this singular mode of interment has been devised. There is, however, another reason. Zartasht said that rich and poor must meet in death; and this saying has been literally interpreted and carried out by the contrivance of the well. The surroundings of the Towers are arranged to foster calm meditation. The mourner at once arrives at the house of prayer, and around is a beautiful garden full of flowers and flowering shrubs, where, under the shade of fine trees, relatives of the deceased can sit and meditate; and the view to the W. and S. over the waters, and to the E. and N. over the harbour and the distant mountains beyond, is enchanting. Even the cypresses, as the Parsis themselves say, tapering upwards, point the way to heaven.

At the S.E. foot of the hill is an **Almshouse** for decayed Parsis of both sexes, erected by the sons of the late Fardonjee Sorabjee Parak, Esq.

The **Parsi Dharmsala**, in the Gam Devi Road, intended for poor Persian Parsis, is passed on the approach to the Towers of Silence from the S. A similar dharmsala close by was erected by Sir Cowasjee Jehangir Readymoney, in memory of his grandfather in 1812.

The **Tata Hydro Electric Scheme** for Bombay, inaugurated by Sir Dorab Tata, bids fair to become one of the most remarkable in the whole world. It is proposed to impound the monsoon rainfall on the Ghats at Lonauli (p. 338), often 500 in., in three lakes at Shirawta, Walwhan, and Lonauli. These have dams 93, 58, and 23 in height, and areas of 3000, 1700, and 720 acres, all 2000 ft. above sea-level; and from them a stream, equal in volume to the Thames, will be led to near the Duke's Nose (p. 338), and will take its plunge of 1740 ft. to the power development house at Khopoli, where 40,000 horse-power will be generated by four great turbines. This power will then be conveyed 42 m. to the receiving station at Sewri. The introduction of electric power will, it is hoped, entirely remove the present smoke nuisance of Bombay, and it is expected that the waste water, after accomplishing its generating purpose, will irrigate 30,000 to 40,000 acres of garden and other crops round the city. The foundation-stone of the Lonauli Lake was laid by Sir George Clarke on 9th February 1911, and it is believed that part of the scheme will come into operation by 1913.

MISSIONS.

The S.P.G., with Church in Kamatipura Road, has four missionary clergy in the town, and a branch of the Ladies' Association working in the zananas.

The **C.M.S.** (established in Bombay since 1820) has a *Church* in Dhanji Street, and large *Schools* for boys and girls at Girgaon.

The **Mission Priests of St John the Evangelist** (Cowley Fathers) serve the Church of St Peter's, Mazagon, and have a Mission House and Schools for boys and girls near it; also a native Mission and Orphanage in Babula Tank Road.

The "**All Saints**" **Sisters** (from Margaret Street) have been working in Bombay since 1878, and nurse in the following Hospitals: European General, Jamsetjee Jeejeebhoy, and Pestonji Kama. They have two High Schools for Girls, in Elphinstone Circle and near St Peter's, Mazagon.

The *American Presbyterian Board of Foreign Missions* or *Maratha Mission, Byculla*, has a considerable staff. The *United Free Church of Scotland* has a strong body of missionaries connected with the Wilson Mission College (p. 16) affiliated to the University.

SIGHTS IN THE VICINITY OF BOMBAY.

1. Elephanta.
2. Vehar Lake.
3. Montpezir Caves.
4. Cave Temples of Kanhari.
5. Jogeshwar Cave.
6. The Tansa Water Supply.
7. Thal and Bore Ghats.
8. Karli.

(1) **Elephanta** is a small island about 6 m. from the Fort of Bombay. For visiting this remarkable place steam launches[1] can be hired at the Apollo Bandar, and make the passage in about 1 or 1½ hrs.; or a bandar-boat may be hired at from Rs.3 to Rs.5, in which case the length of the passage will depend on wind and tide. The boat will pass close to Butcher's Island, which is 3 m. nearly due E. from Mazagon Dock. Persons coming from sea with infectious diseases, such as smallpox, are placed in quarantine at this island. The view in this part of the harbour is very beautiful. To the N. is the hill known as the Neat's Tongue, on Trombay Island, which is 1000 ft. above sea-level. The highest point of Elephanta is 568 ft. There is another hill 400 ft. high to the left of the Caves.

Elephanta is called by the natives *Gharapuri* ("the town of the rock," or "of purification," according to Dr Wilson), or *Garapuri* ("the town of

[1] Consult Messrs T. Cook & Son. Their steam launch makes the excursion several times a week, and makes other excursions in the harbour.

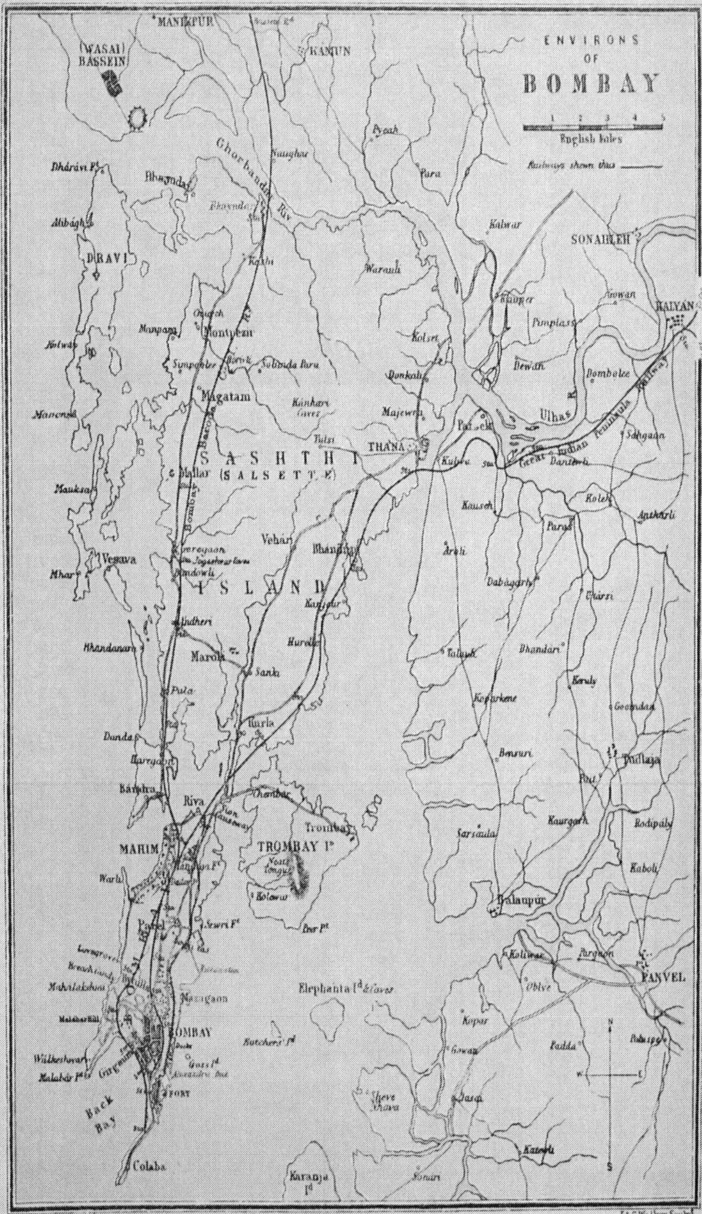

Weller & Graham L^{td} Published by John Murray Albemarle Street, London J & C Walker Sculp^t

excavations," according to Dr J. Stevenson). The caves are called *Lenen* (Lena) by the natives, a word used throughout India and Ceylon for these excavations, most probably on account of the first of them being intended for hermitages of Buddhist ascetics. The island is covered with low corinda bushes and Tal palms. It consists of two long hills, with a narrow valley between them. About 250 yards to the right of the old landing-place, at the S. end of the island on the rise of one of the hills, and not far from the ruins of a Portuguese building, was a mass of rock, cut into the shape of an elephant, from which the place derives its European name. In September 1814 its head and neck dropped off, and in 1864 the half shapeless mass was removed to the Victoria Gardens.

The modern landing-place N.W. of the island is not a very convenient one, as it consists of a rather slippery pier of isolated concrete blocks. The caves are distant about ¼ m., and about 250 ft. above the sea, and are approached by easy steps, constructed in 1853 by a native merchant at a cost of Rs.12,000. There is a bungalow at the entrance, where a fee of 4 annas is paid, and tea can be obtained. The date of the excavation of these caves[1] is now placed about the middle of the 8th century, slightly subsequent to the corresponding cave at Ellora (p. 78). The present main entrance is from the S. side, but the original was from the E., facing the Lingam Shrine. Considered from that aspect the main hall was enclosed by two side colonnades of six columns and two centre colonnades of four columns, the recesses on the N. and S. sides consisting of two aisles separated by two columns, and the outer aisle being much shorter than the inner; the length of the central hall from the pillars at each end is 130 ft., and the breadth from the wall of the south recess to the pillars on the outer side of the north recess is just the same. Of the twenty-six columns, including the sets of two at each entrance to the cave, eight have fallen; satisfactory arrangements have been recently made to save the rest from a like fate. The columns are of a special shape, having a square base, a fluted neck, and a flat cushion capital; the height of the roof varies from 15 ft. to 17 ft.

The *Lingam Shrine*, at the W. end of the hall, stands 4 ft. above the floor of the cave. It is 19½ ft. square, with four doors facing different ways. At the outside of each entrance are two large figures representing Dwarpals or doorkeepers, who lean on dwarfs. The Lingam is a cylindrical stone 3 ft. high, the emblem of Shiva and of reproduction, and is worshipped on great occasions by crowds of devotees.

The *Three-faced Bust, or Trimurti.*—The chief of the mural figures is the immense three-faced bust, 19 ft. in height, at the far end of the Great Cave, facing the N. entrance. It is the representation of Shiva, who is the leading character in all the groups of the cave. The front face is Shiva in the character of Brahma, the creator: the E. face (spectator's left) is Shiva in the character of Rudra, the destroyer; and the W. face (spectator's right) is considered to be Shiva in the character of Vishnu, the preserver, holding a lotus flower in his hand. On either side of the recess is a pilaster with a gigantic dwarpal in front of it.

The *Arddhanarishwar, or half-male half-female Divinity* in the first compartment to the E. of the central figure (spectator's left) represents Shiva, 16 ft. 9 in. high, in the above character. The right half of the figure is intended to be that of a male, and the left that of a female, and thus to represent Shiva as uniting the two sexes in his one person. The bull on which two of the hands of the figure lean, and on which he is supposed to ride, is called Nandi, a constant attendant on Shiva. Brahma, on his lotus throne, supported by five geese, and with his four faces, is exhibited

[1] See *Cave Temples of India*, by Messrs Fergusson and Burgess.

on the right of the figure. On the left, Vishnu is seen riding on what is now a headless Garuda, a fabulous creature, half man half eagle. Above and in the background are found a number of inferior gods and sages of the Hindus, among them Indra, Lord of the Firmament, mounted on an elephant.

In the compartment to the W. of the *Trimurti* are two gigantic figures of *Shiva* and *Parvati,* the former 16 ft. high, the latter 12 ft. 4 in. Shiva has a high cap, on which the crescent and other symbols are sculptured, and from the top of it rises a cup or shell on which is a three-headed figure representing the Ganga proper, the Jumna, and Saraswati, which three streams are fabled to unite at Prayag, or Allahabad, and form the Ganges. According to a well-known Hindu legend, the Ganges flowed from the head of Shiva. The god is standing, and has four arms, of which the outer left rests on a dwarf. In the dwarf's right hand is a cobra, in his left a *chauri* (fly-whisk); from his neck hangs a necklace, with a tortoise ornament. On Shiva's right are several attendants, and above them Brahma, sculptured much as in the compartment on the right of the *Trimurti.* Between Brahma and Shiva is Indra on his elephant.

The *Marriage of Shiva and Parvati* is a sculptured group (greatly damaged) at the S.W. corner of the hall. The position of Parvati on the right of Shiva shows that she is his bride; for to stand on the right of her husband, and to eat with him, are privileges vouchsafed to a Hindu wife only on her wedding-day. In the corner, at the right of Parvati, is Brahma, known by his four faces, sitting and reading, as the priest of the gods, the sacred texts suited to the marriage ceremony. Above, on Shiva's left, is Vishnu. Among the attendants on the right of Parvati is one bearing a water-pot for the ceremony. This is probably Chandra the moon-god. Behind the bashful goddess is a male figure, probably her father Himalaya, who is pushing her forward.

Opposite this in the N.W. corner of the hall is a relief of *Kapalabhrit or Bhairava* with skull and cobra on head and rosary of skulls round neck; two of his eight hands are devoted to the slaughter of a human being, and a third holds up a body for slaughter. At the W. end of the north aisle by which the cave is entered is a relief of *Shiva performing the Tandava dance;* on his left is Parvati, and above is a very perfect Ganesha. Opposite this at the E. end of the aisle is a representation of *Shiva as an Ascetic.* The figure so much resembles Buddha that the early describers of the cave before Erskine thought it to be that personage. The figure has the remains of two arms, which appear to have rested in his lap. It is seated on a lotus, the stalk of which is supported by two figures below. In the aisle behind the east entrance again are two reliefs on the N. and S. ends. The first of these represents *Ravana, the demon king of Lanka,* or Ceylon, attempting to remove Kailas, the heavenly hill of Shiva, to his own kingdom, in order that he may have his tutelary deity always with him, for Ravana was ever a worshipper of Shiva. Ravana has ten heads and twenty arms, and is with his back to the spectator. Shiva is seen in Kailas, with Parvati on his right, and votaries and Rishis in the background. The legend runs that Ravana shook Kailas so much that Parvati was alarmed, whereupon Shiva pressed down the hill with one of his toes on the head of Ravana, who remained immovable for 10,000 years.

The last relief opposite this shows *Shiva and Parvati* seated together, with groups of male and female inferior divinities showering down flowers from above. The rock is cut into various shapes to represent the peaks of Kailas, Shiva's heaven. Behind Shiva and Parvati is a female figure carrying a child on her hip, from which it has been supposed that the sculpture represents the birth of Skanda, the war-god.

Beyond the main hall on the E. side is *the East Wing*, consisting of an open court 55 ft. wide, in the centre of which was a circular platform, probably for a Nandi. On the S. side of the court is a temple on a high terrace, reached by steps with lions at the top of them. The portico of the temple has a chamber at each end, that on the east end with figures of Shiva, Vishnu, and Brahma and of the seven great goddesses or divine mothers (p. 77). The shrine of the temple measures 14 by 16 ft., and has an altar and lingam inside it. The *West wing* of the cave has also an open court with a large cistern on the S. side, and on the W. side a small open chapel with a lingam in it.

Round the hill, a little to the S., are two other excavations fronting the E. These are also Lingam shrines, with *Dwarpals* sculptured outside. On a hill opposite to the Great Cave is a small cave, and an excavation has been commenced but without much progress having been made.

(2) **The Vehar Lake**, on the G.I.P. Rly., can best be visited from Bhandup (17 m.) by arrangement beforehand with the station-master at Bhandup for a pony. The road turns to the right at a signpost, marked 3 m. to Pawe, and from the gateway or Darwazah of Pawe it is 2 m. to the lake; the jungle is very thick part of the way. The lake covers 1400 acres, and measures 2 × 1¼ m.; it was made by Mr Conybeare, C.E. by damming up the Garpur river. It cost £373,650 with the connecting pipes, and can supply 8,000,000 gallons of water a day. The embankment is 30 ft. broad and 30 ft. above the water. The water is 75 ft. deep, of which 50 ft. are available for the supply of Bombay and 25 ft. are kept for *settling*. Fish are numerous, particularly *singara* or "cat-fish." There are also many conger-eels, some of which are 8 or 9 ft. long. There are many teal on the lake, but it is very difficult to get within shot, except in the very early morning. Tigers are scarce now, but many have been killed here. One, shot by Mr Robertson, C.S., had killed sixteen persons.

The *Tulsi Lake*, which lies 2 m. to the N., was formed in 1872, at a cost of £40,000, and water is carried thence to the top of Malabar Hill. 2 m. N. again are the Kanhari Caves.

(3) **Montpezir Caves** (*Mandapeshwar*). — B.B. and C.I. Railway to **Borivli** Station, 22½ m. (good clean waiting-room), thence 1 m. by pony. At the caves is a ruined Portuguese church, with a cross close by. Round the N.E. corner of the church are three Brahmin caves hewn out of the rock, dating from the 8th century. The cave on the E. is 5 ft. 8 in. × 21 ft. Adjoining this cave to the W. is a stone basin for water, of which there is a good supply, said never to fail, and this may be one reason why the Portuguese built here. The next cave is 27 ft. 3 in. × 14 ft. 9 in. In the W. wall is a group of 25 Gana (celestial dwarfs) figures very much mutilated, and a four-armed Shiva. In the corner of the outside wall is half a teak door of the church, with two saints carved on it. The third or W. cave was a vihara (monastery hall) cave in which ten or twelve hermits lived, but was converted into a chapel in 1555 A.D. In the N. part of the E. wall, upside down, is the stone originally over the entrance door, inscribed with the date 1555. At the N.W. are pillared partitions leading to cells, and on the W. side are two pilasters and four pillars about 12 ft. high, with tapering shafts and angular capitals. To the S., on an eminence, is a round tower (40 ft. high), which the priest calls a Calvarium, with a staircase on the outside. There is a good view from the top over the plain.

(4) **Cave Temples of Kanhari**[1] (*Kennery*).—These caves are all excavated in the face of a single hill in the centre of the island of Salsette, and are about 6 m. from the D.B. at Thana (see Route 2). There are one hundred and nine Buddhist caves on the spot; but though so numerous few of them only are interesting as compared with those at Ajanta, Ellora, or Karli. It seems probable that the greater part of them were executed by a colony of Buddhists, "who may have taken refuge here after being expelled from the continent, and who tried to reproduce the lost Karli in their insular retreat." They date from the end of the 2nd century A.D. to about the middle of the 9th, or possibly a little later. The great *Chaitya* is one of the earliest here; those on each side may be two centuries later: the latest is probably the unfinished one, which is the first the traveller approaches by the usual route, and which dates about the 9th or 10th century A.D., or is even still more recent. However this may be, it is at least certain that, to use Heber's words, "the beautiful situation of these caves, their elaborate carving, and their marked connection with Buddha and his religion, render them every way remarkable."

From Thana a cart or light vehicle can proceed between 3 to 4 m. towards the caves to near the shore of the Tulsi lake. From here the path to them is narrow, and winds along the sides of rocks, but it is quite possible to proceed along it on horseback. Most of the surrounding hills are covered with jungle, but the one in which the caves are is nearly bare, its summit being formed by one large rounded mass of compact rock, under which a softer stratum has been denuded by the rains, forming natural caves, which, slightly improved by art, were appropriated as cells. The path runs in a N. direction up to the ravine, lying E. and W., round which the caves are excavated on six ledges in the mountain side connected by flights of steps. Shortly before the end of the ravine is reached, a steep ascent leads up to a platform facing W., where the Great Chaitya Cave (No. 3) and two other caves are situated, and whence steps in the rock lead down to the ravine.

Cave No. 3 entered through a forecourt and a verandah, is a close copy of that at Karli (p. 338), and probably dates from the 6th century. It is 86 ft. long and 40 ft. wide, and has a colonnade of thirty-four pillars, which encircles the dagoba, standing 16 ft. high, at the back. A number of the pillars have bases and capitals carved with elephants, dagobas, trees, worship of sacred feet, etc. At the ends of the great verandah are two later figures of Buddha, 21 ft. high, and over the door is the great arched window, which forms one of the principal characteristics of these structures. In front of the verandah are two pillars, and on the screen of the back wall are Buddhist carvings. In the forecourt are two attached pillars, on which are four lions and three squat figures. On the left of the court is a round cell with a dagoba, and on the right, at the end of a long excavation (No. 2), are three ruined dagobas, with a Buddhist litany (p. 41) on the rock round them.

At a distance of 150 yds. up the ravine N.W. of the Chaitya Cave is the Darbar of Maharaja Cave (No. 10), which was a Dharmsalah or hall of assembly, and not an ordinary vihara. It is 73 ft. × 32 ft. in size, and has two stone benches running down its longer axis, and some cells on the left and back walls. The verandah, which is approached by three flights of steps, has eight columns along the front of it. Nos. 11, 14, and 21 further up the same (left) side of the ravine may also be visited. The first has a small court in front of it, the second has some traces of painting, and the third has columns of the Elephanta type, a Buddhist litany (p. 41), and a figure of Padmapani

[1] Travellers who are able to visit the Caves of Karli and Bhaja, or of Nasik, or Ajanta, or Ellora, need not devote time to any of the Excursions (3) to (5).

crowned by ten adder-heads in a recess on the right of the porch. Above No. 10 on the hill-side is No. 35, a vihara 40 ft. × 45 ft. with benches round it, and four octagonal columns in the verandah; on the walls are reliefs of Buddha seated upon a lotus, of a disciple spreading his cloak for him to walk upon, and of another litany. N.W. from these are caves 56 and 66. From the front of the former is a fine view of the sea—in the latter are some fine sculptures and another litany. Some 400 yards to the south and beyond the Chaitya Cave is a terrace with monuments over the ashes of Buddhist monks. The numbei of cisterns and small tanks round the caves and the flights of steps connecting them are remarkable.

(5) **The Jogeshwar Cave** lies 2 m. N.E. of the village of Jogeshwar (about 1 m. from Goregaon Station on the B.B. and C.I. line). Mr Burgess attributes this Brahmin cave to the latter half of the 8th century, perhaps a quarter of a century after the Elephanta Cave, and half a century after the Sitaki Naháni at Ellora (p. 78). Like the former, it has extensive wings to the central hall, which has a shrine 24 ft. square in the middle, with four doors and a large lingam. The verandah on the S. side is 120 ft. long and has ten columns of the Elephanta pattern, while twenty more such pillars are arranged in a square in the hall. Measured all over, the cave is the largest Brahminical excavation known after Kailása (p. 77).

(6) The **Tansa Water Supply** (D.B. G.I.P. Rly. to Atgaon Station, 59 m.).—The increasing population of Bombay led the Corporation to construct a still larger reservoir on the Tansa River, about 60 m. N.E. of Bombay, which was formally opened by H.E. the Viceroy, Lord Lansdowne, in March 1892. The *Dam* which encloses the valley of the Tansa River, completed 1891, is one of the largest pieces of masonry of modern times. It is of a uniform height of 118 ft. and is 2 m. long, 103 ft. thick at the base, and 24 ft. at the top, where a flagged road runs along it. It encloses a lake 8 sq. m. in area, and is capable of supplying 33,000,000 gallons daily (Engineer, Mr W. Clerke; Contractors, Mr T. C. Glover, and Messrs Walsh, Lovatt, & Co.).

(7) **The Thal and Bore Ghats.**—The ascent of these Ghats passes through some of the prettiest scenery in all India (see pp. 25 and 337); and those who do not intend to leave Bombay by the railway lines which pass up them should make a point of visiting them separately. A visit to the Karli Cave can be combined with the latter expedition. As at present timed, the Panjab and Calcutta mails westwards travel down the Ghats in the daytime.

(8) **Karli.**—85 m. from Bombay; caves 4 m. from railway station (see Route **25**).

ROUTE 2.

BOMBAY TO CALCUTTA by **Kalyan, Nasik, Manmar, Jalgaon** (Caves of Ajanta), **Bhusawal, Khandwa, Itarsi, Jubbulpore, Katni, Manikpur, Allahabad, Mughal-sarai** (Benares), **Patna, Mokamah, Lakhi-sarai**, and **Asansol**, with journeys to **Pachmarhi**, and **Marble Rocks, Buddh Gaya**, and **Parasnath.**

Rail 1349 m. (G.I.P.R. and E.I.R.); mail train 41 hours.

For service to N. India by this route, see p. 97.

The rule for breaking journeys on Indian railways allows the traveller to spend sixteen days on the journey from Bombay to Calcutta with one through ticket. Cost, 1st class Rs.99, as.11; 2nd class Rs.49, as.9, and servants Rs. 13, as. 7. Luggage, free, 120 lbs., 60 lbs., and 30 lbs.—half that amount in seers, the Indian standard of weight. The 85 m. between Bombay and Igatpuri are by far the most picturesque on the whole line between the western and eastern capitals. By the Nagpur and Panjab mails passengers now pass over this portion of the line in daylight; but the Calcutta mail by the E. Indian Railway route traverses it at night.

On leaving Bombay, between Sion and Kurla, the railway passes on a causeway from the island of Bombay to the larger island of Salsette.

9 m. **Kurla** station. Close by (right) are the once famous cotton-mills.

17 m. **Bhandup** station for the Vehar Lake (p. 21).

21 m. **Thana** station, D.B. An early Portuguese settlement, commanding the most frequented passage from the mainland to the island of Salsette. Marco Polo (1298 A.D.) says: "Tana is a great kingdom, lying towards the west. . . . There is much traffic here, and many ships and merchants frequent the place." In 1320 four Christian companions of Friar Odoricus here suffered martyrdom. Friar Jordanus narrates that he baptized about ninety persons ten days' journey from Thana, besides thirty-five who were baptized between Thana and Supara.

The country round Thana was highly cultivated, and was studded with mansions of the Portuguese, when, in 1737, it was wrested from them by the Mahrattas. In 1774 the Portuguese sent a formidable armament from Europe for the avowed object of recovering their lost possessions. The Government of Bombay determined to anticipate their enterprise, and to seize upon the island for the English. A force was prepared under General Robert Gordon, and Thana was taken after a siege of three days. On 6th March 1775 the Peshwa Raghoba, by the Treaty of Bassein, ceded the island of Salsette in perpetuity. In 1816, Trimbakji Danglia, the celebrated Minister of Baji Rao, the last Peshwa, effected his escape from the fort of Thana, though guarded by a strong body of European soldiers. The difficulties of this escape were greatly exaggerated all over the Mahratta country, and it was compared to that of Shivaji from the power of Aurangzeb. The principal agent in this exploit was a Mahratta horse-keeper in the service of one of the British officers of the garrison, who, passing and re-passing Trimbakji's cell, as if to exercise his master's horse, sang the information he wished to convey in a careless manner, which disarmed suspicion. Bishop Heber, who had seen Trimbakji imprisoned in the fort of Chunar, was much interested in this escape, and writes:

"The groom's singing was made up of verses like the following—

"Behind the bush the bowmen hide,
The horse beneath the tree;
Where shall I find a knight will ride
The jungle paths with me?

"There are five-and-fifty coursers there,
And four-and-fifty men;
When the fifty-fifth shall mount his steed,
The Deccan thrives again."

The English Church was being built when he arrived, and on 10th July 1825 was consecrated by him. In the 16th century the *Silk Industry* here employed about six thousand persons. It is now confined to a few Portuguese families and looms.

33 m. **Kalyan** junction station (R.). Here the Madras line through Poona and Raichur branches off S. E. (Route 25). This is a very ancient town, and was once the capital of the Chalukyas. In 1780, the Mahrattas having cut off the supplies from Bombay and Salsette, the British Government determined to occupy the Konkan opposite Thana, as far as the Ghats. Accordingly several posts were seized, and Kalyan amongst them; and here Captain Richard Campbell was placed with a garrison.

Nana Farnavis forthwith assembled a large force to recover Kalyan, on which he set a high value, and attacked the English advanced post at the Ghats, and killed or made prisoners the whole detachment. He then compelled Ensign Fyfe, the only surviving officer, to write to Captain Campbell that, unless he surrendered he would put all his prisoners, twenty-six in number, to death, storm Kalyan, and put all the garrison to the sword. To this Campbell replied that "the Nana was welcome to the town if he could take it." After a spirited defence, he was relieved by Colonel Hartley, on the 24th May, just as the Mahrattas were about to storm. The remains of buildings round Kalyan are very extensive; and Fryer, who visited the place in 1673, "gazed with astonishment on ruins of stately fabrics, and many traces of departed magnificence."

Between Kalyan and Igatpuri, the railway ascends from the Konkan to the Deccan plateau by the mountain pass known as the **Thal Ghat.**

75 m. **Kasara** station (R.). Here a special engine is attached, and the steeper ascent of the Ghat begins. In 9½ m. the line ascends 1050 ft.

59 m. **Atgaon** station for Tansa (p. 23).

At 79½ m. is the Reversing station, and the ascent terminates at 85 m. **Igatpuri** D.B. (R.), where the special engine and brakes are removed.

The ascent of the Thal Ghat is at all seasons interesting; but it is most beautiful in September owing to the wild flowers. The leaves are then bright green, and the country below the Ghats is all streams, pools, and inundations, and the Ghats themselves all cascades and torrents. Igatpuri, properly Wigatpura, "the town of difficulties," so called on account of the precipitous road that preceded the railway, is a pleasant sanatorium and summer resort of Europeans from Bombay. Some large game is to be found in the neighbourhood. There are several European bungalows belonging to railway officials. The line passes through a comparatively level country, with low mountains on either side, to

113 m. **Deolali** station. A halting-place for troops arriving from or proceeding to Europe. There are barracks for 1000 men.

117 m. **Nasik** Road station ✱; D.B. The town, the *Nasika of Ptolemy*, 1900 ft. above sea-level (population 35,000), lies 5½ m. N.W. of the station.

A tramway conveys passengers from the station to it. It is one of the most holy places of the Hindus, owing to its position on the banks of the sacred river Godavery, about 19 m. from its source at Trimbak, and may be called the Western Benares, as the Godavery is termed the Ganga — "Ganges." Thirteen hundred families of Brahman priests are settled here, and all Hindus of rank on visiting it leave a record of their visit with their Upadhya, or "family priest," for each noble family has such a priest at each celebrated place of pilgrimage. In this record are entered the names of the visitor's ancestors, and thus the pedigree of every Hindu chief is to be found in the keeping of these Upadhyas. Even Sir Jang Bahadur, the late *de facto* ruler of Nipal, had his Upadhya at Nasik. The present Gaekwar owes his seat on the throne to this, for when in 1874 the Gaekwar, Mulhar Rao, was deposed, and an heir sought for, the family Upadhya at Nasik supplied proofs of the young prince's legitimate descent from Pratap Rao, brother of Damaji, the third Gaekwar.

At Nasik the river, here 80 yds. broad, is lined on either side for a distance of 400 yds. with flights of steps, and dotted with temples and shrines, and, as in most Indian cities situated near flowing rivers, the view along the banks when hundreds of men and women are bathing is extremely picturesque. The part of the town which stands on the right bank of the river is built upon three hills, and is divided into the New

Town N. and the **Old Town** S. The quarter on the left bank, where are the chief objects of interest, is called *Panchwati.* The manufacture of brass and copper ware, especially of idols, caskets, boxes, chains, lamps, etc., flourishes here. Specimens of the beautiful old work, though rare, are still occasionally to be found in the "old" copper bazaar.

The temples at Nasik, though picturesque, have no striking architectural features. The **Sundar Narayan Temple,** built by one of Holkar's Sardars in 1725, stands at the head of the Ghats on the W. side of the city, close to the Sati gate and ground, and is a miracle of art. Below it may be seen the temples of *Balaji* and of the *White Rama*, and the *Memorial*, erected to the Rajah of Kapurthala, who died in 1870, near Aden, on his way to Europe. From it the river is crossed by a bridge, completed in 1897, which cost Rs. 181,000.

Half a mile to the E., on the Panchwati side, is a fine house of the Rastia family. From here a walk a few hundred yards up a lane leads to five very old and large trees of the *Ficus indica.* Under the largest is a small building. (None but Hindus may pass the vestibule.) It consists of a low front room, from which steps descend to two apartments 5 ft. square and 4 ft. high. In the first room are images of Rama, Sita, and Lakshman. In the second is an image of Mahadeo, 6 in. high, which those three personages are said to have worshipped; hence arises the extreme sanctity of the place, which is quite one of the holiest in Nasik. This hole is **Sita's Gupha**, or Cave, where she found an asylum until lured away by Ravana to Ceylon. Near it is the great temple dedicated to **Kala Rama,** or "Black Rama," which cost £70,000. It stands in an oblong stone enclosure, with ninety-six arches. To the W., up stream, and just before reaching the riverside, is the oldest temple in the place, **Kapaleshwar,** "God of the Skull," a name of Shiva. The ascent to it is by fifty stone steps. It is said to be six hundred years old, but is quite plain and unattractive. Opposite to it the river foams and rushes in a rocky bed. **Rama's Kund** is the place where the god is said to have bathed; hence it is specially sacred, and bones of the dead are taken there to be washed away. Opposite to it and in the river itself is a stone dharmsala, with several arches, roofed over, in which ascetics lodge when the water is low. Down the stream, about 20 yds., are three temples erected by Ahalaya Bai (p. 90). The first is only a few feet high and long, but the next is a large square building, with a stone foundation and brick superstructure, dedicated to Rama; N. of it is a long dharmsala, and a little down the stream is the third temple, all of stone. About 200 ft. down the stream is **Naru Shankar's** temple, with an elaborately carved portico and a large stone enclosure, the last of the temples immediately on the water on the Panchwati side. At the E. end of the city on the S. bank is the hill of **Sunar 'Ali,** and another called **Junagarh,** or Old Fort, on which is a square building, in which Aurangzeb's chief officials used to reside. They command fine views over the city. West of these are the **Jama Masjid,** and the **Hingne Wada,** an old palace of the Peshwa (Chief of the Mahrattas), at present used as a school, and worth a visit for its beautiful carved woodwork.

Sharanpur is the seat of the mission founded by the Church Missionary Society in 1835, in the Junawadi part of Nasik, and moved by Mr W. S. Price in 1855. There was connected with this mission an African Asylum for youths rescued from slavery, and it was from here that Livingstone's *Nasik boys* were drawn. It was closed in 1875, and Mr Price took the boys to the E. coast of Africa, where a colony is established for redeemed slaves. A new church was built here in 1898.

The group of twenty-three **Buddhist Caves**, which vary in age from the 1st century B.C. to the 2nd century A.D., and some of which were altered in the 6th or 7th century of our era, lies 5 m. to the S.W. of Nasik. The caves include three large Viharas or halls, and one fine Chaitya or chapel, and are excavated at the back of a terrace 350 ft. above the level of the plain. The path to the caves,[1] which are numbered from W. to E., reaches the terrace about the middle of them.

Nos. 1 and 2 are damaged and unimportant. No. 3 is a large vihara, measuring 41 ft. by 46 ft., and having a stone bench and eighteen cells round the sides and end walls. In the verandah, behind a decorated screen rail, are six octagonal pillars, carrying four elephants, or bullocks, or horses on their capitals; and above these is a frieze of rail pattern, with a band of animals at the bottom of it. The sculptured door leading into the cave resembles the gateways of the Sanchi tope (p. 98); over it are the three Buddhist symbols of the Bodhi tree (p. 37), the dagoba or tope, and the chakra or wheel of the law, and on each side of it is a guardian dwarpal. In the centre of the end wall of the cave is a large relief of a dagoba. The details of this cave and of No. 10 are almost identical, but the latter is of much earlier date; the carved screens and rail patterns in both of them are specially noticeable. No. 4 is another damaged cave; the next five are marked only by simple rail or other decoration. The Vihara No. 10 measures 43 ft. by 45 ft.; it dates from shortly after the Karli Cave (p. 338), and the carving in it is much more graceful and pleasing than that in the copy of it, No. 3. No. 11 is a small Vihara with six cells off it; the chambers Nos. 12-14, now forming a group, were probably once separate, each forming a small hermitage. Nos. 15 and 16 are much damaged. No. 17 is a smaller Vihara, measuring 23 ft. by 32 ft. The verandah, which is borne by octagonal columns, with elephants and riders, is approached by a flight of steps at one end of it, and not in the centre; on the wall of the back aisle, separated from the cave by similar columns, is a large seated image of Buddha. No. 18 is the Chaitya Cave, the oldest of the group, and nearly contemporary with that of Karli. The front, which is decorated with Buddhist railings, dagobas, serpents, and chaitya windows, is extremely effective; the elaborate carving in the head of the doorway under the great window, which is finished with a representation of wooden beams, simulates the wooden frame-work with which such windows were once fitted. The interior measures 39 ft. by 22½ ft. by 23¼ ft., and is divided by two rows of five plain octagonal columns into a nave and two aisles; at the end of the nave five more columns run round the back of a dagoba 6¼ ft. high and 5½ ft. in diameter. No. 20, at a lower level, is a small Vihara with six side cells. No. 21 is the third largest Vihara, measuring from 37½ ft. to 44 ft. across, and 61 ft. deep. The verandah is carried by four octagonal columns, with bell-shaped capitals. On either side of the hall are eight cells, and in the end wall are three cells and an antechamber, from which two more cells open; all three walls are faced by a low bench. The antechamber to the shrine has two carved columns; the door of the latter is flanked by two gigantic dwarpals. Inside it is a colossal seated image of Buddha, 10 ft. high, attended by two *chauri*-bearers. Nos. 22 and 23, at the extreme east end of the terrace, are both much damaged; the last and No. 2 are Mahayana caves, the rest being older Hinayana works. In addition to the

[1] The detailed account of these caves, as well as those of Ajanta, Ellora, etc., is taken mainly from the monumental work on the *Cave Temples of India*, by Mr J. Fergusson and Mr J. Burgess, published by order of the Secretary of State for India. Those who are specially interested in the subject will find the original work indispensable for them.

caves there are a number of cisterns on the terrace, which affords beautiful views of the country round Nasik.

On the road to **Trimbak** from Nasik (19 m. by road) are several stone-faced wells, and at Nirwadi, on the right of the road, is a beautiful tank lined with stone, and with stone steps and two small pagodas built by Ahalaya Bai. Near Wadi two conical hills, about 900 ft. high, face each other on either side of the road. From these the hills run in fantastic shapes to Trimbak, where they form a gigantic crescent from 1210 to 1500 ft. high. Below this mountain wall, which has near the top a scarp of about 100 ft., is the small town of about 3000 inhabitants. It derives its name from *Tri*, "three" and *Ambak*, "eye," "the three-eyed" being a name of Shiva. The **Fort** stands 1800 ft. above the town, and 4248 ft. above the sea. The **Temple of Trimbakeshwar**, which is on the E. side of the town, not far from where the Nasik road enters, was built by Balaji Baji Rao, third Peshwa. It cost £90,000. It stands in a stone enclosure, which has no corridor, but a portico, which is the music gallery, and is 40 ft. high. The ascent is by steps outside, and strangers are permitted to mount in order to look into the interior of the temple, which none but Hindus may enter. A flight of six hundred and ninety steps up a hill at the back of Trimbak leads to the sacred **source** of the river Godavery where "the water trickles drop by drop from the lips of a carven image shrouded by a canopy of stone" into a tank below. This is the sacred bathing-place of pilgrims, and is called the Kushâwarl. At the S. end is a temple to Shiva.

147 m. **Lasalgaon** station. From this place *Chandor*, an interesting town overhung by a fine hill-fort, is 14 m. N. by a good road. The Maharaja Holkar is hereditary Patel of Chandor. The fort was taken by the British in 1804, and again in 1818.

162 m. **Manmar** junction station, D.B. (R.) This is the junction of the Dhond and Manmar Railway, which forms a cord line between the N.E. and S.E. branches of the G.I.P.R., and of the Godavery Valley branch of the Hyderabad State Railway to Secundrabad (Route 6). About 4 m. S. are the Ankai Tankai Fort, now in ruins, and seven Buddhist caves of some interest. Between the caves and the station rises a curious hill called Ram Gulni, surmounted by a natural obelisk of trap rock 80 or 90 feet high.

204 m. **Chalisgaon** station, branch to 35 m. Dhulia (population 27,400), headquarters of the Khandesh District.

261 m. **Jalgaon** junction of the Tapti Valley Railway (p. 119), and the best station to start from for a visit to the Ajanta Caves (Route 3), is situated in the newly constituted East Khandesh District.

276 m. **Bhusawal** junction station (R.). An important railway colony called into existence by the G.I.P.R. works. Population 16,363. Junction of the Bengal-Nagpur Railway. (Route 7.)

North of Bhusawal the railway passes between the Satpura and Vindhya ranges on the W., and the Mahadeo hills of the former on the E.: these ranges constitute the geographical divisions between Hindustan (N. India) and the Deccan or south country.

278½ m. The **Tapti Bridge**, one of the most important works on the line. The first bridge built was abandoned in consequence of the inferior nature of the stone of which it was constructed.

310 m. **Burhanpur** station, D.B. The city, which is about 2 m. distant, has a population of 33,000. It has been a place of much importance, and is completely walled in. The neighbourhood contains some interesting Mohammedan ruins, and a curious aqueduct still in use. In the town are

two handsome mosques. The *Badshahi Kila*—a ruined citadel and palace—is beautifully situated on a height overlooking the Tapti river. The place was founded in 1400 A.D. by Nasir Khan of the Farukhi dynasty of Khandesh, and was annexed to the Mughal Empire by Akbar in 1600 A.D. It was the capital of the Deccan Province of the empire when in 1614 A.D. Sir Thomas Roe, ambassador from James I. to the great Mogul, passed through, and paid his respects to the Viceroy Prince Parvez, son of Jahangir, and it was here that Shah Jahan's wife, the Lady of the Taj, died in 1629. The place was occupied by the army under General Wellesley on 16th October 1803, and given back to Sindhia the next year. It is now British territory.

322 m. **Chandni** station. About 6 m. by a fair road is **Asirgarh**, an interesting hill-fort on a detached rock standing up 850 ft. from the surrounding plain. It was surrendered on 21st October 1803, after an hour's bombardment, to General Wellesley's army, restored to Sindhia, and again taken in 1819, since when it has belonged to the British. There is a small garrison in the fort, to which an exceedingly picturesque approach of steps and gates leads; on the walls adjoining the gate to the inner fort are several fine native cannon. The only means of conveyance is a country cart —to be ordered beforehand through the station-master. The country around is wild and abounds in large game.

353 m. **Khandwa** junction station, D.B. (R.). A civil station, the headquarters of the district of Nimar in the Central Provinces. From here the metre-gauge system of the Bombay, Baroda, and Central Indian Railway runs N. to Mhow, Indore, and through Western Malwa to Ajmer, and thence to Agra, Delhi, Ferozepore, and the Punjab. (See Routes 8 and 10).

417 m. **Harda** station, D.B. close to station, good (population 16,300). Headquarters of a district, and an important mart for the export of grain and seeds. Here the railway enters the great wheat-field of the Nerbudda Valley, which extends to Jubbulpore.

464 m. **Itarsi** junction station, D.B. (R.) From this the system of the Indian Midland Railway runs N. to Hoshangabad, Bhopal, Jhansi, Gwalior, Agra, and Cawnpore (see Route 9). A railway is under construction from Itarsi to Amraoti and Nagpur (p. 83).

505 m. **Piparia** station. There is a comfortable D.B. close to the station. [A good road leads in 32 m. S. to **Pachmarhi**,* the hill-station of the Central Provinces. There are many bungalows at Pachmarhi and barracks which are occupied by European troops in the hot season. The station is nearly 4000 ft. above sea-level. There is a D.B. on the way at Singhanama; the ascent from here, which is 12 m. long, is very pretty. Good large-game shooting in the forests below the station.]

536 m. **Gadarwara** junction station. A railway 12 m. long leads S. to the **Mohpani** coal-mines, worked by the Nerbudda Coal Co.

Between 590 m. **Bikrampur** and 597 m. **Shahpura** the railway crosses the Nerbudda river.

616 m. **JUBBULPORE** station * (792 m. from Calcutta by Allahabad route). (R.). An important civil and military station, the meeting-place of the G.I.P. and East Indian Railways.[1]

The town (population 100,000) and station are well laid out and well cared for. The Town Hall has a statue of the Queen Empress.

A mile N.E. of the railway station is the Govt. gun-carriage factory.

In the administration of India by the English few subjects have created

[1] A new railway line runs to Nainpur, 60 m. S. of Jubbulpore, and 70 m. further on to Gondia Junction on the Bengal-Nagpur line, 61 m. east of Bhandara Road (p. 85).

more interest than the suppression of the **Thags** (*Thugs*), a fraternity devoted to the murder of human beings by strangulation. The principal agent in hunting down these criminals was Colonel Sleeman,[1] and it was at Jubbulpore that a number of Thag informers and their families were formerly confined,[2] and the once famous "School of Industry" was established in 1835. Originally there were 2500 of these people in confinement here.

Expedition to the Marble Rocks gorge of the Nerbudda.

The Marble Rocks, known to natives as Bhera Ghat, which are 12 m. from Jabalpur, are well worth a visit. Tongas can be hired for the trip, and the road is generally good. About 4½ m. to the west is a remarkable ancient fortress[3] of the Gond Kings, perched on the summit of a huge granite boulder. At 9½ m. a branch road turns to the rocks, the last half m. being often impracticable for vehicles after rain. On the high ground above the lower end of the right side of the gorge are two small D.B.'s and a number of houses, and 100 yds. beyond the bungalow is a flight of 107 stone steps, some of them carved, which lead to the *Madanpur Temple*, surrounded by a circular stone enclosure. All round it are figures of the sixty-four Joginis. Though much mutilated, they are well worth a visit. Three-quarter m. beyond the temple hill the Nerbudda may be reached above the gorge at the point where its waters plunge down the Dhuándhar or Smoke cascade into the cauldron at the upper end of the Marble Rocks. In a recess below the bungalow is the embarkation place for a trip by boat up the gorge. Two men to row and one to steer are enough. The white cliffs of magnesian limestone are only 90 to 105 ft. high, but the effect of the gleaming faces and rifts is extremely picturesque, especially under moonlight; the water is said to be 150 ft. deep in places. Near the entrance to the gorge, which is about 1 m. long, is a spot named the "Monkey's Leap." Further on is an inscription cut on the right side by order of Madhu Rao Peshwa, and near the end of the gorge are some curiously-shaped rocks called the Hathi ka Paon or Elephant's Foot. The gorge is closed by a cascade waterfall over a barrier of rocks. There are usually large nests of wild bees on the rocks, and care must be taken not to excite them by smoking or firing guns. Near the landing-place is a memorial of a young engineer officer who was drowned in seeking to escape the attack of infuriated bees.

673 m. **Katni** junction station. Line S.E. to the coal-fields at *Umaria* 37 m., and thence to Bilaspur on the Bengal-Nagpur Railway (p. 86). Line W. to Saugor (p. 100).

734 m. **Satna** station, D.B. (R.). A town and small cantonment in the Rewah State, also the headquarters of the Baghelkhand Political Agency. A main road runs east to Rewah 30 m. and there joins the Great Trunk Road which runs from Jabalpur to Mirzapur. Near Satna were found the remains of the Bharhut stupa removed to Calcutta Museum (p. 58).

783 m. **Manikpur** junction station. From this place the Indian Midland line runs W. to Jhansi, 181 m. (Route 9 (c).

842 m. **Naini** station (R.). Close by is the **Jail**, one of the largest in India,

[1] Colonel Sleeman's *Rambles and Recollections of an Indian Official*, and *Diaries in Oudh* are among the most fascinating books ever written on India. Meadows Taylor's *Confessions of a Thag* is the finest of all his works.

[2] The Thaggi Reformatory was closed in 1889.

[3] Known as the Madan Mahal.

and there is also a Leper Mission and Asylum here. 2 m. farther the line crosses the Jumna by a fine bridge, 3235 ft. long, and enters

844 m. **ALLAHABAD** station * (Lat. 25° 26′, Long. 81° 55′). The capital of the United Provinces (population 166,000) is situated 316 ft. above sea-level on the left bank of the Jumna, on the wedge of land between it and the Ganges, which the Curzon Bridge and new Bengal and N.W. Railway bridge cross N. and E. of the city.

The Fort stands near the junction of the two rivers. The Civil Station, Cantonments, and City stretch W. and N.W. from this point 6 m. The present Fort and City were founded by Akbar in 1575 A.D., but the Aryans possessed a very ancient city here called Prayag, which the Hindus now call Prag. It is a very sacred place with them, as they believe that Brahma performed a sacrifice of the horse here, in memory of his recovering the four Vedas. The town was visited by Megasthenes in the 3rd cent. B.C., and in the 7th cent. A.D. Hiouen Thsang, the Buddhist pilgrim, visited and described it. It was first conquered by the Moslems in 1194 A.D., under Shahab-ud-din-Ghori. At the end of Akbar's reign Prince Salim, afterwards the Emperor Jahangir, governed it and lived in the Fort. Jahangir's son, Khusru, rebelled against him, but was defeated and put under the custody of his brother Khurram, afterwards the Emperor Shah Jahan. Khusru died in 1615, and the *Khusru Bagh* (see below) contains his mausoleum. In 1736 Allahabad was taken by the Mahrattas, who held it till 1750, when it was sacked by the Pathans of Farukhabad. It changed masters several times, and in November 1801 it was ceded to the British, the Fort having been held by them since 1798.

Allahabad was the seat of the government of the N.W. Provinces from 1804 to 1835, when that was removed to Agra. In 1858, after the suppression of the Mutiny, it again became the seat of the provincial government, of which the title was changed to that of the United Provinces of Agra and Oudh in 1902. The present Lieutenant-Governor is the Honourable Sir J. P. Hewett, K.C.S.I., C.I.E. Previous Lieutenant-Governors have been Mr Thomason, Mr Edmonstone, Sir Wm. Muir, Sir J. Strachey, Sir A. Lyall, and Sir A. MacDonnell, and Sir J. La Touche.

In the spring of 1857 the station, with its magnificent Arsenal and strong Fort, was garrisoned by a single Sepoy regiment, the 6th, to which, on 9th May, a wing of the Ferozepore regiment of Sikhs was added. The officers of the 6th N.I. were confident in the loyalty of their corps, but fortunately a few days later sixty British invalid soldiers were brought in from Chunar. On 5th June most of the Europeans in the place moved into the Fort, thus adding about 100 volunteers to the garrison. The next day the 6th N.I. mutinied and murdered their officers and seven young ensigns who had been posted at Allahabad to learn their drill. The eighty men of the Regiment on duty at the main gate of the Fort were at once disarmed by a fine display of boldness, the 400 Sikhs remaining staunch, under the influence of their C.O., Captain Brayser, though they wavered for a moment. Outside the Fort, anarchy reigned in the city—the jail was broken open, and the prisoners murdered every Christian they met. A Mohammedan Maulvi was put up as Governor of Allahabad, and took up his quarters in the Khusru Bagh. On the 11th of June General Neill arrived in the Fort, and on the morning of the 12th burned Daraganj and got possession of the bridge of boats. On the same day Major Stephenson, with 100 men of the Fusiliers, arrived. General Neill then scoured the neighbouring villages, and produced such a terror in the city that the inhabitants deserted *en masse*, and the Maulvi fled to Cawnpore, and on the 17th June British authority was re-established in the city. General Havelock arrived at Allahabad on 30th June, and left for the relief of Lucknow on 7th July.

The **Khusru Bagh,** close to the railway station, is entered on the S. side by an old archway, nearly 60 ft. high and 46 ft. deep, overgrown with creepers. Within the well-kept garden are three square mausoleums. That to the E. is the tomb of Prince Khusru, W. of it is the grave of a sister of his, and west again that of his mother, a Rajput lady. They are shaded by some fine tamarind trees. The mausoleum of Khusru has been very handsome inside, and is ornamented with many Persian couplets, and with paintings of trees and flowers, which are now faded. The cenotaph of white marble is on a raised platform, without inscription. To the right and left two of Khusru's sons are buried. All three mausoleums have recently been well restored.

E. of the gardens is the **native city,** containing some picturesque corners. On the other side of the railway lies **Canning Town,** the older European quarter, laid out amongst a network of wide avenues. The new **High Court** and **All Saints' Cathedral,** a fine 13th century Gothic structure, 225 ft. long by 40 ft. broad, built of red and white stone, are near the railway station. The throne is a memorial of Bishop Johnson. There are memorial windows of Sir John Woodburn, Lady Muir, C. T. Connell, and others. **Trinity Church** lies N.E. of the Alfred Park. It contains a tablet, which is valuable as a historical record of those who perished in the Mutiny. The **Roman Catholic Cathedral,** in the Italian style, is W. of the Alfred Park, and near it are the **Club** and the Mayo Memorial Hall, and the New University Buildings.

In the Park is also the **Thornhill** and **Mayne Memorial,** with a fine public Library and a Museum. Beyond the Park is the Government House, and to the N. of the Alfred Park is the **Muir College,** a fine building in the Saracenic style. Close by to the W. is the *Mayo Memorial Hall,* a fine structure, with a tower 147 ft. high. The Empress Victoria memorial statue, also in the Alfred Park, is a seated marble figure under a stone canopy. It is intended that the U.P. memorial of King Edward shall take the form of a hospital for consumptives in the hills.

The **Fort** was built by Akbar in 1575. It forms a striking object from the river, but its "high towers have been cut down, and the stone ramparts topped with turfed parapets, and fronted with a sloping glacis. The changes rendered necessary by modern military exigencies have greatly detracted from its picturesqueness as a relic of antiquity. The principal gateway is capped with a dome, and has a wide vault underneath it. It is a noble entrance. The walls are from 20 to 25 ft. high: below them is a moat which can be filled with water at any time. Within the enclosure lie the officers' quarters, powder magazine, and barracks. Access to the **Audience Hall** of the old Palace, though enclosed by the Arsenal, is now possible, thanks to the care of Lord Curzon, by permission of the Local Military Authority. "It is supported by eight rows of eight columns, and surrounded by a deep verandah of double columns, with groups of four at the angles, all surmounted by bracket capitals of the richest design" (Fergusson).

Asoka's Pillar.—In front of the gateway inside the Fort is the Asoka Pillar, which rises 49 ft. 5 in. above ground. It is of stone, highly polished, and is of much interest on account of its great antiquity. On it are inscribed the famous Edicts of Asoka (*circa* 240 B.C.), and also a record of Samudra Gupta's victories in the 2nd cent., and one by Jahangir, to commemorate his accession to

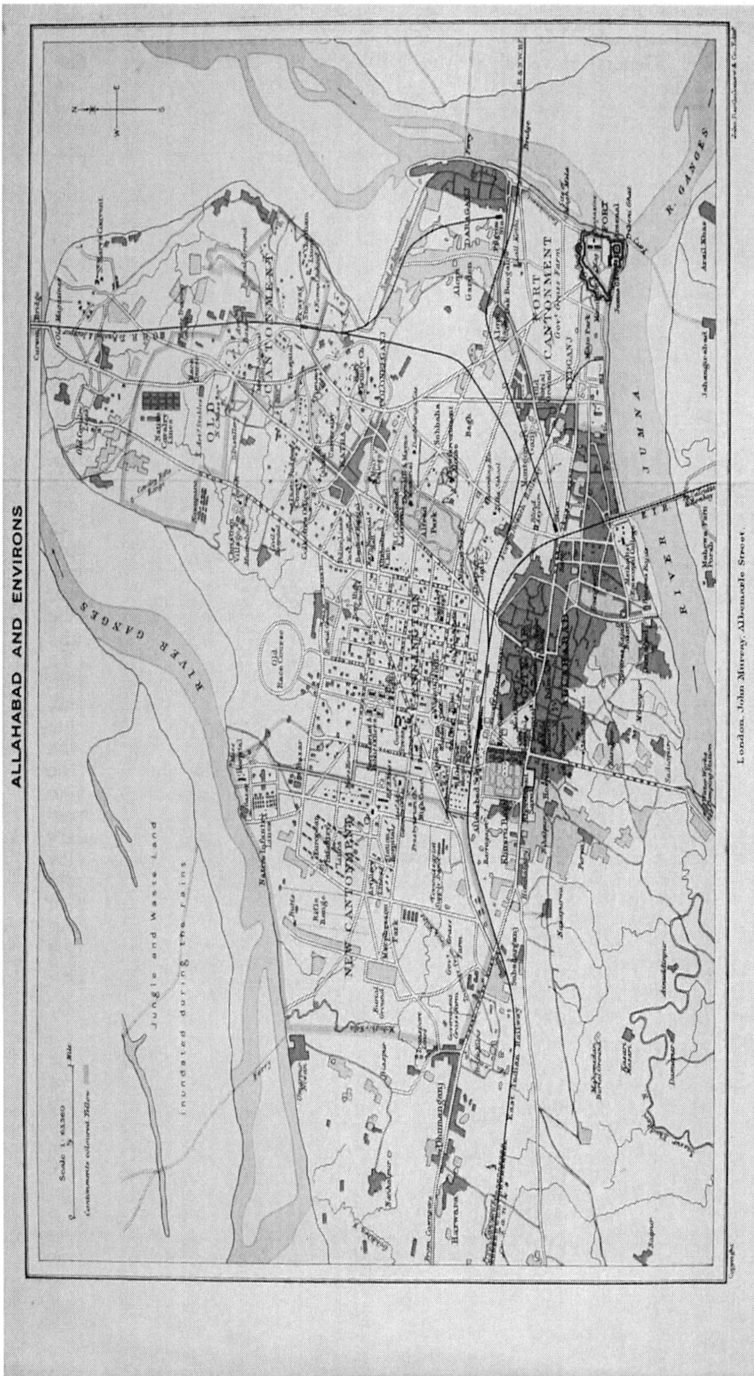
ALLAHABAD AND ENVIRONS
London, John Murray, Albemarle Street.
RIVER GANGES
R. GANGES
RIVER JUMNA
OLD CANTONMENT
NEW CANTONMENT
FORT CANTONMENT
FORT
ALLAHABAD
Old Race Course
Jungle and Waste Land
inundated during the rains
East Indian Railway

the throne. There are also minor inscriptions, beginning almost from the Christian era. According to Mr James Prinsep, who deciphered this and other Asoka inscriptions in 1838 (p. 61), the insertion of some of these inscriptions shows that the pillar was lying on the ground when they were cut.

The **Akhshai Bat (Vata) or undying banyan.**—Hiouen Thsang, the Chinese pilgrim of the 7th cent., in describing *Prayag*, gives a circumstantial description of the undecaying tree. In the midst of the city, he says, stood a Brahmanical temple, to which the presentation of a single piece of money procured as much merit as that of a thousand pieces elsewhere. Before the principal room of the temple was a tree surrounded by the bones of pilgrims who had sacrificed their lives there.

The tree is situated under the wall of the Palace, and is reached by proceeding straight on from the Pillar. Close by is a deep octagonal well flanked by two vaulted octagonal chambers. A few steps lead to a dark underground passage, which goes 35 ft. straight to the E., then S. 30 ft. to the tree. As no tree could live in such a situation, the stump is no doubt renewed from time to time. There are some idols ranged along the passage. In the centre of the place is a lingam of Shiva, over which water is poured by pilgrims. General Cunningham, in his *Ancient Geography of India*, gives an interesting sketch of the probable changes in the locality, and concludes: "I think there can be little doubt that the famous tree here described is the well-known Akhshai Bat or undecaying banyan tree, which is still an object of worship at Allahabad."

The ramparts at the N.E. side of the Fort afford a fine view of the **Confluence of the Ganges,** which is 1½ m. broad, flowing from the N., **with the Jumna,** ½ m. broad, flowing from the W. The Ganges is of a muddy colour, the Jumna is bluer. The **Magh Mela,** a religious fair of great antiquity, to which Allahabad probably owes its origin, occurs every year about the month of January, when a million pilgrims come to bathe at the confluence of the sacred rivers.

The Akbar **Band** runs N.E. from the Fort to Dara Ganj. Here the Bengal and N.W. Railway crosses the Ganges by a fine bridge of 40 spans of 150 ft. each, to Jhusi, and runs 73 m. to Benares. Beyond the old cantonment the new railway line to Jaunpur, Fyzabad, and Lucknow (p. 275) crosses the Ganges by the fine Curzon Bridge.

W. of the Fort is the Minto Park, with the memorial (1910) of the Royal Proclamation of the assumption of the rule of India by the British crown on 1st November 1858. It consists of a stone *lát*, with medallions of Queen Victoria and the late King Emperor, surmounted by four lions bearing the Imperial coronet. Further W. up stream of the Jumna Bridge is the large Methodist Episcopal College.

The trains to Calcutta run back across the Jumna to Naini, and thence to

896 m. **Mirzapur** station. An important, well-built city. Population, 82,500. Before the opening of the East India Railway it was the largest mart on the Ganges for grain and cotton; but much of the trade is now diverted elsewhere. It is still noted for carpets and rugs, dyed with old native vegetable dyes, which are very permanent. There is a handsome river front with fine ghats. The civil station is to the N.E. of the city.

915 m. **Chunar,** with a famous old Fort commanding the Ganges. It was in this stronghold that the Pathan Sher Shah originally strengthened himself against the Mughal Emperor Humayun, and it

was to this that Warren Hastings retreated from Benares in 1781.

931 m. **Mughal Sarai** junction station (R.) for Benares **Cantonment station** 10 m. distant (Route 4), across the Ganges, crossed by the Dufferin steel bridge nearly ¾ m. long.

[From Mughal Sarai some of the express trains to Calcutta now follow the Grand Chord route through Gya to Asansol. The principal stations passed on the Grand Chord line are 62 m. Sasseram (p. 37), 77 m. Sone-East Bank (branch of 80 m. to Daltonganj), 126 m. Gya (p. 36). 204 m. Hazaribagh Road, 232 m. Gomoh junction for the Bengal Nagpur Railway, and 287 m. Asansol (p. 38). The **Japla** station, on the Daltonganj line, is the nearest to Rohtasgarh, the famous fortress of the Emperor Sher Shah (1540 A.D.), which is well worth a visit. From Hazaribagh Road the civil station of that name is about 35 m. distant.]

983 m. **Buxar** station D.B., famous for the great battle won on 26th October 1764 by Major Hector Munro against the Nawab Vazir of Oudh, Shuja-ud-daulah, a battle which, more than Plassey, secured the English possessions in Bengal. It was desperately contended, and while 850 were killed and wounded on the English side, the enemy lost over 2000 in killed alone, and 135 guns, and their whole camp.

1032 m. **Arrah** station, D.B. The special interest that attaches to this spot centres round the defence of the "little house at Arrah" against the mutinous soldiers of Dinapur. The garrison of that place in May and June 1857 consisted of the 7th, 8th, and 40th Regiments of Native Infantry, one company of European, and one company of Native Artillery, and Her Majesty's 10th Foot, under the divisional command of Major-General Lloyd. On 26th July the N.I. troops mutinied and made off for Arrah, unpursued, as in the case of the Meerut mutineers. An unsuccessful attempt was made on the 27th to send troops up the river, and later, on the 29th, a small body of three hundred and forty-three Europeans and seventy Sikhs was despatched to Arrah by steamer, under Captain Dunbar, but was compelled to fall back the next day after having been caught in an ambuscade between the river bank and that place, only fifty men and three officers returning unwounded. For heroic conduct in this attempted relief the V.C. was conferred upon two volunteers of the Bengal Civil Service, Mr M'Donell and Mr Ross Mangles. Private Dempsy of the 10th also won the same reward of valour by his brave conduct on this and on subsequent occasions. Meanwhile Major Vincent Eyre, of the Bengal Artillery, who had previously passed up the river to Buxar, had also learned of the attack on Arrah, and on 30th July advanced with one hundred and sixty men of the 5th Fusiliers, and forty Artillerymen with three guns, to the relief of the place, which lay 48 m. from him. On the 1st August he had a severe engagement with the enemy at Bibiganj, which was only decided by a resolute bayonet charge; and on the morning of the 3rd he effected the rescue of the Arrah garrison. The little house at Arrah, which had been prepared and provisioned for defence by Mr Vicars Boyle, engineer of the railway then under construction, had on that date been held for a week by twelve Englishmen, supported by fifty of Rattray's Sikhs against a body of two thousand mutineers and a large mob. The attack was commenced on 27th July, but the garrison, under Mr Boyle and the Collector, Herwald Wake, met the assailants with so heavy a fire that they speedily fell back to the shelter of trees. On the 28th and 29th the enemy subjected the house to a continuous fire of miscellaneous missiles from two old guns, one of which was finally placed on the top of the larger adjoining house. On the 30th an effort was made to burn the defenders out, but this failed; and an attempt to mine the house was not carried to completion before the relief took place. Towards the end of the attack the provisions of the garrison began to fail, and they were obliged to sink a well 18 ft. deep inside the house to provide themselves with water. The house, which stands in the compound of the Judge, has been converted into an historical monument by Lord Curzon. It is nearly a square, and has two storeys, with a verandah on three sides, supported by arches, which the besieged filled up with sand-bags. The lower storey, which is little over 10 ft. high, was held by the Sikh soldiers.

Arrah is on a branch of the *Son Canal*, the great irrigation work of South Behar.

The Son River is now crossed by a bridge nearly 2 m. long, but little shorter than the Tay Bridge.

1056 m. **Dinapur** Cantonment.

1062 m. **Bankipur**[1] junction station,* (R.), D.B., the headquarters of the Patna district, and forming the western extremity of the city of **Patna** (station 6 m. farther E., 136,000 inhabitants), which covers 10 sq. m., and with its suburbs extends 9 m. along the S. bank of the Ganges. The ancient city of Palabrotha (Pataliputra), on this site, the capital of Chandra Gupta, extended 10 m. along the river, and 2 m. inland from the river bank. The modern city contains nothing of much interest to the traveller, except a building called the **Gola**, which was built for a granary in 1783, but has never been used for that purpose. It is 426 ft. round at the base, built of masonry, with walls 12 ft. 2 in. in thickness, the interior diameter being 109 ft. It is about 90 ft. high, and might contain 137,000 tons. Inside there is a most wonderful echo, the best place to hear which is in the middle of the building. As a whispering gallery there is perhaps no such building in the world. The faintest whisper at one end is heard most distinctly at the other. As a curiosity, if for no other reason, the building should be kept up. The ascent to the top is by steps outside. Sir Jung Bahadur of Nepal rode a pony up the steps outside to the top.

East of the Gola is the fine building of the Patna College, and 3 m. E. of it again the Gulzarbagh quarter, in which the great opium manufactory was situated. The Harmandir is a shrine specially revered by the Sikhs as the birthplace of Guru Govind Singh.

In the city proper, 5 m. from the Gola, and on the right side of the road near the Roman Catholic church, is the grave of the sixty English captives[2] murdered by Mir Kasim and Samru (p. 221) on 6th October 1763, a massacre avenged by the storm of the place exactly a month later.

Till its recent abolition Patna formed with Ghazipur the agency by which the Government monopoly of Behar and Bengal opium was worked. This opium has been famous from time almost immemorial, and was for many years one of the principal sources of income of the E.I. Company. The area under cultivation in Behar has been greatly reduced under the recent agreements with China in 1907 and 1911 for the abolition of the use of the drug in that country. The number of chests exported to China is now limited to 30,000, and this will be gradually reduced until all export ceases in 1917. China can claim this consummation by an earlier date, if she can show that opium cultivation has been effectively stopped throughout the country. The culti-

[1] See also Note, p. 311.

[2] One of these, H. Lushington, aged only 26, who had already escaped from the Black Hole, slew three of his murderers before he was overpowered.

vation was carried out by a system of annual engagements and advances. The crop is sown in November, and matures in February. The following details of the cultivation will be found interesting. "The best soil for growing is loam, so situated that it can be highly manured and easily irrigated. The seed is sown in November. Several waterings and weedings are ordinarily necessary before the plant reaches maturity in February. After the plant has flowered, the first process is to remove the petals, which are used as coverings for the opium cakes. The opium is then collected by scarifying the capsules and scraping off the exudation next morning."

Bankipur is the junction for the Tirhoot State Railway, N.; the Bengal and N.W. Railway leading to Oudh; and the Patna Gaya Railway S. (see p. 311 and below).

Expedition to Gaya.

57 m. from Bankipur.

This journey will chiefly repay the archæologist or the student of Buddhism. The district of Gaya contains many places of great sanctity; and the rocky hills which run out far into the plains of the Ganges valley teem with associations of the religion of Buddha, many of which have been diverted to new objects by modern superstition. The Barábar Caves, 16 m. north of Gaya, are considered to be among the oldest Buddhist monuments in existence. At the present day the chief pilgrims to the temple and sacred tree at Buddh Gaya are Burmese and devout Mahrattas, who come to pray for the souls of their ancestors in purgatory. The Hindu pilgrim, before leaving his home, must walk five times round his native village, calling upon the souls of his ancestors to accompany him on his journey. Arrived at Gaya, he is forthwith placed in charge of a special Brahman guide, with whom he makes the pilgrimage of the place.

Gaya ✱ D.B. is a city of 50,000 inhabitants. The temple of Bishn Pad in the old portion of it is difficult to approach except on foot, owing to the extreme narrowness of the streets. In it is the *Footstep of Vishnu*, or the Bishn Pad, which is 13 in. long and 6 in. broad. It is of silver, and is enclosed in a vessel of silver inserted into the pavement, which has a diameter of 4 ft. Flower and other offerings are made to it.

Buddh Gaya is 7 m. S. of Gaya. For the first 5 m. the road is good, from that point a country road is followed. The origin of the **Temple** *of Buddh Gaya* is of great antiquity (543 B.C.), and is closely connected with events of the life of Buddha. It is built in a hollow, which diminishes its apparent height, and is also shut in by small houses. The figure of Buddha, which, according to Hiouen Thsang, was of perfumed paste, was destroyed centuries ago. Other figures of plaster were subsequently made and also destroyed. To the left is the place where the founder of the present College of Mahants, about 250 years ago, performed *Tapasya*—that is, sat surrounded by four fires, with the sun overhead. The ashes were preserved in a hollow pillar.

Much of the stone railing, which was once supposed to be the work of King Asoka, but is now known to be of a date 100 years later, has been restored to the position which it is supposed to have occupied round the original structure. It has four bars of stone, supported by pillars at intervals of 8 ft. The top rail is ornamented with carvings of mermaids, or females with the tails of fish, inserting their arms into the mouths of Makaras, that is, imaginary crocodiles, with large ears like those ot elephants, and long hind legs. Below this top bar are three others, also of stone, ornamented with carvings of lotus flowers. The pillars are adorned with carvings of various groups, such as a woman and child, a man with a woman who has the head of a horse, Centaurs, and so on. Several additional pillars have been lately recovered and erected in their places. Mr Fergusson pronounces this to be "the most ancient sculptured monument in India." The plinth of the temple is 26½ ft. high, and at the top of it is a clear space 13 ft. broad, which allowed a passage round the tower. At each corner of the platform was a small temple, and outside Asoka's rail were many subordinate temples. Behind the temple, on a raised platform, is the sacred Bo-tree (a pipal or *Ficus religiosa*) under which Buddha sat. The numerous figures and votive models of the temple and of stupas all round the shrine are of late date, *i.e.*, about 800-1000 A.D.

Mr J. C. Oman says: "Defaced by time and the hand of man, transformed a good deal through well-meant restorations, the celebrated temple at Buddh Gaya, even in its modern disguised condition, with its 19th-century stucco about it, and its brand new gilt finial, is an imposing structure, about 180 ft. high and 50 ft. wide at its base. All things considered, it has certainly lasted remarkably well, the material of which it is constructed being only well-burnt brick cemented with mud. Stone has been used only in the door frames and flooring. The building is plastered with lime mortar. It is built in the form of a pyramid of nine stories, embellished on the outer side with niches and mouldings. Facing the rising sun is the entrance doorway, and above it, at an elevation greater than the roof of the porch which once adorned the temple, there is a triangular opening to admit the morning glory to fall upon the image in the sanctuary."

A Burmese inscription records a restoration in 1306-1309. In 1877 permission was granted these Buddhists to again restore the temple, but Raja Rajendralala Mitra, deputed by the Local Government to inspect their work, states that "the Burmese carried on demolitions and excavations which in a manner swept away most of the old landmarks." The remains of the vaulted gateway in front of the temple were completely demolished, and the place cleared out and levelled. The stone pavilion over the Buddha Pad was dismantled, and its materials cast aside on a rubbish mound at a distance. The granite plinth beside it was removed. The drain-pipe and gargoyle which marked the level of the granite pavement were destroyed. The foundations of the old buildings noticed by Hiouen Thsang were excavated for bricks and filled with rubbish. The revetment wall round the sacred tree had been rebuilt on a different foundation on the W. The plaster ornaments on the interior facing of the sanctuary were knocked off, and the facing was covered with plain stucco, and an area of 213 ft. to 250 ft. was levelled and surrounded by a new wall. For further description of the temple, reference may be made to Rajendralala Misra's *Buddh Gaya*, Calcutta, 1878; and Cunningham's *Arch. Surv.*, vol. iii.; and Sir Edwin Arnold's most delightful chapter in *India Revisited*, 1886, "The Land of the Light of Asia."

To the N.W. is a small but very ancient temple, in which is a figure of Buddha standing. The doorway is finely carved.

From Gaya the S. Behar Railway runs E. to Lakhisarai (80 m.). The Grand Chord line as above noted runs S.E. to Asansole, and W. to **Sasseram** (D.B.), (population 2400), where the grand tomb of the Pathan Emperor of Delhi, Sher Shah (1540-45), stands in the middle of a masonry tank. This tomb is one of the finest in all India (see Fergusson's *Indian Architecture,* ii. 218), and should be seen by all interested in Oriental buildings.

1118 m. **Mokamah** junction station (R.). Line to the N., joining the Tirhoot State Railway. To the E. the loop line of the East Indian Railway, which leaves the main line at (262 m.) **Lakhisarai** junction station, runs along the banks of the Ganges *via* **Jamalpur, Sahibganj,** and **Tinpahar** to **Khana** (see p. 39), where it rejoins the main line.

1217 m. **Madhupur** junction station (R.) of the Giridih Line.

[Excursion to Parasnath.

Parasnath Mountain.[1] — From *Madhupur* station to *Giridih* station 24 m. by rail, from the latter place to the foot of mountain 18 m. by hand-drawn dák ghári along a good road. Bearers at Madhuban for the ascent (2¾ hrs.). The sportsman and the lover of mountain scenery will enjoy a visit to this far-famed mountain and place of pilgrimage. It is 4488 ft. above sea-level, and is the Eastern metropolis of Jain worship. According to tradition, Parasnath, who was the 23rd Tirthankar of the Jains, was born at Benares, lived 100 years, and was buried on this mountain. The numerous temples, though most picturesque, are of no great antiquity.

At Madhuban, 1230 ft., is a Jain convent on a tableland in a clearance of the forest—"the appearance of the snow-white domes and bannerets of its temple, through the fine trees by which it is surrounded, is very beautiful." The ascent of the mountain is up a pathway worn by the feet of innumerable pilgrims from all parts of India. Ten thousand still visit the place annually. The path leads through woods with large clumps of bamboo over slaty rocks of gneiss, much inclined and sloping away from the mountain. The view from a ridge 500 ft. above the village is superb. Ascending higher, the path traverses a thick forest of *sál* (*Vateria* or *Shorea robusta*), and other trees spanned with cables of Bauhinia stems. At 3000 ft. the vegetation becomes more luxuriant, and the conical hills of the white ants disappear. At 3500 ft. the vegetation again changes, the trees becoming gnarled and scattered. The traveller emerges from the forest at the foot of a great ridge of rocky peaks, stretching E. and W. for 3 or 4 m. The saddle of the crest (4230 ft.) is marked by a small temple, one of many which occupy various prominences of the ridge, with a beautiful view. To the N. are ranges of low wooded hills, and the Barakar and Aji Rivers. To the S. is a flatter country, with lower ranges and the Damodar River. The situation of the principal temple is very fine, below the saddle in a hollow facing the S., surrounded by groves of plantain and *Ficus Indica.* It contains little but the sculptured feet of Parasnath and some marble cross-legged figures of Buddha, with crisp hair, and the Brahmanical Cord. Many chapels and altars with such reliefs are dotted about the crest. A convalescent depôt for European soldiers was established in 1858, but was abandoned; the officers' quarters are now utilised as D.B.]

1262 m. **Sitarampur** junction station for Barakar, 5 m., and Katrasgarh, 43 m.

1268 m. **Asansol** junction station of the Bengal and Nagpur Railway (see Route 7). Population, 15,000.

1279 m. **Raniganj** station (population 16,000), on the E. edge of the great coal-fields of Bengal, which stretch out 384 m. to the W., and

[1] *See* chap. vi. of Mr Bradley Birt's *Chota Nagpur.*

extend under the bed of the Damodar. The place was formerly the property of the Raja of Burdwan, hence the name. More than thirty species of fossil plants, chiefly ferns, have been found in the coal, of similar species to those in the Yorkshire and Australian coal. The mines afford regular employment to a large number of men and women, chiefly of the Bauri tribe. A vast number of boatmen on the Damodar river are employed in carrying coal to Calcutta. The coal is piled on the banks of the river, and can be carried down only while the Damodar is in flood. The mines are said to have been accidentally discovered in 1820 by Mr Jones, the architect of Bishop's College at Calcutta.

The following information regarding the coal-fields of Bengal will be of interest. "The coal of Bengal is all derived from the rocks of the Gondwana system, and is of the Permian age, or rather younger than the coal of England. The area of the Raniganj field is not less than 500 sq. m., exclusive of its extension under the Ganges Alluvium. The next most important field at the present day is Karharbari, about 11 sq. m. in area, the greater part of which is owned by the E.I. Railway Company. This coal-field yields the best coal in Bengal. A third field" (now the most important of all) "is the Jheria coal-field, about 200 sq. m. in area. It is situated 16 m. to the W. of the Raniganj field. The fourth field is Daltonganj, with an area of about 200 sq. m." The progress of the Bengal coal industry can be judged from the following figures of the output:—1881, 900,000 tons; 1891, 1,747,000 tons; 1907, 8,500,000 tons; 1909, 11,500,000 tons; numbers employed, 130,000. Exports of coal from India have risen to 660,000 tons, and probably twice as much is loaded on steamers for consumption.

1325 m. **Khana** junction station for the loop line (see p. 38).

1334 m. **Burdwan** station. (R.) (population, 35,000), headquarters of a Division and District, and the residence of the Maharaja of Burdwan, the descendant of a Panjab Khatri, who settled at Burdwan soon after the place had been conquered by Prince Khurram, later the Emperor Shah Jahan, in 1624. The Maharaja possesses a fine palace in the place.

1376 m. **Hooghly** junction station for the Eastern Bengal Railway.

1379 m. **Chandernagore** and **Serampore** stations.

1400 m. **Howrah Calcutta terminus** (see Route 5).

ROUTE 3

CAVES OF AJANTA

Jalgaon, 261 m. from Bombay (see p. 28) and 15 m. S. of Bhusawal, is 30 m. by a good road from Fardapur, the nearest rest-house to the Caves of Ajanta. There are two T.B.'s on the road, which can be occupied by permission of the Collector of Khandesh (Dhulia). Practically no supplies are obtainable at it. In fair weather the journey from Jalgaon to Fardapur will be done by a tonga with two pairs of ponies (*if* ordered 2-3 days previously through the kind assistance of the mamlatdar, Jalgaon, cost about Rs. 35) in five hours or somewhat less. Otherwise the journey must be done by country cart, to be ordered through the station-master, Jalgaon, and will occupy eight to ten hours.

The Caves of Ajanta, like those of Kanhari, but unlike the majority of Buddhist caves, are excavated in the scarped side of a deep ravine, at the head of which is a steep waterfall. They lie 3½ m. from the rest-house; and the Warora stream and its affluent from the ravine has to be crossed several times in order to reach them; the crossing is generally a simple matter, but after heavy rain the channels may become impassable torrents for some hours or longer. The ravine is well wooded and pretty, and the view of the curved front of the caves, from the inner entrance to it is extremely picturesque. The caves, which are famous among all such remains for the paintings with which they were once decorated, are twenty-nine in number. Of these, four (Nos. 9, 10, 19, and 26) are Chaitya chapels, and the rest are vihara halls. Six of them belong to the older Hinayana sect, and the rest to the Mahayanas. The oldest and the lowest in position are Nos. 9 and 8, which date from the 2nd century B.C., while the latest are referred to the 7th century A.D. **No. 8**, the first on the left at the end of the path to the caves, is a small vihara, measuring 32 ft. by 17 ft. by 10 ft. It had two cells at each side and two at the sides of the antechamber of the shrine. It is of the same age as the Chaitya Cave, **No. 9**, which is one of the oldest of all the Buddhist caves of India, and is 45 ft. deep, 22¾ ft. wide, and 23 ft. high. In dimensions and in the decoration of its façade it much resembles the Nasik Chaitya Cave (p. 27), but is rather older in date than that. Fourteen plain octagonal pillars on each side separate the nave and aisles, and eleven more continue the colonnade round the dagoba at the end of the cave. The vaulted roof once carried wooden ribs; in front of it is the great horseshoe window, 11½ ft. high, with a terrace and rail in front of it, and a second terrace over the porch, with a guardian *dwarpal* at either end. The dagoba is 11 ft. high to the top of its capital; this is in form of a relic-box, and probably once bore a wooden umbrella. Remains of paintings are still visible on the left and back walls; on each pillar were once painted representations of Buddha, and on the roof of the aisles was painted a pattern of wooden compartments.

No. 10 is a still larger Chaitya, measuring 95 ft. by 41 ft. by 36 ft., and was also once fitted with wooden ribs, the roofs of the aisles having ribs carved in the stone. Its façade has fallen. The dagoba resembles that in No. 9 and, as in that cave, there are considerable remains of the paintings which once covered the walls. The costumes depicted in these resemble those of Sanchi (p. 98).

No. 11 appears to have been remodelled. The roof of the verandah is painted with birds and flowers. The hall measures 37 ft. by 28 ft. by 10 ft., and is carried by four primitive columns. There is a bench along the right side. There are three cells on the left side, and two cells and a shrine in the end wall; in the shrine is a free-cut statue of seated Buddha, with a fine kneeling figure in front of it.

No. 12 is a vihara measuring 36 ft. square, with four cells on each of the three inner sides, and is probably of the same age as No. 9. The cells have two couches with stone pillars. Over their doors are representations of Buddhist windows.

No. 13 is a small hall, 16½ ft. by 13½ ft. by 7 ft., with seven cells, each with a stone couch, round it. This completes the group of the older caves; and with Nos. 7 and 6 begins the group of excavations of the Mahayana school. The **former (7)** is a vihara of unusual shape, in that it has no hall, the verandah, which is preceded by two porches borne by columns of the Elephanta type, leading directly to four cells and to the antechamber to the shrine; both the last are profusely decorated with sculpture. The statue represents Buddha, with his legs crossed under him, and his right hand raised to bless.

No. 6 is the only cave here with two storeys. The lower stage, of which the front has fallen, measures roughly 54 ft. square. It is borne by sixteen plain octagonal columns in four rows, but only seven of these now stand. They are connected above by beams carved on the ceiling. On each side and at the back are cells, and in the middle of the last an antechamber with Elephanta-like columns leads to the shrine containing a seated figure of Buddha. The stair from this storey leads to the verandah of the upper storey, once carried by four columns, with chapels outside it and rooms at the end of it. The hall measures rather less than that of the lower storey, and is carried by twelve columns arranged round a central space. There are cells all round this hall also, and a shrine with a front chamber in the back wall.

Nos. 5 to 1 form with Nos. 21 to 29 the latest group at Ajanta, and belong to the 6th and 7th centuries A.D. **No. 5** has been commenced only, but has a handsome door at the back of the verandah. **No. 4** is the largest of all the viharas, measuring 89 ft. square, and being supported by twenty-eight pillars. It is surrounded by cells as usual, and has a large shrine approached by an antechamber at the back. The verandah was carried by eight octagonal columns, and has three doors and two windows in the back wall leading to the hall, the centre one being decòrated with elaborate carvings. Between it and the right window is a sculptured relief of the Buddhist Litany, in which two figures are represented in each compartment as fleeing to Buddha from danger, from fire, snakes, and wild beasts. **No. 3** is a small vihara, of which again only the verandah is shaped out. **No. 2** is a vihara hall, 48 ft. square, supported by twelve pillars, with five cells on either side and one chapel room at each side of the antechamber and shrine. There are also two chapel rooms at each end of the verandah, the front of which is carried by four pillars with flower-shaped capitals; the roof of the verandah projects 7 ft. to the front of the columns. Between the hall and the verandah are a finely-decorated door and two windows opposite to the side aisles formed by the columns in the hall, which are richly carved. At the end of these aisles are two chapel rooms, that on the E. side with the figures of a king and a queen holding a child, with small figures of sporting children below them; and that on the W. side with two large male figures. A richly carved doorway leads to the shrine; in front of the seated figure in it are kneeling worshippers. Traces of painting exist in this cave on the roofs of the verandah, and the hall and its aisles, and in the shrine and the two side chapels. The scenes on the E. wall of the hall represent a royal procession with elephants, horses, and armed retainers, and a sailing boat laden with jars.

No. 1 is one of the largest and most splendidly decorated viharas of all. In the front is a verandah borne by six columns, once preceded by a porch borne by two. Outside the verandah are three excavations on each wing, and inside is one at each end. The hall measures nearly 64 ft. square, is borne by twenty columns enclosing a central space, and has five cells on either side. At the back an ante-chapel with two columns, flanked by two cells on either side, leads to a large shrine. All along the front of the cave is a sculptured architrave with spirited representations of elephants, hunting scenes, and groups of figures. On the west chapel are representations of the four scenes of sickness, old age, and death, which led Buddha to renounce the world. In the upper part of the frieze are geese under a band of lions' heads. Three doors and two windows open into the hall from the verandah, the centre door being elaborately carved, as are the columns of the back row in the hall, and the sides of the other rows which face inwards. These carvings deserve detailed notice, being among the richest and most ornate known. In the shrine is a colossal statue of Buddha, supported on either hand by Indra. At the sides of the elaborately decorated doorway to it are statues of the goddesses of the Ganges and Jumna above, and of two snake-hooded guardians at the bottom. The whole of the cave was once covered with paintings, of which a certain amount remains. In the four corners of the ceiling are interesting panels which represent groups of foreigners—perhaps Persians. On the front wall is represented the reception of a Persian embassy by a Raja in his palace. On the back wall to the E. of the antechamber is a mountain scene, and between the doors of the two cells a Naga Raja and his wife in conversation with another personage, while high up on the wall is a snake-charming scene; further on is another scene of a Naga Raja and ladies; and between the second and third cell doors, on the E. wall, is a scene of elephants and soldiers. On the back wall of the antechamber to the shrine is a painting of the Temptation of Buddha by Mara, such as is represented in the bas-relief in cave No. 26

Returning to the centre of the path, cave **No. 14** is reached above No. 13, and forms the third of the middle group of Mahayana works. According to Mr Burgess, Nos. 16 and 17 are the finest of the whole series of caves, and with the Chaitya cave, No. 19, date from about 500 A.D. The **first** of these, a vihara, is incomplete. The second, **No. 15**, has a hall 34 ft. square without columns, preceded by a verandah, and with six cells on each side; in the back wall are two cells and a shrine. **No. 16** has a verandah 65 ft. long and nearly 11 ft. wide, borne by six plain octagonal pillars; from the front of it steps descend to a chamber with a representation of a Naga Raja. Here also three doors and two windows open from the verandah into the hall, which is nearly 66 ft. square, and has twenty octagonal pillars, the roof of the front aisle being carved to simulate beams. On each side are six cells. The shrine, which is entered direct from the hall, and has side aisles separated off by two columns, contains in the centre a huge statue of Buddha in the teaching attitude. On the left wall of the hall are paintings of a death scene, and of Buddha with a beggar's bowl, and teaching in a vihara. On the right wall, left of the door of the first cell, are the remains of a representation of Prince Siddhartha drawing the bow. **No. 17** is very similar in size and arrangement to No. 16, but has an antechamber to the shrine, and two cells on either side of the former. Over the central door to the hall are a row of painted Buddhas. There is only one side door and three windows. Between the verandah and No. 16 is a fine cistern. In front of the figure of Buddha in the shrine stand two figures, one with a mendicant's bowl. On the ceiling of the N. end of the verandah is a much damaged circular painting, in the compartments of which human beings and animals are represented; and on the back wall of the E. half is a painting of three females and a male figure flying through the air. The paintings on the side walls of the hall have been ruined by smoke. On the W. portion of the back wall is a picture with scenes in a court of justice, and hunting, and others in which a lion plays the principal part. On the right wall is a scene of the landing of Vijaya in Ceylon, and of female demons devouring victims. **No. 18** is merely a porch. **No. 19** is the third Chaitya cave, measuring 46 ft. by 24 ft. by 24 ft. high. It is therefore of very similar dimensions to No. 9, but, unlike that, is profusely decorated throughout. In front of it was a large court, most of which has fallen; but the porch at the back of the court under the great arched window still stands, and, like the whole façade, is covered with elaborate ornament. Five pillars on each side of the nave separate the aisles from it, and five more run round the dagoba. Outside the first two pillars of each colonnade is another, thus completing an aisle passage all round the cave. The columns have square bases and rounded shafts with bands of carving, and bracket capitals richly decorated. Above the columns on the wall under the curved roof were painted compartments of figures of Buddha, divided by floral arabesques. The roof has stone ribs carved under it. The front of the dagoba bears a figure of Buddha. Outside the cave to the W. is a relief of a Naga Raja with a seven-headed cobra hood, and his wife. **No. 20** has a verandah, of which the roof is carved in imitation of rafters, and a hall 28 ft. by 25 ft.; the antechamber here projects into the hall.

The rest of the caves, from **21** to 29, complete the group of the later Mahayana caves, and lie considerably further W. The verandah of **21**, which has fallen, had at each end of it a chapel chamber with two pillars in front, with the earliest representation, as Mr Burgess believes, of the leaf falling over the corners of the capitals. The jewel or necklace pattern on the frieze above is characteristic of the work of the 7th century. The hall measures 51 ft. square, and has twelve columns; the image in the shrine is attended by huge *chauri* bearers. **No. 22** is a small vihara of 16 ft. square; the image in the sanctuary is represented with its feet resting on a lotus. **No. 23** is another vihara hall about 50 ft. square, with twelve pillars; the sanctuary is incomplete, but all four columns of the verandah are entire. **No. 24** would have been the largest vihara of all, but was never completed. It shows how these caves were excavated by means of long galleries, which were broken into one another; the carving which exists is very elaborate. **No. 25** is a small vihara hall 26 ft. by 25 ft.; the verandah, which has two pillars, opened on a court in front. **No. 26** is the fourth Chaitya cave, and is very similar to No. 29. It is 68 ft. deep, 36 ft. wide, and 31 ft. high. The verandah, borne by four columns, here also opened on to a court with sculptures on the sides of it, one on the east side representing the Buddhist Litany again. Over the verandah was a broad balcony in front of the great window, 9 ft. high; on each side of this are various sculptured reliefs of Buddha. A colonnade of twenty-six pillars forms the aisles, and runs round the dagoba at the back of the cave. The frieze above the colonnade is richly sculptured, and the roof is decorated with stone ribs. The walls of the aisles are also profusely decorated with sculpture; on the left wall near the door from the verandah is a colossal image of the dead Buddha, and further down the wall is the relief of the temptation of Buddha by Mara. The dagoba has representations of Buddha all round it, and is over 20 ft. high. **No. 27** is an unfinished vihara, which would have been 43 ft. wide and 31 ft. deep. **No. 28**, difficult of access, would have been a fifth Chaitya, of which only part of the great window has been excavated. **No. 29** is inaccessible; only part of the verandah of it was ever completed.

ROUTE 4

BENARES

Benares * (p. 34), (lat. 25° 18'. long. 83° 3'), originally Varanási, and commonly called Káshi ("The Splendid"), to which the suffix Ji is added by the Hindus by way of respect (population, 209,000—Hindus, 151,000, Brahmans, 30,000), has been the religious capital of India from beyond historical times. The most generally accepted derivation of the name *Varanasi*, is from the streams Varana (*modern Barna*) and Asi, the former a river of some size on the N. and W. of the city, the latter a rivulet now embraced within its area.

The site of Benares has often been changed, but there is good ground for supposing that the first city was built at *Sarnath*. The past history of this, one of the most ancient cities in India, is involved in obscurity. It is, however, certain that it was a most flourishing and important place six centuries before the Christian era, for Sakya Muni, who was born about 558 B.C., and died in 487 B.C., came to it from Gaya to establish his religion, which he would not have done had it not been then a great centre. Many important writers of the Hindus are first heard of at Benares. Of intermediate events little is known, but the place was sacked by Mahmud of Ghazni. We learn from Husain Nizami's history that in 1194 A.D. Jaichand, Raja of Benares, "whose army was countless as the sand," was defeated and killed by Kutab-ud-din, the general of Shahab-ud-din Ghori, and the Emperor Alla-ud-din destroyed 1000 temples, and built mosques on their sites. From that date Benares was governed by the Moslems, and became part of the province of Allahabad. It is due to the iconoclastic spirit of the conquerors that hardly a single building can be found in Benares which dates beyond the time of Akbar, and there are but few which in their present form date beyond the time of the Mahratta supremacy in the latter half of the 18th century.

In May 1857 the garrison of Benares consisted of the 37th N.I., known to be disaffected, and the Ludhianah Sikh regiment. Upon the arrival of Colonel Neill from Calcutta an attempt was made on 4th June to disarm the regiments on parade, but this miscarried, and in the end it became necessary to turn the guns on the Sikhs, who were driven off by the fire of the battery of Captain William Olpherts, subsequently so distinguished in the first relief of Lucknow.

Benares is still *par excellence* the Holy City of the Hindus, and the great northern centre of the worship of Shiva, and the annual number of pilgrims who visit it is not less than 1,000,000, while the number of Brahmans residing in the place is over 30,000. Every pilgrim, besides visiting the various holy spots in the city, must make the circuit of the Panch Kosi round the sacred territory of Benares, commencing at the Manikarnika Ghat, proceeding by the Asi Ghat and returning by the Barna Ghat (see p. 49). The route, which is nearly 45 m. in length, and the pilgrimage of which occupies six days, is picturesquely lined by fine trees and small shrines, and is marked by several large temples.

The ornamental **Brass-Work** which is met with all over the world is a *specialité* of Benares; but the modern work is far less carefully executed than the old, which is now difficult to procure. Small idols and other images in brass and other materials are made in great quantities in the narrow lanes around the Golden Temple. **Shawls, silks, and embroideries** (Kimkhwab), may also be purchased here.

As the finest view of Benares is obtained from the river Ganges, the banks of which are bordered by **Ghats**, or flights of stone steps, descending to the water from the most famous buildings in the city, the traveller will do well to spend most of his time in a boat, passing along the whole river frontage, where, in the morning especially, he will see crowds of the people coming down to bathe and drink the water of the sacred river.

For those who are pressed for time, it will be sufficient to see the Monkey

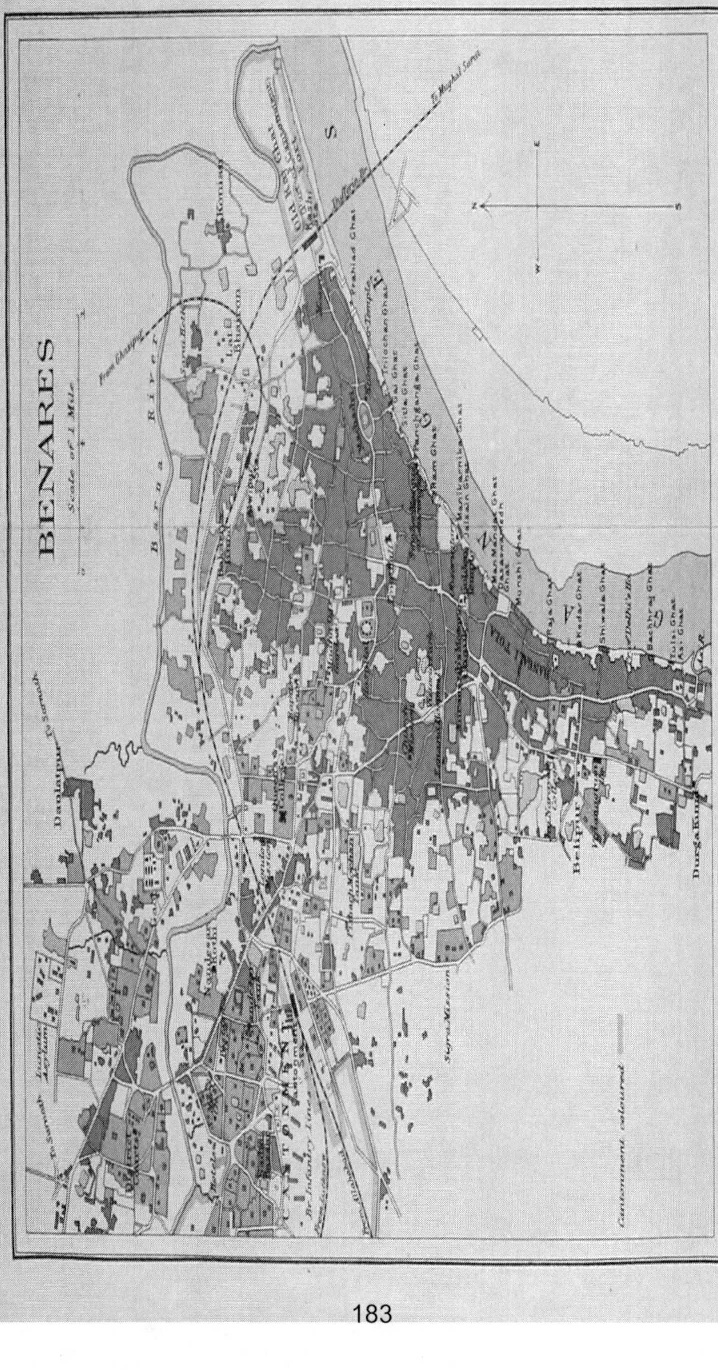
BENARES
Scale of 1 Mile
Barna River
Cantonment coloured
Durga Kund
Bhelupur
Dasaswamedh Ghat
Manikarnika Ghat
Panchganga Ghat
Trilochan Ghat
Prahlad Ghat
Raja Ghat
Kedar Ghat
Tulsi Ghat
Asi Ghat
Secrole
Sigra Mission
Dufferin Br.
To Moghal Serai
From Ghazipur
To Sarnath
Lunatic Asylum
Danlarpur
London. John Murray, Albemarle Street

Temple, the Observatory, and the Ghats, as far as the Panchganga Ghat, disembarking there to see the Golden Temple. The hand-books to Benares by the Rev. Mr Sherring and the Rev. Mr Parker are useful little publications, and Mr E. B. Havell's *Benares the Sacred City* is well edited and illustrated.

The river and native town are nearly 2 m. from the

Cantonment, N. of the railway line, where a detachment of Europeans and a native regiment are stationed. Near the *Hotels* is **St Mary's Church**, with some old tombs; to the N, of these are the Civil Station, and to the E. the Nandeshwar Kothi, the Government College and the garden of Madho Das. The **Queen's College** is a building in the Perpendicular style. The interesting Buddhist and Hindu remains, once here, have been retransferred to Sarnath. To the N. of it is an ancient **monolith**, 31½ ft. high, found near Ghazipur. On the obelisk there is a Gupta inscription and an English record of its removal. In the garden of Madho Das, Warren Hastings was encamped when he attempted to arrest Maharaja Chait Singh of Benares (see below), on 16th August 1781, and it was from here that, five days later, he was obliged to fall back upon Chunar after the repulse of the troops at Ramnagar.

The **Nandeshwar Kothi**, now belonging to the Maharaja of Benares, was the house in which Mr Davis, Judge and Magistrate of Benares, was attacked by the followers of Vazir 'Ali, the deposed Nawab of Oudh, who had just killed Mr Cherry, the British Resident, in the building now occupied by the Collector's Court, on the 14th of January 1799. Mr Davis sent his wife and two children on to the roof, and, with a spear, placed himself at the top of the staircase leading to it, where he successfully defended himself until he was rescued by the arrival of a regiment of cavalry. In the civil station is a house in which Warren Hastings once lived; a sundial constructed by him still exists in the garden of it.

From the Kothi a fine road leads to the Raj Ghat and **Ganj-i-Shahid** Mosque, passing the Bakariya Kund and Bhairon Lat. The first of these, on the right side of the road, was a famous, and still is a picturesque, tank of Buddhist origin; close to it is a Buddhist shrine, known as the Battis Khamba, or Thirty-two Pillars, now a Mohammedan tomb. The Lat of Bhairon, on the left side of the road further on, is another Buddhist relic, and may possibly be one of the Lats erected by King Asoka. The Ganj-i-Shahid on the S. side of the open space in front of the Raj Ghat Railway Station, is an interesting mosque built of fine Buddhist remains, erected as a memorial of the Mussulmans who fell in the early captures of Benares.

The London Mission is close to the Railway Station on the S. side of the line; the Wesleyan Mission is in the middle of the Civil Station; the Zenana and Baptist Missions are near the Queen's College, while the Hospital of the former, and the Church Mission are at Sighra, 1 m. S. of the Railway Station. Further on is the **Vizayanagram's Palace**, built by a Maharaja who died at Benares in 1845 (see p. 334). The house can be visited by permission of the Agent. There is a good view from the terraced roof over the Ganges, in the direction of Aurangzeb's mosque and the Golden Temple. Close to the palace on the W. are several Jain Temples.

The **Central Hindu College and School** in the Kamachcha quarter, started under the auspices of Mrs Annie Besant, has for its object the combination of religious and moral education, with mental and athletic development for Hindu youths. Several lakhs of rupees have been subscribed towards the College, which contains 250 students; the Principal and two Professors are Europeans. The College was visited by King George on 19th February 1906.

NATIVE TOWN.

The **Durga Temple,** sometimes called the Monkey Temple by Europeans, from the numbers of monkeys which inhabit the large trees near it, is about three-fifths of a mile S. of the Vizayanagram Palace. It is stained red with ochre, and stands in a quadrangle surrounded by high walls. In front of the principal entrance is the band room, where the priests beat a large drum three times a day. The central portion is supported by twelve curiously carved pillars, on a platform raised 4 ft. from the ground. Through the doors plated with brass the image of the goddess may be seen; in the porch are two bells. The temple and the fine tank adjoining were constructed by a Mahratta Rani in the 18th century. As Durga is the terrific form of Shiva's wife, and is said to delight in destruction, bloody sacrifices of goats are offered to her here.

From this temple the traveller may proceed to the **Ghats,** embarking either at the upper end of them from the Asi Ghat, or more conveniently from the central **Dasaswamedh** or **Man Mandir** Ghat, and rowing slowly past in front of them. In the following account the Ghats are given in succession from the S., proceeding down stream.

The **Asi Ghat** is one of the five special places of pilgrimage in Benares. The channel of the Asi, which here falls into the Ganges, is dry during the cold weather, but is about 40 ft. broad. The steps at the Ghat are a good deal broken. It is the nearest from which to cross to Ramnagar, the palace of the Maharaja of Benares. The next Ghat is the **Lala Misr Ghat,** which belongs to the Maharaja of Rewah. At the N. end of the **Tulsi Ghat,** which follows, huge masses of masonry have fallen, and lie on the river's edge; this Ghat is named after Swami Tulsi Das, the translator into Hindi of the Sanscrit epic of the Ramayana. The **Janki Ghat** is quite new; at the top of the steps are four Shiva temples with gilded pinnacles, and behind them is the fine Lularik well. At the foot of the Ghat is the pumping station of the Benares Water Works. The **Bachhraj Ghat** belongs to the Jains who have built three temples on the bank of the river. Next comes the **Shivala Ghat,** where the fort in which Chait Sing resided stood. It is a handsome building, and appears as fresh as when first constructed. In the upper part of the N. wall are five small windows in a row, from one of which Chait Sing made his escape, when he fled from Warren Hastings in 1781. It is now called the Khali Mahal, or "empty palace," and belongs to Government. In this vast building two companies of Sepoys and three young officers, who were sent by Hastings to arrest Chait Sing, were massacred by a mob which discovered that the soldiers had come without ammunition. When fresh troops reached the palace, Chait Sing had fled. The graves of the three officers, distinguished by a memorial tablet, lie a short distance to the back of the Palace. The Shivala Ghat is one of the finest and most crowded of all. Part of it is assigned to the religious ascetics called Gusains. The next is the **Dandi Ghat,** and is devoted to the staff-bearing ascetics called Dandi Pants. It is also very fine. The **Hanuman Ghat,** which follows, is large and generally crowded; at the head of it is a temple of the Monkey God. At the **Smashan Ghat,** which is used as a subsidiary cremation ground, wooden pyres may be seen being built, while bodies wrapt up in white or red cloths lie with their feet in the Ganges ready to be burned.

Passing the Lali Ghat, the **Kedar Ghat,** which comes next, deserves attention, as one of the finest and loftiest of all. According to the religious books of the Hindus, the city is divided into three great portions —Benares, Kashi, from whence the popular name, and Kedar. Kedar is a name of Shiva, but it also signifies a mountain, and especially a part of the Himalayan mountains, of which Shiva is the lord, hence called Kedarnath. His temple, at the head of the steps, is much resorted to by the Bengali and Tilanga pilgrims to the city. It is a spacious building, the centre of which is supposed to be the place where Kedarnath dwells: the interior can be seen from the doorway. At the four corners are Shivalas, with cupolas. There are two brass figures, hidden by a cloth, which is removed on payment of a fee. The walls and pillars are painted red or white. There are also two large black figures, which represent *dwarpals*, or janitors; each has four hands holding a trident, a flower, a club, and the fourth empty, to push away intruders. At the bottom of the Ghat is a well called the Gauri Kund, or "well of Gauri," Shiva's wife, the waters of which are considered efficacious in curing fevers, dysentery, etc.; on the steps of the Ghat are many lingam emblems of Shiva. The Mansarovar Ghat (built by Raja Man Singh) leads to the **Mansarovar tank,** round which are sixty shrines. Manas or Mansarovar is a fabulous lake in the Himalayan mountains, near Kailas, or Shiva's heaven. Near the tank at Benares so-called is a stone 4½ ft. high, and 15½ ft. in periphery, which is said to grow daily to the extent of a sesamum seed. In a street to the E. of the tank are figures of Balkrishna, or the infant Krishna, and Chatarbhuj or Vishnu. The head of the **Narad Ghat**, named after the famous Rishi, winds up picturesquely under two fine pipal trees. At the **Chauki Ghat**, under a pipal tree, are many idols and figures of snakes. In a street close by, called Kewal, is a figure of Durga with ten arms.

The next Ghat, where the stairs ascend into a large house or *sarai* built by Amrit Rao for travellers, is the **Raja Ghat.** On leaving it the traveller reaches the **Someshwar Ghat** so called from the adjacent temple of the moon, *Soma* being the "moon," and *Ishwar* "lord." At this Ghat every kind of disease is supposed to be healed. Close by is an alley, in which is the shrine of Barahan Devi, a female Æsculapius, who is worshipped in the morning, and is supposed to cure swollen hands and feet. The **Chausathi Ghat** is one of the most ancient at Benares. The **Rana Ghat,** next to it, built by the Maha Rana of Udaipur, is not much frequented. The **Munshi Ghat** is the most picturesque of all the Ghats at Benares. It was built by Munshi Shri Dhar, Diwan of the Raja of Nagpur, and now belongs to the Maharaja of Darbhanga (p. 311). The fine Ghat between this and the Dasaswamedh Ghat was built by Ahalaya Bai, the famous Mahratta Princess who governed Indore from 1765 to 1795 (p. 90).

The **Dasaswamedh Ghat** is one of the five celebrated places of pilgrimage in Benares, the other four being the junctions (sangam) of the Asi and Barna with the Ganges, and the Manikarnika and Panch Ganga Ghats. It is specially thronged during eclipses. Here Brahma is said to have offered in sacrifice (*medh*) ten (*das*) horses (*aswe*), and to have made the place equal in merit to Allahabad.

At the S. end of the Ghat, which should be visited on foot, is a low whitewashed shrine of Sitla, the goddess of smallpox, and of the presiding deity of the Ghat, figured under a brass lingam. Further on at the Ghat are life-size stone figures in niches of the Ganges, Saraswati and Jumna rivers, and of Vishnu, the Trimurti or Trinity, and the Narsingh or lion-man incarnation of Vishnu, which are passed on the way to the **Man Mandir Ghat** and the **Observatory.** This lofty building gives a fine appearance to the Ghat, and commands a beautiful view of the river. It was erected by Raja Jai Singh, the founder of Jaipur in Rajputana, (see p. 140) with four other observatories—at Delhi, Muttra,

Ujjain, and Jaipur. On entering the Observatory the first instrument seen is the Bhittiyantra, or "mural quadrant." It is a wall 11 ft. high and 9 ft. 1¼ in. broad, in the plane of the meridian; by this are ascertained the sun's altitude and zenith distance, and its greatest declination, and hence the latitude. Then come two large circles, one of stone and the other of cement, and a stone square, used, perhaps, for ascertaining the shadow of the gnomon and the degrees of azimuth. The Samrat Yantra seen next is a wall which is 36 ft. long and 4½ ft. broad, and is set in the plane of the meridian. One end is 6 ft. 4¼ in. high, and the other 22 ft. 3½ in., and it slopes gradually up, so as to point to the North Pole. By this, the distance from the meridian, the declination of any planet or star and of the sun, and the right ascension of a star are calculated. There are also a double mural quadrant, an equinoctial circle of stone, and another Samrat Yantra. Close by is the Chakrayantra, between two walls, used for finding the declination of a planet or star; and near it a Digamsayantra, to find the degrees of azimuth of a planet or star. The instruments are fully described in a leaflet obtainable at the Observatory (see also the account of the Jaipur Observatory, p. 140).

The **Mir Ghat** leads up to the Dharam Kup or Sacred Well, and the Lalita Ghat to the **Nepalese Temple**, a picturesque object, but disfigured by indecent carvings; it does not resemble in the least the Hindu temples.

The famous **Golden Temple** (see p. 49) is between this Ghat and the **Jal Sain Ghat**, or Burning Ghat, which lies beyond the Nepalese Temple on the down-stream side, and is crowned by a mass of temples and spires. Numbers of cremations are usually in progress on the spot, and many sati stones will be noticed all round it; it is naturally regarded by the Hindus as one of the most holy places in the whole of Benares.

The **Manikarnika Ghat** is considered the most sacred of all the Ghats, and in November is visited by multitudes of pilgrims. Just above the flight of steps, which are enclosed by piers running out into the river, is the Manikarnika Well, and between it and the steps is the temple of Tarkeshwara. The well has its name from *Mani*, "a jewel," and *Karna*, "the ear," Devi or Mahadeo having dropped an ear-ring into it. During the eclipse of the sun it is visited by great numbers of pilgrims. The well, or, more properly, tank, is 35 ft. square, and stone steps lead down to the water. Offerings of the Bel tree, flowers, milk, sandal-wood, sweetmeats, and water are thrown into it, and the smell arising from it is in consequence anything but pleasant. Between the well and the Ghat is the Charanapaduka, a round slab projecting slightly from the pavement, on which stands a pedestal of stone: on its marble top are two imprints, said to have been made by the feet of Vishnu. At the second flight of steps of this Ghat is a temple to Siddha Vinayak, or Ganesh. The idol has three eyes, is painted red, and has a silver scalp, and an elephant's trunk covered with a bib. At the feet of the image is the figure of a rat, which is the Vahana or "vehicle" of Ganesh.

The **Sindhia's Ghat** was intended to have been one of the grandest of the whole front, but owing to the great weight of the superstructures the foundations have sunk several feet, and are still gradually sinking. The temple on the left of the S. turret is rent from top to bottom, as are the stairs leading to the curtain between the turrets. It was built about 1830 A.D. by Baiza Bai, widow of Daulat Rao Sindhia, who constructed the colonnade round the Well of Knowledge. Passing two Ghats, the next reached is the **Ghosla Ghat**, which was built by the Nagpur Raja one hundred years ago, and is very massive and handsome. The following picturesque Ghat was built by the last of the

Peshwas. The **Ram Ghat**, which comes next, was built by the Raja of Jaipur.

The next large Ghat is the **Panchganga Ghat**, beneath which five rivers are supposed to meet; it was built by Raja Man Singh, and carries a number of picturesque shrines. Above it rises the small mosque of Aurangzeb, called in old maps "the Minarets." This was built for the Emperor by a Hindu of the name of Madho Das, and the minarets are still called after him. It occupies the site of a temple of Vishnu, and was erected to emphasise the predominance of the Mohammedan religion. The view from the top of the minarets, which rise nearly 150 ft. above the platform of the mosque, and are slightly out of the perpendicular, is extremely fine.

Four unimportant Ghats lie between this and the second Sitala Ghat, below which the Gao or **Gau Ghat**, so called from the number of cows that resort to it, and also from the stone figure of a cow there, stands out into the river.

The **Trilochana Ghat**, the next reached, has two turrets in the river, and the water between them possesses a special sanctity. The pilgrims bathe in the Ganges at this Ghat, and then proceed to the Panchganga and there bathe again. At the head of the Ghat is a temple of Trilochan, or the Three-Eyed, another form of Shiva. The **Prahlad Ghat** is the last of all, and from it a fine view is obtained of the whole river front. Further down the stream is the site of the old Raj Ghat ferry, now spanned by the great Dufferin Bridge, and beyond that the junction of the Barna and Ganges at the **Raj Ghat** near the bridge. Between the junction and the bridge is a piece of high ground which in the Mutiny was strongly fortified, and has ever since been called the Raj Ghat Fort, now dismantled.

The Golden Temple is dedicated to Bisheshwar, or Shiva, as the Poison (*Vish*) God (*Ishwar*), a name given him because he swallowed the poison when the gods and demons churned the ocean, and is known as the Adi (first) Bisheshwar. The temple, which is surrounded by very narrow crowded streets, is in a roofed quadrangle, above which rises the tower. At each corner is a dome, and at the S.E. a Shivala. Opposite the entrance, with its finely wrought brass doors, is a shop where flowers are sold for offerings, from the upper storey of which, on a level with the three towers of the temple, the interior may be seen. The red conical[1] tower (left) is that of Mahadeo's temple; next to it is a gilt dome, and on the right is the gilt tower of Bisheshwar's temple. The three are in a row in the centre of the quadrangle, which they almost fill up. They are covered with gold plates, over plates of copper which cover the stones. The expense of gilding was defrayed by Maharaja Ranjit Singh of Lahore. The temple of Bisheshwar is 51 ft. high. Between it and the temple of Mahadeo hang nine bells from a carved stone framework. One of these, and the most elegant, was presented by the Maharaja of Nepal. The temple of Mahadeo was built by Ahalaya Bai, Princess of Indore (p. 90). Outside the enclosure is the Court of Mahadeo, where on a platform are a number of lingams, and many small idols are built into the wall. They are thought to have belonged to the old temple of Bisheshwar, which stood N.W. of the present one, and of which the remains are still to be seen, forming part of the mosque which Aurangzeb built on them.

In the quadrangle between the mosque and the Temple of Bisheshwar is the famous **Gyan Kup**, "Well of Knowledge," where, according to Hindu tradition, the emblem of Shiva took refuge

[1] These conical towers, almost universal in Hindu temples, are called *Sikras* or *Vimanas*. The origin of their peculiar form is unknown. See Fergusson's *Indian Architecture*, i. 322.

D

when the original temple was destroyed, and still is. The well is protected by a high stone screen and covered by a stone canopy, and the worshippers, an eager and excited crowd, by whom the quadrangle is always thronged, are no longer permitted to cast offerings of flowers, etc., into it. The roof and colonnade of the quadrangle were built in 1828 by Baiza Bai, widow of Daulat Rao Sindhia. On one side of the colonnade is a stone Nandi, given by the Raja of Nipal, 7 ft. high. On another side is an iron railing, within which is a shrine of white marble, and one of white stone, and a carved stone support, from which hangs a bell. Around are many richly carved small temples, particularly one to the S. of Bisheshwar; the gateways of the courtyard are similarly carved, and small gilded spires add to the picturesqueness of the scene.

The great Mohammedan Mosque, usually ascribed to Aurangzeb, but probably built by Jahangir, lies to the N.W. side of the Gyan Kup. The Hindus claim the courtyard between it and the temple wall, and in consequence it is entered from the side. The beautiful columns in the front of the mosque belonged to the destroyed temple, of which further fine remains may be seen at the back of the mosque. During the period of nearly three centuries since the mosque was built not a stone has been loosened. A small number of the faithful assemble here on Fridays; at other times it is generally deserted.

Just outside the Golden Temple is the **Shrine of Sanichar**, or Shani, the planet Saturn or its regent. The image is a round silver disc, from which hangs an apron, or cloth, which prevents one remarking that it is a head without a body. A garland hangs from either ear, and a canopy is spread above. A few steps beyond this is the **Temple of Annapurna**, a goddess whose name is compounded of *Anna*, "food," and *Purna*, "who is filled." She is supposed to have express orders from Bisheshwar to feed the inhabitants of Benares, and in front of this temple are always a number of beggars. It was built about 1725 by the Peshwa of that date, Baji Rao. There are four shrines in this temple dedicated to the Sun, Ganesh, Gauri Shankar, and the monkey-god Hanuman. Near it again is the temple of **Sakhi Vinayak**, the witnessing deity (p. 48). It was built in 1770 by a Mahratta, whose name is not recorded. Here pilgrims, after finishing the Panch Kosi circuit round Benares, get a certificate of having done so. S. of the temple to Shani is that of **Shukareshwar**, *Shukar* being the planet Venus, where prayers are made for handsome sons. Between the Temple of Annapurna, and that of Sakhi Vinayak is a strange **figure of Ganesh**, squatting on a platform raised a little above the path. This ugly object is red, with silver hands, feet, ears, and elephant's trunk.

The narrow streets and lanes which connect the Ghats with one another, and the parts of the city lying more remote from the river front, will be found exceedingly picturesque and interesting; but they cannot be described as clean and sweet, and they must be traversed on foot, though a carriage proceeding along the broader streets at the back can be rejoined at intervals.

Among the remaining objects of interest in Benares may be mentioned the Bhaironath, Dandpan, Bridhkal, and Kameshwar temples, and the Arhai Kangura mosque, all situated on the N.W. outskirt of the city. The first, built by Baji Rao in 1825, is remarkable for a fine tamarind tree. The idol in the temple is considered to be the Kotwal, or magistrate of the city, who rides about on an invisible dog. There is an image of a dog close to the idol, and the confectioners near sell images of dogs, made of sugar, which are offered to it. A Brahman waves a fan of peacock's feathers over visitors to protect them from evil spirits, and they in return must drop offerings into the cocoa-nut shell he holds. The idol is of stone, with a face of silver and four hands. The Dandpan temple close to this contains the staff of Bhairon, a stone shaft 4½ ft. high, and the famous Kal Kup or Well of Fate into which the sunlight falls from a hole in the wall above. The Bridhkal temple contains a well and a small tank renowned for the curing of diseases. Near it is the Alamgiri mosque, constructed in the second year of the reign of Aurangzeb, of pillars from an old temple. The Arhai Kangura Mosque, which, with the Kameshwar temple of the God of Love, lies to the N.W. of Bhaironath and near the Machadri Tank, is built of old Buddhist remains, like the Ganj-i-Shahid (p. 45). In the Victoria Park is a statue of the Queen-Empress.

The palace of the Maharaja of Benares at **Ramnagar,** on the right bank of the Ganges, may be visited by permission, to be obtained from the Secretary to His Highness. It stands above a fine ghat, and affords a splendid view of the river front of Benares. The Maharaja has been recently granted the powers of a ruling chief in his domain.

Sarnath.

Sarnath.—The site of old Benares, where Buddha taught, lies about 4 m. N. of the Civil Station; it can now be reached by the line from Benares to Mau junction and Bhatni, and also by the Ghazipur road, which is left at the third mile-stone. Shortly after turning to the left, two towers are seen, one, the Chaukandi on a hill; the other—½ m., farther N.—the Buddhist Tope figured in Fergusson's *Hist. of Arch.*, which has an excellent account of it, and a representation of the panelling. "The best known as well as the best preserved of the Bengal topes, is" the Dhamek[1] Stupa "at Sarnath. It was carefully explored by General Cunningham in 1835-36, and found to be a stupa—viz., containing no relics, but erected to mark some spot sanctified by the presence of Buddha, or by some act of his during his long residence there. It is situated in the Deer Park, where he took up his residence, with his five disciples, when he first removed from Gaya on attaining Buddhahood, and commencing his mission as a teacher. What act it commemorates we shall probably never know, as there are several mounds in the neighbourhood, and the descriptions of the Chinese pilgrims are not sufficiently precise to enable us now to discriminate between them."

The building consists of a stone basement, 93 ft. in diameter, and solidly built, the stones being clamped together with iron to the height of 43 ft. Above that it is in brickwork, rising to a height of 110 ft. above the surrounding ruins, and 128 ft. above the plain. Externally the lower part is relieved by eight projecting faces, each 21 ft. 6 in. wide, and 15 ft. apart. In each is a small niche, intended apparently to contain a seated figure of Buddha, and below them, encircling the monument, is a band of sculptured ornament of the most exquisite beauty. The central part consists of geometric patterns of great intricacy, but combined with singular skill; and above and below foliage equally well designed, and so much resembling that carved by Hindu artists on the earliest Mohammedan mosques at Ajmer and Delhi, as to make us feel sure that they cannot be very distant in date.

"In his excavations, General Cunningham found, buried in the solid masonry, at the depth of 10½ ft. from the summit, a large stone, on which was engraved the usual Buddhist formula: 'Yedharmma hetu,' etc., in characters belonging to the 7th century." Mr Fergusson writes that he is "inclined to adopt the tradition preserved by Captain Wilford, to the effect that the Sarnath monument was erected by the sons of Mahi Pala, and interrupted by the Mohammedans in 1017 A.D., before its completion. The form of the monument, the character of its sculptured ornaments, the unfinished condition in which it is left,

[1] Dhamek is a corruption of Dharma Desaka, preacher of the Law.

and indeed the whole circumstances of the case," he continues, "render this date so much the most probable, that I feel inclined to adopt it almost without hesitation."[1]

Recent excavations have greatly added to the knowledge of the various buildings at Sarnath. Taking the Dhamek stupa, which stands on high ground, as a centre, the base of the stupa of Jagat Singh (so called after its destroyer) will be found 500 ft. to the W.; this is marked by the peculiarity of an enclosed ambulatory. 120 ft. N. of it, with a number of small stupas between, is the Main Shrine, with a rail on its upper part, standing on a large concrete pavement. W. of this is the broken Asoka pillar, once 51 ft. high, believed to mark the spot where the teacher first preached; its capital of four lions supporting the wheel of the law was found beside it. E. of the Main Shrine is a stupa of the 7th century, with more small stupas on its N. side. In the same direction are the excavations of various large monasteries, one ascribed to the 11th century having an enclosure over 700 ft. long. A museum has been erected on the spot, and contains all important detached finds.

The Chaukandi tower first mentioned above, and passed on the way to the stupa, stands on a very steep mound about 100 ft. high, in which a Buddhist building with several terraces has lately been laid bare. The tower was erected by the Emperor Akbar to commemorate a visit of his father Humayun in 1588 A.D.

Sarnath was visited by the Chinese Buddhist pilgrims, Fa-Hian in 399 A.D., and Hiouen Thsang in 629-645 A.D. The former says: "At 10 li (2 m.) to the N.W. of Benares is the temple, situated in the Deer Park (Mriga dava), of the Immortal." Hiouen Thsang states that to the N.E. of Benares was a stupa, built by Asoka, 100 ft. high, and opposite to it a stone column "of blue colour, bright as a mirror." He says the monastery was divided into eight parts, and was surrounded by a wall, within which were balustrades, two-storeyed palaces, and a Vihara, 200 ft. high, surmounted by an Anmolo or mango in embossed gold. There were 100 rows of niches round the stupa of brick, each holding a statue of Buddha in embossed gold. To the S.W. of the Vihara was a stone stupa raised by Asoka, having in front a column 70 ft. high, on the spot where Buddha delivered his first discourse. W. of the monastery was a tank in which Buddha bathed, to the W. of that another where he washed his monk's water-pot, and to the N. a third where he washed his garments. Close to the tanks was a stupa, then another, and then in the midst of a forest a third. To the S.W. of the monastery at ½ a m. was a stupa, 300 ft. high, resplendent with jewels, and surmounted by an arrow.

[1] Fergusson's *Indian Architecture*, i. 72. This conclusion is now challenged on the basis of recent excavations, and it is considered that the stupa should be referred to the Imperial Gupta era, c. 350 A.D.

ROUTE 5.—CALCULTTA CITY AND ENVIRONS

INDEX.

	PAGE
'Alipur	61
Arsenal	62
Asiatic Society of Bengal	59
Ballygunge	60
Bandel	69
Barrackpur	66
Belvedere (Lt.-Governor's Residence)	61
Bishop's College	60
Black Hole	63
Brahma Somaj	65
Budge Budge	70
Calcutta University Senate House	65
Cathedrals—	
St Paul's	59
Roman Catholic	64
Chandernagore	68
Chinsurah	69
Churches—	
Armenian	64
Greek	64
Old Mission	63
St Andrew's, or Scotch Kirk	63
St John's (Old Cathedral)	63
St Thomas's (Roman Catholic)	59
Synagogue	64
Dalhousie Institute	62
Diamond Harbour	71
Dum Dum	67
Empress, All India Memorial Hall	60
Engineering (Civil) College	66
Forts—	
Old Fort	62
William	62
Garden Reach	61
Gardens—	
Agri-Horticultural	61
Botanical	65
Eden	55
Zoological	61
Government House	56
High Court	56
Hooghly	68
Hospitals—	
Medical College Hospital	64
Ezra	64
Campbell	65
Hospitals—*continued.*	
Dufferin	65
General	65
Military	61
Mayo	64
Eden	64
Howrah	67
Kalighat	60
Jain Temple	65
Maidan or Esplanade	55
Metcalfe Hall	64
Mint	64
Missions	65
Mosque of Prince Ghulam Muhammad	57
Museums—	
Economic	58
Imperial	57
Ochterlony Monument	57
Post-Office	62
Public Buildings	55-59
Race-course	61
Railway Stations—	
Howrah (E.I.R. and B.N. Ry.)	67
Sealdah (E. Bengal Ry.)	64
Mutla and Diamond Harbour	64
Secretariat of Bengal Government	63
Serampore	67
Statues—	
Queen-Empress	56
King Edward	56
Lord Auckland	55
Sir S. Bayley	57
Lord W. Bentinck	55
Lord Canning	56
Lord Dufferin	59
Lord Hardinge	56
Lord Landsdowne	59
Lord Lawrence	56
Lord Mayo	57
Lord Napier	61
Lord Northbrook	55
Sir James Outram	59
Sir W. Peel	55
Lord Roberts	59
Telegraph Office	62
Town Hall	56

History.—The capital of India[1] is of more recent birth than the premier cities of the two sister Presidencies dating only from 1690, when Hooghly, at which a settlement had been established forty-eight years previously, being abandoned in favour of the present site, on which the three villages of Satanati, Kalikata, and Govindpur then stood, Mr Job Charnock being the leader of the merchants who settled here. These estates were formally sold to the East India Company by the Governor of Bengal, Prince Azim, son of the Emperor Aurangzeb, in 1700, some five years after the construction of the

[1] Busteed's *Echoes from Old Calcutta* contains much information about the place at the end of the 18th century. Blechynden's *Calcutta Past and Present*, and Firminger's *Guide to Calcutta* are also full of interest.

Old Fort William (p. 62). Ten years later the place, which then had a population of 10,000, was formed into a separate Presidency; and it continued to flourish, owing to its favourable position at the gate of the principal waterways of N. India, until 1756, when the fort not being defensible, it was attacked and taken by the Nawab of Murshedabad, Suraj-ud-daulah, in return for the burning of Hooghly by British vessels. Most of the British, including the governor, fell down the river in ships to Fulta; those who remained and attempted a defence became the victims of the unintentional tragedy of the Black Hole on 26th June (see p. 63). Early in December Colonel Clive arrived with troops from Madras, and the Nawab's forces being withdrawn north without fighting, the British Flag was run up by Captain Coote—afterwards Sir Eyre Coote—and once more waved above Fort William; and after some negotiations, an agreement was entered into by which the Nawab promised to restore the trading privileges of the Company and return the property plundered in Calcutta. Shortly afterwards a conflict ensued between the Dutch and British, which ended in the capture of Chandernagore by the latter on 23rd March. Encouraged by the French in his service, and by proffers of support from the Mahratta Chief of Nagpur, Suraj-ud-daulah ultimately refused to accept an exclusive alliance with the British, and this led in due course to the Battle of Plassey, on 23rd June 1757. In 1773 the present Fort William was completed. In 1774 Warren Hastings, who had become Governor of Bengal two years previously, was made the first Governor-General of Bengal, and given authority over Bombay and Madras, and the Supreme Court of Calcutta was established. The old Cathedral of St John was built between 1783 and 1787, and the bishopric of Calcutta was created in 1814, the first Bishop being Dr Middleton, and the second (1823), Reginald Heber. Government House was erected between 1797 and 1804, the Town Hall in the latter year, and the Mint between 1824 and 1830, while the Botanical Gardens were created about 1790. It will thus be seen that some of the finest buildings in Calcutta are of much earlier date than those of Bombay and Madras. In 1852 Calcutta was created a Municipality, and in the year following passed with the rest of Bengal under the direct control of a Lieutenant-Governor—Sir F. Halliday being the first to hold this high office—and in 1857 it received its University. In 1861 the Legislative Council of the Lieutenant-Governor was created, and in 1865 the Corporation in lieu of the Municipality. The Chamber of Commerce dates from 1834, and the Port Trust Commission, which consists of fifteen members, from 1870; the latter administers an annual income of £800,000.

The population of the city is now 1,037,000 (with suburbs, 1,216,514). In 1901 it was distributed as follows:—

Hindus . . .	551,000
Mohammedans . .	249,000
Christians . . .	38,000
Jews	1900

The increase has been very large since the first census was taken in 1872, but the area of the city census has also changed greatly. Early in the last century the population was about 200,000, and in 1850, 400,000.

The trade of the Port is valued as follows:—

Imports	£43,000,000
Exports	53,000,000

The former consist mainly of piece-goods, iron and steel, machinery and railway stores, oil, sugar, and liquors, and the latter of jute, tea, opium, oil seeds, grain, hides, indigo, raw silk and cotton, and coal. The record year of trade was 1907-8. There are 202 factories and mills in and, chiefly, round Calcutta, employing over 250,000 daily operatives.

The income of the Corporation amounts to 71 lakhs, derived chiefly from a consolidated rate, a tax on trades and professions, and a tax on vehicles and animals. There is a municipal debt of 350 lakhs in the form of municipal loans.

The Corporation consists now of fifty members — twenty-five elected and twenty-five appointed by Government, or nominated by certain special bodies. The executive duties of the Corporation are discharged by a general committee of twelve members, four chosen by the elected and four by the selected and nominated members, and four appointed by the Local Government. The chairman is also appointed by Government, and has entire control of the executive operations of the Corporation. There is every reason to hope that the present Corporation will prove as capable and go-ahead as the old Corporation was incapable and obstructive.

Calcutta is situated in lat. 22° 34′, long. 88° 24′. It is the headquarters of the Government of the Lower Provinces of Bengal, as well as the winter headquarters (November to April) of the Government of India. The principal Lieutenant-Governors of Bengal since 1858 have been Sir J. P. Grant, Sir R. Temple, Sir Ashley Eden, and Sir C. Elliot. The late Lieutenant - Governor, Sir John Woodburn, died in office in 1902. The present Lieutenant - Governor is the Hon. Sir E. N. Baker, K.C.S.I.

(1). The Maidan and Quarters East and South of it.

The centre of Calcutta is the famous **Maidan** or Esplanade, bounded on the W. side by the Hooghly river and the Strand Road, and on the E. side by Chowringhee Road; it is nearly 2 m. long, and is ¾ m. broad at its head, and 1½ m. broad at the S. end. Government House, the residence of the Viceroy, faces it on the N., while Belvedere, where the Lieutenant-Governor of Bengal lives, is not far removed from the southern limit. In the centre of the W. side is Fort William, and on or near the E. side are the principal hotels, the United Service and Bengal Clubs, and the Imperial Museum; in the N.W. corner are the Eden Gardens, and in the S.E. are the Racecourse, the Presidency Jail, and the Cathedral. The Strand Road above the river bank affords fine views of the shipping and water traffic; another main road, known as the Red Road, runs down the centre of the Maidan from N. to S.

The **Eden Gardens**, for which Calcutta is indebted to the sisters of Lord Auckland, are beautifully laid out, and were for many years the principal evening gathering-place of Calcutta society. In them is the Calcutta Cricket-ground, and on the side of the water is a picturesque Burmese Pagoda brought from Prome, and set up here in 1856. Close to the S.W. gate is the statue of Sir William Peel, the famous commander of H.M.S. *Shannon*, who served with his crew at Lucknow under Sir Colin Campbell (p. 305), and died of smallpox at Cawnpore after the final relief of the Residency; and on the N. side are the statues of Lord Auckland, Lord William Bentinck, and Lord Northbrook. W. of these on the river bank is Babu's Ghat, where is a swimming-bath and the boat-house of the Calcutta Rowing Club, and above it the Chandpal Ghat, affording a fine view of the river; it was at this Ghat that the members of the Supreme Council sent from England, and Sir Elijah Impey and the Judges of the Supreme Court landed in October 1774. A little further up stream the building of the Bank of Bengal faces the Hooghly; and beyond this are the principal jetties extending for ½ m. up to the floating bridge 1500 ft. long and 48 ft. wide, constructed in 1873-74 at a cost of a quarter of a million. From Chandpal Ghat the broad Esplanade Row leads to the E., passing the High Court, the Town Hall, and Government House, and ending at Dharamtolla Street, from which point Chowringhee Road leads S. along the E. side of the Maidan, and Bentinck Street (in which is the

Masonic Hall, continued as Chitpur Road, leads to the extreme N. point of the city on the river bank.

The **High Court,** built in 1872, after the town hall at Ypres, is a fine building with a tower 180 ft. high. The Chief Justice's Court is in the S.W. corner. The Court of First Instance is at the S.E. corner. In the E. face is the Barristers' Library. The Attorneys' Library is in the E. corner; and here is a portrait of Justice Norman. In other public rooms are portraits of Sir Wm. Burroughs, by Lawrence, 1818; Sir William Macnaughten, by Chinnery, 1824; Sir Elijah Impey, by Kettle, 1778; and the Honourable Shambu Nath Pandit, the first Indian Judge. In the Chief Justice's Court are the pictures of Sir R. Garth—Sir H. Russell, by Chinnery, 1872, robed in red; Sir John Anstruther, 1805; and Sir E. Impey, by Zoffany, 1782. At the head of the Chantrey's staircase is a statue of Sir Edward Hyde East, 1821. In the Judges' Library are six pictures of Justices Trevor, H. B. Harrington, and John Russell Colvin, who died at Agra in 1857 (p. 175), and opposite these, of Sir Ed. Ryan, Sir Robert Chambers, and Sir Lawrence Peel. Among the records of the Court is that of the trial of Nand Kumar, by Sir Elijah Impey *and two other judges and a jury.* There is a garden in the centre quadrangle and a fountain.

The **Town Hall,** standing W. of Government House, was built by the inhabitants of Calcutta in 1804, and cost £70,000. The style is Doric, with a fine flight of steps leading to a portico on the S. The carriage entrance is to the N. under a portico. The centre of the building is occupied by a saloon 162 ft. long and 65 ft. broad. In the S. front is a central room, 82 ft. long by 30 ft. broad, and two smaller rooms. In the S. vestibule is a marble statue of Warren Hastings, by R. Westmacott, R.A., standing between a Mohammedan and a Hindu. At the W. end of the lower saloon is a marble statue by J. Bacon, junr., of the Marquis of Cornwallis, who is thus represented in all the three presidential capitals of India. This statue was erected by the British inhabitants of Bengal, 1803 A.D. In the hall is a statue of Maharaja Ramanath Tagore. In the vestibules are busts of the Duke of Wellington, Sir Proby Cautley, and several others; and portraits of Lord Lake, Lord Gough, Sir C. Metcalfe, Sir H. Durand, Dwarkanath Thakur, Bishop Wilson, Mr Wilberforce Bird, Sir Henry Norman, Dr Duff, Bishop Wilson, Sir William Grey, Sir Rivers Thomson, and Babu Keshab Chandra Sen. There are also full-length portraits of Queen Victoria and Prince Albert, presented by Her Majesty to the city of Calcutta.

Government House is situated in a fine enclosure of 6 acres, standing back from the Maidan, which is here dignified by the Jubilee statue of the Queen-Empress Victoria, unveiled in 1902, and the statues of Lord Lawrence, Lord Canning, and Lord Hardinge. The Queen's statue, the work of Mr Frampton, will ultimately be transferred to the Queen-Empress Memorial Hall; and the statue of King Edward, entrusted to Mr Mackennal, will probably be placed here.

Government House was begun under the Marquis of Wellesley (the architect being Captain Wyatt), and finished in 1804, the design being copied from that of Kedlestone Hall, Derbyshire, built by Adam. In the breakfast-room at the head of the fine staircase is a well-executed white marble statue of the Marquis of Wellesley, with portraits of the same Governor-General, and of the Earl of Ellenborough and Marquis of Dalhousie. The *Dining-room* is of white chunam, with a floor of veined white marble. On either side are six well-executed marble busts of the Cæsars, taken from a French ship at the end of the 18th century. The

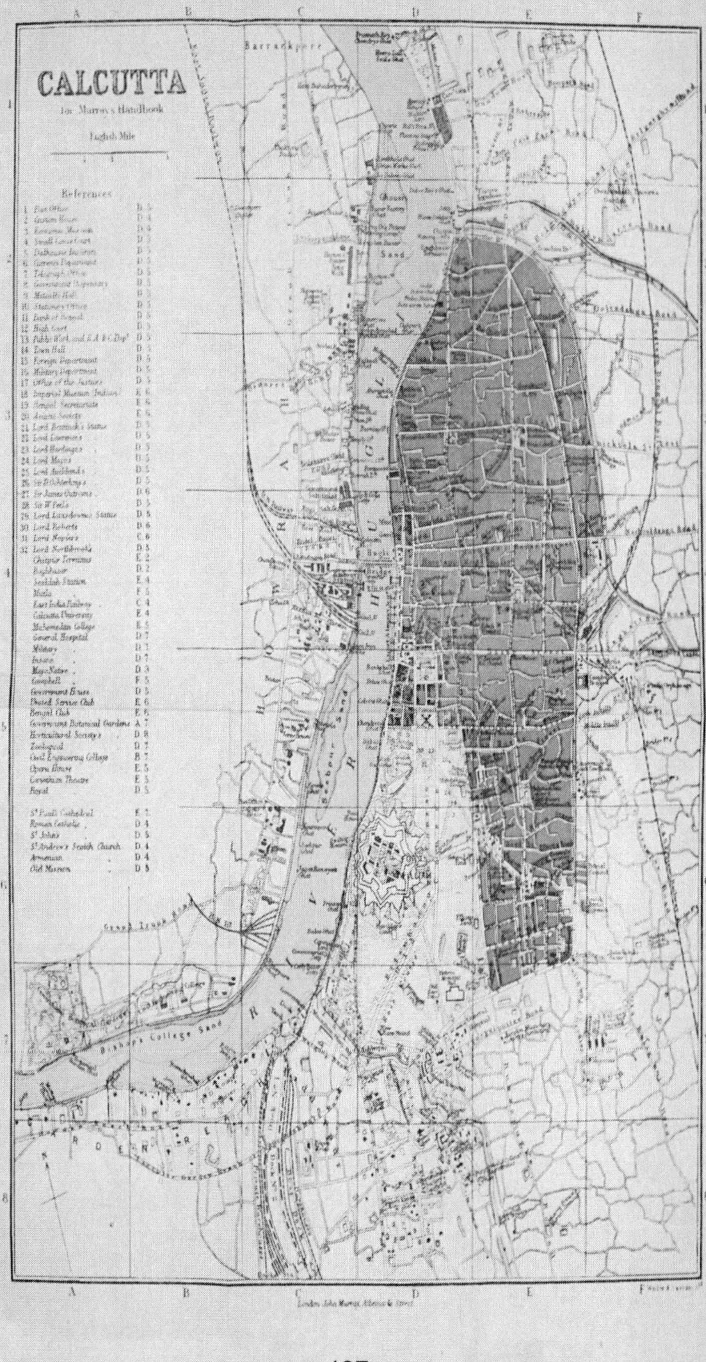
CALCUTTA
for Murray's Handbook
English Mile
References
Barrackpore
Grand Trunk Road
Bishop's College Sand
London: John Murray, Albemarle Street

Throne-room is so called from its containing the Throne of Tipu Sultan. The pictures are—Queen Charlotte, standing; George III. (both supposed to be by Hudson, the master of Sir Joshua Reynolds); General the Hon. Arthur Wellesley, 1803, by Home, R.A. (one of the best in the collection, and extremely interesting); the Earl of Amherst; and the Marquis of Hastings. In the curved passage to the *Council-room* in the E. wing are portraits of the Earl of Auckland, Lord Lawrence, Earl Mayo, the Marquis of Dufferin, Earl Canning, the Marquis of Ripon, Viscount Halifax, and Lord Wm. Bentinck.

In the *Council-room* are pictures of the Earl of Minto, 1807-13; Marquis of Cornwallis, 1786-98-1805; Lord Hardinge, 1844-48, a ¾-length portrait, in blue undress, wearing a Star; Warren Hastings, 1772-85, with a motto, "Mens æqua in arduis," at the top—a fine picture; the Earl of Elgin; the Marquis of Wellesley; Lord Clive, ¾-length, wearing Riband of the Bath, by Nathaniel Dance. The meetings of the Legislative Council of India, as well as of the Supreme Council of the Viceroy, are held in this chamber.

On the staircase from this wing to the upper storey are portraits of Lord Northbrook and Lord Lytton, and on the staircase in the S.E. wing are pictures of Louis XV. and his Queen, by Carle Van Loo; of the Duke of Clarence, the Duke of Wellington, and Sir Jang Bahadur of Nepal; of Lady William Bentinck, by Beechy; of the Nawab S'aadat 'Ali Khan, by Chinnery; Fateh Ali, Shah of Persia, 1798; Jaswant Singh, Maharaja of Bharatpur, by Anger; Amir Sher Ali Khan, by W. M. White; and the surrender of the sons of Tipu Sultan.

Above the dining-room and the adjoining rooms is a splendid ballroom. The floor is of polished teak, and the ceilings are beautifully panelled, after designs by Mr H. M. Locke. The chandeliers and the portrait of Louis XV. are said to have been captured from the French at Chandernagore in 1757.

On the N. side of Government House is a fine brass 32-pounder, taken at Aliwal, and inscribed in Gurmukhi. On either side is a 6-pounder brass tiger-gun, taken from Tipu Sultan. There are also two large brass guns inscribed, "Miani, 17th February," and "Hyderabad, 30th of March 1843"; and another with a carriage representing a dragon, which is a trophy of the peace of Pekin, 1842.

Outside the W. gate is a statue of Sir Stewart Bayley, Lieutenant-Governor of Bengal. At the N. angle of Dharumtolla Road is a large mosque erected during the Government of Lord Auckland, by Prince Ghulam Muhammad,[1] son of Tipu Sultan, killed 1799, in gratitude to God, and in commemoration of the Honourable Court of Directors granting him the arrears of his stipend in 1840; and in the N.E. corner of the Maidan is the large Dharamtolla Tank with the *Ochterlony* monument on the S. side of it. This is a *column* 165 ft. high, raised in 1823 in honour of *Sir David Ochterlony*, who brought the Nepal war (1814-16) to a successful conclusion, and was afterwards Resident in Malwa and Rajputana. From the galleries a fine view over Calcutta is obtained.

Beyond the Royal Theatre and the Continental and Grand Hotels in Chowringhee Road is the Imperial Museum. In front of the former on the Maidan are the Monohar Dus Tank and the statue of Lord Mayo, while to the E. of them lie the municipal office, and the large municipal markets, and beyond them, on Wellesley Road (which with Wellington, College and Cornwallis Roads form the second great thoroughfare from S. to N.) rises the Mohammedan College.

The Imperial **Museum**, 27 Chow-

[1] This gentleman died as lately as 1878.

ringhee Road, is an immense building, with a frontage of 300 ft. and depth of 270 ft., and contains a very fine Geological collection and a Library; but the most important feature is the *Gallery of Antiquities*, well worth inspection, particularly the Buddhist remains brought from the tope at Bharhut (see Fergusson's *Hist. of Arch.*, pp. 86-90); from Buddh Gaya, from Muttra and Gandhara (Panjab). Unfortunately there is no recent catalogue. Some display exquisite feeling, and are executed with a vigour and grace worthy of the Greeks. The Bharhut sculptures are among the most interesting in all India; a number of them are inscribed with the name of the Jataka or Sacred Story which they represent.

The most interesting objects are the carved rails from Bharhut and Buddh Gaya; but among the objects from Muttra may be noticed a figure of Buddha, 6 ft. high, with a halo behind the head, carved with floral devices, and in the Gandhara Collection a portion of a frieze representing six naked boys, quite classic in design, and a domestic scene, suggesting the Stable at Bethlehem.

The archæologist will find here selected pieces from the most famous ancient buildings in India. There are interesting fragments of Buddhist art from the caves of Orissa, from Sanchi, and Buddh Gaya from Muttra, and Sarnath, near Benares; the collection of Greco Buddhist and Indo-Scythian sculptures is very fine. In the separate Asoka Gallery are casts of all the rock edicts of that king.

Amongst the Siwalik Fossil Remains may be observed the Hyænarctos or Hyæna-Bear; the Amphicyon, a dog-like animal as large as the Polar bear; the Machairodus or Sabre-tooth tiger, whose canine teeth were 7 in. long; also the Siwalik cat, which was at least as large as a tiger. There is the skeleton of an elephant 11 ft. high. Amongst Siwalik birds there are the shank-bone and the breast-bone of a wading-bird as big as an ostrich. This bird has been called the Megaloscelornis, and these bones are the only ones belonging to this species existing in the world. In the Upper Paleontological Gallery there are many bones of the Dinornis. Amongst the reptiles, remark a crocodile, from Matlah, 18 ft. long, and a snake of the Python species, of the same length. The remains of the Crocodilus crassidens, are those of an extinct species of enormous dimensions. There is also a specimen of the Siwalik Colossochelys, a gigantic tortoise of prodigious size. It will be noticed that whereas all the species and many of the genera of the Siwalik Mammals and Birds are entirely different from those inhabiting the earth, all the genera of the Reptiles have living representatives in India. The Collection of the Fossil Vertebrata of the Siwaliks is the most complete and comprehensive in the world.

As to Minerals, it may be said that most of the diamonds exhibited are Indian, from Bundelkund, S. India, and Sambalpur. There are also models of the most celebrated diamonds, such as the Regent, the most perfect brilliant in existence, the Koh-i-Nur, the Great Nizam, etc., all of which were obtained in India. Amongst the Meteorites may be remarked the model, No. 16, of one which fell on the 23rd of January 1870, at Nedagolla, in the Madras Presidency. The original weighed over 10 lbs.

The adjoining **Economic Museum** contains fine samples of the products of the native manufactures of the country. It occupies a quadrangular building, in which the Calcutta International Exhibition of 1883-84 was held. The two museums are visited by over half a million of persons annually. Next to the Imperial Museum on the S. side is the Bengal School of Art, an Institution similar to that of Bombay, with 250 pupils.

At the corner of Chowringhee and

Park Street is the United Service Club House, founded in 1845, and just beyond it in the latter street is the **Bengal Asiatic Society** at No. 57. This institution was established in 1784 by Sir William Jones, and led to the foundation of the Royal Asiatic Society in London by Mr H. T. Colebrooke. Visitors can be elected members. The *Asiatic Researches* began to be issued in 1788, and continued to be published until 1839. The *Journal* began in 1832, under the auspices of Professor H. H. Wilson and Mr James Prinsep, who first deciphered the famous rock and pillar inscriptions of King Asoka, and from that time to 1839 both publications were issued. The library contains over 15,000 volumes, and there is a large collection of valuable MS., coins, copper plates, pictures, and busts. The pictures include one of Warren Hastings.

Further down Park Street, in Hare Street on the right, is the Doveton College for the training of Christian students of both sexes. In the S. Park Street Cemetery is buried Landor's Rose Aylmer, d. 1800; the grave is marked by a column spirally fluted. Here also lie Lucia, the wife of Robert Palk, idyllised by Mr Rudyard Kipling, Sir John Clavering, Colonel Monson, Sir William Jones, and Augustus Cleveland (p. 312). In N. Park Street Cemetery opposite is the grave of W. M. Thackeray's father, d. 1815.

In front of the U.S. Club is the fine equestrian statue of Sir James Outram, and further on, facing the E. approaches to Fort William, that of Lord Dufferin, N. of which, on the Red Road, are the statues of Lord Roberts and Lord Lansdowne.

Chowringhee Road runs S. from Park Street, past the Bengal Club (founded 1827, and occupying the house in which Lord Macaulay once lived), and the residential quarter *par excellence* of Calcutta society, to the Cathedral of St Paul's. Off Middleton Street are **St Thomas's Roman Catholic Church**, a handsome building commenced in 1841, and the Convent of Our Lady of Loretto.

St Paul's Cathedral was designed by Major W. N. Forbes in 1819 and commenced in 1839: it is 240 ft. long and 80 ft. broad, and the spire is 200 ft. high. The style is Hindu-Gothic, or spurious Gothic modified to suit the climate of India. In the vestry of the Cathedral is a large folio MS. volume entitled "History of the Erection of St Paul's Cathedral," which contains a plan of the Cathedral at p. 265. Over the porch is a library, left to the public by Bishop Wilson, and here is an excellent bust of that Bishop. The west window, designed by Sir E. Burne Jones, is a memorial to Lord Mayo. The original east window was given by the Dean and Chapter of Windsor, to whom it was presented as a gift by George III. for St George's Chapel. Beneath it are mosaics. The Communion Plate was given by Queen Victoria. The building cost £50,000, of which the Bishop gave £20,000, half of which, however, went to endowment.

On the left side of the vestibule is a black marble tablet to sixteen officers of the Bengal Engineers, who fell during the Indian Mutiny in the years 1857-58. It is ornamented with sixteen bronze medallions, and a relief representing the gallant blowing up of the Kashmir Gate, Delhi, by Lieutenants Salkeld and Home (p. 194). Next are a tablet to fifteen officers who fell in the Bhutan campaign and an elaborate monument in memory of John Paxton Norman, of the Inner Temple, officiating Chief Justice of Bengal, who was assassinated on the steps of the Town Hall when entering the High Court on 20th September 1871. Beyond is the tablet to seven officers of the 68th Regiment N.I., "who died during the Mutiny of the Native Troops, and subsequent operations, from 1857 to 1859, some on the field of battle, some by the hands of their own followers, others from disease—all doing their duty."

Then follows a tablet to Mr William Ritchie of the Calcutta Bar and Inner Temple, a member of the Council of the Governor-General, the inscription by W. M. Thackeray, who was a cousin of Mr Ritchie's. On the left is a tablet to Sir H. M. Lawrence, adorned with a medallion portrait in white marble. In the centre of the left wall of the passage from the vestibule to the transepts and body of the Cathedral is a monument to Lord Elgin, who died at Dharmsalah in 1863.

In the S.E. corner of the S. transept is the *Tomb of Lady Canning*, brought from Barrackpur. It consists of a base of white marble with a sarcophagus, on which is inlaid a cross with flowers. There is also a good statue of Bishop Heber, the second Bishop of the Diocese, by Chantrey.

The upper part of the steeple fell during the great earthquake of 12th June 1897, but has been restored. Among the latest memorials is one of Sir John Woodburn, Lieutenant-Governor of Bengal, 1902, and another erected by Lord Curzon to the members of Lumsden's Horse who fell in the S. African War. The organ is one of the finest ever made by Messrs Willis.

The main road running S. to the E. of the Cathedral leads past the suburb of **Ballygunge**, with the residences of many Europeans. On the right of the road is the London Missionary Society's Institution; and on the Lower Circular road running to the E. of it, and leading to Ballygunge, are the Bishop's College and the Martinière Schools, and, considerably to the N., St James' Church, which can contain a congregation of 700. In the cemetery in the Lower Circular Road are buried Sir Wm. Macnaughten, murdered in Caubul, James Wilson, the Financier, Justice Norman, and Sir John Woodburn.

Kalighat, celebrated as the site of a temple in honour of the goddess Kali, the wife of Shiva, lies about 1½ m. S. of the Cathedral on the bank of the Tolly Nullah, an old bed of the Ganges. The place, after which the present capital of India is named, derives sanctity from the legend that when the corpse of Shiva's wife was cut in pieces by order of the Gods, and chopped up by the disc (*sudarsan chakra*) of Vishnu, one of her fingers fell on this spot. The temple is supposed to have been built about three centuries ago. A member of the Sabarna Chandhu family, who at one time owned considerable estates in this part of the country, cleared the jungle, built the temple, and allotted 194 acres of land for its maintenance. A man of the name of Chandibar was the first priest appointed to manage the affairs of the temple. His descendants have now taken the title of Haldar, and are at present the proprietors of the building. The principal religious festival of the year is on the second day of the Durgapuja, in October, when the temple is visited by crowds of pilgrims.

W. of the Cathedral, on the edge of the Maidan, is the Presidency Jail, near the site of which the All India Memorial Hall of the Queen-Empress Victoria is being erected: the subscriptions for the memorial amount to fifty lakhs of rupees. It has been designed by Sir Wm. Emerson in the style of the Italian Renaissance, and consists of a magnificent building standing on a terrace 6-7 ft. high and surmounted by a dome rising 160 ft. above the Maidan. The whole structure will be cased with white marble. Under the dome will be the Central Empress Hall; other principal apartments will be the Darbar and Princes' Halls. The foundations were begun in 1905, and the foundation-stone was laid by King George on 4th January 1906; and it is hoped the Hall may be completed in 1920. On the further side of the Lower Circular Road are the General and Military Hospitals; and beyond them and opposite the

Race-course the 'Alipur Road, crossing Tolly's Nullah, leads to the Zoological Gardens and Belvedere, and the Agri-Horticultural Gardens. The Zoological Gardens were inaugurated in 1876, and comprise an area of 36 acres well laid out, and a fair show of animals in houses presented by various ruling chiefs and wealthy persons. The tigers, leopards, crocodiles, and snakes are usually the finest. On the S. side of the Gardens is the 'Alipur Observatory.

Belvedere House stands in extensive and well-kept grounds. In the entrance hall are some trophies of Indian arms and full-length portraits of Sir John Peter Grant and Sir William Grey. In the reception room are portraits of H.M. the Queen-Empress Victoria, Sir Cecil Beadon, and Sir Charles and Lady Elliott. At a spot W. of the entrance of Belvedere, on the 'Alipur Road, was fought the duel between Warren Hastings and Sir Philip Francis, in which the latter was wounded. S. of Belvedere are the Agri-Horticultural Gardens commenced here in 1872, and managed by that Society, which was founded in 1820; and still further S. in Judge's Court Road once stood Hastings' private residence, and now stands the State Guest House inaugurated by Lord Curzon.

The **Race-course**, which is 2 m. long, is one of the most famous in India, and the Christmas race meeting, in which the Viceroy's cup is run for, is one of the principal society events of the winter season in Calcutta. The bridge S.W. of it, across Tolly's Nullah, leads to Kidderpur, so called after Colonel Kyd, who constructed the Government Dockyard, near which the Port Trust has excavated magnificent new Docks. Between 1781 and 1821 ships were built at the Kidderpur Docks, at a cost of more than £2,000,000, and in 1818 the *Hastings*, a 74-gun ship, was launched there. The new Wet Docks enclose an area of 10 and 30 acres respectively, in addition to which there are two dry docks; and the sum spent over this improvement has exceeded two and a half crores of rupees. In Kidderpur is St Stephen's Church.

The last bridge near the river, named Hastings Bridge, leads past the Government Dockyard, the docks, and the P. & O. premises, to Garden Reach, once known for its palatial suburban residences, and of late years as the home of the last of the Kings of Oudh, Wajid Ali, who was deposed in 1854, and survived his deposition by more than thirty years. It was considered necessary to place him inside Fort-William during the summer of 1857.

This is the shortest route for visiting the Botanical Gardens (p. 65) on the other side of the river; but unless the boat by which one crosses is detained at the other side, there may be some difficulty in regaining the left bank.

At the W. extremity of Garden Reach, or in its vicinity, was situated the small fort of 'Aligarh, and opposite to it, on the other bank of the river, was the Fort of Tanna, both of which were taken by Clive in the recapture of Calcutta in 1756.

Turning N. from the Hastings Bridge, St George's Gate of Fort William (S.W. corner) is reached in half a mile. On the way is passed Cooly Bazar, near the site of which Nand Kumar was hung for the offence of forgery on 5th August 1775. In front of the gate is a statue of Lord Napier of Magdala, opposite **Prinsep's Ghat.** This, now some distance inland since the reclamation of the foreshore and the excavation of the new docks, is marked by a pavilion of stone, supported by pillars, and inscribed "James Prinsep," in memory of the great Oriental scholar, who died from over-devotion to the pursuits, in which he so greatly excelled, in 1840. Further N., and opposite the Water Gate of the Fort, is the Gwalior Monument, erected by Lord Ellenborough, in 1844, in memory of the officers and men who fell in the Gwalior campaign of 1843, and designed by Colonel W. H. Goodwyn, Beng. Eng. It is of brick faced with Jaipur marble, surmounted by a metal cupola made from guns taken from the enemy. In the centre the names of those who fell at the battles of Maharajpur and Paniar are engraved on a sarcophagus.

Fort-William originally received its name from William III. The site was changed in 1757, after the battle of Plassey, from that now occupied by the Post-Office, to the river bank further S., where Clive commenced a new and much more formidable fortress, which was finished in 1773, at a cost of £2,000,000. It is an irregular octagon, enclosing an area of 2 sq. m., of which five sides look landward and three on the river, and is surrounded by a fosse 30 ft. deep and 50 ft. broad, which can be filled from the river. The garrison consists of two regiments, one British and one N.I., and one company R.G.A. There are six gates—Chowringhee, Plassey, Calcutta, Water Gate, St George's, and Treasury Gate. There is also a sallyport between Water and St George's Gates. Inside the Chowringhee Gate past the Governor's residence, now used as a Soldiers' Institute and Garrison School, is the Fort Church of St Peter, built in 1828. The Catholic Chapel, St Patrick's, was built in 1857. The *Military Prison* behind this is built on a massive storehouse, on which is an inscription relating to the amount of rice and grain deposited there by the authorities in 1782. Over the Treasury Gate are the quarters of the Commander-in-Chief in India while at Calcutta; the offices of the Army Headquarters now remain all the year round in Simla. The *Arsenal* is worth a visit, for which permission must be obtained from the officer commanding the Fort. The sub-marine Mining depôt is also accommodated in the Fort; it cannot be visited.

(2) Quarters North of the Maidan and Government House.

To the W. and E. of Government House lie the Legislative Council Office and the other principal offices of the Government of India. N. of Government House, Old Court House Street on the E., Wellesley Place in the centre, and Council House Street on the W., lead to **Dalhousie Square**,[1] with a fine garden and tank in the middle of it, the second entering the Square opposite the **Dalhousie Institute.** This was built "to contain within its walls statues and busts of great men." The foundation stone was laid in 1865, but the entrance portico preceded it, having been built in 1824. The hall is lined with marble, and measures 90 by 45 ft. It contains a statue of the Marquis of Hastings, by Flaxman, and also statues of the Marquis of Dalhousie, and of the Rt. Hon. James Wilson, and busts of Edward E. Venables, of Brig.-General Neil, C.B., and Sir Henry Havelock, by Noble; and of Sir James Outram and General John Nicholson, by Foley. On the E. side of the Square is the Currency Office, in the S.E. corner is the fine **Telegraph Office**, and on the W. side is the large domed building of the **General Post Office**, occupying part of the site of the Old Fort. It cost Rs.630,510, and occupies an area of 103,100 sq. ft. The dome at the S.E. corner is over 220 ft. high. The **Old Fort-William** lay between Bankshall Street, now Koilah Ghat Street, on the S., and Fort Ghat Street, now Fairlie Place, on the N. Its W. side fronted the river. The W. and E. walls were 710 ft. long, the N. side measuring 340 ft., and the S. side 485 ft. After it was abandoned as a Fort it was used as a Custom-house until the river moved away from the site. Part of the original arcades which served as warehouses on the S.W. side of the interior may still

[1] This was formerly known as the Lal Bagh, and the tank is still known as the Lal (red) Digbi.

be seen inside the yard of the Post-Office, where they are used as a waggon-shed; and where possible the outlines of the Fort have been indicated on the ground. At the N.E. corner of the Post-Office is a tablet inside an arch, which indicates the actual site of the **Black Hole**[1] of 1756, which by the care of Lord Curzon has been paved with black marble. The exact size of the Hole was 22 by 14 ft., and its height was probably 16 to 18 ft.; and into it 146 human beings were forced on the night of 20th June, of whom twenty-three only survived the next morning. The old obelisk memorial of the tragedy erected by the principal survivor, Mr J. Z. Holwell, was renovated in front of the Post-Office, at the expense of Lord Curzon in 1902; the inscription originally borne by it has been modified in the restoration. Mr Holwell, who was on the Calcutta Council from 1768-1772, and was most unjustly removed from the Service by the Directors of the E.I. Company, died in England at an advanced age in 1798.

From the N.W. corner of Government House Hastings Street leads towards the river, past the old **Cathedral Church of St John**, in an enclosure shaded with trees. Outside the church to the N. of the W. entrance is a domed pavilion about 50 ft. high, with twelve pillars. It is said to have been erected in commemoration of those who fell in the Rohilla War, but strangely enough is without inscription.

The church, which was begun in 1783, and opened in 1787, is 136 ft. long and 70 ft. wide.

The W. vestibule has on the left a large picture of the Last Supper, painted and presented to the church by Sir John Zoffany, in which the Apostles are all portraits of certain well-known inhabitants of Calcutta. In the E. end of the nave is the grave of Bishop Middleton, first Bishop of Calcutta (died 1822), and among the memorials are those of Colonel Kirkpatrick, Resident at Hyderabad at the end of the 18th century, Mr Alexander Colvin, Dr James Ward, and others.

In the N.W. corner of the graveyard is the large octagonal mausoleum of Job Charnock, the founder of Calcutta, who died in January 1692. In this is also now a tablet to Surgeon William Hamilton, who in 1716, having cured the Emperor Farrukhsiyar, obtained for the E.I. Company the right of importing their goods free of duty, and other great privileges.

A few yards to the S. is the tomb of Admiral Watson, who with Clive retook Calcutta. It has a large square base supporting an obelisk, inscribed to his memory.

On the N. side of Dalhousie Square are the buildings of the **Bengal Secretariat**, on the site of the Old Writer's Buildings, where so many illustrious Indian statesmen commenced their career. Opposite these is the statue of Sir Ashley Eden.

Just beyond these is the **Scotch Kirk**, *St Andrew's*, situated in Radha Bazaar, and called by the natives *Lal Girjah* or Red Church. It cost £20,000, and was opened in 1818, and seats 500 persons. In the vestry there is a portrait of Dr James Bryce, the first minister, by Sir John Watson Gordon, and there are some handsome monuments within the church. It sends a representative to the General Assembly at Edinburgh.

A little to the E. of the Square in Mission Row is the **Old Mission Church**, called the Purana Girjah or *Old Church* by the natives. It is 125 ft. long from E. to W., and 81 ft. 10 in. broad, and seats 450 persons. It was built by the celebrated mission-

[1] The so-called Black Hole was merely a lock-up for drunken or disorderly soldiers of the garrison of the Fort, and was simply a portion of a sleeping barrack in the S.E. corner of the Fort, enclosed from the rest of the building. The barrack was situated just to the N. of the S.E. bastion, and the Black Hole was therefore between the bastion and the barrack. Views of the Old Fort and of Holwell's monument are among Daniell's drawings of Calcutta.

ary, Johann Zacharias Kiernander, who was born at Azted, in Gothland, Sweden, in 1711, and educated at the University of Upsala. Being offered a post as missionary, he left England in 1758, and opened a school in Calcutta. His second wife on her death left valuable jewels, with which he founded a school. He called his church Beth Tephillah, "House of Prayer." When blind, he was deceived into signing a bond which ruined him, and the church was seized by his creditors, but redeemed by Mr Charles Grant for Rs. 10,000. Mr Kiernander then went to Chinsurah, and died there in 1799. There is a window in the church presented by his grandson; and there is a good engraving of him in the Mission Room, with an inscription in German. There are many interesting tablets in the church, particularly one to Mr Charles Grant, and one to the Rev. Henry Martyn, also to Bishop Dealtry of Madras, to Bishop Wilson, and to an Arab lady of distinction who was converted to Christianity.

The steeple was so seriously injured by the great earthquake of 12th June 1897 that it has been necessary to rebuild it.

From the S.W. corner of Dalhousie Square, Hare Street leads also towards the river, and passing the Small Cause Courts to the **Metcalfe Hall**, founded in honour of Sir Charles Metcalfe by public subscription, and built 1840-1844. The design is copied from the portico of the Temple of the Winds at Athens. The building, which formerly contained a neglected Public Library, was in 1903 converted into an effective Imperial Library of Reference, at the instance of Lord Curzon. Tickets of admission to the reading-room are freely granted to strangers. On the river front, to the N. of this, is the Sailors' Home, and to the S. the office of the Port Trust.

N. of Dalhousie Square and S. of Harrison Road, a new broad thoroughfare, leading from the Hooghly Bridge to the **Sealdah** Station of the Eastern Bengal Railway, are the Synagogue, the Armenian Church, and the Roman Catholic Cathedral, and in the same neighbourhood are a Greek church built in 1780, and a Parsi place of worship; while N. of this road are the Mint and Mayo Native Hospital. The first Portuguese came to Calcutta in 1689, and the English granted them a piece of land in Portuguese Church Lane, on which the friars of the order of St Augustine erected a chapel in 1700. Its successor, the **Roman Catholic Cathedral**, was built in 1797, and is dedicated to the Virgin Mary of the Rosary.

The **Mint**, at the W. end of Nimtolla Street, was built 1824-1830, the architect being Major W. N. Forbes. The style is Doric, the central portico being copied from the Parthenon at Athens. The area of the building and grounds is 18½ acres.

From the N.E. corner of Dalhousie Square, Bow Bazaar, one of the principal trading centres of the city, also leads to the **Sealdah** Station, with the railway station for Mutla or Port Canning, and for Diamond Harbour, and the Campbell Hospital lying to the S. of it. Half-way down it College Street leads to the N., past the Eden, Ezra, and Medical College Hospitals and the Medical College to College Square, also with a fine tank in the middle of it.

The Ezra Hospital is for Jews only. The **Medical College Hospital**, with accommodation for over 300 patients, was erected in 1853, and the **Eden** Hospital for women and children in 1882. The nursing here and in some of the other hospitals is under the Sisters of St John, at Clewer. Behind the Hospital is the **College**, with 500 students, one of the principal institutions of the kind in India. It is intended that the principal memorial of King Edward shall take the form of an endowment fund for medical research, relief, and education.

The Dufferin Zenana Hospital lies considerably to the E., in Upper Circular Road. On the W. side of College Square are the **Calcutta University**, the Hare School, and the Presidency College. The University Senate House is a grand hall, 120 ft. by 60 ft., in which the Convocations for conferring degrees take place. It has a portico supported by six lofty pillars. Close by is the **Hare School**, which is self-supporting. It was erected out of the surplus fees of students. **The Presidency College** was developed in 1855 from the Hindu College founded in 1824, and opened in 1827, at a cost of Rs. 170,000. The foundation-stone of the new building of this College was laid in 1872 by Sir George Campbell.

Somewhat to the E. of College Square are the quarters of C.M.S.; and N. in **Cornwallis Square** are those of the *Free Church of Scotland Mission*, begun by Alexander Duff in 1830. The Scottish church is in Wellesley Square. E. of Cornwallis Square and N. of the end of Beadon Street (abutting on Circular Road, which in its upper portion marks the line of the Mahratta ditch hastily dug in 1742 when these marauders invaded Orissa and Behar), is Halsi Baghan Road, so-called from the gardens of the well-known Omichand (Amin Chand) who was tricked by Colonel Clive, in a lane off which are the marble **Jain** temples in the garden known by the name of Badri Das. The temples, dedicated to the 10th Tirthankar-Sitalnath Ji and the garden form one of the prettiest spots in the whole of Calcutta, and should be visited by all who have a spare half-hour to give to them.

There is also a Chinese Temple in Calcutta.

Missions of the Church of England.—The *Oxford Mission*, 42 Cornwallis Street, works chiefly among the high-caste natives, and has charge of Bishop's College in Circular Road, a Boys' High School, and Industrial School.

S.P.G., headquarters Bishop's College, Lower Circular Road: Mission Church, St Saviour's, Wellesley Square, with a Boarding School.

S.P.G. Ladies' Association have charge of the Millman Memorial School for Girls.

Sisters of St John (Clewer) have charge of the **Government General Hospital**, the **Medical Staff Hospital**, the **Eden Hospital**, and the **Lady Canning Home** for **Nurses**. Also of native mission work at *Peepulpatti* in the rice-fields 3 m. distant.

The **Brahma Somaj** is the reformed Theistic sect of Hindus. It has very little hold on the general population, the few members being generally men of good social position. The church was founded by Raja Ram Mohan Rai in 1830. In 1858 Keshab Chandra Sen joined the Somaj, being then twenty years of age. In 1862 he was ordained minister of the Calcutta Brahma Somaj. In October 1865 he seceded from the original church, and next year a new body was organised by him, entitled the Brahma Somaj of India, and in January 1868 the first stone was laid of a new church for the progressive Brahmas. The creed of the church is an elective Theism drawn from the religious books of the Hindus and Buddhists, the Bible and the Koran; inter-caste marriages are recognised by it, and in 1872 a Native Marriage Act was passed to meet the case of such unions. Before the death of Keshab Chandra Sen a further separation took place in the new church which now consists of three communities.

(3) The W. Bank of the Hooghly River.

The **Royal Botanical Gardens**, on the W. bank of the river, opposite Garden Reach, were founded in 1786, on the suggestion of Colonel Kyd, who was appointed the first Superintendent. The visitor may drive to the Gardens across the bridge and through Howrah, or to Garden Reach, and cross the river Hooghly in a boat. There is also a steamer service from Chandpal Ghat to Shibpur Ghat, and sometimes from the first direct to the Botanical Gardens. At Sibpur is the Engineering College, with its classes of mining instruction. The area of the Gardens is 272 acres, with river frontage of a mile.[1] At the N.W. corner is the Howrah Gate, where are three fine trees—a *Ficus indica* in the centre, with a *Ficus religiosa* on either side. From here an avenue of almond-trees runs along the river front; while an avenue of Palmyra palms to the right of the entrance, and one of mahogany trees to the left, lead to the centre and the memorial of Colonel Kyd, passing the palm plantation which is separated off by a canal crossed by pretty bridges. From the memorial an avenue of palms leads S. to the Landing-Place Gate on the river; and close by it are the three conservatories for orchids, large plants, and palms. Leaving the above avenue to the left, the Great Banyan Tree[2] (*Ficus indica*), which covers ground nearly 1000 ft. in circumference, and has nearly 250 aerial roots, will be reached, and will be found a wonderful sight.

"The fig-tree at this day to Indians known
In Malabar or Deccan, spreads her arms,
Branching so broad and long, that on the ground
The bended twigs take root, and daughters grow
About the mother tree, a pillar'd shade,
High over-arched and echoing walks between."—MILTON, *Paradise Lost.*

On the left of an avenue near it is a monument to Roxburgh, with a Latin epitaph by Heber. Sir J. Hooker writes of these gardens in his Himalayan Journals that, "they have contributed more useful and ornamental tropical plants to the public and private gardens of the world than any other establishment before or since." He says also, "that the great Indian Herbarium, chiefly formed by the Staff of the Botanic Gardens, under the direction of Dr Wallich, and distributed in 1829 to the principal Museums of Europe, was the most valuable contribution of the kind ever made to science"; and adds, "that the origin of the tea-culture in the Himalayas and Assam was almost entirely the work of the Superintendent of the Gardens at Calcutta and Saharanpur." The Superintendent has a house in the Gardens. Near it is the Herbarium, or collection of dried plants, probably the only one in Asia of the first class. There are from 30,000 to 40,000 species represented in it. Attached to the Herbarium is a very fine Botanic Library.

1 An excellent little Guide to the Gardens, with a plan of them, can be bought in Calcutta.

2 The Banyan (which is the Indian Bar or Bor tree) derives its name from the fact that the Hindu traders (baniyas) used to worship under such trees at Gombroon (Ormuz).

(4) Excursions in the Vicinity of Calcutta.

Barrackpur station is called by the natives Charnock, from Job Charnock. The journey may be made by rail (14 m.), carriage, or river, if the traveller can procure a steam launch, or can utilise the local river steamer services. The trip up the river takes three hours, and is interesting and picturesque. The river excursion may pleasantly be extended to Serampore, Chandernagore, Chinsurah, and Hooghly (see p. 67).

Just before reaching Barrackpur, there are some handsome modern temples on the left bank. Then comes the beautiful park (right), with noble trees and a small pier as landing-place, at which the Viceroy's yacht very often lies. At 300 yds. to the S. of the house, under a fine tamarind tree, is a polygonal enclosure, within which is a white marble monument to Lady Canning; it replaces that removed to the Cathedral at Calcutta. A Hall, built by the Earl of Minto in 1813, stands 100 yds. to the N. of the house, within a colonnade of

Corinthian pillars. Over the outside entrance is a black slab, inscribed—

To the Memory of the Brave.

On the walls are four Tablets erected by different Governors-General to the memory of British soldiers who fell in Mauritius and Java, 1810-11, in the Isle of France, and at Maharajpur, and Paniar, 1843.

The House, which is the Viceroy's country residence, was commenced by Lord Minto, and enlarged to its present size by the Marquis of Hastings. It contains some interesting pictures of native princes. N. of the park is Barrackpur **Cantonment.** Troops were first stationed here in 1772, when the place received its name. In 1824, during the Burmese War, the 47th B.N.I., which was ordered on service, mutinied here on the 30th October, on which the Commander-in-Chief, Sir Edward Paget, proceeded to the cantonment with two European regiments, a battery of European artillery, and a troop of the Governor-General's Bodyguard. The mutinous regiment was drawn up in face of these troops, and was ordered to march, or ground arms. On the sepoys refusing to obey, the guns opened upon them, when, throwing away their arms and accoutrements, they made for the river. Some were shot down, some drowned, and many hanged, and the regiment was struck out of the "Army List." In March 1857 there were again mutiny troubles here, and though these were checked for the moment by the personal bravery of General Hearsey[1] commanding the troops, it became necessary to disarm all the native troops at the station on 14th June.

Dum Dum station, 4½ m. from Calcutta. A municipal town and cantonment. It was the headquarters of the Bengal Artillery from 1783 till 1853, when they were removed to Meerut; and their mess-house is now the Soldiers' Club, and is known as the *Outram Institute*. A bust of Sir James Outram stands in the verandah.

In the centre of the Barrack Square is a huge gun. Near this is a monument to the officers and men killed in the Khaibar whilst returning from Kabul in 1841. The Treaty, which restored the British settlements after the recapture of Calcutta ,was signed at Dum Dum. Lord Clive had a house here, and Fairley Hall was occupied by Sir Henry Lawrence, when a Lieutenant. There is an English Church—St Stephen's—a Roman Catholic Chapel, and a Wesleyan Chapel. There is a *Small Arm Ammunition Factory*, which is guarded by British soldiers.

Howrah (population 179,000) is a large and flourishing city on the right bank of the Hooghly, opposite Calcutta, with over 60 mills employing 50,000 hands, chiefly from Calcutta. It is also at present the terminus of the E.I.R., of the Bengal and Nagpur Railway. At the end of the 18th century it was a small village; now it stands sixteenth among all the cities of India.

The following places may be visited by the E.I. Railway.

12 m. **Serampore** station, the headquarters of the subdivision of the same name, is on the W. bank of the Hooghly, opposite Barrackpur (44,500 inhabitants). Serampore was formerly a Danish settlement, and was then called Fredericksnagar. The fine mansion of the Danish Governor now forms the Courts of Justice and administrative offices. In 1845 a treaty was made with the King of Denmark, by which all the Danish possessions in India, namely, Tranquebar, Fredericksnagar, and a small piece of ground at Balasore were transferred to the

[1] General Hearsey, who as a subaltern had taken part in the defence of Sitabaldi (p. 84), had previously shared in the suppression of a mutiny of Native Troops at Wazirabad in 1849.

E.I. Company for £125,000. The chief claim of Serampore to notice arises from its having been from 1800 onwards the scene of the labours of Carey, Marshman, and Ward. The zeal and success of the Baptist missionaries of Serampore, form one of the brightest episodes of Evangelistic efforts in India. From its press proceeded forty translations of the Scriptures.

The old *Danish Church* (1805) cost Rs. 18,500 of which 1000 were given by the Marquis of Wellesley; it is now Anglican. In it there are tablets in memory of the above-mentioned Baptist missionaries. Their tombs are in the native Christian cemetery, on the right hand of the road from the railway station.

The *College* is a handsome building on the banks of the river, and commands a fine view across it over Barrackpur Park. On the ground floor are the Lecture-rooms, and on the floor above the Great Hall, which is 103 ft. long and 66 ft. broad. In the Library are portraits of Madame Grand (who afterwards married Talleyrand) and Dr Marshman, by Zoffany; Frederick VI. of Denmark, and his wife, Queen of Denmark; and the Rev. W. Ward, by Penny. The library contains first editions of Carey and Marshman's forty translations of the Bible; also some curious Sanscrit and Thibetan manuscripts, and an account of the Apostles drawn up by Xavier's nephew for Akbar. In the College compound is the house in which Carey lived and died, now inhabited by the Principal of the College.

The fine mansion next to the chapel, which was the common centre of the Serampore brotherhood, with all Carey's Park and botanic garden, is now the property of the India Jute Company. Here, from 1835 to 1875, the weekly *Friend of India* was edited.

21. m. **Chandernagore**[1] station. Area, 3 sq. m., population, 25,000.

[1] See p 421.

The French settled here in 1673, and under Dupleix, of whom the place has a statue, over 2,000 houses were built, and a considerable trade arose. In 1757 the town was bombarded by the British Fleet under Admiral Watson, and captured, and the fortifications were demolished; but in 1763 the town was restored to the French. In 1794 it was again captured by the British, and held till 1815. when it was again restored to the French. The railway station is just outside the French boundary. A church stands on the bank of the river, built by Italian missionaries in 1726.

24 m. **Hooghly** station. At Hooghly, the E. I. R. and the Northern Bengal Railway are linked across the great cantilever, Jubilee Bridge, which is 1213 ft. long, and ranks as one of the greatest engineering feats in India. The linking line, 3 m. long, joins the Northern Bengal Railway at **Naihati.** Hooghly and Chinsurah (2 m. from Hooghly station, see below), are bracketed together as one in the Census Report, and together cover an area of 6 sq. m. The population is 29,000. Hooghly town is the administrative headquarters of the district of the same name. It was founded by the Portuguese in 1547 A.D., when the royal port of Bengal, *Satgaon,* began to be deserted, owing to the silting up of the Saraswati, on which river it was situated. They commenced by building a fortress at Gholghat, close to the present Hooghly jail, some vestiges of which are still visible in the bed of the river. When Shah Jahan came to the throne, complaints were made to him of the conduct of the Portuguese at Hooghly. The Emperor bore them a grudge, as they had refused to assist him against his father, and he sent a large force against the fort, which, after four and a half months' siege, was stormed. More than 1000 Portuguese were slain, and 4000 men, women, and children were captured. Out of 300 Portuguese vessels, only three escaped. The prisoners were sent to Agra, and forcibly converted to Islam. Satgaon

was then abandoned for Hooghly, which was made the royal port, and was also the first settlement of the English in Lower Bengal. The E.I. Company established a factory there in 1642, under a *farman* from Sultan Shuja', Governor of Bengal, and second son of Shah Jahan. This *farman* was granted, according to tradition, to Dr Broughton, who had cured a favourite daughter of the Emperor, and asked for this reward. In 1669 the Company received permission to bring their ships to Hooghly to load, instead of transporting their goods in small vessels, and then shipping them into large. In 1685, a dispute took place between the English at Hooghly and the Nawab of Bengal, and the Company sent a force to protect their Hooghly factories. It chanced that a few English soldiers were attacked by the Nawab's men in the bazaars, and a street fight ensued. Colonel Nicholson on this bombarded the town, and 500 houses were burnt, including the Company's warehouses, containing goods to the value of £300,000. The chief of the English factory was obliged to fly to Satanati,[1] and take shelter with some native merchants. In 1742 Hooghly was sacked by the Mahrattas.

The principal sight at Hooghly is the **Imambarah**, built by Karamat'Ali, the friend and companion of Arthur Connolly, at a cost of Rs.300,000 from funds bequeathed by Muhammad Muhsin, who owned a quarter of the great Saiyadpur estate, in Jessore district, and died in 1814, without heirs, leaving a property worth £4500 a year for pious purposes. The trustees quarrelled, and Government assumed charge of the estate. During the litigation a fund of £86,110 had accumulated, and with this the Hooghly College was founded in 1836. The façade of the Imambarah is 277 ft. × 36 ft.; and in its centre is a gateway flanked by two minarets, or towers, 114 ft. high. On either side of the door are inscriptions. Within is a quadrangle, 150 ft. × 80 ft., with rooms all round, and a fine hall paved with marble, having a pulpit with sides covered with plates of silver, and a verse of the Koran inscribed in each plate. The library was bequeathed by Karamat 'Ali, but a few books have since been added by other people. Among them are 787 MSS., including a fine folio Koran, in two vols. given by Prince Ghulam Muhammad, son of Tipu Sultan. On the opposite side of the road from this Imambarah is the old Imambarah, built in 1776-77. In the W. corner lie the remains of Karamat 'Ali, and there is a white marble tablet placed against the wall, with an extract from the Koran, but no tomb.

[1] See p. 53.

Chinsurah, 1 m. S. of Hooghly, was held by the Dutch for 180 years, and ceded by them to the British in exchange for Sumatra in 1826. The old *Dutch Church*, of brick, is said to have been built by the Governor in 1678. In it are fourteen escutcheons, dating from 1685 to 1770, with inscriptions in Dutch. Between Chinsurah and Chandernagore is **Biderra**, where the British obtained a decisive victory over the Dutch. It is said that the British commander was aware that his nation and the Dutch were at peace, and wrote to Clive for an order in council to fight. Clive was playing cards, and wrote in pencil: "DEAR FORDE,—Fight them to-day, and I will send you an order to-morrow.—*Thursday, 17th*, 1.30 P.M."

The *Hooghly College* is to the S. of the church. There are 600 students. The cemetery is 1 m. to the W. of the church: the new part is tolerably well kept, but not so the part where the old tombs are. Many of them are of Dutch officials.

Bandel, 1 m. N. of Hooghly. A Portuguese monastery and church were built here in 1599, and the keystone with the date was erected in the new one, which is of brick, and very solidly built. It is dedicated to Nossa Senhora de Rosario. There are fine cloisters on the S., and a priory, in which is a noble room called St Augustine's Hall. The church was founded by the Augustinian Missionaries, demolished by Shah Jahan in 1640, and rebuilt by John Gomez de Soto.

About 6 m. above Hooghly is **Satgaon**, where there is a ruined mosque, which, together with a few tombs near it, is the only remnant of the old capital of Lower Bengal. It was built by Saiyad Jamal-ud-din, son of Fakhr-ud-din, who, according to inscriptions in the mosque, came from Amel, a town on the Caspian. The river of Satgaon, up to Akbar's time, formed the N. frontier of Orissa, and Satgaon flourished for 1500 years. Three centuries ago the Hooghly flowed by the town.

Down the Hooghly River from Calcutta to Saugar Island.

The Calcutta pilots who number fifty-eight, and who are responsible for the safety of some 3100 vessels, with a tonnage of 6,500,000 yearly up and down the river, occupy a higher position than any of their profession. Pilotage receipts amount to 14 lakhs yearly. The Hooghly is a most dangerous and difficult river to navigate, as, apart from the chance of cyclones, which take place in any month except February, there is the normal danger of shoals and tides, which is a very real and a very great one. New shoals are continually forming, and nothing but a daily experience of the river can enable a pilot to take a vessel up safely. The most dangerous shoal, called the "**James and Mary**," is 30 m. S. of Calcutta, just above the Rupnarain; but from the Damodar River to Hooghly Point, a distance of 6 m., the whole river is full of dangers, and the crews of passenger steamers are generally all mustered on deck during the passage of this reach. The name of the above shoal dates from the wreck of a vessel called the *Royal James and Mary* on that bank in 1694. It appears first under it in a chart dated 1711. The Hooghly cannot be navigated at night, nor until the tide makes can it be ascended. It is usual, therefore, for vessels proceeding up the river to anchor near Saugar Island until occasion serves. The ordinary fall and rise of the river is 16 ft. A special feature of the rising tide is the bore, which sometimes attains a height of 7 ft., and reaches as far up the river as Hooghly city.

The view of the river, crowded with ships at anchor many rows deep all the way along the Landing-place, is very striking; and the forest of masts, the plain of the Esplanade, the Fort, and the fine buildings in the background, all give the idea of a great capital.

The vista to the N. from between Garden Reach and the Botanical Gardens is especially fine when the atmosphere is clear. Seven miles from Calcutta the last sight of the capital of India is lost; 5 m. further Budge Budge (Bajbaj; Railway to Calcutta, 16 m.) is passed on the left; at a similar distance further on **Ulubaria**, a small town, is passed on the right. Here the main road from Calcutta to the temple of Jagannath at Puri crossed the Hooghly, and here begins the Midnapur High-Level Canal. The river, which has hitherto followed a S.W. course, now turns due S. to Hooghly Point.

At 27. m., a little above the mouth of the Damodar, is (left) **Falta**, the site of an old Dutch factory, and the place to which the British ships sailed on the capture of Calcutta by Suraj-ud-daulah, and from which Clive advanced to avenge the shedding of innocent blood.

The *Damodar* is navigable as far as Ampta, which is 25 m. from its mouth, by boats of from 10 to 20 tons, and large quantities of coal are brought by it from the Raniganj mines.

Five m. below Falta the Rupnarain River enters the Hooghly nearly opposite Hooghly Point, and from here the river turns S.E. to Diamond Harbour, and then S. again.

At 12 m. up the Rupnarain river, on the right bank, is **Tamluk**, a very famous city in ancient times, and a maritime port of the Buddhists, where the Chinese pilgrim Fa Hian embarked for Ceylon in the beginning of the 5th century A.D. Hiouen Thsang 220 years later speaks of it as an important Buddhist harbour. It is now a long way from the ocean, but reached by the tide. There is a *Temple* here known in the locality by the name of Dargah Bhama or Bhenna, which was originally a Buddhist temple. The shrine is surrounded by a curious triple wall.

At 41 m. from Calcutta is **Diamond Harbour** (left), marked by a large number of trees, where the E.I. Company's ships used to anchor. There is a Custom House here, and the officers board ships proceeding up the river. There is also a railway to Calcutta (39 m.) with five or six trains daily, in three or four hours.

At 48 m. is the town of **Kalpi** (left), which contains a large market-place for the sale of rice grown in the interior, and from which there is a road to Calcutta. Here the estuary of the Hooghly begins, and at 68 m. between Kedgeree and Saugar Island it is 15 m. broad. At this island where the Ganges is considered to join the sea a gathering of from 100,000 to 200,000 pilgrims from all parts of India, but principally from the Bengal districts, takes place in the early part of January, the date of the great Bathing Festival of Bengal. The bathing cermony, as a rule, lasts for three days, though the fair lasts for a couple of days longer.

Sport is abundant. Deer, wild boar, and a great variety of sea-birds are found throughout the year.

Tigers are to be met with in the jungle ; but this sport is very dangerous, and should not be attempted by inexperienced persons.

The sea is reached at 80 m., where there is a lighthouse of iron, 76 ft. high, commenced in 1808, on Middleton Point at the S.W. end of the island. The floating light is 30 m. below this, and the outermost buoy 10 m. further on, and 130 m. from Calcutta.

ROUTE 6.

Manmar to Daulatabad, The Caves of Ellora, Aurangabad, Jalna, and Secunderabad.

Manmar (p. 28). — The railway passes near the S. side of the great rock of Deogiri or Daulatabad, affording a fine view of three sides of it. Permission to visit the fort must be obtained from the First Talukdar, Aurangabad, and a tonga for the journey from the Daulatabad Station to Ellora must be ordered beforehand from the Tonga Mail Agent, Aurangabad. The charge for a tonga is Rs. 10, and a fee of Rs. 2 additional is charged for each day's halt. It is impossible to see the caves properly in less than two days. Travellers who do not wish to visit Daulatabad may order their tonga for Ellora Road, the previous station.

50 m. **Daulatabad*** (*Deogiri*), a 13th-century fortress, is built on a huge isolated conical rock of granite, about 500 ft. high, with a perpendicular scarp of from 80 to 120 ft. all round. On the east side of the fortress were two outer lines of defence, and beyond these stood the walled city now in ruins, and crossed from S. to N. by the road to Roza and Ellora. On the left of the road stands the entrance to the outer line of defence, consisting of a hornwork with three gateways inside it protected by a bastion 50 ft. high. Beyond the gate are (*r*) a Hindu temple with a lamp tower 13 ft. high ; and (*l*) a small shrine of the Pir-i-Kudas. On the latter side a little further on are a large masonry tank, now dry, and a mosque converted out of a Jain temple, which has also served as a Hindu place of worship. Opposite these the Chand Minar, a minaret of Turkish form rises 100 ft., it bears the date of 1435 A.D. The inner line of defence is now passed by a gate similar to that in the outer line, the first gate

in both cases being defended by iron spikes against battering by elephants; and a steep flight of steps leads onwards to a third gate giving access to a platform on the edge of the ditch, 40 ft. wide. On the right here is the *Chini Mahal*, with encaustic decoration, in which Abul Hasan, Tana Shah, the last king of Golconda spent thirteen years of imprisonment; close by on a bastion is a gun 21′ 10″ long called the Kila Shikan, or Fort Batterer. The moat is crossed by a narrow stone bridge, at the end of which the road ascends to the Balakot by rock-cut chambers and passages, and emerges into the air 50 ft. higher up. This point was formerly covered with an iron shutter, 20 ft. long and 1 in. thick, made in ribs (part of it is gone), which in case of siege was heated red hot, so that if assailants could have penetrated so far, they would have encountered a fiery roof quite unapproachable. To provide ventilation for the fire a large hole has been tunnelled through the rock close by. Passing a gateway and the shrine of the Fakir Sukh Sultan, the path leads to a Barahdari, or pavilion, from which there is a fine view. It is believed to have been the residence of the Hindu Princess of Doegiri, and was a favourite resort of the Emperor Shah Jahan[1] in 1636. The pavilion has a wide verandah, with a precipice of from 100 to 200 ft. in front, and a view to Aurangabad on the E. and to Roza on the N. One hundred steps more must be climbed to reach the Citadel itself, on a platform 160 ft. by 120 ft. At the W. corner is a one-gun battery, 60 ft. by 30 ft. The gun is 19 ft. 6 in. long, with a bore of 7 in. On a bastion is a large gun, on which is a Guzerati inscription, saying that the funds for its construction were provided by certain Banias, and also a Persian inscription, naming the gun "Creator of Storms." Tavernier says that the gun on the highest platform was raised to its place under the directions of a European artilleryman in the service of the Great Mughal, who had been repeatedly refused leave to return to his native land, and was promised it if he could mount the gun on this spot.

1 The Emperor's historian recorded a most exact account of the defences.

The place was the capital of the Yadava dynasty, after the fall of the Western Chalukyas. In the year 1293 'Ala-ud-din, afterwards Emperor of Delhi, took the city. The citadel still held out, and he finally raised the siege of it on receiving a ransom of 15,000 lbs. of pure gold, 175 lbs. of pearls, 50 lbs. of diamonds, and 25,000 lbs. of silver. In 1338 A.D. Muhammad Shah Tughlak attempted to establish his capital in the Deccan, removed the inhabitants of Delhi to Deogiri, strengthened the fortifications, and changed the name to Daulatabad; but his plans ended in complete failure.

The road from Daulatabad to Roza (8 m.) and the caves of Ellora ascends the steep hill called Pipal Ghat. It was paved by one of Aurangzeb's courtiers, as recorded on two pillars about half-way up the hill, where there are fine views.

Roza or **Khuldabad** is a walled town (2218 inhabitants), 2000 ft. above the sea, and is 2 m. from the caves of Ellora. It is the *Karbala* (holy shrine) of the Deccan Mussulmans, and is celebrated as the burial-place of many distinguished Mohammedans, amongst whom are the Emperor Aurangzeb and his second son, Azim Shah; Asaf Jah, the founder of the Hyderabad dynasty; Nasir Jung, his second son; Malik Ambar, the powerful minister of the last of the Nizam Shah kings; Hasan Shah, the exiled and imprisoned king of Golconda; and a host of minor celebrities.

Roza once contained a considerable population, but the place is now in great part deserted. It is surrounded by a high stone wall (built by Aurangzeb) with battlements and loopholes. Old and ruinous mosques and tombs abound in every direction on each side of the road.

Midway between the N. and S. gates of the city is the **grave of Aurangzeb** in the Dargah of Saiyad Zain-ud-din on the right side of the road. An ascent of 30 yds. leads to a domed porch and gateway, erected about 1760 by a celebrated dancing-girl of Aurangabad, within which is a large quadrangle. Some of the surrounding buildings are used as rest-houses for travellers, and one as a school. In the centre of the S. side is an exquisite little Nakar Khana, or music hall, from the galleries of which music is played when festivals or fairs are celebrated. The W. side is occupied by a large mosque, the roof of which is supported on scalloped arches. Facing the N. end of the mosque is a small open gateway leading into an inner courtyard, in the S.E. angle of which is the door of Aurangzeb's tomb itself. Above the door is a semicircular screen of carved wood. The grave, which is uncovered, lies in the middle of a stone platform raised about half a foot from the floor. It is overshadowed by the branches of a tree (*Bukuli*) which bears sweet-smelling flowers, otherwise it is quite open to sun and rain, as it should be, according to orthodox Mohammedan ideas. This emperor, who was a man of austere piety, is said before his death to have desired that his sepulchre should be poor and unpretentious, in accordance with the tenets of the Koran, and to have expressly "desired in his will that his funeral expenses should be defrayed from the proceeds of caps which he had quilted and sold, an amount that did not exceed Rs.10; and that the proceeds of the sale of his copies of the Koran, Rs.805, should be distributed to the poor."

Fifteen or twenty paces to the E. of Aurangzeb's tomb is a small quadrangular enclosure of marble, within which are three graves, the one on the right being that of the daughter of the Mohammedan saint buried close by; the next that of **Azim Shah**, Aurangzeb's second son, attached to which is a small marble headstone carved with floral devices; and the one beyond the grave of *Azim Shah's wife*. The whole is surrounded by a plain screen of white marble. Midway between these tombs and that of Aurangzeb is the mausoleum of *Saiyad Zain-ud-din*, on the E. side of which are inscribed a number of verses from the Koran, and the date of the Saiyad's death, 1370 A.D. This tomb, however, was erected many years after that period by one of his disciples. The doors of the shrine are inlaid with silver plates of some thickness; the steps below it are embellished with a number of curiously cut and polished stones, said to have been brought here from time to time by fakirs and other religious devotees of the shrine. A little distance to the rear of this tomb is a small room built in an angle of the courtyard wall, which is said to contain a robe of the Prophet Mohammed. It is carefully preserved under lock and key, and is only exhibited to the gaze of the faithful once a year, the 12th Rabi-ul-Awal.

Opposite this dargah, on the left side of the road, is that of Saiyad Hazrat Burhan-ud-din, with the grave of *Nizam-ul Mulk Asaf Jah*, the first of the Nizams of Hyderabad. The entrance is through a large quadrangle, having open-fronted buildings on all sides, and a Nakar Khana (music gallery), at the E. end. The W. end is used as a school for instruction in the Koran. A door at this end gives access to an inner courtyard in which are a number of graves. Facing the entrance are the tombs of Asaf Jah and Nasir Jang, surrounded by a lattice screen of red sandstone, and that of *Saiyad Hazrat Burhan-ud-din*, a saint who died at Roza, 1344. He was the successor of Muntajib-ud-din sent by Nizam-ud-din Aulia (p. 206), from Upper India with 700 disciples a few years before the first invasion of the Deccan by 'Ala-ud-din, 1294, and was succeeded by Zain-ud-din. Deposited within the shrine are some hairs of the Prophet's beard, which are said to increase yearly in number. The shrine, however, boasts of a still more remarkable treasure, which is described by the attendants as follows: "For some years after its erection, the disciples of the Saiyad were without means to keep it in repair, or to provide themselves with the necessaries of life. Supplication to the deceased saint, however, produced the following remarkable phenomenon. During the night small trees of silver grew up through the pavement on the S. side of the shrine, and were regularly removed every morning by the attendants. They were broken up and sold in the bazaars, and with the proceeds thus realised the Saiyad's disciples were enabled to maintain the shrine and themselves. This remarkable production of silver is said to have continued for a number of years, until a small jagir was allotted to the shrine, since which time the pavement has only yielded small buds of the precious metal, which appear on the surface at night and recede during the day." In proof of these assertions the visitor is shown a number of small lumps of silver on the surface of the pavement. The shrine doors are covered with plates of white and yellow metal wrought into designs of trees and flowers.

Among the tombs between these two shrines and the Ellora D.B. are those of Saiyad Raju Ḳattal, Malik Ambar, and the last king of Golconda. The D.B. is situated above the cliff in which the

CAVES OF ELLORA

are, and the road to them begins to descend immediately beyond it.

The Ellora group of **Cave Temples** is the largest and most varied of all, and comprises twelve Buddhist, fifteen Brahmin, and five Jain works. The road down the Ghat passes the south side of the Kailasa Temple, and divides the caves into two groups of eighteen to the left and fourteen to the right of it. The Buddhist caves lie at the S. end, and the Jain caves at the N. end of the hill face, which is nearly 1½ m. long, the Brahmin caves and Kailasa being situated between the two groups. The local Brahmins are apt to be rather troublesome in pressing their claims on strangers as guides and recipients of alms.

Buddhist Caves.—The first of these, to the S. of the Ghat road, and lying beyond three Brahmin caves, is known as the Tin Thal (No. 12) or Three-Storied, and the furthest group at the S. end is named the Dherwara or Outcasts' quarter; the date of the latter extends from 350 to 550 A.D., and of the former from 650 to 750. **No. 1** is a vihara, measuring 41½ ft. by 42¼ ft., and having eight cells round it. **No. 2,** which was a hall for worship, is approached by a flight of steps, and is reached through a verandah carved with figures, and having large *dwarpal* guardians at the door to the cave, which is flanked by a window on either side. The interior measures 48 ft. square, and has a raised lateral gallery on each side; the roof is supported by twelve columns arranged in a square with high bases and cushion capitals, and the two galleries have four pillars in front of them, all richly decorated. A shrine, with huge *dwarpals* and a colossal seated Buddha in the centre of it and two standing Buddhas on either hand, occupies the middle of the back wall, and on each side of the shrine is a double cell elaborately carved. **No. 3** was a vihara or monastery, measuring 46 ft. square, and having twelve cells round it; the twelve columns which support it have a drooping leaf or ear over their circular necks. In the N. end of the verandah is a chapel with a Buddha seated on a lotus supported by snake-hooded figures, and on the right of this is a pictorial litany.[1] **No. 4** is a much ruined vihara, now measuring 35 ft. by 39 ft. deep. At the inner end is a cross aisle, beyond which a shrine, with a statue of Buddha under the Bo-tree, and two cells were excavated; the columns are similar to those in No. 2. **No. 5,** known as the Mahawara, and formerly as the Dherwara cave, is again reached by steps. It is the largest single-storeyed vihara cave here, measuring 58½ ft. by 117

[1] See p. 41.

ft. deep. The roof is carried by two rows of ten columns, similar to those in No. 2, with two more between them at each end, and two stone benches run down the cave parallel to the ranges of pillars. On either side of the cave is a recess with two pillars and a number of cells, and at the end is a shrine. From its peculiar arrangement it has been conjectured that this cave was a Hall of Assembly. **No. 6,** to the N. of No. 5, is reached through a lower hall with three cells on the E. side; it measures 26½ ft. by 43 ft., and has an antechamber and shrine at the back of it, the former richly carved and the latter containing a large seated Buddha. The figure on a stone at the foot of the goddess Saraswati on the S. wall of the antechamber deserves notice. Beyond it is yet a third hall measuring 27 ft. by 29 ft., with three cells on the E. and N. sides. **No. 9** lies in the N.W. angle beyond the third hall, and is reached from the central hall of No. 6; it has a well-carved façade. **No. 7,** to which the stairs in the first hall of No. 6 lead, is a large vihara, 51½ ft. by 43½ ft., supported by four columns only. **No. 8** is entered from this, and is a hall measuring 28 ft. by 25 ft., with three cells on the north side, a shrine with a passage round it, and a seated image of Buddha in it, and a smaller hall on the W. side. On the face of the rock by this is a group of the

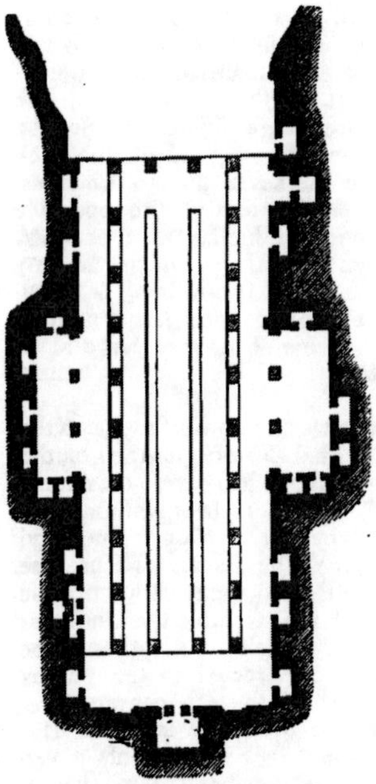

The Mahawara Dherwara Cave.

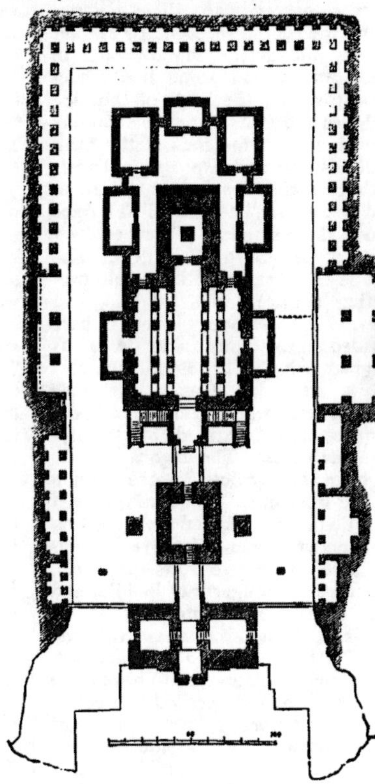

The Kailasa Temple.

child Buddha with his mother and father. The next excavation, **No. 10,** is the only Chaitya or chapel cave of the group, and lies some way to the N. It is known as the Viswakama or Carpenter's cave, and is considered to date from the end of the 7th century A.D. In front of it is a large court, which is reached by steps, and from which a second flight of steps leads to the verandah. The galleries round the court are borne by elegant pillars, and at the foot of each of these was a fine stone lion facing outwards. At the back of the side galleries are two chapels elaborately carved, and at the ends of the back gallery or verandah are two chapels with two columns in front of them and two cells. The fine railed terrace above the verandah is reached by a flight of steps in the N. gallery. The façade is surmounted by a bold projecting cornice cut in the rock, and the great horseshoe window is here divided into lights, and loses its original shape. The interior measures 86 × 43 × 34 ft., and the nave and aisles, which run round the dagoba, are separated by twenty-eight columns. The dagoba is 27 ft. high, and has a colossal seated Buddha in the front of it. The roof is carved in imitation of ribs, and the projecting wall under it and the above columns is carved with two rows of panels, the upper with figures of Buddha and the lower with representations of ganas or dwarfs. Further N. is the Do Thal[1] cave **(No. 11),** which was subsequently discovered to have three storeys; it is also preceded by a court. The lowest storey consists of a verandah only, with a shrine and two cells at the back of it. The middle storey has eight pillars in front and five chapels or cells, of which only the three richly carved ones in the middle are completed. The centre chapel is a small hall with two pillars and a statue of Buddha in the shrine. N. again of the Do Thal is the Tin Thal[2] cave (No. 12), dating probably from about 700 A.D. This again has a fine fore-court (a feature which adds great picturesqueness to the Ellora caves), but in this instance without side galleries. Steps lead from the court into a great hall, 115 ft. × 43 ft., with three rows of columns; beyond this a second hall, 42 ft. × 35 ft., borne by six columns, extends up to the shrine, with a seated statue of Buddha on either wall. The shrine contains a colossal seated Buddha and a number of other figures. On the walls of the front hall a relief of Buddha with attendants and chauri bearers is repeated in many places.

Steps at the S.W. corner of the front hall lead to the middle storey, borne by two rows of eight pillars. The shrine is elaborately carved and two fine *dwarpals* guard its door. The topmost floor is carried by five rows of eight columns, the hall measuring 115 ft. × 70 ft. Along both side walls are large figures of Buddha seated on a throne, and on the back wall are the seven human Buddhas, seated under trees at the one side and under umbrellas at the other. The antechamber, which is very large and has two pillars, is sculptured all round with large figures; in the shrine is a very large squat Buddha.

Brahman Caves.—Fifty yds. N. of the Tin Thal Cave begins the group of fifteen Brahmanical caves, or sixteen, including the Temple of Kailasa. The first of these is a plain room only; next comes the Ravan ka Khai[1], and then the Das Avatára, between which and the Kailasa temple the Ghat road reaches the plain. All these were probably constructed in the 7th and early part of the 8th century A.D., the temple being the latest in date. The Ravan ka Khai presents a very different arrangement from that of any of the Buddhist caves. At the entrance were four columns making a front aisle; behind, twelve columns enclose the central space of the hall; and beyond these is a shrine standing free at the end of the hall. The pillared portion measures nearly 55 ft. sq., and the depth of the cave to the back wall behind the shrine chapel is 85 ft. The S. wall bears

[1] Do Thal = Two storeys.
[2] Tin Thal = Three storeys.

[1] Ravan ka Khai = Excavation of Ravana.

Saiva sculptures of the slaughter of the buffalo demon, Shiva and Parvati playing chess, Shiva dancing the tandava, Ravana shaking Kailasa and Bhairava;[1] while the N. wall has **Vaishnava** representations of Durga, Lakhshmi, wife of Vishnu, the Varahani, or boar incarnation of Vishnu, a four-armed Vishnu, and Vishnu seated with Lakhshmi. Inside the shrine is an altar and a broken figure of Durga; in the passage outside it on the S. side is a group of three Skeleton demon gods, Ganesh, and the seven great goddesses, each with a child, and her cognisance below, viz. Chamundi[2] and owl, Indráni and elephant, Varahani and boar, Lakhshmi and Garuda eagle, Kaumari and peacock, Maheswári and buffalo, Bráhmi and hans or goose. The **Dás Avatara[3] Cave** is next reached by a considerable flight of steps in the rock. It stands at the end of a large court hewn in the rock, which in this instance has a chapel in the middle of it and smaller shrines and cisterns round it; inside the chapel are four columns on a platform which perhaps once had an image of a bull (Nandi) on it. The cave has two storeys, of which the lower is carried by two rows of eight plain pillars, two more standing between four cells in the back wall. From the N.W. corner of the cave a staircase leads first to a landing with eleven reliefs of Hindu gods, beginning with Ganesh and ending with Durga, and then to the upper storey, which measures 95 ft. by 109 ft. deep, and is supported by seven rows of six columns, those in the front row being richly carved. The sculptured scenes on the walls are mainly similar to those in the preceding cave; among other noticeable scenes are Bhairava with a necklace of skulls, and the marriage of Shiva and Parvati on the N. wall; Shiva springing from a lingam and Lakhshmi with elephants pouring water over her, on the back wall; and Vishnu, resting on the five-hooded serpent, and incarnated as a dwarf and as Narasingha (man-lion) on the S. wall. In the shrine behind an antechamber with two columns was a lingam or emblem of Shiva.

The **Kailasa temple** is a marvellous structure, shaped and carved wholly out of rock *in situ*, the back wall of the court-pit in which it stands being over 100 ft. high, while the court itself is 276 ft. long and 154 ft. broad. A rock screen pierced by a fine entrance passage closes the court on the W. side; near it stand two gigantic stone elephants. Between the screen and the temple, and connected with both, is a fine Nandi shrine, 26 ft. square and two storeys high, with a stone flagstaff on either side; and beyond this is the temple measuring 164 ft. from front to back, and 109 ft. from outside to outside of the side porches, and rising 96 ft. above the floor of the court. It consists of three parts—a porch, a central hall measuring 57 ft. × 55 ft., and borne by sixteen massive square columns arranged in four groups of four each, with broad aisles between, from W. to E. and from N. to S., and a dark shrine, 15 ft. square inside, with the Ganges and Jumna as guardians at the door. A passage leads all round the shrine and to five chapels placed at the sides and back of it; these illustrate the shape of the cells on the terraces of structural Buddhist viharas. The solid basement on which the temple stands is carved with a splendid series of immense elephants and monsters projected from the wall, and forms quite one of the finest remains of antiquity in the whole of India. At the sides of the bridge connecting the porch and Nandi chapel, and of the staircases leading to the former, are large sculptures and reliefs, the latter representing scenes from the Ramayana. On the S. side of

[1] See pp. 19, 20.

[2] The name of this goddess, a specially ferocious form of Durga, is derived from the two giants Chanda and Munda whom she slew. She wore an elephant hide and a necklace of corpses, and used to rejoice in human sacrifices. See play of Malati and Madhava in Wilson's *Theatre of the Hindus*.

[3] Dás Avatara = Ten Incarnations.

the court opposite the porch is a rock-cut gallery, borne by two columns, with statues of the seven great goddesses and Ganesh, and E. of this is a plain cave, 55 ft. × 34 ft., borne by four pillars, and with a verandah also with two columns. There is also an upper storey to this cave, once connected with the temple by a flying bridge, under which on the temple wall is a relief of Ravana shaking Kailasa. From this point the E. half of the court round to the N. side porch of the temple is encircled by a corridor cut in the rock, with twelve large compartments of sculpture on the S. side, nineteen on the E., and twelve again on the N., representing various Saiva and Vaishnava scenes. The view of the temple from under the great cliff at the E. end is extremely impressive. W. of the N. corridor is another, but plain, one, under the large Lankeshwar cave. This is 108 ft. by 60 ft., exclusive of a Nandi chapel in front of it, and is reached by a dark winding staircase from yet a fifth corridor W. of the fourth. The cave is borne by sixteen pillars arranged as in the Kailasa temple, and by two rows of five and four more columns on the outer edge of the S. and W. sides, two in front of the shrine completing the whole number of twenty-seven; between the columns of the outer lines is a sculptured rail, and in the back aisle of the cave are a number of large sculptured scenes. At the sides of the door to the shrine are female guardians; the altar inside has been broken. In the N.W. corner of the court is a small cave shrine with two pillars in the front decorated with representations of the three river goddesses of the Ganges, Jumna, and Saraswati; and above this is a small unfinished excavation.

A footpath near the N. side of Kailasa leads up to the plateau past a cave with a Trimurti, or Triad figure of Shiva in it (p. 19). Further N. are four unimportant Brahmin caves, beyond which the Rameswara cave is reached. This is a Saiva temple, once with a porch in front of it, borne by three rows of four pillars very varied in design; it has but few carved scenes. A corridor formerly ran round three sides of the forecourt. The next important cave is known as the **Nila-kantha**; it has a small ruined chapel in the forecourt, from which thirteen steps lead into the cave, measuring 70 ft. by 44 ft. In the shrine is a lingam. The **Khumbarwada** cave, 95 ft. by 27 ft. including the smaller hall at the back, has a figure of the sun god in his seven-horse chariot in the vestibule to the shrine. The next temple is a large hall with several chapels measuring 112 ft. by 67 ft., and supported by columns of the Elephanta type: at the door of the shrine are very large *dwarpals*. The path now reaches a fine ravine, over the scarped head of which a waterfall descends after rain. On the S. side of this is the Vaishnava, Milkmaid's, or **Gopi cave**, and on the N. side the cave named **Sitaki Nahâni** (or bath), which is the last of the Brahmin caves. The verandah of the former is ruined, but on the back wall of it, pierced by a door and four windows, are various carved scenes: the inner hall measures 53 ft. by 22 ft. The second is an extremely picturesque excavation which will remind every one of the great cave at Elephanta, believed to be slightly more modern than this, which dates from about 650-725. It consists of a principal hall, facing nearly W., with a recess on the S. side opening on to the ravine, and a larger recess of irregular shape on the N. side. The central hall measures 149 ft. in depth and 95 ft. in breadth, including the two side aisles which lead to the recesses, and is borne by four rows of four columns, the two eastward of the middle rows being merged in the walls of the free shrine, while two more stand at the W. end of these rows and correspond with those at the sides of the entrance. The steps to this are guarded by two lions, and in front of them is a circular platform for a *nandi*. In the verandah and front aisles of the cave are carved reliefs much as at Elephanta. The shrine is a small square room, approached by four doors as in that cave, and contains a lingam. From the S. recess steps descend to the ravine, of which a charming view is obtained at this point. The N. recess is also reached by steps guarded by lions; a small low cave exists at the E. end of this, and from the S.W. corner of the recess a passage has been broken into an excavation with six pillars; there is usually water in this wing, which prevents any close examination of it.

Jain Caves.—The five Jain caves, dating from the 8th to the 13th century, lie about 200 yds. beyond the most northerly of the Brahmin caves, the first being the **Chhota Kailasa**, some way up the face of the hill and not easily found without a local guide. This temple is in a pit measuring 130 ft. by 80 ft., and has a hall 36 ft. square borne by sixteen columns, and a shrine 14½ ft. by 11¼ ft. It was imitated from the great Kailasa temple and left incomplete. The **Indra Sabha** is entered through a rock screen facing S., in front of which to the E. is a temple with statues of Parasnath, Gotama Swami with creepers round his limbs, and the last Tirthankar, Mahavira. In the S.E. corner of the court is a large elephant, and opposite it was a monolithic column, in front of a cave with six columns, containing reliefs of the same three Tirthankars. In the centre of the front of the court is a chapel with a quadruple image of a Jain saint: at the back of the court is an incomplete hall borne by twelve columns, with two more between the S. and N. colonnades and the verandah and shrine. Over this, reached by a staircase in the verandah, is a second hall with wings to the front of it, each with a small temple borne by four columns. The hall measuring 55 ft. by 65 ft. is supported by twelve pillars, in the centre of which was once an image; the walls all round are divided into compartments filled with Jain saints, and the shrine has a statue of Mahavira. The figures at the ends of the verandah are noticeable, as is the cornice round the shrine door. The **Jagannath Sabha**, a little further on, is also a double cave with a court in front of it. On the W. wing of this is a small hall, and at the side of the main cave is a small chapel; the cave is supported by four columns in front and by four more inside; the sculptures in it are in an unusually perfect condition. The outside staircase to the upper storey leads to another hall 55 ft. by 45 ft., the ceiling of which was once painted in concentric circles, and the walls of which are sculptured all over with figures of Mahavira and Parasnath. This cave connects internally with the Indra Sabha, and also with another to the W. of it consisting of a verandah with two columns and a small hall with four. On the top of the hill in which the Jain caves are excavated is a rock-hewn statue of Parasnath 16 ft. high, protected by a structural building raised over it some 200 years ago.

It will probably be found more convenient to proceed by tonga from Ellora to Aurangabad, 16 m. (a small extra charge is made for this), than to go there by railway from Daulatabad.

63 m. **Aurangabad**, D.B. This thriving city (population 37,000), which has a considerable trade in cotton and wheat, was first called Khirki, and was founded in 1610 by Malik Ambar, the head of the Abyssinian faction in the Ahmadnagar State. The town lies to the E. of the cantonment. 1 m. N.E. of it is the grand **Mausoleum of Rabi'a Durrani**,[1] wife of Aurangzeb. The great door at the gateway is plated with brass, and along the edge is written, "This door of the noble mausoleum was made in 1089 A.H.,

[1] The proper name is Rubia ud Daurani. By some writers the lady is said to have been a daughter of the Emperor. The gravestone is nameless.

when Atau'llah was chief architect, by Haibat Rai." Near the inscription is an infinitesimally small figure, which is said to be a bird, indistinctly carved, and there is a similar carving on the door of the mausoleum itself. It is a common joke amongst natives, when any man asserts that he has been to this mausoleum, to ask if he saw the bird there, and if he answers in the negative, to dispute his having seen the mausoleum at all. The curious roof of the gateway of the mausoleum should be observed. In the garden is a long narrow basin of water, in which fountains used to play and on either side of the water is a walk and ornamental wall. The main fault of this otherwise beautiful building, which is compared to the Taj, is the want of sufficient height in the entrance archway. In the wall of the mausoleum is a second but much smaller door, only 6 ft. high, plated with brass, where the second bird is pointed out. The carving of the flowers on this door is curious, and that of the dragons particularly so. The bird is on the edge of the door close to the upper central knob. Those who wish to enter the tomb are expected to take off their shoes. The cenotaph is enclosed in an octagonal screen of white marble lattice-work exquisitely carved, and stands on a raised marble platform.[1] The place for the slab is empty, and nothing but earth appears. This is much approved by Moslems, as showing humility. In the gallery above the tomb is a marble door exquisitely carved. The Government of the Nizam has gone to great expense in restoring this mausoleum. Below the right corner of the platform is a second tomb, said to contain the remains of Rabi'a Durrani's nurse. There is no inscription. To the W. of the mausoleum is a mosque of brick faced with cement (*chunam*) of a dazzling whiteness. The pavement is covered with tracings of prayer-carpets. The *mimbar*, or pulpit, is of marble.

[1] Tavernier mentions this tomb in his travels, and states that he met carts coming down from N. India with white marble for it.

The **Pan Chakki** or **water-mill**, the shrine of Baba Shah Muzaffar, a *Chishti* (p. 138), and spiritual preceptor of Aurangzeb, is perhaps the prettiest and best-kept shrine in this part of India. It is situated on the right of the road from the cantonment to the Begampura bridge, and on the very edge of the Kham, the river of Aurangabad. In the garden is a brimming tank of clear water, full of fish from 1 ft. to 3 ft. long, of a species called *Khol*. This tank overflows into a lower one, and that again into a narrow conduit. Beyond the first tank and the ornamental garden is a second and much larger one. It is entirely supported on vaults, with two rows of massive pillars. Below is a noble hall reached by steep steps down to the level of the river. On the right of the second tank is a fine mosque, the roof of which is supported by four rows of massive pillars. In two of the rows the pillars are of teak, and in two of masonry. At the S.W. corner of this mosque, in a little garden, is the diminutive **Tomb** of the saint, of beautiful light-coloured marble.

¼ m. N. from the *Pan Chakki*, is the *Mecca Gate* of the city and the *Mecca Bridge*, which are probably some centuries old. The top of the parapet of the gateway is 42 ft. above the road which passes over the bridge. The flanking towers are surmounted by domes. Inside the gate there is a black stone mosque built by Malik Ambar. In the centre is a niche with the Divine Name, and "Victory is near." Above that is the *Kalimah*, and some verses of the Koran written in difficult *Tughra*. Close by is a recess with a bell-shaped ornament. This is perhaps the oldest mosque in the city.

The **Government Offices** are two m. to the S.E. of the cantonment, and in or near the *Arkilla* or citadel built by Aurangzeb. This spot not long ago was entirely covered with cactus and jungle, the haunt of hyenas and other wild animals. It was, however, the site of gentlemen's houses in the reign of Aurangzeb, when Aurangabad was the capital of the Deccan. Sir Salar Jang ordered the site to be cleared, and when this was done, numerous reservoirs, fountains, and other works of interest were discovered. These have been repaired, and the wilderness has literally been changed into a blooming garden. Only one archway of Aurangzeb's citadel remains, but here fifty-three great princes, like the Maharajas of Jaipur and Jodhpur, attended the court of the Emperor with thousands of armed retainers, and Aurangabad was then the Delhi of the South. As soon as Aurangzeb died the princes departed, and Aurangabad sank at once into comparative insignificance. The **Jama Masjid** is on the right of the road, amid a grove of some of the finest trees in India. One immense *Ficus indica* stands close on the road and shades some 300 ft. of it. The Mosque and minarets are low, but the façade is rendered striking by an ornamental band of carving 2 ft. broad along the whole front. Over the central niche are the *Kalimah* and inscriptions in Tughra writing as in Malik Ambar's Mosque. This mosque is wonderfully well kept, and there is, what is not seen anywhere else, a net covering the entire façade, so that no birds or other creatures can enter. Malik Ambar built half this mosque, and Aurangzeb the other half.

The **Caves** of *Aurangabad* are beyond the N. outskirts of the city near Rabi'a Durrani's mausoleum, from which it is necessary to ride or walk to the foot of the hills, which are here about 700 ft. high. The ground at the base of the hill is very rough, and intersected with deep ravines, and the climb up to the caves is over a rough and slippery rock for about 250 ft. The nine Buddhist caves here are the latest of all Buddhist works in India, and date principally from the 7th century: there are five in the W. group, and four in the other lying ¾ m. further E.. **No. 1** at the W. end of the first group is a vihara, a good deal higher up than the other four caves adjoining it, and the path to it is rather difficult. Only the porch and verandah (76½ ft. by 9 ft.) were completed, and the former has been crushed by the fall of a mass of rock; the hall was intended to be one of 28 pillars. **No. 2** was intended to be a hall for worship only. At the back of the verandah, 21½ ft. by 13 ft., is an aisle, and behind this is a shrine with a passage all round it: at the sides of the shrine door are two tall figures standing on a lotus flower and *nága* figures, and inside is a seated figure of Buddha, 9 ft. high, in the teaching attitude. Many reliefs of similar figures are on the walls of the shrine and the passages. **No. 3** is a vihara hall, 41½ ft. by 42½ ft., with twelve columns splendidly decorated as in the late caves at Ajanta; there is a decorated recess also, and on each side two cells. In the front corners of the shrine are a number of life-sized worshipping figures with garlands and elaborate head-dresses. **No. 4** is a chaitya or chapel cave, much ruined. It was only 38 ft. long and 22½ ft. broad, and was carried by seventeen plain columns: the dagoba was nearly 6 ft. in diameter. It dates probably from the middle of the 4th century. Of **No. 5** only the shrine remains, now dedicated to the Jain Parasnath. **No. 6**, the first of the E. caves is again much higher up the hill face than the other three caves in that group. The hall was borne by four columns, and the antechamber of the shrine by two more: in the side walls are four cells, and in the back wall two. The shrine has a passage round it, and a smaller Buddha with smaller worshippers in front. There are traces of painting on the roof of the front of the cave. **No. 7** has a verandah with four columns and a chapel at either end, and a hall 38 ft. by 28 ft., in the centre of which the shrine has been placed; while three cells have been excavated in each side wall, and two chapels with sculptures in the back wall. To the left of the entrance to the hall is one of the best representations of the Buddhist Litany (p. 41): to the right is a figure of Manjusri, patron of the Maháyana sect. The front of the shrine has three large female figures on either side: on the left of the figure of Buddha in the shrine is the representation of a dance and of female musicians. **No. 8** consists of a ruined lower storey and an incomplete upper storey with a hall 27 ft. by 20 ft. **No. 9** is also higher up in the cliff. It consisted of a long verandah hall with three chambers and shrines opening from it. On the W. wall is a sculpture of the dead Buddha 16 ft. long. The sculptures and arrangements of these caves show a distinct approximation to the Brahmin caves of Ellora.

102 m. **Jalna** D.B., a cantonment of the late Hyderabad contingent (population 20,000). From this place the battle-field of **Assaye**, 30 m. distant, may be visited in the inside of a day, if arrangements are made beforehand for a tonga and two relays of horses on the road, through the Tonga Mail Agent of the place. Several old forts, such as once covered all the Deccan, are passed *en route*, and the two fortified villages of Pipalgaon and Waroor on the Kaitna river which showed the Duke of Wellington where the ford was, still stand on either side of the stream. A fine view of the field of battle fought on 23rd September 1803 is obtained from the tower of the fort of the village of Assaye, on the bank of the Juah, between which and the Kaitna the Mahratta army was drawn up, after it was compelled by the British manœuvre to change front from the line of the Kaitna, which it originally faced. The forces of Scindia and of the Bhonsla Raja of Nagpur consisted of 16,000 infantry and 20,000 cavalry, and the British force of 4,500 men all told: the killed and wounded on either side were 12,000 and 1,600. North of it lies the spot where the British who fell in the battle were buried. It is under contemplation to erect a memorial here.

386 m. Secunderabad (p. 379).

ROUTE 7.

BHUSAWAL to CALCUTTA **(HOWRAH) BY AKOLA WARDHA** (expedition to **Warora**, and **Chanda**), **Nagpur, Kampti, Raipur, Bilaspur,** and **Sini,** and from Sini to (*a*) **Purulia** and **Asansol, and** (*b*) **Kharagpur.**

By this line a new route from Bombay to Calcutta (1223 m., or about 130 m. shorter than any other) is opened up. The fares are Rs.91.1, Rs.45.9, and Rs.13.13 by the mail train. The time occupied by this is 40 hours.

It taps an immense territory of the Central Provinces which has hitherto been inaccessible to external trade, and provides an outlet for the great wheat and seed-producing district of *Chattisgarh* (the thirty-six forts), one of "the granaries of India." The scenery in parts of the line, notably at *Darekassa*, *Dongargarh*, and *Saranda* (p. 87), is very fine.

The route from Bombay to

276 m. **Bhusawal** junction (R.) is described in Route 2.

Soon after leaving Bhusawal the traveller enters the districts of **Berar** (population, 2,754,000), which continue almost all the way to Nagpur. They belong to H.H. the Nizam, but were assigned to the British by a treaty, in 1853, for the support of the Hyderabad Contingent force. This treaty was remodelled in December 1860, by which, for the Nizam's services in the Mutiny of 1857, his debt of 50 lakhs was cancelled, the districts of Dharaseo and the Raichur Doab were restored, and the confiscated territory of Sholapur was ceded to him. By a recent arrangement made with H.H. the Nizam, involving a fixed payment of 21 lakhs yearly to the Hyderabad State, the permanent administration of the Berar districts by the British Government has been secured, and they have been added to the Government of the Central Provinces; while the Hyderabad Contingent Force has been formally added to the Indian Army.

The fertility of the Berar districts, which form one of the richest and most extensive cotton-fields in India, is very striking. The soil is black loam overlying basalt. The rainfall is regular and abundant, and at harvest-time the whole surface is one immense waving sheet of crops. The districts are Akola, Amraoti, Elichpur, Buldana, Wun, and Basim.

333 m. **Jalamb** junction station.

[Branch 8 m. S. to *Khamgaon* station, where there is an important cotton-mart.]

363 m. **Akola** station is the headquarters station of the West Berar district of that name.

[A road from Akola runs S. 72 m. to the important town and military station of *Hingoli*. About 30 m. from Akola is the town of *Mehkar*, and 15 m. S. of Mehkar is a curious soda lake called *Lonar*, formed in the crater of an extinct volcano. The salt is used for washing and dyeing purposes, and is exported in considerable quantities.]

413 m. **Badnera** junction station (R.), D.B.

[Br. 6 m. N. to **Amraoti** station (R.), D.B. Both places have cotton-marts, and there are cotton-gins and warehouses. Amraoti is the headquarters of the district of that name, and was that of the Revenue Commissioner, who was formerly the head of the Berar Administration.

472 m. **Wardha** junction station (R.), D.B. The chief town of the most westerly district of the Central Provinces. The place is quite modern, dating only from 1866, and is a considerable cotton-mart. Here is a Medical Mission of the Free Church of Scotland, with fine hospital and leper asylum.

[Branch S. to the **Warora** coalfields, and Chanda.

21 m. **Hinganghat** station, D.B., a very important old cotton-market.

45 m. **Warora** station, a town in the Chanda district of the Central Provinces, and a considerable cotton-mart. Close to Warora are mines of fairly good coal; the yearly out-turn is about 120,000 tons.

74 m. is **Chanda**, the headquarters of the Chanda district (D.B.), and a most attractive spot. The town is surrounded by a continuous wall of cut stone 5½ m. in circuit. Inside the walls are detached villages and cultivated fields. The foliage is beautiful, and there are extensive forest-preserves near. The tombs of the Gond kings, and the temples of Achaleswar, Maha Kali, and Murlidhar, are all worth a visit. At *Lalpet*, in the town, a large space is covered with monolith figures of gigantic size which appear to have been prepared for some great temple never erected. The branch line is to be extended to Warangal (p. 379*b*.)]

520 m. **Nagpur**,✱ lat. 21° 9′ long. 71° 31′, is the capital of the Central Provinces, which have an area of 100,000 sq. m., and a population of 10,761,630.[1] The present Chief Commissioner is the Hon. Mr R. Craddock, C.S.I. The district of Nagpur itself has an area of 3786 sq. m. Among the inhabitants are upwards of 2,000,000 of aborigines called Gonds; and of these the hill-tribes

1 Inclusive of the recently added Berar districts.

have black skins, flat noses, and thick lips. A cloth round the waist is their chief garment. The religious belief varies from village to village. Nearly all worship the cholera and the small-pox, and there are traces of serpent-worship.

The ancient history of the Province is very obscure. In the 5th century A.D. a race of foreigners, *Yavanas*, ruled from the Satpura plateau, and between the 10th and 13th centuries, Rajputs of the Lunar Race governed the country round Jubbulpore, and the Pramars of Malwa ruled territory S. of the Satpuras. The Chanda dynasty of Gonds reigned probably as early as the 10th or 11th century, and the Haihayas of Chattisgarh were of more ancient date. In 1398 A.D. there were princes reigning at Kherla, on the Satpura plateau, and Ferishtah says "they possessed all the hills of Gondwana." In 1467 they were conquered by the Bahmani kings. The next century the Gonds again rose to power, but in 1741 the Mahratta Bhonslas invaded the country. After the events of 1817 the British annexed the Saugor and Nerbudda territories, and in 1853, on the death of the last Raja, Raghoji III., without heir of his body, Nagpur and other districts were resumed, and in 1861 were formed by Lord Canning into the Central Provinces. On the 13th of June 1857 the native cavalry of the Nagpur Irregular force conspired with the Mohammedans of the city to rise against the British, but the Madras infantry continued loyal, and the outbreak was suppressed by the firmness of Mr George Plowden the Commissioner. The Sitabaldi Hill was prepared as a place of refuge, but fortunately the necessity of using this did not arise.

Nagpur, situated on the small stream called the Nag (population, 101,000), is the headquarters of the Government of the Central Provinces. The municipality includes, besides the city, the suburb and the civil station of *Sitabaldi*. In the centre, W. of the railway station, stands Sitabaldi Hill, crowned by a fort, which commands a fine view. At *Sitabaldi*, on the 26th and 27th of November 1817, the Mahratta troops of the Bhonsla Raja, Apa Sahib, attacked the Resident, Mr, afterwards Sir R. Jenkins, and the few troops he had been able to assemble. After a desperate engagement, during which the Mahrattas for a time got possession of one of the two eminences of the Sitabaldi Hill, the British were at length victorious. But the disbandment of the army was only obtained after a second battle, in which the Mahrattas were completely routed. Apa Sahib escaped and died in exile. A child was raised to the throne under the title of Raghoji III., and on his death, in 1853, the country was annexed by the British.

W. of Sitabaldi Hill is the prettily wooded civil station, in which are the Victoria Memorial Technical Institute, the fine Renaissance Secretariat Offices, the New Club House, the Courts, the handsome English cathedral, a large Roman Catholic cathedral and school, an important branch of the Missions of the Free Church of Scotland, two hospitals for men and women, and a fine Mahratta church. Beyond to the N. are the military lines and bazaars, and the suburb of *Takli*, once the headquarters of the Nagpur Irregular force. There is a fine new Government House on Takli Hill; in the summer the Chief Commissioner resides at Pachmarhi (p. 29). Sitabaldi is the suburb S. of the hill of that name. Below the glacis is the railway station; beyond is the Jumá Talao, a large tank; and more to the E. is the city, hidden in foliage. Three great roads lead from the civil station to the city, one on the N. and one on the S. bank of the tank; the third, which is the most N. of all, crosses the railway by a bridge to the N. of the station. Besides the Jumá Talao, there are two other fine tanks, the Ambajheri and Telinkheri, 3-4 m. W. of the city. The chief gardens are the Maharaj Bagh, in Sitabaldi, the Tulsi Bagh, inside the city, and the Paldi, Shakardara, Sonagaon, and Telinkheri in the suburbs.

Nagpur is famous for its delicious oranges, quantities of which are exported. There are two large spinning mills in the place.

The *Bhonsla Palace*, in the city, built of black basalt, was burned down in 1864, and only the Nakkar Khana, or music hall, remains. Near it are the Morris and Hislop Colleges and tbe Town Hall.

The *Cenotaphs of the Bhonsla Rajas* are in the Shukrawari quarter, to the S. of the city.

The Great Indian Peninsula Railway terminates at Nagpur, and from this point E. to Calcutta the line belongs to the Bengal - Nagpur Railway.

529 m. **Kampti**, D.B. A large town and military cantonment (population 39,000) on the right bank of the Kanhan river, which is spanned by a handsome stone bridge that cost £90,000. Close to it is the railway bridge, a fine iron structure that cost £100,000. Kampti dates only from the establishment of the military station in 1821. The English church was built in 1833, and there is a highly useful Roman Catholic establishment of the Order of St Francis de Sales with a church and convent. There are five mosques and a number of Hindu temples.

559 m. **Bhandara Road** station, D.B., is about 6½ m. from the town, which is close to the Wainganga river. It is the headquarters of a district of the same name, and contains the usual public offices, schools, and institutions. Population 11,000.

601 m. **Gondia** junction. A line runs from here north to Nainpur, 74 m., and Jubbulpore (p. 29), 70 m. further.

615 m. **Amgaon** station (R.).

From 624 m. **Salekasa** and 631 **Darekasa** to

647 m. **Dongargarh** station (R.), the line passes through hills and heavy bamboo jungles, and through a pass with a tunnel at the summit. The jungle near this tunnel is famous for generally having a man-eating tiger in it. During the construction of the railway a large number of natives were killed here, and victims have more recently been carried off. Large game of all sorts abounds. Dongargarh is an engine-changing station, with a considerable European population connected with the railway. The ruins of a fort are on the N.E. face of a detached hill, some 4 m. in circuit. Inside the fortified space there are tanks for water supply, but no buildings.

At Amgaon, 95 m. E. of Nagpur, the **Chattisgarh** country is entered and continues to Raigarh station, at 338 m. The people of this country still consider themselves a separate nationality, and always call themselves *Chattisgarhias*. The Rajas of Ratanpur ruled originally over their thirty-six forts, each the chief place of a district; but about 750 A.D., the kingdom was divided into two, and a separate raja ruled in Raipur. Kalyan Sahi, who ruled between 1536 and 1573, went to Delhi and made his submission to the great Akbar, and this prudent conduct resulted in the Haihaya rulers retaining their country until the Mahratta invasion in 1740.

The tract, which is regarded as one of the richest corn-growing countries in the world, and is known as the "granary of India," is in the shape of a vast amphitheatre opening to the S. on the plains of Raipur, but on every other side surrounded by tiers of hills.

708 m. **Raipur** station. The chief town of a district of the same name, the headquarters of the commissioner of *Chattisgarh*, and a small military cantonment. The population is 32,000. The town is surrounded by tanks and groves of trees, which form its attraction. The *Fort* was built by Raja Bhuvaneswar Singh in 1460, and in its time was a very strong work. Its outer wall is nearly 1 m. in circumference. Large quantities of stone were used in its construction, though

no quarries exist in the neighbourhood. The *Burha Tank*, on the S., the same age as the Fort, covered nearly 1 sq. m.; but in later improvements it has been reduced in extent. The public gardens are on its E. shore. The *Maharaj Tank* was constructed by a revenue farmer in the times of the Mahrattas, and close to it is the temple of Ramchandra, built in 1775 by Bhimbaji Bhonsla. There are several other reservoirs in the suburbs; and in the centre of the town is the *Kankali Tank*, constructed of stone throughout, at the close of the 17th century.

776 m. **Bilaspur** junction station (R.). This place is a large engine-changing centre.

[Branch N.W. through a mountainous district and the coal-fields of *Umaria* to 198 m. **Katni** junction on the E.I. Railway (p. 30). This branch passes at *Pendra* station,[1] under the **Amarkantak** plateau (4000 ft.), where the Nerbudda has its source. There are several temples and a "Kund" or reservoir enclosing the head spring. The plateau is frequented by the "tirath básis," and other pilgrims.]

About 15 m. E. of Bilaspur is the precipitous *hill of Dahla*, 2600 ft. high, affording a grand view.

[20 m. N. of Bilaspur is **Ratanpur**, the old capital of the formerly self-contained kingdom of *Chattisgarh, or the Thirty-six Forts*, in which is included the districts of Raipur and Bilaspur. The town lies in a hollow surrounded by the Kenda hills. It ceased to be the capital in 1787, but the crumbling arches of the old fort, the broken walls of the ancient palace, and the half-filled-up moat which surrounded the city, recall its former condition. The population is under 6000. The Brahmins of Ratanpur are still the leaders of their class all over Chattisgarh. The town covers an area of 15 sq. m., and contains within its limits a forest of mango trees, with numerous tanks and temples scattered amidst their shade. Mixed up with temples, great blocks of masonry of uniform shape commemorate distinguished satis (*suttees*). The most prominent of these is near the old fort, where a large building records that there in the middle of the 17th century twenty ranis of Raja Lakshman Sahi devoutly fulfilled the duty of self-immolation. *Kota* station on the Katni branch is a few miles from Ratanpur.]

[1] The scenery between Khongsara and Khodri, east of Pendra, is of exceptional beauty.

Before reaching

809 m. **Champa** station the Hasdu river is crossed. The stream cuts the coalfields of **Korba**, some 20 m. N. of the railway; and in the jungles on its banks are to be found some of the few herds of wild elephants still roaming through the forests of the Central Provinces.

The line continues E. through a thinly-inhabited flat country to

858 m. **Raigarh.**

890 m. **Belpahar** station, on leaving which the Eeb river, which flows S. into the Mahanadi river, is crossed by a considerable bridge. The scenery at the crossing is very fine.

903 m. **Jharsuguda** junction station.

[Branch for the civil and military station of **Sambalpur**, distant 31 m. Near here, at different times, diamonds of considerable value have been procured. They are said to be found in the bed of the Mahanadi up-stream from the town, but whether the source of supply is the Mahanadi or the Eeb river is perhaps not clearly known.]

From Jharsuguda the railway takes a N.E. course, and continuing through a well-inhabited plain country to

916 m. **Bagdehi** station, it enters the hills, in which it continues until the plains of Bengal are reached.

936 m. **Garpos** station. Hereabouts the forests are very dense, and in the rainy season they are largely resorted to by wild elephants. Between this and

957 m. **Kalunga** station, the Brahmeni river is crossed. The natives here earn a very fair living by washing the river-sands for gold. The view up-stream is very grand when the river is in flood.

991 m. **Manharpur** station. Here the railway enters the **Saranda** forests, which contain some of the finest Sal trees (*Shorea robusta*) in India. The line winds round hills, passing close under them on both sides. The summit of the range is reached through a heavy cutting leading into a tunnel. During the construction of the Bengal-Nagpur Railway through these forests and heavy jungles very great difficulty was experienced in procuring labour, as they have a very bad reputation for unhealthiness. The few inhabitants of these wilds are nearly all *Kols*, an aboriginal race.

1029 m. **Chakardarpur** station. Here the hills recede. The country is well cultivated. This is a considerable railway settlement and engine-changing station.

[**Chaibasa,** a civil station, is distant about 16 m. to the S.E. A great fair is held here at Christmas-time, to which the people of the country flock. Athletic sports, races, and national dances take place on the last day of the year, and no better opportunity can be taken for seeing the people.]

1052 m. **Sini.** From here (*a*) the old line of the Bengal-Nagpur Railway runs N.E. to Asansol on the E.I.R., while (*b*) the new direct line runs E. to **Kharagpur,** 1151 m. (p. 322), and **Howrah** (1223 m). On the former are the following stations:—

1068 m. **Chandil** station. Before this place is reached, the hills again close in on the line. Dalma Hill, 3407 ft. above sea-level, is seen 12 m. E. It is from the country about here that the labourers for the tea-cultivation in Upper Assam and Cachar are mainly recruited.

1102 m. **Purulia** station. The headquarters of the Manbhum District, through which the traveller has been passing for many miles. The place has nearly 10,000 inhabitants and the usual offices of a civil station. [From here a branch line runs to

73 m. **Ranchi** (D.B., population 26,000), 2100 ft. above the sea. This place is the headquarters of the Chota-Nagpur Division.

Chota-Nagpur[1] is the seat of a Missionary Bishop of the Church of England. There are a handsome *Church, good Schools,* and a *Native Mission* in the town of Ranchi; and there are communities of *Christian Kols,* the result of extensive S.P.G. missions, conducted by a brotherhood from Trinity College, Dublin.]

1116 m. **Adra Junction,** junction for the E.I.R. Grand Chord, and Kharagpur.

1126 m. **Adra Junction,** junction for the E.I.R. Grand Chord, and Kharagpur (p. 34).

1152 m. **Asansol** junction station. About 6 m. before Asansol is reached the river Damodar (p. 70) is crossed on a very fine bridge. From Asansol to Calcutta, a distance of 132 m., the traveller proceeds by the East Indian Railway (see p. 38), this route being 60 m. longer than the Kharagpur route.

ROUTE 8.

KHANDWA to AJMER **by Mhow, Indore, Neemuch, Chitorgarh, and Nasirabad,** with expeditions by road to **Unkarji** and **Mandu,** and by rail to **Udaipur.**

353 m. **Khandwa** (p. 29). Here the broad gauge is changed for the narrow gauge railway, commencing with the Holkar State Railway. At 38 m., **Mortakka** station, the Nerbudda river is crossed by a fine bridge, with a cart-road under the rails. The only accom-

[1] For this interesting part of India Mr Bradley Birt's *Chota Nagpur* may be consulted.

modation is at the Railway Inspection bungalow, for which permission must be obtained from the Engineer-in-Chief, Indore State Railway, Mhow.

This neighbourhood abounds in large game of every sort.

[A good cart-road of 6 m. leads to **Unkarji**, more properly Omkarji, a place well worth visiting.

The *Great Temple of Omkar* is situated in the island of Mandhata in the Nerbudda. It is said that the island was originally called Baidurya Mani Parvat, but its name was changed to Mandhata as a boon from Shiva to Raja Mandhatri, the seventeenth monarch of the Solar Race, who performed a great sacrifice here to that deity.

The area of the isle is about five-sixths of a sq. m., and a deep ravine cuts it from N. to S. At the N. the ground slopes gently, but terminates at the S. and E. in precipices 500 ft. high. At this point the S. bank of the Nerbudda is equally steep, and between the cliffs the river is exceedingly deep, and full of alligators and large fish.

On both sides of the river the rocks are of a greenish hue, very boldly stratified. It is said that the Temple of Omkar and that of Amreshwar on the S. bank of the river are two of the twelve great temples which existed in India when Mahmud of Ghazni destroyed Somnath in 1024 A.D. During the wars of the 17th and 18th centuries, the S. banks were deserted and overgrown with jungle, and when the Peshwa desired to repair the temple it could not be found, so a new one was built, with a group of smaller ones. Afterwards part of it was found, and the late Raja of Mandhata built a temple over it; but its sanctity and even its name have been appropriated by that which the Peshwa built.

The Raja of Mandhata, who is hereditary custodian of the temples, is a Bhilala, who claims to be the direct descendant of the Chauhan Bharat Singh, who took Mandhata from Nathu Bhil in 1165 A.D. The old temples have suffered from the Mohammedans, and every dome has been overturned and every figure mutilated. The gateways are finely carved. The oldest temple is that on the *Birkhala rocks* at the E. end, where devotees used to cast themselves over the cliffs up till the year 1824, when the custom was abandoned. The temple consists of a courtyard, with a verandah and colonnades supported by massive pillars boldly carved. On the hill are the ruins of a very fine *Temple to Siddeshvara Mahadeva*, which stood on a plinth 10 ft. high. Round the plinth was a frieze of elephants, 5 ft. high, carved in relief with remarkable skill, on slabs of yellow sandstone, but all but two of the elephants are mutilated.

In front of the *Temple to Gauri Somnath* is an immense bull carved in a fine green stone, and 100 yds. farther is a pillar 20 ft. long. On the island itself all the temples are Shivite, but on the N. bank of the Nerbudda are some old temples to Vishnu, and a group of Jain temples. Where the river bifurcates are some ruined gateways, and a large building on which are twenty-four figures of Vishnu, well carved in green stone. Among them is a large figure of the boar Avatar. On a image of Shiva, in the same building, is the date 1346 A.D. Farther down the bank, in the Ravana ravine, is a prostrate figure 18¼ ft. long, with ten arms holding clubs and skulls. On its chest is a scorpion, and at its right side a rat, and one foot rests on a prostrate human figure.

The bed of the ravine is covered with huge basalt blocks slightly carved. The *Jain Temples* stand on an eminence a little back from the river. The largest is on a plinth of basalt, 5 ft. high. The E. wall is still complete. On each side of the doorway is a figure with Shivite and Jain emblems curiously intermixed. The hills near these temples, as well as the island, are covered with remains of habitations.

A great fair is held at the end of

October, attended by 15,000 persons. According to a prophecy, the fulfilment of which the Brahmans at Mandhata anxiously expect, the sanctity of the Ganges will expire in due course and be transferred to the Nerbudda.]

58 m. **Choral** station. From this point the ascent of the Ghat of the Vindhya Range commences and continues almost into Mhow. The scenery is very fine. On approaching,

71 m., **Patal Pani** station, the waterfall of that name is passed.

74 m. **Mhow station** (R.), D.B., in the territory of the Maharaja Holkar, an important military cantonment of British and native troops, headquarters of the fifth Army Division, 1900 ft. above sea-level, population 36,000. Troops are stationed here as provided in the Treaty of Mandsaur of 1818. Mhow has no special interest for a traveller. The buildings and institutions are those common to all places where troops are stationed.

[From Mhow an expedition of 55 m. may be made S.W. to the ruined city of Mandu, the ancient capital of the kingdom of Malwa. It is in the territory of the Maharaja of Dhar, and the best route is by tonga or carriage to the town of Dhar (33 m.), D.B. An introduction to the Political Agent will be found useful in making arrangements for the remaining 22 m. of the journey. Dhar is a walled town of some historical and archæological interest, containing several fine half-ruined mosques. In front of one of them is an iron pillar, which the Emperor Jahangir ordered to be removed to Agra.

Mandu[1] (1944 ft.) occupies 8 m. of ground, extending along the crest of Vindhyas; and is separated from the tableland, with which it is on a level, by a deep valley, above the southern side of which the battlemented walls and gates of the old city rise very finely. The best place in which to pass the night is the gateway of the Jama Masjid; supplies of every kind must be taken from Dhar, as practically none are procurable on the spot. Paths have been cut through the jungle to all the ruins of interest, the chief being the *Jama Masjid* (1431-54 A.D.), less injured than any of the others, and said to be the finest and largest specimen of Afghan architecture extant in India.[1] Between it and the great arched gateway in the northern wall of the city are a number of ruined palaces and courts, including the Water Palace with a fine tank on either side of it and a splendid view of the whole city from its roof, and the marble *Mausoleum* of *Hoshang Ghori.* Two miles to the S.E., on the edge of the Nerbudda Valley, of which there is a splendid view, is the *Palace of Baz Bahadur*, Bayazid, the last king of Malwa, with the pavilion of Rupmati (p. 211). S.W., near an inner citadel in that quarter, is a quaint ravine with temples and a small tank, specially mentioned in the memoirs of the Emperor Jahangir. These once magnificent buildings are still, in their ruined state, very striking on account of their massive proportions. The fortifications were constructed by Hoshang Ghori, who reigned in the beginning of the 15th century, and in whose time the city attained its greatest splendour. In 1526 Mandogarh was taken by Bahadur Shah, ruler of Guzerat, and annexed to his dominions, of which it remained part until their conquest by Akbar in 1570. Of late years measures have been taken for the preservation of some of the most interesting ruins. According to Malcolm, Mandu was founded in 313 A.D. Sir Thomas Roe, the Ambassador of James I. of England, entered Mandu in the train of Jahangir, part of the triumphal pro-

[1] A most interesting account of the ruins of Mandu was published by the late Sir James Campbell in the Gujerat Volume of the *Bombay Gazette.*

[1] See Fergusson, *Indian Architecture*, ii. 247.

cession of the Great Mughal being 500 elephants. He complains in his *Memoirs* of the lions which then infested the country, and killed one of his baggage ponies. The Rajas of the towns Mandu and Chitor were at feud with each other for many years (see p. 93.) From June till November the locality is very unhealthy.

87 m. **Indore** station D.B. This place is the capital of the state, and the residence of the Maharaja Holkar (population 87,000) and of the Agent to the Governor-General for Central India. The present chief is His Highness Maharaja Tukaji Rao Holkar.

Indore stands on an elevated and healthy site. Of recent years modern improvements have been introduced. Roads have been metalled, drains built, the water supply cared for, and the principal streets lighted. Among the chief objects of interest are the Lal Bagh or garden, the mint, high school, market-place, reading-room dispensary, and a large cotton-mill. There is considerable export trade in grain. To the W. of the city is an antelope preserve. Adjoining the town, on the other side of the railway, is the *British Residency*, an area assigned by treaty, and containing not only the house and park of the Governor-General's Agent and the bungalows occupied by his staff and other officials, but a bazaar of some importance, and the central Opium stores and weighing agency. The barracks for the escort of the Agent of the Governor-General and the Rajkumar College[1] for the education of young native chiefs and nobles are also within the Residency limits. Here too is a Mission of the Presbyterian Church of Canada.

The palace of the Maharaja (1 m. from the railway station), with its lofty, many-storeyed gateway, is situated almost in the centre of the city, and is a conspicuous object from every part of it. It faces E., and is in a small square, with the Gopal Mandir to the S., which was built by the Mahorani Krishna Bai. The fine King Edward Hall was opened by King George on 17th November 1905. His Majesty's visit will be commemorated by the new Courts of Justice. To the W. of the palace is the Sharafa Street, of the Marwari money-lenders. Close by is the Haldi Bazaar, where the dealers in opium live, and the Itwar, or Sunday Street, where a market is held on Sundays. H.H. sometimes receives guests in the Lal Bagh mentioned above. This is on the banks of the Sirsuti river, which is dammed up here and which divides the city, and contains a handsome villa. At one end is a house where several lions are kept, and there is also an aviary.

The State troops revolted in 1857 and attacked the Residency, and also the cantonment of Mhow on 1st July. The Resident Colonel Durand, who had arrived at Indore only on 14th May, and the Europeans with him, were compelled, after a fight, to retreat to Sehore, and Hoshungabad; but Captain Hungerford in Mhow drove the mutineers off his guns and remained there until a Bombay force reached that place.

The old capital of the Holkar family was Maheshwar in Nimar, on the banks of the Nerbudda, where is the magnificent **Chhatri** of Ahalaya Bai, widow of the son of Mulhar Rao Holkar, d. 1795. Sir John Malcolm says of this lady: "The character of her administration was for more than thirty years the basis of the prosperity which attended the dynasty to which she belonged. She sat every day for a considerable period in open durbar transacting business. Her first principle of government appears to have been moderate assessment and an almost sacred respect for the native rights of village officers and proprietors of land. She heard every complaint in person, and although she continually referred causes to courts of equity and arbitration, and to her ministers for

1 The Rajkumar College has been closed, and the pupils transferred to the Mayo college, Ajmer.

settlement, she was always accessible; and so strong was her sense of duty on all points connected with the distribution of justice, that she is represented as not only patient, but unwearied in the investigation of the most insignificant causes when appeals were made to her decision. It appears, above all, extraordinary how she had mental and bodily powers to go through the labours she imposed upon herself, and which from the age of thirty to that of sixty, when she died, was unremitted. The hours gained from the affairs of the state were all given to acts of devotion and charity, and a deep sense of religion appears to have strengthened her mind in performance of her worldly duties. Her charitable foundations extend all over India, from the Himalayas to Cape Comorin, and from Somnath to the Temple of Jagannath in the East." Ahalaya Bai is certainly the most distinguished female character in Indian history. It is recorded of her that she had the courage to watch her daughter become *sati*, after vainly seeking to dissuade her from this act.

112 m. **Fatehabad** junction station (R.). From here a short branch line of 26 m. runs to

[**Ujjain** (D.B.). This famous city (the Greek Οζήνη) is situated on the right bank of the river Sipra, which falls into the Chambal after a total course of 120 m. Ujjain is in the dominions of the Maharaja Sindhia of Gwalior in Malwa, of which it was once the capital. It stands in N. lat. 23° 11′ 10″, and is the spot which marked the first meridian of Hindu geographers. It is said to have been the seat of the viceroyalty of Asoka, during the reign of his father at Pataliputra, now Patna, about 263 B.C. It is, however, best known as the capital of the legendary Vikramaditya (Valour's sun), of Jain story, long believed to be the founder of the Samvat era. He was fabled to have driven out the Scythians, and to have reigned over almost all N. India, and at his court were said to have flourished the Nine Gems of Hindu literature, viz., Dhanvantari, Kshapanaka, Amarasinha, Shanka, Vetalabhatta, Ghata-karpara, Kalidasa, of European celebrity, Varanruchi, and Varaha-mihira. Ujjain, as well as the whole province of Malwa, was conquered by Ala-ud-din Khilji, who reigned at Delhi 1295-1317 A.D. In 1387 A.D. the Mohammedan Viceroy, Dilawar Khan Ghori, declared himself independent, and ruled from 1387 to 1405; he made Mandu his capital. In 1531 Malwa was conquered by Bahadur Shah, King of Guzerat, and in 1571 by Akbar. In 1658 the decisive battle between Aurangzeb and Murad and their elder brother Dara, was fought near this city. In 1792 Jaswant Rao Holkar took Ujjain, and burned part of it. It then fell into the hands of Sindhia, whose capital it was till 1810, when Daulat Rao Sindhia removed to Gwalior.

The ruins of ancient Ujjain are situated about 1 m. to the N. of the modern city, which is oblong in shape, and 6 m. in circumference, surrounded by a stone wall with round towers, and on all sides by a belt of groves and gardens. The principal bazaar is a spacious street, flanked by houses of two stories, and having also four mosques, many Hindu temples, and a palace of Maharaja Sindhia. Near the palace is an ancient gateway, said to have been part of Vikramaditya's fort. To the S.W. of this are the picturesque ghats and temples on the river; and outside the city to the S.E. are the remains of the **Observatory**, erected by Maharaja Jai Singh, of Jaipur (p. 140). 5 m. to the N. of the town is a picturesque Water Palace resembling some of those of Mandu.]

161 m. **Rutlam** junction station (R.), (D.B.—Branch line W. by Godhra and Anand to Baroda and

Ahmedabad (p. 122), E. to Ujjain), is the capital of a native state and the residence of the chief. It was founded by Ratna, great-grandson of Udai Singh, Maharaja of Jodhpur. Ratna was at the battle of Fatehabad, near Ujjain, in which Jaswant Rao Rathor, with 30,000 Rajputs, fought Aurangzeb and Murad, with the whole Mughal army. Tod, vol. ii., p. 40, says: "Of all the deeds of heroism performed that day, those of Ratna of Ratlam by universal consent are pre-eminent." The palace in which the Prince resides is within the walls, and is a fine new building, with a handsome reception-room. The town is a great emporium for opium. There is a Chauk or square built by Munshi Shahamat 'Ali. Beyond this is the Chandni Chauk of the bankers which leads to the Tripuliya Gate, and the Amrit Saugar tank.

213 m. **Mandsaur** station. A fortified town remarkable as being the place where in 1818, at the end of the Pindari War, a treaty was made between the British Government and Holkar. Severe fighting occurred here in 1857 between the rebels and a brigade of British troops, moving from Mhow to relieve Neemuch.

[The two short lines from Ujjain and Rutlam unite at **Nagda**, whence the most direct route to Delhi and the Punjab proceeds N. (p. 122).]

244 m. **Neemuch** station. ✱ (R.) D.B., is a cantonment of British troops. Neemuch was about the most southerly place to which the mutiny extended. In 1857 the place was garrisoned by a brigade of native troops of all arms of the Bengal army. This force mutinied and marched to Delhi, the European officers taking refuge in the Fort, where they were besieged by a rebel force from Mandsaur, and defended themselves gallantly until relieved by a brigade from Mhow. Some forty-two ladies and non-combatants found refuge at Udaipur.

278 m. **Chitorgarh** ✱ station. ✱ (Branch line to Udaipur, 54 m.). The Gambheri river below the famous fort is crossed by a massive old bridge of grey limestone, with ten arches all of pointed shape, except the sixth from the W. bank, which is semi-circular. The gateways and towers which existed at either end of the bridge have now disappeared. The builder is popularly said to have been Ajai Singh, son of Rana Lakhshman, in whose reign Ala-ud-din Khilji besieged Chitor (1303 A.D.) on account of the beautiful Padmani, wife of the Rana's uncle, Bhim Singh. The first siege failed, though, according to tradition, Bhim Singh was treacherously captured for a time. When the second was about to prove successful in spite of the sacrifice of eleven royal princes, each made Rana for one day, all the Rajput women proceeded to an underground cave, Padmani entering last, and were there immolated by fire (*johar*), and Bhim Singh and his clansmen fell before the swords of the Mohammedans.

When Chitor was the capital of Mewar, the city was situated in the Fort. The modern town of Chitor called the Talaiti or Lower Town is little more than a walled village, with narrow, crooked streets, in front of the principal W. entrance to the **Fortress**. It is now sufficient to obtain the permission of the local magistrate (Hakim) to visit the Fort.[1]

The abrupt rocky hill crowned by this magnificent Fort rises 500 ft. above the surrounding country, and is a very conspicuous object, though its great length of 3⅓ m. makes it look lower than it really is. The whole of the summit is covered with ruins of palaces and temples, and the slopes with thick jungle. An ascent 1 m. long, with two zigzags, leads to the summit, and is defended at

[1] For a striking account of this wonderful Fort, see *The Naulakha* and *Letters of Marque*, both by Rudyard Kipling.

intervals by seven magnificent gateways, large enough to contain guardrooms and even fine halls. They are the Pádal Pol, the newly rebuilt Bhairon or Tuta (Broken) Pol, the Hanuman Pol, the Ganesh Pol, the Jorla Pol, the Lakhshman Pol, and the Main Gate, or Ram Pol.

Immediately outside the Padal Pol on the left is an erect stone marking the spot where Bagh Singh, the chief of Deolia Pratapgarh, was killed during the siege of Chitor by Bahadur Shah of Guzerat, in 1535.

Between the "Broken" and the Hanuman gates there are on the right two chhatris marking the spots where the renowned Jaimall of Bednor and his clansman, Patta of Kailwa, were killed in Akbar's siege, in 1568. Jaimall, though only sixteen years of age, succeeded to the command of the place, which the Maharana Udai Singh had quitted, on the fall of the Salombra[1] chief; and so far was the heroism of the defenders carried that his bride fought beside him with a lance. He was shot by the Emperor Akbar himself, and 8000 Rajputs fell before the place was carried. The thirty-nine memorial stones here are much venerated, as if marking the shrine of some minor deity.

Facing the great gate is a pillared hall, used as a guard-house, and apparently of ancient construction. From the top of this hall, on which there are two four-pillared chhatris, a fine view of the plain is obtained.

The Ram Pol is a large and handsome gateway, crowned by a Hindu horizontal arch, in which the upper courses of either side, projecting inwards, overlap each other till they meet, or nearly so, and are then connected by an overlying slab. This is the construction of all the gateways on the ascent, except the Jorla, though in one, the Lakhshman, the lower angles of the projecting courses are sloped off, giving the whole the outline of a regular pointed arch. Inside the gate, on each side, is a fine hall, supported on square-shaped and slightly tapering antique pillars.

The principal objects of interest among the ruins of the old city are the two Jain Towers of Fame and Victory, known as the two Kirthams. The **Tower of Fame**, which is much the older, stands up grandly near the E. rampart, and is reached by the broad road turning to the left inside the Ram Pol and passing the Kukreswar Kund and Palace of Ratna Singh, or by a path proceeding directly to the E. Mr Fergusson thus describes it: "One of the most interesting Jaina monuments of the age (the first or great age of Jaina architecture, which extended down to about the year 1300, or perhaps a little after that) is the Tower of Sri Allat (Rana Alluji). It is a singularly elegant specimen of its class, about 80 ft. in height, and adorned with sculptures and mouldings from the base to the summit. An inscription once existed at its base, which gave its date as 896 A.D., and though the slab was detached, this is so nearly the date we should arrive at from the style, that there seems little doubt that it was of that age. It was dedicated to Adinath, the first of the Jaina Tirthankars, and his figure is repeated some hundreds of times on the face of the tower; but so far as I could perceive, not that of any of the other Jaina saints. The temple in the foreground, S. side, is of a more modern date, being put together, principally, of fragments of other buildings, which have disappeared."

The tower consists of seven stories, with an internal narrow and cramped staircase; the roof of the open top storey, which rests on pillars, was much damaged by lightning, but has been well restored. Fragments of an inscribed stone are on the ground under a tree just N. of the tower.

S. of the Tower of Fame the very

[1] The Salombra chief had the hereditary right to lead the van in battle, and to command the Surajpol gate of the fortress when besieged. On all old grants the sign of the Salombra lance precedes the Udaipur monogram.

ancient temple of Nilkanth Mahadeo is passed on the right, and the Suraj Pol or Sungate and its tanks on the left. A mile further on is the Raj Tilla or State hill, the loftiest point on the tableland; the broad road passes round this and returns N. by the Mori Tank, but walkers will probably cross from the E. gate to the palace of **Rani Padmani**, a large and beautiful building overlooking a tank. From this or from the palace of her husband, Bhim Singh, Akbar carried off the famous gates now in the fort at Agra (p. 176). From near this point the road leads past the picturesque ruined palace of Jaimall to the Jai Stambha, or **Tower of Victory**. Of this Mr Fergusson says: "To Kumbo, who reigned from 1418-68, we owe this tower, which was erected to commemorate his victory over Mahmud, king of Malwa, in 1439. It is a Pillar of Victory, like that of Trajan at Rome, but of infinitely better taste as an architectural object. It has nine stories, each of which is distinctly marked on the outside. A stair in the centre leads to each storey, the two upper ones being open and more ornamented than those below. It stands on a base 47 ft. square and 10 ft. high, and is 30 ft. square rising to a height of 122 ft., the whole being covered with ornaments and sculptures, to such an extent as to leave no plain part, while this mass of decoration is kept so subdued that it in no way interferes with the outline or general effect. The old dome was injured by lightning, and a new one was substituted by Sarup Singh, 1842-60. The stair is much wider and easier than that in the Jain tower (the small Kirtham), and in the inside are carvings of Hindu deities with the names below. In the top storey are two of the original four slabs with long inscriptions. The tower took seven to ten years to build, from 1458 to 1468. On the road at the corner of the lower platform is a square pillar recording a *sati* in 1468, A.D."

S.W. of the Tower of Victory is the **Mahasati**, a small wooded terrace, the prettiest spot on the hill, which was the place of cremation of the Ranas before Udaipur was founded. Below, on a lower terrace, are the Gaumukh springs and reservoir. The springs issue from the cliff at places carved with a cow's mouth, hence the name. To the S.W. is a large carved stone temple, built by Rana Mukalji. On the back of the wall is a huge carved head.

To the N. of the Tower of Victory rises the **Temple of Vriji**, built by Rana Kumbo about 1450, a massive building with a *Sikra* (or tower) of unusually large proportions. See Fergusson, ii. 151. Hard by is a similar temple, built by his wife, the famous Mira Bai, of which the chief peculiarity is that the procession path round the cell is an open colonnade with four small pavilions at the corners. Between the Tower and the Ram Pol are the Nau Katha Magazine and Nau Lakha Bhandar, or Treasury, and on the wall connecting these is a small pavilion in which the Ranas of Chitor were formerly enthroned. From here the road traverses the old Moti Bazar to the western Gate and completes the circuit of the Fort.

A branch line runs from Chitor to Udaipur. Dabok, where Colonel Tod, the first Resident and author of the *Annals of Rajasthan* lived, lies in ruins a few miles S. of Debari, 8 m. E. of the capital.

About 1 m. before reaching the capital, the Arh river is crossed, with the old ruined town of that name on its banks. This stream collects the whole drainage of the Girwa, the natural outlet from which was dammed up with an immense masonry embankment by Maha Rana Udai Singh, and thus forms the Udai Saugar Lake, the surplus waters from which, escaping, form the Birach river.

Udaipur (2034 ft. above sea level) is the marvellously picturesque capital of the state of Mewar, founded in the Christian era. The ruling family, now known as the Sesodia, and formerly as the Gehlot, is descended from the Suryabansi, or Sun-stock, royal dynasty of Oudh, and is the premier house of India in point of blue blood. The present representative is H.H. Maharana Dhiraj Sir Fateh Singh, G.C.S.I. The city of Udaipur was founded after 1568 by Maharana Udai Singh (who had been saved from being murdered as a baby by the devotion of his nurse, who substituted her own child), on the capture of Chitorgarh, which he left to its fate. The States of Udaipur, Jodhpur (Rathor), Jaipur (Kachhwaha Chauhan), and Boondi (Hara Chauhan) are the four original great states of Rajputana. The rest are either derived from them or had their origin long subsequent to them.

The *City* 3 m. distant from the railway station (population 46,000) is surrounded by a bastioned wall, which towards the S. encloses several large gardens. The W. side is further protected by the beautiful Pichola lake, and the N. and E. sides by a moat supplied from the lake, while on the S. the fortified hill of Eklinggarh rises steep and rugged. The principal gateways are the Hathi Pol or "Elephant Gate," to the N.; the Kishan Gate, to the S.; the Suraj Pol or "Gate of the Sun," on the E.; the Delhi Gate, on the N.E. and not far from the Hotel, and the Chand Pol, or "Moon Gate," on the W., opening on to the bridge across the N. end of the lake.

W. of the Hotel are the Residency and the mission houses, E. is the Victoria Hall and Museum with a statue of the Queen Empress, and 1½ m. N.E. at Ahar, is a fine group of royal cenotaphs. At the W. end of the bridge is the Sujjangarh hill 1100 ft. above the lake, with beautiful views of the lake from it. The Sujjangarh Palace is a striking feature on the hill.

The main street of the city leads from the Hathi Pol Gate to the Maharana's palace, passing a clock tower, the great Jagannath temple (built c. 1640), approached by a fine flight of steps, with an elephant on each side at the head, and the Walter Hospital for Women, named after Colonel Walter, for many years Resident at Udaipur. The temple, though late in date, is a good example of the Indo-Aryan style, figured at pp. 142-147, vol. ii., of Fergusson's *Indian Architecture.* The porch is covered with a low pyramidal roof, placed diagonally on the substructure, and rising in steps. The tower is ornamented by bold figured friezes and other architectural decoration. In front of the temple is a shrine with a brazen image of a Garuda. The Royal Palace (visited on application to the Private Secretary to the Maharana) is an "imposing pile of granite and marble, of quadrangular shape, rising at least 100 ft. from the ground, and flanked with octagonal towers, crowned with cupolas. Although built at various periods, uniformity of design has been well preserved; nor is there in the E. a more striking structure. It stands upon the very crest of a ridge, running parallel to, but considerably elevated above the margin of the lake. The terrace, which is at the E. and chief front of the palace, extends throughout its length, and is supported by a triple row of arches, from the declivity of the ridge. The height of this arcaded wall is full 50 ft., and although all is hollow beneath, yet so admirably is it constructed, that an entire range of stables is built on the extreme verge of the terrace, on which all the forces of the Maharana, elephants, cavalry, and infantry, are often assembled. From this terrace the city and the valley lie before the spectator, whose vision is bounded only by the distant hills; while from the summit of the palace nothing obstructs the view over lake and mountain."[1]

The entrance to the Palace is through the Bari Pol (1600 A.D.) or Great Gate containing the Royal

[1] *Handbook of Mewar*, by Mehta Fateh Lal, son of a Prime Minister of the Mewar State.

drums, and by the inner Tripulia (1725 A.D.); between the two gates are eight carved arches or torans, under which various Maharanas have been weighed in the past against gold and silver, afterwards distributed in *largesse*. Beyond the Tripulia the Ganesh Dauri gate leads S. to the fine old court known as the Rai Angan or Royal courtyard (1571 A.D.), adjoined on the E. side by the Jewel Room, and from this the visitor will be conducted over a number of palace enclosures, all picturesque and some beautifully decorated. Of these the Chhoti Chitra Shali has brilliant mosaics of peacocks, the Manak (Raby) Mahal is filled wiih figures of glass and porcelain, the Moti (Pearl) Mahal is decorated with mirrors, and the Chini ki Chitra Mahal (1711-34) has beautiful ornamentation of inlaid mirror work, and fine tiles of Dutch and Chinese make; the Bari Mahal or Amar Vilas (1699-1711) has a charming garden in the centre of it. On the W. side of the Tripulia are the Karan Vilas (1620-28 A.D.) and Khush Mahal buildings, while southwards lies the Shambhu Niwas Palace to which the present Maharana has added yet another residence. Beyond and below the line of palaces is the embankment of the lake, reached through a series of beautiful gardens, now named the Sajjan Niwas; and from these a road runs past the Dudh Talai down the E. side of the lake to the Odi Khas, built by the late Chief at its southern end, and from which the expedition by boat on the lake is usually made. The feeding at this place of the wild pig every evening affords a very curious sight. Beautiful as the lake is when seen from the Palace and other points, the view on it near the S. end, with the the marble capped islands in the foreground and the lofty palace and city in the distance, is one of still greater loveliness. The southern island is named the Jagmandar (1640 A.D.), and is chiefly notable for the Gul Mahal, a domed pavilion—most of the other buildings date from the 18th cent. On it Prince Khurram, later Shahjahan, lived when in revolt against his father, the Emperor Jahangir, and the refugee ladies from Neemuch were protected in 1857 (p. 92). Further N. is the Jagniwas Palace island (1740 A.D.) with the older Dilaram and Bari Mahal palaces, in beautiful gardens, and also, unfortunately, with a modern palace and villa; and beyond this again to the W. are two small structures in the lake. The view of the city and ghats and palaces from the bridge below the Gangour Ghat is also specially effective. N. of the Pichola lake is the fine Fateh Sagar constructed by the present Maharana. The foundation-stone of the great embankment was laid by the Duke of Connaught in 1889.

The Chhatris or cenotaphs of the Maharaas at *Ahar* containing the royal ashes stand in what is called the Mahasati or royal place of cremation, which is enclosed by a lofty wall, and is adorned by many fine trees. The most remarkable are those of *Sangram Singh II.*[1] (1734), a large and beautiful structure, and of Amar Singh, grandson of Udai Singh (1616). Besides the modern village of Ahar there are ruined temples of an older town.

Special arrangements are necessary to visit the *great lake at Kankroli*, or Rajnagar, called the Rajsamandra,[2] 35 m. to the N. of Udaipur. The retaining wall is of massive masonry, in many places 40 ft. high. The Band or Ghat is 1115 ft. long, with pavilions and torans or ornamental arches all of marble; behind is an embankment 35 yds. wide. It was erected (1660) as a famine work. On the S.E. side of the lake is the town of Kankroli, with a beautiful temple. There is a fair cart-track to this place. 14 m. N. of Udaipur are the Eklingi lake and temple, a beautiful structure of white marble, sacred to the family deity of the Maharana. Near this, at Nagda, are two fine Jain temples, called the Sas Bahu, or Mother and Daughter-in-Law.

1 See Fergusson's *Indian Architecture*, ii. 165.

2 *Ibid.* 134.

The route to the Jaisamand lake, made at the end of the 17th century, and about 25 m. S.E. of Udaipur, runs through a wild country; it is about 9 m. by 5 m., and is one of the most beautiful sights in India. The dam is 1000 ft. in length and 98 ft in height. There is a fair road to it also.

---

378 m. **Nasirabad** station, D.B. (population 22,000). The military cantonment for Ajmer. The station was originally laid out in 1818 by Sir David Ochterlony. Interest is attached to Nasirabad from the fact that when the mutiny broke out in 1857, the 1st Bombay Cavalry were compelled to remain neutral—though loyally inclined—as their families were at the mercy of the Bengal regiment, which mutinied and marched to Delhi.

Deoli, a small cantonment of an Irregular Force lying 57 m. S.E. of Nasirabad, may be reached by tonga ordered from the latter place. The Kotah contingent stationed at Deoli in 1857 marched to Agra, but mutinied there. 25 m. beyond Deoli is the picturesque city of Boondi, D.B.—introduction to Political Agent, Kotah and Boondi, necessary.

393 m. **Ajmer** junction station (see Route 10).

ROUTE 9.

ITARSI JUNCTION to **JHANSI**, by **Bhopal**, **Sanchi**, and **Bina** (line to **Saugor** and **Bárán**) and from Jhansi to

(*a*) **Kalpi** and Cawnpore;
(*b*) **Datia**, **Gwalior**, **Dholpur**, and Agra, Muttra and Delhi;
(*c*) **Orchha**, **Barwa Saugor**, **Banda** and Manikpur, with excursions to **Nowgong** and **Khajurahu**.

Itarsi junction station, 464 m. from Bombay on the G.I.P. Railway (see p. 29). The line followed by this route is that of the Indian Midland, which is managed by the G.I.P. Railway; it formed the speediest route between Bombay and the N.W. of India until the Rutlum-Nagda-Muttra route (p. 122) was opened. Mail from Bombay to Cawnpore and to Agra, 26 hours, and to Delhi, Lahore, and Peshawar, 30, 40, and 53 hours respectively.

Fares to Delhi, Rs.69, Rs.34, and Rs.9.

11 m. **Hoshangabad** station, D.B., named after Hoshang Ghori (p. 89). A town with population of 16,000, and headquarters of a district. Passing this the railway crosses the Nerbudda on a fine bridge. About 4 m. N. of the Nerbudda river the well-wooded, picturesque ascent of the ghat commences, and at the top the line runs on the tableland of Malwa, with an average elevation of 1500 ft.

57 m. **Bhopal** station (R.) D.B. [Branch to Ujjain]. The town (population 55,000) stands on the N. bank of a fine and extensive lake, 4½ m. long and 1½ broad, and is enclosed by a wall 2 m. in circuit. It is the capital of a native state, under the Central Indian Agency, with an area of 8200 sq. m. The dynasty was founded by Dost Muhammad, an Afghan chief in the service of Aurangzeb, who took advantage of the troubles that followed the Emperor's death to establish his independence. His family have always shown their friendship for the British. In 1778, when General Goddard made his famous march across India, Bhopal was the only Indian state which showed itself friendly. In 1809, when General Close commanded another expedition in the neighbourhood, the Nawab of Bhopal applied to be received under British protection, but without success. The Nawab then obtained assistance from the Pindaris, in the gallant struggle he maintained to defend himself against Sindhia and Raghoji Bhonsla, in the course of which his capital underwent a severe but ineffectual siege.

In 1817 the British Government intervened and formed an alliance with the Nawab, who was, in

1818, guaranteed his possessions, by treaty, on condition of furnishing 600 horse and 400 infantry, to maintain which five districts in Malwa were assigned to him. He was soon afterwards killed by a pistol accidentally discharged by a child. His nephew, a boy, was declared his successor, and betrothed to his infant daughter, but the Nawab's widow, Kudsia Begam, endeavoured to keep the government in her own hands, and the declared heir resigned his claim to the throne and to the hand of the Nawab's daughter, Sikandar Begam, in favour of his brother Jahangir Muhammad. After long dissensions, Jahangir Muhammad was installed as Nawab, in 1837, through the mediation of the British. He died in 1844, and was succeeded by his widow, Sikandar Begam, who ruled till her death in 1868. She left one daughter, Shah Jahan Begam, who ruled till 1900, and was succeeded by Nawab, Her Highness Sultan Begam, G.C.S.I., G.C.I.E. The State maintains 694 horse, 2200 foot, 14 field guns, and 43 other guns, with 291 artillerymen, and pays £20,000 to the British Government in lieu of a contingent.

The name of Bhopal is said to be derived from that of its founder, Raja Bhoj, and the dam by which he formed the Tank; dam being in Hindi *pal*. Thus Bhojpal has been corrupted into Bhopal.

The *Palace of the Begam* is not of much architectural beauty, but is a large and imposing building. The *Citadel* walls afford a fine view of the lake and surrounding country. The *Jama Masjid* was built by the late Kudsia Begam, and the *Moti Masjid*, which somewhat resembles the Mosque at Delhi, by the late Sikandar Begam. The *Mint* and *Arsenal*, and the *Gardens* of the Kudsia and Sikandar Begams also deserve a visit.

The Water-works of the town were built by the Kudsia Begam.

91 m. **Bhilsa** station. A fortified town in the Bhopal state. Population 7000. In the fort lies an old gun, 19½ ft. in length, with a bore of 10 in., said to have been made by order of the Emperor Jahangir. Bhilsa is now chiefly noteworthy as a famous place of Hindu pilgrimage to the temples, picturesquely situated in the bed of the Betwa river, and as giving its name to the remarkable and interesting series of Buddhist Topes found in its neighbourhood.[1] The principal of these is at

85 m. **Sanchi**,[2] the station before Bhilsa. There is a good D.B. of the Bhopal state near the station, and fast trains can be stopped here by communication beforehand to the station-master of Bhopal or Bina.

The Great Tope at Sanchi, anciently called Chaitya giri, the Chapel Hill, and the ruined buildings surrounding it are situated on a level platform upon the top of the hill, which is about 350 ft. above the plain, and is approached by an easy path. The Tope with its rail and gateways were carefully and satisfactorily restored in 1883. They now form one of the most picturesque as well as one of the most interesting monuments of India. The dome, which is 42 ft. high and 106 ft. in diameter, rises from a plinth of 14 ft.; this is surmounted by a terraced path, reached by steps on the S. side, used by worshippers for the perambulation of the Tope and the relic buried in it. The Tope was crowned by an altar or pedestal surrounded by a rail, and must once have been nearly 100 ft. high, but these have not been restored; the pillars of the rail will be noticed on the ground at

1 These are described in General Cunningham's *Bilsa Topes*, 1 vol. 8vo. 1854; also in Fergusson's *Tree and Serpent Worship*. One half of this book and forty-five of its plates, besides woodcuts, are devoted to the illustration of the Great Tope. Casts of the E. gateway are in the South Kensington and Edinburgh Museum.

2 General Maisey's *Sanchi and its Remains* (in 1850-51) published in 1892, and a selection of photographs published under the orders of Sir Lepel Griffin, K.C.S.I., when Agent to the Governor-General for Central India, contain full illustrations of the tope and its sculptures.

the N.E. side of the level platform. The Tope was enclosed below at a distance of 9½ ft. from it by a great railing slightly elliptical in shape, the diameter from W. to E. being

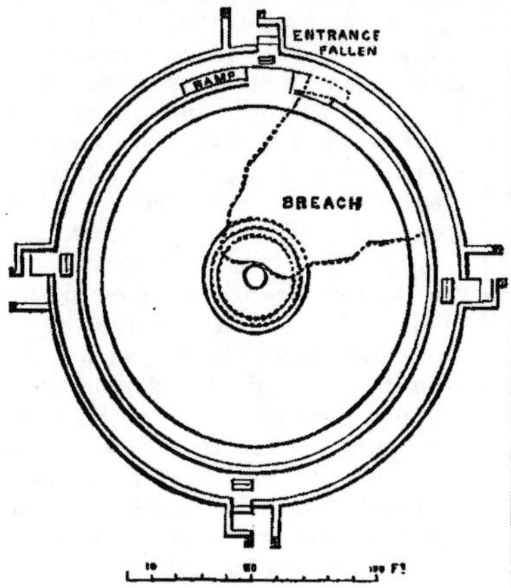

Plan.

144 ft. and from N. to S. 151 ft. The railing is formed of pillars nearly

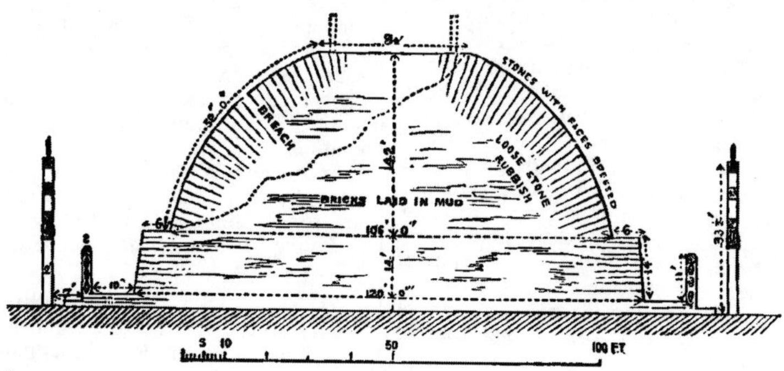

Section. Great Tope at Sanchi.

10 ft. high, carrying three bars, each 2 ft. 2 in. long, and separated by an interval of 3 in., let into them; a rounded coping stone surmounts the whole. At each cardinal point the railing is broken by a splendidly decorated gateway 18 ft. high and 7 ft. bread, crowned by a superstructure of three stages of cross-beams, surmounted by a wheel and other Buddhist emblems; facing each gateway, with its back to the wall of the plinth, is a large seated statue, probably representing the four last Buddhas. The faces of the pillars of the gateways and of the cross-beams are elaborately carved with a series of most interesting scenes, of which the following are the principal.

North Gateway. Pillars surmounted by elephants and riders. *Right pillar*—front face: Staircase and Buddhist railing. Inner face: Worship of tope and trees, monkey worshippers in one scene. *Left pillar*—front face: Worship of tree, procession, scenes at fountain. Inner face: Cave temple, procession, tree worship. The *Architraves* bear scenes of processions with chariots, tree worship, and dagoba worship, and on the back of giants' and of hermits' huts. The floral patterns on the outer sides of these pillars are noticeable.

East Gateway.—Pillars surmounted by elephants and riders. *Right pillar* — front face: Palace scenes, including dance by women. Inner face: Dream of Maya, Prince Siddhartha, and five disciples. *Left pillar* — front face: Worship of symbol of the law (wheel and trident), boat scene of mourning, Buddha leaving his home. Inner face: Kitchen scene, fire worship, hermit scene. *Architraves*—Front: Worship of topes and trees and of impression of Buddha's feet—Back: worship of trees by human beings, various animals, and elephants.

South Gateway. — Pillars surmounted by four lions. *Left pillar*—front: Casket scene in palace, worship of topes, siege, and relic procession. *Architraves* — Siege of a city. The right pillar of this gate has not been found.

Western Gateway. — Pillars surmounted by four dwarfs. *Right pillar*—front: Trial of the bow, tree worship. Back: Worship of trees, one under an umbrella. *Left pillar*—front: Love scenes. Back: Hermits, tree festival, boat scene. *Architraves*—front: Procession with relic-casket, worship of symbol and trees. Back: Worship of topes and temple, triumphal procession.

The railing and the Tope in its present shape are held to date from the time of Asoka, about 250 B.C., and the gates from about 50 A.D. The statues are the latest of the additions made to the Tope, and belong to the 4th or 5th century of our era.

Close to the S. gate are the remains of a fine pillar nearly 40 ft. high, which carried a bell-shaped capital of four lions back to back; another stood near the northern gate. On the platform will be observed many interesting sculptures, and remains, including a huge stone bowl. To the S. of the Tope are the ruins of the only structural chaitya chapel known to exist; the colonnade of the nave and apsidal end can be clearly recognised.

To the W. a path descends steeply to the smaller Tope near the foot of the hill: this also has a very interesting railing, 7½ ft. high, with carved medallions on the pillars, and well-sculptured scenes on the gateways, and should be visited on the way back to the rest-house. In it were found relics of Kasyapa and Mogaliputra, well-known Buddhist apostles in the 3rd century B.C.

Besides the group at Sanchi, there is at *Sonari*, 6 m. off, a group of eight topes, of which two are important structures in square courtyards, and in one of these numerous relics were found. At *Sadhara*, 3 m. farther, is a tope 101 ft. in diameter, which yielded no relics, and one 24 ft. in diameter, in which were found relics of Sariputra and others like those found at Sanchi. At *Besnagar* near Bhilsa was lately found a column referring to the Græco Bactrian King Antialkidas, of the date of 140 B.C.

At *Bhojpur*, 7 m. from Sanchi, are thirty-seven topes, the largest 66 ft. in diameter, and in the next to it important relics were found. At *Andher*, 5 m. W. of Bhojpur, is a group of three small but very interesting topes. "As far as can be at present ascertained," says Mr Fergusson, "there is no reason for assuming that any of these topes are earlier than the age of Asoka, 250 B.C., nor later than the 1st century A.D., though their rails may be later."

143 m. **Bina** junction (R.).

[Hence a line runs N.W. to 73 m. Goona, 147 m. Baran, and 188 m. Kotah (p. 122), on the new direct route between Bombay and Delhi, controlled by the Bombay Baroda and Central Indian Railway, and another 165 m. S.E. to Saugor, Damoh, and Katni on the E.I.R. (p. 30). 8 m. from Bina, at Eran, are some Jain and Buddhist ruins, including two lats or monolithic pillars.

15 m. **Saugor**, D.B. Principal town and headquarters of Saugor district, Central Provinces, and a military cantonment. Population 42,000. Saugor stands 1940 ft. above sea-level, on the borders of a fine lake, nearly 1 m. broad, from which it derives its name. The lake is said to be an ancient Banjara work, but the present city dates only from the end of the 17th century, and owes its rise to a Bundela Raja, who built a small fort on the site of the present structure in 1660, and founded a village called **Parkota**,

now a quarter of the modern town. During the mutiny of 1857 the town and fort were held by the English for eight months, until the arrival of Sir Hugh Rose. During that time the whole of the surrounding country was in possession of the rebels.

Saugor town is well built, with wide streets. The large bathing-ghats on the banks of the lake, for the most part surrounded with Hindu temples, add much to its appearance.

The existing *Fort* at Saugor was completed by the Mahrattas about 1780. It stands on a height N.W. of the lake, commanding the whole of the city and surrounding country, and consists of twenty round towers, varying from 20 to 40 ft. in height, connected by thick curtain walls. It encloses a space of 6 acres, for the most part covered with old Mahratta buildings two storeys high. In 1862 an unhealthy swamp lying N.E. of the lake, which cut off the quarter called Gopalganj from the rest of the city, was converted into a large garden with numerous drives and a piece of ornamental water.]

182 m. **Lalitpur** station, D.B. The headquarters of a district of the same name. Population 11,000.

207 m. **Talbahat** station. A picturesque town with a large piece of artificial water covering more than 1 sq. m. The water is retained by damming the streams that flow through a rocky barrier about 800 ft. high.

238 m. **Jhansi** junction station (R., D.B.) centre of the Indian Midland Railway system. The main line runs N. to Gwalior and Agra, one branch N.E. to Cawnpore, and another E. through Banda to the E.I. Ry. at Manikpur (p. 30). Jhansi (lat. 25° 27′, long. 78° 37′, population 70,000), is one of the main halting-places for troops proceeding up country. It is well worthy of a visit on account of its Fort, which the British Government have exchanged with Maharaja Sindhia for Gwalior; and on account of the various places of interest, Datia, Orchha, Barwa Saugor, which can be reached from it.

The Province of **Bundelkund**, in which Jhansi is situated, was for ages one of the most turbulent and difficult to manage in all India. In the early part of the 17th century the Orchha state was governed by Bir Singh Deo, who built the Fort of Jhansi, 8 m. to the N. of his capital, which is situated on an island in the Betwa river. He incurred the heavy displeasure of Akbar by the murder of Abul Fazl, the Emperor's favourite minister and historian, at the instigation of Prince Salim, afterwards known as the Emperor Jahangir. A force was accordingly sent against him in 1602; the country was ravaged and devastated, but Bir Singh himself contrived to escape. On the accession of his patron, Salim, in 1605, he was naturally pardoned, and rose into great favour; but when, on the death of that emperor in 1627, Shah Jahan mounted the throne, Bir Sing revolted. His rebellion was unsuccessful, and although he was permitted to keep possession of his dominions, he never regained all his former power and independence. During the troubled times which succeeded, Orchha was sometimes in the hands of the Mohammedans and sometimes fell under the power of Bundela chieftains. In 1732 Chatar Sal found it expedient to call in the aid of the Mahrattas, who were then invading the Central Provinces under their first Peshwa, Baji Rao. They came to his assistance with their accustomed promptitude, and were rewarded on the chief's death, in 1734, by a bequest of one-third of his dominions. The territory so granted included portions of the modern division of Jhansi, but not the existing district itself. In 1742, however, the Mahrattas found a pretext for attacking the Orchha state, and annexing that amongst other territories. Their general founded the city of Jhansi, and peopled it with the inhabitants of Orchha.

The district remained under the rule of the Peshwas until 1817, when their rights passed to the E.I. Company. Under British protection, native Rajas ruled until their folly and incompetency ruined the country, and when the dynasty died out in 1853 their territories lapsed to the British Government. The Jhansi state, with Jalaun and Chanderi districts, were then formed into a Superintendency, while a pension was granted to the Rani or widow of the late Raja Rao. The Rani, however, considered herself aggrieved, both because she was not allowed to adopt an heir, and because the slaughter of cattle was permitted in the Jhansi territory.

The events of 1857 accordingly found Jhansi ripe for rebellion. In May it was known that the troops were disaffected, and on the 5th of June a few men of the 12th Native Infantry seized the fort containing the treasure and magazine. Many European officers were shot the same day. The remainder, who had taken refuge in a fort, capitulated a few days after, and were massacred with their families to the number of sixty-six persons, in spite of a promise of protection sworn on the Koran and Ganges water. The Rani then attempted to seize the supreme authority, but the usual anarchic quarrels arose between the rebels, during which the Orchha leaders laid siege to Jhansi and plundered the country mercilessly. On the 4th of April 1858 the fort and town were captured by Sir Hugh Rose, who marched on to Kalpi without being able to leave a garrison at Jhansi. After his departure, the rebellion broke out afresh, only the Gursarai chieftain in the N. remaining faithful to the British cause. On the 11th August a flying column under Colonel Liddell cleared out the rebels from Mau, and after a series of sharp contests with various guerilla leaders, the work of reorganisation was fairly set on foot in November. The Rani herself had previously fled with Tantia Topi, and finally fell in a battle at the foot of the rock fortress of Gwalior.

The siege of Jhansi occupied Sir Hugh Rose's army from 21st March till 4th April 1858, and cost 343 in killed and wounded, of whom 36 were officers. The engineers lost four officers leading the attacking parties at the final escalade. Col. Malleson, quoting Sir Hugh Rose, gives the following description of Jhansi at the time of the investment:—

"The great strength of the **Fort** of Jhansi, natural as well as artificial, and its extent, entitle it to a place among fortresses. It stands on an elevated rock, rising out of a plain, and commands the city and surrounding country. It is built of excellent and most massive masonry. The fort is difficult to breach, because composed of granite; its walls vary in thickness from 16 to 20 ft. It has extensive and elaborate outworks of the same solid construction, with front and flanking embrasures for artillery-fire, and loop-holes, of which in some places there were five tiers for musketry. On one tower, called the 'white turret,' since raised in height, waved in proud defiance the standard of the high-spirited Rani. The fortress is surrounded on all sides by the city of Jhansi, the W. and part of the S. face excepted. The steepness of the rock protects the W.; the fortified city wall springs from the centre of its S. face, and ends in a high mound or mamelon, which protects by a flanking fire its S. face. The mound was fortified by a strong circular bastion for five guns, round part of which was drawn a ditch, 12 ft. deep and 15 ft. broad of solid masonry.

"The city of Jhansi is about 4½ m. in circumference, and is surrounded by a fortified and massive wall, from 6 to 12 ft. thick, and varying in height from 18 to 30 ft., with numerous flanking bastions armed as batteries, with ordnance and loopholes, and with a banquette for infantry. The town and fortress were garrisoned by 11,000 men, composed of rebel sepoys, foreign mercenaries, and local levies, and they were led by a woman who believed her cause to be just."

The Fort has been modernised and supplied with strong armament. The views from the top and from the road round the ramparts are very extensive.

The old civil station (**Jhansi Nauabad**) attached to Jhansi before 1861 remains the headquarters of the district.

(1) *Jhansi* to *Cawnpore*. 137 m.

Between Jhansi and Cawnpore the country abounds in black buck. Numerous old fortified villages are seen from the railway train.

308 m. **Orai** (*Urai*) station (R.). A thriving place of 8000 inhabitants, and the headquarters of the Jalaun district.

329 m. **Kalpi** station. The town is situated amongst deep rugged ravines on the right bank of the Jumna, which is here crossed by a fine iron girder bridge.

Tradition says that the town was founded by Basdeo or Vasuveda, who ruled at Kamba from 330 to 400 A.D. During the Mughal period Kalpi played so large a part in the annals of this part of India that it would be impossible to detail its history at length. After the Mahrattas interfered in the affairs of Bundelkund, the headquarters of their government were fixed at Kalpi. At the time of the British occupation of Bundelkund in 1803, Nana Gobind Rao seized upon the town. The British besieged it in December of that year, and, after a few hours' resistance, it surrendered. Kalpi was then included in the territory granted to Raja Himmat Bahadur, on whose death, in 1804, it once more lapsed to Government. It was next handed over to Gobind Rao, who exchanged it two years later for villages farther to the W. Since that time Kalpi has remained a British possession. After the capture of Jhansi, and the rout of the mutineers at Koonch, they fell back on Kalpi, which throughout the previous operations they had made their principal arsenal. Here, on 22nd May 1858, Sir Hugh Rose (Lord Strathnairn) again defeated a force of about 12,000 under the Rani of Jhansi, the Rao Sahib, and the Nawab of Banda, who then fled to Gwalior.

Kalpi was formerly a place of far greater importance than at the present day. The E.I. Company made it one of their principal stations for providing their commercial investments. The western outskirts of the town contain a large number of ruins, notably the tomb called the *84 Domes*, and twelve other handsome mausoleums. The buildings of the old commercial agency crown high ground near the river bank, but are now deserted. A ruined fort, situated on the steep bank of the Jumna above the town overhangs the ghat or ferry, which has a picturesque temple, and is reached by a long flight of steps.

374 m. **Cawnpore** Jn. station (p. 301).

(2) *Jhansi* to *Agra* via *Datia*, *Gwalior and Dholpur*. 137 m.

254 m. from Itarsi, 16 m. from Jhansi, is **Datia** station. The town has 24,000 inhabitants, and is the residence of the Chief of the Datia state, which contains an area of 836 sq. m.

It stands on a rocky height surrounded by a good stone wall, and is full of picturesque houses and palaces. The Raja's present residence stands within the town surrounded by a pretty garden. To the W. of the town, beyond the walls, is a very large palace of great architectural beauty, now untenanted.[1]

262 m. **Sonagir** station. 2 m. off and visible from the railway are a number of Jain temples of modern date, forming an extremely picturesque group well worth a visit.

299 m. **Gwalior** station. (R.), D.B. The capital of Maharaja Sindhia. The present chief is Major-General Maharaja Sir Madho Rao Sindhia, G.C.S.I., G.C.V.O., A.D.C., LL.D.

[1] Fergusson's *Indian Architecture*, ii. 173.

Cantab. The area of the Gwalior state is 25,000 sq. m., the population 3 millions, and the revenue 140 lakhs. The place is famous for its fort, one of the most ancient and renowned strongholds in India. Population 89,000; Lashkar, 47,000.

For many years a strong brigade of British troops was maintained at *Morar*, a few m. E. of the fort. The latter was garrisoned by British troops from 1858 to 1886, when it was restored to the Maharaja's custody, and with Morar was made over to him in exchange for Jhansi.

History.

General Cunningham, in vol. ii. of the *Reports of the Archæological Survey*, gives a most valuable account of Gwalior. It is believed to have been founded in the 3rd century A.D., when Toramana, a tributary prince under the Guptas, rebelled, and became sovereign of all the territory between the Jumna and Nerbudda. In the reign of his son, the Sun Temple was built and the Suraj Kund excavated; and Gwalior was founded by Suraj Sen, a Kachhwaha chief, who was a leper, and coming when hunting to the Gopagiri hill, on which the fort stands, received a drink of water from the hermit Gwalipa, which cured him of his leprosy. Suraj Sen also received a new name, Suhan Pal, from the hermit, with a promise that his descendants should reign as long as they were called Pal; so eighty-three reigned, but the eighty-fourth was called Tej Karn, and having discarded the name of Pal lost his kingdom.

This Kachhwaha dynasty was succeeded by seven Parihara princes, who ruled for 103 years till 1232 A.D., when Gwalior was taken by Altamsh, in the 21st year of the reign of Sarang Deo.

The capture of Gwalior by Altamsh was commemorated in an inscription placed over the gate of the Urwahi, and the Emperor Babar states that he saw it, and the date was 630 A.H. = 1232 A.D. From 1232 onwards the Emperors of Delhi used Gwalior as a state prison. In 1375 A.D. the Tomar chief, Bir Sing Deo, declared himself independent, and founded the Tomar dynasty of Gwalior.

Early in the 15th century the Gwalior chiefs paid tribute to Khizr Khan of Delhi, and in 1424 Gwalior, being besieged by Hoshang Shah of Malwa, was delivered by Mubarak Shah of Delhi. In 1425, Dongar Sing commenced the great rock sculptures at Gwalior, and his son Kirti Sing, 1454, completed them. In 1465 Husain Shah the Sharki king of Jaunpur, besieged Gwalior, and obliged it to pay tribute. Man Sing acknowledged the supremacy of Bahlol Lodi and of Sikandar Lodi of Delhi; the latter in 1505 marched against Gwalior, but fell into an ambuscade and was repulsed with great loss. In 1506, however, he captured Himmatgarh, but passed by Gwalior, which he despaired of reducing. In 1517 he made great preparations at Agra for the conquest of Gwalior, but died before he could accomplish his purpose. Ibrahim Lodi sent an army of 30,000 horse, 300 elephants, and other troops, against Gwalior, and a few days after they reached that place Man Sing died. He was the greatest of the Tomar princes of Gwalior, and constructed many useful works, amongst others, the great tank to the N.W. of Gwalior, called the *Moti Jhil*. His palace in the Fort is the noblest specimen of Hindu domestic architecture in N. India. After Man Sing's death his son Vikramaditya, sustained the siege for a year, but at last surrendered, and was sent to Agra, where he became the friend of the Emperor, and died fighting at his side against Babar on the field of Panipat in 1526 A.D. His widows, according to tradition, presented the Koh-i-nur to Prince Humayun in return for the protection accorded by him to them.

Babar sent Rahimdad with an army to Gwalior, which he took by a stratagem, suggested by the holy Muhammad Ghaus. In 1542 Abul-Kasim, Governor of Gwalior, surrendered his fortress to Sher Shah. In 1545 Salim, son of Sher, brought his treasure from Chunar to Gwalior, and in 1553 died at the latter place. Rana Sah, son of Vikram, tried to seize Gwalior, and fought a great battle there, which lasted for three days, with Akbar's troops, but was defeated, and the fortress remained in the hands of the Mughals till the fall of their power. In 1761 Gwalior was taken by Bhim Singh, the Jat Rana of Gohad, and in 1779 captured by Major Popham from the Mahrattas, into whose hands it had fallen, and restored to the Rana of Gohad. It was again taken by the Mahrattas under Mahadaji Sindhia[1] in 1784, and once more captured by the English under General White in 1803, and restored to the Mahrattas in 1805. In 1844, after the battles of Maharajpur and Paniar, it was a third time occupied by the British.

At the time of the Mutiny Maharaja Sindhia had, besides 10,000 troops of his own, a contingent consisting of two regiments of Irregular Cavalry—1158 men of all ranks—seven regiments of Infantry aggregating 6412 men, and 26 guns, with 748 Artillerymen. This force was officered by Englishmen, and the men were thoroughly drilled and disciplined, and were, in fact, excellent soldiers, as they proved by defeating and almost driving into the river General Windham's brigade at Cawnpore.

The Maharaja and his minister, Sir Dinkar Rao, remained loyal to their fealty; but the contingent troops mutinied on Sunday, 14th June, and murdered their English officers, and a number of women and children; and those who escaped, or had previously taken refuge in the Maharaja's palace, had to be removed to Dholpur, and thence to Agra. After this Gwalior remained quiet for a time; but later the contingent troops joined Tantia Topi at Cawnpore.

On the 22nd May 1858 an important battle was fought in front of Kalpi, in which the mutineers, led by Tantia Topi and the Rani of Jhansi, were severely defeated by Sir Hugh Rose. They retreated in the direction of Gwalior; and on the 1st June Sindhia with all his army moved out from Gwalior to meet them. The engagement took place about 2 m. E. of Morar. Colonel Malleson thus describes it:—"Sindhia had with him 6000 infantry, about 1500 cavalry, his own bodyguard 600 strong, and eight guns, ranged in three divisions—his guns centre. About 7 o'clock in the morning the rebels advanced. As they approached, Sindhia's eight guns opened on them. But the smoke of the discharge had scarcely disappeared when the rebel skirmishers closed to their flanks, and 2000 horsemen, charging at a gallop, carried the guns. Simultaneously with their charge, Sindhia's infantry and cavalry, his bodyguard alone excepted, either joined the rebels or took up a position indicative of their intention not to fight. . . . The rebels then attacked the bodyguard, who defended themselves bravely, but the contest was too unequal, and Sindhia was compelled to fly, accompanied by a very few of the survivors. He did not draw rein till he reached Agra."

The Rani thereupon seized the Fort of Gwalior and proclaimed the Nana as Peshwa. On hearing of this Sir Hugh Rose immediately marched upon Gwalior. As he neared it he was joined by Sir Robert Napier (Lord Napier of Magdala), who took command of the 2nd Brigade, and by the Hyderabad troops. On 16th June he came into touch with the rebels at Bahadurpur, near Morar. In spite of the long and fatiguing march which his force had endured, Sir Hugh attacked the enemy at once, and drove them from their position.

"The main body of the enemy,

[1] This prince was wounded at the battle of Panipat (p. 215), where one of his brothers was killed. Two more brothers fell in other engagements.

driven through the cantonments, fell back on a dry nullah with high banks, running round a village which they had also occupied. Here they maintained a desperate hand-to-hand struggle with the British. The 71st Highlanders suffered severely, Lieutenant Neave, whilst leading his men, falling mortally wounded; nor was it till the nullah was nearly choked with dead that the village was carried. The victory was completed by a successful pursuit and slaughter of the rebels by the 14th Light Dragoons."

Early next morning (the 17th of June), Brigadier-General Smith, marching up from Jhansi, reached Kotah-ki-sarai, 5 m. to the S.E. of Gwalior, without opposition. There he discovered the enemy in great force, and showing a disposition to attack. "Reconnoitring the ground in front of him, he found it very difficult, intersected with nullahs and impracticable for cavalry. He discovered, moreover, that the enemy's guns were in position about 1500 yds. from Kotah-ki-sarai, and that their line lay under the hills, crossing the road to Gwalior. Notwithstanding this, General Smith determined to attack. First he sent his horse artillery to the front, and silenced the enemy's guns, which limbered up and retired. He then sent his infantry across the broken ground, under the command of Colonel Raines of the 95th. Raines led his men, covered by skirmishers, to a point about 50 yds. from the enemy's works, when the skirmishers made a rush, the rebels falling back as they did so. Raines then found himself stopped by a deep ditch with 4 ft. of water," but surmounting the difficulty he gained the abandoned entrenchment. "Whilst he was continuing his advance across the broken and hilly ground, General Smith moved his cavalry across the river Umrah, close to Kotah-ki-sarai. They had hardly crossed when they came under fire of a battery which till then had escaped notice. At the same time a body of the enemy threatened the baggage at Kotah-ki-sarai. Matters now became serious. But General Smith sent back detachments to defend the baggage and rear, and pushed forward. The road, before debouching from the hills between his position and Gwalior, ran for several hundred yards through a defile along which a canal had been excavated. It was while his troops were pressing through this defile that the principal fighting took place. Having gained the farther end of the defile, where he joined Colonel Raines, General Smith halted the infantry to guard it, and ordered a cavalry charge. This was most gallantly executed by a squadron of the 8th Hussars, led by Colonel Hicks and Captain Heneage. The rebels, horse and foot, gave way before them. The Hussars captured two guns, and continuing the pursuit through Sindhia's cantonment, had for a moment the rebel camp in their possession.

"Amongst the fugitives in the rebel ranks was the resolute woman who, alike in counsel and on the field, was the soul of the conspirators. Clad in the attire of a man and mounted on horseback, the Rani of Jhansi might have been seen animating her troops throughout the day. When inch by inch the British troops pressed through the pass, and when reaching its summit General Smith ordered the Hussars to charge, the Rani of Jhansi boldly fronted the British horsemen. When her comrades failed her, her horse, in spite of her efforts carried her along with the others. With them she might have escaped, but that her horse, crossing the canal near the cantonment, stumbled and fell. A Hussar, close upon her track, ignorant of her sex and her rank, cut her down. She fell to rise no more. That night, her devoted followers, determined that the English should not boast that they had captured her even dead, burned her body."

Following up the operations above described late into the night of the 19th June, Sir Hugh regained the whole place—Morar, the city, the Lashkar—everything but the Fort, which was held by a few fanatics, who had fired on our advancing troops whenever they could throughout the day, and recommenced the following morning.

"On the morning of the 20th, Lieutenant Rose, 25th Bombay Native Infantry, was in command with a detachment of his regiment at the kotwali, or police-station, not far from the main gateway of the rock fort. As the guns from its ramparts continued to fire, Rose proposed to a brother officer, Lieutenant Waller, who commanded a small party of the same regiment near him, that they should attempt to capture the fortress with their joint parties, urging that if the risk was great, the honour would be still greater. Waller cheerfully assented, and the two officers set off with their men and a blacksmith, whom, not unwilling, they had engaged for the service. They crept up to the first gateway unseen. Then the blacksmith, a powerful man, forced it open; and so with the other five gates that opposed their progress. By the time the sixth gate had been forced the alarm was given, and when the assailants reached the archway beyond the last gate, they were met by the fire of a gun which had been brought to bear on them. Dashing onwards, unscathed by the fire, they were speedily engaged in a hand-to-hand contest with the garrison. The fight was desperate, and many men fell on both sides. The gallantry of Rose and Waller and their men carried all before them. Rose especially distinguished himself. Just in the hour of victory, however, as he was inciting his men to make the final charge, which proved successful, a musket was fired at him from behind the wall. The man who had fired the shot, a mutineer from Bareilly, then rushed out and cut him down. Waller came up, and despatched the rebel; too late, however, to save his friend. But the rock fortress was gained."

The New City or **Lashkar.**—When Daulat Rao Sindhia obtained possession of Gwalior in 1794 and 1805, he pitched his camp to the S. of the fort, and a new city rapidly sprung up, which still retains the name of Lashkar, or the camp. The *Sarafa*, or merchants' quarter, is one of the finest streets in India. In the *Phul Bagh* is the *Jai Bilas Palace* of Maharaja Sindhia[1] (not shown to visitors). In the centre of Lashkar is the *Barah*, or *Old Palace*, and near it are the houses of the chief Sirdars.

The new buildings worthy of a visit are the *Dufferin Sarai*, the *Jayaji Rao Memorial Hospital*, and the *Victoria College* and *Market*; the foundation-stone of the latter was laid by the Duke of Connaught, and it and the electrical installation were opened by King George in December 1905. The modern *Temple* was erected by the mother of one of the Sindhia chiefs.

The **Old City** has been gradually decaying, and is now only one-sixth as large as the New City. It is a crowded mass of small, flat-roofed, stone houses, lying along the foot of the N.E. and N. end of the rock. Flanking the city to the N. stands a curious old Pathan archway, the remains of a tomb. Outside the gate of the fort is the **Jama Masjid**, with its gilt pinnacled domes and lofty minarets. Sir W. Sleeman says (*Rambles*, i. 347): "It is a very beautiful mosque, with one end built by Muhammad Khan, in 1665 A.D., of the white sandstone of the rock above it. It looks as fresh as if it had not been finished a month."

On the eastern outskirt of the city, is the noble tomb of the **Muhammad Ghaus**, a saint venerated in the time of Babar and Akbar. It is of stone, and is one of the best specimens of Mohammedan architecture[2] of the early Mughal period. It is a square of 100 ft., with hexagonal towers at

[1] The public rooms of the Maharaja's Palace are shown upon application duly made.

[2] See Fergusson's *Indian Architecture*, ii. 292.

the four corners, attached at the angles instead of the sides. The tomb is a hall 43 ft. sq., with the angles cut off by pointed arches, from which springs a lofty Pathan dome. The walls are $5\frac{1}{2}$ ft. thick, and are surrounded by a lofty verandah, with square bays in the centre of each side, enclosed by stone lattices of the most intricate and elaborate patterns. These are protected from the weather by very bold eaves, supported on long stone slabs resting on brackets. The dome was once covered with blue glazed tiles.

The **Tomb of Tansen**, a famous musician, is a small open building 22 ft. sq., supported on pillars round the tombstone, close to the S.W. corner of the large tomb. The tamarind tree near the grave is much visited by musicians, as the chewing of the leaves is alleged to impart a wonderful sweetness to the voice.

To see the **Gwalior Fort**[1] *an order is necessary:* it can be obtained at the Residency Office, or from the keeper of the Maharaja's bungalow for strangers, who will make arrangements for the elephant which the Maharaja kindly puts at the disposal of visitors, to meet them at the foot of the steep ascent to the fort.

"The great fortress of Gwalior," says General Cunningham, "is situated on a precipitous, flat-topped, and isolated hill of sandstone," which rises 300 ft. above the town at the N. end, but only 274 ft. at the upper gate of the principal entrance. The hill is long and narrow; its extreme length from N. to S. is $1\frac{3}{4}$ m., while its breadth varies from 600 ft. to 2800 ft. The walls are from 30 to 35 ft. high, and the rock immediately below them is steeply but irregularly scarped all round the hill.

The **view** from the fort is varied and extensive, but, except during the rainy season, when the hills are green, the general appearance of the country is brown and arid. To the N., on a clear day, may be seen the gigantic temple of Suhania, about 30 m. distant, and still farther in the same direction the red hills of Dholpur. To the W. and within gunshot lies the long flat-topped sandstone hill of Hanuman, with a basaltic peak at the N. end, and a white-washed temple on its slope, whence the hill has its name. Beyond, far as the eye can reach, nothing is seen but range after range of low sandstone hills. The conical peak of the Raipur hill towers over the lower ranges in the S., and to the E. the level plains, dotted with villages, lengthen till they pass out of sight. On the plain below lies the Old City of Gwalior, encircling the N.E. end of the fortress, and to the S., upwards of 1 m. distant is the New City of *Lashkar.*

The *main entrance* to the Fort is on the N.E. The ascent was formerly by many flights of broad steps alternating with pieces of paved level road, but these have been removed, and there is now a continuous road. The entrance is protected by six **Gates** which, beginning from below, are—

The *'Alamgiri* Gate, built by Mu'tamad Khan, Governor of Gwalior, in 1660, and called after Aurangzeb, whose title as Emperor was 'Alamgir. It is quite plain, and the inscription is obliterated. Inside is a small courtyard, and an open hall in which the Mohammedan Governors sat to dispense justice.

The *Badalgarh* or Hindola Gate has its name from the outwork Badalgarh, which was called from Badal Singh, the uncle of Man Singh. This gate is also called Hindola, from *hindol* "a swing," which existed outside. It is a fine specimen of Hindu architecture. An inscription on an iron plate records its restoration by the Governor Saiyad 'Alam in 1648.

Close under the rock to the right is the stately **Gujari Palace**, built for the Queen of Man Singh. It measures 300 ft. by 230 ft., and is two storeys high. It is built of hewn

[1] Permission is no longer required to visit the Gwalior Fort. Visitors sign their names in a book at the entrance to the Fort.

London John Murray, Albemarle Street.

stone, and was once a very fine building.

The *Bhairon* or Bansur gate was the work of one of the earliest Kachhwaha Rajas. It was called Bansur, from *bansur* "archer," lit. a "bamboo-splitter," from the guard which had the charge of it. It has now been removed.

The *Ganesh Gate* was built by Dungar Singh, who reigned 1424 to 1454. Outside is a small outwork called *Kabutar Khana*, or "pigeon-house," in which is a tank called Nur Saugar, 60 ft. × 39 ft. and 25 ft. deep. Here, too, is a Hindu temple sacred to the hermit *Gwalipa*, from whom the fort had its name. It is a small square open pavilion, with a cupola on four pillars. There is also a small mosque with a chronogram giving a date corresponding to 1664 A.D.

Before reaching the *Lakhshman Gate* is a temple hewn out of the solid rock and called *Chatar-bhuj-mandir*, "shrine of the four-armed," sacred to Vishnu, inside which, on the left, is a long inscription, dated Samwat 933=876 A.D. It is 12 ft. sq., with a portico in front 10 ft. by 9 ft. supported by four pillars. There is a tank here, and opposite to it the tomb of Taj Nizam, a noble of the Court of Ibrahim Lodi, who was killed in assaulting this gate in 1518 A.D. Adjoining is an awkward flight of steps leading to the *north-eastern group* of Jain Statues in the cliff under the Mohammedan palaces. The sculptures are small, and unaccompanied by inscriptions, and are, therefore, unimportant; some of the caves are large. Farther S. on the face of the rock are carvings of Mahadeo and his consort, and about fifty lingams. There was also a colossal group of the Boar incarnation, 15½ ft. high, which was one of the oldest sculptures in Gwalior; but it is now quite defaced. A figure of an elephant over the statue has been cut away to form a canopy.

The *Hathiya Paur*, or Elephant Gate, was built by Man Singh, and forms part of his palace. Here was the carving of an elephant, which Babar and Abul-Fazl praised. Inside the Hathiya Paur and under the S. end of the Palace of Man Singh is the Hawa Gate; and the cool draught of air met through the passage here after the long hot ascent in the morning will be found to justify the name.

Turning to the right on reaching the level of the fort, the five palaces under which the ascent has passed may be first visited. The first of these is the **Man Singh Palace** (1486-1516, repaired in 1881), also called the *Chit Mandir*, or painted palace, as "the walls are covered with a profusion of coloured tiles—bands of mosaique candelabra, Brahmini ducks, elephants, and peacocks—enamelled blue, green and gold, giving to this massive wall an unsurpassed charm and elegance. The tiles of the great windowless S. wall possess a brightness and delicacy of tint unblemished by the four centuries which they have weathered. Nowhere do I remember any architectural design capable of imparting similar lightness to a simple massive wall." (Rouselet). The palace was greatly admired by the Emperor Babar also. It is two storeys high, with two storeys of underground apartments, now uninhabitable from the bats. The E. face is 300 ft. long and 100 ft. high, and has five massive round towers, surmounted by open-domed cupolas, and connected at top by a battlement of singularly beautiful open lattice-work. The S. face is 160 ft. long and 60 ft. high, with three round towers connected by a battlement of lattice-work. The N. and W. sides are somewhat ruined. The rooms are arranged round two courts—small but with singularly beautiful decoration.

The *Vikram Palace* lies between the Man and Karan palaces, and is connected with them by narrow galleries.

The **Karan Palace** should be called the Kirti Mandir. It is long and.

narrow, and of two storeys. It has one room 43 ft. by 28 ft., with a roof supported by two rows of pillars. There are smaller rooms on either side, and bath-rooms below, with some fine plaster-work on the domed ceilings. Close by to the S. is a hall (1516 A.D.) 36 ft. sq., with a roof in the form of a Hindu dome supported on eight carved ribs, of which four spring from the side pillars and four from the angles of the building. Internally the top of the dome is a flat square formed by the intersection of the ribs. The roof is flat, and once had a pavilion on it.

The **Mohammedan Jahangiri** and **Shah Jahan Palaces** at the N. end of the fort are of rubble plastered, and are quite plain and of no architectural interest. They are used now as magazines for military stores.

A little to the N.W. of them is the Johar tank, so called from the immolation of Rajput women, which occurred here before the fortress was taken by Altamsh. On the W. wall slightly to the S., and just above the Dhonda Gate, are the ruins of the buildings, known as the Nauchauki or Nine Cells, which constituted the state prison of so many Emperors of Delhi. The narrow, steep staircases leading to the dungeon rooms can still be traversed.

Passing S. beyond the Hawa gate and the guard-house facing it, the next object of interest is the ruined Jain temple (1100 A.D.) on the E. wall, of which but little remains now. Further S. on the same side are the two Sasbahu temples, and from the walls near all three a fine view is obtained of the eastern cliff of the fortress. The names **Sas-bahu** or *Sahasra-bahu* mean "mother-in-law and daughter-in-law," or "1000-armed" temples. The larger temple, said to have been built by Raja Mahipal, is 100 ft. long by 63 ft. broad. The entrance is to the N., and the adytum to the S. The temple is now 70 ft. high, but the top has been broken, and General Cunningham thinks it was once 100 ft. high. It stands on a richly-carved plinth. There is a long inscription inside the portico, with the date 1093 A.D., and there are figures of Vishnu over the main entrances. The central hall is 31 ft. sq. It is crowded with four massive pillars to aid in bearing the enormous weight of its great pyramidal roof. The smaller temple is built in the shape of a cross, and is open on all four sides. The body is 23 ft. sq., supported on twelve pillars. The plinth is 6 ft. high, and is decorated like that of the great temple. The pillars are round, with octagonal bases and bracketed capitals. The lower part of the shafts in both temples are ornamented with groups of female dancers. They are fine specimens of the ornate style of mediæval Hindu architecture.

From this point it is necessary to cross again to the W. side, where the Teli-Ka-Mandir stands, passing the Suraj Kund tank *en route.* This tank is 350 ft. by 180 ft., and is believed to have been constructed about 300 A.D., and to be consequently the oldest reservoir in the fort.

The **Teli-Ka-Mandir**[1] (probable date, 11th century, restored 1881-83) is 60 ft. sq., with a portico projecting 11 ft. on the E. side. The sides slope upwards to 80 ft., where the building ends in a horizontal ridge 30 ft. long. It is the loftiest building in Gwalior. The doorway is 35 ft. high, and has a figure of Garuda over the centre. It was originally a Vishnavite temple, but since the 15th century it has been Shivite. The whole is covered with sculptures. The gateway in front of it was formed out of fragments found in the fort by Major Keith, R.E., who was entrusted with the repairs and restorations made in 1881-83. The interesting archæological fragments placed round the temple were discovered in various parts of the fort during Major Keith's operations. The temple is close to the cliff of the western

[1] See *Indian Architecture*, ii. 139.

Arwahi ravine, outside the southern wall of which General White's breach was made, and every one will proceed past the round Katora tank and the Ek Khamba tank with a pillar in it, as far S. as this, and the point, still called Faringi Pahar, of Major Popham's escalade; while those who proceed to the extreme S. point of the fort will not be disappointed by the interesting tanks there, and the beautiful view of Lashkar.

Returning from the S., the Gangola tank may be visited, and the route may be pursued to the N.W. of the Suraj Kund, opposite the Katora tank to the fine gate which forms the entrance to the Arwahi ravine, on the further side of which is the Mansarovar Tank. The S. end of the ravine is closed by a wall with a double gate, near which are the wells which supply the fort with drinking-water; and on either side of it, from the bottom of the steep descent from the N. gate, are the Jain statues of the Arwahi group.

"These **Rock Sculptures** of Gwalior," writes General Cunningham, "are unique in Northern India, as well for their number as for their gigantic size. They are all excavated in the steep cliff, immediately below the walls of the fortress, and are most of them easily accessible. There are small caves and niches in almost every place where the face of the rock is tolerably smooth and steep, but the more prominent excavations may be divided into five principal groups, which I will designate according to their positions, as 1st, the Arwahi group; 2nd, the south-western group; 3rd, the north-western group; 4th, the north-eastern group; 5th, the south-eastern group. Of these the first and the last, which are by far the most considerable both in number and size, are the only sculptures that have attracted travellers. Most of them were mutilated, by order of the Emperor Babar, 1527 A.D., only sixty years after they were made. Babar himself records the fact in his memoirs: 'They have hewn the solid rock of this *Arwa*, and sculptured out of it idols of larger and smaller size. On the south part of it is a large idol, which may be about 40 ft. in height (really 57). These figures are perfectly naked. *Arwa* is far from being a mean place; on the contrary, it is extremely pleasant. The greatest fault consists in the idol figures all about it. *I directed these idols to be destroyed.*'" The statues, however, were not destroyed, but only mutilated, and the broken heads have since been repaired by the Jains with coloured stucco.

The Arwahi group consists of twenty-two principal figures, which are accompanied by six inscriptions, dated Samwat, 1497, 1510 = 1440 A.D. and 1453, during the sway of the Tomar Rajas. The chief statues are, No. 17, a colossal figure of Adinath, the first Jain Pontiff, who is known by the symbol of a bull on the pedestal. This has a long inscription, dated 1440 A.D., in the reign of Dungar Singh. The largest figure of this group, and of all the Gwalior sculptures, is the colossus, No. 20, which is 57 ft. high, or six and a half times the length of the foot, which is just 9 ft. The extreme W. figure of this group, No. 22, is a seated colossus upwards of 30 ft. high, of Nemnath, 22nd Jain pontiff, known by a shell on the pedestal.

"The *south-western group*, just outside the Arwahi wall, consists of five principal Jain figures. No. 2 is a sleeping female 8 ft. long, lying on her side, with her head to the S. and face to the W. No. 3 is a seated group of a male and female with a child, who are Siddhartha and Trisala, the reputed father and mother of the infant Mahavira, the last of the twenty-four Jain pontiffs. The sleeping female also is probably intended for Trisala." S. of this group is the Ghargharg Gate, at which General White's assault of the fortress was made.

If it is desired to proceed from here to the Jain sculptures on the S.E. face of the fortress, the carriage should be sent round to this point from the N.E. entrance. It is quite impossible, however, to see all the interesting sights of the Gwalior Fort on a single visit, and each visitor must decide for himself what he will see and how he will see it.

The road from the Arwahi ravine to the Lashkar, and round to the nearest point to the south-eastern group which a carriage can reach, is fair; but that N. to the N.W. group of statues is bad, and they had better be visited by passing round the N. side of the city. The figures there are, however, insignificant, and few will care to visit them. The south-eastern group is the most picturesquely situated of all, with trees and undergrowth adjoining it below; it is also the largest and most important group, as there are eighteen colossal statues from 20 ft. to 30 ft. high, and as many more from 8 ft. to 15 ft, which occupy the whole face of the cliff for upwards of ½ m. They are all of date 1468-1473 A.D., and are the latest of such works in India. In many cases a screen-wall has been left in front of the figure as high up as its waist. A few caves are occupied by mendicant Byragis, and cannot always be visited. The following list gives details of each statue :—

Caves.		Sculptures.			
No.	Front depth and height.	Names.	Position.	Height.	Symbol.
	Feet.			Feet	
1	23×21×27	—	—	30	—
2	10×10×10	—	—	—	—
3	15×12×17	Adinath	Standing	7	Bull
		4 others	—	—	—
4	15×14×16	Adinath	—	14	Wheel
		Nemnath	—	—	Shell
5	—	Adinath	—	—	Bull
6	26×12×16	Supadma	Sitting	15	Lotus
7	15×10×20	—	Standing	20	—
8	21×10×20	Adinath	Sitting	6	—
9	16× 7×28	Male Figure	Standing	21	—
10	10× 7×15	Female	Lying	—	—
		Chandra Prabha	Standing	12	—
		2 others	—	12	—
11	12× 8×25	Chandra Prabha	Sitting	21	Crescent
12	31×10×25	Sambhunath	—	21	Horse
13	40×10×25	Nemnath	Standing	21	Shell
		Sambhunath	Sitting	—	Horse
		Mahavira	Standing	—	Lion
14	26×16×32	Adinath	Sitting	29	Bull
15	26×16×33	Adinath	Sitting	28	—
16	24×22×34	—	—	30	—
17	80× 8×30	Kantanath	Standing	26	Goat
		Shantanath	Sitting	26	Antelope
		Adinath	Sitting	26	Wheel
		And 4 others	—	26	—
18	15×10×30	—	Standing	26	—
19	16×10×30	—	—	26	—
20	12× 8×20	Adinath	—	8	Wheel
21	27×35×15	—	—	—	—

[From Gwalior two light lines of State Railway run S.W. to Sipri (74 m.), not far from which in the Narwar jungle the great rebel leader, Tantia Topi, was betrayed and captured on 7th April 1859, and N.E. to Bhind (58 m.).]

336 m. About 4 m. S. of Dholpur there is a very fine bridge over the Chambal, built of the famous red sandstone of Dholpur, a ridge of which, from 560 to 1074 ft. above sea-level, runs for 60 m. through the territory, and has many quarries.

The river Chambal is bordered everywhere by a labyrinth of ravines, some of which are 90 ft. deep, and extend to a distance of from 2 to 4 m. from the river banks. The floods of the river are very remarkable. The highest recorded flood above summer level rose no less than 97 ft.

340 m. **Dholpur** station (R.), the chief town of the native state of that name. In 1658 Aurangzeb defeated his elder brother Dara-Shikoh at Ran-ka-Chabutara, 3 m. E. of Dholpur, and in 1707 Aurangzeb's sons, Azim and Mu'azzim, contending for the crown, fought a great battle at the village of Barehta, near Dholpur, the former being killed, and the latter becoming emperor, with the title of Bahadur Shah.

The Palace of Dholpur is a moderately handsome building. The tank of Mach Kund, about 2 m. from the capital, is about ½ m. long, and contains several islets, on which are pavilions. The banks are lined with temples, but none of them are ancient or remarkable. There are alligators in the tank, but though crowds of pilgrims bathe in the waters, there is no story of any of them being carried off.

373 m. **Agra Cantonment Station,** where travellers by this route alight for the hotels. The M.R. Line runs on to the Raja ki Mandi station, and so to Muttra and Delhi (p. 169).

---

(3) *Jhansi* to *Manikpur*. 181 m.

Jhansi junction station (see p. 101).

7 m. **Orchha** station, at the old capital of the Orchha state, the oldest and highest in rank of all the Bundela Principalities, and the only one of them that was not held in subjection by the Peshwa. It is built on both banks of the Betwa. There is an imposing fortress, connected by a wooden bridge with the rest of the town, containing the residence of Bir Singh Deo (p. 101) and a palace built for the accommodation of the Emperor Jahangir. The Chhatri of Bir Singh Deo (1605-27) is also fine.

Tehri (*Tekamgarh*), the present capital, in the S.W. corner of the state, is about 40 m. S. from Orchha, with which it is connected by road.

13 m. **Barwa-Saugar** station, D.B. The town is picturesquely situated at the foot of a rocky ridge on the shore of the Barwa-Saugar Lake, an artificial sheet of water formed by a masonry embankment ¾ m. in length, constructed by Udot Singh, Raja of Orchha, between 1705-37, and containing two craggy, wooded islets. Below, a tract of land, extending over 4 m., is thickly planted with mango and other trees, many of great age and enormous size. N.W. of the town rises a fine old castle, also built by Udot Singh, but now uninhabited. 3 m. W. stand the remains of an old Chandel temple, built of solid blocks of stone, carved with the figures of Hindu gods, much defaced by Mussulmans.

40 m. **Mau** station, D.B. (population 23,500). Mau Ranipur is, next to Jhansi, the principal commercial town of Jhansi district. Its buildings are remarkably picturesque, in the style peculiar to Bundelkund, with deep eaves between the first and second stories, and hanging balconies of unusual beauty. Trees line many of the streets, and handsome temples ornament the town, the principal being that of the Jains, with two solid spires and several cupolas. An old brick-built fort with bastions adjoins the bazaar, and contains the public offices.

53 m. **Harpalpur** station (R.R.) for **Nowgong** Cantonment, 18 m. distant (population 11,500). A railway is to be made between the two places. This cantonment, next to that of Jhansi, is the chief military station of Bundelkund. In 1857 the troops in it mutinied on the 10th June, and the Europeans who were not murdered were compelled to leave the place, and made their way with numerous losses on the road

to Kalinjar, and thence to Banda or Allahabad.

67 m. **Jaitpur** station. The town was formerly the capital of a native state. It is picturesquely situated on the banks of the Bela Tal, and was probably founded in the early part of the 18th century by Jagatraj, son of the famous Bundela Raja, Chatar Sal, who built the large fort still in existence. There is a handsome temple in the town, and there are also two forts.

The Bela Tal, a tank or lake dammed up with solid masonry by the Chandel rulers of Mahoba in the 9th century, extends for 5 m. in circumference, but is now very shallow, the embankment having burst in 1869.

86 m. **Mahoba** station, D.B. The town, founded about 800 A.D. by Raja Chandra Varmma, stands on the side of the Madan Saugar Lake, constructed by the Chandel Rajas, and consists of three distinct portions —one N. of the central hill known as the Old Fort; one on the top of the hill known as the Inner Fort; and one to the S. known as Dariba. Architectural antiquities of the Chandel period abound throughout the neighbourhood. The Ram Kund marks the place where Chandra Varmma, founder of the dynasty, died; and the tank is believed to be a reservoir into which the united waters of all holy streams pour themselves. The Fort, now almost entirely in ruins, commands a beautiful view over the hills and lakes. The temple of Munia Devi, partially renovated, has in front of its entrance a stone pillar inscribed to Madana Varmma. Of the lakes, confined by magnificent masonry dams, two have greatly silted up, but the Kirat and Madan Saugars, works of the 11th and 12th centuries, still remain deep and clear sheets of water. The shores of the lakes and the islands in their midst are thickly covered with ruined temples, monstrous figures carved out of the solid rock, pillars, broken sculpture, and other early remains, while on the hills above stand the summer-houses of the early Rajas, and shrines overhang the edge. Relics of Jain temples and Buddhist inscriptions also occur. The existing monuments of Mohammedan date include the tomb of Jalhan Khan, constructed from the fragments of a Shivite temple, and a mosque also built of Chandel materials.

[34 m. S. of Mahoba is the ancient decayed town of **Khajurahu**, formerly the capital of the old province of Jahoti; it may also be reached from Nowgong through Chatarpur and Basári, but the distance is 54 m. Hiouen Thsang mentions it in the 7th century, and Genl. Cunningham gives the same date to the graceful pillared porch of the Ganthai temple. A high mound probably covers ruins of a Buddhist monastery. Upwards of twenty[1] temples still stand in the town, and the ruins of at least as many more bear witness to its former greatness. In one alone General Cunningham counted over 800 statues half life-size, and eight sculptured elephants of like proportions. These noble buildings belong mainly to the Chandel dynasty, who ruled at Khajurahu apparently from 870 to 1200 A.D.

119 m. **Banda** station (R.), D.B., is a municipal town and the headquarters of the Banda district. It stands on an undulating plain, 1 m. E. of right bank of the Ken river.

The modern town derived its importance from the residence of the Nawab of Banda, and from its position as a cotton mart. After the removal of the Nawab in 1858 owing to his disloyalty during the Mutiny, the town has declined. There are five Jain temples, some of which possess fair architectural merit.

35 m. S. of Banda, and 16 m. S. of Badausa station, 26 m. E. of Banda, is the famous Fort of **Kalinjar**, at which the Emperor Sher Shah met his death (1545). It is necessary

1 Fergusson's *Oriental Architecture*, ii. 49-54, 95-96, 140.

to use an ekka or country cart for the trip, while that to the Ajaigarh Fort, 16 m. further, can be accomplished only on foot or on horseback. There are rest-houses at both places.

162 m. **Karwi** station (population 4100). In 1805 the town formed a cantonment for British troops, and in 1829 it became the principal residence of the Peshwa's representative, who lived in almost regal state, and built several beautiful temples and wells. Numerous traders from the Deccan were thus attracted to Karwi. During the Mutiny Narayan Rao assumed the government, and retained his independence for eight months. The accumulations of his family constituted the great treasure afterwards so famous as the "Kirwee and Banda Prize Money." It was kept in a vault of the Bara, a large palace. Since the Mutiny the prosperity of Karwi also has gradually declined. There is a fine temple and tank with a masonry well attached, known as the Ganesh Bagh, built by Vinayak Rao in 1837.

181 m. **Manikpur** junction station of E.I. Railway Jubbulpore Branch (see p. 30).

ROUTE 10.

BOMBAY to DELHI by **Bassein**, **Surat**, **Broach**, **Miyagam**, **Baroda**, and thence
(1) by broad gauge direct to Delhi (863 m.) by **Rutlam**, **Nagda**, **Kotah**, **Bharatpur**, and **Muttra**
(2) to **Ahmedabad**, and thence by metre gauge to Delhi (849 m.) by **Mehsana**, **Palanpur**, **Abu** Road, **Marwar** Junction, **Ajmer**, **Phalera** Junction, **Jaipur**, **Bandikui** Junction, **Alwar** and **Rewari**,
with excursions by road to **Mount Abu**; and by rail to (*a*) **Dabhoi**, (*b*) **Luni** Junction (branch line to Hyderabad Sindh), **Jodhpur**, **Bikaner**, and **Phalera** Junction, and (*c*) **Hissar** **Bhatinda**, and **Ferozepore**.

The journey by the first route is the shortest to Delhi, occupying 28½ hrs. as against 35 hrs. by the second route, and 30 hrs. by Route 9, G.I.P. and Midland Railways. Fares, Rs.66 and Rs.62, Rs.33 and Rs.31, Rs.9 and Rs.8. The stations in Bombay city where the mail trains stop are *Colaba*,[1] *Church Gate*, and *Grant Road*, where ample time is given.

9 m. **Mahim** station, where the railway crosses a causeway connecting the island of Bombay with the island of Salsette. The country is flat, and studded with villages and cocoanut groves. The Mahim *band* was constructed largely at the expense of the first Lady Jamsetjee Jeejeebhoy.

10 m. **Bandra** station, left, on seashore, a favourite residence for persons who have daily business in Bombay. Several *chapels* built by the Portuguese still exist here, notably that of *Mount Mary*, held in respect for miles around.

18 m. **Goregaon** station. About 1 m. from the station are the famous Hindu caves of **Jogeshwar** (see p. 23).

22 m. **Borivli** station is near the Caves of Montpezir (see p. 21) and the ruins of a Jesuit monastery of the 16th century. The Caves of Kanhari (see p. 22), 5 m. distant, are more easily visited from Thana.

22 m. **Bhayandar** station, on the S. edge of the Bassein creek, which divides Salsette from the mainland. The railway here crosses the river by a very long bridge. On the right, and for some miles up the stream, the scenery is most beautiful—the Kamandrug Hills and Ghorbandar, with the quiet water between them, forming a tropical landscape as charming as can be seen anywhere in India.

33 m. **Bassein Road** station,[2] D.B. The ruins are distant about 5 m.

The first notice of Bassein is in 1532,

[1] It is advisable to secure places in the train from the Colaba terminus.
[2] Write beforehand to station-master for tonga.

when the Portuguese ravaged the neighbourhood. In 1534 they took Daman,[1] which they still hold, and obliged Sultan Bahadur of Guzerat, then hard pressed by the Emperor Humayun, to cede Bassein in perpetuity. "For more than 200 years Bassein remained in the hands of the Portuguese, and during this time it rose to such prosperity that the city came to be called the Court of the North, and its nobles were proverbial for their wealth and magnificence. With plentiful supplies of both timber and stone, Bassein was adorned by many noble buildings, including a cathedral, five convents, thirteen churches, and an asylum for orphans. The dwellings of the Hidalgos, or aristocracy, who alone were allowed to live within the city walls, are described (1675) as stately buildings" (Hunter). Fryer, describing the town in 1675, says: "Here were stately dwellings graced with covered balconies and large windows, two stories high, with panes of oyster-shell, which is the usual glazing amongst them (the Portuguese) in India, or else latticed." On the 17th February 1739 the Mahrattas invested Bassein, and the town surrendered on the 16th of May, after a most desperate resistance, in which the commandant, Silveira de Mineyes, was killed, and 800 of the garrison were killed and wounded, the Mahrattas' loss being upwards of 5000. On the 13th of November 1780 General Goddard arrived before Bassein, and on the 28th his first battery opened against it. He had very powerful artillery, and one battery of twenty mortars, which shortly after opened at the distance of 500 yds., and did great execution. The place surrendered on the 11th December, on which day Colonel Hartley, with a covering army of 2000 men, defeated the Mahrattas' relieving army of upwards of 24,000 men, and killed its distinguished General, Ramchandra Ganesh.

The *Fort* with the ruins stands on the Bassein Creek, a little away from the sea; it is now entered from the N.

The Old Town, surrounded by walls and ramparts, contains the ruins of the Cathedral of St Joseph and other churches built by Roman Catholic missionaries in the 14th and 15th centuries. Several inscriptions remain, the earliest dated 1536. A guide is necessary to point out the various ruins. Among them are the church of St Anthony, the Jesuits' church, and the churches and convents of the Augustinians and Franciscans.

108 m. **Daman Road** station, ✱D.B. *Daman* (7 m. W.) is a Portuguese settlement subordinate to Goa (area 149 sq. m., population 42,000). It was taken by the Portuguese in 1531, again in 1535, and finally in 1559. The town (population 17,000) is situated on the Daman Gunga river, with a bad bar, and a roadstead. The place in the days of small ships had a very considerable trade. It has a fort on each bank of the river. In the main fort, on the left bank, are the ruins of an old monastery and two churches,—only Christians may reside within the walls. In it are the houses of the governor and his staff and the public offices. The smaller fort of St Jerome opposite is more modern. (See also p. 362.)

114 m. **Udvada** station. Remarkable as containing the oldest *Fire Temple* in India. It is believed that the fire kept alive is that which was originally brought from Persia by the Parsis, and first kindled here in 700 A.D.

124 m. **Balsar** station. This place is occasionally used as a rest-camp, and near it is the village of Tithal on the sea-coast, where many inhabitants of Guzerat resort in the hot season. There are fine sands and a grand rolling sea.

148 m. **Navsari** station (population 21,400). The capital of the Gaekwar's southern possessions, and the headquarters, from the earliest days, of the

[1] The poet Camoens distinguished himself on this occasion.

Parsi community. Here the Zoroastrian Priesthood receive their initiation and confirmation. The *Town Hall* is an imposing building. A Parsi has established here a manufactory of essences and soaps on European principles.

167 m. **Surat** station ✱ (R.). The name is derived by Sir Henry Elliot and others from *Saurastra*, the ancient name of the peninsula of Kathiawar with which it was the principal port of communication. In the 12th century the Parsis, who were driven from Persia 500 years before, and had settled in *Sanjan*, 70 m. from Surat, found their way here on the death of the Sanjan chief. Amongst Indian cities it is not a place of antiquity, but it had a large trade at the end of the 15th century, and in the 18th was one of the most populous and important mercantile cities in India, the port being much frequented by British and other European traders. It is the seat of a collectorate, is situated on the river Tapti, and is surrounded on the land side by a wall about 5½ m. in circuit, with twelve gates. Except the main street running from the station road to the castle, the streets in Surat are narrow and tortuous, and some of them still bear marks of the great fire in 1837, which raged for nearly two days, when 9373 houses were destroyed, and many persons perished. Again in 1889 a fire broke out which raged over twelve hours, and destroyed 1350 shops and houses. In 1896 Lord Elgin inaugurated here the "Rupee Railway," a local joint-stock enterprise, to run up the valley of the Tapti (see p. 119).

The population of Surat as late as 1797 was estimated at 800,000, but as Bombay rose Surat declined, until in 1841 it had only 80,000 inhabitants. It now (1911) numbers 114,000. There are three mills, employing 1200 hands.

The Portuguese found their way to the place soon after their arrival in India, and in 1512 sacked the then open town. On the 19th January 1573 it surrendered to Akbar after a siege of one month and seventeen days. Early in the 17th century the English began to visit it, and in 1612 the Mughal Emperor sent down a *farman*, authorising an English minister to reside at his court, and opening to English subjects the trade at Surat. In 1615 Captain Downton, with four ships, mounting eighty guns, defeated the Portuguese fleet, consisting of four galleons, three other large ships, and sixty smaller vessels, mounting in all 134 guns. This victory established the reputation of the English for war, and their superiority over the Portuguese. The Dutch trade with Surat commenced in 1616, and for some years the Dutch Factory competed successfully with the English there. The French Factory was not founded till 1668, when the agents of the French E.I. Company, which Colbert had established in 1664, settled at Surat. On January the 5th of the same year the prosperity of Surat received a severe blow from Shivaji, the founder of the Mahratta Empire, who with 4000 horse surprised the city, and plundered it for six days. The defenders of the English Factory under Sir George Oxenden, who described the Mahratta leader as "Sevagye ye grand rebell of ye Deccan," showed a bold front throughout, and recommended Shivaji to "save the labour of his servants running to and fro on messages, and come himself with all his army," and in the end were left unassailed. Their courageous defiance so pleased Aurangzeb, that he sent Sir G. Oxenden a robe of honour, and granted the English an exemption from customs. The walls of Surat up to this time were of mud, but they were now ordered to be built of brick. In 1687 the seat of government was transferred by the E.I. Company to Bombay from Surat, which was again partially pillaged by the Mahrattas in 1670, 1702, and 1706. About this time commenced the disputes of the rival London and English Companies; and on the 19th of January 1700 Sir Nicholas Waite, consul for the king, and president of the New Company, arrived at Surat. The struggle of the Companies continued till 1708, when they were united. This marked a new era for the English at Surat, who were fast approaching the period when they were to acquire political influence in the city, then the greatest emporium of W. India.

In 1759 the Nawab signed a treaty by which the castle and fleet were made over to the British for a yearly stipend of Rs. 200,000. This arrangement was confirmed by the Emperor at Delhi, and the British authority was firmly established in Surat, which was definitely taken over in 1800. In 1842 the last titular Nawab died, and the flag of Delhi was removed from the castle.

The *Castle*, so prominent in the early annals of the British in W. India, stands beyond the city, on the banks of the river. It was built by a Turkish soldier about 1546, and is a brick building with walls about 8 ft. thick, much modernised. There is a good view of the city and river from the S.W. Bastion. Over the E. gateway is an inscription, and in front of it is the well-kept *Victoria Garden*, of 8 acres. The adjoining church was consecrated by Bishop Heber.

The remains of the *English Factory* are near the way to the Katargaon Gate, close to the river, on the N. side of the city. The building is now a private dwelling. Near it is the *Portuguese Factory*, where some records are still kept. A wooden cross marks the site of the church. Close to this are the vacant site of the *French Lodge* and the *Persian Factory*. There is a fine view of the town from the *Clock Tower*.

In the *English Cemetery*, N. of the city on the Broach Road, is (on the right on entering) the mausoleum of Sir George Oxenden (d. 1669), and near it the tomb of his brother Christopher. There are also a number of other large tombs; the sites of the graves of Gerald Aungier (d. 1677) and Tom Corryat (d. 1617) are unknown.

The *Dutch Cemetery* is also curious from the great size of the monuments. The most striking is that of Baron van Rheede, the author of the valuable work, *Hortus Malabaricus*, and collector of books and curiosities, which he sent to Holland.

The **chief Mosques** of Surat are—

1. Khwajah Diwan Sahib's Mosque, built about 1530. He is said to have come to Surat from Bokhara, and to have lived to the age of 116. 2. The Nau Saiyad Mosque, "Mosque of the Nine Saiyads," on the W. bank of the Gopi Lake. 3. The Saïyad Idrus Mosque, in Saïyadpura, with a minaret, one of the most conspicuous objects in Surat; it was built in 1639, in honour of the ancestor of the present Kazi of Surat. 4. The Mirza Sami Mosque, built in 1540 by Khudawand Khan, who constructed the castle.

The **Tombs of the Bohras** deserve a visit. There are two chief **Parsi fire-temples**, built in 1823. The Hindu sect of the Walabhacharis has three temples. The **Swami Narayan** temple, with three white domes, is visible all over the city. In the two old temples in the Ambaji ward the shrines are 15 ft. underground, a relic of Mohammedan persecution. The **Shravaks**, or Jains, have forty-two temples, the chief of which are from 150 to 200 years old. There are several steam *Cotton Mills* in Surat; and carved sandalwood and inlaid work form important industries.

Near the Fort the Hope Bridge spans the Tapti, and 3 m. across it is *Rander*, built on the site of a very ancient Hindu city, destroyed by the Mohammedans in the 12th century. The Jama Masjid stands on the site of the principal Jain temple. In the façade the bases of the Jain columns are still visible, and the great idol is placed head downwards as a doorstep for the faithful to tread on in entering the mosque. In another mosque are the wooden columns and domes belonging to a Jain temple, which are the only wooden remains of the kind in India.

[The Tapti Valley Railway runs from Surat to Amalner (147 m.)

through Nandurbar; from Amalner a branch of the G.I.P. Railway, 35 m. long, runs to Jalgaon (p. 28)].

2 m. after leaving Surat the *Tapti* or *Tapi river* is crossed by a very long bridge, and close to Broach the *Nerbudda* or *Narmada river* is passed on the finest *Bridge* on the railway, consisting of 25 spans, with a good view on the left of Broach.

From (193 m.) *Ankleswar* a branch runs 33 m. N.E. to *Nandod.*

203 m. **Broach** (*Bharoch*) station (R.), D.B., is a place of extreme antiquity (population 43,000). The author of the *Periplus*, 60-210 A.D., mentions Broach under the name of Barugaza. It was then ruled by a feudatory Gurjjara prince, and subsequently fell under the rule of the Chalukyas. The Moslems appeared in the 8th century, and Broach was ruled by them from 1297 to 1772. In 1613 A.D. it was first visited by Aldworth and Withington, English merchants, and in 1614 a house was hired for a factory, permission to establish which was granted to Sir Thomas Roe by Jahangir in 1616. The Dutch set up a factory in 1617. In 1686 the Mahrattas plundered Broach. On the 18th of November 1772 the British troops stormed the place with the loss of their commander, General Wedderburn, whose tomb is at the N.W. corner of the fort. On the 29th of August 1803 Broach was again taken by storm by the British.

The *Nerbudda* here is a noble river, 1 m. in breadth. The city with its suburbs covers a strip of land 2½ m. long and ¾ m. broad, hence by its inhabitants it is called Jibh, or "the tongue." The *Fort* stands on a hill more than 100 ft. above the river, and a massive stone wall lines the river bank for about 1 m. In it are the Collector's Office, the Civil Courts, the Dutch Factory, the Jail, the Civil Hospital, the English Church and School, the Municipal Office, and the Library. The streets of the city are narrow and some of them steep. The Jama Masjid, lying at the E. foot of the fort, is constructed of materials taken from a Jain temple, and perhaps on the site of that temple.

The Dutch tombs are 2 m. W. of the fort, and some 100 yds. off the road, left. Two of them are from 16 to 20 ft. high.

Opposite the Dutch tombs are five *Towers of Silence*, one of them about 15 ft. high. The second tower is still in use. Outside the E. gate on the river bank is the *Temple of Bhrigu Rishi*, from whom the town got the name of Brigukackha, contracted into Bharoch.

Broach is celebrated for its cotton: there are four spinning and weaving mills, employing 2000 hands, besides ginning and cotton-pressing factories.

[10 m. to the E. of Broach is the celebrated place of Hindu pilgrimage, **Suklatirth.** It is on the N. or right bank of the Nerbudda, and here Chanakya, king of Ujjain, was purified of his sins, having arrived at this holy spot by sailing down the Nerbudda in a boat with black sails, which turned white on his reaching Suklatirth. Here, too, Chandragupta and his minister, Chanakya, were cleansed from the guilt of murdering Chandragupta's eight brothers, and here Chamund, king of Anhilwada, in the 11th century, ended his life as a penitent. There are three sacred waters—the Kavi, the Hunkareshwar, and the Shukal; at the second is a temple with an image of Vishnu. There is a fair here in November, at which 25,000 people assemble. Opposite Mangleshwar, which is 1 m. up stream from Suklatirth, in the Nerbudda, is an island in which is the famous *Banyan Tree*, called the *Kabir wad*, or "the fig-tree of Kabir," from whose toothpick it is said to have originated. It has suffered much from floods. Forbes, who visited Broach 1776-83, says in his *Oriental Memoirs* (i. p. 26) it enclosed a space within its principal stems 2000 ft. in circumference. It had 350 large and 3000 small trunks, and had been known to shelter 7000 men. Bishop Heber, in April 1825, says though much had been washed away, enough remained to make it one of the most noble groves in the world. A small temple marks the spot where the original trunk grew.]

228 m. **Miyagam** junction station. This is a junction of a system of narrow gauge railways (2′ 6″) owned by the Gaekwar of Baroda and worked by the B.B. and C.I. Railway.

[**Dabhoi**, 20 m. from Mayagam, is a town belonging to the state of Baroda (population 15,000). The ancient hindu architecture of this place is most interesting, but is little known. A full account of it by Mr Burgess will be found in a volume of the *Archæ. Survey of W. India.* The fort is said to have been built by the Vaghela king of Patan in the 13th century. The *Baroda Gate* is 31 ft. high, with elaborately carved pilasters on either side. The carvings represent the incarnations of Vishnu, and nymphs sporting with makras or alligators. Near this are interesting interior colonnades in the fort walls affording shelter to the garrison. The S. or Nandod Gate is 29 ft. high and 16 ft. 4 in. wide. Trees have grown in the walls and fractured them with their thick roots. The Hira Gate in the E. face of the town is 37 ft. high, and a marvel of minute carving. About 10 ft. up in the N. face of the centre, a man and woman are carved 4 ft. high, standing with a tree between them, like the old representations of Adam and Eve. To the left is the tall figure of a devil, with a ghastly leer. High in the centre face is an elephant, under which the builder of the gate is said to have been interred. On the N. side of the town is what was the palace, in which the law courts now sit. On this side there is a fine tank and the Mori Gate. On the left, looking out from inside the tower, is the temple of Maha Kali, and on the right beyond the gate and inside it is a smaller temple, now quite ruined. The former is a wondrous example of carving, which when new must have been very beautiful, but is now much worn by the weather.

From Dabhoi a branch railway runs 10 m. S. to **Chandod** station, a celebrated place of Hindu pilgrimage, owing to its situation at the confluence of the *Nerbudda* and the *Or.* Thousands flock there every full moon.

Another line runs 22 m. E. to Bodeli, and a third connects again with the main line of the B.B. and C.I. Railway at Vishvamitri, 245 m. from Bombay. 15 m. N.E. of Bahadarpur on the Bodeli line is the fortified mountain of *Pawangarh*, and the ruined city of **Champanir.**

An interesting expedition may be made to these, but arrangements must be completed beforehand for the trip. Champanir was long the fortress-city of local Rajput kings. After many vicissitudes it was taken in 1484 by Mahmud Bigara of Ahmedabad, who made it his capital, and in 1535 it was besieged by Humayun, Emperor of Delhi. With others he scaled the precipices of the fort by the aid of iron spikes driven into the rock, and opened the gate to admit his army. There are remains of many mosques, tombs, and tanks in the lower city; and in the forest for miles around may be found the ruins of massive wells, minarets, and palaces, which testify to the former greatness of Champanir.[1]]

247 m. **BARODA**✱ (R.) is the capital of the very important Mahratta state of the Gaekwar, which with its dependencies covers an area of 8570 sq. m., with a population of 2,000,000.

The state was founded by Damaji Gaekwar early in the 18th century; the present chief is H.H. Maharaja Sir Sayaji Rao Gaekwar, G.C.S.I.

W. of the railway station are situated the principal offices of the state and the residences of many high officials, and the State Rest-House for guests of H.H. E. of the station is the city (population 99,000), with the fine College, the *Marchioness of Dufferin's Hospital*, the *State Offices*

[1] For the architecture of Champanir, Mehmadabad, etc., see Burgess's *Mohammedan Architecture of Gujarat* (1896).

and *Library*, by the Juna Kot, the *Central Jail*, etc. The Vishwamitri river flows W. of the town, and is spanned by four stone bridges, which exhibit great contrasts of style. The city proper is intersected at right angles by two wide thoroughfares, which meet in a market-place, where there is a fine pavilion of Mohammedan architecture, a clock tower, and the old Nazar Bagh Palace. Adjoining it is the guard-house, where the gold and silver cannon of the State are kept. They contain 280 lbs. weight each of solid gold, and are drawn by splendid milk-white bullocks, stabled hard by. The new **Lakhshmi Villas Palace** cost 27 lakhs of rupees. Passes to view it must be obtained from the Resident.

N. of the city are the *Cantonment* and *Residency*, well laid out with open well-planted roads. The *English Church* was consecrated by Bishop Heber 1824, and in 1838 was almost entirely rebuilt. There is a good public garden between the Cantonments and the city on the banks of the river.

The palace at **Makarpura** is 4 m. S. of the city. The *Naulakhi Well*, 50 yds. N., is a fine structure of the Baoli class, described below.

Baroda is supplied with water from the artificial *Ajwa Lake*, 18 m. distant, completed in 1892 at a cost of 35 lakhs.

The *Baolis*, in Guzerat, are large wells. The following account of these is given by Mr A. Forbes in his interesting work on Guzerat, the *Ras Mala:* "There remain in different parts of the country examples of two kinds. Some are large circular wells containing galleried apartments; others are more properly described as '*wao's*' or '*baolis*.'[1] The *wao* is a large edifice, of a picturesque and stately, as well as peculiar, character. Above the level of the ground a row of four or five open pavilions, at regular distances from each other, usually square in the interior, but sometimes, in the larger examples, passing into the octagonal form within, is alone visible; the roofs are supported on columns, and are, in the structures of the Hindu times, pyramidal in form. The entrance to the *wao* is by one of the end pavilions; thence a flight of steps descends to a landing immediately under the second dome, which is now seen to be supported by two rows of columns, one over the other. A second flight of steps continues the descent to a similar landing under the third pavilion, where the screen is found to be three columns in height. In this manner the descent continues stage by stage, the number of the columns increasing at each pavilion, until the level of the water is at last reached. The last flight of steps conducts to the most adorned portion of the *wao*, an octagonal structure, in this position necessarily several storeys high, with a gallery at each storey, and covered by a dome. The structure, which is sometimes 80 yds. in length, invariably terminates in a circular well."

[1] A fine model of a *Wao Baoli* at Adalaj (p. 130) may be seen in the Bodleian at Oxford.

(1) Route from Barodah by broad gauge direct route to Delhi.

This service of the B.B. and C.I. Railway diverges N.W. to 292 m. **Godhra**, 337 m. **Dohad**, 408 m. **Rutlam** (p. 91), and 434 m. **Nagda**. Godhra (pop, 21,000) is the headquarters of the Panch Mahals. Dt. Dohad (pop. 14,000) was of note under the Gujerat kings.

From Nagda the line turns N. and runs to 521 m. **Sri Chatrapur**, 17 m. from **Jhalra Patan**, 574 m. **Kotah Jn.**, 754 m. **Bharatpur Jn.** (p. 162), and 775 m. **Muttra Jn.** (p. 169), and thence to 864 m. Delhi. At 545 m. **Darrah** it passes through the famous Mokand-darrah Pass, from which Colonel Monsoon made his disastrous retreat in the summer of 1804 before Jaswant Rao Holkar; the scenery here is striking, and the engineering of the line is very remarkable. **Kotah** (population 35,000) is the capital of the Kotah State, separated from Boondi (p. 97) in 1625, and of which the chief is Raja Umed Singh,

G.C.I.E., K.C.S.I. It is a walled city, picturesquely situated on the right bank of the Chambal; the fine old palace and the royal cenotaphs lie S. of it. The new palace is called the Umed Bhawan. There is a Hospital for women named after the Queen Empress. N. of Kotah the railway passes 641 m. **Siwai Madhopur** (population 11,000; branch line to Sanganer, p. 143), 681 m. Gangapur, and 708 m. **Hindaun**, all in the Jaipur State, and the last once a place of importance, but devastated by the Mahrattas, and Bayana (Biana) (p. 185) on the bank of the Gambhir.

(2) Route to Ahmedabad and by metre gauge to Delhi.

269 m. **Anand** junction station.

[(*a*) One branch line from here runs N.E. to **Godhra**, 49 m. At

18 m. **Dakor** station is a large lake, and a temple with an image much venerated by the Hindus. As many as 100,000 pilgrims assemble in October and November.

About 20 m. N. of **Dakor** is the walled town of

Kapadvanj, D.B., noted for its industry in *soap, glass*, and *leather jars for "ghee."*

Midway between the two places are the hot springs of **Lassundra**, the highest temperature being 115°. The water is slightly sulphurous, and is efficacious in skin diseases.

[(*b*) Another line runs S.W. 15 m. to **Petlad** (population 15,528), and 32 m. to **Cambay**, the capital of the Native State of that name (population 32,090). The town and port are of great antiquity. In A.D. 913 Cambay is described by the Arab traveller Masudi as standing on the shores of a deep bay surrounded by towns, villages, farms, cultivated fields, trees, and gardens. It was governed by the kings of Anhilvara (the modern Patan), up to the end of the 13th century. Mohammedan writers of the period call it the "first city in Hind." The beauty and wealth of the country led to its invasion by the Mohammedan Emperor Ala-ud-din in 1304, when the city was plundered and its temples destroyed.

Cambay reached the height of its glory under the Mohammedans at the latter end of the 15th and beginning of the 16th centuries, and in 1583 letters carried by Fitch, Leedes, and Newberry from Queen Elizabeth, were addressed to Akbar, as king of Cambay. The Portuguese and Dutch had already established factories here; in 1613 when the English appeared it was still a flourishing city, but commenced to decline as Surat increased in importance. In the 18th century it was plundered more than once by the Mahrattas; at the same time the entrance to the harbour began to silt up, and it is now an unimportant place.

Cambay was formerly a stronghold of the Jains, and still possesses some of their *MSS.*, second only to those at Patan. The *Jama Masjid* (1325) was built with fragments of Jain and Hindu temples.

The town is celebrated for the manufacture of agate, cornelian, and onyx ornaments.]

291 m. **Mehmadabad** station. Picturesque view of river from railway station. In the morning and evening troops of grey monkeys play near the line. Mehmadabad was founded by Mahmud Bigara in 1479. There is a fine tomb 1½ m. E. of the town, built in 1484 in honour of Mubarak Saiyad, a minister of Mahmud. For "simplicity about its plan, and solidity and balance of parts in the design, it has rarely if ever been surpassed in any tomb in India."[1] Bigara also constructed the *Bhamara Baoli* well, passed on the way to the tomb. It has two stone arches, on which it was said the king's swing was hung. It is 74 ft. long by 24 ft. broad, is entered by four winding stairs, and has eight underground chambers.

Kaira, 7 m. from Mehmadabad, by a good road shaded by fine trees (population 10,400), is the largest town in the district of that name. It consists of two parts, the town

[1] See Fergusson's *Indian Architecture*, ii. 244.

proper and the suburbs. Kaira is said to be as old as 1400 B.C. Copper-plate grants show that the city was in existence in the 5th century. The chief industry is printing cloth for saris and other native garments. In the centre of the town is the Court House, a building with pillars of a Greek order. Near it is a Jain temple, with beautiful dark wood carving. Outside the E. gate is the new Jail. It was once a military cantonment, but proved so unhealthy for Europeans that the troops were withdrawn. The large church was consecrated by Bishop Heber in 1822, and has a beautiful bell.

Wild hog may still be found in the district and the Nilgai (*Portax pictus*), antelope (*Antilope bezoartica*), and Indian gazelle (*Gazella Bennettii*), are common. The *Sarus* (*Ardea Antigone*) is a tall grey crane with a crimson head. Wild-fowl, bustard (*Eupodotis Edwardsii*), and florican (*Sypheotides auritus*), partridges and quails, sand-grouse, plovers and bitterns, pea-fowl and green pigeon, are found everywhere. The Mahsir (*Barbus Mosal*) is found in the Mahi, Vatrak, Meshwa, and Sabarmati, and afford excellent sport with the rod and fly.

310 m. **Ahmedabad**[1] Jn. ✱ Change to metre gauge railway for Delhi and stations on C.I. line.

This most beautiful city, covering an area of 2 sq. m. (215,000 inhabitants), stands on the left bank of the Sabarmati river, in Lat. 23° 2′, Long. 72° 38′. The remains of an old wall, with twelve gateways, surround it.

Ahmedabad, once the greatest city in Western India, is said to have been from 1573 to 1600 the "handsomest town in Hindustan, perhaps in the world." In Sir Thomas Roe's time, 1615, we are told, "it was a goodly city as large as London." It was founded in 1411 by Sultan Ahmad I., who made Asaval, the old Hindu town now included in the S. part of the city, his capital. It passed through two periods of greatness, two of decay, and one of revival. From 1411 to 1511 it grew in size and wealth; from 1512 to 1572 it declined with the decay of the dynasty of Guzerat; from 1572 to 1709 it recovered under the Mughals; from 1709 to 1809 it dwindled with them; and from 1818 it has again increased under British rule. There are 34 mills in it, employing 20,000 hands.

It is supplied with filtered water obtained from wells sunk in the bed of the river.

The Cantonment lies 3½ m. N.E. of the city, and is reached by a good road lined by an avenue of trees, the haunt of thousands of parrots. Here there is an English Church, and there is another, **Christ Church**, in the *Idaria Quarter*, 500 yds. S. of the Delhi Gate.

It is hard to account for Ahmedabad being so little known to modern travellers from Europe. It certainly ranks next to Delhi and Agra for the beauty and the extent of its architectural remains.[1] Its architecture is an interesting and striking example of the combination of Hindu and Mohammedan forms. "Nowhere did the inhabitants of Ahmedabad show how essentially they were an architectural people as in their utilitarian works (wells [*Baolis*] and inlets to water reservoirs). It was a necessity of their nature that every object should be made ornamental, and their success was as great in these as in their mosques or palaces" (see Fergusson's *Indian Architecture*).

The *Jain feeding-places for birds*, which at the first glance look like pigeon-houses, may be seen in many of the streets, and are a peculiar feature

1 No one should pass this ancient capital, the stronghold of the Northern Jains, without pausing long enough (four hours) to visit the Jama Masjid, the *Tombs of the Queens*, and the Rani Sepree Mosque. The chief objects of interest are marked ✱.

1 The amplest details of the architecture of Ahmedabad will be found in a recent volume of the *Archæological Survey of N. India*, by Mr Burgess.

of Ahmedabad: they are extremely picturesque, ornamented with carving, and often gaily painted. Many of the houses in the streets have fronts beautifully ornamented with wood carving.

The old parts of the city are divided into quarters wholly separated off from one another.

The buildings in the city may be seen in the following order:—

The Jama Masjid and Tombs of Ahmad Shah, and his wives; the Rani Sepree Tomb and Mosque; Dastur Khan's Mosque; the Tin Darwazah; the Bhadr Azam Khan's palace; Sidi Said's Mosque; Ahmad Shah's Mosque; Shaikh Hasan's Mosque; the Rani (or Queen's) Mosque in Mirzapur; Muhafiz Khan's Mosque.

With a second morning to spare, he should start early and see Sarkhej, across the river to the S.W., giving himself *at least* four hours for the trip. A second afternoon could be devoted to the Kankariya Tank and Shah 'Alam, S. of the city, and perhaps the modern Jain Temple of Hathisingh, outside the Delhi Gate.

Near the railway station are the handsome lofty minarets and arched central gateway, which are all that remain of a mosque[1] (1) destroyed in the struggle with the Mahrattas in 1753.

The **Jama Masjid** (3),* or *principal mosque*, stands near the centre of the city, on the S. side of the main street (Manik Chauk), a little E. of the Three Gateways. It was built by Sultan Ahmad I. (Ahmad Shah) in 1424. Mr Fergusson says: "Though not remarkable for its size, it is one of the most beautiful mosques in the East." The mosque is entered from the N. by a flight of steps. On the S. is another porch leading into the street, and on the E. is the enclosure, in which is the tomb of the founder. The court is surrounded by a cloister. To the W. is the mosque proper. On the threshold of the main arch, embedded in the pavement, lies a black slab brought from Chintaman's Temple, which, according to Mr Hope, is a Jain idol turned upside down for the faithful to tread on; and touching it on the E. is a white marble crescent, where the Imam stands to pray. In the right-hand corner on entering is a gallery, which was probably used by the members of the royal family. The roof, supported by 260 columns, has fifteen cupolas with galleries round the three in front. The centre cupola is larger and much higher than the others. The two minarets lost half their height in the earthquake of 16th June 1819. They are now 43 ft. high.[1] On the marble slab above the centre of the three *kiblahs* or prayer-niches are these words in Arabic: "This high and far-stretching mosque was raised by the slave who trusts in the mercy of God, the compassionate, the alone to be worshipped." The Koran says, "Truly mosques belong to God, worship no one else with Him." "The slave who trusts in God, the Aider, Nasir-ud-dunya wa-ud-din Abu'l Fath Ahmad Shah, son of Muhammad Shah, son of Sultan Muzaffar."

Through the E. gate is the **Tomb of Ahmad Shah** (2), (repaired 1587). This domed building has a portico to the S. with eighteen pillars. The windows are of perforated stonework. The central chamber is 36 ft. square. It is paved with marble of different colours. The centre cenotaph is that of Ahmad Shah, the one to the W. is that of his son, Muhammad Shah, and that on the E. is that of his grandson, Kutab Shah, died 1441, 1451, and 1459 A.D.

50 yds. to the E. across the street are the **Tombs of the queens of**

[1] These numbers in brackets refer to the numbers on the accompanying plan.

[1] In 1781 Mr Forbes, in his *Oriental Memoirs*, said of them: "A circular flight of steps led to a gallery near the top of each. A little force at the arch of the upper gallery made both minarets shake, though the roof of the mosque remained unmoved."

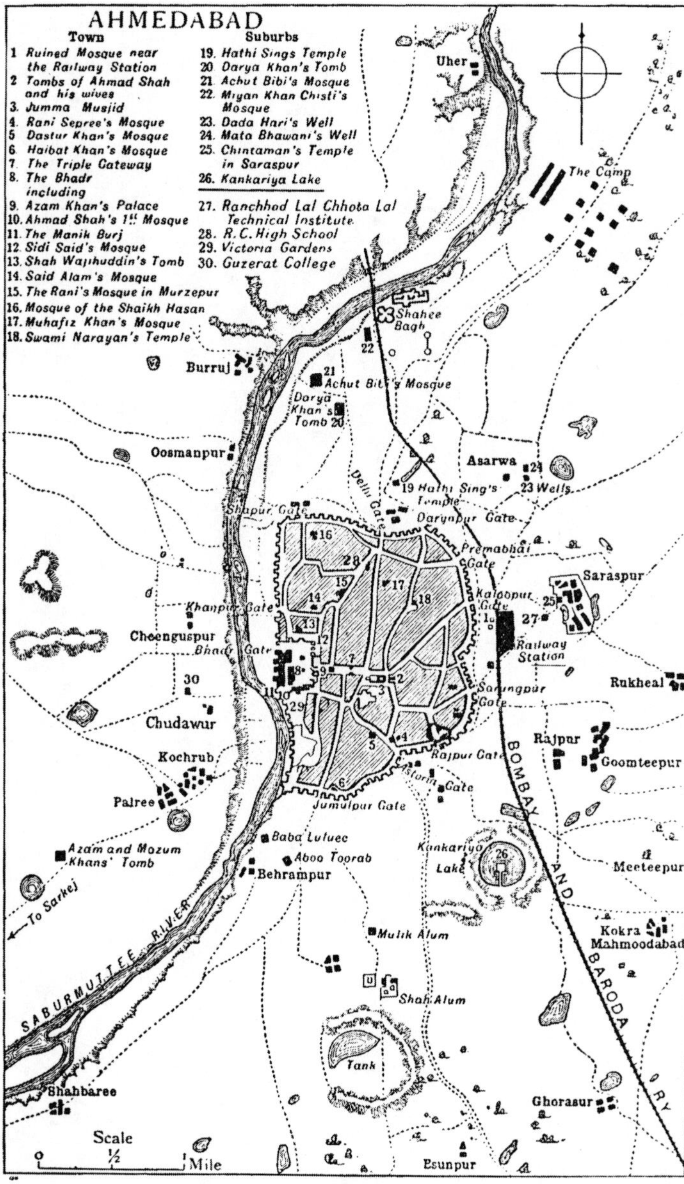
AHMEDABAD
Town
1 Ruined Mosque near the Railway Station
2 Tombs of Ahmad Shah and his wives
3. Jumma Musjid
4. Rani Sepree's Mosque
5 Dastur Khan's Mosque
6 Haibat Khan's Mosque
7. The Triple Gateway
8. The Bhadr including
9. Azam Khan's Palace
10. Ahmad Shah's 1st Mosque
11. The Manik Burj
12. Sidi Said's Mosque
13. Shah Wajihuddin's Tomb
14. Said Alam's Mosque
15. The Rani's Mosque in Murzepur
16. Mosque of the Shaikh Hasan
17. Muhafiz Khan's Mosque
18. Swami Narayan's Temple
Suburbs
19. Hathi Sings Temple
20. Darya Khan's Tomb
21. Achut Bibi's Mosque
22. Miyan Khan Chisti's Mosque
23. Dada Hari's Well
24. Mata Bhawani's Well
25. Chintaman's Temple in Saraspur
26. Kankariya Lake
27. Ranchhod Lal Chhota Lal Technical Institute
28. R. C. High School
29. Victoria Gardens
30. Guzerat College
Uher
The Camp
Shahee Bagh
Burruj
Achut Bibi's Mosque
Darya Khan's Tomb
Oosmanpur
Asarwa
Hathi Sing's Temple
23 Wells
Delhi Gate
Shapur Gate
Daryapur Gate
Premabhai Gate
Saraspur
Kalooput Gate
Khanpur Gate
Cheenguspur
Bhadr Gate
Railway Station
Rukheal
Sarungpur Gate
Chudawur
Rajpur
Goomteepur
Kochrub
Rajpur Gate
Storia Gate
Palree
Jumulpur Gate
Baba Luluee
Azam and Mozum Khans' Tomb
Aboo Toorab
Kankariya Lake
Behrampur
Meeteepur
To Sarkej
Mulik Alum
Kokra Mahmoodabad
SABURMUTTEE RIVER
BOMBAY AND BARODA RY
Shah Alum
Tank
Shahbaree
Ghorasur
Scale
0 ½ 1 Mile
Esunpur

[To face p. 124.

Ahmad Shah (2).* The houses are so close that they quite shut out the façade of the mausoleum, which is raised on a platform. In the façade are thirteen highly ornamented carved recesses. Inside is a rectangular court, with a corridor running round it. In the centre are eight large cenotaphs and several small ones. The centre tombstone is finely carved, and is the tomb of Mughlai Bibi. It is of black stone or marble, inlaid with white. This building is one of the finest in Ahmedabad, but much out of repair

Rani Sepree's Mosque and Tomb (4)* are almost the most beautiful monuments in Ahmedabad. Rani Asni, by whom the mosque and tomb were really built, was one of the wives of Mahmud Bigara, and they were completed in 1514. "They are the first of a series of buildings more delicately ornate than any that preceded."[1] The mosque has two minarets, about 50 ft. high, having four compartments tapering up to the top. The roof is supported by a row of six coupled pillars with single ones behind. The roza, or tomb, is 36 ft. sq.

Dastur Khan's Mosque (5), built in 1486 by one of Mahmud Bigara's ministers. The open stone screenwork that shuts in the cloister round the courtyard is very fine. In the gateway the marks of shot may be seen. A few yds. to the E. of Dastur Khan's Mosque is *Asa Bhil's Mound*, the site of the fort of the Bhil chief, from whom the town of Asaval had its name.

A little to the N.E. of the Jamalpur Gate is **Haibat Khan's Mosque** (6), which is interesting as one of the earliest attempts to combine Mohammedan and Hindu elements. Haibat Khan was one of the noblemen of Ahmad Shah's court. The mosque is very plain. The front wall is pierced by three small pointed arches some distance apart. The minarets are small and without ornament, and rise like chimneys from the roof. The central dome, of Hindu workmanship and of great beauty, is barely raised above the others. The pillars, taken from different temples, display every variety of rich ornament. Except for the form of its dome, the outer porch would suit a Hindu temple.

[1] Mr. T. Hope's *Ahmedabad*.

The **Tin Darwazah**, or **Three Gateways** (7), built by Sultan Ahmad I., is of stone richly carved. It crosses the main street a little to the N. of the Jama Masjid. This gateway led into the outer court of the Bhadr, known as the Royal Square, and was surrounded, in 1638, by two rows of palm trees and tamarinds (J. A. de Mandelso's *Voyages*, 1662, p. 76). Facing the Bhadr Gate is a municipal garden. N. of the garden is the High School, and to the W. the Hemabhai Institute, with a good library and newspapers and periodicals. Near it is the **Mosque of Malik Sha'ban**, with an inscription that says it was built in the reign of Kutab-ud-din, by Sh'aban, son of 'Imad-ul-mulk, in 856 A.H. = 1452 A.D.

The **Bhadr** (8), (pronounced *Bhaddar*), an ancient enclosure or citadel, built by Ahmad Shah, 1411, and named after the goddess Bhadra, a propitious form of Kali, is occupied by public offices. In the E. face is the **Palace**, built by **'Azam Khan** (9), the 23rd Viceroy (1635-42), who was called *Udai*, "the white ant," from his love of building. It is now the Post Office. Over the gate is a Persian chronogram, giving the date 1636 A.D. The *N. entrance to the Bhadr* is very handsome. The gate under an archway is 18 ft. high, and opens into a regular octagonal hall of great elegance, containing, in the upper story, an arched gallery, having in front a low wall of open-cut stone, and each gallery surmounted by a cupola. Underneath this hall is a fine vaulted chamber, entered by a flight of steps at each side, with a reservoir and fountain in the middle. Close to the Jail is a temple to Bhadra Kali Mata. At the N.E. corner is **Sidi Said's Mosque** (12),* which forms part of the wall, and was till lately the Mamlatdar's office. Two of its windows are filled with delicate stone tracery of tree-stems and branches beautifully wrought. Mr Fergusson, who gives an illustration of one of the windows, says in his *History of Architecture:* "It would be difficult to excel the skill with which the vegetable forms are conventionalised just to the extent required for the purpose. The equal spacing also of the subject by the three ordinary trees and four palms takes it out of the category of direct imitation of nature, and renders it sufficiently structural for its situation; but perhaps the greatest skill is shown in the even manner in which the pattern is spread over the whole surface. There are some exquisite specimens of tracery in precious marbles at Agra and Delhi, but none quite equal to this."

In the S.W. corner of the Bhadr is **Ahmad Shah's Mosque** (10), built by him in 1414, twenty years before the Jama Masjid, being perhaps the oldest here. It is said to have been used as the king's private chapel. Left on advancing towards the mosque, was once the **Ganj i-Shahid** or Store of Martyrs, where were buried the Moslems killed in storming the town. The façade is almost bare of ornament, with ill-designed pointed arches. The two minarets are evidently unfinished. The *mimbar*, or pulpit, is adorned with what looks like laurel leaves. The architecture shows the first attempts at building a Moslem edifice in what had been a Hindu city. The pillars still bear Hindu figures and emblems. The N. porch, leading into the latticed ladies' gallery, is Hindu throughout, and may be part of a temple *in situ*.

W. of this mosque is the **Manik Burj** (11) or **Ruby Bastion,** built round the foundation-stone of the city. There is a small round tomb in the yard near the collector's office, which is said to be that of Ibrahim Kuli Khan, a Persian warrior.

Shah Wajihud-din's Tomb (13), built by Saiyad Murtaza Khan Bokhari, 11th Viceroy, 1606-1609, is a very beautiful monument.

Said 'Alam's Mosque (14), was built about 1420 by Abubakr Husaini. The inner details are as rich as Hindu art could make them. S. of this 170 yds. is

The **Rani Masjid (Queen's Mosque)** (15) *in Mirzapur*, a few yds. to the S. of the D.B., built probably in Sultan Ahmad I.'s reign. There are two minarets, unfinished or partly destroyed by an earthquake, and now only 33 ft. high. The roof has three domes, and is supported by thirty-six plain pillars. To the N.E. of the mosque is the roza or tomb (restored). Under the dome are two cenotaphs of white marble; the central one is the tomb of Rupvati, a princess of Dhar. It is in good preservation, while that on the W. side is much injured; both are ornamented with the chain and censer, a Hindu device. Mr Fergusson has given a plan of this mosque, and says: "The lower part of the minaret is of pure Hindu architecture. We can follow the progress of the development of this form from the first rude attempt in the Jama Masjid, through all its stages to the exquisite patterns of the Queen's Mosque at Mirzapur."

The **Mosque of Shaikh Hasan Muhammad Chishti** *in Shahpur* (16) is in the N.W. angle of the city, not far from the Sabarmati, 1565 A.D. The minarets are unfinished. "The tracery in the niches of their bases is perhaps superior to any other in the city." On the S. or left side of the central arch is a Persian quatrain.

This chronogram gives the date 1566 A.D.

East of the Rani's Masjid the **Mosque of Muhafiz Khan** (17) was built in 1465 by Jamal-ud-din Muhafiz Khan, governor of the city in 1471 under Mahmud Bigara. It is the best preserved of all the mosques. According to Mr Hope, "its details are exquisite," and the minarets of the mosque and those of Rani Sepree "surpass those of Cairo in beauty."

S. of this mosque is the modern **Swami Narayan's Temple** (18), finished in 1850. It has an octagonal dome, supported on twelve pillars, and is a fine building.

Close to it is the **Pinjrapol** or *Asylum for Animals.* The enclosure is surrounded by sheds where about 800 animals are lodged. There is also a room where insects are fed. Close to the S. of it are nine tombs, each 18 ft. 3 in. long, called the **Nau Gaz Pirs**, "the Nine Yard Saints." They are most likely the tombs of a number of men killed in some battle.

The **Mosque, Tomb, and College of Shuja'at Khan.** This mosque, which stands 400 yds. N.E. of the Lal Gate of the Bhadr, has two slender minarets, and is divided by piers into five bays, and over the kiblah are written the creed and date = 1695. The walls, up to 6 ft., are lined with marble. The tomb is of brick, with a marble floor, much destroyed. It is called both the Marble and the Ivory Mosque.

Ahmedabad is celebrated for its **Handicraftsmen**—goldsmiths, jewellers, etc., who carry the *chopped* form of jewellery (the finest archaic jewellery in India) to the highest perfection; copper and brass-workers, as instanced particularly in the very graceful and delicate brass-screens and *pandans* (betel-boxes); carpenters, who have long been famous for their superior carving in *shisham*, or mongrel blackwood, of which the finest specimens are to be found here; stone-masons, lacquer-workers, carvers in ivory,—also for the manufacture of "Bombay boxes"; mock ornaments for idols; leather shields; cotton cloth (four monster steam-factories); calico-printing, gold-figured silks, and gold and silver tissues; Kimkhwab (*kinkab*), or brocades (the noblest produced in India); gold and silver lace and thread, and all manner of tinsel ornaments.

Its industrial importance is shown by the fact that "the *Nagar-Seth*," or city lord, of Ahmedabad is the titular head of all the Guilds and one of the highest personages in the city.

Carpets have also become a speciality of Ahmedabad, and the manufactories as well as the workshops of the other crafts are well worth visiting.

ENVIRONS.—For 12 m. round Ahmedabad the country is full of interesting ruins; but here only the principal can be mentioned. Just outside the Delhi Gate, on the N., is the modern **Hathi Singh Temple** (19),* built of white marble and surmounted by fifty-three domes. This and a rest-house and family mansion close by were finished in 1848, at a cost of Rs. 1,000,000. The dimensions of this temple are of the first order; its style the pure Jain; and it stands a convincing proof that the native architecture has not been extinguished by centuries of repression. In its sculptures may be seen representations of the twenty-four holy men, or Tirthankars, and hundreds of other images, all similar, but each labelled on the base with the emblem of some distinct Jain. The entrance is from a courtyard surrounded by a corridor, where woollen slippers are provided before ascending a portico richly carved and supported by pillars. The temple consists of an outer and an inner chamber, both paved with coloured marbles chiefly from Makran in Rajputana: in the latter is the image of Dharmnath, who is represented as a beautiful youth, with a sparkling tiara of imitation diamonds. Mr Fergusson says: "Each part increases in dignity to the sanctuary. The exterior expresses the interior more completely than even a Gothic design, and, whether looked at from its courts or from the outside, it possesses variety without confusion, and an appropriateness of every part to the purpose intended." N.W. of this is the ruined **Tomb** of **Darya Khan** (20), 1453, chief minister of Mahmud Bigara. The dome is 9 ft. thick, and the largest in Guzerat. Not far beyond it is the **Chhota** or small **Shahi Bagh,** of no architectural interest, now a private house, where it is said the ladies of the royal harem lived. Across the railway line is the **Shahi Bagh,** a very fine garden-house, now the residence of the Commissioner of the N. Division. A subterranean passage is said to communicate between the two places. The building was erected in 1622 by Shah Jahan, when Viceroy of Ahmedabad, to give work to the poor during a season of scarcity. In the 16th century this was the great resort for the people of the city. The Shahi Bagh is close to the railway bridge over the Sabarmati, which river it overlooks. Half a m. S.W. of the Shahi Bagh is **Miyan Khan Chishti's Mosque** (22), built in 1465 by Malik Maksud Vazir; and ½ m. more to the S.W. is **Achut Bibi's Mosque** (21), built in 1469 by 'Imadu'l mulk, one of Bigara's ministers, for his wife Bibi Achut Kuki, whose tomb is close by. There were seven minarets here, all of which were thrown down in the earthquake of 1819. Returning from this point, the drive may be continued to the N.E. side of the city, to Asarva, about ½ m. N.E. of the Daryapur Gate, where are the **Baolis** or **Wells of Dada Hari** (23) * and **Mata Bhawani.** The real name of Dada is said by the local people to have been Halim, "mild," and they call him Dada Hari. He is said to have been the husband of the Dai, or nurse of one of the kings. There is an ascent from the road to the platform which surrounds the well's mouth. A domed portico, supported by twelve pillars, gives entrance to three tiers of finely constructed galleries below ground, which lead to the octagonal well, with inscriptions in Sanscrit and Arabic. The well beyond the octagonal one has pillars round it and a fence wall. Beyond this is a circular well for irrigation. A very narrow staircase leads to the level ground, where by the side of the well are two stone kiosks. About 50 yds. to the W. is *Dada Hari's Mosque,* one of the best decorated buildings at Ahmedabad, though no marble is employed. The stone is of a dull reddish-grey colour. The bases of the two minarets are richly carved; a portion of them was thrown down by the earthquake of 1819. To the N. is the *Roza of Dada Hari or Halim.* The N. door is exquisitely carved, but the inside is quite plain.

Mata Bhawani (24).—This well is about 100 yrds. N. of Dada Hari's, but is much older, and is thought to be of the time of Karan, when Ahmedabad was called Karanavati. The descent to the water from the platform is by fifty-two steps and pillared galleries as at Dada Hari. The porticoes are quite plain, and the well is altogether inferior to that of Dada Hari.

Most of the houses in the *Madhavpura* suburb are warehouses, and it is the great business quarter. *Saraspur,* E. of the railway station, is a distinct walled town, the largest of the suburbs. In this suburb is the Jain **Temple of Chintaman** (25), restored in 1868 by Shantidas, a rich merchant, at a cost of Rs.900,000. Aurangzeb defiled it and changed it into a mosque. The Jains petitioned the Emperor Shah Jahan, who ordered his son to repair and restore the temple. But in 1666 Thevonet speaks of it as a mosque (*Voyages,* v. p. 28).

¾ m. S.E. of the Rajpur Gate is the Hauz-i-Kutab, generally called the **Kankariya Lake** (26), or Pebble Lake. This reservoir, one of the largest of its kind in this part of India, is a regular polygon of thirty-four sides, each side 190 ft. long, the whole being more than 1 m. round. The area is 72 acres. It was constructed by Sultan

Kutab-ud-din in 1451, and was then surrounded by many tiers of cut-stone steps, with six sloping approaches, flanked by cupolas and an exquisitely carved water-sluice. In the centre was an island, with a garden called Nagina or the Gem, and a pavilion called Ghattamandal. In 1872 Mr Borrodaile, the Collector, repaired the building, and made a road from the Rajpur Gate. On the E. bank of the lake are some Dutch and Armenian tombs, Saracenic in style, with domes and pillars a good deal ruined. The dates range from 1641 to 1689.

This expedition may be continued to **Batwa**, which is almost 5 m. due S. of the Rajpur Gate. Here Burhan-ud-din Kutab-ul-Alam, the grandson of a famous saint buried at Uch on the Sutlej, is interred. He came to the court of Sultan Ahmad I., settled at Batwa, and died there in 1452. A vast mausoleum of fine design and proportions was erected to his memory. It resembles the buildings at Sarkhej, but the aisles are arched and vaulted, and the dome is raised by a second tier of arches. The workmanship is most elaborate, but the building is unfortunately much out of repair. Adjoining it are a mosque and tank.

The tomb of **Shah 'Alam**, the son of the saint buried at Batwa, is 2 m. S.E. of the town on the Batwa road. Before reaching the tomb the road passes under two plain gateways, and then through one with a Nakar Khana (music gallery) above the archway, and so into a vast court. To the W. is the mosque, which has two minarets of seven stories, handsomely carved and about 90 ft. high. The tomb of Shah 'Alam is to the E., and is protected by metal lattices: he was a spiritual guide of Mahmud Bigara and died in 1475. To the S. is an assembly hall, built by Muzaffar III. (1561-72) and partly destroyed by the British in 1780 to furnish materials for the siege of the city. The tomb is said to have been built by Taj Khan Nariali, one of Mahmud's courtiers. Early in the 17th century Asaf Khan (p. 238), brother of the Empress Nur Jahan, adorned the dome with gold and precious stones. The floor of the tomb is inlaid with black and white marble, the doors are of open brass-work, and the frame in which they set, as well as what shows between the door-frame and the two stone pillars to the right and left, is of pure white marble beautifully carved and pierced. The tomb itself is enclosed by an inner wall of pierced stone. The outer wall in the N. is of stone trellis-work of the most varied design, and here Shaikh Kabir, renowned for his learning, who died in 1618, is buried. The mosque was built by Muhammad Salih Badakhshi. The minarets were much damaged by the earthquake of 1819, but have been repaired, and are now in good order. To the S. of the mosque is a tomb like that of the chief mausoleum where the family of Shah 'Alam are buried. Outside the wall to the W. is a reservoir, built by the wife of Taj Khan Nariali.

Sarkhej is 6 m. to the S.W. of the Jamalpore Gate, whence a good carriage will take two people comfortably in about an hour. Sarkhej is served by the railway line to Dholka (p. 130), but the service is not likely to be suitable to visitors. The road crosses the Sabarmati river, the channel of which is about ½ m. broad, but the water in the dry weather is only 2 ft. deep. On the left bank is the Victoria Garden, of which the site was given by Govt. to the city, with a marble seated statue of the Queen Empress by Mr G. A. Mhatre. The river-bed is dotted with enclosures for the cultivation of melons, potatoes, and other vegetables, and the running water is lined with gaily-dressed women washing their clothes. Garments of every shape and of the brightest colours are laid out to dry. These persons are not professional washerwomen, but belong to many classes of society. The remains of a bridge will be seen near the crossing; both it and the railway bridge were carried away by the great flood in 1875, but the latter was at once restored. Near the bridge the city wall is from 40 to 60 ft. high. The road from the river's bank is good, with rich fields on either side, and at 1¾ m. right is the massive brick.

Mausoleum of'Azam and Mu'azzam, built probably in 1457. These brothers are said to have been the architects of Sarkhej, and to have come from Khorasan. The immense structure which contains their tombs is raised on a platform. About 300 yds. from the principal buildings at Sarkhej there are two brick towers about 30 ft. high, the bases of which, close to the ground, have been so dug away that it seems a miracle they do not fall. After another 200 yds., the road passes under two arches, leading into the courtyard of Sarkhej. To the left on entering is the fine mausoleum of **Mahmud Bigara**[1] and his sons, and connected with it by a beautiful portico another equally magnificent tomb on the border of the tank for his queen Râjabai. To the right is the **Tomb of the Saint** *Shaikh Ahmad Khattu Ganj Bakhsh*, called also Maghrabi. Ganj Bakhsh lived at Anhalwara, and was the spiritual guide of Sultan Ahmad I., and a renowned Mohammedan saint; he retired to Sarkhej, and died there in 1445 at the age of 111, and this magnificent tomb and mosque were erected to his memory. The tomb is the largest of its kind in Guzerat, and has a great central dome and many smaller ones. Over the central door of the tomb is a Persian quatrain. It gives the date 1473 A.D. The shrine inside is octagonal, surrounded by finely-worked brass lattice-windows. The pavement is of coloured marbles. and the dome inside richly gilt; from it hangs a long silver chain which once reached to the ground. The vast adjoining **Mosque** is the perfection of elegant simplicity: it has ten cupolas supported on eighteen rows of pillars. The whole of these buildings, says Mr Fergusson, "are constructed without a single arch; all the pillars have the usual bracket capitals of the Hindus, and all the domes are on the horizontal principle." S. of the saint's tomb is that of his disciple Shaikh Salah-ud-din.

Mahmud Bigara excavated the great tank of 17½ acres, surrounded it by flights of stone steps, constructed a richly-decorated supply-sluice, and built at its S.W. corner a splendid palace and harem (now in ruins).

With the lake, the Sarkhej buildings form the most beautiful group in Ahmedabad. They belong to the best period of the style, and have the special interest of being almost purely Hindu, with only the faintest trace of the Mohammedan style. Numbers of people bathe in the tank in spite of the alligators. A little S. of the lake is the tomb of Baba Ali Sher, a saint even more venerated than Ganj Bakhsh. It is small, ugly, and white-washed. Close by are the remains of Mirza Khan Khanan's Garden of Victory, laid out in 1584 after his defeat of Muzaffar III., the last Ahmedabad king. In the 17th century Sarkhej was so famous for indigo that in 1620 the Dutch established a factory there.

Leaving Ahmedabad, the metre gauge railway crosses the Sabarmati river quite close to the Shahi-bagh on a fine bridge which carries the rails for both gauges and a footway on one side.

At 314 m. **Sabarmati** junction station the narrow gauge continues N. to Delhi, whilst the broad gauge turns W. for Wadhwan and Kathiawar (Rte. 11). There are also branch lines to the S.W. to Dholka (33 m.) passing Sarkhej (above), and to the N.E. to Parantij (41 m.) and Idar (55 m.). The chief of Idar is Major-General Maharaja Sir Partab Singh, G.C.S.I., K.C.B., A.D.C., uncle of the late Maharaja of Jodhpur.

The country going N. is flat and well cultivated. The beautiful and celebrated well at Adalaj is in this direction, but can perhaps be more easily visited by road.

353 m. **Mehsana** junction station. This is one of the most important

[1] Reigned 1459-1513 A.D. Bigara means with horn-like moustaches.

railway centres in Guzerat, as it is the junction for three branch lines constructed by the Gaekwar of Baroda. They are: (1) a line passing through **Visnagar**, **Vadnagar**, and **Kheralu**, total distance 27 m., general direction N.E.; (2) a line to **Patan**, the historic capital of Guzerat, distance 24 m. N.W.; (3) a line to **Viramgam**, 40 m. S.W., made to connect the Rajputana and Kathiawar metre-gauge lines of railway. (For Viramgam see p. 148).

On these branch lines two places only need be noticed here.

[**Vadnagar**, 21 m. N.E. (population 13,700). This place, once very important as the site of Anandpura, is stated to have been conquered by a Rajput prince from Ayodhya in 145 A.D. There are some interesting ruins, including a very fine Kirti Stambha gateway, and the *Temple of Hatkeshvar Mahadeo* is worth a visit. It is now the religious capital of the Nagar Brahmans, a most influential class of men in Guzerat and Kathiawar. It was long the chartered refuge of the Dhinoj Brahmans, a class of robbers who were protected and taxed by successive native governments down to quite a recent date.

Patan, 24 m. N.W. of Mehsana (population 31,500). The city stands on the site of the ancient Anhilvara, capital of the Hindu kings of Guzerat, which was taken by Mahmud of Ghazni on his way to attack the temple of Somnath in 1024 A.D. The site for generations has been a quarry whence beautiful carved stones have been carried to other places. It is still famous for its libraries of Jain MSS. There are no less than 108 Jain temples here.]

366 m. **Unjha** station. A town in the Baroda territory, and the headquarters of the Kadwakanbis, a peculiar caste of agriculturists. Marriages among them take place but once in eleven years, when every girl over forty days old must be married on one or other of the days fixed. Should no husband be found, a proxy bridegroom is sometimes set up and married to a number of girls who immediately enter a state of nominal widowhood until an eligible suitor presents himself, when a second marriage takes place.

374 m. **Sidhpur** station (population 16,224). It stands on the steep northern bank of the Sarasvati river, and the scene in the bed of the stream during the day in the dry weather is specially gay. The place is of extreme antiquity, and contains the ruins of *Rudra Mala*, one of the most famous ancient temples in W. India. It was wrecked by Ala-ud-din Khilji in 1297; and much of it has been carried off since for building purposes. The stones are gigantic, and the carving superb, but very little of it remains. A row of small temples has been converted into a mosque. The more modern temples are very numerous. *Kadi*, the N. division of Baroda, in which Sidhpur is situated, is the only part of the whole of the Bombay Presidency in which *poppies* are allowed to be grown. The opium is manufactured in Sidhpur at the *State Stores*.

390 m. **Palanpur** station (R.), D.B. The chief town of a native state of that name, the residence of a Political Agent. [Railway N.W. to the military station of **Deesa** on the *R. Banas* 20 m. distant.]

425 m. **Abu Road** station * (R.), D.B. This is a well-built, attractive-looking place. Mount Abu looks down on it from the N.W.

[The excursion to Mount Abu is one of the most interesting in India, on account of the Jain temples. The ascent to it, 16½ m., is by a good road, now practicable for tongas — (cost Rs. 10, per seat Rs. 4), which should be ordered beforehand by telegram. An ekka for luggage costs Rs. 4.8 as. Rooms should be secured beforehand at the small Rajputana Hotel. The Dilwarra temples can be visited only in the afternoon—pass necessary from the Magt., Mount Abu. Though part of the Aravalli range, which runs up to Delhi, Abu is detached from that chain by a valley about 15 m. wide. The plateau at the top is about 14 m. by 4 m., and varies in height from 4000 to 5600 ft.

Mount Abu * is the headquarters of the Rajputana administration, and the residence of vakils or agents from a large number of native states. It is also a sanatorium for European troops and a hot-weather resort in the summer season.

At it are the Residency, *Church*, *Lawrence Asylum Schools* for children of soldiers, *Barracks*, *Club*, *Bazaar* of shops, and a considerable number of private houses on the margin of the *Gem Lake*, a most charming piece of artificial water studded with islands, and overhung by a curious rock that looks like a gigantic toad about to spring into the water. The *Railway Schools* for children are outside the station on the plateau. The surface of Mount Abu is very much broken up, so that the carriage roads are very few, but there are many bridle-roads and picturesque footpaths. The views over the plains from various points are exceedingly fine. An attack was made on the place on 21st August 1857 by mutineers from the Erinpura force, but was beaten off.

The **Dilwarra Temples**, the great attraction of Mount Abu, are reached by a good bridle-path (2 m.). *A pass to visit them is necessary.*

In spite of ill-usage and some very bad restoration in parts, the Dilwarra temples are very beautiful, and find a fitting framework in their nest of mango trees, with green fields of barley waving at their feet, and high hills surrounding them on all sides.

"The more modern of the two temples was built by the same brothers, Tejahpala and Vastupala, who erected the triple temple at Girnar.[1] This one, we learn from inscriptions, was erected between 1197 and 1247, and for minute delicacy of carving and beauty of detail stands almost unrivalled, even in the land of patient and lavish labour. It is said to have taken fourteen years to build, and to have cost Rs. 18,000,000, besides a large sum spent in levelling the hill on which it stands.

"The other, built by another merchant prince, Vimala Sah, apparently about 1032 A.D., is simpler and bolder, though still as elaborate as good taste would allow in any purely architectural object. Being one of the oldest as well as one of the most complete examples known of a Jain temple, its peculiarities form a convenient introduction to the style, and serve to illustrate how complete and perfect it had already become when we first meet with it in India.

"The principal object here, as elsewhere, is a cell lighted only from the door, containing a cross-legged seated figure of the saint to whom the temple is dedicated, in this instance Parswanatha. The cell terminates upwards in a sikra, or pyramidal spire-like roof, which is common to all Hindu and Jain temples of the age in the north of India. To this is attached a portico composed of forty-eight free-standing pillars; and the whole is enclosed in an oblong courtyard, about 140 ft. by 90 ft., surrounded by a double colonnade of smaller pillars, forming porticoes to a range of fifty-five cells, which enclose it on all sides, exactly as they do in Buddhist viharas. In this case, however, each cell, instead of being the residence of a monk, is occupied by one of those cross-legged images which belong alike to Buddhism and Jainism. Here they are, according to the Jain practice, all repetitions of the same image of Parswanatha, and over the door of each cell, or on its jambs, are sculptured scenes from his life. The long beams, stretching from pillar to pillar, supporting the roof, are relieved by curious angular struts of white marble, springing from the middle of the pillar up to the middle of the beam" (Fergusson, ii. 36.)

Achilghar is reached by following the bridle-path past Dilwarra for about 4 m. to the village of Uria, where there is a bungalow. From this a bad track turns right for another 1 m. to the first temple. It is surrounded by

[1] See p. 156.

a wall, approached by a flight of steps, and beautifully ornamented. S.E. of this are other temples on higher ground overlooking the valley. The view is magnificent. These are the buildings seen on the right during the ascent from Abu Road. S. of the first temple is the *Agni Kund*, a tank famous in Hindu mythology. On the bank is a marble image of Pramar with his bow, and near him three large stone buffaloes. This figure is superior in style and treatment to most; and the same may be said of the statues in other temples around the Hill of Abu, specially of the brass figure at Gaumukh alluded to below. The Achilghar group is perhaps as attractive as the more renowned temples at Dilwarra, though not comparable in size or finish; but the absence of modern work, and an air of antiquity, solidity, and repose, make them worthy of all admiration.

Other paths lead to the following sites; the beaten way should not be left without a guide or person who knows the country intimately.

Gaumukh, a beautifully situated temple 500 ft. down the S.E. slope, and 3 m. from the church. There is a brass figure facing the temple.

Gautama, on S. side of the hill, W. of Gaumukh; 5 m. from station. Lovely view.

Rishi Krishna, at the foot of the hill, S.E. side, 14 m. from the Civil Station, is easily visited from Abu Road railway station.

476 m. **Erinpura Road** for the cantonment of the Erinpura Irregular Force, lying 6 m. W. The Jodhpur legion there, in 1857, mutinied on 23rd August, but spared its officers. Two weeks later it defeated the troops of the Jodhpur State sent against them, and finally started for Delhi. It was intercepted on 16th October at Narnaul (p. 145), and defeated by Colonel Gerrard, who lost his life in the engagement.

25 m. S.E. of the railway station is the famous marble temple of Sadri, which is really at Rampura, 5 m. S. of Sadri, built by the Kumbo Rana (p. 94), and considered by Mr Fergusson to be the finest Jain temple in all India (*Indian Architecture*, p. 240). It can be visited only by riding and with the assistance of the officer commanding at Erinpura.

528 m. **Marwar Railway** junction station.

Route to Hyderabad Sindh and excursion to Jodhpur.

From this point the Jodhpur-Bikanir Railway branches E. to (44 m.) *Luni Jn.*, and then continues in a northerly direction. From Luni Junction a line 310 m. long runs to Balotra Junction for the salt-works at *Pachbadra* (60 m.), and on through a desolate country to Hyderabad Sindh, in 15½ hours, and to (420 m.) Korachi in 29½ hours—through journey from Bombay in 43 hours. A refreshment car is now attached to the trains on this line, which forms the most direct route between Bombay and Korachi.

Many miles before reaching Jodhpur the Fort can be distinguished rising abruptly out of the bare plain.

64 m. **JODHPUR** station, D.B., the capital of the Rajput state of that name, and of the country known as Marwar, is the residence of the chief and of a Resident, from whom it is necessary to ask permission to see the Fort.

The *State of Jodhpur* or *Marwar* covers an area of 35,000 sq. m., with a population of 2,000,000; the revenue of the state amounts to 49 lakhs. The present chief is H.H. Maharaja Dhiraj Summair Singh. The state was founded from Kanauj, after the defeat of the Rathors there in 1211. The *City* was built by Rao Jodha in 1459, and from that time has been the seat of government. Maharaja Udai Singh, of the Jodhpur House, and his grandson, Maharaja Gaj Singh, were leading nobles at the Court of the Emperors Akbar and Jahangir; and Maharaja Jaswant Singh commanded the armies of Shah Jahan and Dara Shikoh against the forces of Princes Aurangzeb and

Murad in 1658, and died in Kabul, commanding the Imperial Forces there.

The city (population 79,000) stands on the S. end of a range of sandstone hills running E. and W., and is surrounded by a strong wall nearly 6 m. in extent, with seven gates, each bearing the name of the town to which it leads. Some of the houses and temples in the city are of stone richly carved. Amongst the most important buildings are the *Temple* in the Dhan Mandi (wheat market), and the *Talaiti Mal*, an old palace now used as the Jaswant Female Hospital.

The **Fort** stands up boldly some 400 ft. above the city and the plain, and presents a magnificent appearance. The rock is on every side scarped, but especially at the N. end, where the palace is built on the edge of a perpendicular cliff at least 120 ft. high. Strong walls and numerous round and square towers encircle the crest of the hill. A modern engineered road winds up the neighbouring slopes to a massive gateway. Here is the first of seven barriers thrown across the zigzag ascent, having immense portals with separate guards at each. On the wall of the last are represented the hands of fifteen wives of the Maharajas who underwent *sati* at their deaths.

At the top of the rock are the highly interesting *Old Palaces*. There are courtyards within courtyards, all solidly built and surrounded by lattice windows of the most delicate and beautiful designs. Here in the *Treasury* are the Maharaja's jewels, a wonderful collection, and well worth seeing. Some of the pearls, emeralds, and diamonds are unusually fine. The silver trappings for elephants and horses should also be noticed. The view from the palace windows is most interesting and extensive, and shows the town nestling under the huge rock.

There was formerly great scarcity of water in the fort, and the women had daily to walk all the way to Mandor (see p. 135) to fetch it, but now it is brought up to the top of the fort in pipes. There is a well in the fort 450 ft. deep. The principal **Tanks** [1] are—The *Padam Saugar* Tank in the N.W. part of the city, excavated out of the rock, but of small size. In the same quarter is the *Rani Saugar*, at the foot of the W. entrance into the fort with which it is connected by outworks, and is chiefly reserved for the garrison and ladies residing in the fort. The *Gulab Saugar*, to the E., is handsomely built of stone, and is capacious, with a smaller one adjoining it. The *Baiji ka Talao*, S. of the city, is extensive, but not capable of holding water long. 1 m. W. is a lake called *Akherajji ka Talao*, which is a fine sheet of water, clear, deep, and extensive, resembling rather a natural lake than an artificial tank. 3 m. N. of the city is the *Bal-Samand*, a pretty tank, with a palace on the embankment and garden below, used by the Maharaja as a summer residence. The *Canal* from it to the city is a work of much importance.

The chief **Sport** near Jodhpur is *pig-sticking*, the pigs being preserved by the Maharaja.

S.E. of the city are the **Raikabagh Palace**, where the late Chief resided, and the **Jubilee Buildings** or public offices near it, designed by Colonel Sir S. Jacob in the native style. They are extensive and beautiful, and deserve attention.

The Palace of the present chief is further S. at Ratanada.

The **Public Gardens**, and fine stone houses of the officials, have now replaced the barren tract that formerly bounded the city in the S. side. These, and many other improvements, are due to the late Prime Minister, Sir Partab Singh, now Maharaja of Idar.

At about 1½ m. outside the N.E. angle of the city is a suburb of 800 houses called the **Mahandir**, or "great temple." The roof of the temple is supported by 100 pillars, and the interior is richly decorated.

[1] The Kalyan reservoir, 3 m. W. of the town, is the largest of all.

This suburb is defended by a stone wall, with a few bastions. In it are two palaces, in one of which the spiritual adviser of the late Maharaja lives. The other is reserved for the spirit of his predecessor, whose bed is laid out in a state chamber, with a golden canopy over the pillow; and has no living occupant. The priests, called *Naths*, have lost nearly all their former prestige.

Mandor. This was the capital of Marwar before the foundation of Jodhpur. It is situated about 3 m. to the N. of Jodhpur. Here are the *Chhatris* or cenotaphs (much neglected) of the former rulers, erected on the spots where the funeral pyres consumed their remains. Some are fine massive buildings,—that dedicated to *Ajit Singh*, d. 1724, being the largest and finest. These "proud monuments," as Colonel Tod calls them,[1] are built of "a close-grained freestone of a dark brown or red tint, with sufficient hardness to allow the sculptor to indulge his fancy. The style of architecture here is mixed, partaking both of the Shivite and the Buddhist, but the details are decidedly Jain, more especially the columns." Across a little stream not many yards from here is a pantheon called the *Shrine of the 300,000,000 gods* containing a row of gigantic painted figures of divinities and heroes. At the end of the long building where these figures are arranged is a curious fresco of a sea-piece. Near this is the stone palace of *Abhay Singh*, who succeeded Ajit Singh in 1724. It is now quite deserted and given over to the bats. There are some fine bits of trellis screen-work in the garden.

125 m. W. of Jodhpur lies Jaisalmer, the capital of the Bhati Rajputs of the western desert, founded by Jaisal in 1156 A.D. It is famous for buildings constructed of yellow-brown stone, and for its handsome Jain temples.

[1] For full details see Colonel Tod's *Rajasthan*.

128 m. **Merta Road** junction for Bikaner and Bhatinda. **Merta**, a fortified Marwar town of some importance, is some miles from the railway. Near this town was fought a decisive battle between the Mahrattas and Rajputs, in which the former, with the treacherous assistance of a large body of Pindaris under Amir Khan, inflicted a crushing defeat upon the latter.

Excursion to Bikaner.

35 m. **Nagaur.** A fortified town of importance in Marwar, pop. 56,000. The crenellated wall, houses, and groups of temples make an agreeable break in the monotonous desert.

103 m. **Bikaner**, the capital of the state of that name. It was founded by Bika, sixth in descent from Jodha of the royal house of Jodhpur. The state has an area of upwards of 22,300 sq. m., and a population of about 584,000. The ruling chief is H.H. Maharaja Sir Ganga Singh, G.C.I.E., K.C.S.I., A.D.C. A large part of the state is desert, and the great depth (150 ft. to 300 ft.) at which water is found renders irrigation impossible, and the country is much subject to famines, which have been very frequent and severe during late years. The chief wealth of the people is their flocks and herds, which feed on the bushes and scanty herbage.

For a visit to Bikaner the Private Secretary to the Maharaja must be addressed. The Maharaja's old palace itself is picturesque and imposing, viewed from a distance. But, like most Hindu palaces, its interior consists for the most part of a mass of small irregular suites of rooms, due to the custom which forbids a chief to live in the apartments of his predecessor, though the Ganga Nawas built by the present Maharaja is a fine structure. Some of the rooms are lined with willow-pattern plates and tiles set in the walls; there is a fine collection of arms and jewels in it. The modern Lalghar palace lies 2 m. from the city. The town is surrounded by a wall, and contains several houses with handsome fronts of carved stonework, belonging to wealthy Jain merchants. Outside the town are a number of very deep wells constructed as works of charity. One of these should be seen and its depth viewed by a beam of light reflected from a mirror. At Devi Kund on the E. side are the chhatris (cenotaphs) of the Bikaner chiefs.

From Bikaner a branch line now runs on 200 m. to Bhatinda (201 m.) (see p. 146), through (113 m.) Suratgarh, and (144 m.) Hanumangarh.

---

201 m. **Kuchaman Road.** From here a branch of the C.I. Railway runs on 20 m. to Phalera.

216 m. **Sambhar** station.

The Sambhar Lake lies on the border of the Jaipur and Jodhpur states. The surrounding country is arid and sterile, being composed of rocks abounding in salt, and belonging to the Permian system; and the salt of the lake comes from the washing of these rocks. The bottom is tenacious black mud resting on loose sand. The lake is 21 m. long from E. to W. after the rains, and the average breadth at that time is 5 m. from N. to S., and the depth, 1 m. from the shore, is only 2½ ft. The water dries up from October to June, and leaves about an inch of salt in the enclosures, which are constructed only where the black mud is of considerable thickness.

From the 17th century the salt was worked by the Jaipur and Jodhpur Governments conjointly till 1870, when the British Government became lessee of both states. The works are on the E. and N. edges of the lake. The average yearly outturn is from 300,000 to 400,000 tons of salt, and the cost of storage and extraction is ¾d. for every 82$\frac{2}{7}$ lbs. When the salt is formed men and women of the Barrar caste wade through the mud and lift it in large cakes into baskets, in which it is brought to the depôts on the lake side.

221 m. **Phalera** station N. junction of C.I. and J.B. railways (p. 139).]

Proceeding from Marwar junction (p. 133) towards Ajmer, after leaving,

561 m. **Haripur** station, D.B., the line engages in a rocky ascent which continues to close to

582 m. **Beawar** station, D.B., an important town, and reaches

615 m. **AJMER** junction station, ✱ D.B. Lat. 26° 87′ Long. 74° 44′. [From this place a line runs S. to *Nasirabad*, *Chitorgarh*, *Neemuch*, *Rutlam*, *Indore*, *Mhow*, and *Khandwa* (see Route 8).]

Ajmer, the key to Rajputana (population 86,000), is the capital of an isolated British district in the Rajput states. The district comprises two tracts known as Ajmer and Merwara (population 447,000). The Agent of the Governor-General[1] for Rajputana, whose headquarters are at Abu, is ex-officio Chief Commissioner of Ajmer. The city is of great antiquity and celebrity, and is situated in a valley, or rather basin, at the foot of the rocky and picturesque Taragarh Hill (3000 ft. above the sea). It is surrounded by a stone wall with five gateways, and is well built, containing many fine houses of stone with ornamental façades. Ajmer was founded in 145 A.D. by Ajaypal, one of the Chauhan kings. It was sacked in 1024, by Mahmud of Ghazni, on his way to Somnath in Kathiawar, taken again by the Mohammedans in 1200, and finally conquered by Akbar in 1556.

The memory of the Ajmer Chishti was held in particular respect by the great Akbar, who was accustomed to pay a yearly visit to his shrine. Several of these pilgrimages were made on foot from Agra and other

[1] At present the Hon. E. G. Colvin, C.S.I.

places. The road from Fatehpur-Sikri to Ajmer was so much used by Akbar that he caused "Kos Minars" (masonry columns answering to our milestones) to be erected along the route. Several of these minars can still be seen from the railway.

Thomas Coryat, in the 17th century, walked from Jerusalem to Ajmer, and spent £2, 10s. on the journey. Sir Thomas Roe, the Ambassador of James I., gives an account of the city in 1615-16. In about 1720 Ajit Singh Rathor seized the city, which was recovered by Muhammad Shah, and made over by him to Abhay Singh. His son, Ram Sing, called in the Mahrattas, under Jay Apa Sindhia, who, however, was murdered, and in 1756 Ajmer was made over to Bijai Singh, cousin of Ram Singh. In 1787 the Rathors recovered Ajmer, but after their defeat at Patan had to surrender it again to Sindhia. On the 25th of June 1818 Daulat Rao Sindhia made it over by treaty to the English.

Ajmer is the headquarters of about 1800 miles of metre-gauge railway worked by the B.B. and C.I. Railway Company. Near the railway station are very extensive workshops employing many thousand Hindu and Mohammedan workmen, who accomplish their tasks with a wonderfully small amount of European supervision.

The Residency is on the brink of the beautiful artificial lake called the **Ana Saugar**, constructed by Raja Ana in the middle of the 11th century, and lying N. of the city and railway station. It forms the source of the river Luni, which finally unites with the Delta of the Indus. The Emperor Shah Jahan erected a noble range of marble pavilions on the embankment. They were long the only public offices in Ajmer, and the chief one in which the emperor often reposed was used as the official residence of the Commissioner. They have now all been restored by direction of Lord Curzon. The walk along the *band* or embankment (which is public) is very delightful. To the N. is the broad expanse of the lake, and to the S. under the *band* is the *Public Garden*. The city is supplied with water from the new lake, the *Foy Saugar*, formed by an embankment thrown across the valley 5 m. higher up.

Akbar's Palace is outside the city proper, to the E., not far from the railway station. The entrance gate is very fine. It was once an arsenal, and then used as a tehsil building, and is now being restored.

The mosque, called the **Arhai-din-ka-jhompra**, or "The Hut of two and a half Days," is just outside the S. city gate beyond the Dargah. It was built by Altamsh or Kutab-ud-din about 1200 from the materials of a Jain temple. The name is derived from a tradition that it was built supernaturally in two and a half days. Modern archæologists assert that it was probably erected by the same architect who built the Kutab Mosque near Delhi. It is uncertain whether any of the undoubtedly Jain pillars of which the mosque is built were left *in situ*. Their ornamentation is very complex, no two being alike. The mosque is sadly ruined, and only the screen of arches (200 ft. long), and part of the mosque proper behind them, now remains, the whole of the other three sides of the enclosure having disappeared. The mosque was very much larger than that at the Kutab near Delhi (p. 208), the measurements of the exterior being 272 × 264 ft., and of the interior quadrangle 200 ft. × 175 ft. The mosque proper measures 259 ft. × 57 ft., and has ten domes in the roof borne by one hundred and twenty-four columns. The screen in front of it is a work well deserving attention; it is the glory of the mosque, and consists of seven arches very similar to those with which Altamsh adorned the courtyard of the Kutab. In the centre the screen rises to a height of 56 ft. and at the corners above this arch rise two short minarets with Tughra inscriptions. Nothing can exceed the taste with which the Kufic and Tughra inscriptions are interwoven with the more purely architectural decorations and the constructive lines of the design.

The bridle-path to **Taragarh** passes this mosque, and by a steep ascent reaches the summit in 2 m. The view from the top is very fine; but the ascent is somewhat trying and had better be made in the early morning. There is also an interesting graveyard of Mohammedan martyrs, who fell in the assault of the fort on the top.

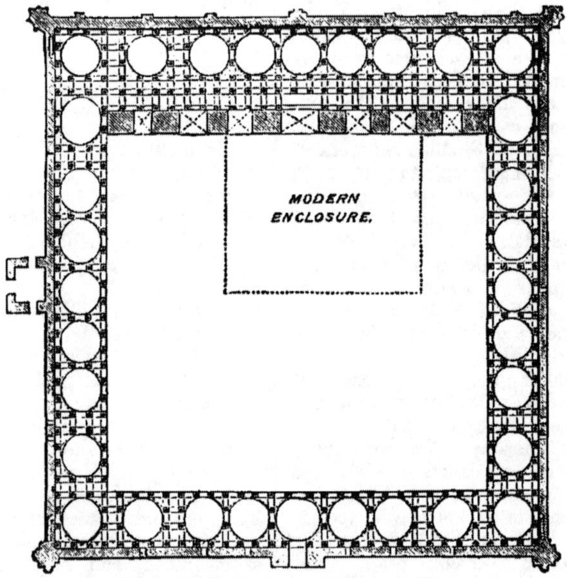

The Arhai-din-ka-jhompra Mosque at Ajmer.

One of the principal points of interest in Ajmer is the **Dargah**, which was commenced by the Emperor Altamsh and completed by Humayun. It is venerated alike by Mohammedans and Hindus, and derives its extreme sanctity from being the burial-place of Khwajah Muin-ud-din Chishti, who was called Aftab-i-Mulk-i-Hind, the Sun of the Realm of India. He died in 633 A.H. = 1235 A.D. He was the son of Khwajah 'Usman, and was called Chishti from a quarter in the city of Sanjar in Persia. Of this family of saints and courtiers, Farid-ud-din is buried at Pak-patan, in the Panjab; Nizam-ud-din, Kutab-ud-din, and Nasir-ud-din at or near Delhi; Shaik Salim at Fatehpur-Sikri near Agra; and Bandah Nawaz at Gulbargah in the Deccan.

Woollen socks are supplied to be worn over one's boots before entering the Dargah. Passing through a lofty gateway, a courtyard is entered in which are two very large iron cauldrons. Rich pilgrims occasionally pay for a feast of rice, ghi, sugar, almonds, raisins, and spices to be cooked in one of these, the contents being ladled out and finally scrambled for by the attendants of the shrine and various families connected with it. On the right of the courtyard is a mosque built by Akbar, with drums and candlesticks from Chitor presented by that Emperor; and further on in the inner court is a white marble mosque, 100 ft. long, and with eleven arches to the front, built by Shah Jahan; a Persian inscription runs along the whole front under the eaves. In the centre of the second court and opposite the marble mosque is the *Tomb* of the Saint, a square building of white marble surmounted by a dome. It has two entrances, one of which is spanned by a silver arch. S. of it in a small enclosure with well-cut marble lattices is the *Mazar* or "grave" of Hafiz Jamal, daughter of the saint, and W. of it, close by her tomb, is that of Chimmi Begam, daughter of Shah Jahan. All these are considered too sacred to be approached by any one except Mohammedans. There are some very fine trees in the enclosure.

At the S. end of the Dargah enclosure is the Jhalra, a deep tank partly cut out of the rock and lined by steep flights of irregular steps. As at Fatehpur Sikri, the doors of the shrine are covered with votive horse-shoes.

S.E. of the city is the **Mayo College** for the education of young Rajput princes, opened by Lord Northbrook in 1875. It contains about a hundred and seventy boys, between the ages of eight and twenty-one years. The central building is a handsome white marble pile: in front of it is a statue of Lord Mayo. The subsidiary buildings have been erected by various States as hostels for the pupils from each state. Perhaps nowhere else in India is so much good modern native architecture to be seen as here. The park round the buildings comprises 200 acres.

[The sacred Lake of **Pushkar** lies about 7 m. W. of Ajmer.

The road skirts the W. shore of the Ana Saugar, and at 3 m. passes the village of Nausar, in a gap in the hills which divide the Ana Saugar from the Pushkar Lake. This striking pass through the hills is 1 m. long. Pushkar, the most sacred lake in India, lies in a narrow valley overshadowed by fine rocky hills, and is said to be of miraculous origin, marking the spot hallowed by the great sacrifice of Brahma. Early in the Middle Ages it became one of the most frequented objects of pilgrimage, and is still visited during the great Mela (fair) of October and November by about 100,000 pilgrims. On this occasion is also held a great mart for horses, camels, and bullocks.

Although the ancient temples were destroyed by Aurangzeb, the five modern ones with their ghats on the margin of the lake are highly picturesque. That to Brahma is usually said to be the only one in India; but there are smaller shrines to Brahma at several old temples. Over the gateway is the figure of the *hans*, or "goose," of Brahma. The D.B. is in a native house on the lake, from which there is a good view.]

658 m. **Naraina** station. The village with a large tank is seen from the railway. It is the headquarters of the Dadupanthi sect of reformers. Their religion, ethics, and teaching are embodied in a mass of poetry written by one Dadu and his disciples. A division of the sect is composed of military monks, who serve in the armies of the Jaipur and neighbouring states.

664 m. **Phalera** junction (p. 136).

A direct chord line, 133 m. long, now runs from Phalera to Rewari (p. 145).

* 699 m. **JAIPUR** station * (population, 136,000). Ambèr is the ancient capital, Jaipur the modern; it is the residence of the Maharaja, whose state covers nearly 15,600 sq. m., with a population of 2,800,000, and yields a revenue of 66 lacs, and the headquarters of the Resident. The present chief, who is head of the Kachhwaha clan of Rajputs,

is H.H. Maharaja Dhiraj Sawai Sir Madho Singh, G.C.S.I., G.C.I.E., Jaipur derives its name from the famous Maharaja Sawai[1] Jai Singh II. (1699-1743), who founded it in 1728. This chief stood by the son of Prince Azim Shah in the struggle for the Empire on the death of Aurangzeb, and drove the Mughals out of Jaipur; he died in 1743 after a very long reign. The town is surrounded on all sides except the S. by rugged hills, crowned with forts. That at the end of the ridge overhanging the city on the N.W. is the Nahargarh, or "Tiger fort." The face of the ridge is scarped and inaccessible on the S. or city side, while on the N. it slopes towards Ambèr.

A masonry, crenellated wall, with seven gateways, encloses the whole city, which is the pleasant healthy capital of one of the most prosperous independent states of Rajputana, and is a very busy and important commercial town, with large banks and other trading establishments. It is a centre of native manufactures, especially those of many kinds of jewellery and of coloured printed cloths and muslins. The enamel-work done here is the best in India, and the cutting and setting of garnets and other stones found in the state is an important industry. The crowded streets and bazaars are most lively and picturesque. The city is remarkable for the width and regularity of its streets. It is laid out in rectangular blocks, and is divided by cross streets into six equal portions. The main streets are 111 ft. wide, and are paved, and the city is lighted by gas.[2]

Passes to view the Maharaja's Palace and stables and the old Palace of Ambèr must be obtained from the Secretary to His Highness.

The **Maharaja's Palace**, with its beautiful gardens and pleasure grounds ½ m. long, adorned with fountains, fine trees, and flowering shrubs, occupies the centre of the city and covers ⅐ of its area. The whole is surrounded by a high embattled wall, built by Jai Singh, but many of the buildings included in it are of a later date. The Chandra Mahal, which forms the centre of the great palace, is a lofty and striking building, seven stories high, looking over the gardens. On the ground-floor is the Diwan-i-Khas, or private hall of audience, built partly of white marble, and remarkable even in India for its noble simplicity. On the top story there is a magnificent view over the centre city. To the left are the gaudily-furnished modern buildings containing the apartments of the Maharaja and his courtiers and the zenana.

E. of the Chandra Mahal is the famous Jantra or **Observatory**, the largest of the five built by the celebrated royal astronomer, Jai Singh, at Benares, Muttra, Delhi, Ujjain, and here. It is not under cover, but is an open courtyard full of curious and fantastic instruments invented and designed by him. It was constructed between 1718-1734 A.D., and has been recently restored by the Maharaja of Jaipur through the agency of Lieutenant A. Garret, R.E., and Pandit Chandradhar Guleri, who have published a most interesting monograph upon it. The principal instruments are first on the W., the two circular Ram Yantras for reading altitudes and azimuths, with twelve horizontal sectors of stone radiating from a round vertical rod; then E. of these, the twelve Rashivalayas for determining celestial latitudes and longitudes; and next, the great Samrat Yantra or gnomon, 90 feet high, situated between two graduated quadrants, with sextants in a chamber outside them. The gnomon's shadow thrown by the sun touches the W. quadrant at 6 A.M., gradually descends this at the rate of 13 ft. per hour till noon, and finally ascends the E. quadrant. To the N. of this is a Dakhshina Bhitti Yantra or meridional

[1] Sawai means 1¼, and was a complimentary title given to Jai Singh by the Emperor of Delhi.

[2] See *Letters of Marque* by Rudyard Kipling.

wall, near which is a large raised platform known as Jai Singh's seat, and near it two brass circles, one of which is a map of the celestial sphere. Between these and the Ram Yantras are a number of other instruments known as the Kranti Yantra, the Kapali, and the Chakra Yantra, the last being a graduated brass circle corresponding to the modern equatorial. For further details regarding the Observatory, reference must be made to the above publication.

Adjoining the Observatory are the royal **Stables**, built round large court-yards; and beyond them is the Hawa Mahal, or **Hall of the Winds**, built by Madho Singh I., a fantastic and elaborate building, decorated with stucco, and overlooking one of the chief streets of the town.

In the central court of the palace are the Raj Printing Office, the Clock Tower, and the Armoury. To the E. of the Diwan-i-'Am is the Parade Ground, girt with open colonnades, behind which are the Law Courts.

Near the chief entrance rises the Ishwari Minar Swarga Sul, the "Minaret piercing heaven," built by Raja Ishwari Singh to overlook the city.

The Public Garden, outside the city wall, is one of the finest in India, 36 acres in extent, and was laid out by Dr de Fabeck at a cost of about Rs.400,000. Attached to it are a fine menagerie and aviary. These gardens cost the Maharaja Rs.16,000 a year to keep up. There is a fine *statue of Lord Mayo* in them, and in the centre is the **Albert Hall**, a sumptuous modern building, of which the Prince of Wales laid the first stone in 1876. It contains a large Darbar Hall and a beautiful museum—an Oriental South Kensington, suitably housed. The collections of modern works of art and industry, and also of antiquities, from every part of India, are very complete and highly interesting. There is a fine view from the top.

The Mayo Hospital beyond the gardens is of rough white stone, with a clock tower. It can house 150 patients.

The **Church** is on the way to the railway station, a little to the W. of the road.

At the **School of Art**, a handsome modern building, are first-rate technical and industrial classes for teaching and reviving various branches of native artistic industry, such as metal and enamel-work, embroidery, weaving, etc.

The **Maharaja's College**.—In Jaipur public instruction has made greater progress than in the other states of Rajputana. The College, opened in 1844 with about 40 pupils, had in 1902 and 1903 a daily class attendance of 1200, and compares favourably with similar institutions of the kind in British India. It is affiliated to the Allahabad University.

The Chhatris, or *cenotaphs of the Maharajas* at Gethur are just outside the N.E. city wall. They are in well-planted gardens, the trees of which are full of solemn-looking, grey-headed monkeys. The first seen on entering is Jai Singh's Chhatri, the finest of all. It is a dome of the purest white marble, supported on twenty beautifully carved pillars rising from a substantial square platform, and profusely ornamented with scenes from Hindu mythology. S.E. of Jai Singh's Chhatri is that of his son Madho Singh, a dome rising from the octagon on arches reversed. The only ornaments are carved peacocks. W. of this chhatri is that of Pratap Singh, his son, completed by the late ruler Ram Singh. It is of white marble brought from Alwar.

The water which supplies Jaipur is drawn from a stream on the W. of the city, running into the Chambal. The pumping-station and high-level reservoirs are nearly opposite the Chandpol Gate.

An expedition for the sake of the *view* may be made by elephant or on foot to the ***Shrine of the Sun God*** at *Galta*, an uninteresting building 350 ft. above the plain, and built on a jutting rocky platform, on the summit of a range of hills, about 1½ m. to the E. of Jeypore, of which by far the finest view is obtained from this point. The way the sandy desert is encroaching on the town should be noticed. It has caused one large suburb to be deserted, and other houses and gardens are going to ruin.

The excursion to **Ambèr** (5 m.), founded in the 11th century, and the capital of Jaipur till 1728, now ruined and deserted, is most interesting, and will occupy a whole morning. A refreshment room has now been opened here.

On the left of the road a line of fortified hills is passed; these culminate in the great *Fort* 400 ft. above the old palace, connected with it and built for its defence. The picturesque situation of Ambèr at the mouth of a rocky mountain gorge, in which nestles a pretty lake, has attracted the admiration of all travellers, including Jacquemont and Heber. It was founded by the Minas, and was flourishing in 967. In 1037 it was taken by the Rajputs, who held it till it was deserted.

The old **Palace**, begun by Man Singh,[1] 1600, ranks architecturally second only to Gwalior, though instead of standing on a rocky pedestal it lies low on the slope of the hill, picturesquely rooted on its rocky base and reflected in the lake below. The interior arrangements are excellent. The suites of rooms form vistas opening upon striking views. It is a grand pile, and though it lacks the fresh and vigorous stamp of Hindu originality which characterises earlier buildings, the ornamentation and technical details are free from feebleness.

[1] Man Singh was the nephew of Raja Bhagwan Das, the friend of Akbar, and the first among the great Rajput chiefs to give a daughter in marriage to the Mughal Imperial House. (See p. 183.)

Entered by a fine staircase from a great courtyard is the Diwan-i-'Am, a noble specimen of Rajput art, with a double row of columns supporting a massive entablature, above which are latticed galleries. Its magnificence attracted the envy of Jahangir, and Mirza Raja,[1] to save his great work from destruction covered it with stucco.

To the right of the Diwan-i-'Am steps is a small temple where a goat offered each morning to Kali preserves the tradition of a daily human sacrifice in pre-historic times.

On a higher terrace are the Raja's own apartments, entered by a splendid gateway covered with mosaics and sculptures, erected by Jai Singh, over which is the *Sohag Mandir*, a small pavilion with beautiful latticed windows. Through this are further marvels—a green and cool garden with fountains, surrounded by palaces, brilliant with mosaics and marbles. That on the left is the *Jai Mandir*, or Hall of Victory, adorned by panels of alabaster, some of which are inlaid, and others are adorned with flowers in alto-relievo, "the roof glittering with the mirrored and spangled work for which Jaipur is renowned." Near the Jai Mandir a narrow passage leads down to the bathing-rooms, all of pale creamy marble. Above is the *Jas Mandir*, "which literally glows with bright and tender colours and exquisite inlaid work, and looks through arches of carved alabaster and clusters of slender columns upon the sleeping lake and the silent mountains."

At the N.E. angle is a balcony, whence there is a fine view over the town of Ambèr and the plain beyond to the hill which overlooks Ramgarh. Some chhatris outside the wall are those of chieftains who died before Jai Singh II. In the palace to the right is a chamber on the right wall of which are views of Ujjain, and on the left views of Benares and Muttra. That opposite the Jai Mandir is called the *Sukh Niwas*, "Hall of

[1] Raja Jai Singh I., nephew of Man Singh, was known by this title.

Pleasure." In the centre of the narrow dark room is an opening for a stream to flow down into the groove or channel which runs through the hall. The doors are of sandal-wood inlaid with ivory.

A steep path leads down to the Khizri Gate, beyond which, as it leads to one of the forts, Kantalgarh, no one is allowed to pass without an order. At the bottom of this path there is a temple to Thakurji, or Vishnu. It is white and beautifully carved, and just outside the door is a lovely square pavilion exquisitely carved with figures representing Krishna sporting with the Gopi milkmaids.

Ambèr formerly contained many fine temples, but most are now in ruins.

[**Sanganer**, about 7 m. to the S. of Jaipur, also deserves a visit, and may be reached by a nice drive past the Residency and the Moti Dongari, or by the railway from Jaipur to Siwai Madhopur (p. 122).

The road into the town is through two ruined Tripuliyas, or triple gateways of three storeys, about 66 ft. high. The second story has an open stone verandah, supported by four pillars on either side of the archway. On the right, ascending the street, is a small temple sacred to *Kalyanji* or *Krishna*, the door of which is handsomely carved. Opposite is a temple to Sitaram, with a pillar, 6 ft. high, of white Makrana marble called a Kirti Khambh. On the four sides are Brahma with four faces, Vishnu, cross-legged, holding the lotus, Shiva holding a cobra in his right hand and a trident in his left, with Parvati beside him and Ganesh.

Higher up, on the left, are the ruins of the *Old Palace*, which must once have been a vast building. N. by E. from this is the *Sanganer Jain Temple* with three courts, and finely-carved marble work. Visitors are not allowed to enter the third.

755 m. **Bandikui** junction station (R.) Here are railway workshops, church institute, and a considerable station for railway employés. The line for *Bharatpur Junction*, *Muttra Junction* and *Agra* branches off E. (see Route 12).

792 m. **ALWAR** (Ulwar) station, * D.B., is the capital of the native state of that name, founded only in 1771, and known formerly as Macheri. The present chief, by race a Naruka Rajput, is H.H. Maharaja Siwai Jai Singh. It has an area of 3024 sq. m., a population of 828,000, and a revenue of about 27½ lakhs. The dress of the people is highly picturesque. The men often carry long matchlocks or staves, and the sarhis of the women are embroidered and of bright colours.

The **City** (58,000 inhabitants) is the residence of the Chief and of a Political Agent. It is beautifully situated on rising ground, dominated by the fort, which crowns a conical rock 900 ft. high, and is backed by a range of rugged mountains. A shady road between fields and native houses, and passing left the small Roman Catholic Church, and then the pretty Scottish Mission Church, and the Company Bagh, leads in 1 m. from the railway station to the chief of five vaulted gateways which pierce the city wall. At the gate is a formidable-looking brass gun. Inside an irregular whitewashed street stretches to the high fort at the end. About half-way along it, at the junction of four ways, the streets are spanned by a four-sided vaulted archway called the Tripuliya, supporting the tomb of Tarang Sultan, d. 1350, brother of Feroz Shah.

At the end of the street is a temple of Jagannath, and leaving it (left) and passing round and up a slight incline the **Royal Palace** is reached. Permission to visit it must be obtained from one of the members of Council, or through the Political Agent. It is a group of buildings partly detached, and built in a variety of styles, separated from the base of the mountains by a Tank. In the centre of the wall of the large court of the palace is an elegant building called an Aftabi, and two chhatris or cenotaphs of marble, adorned with carved lattice-work. The darbar-room is 70 ft. long, with marble pillars. The handsome Shish Mahal overlooks the tank. Besides other state rooms, the palace contains a valuable *Library*, kept in excellent order, and rich in Oriental manuscripts. The chief ornament of the collection is a matchless *Gulistan*, which cost about £10,000 to produce; it is beautifully illustrated with miniature paintings, the joint work of three men. The MS. was written by Agha Sahib, the miniatures were painted by a native of Delhi, and the scrolls are by a Panjabi; it was finished in 1848 by order of Maharao Raja Bani Singh. Another beautiful book is the *Dah Pand*, written by Rahim 'ullah, in 1864.

The *Toshah Khana*, or Jewel House, is rich in magnificent jewels, shown only when both the Prime Minister and the Political Agent are present. There is an emerald cup of large size, and also one said to be a ruby, some curious cameos, and massive silver trappings for horses and elephants.

The *Armoury* contains a splendid cellection of sabres and other weapons finely wrought and finished and studded with jewels; also fifty handsome swords with hilts of gold. One or two are from Persia, but most of them were made at Alwar, and the imitation of the Ispahan steel is excellent. The arms of Bani Singh[1] could only be worn by a man of great stature. His coat of mail weighs 16½ lbs., and his sword 5 lbs. They are studded with large diamonds. A Persian helmet and cuirass of the 16th century, and large enough for a man 7 ft. high, are both perforated with small bullets. The Maharaja resides at the Moti Dongari, 1 m. to the S. of Alwar, surrounded by fine gardens, and fitted with every kind of electrical appliance.

The **Palace Tank**, with the buildings that surround it, and the fort in the background, forms one of the most picturesque spots in India. To the E. are the palace and zenana; on the W. are a number of temples to Vishnu; on the N. are smaller temples and shrines, shrouded by trees; and raised upon the centre of a platform on the S. is the cenotaph or mausoleum of **Bakhtawar Singh**,[1] a pavilion with white marble pillars. In the centre of the pavement are four small feet cut out in the marble, and at one corner is a gun, at the next a dagger, and at the third a sword and shield. Visitors who care to enter are required to take off their shoes.

Myriads of rock-pigeons fly about these sacred precincts, making the ground blue when they alight, and numbers of stately peacocks strut unmolested about the marble pavements.

The **State Stables** are well worth a visit. There are 500 horses, some of them very fine.

In the city the house may be visited in which the **Elephant Carriage** is kept. It was built by Bani Singh, and is used by the Raja at the Festival of the Dasahra. It is a car two storeys high, and will carry fifty persons. It is usually drawn by four elephants.

There is nothing to see in the **Fort**, but if the visitor desires to ascend for the purpose of enjoying the magnificent view over the valley and adjoining hills, he should do so in the early morning. This ascent is steep and is paved with slippery and rugged stones. At about 150 ft. up there is a fine *Ficus indica* and a hut, and here the steepest part of the ascent begins. It is called the Hathi Mora, "Elephant's turn," because those animals cannot go beyond this point. There is another hut further up at a place called Ghazi Mard. It takes about thirty-eight minutes to walk from that place to the gate of the fort. The scarp of the rock is 27 ft. high. Inside the fort is a large ruined mansion

[1] Ruled, 1815-1857.

[1] See Fergusson's *Indian Architecture*, ii. 168. This chief ruled 1781-1815.

of Raghunath, formerly governor of the place. On the left hand is a cannon 12 ft. long. Thence to the inner fort is 100 yds. further up.

The **Tomb of Fateh Jang**, a minister of Shah Jahan, near the station on the Bharatpur road, is a conspicuous object with an immense dome, and bears the date, in Nagri, 1547; the outside is poor in design compared with the interior, which is good. The building possesses a considerable amount of fine plaster-work in relief, with flat surface patterns and rectangular mouldings.

1 m. N. of the city is the **Jail**, and 2 m. to the S. is the **Artillery Ground** and Top Khana, "artillery arsenal." On returning, a visit may be paid to a ravine, where at the distance of 1 m. is the chhatri of Pratap Singh, and a spring of water, as also temples to Shiva, Sitaram, and Karanji, and a small monument to the Queen of Pratap Singh, who became *sati*.

Alwar and the neighbourhood are supplied with water from the artificial **Lake of Siliserh**, 6 m. S.W. of the city, a charming spot. There is a palace of Bani Singh on the hill and an unfinished water palace on the lake.

There is a great deal of game, including tigers, in the neighbourhood of Alwar, but the tigers are strictly preserved.

20 m. E. of Alwar, and adjoining the Mewati hills, is the battlefield of Laswari, where Lord Lake annihilated the Deccan battalions of Daulat Rao Sindhia's European trained army on 1st November 1803, the British losses being 172 killed and 652 wounded, and the Mahratta losses 5000-7000. Later events have unduly obscured the achievements of this great British leader, who within a space of two months, and with a force never exceeding 8000 men, crushed 31 battalions of Sindhia's troops in four pitched battles, captured 426 guns, took two fortresses (Aligarh and Agra), and entered the capital of India (Delhi) as a conqueror.

838 m. **Rewari** junction station (R.), D.B.

Rewari was founded in 1000 A.D. by Raja Rawat. There are the ruins of a still older town E. of the modern walls. The Rajas of Rewari were partially independent, even under the Mughals. They built the mud fort of Gokulgarh, near the town, which is now in ruins, but was once very strong. They coined their own money, and their currency was called Gokul Sikkah. Rewari is a place of considerable trade, particularly in iron and salt. The Town Hall is handsome, as are the *Jain Temples*, close to the town.

[30 m. S.W. of Rewari lies **Narnaul**, the principal town of the possessions of the Patiala State in this quarter, made over to the State for loyal services rendered in 1857. This is on the Chord line lately constructed from here to Phalera (p. 139).

From Rewari a branch of the narrow gauge line runs N.W. to Hissar and Ferozepore, and so to Lahore, passing the following places.

52 m. **Bhiwani** station with 30,000 people, chiefly Hindus, formerly a great market for all North Rajputana.

74 m. **Hansi** station, D.B., a modern town of 14,000 inhabitants, on the W. Jumna Canal. It is said to have been founded by Anangpal Tomar, king of Delhi, and was long the capital of Hariana. There are ruins of an ancient *Citadel* and some remains of gateways, and a high brick wall, with bastions and loop-holes. In 1795 the famous sailor adventurer, George Thomas, fixed his headquarters at Hansi, which forthwith began to revive. In 1802 British rule was established, and a local levy was stationed here, and Colonel Skinner, C.B., settled in 1829. In 1857 the troops of this town mutinied, following the mutineers at Hissar.

At **Tosham**, 23 m. S.W., are some ancient inscriptions. They are cut in the rock half the way up the hill near a tank much visited by pilgrims, who come from great distances to the yearly fair there.

89 m. **Hissar** station (R.), D.B. (population, 17,700). The Hissar branch of the *W. Jumna Canal*, made originally by the Emperor Firoz Shah, to irrigate his hunting-seat at this place, terminates here. In 1826 it was restored by the British. In this place also the local levies revolted during the Mutiny of 1857, and murdered the Collector and fourteen Christians, to whom a monument is erected beside the little church; but before Delhi was taken, a body of Sikh levies, aided by contingents from Platiala and Bikaner, under General Van Cortlandt, had restored order.

The city and the fort on the W. side of it were founded in 1354 A.D. by the Emperor Firoz Shah, who made it his favourite hunting-seat. Lying on the main track from Mooltan to Delhi it became a place of importance, of which there are only buried remains now besides the old walls and gates. In the fort are the ruins of a Mohammedan building constructed of Jain remains; and E. of the city is a fine stone building called the Jahaz or Ship from its shape, now used as a workshop of the W. Jumna Canal. A large cattle fair is held at Hissar twice a year. S. and W. of the city there is a Government cattle-farm (*Bir*), managed by a European superintendent, and attached to it is an estate of 43,287 acres for pasturage.

The *District of Hissar* borders on the Rajputana Desert, and in parts is itself little better than a waste, scattered over with low bushes. The water supply is inadequate, the average rainfall being only 10 in., and the country is sadly subject to famines. The *Ghaggar*, with scant verdure along its banks, winds through the N. of the district like a green riband.

140 m. **Sirsa** station (population 15,800). The town and fort are supposed to have been founded by one Raja Saras, about the middle of the 6th century. It was formerly well known as Sarsuti. A great cattle fair is held here in August and September, at which 30,000 head of cattle are exposed for sale.

187 m. **Bhatinda** junction station. From this place lines run E. to Patiala, Rajpura, and Umballa, and W. to Samasatta (Bahawalpur), Hyderabad and Karachi, S.E. to Rohtak and Delhi, and S. to Bikaner. There is a very high picturesque fort seen well from the railway, but the modern town contains nothing of special interest.

213 m. **Kot-Kapura** junction station (R.). From here a branch line of 50 m. runs W. to Fazilka on the Sutlej river.

221 m. **Faridkot** station, capital of the Sikh State of that name. The chief is of a different Jat family from those of the Phulkian States (p. 223).

241 m. **Ferozepore**[1] station (R.), D.B. (population 49,000). The fort with an arsenal and the cantonment lie 2 m. to the S. The city was founded in the time of Firoz Shah, Emperor of Delhi, 1351-87 A.D. When it lapsed to the British in 1835 it was in a declining state, but through the exertions of Sir Henry Lawrence and his successors it has increased to its present importance as a market of raw produce, much of which is due to the Sirhind canal, extended to the district in 1882, and the Grey inundation canals along the Sutlej, inaugurated by Colonel Grey, C.S.I., in the years 1874-78. The main streets are wide and well paved, while a circular road which girdles the wall is lined by the gardens of wealthy residents.

It was at Ferozepore that the Governor-General, Lord Auckland, met Maharaja Ranjit Singh in December 1839, only six months before his death, to make arrange-

[1] A memorial has been recently erected at Ferozepore to the Sikh garrison of Saraghari on the Orakzai Samana range (p. 245), which fell to a man defending the post in 1897.

ments for the advance of the British army on Kabul; and it was here also that, just three years later, Lord Ellenborough received the so-called victorious army on its return to British India, General Sale and the Jelalabad garrison crossing the bridge over the Sutlej at the head of the force.

On the 10th of December 1845 the Sikhs invaded the district, but, after desperate fighting, were driven back across the Sutlej. Since then peace has prevailed, except during the Mutiny of 1857. In May of that year one of the two Sepoy regiments, stationed at Ferozepore, revolted, and in spite of the presence of a British regiment and some British artillery, partly destroyed the cantonment.

The *Fort*, which contains the principal arsenal in the Panjab, was rebuilt in 1858, and greatly strengthened in 1887. The railway and the trunk road to Lahore separate it and the town from the cantonment.

The *Memorial Church*, in honour of those who fell in the Sutlej campaign of 1845-46, was destroyed in the Mutiny, but was subsequently restored. In the cemetery on the G. Trunk Road to Ludhianah lie many distinguished soldiers, amongst them Major George Broadfoot, C.B., Governor-General's Agent, N.W. Frontier, General Sale, and General Dick.

The three great battlefields of the First Sikh War, fought by Lord Gough, can best be visited from this point. **Mudki** (18th December 1845) lies 22 m. to the S.E.; **Ferozeshah** (21st and 22nd December) 16 m. E., and on the railway to Ludhianah and 8 m. from Mudki; and **Sobraon** (10th February 1846) 20 m. N. It was at the Hariki Ford, near Sobraon, that the Sikh army entered British territories, and in this last battle they lost 10,000 men killed or drowned in attempting to escape across the river. The losses of the British in killed and wounded in these battles,[1] in which they met in the Sikhs a foeman worthy of their steel, were terrible, viz., at Mudki, 872 killed and wounded; at Ferozeshah (where the troops failed in the first attack on the entrenchments, which were carried the next day), 2415; and at Sobraon, 2299. Generals Sale and M'Caskill were killed at Mudki, Major Broadfoot at Ferozeshah, and General Dick at Sobraon. The Governor-General, Lord Hardinge, was present at the battles of Mudki and Ferozeshah. A plain obelisk has been erected on each of the battlefields.

[1] See *The Sikhs and the Sikh Wars*, by General Sir H. Gough, V.C., and A. D. Innes; also *Life and Campaigns of Hugh, 1st Viscount Gough, Field-Marshal*, by R. S. Rait.

Beyond Ferozepore the railway crosses the Sutlej river by a fine bridge, and proceeds past Kasur (257 m.), an old Pathan stronghold, to (274 m.) Raiwind, on the N.W. Railway (Route 18).] **Kasur** is connected on the N. with Patti, Taran Taran and Amritsar (p. 228), and on the S. with Lodhran and Bhawalpur (p. 261).

Beyond Rewari the railway passes

870 m. **Gurgaon**, the headquarters of the south-easternmost district of the Panjab, and then W. of the Kutab Minar and the tombs and ruins S. of Delhi, shut off from view by the line of hills, and when near the city turns E. to it. (Here the Delhi, Umballa, and Kalka Railway turns N. and the S. Panjab Railway to Rohtak (44 m.) and Bhatinda (168 m.) W.). The line passes through the W. wall of the city near the Ajmer Gate, meeting in a fine central station the E.I. Railway and N.W. Railway, which enter the city over the Jumna river bridge from the E. The new direct line of the Midland Railway from Agra (p. 169) also joins the station from the S.

890 m. **DELHI** junction station.*

ROUTE 11.

From AHMEDABAD through **KATHIAWAR by Viramgam, Kharaghoda, Wadhwan, Bhaunagar, Junagarh, Girnar, Somnath, Porbandar, Rajkot,** and back to **Ahmedabad,** with expedition by road to **Palitana.**

Leaving **Ahmedabad** (Route 10), 310 m. from Bombay the Sabarmati is crossed on a fine bridge, with a footway for passengers alongside, and carrying the rails for both broad and narrow gauges. From 4 m., **Sabarmati** (junction station), on the N. bank of the river of that name, the narrow gauge continues N. to Delhi and Agra, whilst the broad gauge turns W., and passing through a well-cultivated country, reaches 40 m. **Viramgam** junction station,*—a walled town, population 19,000. The Mansar tank dates from the end of the eleventh century. It is shaped like a shell, and surrounded by flights of stone steps; round the tops of the steps runs a row of small temples. The inlet is much ornamented. The neighbourhood abounds in black buck, grouse, and all manner of water-fowl. From this place a branch line runs N.W., passing at 19 m. Patri, D.B., a small walled town with a Citadel; and, at 29 m., reaches **Kharaghoda,** where there are very extensive salt-pans on the edge of the **Little (Runn) Ran of Cutch.**[1] In the dry season the Runn presents the appearance of a hard, smooth bed of dried mud, and may be ridden over at any place. There is absolutely no vegetation except on some small islands which rise above the level of the salt inundation; the only living creatures that inhabit it are some herds of wild asses, which feed on the lands near its shores at night, and retreat far into the desert in the daytime. With the commencement of the S.W. monsoon in May, the salt water of the Gulf of Cutch invades the Runn, and later in the season the rivers from Rajputana pour fresh water into it. The sea is now encroaching rapidly on the Runn at its junction with the Gulf of Cutch, and there is reason to suppose that serious changes of level are taking place. The centre of the Runn is slightly higher than the borders, and dries first. The railway has many sidings extending into the Runn, to facilitate the collection of the salt, which is stacked at the station in very large quantities under the custody of the Salt Customs Department. Originally, it was considered necessary to erect expensive roofs over the salt stacks, but experience has shown that this can be dispensed with. The salt is evaporated by the heat of the sun from brine brought up in buckets from depths of 15 to 30 ft. Wonderful mirages are seen in the Ran, and in the winter season the flights of flamingoes and other birds are extraordinarily large. There are sand grouse to be had round about.

[1] Bhoj, the principal town of Cutch, renowned for the work of its silversmiths, lies on the N. side of the Ran, and is at present difficult of access. Ran means a desert. The Great Ran lies N.W. of Bhoj.

80 m. **Wadhwan** junction station D.B. To the W. runs the *Morvi State Railway,* the exclusive property of the Morvi State, constructed on 2½ ft. gauge to maintain communication with *Morvi,* but now being converted to the standard narrow gauge, *Jetalsar* and *Rajkot.* To the S. the line is continued by means of the *Bhaunagar Gondal Railway,* a portion of the metre-gauge system, which opens up a large number of places in South Kathiawar. These railways are under a central administration, but are the property of the State through which they pass.

The *Civil Station of Wadhwan,* on which the railway station is built, is a plot of land rented by Government in perpetuity from the Wadhwan State, for the location of the establishments necessary for the administration of the N.E. portion of Kathiawar. A small town has sprung up close to the railway station.

The only institution of special interest in the place is the *Talukdari*

School, where the sons of *Girassias,* or land-owners, are educated when their parents are unable to afford the heavy cost of sending them to the *Rajkumar or Princes' College at Rajkot.* In many cases elder brothers are placed at the Rajkumar College, and the younger at the Talukdari School.

The *Province of Kathiawar* which is now entered, exists under circumstances quite exceptional. It consists of 187 separate states, ranging in extent from considerable tracts of country, with chiefs enjoying great executive freedom, to mere village lands, which are states only in name. Almost without exception the capitals of these states are places of interest which will repay a visit.

For purposes of administration the Province is divided into *four Prants,* or divisions. The arduous task of administering it is entrusted to a *Political Agent* who resides at *Rajkot,* and has assistants distributed through the country.

Everywhere in Kathiawar the traveller will remark long lines of *palias,* or memorial stones, peculiar to this Province, on which men are usually represented as riding on a very large horse, whilst women have a wheel below them to indicate that they used a carriage. A woman's arm and hand indicate here, as in other parts of India, a monument to a lady who became *sati.*

Proceeding S. by the Bhaunagar Gondal Railway, the river is crossed close to the station.

At 83 m. **Wadhwan City** station is reached. The town wall is of stone and in good order. Towards the centre, on the N. wall, is the ancient temple of **Ranik Devi.** She was a beautiful girl, born in the yunagarh territory when Sidh Raja was reigning at Patan, and was betrothed to him. But Ra Khengar, who then ruled Junagarh, carried her off and married her, which caused a deadly feud between him and Sidh Raja, whose troops marched to Junagarth. Khengar was betrayed by two of his kinsmen, and was slain by Sidh Raja and his fortress taken. The conqueror wanted to marry Ranik Devi, but she performed *sati,* and Sidh Raja raised this temple to her memory. It bears marks of extreme old age, the stone being much worn and corroded, and all but the tower is gone. Inside is a stone with the effigy in relief of Ranik Devi, and a smaller one with a representation of Ambaji. N. of this temple, and close to the city wall, is a *sati* stone dated 1519. Near the Lakhupol Gate is a well with steps, ascribed to one Madhava, who lived in 1294 A.D.

The *Palace* is the centre of the town, has four stories, and is 72 ft. high. It stands in a court facing the entrance, on the right of which is a building called the Mandwa, where assemblies take place at marriages.

96 m. **Limbdi** station. Chief town of the cotton-producing state of that name. Population 13,000. A well-cared-for place, with a very handsome palace.

126 m. **Botad** station. Frontier of the Bhaunagar State.

152 m. **Dhola** junction station (R.) Here the line turns W. to Dhoraji and Porbandar, and E. to Bhaunagar, passing at

165 m., a little N. of **Songad,** * the residence of the Assistant Political Agent for the eastern portion of the Province.

[Excursion to Palitana and the Satrunjaya Hills.

(Arrangements for a conveyance can be made, by applying to the Deputy Assistant Political Agent at Songad. No public conveyances can be depended upon.)

Palitana, * about 15 m. S. of Songad, the latter part of the road over a barren country between low rocky hills, is the residence of the chief, and is much enriched by the pilgrims who reside in it during their visit to the *Holy Mountain*, and its famous Jain temples.

The distance from Palitana to the foot of **Satrunjaya**, or the **Holy Mountain**, 1977 ft. above sea-level, is 1½ m. The road is level, with a good water supply, and shaded by trees. The ascent begins with a wide flight of steps, guarded on either side by a statue of an elephant. The hillside is in many places excessively steep, and the mode of conveyance is a *dholi*, a seat or tray 18 in. square, slung from two poles and carried by four men. Few of the higher-class pilgrims are able to make the ascent on foot, so there is an ample supply of *dholis* and bearers.

The Satrunjaya hill is truly a city of temples, for, except a few tanks, there is nothing else within the gates, and there is a cleanliness withal about every square and passage, porch and hall, that is itself no mean source of pleasure. The silence too is striking. Now and then in the mornings you hear a bell for a few seconds, or the beating of a drum for as short a time, and on holidays chants from the larger temples meet your ear; but generally during the after-part of the day the only sounds are those of vast flocks of pigeons that fly about spasmodically from the roof of one temple to that of another. Paroquets and squirrels, doves and ringdoves abound, and peacocks are occasionally met with on the outer walls. The top of the hill consists of two ridges, each about 350 yds. long, with a valley between. Each of these ridges, and the two large enclosures that fill the valley, are surrounded by massive battlemented walls fitted for defence. The buildings on both ridges again are divided into separate enclosures called *tuks*, generally containing one principal temple, with varying numbers of smaller ones. Each of these enclosures is protected by strong gates and walls, and all gates are carefully closed at sundown.

No attempt is made to describe the shrines in detail; their general character is so often repeated that it would only be possible to do so with the aid of profuse illustrations. The area enclosed on the top is small enough for any one of ordinary activity to see all over it in the course of a two hours' visit. Mr Burgess' little book on the place is excellent.

There is one gate leading into the enclosure, but there are nineteen gates within, leading to the nineteen chief Temples. Not far from the *Ram-pol* (pol means gate) is a resting-place used by persons of distinction, with a tolerable room surrounded by open arches.

Mr James Fergusson says:—

"The grouping together of these temples into what may be called 'Cities of Temples,' is a peculiarity which the Jains practised to a greater extent than the followers of any other religion in India. The Buddhists grouped their stupas and viharas near and around sacred spots, as at Sanchi, Manikyala, or in Peshawur, and elsewhere; but they were scattered, and each was supposed to have a special meaning, or to mark some sacred spot. The Hindus also grouped their temples, as at Bhuvaneshwar or Benares, in great numbers together; but in all cases because, so far as we know, these were the centres of a population who believed in the gods to whom the temples were dedicated, and wanted them for the purposes of their worship. Neither of these religions, however, possesses such a group of temples, for instance, as that at Satrunjaya, in Guzerat. It covers a very large space of ground, and its shrines are scattered by hundreds over the summits of two extensive hills and in the valley between them. The larger ones are situated in *tuks*, or separate enclosures, surrounded by high fortified walls; the smaller ones line the silent streets. It is a city of the gods, and meant for them only, and not intended for the use of mortals.

"All the peculiarities of Jain architecture are found in a more marked degree at Palitana than at almost any other known place, and, fortunately for the student of the style, extending through all the ages during which it flourished. Some of the temples are as old as the eleventh century, and they are spread pretty evenly over all the intervening time to the present century."

Mr James Burgess in his report gives the following general description:—

"At the foot of the ascent there are some steps with many little canopies or cells, 1½ ft. or 3 ft. square, open only in front, and each having in its floor a marble slab carved with the representation of the soles of two feet (*charan*), very flat ones, and generally with the toes all of one length. A little behind, where the ball of the great toe ought to be, there is a diamond-shaped mark divided into four smaller figures by two cross lines, from the end of one of which a curved line is drawn to the front of the foot.

"The path is paved with rough stones all the way up, only interrupted here and there by regular flights of steps. At frequent intervals also there are rest-houses, more pretty at a distance than convenient for actual use, but still deserving of attention. High up we come to a small temple of the Hindu monkey god, Hanuman, the image bedaubed with vermilion in ultra-barbaric style. At this point the path bifurcates to the right leading to the northern peak, and to the left to the valley between, and through it to the southern summit. A little higher up, on the former route, is the shrine of Aengar, a Mussulman *pir*, so that Hindu and Moslem alike contend for the representation of their creeds on this sacred hill of the Jains.

"On reaching the summit of the mountain, the view that presents itself from the top of the walls is magnificent in extent; a splendid setting for the unique picture. To the E. the prospect extends to the Gulf of Cambay near Gogo and Bhaunagar; to the N. it is bounded by the granite range of Sihor and the Chamardi peak; to the N.W. and W. the plain extends as far as the eye can reach. From W. to E., like a silver ribbon across the foreground to the S., winds the Satrunjaya river, which the eye follows until it is lost between the Talaja and Khokara Hills in the S.W."]

[Excursion to Valabhipur.

The antiquarian who is not pressed for time may care from Songad to visit the site of the ancient city of **Valabhipur**, which is nearly identical with the modern town of Walah, and is 12 m. distant by road. The authorities at Songad will arrange for the journey. Valabhipur was perhaps as old as Rome, and was the capital of all this part of India. The present town (under 5000 inhabitants) is the capital of one of the small Kathiawar states. It has been very much neglected. There are scarcely any architectural remains at Walah, but old foundations are discovered, and sometimes coins, copper plates, mud seals, beads, and household images have been found in some abundance. The ruins can be traced over a large area of jungle.]

Resuming the journey from Songad to Bhaunagar, the railway passes 90 m. **Sihor** station D.B. This was at one time the capital of this state. The town, well situated 1½ m. S. of the railway, has some interesting Hindu temples.

103 m. **Bhaunagar.*** The city of 56,400 inhabitants, founded 1723, stands on a tidal creek that runs into the Gulf of Cambay. The head of the gulf above this creek is silting up so rapidly that it is very difficult to maintain the necessary depth of water for native trading vessels and coasting steamers. The Bhaunagar State has from its first connection with the British Government been administered by men of intelligence, and the town will be found a most pleasing

sample of the results of native Indian government going hand in hand with European progress. The staple export is cotton. There are no interesting ruins, but abundance of very handsome modern buildings on Indian models, water works, reservoirs, and gardens; and at the port will be seen an intelligent adoption of modern mechanical improvements.

To visit Junagarh, Somnath, Porbandar, or any places in the W., it is necessary to return to *Dhola junction* and change there.

Jetalsar junction station (R.), 152 m. from Wadhwan, is the residence of the Assistant Political Agent for the S. or *Sorath* division of the Province of Kathiawar. Here the line branches (1) S. to *Verawal* for *Somnath*, (2) W. to *Porbandar* (p. 161), and (3) N. to *Rajkot*, *Vankaner* and *Wadhwan* (p. 162).

(1) *Jetalsar to Junagarh and Verawal.*

16 m. from Jetalsar is **Junagarh** station,* (D.B. W. of the town, opposite a modern gate-way, called the *Reay Gate*), the capital of the state, and the residence of the Nawab. The name means Old Fort. Population, 34,000.

Situated as it is under the Girnar and Datar Hills, Junagarh is one of the most picturesque towns in India, while in antiquity and historical interest it yields to few. The scenery from the hills around is most pleasing, and the place has attractions wanting in most ancient Indian towns, which, as a rule, are situated in uninteresting plains. There is a great deal of game in Kathiawar, and specially in the **Gir**, the large uncultivated tract to the S.E. of Junagarh; but the Gir is very unhealthy in the early part of the autumn, and again at the beginning of the rains. The few remaining lions are now strictly protected.

The fortifications of the present town were all built by the Mohammedans after the capture of the place by Sultan Mahmud **Bigara**, of Guzerat, about 1472. The *Nawab's Palace* is a fine modernised building. In front of it is a good circle of shops called the *Mahabat Circle*. The *Arts College* was designed and built by a local architect, and was opened by Lord Curzon in November 1900.

The **Tombs of the Nawabs** are highly finished buildings. Mr Fergusson says:—"There is a cemetery at Junagarh where there exists a group of tombs all erected within this century, some within the last twenty or thirty years, which exhibit, more nearly than any others I am acquainted with, the forms towards which the style was tending. The style is not without a certain amount of elegance in detail. The tracery of the windows is executed with precision and appropriateness." Entering the enclosure by the N. gate, the tomb of Bahadur Khan II. is in front on the left, next to it the tomb of Hamed Khan II., and on its left that of Ladli Bu, a lady whose marriage, and the influence she gained, caused no slight difficulty to this state, and no little trouble in the Political Agency. Beside these is the tomb of Nawab Mahabat Khan, in Saracenic style, and finely carved. ½ m. beyond the N. gate of the town is the **Sakar Bagh**, a well-laid-out garden that belongs to the Vazir. There is a two-storied villa, surrounded by a moat full of water. About 50 yds. from the house is a menagerie, in which are lions, panthers, deer, etc. In a still finer garden at the S. of the town, the **Sardar Bagh**, are kept a number of lions and lionesses from the Gir forest. There are no tigers in the Kathiawar peninsula, but up to the middle of the present century lions inhabited all the large jungles, and were shot in the Choteyla Hills E. of Rajkot. Now the animal is confined to the Gir. The lion is in no way inferior to the African species, although the mane is not so large. The Gir lion is not a man-eater usually, but Col. J. W. Watson has heard of one or two well-authenticated instances of his killing men.

The soft sandstone which everywhere underlies Junagarh is an interesting study. Formed apparently in very shallow water, it shows on all sides complicated lines of stratification. The facility with which it is worked may be one reason why it has been largely excavated into cave-dwellings in Buddhist times.

The **Caves**—In the N. part of the town enclosure, near the old telegraph office, is the group called the *Khapra Khodia.* These caves appear to have been a monastery, and bear the cognizance of the then ruling race, a winged griffin or lion. They appear to have been two or three storeys high. They are, however, excavated in good building stone, and the modern quarrymen have been allowed to encroach and injure them; the lower ones have never been systematically cleared out. The most interesting caves of all in the Uparkot (see below) about 50 yds. N. of the great mosque. They are now protected by an iron gate. They consist of two storeys, the lower chambers being 11 ft. high. The upper storey consists of a tank surrounded by a corridor, and of a room 36 ft. by 28 ft., supported by six columns, beyond which is a small kitchen. From here a winding staircase leads to the lower storey, measuring 39 ft. by 31 ft. with broad recesses all round it, and over them a frieze of chaitya windows. Of the columns, Mr Burgess says:—"Few bases could be found anywhere to excel in beauty of design and richness of carving those of the six principal pillars." Inside the Wagheshwari Gate, through which the Girnar Mount is reached, are the caves known by the name of *Bawa Piara*, a comparatively modern Hindu ascetic who is said to have resided in them. These caves date from about the time of Asoka (263-225 B.C.), are among the very oldest in all India, and are nearly all small and plain. They are situated in the scarp of a circular detached mass of rock and face S. and E., a third line to the N. also facing S. being excavated on a higher level than the S. line. The most interesting group is that facing E., where a number of caves were dug round a central space.

The **Uparkot**, on the E. side of the city, used as a jail until 1858, is now practically deserted. It was the citadel of the old Hindu princes, and is probably the spot from whence Junagarh derives its name. Permission to visit it must be asked. Without presenting any very special features to describe, the Uparkot is one of the most interesting of old forts. The parapets on the E., where the place is commanded by higher ground, have been raised at least three times to give cover against the increasingly long range of projectiles. The views from the walls are delightful. Here were quartered the lieutenants of the great Asoka, Buddhist king, and, later, of the Gupta kings. The entrance is beyond the town in the W. wall, and consists of three gateways, one inside the other. The fort walls here are from 60 to 70 ft. high, forming a massive cluster of buildings. The inner gateway, a beautiful specimen of the Hindu Toran, has been topped by more recent Mohammedan work, but the general effect is still good and, with the approach cut through the solid rock, impressive. On the rampart above the gate is an inscription of Mandalika V., dated 1450. About 150 yds. to the left, through a grove of *sitaphal* (custard apples) may be seen a huge 10-in. bore **cannon** of bell-metal, 17 ft. long and 4 ft. 8 in. round at the mouth. This gun was brought from Diu, where it was left by the Turks. There is an Arabic inscription at the muzzle, which may be translated: "The order to make this cannon, to be used in the service of the Almighty, was given by the Sultan of Arabia and Persia, Sultan Sulaiman, son of Salim Khan. May his triumph be glorified, to punish the enemies of the State and of the Faith, in the capital of Egypt, 1531." At the breech is inscribed: "The work of Muhamman, the son of Hamzah." Another large cannon called Chudanal, also from Diu, in the southern portion of the fort, is 13 ft. long, and has a muzzle 4 ft. in diameter. Near this is the **Jama Masjid**, evidently constructed from the materials of a Hindu temple built by Mahmud Bigara. One plain slim minaret remains standing, but the mosque is much ruined. The ascent to the terraced roof is by a good staircase outside.

The **Tomb of Nuri Shah**, close to the mosque, is ornamented with fluted cupolas, and a most peculiar carving over the door. There are two **Wells** in the Uparkot—the *Adi Chadi*, said to have been built in ancient times by the slave girls of the Chudasama rulers, is descended by a long flight of steps (the sides of the descent show the most remarkable overlap-

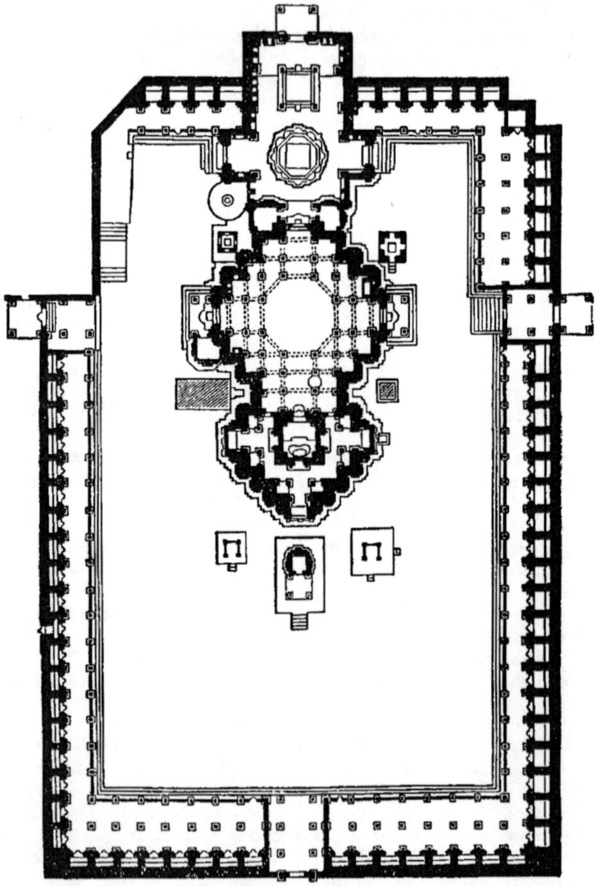

Temple of Nemnath, Girnar.

GIRNAR.

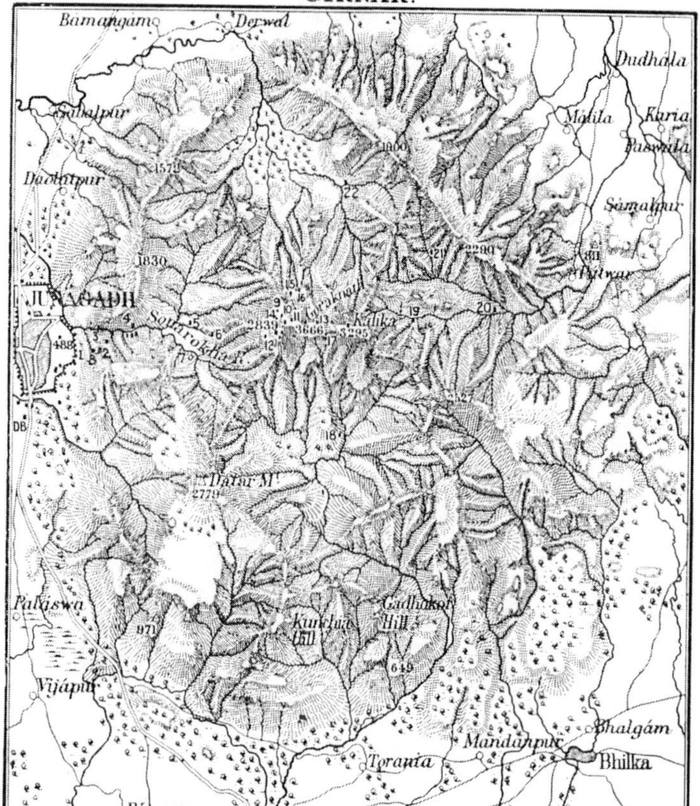

Scale of Miles

Stanford's Geog^l Estab^t

1. Wagheshwari Gate.
2. Asoka's Stone.
3. Bridge.
4. Temple of Damodar.
5. ,, ,, Savanath.
6. ,, ,, Bhavanath.
7. Chadá-ni-wao Well.
8. Wagheshwari Temple.
9. Bhairo-Thumpa.
10. Gaomukhi Temple.
11. Amba Deva Temple.
12. Máliparab Khund.
13. Datátari.
14. Háthi pagla Khund.
15. Sesáwan Temple.
16. Hanmandhára Khund and Temple.
17. Kamandal Temple.
18. Sakri ámbli.
19. Malbela.
20. Suraj Khund.
21. Sarkharia.
22. Bawaha Madhi.

[*To face p.* 155.

pings and changes of lie in the strata, for which alone it is worth a visit to any one with geological tastes); and the *Naughan*, cut to a great depth in the soft rock, and with a wonderful circular staircase.

There is a fine dharmsala belonging to the goldsmiths near the Wagheshwari Gate.

The mountain **Girnar** is the great feature of Junagarh, and the Jain temples upon it are amongst the most ancient in the country. It is 3666 ft. high, and is one of the most remarkable mountains in India. From the city of Junagarh only the top of it can be seen, as it has in front of it lower hills, of which Jogniya, or Laso Pawadi, 2527 ft., Lakhshman Tekri, Bensla, 2290 ft. high, and Datar, 2779 ft. high, are the principal. Girnar was anciently called Raivata or Ujjayanta, sacred amongst the Jains to Nemnath, the 22d Tirthankar, and doubtless a place of pilgrimage before the days of Asoka, 250 B.C.

The traveller, in order to reach Girnar, will pass through the Wagheshwari Gate, which is close to the Uparkot. At about 200 yds. from the gate, to the right of the road, is the Temple of Wagheshwari, which is joined to the road by a causeway about 150 yds. long. In front of it is a modern temple, three stories high, very ugly, flat roofed, and quite plain. About a furlong beyond this is a stone bridge, and just beyond it on the right is the famous **Asoka Stone**, a round boulder of granite, measuring roughly 20 ft. × 30 ft., and covered with inscriptions, which prove on examination to be 14 Edicts of Asoka (250 B.C.)[1] Nearly identical inscriptions have been found at Dhauli, and Shahbazgarhi (pp. 328 and pp. 246), and elsewhere. The character is Pali.

On leaving Asoka's Stone, the route crosses the handsome bridge over the Sonarekha, which here forms a fine sheet of water, then passes a number of temples, at first on the left bank of the river and then on the right, where Jogis go about entirely naked, to the largest of the temples dedicated to **Damodar**, a name of Krishna, from Dam, a rope, because by tradition his mother in vain attempted to confine him with a rope when a child. The reservoir at this place is accounted very sacred. The path is now through a wooded valley, with some fine Indian fig-trees. Near a cluster of them is an old shrine called **Bhavanath**, a name of Shiva, and round it are a number of large monkeys, who come on being called. Most persons who are not active climbers will probably proceed up the mountain in a swing *dholi* (p. 150), for which Rs. 4 or 5 will be paid according to tariff. A long ridge runs up from the W., and culminates in a rugged scarped rock, on the top of which are the temples. Close to the old shrine is a well called the Chadáni-wao. The paved way begins just beyond this and continues for two-thirds of the ascent; the first resthouse, Chodia-paraba, is reached, 480 ft. above the plain, and the second halting-place at Dholi-deri, 1000 ft. above the plain. From here the ascent becomes more difficult, winding under the face of the precipice to the third rest-house, 1400 ft. up. So far there is nothing very trying to any one with an ordinarily steady brain. But from this point the path turns to the right along the edge of a precipice, which, though improved of late, is still very narrow, so that the *dholi* almost grazes the scarp, which rises perpendicularly 200 ft. above the traveller. On the right is seen the lofty mountain of *Datar*, covered with low jungle. At about 1500 ft. there is a stone dharmsala, and from this there is a fine view of the rock called the *Bhairav-Thampa*, "the terrific leap," because devotees used to cast themselves from its top, falling 1000 ft. or more.

At 2370 ft. above Junagarh the gate of the enclosure known as the **Deva Kota**, or Ra Khengar's Palace, is reached. On entering the gate, the large enclosure of the temples is

[1] See *Life of John Wilson, F.R.S.*, by Dr. G. Smith, for picture and account of the stone; or Mr Burgess, *Second Archæol. Report*.

on the left, while to the right is the old granite temple of *Man Singh*, Bhoja Raja of Cutch, and farther on the much larger one of *Vastupala* (see below). Built into the wall on the left of the entrance is an inscription in Sanscrit. Some 16 Jain temples here form a sort of fort on the ledge at the top of the great cliff, but still 600 ft. below the summit. The largest temple is that of *Nemnath* (see plan, p. 154) standing in a quadrangular court 195 × 130 ft. It consists of two halls (with two porches, called by the Hindus *mandapams*), and a shrine, which contains a large black image of Nemnath, the 22d Tirthankar, with massive gold ornaments and jewels. Round the shrine is a passage with many images in white marble. Between the outer and inner halls are two shrines. The outer hall has two small raised platforms paved with slabs of yellow stone, covered with representations of feet in pairs, which represent the 2452 feet of the first disciples. On the W. of this is a porch overhanging the perpendicular scarp. On two of the pillars of the mandapam are inscriptions dated 1275, 1281, and 1278—dates of restoration, when Mr Burgess says it was covered with a coating of chunam, and "adorned with coats of whitewash" within. The enclosure is nearly surrounded inside by 70 cells, each enshrining a marble image, with a covered passage in front of them lighted by a perforated stone screen. The principal entrance was originally on the E. side of the court; but it is now closed, and the entrance from the court in Khengar's Palace is that now used. There is a passage leading into a low dark temple, with granite pillars in lines. Opposite the entrance is a recess containing two large black images; in the back of the recess is a lion rampant, and over it a crocodile in bas-relief. Behind these figures is a room from which is a descent into a cave, with a large white marble image, an object of the most superstitious veneration by the Jains, which the priests usually

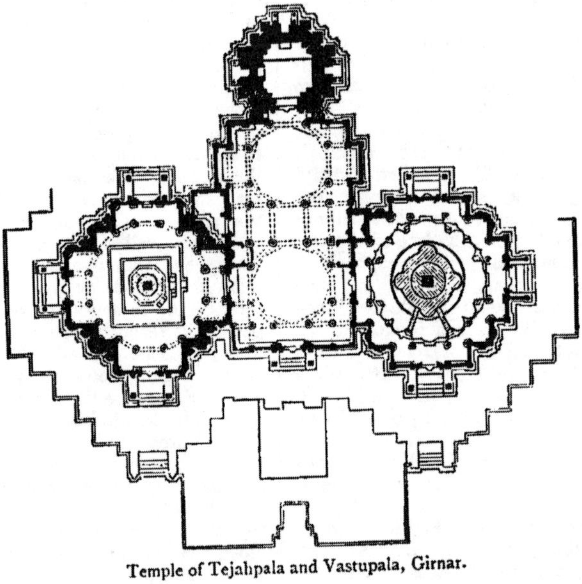

Temple of Tejahpala and Vastupala, Girnar.

try to conceal. It has a slight hollow in the shoulder, said to be caused by water dropping from the ear, whence it was called *Amijhera*, "nectar drop." In the N. porch are inscriptions which state that in Samwat 1215 certain Thakurs completed the shrine, and built the Temple of Ambika. After leaving this there are three temples to the left. That on the S. side contains a colossal image of Rishabha Deva, the 1st Tirthankar, exactly like that at Satrunjaya, called Bhim-Padam. On the throne of this image is a slab of yellow stone carved in 1442, with figures of the 24 Tirthankars. Opposite this temple is a modern one to Panchabai. W. of it is a large temple called *Malakavisi*, sacred to Parasnath. N. again of this is another temple of Parasnath, which contains a large white marble image canopied by a cobra, whence it is called *Sheshphani*, "an arrangement not unfrequently found in the S. but rare in the N."[1] It bears a date = 1803. The last temple to the N. is **Kumarapala's**, which has a long open portico on the W., and appears to have been destroyed by the Mohammedans, and restored in 1824 by Hansraja Jetha. These temples are along the W. face of the hill, and are all enclosed. Outside to the N. is the Bhima Kunda, a tank 70 ft. by 50 ft., in which Hindus bathe. "Immediately behind the temple of Nemnath is the triple one erected by the brothers **Tejahpala and Vastupala** (built 1177)." The plan is that of 3 temples joined together. The shrine has an image of Mallinath, the 19th Tirthankar. Farther N. is the temple of **Samprati Raja.** This temple is probably one of the oldest on the hill, date 1158. Samprati is said to have ruled at Ujjain in the end of the third century B.C., and to have been the son of Kunala, Asoka's third son. S. of this, and 200 ft. above the Jain temples, is the *Gaumukhi Shrine*, near a plentiful spring of water. From it the crest of the mountain (3330 ft.) is reached by a steep flight of stairs. Here is an ancient temple of Amba Mata, which is much resorted to by newly-married couples of the Brahman caste. The bride and bridegroom have their clothes tied together, and attended by their male and female relations, adore the goddess and present cocoa-nuts and other offerings. This pilgrimage is supposed to procure for the couple a long continuance of wedded bliss. To the E. not far off, are the 3 rocky spires of the Gorakhnath, the Nemnath or Gúrú-dattáraya, and the Kalika Peaks.

[1] Fergusson's *Indian Architecture*, ii. 34.

S.E. of the Verawal Gate of Junagadh is the **Shrine of Jamal Shah or Datar.** After passing under a low arch near the city, the house of the Mujawir or attendant of the shrine is seen in front. To the right is a stone platform surrounding an unusually fine mango tree, with a tank just beyond, and the shrine of Datar, a building 30 ft. high with a fluted cone at top. Here it is necessary to take off one's shoes. The shrine and the whole place are very attractive.

There is a **Leper Asylum** near the Datar Temple for 100 lepers of both sexes, built at the expense of the Vazir Sahib Bahu-ud-din. H.R.H. Prince Albert Victor laid the foundation stone in 1890. Above it, 4 m. in S.E. direction, is the *Datar Peak* (2779 ft.). On the summit of the hill is a small shrine, and from it a very beautiful view. The hill is held sacred by Mohammedans and Hindus alike, and is supposed to have a beneficial effect on lepers, who repair to it in considerable numbers.

61 m. from Jetalsar is **Verawal** station. The railway terminus is on the W. side of the city (population, 17,000), close to the walls, and about ½ m. from the lighthouse at the landing-place. This is a very ancient seaport, and probably owes its existence to its more celebrated neighbour *Patan Somnath.* It rose into notice during the time of the Guzerat sultans, and in their

reigns became, until superseded by Surat, the principal port of embarkation for Mohammedan pilgrims to Mecca. It is still a flourishing little seaport. In the Temple *Harsad Mata* is a celebrated inscription (1264), recording that a mosque was endowed in that year, and bearing dates in four different eras. It was from this inscription that it was discovered that the Valabhi era commenced in 319 A.D., and the Shri Singh era from 1113 A.D. The river Devka flows to the N. of Verawal, and joins the sea at a place called Dani Baru. The *Jaleshvar Temple*, about 2 m. N.W. from the town, at the mouth on the right bank, is of great antiquity. Half way to it on the sand dunes is the Rest-House of the Junagarh State. On the S.W. face of Verawal there is a modern sea-wall and an unfinished stone pier with a lighthouse at the end of it. A large *Custom House* has been built on the sea face, and near it is a *dock* established on reclaimed land.

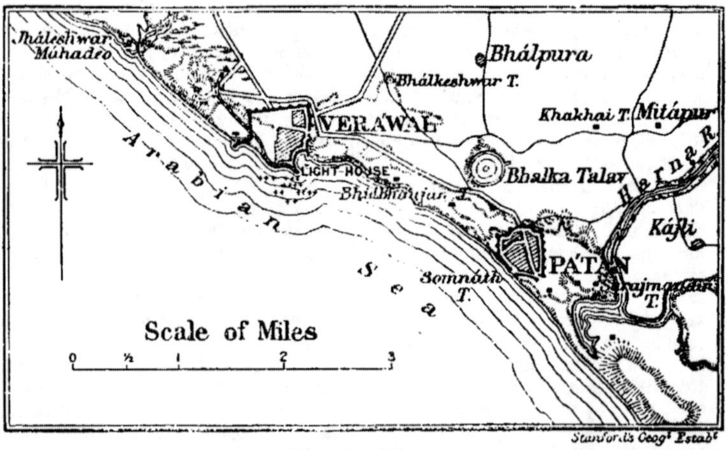

Verawal and Patan.

On the sea-shore, nearly 3 m. to the S.E., is **Patan Somnath**, also known as Prabhas Patan, or Deva Patan, the *Semenat* of Marco Polo. The anchorages at Verawal and Patan are so bad that it is hard to account for the undoubted fact that from the earliest times they carried on a trade with the Red Sea, Persian Gulf, and African coast. The place is renowned in Hindu mythology. It was here the Jadavs slew each other, and here Krishna, the late legends of whom are connected with Kathiawar as the earlier ones are with Muttra (p. 166), was shot by the Bhil. In the Gir Forest, inland from Patan, is the only place in India where there are one or two separate communities of African negroes. Mahmud of Ghazni conquered the town in 1025 A.D., and it appears that he left behind a Mohammedan Governor. Subsequently the Hindus recovered their power, but it was again cast down by Alauddin *circa* 1300 A.D., and the coast belt or Nagher kingdom conquered. From this date Mohammedan supremacy prevailed throughout the belt, and from the reign of Muhammad Tughlak governors were regularly appointed. Through the gallantry and statesmanship of Diwan Amarji, it was conquered by the Nawab of Junagarh in whose hands it remains.

Proceeding from Verawal to Patan (population 8,500), to the right is a vast burial ground, with thousands of tombs, and *palias*. There are also buildings which well deserve examination after the traveller has seen the city. The Junagarh or W. Gate, by which Patan is entered, is a triple gate of Hindu architecture. The centre part of the first division of the gateway is very ancient, and has a carving of two elephants on either side pouring water over Lakshmi, whose figure is almost obliterated.

After passing the second gate the W. wall of a mosque of the time of Mahmud is seen on the left. There is no inscription in it, but its antiquity is so credited that the Nawab has assigned the revenue of three villages for keeping it in order. After passing the third portal of the Junagarh Gateway, there are four stones on the right hand, of which two have Guzerati, and two Sanscrit inscriptions. Driving on straight through the bazaar, which is very narrow, and has quaint old houses on either side, the *Jama Masjid* is reached. The entrance is by a porch, which has been a mandir in front of a Hindu temple. The most interesting part of this very ancient building is, that in each of the four corners is a carving of two human figures with the Bo tree between them. A low door in the W. side of the porch leads into the court of the Mosque, which was deserted for 25 years, and inhabited by Moslem fishermen, who dried their fish in it, but is now used again.

To reach the **Old Temple of Somnath** it is necessary to drive to the end of the bazaar of Patan and turn to the right. The structure is close to the sea. Mr Fergusson considers that it was probably never a large temple, but adds that the dome of its porch, which measures 33 ft. across, is as large as any we know of its age. The interior of the porch is even now in its ruins very striking. "From what fragments of its sculptured decorations remain, they must have been of great beauty, quite equal to anything we know of this class of their age." It was, no doubt, like the temple of Nemnath, on Girnar, surrounded by an enclosure which would make it a strong place. Now the temple stands alone, stripped even of its marble, like, but superior

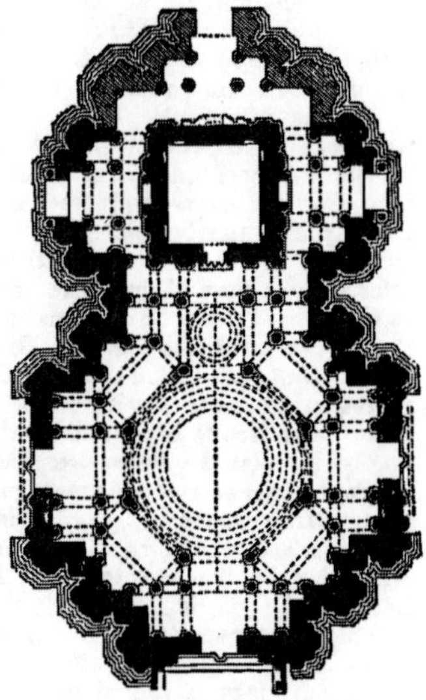

Plan of Temple of Somnath, by Mr J. Burgess.

to, the temples of Dabhoi and Lakkundi. There are three entrances to the porch, and a corridor round the central octagonal space, which was covered by the great dome. There are four smaller domes. The dome in the centre is supported by eight pillars and eight arches. The pillar on the right hand, looking from the E., next but one before reaching the adytum, has an inscription, which is illegible except the date, Samwat 1697 = 1640 A.D. The walls on the N., S., and W. sides have each two handsomely carved niches, in which there have been idols.

The temple is said to have been first built of gold by Somraj, then of silver by Ravana, then of wood by Krishna, and then of stone by Bhimdeva. Though three times destroyed by the Mohammedans, it was nevertheless three times rebuilt, and so late as 1700 A.D. was still a place of great sanctity. But in 1706 Aurangzeb ordered its destruction, and there seems every reason to believe that this order was carried out.

The celebrated expedition of Sultan Mahmud of Ghazni to Somnath took place in 1025 A.D. He marched with such rapidity, by way of Guzerat, that the Hindu rajas were unable to collect their forces for its defence, and after a sharp fight for two days conquered both the city and the temple. Immense spoil was found in the temple, and after a short stay Mahmud returned to Ghazni. It was on this occasion that he carried off the famous "Gates of Somnath," of which the so-called representatives are now in the fort at Agra. Sir Henry Elliot records that 10,000 populated villages were held by the temple as an endowment, and that 300 musicians and 500 dancing-girls were attached to it. There were also 300 barbers to shave the heads of the pilgrims.

The **confluence of the Three rivers**, or *Triveni*, to the E. of the town, has been, no doubt, a sacred spot from times of remote antiquity. It was near this that, according to tradition, Krishna sleeping under a deer skin was accidentally shot by a Bhil and killed. The road to it passes through the E. gate, called the *Nana*, or "small," also the *Sangam*, or "confluence gate." It has pilasters on either side, and on the capitals figures are represented issuing out of the mouths of Makaras, a fabulous crocodile, which in Hindu mythology is the emblem of the God of Love. About a ¼ m. outside the gate is a pool on the right hand, called the Kund, and a small building on the left called the Adi Tirth, and next to these is a temple and the Tirth of Triveni, where people are always bathing. The stream here is from 100 to 200 yds. broad, and runs into the sea. N. of this, about 200 yds. off, is the **Suraj Mandir**, or temple to the Sun, half broken down by Mahmud, standing on high ground, and wondrously old and curious. Over the door of the adytum are groups of figures, with a tree between each two. Inside the adytum is a round red mark for the sun, not ancient; and below is a figure of a goddess, also coloured red. On the W. and S. outer walls are masses of carving much worn. At the bottom there is a frieze of *Keshari* lions, that is, lions with elephants' trunks. This temple is probably of the same age as that of Somnath. About 250 yds. to the W. is a vast tomb, quite plain; and below, in a sort of quarry, is a subterraneous temple, which is called Ahdi Shah's. The same name is given to a mosque with six cupolas to the N., which has been a Hindu temple.

200 yds. to the N.W., inside the Nana Gate, will be found the temple built by Ahalaya Bai, to replace the ancient Somnath. Below it is another, reached by descending 22 steps. The dome of this subterraneous building is supported by 16 pillars. The temple itself is 13 ft. square. It is of no interest except on account of its builder, Ahalaya Bai (p. 90).

Returning towards Verawal, about ½ m. outside the Junagarh Gate is the **Mai Puri**, which in ancient times was a temple of the sun. The carving of this building is exquisite, and in better preservation than that of the temple of Somnath. In the centre of the building is an enclosure 6 ft. square, in which Mai Puri, "the Perfect Mother," is buried. A legend is told about her, which states that she brought about the siege of Somnath by Mahmud. The temple (or mosque, as the Moslems have made it) contains a mass of old Hindu carving, still beautiful though mutilated. Not far from the Mai Puri is the tomb of Silah Shah. There is a curious stand for lamps here carved in stone, in the shape of a crown. To the S.E., about 50 yds., is the tomb of Mangroli Shah, which has been restored. Before reaching the shrine you pass through the porch of an ancient Hindu temple.

Not far from this spot is the *Bhid Bhaujan Pagoda* on the sea-shore, locally known as Bhidiyo, very old, perhaps of the 14th century. It is 60 ft. high, and forms a good mark for sailors. To the E. of the Pagoda is a clear space, where Englishmen coming from Rajkot pitch their tents.

Various coasting steamers call at Verawal regularly, and a traveller can go by sea to Bombay or to Porbandar, Cutch, or Karachi.

(2) *Jetalsar to Porbandar.*

9 m. **Dhoraji**, an important commercial town.

79 m. **Porbandar** terminal station, D.B. (population, 26,420), E. of the town, the capital of the state of that name, and a place of some interest. It is identified with the ancient city of Sudâmpuri, known to the readers of the *Bhagavata*. Near this is an old temple of Sudâma. The line is continued for goods traffic along the shore to the creek W. of the town, where it terminates in a wharf. The place is a very old-world corner, not recommended to visitors in a hurry, but very interesting to those who have leisure, or to sportsmen. The coasting steamers between Bombay and Karachi touch at Porbandar.

[The places of interest in the neighbourhood are—

(*a*) *Shrinagar*, 9 m. N.W. of Porbandar, believed to have been the first capital of the Jethwa Rajputs. There are remains of an ancient temple of the sun.

(*b*) *Miani*, a very ancient seaport 18 m. N.W. of Porbandar. To the extreme N.W. in the district of **Okhamandal**, directly under the Gaekwar of Baroda are some of the most sacred *Hindu Temples* in India, viz., those at **Dwarka** ("door") and **Bet** ("island"). The original possessors of the place were a war-like tribe of Rajputs, called "*Whagire*," who were notorious pirates up to the early part of the 19th century, and though reduced at that time by the British Government, still clinging to their former traditions by which each man believes that he is a prince in his own right.

(*c*) *Chaya*, a village 2 m. S.E. of Porbandar, was once the capital. The old palace is still there.

(*d*) *Bileshwar*, 8 m. N. of Ranawao station, a small village E. of the Barda Hills. There is here a fine temple of considerable antiquity, and in good preservation.

(*e*) *Ghumli* or *Bhumli*, is about 12 m. N. of Bileshwar, or 24 m. from Porbandar by the road passing W. of the Barda Hills. This place is now absolutely ruined and deserted; it was the capital of the Jethwas when at the zenith of their power. It lies in a gorge of the Barda Hills; the ruins are of the 11th or 12th century. The most interesting remains are the Lakhota, the Ganesh Dehra, the Rampol, the Jeta Wao, and the group of temples near the Son Kansari Tank, and some ruins on the summit of the Abapura Hill. It is about 4 m. S. of Bhanwar, a fort belonging to the Jam of Nawanagar.[1]

40 m. S.E. from Porbandar, at **Madhavapur**, Krishna is said to have been married. There is an important temple dedicated to him there.]

(3) *Jetalsar to Rajkot, Vankaner and Wadhwan.*

23 m. **Gondal** is the capital of the state of that name, and the residence of the chief. It is a cheerful, well-cared-for town, with many handsome temples. The public offices are situated outside the town on open sites surrounded by gardens. The courtyard of the palace is very handsome.

46 m. **Rajkot** station, a civil and military station, the residence of the Political Agent, and the headquarters of the administration (population, 36,000).

[1] Ghumlí is illustrated in Mr Burgess's *Second Archæol. Rep.*

The most important public work in Rajkot is the *Kaisar-i-Hind Bridge* over the Aji river, built by Mr R.B. Booth, whose name is connected with nearly every important modern building in the Province. The total cost of the bridge was Rs. 117,500, of which the Chief of Bhaunagar paid all but Rs. 7500. The munificent donor of this bridge was educated at Rajkumar College, on which he bestowed Rs. 100,000, to build a wing and a residence for the Principal, and further contributed Rs. 50,000 to the Endowment Fund.

The *Rajkumar College* deserves a visit, as the place where the young princes of Kathiawar are educated. It was opened in 1870. On the ground floor is a fine hall, which gives access to the class-rooms. Some good portraits hang on the walls. Along both fronts is a massive verandah, and over the E. entrance a rectangular tower 55 ft. high. The entrance is on the W., and is flanked by two circular towers. The N. and S. wings contain 32 suites of bedrooms and sitting-rooms, bath-rooms and lavatories. To the W. of the N. wing is a chemical laboratory, and on the opposite side a gymnasium and racquet-court. N. of the laboratory are extensive stables. The young princes, beside playing all manly games, are drilled as a troop of cavalry. W. of the quadrangle are the houses of the Principal and Vice-Principal, with extensive gardens. S. of the buildings is the cricket-field of 19 acres. The college was founded by Colonel Keatinge.

The *High School* was opened in January, 1875. It was built at the expense of the Nawab of Junagarh and cost Rs. 70,000. In the centre is a fine hall.

N.E. of Rajkot are the *Jubilee Water Works*, which supply the town.

A branch line runs to (54 m.) *Nawanagar* or **Jamnagar**, capital of the state of that name, of which the famous cricketer, H. H. Jam Shri Ranjitsinghji, is chief. Hence *Mandvi* can be reached by native craft, but is best reached by steamer direct from Bombay about twice a week. Small steamers occasionally ply between Beoi, near Nawanagar, and Bombay.

From Rajkot the *Morvi State Railway* (a narrow gauge (2·5) line) runs N. E. to Wadhwan, *viâ* **Vankaner** junction station (25 m.). This is the capital of a small state and the residence of the chief. The country around is undulating, rising into hills W. and S. of the town. From Vankaner the line runs E. to (51 m.) Wadhwan, and (91 m.) Viramgam (see p. 148). From this point a line runs to Mehsana (see p. 130) for Ajmer, Delhi, etc.

ROUTE 12.

(*a*) BANDIKUI JUNCTION to **BHARATPUR Junction, Achnera Station,** and Agra, and

(*b*) **Achnera Station to Muttra, Brindaban,** and **Hathras Road,** and by road to **Mahaban, Govardhan** and **Dig.**

(*c*) **Agra** to **Delhi,** direct route by Midland Railway, through Muttra.

61 m. **Bharatpur Junction,** D.B. Here the C.I. Railway is joined by the B.B. Railway broad gauge route from Rutlam and Kotah to Muttra and Delhi (p. 121). Bharatpur is the capital of a Jat State (33,000 inhab.); the Maharaja, however, usually resides at Sawari, 3 m. from Bharatpur. The ruling family is descended from a Jat Zamindar named Churaman, who harassed the rear of Aurangzeb's army during his expedition to the Deccan. He was succeeded by his brother, and after him by his nephew, Suraj Mal, who fixed his capital at Bharatpur (1733), and subsequently (1761) drove out the Mahratta governor from Agra, and made it his own residence.

In 1765 the Jats were repulsed before Delhi and driven out of Agra.

In 1782 Sindhia seized Bharatpur and its territory; but restored 14 districts, and when he got into difficulties he made an alliance with the Jat chief Ranjit Singh.[1] The Jats, however, were defeated by Ghulam Kadir at Fatehpur-Sikri, and were driven back on Bharatpur, but being reinforced at the end of the same year, 1788, they raised the blockade of Agra, and Sindhia recovered it. In 1803 the British Government made treaty with Ranjit Singh, who joined General Lake at Agra with 5000 horse, and received territory in return. Upon Ranjit Singh intriguing with Jaswant Rao Holkar, Bharatpur was besieged by General Lake, but four assaults on the fort were repulsed with a loss of 3000 men. The chief then made overtures for peace, which were accepted on the 4th of May 1805. On troubles breaking out regarding the succession, Bharatpur was again besieged by General Lord Combermere, and on the 18th of January 1829, after a siege of six weeks, the place was stormed. The loss of the besieged was estimated at 6000 men killed and wounded. The British had 103 killed, and 477 wounded and missing. On this occasion again the British artillery was unable to make any real impression on the mud defences of the fort, and the breach was made by the explosion of mines.

The Walled City of Bharatpur is an irregular oblong, lying N.E. and S.W. The **Inner Fort**, surrounded by a ditch and a lofty mud wall, is contained in the N.E. half of the outer fort. Three palaces run right across the centre of the inner fort from E to W., that to the E. being the Raja's Palace. Next is an old palace built by Badan Singh. To the W. is a palace which is generally styled the Kamra; it is furnished in semi-European style.

There are only two gates to the inner fort, the Chau Burj Gate on the S., and the Assaldati on the N. The fine bastion at the N.W. corner of the inner fort is called the *Jowahar Burj*, and is worth ascending for the view. N. of the Kamra Palace is the Court of Justice, the Jewel Office, and the Jail. On the road between the Chau Burj Gate of the inner fort and the Anah Gate of the outer fort are the Gangaka Mandir, a market-place, a new mosque, and the Lakhshmanji temple.

[1] Ruled 1763-1805. The Jats had successfully defended their mud forts on previous occasions.

78 m. **Achnera** junction station (R.), of the line of railway passing through Muttra to Bindraban and to Hathras on the East Indian Railway and to Farukhabad, Fatehgarh, and Cawnpore. (See p. 300.)

93 m. **AGRA Idgah Station,** junction of the Indian Midland Railway from Gwalior and Jhansi, likely to be abolished when the B.B. Railway broad gauge is continued from Bayana to Agra Cantonment Station. The direct route of that line to Delhi (p. 169) crosses our line W. of the station. Travellers for the hotels alight at

94 m. **AGRA Fort Station** (R.), just outside the Delhi Gate of the Fort.

(*b*) Achnera Station to Hathras Road.

23 m. **MUTTRA** (or Mathura) junction station, D.B., in the cantonments S. of the city (the town station is on the branch line to Brindaban). Population 60,000. The city, the Μόδουρα ἡ τῶν Θεῶν of Ptolemy, stretches for about 1½ m. along the right bank of the Jumna. Fa Hian, in the beginning of the 5th century A.D., found that there were 20 Buddhist monasteries with 3000 monks at Muttra; but when Hiouen Thsang visited the place in 634 A.D. the number had declined to 2000. The Buddhists had disappeared when Mahmud of Ghazni came to Muttra in 1017 A.D. He remained there 20 days, pillaged and burned the city, and carried off five golden idols, whose eyes were of rubies, worth 50,000 dinars—£25,000. A sixth idol

of gold weighed 1120 lbs., and was decorated with a sapphire weighing 300 *Mishkals*, or 3½lbs. There were also 100 idols of silver, each of which loaded a camel. The idols together were worth not less than £3,000,000. The Brahman temple of Kesava Rao was built on the very site where the great Buddhist monastery Yasa Vihara stood.

The Fort, rebuilt in Akbar's time, is in the centre, but only the substructure now remains. In May, 1857, the troops on the Treasury at Muttra mutinied and carried off the money which was about to be sent to Agra. The Europeans of the place retreated north to Hodal, to which place some troops of the Bharatpur State had passed on, and upon these proving faithless took refuge elsewhere. The Magt. of the District, Mr Mark Thornhill, remained at Muttra till 14th June, but as Agra was unable to send him any assistance he was finally compelled to fall back there.

The Jail and Collector's Office are 1¾ m. to the S. beyond the town. 1 m. to the W. of the Katra (see below) is a **Jain temple** and a large mound of bricks called **Chaurasi Tila**, and about ½ m. to the S. is another mound called **Kankali**, while to the S.W., at distances varying from ½ m. to 1 m., are five mounds called the **Chaubarah** mounds.[1] There are three **Churches** — the Anglican "Christ Church," the Roman Catholic Church, and a Presbyterian Church. The first contains several interesting monuments.

The city is entered by the Hardinge Gate, also called Holi Gate, built by the municipality. The finely-carved stonework façades of the better class of houses are well worthy of inspection, and are one of the peculiarities of the city.

The **River** and **Ghats**.—The Jumna is about 300 yds. broad. There is a paved street the whole way along it, with bathing ghats, descending to the water, and ornamental chabutarahs, or platforms, and small but well-proportioned pavilions.

The river is full of turtles, some of them very large, poking their long necks and heads out to be fed. About 80 yds. N. of the bridge is the fine **House of the Guru Parshotamdas.** Then comes another belonging to a Guzerati merchant **Ballamdas.** Opposite to this, on the farther bank of the river, is the flourishing village of **Hans Ganj**, or "Swan borough." N. again is a stone tower, 55 ft. high, called the **Sati Burj**, because when Hans was killed by Krishna, his widow became *sati* here. M. Growse, to whose instance Muttra owes much of its best modern architectural work, says it was the wife of Raja Bhar Mal, of Ambèr, mother of Bhagwandas (p. 142), who built it in 1570 A.D. The traveller now descends several steps to the Bisraut Ghat, a little N. of the Sati Burj, and so to a sort of square, where Rajas are weighed against gold. There is a small white marble arch here, close to the river. Beyond this is a ghat built by Jai Singh, of Jaipur, and the enormous house and temple belonging to the well-known late Seth Lakshman Das, son of Seth Govind Das.

Close by in the centre of the town, on an isolated site, rises the Jama Masjid, once covered with encaustic tiles; its court is 14 ft. above the level of the street. On either side of the façade of the gateway are Persian lines. The chronogram gives the date 1660-61. Over the façade of the mosque proper are the 99 names of God. At the sides are two pavilions roofed in the Hindu manner. There are four minarets, which are 132 ft. high. At the entrance to the W. of the town is the **Idgah** (the glazed tiles should be observed), and about ¼ m. beyond is the **Katra**, which is an enclosure like that of a sarai, 804 ft. long by 653 ft. broad. Upon a terrace 30 ft. high stands a great red stone **mosque**, built by Aurangzeb, and the most con-

[1] All these places will be found mentioned by General Cunningham in vol. iii. of his *Arch. Survey Reports*, p. 13, and also in vol. i. p. 233.

spicuous object in a distant view of Muttra. There is another terrace 5 ft. lower, where are votive tablets in the Nagri character, dated Samwat 1713-20. On this site stood the great temple of **Kesava Rao**, which Tavernier saw in the beginning of Aurangzeb's reign, apparently about 1659 A.D., and which he describes as very magnificent, adding that it ranked next after the temples of Jagannath and Benares (*Travels*, pt. ii., book iii., ch. 12, French ed., and Cunningham, *Reports*, vol. iii. p. 15). In the **Katra** mound a number of Buddhistic remains have been found by General Cunningham and others, including a broken Buddhist railing pillar, with the figure of Maya Devi standing under the *Sal* tree, and also a stone on which was inscribed the well-known genealogy of the Gupta dynasty, from Shri Gupta, the founder, down to Samudra Gupta, where the stone was broken off. At the back of the Katra is a modern temple to Kesava, and close by is the **Potara-Kund**, a tank in which Krishna's baby linen was washed. This tank is faced throughout with stone, and has flights of stone steps down to the water. There is also a very steep ramp for horses and cattle.

To the S. of the city is the **Museum**, erected by public subscription, at the suggestion of Mr Mark Thornhill, decorated by stone carving which Mr Growse calls "the most refined and delicate work of the kind ever executed." It contains a number of interesting Buddhist remains found in Muttra, but the finest of these are now in the Imperial Museum, Calcutta, and the Museum at Lucknow.

Immediately opposite are the **Public Gardens**, and a little farther on is the **Jail**, between which and the Collector's Office and Magistrates' Courts, extensive discoveries were made. It appears that on this site stood two Buddhist monasteries, the Huvishka and the Kunda-Suka Vihara—the latter the place where the famous monkey which made an offering to Buddha jumped into the tank and was killed. At this mound statues of all sizes, bas-reliefs, pillars, Buddhist rails, votive *stupas*, stone umbrellas, and inscriptions have been found, one inscription being of the 1st century B.C.[1]

The most important discoveries at Muttra were made by Dr Führer during his excavations at the **Kankali Tila** or mound, which he looks upon as the site of the Upagupta monastery mentioned by Hiouen Thsang. The remains of one Vaishnava and two Jain temples, and a Jain stupa, some 49 ft. 8 in. in diameter, were brought to light, and besides some hundreds of most valuable sculptures, stupa railings, panels, etc., on many of which are inscriptions dating back before the Christian era. The discoveries prove that the *national* Indian arts of architecture and sculpture flourished in a high degree at Muttra, and have led to the conclusion that play-acting was practised very early in the city of the gods. All the objects discovered have been deposited in the Lucknow Museum,[2] where they can be examined by visitors.

[**Mahaban** is about 6 m. S.E. of Muttra, on the left bank of the Jumna, and is reached by a good road. It is a very ancient town and place of pilgrimage, and first emerges into modern history in the year 1017 A.D., when it shared the fate of Muttra, and was sacked by Mahmud of Ghazni. The Hindu prince is said, when the fall of the town became inevitable, to have solemnly slain his wife and children, and then committed suicide. In 1234 a contemporary writer mentions Mahaban as one of the gathering places of the army sent by Shams-ud-din Altamsh against Kalinjar. It is incidentally

1 For the many other discoveries made in different mounds near Muttra reference must be made to General Cunningham's *Report*, vol. i. of the Archæological Survey, where they are detailed at great length.

2 See Illustrated description in *Proceedings of the Archæol. Dept. of the N.W.P.*

referred to by the Emperor Babar in 1526.

The country round about it, although now bare of woods. appears to have once been literally *Mahaban*, "a great forest." Even as late as 1634, the Emperor Shah Jahan held a hunt here, and killed four tigers. This ancient woodland country fringing the sacred Jumna is the scene of very early religious legends. In Sanscrit literature it is closely associated with **Gokul**, about a mile off, overhanging the Jumna. Indeed, the scenes of the youthful adventures of Krishna, actually shown at Mahaban, about a mile from the river, are ascribed in the Puranas to Gokul. Gokul seems to have been originally the common name for the whole, although it is now restricted to what must have been the waterside suburb of the ancient town.

The ruins of Mahaban, which rise as a hill of brick and mud, covering about 30 acres, are on the site of the old fort. The architectural remains combine Buddhist and Hindu forms.

The most interesting relic at Mahaban is the so-called **Palace of Nanda**, the foster-father of the changeling Krishna. It consists of a covered court, re-erected by the Mohammedans in the time of Aurangzeb from ancient Hindu and Buddhist materials to serve as a mosque, and is divided into 4 aisles by 5 rows of 16 pillars, 80 in all, from which it takes its popular name of Assi Khamba, or the "Eighty Pillars." Many of the capitals are curiously carved with grotesque heads and squat figures. Four of them are supposed to represent by their sculptures the four ages of the world. The pillar known as the Surya Yug, or "Golden Age," is covered with rich and beautiful carving; that known as the Treta Yug, or "Second Age" of the world, is adorned with almost equal profusion. The Dwapar Yug, or "Third Age," is more scantily carved; while the Kali Yug, or present "Iron Age" of the world is represented by a crude unsculptured pillar.

In the Palace of Nanda are laid the scenes of Krishna's infancy. His cradle, a coarse structure covered with red calico and tinsel, still stands in the pillared hall, while a blue-black image of the sacred child looks out from under a canopy against the wall. The churn in which Krishna's foster-mother made butter for the household is shown, and consists of a long bamboo sticking out of a carved stone. A spot in the wall is pointed out as the place where the sportive milkmaids hid Krishna's flute. One pillar is said to have been polished by his foster-mother's hand, as she leant against it when churning, and others have been equally polished by the hands of generations of pilgrims. From the top of the roof there is a view over mounds of ruins, with the Jumna beyond showing its waters, at intervals, amid an expanse of sand, high grasses, and rugged ravines. Mahaban is still a very popular place of pilgrimage among the Hindus. Thousands of Vishnu worshippers, with yellow-stained clothes, yearly visit the scenes of the infancy of the child-god. The anniversary of Krishna's birth is celebrated during several days in the month of Bhadon (August) by a vast concourse of people.

The riverside village of Gokul, where Vishnu first appeared as Krishna, has few relics of antiquity. Its shrines and temples are quite modern. It is approached, however, by a lofty and beautiful flight of steps (ghat) from the river, and for more than three centuries it has been the headquarters of the Vallabhacharya sect, or Gokulastha Gusains, whose founder preached here. Many thousands of pilgrims, chiefly from Guzerat and Bombay, yearly resort to this centre of their faith, and have built numerous temples of a rather tasteless type.]

[From Muttra an expedition may be made to **Dig** (D.B.), a town in the territory of the Raja of Bharatpur, 24 m. West of Agra. It is well to intimate an intended visit to the Political Agent, Bharatpur. The journey may be continued to the latter place, 22 m. from Dig, or the whole journey may be made the reverse way from it to Muttra. At **Govardhan**, about 14 m. from Muttra, is the celebrated hill which was upheld by Krishna on one finger to shelter the cowherds from a storm excited by Indra as a test of Krishna's divinity. Here, on the right, are the "chhatris" of the Bharatpur Rajas, a striking group of tombs, temples, and ghats built on the margin of two vast tanks, one of which, called the Munusa Ganga, is the resort of thousands of pilgrims during the annual autumn fair. The chief chhatris are those of Buldeo Singh, and of Suraj Mal, the founder of the dynasty, and his wives, of Randhir Singh[1] and Bela Diva Singh. Most of them show good carving. Mr Fergusson says of the temple of Hardeo-ji, built in Akbar's reign: "It is a plain edifice, 135 ft. long by 35 ft. wide, externally, and both in plan and design singularly like those Early Romance churches that are constantly met with in the S. of France, belonging to the 11th and 12th centuries."

For 3 m. before reaching Dig, the road forms a sort of causeway above a very low flat country, which was once a morass and formed the principal defence of the Fort.

At **Dig** (or Deeg) the chief object of interest is the splendid **Palace**, or rather group of palaces, built by Suraj Mal of Bharatpur. Though his great design was never completed, it surpasses all the other modern palaces for grandeur of conception and beauty of detail. Mr Fergusson greatly admired this palace, and says of it: "The glory of Deeg consists in the cornices, which are generally double, a peculiarity not seen elsewhere, and which for extent of shadow and richness of detail surpass any similar ornaments in India, either in ancient or modern buildings. The lower cornice is the usual sloping entablature almost universal in such buildings. . . . The upper cornice, which was horizontal, is peculiar to Deeg, and seems designed to furnish an extension of the flat roof which in Eastern palaces is usually considered the best apartment of the house; but whether designed for this or any other purpose, it adds singularly to the richness of the effect, and by the double shadow affords a relief and character seldom exceeded even in the East." The palace enclosure is 475 ft. by 350 ft., and has two pavilions on each side and one at each end. Several of these are figured in vol. ii. p. 82 of the *Rambles of Sir Wm. Sleeman*, who was much struck with them. The chief pavilions are the **Gopal Bhawan** (1763), flanked by two smaller pavilions and faced by an arch for a swing and two marble thrones, which stands E. of the fine unlined Tank; the **Nand Bhawan**, N.E. of this, a fine hall, 150 x 80 x 20 ft.; the **Suraj Bhawan** and the **Harde Bhawan**, S.; and the **Kishan Bhawan**,[1] E. again of these. All are highly decorated, and between them are lovely gardens surrounding a small tank. Beyond and adjoining the gardens is the large **Rup Saugar Lake**, and beyond it the N. gate of the Fort. This has 12 bastions, and a ditch 50 ft. broad. Beyond this is a natural mound, about 70 ft. high, and a building which serves as a prison. The walls are very massive and lofty. There are 72 bastions in all; and on the N.W. bastion, about 80 ft. high, is a very long cannon.

Dig is celebrated for the battle fought on the 13th November 1804, in which General Frazer defeated Jaswant Rao Holkar's army. The British took 87 pieces of ordnance in this battle, and lost in killed and wounded about 350 men. The remains of Holkar's army took shelter in the Fort of Dig. On the 1st December following, Lord Lake joined the army before this place, and immediately commenced

[1] Ruled 1823-1858.

[1] The Suraj Bhawan is built of white marble and mosaic work; the other halls are of cream-coloured sandstone.

operations to reduce it. On the night of the 23rd his troops captured an eminence which commanded the city, but not without considerable loss. The enemy then evacuated Dig on the following day and the fort on the succeeding night, and fled to Bharatpur.]

6 m. from Muttra by railway is **Brindaban** (properly Vrindaban, meaning a forest of basil plants), the place to which Krishna removed from Gokul.

There is no reason to believe that Brindaban was ever a great seat of Buddhism. Its most ancient temples, four in number, date only from the 16th century, "while the space now occupied by a series of the largest and most magnificent shrines ever erected in Upper India was 500 years ago belt of woodland" (see Growse's *Muttra*, p. 174). The four chief temples are those of Gobind Deo-ji, Gopi Nath, Jugal Kishor, and Madan Mohan. Brindaban is famous as the place where Krishna sported with the Gopis (milkmaids), and stole their clothes when they were bathing. The Jumna bounds the town to the E., and winds pleasantly round it. At the entrance to the town, on the left, is the large **red temple**, dating from 1590, sacred to **Gobind Deo-ji**, which was almost destroyed by Aurangzeb, but has been somewhat restored by the British Government. "It is one of the most interesting and elegant temples in India, and the only one, perhaps, from which an European architect might borrow a few hints. The temple consists of a cruciform porch, internally nearly quite perfect, though externally it is not quite clear how it was intended to be finished. The cell, too, is perfect internally—it is used for worship—but the sikra is gone; possibly it may never have been completed. Though not large, its dimensions are respectable, the porch measuring 117 ft. E. and W. by 105 ft. N. and S., and is covered by a true vault, built with radiating arches —the only instance, except one,[1] known to exist in a Hindu temple in the N. of India. Over the four arms of the cross the vault is plain, and only 20 ft. span, but in the centre it expands to 35 ft. and is quite equal in design to the best Gothic vaulting known. It is the external design of this temple, however, which is the most remarkable. The angles are accentuated with singular force and decision, and the openings, which are more than sufficient for that climate, are picturesquely arranged and pleasingly divided. It is, however, the combination of vertical with horizontal lines, covering the whole surface, that forms the great merit of the design."[1]

E. is a modern *Temple*, built by Seth Radha Krishna and Seth Govind Das in the Dravidian style. Europeans are not allowed to enter, but above the W. gate is a terrace, commanding a view of the temple, which consists of a vast enclosing wall, with three gopurams, which are 80 to 90 ft. high, while the gates are about 55 ft. It is dedicated to Sri Ranga, a name of Vishnu (pp. 391, 429); and figures of Garuda, the man-bird of Vishnu, are very conspicuous. In the great court are two white marble pavilions, one E. and W. of the tank, and a stone pavilion with a flat roof, supported by sixteen pillars, opposite the E. gopuram.

At the back of the red temple on the W., are, at two corners, two other temples which resemble each other. There is a new temple adjoining this to the W., built by a Bengali Babu. It is not tasteful, but has a finely carved door.

The **Madan Mohan Temple** stands above a ghat on a branch of the river. Under two fine trees, a *Ficus indica* and a *Nauclea orientalis*, is a pavilion, in which many cobras' heads are represented. Shiva is said to have struck Devi with a stick here, when she jumped off this ghat, and made it a place for curing snake-bites. On the ghat is a Salagram (a species of Ammonite worshipped as a type of Vishnu), with two footprints,

[1] *I.e.* the temple of Hardeo-ji at Govardhan.

[1] Fergusson, *Architecture of India*, ii. 157

$2\frac{1}{4}$ in. long. This temple is 65 ft. high, and is in the shape of a cone.

The **Temple of Gopi Nath** is thought by Mr Growse to be the earliest of the series. It was built by Raesil Ji, who distinguished himself under Akbar. It resembles that of Madan Mohan, but is in a ruinous condition. Its special feature is an arcade of three bracket arches.

The **Temple of Jugal Kishor** is at the lower end of the town, near the Kesi Ghat. It is said to have been built by Neo-Karan, a Chauhan chief, in 1627 A.D. The choir has pierced tracery in the head of the arch, and above it a representation of Krishna supporting the hill of Govardhan.

The **Temple of Radha Ballabh**, of which the shrine was demolished by Aurangzeb, is also a picturesque ruin.

---

47 m. **Hathras City** (population 42,600).

52 m. **Hathras Road**, Station, Junction of E.I. Railway (p. 300).

(*c*) Agra Cantonment Station to Delhi, direct route by Midland Railway through Muttra. The route between these places was formerly by E.I. Railway through Tundla (Route 22), Aligarh and Ghaziabad Junction, and the journey occupied 5-7 hours. The direct route, occupying $3\frac{1}{2}$-6 hours, runs through—

34 m. **Muttra** (see above).

59 m. **Kosi.**

85 m. **Palwal**, and

110 m. **Tughlakabad** to

123 m. Delhi. (957 m. from Bombay by this route, and 864 m. by the B.B. and C.I. direct broad gauge route.)

From Tughlakabad onwards the line passes through the ruins of old places S. of Delhi (p. 187), the Kutab Minar, 7 m. to the W., being at first in full sight.

ROUTE 13. AGRA AND FATEHPUR-SIKRI.

AGRA.✱ There are a number of railway stations at Agra, but visitors are concerned only with the Fort Station (p. 300) and the (new) Cantonment Station (p. 113), lying W. of the Cantonment (p. 169), where conveyances will always be found.

The city was renamed Akbarabad in the 16th century, but the old name has prevailed over the new one. In size and importance it is the third in the United Provinces, and has a population of 182,000. It stands on the right bank of the Jumna, in lat. 27° 10′ and long. 78° 5′. It is 842 m. distant from Calcutta by rail, 849 m. from Bombay, 142 m. from Delhi, and 779 m. from Peshawar.

Though a week might very pleasantly be spent in visiting the sights in and around Agra, they can be seen in shorter time, and for those persons who have not so many days at their disposal the following Itinerary may be of service:—

1st Day, *Morning.* — Fort and Palace. *Afternoon.*—Drive to the Jama Masjid and on to the Taj.

2nd Day, *Morning.*—Drive to Sikandara. *Afternoon.*—To Itimad-ud-daulah, and Chini ka Roza on the left bank of the Jumna.

Most people will like to visit some of these places more than once. A full day, or, better still, 24 hours should be devoted to the excursion to Fatehpur-Sikri.

The hotels are situated at the N.W. corner of the Cantonment, below the S.W. corner of the city. Near them are the post-office, banks, and club, the last at the W. end of the Mall, which bounds the principal part of the Cantonment on the N. and leads E. to the Taj Road and the Macdonnell Park, laid out between the Taj and the Fort, and enclosing at its N. end the memorial statue of the Queen Empress. S. of the telegraph office are the fine public gardens. N. of the hotels and on the S.W. and N.W. side of the city are the District Courts and the Agra College, and 1½ m. beyond the latter the City Jail. To the E. of this and on the N. side of the city are the R.C. Cathedral, College, and Convent, and 1 m. to the N. are the Courts of the Commissioner and Judge and the R.C. Cemetery. The road to Sikandara, which is the main road to Muttra, runs N.W. from Agra past the District Jail, and the road to Fatehpur-Sikri runs S.W. No one should miss the last, as the buildings of the Emperor Akbar's palace are unique, and afford one of the most interesting sights in all India. The Jumna flows past the city in a direction from N. to S., but opposite the Fort it turns on a great elbow, and in consequence the Taj is nearly due E. of the S. end of the Fort. It is desirable to visit the Agra Fort before Delhi, as otherwise it is difficult to understand the exact relation of the more isolated buildings of the latter palace.

The old **Native City** covered about 11 sq. m., half of which area is still inhabited. It is clean, and has a fine bazaar. The chief **Articles of Native Manufacture** are gold and silver embroidery, carving in soapstone, and imitation of the old inlay work (*pietra dura*) on white marble.

History.—Nothing certain is known of Agra before the Mohammedan

AGRA AND ENVIRONS

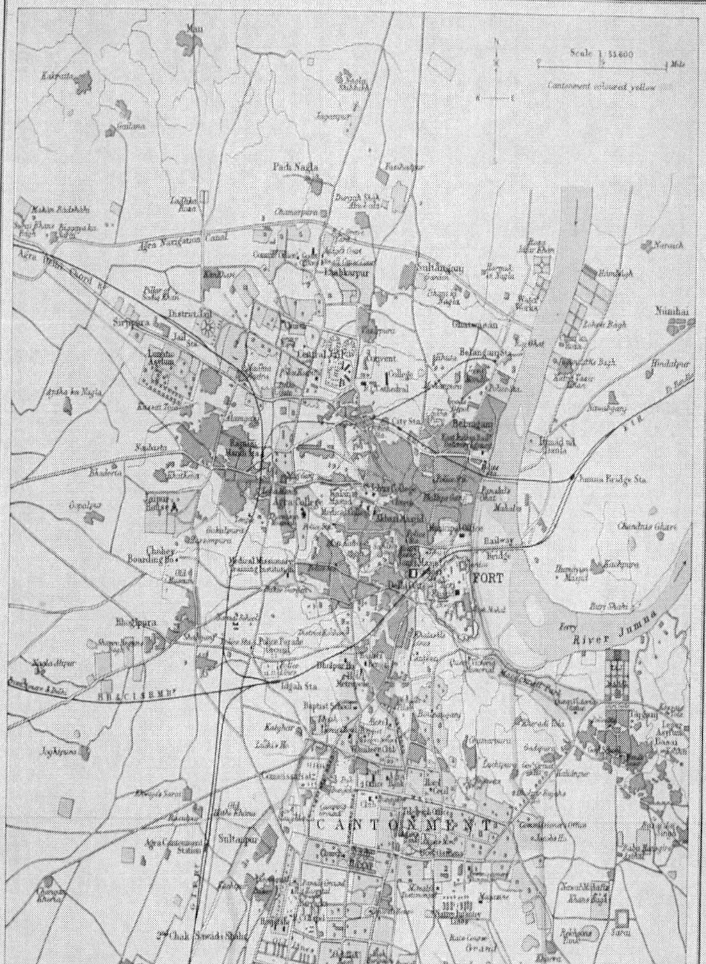

London John Murray, Albemarle Street

period. The house of Lodi was the first Mohammedan dynasty which chose Agra for a settled residence. Before their time Agra was a district of Biana. Sikandar Lodi died at Agra in 1515 A.D., but was buried at Delhi; he built the Barahdari Palace, near Sikandara, which suburb received its name from him. Babar is said to have had a garden-palace on the E. bank of the Jumna, nearly opposite the Taj, and there is a mosque near the spot, with an inscription which shows that it was built by Babar's son, Humayan, in 1530 A.D.

The Emperor Akbar resided at Agra in the early years of his reign, and removed there from Fatehpur-Sikri about 1568. The only buildings that can now be attributed to him are the walls and the red palace in the Fort. He died at Agra in 1605. Jahangir left Agra in 1618, and never returned. Shah Jahan resided at Agra from 1632 to 1637, and built much of the Fort and constructed the principal buildings of the Palace and the Taj. Between 1638 and 1650 he caused the Palace at Delhi and the Jama Masjid to be erected, and he doubtless intended to remove the capital to that place. Before this was finally done he was deposed by his son Aurangzeb in 1658, but lived as a State prisoner seven years longer at Agra. Aurangzeb removed the seat of Government permanently to Delhi. In 1764 Agra was taken by Suraj Mal, of Bharatpur and Samru, with an army of Jats, who did much damage to the town. In 1770 the Mahrattas captured it, and were expelled by Najaf Khan in 1774. In 1784 when Muhammad Beg was Governor, Agra was besieged and taken by Mahadaji Sindhia, and the Mahrattas held it till it was captured by Lord Lake, 17th October 1803, Colonel Hessing, who commanded, surrendering after a brief bombardment. Between 1835 and 1858 the seat of government of the N.W. Provinces was at Agra.

When the mutiny broke out at Meerut and Delhi on 10th and 11th May 1857 there were in Agra one British Regiment and some British Artillery, and two N.I. Regiments, the 44th and 77th. The Fort was at once secured by the Europeans, and after the two companies of the 44th, which had been sent to Muttra to bring the treasure there into Agra, mutinied and marched off to Delhi, their comrades in Agra were ordered to pile their arms on 31st May, and did so. On 4th July the Kotah contingent mutinied, and went off to join the Neemuch mutineers, consisting of a strong brigade of all arms, 2 m. from Agra. On 5th July, Brigadier Polwhele moved out with 816 men to attack them. The battle began with artillery, but the enemy were so well posted, sheltered by low trees and walls and natural earthworks, that the British guns were able to do them but little damage. At 4 P.M. the British ammunition was expended; Colonel Riddell advanced with the English soldiers, and captured the village of Shahganj, but with such heavy loss that they were unable to hold their ground, and were obliged to retreat into the Fort of Agra.[1] The rebels burnt the cantonments, murdered all Europeans who were found outside the Fort, and then marched to Delhi.

There were now 6000 men, women, and children, including 1500 natives in the Fort which was put in a thorough state of defence, Colonel Cotton assuming command. On the 20th of August he sent out Major Montgomery with a small column, which on the 24th defeated the rebels at Aligarh, and took that place. On the 7th September Mr Colvin, Lieut.-Governor of N.W. Provinces, died. When Delhi was captured by the British in September, the fugitive rebels, together with those of Central India, advanced, on 6th October, upon Agra. At this very time Colonel Greathed's force from Delhi arrived without their knowledge, and when they attacked the place, they were

[1] An appalling picture of confusion, insubordination, and insanitation in the Fort is given in Mr M. Thornhill's *Personal Adventures and Experiences of a Magistrate in the Indian Mutiny.*

completely routed on 10th October, and Agra was finally relieved from all danger.

The **Taj Mahal** should be seen repeatedly. The best time for a first visit is late in the afternoon. The building is properly named *Taj bibi ka Roza*, or "The Crown Lady's Tomb." It was commenced in 1040 A.H., or 1630 A.D., by the Emperor Shah Jahan, as a tomb for his favourite queen, Arjmand Banu, entitled Mumtaz-i-Mahal, the "Chosen of the Palace," or more freely, "Pride of the Palace." She was the daughter of Asaf Khan, brother of Nurjahan, the famous empress-wife of Jahangir. Their father was Mirza Ghiyas, a Persian, who came from Teheran to seek his fortune in India, and rose to power under the title of Itimad-ud daulah. (See p. 178) Mumtaz-i-Mahal married Shah Jahan in 1615 A.D., had by him seven children, and died in child-bed of the eighth in 1629, at Burhanpur, in the Deccan. Her body was brought to Agra, and laid in the garden where the Taj stands until the mausoleum was built. The Taj cost, according to some accounts, Rs. 18,465,186, and according to others, Rs. 31,748,026, and took upwards of twenty-two years to build, according to Tavernier, who records that he saw both its commencement and completion, and that the scaffolding used was constructed of brick. There were originally two silver doors at the entrance, but these were taken away and melted by Suraj Mal and his Jats. Austin of Bordeaux was then in the Emperor's service, probably took part in the decoration, and especially in the inlaid work, of the mausoleum.

Before reaching the Taj the recently built State Circuit House will be seen on the left. The surroundings outside the enclosure have been well restored of recent years, and both the tomb and the Fattehpuri mosque of red sandstone in front of the approach from the Fort now form extremely picturesque features in the scene. The approach to the Taj is by the *Taj Ganj Gate*, which opens into an outer court 880 ft. long and 440 ft. wide. Inside the court are two tombs, and in the N.W. corner a small caravanserai—all of which have been satisfactorily repaired. On the right is a gate which leads into the quarter S. of the Taj, and on the left is the **Great Gateway** of the garden-court, built 1648, which Mr Fergusson calls "a worthy pendant to the Taj itself." It is indeed a superb gateway of red sandstone, inlaid with ornaments and inscriptions from the Koran in white marble, and surmounted by 26 white marble cupolas.

Inside is the beautiful Taj garden. This is laid out in formal style, the whole to the S. of the platform of the Taj and the buildings which support it architecturally being divided by two main thoroughfares into four portions, which are again subdivided into four. The principal vista, which has a marble water-course all down it interrupted in the middle by a marble platform, leads directly to the Taj, which rises in all its peerless beauty at the end, and is mirrored in the water below. The cypresses which lined the vista have been lately removed, as the size to which they had grown obstructed the view of the Taj, but others have been planted, and will take their place in the scene in due course. The trees of the garden generally have also been wisely thinned, and now admit of endless beautiful views and peeps of the marble dome, the marble walls and the marble minarets, which can be enjoyed at leisure from the seats placed about the gardens. Very fine views are also obtained from the top of the great gate and from the halls in the centre of the side walls. Along the S. wall on either side of the great gate is an extremely fine pillared gallery of red sandstone. The beauty of the Taj is perhaps most perfect immediately after sunset, or under the moonlight; but every change of light seems to lend new graces to it. Those who linger for

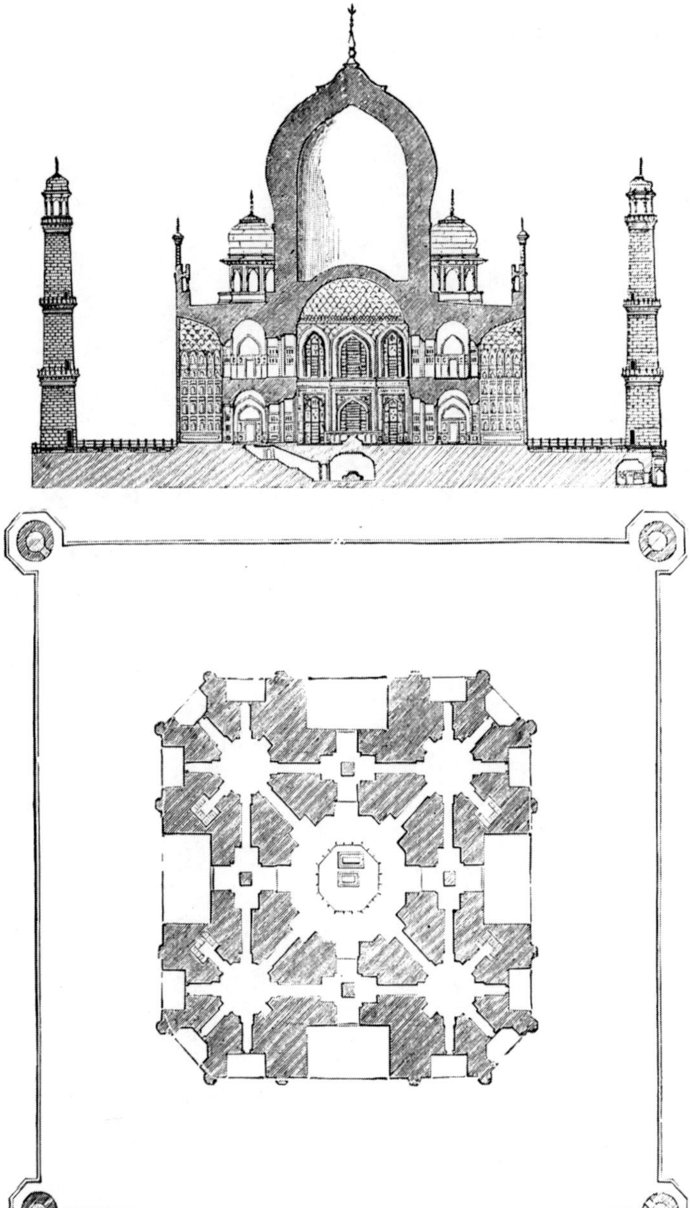

Section and Plan of the Taj Mahal.

[*To face p.* 172.

evening or night effects must take precautions against a possible chill in such damp surroundings.

The central marble platform on which the tomb stands is 22 ft. high and 313 ft. sq. At each corner is a minaret of white marble picked out by black lines, 137 ft. high. The tomb itself measures 186 ft. on each side, the corners being bevelled off and recessed into a bay. On either side of each angle corner is another small bay, and in the centre of each side is a splendid deep bay 63 ft. high. The height of the walls and parapet over them is 108 ft.; at each corner above them rise smaller marble domes, and in the centre soars the great central dome, which rises to a height of 187 ft., the metal pinnacle adding yet 30 ft. to the whole: the height of the top of the dome above the level of the garden is just 25 ft. less than that of the Kutab Minar, and of the top of the pinnacle a few ft. higher than that. "The building," writes Mr Fergusson, "is an exquisite example of that system of inlaying with precious stones which became the great characteristic of the style of the Mughals after the death of Akbar." All the spandrels of the Taj, all the angles and more important details, are heightened by being inlaid with precious stones. These are combined in wreaths, scrolls, and frets as exquisite in design as beautiful in colour. They form the most beautiful and precious style of ornament ever adopted in architecture. Though of course not to be compared with the beauty of Greek ornament, it certainly stands first among the purely decorative forms of architectural design. The judgment with which this style of ornament is apportioned to the various parts is almost as remarkable as the ornament itself, and conveys a high idea of the taste and skill of the Indian architects of the age.

The delicately sculptured ornamentation, in low relief, to be found on all exterior walls and the recesses of the building, is in its way as beautiful as the pietra dura work itself.

In the centre of the tomb is an octagonal chamber surrounded by a series of other rooms. Each side of the central room measures 24 ft. The dome rises 80 ft. above the pavement, and is 58 ft. in diameter. Under the centre of the dome, enclosed by a trellis-work screen of white marble, which Mr Fergusson considers "a *chef d'œuvre* of elegance in Indian art," but which most people will rate less highly —it probably dates from the reign of Aurangzeb—are the tombs of Mumtaz-i-Mahal and Shah Jahan; the simple inlay work on these and the more elaborate work on the screen deserve special examination. "These, however, as is usual in Indian sepulchres, are not the true tombs—the bodies rest in a vault, level with the surface of the ground, beneath plainer tombstones placed exactly below those in the hall above." Over the two tombs hangs a fine Cairene lamp, the graceful gift of Lord Curzon. The inscriptions on them are "Markad-i-Munawwar i Arjmand Banu Begam, Mukhatib ba Mumtaz-i-Mahal, taufiyat san 1040" (the resplendent grave of Arjmand Banu Begam, called Mumtaz-i-Mahal, deceased in 1040), and "Markad i Mutahhar i Ali i Hazrat i Fardausashyani Sahib Kiran i Sani, Shah Jahan Badshah, Taba Sarrahu" (the famous grave of his Imperial Highness, the resident of Paradise, the second Alexander (Lord of the two horns), King Shah Jahan. May his grave be fragrant). The Queen's tomb bears the 99 names of God. "The light in the apartment where the tombs are," says Mr Fergusson, "is admitted only through double screens of white marble trellis-work of the most exquisite design, one on the outer and one on the inner face of the walls. In our climate this would produce nearly complete darkness; but in India, and in a building wholly composed of white marble, this was required to temper the glare that otherwise would have been intolerable. As it is, no words can express the chastened beauty of that central chamber, seen in the soft gloom of the subdued light that reaches it through the distant and half-closed openings that surround it.[1] When used as a Barahdari, or pleasure-palace, it must always have been the coolest and the loveliest of garden retreats, and now that it is sacred to the dead, it is the most graceful and the most impressive of sepulchres in the world." There is a most wonderful echo in the dome. It was seriously proposed by a Governor-General of India to demolish the Taj and sell the marbles; but that was many years ago, and the mausoleum and its surroundings now receive far more loving care than would ever have been the case under a Mohammedan Emperor. For the excellent work done in this connection at Agra and at Fatehpur-Sikri and Sikandarah of late years, the public have to thank, in the first place, Sir John Strachey, and next, Sir Antony, now Lord MacDonnell, and his able assistant, the late Mr E. W. Smith.

On a lower level at either side of the mausoleum are two fine buildings of red sandstone, that on the W. side being a mosque, and that on the E. side forming a *jawab* or complement, a hall. On the pavement in front of the former, which bears the unusual decoration of flowers, is a representation of the finial of the Taj. The Taj was intended to be seen balanced between these two buildings, and every one should cross the river by the ferry boat, which will be found at the end of the road which runs outside the W. wall from the entrance to the outer court, in order to realise this beautiful view. From the further side various paths lead to the E. end of the Jumna Bridge, if it is desired to return by that route.

The **Fort.**—Most of the magnificent Mughal buildings which render Agra so interesting in the eye of the traveller are situated within the Fort, which has a circuit of over a mile. The walls and flanking defences are of red sandstone, and have an imposing appearance, being nearly 70 ft. high; the finest portion of them is along the N. side and to the S. of the N.E. bastion. The ditch is 30 ft. wide and 35 ft. deep. The Water Gate on the E. is closed, but there are still two entrances—the Amar Singh Gate on the S., the Delhi Gate on the W. Outside the latter and connecting it with the Jama Masjid was the fine Tripulya court, removed after 1857; in it was the Nakkar Khana music gallery. Crossing the draw-bridge to the Delhi Gate, and passing the outer and inner archways, the latter with a date of 1600 A.D., a somewhat steep slope between red sandstone walls will be found to lead to another gateway called the *Hathi Pol*, or "Elephant Gate." There used to be two stone elephants here with figures of Patta and Jaimall (p. 93), the two famous Rajputs of Chitorgarh, said to have been removed to Delhi (p. 199), and the marks where their feet were fixed may still be traced on the platforms on either side of the archway. This is flanked by two octagonal towers of red sandstone, relieved with designs in white plaster. The domed interior of the gateway, with a raised platform for the guard on either side, is very striking.

Inside the gate one broad road sweeps to the left, and, passing the magazine, turns to the front of the Moti Masjid and the N. gate of the court in front of the Diwan-i-'Am, while another, passing to the right as far as the head of the descent to the Amar Singh Gate, then turns to the S. gate of that court. A short way down the latter on the left a road, not always open, leads to the Mina Bazaar, between the mosque and court.

The **Moti Masjid**, the "Pearl Mosque," is described by Mr Fergusson as "one of the purest and most elegant buildings of its class to be

[1] The light in the interior is hardly sufficient now that the marble grilles are fitted with glass. It is not probable that the Taj was ever used as a pleasure house.

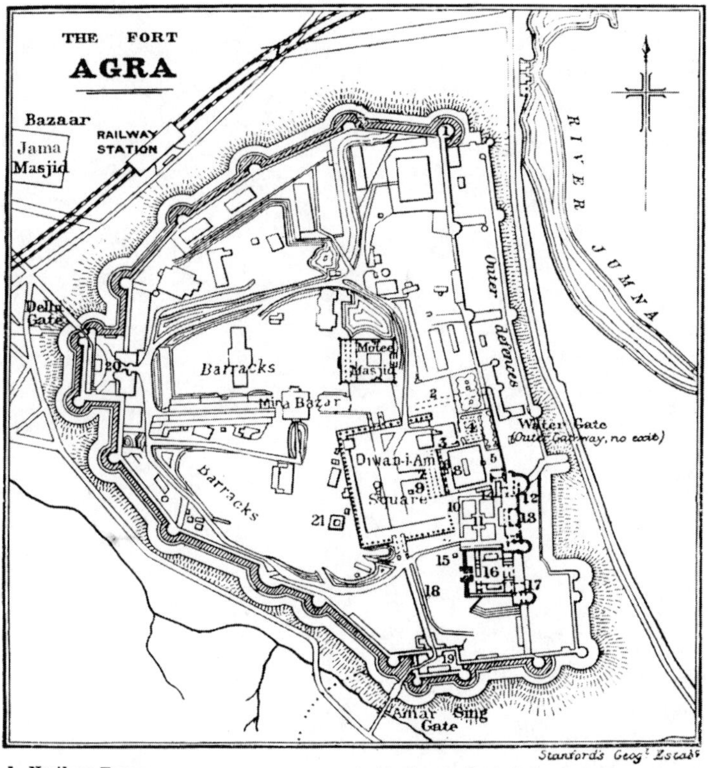

Stanford's Geog[l] Estab[t]

1. Northern Tower.
2. Descent to Water Gate.
3. Naginah Masjid and ladies' private Bazaar.
4. Small Courts and ruins of Baths.
5. Open Terrace with Diwan-i-Khas on S. side.
6. Recess where the Emperor's Throne stood.
7. Diwan-i-'Am (Hall of Public Audience).
8. Machchi Bhawan.
9. Mr Colvin's Grave.
10. Mina Mosque.
11. The Anguri Bagh (Grape Garden).
12. Saman Burj (Octagon Tower). At N. angle is an outlet by secret passage.
13. Khas Mahal.
14. Shish Mahal (Mirror Palace).
15. Well.
16. Palace of Jahangir (or Akbar).
17. Tower. At the base is an entrance to a secret passage.
18. Incline from Amar Sing's Gate
19. Court of Amar Sing's Gate.
20. Elephant Gate.
21. Kiosk of Salimgarh.

[*To face p.* **174.**

found anywhere." It was commenced 1056 A.H.=1648 A.D., and finished 1063 A.H.=1655 A.D., and is said to have cost Rs.300,000. It was built by Shah Jahan on ground sloping

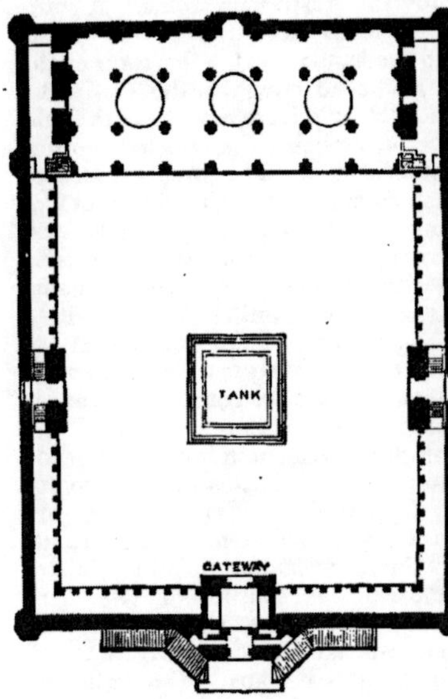

Moti Masjid.

from W. to E., and the fine entrance gateway of red sandstone makes a trihedral projection from the centre of the E. face: it is approached by a double staircase with a restored railing. The exterior is faced with slabs of red sandstone, the interior built of marble — white, blue, and grey veined. "The moment you enter the effect of its courtyard is surpassingly beautiful."

In the centre there is a marble tank, 37 ft. 7 in. sq., for ablutions, and between it and the S.E. inner corner of the mosque there is an ancient sundial, consisting of an octagonal marble pillar, 4 ft. high, with no gnomon, but simply two crossed lines and an arc. A marble cloister runs round the E., N., and S. sides of the court, which measures 234 and 183 ft., interrupted by archways, of which those in the N. and S. sides are closed. The mosque proper, or liwan, measures 149 ft. by 56 ft., and consists of three aisles of seven bays opening on to the courtyard, and surmounted by three domes. On the entablature over the front row of supporting pillars, *i.e.* on the E. face, there is an inscription running the whole length, the letters being of black marble inlaid into the white. The inscription says that the mosque may be likened to a precious pearl, for no other mosque is lined throughout with marble like this. Narrow flights of steps lead to the top of the gateway and to the roof of the mosque, from which there is a fine view. During the Mutiny this mosque was used as an hospital.

Beyond the Mina Bazaar on the right and the descent to the closed Water Gate on the left, is the entrance to the fine court of the Diwan-i-'Am, with colonnades lately restored. In front of the Durbar Hall is the tomb of Mr Colvin, Lieut.-Governor of the N.W. Provinces, who died in the fort on 7th September 1857. The **Diwan-i-'Am**, or Hall of Public Audience, is 208 ft. long by 76 ft. deep, and consists of three aisles of nine bays open on three sides. The roof is supported by graceful columns of red sandstone, which have been subjected to judicious restoration. Along its back wall are grilles, through which fair faces could watch what was going forward in the hall below, and in its centre is a raised alcove of white marble richly decorated with *pietra dura* work and low reliefs, which bear evident traces of Italian design. It is probably the work of Shah Jahan, though lacking the elegance of most of the buildings of that Emperor.

The entrance to the inner courts of the palace from this side is by a passage and steps to the N. of the Diwan-i-'Am; it was within these courts and the Diwan-i-'Am that the scenes which

Captain Hawkins so graphically describes in connection with the Emperor Jahangir took place. The first enclosure entered is the **Machchi Bhawan**, or "Fish Square," which formerly possessed a large tank. A two-storied cloister runs all round it, except on the side which fronts the Jumna, where the upper storey gives place to an open terrace. In the N. side are two very fine bronze gates taken by Akbar from Chitorgarh (page 94), and at the N.W. corner is a beautiful little three-domed mosque of white marble, called the **Naginah Masjid**, or "Gem Mosque." This was the private mosque of the royal ladies of the court, and was built by Shah Jahan, who was afterwards imprisoned there by his successor Aurangzeb. Beneath, in a small court-yard, was a bazaar where the merchants used to display their goods to the ladies of the court. On the terrace on the river side is a **black throne** with a white seat opposite it. The former has a long fissure, which is said to have appeared when the throne was usurped by the Jat chief of Bharatpur. There is a reddish stain in one spot which the natives pretend is blood. An inscription runs round the four sides, stating that, "when Salim became heir to the crown his name was changed to Jahangir, and for the light of his justice he was called Nur-ud-din. His sword cut his enemies' heads into two halves like the Gemini." The date given is 1011 A.H. = 1603 A.D. Beneath this terrace is a wide enclosure within the outer walls where contests between elephants and tigers used to take place. On the N. of the terrace is the site of a hall of green marble, and of various rooms of the Bath or **Hammam**, now in a ruinous condition, and on the S. is the **Diwan-i-Khas**, or Hall of Private Audience. The hall, which consists of an open colonnade in front and an enclosed room at the back, measures 65 ft. by 34 ft. by 22 ft. high, and is a miracle of beauty. The carving is exquisite, and the flowers inlaid on the white marble with red cornelian, and other valuable stones, are introduced with better because more sparing effect than in the Diwan-i-Khas of Delhi. The date of the building is 1046 A.H. = 1637 A.D. It is contained in the title Sa'adat Sarai wa Humayun Asas, the Abode of Joy and Auspicious Home. A staircase leads from the Diwan-i-Khas to the **Saman Burj**, a few steps on the right conducting to the tiny **Mina Masjid**, or private mosque of the Emperor, probably the smallest mosque in existence. The proper name of the Saman Burj is Musamman or Octagon, but it is generally known by a corruption of its name as the Jesamine (Yâsmin) Burj; the chief Sultana lived in the beautiful pavilion, with a fountain and retiring-room, over the river. The lovely marble lattice-work seems to have been broken by cannon-shot in some places. Part of the marble pavement in front of it is made to represent a Pachisi or chess-board.

Opposite the Saman Burj, but usually entered from the next court, is the **Shish Mahal**, literally "Mirror Palace." It consists of two dark chambers furnished with fountains and an artificial cascade arranged to fall over lighted lamps. The walls and ceilings are decorated with pounded talc, and with innumerable small mirrors, which were restored in 1875.

Above the buildings at this spot and approached by steps above the Mina Masjid are the remains of reservoirs and waterducts, and arrangements for the raising of water from below. From the roof a fine view is also obtained of the courts on either side of it, of the Moti Masjid and the Taj. Of the the latter, many fine views and peeps are obtained along the river from the terrace of the Machchi Bhawan to the palace of Akbar.

The **Anguri Bagh** or "Grape Garden," now entered is a fine square of 280 ft., now planted with grass. In the centre of the E. side is a lovely hall called the **Khas Mahal**, the gilding and colouring of which were in part restored in 1875. In front are small tanks and fountains. The Khas Mahal undoubtedly formed the model upon which the Diwan-i-Khas at Delhi was built: it measures 70 ft. by 40 ft. In the platform under it are subterranean apartments for use in the summer heats, from which passages lead to still cooler rooms round the baoli in the S.E. corner of the Fort. On either hand also facing the river are the **Golden Pavilions**, so called from their curved roofs being covered with gilded plates of copper. In them are bedrooms for ladies, with holes in the wall, 14 in. deep, into which they used to slip their jewels. These holes are so narrow that only a woman's arm could draw the contents out. In the S.E. corner of the Anguri Bagh will be found three rooms, beautifully decorated in fresco, which were the private apartments of Shah Jahan. The room nearest the river is an octagonal pavilion, and very beautiful. In it, according to tradition, Shah Jahan died, gazing upon the **Taj**. To the W. of the rooms is another in which stand the so-called Gates of Somnath, 12 ft. high, and finely carved: they are of Deodar, not sandal, wood, and of Mohammedan work. There is a Kufic inscription running round them in which the name of Sabuktagin has been read. They were captured by General Nott at Ghazni and brought here in 1842.

The Jahangir Mahal, a beautiful red sandstone palace now entered was built either by Jahangir or Akbar. It stands in the S.E. part of the Fort, between the palace of Shah Jahan and the Bangali bastion, the principal façade being on the E. This is handsomely decorated with bright tiles in the upper portion, and is pierced in the centre by a fine entrance gateway. This leads through a vestibule into a beautiful domed hall, 18 ft. sq., the ceiling of which is elaborately carved, and from which a corridor leads into the grand central court, which is 72 ft. sq. The design of this court, its pillars, the carving and ornamentation, are all pure Hindu, and for minute and exquisite ornamental carving in stone it is pre-eminent.

"On the N. side of the court is a grand open pillared hall, 62 ft. long and 37 ft. broad. The pillars support bracket capitals, richly carved and ornamented with pendants. The front brackets support broad sloping eaves of thin stone slabs. But the stone roof or ceiling of this pillared hall is the most remarkable feature about it. It is supported most curiously by stone cross-beams, which are ornamented with the quaint device of a great serpent or dragon carved on them lengthways. A covered passage or corridor runs round the top of this hall, from which one can look down into it. The other pillared hall on the opposite or S. side of the grand court is somewhat less in size."

From the grand court, a large chamber to the E. leads to a recessed portico in the centre of a quadrangle which faces the river, supported by two lofty pillars and two half pillars of the more slender and graceful Hindu kind. Some of the chambers are lined with stucco, which has been painted, and has lasted better than the stone-work. The palace ends on the side facing the river with a retaining wall and two corner bastions, each surmounted by an ornamental tower with a domed cupola. There are many vaulted chambers underneath the palace, used as places of retreat during the summer heats. The palace has lately been most successfully restored, a process rendered necessary by the bad quality of the red sandstone originally used. This process is being extended to the building S. of it, which contains a court 140 ft. square.

In the space in front of the palace is the *Hauz* of Jahangir, an enormous monolithic cistern of light-coloured porphyry, externally nearly 5 ft. high, and internally 4 ft. deep, and 8 ft. in diameter at top; and at the N.W. corner is the head of the descent to the Amar Singh Gate, so called from the elder brother of Maharaja Jaswant Singh of Jodhpur, who was disinherited by his father for his turbulence, and was killed here in 1648 with all his followers after a fatal brawl within the royal precincts. Outside the Gate is the half-buried figure of a horse in red sandstone, and on rising ground to the S.W. are the cemeteries in which many who died in the Fort during the summer of 1857 were buried. Near it is the N. end of the Macdonnell Park, and the fine memorial of the Queen Empress, by Thorneycroft. The bronze statue, which is of a standing figure on a high base, was unveiled by King George on 18th December 1905. It was the S.W. bastion which was battered by Lord Lake in 1803 so successfully that the Mahratta garrison at once surrendered. Before descending to the Gate, the beautiful little Hindu Pavilion, situated on high ground, outside the S.W. corner of the Diwan-i-'Am court, should be visited. It is perhaps the most ornamental structure of all in that style at Agra, and is probably the work of Salim Shah, son of the Emperor Sher Shah.

The **Jama Masjid** faces the Delhi gate of the Fort, close to the Fort railway station, and a fine view of it is obtained from the footbridge to the station. It stands upon a raised platform, 11 ft. high, reached by flights of steps on the S. and E. sides. The mosque proper measures 130 ft. by 100 ft., and is divided into five compartments, each of which opens on the courtyard by a fine archway. The inscription over the main archway sets forth that the mosque was constructed by the Emperor Shah Jahan in 1644 in the name of his daughter, Jahanara, who afterwards shared her father's captivity (p. 206). The great peculiarity of this Masjid consists in its three great full-bottomed domes without necks, built of red sandstone, with zigzag bands of white marble circling round them.

On the W. side of the city is the **Agra College**, which owes its origin to the Gwalior State, of which the Maharaja at the end of the 18th century made over certain villages in the districts of Muttra and Aligarh to a learned Brahman for the twofold purpose of keeping up a Sanscrit School, and of supplying the wants of pilgrims visiting the shrines around Muttra. In 1818 the original grantee left his lands in trust to the E. India Co., who devoted two-thirds of the proceeds to the establishment of this college, and one-third to hospitals at Muttra and Aligarh. The College, opened 1835, consists of a high school, with 700 pupils, and a college proper with 175 undergraduates and 7 professors, besides 45 law students. It is managed by a board of trustees. E. of the College and situated in the western outskirts of the city are the Medical School, the Kalan Masjid, and St John's College, the centre of the C.M.S. Mission, nearly as large as the Govt. College. The mosque was probably built by Sikandar Lodi, and is the oldest building in Agra.

E. of the **Central Jail** are the **Roman Catholic Cathedral, Convent, and Schools**, dedicated to the Virgin Mary, the first with a tower about 150 ft. high. The buildings are large, but not architecturally interesting. The Mission was founded in the time of Akbar, and has long been celebrated for its school, where the children of soldiers and others are educated. The earliest tombs connected with the settlement of Christians at Agra are in the R.C. cemetery, which lies ¾ m. to the N. The most ancient epitaphs are in the Armenian character. Among the tombs are those of John Hessing, and John Mildenhall (died 1614), and the notorious Samru, Walter Reinhardt (see p. 221). N.W. of the Cathedral is the Kandahari Bagh, where Shah Jahan's first Persian wife was buried, now Bharatpur House, and N. of it again the Seth's Garden, once containing the graves of Faizi and Abul Fazl (p. 185), and their sister, Ladli Begam.

The **Tomb of I'timad-ud-daulah** lies about 250 yds. to the N. from the E. end of the new E.I.R. bridge. It is the mausoleum of Ghiyas Beg, a Persian, who was the father of Nur

Jahan, and her brother, Asaf Khan, and a grandfather of the lady of the Taj, and who became high treasurer of Jahangir. The tomb stands in a beautiful garden, which receives much attention, on a platform 4 ft. high, and measuring 150 ft., and is itself 69 ft. square. At each corner is an octagonal tower 40 ft. high, and on the terrace of the roof is a pavilion 25 ft. square; and the design of the mausoleum clearly served for that of the Emperor Jahangir also built by Nur Jahan at Shahdara, near Lahore (p. 238). The centre room below, measuring 22 ft., contains the two tombs of I'timad-ud-daulah and his wife, made of yellow coloured marble; the side rooms round it display paintings of flower vases, fruits, etc., which were also reproduced in the Shahdara mausoleum. The marble lattice work of the passages admitting light to the interior is extremely fine. The pavilion on the terrace of the tomb has a curved roof and broad sloping eaves, and contains two marble cenotaphs corresponding to those below. The whole of the exterior and much of the interior is of white marble with beautiful inlay work. The inlay work here is the earliest known in India (1628 A.D.), and will appear to many more pleasing than the less simple work in the buildings of the Emperor Shah Jahan.

Half-a-mile N. of this is the **Chini ka Roza**, or china tomb. It has one great dome resting on an octagonal base. In the centre of the octagonal domed chamber, much ruined, are two tombs of brick, which have replaced marble tombs. Externally it is decorated with glazed work, such as was so successfully used on the public buildings at Lahore; the flower patterns of many of the panels are very effective, and must once have been very beautiful. The tomb was probably erected in the reign of Aurangzeb.

Further up the left bank of the river again is the Ram Bagh, where the Emperor Babar was buried pending the erection of his mausoleum at Kabul. The river terrace of this garden is extremely picturesque, and a very pleasant return journey may be made from it by boat to the city.

The mausoleum of the **Emperor Akbar** at **Sikandarah**, so named from Sikandar Lodi, who reigned from 1489 A.D., is $5\frac{1}{2}$ m. from the cantonment at Agra. There are many tombs on the way, and on the left side of the road, about 4 m. from Agra, and nearly opposite the lofty arched gateway of an ancient building called the Kachi ki Sarai, there is a poorly sculptured horse. At $\frac{1}{2}$ m. farther on, a little back from the road on the E. side, is a tank of red sandstone, with ornamental octagonal towers, called Guru ka Tal. On the S. side are three flights of steps, and E. of them is a long and broad channel of masonry, which brought water to the tank. $\frac{1}{2}$ m. beyond the mausoleum is a red sandstone two-storeyed building, called the Barahdari, and built by Sikandar Lodi in 1495 A.D. The ground floor contains forty chambers. Each corner of the building is surmounted by a short octagonal tower. It was made the tomb of Mariam uz Zamani, wife of the Emperor Akbar, whom tradition has converted into a Christian (p. 183), and is now occupied by a part of the establishment of the Agra Orphan Asylum.

A fine gateway leads to the great garden enclosure in which the mausoleum of the Emperor Akbar is situated: on either side of it in flanking walls are boldly pierced sandstone grilles. It is of red sandstone, inlaid with white marble in various polygonal patterns, very massive, and with a splendid scroll of Tughra writing a foot broad adorning it. On the top of the gateway, at each corner, rises a white minaret of two storeys; the cupolas destroyed over 120 years ago have been restored. There is a fine view from the platform at the top. A broad paved path leads to the mausoleum. It is a pyramidal building, 74 ft. high, of four storeys, three of which are of red sandstone, the fourth, enclosing the cenotaph, being of white marble. The basement measures 320 ft. each way, and the top storeys, 157 ft. Mr Fergusson was of opinion that the idea of the arrangement was taken from that of a structural Buddhist monastery, but this hardly seems probable. A massive cloister runs round the lower storey, broken S. and N. by high central arches, that on the S. forming the entrance to the tomb chamber. The vaulted ceiling of the vestibule was elaborately frescoed in gold and blue, and a section of this has been restored. The Surah-i-Mulk[1] runs under the cornice in a scroll 1 ft. broad. A gentle incline leads to the dark vaulted chamber in which the great Akbar rests. On either side of the main arch some bays of the cloister are screened off and contain tombs, with inscriptions in beautiful characters. In a niche in the side of the room, farthest from the entrance, is an alabaster tablet inscribed with the 99 divine names.

Narrow staircases lead to the platforms and terraces above. The fourth is surrounded by a beautiful cloister of white marble, carved on the outer side into lattice-work in squares of 2 ft., every square of a different pattern. In the centre is the splendid white monolith cenotaph of the Emperor, engraved with the 99 glorious names of the Deity, just over the place where his dust rests in the vaulted chamber below. On the N. side of the cenotaph is inscribed the motto of the sect he founded, "Allahu Akbar," "God is greatest"; and on the S. side "Jalla Jalalahu," "May His glory shine." To the N. of it, at the distance of 4 ft., is a handsome white marble pillar 2½ ft. high, which, according to tradition, was once covered with gold and contained the Koh-i-Nur. The wind sighing through the pierced screens maintains a perpetual solemn requiem over the great Emperor. The gateway recesses in N., E. and W. walls of the garden are also decorated with marble mosaics. The cost of the tomb was 15 lakhs.

1 A Chapter of the Koran.

A good shady road—the one used by the great Akbar himself—leads S.W. from Agra to 22½ m.

FATEHPUR-SIKRI, D.B.—(Motors for the trip can be hired in Agra). The B.B. Railway broad gauge system is about to be extended from Agra Cantonment Station to Bayana (p. 122) through Fatehpur-Sikri.—At the entrance to Shahganj are the ruins of a mosque, with an inscription saying it was built in 1621. It marks the site of the old Ajmer Gate. Farther on is a Moslem cemetery, with a tomb said to be that of Mirza Hindal, son of Babar, father of Akbar's chief wife. At the foot of the tomb is a monolith 7 ft. high, with the date 1570.

The royal but long deserted city of Fatehpur-Sikri, standing on a low sandstone ridge, was the creation of Akbar, who built every structure in it, but abandoned it for Agra. Owing to this fact and on account of its very perfect preservation it forms an unique specimen of a city in the exact condition in which it was occupied by the Great Mughal and his court. The alleged reason for its construction was the presence on the spot of the Chishti Saint, Shaikh Salim; and the undoubted reason of its desertion was the difficulty of obtaining good water in the place and the unhealthiness of its surroundings.

From the arrangement of the buildings it is evident that Akbar had the whole carefully planned out. This will be seen by the position of the Khwabgah, Akbar's private room, which commands the *Daftar Khana*, Record Office, and the whole of the principal buildings, and from which he could reach, without being observed, the "Jodh Bai" Palace—by a covered way pulled down during nineteenth century restorations—Miriam's House, Bir Bal's House, the Panch Mahal, Turkish Sultana's House, Council Chamber, etc., etc. Inside the old walls of the city and about 1½ m. from Fatehpur and

Sikri the road divides, that to the left passing under the ridge, and to the village at the foot of the steps below the Buland Darwazah, and that going straight on gradually ascending the ridge to the palace. This passes beneath the Naubat Khana, from the upper rooms of which musicians played as Akbar entered the city. Farther left are the remains of the **Treasury,** and opposite it what is known traditionally as the **Mint**, a large quadrangular building. Near the mint a new Traveller's Rest House has been built. Beyond this the road enters the inner enceinte of the palace[1] and the court in front of the **Diwan-i'-Am**, measuring some 366 ft. from N. to S. by 181 ft. from E. to W., and surrounded by a flat-roofed cloister. On the W. side is the Audience Hall, with a deep verandah in front, and an isolated space for the Emperor between two pierced stone screens of fine geometric design. The room behind has a peculiar roof, which was painted. The road leads through the courtyard to the **Daftar Khana**, or Record Office, once the D.B. On the back is a staircase leading to the roof, from which there is a fine view of the city. The inner stone partition walls are modern. In front, facing N., is Akbar's **Khwabgah**, or Sleeping Apartment, literally "House of Dreams." Written on the internal walls over the architraves of the doors are some Persian complimentary verses (much defaced). The remains of the paintings which once

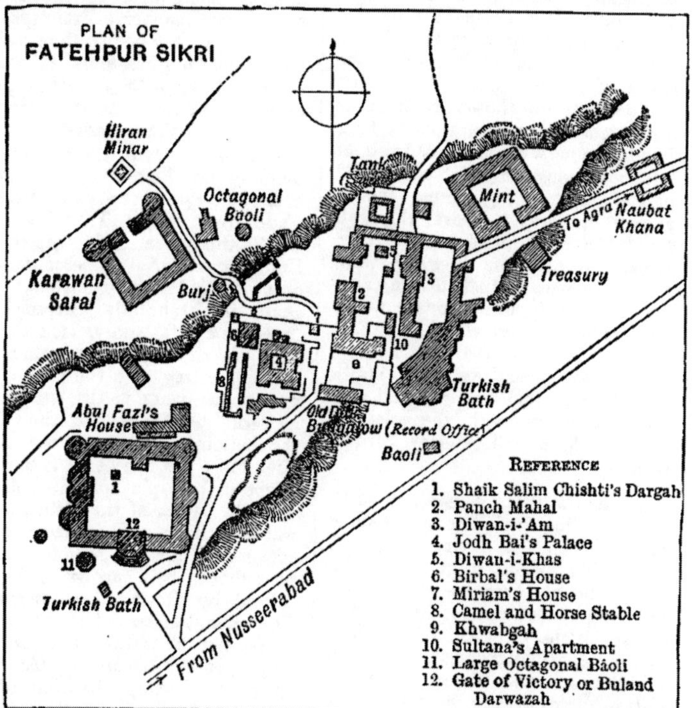

Walker & Boutall sc.

[1] The four vols. published by the late Mr W. E. Smith upon Fatehpur-Sikri are the finest ever produced by the Archæological Survey of the Government of India, and show exactly how the work of that Department should be done.

decorated it are now very slight. Below is a room, and at the E. end of it a platform supported by two splendid red sandstone shafts beautifully carved. Probably a Hindu priest lived here. The space to the N. formed the **Khas Mahal.**

At the S.E. corner of this courtyard is the "**Turkish Queen's" House**,[1] which many may consider the most interesting apartment of all. As it *now* stands it consists of only one small chamber, 15 by 15 ft. Every square inch is carved, including the soffits of the cornices. The ceiling and decoration of the verandah pillars and pilasters are exceptionally fine. Inside is a most elaborate dado about 4 ft. high, consisting of 8 sculptured panels representing forest views, animal life, etc. Above, the wall takes the form of a stone lattice screen, the divisions of which were used as shelves. Much of the carving is curiously like Chinese work, and reminds one of what Abul Fazl says of the local red sandstone—"Clever workmen chisel it so skilfully as no turner could do with wood, and their works vie with the picture-books of Mani (a legendary Persian painter)."

W. is the **Girls' School**, a small plain building carried on square stone piers. Upon the paving stones of the open space in front (E.) is the Pachisi-board, or chess-board, with the Emperor's stone seat in the centre, in the form of a cross laid out in coloured pavement, and it is said the game was played with slave girls as pieces to take the moves.

Just to the N. of this is the **Panch Mahal**, a building of five storeys borne by open colonnades, each tier being smaller than the one below, till nothing but a small kiosque remains a-top. It was probably erected for the ladies of the court as a pleasure resort, as the sides were originally enclosed with stone screens. The first floor is remarkable on account of the variety of the 56 columns which support the storey above, no two being alike in design. Many of the shafts are similar, but the caps vary: at the angles of one are elephants' heads with interlaced trunks, on another is a man gathering fruit. On the N.W. angle is a group of four columns which should be examined. From the topmost floor there is a splendid view.

[1] Rumi Sultana.

At the N. of the quadrangle is the **Diwan-i-Khas**, or "Private Hall," or Council Chamber. From the outside it appears to be two storeys high, but on entering it is found to consist of one only, with a central pillar crowned by an immense circular corbelled capital, radiating from which to the four corners of the building are four stone causeways enclosed by open trellis stone balustrades (restored). Tradition says that in the centre of this capital the Emperor sat whilst the corners were occupied by his four ministers. The shaft is beautifully carved, and deserves careful study. On the E. and W. sides are stone staircases communicating with the roof. The open screen-work in the windows is modern. A few feet to the W. is the building known as the **Ankh Michauli**; the story told is that the Emperor here played hide-and-seek with the ladies of the Court, but it was most likely used for records. It consists of three large lofty rooms, surrounded by narrow passages, lighted by stone screen windows. The ceilings of two of the rooms are coved, but the third is flat and supported on struts ornamented with grotesque carving. In front of the S.E. corner is a small canopied structure used by the astrologer, who probably was a Hindu Guru, or "teacher." It is in the style of architecture used by the Hindus during the eleventh and twelfth centuries. Under the architraves are curiously carved struts issuing from the mouths of monsters dowelled into the shafts at the corners. The under side of the dome was painted. Adjoining these buildings to the W. is the Hospital with some of the stone partitions forming the wards still extant. The ceilings are of solid slabs of stone, carved on the exterior to represent tiles.

Outside the west side of the Khas Mahal enclosure is the **House of Miriam** (traditionally a Portuguese Christian, but really the Jaipur princess, who bore the title Mariam uz Zamani, and was mother of Prince Salim, afterwards the Emperor Jahangir), a small building with defaced frescoes in the niches and upon the walls, and piers of verandah. One, in which the wings of angels are distinctly visible, has been thought to suggest the Annunciation. At one time the whole house was painted inside and out. The original name Sonahra Makan, or "Golden House," was given it on account of the profuse gilding with which its walls were adorned. On the N.W. is Miriam's Garden, and at S.E. angle her bath, with a large column in the centre. On the W. side is the **Naginah**, or Ladies' **Mosque**, and the remains of a small Turkish bath. At the S. end of the garden is a small fish tank, which, together with the stone pavement of the garden, was brought to light by Mr E. W. Smith.

To the N.W. a road leads to the **Hathi Pol** (Elephant Gate) on the N. of the city. Over the W. archway, 20 ft. from the ground, are two life-sized elephants much mutilated, probably by Aurangzeb. To the left is the **Sangin Burj**, a groined bastion or keep, said to have been the commencement of the fortifications planned by Akbar, but abandoned on account of objections raised by Shaikh Salim Chishti. Down the old stone paved road on the left is the **Karawan Sarai** (caravanserai). It consists of a large court 272 by 246 ft., surrounded by the merchants' hostels. Formerly the S.E. side was three storeys high. At the N. end, beyond the Sarai, stands the **Hiran Minar** (Deer Minaret), a circular tower some 70 ft. high studded with protruding elephants' tusks of stone. Tradition says that it is erected over the grave of Akbar's favourite elephant, and that from the lantern in the top the Emperor shot antelope and other game driven under it by beaters. The land to the N. and W. was a large lake in Akbar's time.

On the left of the road returning to the Hathi Pol is a very fine stone well surrounded by rooms and staircases which formed a part of the waterworks. The water was lifted from this level by a series of Persian wheels and a system of reservoirs to the arched gate on the N.W. corner of Bir Bal's House, and thence dispensed throughout the palace.

The palace of **Birbal** stands to the S.W. of Miriam's Garden, near the N.W. corner of the Jodh Bai palace. It is the finest in Fatehpur-Sikri, and is said to have been built by Raja Bir Bal for his daughter, who, however, was not one of the wives of Akbar. It is a two-storeyed building of red sandstone standing on a raised platform, and consists of four rooms 15 ft. square, and two entrance porches on the ground floor and two above with small terraces in front of them, enclosed by stone screens, forming a ladies' promenade. Over the upper rooms are flat-ribbed cupolas, carried on octagonal drums and supported on richly ornamented corbel brackets stretching across the angles of the rooms; and the stone panelled walls and niches are covered with intricate patterns. The ceilings of the lower rooms are supported on a fine and unique frieze, and the whole of the interior, pilasters, recesses. walls, and cusp-arched doorways are elaborately and beautifully carved with geometrical patterns. The exterior walls are almost as profusely ornamented. No wood has been used in the construction of this extraordinary building, to which the words of Victor Hugo have been applied: "If it were not the most minute of palaces, it was the most gigantic of jewel-cases." Raja

Birbal was celebrated for his wit and learning, and was the only Hindu of eminence who embraced the new religion of Akbar, whose favourite courtier he was. He perished with the whole of the army he was commanding in the Yusafzai country to the N.E. of Peshawar in 1586.

S. of Bir Bal's house are the **Stables** for 102 horses and nearly as many camels. In some of the mangers stone rings for the horses' halters still remain, and on the N.W. side one of the old doors. The camel stables are lighted by openings in the roof.

The **Palace of Jodh Bai** is probably erroneously so called, as it is more likely that it was used by the Emperor or by his chief wife Sultana Rakiyah, his first cousin. The entrance is on the E. from the open space in front of the *Record Office*. It is a quadrangular building, 232 by 215 ft. The courtyard within has reception rooms on the N., S., and W. sides connected by a flat-roofed corridor partly closed by stone walls. The room on the W. is more ornate than the others, and in the rear wall is a fireplace. There are chambers above, and those on the N. and S. sides rise to two storeys: they are gable-roofed and ornamented with blue enamelled tiling, recalling the Manmandir Palace of Gwalior (p. 109). At the angles the chambers are surmounted by cupolas, originally painted. Overlooking Miriam's garden is a small projecting room, the walls of which are entirely composed of beautiful stone lattice-work. From the mezzanine floor on the N. side a closed passage leads to a garden abutting on the waterworks, beside which a gallery passed to the N. side of the Sarai near the Hiran Minar. It is now in ruins, and not easy of identification. In the passage, and just before the garden is reached, is a very fine stone screen beneath a small cupola.

The **Dargah Mosque** lies S.W. of the Jodh Bai palace. The E. gate, called the Badshahi, or "royal" gate, opens into the quadrangle, which measures 433 ft. × 366 ft. To the right is the Tomb or Dargah of Shaikh Salim Chishti, grandson of the Shakkar Ganj Pir, who is buried at Pak Patan (*see* pp. 138 and 259). It is surrounded by beautiful white marble lattice-work screens, and has doors of solid ebony, ornamented with brass. The canopy over the tomb of the saint is inlaid with mother-of-pearl, hung with the usual display of ostrich eggs. On the cenotaph is written the date of the saint's death and the date of the completion of the building, 1580, "May God hallow his tomb! The beloved helper of the sect and its saint, Shaikh Salim, whose miraculous gifts and propinquity to the Divine Being are celebrated, and by whom the lamp of the family of Chishti is illuminated. Be not double-sighted, looking to the transitory self, as well as to the everlasting Deity. The year of his decease is known throughout the world."[1] The brackets which support the drip-stone or eaves of the tomb are copies of those in the old mosque[2] of the stone-masons. Childless women, both Hindu and Mohammedan, resort to the tomb and pray the saint to intercede in their favour. On the N. of the quadrangle is also the tomb of Islam Khan, surmounted with a cupola; he was the grandson of the saint, and Governor of Bengal.

The **Mosque** proper (liwan), to the W., is said to be a copy of the one at Mecca. It is about 70 ft. high, and very beautiful. It consists of three interior square chambers surrounded by rows of lofty pillars of Hindu type. At the N. and S. ends are

[1] All the inscriptions here may be found in the *Miftah-ul-Tawarikh*, by John Ellis, printed at Agra.

[2] This is outside the quadrangle and W. of the mosque, where Shaik Salim lived his hermit life in a cave now covered by a room. In a portico on the right of the old mosque the saint taught his disciples before the place had attracted the notice of royalty.

zenana chambers. Going out by a door at the back of the mosque, in an enclosure on the right is an infant's tomb, said to be that of the saint's son, whose life was sacrificed at the age of 6 months in order that Akbar's son (Jahangir) might live when born. In the S. wall of the quadrangle is the **Gate of Victory**, **Buland Darwazah** ("high gate"), which towers to the height of 130 ft. Mr Fergusson expresses the opinion that when looked at from below its appearance is noble beyond that of any portal attached to any mosque in India, perhaps in the whole world. The grandeur of this great height is increased by a fine flight of steps on the outside, giving a total height of 172 ft.[1] There is a grand view from the top.

In the archway is an inscription on the left hand going out, which says that the "King of Kings, Shadow of God, Jalal-ud-din Muhammad Akbar, the Emperor, on his return from conquering the kingdoms of the S., and Khandesh, formerly called Dhandesh, came to Fatehpur in the 46th year of his reign (corresponding to 1601 A.D.), and proceeded from thence to Agra." On the opposite side is inscribed "Isa (Jesus) on whom be peace, said: 'The world is a bridge, pass over it, but build no house on it. The world endures but an hour, spend it in devotion.'" The doors of this great gateway are studded with horse-shoes, affixed by the owners of sick horses who implore the prayers of the saint for their recovery. From the steps, or better still, from the summit of the gate, may be seen the villages of Sikri and Fatehpur, and the surrounding tract of barren country. To the W. of the steps is a large well, into which boys and men used to spring from the walls, from heights varying from 30 to 80 ft.; but the practice has now been prohibited. A **Mela** or fair commences on the 20th of *Ramzan*, the anniversary of the saint's death, and lasts for eight days. In front of the steps are some **Turkish baths**.

[1] The gate and shrine are specially noticed by the traveller Finch.

Outside the N. wall of the Dargah are the houses of the brothers **Abul Fazl** and Faizi, the learned favourites of Akbar and followers of his new religion, now used as a boys' school. They consist of several rooms: what is now the English class-room was the zenanah. A little to the N.E. of the Record Office, to the right of the road to the Diwan-i-'Am, is the **Hakim's**, or doctor's house, and a very large and fine **Hammam**, the walls and ceilings of which are richly ornamented with stamped plaster-work. To the right on leaving and adjoining the high road below is a spacious and interesting **Baoli**, from which the baths and this part of the city were supplied. Leading to a well at one end is a broad staircase enclosed on each side by rooms. Around the well are chambers for Persian wheels for drawing the water.

25 m. S.W. of Fatehpur-Sikri is **Bayana** (p. 122), once a famous city, near which Babar defeated the Sanga Rana (Singram Singh) of Chitorgarh on 16th March 1527, after sustaining a severe check from this prince in the previous month; it was from Baber's victory that Sikri received the name of Fatehpur. The Rana, who was the bravest Hindu warrior of his day, is said by Colonel Tod to have borne 80 wounds on his body. He refused to return as a defeated chief to Chitor; and his grandson Maharuna Udai Singh deserted that place for Udaipur after its capture by Humayun (p. 93). It belongs to the Bharatpur State, and has a population of 7000. Biana was taken by Syad Salar Masaud, nephew of Mahmud of Ghazni, in 1004 A.D. In the Fort is a pillar of the date of 372 A.D.

ROUTE 14—DELHI.

INDEX.

PAGE

Alai Darwazah 211
Badarpur 214
Badli-ki-Sarai 190 and 203
Batteries of 1857 192, 202
Cemeteries—
  Nicholson 202
  Old Magazine 195
  Rajpur 202
Chandni Chauk 200
Chitor Elephants 199
Coronation Durbar, 1903 203
Dariba 200
Firozabad 204
Flagstaff Tower 203
Fort and Palace 195
Gardens—
  Kudsia 202
  Nicholson 202
  Queen 201
  Roshanara 204
Gates—
  Ajmer 200
  Delhi 204
  ,, of Fort 198
  Kabul 201
  Kashmir 195
  Lahore 201
  ,, of Fort 195
  Mori 201
Turkman 200
Hauz Khas 208
Hauz Shamsi 212
Hindu Rao's House 203
Idgah 201
Imperial Assemblage 203
Indrapat 204
Jahanpanah 208
Jain Temple 200
Kila Rai Pithora 208
Kutab Minar 210
Lal Darwazah 204
Lal Kot 208
Lat, Ridge 203
,, Firozabad 204
Magazine, Old 195
Mahrauli 212
Missions—
  Cambridge 201
  Baptist 199
Memorials—
  Magazine 195
  Mutiny 203
  Kashmir Gate 195
  Telegraph 195
Mosques—
  Begumpur 207
  Chauburji 203
  Fatehpuri 201
  Firozabad Kotila 204

PAGE

Mosques—*continued.*
  Jama 199
  Jamali 211
  Kalan 200
  Khirki 212
  Kuwat ul Islam, Kutab 208
  Moti Masjid, Fort 198
  ,, Mahrauli 212
  Nizam-ud-din 206
  Sher Shah, Purana Kila 205
  Sonahri, Fort 199
  ,, Chandni Chauk 201
  Zinat-ul-Masajid 199
Observatories—
  Jai Singh 207
  Ridge 203
Palace and Fort 195
Purana Kila 204
Ridge 202
Sabzi Mandi 203
St James' Church 195
Shahlimar 203
Shrines—
  Chiragh Delhi 213
  Kutab-ud-din 212
  Nizam-ud-din 206
  Shah Alam 203
Siri 207
Statues—
  Queen-Empress 201
  Brigadier-General Nicholson 202
Tombs, Graves, and Mausolea—
  Adham Khan 211
  Altamsh, Emperor 210
  Amir Khusrau 206
  Azam Khan 206
  Bahadar Shah, Emperor 212
  Bahlol Lodi 213
  Balban 211
  Barnard, Major-General Sir H. 202
  Chausath Khambe 208
  Firoz Shah 207
  Ghazi-ud-din 200
  Greathed, Mr 202
  Hauz Khas 208
  Humayun, Emperor 205
  Isa Khan 205
  Kadam Sharif 201
  Khanan Khan 205
  Jahanara Begam 206
  Muhammad Shah 206
  Nicholson, Brigadier-General 202
  Roshanara Begum 204
  Safdar Jang 207
  Saiyad Kings 207
  Sikandar Lodi 207
  Skinner, Col. 195
  Tughlak Shah 213
  Zabita Khan 212

Delhi ✱ (Lat. 28° 39′, Long. 77° 16′). Population 233,000. The old Mughal capital, and ninth among the cities of India in point of inhabitants. The place is famous for its jewellers, silversmiths, and embroiderers, and many artistic products of other parts of India will be found

DELHI AND ENVIRONS

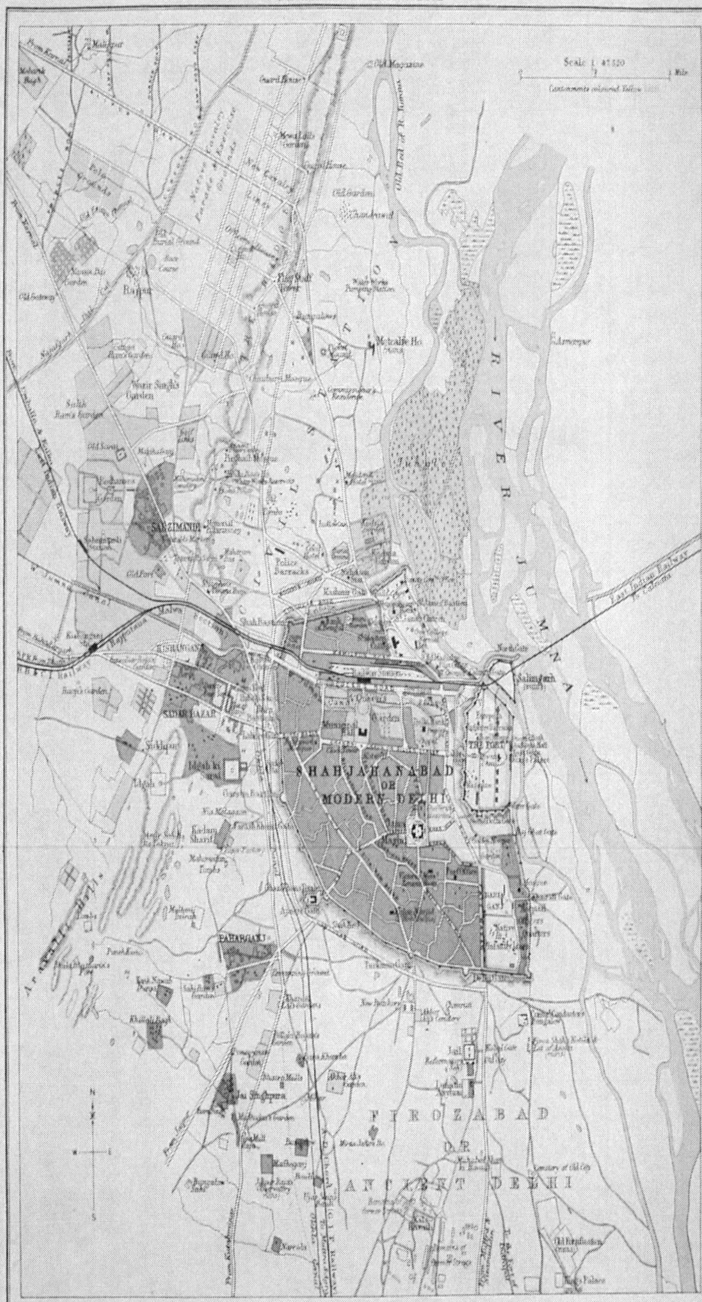

London John Murray Albemarle Street.

in its shops, the principal ones being situated in the centre and E. end of the Chandni Chauk.

The railway station, now one of the largest in India, lies on the N. side of the city; the Queen's Gardens separate it from the Chandni Chauk, which forms a street running E. and W. from the Fort and Palace on the Jumna, to the Fatehpuri Mosque, near the Lahore Gate. Facing the S.W. angle of the Fort is the great Jama Masjid, and further down the river from the Fort is the small cantonment of Daryaganj. In the N. wall of the city are the Kashmir and Mori Gates; at the N.W. corner the Kabul Gate; below it the Lahore Gate; and at the S.W. corner the Ajmer. Outside the N. wall lies the civil station, bounded on the E. by the river, and on the W. by the Ridge, beyond which the cantonment lay in 1857. S. of the modern city, which should properly be known by the name of Delhi-Shahjahanabad, the ruins of old cities and fortresses stretch for 12 m. to the S.; first Firozabad, then Indrapat, with the tomb of the Emperor Humayun and the Shrine of Nizam-ud-din Aulia beyond it; then, at a considerable interval further to the S.W., the ruins of the defences of Siri, Jahanpanah, and the Fort of Rai Pithora, in the citadel of which are situated the Kutab Mosque and Minar, 11 m. from Delhi, and, finally, 5 m. E. of the Kutab, the remains of Tughlakabad and the fortresses round it.

The sights of Delhi cannot be comfortably seen in less than four or five days. For those who can spare only three days to them, the following itinerary may be of use:—

1st Morning.—Fort and Palace, Jama Masjid, Kalan Masjid, Jain Temple, and Chandni Chauk.

Afternoon.—Firozabad and Indrapat.

2nd Morning.—Visit sights outside the city in connection with the Mutiny and Siege, driving out by the Kashmir Gate and returning by the Mori Gate.

Afternoon.—Drive by the mausoleum of Ghazi-ud-din to Jai Singh's Observatory and Safdar Jang's Tomb, and round by the tomb of Nizam-ud-din Auliya to that of Humayun, and so back past Indrapat.

3rd Day.—Starting early, drive to Kutab (perhaps stopping *en route* to see the tank of Hauz-i-Khas). After an early luncheon, proceed to Tughlakabad, and back by the Muttra Road to Delhi. (A long day—but perhaps the new railway from Delhi to Muttra will allow of the driving portion being shortened, and motors will greatly lessen the time spent on the road.)

History.[1] — Though the country round Delhi was connected with the early history of India, as recorded in the *Mahabharata* or *Great War* (Introd. p. lviii.), but little is known of the place prior to the Mohammedan conquest in 1193 A.D. According to tradition, a city called Indraprastha was founded by the early Aryan immigrants, under a king called Yudhisthira, and the fort of Indrapat, also called Purana Kila, or "Old Fort," stands on the site of this. The extensive ruins lying S. of modern Delhi, and covering an area of about 45 sq. m., are the remains of many forts or cities, built by different kings. The oldest are the Hindu forts of Lalkot, built by Anang Pal Tomar in 1052 A.D., and of Rai Pithora, Chauhan, the Prithvi Raja, built by the king of that name, about 1180 A.D. These two forts, and the iron pillar at the Kutab, are the only remains of the Hindu period. The earliest Mohammedan forts or cities were Siri, built by 'Ala-ud-din in 1304 A.D.; Tughlakabad, built by Tughlak Shah, in 1321 A.D.; and Jahanpanah, enclosed by Muhammad Tughlak, about 1325 A.D. Subsequently Firozabad was constructed by the Emperor Firoz Shah Tughlak, and the Purana Kila was founded and built by Humayun and Sher Shah. This new Delhi was not favoured by

[1] Those interested in the history and archæology of Delhi will find the fullest details in *Delhi Past and Present*, by Mr H. C. Fanshawe, C.S.I., late Commissioner of the Delhi Division. John Murray.

the Emperors Akbar and Jahangir, and the modern town dates from the commencement of the fort by Shah Jahan in 1638, whence it was called Shahjahanabad. Delhi has been frequently attacked, and often captured, since it was conquered by the Mohammedans of Ghor and became the temporary capital of the Mohammedan empire of India. It was sacked by Timur, the Mughal, in 1398; by Nadir Shah, the Persian, in 1739; and by Ahmad Shah Durani, the Afghan, in 1756. On the 10th March 1739, the small Persian garrison which Nadir Shah had introduced into the city when he occupied it was almost entirely put to the sword by the people. On the 11th he gave his troops, who had been summoned from the encampment outside the city, orders for a general massacre. From sunrise till 12 o'clock Delhi presented a scene of appalling carnage, the horrors of which were increased by the flames ignited in almost every quarter of the capital. The Mughal Emperor Muhammad Shah then interceded for the people, and Nadir Shah replied, "The Emperor of India must never ask in vain," and commanded the massacre should cease. A vast multitude of persons had, however, perished, and Nadir Shah carried with him from Delhi treasures, estimated at from 30 to 70 millions sterling, the famous Peacock Throne, and the Koh-i-Nur diamond.

In 1759 the Mahratta chief, Mahadaji Sindhia, captured Delhi, and the Mahrattas held it till, in September 1803, when Genl. Lake defeated Louis Bourquin, commanding Sindhia's army, and gained possession of Delhi and of the family and person of the Emperor Shah 'Alam. In October 1804 Delhi was besieged by the Mahratta, Jaswant Rao Holkar, but was successfully defended by the British under Generals Burn and Ochterlony. From that time to 1857 the old capital of India remained in the possession of the British, although the descendants of the Mughal were allowed some show of royalty, and the name of king. The last king, Bahadur Shah, succeeded in 1837, and was about eighty years old when the Mutiny broke out. With his death at Rangoon, in 1862, the last vestige of the Mughal dynasty disappeared.[1] Till 1857 Delhi and the surrounding districts as far as Gurgaon, Hissar, and Karnal, were under the administration of the N.W.P., but in 1858 they were placed under the Punjab Government.

The buildings in and round Delhi may be conveniently classified as follows, according to their dates and styles. The so-called early Pathan style is really Turki, but the old nomenclature is generally followed.

(1)

Early Pathan, 1193-1320.

The Kutab Mosque and Minar—the tomb of Altamsh; the Alai Darwazah (p. 211), and the Khizri or Jamat Khana Mosque at Nizam-ud-din (p. 206).

At first, adoption and adaptation of Hindu materials and style; then developments of elaborate and beautiful decoration from Hindu prototypes.

(2)

Middle Pathan, 1320-1414.

Earlier style.—Tughlakabad and tomb of Tughlak Shah (p. 213).

Later and Severer Style.—Kalan Masjid of Delhi (p. 200); mosque of Kotila Firoz Shah (p. 204); Kadam Sharif (p. 201); ruined buildings on the Ridge (p. 203); Hauz Khas tomb (p. 208); mosques at Nizam-ud-din, Begampur and Khirki (pp. 206, 207, and 212).

First buildings of finely-cut stone, or of red sandstone with sloping walls; then buildings with sloping walls of stone and mortar

[1] A list of sovereigns who reigned at Delhi from 1193 will be found on p. liii Introd.

plastered all over, and borne by rough columns of simple rectangular stones; arches usually flat Hindu arches; mosques generally built on high raised platforms.

(3)

Later Pathan Style, 1414-1556.

Tombs of Saiyad and Lodi kings (p. 207); Purana Kila and Mosque (p. 204); Jamali Mosque (p. 211); tomb and mosque of Isa Khan (p. 205).

Buildings usually with fine domes, and decorated with coloured marbles and tiles, and in some cases inside with fine plaster ornamentation; arches still often of the Hindu type.

(4)

Mughal, 1556-1660.

Earlier.—Tomb of Humayun (p. 205); tomb of Azam Khan (p. 206); Fort and Palace of Delhi (pp. 195-198); Jama Masjid, Delhi (p. 199); Fatehpuri Masjid, Delhi (p. 201).

Later decadent style.—Zinat-ul-Masajid Mosque (p. 199); Moti masjid at Mahrauli (p. 212); Sonahri Masjids in Chandni Chauk (p. 201), and of Javed Khan (p. 199); mosque, tomb and college of Ghazi-ud-din Khan (p. 200); tomb of Safdar Jang (p. 207).

Buildings at first of red sandstone and white marble, later of fawn coloured sandstone; white marble used more and more. Fine domes, true arches, and lofty minarets are special characteristics of the style.

The Mutiny, 1857.

As the principal events of the great mutiny of the Bengal army in 1857 centred originally round Delhi, it is desirable to give a somewhat detailed account of them in this connection.

On the 10th of May 1857 there was in the large cantonment of Meerut, 40 m. N.W. of Delhi, a British force consisting of a battalion of the 60th Rifles, a regiment of Carbineers, and a large force of Artillery, though only two field-batteries were fully equipped. The Native troops were one regiment of Cavalry—the 3rd, and two regiments of Infantry—the 11th and 20th—in all about 2500 strong.

On the evening of that date, Sunday, the troopers, and after them the two regiments, broke into mutiny, and released eighty-five men of the 3rd Cavalry, who had been imprisoned the previous day. The mutineers were not attacked by the British troops, and after a brief period of murder and robbery they started unpursued for Delhi, where there were three Native regiments and a battery of Native Artillery, but no British troops. On reaching that place early the next morning, the troopers who arrived first called upon the King from below the palace walls to join them, and then made their way into the city and attacked the civil officers, who had received news of the outbreak at Meerut, and were attempting to prevent the mutineers from entering. These officers, the Commissioner Mr Simon Fraser, the Collector Mr Hutchinson, and Captain Douglas, Commandant of the Palace, were compelled to fall back into the fort, and were there shortly afterwards murdered by the mob. When the 54th Regiment marched down from the cantonment to the Kashmir Quarter Guard at the N.E. corner of the city, most of the officers were shot down by the troopers, and the men of the regiment refused to act, an example followed by the 74th Regiment, which was sent down later. Meanwhile the officer in charge of the Arsenal, Lieutenant Willoughby, who had been forewarned by the civil magistrates, made a desperate attempt with his subordinates to hold that place against the mutineers until aid should arrive from Meerut; and when defence was no longer possible, blew up the magazine, and managed to escape to the Kashmir Gate with some others. After the explosion the troops there broke out into open mutiny, and shot most of the remaining officers, a few escaping over the face of the Kashmir Bastion. The Europeans in the cantonment, who had collected at the Flagstaff Tower, were then compelled to take flight to Karnal. Before nightfall every vestige of British power had disappeared from Delhi.

Measures were at once taken by General Anson, the Commander-in-Chief of the army, who was at Simla, to collect troops for the recapture of Delhi, and by Sir John Lawrence and the officers of the Panjab to anticipate the mischief of further mutiny. With what success the latter acted will be found under various heads in Routes 15 and 16. The troops collected were unable to advance for some time, owing to the usual state of unpreparedness prevailing at that period, and reached Alipur, 10 m. from Delhi, under the command of Major-General Sir H. Barnard (General Anson having died of cholera at Karnal on 27th May) only on 5th June. There the Umballa force was joined by that from Meerut under Brigadier-General Archdale Wilson, who had defeated the rebels twice near Ghaziabad (p. 220).

On the following day the combined forces marched on Delhi, and found the rebels well posted and supported by thirty guns 6 m. N. of Delhi, at the village of Badli-ki-Sarai. Attacking the mutineers, General Barnard gained a complete victory. The most important result of this success was to give the British possession of "the Ridge," from which all subsequent operations against Delhi were made.

"The tents of the British were pitched a little to the rear of their old houses, behind the left and centre of the Ridge, obliquely to the front of attack, and effectually concealed from the besieged. The position on the extreme right invited attack. It was surmounted by an extensive building known as Hindu Rao's House. A strong body of troops was posted here, and in an old Observatory near it. About 800 yds. to the N. of Hindu Rao's House, and on the Ridge, was an old mosque, and again 800 yds. to the N. was the Flag-Staff Tower, a double-storeyed circular building—a good post for observation, and strong enough to afford shelter to troops. At these four points General Barnard established pickets supported by guns. Below Hindu Rao's House, on the right flank, was the suburb of Sabzi-mandi, which, with its houses and walled gardens, afforded shelter to the enemy, and was in fact the key of the English position. Beyond Sabzi-mandi, towards the Kabul Gate, were the suburbs of Kishanganj, Trevelyanganj, Paharipur, and Teliwara, all strong positions which covered the enemy when they advanced to the attack, but were too near the city walls for us to occupy. Opposite the mosque picket, to the E., was Metcalfe House, on the banks of the Jumna, with substantial outbuildings, and a mound in their rear, which seemed to recommend it for occupation. Between it and the city was an old summer palace of the Emperor, the Kudsia Garden, with lofty gateways and spacious courtyards, and in a line between the latter and Hindu Rao's house was Ludlow Castle, the house of the late Commissioner Simon Frazer."[1]

To take this great walled city General Barnard had a force of about 3000 British, one Goorkha battalion, the Corps of Guides, the remnant of certain native regiments, and twenty-two guns. At first it was intended to assault the city by night, but as failure would have been disastrous,

[1] The best account of the Siege of Delhi is Captain Norman's Narrative, republished in *Delhi Past and Present*. Those who desire a concise account, without military technicalities, cannot do better than refer to Holmes' *Indian Mutiny*.

it was considered best to delay till the expected reinforcements had arrived. Between the 12th and 18th June the rebels attacked the British position four times, in front and rear. Again on the 23rd, the anniversary of Plassey, they attacked fiercely, having been reinforced by the mutineers from Nasirabad; fortunately the British by that time had received an additional 850 men.

On the 24th General Chamberlain arrived, and with him the 8th and 61st Europeans, the 1st Panjab Infantry, a squadron of Panjab Cavalry, and four guns, raising the British strength to 6600. The rebels also received an accession of about 4500 from Bareilly.

On the 5th July General Barnard also died of cholera, and was succeeded by General Reed.

On the 9th and 14th of July fierce engagements were fought on the right of the British position, near Hindu Rao's house, in and about the Sabzi-mandi, in which 25 officers and 400 men of our force were killed and wounded.

"On the 17th of July General Reed resigned the command to Brigadier-General Archdale Wilson. At this time the besieging force was in great difficulties; two generals had died, a third had been compelled by illness to resign, the Adjutant-General and Quartermaster-General lay wounded in their tents; and the rebels had attacked so often, and with such obstinacy, that it had come to be acknowledged that the British were the besieged and not the besiegers. On the 18th of July the rebels made another sortie, which was repulsed by Colonel Jones of the 60th Rifles. The Engineer officers now cleared away the walls and houses which had afforded cover to the enemy, and connected the advanced posts with the main pickets on the Ridge. After this there were no more conflicts in the Sabzi-mandi. On the 23rd of July the enemy streamed out of the Kashmir Gate, and endeavoured to establish themselves at Ludlow Castle. They were driven back, but the English were drawn too near the city walls, and suffered severe loss.

Reinforcements were now on their way from the Panjab, commanded by one of the best soldiers that India had ever produced — Brigadier-General Nicholson. "On the 7th of August Nicholson stood on the Ridge at Delhi. He had come on in advance of his column of 2500 men, which arrived on the 14th.[1] On the 25th he marched out to the S.W. towards Najafgarh with a strong force to attack the mutineers, who had moved to intercept the siege train coming from Ferozepore. The march was a difficult one, through deep mud. He found the mutineers in three bodies, occupying two villages and a garden in front, all protected by guns. Crossing a ford where the water was breast-high, Nicholson, at the head of the 61st Regiment and the 1st Bengal European Fusiliers, stormed the garden, and captured the guns; but the Sepoys fought well, and sold their lives dearly. Those who survived made for the bridge crossing the Najafgarh Canal, and fled to Delhi; in all 800 were killed and thirteen guns were captured. General Nicholson blew up the Najafgarh Bridge, and returned to camp next day.

"On the morning of the 4th of September the siege guns, drawn by elephants, with an immense number of ammunition wagons, reached the camp. On the 6th, the rest of the Rifles from Meerut marched in. On the 8th the Jammu contingent arrived, with Colonel R. Lawrence at their head. Many, and amongst them foremost of all Nicholson, chafed at the delay which occurred in storming Delhi. The responsibility of the attack rested with General Archdale Wilson, who had thus stated the magnitude of the enterprise in a letter to Colonel Baird Smith, commanding the En-

[1] Between 15th and 22nd August, Lieutenant Hodson made his successful cavalry raid to Rohtak, and cut up and scattered the rebels there.

gineers, on the 20th of August: 'Delhi is 7 m. in circumference, filled with an immense fanatical population, garrisoned by full 40,000 soldiers, armed and disciplined by ourselves, with 114 heavy pieces of artillery mounted on the walls, with the largest magazine of shot, shell, and ammunition in the Upper Provinces, besides some 60 pieces of field artillery, all of our own manufacture, and manned by artillerymen drilled and taught by ourselves; the Fort itself having been strengthened by perfect flanking defences, erected by our own engineers, and a glacis which prevents our guns breaching the walls lower than 8 ft. from the top.' These circumstances led General Wilson to write that the chances of success were, in his opinion, anything but favourable, but that he would yield to the judgment of the chief engineer. Many condemned his apparent reluctance to order the assault, but they have since acknowledged that they did him less than justice, for the principles of warfare were upon his side.

"Investment by the British, with their limited means, being impossible, it was necessary to concentrate all their breaching power on a portion of the walls. This consisted of the Mori, Kashmir, and Water Bastions, with their connecting curtains. This front was chosen because the fire of the Mori Bastion alone commanded the approach to it, and because there was excellent cover to within a short distance of the walls. On the evening of the 6th of September, a light battery,[1] consisting of six 9-pounders and two 24-pounders, under the command of Captain Remmington, was constructed on the plateau of the Ridge to protect the operations going on below. On the night of the 7th the first heavy battery[2] was constructed at 700 yds. from the wall. It consisted of two parts connected by a trench. The right portion held five heavy guns and a howitzer, the function of which was to demolish the Mori Bastion. The left held four guns to keep down the fire of the Kashmir Bastion. While darkness lasted the enemy only fired twice, but when the morning revealed the British plans, the rebels poured in a shower of shot and shell; but the British persevered in their work, and before sunset the rebel battery was silenced. The British had lost 70 men in the trenches. The left section of their battery maintained a fire on the Kashmir Bastion during the greater part of three days, but at noon on the 10th it took fire, and the guns were of necessity withdrawn. By that time No. 2 Battery had been finished—the left section immediately in the front of Ludlow Castle, and the right section 90 yds. to the S. of it. Both were within 600 yds. of the city; the right section had seven howitzers and two 18-pounders, and the left section nine 24-pounders.

"This battery did not open fire till No. 3 Battery was completed. It was built in the Kudsia Garden, behind part of the Custom House, at 180 yds. from the Water Bastion, on which it was to play. The enemy poured in such an incessant fire of musketry, with occasional shells, that it was impossible to work in the day, and difficult at night. Meantime a powerful mortar battery was also constructed in the Kudsia Garden. At 8 A.M. on the 11th of September, the nine 24-pounders in the left section of No. 2 Battery opened with terrific effect on the Kashmir Bastion. The enemy replied, and severely wounded the commandant of the heavy guns, but their fire was soon silenced by No. 2 Battery, aided by the mortars in the Kudsia Bagh. Then the walls of Delhi began to fall, and whole yards of parapet came down. At 11 A.M. on the 12th No. 3 Battery unmasked and pounded the Water Bastion into

[1] This was known as the Sammy House Battery, and lies 400 yds. E. of the Mutiny Memorial.

[2] The sites of this battery, 400 yds. to the E. of the foot of the slope of the Ridge below the Mutiny Memorial, will be found inside the Police Lines, and behind a house to the N. of these.

ruins. All through the 12th and 13th the roar of fifty heavy guns was heard day and night, without intermission. On the 13th, Alexander Taylor, of whom Nicholson said, 'If I survive to-morrow I will let all the world know that Aleck Taylor took Delhi,' announced that the breaches were practicable.

"The arrangements for storming Delhi were forthwith made. The 1st Column under Nicholson consisted of 300 men of the 75th Foot, 250 of the 1st Fusiliers, and 450 of the 2nd Panjab Infantry. It was to storm the breach in the curtain near the Kashmir Bastion. The 2nd Column, under Brigadier Jones, C.B., was to storm the breach at the Water Bastion, and it consisted of 250 men of the 8th Foot, 250 of the 2nd Fusiliers, and 350 of the 4th Sikhs. The 3rd Column, under Colonel Campbell of the 52nd, was to assault the Kashmir Gate, and consisted of 200 men of the 52nd Foot, 250 of the Kumaon Battalion, and 500 of the 1st Panjab Infantry. The 4th Column, under Major Charles Reid, who so long and gallantly held the post at Hindu Rao's house, was to enter the city by the Lahore Gate. It consisted of 860 men of the Sirmur Battalion, the Guides, and other corps. The 5th Column, the Reserve, was commanded by Brigadier Longfield, and consisted of 1700 men. Besides these five columns, Colonel Hope Grant with 600 sabres of the 9th Lancers and Sikh Horse, whose duty it was to prevent sallies from the Lahore and Kabul Gates, were for long under heavy fire.

"On the night of the 13th, Lieutenants Medley and Lang explored the Kashmir breach, and Lieutenants Greathed and Home that of the Water Bastion. The morning of the 14th was fine and still. Nicholson laid his arm on Brigadier Jones's shoulder, and asked him if he was ready. He then rejoined his own Column, gave the order to storm, and immediately the heavy guns, which were roaring at their loudest, became silent. The Rifles sounded the advance, and the 1st and 2nd Columns ascended the glacis. The fire of the enemy was terrible, and the Engineers Greathed and Ovenden were the first to fall. The stormers, carrying the ladders, were led by Captain Baines and Lieutenant Metje. When Baines reached the Water Bastion he had only twenty-five men left out of seventy-five. Both he and Metje were carried disabled to the rear. The 1st Column was divided into two sections. Nicholson himself led one, and Colonel Herbert of the 75th the other. Nicholson was the first to mount the wall. In the other section Lieutenant Fitzgerald, who was the first to ascend, was shot dead. Another took his place, and soon both sections of the 1st Column had carried the breach near the Kashmir Bastion, and taken up their position at the Main Guard. The 2nd Column entered by the breach at the Water Bastion, and joined the 1st Column at the Quarter Guard. These Columns then proceeded along the inner side of the city wall to the Mori or Shah Bastion at the N.W. angle, where the rebel gunners fought gallantly, and were bayoneted at their guns. The Columns then advanced and took the Kabul Gate, on which a soldier of the 61st planted a flag. The enemy kept up a galling fire on this from the Lahore Gate. Nicholson collected a number of men to storm it. As he advanced he found himself in a long narrow lane lined with marksmen on both sides. Some of the enemy's guns were brought to bear on the attacking column, and the men fell fast. Major Jacob of the 1st Fusiliers received his death-wound, Captain Greville and Lieutenant Speke were struck down. The Column wavered; Nicholson rushed forward, his lofty stature rendered him conspicuous, and in a moment he was shot through the body, and in spite of his remonstrances was carried to the rear to die, and the Columns fell back to the Kabul Gate. He died of his wound ten days later.

"The 3rd Column had been appointed to enter the city through the Kashmir Gate, which was to be blown open by Lieutenants Home and Salkeld, Sergeants Carmichael, Burgess, and Smith. Home, with Bugler Hawthorne, was first down into the ditch. He planted his bag, but as Carmichael advanced with his, he was mortally wounded. Smith then advanced, and placed his dying comrade's bag as well as his own, and prepared the fuses for ignition. Salkeld was ready with a slow match, but as he was lighting it he received two bullets, and falling he called on Smith to take the match, which was taken by Burgess, and Smith was in the act of giving him a box of lucifers when Burgess also fell with a bullet through his body. Smith was now alone, but he had struck a light, and was applying it when a portfire went off in his face. There was a thick smoke and dust, then a roar and a crash, as Smith scrambled into the ditch. There he placed his hand on Home, who said he was unhurt, and having joined the column went forward. The gate had been shattered, but not so destroyed as had been anticipated; but the 3rd Column passed through it. Smith then obtained stretchers, and had Burgess and Salkeld carried to the camp, but both of them died—Burgess on the way, and Salkeld a few days afterwards."

The 3rd Column, which was immediately joined by the reserve, pushed across the Queen's Garden and Chandni Chauk to the Kotwali, under the guidance of Sir T. T. Metcalfe, and then down the Dariba to the Jama Masjid. This, however, was strongly defended and held, and as the column was without guns or means of blowing in the gates, it was compelled to fall back when the advance on the Lahore Gate failed. In spite of the losses of the assault (66 officers and 1100 men), the British force maintained itself in the N.W. corner of the city, as far S. as the College, and in spite of regrettable excesses on the part of the troops, gradually captured the whole city. On the 16th the Magazine was taken, and posts were established from it to the Kabul Gate during the 17th and 18th, the troops working from house to house under cover. On the 19th the Burn Bastion, between the Kabul and Lahore Gates, was seized, and on the next morning the latter gate was captured, and cavalry entering by the Delhi Gate on the S. occupied the Jama Masjid; and on the 20th the Fort and Palace were taken, very little opposition being offered by the few rebels left in it. On the 21st the king was captured by Lieutenant Hodson at Humayun's tomb, and on the following day the same officer received the surrender of the king's sons at the same place, and shot them in front of the Delhi Gate. On 24th September a column under Colonel Greathed marched S. from Delhi, and on 10th October relieved Agra (p. 172); on the day that it left, Brigadier-General Nicholson was buried in the Kashmir Gate Cemetery.

The number of troops engaged on the Siege of Delhi from first to last was 9866, of which no less than 3837 were killed or died of wounds or were wounded. These included 46 European officers killed and 140 wounded. No more marked display of endurance and steady courage than that shown by the Delhi Field Force during the summer of 1857 can be found in the whole splendid record of the British and Indian Armies.

For the convenience of sight-seeing, Delhi and the adjoining country may be divided as follows:—

(1) The city, including the old Magazine, the Fort and Palace, the Jama Masjid and Kalan Masjid, and the Chandni Chauk.

(2) The tract lying N. of the city walls with which the principal incidents

of the Siege of Delhi and the Imperial Assemblages are concerned.

(3) The tract lying immediately S. of the city and including the ruins of Firozabad, the Purana Kila, the Mausolea of the Emperor Humayun and Nawab Safdar Jang, and Nizam-ud-din Aulia, the Saiyad and Lodi tombs, and Jai Singh's Observatory.

(4) The tract lying still further S., including the tomb of the Emperor Firoz Shah at Hauz Khas, Siri, Jahanpanah, Kila Rai Pithora, the citadel of Lal Kot, with the Kutab Minar and Mosque, and Tughlakabad 5 m. to the E. of these.

(1) The City.

On the outer face of the **Kashmir Gate** is a memorial tablet of the Explosion Party. The first was erected by Lord Napier of Magdala, the present one by Lord Minto in 1910. On the inside, the outlines of the **Quarter Guard**, in which so many European officers were murdered on the 11th May 1857, are still traceable; on the N. side a ramp leads on to the walls just above the main breach, and from here and from the adjoining bastion a fine view is had of the vistas cut to the points where No. 1 and No. 2 Siege Batteries were established. E. of the Quarter Guard are the District Courts and the second breach at the side of the Water Bastion.

In front of the gate is **St James' Church**, built by Colonel Skinner, C.B., whose Delhi residence stood on the opposite side of the clear space here; in the churchyard are the old dome-cross bearing the marks of bullets fired at it in 1857, a memorial cross to the victims of the Mutiny, and the graves of the Skinner family and of Mr William Fraser, murdered in 1835, and of Sir T. Metcalfe; and inside the church are a number of memorial tablets. 200 yds. S. of the gate is the Cambridge Mission College on the right, and 200 yds. further upon the left the High School building, once the Delhi College, and before that the Residency. Beyond again is the Telegraph Office, and in front of it a granite memorial of the officers of the Department who fell in 1857; and adjoining is the Post Office situated inside the enclosure of the old **Magazine**. Over the central gate of the Magazine is a memorial of Lieutenant Willoughby[1] and the eight heroic men who shared in its defence; in the S.E. corner at the back may still be seen the steps by which the survivors escaped to the Kashmir Gate. The road now passes the oldest cemetery in Delhi on the left; and beyond the arch of the railway bridge the main thoroughfare (which branches to the railway station on the right, and on the left to the ghats and the Jumna bridge) ascends the slope in front to the **Mughal Fort and Palace**, built by the Emperor Shah-jahan between 1638-48.

There are two fine gates to the fort as at Agra, the one in the centre of the W. side, and facing the E. end of the Chandni Chauk, being called the Lahore Gate, and the other at the W. corner of the S. side, and named the Delhi Gate. A fine view of the magnificent red sandstone wall (from whence the name Lal Kila or Red Fort) is obtained by walking along the ditch to the N.W. corner, where the three bridges between the fort and the Salimgarh may be seen, and the picturesque **Ghats**, which include among them the traditional Dasaswamedh and Nigambodh ghats where the Imperial Horse sacrifice was performed by Yudisthara (Introd., p. lviii.), and the sacred Vedas were recovered from the bottom of the ocean.

Entering the forework erected by the Emperor Aurangzeb in front of the **Lahore Gate**, and passing under its grand archway, it will be found that the route beyond leads under a vaulted arcade (see plan of Fort and

[1] Lieutenants Raynor and Forrest, Conductors Shaw, Scully, and Buckley, Sub-Conductor Crow, Sergeants Edwards and Stewart.

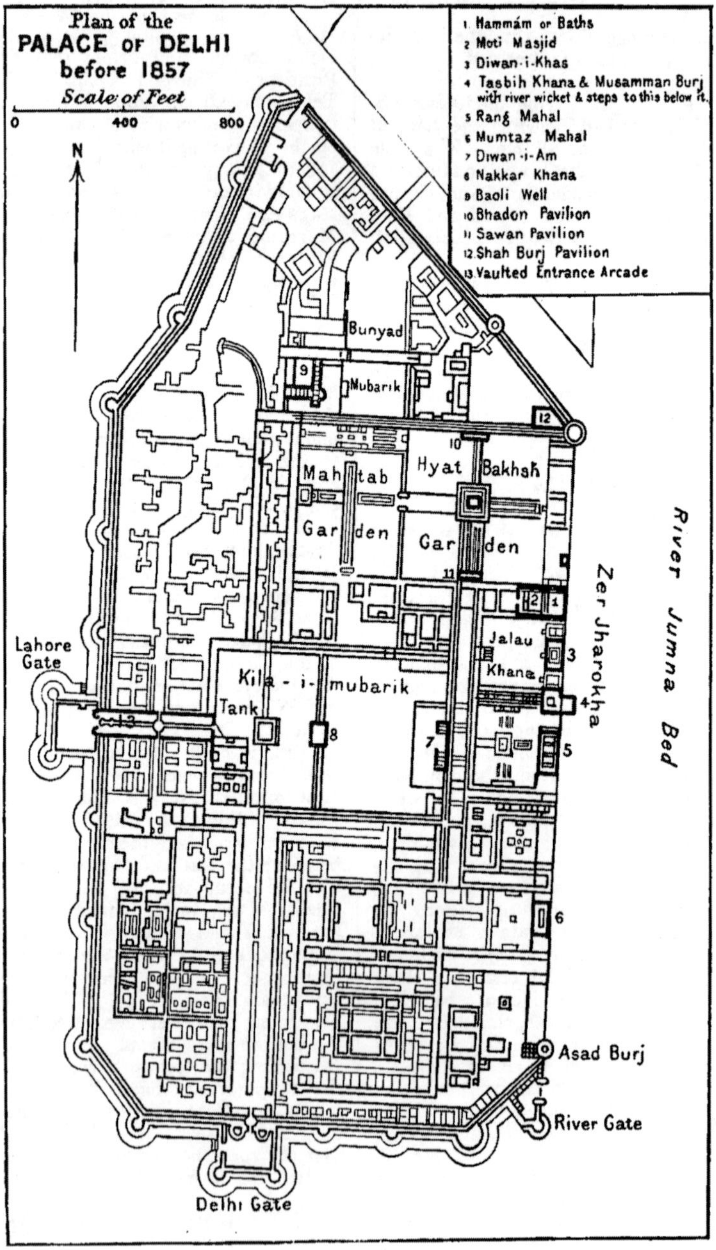
Plan of the
PALACE OF DELHI
before 1857
Scale of Feet
0 400 800
N
1 Hammám or Baths
2 Moti Masjid
3 Diwan-i-Khas
4 Tasbih Khana & Musamman Burj with river wicket & steps to this below it.
5 Rang Mahal
6 Mumtaz Mahal
7 Diwan-i-Am
8 Nakkar Khana
9 Baoli Well
10 Bhadon Pavilion
11 Sawan Pavilion
12 Shah Burj Pavilion
13 Vaulted Entrance Arcade
Bunyad
Mubarik
Mahtab Garden
Hyat Bakhsh Garden
River Jumna Bed
Zer Jharokha
Jalau Khana
Kila-i-mubarik
Tank
Lahore Gate
Asad Burj
River Gate
Delhi Gate

Palace), which Mr Fergusson considers to be the noblest entrance known to belong to any palace. From the octagon in the centre of it a gateway to the left conducts to the steps leading up to the rooms (now private quarters) over the Lahore Gate. At the foot of these, on the 11th May 1857, was killed the Commissioner of the Division, and in the rooms above were murdered the wounded Collector and Commandant, the Chaplain and two ladies. The vaulted arcade ends in the centre of the outer court, which measured 540 ft. by 360 ft., of which the side arcades and central tank have been removed; round the edge of the latter were murdered, on 16th June 1857, some fifty Christians who had escaped the massacre of the 11th. In the E. wall of the court was the now isolated **Naubat or Nakkar Khana**, the band gallery of which is 100 ft. by 80 ft.; and here every one except princes of the royal blood was required to dismount. The gate is now used as a **Palace Museum**,[1] and contains parts of the old stone elephants, portraits of the Mughal Emperors, and some views and plans of old Delhi. The carving of the flowers on the red sandstone dado is unusually good. The inner main court to which this gateway led was 540 ft. broad and 420 ft. deep, and was also surrounded by arcade galleries, where the great feudatories used to mount guard. This space has been recently cleared of the modern military structures which so long defaced it. On the further side of it is the splendid Hall of Public Audience, **the Diwan-i-'Am** (100 ft. by 60 ft.). The proportions of this hall and of its columns and of the engrailed arches are extremely beautiful, and so far as the expression of power goes it is probably the finest of all such works; the whole of it was originally covered with brilliant chunam. At the back in the raised recess the Emperor used to be seated on the peacock throne. Below it is the marble seat of the Wazir, and around it above are the inlaid panels executed by Austin of Bordeaux, including that of the artist as Orpheus, lately recovered by Lord Curzon from the S. Kensington Museum. The hall has been thoroughly restored by the care of that Viceroy, and a Florentine artist, Sr. Mennegatti, has renewed the inlay work of the throne recess, and the plaques of the arch to the W. side of the throne. Bernier gives a full account of the splendid appearance of the Hall in the time of Aurangzeb, and Tavernier records a minute description of the glories of the peacock throne, which was carried off by Nadir Shah. The following description is from Mr Beresford's *Guide of Delhi*:—"It was so called from its having the figures of two peacocks standing behind it, their tails being expanded, and the whole so inlaid with sapphires, rubies, emeralds, pearls, and other precious stones of appropriate colours, as to represent life. The throne itself was 6 ft. long by 4 ft. broad; it stood on six massive feet, which, with the body, were of solid gold, inlaid with rubies, emeralds, and diamonds. It was surmounted by a canopy of gold, supported by twelve pillars, all richly emblazoned with costly gems, and a fringe of pearls ornamented the borders of the canopy. Between the two peacocks stood the figure of a parrot, said to have been carved out of a single emerald."

A gate on the N. side of the Hall led to the innermost court of the palace, called the **Jalau Khana**, and the **Diwan-i-Khâs**, or Hall of Private Audience. Though the general effect of this has been spoilt by the unnecessary removal of the marble pavement in front of it, and of the arcaded court which once enclosed it like the Khas Mahal at Agra (p. 176), it is still one of the most graceful buildings in the world, though its elegance shows a certain amount of approach to weakness. It measures 90 ft. by 67 ft., and is built wholly of white marble inlaid

[1] The Museum will be transferred to the Mumtaz Mahal, p. 198.

with precious stones; the ceiling, which was once of silver, and was removed by the Jats or Mahrattas, has been restored in wood. At either end of the Hall, over the two outer arches, is the famous Persian inscription :

"Agar Fardaus bar rué zamin ast
Hamin ast wa hamin ast wa hamin ast."

"If heaven can be on the face of the earth,
It is this, oh! it is this, oh! it is this."

The Hall has many historical connections—the presence of Nadir Shah the Persian and Ahmad Shah the Afghan, the blinding of the Emperor Shah Alam by the brutal Ghulam Kadir, the reception of Lord Lake after the battle of Delhi in 1803, the thanksgiving service of the Delhi Field Force on the 27th Sept. 1857, the trial of the last King of Delhi in January and March 1858, the ball given to H.R.H. the Prince of Wales by the Indian army in January 1876, and that on 6th January 1903, in honour of the Coronation of his present Majesty. In the river-bed below the Hall and the connected buildings was the space known as Zer-Jharokha or Beneath the Lattices. It was here that the mutinous troopers from Meerut called upon the king on 11th May, and it was from the terrace above, between the Hall and the **Royal Private Apartments**, that Captain Douglas bade them remove themselves to the south of the city. These apartments consist of three sets of rooms and of a tower called the Mussamman (octagon) Burj, projecting over the river. In the centre room is a fine alabaster panel with a representation of the heavens round the Scales of Justice, Mizan-i-adal, and in others will be found the most beautiful decorations and pierced grilles now left in Delhi. S. of these apartments is the **Rang Mahal** or Painted Palace, the residence of the Chief Sultana, till lately used as a mess-house, and now restored: the marble water channel (see below) runs under this also. Further S. is another hall, the **Mumtaz Mahal**, till recently used as a prison room. On the N. side of the Diwan-i-Khas, and connected with it by a shallow water channel, which also passed through the Royal Apartments, are the **Royal Baths**. These consist of three large rooms, floored with white marble, elaborately inlaid with *pietra dura* work, and crowned with domes, unhappily whitewashed. They were lighted by windows of coloured glass in the roof. In the centre of each room is a fountain, and in the wall of one of them a reservoir of marble.

Opposite to them, to the W., is the **Moti Masjid** or the "Pearl Mosque," of white and grey marble. A bronze door covered with designs in low relief leads to the courtyard, 40 ft. by 35 ft. The mosque proper has three arches, and is divided into two aisles. The walls are decorated with low reliefs. It was built in 1659 A.D. by Aurangzeb, and cost Rs. 160,000. Certain details in the decoration show that the elegance of late Mughal work was already beginning to degenerate into weak floridness.

To the N. of these buildings lay the fine **Hyat Bakhsh**, or Life-giving, garden-court, 200 ft. square, of which till lately only the Shah Burj pavilion in the N.E. corner, and the Bhadon and Sawan Pavilions on the N. and S. sides remained. The tank and water channels have been restored as far as possible, and all modern unsightly excrescences have been removed by the influence of Lord Curzon. Beyond these the road to the N. leads to the Salimgarh, built by Salim Shah in A.D. 1546; except for the view over the river, this outwork scarcely deserves a visit. W. of the above garden was another called the Mahtab (moon) Bagh, and near what was the N.W. corner of it is a picturesque baoli tank. Nothing else remains of the courts and beautiful buildings of the old palace which were so barbarously and unnecessarily removed after 1857. The road from the baoli leads due S. to the **Delhi Gate** of the Fort which is inferior to the Lahore Gate; near it, on the right, the King of Delhi was imprisoned after September 1857. Between the inner and outer gates stand two large stone elephants (p. 174), without riders, replaced here by the gift of Lord Curzon. Beyond the southern glacis of the Fort, on which a cross marks the site of the old cemetery, are the gardens and cantonment of Daryaganj. The latter is bounded on the W. by the Faiz Bazar leading to the Delhi Gate; over the Khairati Gate in the N.E. corner is the **Zinat-ul-Masajid Mosque**, built by a daughter of Aurangzeb in 1710. The house in the cantonment numbered 5, just beyond the road to the gate, was defended for 48 hours after 11th May 1857 by a party of Europeans, of whom only two escaped finally.

From the Delhi Gate of the Fort the Khas Bazar once led to the **Jama Masjid**, and on the open space now on this side stood a number of the principal private palaces. It is intended that the All India Memorial of King Edward, an equestrian statue, should be erected here, a truly noble and imperial site. To the S. of it are the Schools and Hospital of the Baptist Mission, and the Empress Victoria Memorial Hospital for women, and to the W. of it are the Jama Masjid and Dufferin Municipal Hospital. On the left of the road and in front of the Delhi Gate is the graceful **Sonahri Masjid** of Javed Khan, built in 1751. Of the Jama Mosque Mr Fergusson wrote: "It is not unlike the Moti Masjid in the Agra Fort in plan, though built on a very much larger scale, and adorned with two noble minarets, which are wanting in the Agra example; while from the somewhat capricious admixture of red sandstone with white marble it is far from possessing the same elegance and purity of effect. It is, however, one of the few mosques, either in India or elsewhere, that is designed to produce a pleasing effect externally. It is raised on a lofty basement, and its three gateways, combined with the four angle towers and the frontispiece and domes of the mosque itself, make up a design where all the parts are pleasingly subordinated to one another, but at the same time produce a whole of great variety and elegance. Its principal gateway cannot be compared with that at Fatehpur-Sikri, but it is a noble portal, and from its smaller dimensions more in harmony with the objects by which it is surrounded." The three noble gateways are approached by grand flights of steps, unrivalled elsewhere, except at Fatehpur-Sikri. As of old the great doors of the main (E.) gateway were opened only for the Mughal Emperor, so now they are opened only for the Viceroy of India and the Lieutenant-Governor of the Panjab; but other visitors can enter from this side by the wicket in the doors. These are massive and overlaid with brass arabesques half an inch thick. Inside them is the stately quadrangle, 325 ft. square, in the centre of which are a marble basin and fountain. Round three sides of the quadrangle runs an open sandstone cloister, 15 ft. wide, with pillars of the same material. The mosque proper is 200 ft. long and 90 ft. broad. The inscription on the front gives the date in Arabic as 1658 A.D., the year in which Aurangzeb deposed his father, Shah Jahan; it is found in the single word "Ya Hadi," "Ah the Guide," on the centre panel. Visitors entering this part of the mosque are required to envelop their boots with covers provided there. The three white marble domes are relieved by thin vertical lines of black marble. The two minarets rise to the height of 130 ft. They are reached from the S. gate over the roof of the arcade. At the N.E. corner of the court is a pavilion in which are placed relics of the Prophet Mohammed. The view of the Fort walls from the galleries on the E. side of the court is very fine; and that of the outside of the back wall of the mosque from the W. is most impressive. From there the Chaura Bazar leads S.W. to the Kazi Hauz and the Lal Kua Bazar, which is the principal thoroughfare of the S.W. side of the city and extends up to the Fatehpuri Masjid. S. from the Kazi-ka-Hauz one main street runs past the Kalan Masjid to the Turkman Gate, and another continues W. to the Ajmer Gate and the mausoleum of Ghazi-ud-din Khan outside it. The **Kalan** (Great) **Masjid**, popularly known as the Kala (Black) Masjid, was once included within the limits of Firozabad, and was built by the Emperor Firoz Shah in 1386. The outside consists of two storeys, of which the lower, forming a kind of plinth to the actual place of worship, is 28 ft. high, the total height to the top of the battlements being 66 ft. "The sloping style of the architecture seems peculiarly illustrative of the buildings of that and earlier periods. The sloping pilasters on each side of the main entrance give somewhat of an Egyptian appearance to the front of the building, which is not dissimilar from those of the more ancient remains of Hindu architecture.... The peculiar construction of the arches and domes, the stones of which are held together by the wonderful adhesive qualities of the lime used in those days, without any keystones, is characteristic of the Mohammedan Indian buildings of the 14th century" (Carr Stephen). The walls, which are very thick, have in the upper storey a number of openings, filled with red stone screens, now much mutilated: the arcades are supported by plain square columns of stone. There is a stern look about this sombre building, the plan of which, Bishop Heber says, "is exactly that of the original Arabian mosques—a square court surrounded bv a cloister, and roofed with many small domes of the plainest and most solid construction." To the E. of the mosque is the tomb of Turkman Shah, who was styled the "Sun of Devotees." He died in 638 A.H. = 1240 A.D., in the time of Muizz-ud-din Bahram Shah, and his grave is therefore one of the oldest of those near modern Delhi. Near the Turkman gate is the successful Christian church built in 1904.

A little to the N. of this saint's grave in the Bulbuli Khana is the tomb of **Sultan Raziyah,** daughter of the Emperor Altamsh, and the only Mohammedan Queen Empress of India, who ruled from 1236 to 1240; she was killed in flight from a battle in which she sought to recover her throne. The mausoleum at the **Ajmer Gate** is enclosed in a modern hornwork. It was constructed about 1710 by **Ghazi-ud-din Khan,** father of the first Nizam of Hyderabad, whose son, Ghazi-ud-din, is also buried here, and whose grandson, Ghazi-ud-din (Imad-ul-Mulk), played a prominent part in the saddest events connected with the fall of the Mughal empire. In addition to the graves standing in a small enclosure surrounded by panels of pale-coloured sandstone, some pierced and some carved with flowers, there are a mosque and a college, the latter now occupied by the Anglo-Arabic School. The wooden doors in the Ajmer gateway are interesting as being similar to those of the Kashmir Gate, blown in on 14th September 1857.

Close to the Jama Masjid on the N.W. side is a **Jain Temple,** approached by narrow streets. It stands upon a high walled platform, gained by narrow steps, and consists of a small marble court surrounded by a stucco colonnade in front of the temple proper, which is surmounted by an oblong dome. Within, the ceiling and walls are richly gilded, and are supported by two rows of small marble columns. In the centre of the temple is a pyramidal platform in three tiers, upon which rests the small figure of a Jain saint, seated beneath an elaborate ivory canopy. Mr Fergusson[1] draws particular attention to the exquisite device in the porch of filling in the back of the struts which support the architrave beneath the dome with foliated tracery. To the N. the **Dariba** passes the Dufferin Hospital on the right, and leads to the **Chandni Chauk.** The portion of that famous street between this point and the Fort was called the Urdu, or Camp. On the N. side of it is a large

[1] *Indian Architecture*, ii. 67.

residence, occupied by the **Delhi Bank**; this formerly belonged to the Begam Samru, and here Mr Beresford, the manager of the bank, desperately defended himself and his family on 11th May 1857. W. of the Dariba came the Flower Market and the Jewellers' Market in the main street, and then the Chandni Chauk proper, which has swallowed up all the other names. Houses were built both across it and down it during the last years of Mughal rule; they were all removed early last century, and the branch of the W. Jumna Canal running down was closed over after the Mutiny. Opposite a fountain and the S.E. gate of the Queen's Gardens is the **Kotwali**, where many executions took place after September 1857, and on the W. side of the open space in front of it is the **Sonahri Masjid** of Roshan-ud-daulah, on the platform of which Nadir Shah sat in stony silence while the inhabitants of Delhi were being massacred by his troops. Further on, in the centre of the square in front of the famous **Karawan Sarai**, built by **Jahanara Begam**, daughter of the Emperor Shah Jahan, and held by Bernier to be one of the wonders of Delhi, rises the Northbrook Clock Tower; while on the N. side of the street, between it and the Municipal Buildings, is the **Statue of the Queen Empress**, presented to his fellow-citizens by Mr James Skinner, grandson of the famous Colonel Skinner, C.B., as a memorial of her late Majesty. (The excellent Empress Victoria Memorial Hospital for Women, built on the S. side of the space in front of the Jama Masjid, was opened in 1908.) Behind the buildings are the Begam or Queen's Gardens with a fine monolithic marble bath. The Chandni Chauk proper ends at the **Fatehpuri Mosque** constructed by Begam of Shah Jahan in 1650; it is built of red sandstone and is surmounted by a single dome. On the S. side of the mosque a street leads to the Lal Kua Bazar, and on the N. side another leads to the **Lahore Gate** and the smaller Sarhandi Mosque, erected by another wife of the Emperor, in front of it. Beyond the channel which connects the western Jumna Canal with the Agra Canal at Okhla, near the Sadar Bazar, are the quarters of Paharipur and Kishanganj (p. 190). To the S., on the crest of the ridge, is the **Idgah**, seen so clearly from the Mutiny monument; and to the S.W., at the foot of the ridge, is the picturesque enclosure of the **Kadam Sharif** or Sacred Foot, in which Prince Fateh Khan, eldest son of the Emperor Firoz Shah, was buried in 1373. The name is derived from the imprint of the feet of the Prophet Mohammed on a small slab preserved at the tomb. The road running from the front of the Fatehpuri Masjid past the W. end of the Queen's Gardens and the Cambridge Mission Church leads to the main road coming past the N. side of the gardens to the Kabul Gate. On the left side of the road, in a large house which once belonged to Nawab Safdar Jang, the **Cambridge Mission** is located. Besides the college and school under this mission, there is a large female Hospital at Tis Hazari, below the S. point of the Ridge. The lady workers of the mission, and the members of the Baptist Mission, reside in the Civil Station. Further on, just before arriving at the site of the **Kabul Gate**, now removed, a road inside the walls, reached by a bridge over the canal, leads to the spot where **Brigadier-General Nicholson** was mortally wounded, in pushing towards the Lahore Gate, on 14th September 1857.

(2) Tract lying N. of the City.

The Dufferin Bridge, crossing the railway from the above road, leads to the Mori Gate and the Civil Station. The **Mori** or **Shah Bastion**, 200 yards to the W. of the gate, affords a fine view of the S. end of the Ridge and of the N. wall front down to the Kashmir Gate. The present walls of Delhi were constructed by the British after the attack of the city by Jaswant Rao Holkar, in October 1805. The repulse of 70,000 Mahrattas, with 130 guns, by Colonel Burn, with two and a half battalions of Sepoys and two corps of irregular cavalry, was a most notable feat of arms, though now forgotten like the battle of Delhi in 1803 (p. 220). On the right, just outside the Kashmir Gate, is the **Kudsia Garden**, and on the left the Nicholson Garden, with the newly erected statue of General Nicholson by Sir T. Brock, R.A. He is buried in the cemetery N. of it. The grave is 50 yds. to the right of the entrance, and bears the brief soldierly inscription:

The Grave of
Brigadier-General JOHN NICHOLSON,
Who led the assault of Delhi, but fell
In the hour of victory
Mortally wounded,
And died 23rd of September 1857,
Aged 35 years.

To the left of the path leading straight from the gate is the grave of Mr Harvey Greathed, Political Officer with the Force before Delhi, who died of cholera four days after the assault. Just beyond the back (W.) wall of the cemetery is the right section of **No. 2 Siege Battery.** Passing, in the Kudsia Garden, the Flagstaff which bore the Royal Standard at the Coronation Durbar of 1st January 1903, the site of **No. 3 Battery** will be found to the S. of the mosque there, which still bears marks of the siege, and the **Mortar Battery** to the left of the N. entrance of the Gardens from the Grand Trunk Road. Just beyond this, on the opposite side, is **Ludlow Castle**, the residence of Mr Simon Fraser in 1857, and now the Delhi Club, with the left section of **No. 2 Battery** in the grounds close to the wall of the main road. Passing the offices of the W. Jumna Canal and Maiden's Hotel, the present residence of the Commissioner will be seen on the left hand. Close behind was the **Telegraph Office** in 1857, of which the staff remained on the spot till late in the afternoon of 11th May, and of which one member returned still later with an officer to send an official message to Amballah. It was the irresponsible talk of the office clerks along the line which really conveyed the news of the mutinies of Meerut and Delhi to Amballah, and so to Lahore, and enabled steps to be taken to check worse mischief in the Panjab. A quarter of a mile further on, across a small drainage ravine from the Ridge, is a high mound, on the crest of which defensive works are still discernible. This was the **Mound Picket**, and **Metcalfe House**, which formed the extreme left of our position before Delhi, lies 500 yds. E. of it, on the bank of the Jumna. The walk to the house, though now in utter ruin, will be found to well repay the trouble of it. The road now proceeds N. for ¾ m. and then turns W. through the Ridge, the northernmost outlier of the Aravallis, the Ridge Road to the left, leading past the grave of some of the officers of the 54th, murdered on 11th May 1857, to the **Flagstaff Tower**, to which another steeper road leads direct from the S. From the Tower a complete view is obtained of the whole position before Delhi, and of the encampment of the British Force below the Ridge, the pale dome of St James' Church marking the site of the Kashmir Gate, and the square roof of a factory that of the Mori Bastion. The large house to the West from the Flagstaff Tower is the Circuit House, built for the Viceroy at the Coronation Durbar, and occupied by the Prince of Wales in 1905. A pleasant walk may be taken through the old Cantonment, in which the lines of a native cavalry regiment and residences for the officers have been recently built, and which the Najafgarh Canal bounds on the further side. Near this is the **Rajpur Cemetery** where Major-General Sir H. Barnard and so many of the brave men who fell before Delhi lie buried.[1] There is a memorial cross of grey Aberdeen granite. Beyond

[1] This walk can be prolonged by 4 m. by walking N. through the old Cantonment to

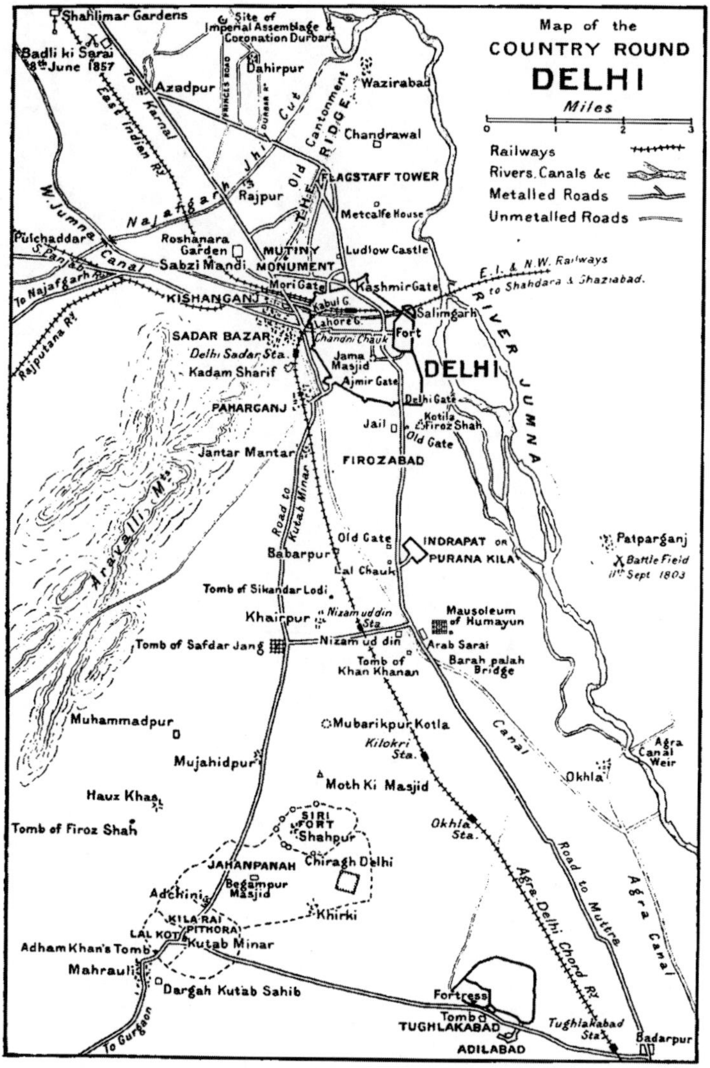
Map of the
COUNTRY ROUND
DELHI
Miles
0 1 2 3
Railways
Rivers, Canals &c
Metalled Roads
Unmetalled Roads
Shahlimar Gardens
Site of Imperial Assemblage & Coronation Durbars
Badli ki Sarai 8th June 1857
Azadpur
Dahirpur
Wazirabad
Chandrawal
FLAGSTAFF TOWER
Rajpur
Metcalfe House
Pulchaddar
Roshanara Garden
MUTINY MONUMENT
Ludlow Castle
Sabzi Mandi
Mori Gate
Kashmir Gate
KISHANGANJ
Kabul G.
Lahore G.
Salimgarh
Fort
SADAR BAZAR
Chandni Chauk
Delhi Sadar Sta.
Jama Masjid
Kadam Sharif
Ajmir Gate
DELHI
Delhi Gate
PAHARGANJ
Jail
Kotila Firoz Shah
Old Gate
Jantar Mantar
FIROZABAD
RIVER JUMNA
E. I. & N. W. Railways to Shahdara & Ghaziabad.
Aravalli Mts.
Old Gate
INDRAPAT OR PURANA KILA
Patparganj
Battle Field 11th Sept 1803
Babarpur
Lal Chauk
Tomb of Sikandar Lodi
Khairpur
Nizam ud din Sta
Mausoleum of Humayun
Tomb of Safdar Jang
Nizam ud din
Arab Sarai
Tomb of Khan Khanan
Barah palah Bridge
Muhammadpur
Mubarikpur Kotla
Kilokri Sta.
Agra Canal Weir
Mujahidpur
Okhla
Moth Ki Masjid
Hauz Khas
Tomb of Firoz Shah
Okhla Sta.
SIRI FORT
Shahpur
Chiragh Delhi
JAHANPANAH
Begampur Masjid
Adchini
Khirki
KILA RAI PITHORA
LAL KOT
Adham Khan's Tomb
Kutab Minar
Mahrauli
Dargah Kutab Sahib
Fortress
Tomb
TUGHLAKABAD
ADILABAD
Tughlakabad Sta.
Badarpur
To Gurgaon
To Karnal
East Indian Ry
W. Jumna Canal
Najafgarh Jhil Cut
Old Cantonment
THE RIDGE
Punjab Ry
To Najafgarh Rd
Rajputana Ry
Road to Kutab Minar
Canal
Road to Muttra
Agra Delhi Chord Ry
Agra Canal

To face p. 202.

the Canal was a battery, erected to protect the rear of our position. Four m. further down the road is the field of the battle of Badli-ki-Sarai, fought on 8th June 1857 (p. 190). A m. to the W. of the fine old Mughal Sarai are the ruins of the glorious Shahlimar Gardens of the Emperor Shah Jahan, the scene of the coronation of his usurping son, Aurangzeb. Half way to Badli-ki-Sarai, and removed some 2 m. to the N. side of the road, is the Plain of Barwari, on which the Imperial Assemblage of 1st January 1877 and the Coronation Durbar of 1st January 1903 were held, and presented scenes of splendour such as were never seen under the greatest of the Mughal Emperors. The Coronation Durbar of 1911 will also be held here.

Returning to the **Flagstaff Tower**, in which the ladies and children of the Cantonment were gathered, all the long afternoon of 11th May '57, and looked in vain for the troops from Meerut, and proceeding S. down the Ridge, the old mosque of the time of Firoz Shah, known as the **Chauburji Mosque**, is reached in half a mile. This formed the left of the British position on the Ridge, and round it traces of the breastworks may still be seen. The dark building that rises ½ m. further S. is the so-called **Observatory**, possibly the clock tower of the palace of Firoz Shah, known generally as the Pir Ghaib Mosque; to the E. of it the earthworks of a battery are still visible, and just beyond it is **Hindu Rao's House**, the key of the position on the Ridge which was so gallantly held by Major Reid (afterwards Sir Charles Reid, G.C.B.) with his little Goorkhas, supported by the 60th Rifles and the Guides. From the N. side of this, on the edge of the reservoir of the Delhi Water Works, a fine view is obtained of the slope from the Mori Gate up to the right of our position, to which the mutineers so often advanced. At the bottom of the slope, on the W. side, is a fine "baoli," which no doubt also belonged to the Hunting Palace of Firoz Shah, called Kushk-i-Shikar and Jahannuma, in which the **Lat of Asoka**, 250 yds. S. of Hindu Rao's house, was erected. The history of this column is given in the *inscription* on the base of it. Three hundred yards further S. again rises on a lofty platform the ungainly **Mutiny Memorial**, occupying the site of the right batteries of our position; on the poor panels round the base of the memorial are records of the troops who served before Delhi, of the various actions fought by them, of our losses, and the names of the officers who fell in them. Behind it to the W. was the Crow's Nest over the old flooded quarry, and in front of it, to the S.E., was the Sammy House. It was at this end of the Ridge that Timur entrenched himself after crossing the Jumna in December 1399, and repulsed an attack made on him by the minister of Mahmud Khan Tughlak. From it a fine view is obtained of the sites of the actual siege, the Sammy House Battery being in full view 400 yds. to the W., and the smashed face of the Mori Bastion 1000 yds. off, while the buildings of the Police Lines and Ludlow Castle and St James' dome indicate the position of the Siege Batteries. The Sammy House, quaintly named from the image of a deity (Swámi), in the court of a monastery, was held in order to check the attacks on the right, and round it some of the severest fighting took place; the Sammy House Battery was erected 100 yds. to the N. of it. In the dip of the Ridge which occurs at this point are seen the suburbs of Paharipur and Kishanganj, and further to the W. that of **Sabzi Mandi**,[1] through which the enemy so often attacked the British position, and even their right rear; while full in view, on the Ridge beyond the gap, are the walls of the great **Idgah**. W. of Sabzi Mandi

the end of the Ridge and the picturesque shrine of Shah Alam situated near Wazirabad, on the bank of a nullah spanned by an old Pathan bridge.

[1] Vegetable Market.

are the **Roshanara Gardens**, created by the daughter of Shah Jahan, who lies buried here. She died in 1671—three years before her sister, Jahanara Begam (p. 206).

(3) Tract lying immediately to the S. of the City.

It is more interesting to make the proposed round of this tract by starting on the E. side from the **Delhi Gate** and returning on the W. side to the **Ajmer Gate.**

Not far from the Delhi Gate were shot the rebel Princes whom Lieutenant Hodson had captured at the tomb of Humayun. 400 yds. from the gate a side road on the left leads from the Grand Trunk Muttra Road to the **Kotila of Firoz Shah,** which formed the citadel of the city of Firozabad founded by that Emperor. In the Kotila built up on the top of a lofty platform rises the second **Lat of Asoka,** which was brought here from Topra on the bank of the Jumna in the Umballa District. The pillar is 10 ft. 10 in. round where it leaves the platform, and the total height is 42 ft. 7 in., of which 4 ft. 1 in. are sunk in the masonry. At 10 ft. 1 in. from the base are some Nagri inscriptions, with the date in two of them, of Samwat 1581=1524 A.D. These must have been inscribed after the removal of the pillar to Delhi. Above these Nagri inscriptions is the Pali inscription, which contains the edict of Asoka, prohibiting the taking of life. This dates from the middle of the 3rd century B.C., and the characters are of the oldest form that has yet been found in India (see Introd., p. lxiii.). It is very clearly written, but when Feroz Shah assembled all the learned of the day to decipher the inscription, they were unable to do so. There is a second inscription, which records the victories of the Chauhan Prince Visaladeva, whose power extended from Himadri to Vindhya. This record consists of two portions, the shorter one immediately above Asoka's edicts, and the longer immediately below them. Both are dated Samwat 1220=1163 A.D., and refer to the same prince. The minor inscriptions are of little interest.

To the S. of the Lat is a **Mosque,** now much ruined, but which must once have been a very fine one; it was surrounded by arcades and by a covered hall borne by plain stone columns like those of the Kalan Masjid in Delhi. To the S. of it again are the large enclosures shut in by the very lofty walls which look so imposing from the Grand Trunk Road. Returning to this a fine Pathan gate of decorated stonework is passed on the left: it is known as the **Lal Darwazah** or Red Gate, and was apparently the northern gate of the short-lived capital of Sher Shah which probably was left incompleted. The ruins of **Firozabad** were extensively used for the construction of it and of the Delhi of Shah Jahan, and but little remains of that now, though scattered ruins show that its area must have been larger than that of the present city. Two miles to the S., on the site of the old Indrapat, rise the lofty walls of the **Purana Kila,** built by that prince or by him and Humayan, with their graceful high gates. The S. gate, by which the Fort is most conveniently entered, is reached by a bridge across an old branch of the Jumna here; opposite the point where the road to it turns back N. is a large red sandstone building known as the **Lal Chauk** or Red Enclosure with a fine gate and fine mosque built by Maham Anagah, foster-mother of the Emperor Akbar and mother of Adham Khan (p. 211). To the side of this is another gate similar to the Lal Darwazah, which formed the entrance of a large market. It is worth while to ascend the gate of the Purana Kila for the sake of the splendid view to the S., and to visit some of the large rooms under the inner wall in which the garrison was quartered. The narrow road running straight on from the gate leads in 300 yds. to the **Mosque of**

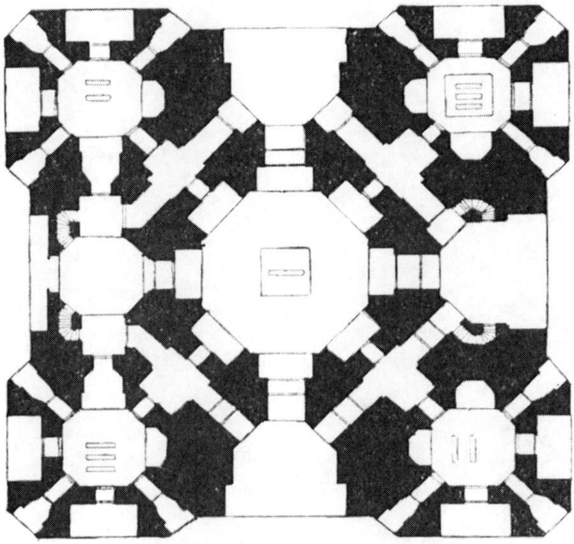

Plan of the Tomb of Humayun.

[To face p. 205.

Sher Shah, which is one of the handsomest and most picturesque structures at Delhi: the colour of the red sandstone, the brackets under the balconies, the floral carving round the arches, and the pendentives of the domes of the interior are all worthy of special notice. A little to the S. of the mosque is a red octagonal building called the Sher Mandal, on the steps of which the Emperor Humayun slipped in rising from the evening prayer, and received injuries of which he died a few days later (1550 A.D.).

Two miles further down the Grand Trunk Road[1] again, at a tomb with a dome of green glaze, side roads run left and right to the **Mausoleum of Humayun** and the shrine of Nizam-ud-din Aulia. The branch to the mausoleum runs round the **Bu Halima Garden** and its picturesque corner kiosks, and affords a partial view of the tomb and mosque of Isa Khan, inside the walls of **Arab Sarai**. Opposite the fine gate of this place, built, like the mausoleum, by the widow of the Emperor, the road turns back again to the noble portal of the enclosure of the tomb, the first important architectural work of the Mughals in India. The wings of the gate are sloped backwards at the sides, as are the angles of the corner rooms of the mausoleum. Each side is 156 ft. long, and the height to the top of the dome is 125 ft. It stands upon a high platform of red sandstone, and consists of a large central octagon surmounted by a dome with octagon towers of unequal sides at the angles. "Its plan is that afterwards adopted at the Taj, but used here without the depth and poetry of that celebrated building. It is, however, a noble tomb, and anywhere else must be considered a wonder" (Fergusson). The red sandstone of the exterior is most artistically picked out in relief with white marble.

[1] Left of the road will be seen a kos minar pillar or Mughal milestone. The kos of Akbar was 2 m. 1000 yds.

The windows are recessed, and the lower doors are filled in with beautiful lattices of stone and marble. In the centre of each side of the main octagon is a porch 40 ft. high, with a pointed arch. From the S. porch a door leads to the central octagonal chamber, with a diameter of 48 ft., in which is the cenotaph of the Emperor—it is of white marble, and quite plain, without any inscription. The actual grave chamber can be entered by a long, dark passage in the S. face of the platform. In the N.E. corner above is the tomb of his wife, Haji Begam,[1] and among the tombs in other chambers are believed to be those of Dara Shikoh, two brothers of Bahadur Shah, and the Emperors Jahandar Shah and Alamgir II. Steps lead from the side of the E. and W. bays, first up to a gallery round the upper portion of the central chamber, and then to the terrace round the neck of the great dome. The buildings on the terrace which once formed a small college afford a splendid view of the country on all sides. Inside the garden of the mausoleum, which measures 13 acres, is a pretty tomb of red sandstone, with some beautiful grilles; outside at the S.E. corner rises the blue dome of the tomb of Fahim Khan, while half a mile away to the S.W. is the huge half-ruined tomb of **Khanan Khan**. Outside the N.E. corner of the garden, but not visible from here, is an interesting enclosure and mosque, said to have been the abode of Nizam-ud-din Aulia. It was at the mausoleum of Humayun, it will be remembered, that Lieutenant Hodson received the surrender of Bahadur Shah, ex-King of Delhi, and of two of his sons and a grandson, after the capture of the city. The garden of the tomb, and those of Isa Khan and Safdar Jung are being well restored now. Every one who can should visit the tomb and mosque of **Isa Khan**, now in satisfactory surroundings, of Khanan Khan (despoiled by a Nawab of Oudh), and the old Barahpalah Bridge beyond it.

[1] Her title was Mariam Mukami.

The **Dargah** or **Shrine of Nizam-ud-din Aulia**, stands on the left side of the branch road to the W. On the N. side, are the Lal Mahal or Red Palace, possibly of Ala-ud-din Khilji, and the Barah Khambe or Twelve Columns; and on the S.E. side, in the village, a fine but ruined mosque, with four arcaded courtyards, similar to that at Khirki (p. 212), and of the date of 1372 A.D. The gateway of the shrine leads directly on to the tank, a special feature at Chishti Dargahs, and in this instance the traditional cause of the quarrel between the Emperor Tughlak Shah and the Saint, who lived to the age of ninety-two, and died in 1324 A.D. The story runs that the Emperor requisitioned the workmen on the tank for labour on his fortress at Tughlakabad, and that when the Saint arranged to carry on his work at night, the Emperor forbade the sale of oil to him. Thereupon the water of the tank miraculously served as oil, and was duly cursed by the incensed King, in return for which the Saint cursed Tughlakabad. Be the cause what it may have been, there can be no reasonable doubt that Nizam-ud-din was concerned with Ala-ud-din in the plot against the Emperor; and the saying with which he comforted his disciples when told that the King was returning to punish him, and, indeed, was only a few miles distant—"Dilli hanoz dur ast" ("Delhi is still far off")—has passed into the currency of a proverb. On the right side of the tank are some tombs, and from these and from the enclosure walls men and boys dive into the water. On the left side a covered passage leads to an inner gate, and yet to another, which gives admittance to the court in which the **Tomb of the Saint** stands. This is built of white marble, and is 18 ft. square, and surrounded by a broad verandah: it has been restored and altered on many occasions, and there is very little of the original structure left in it now. Round the covered grave is a low marble rail, and over it is a canopy inlaid with mother-of-pearl: in the walls are fine pierced screens. To the W. of the tomb is a fine red sandstone mosque called the **Jamat Khana**, with a large central compartment and two side bays, somewhat in the style of the Alai Darwazah; and at the N. end of the enclosure is a Rest House built by the Emperor Aurangzeb. S. of the tomb of the saint are from W. to E. the grave enclosures of **Jahanara Begam**, sister of that Emperor; of **Muhammed Shah**, Emperor 1719-1748; and **Prince Jahangir**, son of Akbar Shah. The grave of the first is open to the sky and has grass planted in the hollow in the top of it: the erect gravestone at the head embodies the sentiment of this humble arrangement. This was the lady successfully treated by Mr Gabriel Broughton, who asked as his reward certain trade concessions to the English in Bengal. The other two tombs have elaborately carved marble doors in the archways in the screens of beautiful pierced marble work which surround them. Beyond the central court is another called the **Chabutarah Yarani** or Seat of the Friends, where the Saint used to sit with his disciples; the beauty of both these courts is greatly enhanced by the fine trees in them. To the right in this enclosure is the tomb of the famous poet, **Amir Khusrau**, the friend of the Saint, whom he survived for a few days only. In the inscription on the walls he is termed the Tuti-i-shakar makál or sweet-tongued parrot. The grave chamber is surrounded by two galleries, and only a very subdued light reaches it.

E. of the tank, on a higher level, is the picturesque polychrome tomb, well restored, of **Azam Khan**—known also as **Atgah Khan**, who saved the life of the Emperor Humayun at the battle of Kanauj, and was a foster-father of the Emperor Akbar. He defeated Bairam Khan when that general rebelled, and was murdered at Agra in 1556 by Adham Khan (p. 211). Two hundred yds. further to the S.E. is the Hall known as the **Chausath Khambe**, or Sixty-four Pillars, which forms the family vault of the sons and brothers of Azam Khan, who were known as the Atgah Khail or Gang, from the royal favours which were showered on them. It was built by Aziz Kokaltash, foster-brother of Akbar, who died in 1624 A.D.

About 2 m. from Dargah towards the Tomb of Safdar Jang will be seen a fine domed mausoleum on the left, and four similar buildings on the right. The first is that of **Mubarik Shah**, murdered in 1433. Of those on the N. side of the road the nearest figured in Fergusson's *Architecture of India* covers the grave of another Saiyad King **Muhammed Shah**; the next is the fine gateway to a mosque beautifully decorated with plaster, and the most splendid specimen of this work in all India; the third is a nameless tomb, and the fourth, N. of the village and close to a fine stone bridge, is the mausoleum of **Sikandar Lodi** (1489-1517), built in the middle of a fine fortified enclosure. No one who can by any means make an hour available should fail to visit these northern buildings.

Half a mile to the W. and facing the end of the road is the mausoleum of **Nawab Safdar Jang** (d. 1754), by which title Mansur Ali Khan, the second prince of Oudh and first Nawab Vazir, was known. The large garden enclosure is entered by a fine gateway, to the N. of which is a mosque opening to the outside of the garden. The tomb stands on a high platform at the end of a paved walk, once with water down the centre of it as at the Taj. It is 90 ft. sq., and is arranged in three storeys; some of the fawn-coloured stonework on it is very effective, but the marble decoration inlaid on the corner red towers greatly spoils the general effect. In the centre chamber is the carved tomb of Safdar Jang, and in the chamber below are two earthen graves. The plaster decoration of this chamber and the rooms round it is perhaps the weakest feature of the building. The view from the top of the roof is very fine. The garden which was once much neglected has been improved of late years. Three miles to the N. on the road to Delhi is a ruined **Observatory**, erected like those at Ujjain, Jaipur, and Benares by Maharaja Jai Singh of Jaipur about 1725 A.D. (See Jaipur Observatory, p. 140.) The largest of the buildings is an immense equatorial dial, named by the Raja the Samrat Yantra, or "Prince of Dials," the dimensions of the gnomon being as follows:—

	ft.	in.
Length of hypothenuse .	118	5
,, base . .	104	0
,, perpendicular	56	7

To the S. of the gnomon are two circular structures, with niches in the walls to enable the ascension and declension of the stars to be marked on them. Two m. N. of the Observatory is the Ajmer Gate of the city.

(4) The extreme S. of the Surroundings of Delhi, including the Kutab (11 m. from Delhi) and Tughlakabad (5 m. from the Kutab).

Immediately S. of the tomb of Safdar Jang is the field of battle upon which Timur utterly defeated Mahammad Shah Tughlak and his minister on 12th December 1398, and became master of Old Delhi. A mile further S. on the left side of the road is seen the dark wall of the Idgah, where Timur encamped the day after the battle. E. of this rise the walls of **Siri**, and to the S. of them a lofty platform known as the Badi Mandal, and the **Begumpur Mosque** with its many domes. This mosque had an extremely fine court, and was built by the Wazir Jahan Khan in the reign of the Emperor Firoz Shah: it is now occupied by a village in which some Europeans were concealed in 1857. A little further on, and about 1½ m. to the W. of the road, a gleaming dome rising above trees indicates the **Mausoleum** of that Emperor, who died in 1389. It is built on the S.E. corner of the **Hauz Khas**, constructed by 'Ala-ud-din Khilji, and is well deserving of a visit on account of its picturesque situation. It was here that Timur first rested after his victory. At the ninth milestone from Delhi the road passes through the **Jahanpanah** defences, which were constructed to connect Siri, the new city of 'Ala-ud-din, with the older Delhi to the S. of it. The wall of this, originally the **Fort of Rai Pithora,** is crossed at the 10th m., whence the northern wall of the citadel of **Lal Kot** is well seen. In the middle of the E. side of the Lal Kot is the Kutab enclosure, and on the S. wall is the tomb of Adham Khan. Rai Pithora is the local name of the Prithvi Raja, the gallant Chauhan Prince of Ajmer, grandson of both Anang Pal II. Tomar and his conqueror Bisal Deo, Chauhan, who checked Shahab-ud-din Ghori near Thanesar in 1191, but was defeated and put to death the next year, his fortress falling in 1193.

The arrangement of the buildings of the **Kutab Minar Enclosure** will be readily understood from the accompanying plan. The original **Kuwat ul Islam Mosque** was begun by Kutab-ud-din Aibak when Viceroy of Shahab-ud-din Ghori, after the capture of Delhi in 1193 A.D., as recorded by the King himself in the long inscription over the inner archway of the E. entrance. Even in ruins it is a magnificent work. It was seen by Ibn Batuta about 150 years after its erection, when he describes it as having no equal, either in beauty or extent, and was extolled by the poet, Amir Khusrau, who specially mentions the extension of 'Ala-ud-din. It is not so large as the great mosques of Jaunpur and others, but is still unrivalled for its grand line of gigantic arches, and for the graceful beauty of the flowered tracery which covers its walls. It occupies the platform on which stood Rai Pithora's Hindu Temple, demolished by the Mohammedans. Altamsh in 1210-1230 surrounded it by a larger cloistered court, in the S.E. corner of which stands the Kutab Minar, and extended the great screen of arches N. and S. across the extensions on these sides; and in 1300 'Ala-ud-din appended a further eastern court, entered by his great S. gateway, the Alai Darwazah, and designed a great addition, with a further extension of the screen on the N. side, in which the Alai Minar was to correspond to the Kutab Minar: ruined piers of these still remain on the W. and N. sides. The main entrance to the original mosque is an arched gateway in the centre of its E. wall. Steps ascending under this lead to the courtyard (142 ft. by 108 ft.), which is surrounded by cloisters formed of Jain pillars placed one upon another. Most of these are richly ornamented; many of the figures have been defaced by the Mohammedans, though some may still be found in unnoticed corners. The Arabic inscription over the E. gate states that the materials were obtained from the demolition of twenty-seven idolatrous temples, each of which had cost twenty-seven lakhs of dilials, fifty dilials being equal to one rupee. The domed pavilions in the angles of the cloisters are worthy of notice.

The famous Iron Pillar (see p. 210) stands in front of the central opening to the mosque proper, a building of small proportions, and now in ruins, overtopped and hidden by the grand screen of lofty arches which occupies the whole of the W. side. This screen was erected by Kutab-ud-din later than his other work, and was extended beyond on either side for 115 ft. by Altamsh. The central arch is 53 ft. high by 22 ft. wide. "The Mohammedan conquerors had a tolerably distinct idea that pointed arches were the true form of architectural openings, but being without science sufficient to construct them, they left the Hindu architects and

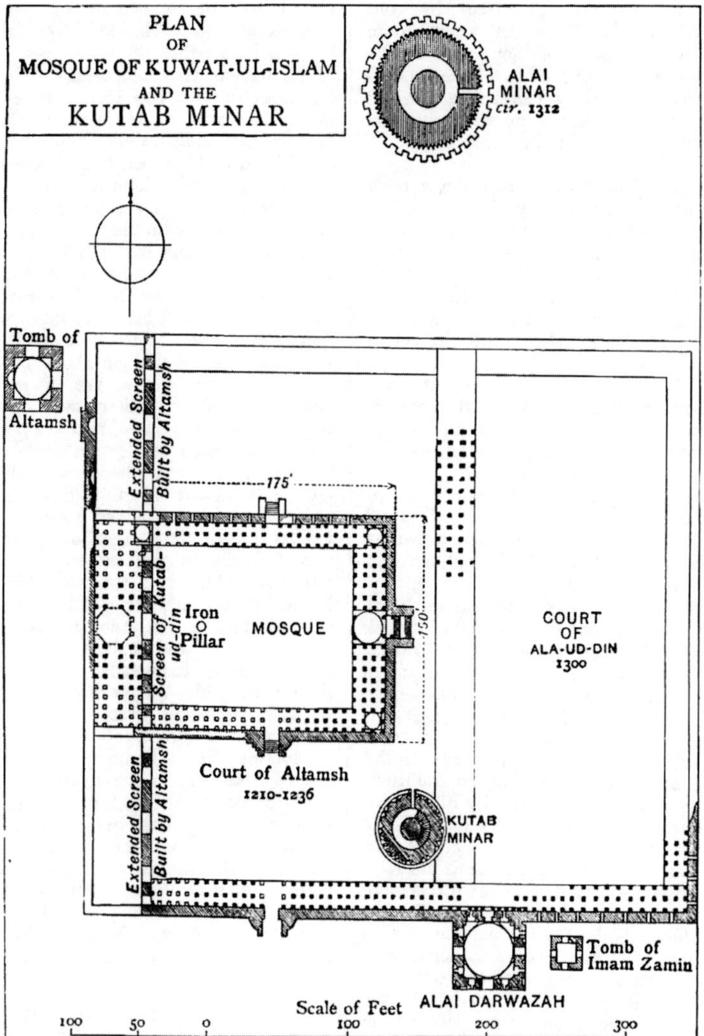

Walker & Boutall sc.

builders to follow their own devices as to the mode of carrying out the form. Accordingly they proceeded to make the pointed openings on the same principle upon which they built their domes—they carried them up in horizontal courses as far as they could and then closed them by long slabs meeting at the top." The impost in the central arch was added by the British restorers. The ornamentation, interspersed with texts from the Koran, is evidently taken from that on the old pillars of the cloister. Fragments of the roof of the mosque still remain, supported by old columns, and do not reach more than one-third of the height of the screen in front of it. When Delhi was captured by Timur, the Mughals massacred all the persons who had taken refuge in the mosque.

The **Iron Pillar** is one of the most curious antiquities in India. It is a solid shaft of wrought iron, more than 16 in. in diameter, and 23 ft. 8 in. in length. The height of the pillar above ground is 22 ft., but the smooth shaft is only 15 ft., the capital being 3½ ft. and the rough part below also 3½ ft.

"The Iron Pillar records its own history in a deeply cut Sanscrit inscription of six lines on its W. face, which was translated by Mr James Prinsep (*B.A.S. Journ.*, vol. vii. p. 630). The pillar is called 'the Arm of Fame of Raja Dhava.' It is said that he subdued a people on the Sindhu, named Vahlikas, and obtained, with his own arm, an undivided sovereignty on the earth for a long period." The pillar which was probably brought from Muttra, once no doubt bore the eagle of Vishnu. Other masses of welded iron exist at Dhar and Kanarak.[1] Mr Prinsep assigns the 3rd or 4th century after Christ as the date of the inscription. According to tradition, the pillar was erected by Bilan Deo, or Anang Pal, the founder of the Tomar dynasty, and rested on the head of a great snake until the Raja unwisely moved it to see if this were so, an act which cost the Tomars their kingdom. The name of Anang Pal also is inscribed on the shaft, with the date Samwat 1109=1052 A.D. Four ft. above the inscription is a deep indentation, said to have been made by a cannon-ball fired by the troops of the Bharatpur Raja.

The **Kutab Minar** is a grand monument, and looks what it is intended to be—a tower of victory. It has been a question whether it was not originally Hindu, altered and completed by the Mohammedan conquerors, but the conclusion of General Cunningham, that it is a purely Mohammedan structure, seems to be the right one.[1] The lowest storey bears the name of Muhammed bin Sam (Shahabuddin), and of Kutab-ud-din Aibak, and the next three storeys contain that of Altamsh. At the entrance door is an inscription of Sikander Lodi with the date 1503. As seen at present, it is 238 ft. high, and rises in a succession of five storeys, marked by corbelled balconies and decorated with bands of inscription. The base diameter is 47 ft. 3 in., and that of the top about 9 ft. The three first storeys are of red sandstone with semicircular and angular flutings; the two upper storeys are faced chiefly with white marble, and were almost entirely rebuilt by Firoz Shah Tughlak in 1368, when he also added a cupola. On 1st August 1803, the whole pillar was seriously injured by an earthquake and the cupola thrown down. It was injudiciously restored in 1829, the battlements of the balconies being removed and replaced by the present flimsy balustrades. Notice should be taken of the honeycomb work beneath the brackets of the first-storey balconies, of which the "structure differs in no perceptible degree from that in the Alhambra." The lowest great band of text inscription is extremely beautiful, and is well seen from the top of the cloister of the mosque or of the Alai Gate. A magnificent view is obtained from the summit, reached by 379 steps; but that from the first gallery, 95 ft. above the ground, is nearly as fine.

The **Tomb of Altamsh** (who died in 1235 A.D.) stands outside the N.W. corner of his extension of the mosque. It is of red sandstone. The main

[1] See pp. 89 and 332.

[1] For particulars regarding the discussion, see *Archæo. Reports*, vol. i. p. 190.

entrance is to the E., but there are also openings to the N. and S. The interior is almost completely covered with beautiful decoration, and is inscribed with finely written passages of the Koran; in the centre of the W. side is a Kiblah of white marble discoloured with age. The tomb is in the centre, and stands on a high base; the top part is of modern masonry. General Cunningham notes that though there is no roof, "there is good reason to believe that it was originally covered by an overlapping Hindu dome. A single stone of one of the overlapping circles, with Arabic letters on it, still remains." Mr Fergusson points out, "In addition to the beauty of its details, it is interesting as being the oldest tomb known to exist in India."

The **Alai Darwazah**, 40 ft. to the S.E. from the Kutab Minar, is the S. entrance of the great or outer enclosure to the mosque. It was built of red sandstone richly ornamented with patterns in low relief, in 1310 A.D., by 'Ala-ud-din. Over three of the entrances are Arabic inscriptions, which give 'Ala-ud-din's name, and his well-known title of Sikandar Sani, the second Alexander, with the date 710 A.H. The building is a square with lofty doorways, with pointed horse-shoe arches on three sides, and a rounded arch curiously decorated on the inner side. In each corner there are two windows closed by massive screens of marble lattice-work. The gate stands high above the ground to the S. of it, and should be viewed from that side. A few yards to the E. stands the richly-carved building in which is the tomb of **Imam Zamin.** He came to Delhi in the reign of Sikandar Lodi, and died in 944 A.H.=1537 A.D. The tomb is a small domed building, about 18 ft. square, of red sandstone covered with chunam. There is an inscription in the Tughra character over the door.

The **Alai Minar** stands 150 ft. N. of the original Kutab enclosure. The inner tower and outer wall are of very coarse work, of large rough stones: the flutings in the exterior show the shape which the Minar would have assumed when lined with red sandstone. The total height as it now stands is 70 ft. above the plinth, or 87 ft. above the ground level. Had this pillar been finished it would have been about 500 ft. high. In the S.W. corner of the *outer* enclosure corresponding with the tomb of Altamsh are a group of ruined buildings. That on the S. side is believed to have been the tomb of 'Ala-ud-din, whose grave was in the centre room of it.

To the S.E. of the Kutab Minar is a tomb of a brother of Adham Khan, once used as a country house by Sir T. Metcalfe, and 500 yds. beyond it is a fine mosque of the latest Pathan style, known as the **Jamali** Mosque. At the N.E. corner of it in a separate enclosure is the pretty tomb of Shekh Fazl-ullah decorated with bright tiles. 200 yds. due E. of the mosque in the midst of mounds of ruins are the broken massive walls of the **Tomb of the Emperor Balban** (1287 A.D.), which formed a Dar-ul-Aman or House of Refuge in his life-time.

To the W. of the Kutab enclosure which is bounded by the road from Delhi to Mahrauli a paved way leads to a well-known Hindu temple called the Jog Maya. 200 yds. further S. the tomb of **Adham Khan** rises high on the S. wall of Lal Kot. Adham Khan, who was half-brother as well as foster-brother of Akbar, murdered Azam Khan, whose wife was also foster-mother to the Emperor, in the palace of Agra, and was thrown down from the terrace there by the Emperor, who himself felled him with a blow of the fist as he issued from his private apartments. Adham Khan had previously distinguished himself by driving the mistress of the last King of Malwa to suicide upon capturing Mandu, while his mother, not to be outdone, put to death two of that prince's daughters for fear that they might complain to the Emperor. She is said to have died of a broken heart a few days after her son, and to have been buried here too. The tomb is entirely constructed of materials taken from some Pathan tomb of the middle period.

A short distance to the S.E. of the tomb across the road, is a large round well into which also men and boys dive. Not far from this is the northern entrance of the **Dargah** or shrine of **Kutab-ud-din** Bakhtiar Kaki; the inner gateway and the ruined music-gallery gate on the right of the approach date from the time of Salim Shah. Close to a third gateway is the grave enclosure of the Nawabs of Jhajjar, the last of whom was hung in 1857. In the main courtyard, which is but small, are a mosque and the tomb of Mohamed Khan; on the right and standing back from them is a gate to another court and the main W. approach to the shrine. South of this western court is an enclosure with a pretty but feeble **Moti Masjid** of white marble, built by Bahadur Shah, eldest son of Aurangzeb, in 1709, and beyond it in a separate court are the simple graves of the Kings of Delhi Akbar Shah II. (died 1837), of the blind Shah Alam (d. 1806), and of the **Emperor Bahadar Shah** (d. 1712). The space between the last two was to have been the resting-place of the last King of Delhi, who died at Rangoon in 1862. From the Eastern courtyard a passage paved and lined with marble and with a fine pierced marble screen on the right hand leads past the **Grave of the Saint** which stands in the open protected by an awning above it: on the back wall of this enclosure, which may be entered only with uncovered feet, is some fine work of glazed tiles dating from the time of Aurangzeb. The saint, who was born at Ush in Turkestan, and perhaps came to Delhi before the Mohammedan conquest, died during the reign of Altamsh in 1235 A.D.: his name Káki is derived from the alleged miracle of his having been fed by heavenly food—*kák*=cake. Outside the innermost shrine is the mosque where the saint used to pray, and beyond it is a picturesque baoli tank, now dry. At the W. end of this is the grave of **Zabita Khan,** and another said to be that of Ghulam Kadir Khan, who thus, if the grave be really his, rests near his unhappy victim Shah Alam. To the S. of these is a small court with the graves of the family of the Nawab of Loharu.

Outside the W. gate are a fine gateway known as the Mahal Sarai, and beyond it a pretty mosque standing on a high platform built by Ahsanullah Khan, physician of the last King of Delhi. Turning S. from here for 400 yds. along the main picturesque street of Mahrauli the **Shamsi Hauz,** the great tank of Shams-ud-din Altamsh, will be reached on the right. It was constructed by that Emperor, and has a ruined pavilion in the centre like the Hauz Khas of 'Ala-ud-din, and must have been very picturesque when full of water. On the E. bank is an interesting building of red sandstone called the Jaház or Ship, and beyond it the **Aulia Masjid** where according to tradition thanks were offered up on the capture of Delhi in 1191. On the opposite side of the road here is the picturesque Jhirna (Spring) garden through which the water of the tank descended and found its way past the tomb of Balban to Tughlakabad. The walk down the depression to the tomb is exceedingly pretty.

The Fort of **Tughlakabad** lies 5 m. to the E. of the Kutab. The road descends from the Lal Kot just beyond the removed modern cupola of the Kutab, and passes through the eastern wall of Kila Rai Pithora, a mile further on. The N.E. portion of this wall runs 1¼ m. up to **Khirki,** where there is a most interesting covered mosque with four open courts, each 32 ft. sq., built by Jahan Khan in 1380; it must be visited on foot, but is well worth a visit. Adjoining the mosque on the E. is a fine sluice of seven bays, and ¾ m. N.E. again is the Dargah of Chiragh Delhi, the last great Delhi Saint, who died in 1356, and the tomb of Bahlol Lodi (d. 1488). Long before it is reached the great Fort of Tughlak Shah is seen rising high above the plain to the left of the road. General Cunningham writes that "it may be described with tolerable accuracy as a half hexagon in shape, with three faces of rather more than ¾ m. in length, and a base of 1½ m., the whole circuit being only 1 furlong less than 4 m. It stands on a rocky height, and is built of massive blocks of stone, so large and heavy that they must have been quarried on the spot. The largest measured was 14 ft. in length by 2 ft. 2 in., and 1 ft. thick, and weighed rather more than 6 tons. The short faces to the W., N., and E. are protected by a deep ditch, and the long face to the S. by a large sheet of water, dry, except in the rainy season, which is held up by an embankment at the S.E. corner. On this side the rock is scarped, and above it the main walls rise to a mean height of 40 ft., with a parapet of 7 ft., behind which rises another wall of 15 ft., the whole height above the low ground being upwards of 90 ft." It had thirteen gates, and there are three inner gates to the citadel.

Opposite the causeway to the tomb, a gateway with a Hindu arch leads into the fort at the point where the largest of the tanks in it was excavated. Beyond this, to the N.W. and N., are ruins of the palace and a mosque, and high above it, in the S.W. angle, is the citadel, which occupies about one-sixth of the area. It contains the ruins of an extensive palace, surmounted by an inner citadel from which there is a splendid view. The ramparts are raised on a line of domed rooms, which rarely communicate with each other, and which formed the quarters of the garrison. One dark passage near the S.E. corner below the inner citadel leads to a small sally-port in the outer wall. The walls slope inwards, and the vast size, strength, and visible solidity of the whole, give tc Tughlakabad an air of stern and massive grandeur that is both striking and impressive.

In the N. part of the fort below are the ruined walls of a Jama Masjid. The curse of the Nizam-ud-din Aulia upon Tughlakabad was:

"Ya base Gujar
Ya rahe ujar"

("May it be inhabited by Gujars
or may it remain desolate")

and while it is impressively desolate now, it also contains small Gujar colonies in the midst of its desolation.

The fine *Tomb of Tughlak Shah* is outside the S. wall of Tughlakabad, in the midst of an artificial lake, and surrounded by a pentagonal outwork, which is connected with the fort by a causeway 600 ft. long, supported on twenty-seven arches. Mr Fergusson says: "The sloping walls and almost Egyptian solidity of this mausoleum, combined with the bold and massive towers of the fortifications that surround it, form a picture of a warrior's tomb unrivalled anywhere." The outer walls have a slope of 2·333 in. per foot; at base they are 11½ ft. thick, and at top 4 ft. The exterior decoration of the tomb itself depends chiefly on difference of colour, which is effected by the use of bands and borders of white marble inserted in the red sandstone. In plan it is a square, and three of its four sides have lofty archways, the space above the doorway being filled with a white marble lattice screen of bold pattern. It is surmounted by a white marble dome. In the S.W. corner of the enclosure is a small domed chamber with a number of graves.

"Inside the mausoleum there are three cenotaphs, which are said to be those of Tughlak Shah, his Queen, and their son Juna Khan, who took the name of Muhammad when he ascended the throne." This King was, and is still, known as the Khuni Sultan, "the bloody King." Firoz

Shah, his successor, bought acquittances, from all those he had wronged, and put them in a chest at the head of his tomb, that he might present them when called to judgment.

Opposite the S.W. corner of Tughlakabad a fine embankment which held up the waters of the lake connects **Adilabad** with it; there is a sluice between it and the rocky ground at the N. end. Adilabad is said to have been built by Muhammed Tughlak; there is a fine gate in the Hindu style in the W. face, and a magnificent view from the top of the mausoleum and fort, and the Kutab Minar. A little further to the E. is an isolated fortified residence, called the Nai's (Barber's) Fort, which seems to have been a college or the residence of some saint. 2½ m. further on, and 8 m. from the Kutab, is **Badarpur**, on the Grand Trunk Road and railway from Delhi to Muttra. Tilpat lies 4 m. S.W. of Badarpur. From this place it is 7 m. to the mausoleum of Humayun and shrine of Nizam-ud-din.

ROUTE 15.

(*a*) DELHI to **KASAULI** (171 m.), and **Simla** (219 m.) by **Panipat**, **Thanesar**, **Umballa** and **Kalka** (162 m.).

(*b*) DELHI to **LAHORE** by **Ghaziabad** Junction, **Meerut**, **Sardhana**, **Saharanpur**, **Umballa**, **Sirhind**, **Ludhiana**, **Jullundur**, **Amritsar** and **Lahore Cantonment** (349 m.).

There are two railway routes from *Delhi to Umballa*, and to further N., viz.:

(1) The direct E.I. Railway line on the W. bank of the Jumna through Panipat and Karnal, 123 m., in 4 to 6 hrs.—fares, Rs. 10, Rs. 5, Rs. 1 As. 12.

(2) The N.W. Railway line on the E. bank of the river, crossing it twice, and passing through Ghaziabad, Meerut, and Saharanpur, 162 m. in 6 to 8 hrs.—fares, Rs. 15, Rs. 7½, Rs. 2.

(1)

Leaving the central station at Delhi, the railway proceeds over a level plain to

9 m. **Bádli.** Before reaching this station, the ruins of the Shahlimar gardens (p. 203) are seen on the left, and the battlefield of Badli-ki-Sarai (p. 190) on the right. From here the tract irrigated by the W. Jumna Canal is entered.

27 m. **Sonepat**, an ancient place, and with Panipat (see below), Baghpat (lying E. on the Jumna), Indrapat (p. 204), and Tilpat (see above), one of the five estates or pats over which the traditional conflict of the Mahabharata took place about 1000 B.C. (p. lviii. Introd.).

55 m. **Panipat** station, D.B. (Population, 27,000). The modern town stands near the old bank of the Jumna, upon a high mound consisting of the *débris* of earlier buildings. In the centre the streets are well paved, but the outskirts are low and squalid. There are the usual civil offices.

Panipat is famous as the place where three of the most decisive battles in India have been fought; but the silent plain tells no tales, and shows scarcely any sign of the events that have happened on it.

Here, on the 21st April 1526, Babar encountered Ibrahim Lodi, King of Delhi. On the night before the battle Babar had sent out 5000 men to make a night attack on the Indian army, but this had failed, owing to a delay on the part of the attacking force, which did not reach the enemy's camp till dawn. With the first streaks of light next day the Mughal pickets reported that the Indians were advancing in battle array. Babar immediately prepared for action, and stationed strong flanking parties of Mughals on the right and left of his line, who, when ordered, were to wheel round, and take the enemy in flank and rear. When the Indians arrived at the Mughal lines they hesitated for a moment, and Babar availed himself of their halting to attack them, at the same time sending his flanking parties to wheel round and charge them in the rear. Babar's left wing was roughly handled, but he supported it by a strong detachment from the centre, and the Indians in the end were driven back. On the right, too, the battle was obstinately contested, but Babar's artillery was the more effective, and at last the Indians fell into confusion. They maintained the battle till noon, when they gave way in all directions. The rest was mere pursuit and slaughter. According to Mughal accounts, 15,000 Indians were left dead on the field of battle, and those who fled from the field were chased as far as Agra. The body of Ibrahim Lodi[1] was found the same afternoon amidst 5000 or 6000 of his soldiers lying in heaps around him, and was specially honoured by the victor. Babar reached Delhi on the third day after the battle, and on the Friday following his name as Emperor was read in the public prayers.

The **Second** Great battle was fought in the latter part of 1556 A.D., when the youthful Akbar, who had just succeeded his father the Emperor Humayun, and his general, Bahram Khan, defeated Himu,[2] the general of Sultan Muhammad Shah 'Adil, nephew of Sher Shah. Himu had 50,000 cavalry, and 500 elephants, besides infantry and guns; but after a well-contested battle he was wounded in the eye by an arrow, taken prisoner, and put to death. This battle was decisive of the fate of the Pathan dynasty called the Sur, founded by Sher Shah, 1540-45, and finally established the fortunes of the House of Timur.

The **Third** Battle took place on the 7th of January 1761 A.D., when the whole strength of the Mahrattas was crushed with terrible slaughter by Ahmad Shah Durani, the Afghan King. All the Mahratta chieftains of note, Holkar Sindhia, the Gaekwar, the Peshwa's cousin and son, were present with their forces. The Mahratta army is said to have amounted to 15,000 infantry, 55,000 cavalry, 200 guns, and Pindaris and camp-followers numbering 200,000 men. The Afghan force consisted of 38,000 infantry, 42,000 cavalry, and 70 guns, besides numerous irregulars. The Mahrattas had allowed themselves to be cooped up in their camp for many days, and were compelled to fight by impending starvation. On the morning of the battle they marched out with the ends of their turbans loose, their heads and faces anointed with turmeric, and with every other sign of despair. Seodasheo Rao, the cousin and generalissimo of the Peshwa, with Wishwas Rao, the Peshwa's eldest son, and Jaswant Rao Holkar, were opposite the Afghan Grand Vazir. The great standard of the Mahratta nation, the *Bhagwa Jhanda*, floated in the Mahratta van, and there were three *Jaripatkas*, or Grand Ensigns, of the Peshwa in the field.

The Mahrattas made a tremendous charge full on the Afghan centre, and broke through 10,000 cavalry under the Vazir, which unwisely received them without advancing. The dust and confusion were so great that the combatants could only distinguish each other by their war-cries. The Vazir Shah Wali Khan, who was in full armour, threw himself from his horse to rally his men, but most of them here gave way; while Ibrahim Khan Gardie, who commanded the Mahratta artillery, broke the Rohillas who formed the right wing of the Mohammedan army, and killed or wounded 8000 of them. Ahmad Shah now evinced his generalship; he sent his personal guards to rally the fugitives, and ordered up his reserves to support the Vazir. In this protracted and close struggle the physical strength of the Afghans proved an overmatch for the slighter frames of the Hindus. A little after 2 P.M. Wishwas Rao was mortally wounded,

[1] The alleged grave of the King lies on the N.W. side of the city.

[2] Himu, who had driven Humayun's Governor out of Delhi, had the misfortune to lose his guns before the battle.

and Seodasheo Rao, after sending a secret message to Holkar, charged into the thickest of the fight, and disappeared. Whatever the message to Holkar was, it proved instantaneously fatal, for he went off, and was followed by the Gaekwar. Scindiah, who left the field last, was cut down by an Afghan horseman many miles from it; he used to say that for long years afterwards he constantly saw in his dreams his grim pursuer gaining and gaining on him, and finally leave him for dead. The Mahrattas then fled; thousands were cut down, and vast numbers were destroyed in the ditch of their entrenchment. The village of Panipat was crowded with men, women and children, to whom the Afghans showed no mercy. They took the women and children as slaves, and after ranging the men in lines, amused themselves with cutting off their heads.

76 m. **Karnal** station, D.B. (Population, 23,000). This town is traditionally of great antiquity, being said to have been founded by Raja Karna, champion of the Kauravas, in the great war of the Mahabharata. It was seized by the Raja of Jind in the middle of the 18th century, and wrested from him in 1795 by the adventurer George Thomas. It was conferred by Lord Lake in 1803 upon Nawab Muhammud Khan, a Mandil Pathan. A British cantonment was maintained here until 1841, when it was abandoned, probably owing to the unhealthiness of the site, as the W. Jumna Canal, passing the city, intercepted the drainage and caused malarial fever. The Canal has since been re-aligned. A wall 12 ft. high encloses the town. A Government Grass Farm has been established in the old cantonment lands. There is fair small-game shooting near, and fine black buck shooting 20 m. to the W.

Karnal is famous as being the place where the Persian Nadir Shah defeated the Mughal Emperor Muhammad Shah in 1739. The battle lasted two hours, 20,000 of the Indian soldiers were killed, and a much greater number taken prisoners. An immense treasure, a number of elephants, part of the artillery of the Emperor, and rich spoils of every description fell into Nadir Shah's hands. The Persian loss is variously stated at from 500 to 2500 killed. The next day Muhammad Shah surrendered himself to his conqueror, who marched to Delhi, and after a massacre in the streets and a fifty-eight days' sack returned to Persia with a booty estimated at £30-70,000,000 (see p. 188).

97 m. **Thanesar** (D.B.) (population, 5000) is a famous place of Hindu pilgrimage and a very ancient town, near which Shahab-ud-din Ghori was defeated by and subsequently defeated the Prithvi Raja in 1192 A.D. As many as 100,000 persons have been known to assemble here on the occasion of an eclipse of the moon, when it is believed that the waters of all other tanks visit the one here, so that he who bathes in it at the moment of eclipse obtains the additional merit of bathing in all the others. This **Brahmasar Tank** lies about 1 m. W. of the railway station, and is reached by passing through part of the town. It is an oblong sheet of water 3546 ft. in length, and is not only the centre of attraction to pilgrims, but also the haunt of innumerable wild-fowl from the pelican to the snipe. It is surrounded by temples in every stage of decay, overshadowed by great trees, and flights of dilapidated steps lead down to the water on all sides. On the W. a causeway stretches out to an island where, partly hidden by trees, the most perfect of the temples stands. The ruins of this causeway extend farther S. to the remains of other temples. The area round it is known to the Hindus as the Dharma Kshetra or the Holy Field, which was the centre of Kuru Kshetra, the great plain of the Mahabharata battle of the Kauravas and Pandavas (Introd. p. lviii.). Traditionally the latter is 40 kos. (50 m.) in length, and extends W. to Pihewa and Kaithal,

which are both sacred places. On the Sirsuti, a mile N. of the town and a mile W. of the tank, and all round at various distances, are a number of sacred sites, some identified with places actually mentioned in the *Mahabharata*.

The **Town** is about ¼ m. N. of the tank, and beyond it are extensive remains of the Mohammedan **Fort**. The chief building of interest, and that in best repair, is the white-domed **Tomb of Shaikh Chilli**. It is an octagon of drab-coloured marble, lighted by trellis-work windows of fine design. It stands upon a small octagonal platform in the centre of a larger square one surrounded by cupolas. In the centre of the W. side is a small pavilion with deep caves, which also forms a tomb.

S.W. from here, within a stone's throw, is a small mosque of red sandstone (the **Lal Masjid**), supported on eight columns. The carving on the domes and elsewhere is very beautiful, and resembles that at Fatehpur-Sikri. Some of the trees in the neighbourhood are very fine.

Between Thanesar and Umballa are passed the Sarsuti (ancient Saraswati) Markanda and other torrents issuing from the Siwaliks, and above Umballa the Ghaggar or Drishadvati.

The strip of country included between the first and last is "the Holy Land" of the Hindu faith, the first permanent home of the Aryans in India, and the spot in which their religion took shape. Hence the sanctity of the waters of the Sarsuti, to which worshippers flock from all parts of India.

123 m. **UMBALLA** Cant. Jn. station. Headquarters of the 3rd Army Division. Umballa **City** and **Civil Station*** are 5 m. farther N.W. (total pop. 80,000). The important cantonments were formed in 1843: they cover 7220 acres, and are laid out with good roads and fine trees. The centre is occupied by the bungalows of the residents, and to the W. are the military lines, and the whole is surrounded by extensive Maidans.

The **Race-Course** is on the E. Maidan; **Paget Park**, a favourite resort, is on the N. There are various good European shops in the cantonment. The city is a second-class municipal town, and the headquarters of the district.

The **Cantonment Church**, which is in the Gothic style, was consecrated in 1857, and is one of the finest in India. There is also a **Presbyterian Church**, a **Hospital**, **Charitable Dispensary**, and a **Leper Asylum**.

162 m. **Kalka** station, * D.B. (R.), the terminus of the broad gauge railway, 2400 ft. above sea-level. A few miles S.E. of Kalka is the old Mughal palace of Pinjor in picturesque gardens.

The mountain railway from Kalka to Simla has now been open for five years. Following the line of the old Tonga Road most of the way, it passes round the W. and N. sides of the Jutogh Hill, and reaches Simla on the N. side, carried to the S. face of the Ridge by a tunnel. The gradient of nearly half the line is 1 in 33; there are 103 tunnels on it.

The fares to Simla are Rs.18, Rs.10, and Rs.3 4½ annas. The journey up occupies 7 hours, down 6 hours. It is wise to put on warmer clothing at least at Solon, whenever the upward journey is made in the summer. It is under consideration to convert the line into one worked by electricity.

Only hand-luggage can be taken into the carriages.

[(1) *Kasauli* is still usually reached from Kalka along a bridle-path, once the *old* Simla road. It can also be reached by the railway to Dharmpur (p. 218), and from there by tonga up a steep road passing up under Sanawar.

9 m. **Kasauli**.* This is a cantonment and convalescent depôt on the crest of a hill overlooking the Kalka Valley, and 6322 ft. above sea-level. The views from it are very grand and extensive. Kasauli is the Pasteur Institute of India, at over 10,000

cases have been treated since its opening.

The bridle-road continues on through *Kakarhatti Sairi* and *Jutogh* (see below) to Simla (41 m.).

3 m. off across a dip the road rises to **Sanawar**, which, however, is not quite so high as Kasauli. Here is the **Lawrence Military Asylum**. From it may be seen Dagshai and Sabathu, and in the far distance Simla. The ground was made over to the Asylum in 1858, in fulfilment of the wish of Sir H. Lawrence. There are separate barracks for boys, girls, and infants, and a chapel. Children of pure European parentage take precedence as candidates for admission, orphans have the preference over all others. The boys qualify for the service of Government in various departments.

(2) The railway to Simla passes first 20 m. **Dharampur** (D.B. good) in the territory of the Maharaja of Pattiala, 4500 ft. The King Edward Consumption Hospital here is due to the initiative of Mr Malabari, and the liberality of the Maharaja. From near here a road leads N. 10 m. to the summer cantonment of **Sabathu** lying between the old tonga and bridle-roads. The next station

24 m. **Kumarhatti** serves the cantonment of **Dagshai**. The railway now passes under the Barogh Ridge by a tunnel of 3750 ft., the longest in India, and runs high above the fine valley of the Giri, famous for its mahseer fishing, to the smaller cantonment of

28 m. **Solon** (H. and D.B.) in the State of the Rana of **Baghat**, 4900 ft. It then turns N. and ascends the slopes high above Sabathu and until it reaches a level run round to

52 m. **Tara Devi**, passing under the bold cliffs of that peak. It then winds round the W. and N. faces of the Jutogh Hill, the Tonga Road rising 1500 ft. up the S. face, through fine woods of pines and rhododendrons, and reaches

55 m. **Jutogh**, the fifth hill cantonment served by it. Curving round the N. side of the hill the railway passes Summer Hill and by a tunnel to Simla 60 m. on S. of the Ridge. It will be continued ½ m. further east from the present terminus.

The station at **Simla** consists of the lofty (8048 ft.) mountain of Jakko to the E., which is connected with Observatory Hill and Prospect Hill on the W. by a long Ridge. On the N. side of Jakko is Elysium Hill, so called in compliment of the sisters of Lord Auckland, who resided on it with their brother, and on the S. side the long slope of Chhota Simla, with the residence of the Lieutenant-Governor of the Panjab at Barnes Court, leads through that quarter to the stream which drains the amphitheatre formed by the Mahasu range, and to Junga, capital of the Keunthal State. On the S. face of the Ridge where it starts from the slope of Jakko is the native bazaar, and above this are the principal European shops, the Station Church, and the Town Hall. W. of these again are the Post Office and Telegraph Office, while below the main road, called the Mall, are the District Courts, and westward of them large blocks of Government of India offices, including those of the Army Headquarters, near the railway terminus. Further on again on a rocky summit are large new offices of the Government of India, below which on the S. side is a link between the Mall and the Tonga Road, and on the N. side are the paths leading to Annandale (see p. 219.) Half a mile further W. again is Peterhoff Hill, on which the old Government House stood, with the office of the Foreign Department of the Government of India at its base. The Mall winds round this Hill to Observatory Hill, on which stands the Viceregal Lodge, the ordinary summer residence of the Viceroy. W. of this again is Prospect

SIMLA AND JUTOGH

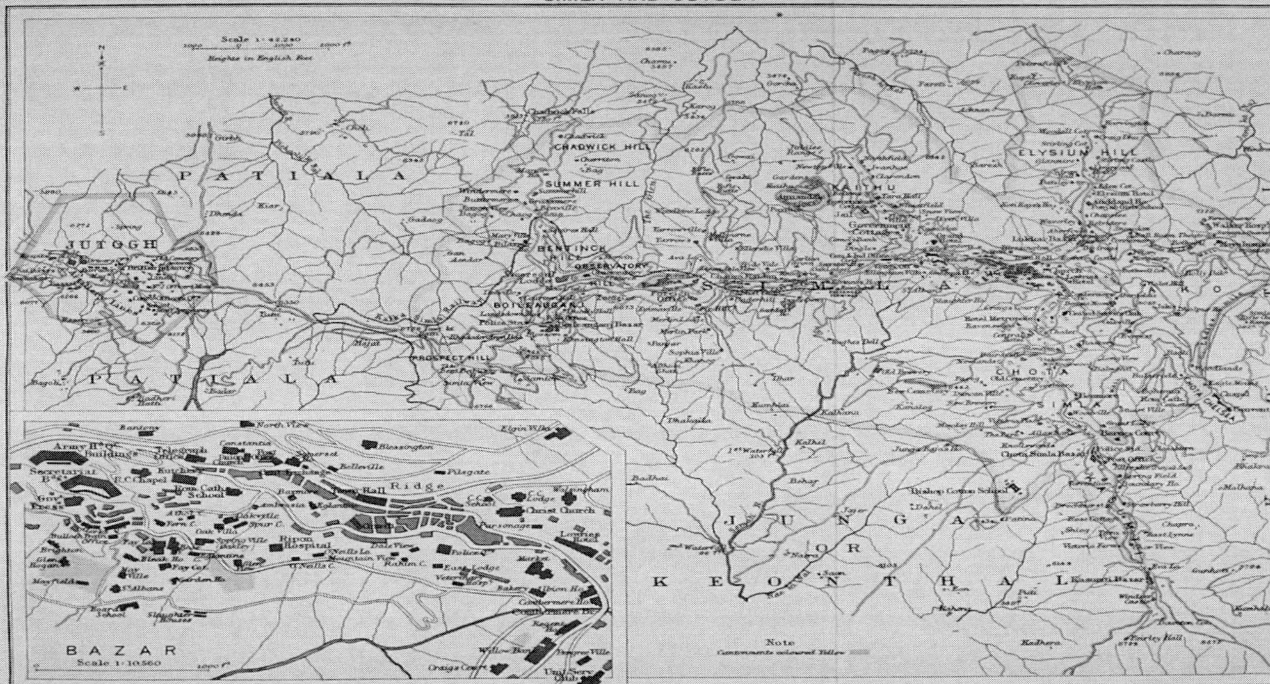

London. John Murray, Albemarle Street.

Hill (7140 ft.) with a grand view down to Sabathu and up to Kasauli; beyond it (3 m.) is **Jutogh**, and north of it is Summer Hill. There are many beautiful walks round Jakko and some of the other hills: from the top of Jakko, famous for its fakir and the monkeys which haunt the temple, there are fine views of Chor mountain (10,000 ft.) to the S.E., and of the snows when the weather is clear. One of the prettiest walks leaves the Mall near the S. approach to the U.S. Club (which stands over the Combermere ravine running down the W. face of Jakko to the S. side of the Ridge), and winds down the lower slopes of the Chhota Simla spur as far as Bishop Cotton's school. Snowdon, the residence of the Commander-in-Chief, the Walker Hospital founded by Sir James Walker, C.I.E., and the Mayo Orphanage are on the Mall on the N. side of Jakko, and the Convent schools are situated at the S.W. corner.

The land upon which Simla stands was retained by the British Government as a sanatorium at the close of the Goorkha War in 1815-16, when most of the surrounding district was given or restored to various Native States. Lieut. Ross erected the first residence, a thatched wooden cottage, in 1819. His successor, Lieut. Kennedy, in 1822 built a permanent house.[1] Other officers followed the example, and in 1826 Simla became a settlement. In 1829 Lord Amherst spent the summer there, and from that date the sanatorium grew rapidly in favour with Europeans. Since the government of Sir John Lawrence in 1864, Simla has been the summer capital for India. As soon as the hot weather sets in, at the end of March, the Viceroy and the Officers of the Supreme Government quit Calcutta for Simla, which is largely deserted in the winter,[2] though the Army Headquarters Offices now remain there all the year round.

The distances at Simla, taken from Christ Church, are—Round Jakko, 5 m.; Boileauganj, 2½ m.; to the end of Chhota Simla, 2 m.; round Elysium Hill, 2¼ m.

Annandale is a fairly extensive plain, in a valley 1200 ft. below the Ridge on the N.W. of the station. The *Race-course* surrounds it, and it contains *Gardens*, and the *Cricket Ground*, and some very fine deodar trees. West again of Annandale is the **Glen**, a charming wooded valley with some grassy slopes and fine timber.

Mashobra and **Mahasu** (5 m. and 8 m. from Simla) are pleasant places. The Viceroy has a summer retreat at the former. 8 m. beyond it is Nal Dera, a fine wood of deodars with a picturesque timber temple, from which a glimpse of the Sutlej may be obtained 5000 ft. below.

A magnificent view of the snows E. of Kullu is obtained from Narkanda (9600 ft.) and from the Bhági Forest beyond it. The stages of the route, each with a D.B., are as follows:—

Name of Stage.	M.	Above Sea-level.
Mahasu from Simla	8	8200 ft.
Fagu . . .	15	8200 ,,
Theog . . .	22	7700 ,,
Mattiana . .	38	7720 ,,
Narkanda . .	45	9500 ,,
Kotgarh . .	54¾	6000 ,,

Six marches up the Sutlej Valley from Narkanda, is Rampur, from which the fine wool used in Rampur *chadars* used to come. 120 m. beyond Rampur is Chini, east of which two routes crossing the Shipki and Sholarang passes lead to the uppermost course of the Sutlej and Gartok (14,200 ft. high). The present track will be gradually improved so as to make it a fairly passable route for trade with Thibet.

Sultanpur, the old residence of the chiefs of Kullu, in the **Kullu** Valley, is approached by way of Simla: it

[1] Mr E. J. Buck's *Simla, Past and Present*, may be consulted.

[2] The summer population of Simla is over 40,000—the winter, perhaps, 7,000.

is a long and somewhat tedious expedition, but the scenery cannot be surpassed for grandeur, and the Deodar Forests abound in pheasants and other game. Farther up amongst the high peaks sportsmen will find ibex and bears. The following are the marches (see map, 250):—

From	To	Height above Sea-level.	Accommodation.	Country.	Distance.
		Feet.			Ms.
Narkanda	Kumharsen	5200	Vil. good bungalow	All down hill.	8
Kumharsen	Dalarsh	6500	" bungalow	Cross Sutlej. Steep ascent and descent.	11
Dalarsh	Chawi	6100	" small bungalow	Cross a ridge.	7
Chawi	Kot	7700	" " "	Cross valley, steep ascent and descent.	9
Kot	Jibhi	5900	" " "	Cross Jalaori pass (10,500 ft.)	11
Jibhi	Manglaur	3800	" " "		8
Manglaur	Larji	3100	" " "		8
Larji.	Bajaora	3600	" " "		11
Bajaora	Sultanpur.	4043	" good bungalow		9

At Bajaora are two fine stone temples, one half buried in the ground. One march N. of Sultanpur is Nagar, the headquarters of Kullu, and two marches [Manauli (6300 ft.) and Rahla (8850 ft.)] further on, through the lovely scenery of the Upper Beas Valley, is the Rohtang Pass (13,000 ft.) into Lahaul.

(2)

Delhi to Lahore *viâ* Ghaziabad.

4 m. **Shahdara.** 4½ m. S. of this and near the once flourishing market of Patpargarj is the field of the battle of Delhi, in which Lord Lake defeated the Mahratta troops under M. Bourquien on 11th September 1803 after a brief but severe fight. An obelisk on the spot commemorates the officers who fell in the engagement.

13 m. **Ghaziabad** junction station.✱ From this point the E.I. Railway runs S.E. to Allahabad and Calcutta, and the Oudh and Rohilkand Railway E. to Moradabad (100 m.) (see p. 273). Near this place, then called Ghazi-ud-din-nagar, the small force under Brigadier-General Archdale Wilson twice defeated the Meerut and Delhi mutineers on 30th and 31st May 1857.

41 m. **Meerut** city station and

44 m. **Meerut** Cantonment (✱) (combined population, 115,000). This **Cantonment** is the headquarters of the 7th Army Division, and is known in history as the scene of the outbreak of mutiny of the Indian Army (on Sunday, 10th May 1857). This began with the 3rd Bengal Cavalry, eighty troopers of this regiment having been imprisoned the previous day with unnecessary degradation for refusing to receive cartridges of the old pattern, and was calculated to ensure the murder of all the Europeans of the place while at evening service, but miscarried by a happy accident. A number of officers and others were however murdered, and most of the houses of the S. cantonment were burned; and finally the mutineers (consisting of the 3rd Bengal Cavalry and the 11th and 20th regiments Native Infantry) marched off to Delhi unpursued. The English force in Meerut consisted of the 60th Rifles, the Carbineers, and one battery of Royal Artillery, of Horse Artillery, and of Foot Artillery, and the native force of about 2500 men. Every one should read the story of the Mutiny ot Meerut, as told in Colonel A. R. D. Mackenzie's *Mutiny Memoirs.*

The Station is very extensive

measuring 3½ m. from the railway on the W. to the Police Lines on the extreme E., traversed by the **Mall**, one of the finest in India, and 3 m. from where the Bulandshahar Road, on the S., leaves the station, to the end of Church Street. The European Cavalry Barracks are of remarkable extent. As in 1857, these and the other British Barracks lie to the N. of the church, and the lines of the native troops to the S.

St John's Church, completed 1821, in the Italian style, was the first church erected in the Upper Provinces of India. There are tablets in it to a great number of officers who have been killed in action or have died in Upper India.

The large **Cemetery**, which lies to the N.W. of the church is divided into two parts—the new being marked by crosses and English tombs, the old by cupolas and pyramids. The pillar, 50 ft. high, was erected to Sir R. Rollo Gillespie, who subdued the Mutiny at Vellore (p. 396), and fell in the Goorkha war. Sir D. Ochterloney is also buried here.

The **Central Jail**, completed in 1891, is capable of holding 4600 prisoners. The District Jail is a little farther to the E.

Temples. — The *Suraj Kund*, commonly called by Europeans the "Monkey Tank," lies to the W. of the Jail. "It was constructed by Jowahir Mal, a wealthy merchant of Lawar, in 1714. There are numerous small temples, dharmsalas, and *sati* pillars on its banks, but none of any note." The *Bholeshwar Nath Temple* is the oldest in the district, and dates from before the Moslem invasion. The *Dargah*, in the Nau Chandi Mahallah, is said to have been built by Kutab-ud-din, from the remains of a Hindu temple which he pulled down. The *Dargah of Shah Pir* is a fine structure of red sandstone, erected about 1620 A.D. by Nur Jahan, in memory of a pious fakir of that name. The *Jama Masjid* is said to have been built in 1019 by Hasan Mahdi, Vazir of Mahmud Ghaznavi, and was repaired by Humayun. The *Makbarah* of Salar Masa-ud Ghazi is attributed to Kutab-ud-din Aibak in 1191. There are two large *Imambarahs*, one near the Kamboli Gate, and another in the Zabidi Mahallah, and an *'Idgah*, on the Delhi Road, built in 1600. There is a mosque built by Nawab Khairandesh Khan in the Saraiganj. And besides those already mentioned, there are 62 mosques and 60 temples in the city, none of which, however, deserve any particular notice.

Before reaching Sardhana the Ganges Canal, made by Sir Proby Cautley, is crossed.

51 m. **Sardhana** station, D.B., is connected with Walter Reinhardt, known as Samru, of Walloon origin, who came out to India as a carpenter in the French navy. He became leader of a band of European deserters and Sepoys, whom he brought to an unusual state of discipline; and after serving under several native chiefs, he joined one Gregory, an Armenian, who was high in the favour of Mir Kasim,[1] the Nawab of Bengal. It was after the fall of Monghyr (p. 310) that he did his employer the base service of putting to death all the sixty English prisoners who had been collected at Patna (p. 35). He next joined the Bharatpur chief, and from him finally went over to Najaf Khan, from whom he received a grant of the Parganah of Sardhana, then valued at 6 lakhs a year. He died in 1778, and his Begam, originally a Kashmir dancing-girl, was recognised as his widow, and succeeded to his domains. She became a Roman Catholic in 1784, and married a French adventurer named Le Vaisseau (1792), who, having shown himself

[1] Less fortunate than Samru, Mir Kasim died a beggar in Delhi, his last shawl being sold to defray his funeral expenses.

incompetent, was induced to commit suicide. The revolt which he had caused was quelled by the aid of the Englishman, George Thomas, and by a son of Samru, Zafar yab Khan. At his death (1802) the Begam gave her daughter in marriage to Mr Dyce, one of her officers, afterwards Colonel Dyce, and their son, Dyce Sombre, in 1840 married Lady Mary Jervis, daughter of Earl St Vincent, afterwards Lady Forester. The Begam was a woman of shrewd ability, and after keeping up a good understanding with the British Government, her forces were received into British pay. She died in 1836. The Begam was thus described by Major Thorn, who saw her in 1806. "She appeared to be about fifty-three years of age, of middling size and fair complexion. She was the constant attendant at headquarters, dressed in the European style with a hat and veil, sometimes riding in a palanquin, and at other times on a horse or an elephant"—(*Memoir of the War in India*).

E. of the town is a modern English mansion, built 1834, and called the Palace, with a grand flight of steps at the entrance. It stands in a garden of 50 acres, and is commonly known as the **Kothi Dilkusha.** Within it were two framed inscriptions recording the charities of H.H. the Begam Samru in Sardhana, and portraits of the Begam and her friends, with George Thomas, General Ochterlony, Sir C. Metcalfe, Lord Combermere, Colonel Boileau, General Ventura, her butler, etc. The house has lately been sold by the family.

The **R.C. Cathedral** is outside the town on the S. It is an imposing building, standing in an enclosure, surrounded by an ornamental wall. By the side entrance, on the right, is the Begam's white marble monument, made at Rome. Close by is the **R.C. College**, a low masonry house, which was once the Begam's own residence. It is intended for the instruction of native priests, and endowed by the Begam. There are fifty pupils taught by the Italian priest and his curate.

112 m. **Saharanpur** junction station ✱ (R.) D.B. From here the Oudh and Rohilkand Railway runs S.E. to Lucknow, and Benares. (See Route 20.) Population, 60,000.

The town was founded in the reign of Muhammed Tughlak about 1340, and named from Shah Haran Chishti, whose shrine is still much visited by Mohammedans. It was a favourite place of summer resort of the Mughal court. In the reign of Shah Jahan a royal hunting-seat, called Badshah Mahal, was built by 'Ali Mardan Khan, the projector of the **Eastern Jumna Canal.** The canal was neglected during the decline of the Mughal Empire, and was never of much utility till the district came under British rule, when Sir P. Cautley reconstructed it, and since then cultivation has spread on every side. In 1857 the station was successfully held by the Collector, Mr Spankie, with assistance afforded him from Umballa.

There is an Anglican church, consecrated in 1858, and an American Presbyterian church, and a mission from that body. An old Rohilla fort is used as a Court-House. A handsome modern mosque has been erected on the plan of the Jama Masjid at Delhi. The main attractions of the place, however, are the extensive **Government Botanical Gardens**, where many valuable plants have been acclimatised. Near the entrance by the N. gate is the Agricultural Garden, and beyond it to the E. the Medicinal Garden; beyond this to the S. is the Linnæan Garden. The main working divisions are the horticultural department, the Doab Canal tree nursery, the nurseries for cuttings, bulbous plants, fruit-trees, and seedlings. There are also a Hindu temple and a tank and wells in the gardens, and the S.E. gate leads to some *sati* monuments and *chhatris*. The most picturesque spot in it is an island shaded by clumps of bamboo and surrounded by lotus.

Saharanpur is celebrated as the station whence the **Trigonometrical Survey** of the Himalayas was commenced. The snowy peaks add much sublimity to the view to the N.

162 m. **Umballa** Cantonment station (p. 217).

179 m. **Rajpura** junction station. D.B. [From here a branch line runs S.W. 16 m. to Patiala, and 32 m. to Nabha, the capitals of the two Jat Sikh States so named; the Chief of the latter is H.H. Raja-i-Rajagan Colonel Sir Hira Singh, G.C.S.I., G.C.I.E. These two Chiefs and the Raja of Jind are the Phulkian Chiefs of the Malwai Sikhs, who lie S. of the Sutlej, the Manjha Sikhs occupying the Bari Doab across that river. From Nabha the line runs W. to Bhatinda on the Rewari-Ferozepur line, and is crossed at Dhuri by the line from Ludhiana (see p. 224) to Jakhal on the S. Panjab line (p. 147), 108 m.]

195 m. **Sirhind** station. The name of this town was formerly applied to a very extensive tract, which included the Umballa district and the native states of Patiala, Jind and Nabha. In Cunningham's *Archæological Survey* (vol. ii. p. 205), a very interesting account of it will be found. It is the place where many Afghan princes of Shah Shuja's family and other Mohammedans of note are buried.

It is mentioned by Firishtah as the most eastern possession of the Brahman kings of Kabul. After they were conquered by Mahmud, it became the frontier town of the Moslems, whence its name of Sirhind or Sar-i-hind, "Frontier of Hind." It must have been a place of importance as long back as 1191 A.D., when it was taken by Shahab-ud-din Ghori, and besieged by Rai Pithora (Pirthvi Raja) for 13 months. At that early date it had a separate governor.

For the century and a half that intervened between the accession of Akbar and the death of Aurangzeb, Sirhind was one of the most flourishing cities of the Mughal Empire. Many tombs and mosques are yet standing, and heaps of brick ruins surround the old city for several miles. In 1709 the city was taken and plundered by the Sikh chief Banda, who put the governor Vazir Khan to death in revenge for the murder of Guru Govind's mother and children. In December 1763, Sirhind was taken and totally destroyed by the Sikhs. Even to this day every Sikh, on passing through Sirhind, carries away a brick, which he throws into the Sutlej in the hope that in time the detested city will thus be utterly removed from the face of the earth. The finest and oldest building is the

Tomb of Mir Miran. This is of stone, and is surmounted by a large central dome on an octagonal base, with a smaller dome at each of the four corners on a square base. Each of the four sides is pierced by a recessed doorway with a pointed arch covered by a second loftier and larger arch. The dead walls are relieved by squares of blue enamelled tiles. The general effect is decidedly good, and altogether this tomb is one of the most pleasing and perfect specimens of the later Pathan architecture.

The **Largest Tomb** is a plain brick building. At the four corners are very small turrets, which look mean beside the lofty central dome of 40 ft. diameter which crowns the building. The next tomb in size is another red brick building, attributed to *Khoja Khan*. The great dome is 36 ft. in diameter outside. This building is probably of the 15th century. There is a pretty little octagonal **Tomb of Pirbandi Nakshwala** (or the painter). It is on open arches, and is surmounted by the pear-shaped dome of the Mughal period. The body of the building is profusely covered with paintings of flowers, and the roof with glazed tiles, arranged so that the melon-like divisions of the dome are marked by dark blue lines, and the intervals by coloured tiles laid herring-bone fashion, beginning with yellowish pale green at the top, and ending with dark green at the bottom. The only mosque worth mentioning is that of *Sadan Kasai*, to the N. of the present town. The W. end has fallen down. The centre space is covered by a dome 45 ft. in diameter.

The *Haveli* or mansion of Salabat Beg is perhaps the largest specimen of the domestic architecture of the Mohammedans of the Mughal Empire. It consists of two great piles of brick, each 60 ft. sq. and about 80 ft. high, connected by high dead walls.

The great *Sarai* of the Mughal emperors is to the S.E. of the city. It is now used as a public audience-hall by the Patiala authorities, and is called the *Amkhas*.

Beyond Sirhind the railway crosses the **Great Sirhind Canal** (opened in 1882), one of the largest irrigation canals in the world. It draws its water from the Sutlej at Rupar (20 m. distant from Doraha), and passing through Ludhiana and Patiala, with side branches to Nabha, Jind, and other native States of the Panjab, eventually irrigates the S. half of the Ferozepore district. At Rupar Lord Wm. Bentinck had a famous meeting with Maharaja Ranjit Singh in October 1831.

233 m. **Ludhiana** junction, D.B. This is a municipal town and head-quarters of a district of the same name. (Population, 49,000, of whom much the greater portion are Mohammedans.) It is a great grain market, and famous for its shawls made from Pashmina wool, also for the manufacture of Rampur chaddars. It is situated near the S. bank of the Sutlej, 8 m. from the present bed of the river. The Fort lies to the N.W. of the city, and under it is a **Shrine of Pir-i-Dastgir**, or 'Abdul Kadir Gilani.

Ludhiana was founded in 1480 by two princes of the Lodi family. In 1809 General Ochterlony occupied it as Political Agent for the Cis-Sutlej States, and from 1834 to 1854 the town was a military station. The **Church** and **Public Gardens** are to the S. of the city. There has been an American Presbyterian Mission here since 1840. Three of the great battles of the first **Sikh War** were fought between Ludhiana and Ferozepore, viz., Moodki, Ferozeshah, and Aliwal. The first two are noticed at page 147. Aliwal lies 16 m. W. of Ludhiana, and must be reached by riding. In the battle here Sir Harry Smith, with a force of 10,000 men, defeated a body of 20,000 Sikhs under Sirdar Ranjodh Singh, who had slightly worsted him a week previously at Budhowal. There is there an *Obelisk* with the inscription, "Aliwal, 26th January 1846," repeated in Persian and Gurmukhi.

A line of railway now runs from Ludhiana to Ferozepore, p. 147.

241 m. **Phillaur.** Beyond the Sutlej, crossed by a fine bridge, of which it was necessary to sink the foundations to an extraordinary depth, is the old Mughal Sarai and Sikh Fort of Phillaur, now used as a Police Training School. It was just saved from the mutineers in May 1857, by the despatch of British troops from Jullundur, and was held successfully when the N. regiments in the latter station mutinied on 17th June. The Civil authorities in Ludhiana did all in their power to prevent the mutineers crossing the Sutlej, Mr Thornton (C.S.I.), an Assistant Commissioner of a few weeks' standing, cutting the bridge of boats, and Mr Ricketts, the Deputy Commissioner, boldly facing them with a few of Rattray's Sikhs; but the mutineers got past them, and, after looting the Ludhiana Station, went on to Delhi.

265 m. **Jullundur City** station.

265 m. **Jullundur Cantonment station,** ✱ D.B. A municipal city, cantonment, and headquarters of a division and district. The city itself (station 3 m. farther N.) has a population of 68,000, of whom the greater number are Mohammedans. Anciently it was the capital of the Rajput Katoch kingdom, before Alexander's invasion. Hiouen Thsang, the Chinese pilgrim of the 7th century A.D., describes the town as 2 m. in circuit; now two **ancient Tanks** are all that are left of this. Under the Mughal Empire it formed the capital of the country between the Sutlej and the Beas. The modern city consists of a cluster of wards, each formerly surrounded by a wall. There is a fine *Sarai* built by Karim Bakhsh.

The **Church,** ½ m. W. of the artillery lines, is a long building without any tower.

The **American Presbyterian Mission** maintains an excellent school. The **Cantonment,** which is considered a healthy one, was established in 1846, and has an area of 7½ sq. m. Two regiments and a battery of artillery are stationed here. Though a British regiment (the 8th King's), and a battery of artillery were present here in May 1857, and though the Phillaur Fort was secured by the former under the orders of Colonel Hartley, no steps were taken by Brigadier-General Johnstone to disarm the 36th and 61st regiments of Native Infantry, and when these mutinied on 7th June and started for Delhi, no pursuit of them was ordered until it was too late.

The **Public Gardens** in the military cantonment are nicely laid out.

[The native state of **Kupurthalla** lies 15 m. S.W. Good road. From the Kartarpur Station to Kupurthalla is only 7 m.]

288 m.-291 m. Between **East Bank** and **Beas** the river of that name is crossed.

317 m. **AMRITSAR** junction station, ✱ D.B., about ¾ m. W. of the city. A branch line from here goes N.E. 67 m. to Pathankot for **Dalhousie,** etc. (see p. 228).

Amritsar is a city with a population of 152,000. It is the wealthiest next to Delhi, and after that place and Lahore, the most populous city of the Panjab, and the religious capital of the Sikhs. It was founded in 1574 by Ram Das, 4th Guru of the Sikhs, upon a site granted by the Emperor Akbar around a sacred tank, from which the city takes its name, "Pool of Immortality." Ahmad Shah Durani destroyed it in 1761, blew up the temple, and defiled the shrines. After his retirement, the city was divided amongst the various Sikh chiefs, to each of whom was assigned a separate ward; but it gradually passed into the power of the Bhangi Misl, who remained supreme till 1802. In that year Ranjit Singh seized it, and roofed the great shrine with sheets of copper gilt, whence it was called the Golden Temple. He also built on the S.W. the Fort of Govindgarh in order to overawe the pilgrims, and surrounded the city with a massive wall, the greater part of which has been demolished since the British occupation.

Amritsar is a centre of local manufacturing industry. Its staple was the weaving of **Kashmir shawls** from the inner soft wool of the goat, on which 4000 Kashmiris were engaged, but most of them are now employed in carpet factories, which have been greatly developed since the Jail carpet workshops were mainly done away with, and of which the principal, and perhaps the principal in all India, is that of Messrs Devi Sahai and Chamba Mal, lying to the right of the Hall Gate of the city. *Rampur chaddars* are also made here and silks of solid texture and beautiful patterns. **Carving** in ivory also employs a few artists.

The materials for these manufactures are, in a great measure, brought from all parts of Central Asia, and the merchants who bring them—Kashmiris, Afghans, Nepalese, Bokhariots, Beluchis, Persians, Turcomans, Tibetans, Yarkandis, and others—may be seen in their national and highly picturesque costumes about the town, but more especially in the caravanserais. Besides the raw materials they bring fine specimens of their own national manufactures and embroideries, which may be purchased from dealers in this town as well as in the other chief cities of India. Amritsar is also the depôt for piece-goods, copper, brass, etc., for the Central Asian markets.

The City has twelve gates, of which the only old one is that on the N. side facing the Ram Bagh. The direct road from the railway station to the Great Temple, called the Darbar Sahib, in the centre of the town, passes two of the large above-noticed modern **Sarais,** the principal **Carpet Factory,** and several small mosques, and finally through a deep archway in the centre of the municipal buildings enters the **Kaisar Bagh,** where stands a white marble statue of the Queen-Empress Victoria. At the entrance to the temple precincts, just beyond this, rises the **Clock Tower,** which overlooks the tank and the temple in the centre. The view from here is wonderfully picturesque. Before visiting the temple it will be necessary for the visitor to take off his boots and put on soft slippers provided for him at the entrance on payment of a trifle. It is also necessary for a policeman to accompany him, in accordance with Government rules. The Sacred Tank is surrounded by a tesselated pavement[1] of white marble 24 ft. broad, with ribs of black and brown, brought from Jaipur. It is 470 ft. sq.[2] The buildings around it are called **Bungahs,** and are the hostels and chapels of great chiefs who come to worship. To the N.W. of the Darbar Temple is that of Takht Akal Bungah Sahib (see p. 227), with a gilt dome, and adjoining it, to the S., is the bungah of Dhiyan Singh, a plain brick building. Next to it on the S. is the gorgeous bungah of Sher Singh, and in the same direction beyond it is the bungah of Lehna Singh. In the N.E. is the white bungah of the Chiefs of Patiala and Nabha, and beyond, to the E., are the two gigantic minars of Mangal Singh's family, called the Ram Garhia Minars. A local guide by Sirdar Sundar Singh gives full details.

The **Darbar Sahib** or **Golden Temple** stands in the centre of the tank on a platform 65 ft. sq. It is approached from beneath an archway on the W. side by a white marble causeway 204 ft. long, flanked on either side by gilded standard lamps.

Except for the lower part of the walls, which are of white marble, the whole of the building is encased in gilded copper, inscribed with verses from the *Granth Sahib*, written very clearly in the Panjabi character. It is entered by four doorways, one on each side, with doors plated with silver finely wrought. That on the N. side is the only one through which Europeans may pass. The scene within is a most picturesque one. The walls are richly gilded and painted with representations of flowers, etc. On the E. side is seated the high priest, either reading from a copy of the *Granth Sahib* on an ottoman before him, or waving a *chauri* over it, whilst pilgrims throw offerings of cowries, money, or flowers into a sheet spread in the middle of the floor to receive them, and then taking their places around it, sit down and join in chanting verses of the sacred volume to the music of stringed instruments.

Cups of sugar are presented to visitors, who may in return make an offering of Rs. 1-2. On the roof above there is a small but richly decorated Shish Mahal or pavilion, where it is said the Guru used to sit.

1 Along this pavement sit hawkers who sell beads and miniature spear-heads and quoits, which the Sikhs are now content to wear in their turbans in place of the real weapons.

2 See Sir G. Birdwood's *Industrial Arts*.

The brooms kept to sweep it out are made of peacocks' feathers.

Returning to the gateway, which has doors covered with massive silver plates, a staircase will be found to lead up to the **Treasury**, in which is a large chest. This place has thirty-one pillars or poles of silver 9 ft. long and 4½ in. in diameter, and four large ones. In the chest are kept three gilt maces, a *pankhah*, two *chauris*, all with gilt handles, a *canopy*, weighing 10 lbs., of pure gold, set with emeralds, rubies, and diamonds, a pendant of gold, a coloured plan of the temple, and a magnificent diadem of diamonds with strings of pearl pendants, which used to be worn by Nau Nihal Singh. There is also a sort of gilt arch 6 ft. high. All these are used when the *Granth* is carried in procession.

On the W. side of the small square facing the gateway is the **Akal Bungah**, with its gilt dome. This temple was built in the time of Arjan, the fifth Guru. A low staircase leads to a room with a projecting window. In the room is a gilt ark, on the floor of which are a number of things covered with a cloth; this is partly removed, and a large sword is taken out and shown. It is a falchion 4 ft. long and widening towards the end. It is said to be the sword of Guru Govind; a mace also is shown, which was wielded by one of the Gurus. In the ark are also the vessels for the initiation of new members into the Sikh Brotherhood.

On passing round to the S. side of the enclosure, the **Temple Garden**, Guru ka Bagh, is reached. It is 30 acres in extent, and contains pomegranate, orange, and other fruit trees, a tank called Kaulsar, and several small pavilions. At the S. end of the garden is the picturesque **Baba Atal Tower**. The lower room is richly painted with frescoes representing scenes from the life of Guru Nanik, a good and interesting example of modern Sikh art. A staircase leads up to seven galleries; there is then a wooden ladder which ascends to an eighth — the entire height of the building is 131 ft.

This tower is dedicated to Atal Rai, the younger son of Guru Har Govind, who is said to have been reproved by his father for raising the deceased child of a widow to life, on the ground that the supernatural powers ought to be displayed in purity of doctrine and holiness of life, and not in miracles. Thereupon Atal Rai said that as a life was required and he had withheld one, he would yield up his own; and so lay down and died.

Outside the Temple enclosure on the E. are the lofty plain **Ramgarhia Minars**. The one to the N. may be ascended. At the top there is a good view to the N.W., taking in a white temple to Shiva at the extremity of the city, built by Sardar Tej Singh. To the N.E. at 1 m. off, **St Paul's Church** is seen peeping out among woods, close to the D.B. Govindgarh Fort appears to the S.W.

The return journey may be made by the Ram Bagh Gate (the only remaining old one) of the city to the Kotwali Chauk. The Kotwali, or Police Office, has a handsome front. To the left is the mosque of Muhammad Jan, with three white domes and slender minarets. Farther to the N. is the 'Idgah; and close to it is the mosque of Khan Muhammed. In front of the Gate are the pretty Rambagh **Public Gardens**, which are about 40 acres in extent. In the centre is a pavilion in which Ranjit Singh used to stop when he came to Amritsar.

The **Fort of Govindgarh** is a short distance to the S.W. of the city. It is garrisoned with a battery of artillery and a company of British infantry. It was built by Ranjit Singh in 1809, the fortifications being traced by the French officers in his service. In May 1857 it was secured by British troops sent over from Lahore in ekkas. French names are still on the walls, *e.g.* Ronde de l'Est.

There is a large Church Mission establishment at Amritsar with a well-known school and hospital. 2½ m. W. of the place is the Sikh Khalsa College, founded in 1882, which was honoured by a visit by King George on 11th December 1905.

[14 m. to the S. of Amritsar is **Tarn Taran,** D.B., a place very holy to the Sikhs, through which a line runs to Patti and Kasur (p. 147).

The **Temple** and **Tower** are situated on the E. side of a magnificent tank, which is kept full of water from the Bari Doab Canal. This tank was made by Maharaja Ranjit Singh when he built the temple. Boots must be taken off and cloth slippers put on before descending into the enclosure. The lower room of the temple has been handsomely painted with representations of trees, while the outside walls have paintings of gods and goddesses. The room has a corridor round it, on the S. side of which is the *Granth,* enveloped in silk wrappers, and fanned by an official with a *chauri.*

This place was the residence of the Guru Arjan, and is older than Amritsar; unlike the temples at that city, it has no writings on the walls. There is a small pavilion with open sides on the roof. The tank is said to possess miraculous powers to cure the lepers who can swim across it. At its N. corner is a tower built by Nau Nihal Singh.

The neighbourhood is famous as the stronghold of the Manjha Sikhs, and the former recruiting-ground for their army. There is a leper asylum outside the town, and a suburb inhabited by those infected with the disease, from which it is said the Guru Arjan himself suffered.]

At Amritsar passengers for Dalhousie, Chamba Kangra and Dharmsala change on to the Amritsar-Pathankot Railway.

24 m. **Batala.**

47 m. **Gurdaspur,** headquarters of a District.

[9 m. N.W. of **Gurdaspur** is the Trimmu Ghat of the Ravi, where Brigadier-General Nicholson defeated the Sialkot mutineers (p. 240), on 12th July. Four days later the remnants of them were attacked on an island in the river, and all destroyed or captured. General Nicholson had been obliged by events to return from Phillaur to Amritsar with the moveable column, having disbanded the Native Infantry regiments with it at the former place, and the 59th Regiment at the latter.

67 m. **Pathankot** terminus station (R.), D.B. A picturesque town with a 16th-century Fort. Here a tonga may be procured for, 34 m., **Danera,** D.B. Thence by pony or ricksha (Rs. 5), or dhooly (Rs. 10) to, 22 m., **Dalhousie,** ✱ a charming hill-station and sanatorium 7700 ft. above the sea, surrounded by forests. The scenery is very fine, especially in the neighbourhood of **Chamba,** D.B., 12 m. distant across the Ravi.

The tonga route from Pathankot to **Dharmsalah** (50 m.), headquarters of the Kangra District, passes through very pretty country to Nurpur and Shahpur, and then ascends considerably to the lower station, 4560 ft., where the small Goorkha cantonment of Bhagsu is situated. The higher station lies 3000 to 4000 ft. above this, in the midst of fine forest trees and overshadowed by the great rock wall of the Daola Dhar, which rises to 16,000 ft. In the centre of it is the church, and in the churchyard is the tomb of Earl Elgin, Viceroy, 1862-63, who died here, at the end of a tour in Kulu. The station and Kangra, 15 m. S., suffered terribly in the earthquake of 1903. Kangra, formerly known as Nagar Kot (2500 ft.), is picturesquely situated on a bold rocky promontory between two rivers; the old temples in it were ruined by the earthquake. It was captured, and an enormous spoil was taken, by Mahmud of Ghazni in 1008 A.D. Some 21 m. S.E. of Dharmsalah is the pretty little settlement of Palampur, the centre of the Kangra tea plantations of 10,000 acres.

LAHORE AND ENVIRONS

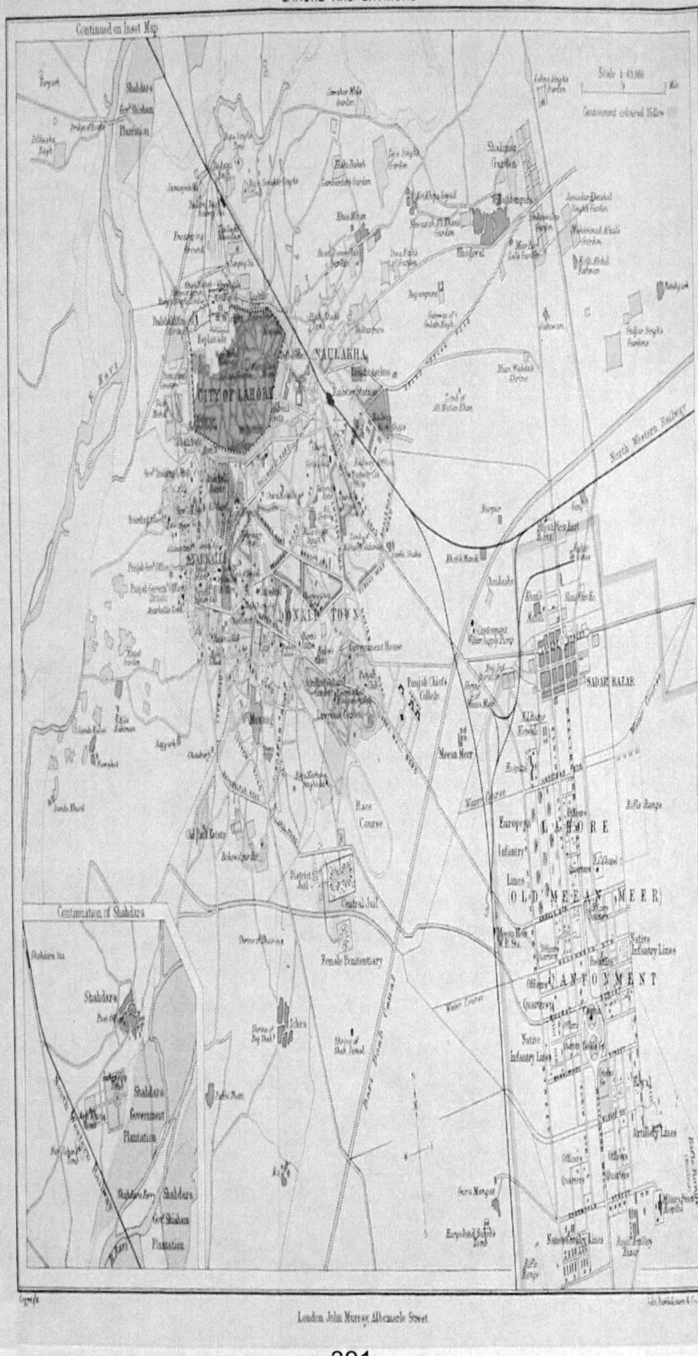

London, John Murray, Albemarle Street.

9 m. E. again are the interesting temples of Baijnath—see i. 300, of Fergusson's *Indian Architecture*—and from here a road, dividing at the next stage, Jatingri, leads to Sultanpur in Kullu, 80 m. from Dharmsalah (p. 219), by either the Dulchi (7000 ft.) or Babbu pass (10,000 ft.), with a D.B. at each stage: the former joins the road from Simla at Bajaora. The shooting round Kulu is excellent—full details will be found in Colonel Tyacke's little *Sportsman's Manual in Kulu, Lahaul, and Spiti*, 21 m. S.E. of Kangra is the famous temple of Joalla Mukhi picturesquely built up against a rocky cliff, from a cleft in which an inflammable gas issues. This was once one of the most popular Hindu shrines in all N. India, and the autumn fair is still sometimes attended by 50,000 people.

---

346 m. **Lahore Cantonment E.**, formerly Meean Meer, station.

349 m. **LAHORE** junction station * (R. good). Lines run N.W. to Rawal Pindi and Peshawar, and S.W. through Sind to Karachi. The railway *workshops* are very extensive, covering 126 acres, and employing over 2000 men. A very large new railway quarter is now being extended towards Lahore Cantonment.

If only a few hours can be devoted to Lahore, a selection of the objects of greatest interest may be made from the following route. The Mosque of Wazir Khan, the Fort, and the Badshahi Mosque should be seen in any case. Then drive to the Queen's Jubilee Statue at the cross-roads (Charing Cross) and driving E. along the **Mall** passing (in the order in which they are named), right, the entrance to the **Lawrence Gardens**; left, **Nedon's Hotel**; right, the combined **Lawrence** and **Montgomery Halls**; left, **Government House**, the residence of the Lieutenant-Governor; left, the **Panjab Club**, and **Aitchison or Chiefs' College**; 3 m. further on is the desolate old **Meean Meer Lahore Cantonment.** Driving along the Mall W. from Charing Cross the route passes several good shops; left, **R.C. Cathedral**; left Lord **Lawrence's Statue**; right, the **Cathedral**; left, the **Chief Court** and the Accountant-General's Office; several **Banks**, and then, right, the **Telegraph Office**, with the statue of the King in front of it, and left, the **Post-Office.** Near a slight turn in the road are, the **Market**, the **Jubilee Museum**, the **Mayo School**, and the **Town Hall**, and beyond the entrance to the **Anarkali Gardens**; the tomb of Anarkali and the Principal Panjab Government offices lie to the S.W. of these, the rest of the offices and the Senate Hall of the University being situated to the N. of the Museum and Town Hall. Turning N. from the Gardens the **Government College** is passsd right; left, **Deputy Commissioner's** Court, **Model School** and **Government School.** Further E. are the **Mayo Hospital**, etc. Proceeding round the W. side of the city the **Cemetery** is passed left, and a little further on the road divides; that, left, leading to **Shah Dara** (p. 238) across the bridge of boats, and that right passing the Badshahi Mosque, the **Fort**, and the N. of the city to the railway station.

In the new Public **Buildings** of Lahore an attempt has been made to adopt Hindu and Mohammedan styles of architecture to the requirements of modern buildings. The success of these is largely due to the late Mr J. L. Kipling, C.I.E., Principal of the School of Art, and R. B. Ganga Ram, C.I.E., Ex-Engineer.

Lahore[1] is a municipal city, capital of the Panjab headquarters of the Panjab Government, the seat of an episcopal see, and headquarters of a division and district of the same name (population with Mian Mir 228,000. Lat. 31° 34′; long. 74° 21′). Tradition says that Lahore was founded by Loh, the elder son of

[1] Thornton's *Lahore*, and Syad Mahammad Latif's *Lahore* give very full accounts of the place.

Rama; no mention of it, however, is made by Alexander's historians, and no Græco-Bactrian coins are found among the ruins.

The first reference to it is in the Itinerary of the Chinese pilgrim Hiouen Thsang, in the 7th century. It seems then to have been governed by a family of Chauhan Rajputs, from whom it was wrested by Mahmud of Ghazni, whose famous slave, Malik Ayaz, was Governor here. It did not, however, attain to magnificence till the rule of the Mughals. Akbar enlarged and repaired the fort, and surrounded the town with a wall, portions of which still remain, built into the modern wall of Ranjit Singh. Jahangir often resided at Lahore, and during his reign Arjan Mall, Guru of the Sikhs, compiler of the *Adi Granth*, died in prison here. The mausoleum of Jahangir is at Shah Dara, 4 m. from Lahore (see p. 238). Shah Jahan built the palace of Lahore, and Aurangzeb built the great mosque, but in his time the city began to decline, and was much ruined by the invasions of Ahmad Shah Durani. Of its glory in its prime the proverb ran: "Isfahan and Shiraz united would not equal the half of Lahore." For half a century after the Mughal capital was utterly effete, vigorous Mohammedan governors, Abdul Samand Khan, Zakaria Khan (1717-1738), Yahia Khan (1738-1748), the son of the latter, and nephew of the Delhi Wazir Kamar-ud-din Khan, and Mir Mannu, son of the last (1748-1752), maintained themselves in the Panjab, and fought with the Sikhs, and submitted to the Persians under Nadir Shah, and the Afghans under Ahmad Shah. When the widow of Mir Mannu, Murad Begam, was treacherously entrapped by the Wazir Ghazi-ud-din, Adina Beg (1755-1758), was made Governor of the Province; and it was his summoning the Mahrattas to protect him against the Sikhs that ultimately led in 1761 to the battle of Panipat, in which Ahmad Shah utterly crushed the Hindu forayers of the south for the moment. From 1775 onwards, the Sikhs were the real rulers of Lahore.

Under Ranjit Singh Lahore regained some of its former splendour, and since the period of the British rule, which commenced in 1849, buildings have greatly multiplied. The modern city covers an area of 640 acres, and is surrounded by a brick wall cut down to 15 ft. The moat has been filled in and changed to a garden, which encircles the city on every side except the N.W. A metalled road runs round the rampart, and gives access to the city by thirteen gates.

Within the ramparts that surround the city, in the N.W. corner, is the *Citadel*, usually called the Fort. The **Ravi** river flowing W. once washed the walls of the city, and in 1662 made such encroachments as to necessitate the construction of a massive embankment 4 m. long. It now sweeps round Lahore and passes to the S. at about 1 m. W. of the city.

The **Lawrence Gardens**, which cover 112 acres, contain a large variety of trees and shrubs of different species. The visitor will remark the *Pinus longifolia*, the Australian gum-tree, and the carob tree of Syria. There is also a menagerie at the W. end, and a cricket ground at the E. end.

At the N. side is the **Lawrence Hall**, built in memory of Sir John Lawrence in 1862, fronting the **Mall**; and the **Montgomery Hall**, built in 1866, in memory of Sir R. Montgomery, facing the central avenue of the gardens. A covered corridor connects them. The Montgomery Hall contains portraits of Sir Henry Lawrence, Sir John Lawrence, and other Lieutenant-Governors of the Province, and celebrated Englishmen, including Brigadier-General John Nicholson.

Government House stands on the opposite side of the Mall, N. of the Lawrence Gardens. It was the tomb of Muhammad Kasim Khan, cousin of the Emperor Akbar. He was a great patron of wrestlers, and his tomb used to be called *Kushtiwala Gumbaz*, or Wrestler's Dome. The present Lieutenant-Governor of the Panjab is Sir Louis W. Dane, K.C.I.E., C.S.I.

E. of this is the **Panjab Club**, and E. again the **Aitchison Chiefs' College**, which owes its inception to Sir C. U. Aitchison (Lieutenant-Governor, 1882-1887), and of which the foundation stone was laid by Lord Dufferin in 1888, intended for the education of the sons of the Native Princes and leading Chiefs of the Panjab. The Central Building is a very fine one, and the number of students varies from eighty to one hundred.

The Jubilee **Statue of the Queen** in the centre of the Mall, at the spot known as Charing Cross, is a pleasing one. The **R. C. Cathedral** is a very fine building: the **Anglican Cathedral** is a large red brick Gothic church, erected in 1884-87. Beyond is an ineffective statue of Lord Lawrence, Chief Commissioner and Lieutenant-Governor of the Panjab, 1853-1859. The **Chief Court** is a pleasing structure built in the late Pathan style of the 14th century. The Telegraph Office, the Post-Office, and the Bank of Bengal, are all handsome buildings. In front of the first is a statue of H.M. King Edward VII.; adjoining the last is the American Presbyterian College. The new **Jubilee Museum** is perhaps the most effective of all the public buildings in Lahore; the foundation stone of it was laid by H.H. the Duke of Clarence in February 1890.

Opposite this is the New University Hall, and in front of it is the famous gun, "Kim's" gun, called the Zamzamah, "Hummer" or Lion's roar. The Sikhs called it the Bhangianwali Top, that is the cannon of the Bhangi confederacy. The gun was made by Shah Wali Khan, Vazir of Ahmad Shah Durani, and was used by him at the battle of Panipat. After Ahmad Shah left India it came into the hands of the Bhangi Misl, and Maharaja Ranjit Singh eventually got possession of it, and used it at the siege of Mooltan in 1818. It was then placed at the Delhi Gate of Lahore until 1860, when it was removed to its present site. The Persian inscriptions on it give the date of casting, 1762 A.D.

The Museum contains specimens of the antiquities, arts, manufactures, and raw products of the Panjab.

In the archæological department there is a stone with an inscription of the time of King Gondophares, who by tradition put St Thomas to death (see p. 409); the bases of two pillars brought by General Cunningham from Shah ka Dera, probably the ancient Taxilla; numerous Buddhist sculptures from the Yusafzai country and elsewhere, in which classical influence is plainly discerned; a Buddhist pillar about 9 ft. high, with a huge head projecting on one side, dug up near Jhelum; also two old brass cannon found buried in a mound of Anandpur in the district of Hoshiyarpur, thought to be of the time of Guru Govind. There are also two relics of the prehistoric age, two finely finished celts of porphyritic greenstone, found in Swat. There is a very fine collection of the coins of India which can be seen on application to the Curator.

The series of portraits, representing princes and chiefs of the Panjab, will probably be found interesting, though as specimens of art they cannot be much praised. Among ornaments worn by the people may be noticed the *perak*, a sort of coif used by maidens in Lahaul and Spiti, in which a number of turquoises are sewn. There is also a good collection of musical instruments of the country; specimens of pottery and Panjab glass, and of the *Koftgari* work of Gujrat and Sialkot; cups and ornaments of vitreous enamel from Bahawalpur; silver inlaid in pewter, and perforated metal-work from Delhi. A dagger with small pearls set loosely in the blade is noticeable.

There are good specimens of the

silk manufactures of Bahawalpur and Mooltan, and the satinettes are excellent. The embroideries called *shishadar phulkaries*, of soft floss silk on cotton, interspersed among which are small bits of glass, are special to the Panjab; the rude idols hideously painted were worshipped by the ladies of the Sikh Court. There are also collections of the leathern ware of the Punjab; of ethnographical heads by Messrs Schlagentweit; lay figures habited in the costumes of the people of Lahaul, Spiti, and Ladakh; and Thibetan curiosities, such as prayer-wheels.

In the mineral section will be seen the model of the *Koh-i-Nur*, made for the Exhibition of 1851. According to the Hindus, this diamond belonged to Karna, King of Anga, and according to the Persians, it and its sister diamond, the Darya-i-Nur, or "Sea of Light," were worn by Afrasiyab. The Sea of Light is now at Teheran in the Shah's treasury. It is said that Prince, afterwards the Emperor Humayun, received the Koh-i-Nur from the widows of the Gwalior Chief; Nadir Shah brought it from Delhi, and when he was killed it fell into the hands of Ahmad Shah Durani, and from him descended to Shah Shuja'a, his grandson, from whom Maharaja Ranjit Singh took it in 1813. In 1849 it was made over to the British, and delivered to the Queen in 1850. It was re-cut in London, and its weight was diminished from 186 carats to 102¼.

There are also specimens of the mineral resources of the country. Among them will be seen iron ore from Bajaur. It is a magnetic oxide of singular purity. Antimony and lead are also shown, and gold found in the sands of the Panjab rivers in small quantities. Specimens of rock-salt of two kinds, one from the hills between the Jhelum and the Indus, and the other from the hills beyond the Indus are exhibited too.

The **Lahore School of Art** attained considerable eminence under the late Mr J. Kipling, C.I.E. Sirdar Bahadur Ram Singh, a pupil of Mr Kipling, and now Deputy-Principal, is well known for the fine carved work which he executed for the late Queen Empress and H.R.H. the Duke of Connaught.

W. of the new Museum is the **Town Hall**, opened by H.R.H. the late Duke of Clarence in 1890, and S. of this is the **Panjab Library**, said by some to have been built by Wazir Khan, by others by Ilahi Bakhsh. It is a handsome building, with four white cupolas, and contains many valuable books.

Not far off on the E. outskirts of the Anar Kali Bazaar is the Nila Gumbaz or Blue Dome, the tomb of Abdul Razak, a saint of the time of Humayun. Further S., near the Presbyterian Church, is the shrine of another Mohammedan saint called **Mauj-i-Darya.** Over the door is a Persian inscription which says it is the tomb of Saiyad Muhammed Shah Mauj-i-Darya, son of Nuru'llah, who was a spiritual guide in the time of Akbar.

The **Tomb of Anar Kali**, "Pomegranate Blossom" (a name given to a favourite lady in the harem of Akbar, who was also called Nadirah Begam, or Sharafunnissa), is an octagon cased in plaster and surmounted by a dome. It was for many years the church of the civil station (St James), but it is now used as the Secretariat Library. The cenotaph, now placed at the E. end of the central chamber, is of the purest white marble, and the ninety-nine names of God carved on it are so exquisitely formed as to surpass anything of the kind in India. On the side, below the names of the Deity, is written *Majnun Salim Akbar*, "The enamoured Salim, son of Akbar," Salim being the name of Jahangir. On the W. side is a date, above the words "In Lahore," corresponding to 1615, which is probably the date of the building of the tomb. The story is that Anar Kali was beloved by Salim, and was seen by Akbar, his father, to smile when the Prince entered the harem. As a punishment for this it is said that she was buried alive; and the pathetic distich engraved on her sarcophagus certainly indicates that Salim was her lover.

"Ah gar man baz binam rue yar-i-khwesh ra
Ta Kiamat shukar goyam Kardagar-i-khwesh ra."

"Ah, if I could again see the face of my beloved,
To the day of judgment I would give thanks to my Creator."

In front of the Civil Secretariat Office adjoining the tomb is a cross to the memory of Sir Donald M'Leod, Lieutenant-Governor, 1865-1870.

The **Government College** Buildings rise finely on the right side of the road from Amarkali to the city; the convocation meetings of the Panjab University are held in the great Hall of the College, and there is a large boarding-house attached to it.[1] On the opposite side of the road are the District Courts, which possess more architectural merits than buildings of this class usually do in India. Further back to the W. from here is the noted shrine of **Data Ganj Bakhsh**, a saint of the time of Mahmud of Ghazni. Passing round the W. side of the city a fine view is obtained at the N.W. corner of the great mosque and the Sikh sacred places to the N. of it and the Fort rising above it. The first of the shrines is that of **Guru Arjan**, the fifth Guru, and compiler of the *Adi* (original) *Granth*. The *Granth* is read here daily, in a huge volume over which attendants reverently wave *chauris*. According to Sikh legend he disappeared in the Ravi on this spot, upon which Maharaja Ranjit Singh accordingly built this memorial. Between this and the Hazuri Bagh is the **Samadh** or cenotaph of Maharajas Ranjit Singh, Kharak Singh, and Nau Nihal Singh, a glittering white building rather out of keeping with the solemn mosque. It faces the W. wall of the Fort, and is a square stucco building, restored in part in 1840, on a high platform of marble. The ceilings are decorated with traceries in stucco inlaid with mirrors. The arches of the interior are of marble, strengthened with brick and *chunam*, and clamped with iron, by order of Sir D. M'Leod when Lieutenant-Governor of the Panjab. In the centre is a raised platform of marble, on which is a lotus flower carved in marble, surrounded by eleven smaller flowers. The central flower covers the ashes of the great Maharaja; the others those of 4 wives and 7 concubines who became *satis* with his corpse.

[1] The Oriental College is also included in these. It contains 90 students, and the Government College 200.

On entering the **Hazuri Bagh**, through the gate which fell on Maharaja Nau Nihal Singh on 5th November 1840 as he returned from his father's cremation, the high crenellated wall of the Fort rises on the left, and in its centre the **Akbari Darwazah**, built by the Emperor Akbar, and now closed. The Hazuri Bagh forms an outer court to the mosque on its W. side. In its centre is the *Barahdarri*, a beautiful pavilion, built by Maharaja Ranjit Singh with white marble taken from the tombs of the Emperor Jahangir and the Empress Nur Jahan at Shahdara.

A fine flight of steps leads up to the gate of the **Jama** or **Badshahi Masjid**, raised on a lofty platform supported by arches. In a chamber above the archway are preserved certain relics of the Prophet and his family. They consist of turbans of 'Ali and of his sons Hasan and Husain, a cap with Arabic writing on it, the prayer-carpet of Fatima, a slipper of Mohammed, and the mark of his foot impressed in a stone. There are also a vestment of the Prophet, his prayer-carpet, a green turban, and a hair of the Prophet's beard. The mosque was built by Aurangzeb with the funds derived from the confiscated estates of his eldest brother Dara Shikoh, whom he put to death, and it has consequently never been popular as a place of prayer. Over the entrance is written the Moslem creed, and then in Persian the date=1674. Of the four minarets, all of which are disfigured by the loss of one storey, only that to the S.W. is open. The cupolas were so much injured by an earthquake that it was necessary to take them down. The mosque is built of red sandstone, and the façade of the mosque proper is beautifully adorned with white marble flowers. It has one large and ten smaller archways facing the court, under three white marble domes. Unlike any other in India the courtyard is made beautiful by the fine trees in it. It was a magazine under the Sikhs, and was restored to the Mohammedans after the visit of King Edward in 1876.

Facing the Samadh of Maharaja Ranjit Singh is the Hathi Paon Gate of the **Fort**. A steep incline,[1] made by the British, leads into the interior, but before ascending it attention should be paid to the peculiar decoration of the walls of the **Palace of Akbar**, which face the gate. The façade is inlaid with a mosaic of encaustic tiles, representing grotesque figures of men, horses, and elephants, engaged in hunting, and also the angels, who, according to old Persian mythology, preside over the days and months. In spandrels over arcaded compartments in front of the part of the palace attributed to Jahangir are four representations of the rising sun. Other spandrels show cherubs like those in Christian churches, which were perhaps borrowed from the Portuguese Jesuit church at Lahore.

The *Palace of Akbar* is on the extreme E. of the Fort. To it succeeds a part built by Jahangir, and then a curtain wall between two hexagonal towers ascribed to Shah Jahan, to which Aurangzeb and the Sikhs made additions. The Fort was visited and described by Sir Thomas Roe and Sir Thomas Herbert in 1615 and 1626.

On the left near the top of the incline is the **Moti Masjid**, or Pearl Mosque, of white marble, with three domes. Over the arched entrance into the outer court are a Persian inscription and date corresponding to 1598 A.D. Maharaja Ranjit Singh kept his treasure here, and the British long used it for the same purpose. It is the most elegant of Jahangir's works here, and has been well restored.

N. of the Moti Masjid is the enclosure of the **Shish Mahal**, or Palace of Mirrors, which is the joint work of Shah Jahan and Aurangzeb. The E. wall of this building did not exist in Maharaja Ranjit Singh's time, and there was an extensive court into which he used to pass from it to the Moti Masjid.

The Shish Mahal building which stands on the N. wall was the place where the sovereignty of the Panjab was transferred to the British Government, and where Maharaja Ranjit Singh held Darbar. In the small rooms leading to the upper tower the ceilings are cut into geometrical patterns. These paintings and the mirror-work with which the walls and ceilings are ornamented were done by the Sikhs, and ill agree with the chaste beauty of the Mughal architecture. The windows look out on the *Badami* ("almond") *Garden* plain to the N., where Maharaja Ranjit Singh used to hold reviews. The basins of the fountains, formerly in the centre of the quadrangle, still remain.

In the centre of the W. side of the quadrangle is a graceful white marble pavilion called **Nau Lakha**, as it is said to have cost 9 lakhs or Rs.900,000. This beautiful work of

[1] The old elephant route into the Fort has now been reopened. Visitors following its windings to the left arrive first at the Shish Mahal Court, and then, passing the Moghal buildings, leave the Fort at the Diwan-i-Khas and pass under the walls to the gate of entrance.

THE FORT, LAHORE.

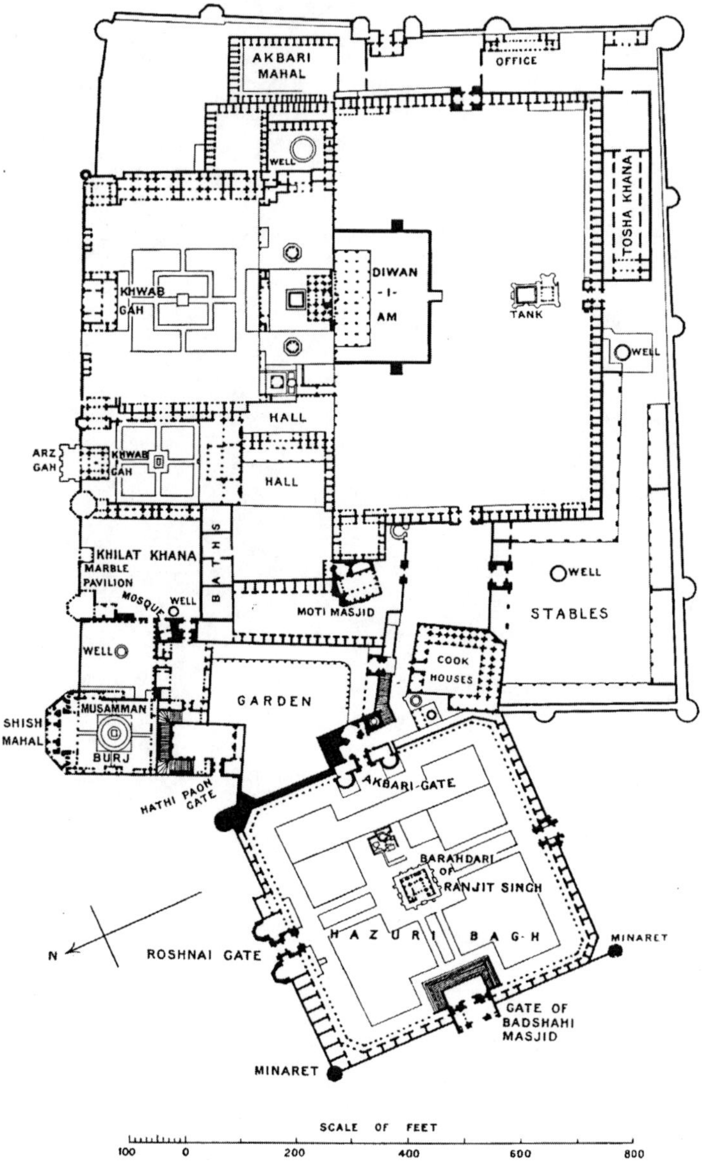

[*To face p.* 234.

art is inlaid after the fashion so well known at Agra. Between the pillars on the S. side of the quadrangle walls have been erected, and thus a large **Armoury** has been formed. In it is the round shield of Guru Govind. It is of rhinocerous hide, and has a single boss. His battle-axe is also shown, the blade of which is of fine Damascus steel. Here too will be seen the arms taken from the Sikhs by the English; some of the helmets are inscribed "Akal Sipahi." The long gauntleted swords were merely used in fencing. There are many cuirasses which belonged to the regiments commanded by French officers, with brass cocks upon them. There are also rings of steel which were used as missiles in war, particularly by the Akalis. The crests of these soldiers, called Jikars, in the shape of a bar passing through two semicircles, and crowned with a ball, are exhibited. There are also some cannon with barrels which turn like those of a revolver, and a number of camel guns and an obus, inscribed in Persian, "Fath ya shahid, 1815"—"Victory or death." Many coats of mail will also be observed.

Parallel with the tower of the Shish Mahal was once another tower, the **Musamman Burj**, of great height.

To the E. from here is the enclosure of the Akbari Mahal with the **Diwan-i-Khas** and Khwabgah on the N. side of it. The Diwan-i-Khas is a beautiful building of white marble, supported on thirty-two columns, and till lately used by the English as a church. There is an aperture in the Jali or perforated screen, on the N., about 2 ft. sq., at which the Emperor sat and heard his *Arzbegi* read the petitions from the roof of a building now ruined, 24 ft. below. This and the Diwan-i-'Am were built by Shah Jahan.

From the Diwan-i-Khas sixty-seven steps lead down to the ditch between the outer wall and the N. wall of the palace. About 20 yds. from this is the *Khwabgah-i-Kalan*, of red sandstone, which has been whitewashed. The architraves of the pillars are well carved in the Hindu fashion, with representations of elephants and birds, as are also those of the **Akbari Mahal**, an ornamented Hindu pavilion. Further E. again on the wall of the Fort is the Jahangiri Khwabgah, reminding one of Akbar's red palace at Agra (p. 177).

S. of the Akbari Mahal and near the centre of the Fort is the **Diwan-i-'Am** (now used as barracks). The building is of red sandstone, supported in the centre by twelve columns. The outer arches have been filled in to form walls, and the whole has been whitewashed. In the centre is the Takhtgah, or "throne place," where the Emperor sat. The ascent is by twelve steps, and there are several rooms behind. In the front of the building are the remains of a red sandstone railing, inside which only the nobles could come. N. of this, where now stands a clump of trees, was a tomb, out of which a holy man used to warn the Emperor that he was mortal.

To the E. is the Hammam building which was used by Maharani Chand Kanwar, widow of Nau Nihal Singh, for her residence: in it she was confined by order of Sher Singh, and put to death according to his commands by her handmaidens. It is now used as a hospital. E. of the Diwan-i-'Am and adjoining it is the house of Sher Singh, which was four storeys high, two of which only now remain. In the N.E. corner of the Fort is the insignificant temple of Loh, from which the name Lahore is derived. Outside this corner is a mosque built by Mariam-uz-zamáni (p. 183), mother of the Emperor Jahangir.

Leaving the Hazuri Bagh by the S. Gate and turning E. past the reservoir of the Water-works, the **Sonahri Masjid** or Golden Mosque is reached. This has three gilt domes, and was built in 1753 A.D. by Bikhari Khan, a favourite of the widow of Mir Mannu, a lady who governed Lahore a short time after her husband's death. He is said to have displeased the lady, whose female attendants beat him to death with their shoes. The situation of this mosque at the junction of two streets is picturesque.

In a courtyard behind the mosque is a large **well**, with steps descending to the water. It is said to have been dug by Arjan, the fifth Guru.

A street with some fine balconies leads E. again from here to a *chauk* or square, where is the very beautiful **Mosque of Wazir Khan.** It was built in 1634 by Hakim 'Alau-ud-din of Chiniot, Governor of the Panjab under Shah Jahan. The brick walls are covered with inlaid work called Nakkashi, a kind of mosaic of glazed tiles, lately renewed where necessary. The colours of the tiles are burnt in, and they are set in hard mortar. The yellow ground of the tile-work is extremely effective and beautiful. Over the noble entrance is written in Persian, "Remove thy heart from the gardens of the world, and know that this building is the true abode of man." It was completed in 1634 A.D. The architect was Hidayat-ul-lah, the faithful servant of Wazir Khan. In the centre front of the mosque is the Moslem creed, and in panels along the façade are beautifully written verses from the Koran. From the gallery round the minarets, about 3 ft. broad, there is a very fine view over the city, which is truly Oriental and picturesque. Beyond the *chauk* is the Delhi Gate of the city, from which the Landa Bazaar now leads to the Railway Station. The magnificent palace of Dara Shikoh and the great Tripulia Bazaar lay between the city and the station; and the houses and gardens and tombs of the nobles extended along the Ravi, as far E. as Shahlimar. The ruined tomb of Mir Mannu adjoins the open space W. of the railway station; the mosque E. of the station, now used as a railway office, was built by a foster-mother of Shah Jahan in 1635.[1]

[1] This mosque, the Mai Anagah, has been lately restored to the Mohammedans at the instance of Lord Curzon.

The picturesqueness of the old town must appeal to every one, but to artists it will be found of especial interest. The balconies and projecting oriel windows of the irregular brick houses, together with the variety and colour of the costumes of the people, form a striking picture. The most effective corners will be found at the N. ends of the streets leading from the Mori and Lohari Gates. In front of the latter the Anarkali Bazaar runs for ¾ m. down to the Panjab Museum. To the E. of it lie the Mayo Hospital, with the Albert Victor Memorial wing, the Lady Aitchison Female Hospital, and the Lady Lyall Nurses' Home. It is intended to rebuild the Mayo Hospital and Medical College at a cost of 6 lakhs (£40,000) as a memorial of King Edward. A college for girls is being started in memory of the visit of Queen Mary.

Near the S.W. corner of the Civil Station is the Chauburji ("Four Towers") gateway. This beautiful but ruined building, which led to the garden of Zebunnissa Begam, a daughter of the Emperor Aurangzeb, is faced with blue and green encaustic tiles. This lady, who died in 1669 A.D., long before her father, and who was a poetess under the name of Makhfi (Hidden), is buried at Nawan Kot, 2 m. S. from this garden.

Excursions from Lahore.

The **Shalimar Gardens** are **5 m.** E. from the railway station. About half-way to them is the gateway to the **Gulabi Bagh** or Rose Garden, laid out in 1655 by Sultan Beg, Admiral of the fleet to Shah Jahan. The Nakkashi work of coloured tiles on the gate is very beautiful, and hardly inferior to that on Wazir Khan's Mosque. On the gateway is inscribed in Persian:

"Sweet is this garden; through envy of it
the tulip is spotted,
The rose of the sun and moon forms its
beautiful lamp."

Close to this is the tomb of Sharf-unnissa Begam, sister of Zakariah Khan, with paintings of cypress trees.

There are many dargahs and gardens near this building to which on holidays crowds of people go on pilgrimage. Between them and the river is the village of Begampur. The ruined octagonal tomb to the E., known as the Bagga Gumbat, or White Dome, is the tomb of Yahia Khan, and not far off are the mosque and grave of Zakariah Khan and his father, in a garden of the former, whose palace was at this place. Nearer the river again is the garden tomb of Shah Bilawal, a saint honoured by Shah Jahan, where Maharaja Sher Singh was murdered in 1843.

Opposite to the Gulabi Bagh, across a field on the S. side of the road, is the **Tomb of 'Ali Mardan Khan**, the celebrated engineer, who also created the Shalimar Gardens. Its lofty archway retains traces of exquisitely coloured tiles. 50 yds. S. of this is the octagonal tomb, built of brick, now much ruined.

The *Shalimar Gardens* were laid out in 1637 A.D. by order of Shah Jahan. They are divided into three parts, in tiers of different levels: the highest was known as the Farhat Bakhsh, and the two lowest as Faiz Bakhsh. The whole extent is about 80 acres, surrounded by a wall, with a large gateway and pavilions at each corner. Canals traverse the garden, and there is a tank in the centre with an island and a passage across to it. There are one hundred small fountains in the first garden, and double that number in the tank. The trees are chiefly mangoes, and the garden is laid out in monotonous square beds. Once, when the cement was intact and the frescoes new, it must have been a very pretty place, but now it strikes one as rather decayed and shabby.

On the opposite side of the road are two other gardens, the **Sindhanwala** and **Misr Brij. Lal's**; to the E. is the fine garden of **Jamadar Khushhal Singh**, and across the road to the N.E. that of **Lehna Singh**.

The Lahore cantonment, formerly **Meean Meer**, lies 5 m. to the S.E. of the Civil Station. It is the head-quarters of the 3rd Army Division. Six of the nine Army Divisions, it may be noted, are in the corner of India, N.W. of Lucknow.

The cantonment, built in the middle of graveyards, and upon them, has always been very unhealthy; the dust and heat of the place in summer render it one of the most unpopular in India.

About ¾ m. to the N.W., on the right of the road from the railway station to the cantonment, is the *Shrine of Meean Meer*, a saint from whom the cantonment has its name, and who was honoured by the Emperors Jahangir and Shah Jahan, his real name being Mahomed Mir. It stands in the centre of a quadrangle, 200 ft. sq., on a marble platform. Over the entrance are an inscription in Persian and the date = 1635 A.D. The left side of the enclosure is occupied by a mosque.

The disarmament of the Native Regiments at Meean Meer, on 13th May 1857, by Brigadier-General Corbett, was perhaps the most important of all the steps taken at the commencement of the Mutiny to secure the Panjab and ensure the taking of Delhi. It was carried out quietly and effectively by the 81st Regiment and the artillery of the station, in the presence of the Judicial Commissioner, Mr Robert Montgomery, Sir John Lawrence being at the time in Rawal Pindi. The 81st also occupied the Fort of Lahore and the Govind Garh Fort at Amritsar.

Returning towards the city, the traveller will pass on the right the village of **Shahu-ki-Ghari**, where are a number of large tombs, some with cupolas, but all more or less ruined. Some way W. of the village is Kila

Gujar Singh, so called from one of the Bhangi Sirdars, and near it and upon the main road from the Civil Station to the railway station, is the most venerated tomb in Lahore or its vicinity. It is called the **Tomb of Bibi Pakdaman,** "The Chaste Lady." According to tradition, this saint was the daughter of the younger brother of 'Ali by a different mother. Her real name was Rakiyah Khanum, and she was the eldest of six sisters, who are all buried here, and who fled with her from Bagdad, after the massacre at Karbala; she died in 728 A.D., at the age of ninety. Visitors are expected to take off their shoes. There are five enclosures, and the tomb of Rakiyah is in the fifth. It is of brick, whitewashed.

Shah Dara is situated beyond the Bridge of Boats on the right bank of the Ravi, about 1¼ m. to the N. of the railway bridge over that river. The journey by rail is 5 m. to the Shah Dara station, from which the **Tomb of the Emperor Jahangir** is 1¼ m. It is more convenient to go in a carriage (about 5½ m. drive).

Before crossing the railway, is seen, right, the tomb of **Nur Jahan,** wife of Jahangir, a plain building of one storey. A fund is being raised for its restoration, to which the Maharaja of Burdwan has given 5000 Rs.

After crossing the railway a domed building is passed on the left. This is the tomb of Asaf Khan (see below); and immediately E. of it is the enclosure, which was the sarai or outer court of the mausoleum. An archway of white marble, and 50 ft. high, leads into the garden court of the mausoleum, once the Dilkusha garden of the Empress Nur Jahan. The Mausoleum consists of a fine terraced platform, not unlike the lowest terrace at Sikandara (p. 179), with four minarets at the corners and a small pavilion over the tomb chamber in the centre.[1]

[1] The model of the tomb was that of Itmad-ud-daulah at Agra (see p. 179.)

The passage to the tomb chamber is paved with beautifully streaked marble. The cenotaph is of white marble, inlaid with *pietra dura* work, and stands in the centre of an octagonal chamber. On the E. and W. sides are the ninety-nine names of God, most beautifully carved, and on the S. side is inscribed, "The Glorious Tomb of His High Majesty, Asylum of Protectors, Nur-ud-din Muhammad, the Emperor Jahangir," 1627 A.D. On the four sides are exquisite screens of lattice-work. The lamp over the tomb was presented by the Maharana of Kotah.

Outside the entrance a staircase leads up to the flat roof of the terrace covered with a fine marble tessellated pavement. The minaret at each corner is 95 ft. high from the platform. The marble parapet which ran round the pavement was taken away by Maharaja Ranjit Singh, but has been restored. The minarets are four storeys high, and are built of magnificent blocks of stone 8 ft. long. From the top there is a fine view over the Ravi to the city of Lahore.

The **Tomb of Asaf Khan,** brother of the Empress Nur Jahan, is an octagon surmounted by a dome. It has been utterly ruined and almost entirely stripped of the lovely Nakkashi work which once adorned it. In the portals some fragments still remain to show how splendid it once was. The cenotaph is of white marble. The Tughra writing on it is extremely fine, and resembles that on the tomb of Jahangir. The gardens here and round the Emperor's Tomb have been much improved of late. Asaf Khan and his sister had entire control over the indolent Jahangir during the last years of his life. On his death Nur Jahan wished a younger son of the Emperor married to her daughter by her Afghan husband to succeed him; but Asaf Khan stood by Shah Jahan, and the ex-Queen at once retired into private life. Asaf Khan died six years later, having attained to the rank of Khan-i-Khanan and Governor of Lahore; and his tomb was erected by the Emperor, who was himself born at Lahore. Nur Jahan survived her brother for four years.

---

18 m. W. of Lahore is **Shekhupura**, formerly Jahangirabad, the hunting-seat of Jahangir and of Dara Shikoh, the eldest brother of Aurangzeb.

The road crosses the bridge over the Ravi, near the ruins of the river-pavilion of Kamran, brother of the Emperor Humayun, and at about 4 m. enters a dreary tract of long grass and jungle. A bridge over the Bagh Bachcha (Tiger Cub), a branch of the Dig, is then passed. At Mandiali there is a good Road Chauki, standing 100 yds. back from the road.

On the left at Shekhupura is a garden-house, built by Rani Nakayan, queen of Ranjit Singh. At the S.W. corner of the garden is her *Samadh*, an octagonal building. Over the door is a picture of the ten Gurus, with an inscription. Across the road is a very clean and comfortable house which belongs to the Raja Jagirdar, grandson of Maharaja Teja Singh, and is lent by him to travellers.

The Raja resides in the fine old fort here.

There is good shooting round about. 3 m. from the town is a large tank surrounded by flights of steps with a three storeyed *barahdarri* in the centre. A tall minaret, Hiran Minar, or Deer Tower, stands near an entrance gateway N. of the tank.

ROUTE 16.

Lahore to **PESHAWAR** by **Gujranwala, Wazirabad** Junction, **Gujrat, Lala Musa** Junction, **Jhelum, Rohtas, Manikyala, Rawal Pindi, Golra, Attock,** and **Nowshera,** with expeditions by rail from Wazirabad to **Sialkot** and **Jammu,** from Lala Musa to **W. Panjab,** from Golra to **Khushalgarh** and **Kohat,** and from Nowshera to **Hoti Mardan and the Malakand.**

Lahore to Peshawar is 288 m. by the North-Western Railway, and the time occupied in transit eleven hours. Fares, Rs.28, Rs.14, Rs.3, as.10.

5 m **Shah Dara** station. The tomb of the Emperor Jahangir, 1½ m. off, is described on p. 338. From here a branch line runs 56 m. tc Sangla, p. 241.

42 m. **Gujranwala** station (R.) D.B. (population 29,600). Headquarters of a district and the birthplace of Ranjit Singh. At ¼ m. beyond the station is the *Samadh of Mahan Singh*, father of the great Maharaja. It is an octagonal building, 81 ft. high to the top of the gilt ornament on the summit. Within are the sculptured rosettes or knobs which mark where the ashes are deposited. The large rosette surrounded by twelve smaller ones is inscribed Sarkar Ranjit Singh. That nearest the entrance is in memory of a blue pigeon that fell down into the flames in which Ranjit Singh and his concubines were being consumed. Other rosettes mark the ashes of Mahan Singh Padshah, Maharaja Sher Singh, and Sarkar Nau Nihal Singh Ji. There is a narrow but lofty pavilion, covered with mythological pictures, among which is one of Duryodhana ordering Draupadi (p. lviii) to be stripped. As fast as the clothes were pulled off her she was supernaturally re-clothed. At 100 yds. to the E. is the pavilion of Mahan Singh, a handsome building, now

used as the reading and meeting room of the Anjuman of the town. Close to the market-place is the **house where Ranjit Singh was born**, with a frieze of geese round the courtyard.

N.E. of the town is the *Barahdarri*, or pavilion, of the famous general, Hari Singh Nalwa. It stands in 40 acres of garden and grounds. To the E. is a pavilion 12 ft. high, full of small niches for lamps. On the E. wall is a painting of warriors and elephants, now almost gone. At 70 yds. to the N. of the house is the samadh of Hari Singh (see p. 249). The place where the ashes lie is marked by a knob shaped like a budding flower. There are no *sati* memorials. A picture on the wall inside is a portrait of Hari Singh hawking, with a string of ducks passing over his head. The gardens round Gujranwala are famous for oranges.

62 m. **Wazirabad** junction station (R.), D.B. (15,200 inhabitants). From here a line runs N.E. to *Sialkot* and *Jammu* (see below). This place, founded by Wazir Khan in the reign of Shah Jahan, became, under the rule of Ranjit Singh,[1] the headquarters of General Avitabile, who built a completely new town on the plan of a parallelogram, surrounded by a wall. A broad bazaar runs from end to end. Close to the town is one of the most famous **gardens** in the Panjab, laid out by Dewan Thakur Das Chopra. N. of Wazirabad is the great *Alexandra Bridge* over the Chenab, opened on 27th January 1876 by King Edward.

The Chenab was a most difficult stream to deal with, owing to the sudden furious floods to which it is subject, and the absence of a well defined river-bed.

[An expedition may be made by branch line from Wazirabad to

27 m. **Sialkot** station, D.B. A town with military cantonment 1 m. N. (population 58,000). The *Church* is a striking object, having a steeple 150 ft. high. Near the railway station and the city is a lofty old Fort, in which the British residents took refuge on the mutiny of the two native regiments on 9th July 1857. A number, however, were killed before they could make their escape, and Brigadier-General Brind commanding the station died, after reaching the Fort, of the wounds inflicted on him. The mutinous regiments spared most of their officers, and even offered them higher pay to lead them to Delhi! The present garrison includes a regiment of British Infantry and Cavalry, two batteries of Artillery and a regiment of Native Infantry. The railway continues to

52 m. **Jammu** station, D.B. (population, 36,000). This is the winter capital of the Maharaja of Jammu and Kashmir State, which has an area of 81,000 sq. m., and a population of 2,000,000 persons. The present Chief of the State (of which the annual revenue is 70 lakhs) is His Highness Major-General Maharaja Sir Partab Singh, G.C.S.I., grandson of the famous Dogra Maharaja, Gulab Singh, to whom Kashmir was made over in 1846, after the first Sikh war.

The **Old Palace** at Jammu, in the N.E. corner of the city, has no special pretensions to beauty. It is entered by a large irregular quadrangle, on the right side of which is a vast reception-room. The verandah of the small reception-room overlooks the Tawi.

W. of the city is a temple covered with plates of copper-gilt. A little to the N. of it is the new palace built for King Edward's visit on 20th-22nd January 1876: the Prince of Wales College commemorates that of King George V. on 10th December 1905. Close by to the E. is the old parade-ground, with the hospital and college to the S.E. The *Gumit Gateway*, by which the city is entered from the river Tawi, is approached by a very picturesque flight of rough stone steps. A new road leads from

[1] See p. lxvi.

below it to the Residency Rest-House in the S.E. corner of the city. 2 m. S. of this gate is a fine garden belonging to the Maharaja.

The Banihal route to the Kashmir Valley starts from Jammu (see Route 17).

From Wazirabad another branch line runs down the colony settled on the waste lands now irrigated by the Chenab Canal through Sangla, 68 m. and Lyallpur, 97 m. (so named from Sir J. B. Lyall, G.C.I.E., Lieutenant-Governor, 1887-1892), to Mooltan (232 m.). This colony is unique in the whole of India, and contains a specially selected population averaging 212 per sq. m., and an irrigated area of 1½ million acres, producing crops valued at £3,500,000. A similar colony is being established on the Jhelum Canal. The Panjab Agricultural College is at Lyallpur.

71 m. **Gujrat** station. This pretty place is the administrative headquarters of a district of the same name. The town (19,400 inhabitants) stands on the ancient site of two earlier cities. The second, according to General Cunningham, was destroyed in 1303 A.D. Two centuries after this Sher Shah was in possession of the country, and either he or Akbar founded the present town. Akbar's fort stands in the centre of the city. It was first garrisoned by Gujars, and took the name of Gujrat Akbarabad. Akbar's administrative records are still preserved in the families of the hereditary registrars. During the reign of Shah Jahan, Gujrat became the residence of a famous saint, Pir Shah Daulah, who adorned it with numerous buildings. In 1741 the Ghakkars established themselves at Gujrat, and in 1765 the Sikhs acquired the country. The **Civil Station,** in which is the D.B., lies to the N. In it are a Church of Scotland Mission Church and Schools.

The Battlefield.—The decisive battle of Gujrat, which ended the second Sikh War, was fought on the 21st of February 1849. The villages of Kalra, 2½ m. S. of the D.B., were the key of the Sikh position. The villages are situated in a flat plain, where there are no natural advantages to assist an army in maintaining its position. Lord Gough's camp, which had been at Wazirabad, where he was joined by the force which had captured Mooltan under General Whish, was moved to Shadiwal between 17th and 19th February. Thence at 7 A.M. on the morning of 21st February the British force advanced on the Sikh position at Kalra. The artillery went to the front and poured their fire on the Sikh army, which comprised six brigades of infantry with fifty-nine guns, and four great bodies of Sikh cavalry with 4000 Afghan horse, the British army consisting of 25,000 men and nearly 100 guns. The heavy English guns opened on the Sikhs at 1000 yards, and crushed their lighter metal. As the Sikh fire ceased, the British field-batteries were constantly pushed forward. By 11.30 A.M. most of the Sikh guns had been withdrawn, dismounted, or abandoned. The British infantry then advanced, deployed, and drove the Sikhs from their position in the two villages of Kalra. There was no attempt to make a further stand at Gujrat, and the Sikh army streamed away in utter defeat to the E. and W. of the town, which was occupied by one o'clock. The British losses were only 766.

Next day General Gilbert, with 12,000 men, started in pursuit of the enemy, and at Rawal Pindi received the submission of the entire Sikh army.

In the cemetery at *Shah Jahangir*, called after a fakir of that name, are the tombs of those who fell in the battle. Beyond to the E. are two mosques, one of which is rather remarkable. Gujrat is one of the starting-places for Kashmir. (See Route 17.)

83 m. **Lala Musa** junction station (R.).

[The Sindh-Sagar line runs 346 m. from here to Sher Shah junction, south of Mooltan (p. 261), passing Chillianwalla, Malakwal junction, (from which a short line runs to Bhera and a longer one to Sargodha, 47 m., and Jhang, 116 m., in the Jhelum Canal colony, and thence Mooltan); Haranpur (for the Khewra salt mines), Pind Dadan Khan, Khushab (for Shahpur), Mitha Tiwana (the headquarters of the famous Tiwana horsemen), Kundian (where the line from Campbellpur (p. 245) joins in), Darya Khan (for **Dera Ismail Khan**, 12 m. distant across the Indus, population 32,000, headquarters of a frontier district: Sir H. M. Durand, Lieutenant-Governor of the Panjab, 1870-71, who lost his life from an accident at Tánk, is buried in the churchyard here), Mahmud Kot (for Dera Ghazi Khan, population 24,000), also on the right bank of the Indus, now almost destroyed by the river, and Muzaffargarh. Between Kundian and Mahmud Kot the table-rock of the Takht-i-Sulaiman, the throne of Solomon, 12,300 ft., will be seen on the W. horizon on clear days.

At **Chillianwalla** was fought in the second Sikh War, on 13th January 1849, the most desperate of all the battles between the British and the Sikhs. The Sikhs advanced from their position on high ground between Rasul on the N. to Moong on the S., and opened a heavy fire on the British troops, and Lord Gough ordered a general attack on them, though only a very short time of daylight remained. In making this the two brigades on the left under Sir Colin Campbell became separated, and that of General Pennycuick was badly checked, and finally had to fall back, while the absolute failure of the cavalry on the right of the British line exposed the divisions there to a flank attack, which prevented their advance. Finally the troops were recalled, the British losses being 2238, and several British guns being captured. On the Sikh side from 20,000 to 25,000 men were engaged, and on the British side 14,000. A full view of the field may be obtained from the obelisk erected on the mound to the E. of it, from which Lord Gough watched the battle. Alongside of the obelisk is a cross and a small cemetery in which General Pennycuick and his son and the officers of the 24th Regiment, which suffered most of all, and other officers who fell at Chillianwalla, are buried. On the news of the battle reaching England Lord Gough was recalled; but before the orders of recall reached him he had won the final victory of Gujrat.

According to General Cunningham, Alexander crossed the Jhelum somewhere in the neighbourhood of Rasul and Moong, and defeated Porus in 327 B.C., not very far from the field of Chillianwalla.

Those interested in geology and in picturesque sights will find a visit to the famous Khewra salt mines (D.B.) will well repay the trouble of the journey. It would be well to write beforehand to the Superintendent of the Mines for facilities to visit them.

20 m. from Pind Dadan Khan, and high up in the Salt Range, is the picturesque village and garden of Choya Saidan Shah, and near it are the temples of Katas, a very holy place of Hindu pilgrimage. Khushab, on the right bank of the Jhelum, is a place of great antiquity.]

Beyond (92 m.) **Kharian** the line traverses a curiously broken tract, known as the Pabbi, which is being afforested, and crosses the Jhelum river by a fine bridge, affording a grand view of the snows of the Pir Panjal and of the town on the north bank.

103 m. **Jhelum** station (R.), D.B., is a modern town (population 15,000), and the administrative headquarters of a district of the same name, built on an ancient site. The Civil Lines and Cantonment lie 1 m. E. and W. of the town respectively. The attempt to disarm the Native Regiment here on 7th July 1857 was badly mismanaged, and resulted in the loss of valuable lives. Many ancient pillars have been dug up near the railway station, and amongst them one with a human face in the Greek style, which is now in a Lahore Museum. Another is to be seen in the railway engineer's compound.

[**Rohtas** is 11 m. N.W. of Jhelum. Carriage-road to the Kahan river, 8 m., and after that cart-track along the river, and then a bridle-path below barren hills 200 ft. high. This famous fort, which is partly visible from the railway, stands on a hill overlooking the gorge of the Kahan river. Its walls extend for 3 m., in places from 30 to 40 ft. thick, and enclose about 260 acres. It was built by Sher Shah, in 1452, as a check on the Ghakkar tribes.

The entrance, up a steep path, is by the Khawas Khan Gate, on the N.E. of the hill. The Suhali Gate (where is the D.B.) is on the S.W., and is reached through the town, with a deep fissure on the left, and on the right an inner wall with a lofty gateway, called after Shah Chand Wali. Within this stand the ruins of Man Singh's palace, built after he reduced Kabul (p. 142). The S.W. corner is a lofty barahdarri, with a stone finely carved with figures of birds, etc. In the S.E. corner, 150 ft. off, is a smaller barahdarri, about 25 ft. high. The wall between the two is gone. There were twelve gates to the fort, but they are now nearly all in ruins. The Shisha Gate (an inner gate) was so called from the Harim's Hall of Mirrors, which adjoined it.]

The gradients of the line between Jhelum and (135 m.) **Sohawa** are very considerable, and the alignment has been several times changed. The scenery of the east extremity of the Salt Range through which the line passes is very wild in parts.

163 m. **Mankiala** station is the nearest point to Manikyala Tope, which is 1 m. distant.[1]

[**Manikyala** was first noticed by Mountstuart Elphinstone in 1815, and afterwards thoroughly explored by General Ventura in 1830. In 1834 the stupa was explored by General Court, and thirty years after by General Cunningham. The date is uncertain. There are coins taken from it of Kanishka and Huvishka, which date from the beginning of the Christian era, but with them was found a coin of Yaso Varmma, who reigned not earlier than 720 A.D., and many silver Sassano-Arabian coins of the same period. General Cunningham thinks that the stupa may have been originally built by Huvishka, who deposited coins of his own reign and of his predecessor Kanishka, and that the stupa, having become ruinous, was rebuilt in its present massive form by Yaso Varmma, who redeposited the relic caskets with the addition of a gold coin of himself and several contemporary coins of Arab governors.

The dome of the stupa, which was probably about 100 ft. high, is an exact hemisphere, 127 ft. in diameter. The outer circle measures 500 ft. in circumference, and is ascended by four flights of steps, one in each face, leading to a procession path 16 ft. in width, ornamented both above and below by a range of dwarf pilasters, representing the detached rail of the older Indian monuments.

Mr Fergusson says: "It is, indeed, one of the most marked characteristics of these Gandhara topes that none of them possess, or ever seem to have possessed, any trace of an independent rail; but all have an ornamental belt of pilasters, joined generally by arches simulating the original rail. This can hardly be an early architectural form, and leads to the suspicion that, in spite of their deposits, their outward casing may be very much more modern than the coins they contain."

At 2 m. to the N. of Ventura's tope is **Court's Tope**. Here the earth is of a bright red colour, and General Cunningham identifies this stupa with that mentioned by Hiouen Thsang as "the stupa of the body-offering"; while at 1000 ft. to the S. of it is Hiouen Thsang's "stupa of the blood-offering," which that pilgrim ignorantly attributed to its being stained with the blood of Buddha, who, according to a curious legend, is said[1] to have offered his body to appease the hunger of seven tiger cubs. The stupa of the body-offering was opened by General Court, who

[1] Cunningham's *Arch. Rep.*, vol. ii. p. 152; Fergusson's *Indian Arch.*, i. 95; James Prinsep's *Journal*, vol. iii.

[1] This was in a previous existence.

found in a stone niche, covered by a large inscribed slab, three cylindrical caskets of copper, silver, and gold, each containing **coins** of the same metal; four gold coins of Kanishka were found in the gold box; in the silver box were seven silver Roman denarii of the last years of the Republic, the latest being M. Antonius Triumvir, and therefore not earlier than 43 B.C. The eight copper coins in the box belonged to Kanishka and his predecessors. The inscription has been deciphered by Mr Dowson, who made out the date to be the eighteenth year of Kanishka, and that it was the record of the monastery of the Huta-Murta, or "body-oblation."

General Cunningham ran trenches across the mound, which now represents the monastery, and brought to light the outer walls and cells of the monks, forming a square of 160 ft.

174 m. **Rawal Pindi** Cantonment junction station,* D.B., Hotels (R.). This is the headquarters of a civil division and district, and of the 2nd Army Division. The Cantonment is the largest military station in India, and has lately been surrounded by a chain of detached forts. The city and Cantonment have a population of 87,000, the majority of whom are Mohammedans. It received its name from Jhanda Khan, Ghakkar chief, who restored the town of Fatehpur Baori, destroyed by an invasion of the Mughals in the 14th century. A very fine Mall runs for 4 m. through the station from the W. Ridge to the Fort. In front of the club is a memorial statue of the Queen Empress. The *Church* is about 1 m. from the Railway Station, and the *Fort* is about ½ m. S. of that again. The *Public Garden* by this is a park of 40 acres, with a low forest well preserved. The town has nothing very remarkable in it.

[Rawal Pindi is the starting-place for **Murree,*** 37 m. distant: there is now a motor as well as a tonga service to it. Murree[1] is the N. sanatorium of the Panjab and the headquarters of the Northern Army. Barracks were erected in 1853. The houses are built on the summit and sides of an irregular ridge, and command magnificent views over forest-clad hills into deep valleys, studded with villages and cultivated fields, with the snow-covered peaks of Kashmir in the background. The station is 7507 ft. above the sea-level, and the loftiest peaks behind the sanatorium attain a height of over 9000 ft. The climate is well adapted for Englishmen, the lowest recorded temperature being 21°, the highest, 96°.

The stationary population is only about 3000, but in the height of the summer it rises to 14,000 or 15,000. There is very little game now to be found in the hills. The camps and small stations in the hills, N.W. of Murree, known as the Gallies (Thoba, Changlagalli, Khairagalli, Nathiagalli), are most conveniently reached from Murree. The most northerly of them, Nathiagalli, is the summer residence of the Chief Commissioner of the N.W. Frontier Province. The walls through the Gallies are lovely in spring—nothing in the whole Himalayas is more beautiful.

Rawal Pindi is also the starting-place for **Kashmir** by Murree and the Jhelum Valley. This is the best route into the country (see Route 17).]

It is proposed to construct a railway from Pindi to Murree, and on to Kashmir, to be worked by electric power from the Jhelam falls.

9 m. beyond Rawal Pindi, on an eminence above the little Margala Pass, is the monument of General John Nicholson, with the following inscription:

"Erected by friends, British and Native, to the memory of Brigadier-General John Nicholson, C.B., who, after taking a hero's part in four great wars, fell mortally wounded, in leading to victory the main column of assault at the great siege of Delhi, and died 22nd September 1857, aged 34."

185 m. **Golra** junction for the line to Khushalgarh, Kohat, 109 m. Hangu, 138 m., and Thal, 171 m., at the

[1] At the S.E. point of the station lies the Murree Lawrence Asylum.

MURREE

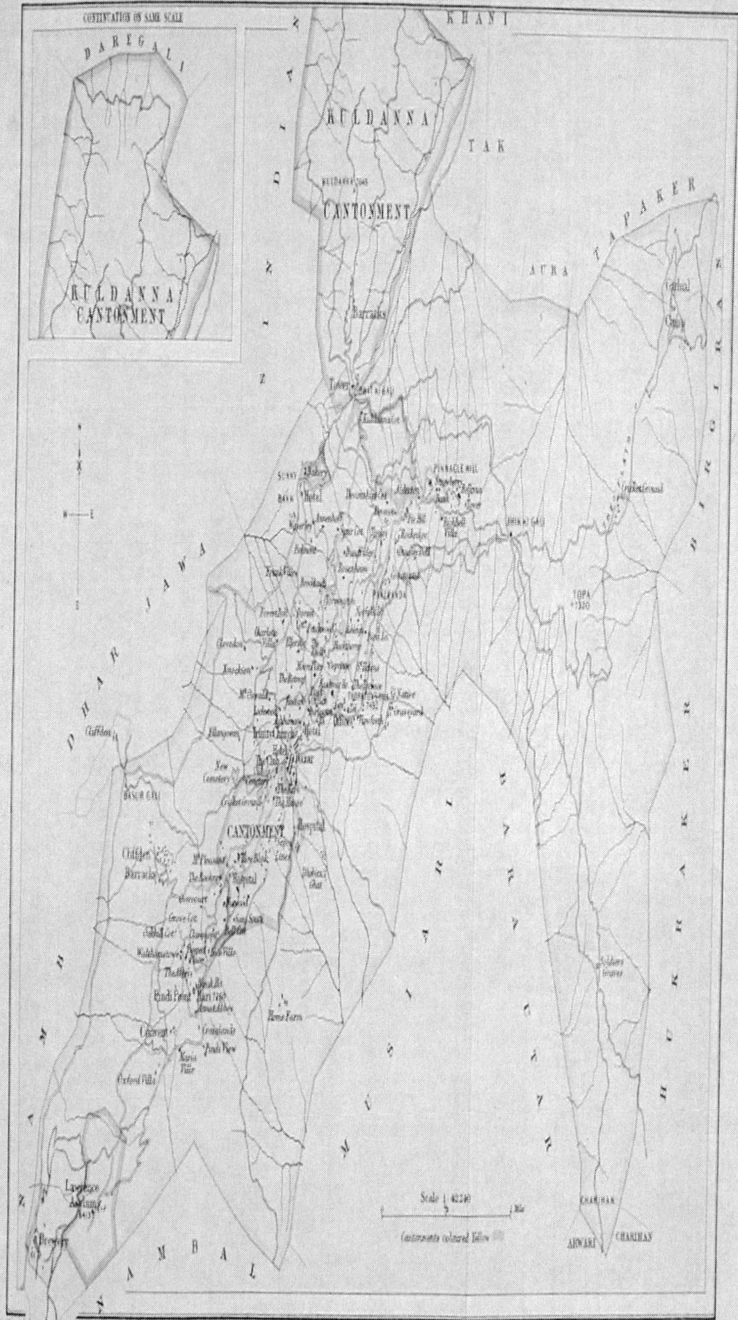

London: John Murray, Albemarle Street.

entrance to the Kurram Valley. [At Basal (56 m.) the line is crossed by that from Campbellpur (p. 242), which with the Sindh-Sagar Railway serves the whole of the position of the left bank of the Indus. From Kalabagh, on a short branch line from Kundian, a light railway is being constructed to (83 m.) **Bannu**, commanding the Tochi route.] At Khushalgarh (83 m.) the Indus is crossed by a cantilever bridge, with a roadway over the railway, the river flowing through a deep, bold gorge; the railway from this point to Kohat has been converted to the broad gauge, on to Thal. Thal is of the 2 ft. 6 in. gauge. On the N. side of the road to Kohat are the hills of the Jowakhi Afridis, against whom a campaign was waged in 1875-76, and N. beyond Kohat is the Samana Range of the Orakzai, against whom campaigns were undertaken in 1889 and 1892, and again on the occasion of the Tirah Afridi expedition in 1897. The Kurram Valley, to which the route beyond Thal leads, was detached from Afghanistan in 1879, but was not taken under direct British management till thirteen years later. The Safed Koh Mountains, with the grand peak of Sika Ram, rise magnificently along the N. side of the valley.]

194 m. **Kala ki Sarai** station, D.B. About a mile from the station are the extensive ruins of a fortified city, which have been identified by General Cunningham with the **Taxila** of Alexander the Great, later the capital of the Scythian Buddhist King Kanishka and his successors, from about A.D. 100 onwards.

203 m. **Hasan Abdal** station, D.B., famous for the so-called *Lalla Rookh's*[1] tomb, which is close by; also on account of the spring of *Baba Wali*, or, as the Sikhs call him, Panja Sahib. This is one of those attractive places to which each religion in succession has attached its legends, and it has been appropriated in turn by Buddhist, Brahman, Mohammedan, and Sikh. The shrine of this saint is on the peak of a lofty and precipitous hill, at the N.W. foot of which numerous springs of limpid water gush out of the ground.

At the E. entrance into the town on the right hand, about ½ m. from the D.B., is the tomb of (?) one of Akbar's wives, popularly said to be that of Nur Jahan. The road to it passes through roughly-paved streets, and then leads down to a clear rapid brook, crossed by stepping-stones, a few yards beyond a *Sikh temple*, near a beautiful pool of water, canopied with mulberry and pipal trees of large size and full of mahsir, some of them as big as a 20-lb. salmon. The walk now leads 250 yds. along the stream, past some ruins of the time of Johangir, and past another pool to the **Tomb**, which is very plain, and stands in a garden surrounded by a wall, with four slim towers, one at each corner: the enclosure is well filled with trees, amongst which is a cypress more than 50 ft. high.

[From Hasan Abdal branches off one of the roads to Kashmir (Route 17) *viâ* **Abbotabad**, D.B., a pretty hill-station (4200 ft.), and headquarters of the Frontier Force Command, famous for its gardens. It is named from Lieutenant James Abbot, who reduced the district to order in 1845-48. At Haripur (20 m.) from Hasan Abdal, is a memorial to Colonel Canara, who was killed defending his guns against the Sikh insurgents in 1848. It is under contemplation to construct a railway line to Kashmir by this route or from Kala Ki Sarai, joining that from Murree at Muzafferabad.]

222 m. **Campbellpur Cantonment** Junction. Line to Kundian (p. 242).

232 m. **Attock Bridge** station (D.B.), 1 m. below the town and Fort. Attock is a small town (population, 2800) and fortress of some military

[1] The last poem in *Lalla Rookh*, that of the "Fair Nurmahal," was recited by the disguised prince at Hasan Abdal.

importance. The railway crosses the Indus by a very fine *Iron Girder Bridge*, which was difficult to construct, owing to the rapidity of the current and the height above the water. The rails are on the top of the girders, and there is a passage for road-traffic below. Each end is protected by a fortified gate. The river has been known to rise 90 ft. in flood near the Fort, where the channel becomes very narrow.

The **Fort**, situated on a commanding height, overhanging the E. bank of the Indus, and a little to the S. of the point where it receives the *Kabul river* on the W. bank, is very extensive and has a most imposing appearance. It was built by the Emperor Akbar in 1583, who also established the ferry which it commands. Maharaja Ranjit Singh occupied the place in 1813, and it remained in the hands of the Sikhs till the British conquest of 1849. It is now held by a small European detachment. Leave can be obtained to walk round the ramparts; this is well worth doing on account of the picturesque views to be obtained, which extend N.W. as far as the distant peaks of the Safed Koh.

To the N. of the Fort is an old sarai, converted into the artillery officers' mess-room.

A ravine to the S. divides the sarai from the higher hill on which the Fort stands.

S. of the Fort is another ravine, which separates it from the village of Mullah Tolah, the ferrymen's quarter.

The hills that line the river near Attock have old round towers and ruined forts dotted about them, and the Attock Fort, seen from them, resembles an ancient baronial castle. Of late years a very strong fortified position has been created on the hills on both sides of the river.

Outside the Fort to the W. is the tomb of a Diwan of the saint Abdul-Kadir Gilani. It stands in a small enclosure on the edge of a cliff.

A trip by boat down the Indus to Khushalgarh, or to Kalabagh and Mari, will afford picturesque views of the deep dark gorges of the Indus. Application should be made some days beforehand to the Assistant Commissioner at Attock, for a boat and crew for the voyage.

235 m. **Khairabad** station (R.), fine retrospect of a railway bridge and the Attock Fort.

251 m. **Nowshera** station, D.B., is the headquarters of a sub-district of the same name in Peshawar district, on the right side of the Kabul river. The cantonment is on the banks of the river. About 2 m. distant on the Grand Trunk Road is a ruined fort built by the Sikhs.

[From Nowshera a railway 2 ft. 6 in. gauge, runs past a new cavalry cantonment, and 15 m. Hoti Mardan, to Dargai (40 m.) at the foot of the Malakand Pass, now a fortified position, which was the scene of severe fighting in the Chitral campaign of 1896, and in the subsequent rising of the Swat tribes. 8 m. beyond the Malakand crest, on the further bank of the Swat river, is the Fort of Chakdarra, so desperately defended against the Swat tribes in 1896. The country round is full of ruined Buddhist remains and sculptures, of which many beautiful specimens were secured by Sir Harold Deane, late Chief Commissioner of the N.W. Frontier Province.

Hoti Mardan, the headquarters of the King's Own *Corps of Guides*.

7 m. N.E. of Hoti Mardan is the famous rock of Shahbazgarhi, 24 by 10 ft., situated about 80 ft. up a slope, with one of the great Asoka inscriptions, Introd. p. lxiii.

At 24 m. from Nowshera at Takht-i-Bahi, an isolated hill rising 650 ft., are the remains of a Buddhist monastery (see Fergusson's *Indian Architecture*, i. 110), and another at Sahri Bahlol at its foot. Many fine Buddhist carvings, now in Lahore and Calcutta, were found here.

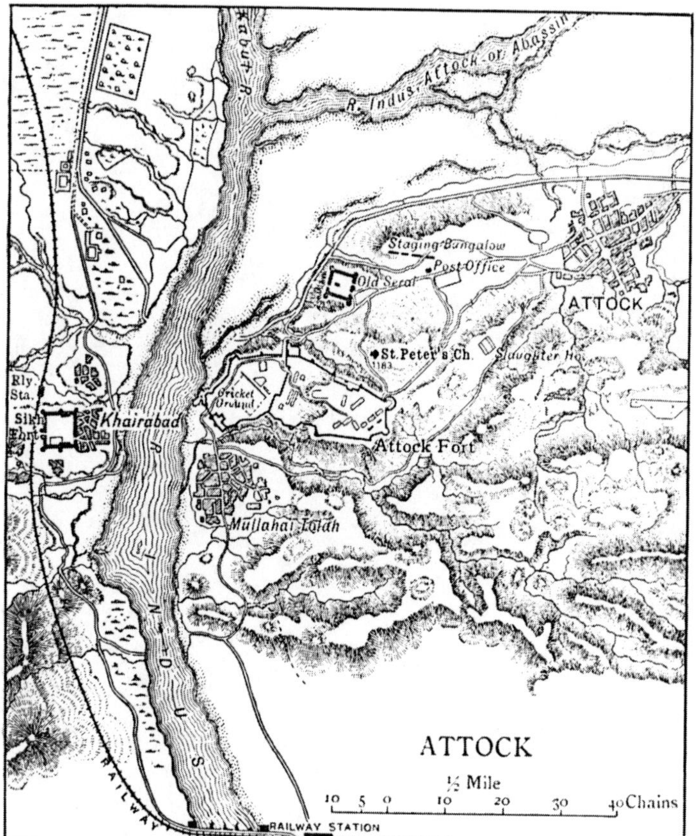

Attock.

[To face p. 246.

267 m. **Pabbi** station. [18 m. from here is **Cherat**, D.B., a hill cantonment and sanatorium for Peshawar, 4500 ft. above sea-level. The temperature seldom exceeds 90°, even in the hottest season. A tonga runs between Pabbi and the foot of the hills, whence a bridle-path of about 5 m. leads into Cherat.]

276 m. **Peshawar City** station.

278 m. **Peshawar Cantonment** station,* D.B., lat. 34° 1′, long. 71° 37′ (97,400 inhabitants, chiefly Mohammedans). This place, the headquarters of the first Army Division, the most important frontier city of India, and the residence of the Chief Commissioner of the N.W. Frontier Province, at present the Hon. Lieutenant-Colonel Sir G. Roos Keppel, K.C.I.E., is both interesting and picturesque. It stands upon a ridge above the plain, stretching towards the mountains, on the left bank of the Bara stream, 15½ m. S.W. of the junction of the Swat and Kabul rivers, and 10½ m. E. of Jamrud Fort, at the entrance of the Khaibar Pass. Kabul is 190 m. distant from here. The N.W. Frontier Province includes the districts of Hazarah, Peshawar, Kohat, Bannu, and Dera Ismail Khan, and the Agencies of Chitral and Swat, the Khaibar Pass, Kurram, the Tochi, Goomul, and Wana.

Peshawar is the ancient capital of the Gandara Province, in which the Mahayana Buddhists (p. lxiv.) arose. To the E. of the city are the mounds of Shahjiki dheri, covering ruins of the largest Buddhist stupa in all India (285 ft. from side to side), in which a relic casket of King Kanishka, containing some of the ashes of Buddha, was discovered in 1909. The Pathans made their appearance about the 8th century, and the present tribes settled in the 15th century. Sabaktagin, Prince of Ghazni, conquered Raja Jaipal here in 978, and his more famous son Mahmud conquered this prince again and his son Anandpal in 1001 and 1008, and Babar passed through it in 1519 A.D. The old name of Parashawar was changed by the Emperor Akbar; and till the reign of Aurangzeb the place was of great importance as commanding the route to the Mughal Province of Kabul. The houses of the city are built of small bricks or mud, held together by a wooden framework to protect them from earthquakes, and the streets are irregular and tortuous. The Edwardes, or Kabul, Gate leads to the main Kissa Kahani street. The *Ghor Khatri*, which stands high in the N.E. corner of the city, was successively a Buddhist monastery and Hindu temple, and is now the Tehsil. The C.M.S. has an important school in the city, and a pretty mission church; the Zenana Hospital is named after H.R.H. the Duchess of Connaught. Outside the city, N., is the square Bala Hissar fort, with earthen walls 92 ft. high. From it and from the Ghor Khatri there is a very good view of the Peshawar Valley and hills. At the Bajauri Gate is a fine Govt. Hostel for Indians of rank. The cemeteries are very numerous, and quite surround the city.

Peshawar has a great transit trade from Kabul and Bokhara and Central Asia. The **Bazaars** are well worth a visit, both for the objects they contain—many of them not seen in Central India—and for the fierce-looking and picturesquely-dressed natives from Afghanistan and Central Asia.

The special manufacture of Peshawar is bright-coloured scarves or *lungis*, worn as turbans. Wax-cloth work and some ornamental needle-work are also made here, as well as knives and small-arms; a special form of wood-carving also flourishes.

The **Cantonments**, 2 m. W. of

the city, and 3½ m. long by 1¼ m. broad, are situated on a slope towards the Khaibar Pass. In them are a *Public Garden*, the Govt. House, and the Victoria Memorial building, now containing a museum of Buddhist remains; and the main roads are lined with trees, and in the spring, when the roses and fruit-trees are in bloom, and the fresh winter snows stand up grandly to the N. and W., the place is extremely beautiful. The lines of the Native troops are situated in the eastern portion of the cantonment, and the barracks of the British troops in the western and on the N. side. The Roman Catholic and Anglican churches lie towards the west end of the Mall, and the Club is close to the latter. Near the railway station is the grave of a *Naugaza* (nine yard) saint. And not far off, at the E. end of the Mall, is an obelisk to the memory of Colonel Mackeson, C.B., Commissioner of the Peshawar Division, who was murdered by an Afghan in 1853. Further on, beyond the pretty cricket-ground, were the District Courts, partly accommodated in the old Residency, and surrounded by a garden: the former have been moved to near the Jail, and the latter will be superseded by a residence for the Lieutenant-General commanding the Division.

On the outbreak of the mutiny in May 1857, Brigadier-General Sydney Cotton was in command at Peshawar, Colonel (afterwards Sir Herbert) Edwardes being Commissioner, and John Nicholson Deputy Commissioner. These decided that the formation of a movable column was necessary. Sir John Lawrence approved of this, and the column was at once constituted under the command of Colonel Neville Chamberlain (afterwards Field-Marshal Sir Neville Chamberlain, G.C.B.), then commanding the Panjab Frontier Force; and later, under General Nicholson, was responsible for rendering harmless or destroying most of the dangerous mutinous elements still left in the Panjab. Besides the native troops in the Peshawar cantonment there were large numbers elsewhere in the valley, amounting in all to nearly 10,000, against which, fortunately, could be set a force of 2500 British at Peshawar and Nowshera. On the news of the half-hearted mutiny of the 55th Native Infantry at Nowshera on 21st May, it was determined to disarm the native regiments in Peshawar, and this was quietly and effectually done at two separate parades on the 24th, under the rifles of a British regiment supported by guns. The Nowshera men allowed themselves to be led to Mardan, where two companies had already taken the place of the Guides marching to Delhi; and on a flying column advancing from Peshawar, with John Nicholson as Political Officer, to disarm them, the whole regiment broke away in wild flight to the hills, many being captured or killed on the way, and most of the rest perishing in Swat and Boner.

There is capital *hunting* at Peshawar throughout the winter. The climate at this season is often very cold, and demands warm clothes.

(1) The Khaibar (Khyber) Pass.

If permission can be obtained this expedition should not be omitted, as no description can convey a real idea of the natural strength and wildness of the Pass. Application must be made to the Political Officer. A tonga can now proceed all the way to Landi Kotal;[1] the railway itself extends to Jamrud, and the tonga can be joined there if some train is convenient for this. The Pass is open only on certain days in the week for the benefit of caravans, when it is guarded by the corps of *Khaibar Rifles*, Afridis enlisted for the purpose. Several fortified posts, the chief of which are Ali Masjid and Landi Kotal (1700 ft. above sea-level), are held by them. Pictur esque convoys of camels, oxen, and

[1] A railway will probably be constructed to below Landi Kotal along the line of the Kabul river valley.

asses, heavily laden with well-poised loads, of goats and sheep, and of wild-looking men, women, and children, will be seen in the defiles.

The *Fort of Jamrud* (1670 ft.), 10½ m., was rebuilt by Sirdar Hari Singh, and gallantly held against the Afghans till April 1837, when he was killed in battle against troops sent by Dost Muhammad. Between it and Peshawar is Burj Hari Singh, near which the body of the fallen Sikh leader was cremated.

To the S. of the Fort is the defensible post occupied by the Khaibar Rifles here, and towards the hills on this side are seen a large number of Afridi villages. The road first passes a small Mohammedan shrine with fine heads of Markhor placed on the tomb, and ascends a ravine to the crest known as **Mackeson's Ridge**, from which it descends again to the bed of the real Kaibar stream, which enters the plains some way S. of Jamrud. From here the heights of Tartarra (6800 ft.) on the N. side of the real Khaibar Pass are finely seen, and further on from the Shagai Ridge, the cliffs and Fort of **Ali Masjid** (2433 ft.). The Pass is exceedingly narrow, and is hemmed in by cliffs on either side, those on the Ali Masjid side being extremely fine. The road goes up the Pass along the left bank, and above it runs through the desolate narrow valley of Lalabeg[1] till **Landi Kotal** (3373 ft.) is reached. From here a steep descent of 2000 ft. leads to Landi Khana in Afghan territory, the boundary being 6 m. from the Kotal. A fine view of the valley which runs from Dakka up to Jellalabad, named after Akbar, and renowned for its defence by Sir R. Sale from 12th November 1841 to 7th April 1842, is obtained from the **Pisgah Peak** (4500 ft.), to the N.W. of Landi Kotal. The start on the return journey to Peshawar must be made in good time on short winter days.

[1] Below Ali Masjid and at Lalabeg are some Buddhist stupas.

The Khaibar Pass, of which the Sikhs and the native troops of the British army had a great dread, was forced by General Pollock, with an army 8000 strong, early in April 1842, the heights on both sides being carefully crowned; and the same measures protected our army on its retirement in November of the same year. At the opening of the second Afghan War in November 1878, Ali Masjid was attacked by the force under General Sir Sam Browne on 21st November, and was deserted at night by the enemy. It was held by the Khaibar Rifles from 1890-1896, when it was allowed to be taken by the Khaibar tribesmen, and is now held again by the reconstituted Rifles; Landi Kotal, is, however, the more important post. The Khaibar Rifles, furnished by the various clans of the Afridis, now consist of two battalions of 600 men each, under English officers.

The clans of the Khaibar Afridis are the Zakka Khel, Kuki Khel, Malikdin, Kamrai, Kambar Khel, and Sipah, numbering 20,000 fighting men. Besides these this great tribe includes the Aka Khels and the Adam Khel, who are not directly connected with the Khaibar Pass. N. of the Kabul river above the Pass is the Mohmand tribe, and S. of Tirah are the Orakzais, separated from the Kohat District by the Samana Range.

(2) **Bara**, D.B.—A visit may be paid to Bara (7 m.), from which place good water has now been brought to Peshawar in a conduit made of blocks of concrete. At intervals of ½ m. there are small towers for ventilation. There is a mud fort at 6 m. S.W. of the cantonment, close to the pass from which the water comes. At Pusht-i-Khar, halfway between Peshawar and Bara, is an aqueduct bridge.

There are other forts at the mouths of passes into the hills, such as Michni, Shabkadar, and Abazai, but permission to visit them is necessary.

Abazai protects the headworks of

the canal from the Swat river, which joins the Kabul river at Nisatha, 15 m. N.E. of Peshawar.

(3) Persons accustomed to a hard day in the saddle will enjoy a ride of 37 m. from Peshawar through the Kohat Pass to **Kohat** (1767 ft.), D.B., 5 m. from the S. base of the Afghan mountains. The crest of the Pass is 2800 ft. high.

There is a Rest-House at Aimal Chabutra, 20 m. from Peshawar. Fort Mackeson lies on the left of the road, N. of the Aimal Chabutra. A railway will probably be constructed over this route.

ROUTE 17.

KASHMIR and some of the routes into that country.[1]

General description.—The *valley* of Kashmir is an oval plain, some 84 m. in length and 20 to 25 m. in breadth, at an average height of about 6000 ft., and entirely surrounded by the lofty snowy outer ranges of the Karakoram and Himalaya. Up to the end of May, and sometimes by the beginning of October, there is a continuous ring of snowy peaks around the valley, the principal being N. of the Wular Lake, Nanga Parbat, 26,620 ft.; E., Haramukh, 16,900 ft., and Amarnath, 17,320 ft.; S., the Panjal range with peaks of 15,000 ft.; and W., Kazi Nag, 12,125 ft. These are all visible from the valley. Farther distant, but still in the territory of His Highness Maharaja Sir Pratab Singh, of Jammu and Kashmir, G.C.S.I., are many peaks of over 20,000 ft., the highest of which is probably Mt. Godwin Austen, 28,278 ft. In the Chitral State, about 200 m. N.W. of Srinagar, is the peak, Agram, 25,426 ft., in the Hindu Kush range.

The valley of Kashmir is watered by the Jhelum and its tributaries, which find an outlet in the gorge at Baramula, and finally join the Chenab and Indus in the Panjab. The soil is fertile. Rice and maize are the chief crops; then come wheat, barley, and orchard or garden produce. The saffron (*Crocus sativus*) is famous for its bouquet, and its cultivation is an ancient industry. The floating gardens of the Dal Lake are made of long strips of the lake reed, which are moored at the four corners by poles driven into the lake bed, heaps of weed and mud being then formed into small cones, on the reeds. Melons, tomatoes, and cucumbers grow upon these cones with astonishing vigour. The *singhara*, or water chestnut, grows wild in the Wular and Dal lakes; the kernel, which is white and mealy, is either ground into flour, or parched, and so eaten. All the fruits and vegetables of temperate climes grow well in the valley. The mulberry, bitter cherry, plum, apple, pear, grape, walnut, and pomegranate are indigenous; the apricot and peach have spread all over the valley since their introduction. The forest trees grow to a great size. The principal among them are the deodar (the best, but not common), the blue pine, spruce, and silver fir; the elm, walnut, poplar, maple, willow, mulberry, horse-chestnut, and plane (or *chenar*), which is the special glory of the valley.

The climate is delightful in the early summer. In July and August, although the thermometer does not rise above 80° or 85°, the stillness of the air causes the heat to be oppressive in the valley, and then the mosquitoes make up for their comparatively mild sting by their enormous numbers. At this period visitors are glad to ascend to the upland plateaus, Gulmarg; Sonamarg, in the Sindh valley; Nagmarg; Pailgam, at the head of the Liddar valley, and Gurais. The pleasantest

[1] The best guide-book of Kashmir is that by Dr Arthur Neve. Lieut.-Colonel J. Duke's guide, recently revised by the author, may also be commended.

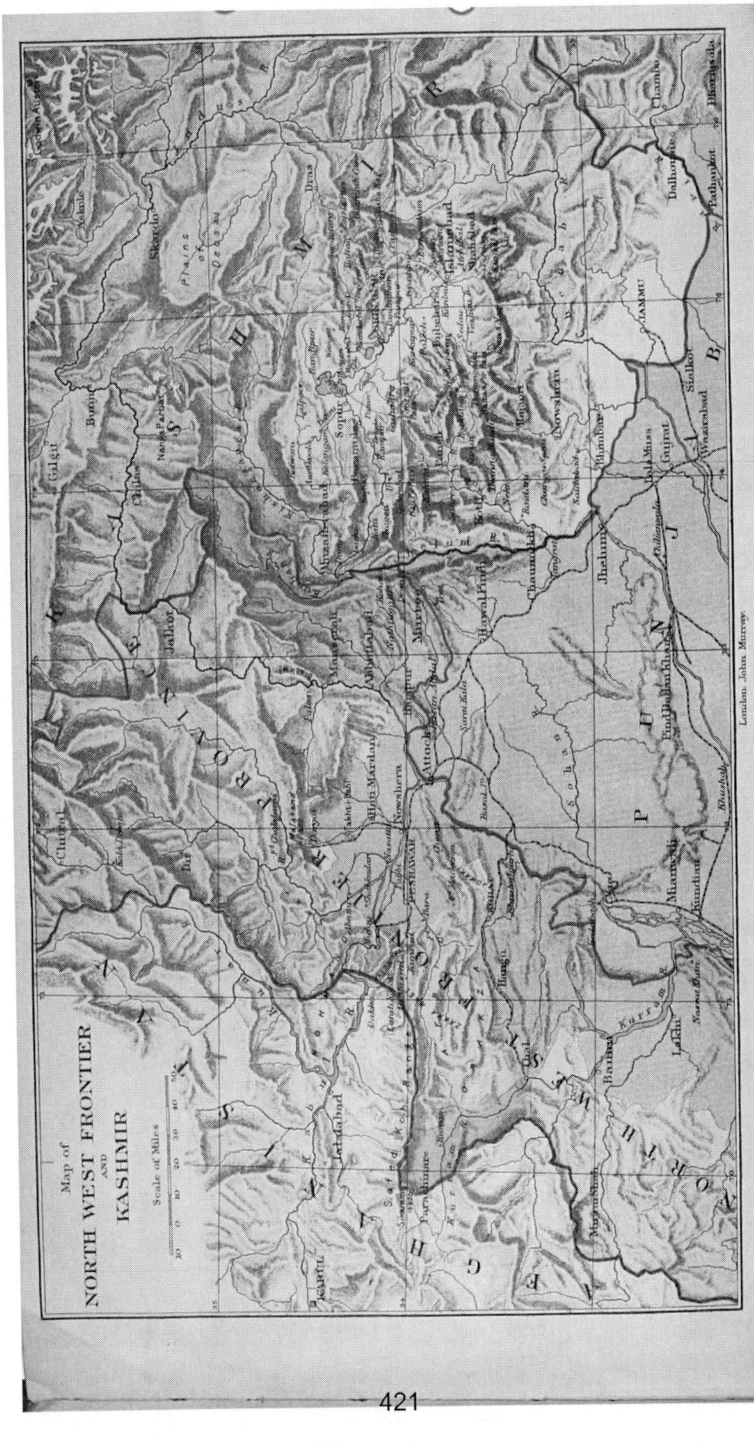
Map of
NORTH WEST FRONTIER
AND
KASHMIR
Scale of Miles
London: John Murray.

months in Srinagar, with a latitude of 34° 5′ N., are April, May, June, October and November. The spring months are showery, July and August are sometimes rainy, and the snows set in about Christmas time. The cold in winter is sometimes severe. In 1890-1 the thermometer fell below zero. In January and February 1893 there was skating all over the Dal Lake.

One of the latest writers, Sir Walter Lawrence, says: "The valley contains nearly everything which should make life enjoyable. There is sport varied and excellent, there is scenery for the artist and layman, mountains for the mountaineer, flowers for the botanist, a vast field for the geologist, and magnificent ruins for the archæologist. The epicure will find dainty fruits and vegetables cheaper here than perhaps in any part of the world, while the lounger can pass delightful days of *dolce far niente* in the mat house-boats moored under the shady chenar tree."

The population of the valley is 900,000, of whom 126,000 inhabit the capital, Srinagar. The Mohammedans number 850,000, and the Hindus 50,000.

History. — For many centuries Kashmir was ruled by Scythian Hindu princes, who were succeeded by Tartars. In 1587 the country was conquered by the great Mughal Akbar and annexed to his Indian Empire. Akbar built the fort on Hari Parbat hill. His successor, Jahangir, made many expeditions to Kashmir, where he planted chenar trees, and constructed lovely pleasure-gardens. In 1753 Kashmir passed into the hands of the Durani Chiefs from Kabul, and in 1819 Maharaja Ranjit Singh's general, Misr Chand, defeated the Pathan Governor, Jabbar Khan, and annexed the country. In 1846, on the close of the first Sikh War, Kashmir was assigned by treaty to Maharaja Gulab Singh.

Antiquities.—The chief ruins of Kashmir are those at Bhaniyar Patan, Pandrathan, Payech, Avantipore, Martand, and Wangat. They exhibit traces of Greek influence, and are of great archæological interest. See Fergusson's *Indian Architecture*, i. 255-270.

The **Coins** of Kashmir are worthy of notice.[1]

There are many **Routes** into Kashmir, mostly from the S. and W. The following are the most frequented:—

1. From Rawal Pindi *viâ* Murree (p. 244) and the Baramula Pass.
2. From Gujrat (p. 241) *viâ* Bhimber and Pir Panjal (see p. 256).
3. From Jhelum (p. 242) *viâ* Punch (see p. 257).
4. From Hasan Abdal *viâ* Abbotabad (p. 245) (see p. 258).
5. From Jammu (p. 240) (see p. 258).

(1) *Murree Route to Kashmir.*

Rawal Pindi

By tonga to

25 m. **Tret** (D.B.)
37 m. **Murree** (Hotel)
64 m. **Kohala** (D.B.)

(From Murree there is a short cut (bridle-path) to Kohala *viâ* Dewal, 18 m. instead of 29 m.)

75 m. **Dulai** (D.B.)
85 m. **Domel** (D.B.)
99 m. **Garhi** (D.B.)
108 m. **Hatti.**
119½ m. **Chagoti** (D.B.)
133 m. **Uri** (D.B.)
146 m. **Rampur** (D.B.)
162 m. **Baramula** (D.B.)
195 m. **Srinagar** (D.B.)[2]

The above are easy stages. There is a D.B. at every stage (except Hatti) with a Khansama and European supplies.

[1] The best book on the subject is *Coins of Kashmir*, by Mr Rogers of Amritsar.

[2] If the traveller intends to go beyond Srinagar, it will be necessary for him to get a camp kit, ponies, etc. All this can be arranged at Srinagar, or by writing beforehand to Cockburn's Agency, Srinagar. The ponies are procured from the State Stables.

The usual time for the journey is three days, but it can be accomplished in two days from Murree.

It is advisable to spend a day at Rawal Pindi or Murree to make arrangements for the journey.

The road is well metalled all the way, though liable to interruptions from landslips in wet weather.

Fare for *Tonga* (three seats) Rs. 112, one seat Rs. 35. Mail tongas do not travel by night. *Ekkas* can be procured for servants or baggage for Rs. 22. These prices are from Rawal Pindi to Srinagar. Apply to Messrs Dhanjibhoy & Son, Rawal Pindi. The head of the firm is Khan Bahadar Camador Dhanjibhoy, C.I.E.

If the traveller intends to march into Kashmir by stages he can engage coolies at 4 an. a stage, baggage ponies at 12 an. a stage, and riding ponies with saddles at Rs. 2 a stage.

The road ascends steadily from Barakao to 25 m. Tret (4000 ft.) and to

37 m. **Murree** * (see p. 244) (7700 ft.), and then descends until the *Jhelum River* is reached at

27 m. **Kohala** (2000 ft.), D.B. good. The bridle-path by Dewal from Murree to Kohala is 11 m. shorter than the tonga route. The road along the Jhelum valley is hot in the summer months, so that travelling in the early morning or evening will be found the most agreeable. In addition to the very fine near scenery along this road, grand views of the snows may be obtained in April and May.

After crossing the river by a large suspension bridge, where toll is levied, the road ascends the left bank all the way to Baramula. There is a good picturesque little D.B. at

11 m. **Dulai.** From here the road is cut in the face of the cliff, and is liable to be blocked by landslips after rain.

10 m. **Domel,** D.B., where the route from **Hasan Abdal** (4) joins in left. Here the road turns E. at an acute angle, where the Jhelum is joined by the Kishanganga. About a mile N. is seen the town of Muzafferabad, with one or two temples, and beyond it is the Sikh fort.

14 m. **Garhi,** D.B. good. Late in the afternoon this march is shaded by the high hills.

9 m. **Hatti.** The scenery is bolder and more beautiful.

11½ m. **Chagoti,** D.B. There is a swing bridge below the bungalow. Soon after leaving Chagoti the ruins of a mosque are passed, the carving of which was copied, and sent to London for the Colonial Exhibition.

13½ m. **Uri,** D.B. good. The *Haji pir* river which falls into the Jhelum from the S., is here crossed. For the sake of the gradient the road makes a long detour.

13½ m. **Rampur,** D.B. From here the road is comparatively level. An ancient temple is passed at Bhaniyar, standing in a fine cloister, one of the most complete and interesting of all in Kashmir, and then the fort and village of Nowshera.

15½ m. **Baramula,** D.B. good. Near here is the Water Power scheme which provides the electric power used in Kashmir. Here Kashmir doongas, or house-boats, can be procured for the life on the river; if it is desired to make the journey on to Srinagar by such a boat, it is best to arrange for one beforehand through the above Agents. The larger doongas may be hired for Rs. 20 a month; the smaller, generally used for kitchen and servants, cost Rs. 15 a month. These prices include four boat people to each boat. English house-boats cost Rs. 30 to Rs. 150 a month, according to accommodation and whether furnished or not, or from Rs. 200 to Rs. 400 for the season, exclusive of

SRINAGAR AND ENVIRONS.

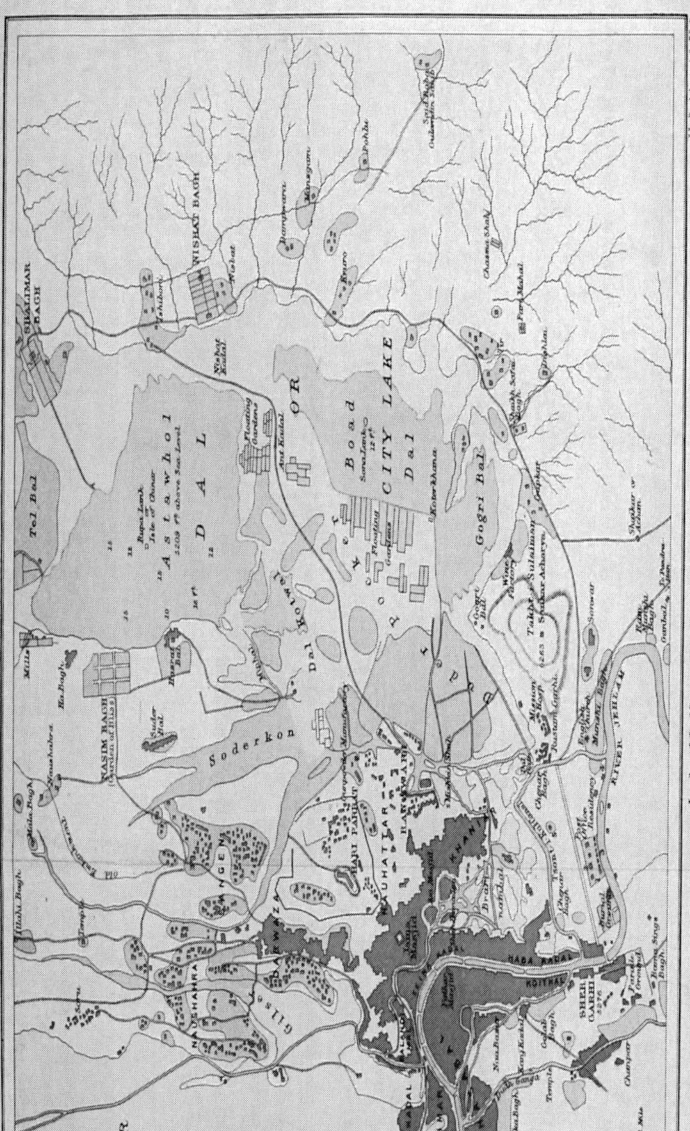

London, John Murray, Albemarle Street.

the wages of the crew. Some of them have every comfort.

[On leaving Baramula *by boat*, **Sopor** is passed at the entrance to the Wular Lake. Fair mahsir fishing may be obtained here. Sopor is the starting point for the Lolab Valley and Nagmarg. When the river is high boats go from Sopor to **Shadipore** by the Naru Canal. If the water is insufficient for the canal, the **Wular Lake** should be crossed early in the day, as dangerous storms sometimes arise later. The Wular Lake is the largest in India, being 12½ m. long by 5 m. broad. From the Wular the boats join the river by a small canal, which leaves the river at Hanjan. 5 m. N. of this is the Lanka Island, with the ruins of an old temple. 8 m. up stream from Hanjan is **Sambal.** This is the starting point for the trip by boat to the exquisitely beautiful **Manasbal Lake,** with an old temple immersed in the water at the S.E. end of it. Shadipore is 6 m. up the river from Sambal, and Srinagar about 10 m. farther by the river. From Baramula to Srinagar by the Naru Canal takes little more than one day; by the Wular Lake two to three days.

From Baramula the traveller can go by boat up the Pohru River to **Sunawin,** the next day to **Kolangam,** and the third day, if the river is full, to **Awatkoola**—very pretty scenery. Sending the boat back to Sopor, a pleasant march may be made through the **Lolab Valley** as follows ;—Awatkoola to *Kofwara* (8 m.) ; to *Lalpoor* (18 m.), the capital of the Lolab Valley ; to *Harwan* (18 m.) ; back to *Sopor* (10 m.) ; and then on to Srinagar as above. The Lolab Valley is very pretty, and the marches easy. Formerly black bears were numerous, especially during the mulberry season, but they are not now so common.]

The journey by tonga from Baramula to Srinagar (33 m.) occupies 4½ hours. At 14 m. from Baramula is Patan, in which are ruins of two temples of the 9th century.

Srinagar*(originally Suryanagar, or Sun City), lat. 34° 5′, long. 74° 51′, 5250 ft. above sea-level, is the capital of Kashmir State. It is beautifully situated in the centre of the "Happy Valley," has a population of 123,000, and is divided into two parts by the river *Jhelum*, along the banks of which it stretches for nearly 2 m. The river is crossed by quaint wooden bridges, and its banks are lined with carved blocks of limestone, now unfortunately much defaced by time and neglect.

The city, traversed by canals, was built by the Raja Pravarasen in the 6th century, and consists chiefly of wooden houses, some of them several storeys high, surmounted by sloping roofs covered with earth. Within the *Sher Garhi*, surrounded by massive walls, are the City *Fort* and one of the **Summer Residences** of the Maharaja. The **Jama Masjid,** near the Mar Nullah, is of considerable size, and of interest as being designed to be constructed in wood. All the pillars which support the cloisters of the courtyard are of deodar pine, "honest wooden forms," with the remains of rich and beautiful carving. There is another wooden mosque in the city, the **Shah Hamadan,** the roof of which is probably similar to that which covered the Temple of Martand. Not far from it, on the opposite (left) bank of the river is the stone mosque built by Nur Jahan, wife of the Emperor Jahangir, while below the fourth bridge is the tomb of Zain-ul-ab-uddin. His Highness is constructing a Zenana Hospital in memory of King Edward.

A fine view of the city and its neighbourhood is obtained from the top of the **Takht-i-Suleiman** (Throne of Solomon), 6263 ft., *i.e.* 987 ft. above the city, where there is a fine stone **Temple,** said to be of great antiquity, but in its present form probably not earlier than the 16th century. The road to it lay along a famous **Poplar Avenue,** more than 1 m. in length ; but this was cut down some years ago. The **Hari Parbat,** an isolated hill on the N. outskirts of the city, and 250 ft. above it, should also be ascended. It is surrounded by an extensive wall, and surmounted by the **Fort** built by Akbar at the end of the 16th century.

Many good subjects for the artist may be found in Srinagar, but the smells in the town are often very trying.

The chief **industries** are those of the wood-carvers, shawl-makers, gold, silver, and copper smiths, papier-mâché makers, leather workers, and dealers in precious stones.

The Residency and the European quarter lie above the city and the highest bridge on the river. In the centre of it is a fine ground for cricket, polo, and races, provided by the Maharaja: on the N. side of this is Nedou's Hotel; and at the N.E. corner is the Takht-i-Suleiman, with the entrance to the Dal Lake at its foot, not far from the C.M. Hospital. As a matter of etiquette, a call should be paid by visitors to the Resident.

Excursions.

(1) The first excursion should be to the **Dal Lake**, which is close to Srinagar, on the N.E., and is one of the most beautiful spots in the world. The lake is about 4 m. long and 2½ m. broad. Skirting the W. and N. sides of the Takht-i-Suleiman from the Dal Gate, and passing through a stretch of floating gardens, the **Nishat Bagh** will be first reached on the E. side of the lake. The terraces in this, the flights of steps ascending them, and the water falling down them are extremely beautiful, and the first afford delightful glimpses of the lake. 2 m. further on is the **Shalimar Bagh**, built by Jahangir, who lived there in the summer months with Nurmahal,[1] "The Light of the Harem." They are fully described by Bernier. In crossing the lake to the W. side a fine view is obtained of the mountains behind these two gardens. Beyond a small island with chenar trees lies the **Nasim Bagh**, a delightful, fine, park-like expanse, closely planted with magnificent chenar trees. Well raised above the lake, it catches the breeze, whence its name is derived. On the way back to Srinagar are passed a village with a large mosque, called Hazrat Bal; further on is a fine view of the picturesque Hari Parbat, from which the Nasim Bagh Canal leads to the Dal Gate. The name of Hazrat Bal is derived from a hair of the Prophet Muhammad, believed to be preserved in the mosque.

[1] Better known as Nur Jahan, p. 238.

The eastern shores of the lake may also be reached on foot. Starting from the Munshi Bagh, the road leads S. of the Takht-i-Suleiman to the edge of the lake. To the left is a wine factory. A massive building, high up the mountain-side farther on, is the Pari Mahal, probably originally erected for astrological purposes. Beyond are vineyards, and then higher up the Chashma Shahi, a garden of the usual Mughal plan. The Nishat Bagh is 2 m. farther, and 3 m. from the Munshi Bagh, and Şhalimar 2 m. beyond that.

(2) Starting again from the Dal Gate below the C.M.S. Mission Hospital, and turning to the left, the Mar Nullah leads through the northern side of the city to the west of Hari Parbat and the Anchar Jhil, across which a boat can proceed to Gandarbal, 14 m. from Srinagar. Beyond the Dilawar Khan Bagh the canal passes under a series of bridges and balconied houses, and affords some of the most picturesque, but often also the most malodorous, views in the whole city. Near the end of it is the Idgah. From outside the Dal sluice-gate the Tsont-i-Kul, or Apple Canal, leads past the Chenar Bagh (one of the prettiest spots near Srinagar, but by no means a healthy one to camp on) to the river opposite the Sher Garhi, presenting varied and beautiful views all the way. Both of these expeditions may be often repeated with increased pleasure.

(3) The **Temple of Pandrathan** lies about 3 m. E. of the Residency by road, but very much farther by boat, owing to the loops of the river above Srinagar, which form so singular a feature in the views from the Takht-i-

Suleiman. It is about 18 ft. square and 30 ft. high, and stands in a tank which covers the water-court that once surrounded it. A small boat kept on the tank enables one to examine the carvings of the interior; but the real beauty of the temple lies in its proportions and in the trefoil-headed arches and roof which form the chief characteristics of the Kashmir style, unknown elsewhere, except from a few out of the way places in the Panjab. The temple was built in 921 A.D. On the N. side of the tank are some broken remains, including a square pillar with figures on each side of it.

(4) **Islamabad, Martand, Vernag,** and the **Liddar Valley.** Proceeding by boat up the river, and passing Pandrathan, and, 8 m., *Pampur*, *Karkapur*, the starting-place for the **Temple of Payech,** is reached 6 m. further on. This tiny temple (only 8 ft. square) is in excellent preservation, and, being complete, gives a good idea of what the beauty and elegance of the larger temples must have been. It is constructed of eight stones only. It has been ascribed by General Cunningham to King Narendraditya, who reigned from 483 to 490 A.D. In the interior is a large stone *lingam.*

About 6 m. above Karkapur is **Avantipore,** once a famous city and the capital of King Avanti-varmma, who reigned 858 to 883 A.D. He built here two temples, now shapeless masses of ruins, but the gateways of both are standing, and are richly decorated, and the colonnade of the smaller one has been partially excavated. About 10 m. further is *Bijbehara*, where there is fair fishing, and a good encamping ground above the town and bridge. From here it is 6 m. to Kanbal for **Islamabad,** the second town in Kashmir, with 9000 inhabitants, and originally the capital of the valley. The springs in the town are exceedingly picturesque, and the Wazir Bagh to the S. of it is an extremely pretty place to camp in. From Islamabad it is necessary to proceed by road to the **Ruins of Martand,** which are 5½ m. N.E., and stand isolated on an elevated plateau above the valley. The temple, which is the largest in Kashmir—being 63 ft. long and over 70 ft. high when complete—is "interesting as a typical example of a quasi-classical style, with a Western impress on its details unusual in the East." Its date is uncertain, but it may be probably ascribed to the 5th century A.D. It has suffered much from earthquakes and neglect, and it is to be regretted so little has been done to preserve it. The colonnade was built by the famous King Lalitaditya, who reigned from 693 to 729 A.D.

From Martand a path leads to 5 m. **Atchibal** (7 m. from Islamabad), with its beautiful streams and cascades, groves of magnificent chenar trees, and the old pleasure garden of Jahangir. There is a bungalow for visitors, and an excellent camping ground.

From Atchibal a path leads *viâ Shahabad* to (12 m.) **Vernag.** Here are the celebrated springs, the source of the river Jhelum, which rises in an octagonal tank in a garden near the foot of the Banihal Pass (9763 ft.). One of the recesses of the enclosure round the tank bears an inscription by Jahangir. This spot was a favourite haunt of his empress, Nurmahal. The tank is full of sacred fish.

2 m. E. of Martand, in the lowlands of the valley, is **Bawan,** where there are celebrated chenars and tanks, and excellent camping grounds. From here it is 12 m. up the Liddar valley to *Eishmakam*, where there is an old ziarat from which a fine view is obtained. The next march reaches (14 m.) **Pailgam** (8500 ft.), a favourite summer resort, with good camping ground under the pines.

From Pailgam an expedition may be made farther up the valley to (12 m.) *Tanin* (10,500 ft.), whence it is a stiff climb to (11 m.) *Shisha Nag* (13,000 ft.), a fine sheet of water covered with ice till the month of June. From Shisha Nag it is 16 m.

to the *Amarnath Cave*, but the path is not easy and should be attempted by experienced mountaineers only. The cave is a famous resort of pilgrims.

From Pailgam another route leads N. through Aru and Lidarwat into the Sindh valley. This route also is not an easy one, and as it ascends over 14,000 ft. it is often under snow till July. The descent into the Sindh valley may be made either to Sakwas or Suphrar near Gund—see below.

(5) Another beautiful expedition may be made from Srinagar up the **Sindh Valley.** The first stage is either by boat, or by land, to (14 m.) *Gandarbal*, a small village at the mouth of the valley. Gandarbal is 9 m. by road from the Nasim Bagh in the Dal Lake. From Gandarbal the marches up the valley are to *Kangan* (11 m.), to *Gund* (14 m.), to *Gagangair* (9 m.), and **Sonamarg** (9 m.). From Kangan a detour may be made N. to (8 m.) the temples of Wangat, or Naghal, placed in an exceedingly beautiful situation above the stream, and now the most picturesque of all the ruined temples of Kashmir. The route from Gund onwards is extremely beautiful, and the torrent pass, in which small snow glaciers will have to be crossed early in the season, leading up to Sonamarg, is extraordinarily fine. Sonamarg (8500 ft.) contains lovely meadows, and was once the chief sanatorium of Kashmir. The next stage, *Baltal* (9 m.) 9282 ft., is at the foot of the Zojila Pass (11,300 ft.), which leads to Dras, and thence to **Leh**, the capital of Ladakh (nineteen marches from Srinagar). From Baltal the Cave of Amarnath (see above) may be reached in the spring or early summer before the snow bridges have melted. Provisions are not easily obtained in the Sindh valley, and there are no bungalows.

(6) There are several routes from Srinagar to **Gulmarg**,* the favourite resort when the valley becomes hot, but the best is by road and tonga to (*a*) Margan (D.B.), 15 m., and (*b*) to the foot of the final ascent, 10 m., whence it is 2 m. on to the plateau itself. The other possible routes are.

1. By boat to Palhallan, then by road, 16 m.
2. By boat to Sopor, then by road, 18 m.
3. By boat to Baramula, then by road, 17 m.

Gulmarg (or "Meadow of Roses") is a lovely, but somewhat rainy, spot at an elevation of 8500 ft. Above it is the ridge of the Firozpur Pass and the Apharwat Mountain, 14,500 ft. The fine snowy peak of Nanga Parbat, nearly 26,600 ft., is beautifully seen. Gulmarg offers the attractions of polo, racing, cricket, golf, and other amusements.

(2) *Pir Panjal Route to Kashmir.*

Riding or on foot.	**Gujrat** to	
28 m.	**Bhimbar**, D.B.	
43 m.	**Saidabad**, D.B., crossing Aditak Range.	
56 m.	**Nowshera**, D.B.	
70 m.	**Changas Sarai**, D.B.	
84 m.	**Rajaori**, D.B.	
98 m.	**Thanna Mandi**, D.B.	Crossing Rattan Pir.
108 m.	**Baramgalla**, D.B.	
118 m.	**Poshiana**.	Crossing Pir Panjal.
129 m.	**Aliabad Sarai**.	
150 m.	**Shupiyan**, D.B.	
180 m.	**Srinagar**.	

This is one of the finest routes into Kashmir, but is practicable only for riding or walking, as it is impossible to drive.

Gujrat, p. 241.

28 m. **Bhimber**, D.B., a considerable town, situated near the right bank of the stream of that name, and surrounded by wooded hills. The road, which is fairly easy for 20 m., crosses over the *Aditak* range (2000 ft.) to

15 m. **Saidabad**, D.B., where the *Samani Serai* is worth a visit. The road then crosses the *Kaman Goshi* range (3000 ft.), from the top of which the snows first come in sight.

15 m. Nowshera, D.B., and camping ground on the *Tawi river*, in which there is mahsir fishing.

14 m. Changas Sarai, D.B. The shorter road fords the Tawi twice on the way. The D.B. is built on the right bank, about 200 ft. above the river, on an old Mughal Sarai. Here is a very fine view of the snows.

14 m. Rajaori, D.B. (3200 ft.), a day's march to the E. of which there are two hot sulphurous springs. The D.B. is in an old pleasure garden on the left bank of the river, overlooking on the right the picturesque town.

14 m. Thanna Mandi, D.B., along the *Tawi*, which becomes very narrow, the valley also contracting considerably. It is situated at the foot of the *Rattan Pir* Pass, with a good road running through it from Punch to Jammu.

8 m. Baramgalla, D.B., crossing the *Rattan Pir* (8200 ft.), easy ascent, very fine scenery. From this point ponies cannot be taken early in the year.

10 m. Poshiana. From Baramgalla the road passes along a deep valley, crossing the *Sooran* torrent several times by log bridges, and ending with a steep climb. Poshiana (8200 ft.) is covered with snow till the end of May, and consists of a few shepherds' huts, which are flat-roofed. Tents may be pitched on the roofs, or the huts may be occupied, but they are roughly made and draughty.

11 m. Aliabad Sarai.

The road, very rough, now runs up the *Nilana Valley* to the summit of the **Pir Panjal** (11,400 ft.), from which there is a magnificent view of the Wardwan and Astor range. There are huts of refuge on either side of the Pir in case of storms. The Sarai is not habitable until May, owing to the snow.

20 m. Shupiyan, D.B., in the Kashmir valley, a pleasant, easy walk, passing *Hirpur*, R.H., on the way. There is camping ground here, and supplies are procurable for the first time since leaving Baramgalla. Hence it is a couple of easy marches (Ramu 12 m.) to Srinagar. Or the route through *Mohanpoora* to *Kanbal*, D.B., for Islamabad (19 m.) may be followed and a boat be taken (p. 252) down the Jhelum river to Srinagar, about fourteen hrs. From Shupiyan, 15 m. distant by Sedau, may be visited the Haribal Falls (40 ft. high) of the Veshau river. From Sedau it is two marches (12 m.) to the Konsa Nag mountain lake.

(3) *Jhelum and Punch Route to Kashmir*

Jhelum to

13 m. **Shikarpur**, D.B.	89 m. **Sahri.**
26 m. **Tangrot**, D.B.	105 m. **Punch**, D.B.
36 m. **Chaumukh.**	115 m. **Kahoota**, D.B.
46 m. **Raidani.**	130 m. **Hyderabad**, D.B.
58 m. **Neki.**	140 m. **Uri.**
66 m. **Berarli.**	
74 m. **Kotli.**	

This route is long, the marches somewhat difficult, and supplies scarce. Owing to the steepness of the road in places, the traveller is recommended to take coolies rather than ponies.

Jhelum, p. 242.

13 m. Shikarpur, D.B. The road is unmetalled, but in good order and level the whole way.

13 m. Tangrot, D.B. The road lies, for the most part, in the bed of the Jhelum, so can only be used when the river is low. The fishing here is probably the best in India.

10 m. Chaumukh crossing the Punch by a ferry. The ascent is by a very rough path (only walking being possible) to the village of

10 m. **Raidani**, prettily situated in a valley. Thence by the worst march in the route to

12 m. **Neki**, which is the residence of a few cowherds. No supplies obtainable.

8 m. **Berarli**, a small village, where there is good spring water, and supplies and coolies plentiful.

8 m. **Kotli**, on the left bank of the Punch. The camping ground is through the town, under some trees, among a lot of streams working twenty flour mills. Supplies, coolies, ponies, etc., abundant.

15 m. **Sahri**, where black partridges abound. The scenery here is very pretty.

16 m. **Punch**, D.B., a largish town, on the right bank of the Sooran, the conspicuous features of which are the *Raja Buldeo Singh's palace*, and the *Fort*. Punch may also be reached in three marches—Sooran, 16 m., Sahri, 11 m.—from Thanna Mandi (p. 257).

10 m. **Kahoota**, D.B., a cluster of huts up the Bitarh valley, commanding a magnificent view of the surrounding mountains.

15 m. **Hyderabad**, D.B., a small mountain village beyond the Haji Pir Pass (8500 ft.), where supplies are very scarce.

10 m. **Uri**, thence (see p. 252) to Baramula and Srinagar.

(4) *Hasan Abdal and Abbottabad Route to Kashmir.*

12 m. **Dedur**, D.B.
8 m. **Haripur**, D.B.
22 m. **Abbottabad**, D.B.
16 m. **Manserah**, D.B.
18 m. **Garhi Habibulla**, D.B.
22 m. **Domel**, D.B.
(For continuation *viâ* Uri, see p. 252)

The stages to Abbottabad can be done by tonga. The road from Abbottabad is a fair one, and is being gradually improved.

Hasan Abdal, D.B. (p. 245).

12 m. **Dedur**, R.H., a roadside sarai and camping ground.

20 m. **Haripur**, D.B., a large and flourishing native town, lying in a richly cultivated valley.

42 m. **Abbotabad**, D.B. (p. 245).

58 m. **Manserah**, D.B.

76 m. **Garhi Habibulla**, D.B.

88 m. **Domel**, D.B., thence to Garhi, Uri, etc. (p. 252).

(5) *Jammu* (p. 240) *to Srinagar.*

This route is practically the private one of the Maharaja, and travellers are not permitted to use it except with special permission from the Resident in Kashmir—winter headquarters at Sialkot. It is 178 m. long, divided into nineteen stages, and crosses the Chenab near Ramband and the Banihal Pass (9000 ft.) above Vernag (p. 255). Should an electric railway to Kashmir be ever made, the circuit of the country may be completed by a prolongation along this route.

ROUTE 18.

LAHORE TO **KARACHI** by **Mooltan, Sher Shah** Junction, **Bahawalpur, Samasatta, Rohri, Khairpur, Hyderabad** and **Kotri,** with expedition by road from Jungshahi to **Thatta**, and from Rohri to **Sukkur, Ruk** Junction, **Larkana, Sehwan** and Kotri by the right bank of the Indus.

The journey occupies 24½ hrs.
Fares, Rs.58, Rs.29, Rs.9.

General Note on Sindh.

Wherever there is any shooting there is no difficulty in obtaining local shikaris and camels, but they should be engaged beforehand by writing. The beaters and camel men are all keen sportsmen, but the tariff should be arranged before starting. Camels cost about Rs.1.8 per day, beaters 4 annas to 8 annas. In nearly all parts of Sindh there is good small-game shooting—many varieties of duck, quail, snipe, kunj, bustard; and a good shot should have no difficulty in getting over fifty brace a day.

---

4 m. **Lahore Cantonment** W., second station of this cantonment.

26 m. **Raewind** junction station (R.) for 33 m. *Ferozepore* and *Rajputana* (see Route 10).

104 m. **Montgomery** station (R.), D.B. This place, created under British rule is, since 1855, the headquarters of a district formerly known as Gugaira, and received its present name from Sir R. Montgomery, Lieutenant-Governor of the Panjab (1859-1865). [From this point may be reached **Pak Pattan**, 30 m. S., near the Sutlej river, an extremely ancient place, first known in history as *Ajudhan*, and identified by General Cunningham with one of the towns belonging to the Sudrakœ or Oxudrakœ of Alexander's historians. It was important at a later date as the chief ferry over the Sutlej, which formed the principal approach to Delhi from Ghazni and Multan up to the time of the Mughal conquest. Now it is best known on account of the tomb of Farid-ud-din, a saint of the famous Chishti family (p. 138). A great pilgrimage of Mohammedans takes place here at the time of the *Muharram*, as many as 60,000 attending.]

116 m. **Harapa** station. A hamlet now of no importance, but identified by General Cunningham with the site of a town in the territory of the Malli attacked and taken by Alexander the Great. The ruins, which are the most extensive of any along the banks of the Ravi, lie to the N. of the line and close to it.

General Cunningham attributes the destruction of Harapa to Muhammad-bin-Kasim in 715 A.D. The site has yielded thousands of Indo-Scythian coins, but not a single Greek one.

207 m. **Mooltan** (*Multan*) **City** and

208 m. **Mooltan Cantonment** (R.) D.B. * station.

Mooltan City (D.B. 1¼ m. N. of railway station) is a municipal town, with a population of 87,000, of whom the majority are Mohammedans; lat. 30° 12′, long. 71° 31′. It is the headquarters of a division and district of the same name, and is 4 m. from the left bank of the Chenab, and not far from the old bed of the Ravi. It is a place of great antiquity and supposed to be the capital of the Malli mentioned in Alexander's time. It is said to have been founded by Kashipa, the father of Hiranya-Kashipa, and was probably the Kaspeira of Ptolemy.

The first mention of Mooltan by name is by Hiouen Thsang in 641 A.D.

Istakhri, who wrote in 950 A.D., describes the temple of the idol of Mooltan as a strong edifice between the bazaars of ivory dealers and the shops of the coppersmiths. The idol was of a human shape, with eyes of jewels, and the head covered with a crown of gold. Shortly after, Mooltan was taken by the Karmatian chief, Jelem, son of Shiban, who killed the priests and broke the idol in pieces. It was restored in 1138. In 1666 A.D. Thevenot describes the temple of the Sun God as still standing, and the idol as clothed in red leather, and having two pearls for eyes. This idol was destroyed by the orders of Aurangzeb.

Muhammad Kasim conquered Mooltan for the Khalifs, and it was afterwards taken by Mahmud of Ghazni, in 1005, and by Timur in October 1398. Subsequently it formed part of the Mughal Empire, and then of the Durani kingdom. In 1779 Muzaffar Khan, a Sadozai Afghan, made himself ruler, but was killed with his five sons when Ranjit Singh stormed the place in 1818. In 1829 Sawan Mall was appointed governor. He was shot in 1844, and was succeeded by his son Mulraj. Upon his resignation after the first Sikh War Mr Vans-Agnew and Lieutenant Anderson, who were sent down to receive the surrender of his office, were attacked in the Fort and subsequently murdered at the Idgah on 19th April 1848, whereupon Mulraj went into rebellion. His forces were twice defeated by Major Herbert Edwardes, and he was shut up in the Fort; but owing to the delay with which the British authorities took action, the Sikh forces before the place, under the command of Maharaja Sher Singh, also went into rebellion, and this led to the second Sikh War. On the 2nd of January 1849 the city was stormed by the army under General Whish, and the Fort was surrendered by Mulraj, and since then the whole district has been under English rule. At the time of the mutiny in 1857 the garrison consisted of two Native Infantry regiments and a Mounted Battery without a single European company. On the 10th June these troops were induced to give up their arms by the courage and adroitness of Major Crawford Chamberlain; but on the 31st August the men rose in unreasoning mutiny, and having attacked the Bombay and Panjab troops, which had meanwhile arrived on the scene, were almost wholly exterminated. The importance of Mooltan as the connecting link with Sindh, from which the first outside assistance against the mutineers was received in the Panjab, was at the time almost supreme.

The heat of Mooltan is notorious, and the rainfall is little above 7 in. The saying is—

> Dust, beggars, and cemeteries
> Are the three specialities of Mooltan.

The *Cantonment*, to the W. of the town, was extended to the S.W. and made more defensible in 1888. The Lines of the Native Cavalry are to the extreme S., outside the cantonment, with the Artillery Lines to their N., and beyond these, in the same direction, are the *Hospital* and D.B., with the Roman Catholic cemetery to the N.W., and the Mohammedan cemetery, the Parsi cemetery, and the English church in succession to the N.

The **Old Fort** rises near the N. of the city. The entrance is by the De (Dewal=temple) Gate, so called because it leads to the famous temple of the Narsingh (Lion Man) form of Shiva or Prahladpuri. The original temple stood in the middle of the fort, and was destroyed by Aurangzeb; while the mosque built upon its site was totally blown up in the siege of 1848. Inside the enclosure, on the left, is the modern small temple, and further on the **Shrine of Rukn-ud-din**, grandson of Bhawal Hakk, commonly known as Rukn-i-'Alam, "Pillar of the World." This is an octagon of red brick, bonded with beams of Sisu wood, and supported by sloping towers at the angles. Over this is a smaller octagon, leaving a narrow passage all round for the muezzin to call the faithful to prayers.

Above this is a hemispherical dome. The total height is 100 ft., but as the tomb stands on high ground, it is visible for 30 m. round. One of the towers was thrown down when the powder magazine blew up in the siege of 1848, and was rebuilt in faithful imitation of the old one, including the timber bonds. The whole outside is ornamented with glazed tile patterns and string courses and battlements. The colours used are dark blue, azure, and white, which, contrasted with the deep red of the finely polished bricks, give a most pleasing effect. The mosaics are not like those of later days, mere plain surfaces, but the patterns are raised from half an inch to two inches above the background.

The tomb was built by the Emperor Tughlak Shah (1340-50) for himself, but given by his son Muhammad Tughlak as a mausoleum for Rukn-ud-din.

Farther on to the right is an *Obelisk* about 50 ft. high, erected in memory of Vans-Agnew and Anderson. On a white tablet on the W. face of the pedestal is an inscription which tells briefly an important chapter of the history of the Panjab. The concluding words are—

The annexation of the Panjab to the Empire
Was the result of the War,
Of which their assassination
Was the commencement.

The Tomb of Baha-ud-din Zakhariya, "The Ornament of the Faith," commonly called Baha-ul-Hakk, or Bhawal Hakk, is as old as the reign of the Emperor Balban (1264-86), of which period there are few other architectural specimens. It was almost completely ruined during the siege of 1848. It was afterwards repaired and plastered over, but some glazed tiles remain outside. The lower part is a square; above this is an octagon half the height of the square, and above that a hemispherical dome. The son of Bhawal Hakk, whose name was Sadar-ud-din, is buried in the same tomb. His cenotaph is adorned with green tiles. Opposite, in the corner of the vestibule, is the tomb of **Nawab Muzaffar Khan.**

About ¾ m. to the **N.W.** of the Fort is the Idgah in which Vans-Agnew and Anderson were murdered in 1848. It has been restored to the Mohammedans as a place of worship.

The **Tomb of Shams-i-Tabriz,** who lived in the time of Shah Jahan, stands ½ m. to the E. of the Fort on the high bank of the old bed of the Ravi. The main body of the tomb is a square surrounded by a verandah, with seven openings in each side. Above is an octagon, surmounted by a hemispherical dome, covered with glazed sky-blue tiles. The whole height is 62 ft. To the left of the entrance is a small square building, dignified as the Imambarah.

219 m. **Sher Shah** junction station, D.B., whence the Sindh-Sagar Railway (p. 241) branches off W. and N., and crosses the Chenab, about 1 m. broad, on a splendid bridge of seventeen 200-ft. girders.

262 m. **Lodhran** junction (p. 147).

270 m. The **Adamwahan Bridge,** 4224 ft. long, carries the North West Railway across the Sutlej river, at a height of 28 ft. above the stream.

272 m. **Bahawalpur** (D.B.), is a town with about 15,000 inhabitants, and the capital of a native State under the political direction of the government of the Panjab. Its area is about 22,000 sq. m., with a population of nearly 600,000, of whom four-fifths are Mohammedan. The Nawab of Bahawalpur, by race a Daudputra, ranks on the list of Panjab chiefs next after the Maharaja of Patiala. His ancestors came from Sindh, and assumed independence after the first expulsion of Shah Shuja from Kabul.

In 1847-48, Bhawal Khan, the then Nawab, assisted Sir Herbert Edwardes during the Mooltan rebellion, for which he was rewarded and a life-pension of a lakh of rs. and the gift of the districts of Sabzalkot and Bhaungbara. His son, S'aadat Khan, was expelled by his elder brother, and died a refugee in British territory in 1862. In 1863 and 1865 rebellions broke out, but were crushed by the Nawab, who died soon after. Since then there have been two long minorities and the State is now under a third.

Palace of the Nawab, which is to the E. of the town, cost about £30,000. It is a square pile, with towers at each corner. In the centre is a hall for holding receptions. There is a fountain in front. At the side are underground rooms where the thermometer remains at 70°, while it rises from 100° to 110° in the upper rooms. Ascending to the roof, the visitor will have an extensive view E. towards the vast *Desert of Bikaner* which stretches, waterless, away for 100 m.

292 m. **Samasata,** junction for Bhatinda and thence for Umballa, Delhi, Rewari and Bikaner.

Following the course of the Indus, through an uninteresting tract, the railway reaches

417 m. **Reti** station (R.). A rest-camp for troops between Karachi and Lahore has been established here. 4 m. S. of Reti are the vast ruins of *Vijnot*, a leading city before the Mohammedan conquest. A mouth of the *E. Nara Canal* (see below) is crossed 2 m. before reaching Rohri, and from Rohri runs due S. through Khairpur, and enters the Thar Parkar district.

488 m. **Rohri** station, D.B., a municipal town (population, 9600), the capital of a subdistrict of the same name, which has an area of 4258 sq. m. It is on the left, or E. bank of the Indus, on a rocky eminence of limestone, interspersed with flints, and seen from a distance has a striking appearance, the houses being four and five storeys high, with flat roofs surrounded by balustrades. It is said to have been founded by Saiyad Rukn-ud-din Shah in 1297 A.D., which was more than 300 years after the Indus deserted its former bed at Alor and came to Rohri. The rocky site of Rohri ends on the W. side in a precipice 40 ft. high, rising from the river bank. In the latter part of the rains the water rises 16 ft. above its lowest level.

The *Jama Masjid* is a fine building of red brick, with three domes, and coated with glazed porcelain tiles. A Persian inscription records that it was built by Fateh Khan, an officer of the Emperor Akbar, about the year 1572 A.D. One of the sights of the place is the *Mui Mubarak*, or "a hair of the Prophet," in amber and preserved in a gold tube adorned with rubies. It is said that the War Mubarak, a building 25 ft. sq., on the N. of the town, was erected about 1545 by Mir Muhammad for the reception of this. It appears it was brought from Constantinople by one Abdul Baki, whose descendants have still the keeping of it. The *'Idgah* was erected in 1593 A.D., by Mir Muhammad M'asum. Near Rohri are three forests covering 58,000 acres, or about 90 sq. m., which were planted in 1820 by the Talpur Amirs, and are now under the control of the Sindh Forest Department.

½ m. from Rohri at the mouth of the **Eastern Nara Canal,** 156 ft. wide, are the powerful Sluice Gates which regulate the supply of water from the Indus. When these gates are closed during inundations it is a wonderful sight to see the fish trying to pass them. Millions collect on these occasions, and in attempting to leap the falls, fall back upon common Indian cots, made of rope, which are suspended from the arches of the regulator. The fishing is let out by yearly contract and yields a handsome revenue.

[**Excursion to Alor.**—While at Rohri, a visit may be paid to the very ancient town of Alor, which is only 5 m. distant to the E. This was the capital of the Hindu Rajas of Sindh, and was taken from them by the Mohammedans, under Muhammad Kasim, about 711 A.D. At that time the Indus washed the city of Alor,[1] but was diverted from it by an earthquake about 962 A.D., at which time the river entered its present channel.

The road from Rohri passes over a bridge about 600 ft. long, across the ancient channel of the Indus. On the farther side is a village with about 100 inhabitants, and from this an extensive ridge of ruins runs in a N.E. direction. That which bears the name of 'Alamgirs Mosque is picturesque. Two of them are shrines, one to Shakarganj Shah and the other to Kutb-ud-din Shah. To the former tomb people of the neighbouring villages still make pilgrimages. It has no dome or building over it, but is a plain, white, neat tombstone, with a border of carved flowers.]

From Rohri the loop line to Kotri (p. 267) crosses the Indus, and the direct line to Karachi (784 m. distant from Lahore by this route) runs down the left bank of the Indus to

504 m. **Khairpur** (population, 14,000), founded 1783, the seat of the last Amirs of Sindh the Talpuras, and the capital of the native State of that name, over 6000 sq. m.

674 m. **HYDERABAD** (Haidarabad), D.B., has a population of 76,000 inhabitants. It is situated on a high part of the rocky ridge called the Ganjah Hills, in an island formed by the Indus and the Fuleli, a branch which, leaving the main stream 12 m. above the town, rejoins it 15 m. below. The old city was for centuries the capital of the Kalhoras. The modern city of Hyderabad was founded by Ghulam Shah Kalhora in 1768. His tomb is at the N.W. of the plateau on which the town stands.

The **Fort** of Hyderabad is of a very irregular form, and about ¾ m. in circumference; at the S. extremity is the huge round tower, erroneously supposed to have been the treasury of the Amirs. On the N. side a trench separates the citadel from the town. It is crossed by a bridge leading to one of these intricate gateways which have so often yielded to a *coup de main*. Where the walls do not rise immediately from the edge of the declivity, the defence is strengthened by a ditch 10 ft. wide and 8 ft. deep. The residences of the principal Amirs, formerly within the walls of the Fort, have now almost disappeared, and the Commissary of Ordnance and the Executive Engineer divide the Fort between them as an arsenal and storehouse. Mir Nasir Khan's palace alone is kept up, and is occupied by the Commissioner in Sindh on his tours, and by other officers of rank when visiting Hyderabad. Sir C. Napier frequently resided in this palace, and in it he held his Grand Darbar on 24th and 25th May 1844, when every chief in Sindh came from far and near to submit himself to the conqueror. One room in Mir Nasir Khan's palace, styled the Painted Chamber, is still tolerably perfect, and gives some idea of what the effect must have been when all was uninjured. In the recesses various historical subjects connected with the Talpura family are delineated. In one recess is a very indifferently-executed picture of an English gentleman and an Amir, the work of a native artist, who obliterated one of the least popular subjects, and introduced these figures, one of which is intended for Colonel (Sir James) Outram. Above the gateway of the fort is a room which looks down on the principal bazaar. From this room, in the afternoon, it is worth while to watch the motley crowds of all nations, in various costumes, which throng the mart below. The visit to the Fort should conclude with a walk round the ramparts and an ascent to the top of the circular tower, whence a fine view of the surrounding country with

[1] Alor, Uch, and Hyderabad are believed to have been the sites of three of many Alexandrias founded in the Panjab.

the Fuleli, on one side, winding through the dusty plain, and on the other side, of the rapid Indus, with its buttress of rock in the background, will be obtained.

The *Tombs of the Kalhoras and Talpuras* cover the northern portion of the hill on which Hyderabad is built. The tombs of the Talpuras are very beautiful, but are not in such exquisite taste as that of *Ghulam Shah Kalhora*, the description of which may serve for all. On entering the enclosure by a small but richly carved door, the visitor is impressed by the beautiful symmetry of the mausoleum, and the religious feeling displayed in the decorations. Latticed windows in the lofty dome sparingly admit the light, and shed a subdued lustre over an exquisitely carved marble tomb, at the same time revealing the rich fresco paintings on the walls, without giving them too much prominence. Over one of the archways is an inscription in Persian written by the orders of his son *Sarfaraz*, whose tomb adjoins, and was built in 1785 A.D. It is painted inside, and is in good repair. There are four other tombs of the Talpura family—that of *Mir Karam Ali*, a domed rectangular building, with a turret at each corner, built in 1812, with marble fretwork, and roofed with coloured tiles; that of Mirs Murad 'Ali, Nur Muhammad, Nasir Khan, and Shahdad Khan, built in 1847, with white marble tombs inside; that of Mir Ghulam Shah and Fazl 'Ali, erected in 1855; and that of Mir Muhammad, built in 1857. All the Talpura tombs, except Karam 'Ali's, are kept in good order, at the cost of surviving members of the family.

The **Cantonment** lies to the N.W. of the town. There is a fine range of *Barracks* for Europeans. Not far off is the *Church* of St Thomas, built in 1860, at a cost of Rs.54,000. It can hold 600 persons. It has several memorial windows, and on the N. side of the communion-table is a brass showing the number of officers and men who fell at Miani and Dabo (1843).

The Roman Catholics have had a church at Hyderabad from the time of the conquest.

Hyderabad is famous for its *embroideries* in silk and gold and its silver tissues. There are four or five famous fabricants, each working with a different stitch. The patterns are of endless variety. All the work is made on a simple wood frame.

In the Amirs' time there was a great demand for **Enamelling**, the principal sardars vying with each other in the beauty and costliness of their swords, matchlocks, and horse-trappings, which were profusely decorated with enamelled ornaments. In enamelling on gold, the colours red and crimson are chiefly used, and blue and green are the favourite colours with silver.

A visit can be made to the famous *battle-fields of Miani and Dabo*, on which, in 1843, was decided the fate of Sindh. The three places form a triangle, Miani being 6 m. to the N.W. of Hyderabad and Dabo 5½ m. to the E. of Hyderabad.

On the E. side of the monument at Miani, enclosed in a well-kept garden, are the names of the officers who fell.

(From Hyderabad a branch line runs by Shadipalli to 310 m. Luni junction (p. 233). At Mirpur Khas, 42 m. E. of Hyderabad, a stupa 50 ft. each way, with terra-cotta figures of Buddha, has been lately excavated.)

The main line now crosses the Indus to

679 m. **Kotri**, D.B. (loop line to Rohri, p. 267), a place of some importance (population, 7600), and for a time the terminus of the Sindh railway and the Indus Flotilla. Goods for Karachi brought down the river by country boats from the Panjab are still largely transferred to the railway here, which at this point quits the Indus for that port

lying some 50 m. N.N.W. of its mouths.

731 m. **Jungshahi** station (R.).

Thatta, D.B. (no provisions procurable), which lies 13 m. S. of Jungshahi on the Makkalli Hills, was once a place of some importance (present population, 10,800). A camel carriage will make the journey in about three hours. It was while seeking to reduce Thatta in 1351 A.D. that Muhammad Tughlak died, and his successor, Firoz Shah (p. 204), twice lost an army and nearly lost his life, before he effected the conquest of the place. In the Mughal times it was the headquarters of a Province, and an English factory was established at it in 1758.

The *most remarkable sights* at Thatta are the Grand Mosque; the manufactures of silk *lungis* and stamped cottons; the tombs at the *Makkalli Hill*, and Kalyan Kot.

The *Grand Mosque*, near the centre of the town, was begun by Shah Jahan in 1647 A.D. and finished by Aurangzeb. It has been a magnificent edifice, but is now much decayed. The roof is surmounted by 100 domes, each painted in a different way. The inscriptions carved round the great stone arch, and those upon the two stones bearing the date of the edifice, are admirably executed in large letters. Not far from this is the old house inhabited by Mr Crowe, the first British Resident in Sindh.

The *Makkalli Hill* Cemetery is about 1½ m. W. of the town. The area of it is said to be 6 sq. m. and to contain 1,000,000 graves, the custom of Mohammedans requiring that all tombs shall be single, and that none be re-opened to receive more than one body. This place began to be used for interment about 1500 A.D. The summit of the rocky ridge looking towards Thatta is crowned by an immense *'Idgah*. The building consists of a long wall, with a low flight of steps leading to the mihrab and the mimbar (or pulpit). Tall slender minarets of elegant form spring from either extremity. The date, 1633 A.D., is inscribed in beautiful large *Nast'alik* characters.

Behind this building vaulted domes, arches and towers, porticos, gateways, and vast colonnades rise in apparently endless succession above shapeless mounds of ruins. In some the cupola is surrounded by a ring of smaller domes, with a single or double colonnade, enclosing a gallery and platform, broken by pointed arches in each of the four fronts. Others are girt by lofty stone walls, forming square courtyards, with entrance gates leading to the different doorways. Some consist of heavy marble canopies, on fantastic columns. Many are built of coloured and glazed tiles and bricks, the work probably of Persian bricklayers, who are renowned for their skill. Nothing can be richer than the appearance of the inscriptions on the bricks, in large white letters, upon a dark purple ground.

Kalyan Kot, "Fort Prosperous," is called by the Mohammedans Tughlakabad. It is a ruin of great antiquity, somewhat less than 2 m. S. of Thatta, and according to some it was erected by Alexander the Great.

750 m. **Dabheji** station is the place from which Bambura may be visited; it is 6 m. distant.

[**Bambura** is supposed by the natives to be the site of the most ancient seaport in Sindh. It may have been the ancient Debal, the first city captured by Muhammad Kasim, having its name from a temple in the fort of great celebrity. It is unquestionably of great antiquity, and the remains of ramparts, bastions, towers, etc., prove its former importance. Many coins also have at different times been found among its ruins. The town of Gharo is about 3 m. to the E.]

782 m. **KARACHI** (*Kurrachee*) **Cantonment (or Frere Street)** station * —The **M'Leod or City** station is 2 m. farther on towards the harbour.

Karachi (lat. 24° 51′, long. 67° 4′ E.; population, 159,000; distance from London, 6283 m.) is the chief town in Sindh. It is situated at the N.W. extremity of the delta of the Indus, and is the headquarters of the Commissioner, the Judicial Commissioner, and the General commanding the District. It existed as a mere fort from 1725 to 1842, when it was yielded up by the Talpura Amirs to the British. Then it began to rise rapidly as a flourishing sea-port with a trade whose exports have now an annual value of £15,000,000 (subject to great variations, however) and imports of £7,000,000. The steamers using the port number about 1050 with a tonnage of 1,500,000 tons; the income of the Port Trust is £170,000, and of the Municipality 16 lakhs. N. of the station are the **Napier Barracks**, a fine block of buildings extending over the maidan for 1 m., with accommodation for 1500 European troops. E. of the Lines are the **R.C. Church and General Hospital**. W. of Frere Road from the railway station is the **Frere Hall**, built in 1865 in honour of Sir Bartle Frere. The building contains a large ballroom, a public meeting-room, and the Karachi General Library. In the grounds is a fine statue of the Queen Empress, unveiled by King George on 18th March 1906. It is intended to erect a statue as the memorial of the late King Emperor. Adjoining the Frere Hall compound are the handsome buildings of the *Sindh Club*. Passing beyond it is the **Masonic Hall**, and in front of it is the **Gymkhana** and Ladies' Club.

Close by W. is **Government House**, built by Sir C. Napier, bought from him by Government, and now the residence of the Commissioner in Sindh. Behind it is **Trinity Church** (the garrison church), with its square campanile, 150 ft. high. It was built at the instigation of Sir Bartle Frere, and contains a fine stained glass window put up in honour of Sir C. Napier and the victors of Miani. Beyond, W., are the Artillery Messhouse, **Barracks, and Arsenal**; and a few yards farther is **St Andrew's Scotch Church.**

On the N.W. side of the cantonment are the **Zoological Collection** in the Gardens, considered the best in India, and well worth a visit.

From Government House, M'Leod Road to the sea leads to a fine block of buildings containing the quarters of the **European** and **Persian Gulf Telegraph Staff**, the **General Post Office**, and the **Municipal Offices**. On the left of the road is the Karachi **City Railway Station**. Beyond are the **Court House**, containing the Judicial Commissioner, District Judges, and Town Magistrate's offices, the **Bolton Market**, the Chamber of Commerce, the **Custom House**, and the offices and godowns of the European merchants, Banks, and Steamship Agencies, and N.W. of these lies the native city. The native city lies to the N. of M'Leod Road, between it and the Layari River, and is traversed by Bandar Road, which joins the former near the memorial clock tower of Sir Wm. Merewether.

2 m. along the Napier Mole is **Kiamari** (4 m. from the cantonment; carriage fare, Rs. 2) a busy shipping port, with its long line of wharves, and connected with the cantonment and native town by rail, tram, road, telegraph or telephone. In the old days this was an island. At Kiamari the **Karachi Harbour** commences. It is a first-class harbour, capable of accommodating the largest steamers, and owes its existence to the strenuous exertions of Sir Bartle Frere. It was designed by Mr Walker, commenced in 1854, and completed in 1883, since when additional railway facilities have constantly been added. There is very good sea-fishing to be had in the harbour, which is famed for its fish and oysters. Near the Napier Mole, on the back-water, is the **Sindh**

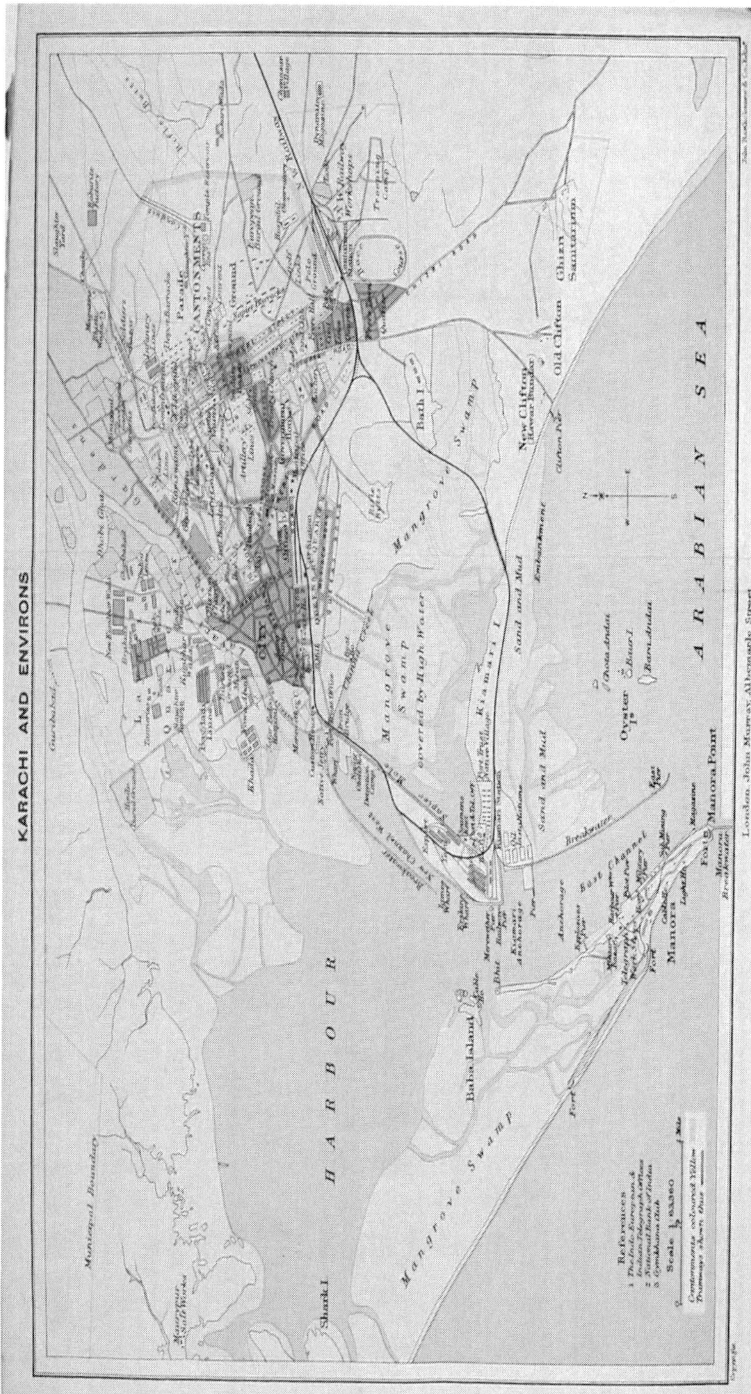
KARACHI AND ENVIRONS
HARBOUR
ARABIAN SEA
Manora Point
Manora
Baba Island
Shark I.
Oyster I.
Mangrove Swamp
CANTONMENTS
CITY
New Clifton
Old Clifton
Kiamari I.
Sand and Mud
Breakwater
Municipal Boundary
London, John Murray, Albemarle Street

Boat Club House. The **Defences** of the harbour consist, beside the marine defences, of three large forts, the largest on the *Manora* headland, at the entrance to the harbour on the W. The **lighthouse** near this shows a fixed light 148 ft. above sea-level, visible 17 m. in clear weather. On the meridian of Karachi there is no land between Manora and the South Pole.

The cheapest route from London to Quetta, Mooltan, Lahore, and North-West India is *viâ* Karachi. Through tickets by the P. & O. and other steamer lines to Karachi, 483 m. (P. & O. passengers change to B.I.S.N. mail steamer in Bombay harbour), are issued at the same price as tickets to Bombay. There is a quick weekly service by the B.I.S.N. from Karachi to Muscat, Bandar Abbas, Bushire and Basrah on the Persian Gulf.

Clifton, 3 m. S. of the cantonment, a favourite afternoon ride and drive, stands on the sea, and is approached by a good road. There is a fine sandy beach here extending S.E. for miles—on this beach thousands of turtles in August, September, and October, come up at night to lay their eggs; and the turtle-turning picnic parties arranged for moonlight nights are among the standing amusements of the place. During the cold weather the tanks and jeels about Karachi swarm with small game birds, while in the Baluch Mountains, 25 m. W. of Manora, good shooting is obtainable. In the Hub river, ✱ the boundary between India and Baluchistan (20 m. from Karachi), good mahsir fishing can be had.

[**Magar Pir,** 7 m. N. of Karachi, is well worth a visit. For a detailed account of this curious place see *Dry Leaves from Young Egypt*,[1] p. 218, and Burton's *Sind*, vol. i. p. 48. As the place can be comfortably seen in an afternoon from Karachi, there is no necessity to stop there; as a matter of fact the *dharmsala*, or rest-house, is not comfortable for Europeans. The road out in parts being very sandy, an extra horse is attached to the carriage; the charge for the trip is generally Rs. 12.

From the roots of a clump of date trees gushes out a stream of hot water, the temperature of which is 133°. On the W. side of the valley is a temple surrounded by a thick grove, and close to a swamp caused by the superfluous waters of the spring. There is also a tank surrounded by a 5-ft. mud wall, and containing some eighty or ninety alligators, which, as they attract a considerable number of visitors, the Mohammedans in charge of the Pirs Tomb regard as sacred, for a brisk and remunerative business is done by these custodians in killing goats for visitors to see the alligators fed. It is a curious fact that the so-called alligators are really crocodiles, and are a different species from the long-snouted *Gharial* of the Indus.]

[1] In the Library in the Frere Hall.

---

487 m. **Rohri** (p. 263) to Kotri by the right bank of the Indus—228 m.

Opposite to Rohri, in the Indus, is the *Island of Khwajah Khizr*. Here is a mosque of great apparent antiquity. It has an inscription, the date 952 A.D. The shrine of Khizr, who was also called Zindah Pir, or "the living saint," is venerated by Hindus and Mohammedans alike.

A little to the S. of the isle of Khizr is the larger **Island of Bhakkur.** It is a limestone rock of oval shape, 800 yds. long, 300 yds. wide, and about 25 ft. high. Almost the whole of it is occupied by a fortress, which has two gateways, one facing Rohri on the E., the other Sukkur, on the W. The Amirs attached much importance to this fort. But on our advance to Kabul in 1838, it was placed at the disposal of the British Government, and was used, first as an arsenal and then, until 1876, as a prison for Baluchi robbers.

So early as 1327 A.D., Bhakkur seems to have been a place of note, for the Emperor Muhammad Tughlak sent persons of importance to command there. Under the Samma princes the fort changed hands several times, being sometimes under their rule and sometimes under that of Delhi. During the reign of Shah Beg Argun the fortifications were rebuilt, the fort of Alor being destroyed to supply the requisite material. In 1574 it was delivered up to Keshu Khan, an official of the Emperor Akbar. In 1736 it fell into the hands of the Kalhoras, and subsequently into those of the Afghans, who retained it till it was taken by Mir Rustam of Khairpur.

The Indus, which runs here with great rapidity, is crossed by the grand *Lansdowne Bridge*, erected on the *cantilever principle*, connecting Rohri with the Island of Bhakkur: the line then crosses the island, and is connected with Sukkur (see below) by another bridge of a single span. The span is 840 ft. from centre to centre of the cantilevers; each cantilever is 320 ft. long, and the central girder connecting them is 200 ft. long. The roadway is 18 ft. wide in the clear, or enough for a line of carts in each direction. A single line of railway is laid in the centre. A path 4½ ft. wide for foot and pony traffic is also provided on each side outside the railway, and can be used at all times. The total weight of steel and iron employed was nearly 3000 tons.

3 m. **Sukkur** station (R.), D.B.✱ The headquarters of the Sukkur and Shikarpur subdistrict, standing on the right bank of the Indus, has a population of 31,300, and is well drained and clean. There are also some locomotive shops of the North-Western Railway here. A series of low bare limestone ridges slope down to the Indus, and on them, about 1 m. off, is the European quarter called **New Sukkur**, to distinguish it from the old town of the same name. The only sights are the tombs of Shah Khair-ud-din, built about 1758, and *Muhammad M'asum*, in the cantonment at the foot of a tower 90 ft. high which he erected, and which overlooks the country for many miles. The town was ceded to the Khairpur Amirs, between 1809 and 1824. In 1833 Shah Shuja'a defeated the Talpuras here with great loss.

11 m. **Ruk** junction station (R.). From here the Sindh, Pishin, and Quetta Railway branches N. (see Route 19).

49 m. **Larkana** station, D.B., is a municipal town (population, 14,500), the capital of a subdistrict of the same name. The country surrounding it is fertile and populous, and perhaps the finest tract in the whole of Sindh.

The fort served in the time of the Talpuras as an arsenal, and under British rule it has been turned into a hospital and jail.

141 m. **Sehwan** station. (D.B. in the old Fort.) ✱ The chief town (population, 53,000, 117 ft. above sea) of a subdistrict of the same name in the Karachi district. The river Aral, which is crossed by a bridge with iron girders, formerly flowed close to the town, but has now quite deserted it. The tomb of *Lal Shahbaz* is enclosed in a quadrangular building, which has a dome and lantern, and is adorned with beautiful encaustic tiles, with Arabic inscriptions. Mirza Jani, of the Tarkan dynasty, built a still larger tomb to this saint, which was completed in 1639 A.D. by Nawab Dindar Khan. The gate and balustrade are said to have been of hammered silver, the gift of Mir Karam 'Ali Talpura, who also crowned the domes with silver spires. The chief object, however, of antiquarian interest in Sehwan is the **Fort** ascribed to Alexander the Great. It is an artificial mound in the N.W. part of the town, said once to have been 250 ft. high, but now only 60 ft., measuring round the summit 1500 ft. by 800 ft., and surrounded by a broken

wall. The remains of several towers are visible, but the fortifications are ruined.

Sehwan is the centre of the Government system of *Canals*, thirty-seven in number, of which the principal are the *W. Nara*, 30 m. long, and over 100 ft. wide at its mouth; the *Ghar*, 22 m. long, and 80 ft. wide; the *Naurang*, a continuation of the Ghar, 21 m. long, and 90 ft. wide; the *Birei-ji-Kur*, 27 m. long, and 48 ft. wide; and the *Eden Wah*, 23 m. long.

There is good **Shooting** to be had in the Sehwan district; hyenas, wild hog, wolves, foxes, jackals, the hog-deer, and the *chinkarah*, or "ravine antelope," being common.

[The **Manchhar Lake** * is not very far from Sehwan to the W. It is formed by the expansion of the W. Nara Canal and the Aral river, covering an area of 160 sq. m. in the wet season, but shrinking to about half that size at other times. In the cold weather there is abundance of water-fowl shooting, and excellent snipe, quail, and partridge shooting round the edge of the lake, and an extraordinary number of fine fish.

The fish are generally caught with spears or nets. The boat, which is flat-bottomed, is propelled by one man, while another, armed with three or four light cane spears, 8 ft. long, and barbed at the tip, stands at the prow watching the water; as soon as he sees a fish flash through the weeds, with which the lake is covered, he hurls a handful of spears in that direction, and is sure to strike one or two fish, which, as the spear becomes entangled in the weeds, cannot go far, and are followed and lifted into the boat.

For the other method of catching the fish, an ingenious circular enclosure of nets supported by poles is laid down in the lake. A flotilla of small boats containing men with drums and other noisy instruments surrounds the enclosure at some distance and gradually draws nearer.

"The fish, frightened by the din, and not daring to escape through the boats, press heavier and nearer to the net. Then when the boats approach, huge *dambhros* are seen flinging themselves into the air to a height of from 3 to 4 ft., hoping to jump over the lower net, but only to strike against the upper one and fall into the bag below, a self-made prey. In the meantime, men with spears hurl them at the huge *gandams*, which are unable to leap, and lifting them high in the air over the net, deposit them in the boats. Divers then go inside the net, and examine it carefully under water, securing such fish as may be endeavouring to force a passage through it. These men in their habits seem almost amphibious" (*Gaz. of Sindh*, p. 710).]

163 m. **Laki** station (R.), good quail, duck, and snipe shooting in the neighbourhood. The railway runs through the Laki Pass, at an elevation of 200 ft., the Indus lying below. This range of hills contains several hot springs, and shows many signs of volcanic action. There are also lead, antimony, and copper in them, though not in great quantities.

228 m. **Kotri** station (R.) (p. 264).

ROUTE 19.

RUK JUNCTION TO **CHAMAN** on the frontier of **Afghanistan** by **Shikarpur, Jacobabad, Sibi** Junction and **Quetta**, returning by the **Harnai** route.

Ruk junction station (R.), D.B., 15 m. on the Karachi side of Sukkur (see p. 268). The first station on the Sindh-Pishin Railway is

11 m. **Shikarpur** station, D.B., ✱ a municipal town and headquarters of a district of the same name, founded 1617. The population is 49,000, of whom 16,000 are Mohammedans. The great road to Baluchistan, Kandahar, and Central Asia passes through it, and Shikarpur was long a great trade depôt. These conditions have, however, been changed by the opening of the railway, and consequent facilities for direct trade.

The bazaar is covered in on account of the heat in summer, Shikarpur, Jacobabad, and Sibi being about the hottest places in India. The old bazaar has been lengthened, and the prolongation of it, called the *Stewart Ganj Market*, after a popular district officer, is well built and commodious, and is the best bazaar in Sindh. To the E. of the town are three large tanks, called Sarwar Khan's tank, Gillespie, and Hazari tanks. There is abundance of water for irrigation and other purposes, but the climate is very hot and dry, and the rainfall for twelve years averaged only 5.15 in.

37 m. **Jacobabad** station, D.B. (population, 7700). This was the chief military frontier station before Quetta was occupied.

The town was planned and laid out on the site of the village of Khangarh by General John Jacob, the distinguished frontier officer and commander of the Sindh horse, who built the Residency, and is buried here under a massive tomb. When he arrived in Upper Sindh, the whole country about Khangarh was in a state of anarchy, bodies of mounted robbers—Bugtis, Dumkis, Burdis, or Maris—swept the plains and robbed and murdered those they encountered. Khangarh itself offered a stout resistance to the 5th Bombay N.I., but General Jacob's rule put an end to all these troubles, and to him the peace of Upper Sindh was originally due. Of late years Jacobabad has decreased in population and importance. It is garrisoned by a Native cavalry regiment.

122 m. **Mithri** station.

134 m. **Sibi** junction station (R.), D.B. This place is in the valley of the river Nari, near the entrance of the Bolan Pass. Sibi was occupied by the British in the name of Shah Sujah from 1839-42, the old fort being used as a commissariat depôt. The place was ceded to the British by the Treaty of Gandamak in 1879. The Victoria Memorial Hall for jirgas is a fine building.

From *Sibi* to *Bostan junction* there are two lines—the Northern or *Harnai* Loop Line, which has maximum gradients of 1 in 45, and traverses a country inhabited by Pathans, and the Southern, or direct, Mushkaf-Bolan Line. A word of warning is necessary to a visitor starting on these journeys. In the winter cold of from 22° to 23° F. *below* zero is not at all uncommon on the higher parts of the line, whilst in summer 128° inside the house is not an unfrequent temperature at Nari. It is scarcely necessary to say that the consequences of insufficient clothing may be very serious to travellers who make this trip as part of a cold weather tour.

1. The Mushkaf-Bolan Direct Route.

The original alignment of this railway along the Bolan was afterwards abandoned in favour of the present line. As far as Rindli, at the mouth of the Bolan Pass, the old line is still kept up, but no trains are run upon it.

From **Mushkaf** (145 m.) the line runs for 28 m. up the Mushkaf Valley with easy gradients. It then passes by the Panir tunnel, 3000 ft. long, into the upper Bolan, and ascends by very steep gradients, some as much as 1 in 25, to **Kolpur** (196 m.). For 6 m. beyond the tunnel the works are exceptionally heavy, but from there up to **Mach** (181 m., 3250 ft.—engine-changing station) they are lighter. From **Hirak** (189 m.) they become very heavy again, and the Bolan is crossed nine times.

222 m. **Quetta**[1] (Kotah) station * (R.), D.B. At Quetta are the headquarters of the Agent to the Governor-General, Bauchistan, and of the 4th Army Division. The garrison consists of 2500 British and 6500 native troops. It is situated at the N. end of the Shal Valley in lat. 30° 12′, long. 66° 55′, 5000 ft. above the sea-level and 103 m. N. of Khelat. The Civil Station, with the Residency, the Club, and the fine Sandeman Hall, a design of Col. Sir S. Jacob, and a statue of Sir Hugh Barnes, lies E. of the railway, and beyond these is the city (population, 30,000). N. of both, on the further side of the deep Habib Nalla, are the Cantonments. To the N.E. stands the *Miri* or Fort, a former residence of the Khan of Khelat, from which there is a very extensive view of the neighbouring valley. In the same direction is the Staff College. The place is surrounded by fortified lines, and commanding, as it does with its strongly-fortified outpost of *Baleli*, both the *Khojak* and *Bolan* Passes, it forms one of the most important Indian frontier posts. It has rapidly increased since 1880, and now contains 50,500 inhabitants. In winter the cold is very severe. Numerous gardens and orchards abound in the suburbs, and the water-supply is good.

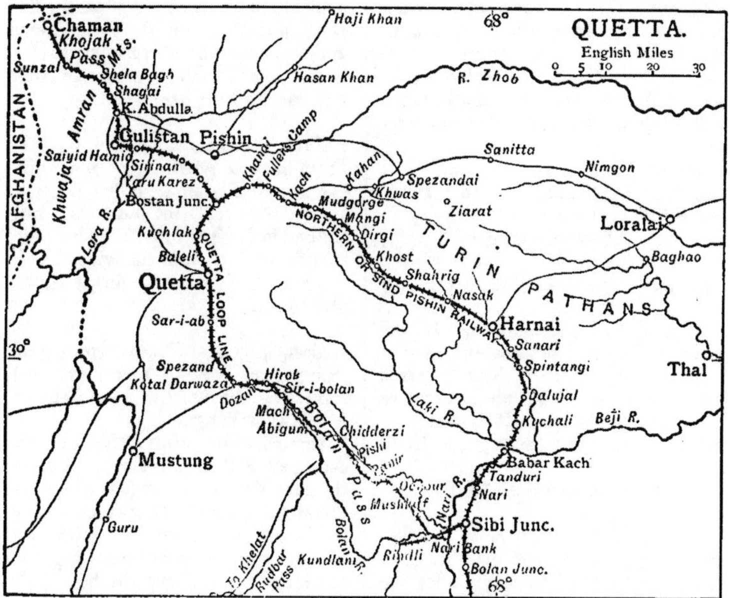

Walker & Boutall sc.

Quetta was occupied by British troops in the first expedition to Kabul. In 1877 a British political officer was again posted at Quetta, which was annexed in 1880, since when there has been a Governor-General's Agent for Baluchistan, Sir R. Sandeman, K.C.S.I., being the first to bear the title. The present

[1] From Spezend, 23 m. below Quetta, a railway has been constructed over 83 m. of desert to Nushki.

Agent is the Honble. Col. J. Ramsay, C.I.E. During the Afghan campaigns of 1878-1880, Quetta formed the base of operations for the Bombay column.

The line now proceeds up the Quetta Valley by Baleli and Kuchlak to

242 m. **Bostan Junction** for Harnai Route (see below).

About 14 m. beyond Bostan junction the Lora river is passed, the first stream the traveller will have seen on the Central Asian watershed, all the rivers he has hitherto crossed draining into the Arabian Sea.

249 m. **Yaru Karez**, the station for **Pishin**, 6 m. distant; tonga service. Since the opening of the railway to Chaman, the importance of Pishin, which is the principal place of the Achakzai country has much decreased.

273 m. **Gulistan** station. In the infancy of these lines a short surface railway was laid from here towards the Ghwa-zha Pass, an alternative route to Kandahar. It is not now used, the main line turning due N. to

281 m. **Killa Abdullah** (R.).

292 m. **Shela Bagh** is at the foot of the *Khojak Pass*, and near the S.E. end of the tunnel passing under the Kwaja Amran Mountains. This tunnel is 2⅔ m. long. Passing through it we reach the present ending of the line at

310 m. **Chaman** station, where there is a small military outpost.

The Khojak Pass is surmounted by a fine military road, and those who have the opportunity should ascend it (7500 ft.) to see the magnificent view W. over the Kadanai Plain and N. to beyond Kandahar, which is hidden by intervening hills.

When the line is continued to Kandahar it will necessarily make a long bend to the N. to obtain length for the descent into the Kadanai Valley, which lies far below Chaman, and the distance to Kandahar, the Arachosia of Alexander, will be about 85 m.

2. Bostan to Sibi, Harnai Route.

The scenery of this route, which is unsurpassed for weird grandeur in the whole world, is best seen by taking the downwards route from Bostan, and should at any sacrifice of time be seen by daylight. Leaving **Bostan** the line skirting the northern slopes of Takatu mountain on a gradually rising gradient, in one place forming a complete circle and passing over itself runs to

Kach ✱ 110 m. from Sibi, 6357 ft. From here a good tonga road goes (33 m.) to Ziarat, a valley 8000 ft. above the sea, set amongst hills clothed in Juniper forests. This place is entirely shut up in the winter.

From Kach the line drops all the way to Sibi.

Mangi, 97 m. From here a good riding road goes to Ziarat (22 m.), traversing the narrow deep defile of Mir Kásim Tangi.

Immediately after Mangi the **Chappar Rift** is traversed. This is the shoulder of a mountain which has the appearance of being cracked from top to bottom through the solid mass of limestone. The Rift itself is passed at nearly 300 ft. above the bed of the stream, and the train at several places seems suspended in the air. The line near the Rift constantly runs through tunnels and across high bridges. On leaving it a magnificent view is obtained of the Khalifat Range (11,440 ft.) rising sheer out of the valley on the N.W.

Harnai (R.) 58 m. from Sibi. From here the tonga road to Loralai and Fort San St Deman takes off

Nari (7 m.). The line leaves the hills and runs over a flat alluvial plain to Sibi (p. 270).

ROUTE 20.

(*a*) SAHARANPUR by the Oudh and Rohilkand Railway to Mughal Sarai through **Lhaksar** Junction, **Moradabad**, **Bareilly** Junction, Lucknow, and thence to Benares by (1) **Fyzabad** and **Jaunpur**, and (2) **Rae Bareli.**

(*b*) **Lhaksar** Junction to **Hardwar**, **Dehra Dun**, and the **Mussooree Chakrata** hill station.

(*c*) Bareilly Junction to **Naini Tal**, **Almora**, and **Ranikhet.**

Journey in 16¼ hrs.

Fares, Rs. 47, Rs.23½, Rs.5.

(*a*)

Saharanpur Junction (see p. 222).

22 m. Roorkee station (*Rurki*), D.B., a modern manufacturing town and military station, stands on a ridge overlooking the bed of the Solani river. Up to 1845 it was merely a mud-built village; it is now a flourishing town of 17,000 inhabitants, with broad metalled roadways meeting at right angles, and lined with excellent shops. It is the headquarters of the Ganges Canal workshops and iron foundry, established in 1845-1852. The *Canal* passes to the E. of the town between raised embankments.

The Thomason Civil Engineering College was founded in 1847. The students are partly English youths born in the country, partly Anglo-Indians and natives; and there are also special classes for soldiers picked for their ability. The whole number is about 350.

33 m. **Lhaksar** junction station. [A branch line from here runs N. 16 m. to **Hardwar** and **Dehra Dun**, giving access to the hill stations of Mussooree, Landour, and Chakrata (see (*b*) p. 279).]

59 m. **Najibabad.** [Branch line to *Kotawara*, 15 m., whence by road 18 m. to the military hill station of *Lansdowne*, which is garrisoned by Goorkha regiments.]

73 m. **Nagina** station (R.), noted for its work in ebony.

120 m. **Moradabad** junction (line to Ghaziabad and Delhi, p. 220),✱ D.B., lies at the S.E. of the city (population, 78,000), which is on the right bank of the Ramganga river. To N.W. of the town are the Cantonments and civil station. It is noted for its metal work, some of the designs of which are extremely good, though the cheaper articles are poor in all respects.

About ½ m. N. of the railway station are the *American Church*, and the office of the Tahsildar, and 1 m. from this church is the District School, on the banks of the Ramganga, which is here crossed by a bridge of boats. To the W. of the school is the Badshahi Masjid, dating from 1634 in the reign of Shah Jahan, after whose son, Murad Bakhsh, the place was named. N. are the ruins of the fort of Rustam Khan the Rohilla.

On the outbreak of the mutiny at Meerut on 10th May 1857, the Judge of Moradabad, Mr Cracroft Wilson, and the Collector, Mr C. B. Saunders, afterwards Commissioner of Delhi, maintained themselves in Moradabad till 3rd June, but were then obliged to fall back on Meerut.

176 m. **Bareilly** junction station ✱ (R.), D.B. (population, 127,500). [From here one branch of the Rohilkand and Kumaon Railway runs N. to 66 m. *Kathgodam*, under Naini Tal, and 30 m. to *Pilibhit*, D.B. (see p. 281), and another runs to Chandausi and Aligarh on the E.I. Railway (see p. 299).

The city of Bareilly, the capital of the country of Rohilkand known in the early history of India as Kather, was originally founded by one Baral Deo in 1537, and was refounded a hundred years later. Ali Muhammad Khan, the first chief who united the Rohillas under him, between 1707 and 1720, made Bareilly his headquarters, and Hafiz Rahmat Khan, who ultimately succeeded him, extended his power from Almora in the N. to Etawah in the S.W. The Rohillas, who were no whit less turbulent than the other fighting elements in India at that period, and who took a prominent share in the dismemberment of the Mughal Empire, ultimately provoked an invasion of the Mahrattas, and to buy them off executed a promise to pay an indemnity of 40 lakhs, for which the Nawab Wazir of Oudh stood surety. These transactions led to the Rohilla War, 1772-74, in which the ruler of Oudh, with the support of British troops, conquered Rohilkand, Hafiz Rahmat being killed in battle fighting valiantly.[1] Feiz Ullah, son of Ali Muhammed Khan, succeeded to the chiefship of the Rohillas, and from him the present chief of the *Rampur* State is descended. In 1816 an insurrection broke out, in consequence of the imposition of a new tax on houses, and was suppressed only with the loss of several hundred men killed and wounded.

On the outbreak of the mutiny in 1857 there were no British troops at Bareilly, but only a native garrison consisting of two Native Infantry regiments, one Native Cavalry regiment, and one Battery. These revolted on 31st May, shortly after the arrival of fugitives from Ferozepore (p. 147), and the Europeans in the station were obliged to fly for their lives, after a certain number, including the Brigadier-General, had been murdered: the few who remained in the place were afterwards massacred by the order of Khan Bahadur Khan, grandson of Hafiz Rahmat Khan, who had been proclaimed ruler of the country, and who induced the Bareilly Brigade, under Subahdar Bakht Khan, to march on 10th of June to Delhi, where their leader was appointed General of the rebel army.

The city of Bareilly contains some fine bazaars and mosques. The place is famous for its splendid rows of bamboos, from which it is commonly called Bans Bareilly. In the churchyard of the station church is the tomb of Mr Thomason, Lieutenant-Governor of the Province of Agra between 1843 and 1853, to whom perhaps more than to any one else the present systems of land revenue and administration of N. India are due.

219 m. **Shahjahanpur** junction. (A branch line runs from here to 38 m. Mailani junction on the Rohilkand Kumaon line from Bareilly to Lucknow) (R.). Chief town of a district with civil station and military cantonment (population, 68,000). The station contains an English church and three churches for native converts belonging to the American Methodist Mission, which also supports several schools. The principal local manufacture is sugar. The Rosa sugar factory and rum distillery is situated on the Garra river a few m. from the city, with which it is connected by railway.

In 1857 the Europeans at the station were attacked by mutineers while at morning service on 31st May, but managed to defend themselves in the church with the aid of some faithful Sepoys, and to fall back on Muhamdi in Oudh, where, however, they were all murdered shortly afterwards.

258 m. **Hardoi** station (R.), D.B.

322 m. **Lucknow** junction station (R.) [Branch S.W. to Cawnpore; S.E. to *Rae Bareli*, E. to Fyzabad, and by the Bengal and North-Western Railway to Bahramghat (Chauka Ghat, and Gogra Ghat), and N. to Sitapur and Bhojeepura (p. 281).

From Lucknow two lines run to Benares, the direct 187 m. by Rae Bareli, 370 m. from Saharanpur and Pertabgarh, 420 m., both the headquarters of districts, and the older and longer, 209 m., by Fyzabad, 79 m. from Lucknow, and Jaunpur, 163 m. There is nothing of special interest

1 The true narrative of the Rohilla War, which formed one of the articles of formed ment against Warren Hastings, may be read in Sir John Strachey's *Hastings and the Rohilla War*.

to note on the former route, though Rae Bareli, named from the once important tribe of Bhars, contains an old fort of Ibrahim Sharki.

The Bengal and N.W. Railway connecting Oudh with Gorakhpur and Behar (p. 311) runs alongside of the loop route to 17 m. **Barabanki Junction**, and then diverges to 22 m. Bahramghat. From Gonda, 31 m. beyond the Gogra, two branches turn N. to 38 m. Bharaich, Naipalganj Road and Katarnian Ghat, and 23 m. Balrampur, 93 Uska Basar, and Gorakhpur. Bharaich is famous for the tomb shrine of Syad Salar Masaud, nephew of the great Mahmud of Ghazni, who was killed here in 1033 A.D.

79 m. **Fyzabad** junction station (R.), D.B.

[Branch to *Ajodhya Ghat*, 6 m. and thence to Bengal and N.W. Railway. A line now connects Fyzabad and Allahabad running through Sultanpur and Pertabgarh.]

Fyzabad (population 55,000) is the headquarters of a district and of a Division. Once the capital of Oudh, the city has fallen into decay since the death, in 1816, of Bahu Begam, who resided here for many years. The first Nawab of Oudh, S'aadat Khan, seldom resided at Fyzabad, though it was his nominal capital, nor did his successor Safdar Jang; but in 1776 Shuja-ud-daulah, who succeeded, took up his permanent residence there. When defeated at Buxar he fled to Fyzabad and constructed the lofty entrenchment whose ramparts of rammed clay still frown over the Gogra. At his death, in 1775, his widow, the Bahu Begam, remained at Fyzabad, while Asaf-ud-daulah, the then Nawab, removed to Lucknow. The city is bounded to the N. by the Gogra river, which here divides into two streams, both crossed by pontoon bridges. The **Cantonment** lies to the N.W. of the Indian city, at the S.W. corner of which the railway to Benares passes. The **Mausoleum of the Bahu Begam**, wife of Shuja-ud-daulah, Nawab of Oudh, and mother of Asaf-ud-daulah, is the finest mausoleum in the province of Oudh and its neighbourhood. The cenotaph is of marble without inscription. The total height may be taken at 140 ft. There is a very fine view from the top. This lady was one of two Begams of Oudh whose alleged ill-treatment formed a subject of indictment of Warren Hastings on which Burke and Sheridan wasted much misplaced oratory. As a matter of fact, although Asaf-ud-daulah and the British officials acting with him did put considerable pressure on the servants of the two Begams (of whom the mother of Shuja-ud-daulah was known as the Mani Begam), to compel them to disclose where the State money of which the ladies had possessed themselves was hid, the ladies themselves were left untouched. It may be added that they wrote letters of condolence to Warren Hastings on his trial! The **Mausoleum of Shuja-ud-daulah** is close by, and is something like the Begam's, but not nearly so grand or imposing. At each of the four corners of the building are an oblong and a square reservoir. In the centre space on the ground floor are three tomb-stones without inscription. The middle slab is that of Shuja-ud-daulah. His mother's is to the W., and that of his son, Mansur 'Ali, to the E. In the W. side of the enclosure is a mosque at the N. end, with an Imambarah on the S. The Civil Station cantonments and environs are beautifully wooded with innumerable tamarind, mango, and other trees.

The **Gupta Park** is prettily laid out: at the S. end of it is a temple where the Rama is said to have disappeared.

[6 m. **Ajodhya** ancient Sanscrit *Ayudhya*, on the banks of the Gogra, is the place where the great Ram Chandra once reigned. The ancient city is said to have covered an area of 48 kos, or 96 m., and to have been the capital of Koshala, "the resplendent," the country of the Solar race of kings, of whom Manu was the first. A copper grant of Jai Chand, the last of the Kanauj Rathors, dated 1187 A.D., was found near Fyzabad. Koshala was the cradle of Buddhism, for Sakya Muni, its founder, was born in the Gorakhpur district (see p. 311). and preached at Ajodhya. The Chinese traveller, Hiouen Thsang, found at Ajodhya twenty Buddhist monasteries with 3000 monks. According to him, the celebrated Toothbrush Tree of Buddha grew here.

The road from Fyzabad cantonment to Ajodhya (4 m.) is excellent, and it may be found more convenient than the railway. On entering Ajodhya, the **Janam Sthan Temple** will be found on the left. In the sanctum, the door of which has a silver frame, are images of Sita and Rama. Rama has a gleaming jewel of large size, which looks like a light-coloured sapphire. The temple is an oblong of about 200 ft. by 150 ft. The walls are 45 ft. high, and seem strong enough for a fortress; which justifies its name of *Hanuman Garhi*; "Hanuman's fortress." The neighbouring trees swarm with gray monkeys.

To the N.W. is the temple of **Kanak Bhawan**, or Sone Ka Garh, with images of Sita and Rama crowned with gold, whence the name "Hall of Gold." This is said to be the oldest temple of all.

The **Janam Sthan**, or place where Ram Chandra was born, is ½ m. W. of the Hanuman Garhi; it is a plain masonry platform, just outside a temple, but within the enclosure on the left-hand side. The primeval temple perished, but was rebuilt, and was converted by Baber into a mosque. Europeans are expected to take off their shoes if they enter the building, which is quite plain, with the exception of twelve black pillars taken from the old temple, On the pillar on the left of the door on entering may be seen the remains of a figure.

At about ¼ m. to the N. of Janam Sthan is **Swarga Dwara**, or Ram Ghat, where Rama was cremated. S.W. is **Lakshman's Ghat**, where Lakshman, the half-brother of Rama, used to bathe. 1 m. to the S. of Hanuman Garhi is the *Mani Parbat*, and to its S. again are the *Kuver Parbat* and *Sugriv Parbat*, mounds of great antiquity. The **Mani Parbat** Hill is 65 ft. high, and is covered with broken bricks and blocks of masonry. The bricks are 11 in. sq. and 3 in. thick. At 46 ft. above the ground, on the W. side, are the remains of a curved wall faced with *Kankar* blocks. General Cunningham supposes that the great monastery described by Hiouen Thsang is the **Sugriv Parbat**, which is 560 ft. long by 300 ft. broad, and that the Mani Parbat is the Stupa of Asoka, built on the spot where Buddha preached the law during his six years' residence at Saketa.]

163 m. **JAUNPUR City**, station (R.), D.B. (There are two stations at Jaunpur—the Civil Lines, or Zafarabad station is 4 m. farther on.)

Jaunpur[1] (population, 30,400), named after Juna Khan, known as Muhammad Tughlak, 1325-51), and founded by Firoz Shah Tughlak in 1360, (p. 208), is a place of much interest, and was the capital of an independent Mohammedan kingdom (the Sharki or Eastern dynasty) from 1397-1478, and retained a partial independence until finally conquered by Akbar. The stone **Bridge**, 714 ft. long, over the Gumti, was erected in the reign of that Emperor. It consists of ten spans besides those standing on the land, the middle group of four being larger than the three at each end. It was designed by 'Afzal 'Ali, a Kabuli

1 For the architecture of Jaunpur a volume published by Messrs Führer and Smith of the Archæological Survey of India, entitled the *Sharki Architecture of Jaunpur* (Trübner), may be consulted and Fergusson's *Indian Architecture*, ii 222.

architect, at the expense of Munim Khan, one of Akbar's high officers. It was commenced in 1564 and completed in 1568, and is said to have cost £300,000. Formerly there were shops on either side, but these were destroyed during the flood of 1774. At a market-place at the S. end of the bridge is a stone lion somewhat larger than life, which was found in the fort. Under it is a young elephant, which it is supposed to have seized. From this all distances in the city and province were calculated.

Near the bridge on the left bank is the **Fort** of Firoz containing the Fort Masjid, almost entirely constructed from ruined temples. The entrance gate, 47 ft. high, is covered with *kashani hak*, a sort of blue and yellow enamelled bricks, of which beautiful portions remain. The inner gate has many stones of Hindu temples built into the walls, on some of which is carved a bell. At 200 ft. from this gate is a low mosque, 130 by 22 ft., divided into three chambers by lateral walls, with a reservoir in front, and a remarkable Lat, or *minar*, apparently unaltered since its erection, and beautifully inscribed. The river-face of the Fort is 300 ft. beyond this pillar. It is 150 ft. in perpendicular height, and commands a noble view of the country and city. Before reaching it, a round tower called the magazine will be noticed, with a *hammam*, or bath, on the left.

Some 400 yds. to the N. of the bridge and Fort, and not far from the *Post Office* and *Town Hall*, is the N. entrance of the **Atala Masjid**,[1] erected on the site of an old Hindu temple dedicated to the goddess Atala Devi, which was destroyed in Sultan Ibrahim's reign (1401-1440) and the materials used up for the mosque. On the principal **Mihrab**, built of black marble, immediately in the centre of the main W. wall of the Masjid proper in which the prayers are said, is a verse from the Koran, and above it the creed. The façade is 75 ft. high. Almost in the centre of the large courtyard and to the N.E. of the musallah or praying-ground is a well with a fine citron-leaved Indian fig-tree (*Ficus venosa*). At the S.W. corner of the large square is a chamber screened by a lattice of stone, intended for the women. Leading from it to the roof is a staircase. Behind the propylon screening the dome from the courtyard

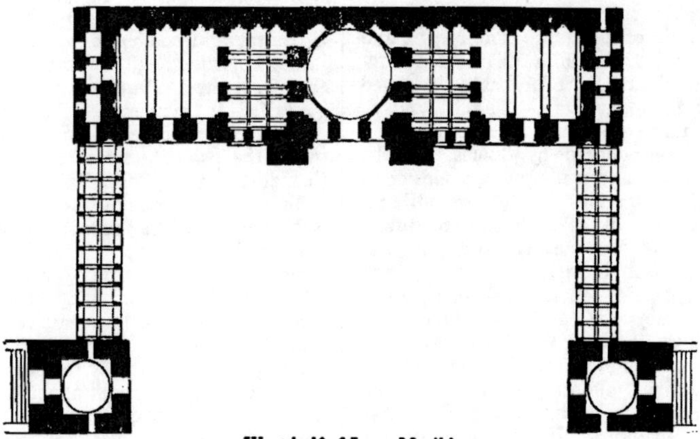

West half of Jama Masjid.

[1] The chief features of the Jaunpur mosques are the use of Jain materials, the two storeyed arcades, the great gates, and the large central screen arches of the mosque proper.

and surrounding three sides of the drum of the dome, is a chamber some 11 ft. high and 6 ft. wide.

½ m. N.W. of the Atala mosque, raised on a platform some 20 ft. in height, is the splendid **Jama Masjid**, built by Sultan Hasan, 1452-1478,[1] commenced 1438, finished after 1478. Some attribute the design to Ibrahim, as his family lie in the cloistered court of a building adjoining the N. side of the Masjid. On entering the S. gate an inscription (upside down) in Sanscrit of the 8th century will be seen on one of the outer voussoirs of the exterior arch, another in Tughra characters over the top of the central *mihrab*, and a third in Arabic characters around the outer margin of the arch. The N., S., and E. sides are in a dilapidated condition, and were probably destroyed by Sikandar Lodi. The N. and S. entrance gates have been restored and are surmounted by domes. In the cloisters and walls many stones from Hindu temples have been utilised. Its general arrangement resembles that of the Atala and the Lal Darwazah Mosque (see below), and the façades are not unlike, although the cloisters here have three tiers, whilst those at the Atala have only two. The mosque proper is very massive, almost fort-like in construction. It measures 59 ft. by 235 ft., including the thickness of the walls, but not the bastions at the angles. It is divided into five compartments on the ground floor, and above are two zenana chambers, one on each side of the grand dome, with splendid stone carved ceilings. On the E. side is an immense propylon 80 ft. high, divided by string courses into five storeys.

N. of the mosque is the **burial ground** of the **Sharki kings**, the walls of which approach the N. wall of the mosque within 30 ft. In the quadrangle is the tomb of *Ghulam 'Ali* with a fine Persian inscription. In the centre, beyond this tomb, is that of *Sultan Ibrahim Shah.* The only inscription is on a round stone in the centre which has the Kalimah.

Next to the tomb of Ibrahim is that of his grandson Sultan Hasan Shah.

Besides those already mentioned, six other mosques deserve visiting: 1. The Charungli or **Mosque of Malik Khalis Mukhlis**, built on the site of the favourite temple of Vijaya Chandra, which was broken down by Malik Khalis and Malik Mukhlis, by order of Sultan Ibrahim. In one of the pillars is a black stone, still worshipped by the Hindus. 2. **Chachakpur Mosque**, called Jhanjhri Masjid, on account of the "screen-like" appearance of its ornamentation, was a temple built by Jai Chandra, and converted by Ibrahim into a mosque. 3. To the W. of the city is the **Lal Darwazah Mosque**, so called in memory of the "high gate painted with vermilion" belonging to the palace erected close by at the same time by Bibi Rajo, Queen of Sultan Mahmud, 1440-1452. This is the smallest of the Jaunpur mosques. The style of architecture is the same as that of the Jama and Atala Masjids, but the building throughout is on a less massive and much lighter scale. The date is uncertain, though probably the cloisters of the court were erected about 1447. On the N., S., and E. sides of the court are massive gate entrances. The cloisters are two bays deep, and the W. walls as well as the cloisters are panelled. The columns deserve study on account of their variety. The propylon, the principal feature of the building, standing in the centre of the W. façade, is 48 ft. 6 in. high, and is wider at the base than the top. The towers contain staircases leading to a mezzanine floor, on each side of the dome. The principal mihrab is of black stone. On the top of the architrave is an Arabic inscription. 4. **Mosque of Nawab Muhsin Khan.** Sukh Mandil, who was the Diwan of Khan Zaman Khan, had built a temple where this mosque stands. When Khan Zaman was killed the building came into the hands of

[1] This King was conquered by Sultan Bahlol Lodi of Dehli, but was allowed to remain in Jaunpur.

Muhsin Khan, one of Akbar's courtiers, who destroyed the temple and built a mosque. 5. The **Mosque of Shah Kabir,** built by Baba Beg Jalagur, governor of Jaunpur in Akbar's reign, in 1567, in honour of the saint Shah Kabir. 6. The **'Idgah Mosque,** built by Sultan Hasan, and repaired in Akbar's reign by Khan Khanan. Afterwards it fell into a ruinous state, and was deserted till restored by Mr Welland.

167 m. **Zafarabad** station for the Civil Lines of Jaunpur. The **Church** (Holy Trinity) contains a tablet to Manton Collingwood Ommaney, B.C.S., Judicial Commissioner of Oudh, who rebuilt it in 1852, and died at Lucknow during the siege. A few officers were killed on the outbreak of the Mutiny at Jaunpur in 1857, but the majority of the Europeans escaped safely to Benares.

The mosque of Shaikh Barha in Zafarabad composed wholly of Jain materials is the oldest at Jaunpur.

519 m. from Saharanpur by Rae Bareli, **Benares** station (See Route 4).

530 m. **Mughal Sarai** junction station with the East Indian Railway (see p. 34).

(*b*)

Lhaksar, p. 273.

16 m. **Hardwar** station (population, 26,000—height above sea-level is 1024 ft.) is situated on the right bank of the Ganges, at the southern base of the Siwalik range, at the mouth of a gorge through which that great river enters the plains. The Ganges here divides into several channels, intercepted by large islands, many of which are placed beyond the reach of high flood-water. One of these channels commences about 2½ m. above Hardwar, and flows by it, and by Mayapur and Kankhal, rejoining the parent stream a little below the last town. The Ganges Canal system commences at Hardwar, the head-waters being taken from a spot on this bank between Mayapur and Kankhal.

The town is of great antiquity, and has borne many names. It was originally known as Kapila, or Gupila, from the sage Gupila, who passed a long period here in religious austerities, at a spot still called Kapila Sthana.

In the 7th century A.D. the Chinese pilgrim Hiouen Thsang visited a city which he calls Mo-Yu-Lo, which General Cunningham identifies with Mayapur, a little S. of the modern Hardwar.[1] Timur sacked the place in January 1399. The name of Hardwar "Door of Hari or Vishnu," is comparatively modern, and probably does not date farther back than 1400 A.D.

The great object of attraction is the temple of *Gangadwara* (see p. 280), and the adjoining bathing ghat. This ghat has its name from the *Charan*, or footprint of Hari, impressed on a stone let into the upper wall, which is an object of great veneration at the annual gathering. Each pilgrim struggles to be first to plunge into the pool after the propitious moment has arrived, and stringent police regulations are required to prevent the crowd from trampling one another to death and drowning each other in the sacred water. In 1819, 430 persons lost their lives in this manner, after which accident Government built the present enlarged ghat of 60 steps, 100 ft. wide. The advantages supposed to be derived from bathing in the Ganges are the cleansing from all sins. The great assemblage of pilgrims takes place on the 1st of Baisakh (March-April), the day on which the Ganges is said to have first appeared, and when the Hindu solar year begins.

Every twelfth year the planet Jupiter being in Aquarius, a feast of peculiar sanctity occurs, called a *Kumbh-mela*, attended by enormous crowds. In ordinary years the

[1] For the ancient history of Hardwar, see *Arch. Rep.*, vol. ii. p. 231.

pilgrims amount to 100,000, and at the *Kumbh-mela* to 300,000. Riots and bloody fights used to be common; in 1760, on the last day of bathing (10th April), the rival mobs of the Gusain and Byragi sects had a battle, in which 18,000 are said to have perished. In 1795 the Sikh pilgrims slew 500 Gusains.

Gangadwara is celebrated in the Puranas as the scene of Daksha's sacrifice, to which he neglected to invite Shiva, the husband of his daughter Sati. Sati attended the sacrifice in spite of Shiva's warning not to do so, and was so shocked at her father's disrespect that she went to the bank of the Ganges, and by her own splendour consumed her body. Enraged at Sati's death Shiva produced Vira-Bhadra, who cut off Daksha's head and threw it in the fire. Shiva restored Daksha to life, but as his head had been consumed, replaced it with that of a goat or ram. The spot where Daksha is supposed to have prepared his sacrifice is now marked by the *Temple of Daksheshwara*, a form of Shiva. It is at the S. end of Kankhal, 2½ m. below the bathing *ghat*. Around the temple are several smaller ones, of no interest.

There are three *old temples* at Hardwar, to Narayana-shila, to Maya-devi, and to Bhairava.

The *Temple of Narayana-shila* is made of bricks 9½ in. square and 2½ in. thick, and is plastered on the outside. The *Temple of Maya-devi* is built entirely of stone, and General Cunningham thinks it may be as old as the 10th or 11th century. The principal statue, which is called Maya-devi, is a three-headed and four-armed female, in the act of killing a prostrate figure; in one hand is a discus, in another what resembles a human head, and in a third a trident. Close by is a squatting figure with eight arms, which must be Shiva, and outside the temple is the bull Nandi. Outside the *Temple of Sarvvanath* is a statue of Buddha under the Bodhi tree accompanied by two standing and two flying figures. On the pedestal is a wheel with a lion on either side.

From Hardwar many pilgrims proceed to visit the shrine of Kedarnath, a name of Shiva, and that of Bhadrinath far up in the Himalaya Mountains.

48 m. **Dehra Dun (or Doon)** is the headquarters of the Dehra Dun district. Dehra itself (28,000 inhabitants) is prettily situated in the midst of a mountain valley, 2300 ft. above sea-level. It was founded by Guru Ram Rai, who settled in the Dun at the end of the 17th century. His temple, on the pattern of the mausoleum of the Emperor Jahangir at Shah Dara, forms the chief ornament of the town. At Dehra Dun is the Indian Forest School, to which is attached an exceedingly pretty Botanical Garden. The place is also the summer headquarters of the Viceregal Bodyguard.

In the earliest ages of Hindu legend Dehra Dun formed part of a region known as Kedarkhand, the abode of Shiva, from whom also the Siwalik Hills are called. Here Rama and his brother are said to have done penance for killing Ravana, and here the five Pandus stopped on their way to the snowy range where they immolated themselves. Authentic history knows nothing of Dehra Dun till the 17th century when Ram Rai was driven from the Panjab and the Sikh Guruship on account of doubts as to his legitimacy. In 1757 Najib-ud-daulah, Governor of Saharanpur, occupied the Dun, but he died in 1770, when the country was swept by various invaders, last of all the Goorkhas. At the end of the Goorkha War in 1815 these ceded the country to the British, who had easily occupied Dehra, and taken the strong hill fortress of Kalanga after a gallant defence, in which Sir Rollo Gillespie, a gallant soldier who suppressed the mutiny at Vellore (p. 396), was killed. There is a monument to the slain a short distance from Dehra.

The approach to Mussooree from Dehra is by *Rajpur* ✱ (6 m.), a large

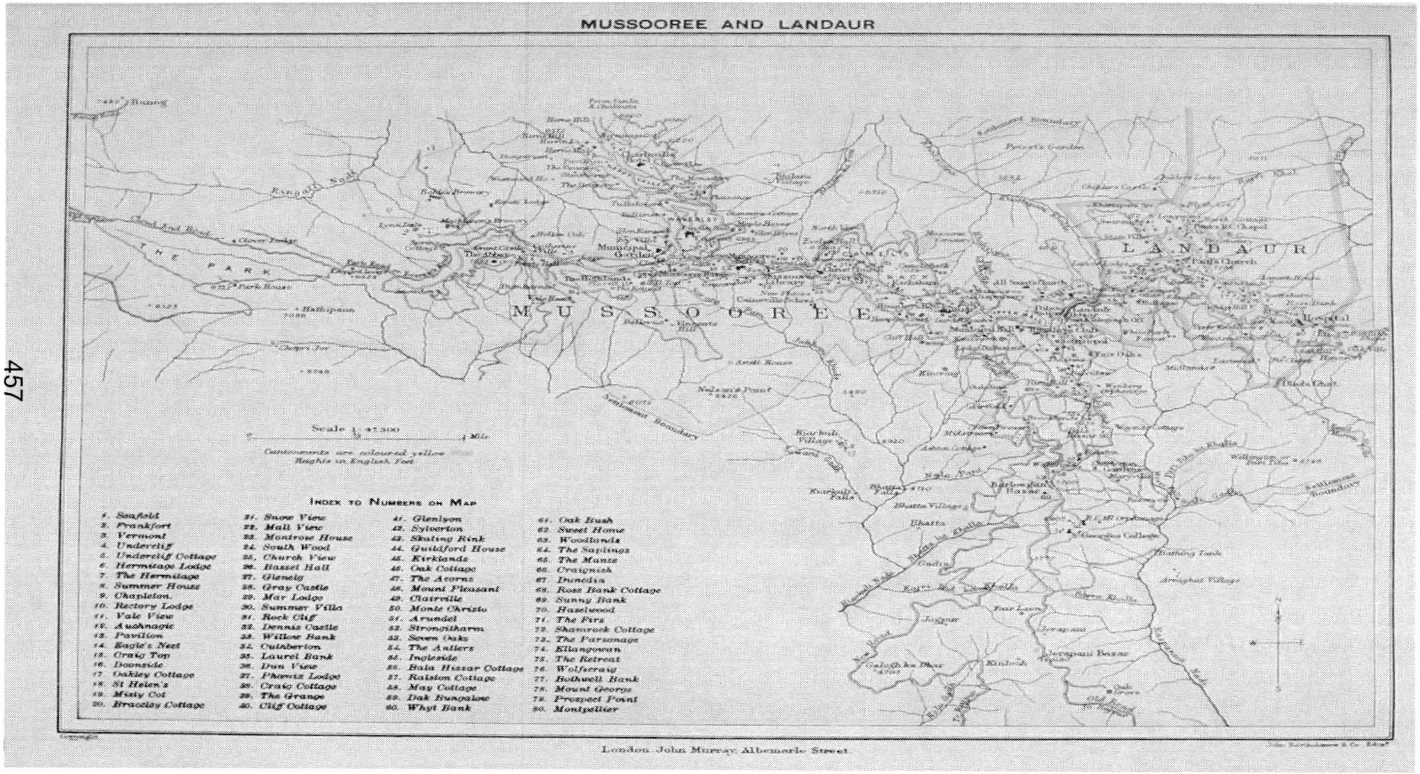
MUSSOOREE AND LANDAUR
MUSSOOREE
LANDAUR
Scale 1/47,500
Mile
Cantonments are coloured yellow
Heights in English Feet
INDEX TO NUMBERS ON MAP
1. Seafield
2. Frankfort
3. Vermont
4. Undercliff
5. Undercliff Cottage
6. Hermitage Lodge
7. The Hermitage
8. Summer House
9. Chapleton.
10. Rectory Lodge
11. Vale View
12. Auchnagie
13. Pavilion
14. Eagle's Nest
15. Craig Top
16. Doonside
17. Oakley Cottage
18. St Helen's
19. Misty Cot
20. Bracelay Cottage
21. Snow View
22. Mall View
23. Montrose House
24. South Wood
25. Church View
26. Bassett Hall
27. Glenelg
28. Gray Castle
29. Mar Lodge
30. Summer Villa
31. Rock Cliff
32. Dennis Castle
33. Willow Bank
34. Cuthberton
35. Laurel Bank
36. Dun View
37. Phœnix Lodge
38. Craig Cottage
39. The Grange
40. Cliff Cottage
41. Glenlyon
42. Sylverton
43. Skating Rink
44. Guildford House
45. Kirklands
46. Oak Cottage
47. The Acorns
48. Mount Pleasant
49. Clairville
50. Monte Christo
51. Arundel
52. Strongitharm
53. Seven Oaks
54. The Antlers
55. Ingleside
56. Bala Hissar Cottage
57. Ralston Cottage
58. May Cottage
59. Dak Bungalow
60. Whyt Bank
61. Oak Bush
62. Sweet Home
63. Woodlands
64. The Saplings
65. The Manse
66. Craignish
67. Dunedin
68. Rose Bank Cottage
69. Sunny Bank
70. Hazelwood
71. The Firs
72. Shamrock Cottage
73. The Parsonage
74. Ellangowan
75. The Retreat
76. Wolferaig
77. Bothwell Bank
78. Mount George
79. Prospect Point
80. Montpellier
London. John Murray, Albemarle Street.

native village, and at an elevation of about 3000 ft. (tonga, Rs. 5). The road from Rajpur to Mussooree is very steep, and the journey can be made only by pony (Rs. 4) or jampan (Rs. 5).

About half-way up is *Jarapani*, a halting-place where there is water and a bazaar; and here, at an elevation of 5000 ft., are the first houses of the European residents.

4 m. **Mussooree**, ✱ a hill station, and *Landour*, the adjacent Convalescent Depôt for British troops, are situated upon one of the outer ranges of the Himalayas, which lie to the N. of Dehra Dun. The hill on which Mussooree is built rises from the plains in the form of a horse-shoe, gradually ascending to the centre, and enclosing in the hollow a number of ridges which lose themselves in the mass above. Ridges also run down from the back of a hill to a valley in which flows a tributary of the Jumna; between the ridges N. and S. are deep wooded gorges. The greater number of the houses are built at an elevation of from 6000 to 7200 ft., mainly on the S. side of the hill. The view from Mussooree over the valley of the Dun and across the Siwalik Hills to the plains is very beautiful, as also is the view towards the N., which is bounded by the peaks of the snowy range. The hills, on the side nearest the plains exposed to the prevailing winds, are nearly bare, and the visitor misses the pine and deodar forests which form so beautiful a feature at Simla and other Himalayan stations. To the N., however, not far below the ridge, trees are plentiful. They are principally oak, rhododendron, and fir. In sheltered places apricots, apples, pears, and cherries flourish, together with many English annual and perennial plants. The climate is delightful.

Landour ✱ is a little to the S.E. of Mussooree, connected with it by a narrow spur 200 yds. long, and from 20 to 30 yds. in breadth, with a sheer precipice of from 80 to 100 ft. on either side. It rises rather abruptly to the Landour hill, the highest point of which is about 900 ft. above the average of the Mussooree ridge. The houses and barracks are built upon the ascending slope of the spur, and upon the precipitous slopes of the ridge. The barracks face the S. There is a permanent Anglo-Indian population at Landour and Mussooree, and a large influx of visitors during the hot season. English and Roman Catholic churches exist at both places, with numerous schools and boarding-houses, and at Mussooree a public library, masonic lodge, club, brewery, and three banks.

There is a good road from Mussooree (148 m.) to Simla *viâ* **Chakrata**, a military hill-station 7000 ft. above the sea in the centre of the district called Jaunsar Bawar (21 m.). The accommodation on the way is, however, but scanty, and tents, food, and servants should be taken. The number of marches is twelve. The highest point crossed is the Patemalla Mountain (9368 ft.), 33 m. from Simla.

(*c*)

Bareilly (see p. 273).

12 m. **Bhojeepura** junction. The main line runs from here E. and S. to 63 m. Pilibhit, 115 m. Lakhimpur, 143 m. **Sitapur**, and passing through the old cantonment of Mariaon, to 198 m. Lucknow. One of the saddest incidents of 1857 occurred in connection with the Europeans at Sitapur, where the troops mutinied on 3rd June. Those who escaped suffered the extremity of distress, for four months at one time in the jungles, at another in the custody of false friends; and the few who remained were ultimately sent to the Kaisar Bagh in Lucknow (p. 294). Of the whole number only one child, smuggled into the Alam Bagh by a trusty native, and two ladies were finally saved.

The Rohilkand Kumaon line runs N. to

66 m. **Kathgodam** (R.) terminus station.* The journey from here to Naini Tal takes 3 hrs.: the distance is 15 m. The first 12 m. are done in tongas, Rs.11; the last 3 m. in dandies or on ponies, Rs.3 or 2. From the railway station the country is flat for 2 m. as far as *Rambagh* D.B. The road then ascends the valley of the Balaya, amidst picturesque scenery, with waterfalls flowing down deep ravines, to (12 m.) *Brewery*. Here the steep ascent of the ghat (3 m. to Naini Tal) commences. On the way up, "Douglas Dale," a pleasant halting-place, is passed.

Naini Tal,* D.B., is a favourite sanatorium of the United Provinces, and the summer residence of the Lieutenant-Governor, and of the Lieutenant-General of the Bengal Command. It is extremely picturesque, the lake forming a most striking feature; but for travellers with a limited time at their disposal it does not possess the attractions of Darjeeling or Simla. The highest peaks are to the N.W., as China, which is 8568 ft. above sea-level, Deopathar, 7589 ft. etc.

The *Lake* is nearly 1 m. long, and 400 yds. broad, with an area of 120 acres. The flood-level is 6410 ft. above the sea. The depth ranges from 5 fathoms at the N. end to 15½ in the broadest part; and there are *Sulphur Springs* at the end near the Convalescent Depôt.

The principal residences lie to the N.W. of the lake, where close to the shore are the *Assembly Rooms* with *Library*, and the *Masonic Hall*, the *Club* about ½ m. farther, the *Post Office* lying on the way, and some *European shops*. The *Cricket*, *Polo*, and *Lawn Tennis Grounds*; the *Racquet-court*, *Bathing Sheds*, *Billiard Rooms*, and *Public Gardens* are all near the Assembly Rooms. There are numerous *Educational Institutions*, including a *Kindergarten*. The Lady Dufferin *Hospital* was opened in 1890.

The *Church of St John in the Wilderness*, ½ m. beyond the Club, is built of stone. It has a roof of dark-coloured wood, and has two stained-glass windows. There is a handsome brass under the window, on the N. side of the communion-table, in memory of Cuthbert Bensley Thornhill, C.S.I.

On 18th September 1880 a sad catastrophe occurred at Naini Tal. On Thursday the 16th of September rain fell in torrents, and continued during Friday, and Saturday, by which time 33 in. had fallen in the twenty-four hours. The Victoria Hotel, which stood about 280 yds to the N. of the N. corner of the lake, had a lofty hill at its back. At ten o'clock on the morning of Saturday, the 18th, a slight landslip occurred on the spur of the hill behind the hotel, crushing in the outhouses and a portion of the rear of the premises, and burying several natives and one European child. The Assistant-Commissioner, Mr Leonard Taylor, with some police and labourers, came at once to render assistance, and sent for the military, who hastened to the spot under the command of Captain Balderstone. The work of extricating the dead and wounded went on till 1.30 P.M., when in a moment the whole precipitous cliff overhanging the spot fell with a tremendous roar, burying at once the hotel, the soldiers, the assembly rooms, library, orderly room, road, and garden. Almost every person in the buildings and grounds was entombed, and it was utterly impossible to extricate any of them.

There is a pretty ride on the W. side of the lake, where the visitor may ascend to a considerable height. But the finest views will be obtained on the E. side, *e.g.* from Sher ka Danda, whence the snowy mountains beyond Almora and Ranikhet may be seen.

An excursion may also be made by a very pretty road from Naini Tal to **Bhim Tal**, 12 m. (Bungalow and

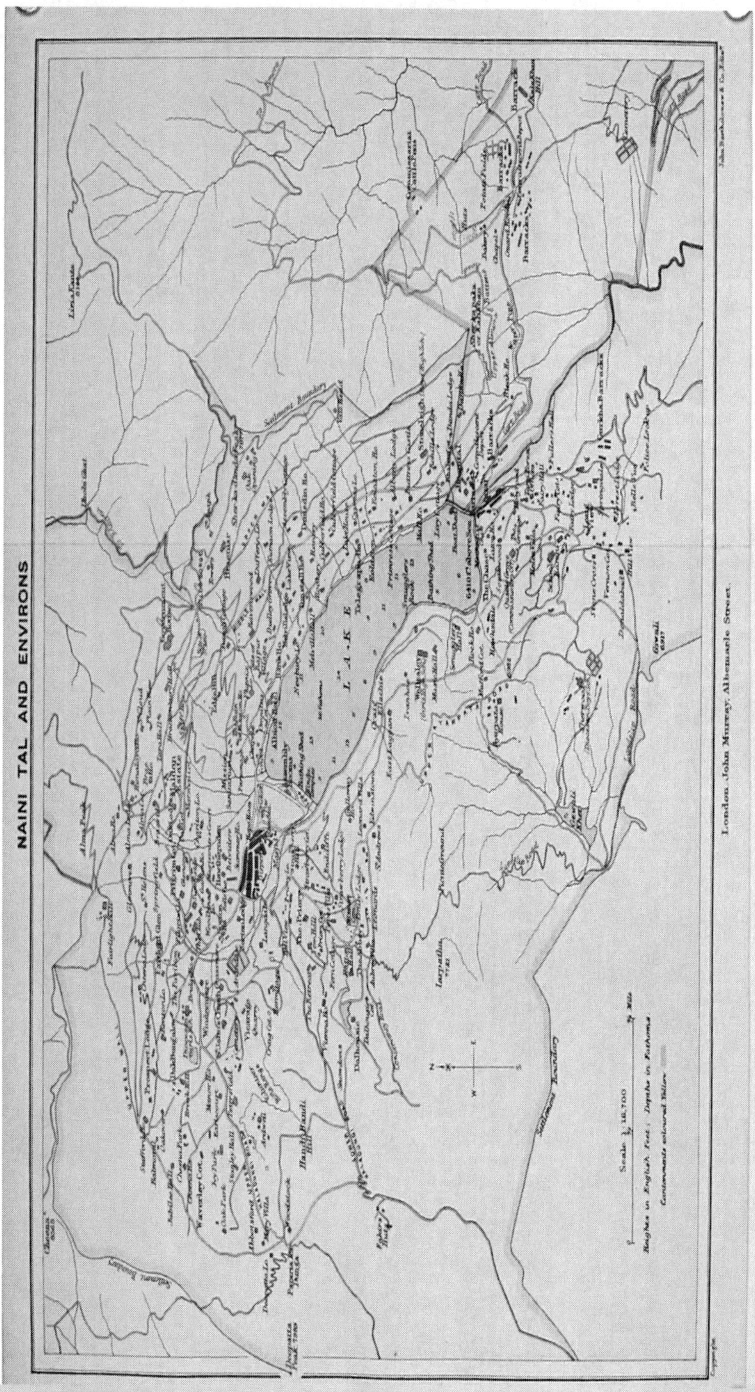
NAINI TAL AND ENVIRONS
LAKE
Scale 1/16,700
Heights in English Feet : Depths in Fathoms
Cantonments coloured Yellow
London, John Murray, Albemarle Street.

fishing), to **Nankulchia Tal**, 2 or 3 m. from Bhim Tal (camping-ground and fishing), and to **Malwa Tal** 10 m. from Bhim Tal over the hills, a very pretty lake (bungalow ; fishing, and good shooting procurable). From Bhim Tal it is possible to return direct to **Kathgodam** (7 m.) A through tonga service now runs between Kathgodam and Ranikhet.

The stages on the round route to Ranikhet and Almora are as below—the direct route from Kathgodam to these places is by Bhim Tal. There is a good cart-road from Naini Tal to Ranikhet. Pony to Ranikhet or Almora, Rs.7, an.8, dandy Rs.3, an.2.

Nos.	Names of Stages.	Miles from Stage to Stage.
1	From Naini Tal to Khyrna D.B. . .	12
2	From Khyrna to Ranikhet D.B. . .	18
3	From Ranikhet to Maykhali D.B. .	8
4	Maykhali to Almora D.B. . . .	16
5	From Almora to Peora D.B.	9
6	From Peora to Ramgarh D.B. . . .	12
7	From Ramgarh to Naini Tal	13
	Total . .	88 m.

At **Khyrna** on the Casi River is mahsir fishing, also gooral shooting, and a few leopards in the hills. From Khyrna to **Almora** by the river is rough going but fair fishing.

Ranikhet, D.B., an important military hill station. Population, 6000. Elevation between 6000 and 7000 ft. The views of the Himalaya snows from this station are very grand.

Almora, ✱D.B., the chief town of the Kumaon district, 5500 ft. above sea-level, population 7500; there was much severe fighting round Almora in the Goorkha War, and the place is now a station for two battalions of Goorkhas. **It is famed as a residence for persons with weak lungs.** The views of the snows are fine. In the neighbourhood are the *Julna* and *Binsur fruit orchards*.

Almora to *Pindri Glacier*, six marches; D.B. on the way, but no supplies or attendance. Best time of year September or October. *Shooting* plentiful.

ROUTE 21.

LUCKNOW (Lakhnao), p. 274 (R.)✱ The city covers 36 sq. m., and has a population of 260,000, including the cantonments, of whom three-fifths are Hindus. It is situated in lat. 26° 51′, long. 80° 58′, and is the largest city in the Indian Empire after Calcutta, Madras, Bombay and Hyderabad. It has been the capital of Oudh since 1775, but contains very little of interest outside the Chauk Bazaar on the N. side opening on to the Machhi Bhawan, and the shrine of Hazrat Abbas to the S.W. of this. The chief art products of the city are silver work, "bidri" work of silver inlaid on iron, and embroideries, to which may be added terra-cotta figures. There is a good show of these in the Museum (p. 294), where duplicates at a fixed price can be ordered. Lucknow, by reason of its climate, parks and gardens, and its many interesting sites, is a charming place at which to make a stay. The sights of it cannot possibly be well seen under two and a half days.

Short description of Lucknow and of the places of interest in it.

Lucknow stands in a bend of the Gumti ("Serpentine"), the Residency on the N. and the Martinière on the E. being equidistant (2½ m.) from the Char Bagh. West of the northern line from this point is the city, with the Machhi Bhawan, the Imambarah and the Jama Masjid between it and the river ; and E. of it is the Civil Station with the palaces and other buildings of the Kings of Oudh on the N. up to the river-bank, and the present Cantonment, Headquarters of the 8th Army Division, with the Martinière and Dilkusha Park on its N.E. side on the S. The Royal buildings from the Residency to the E. are the Tehri Kothi ; the Farhat Bakhsh and Chhatar Manzil Palaces ; the Kaisar Bagh with its mausolea standing back a little to the S. : the Moti Mahal on the river, with the Khurshaid Manzil and Tara Kothi S. of it ; and the Shah Najaf, Kadam Rasul, and Sikandra Bagh at the extreme E. end. Here the river takes a sharp bend to the S., and W. of this and S. of the Sikandra Bagh come in succession the Wingfield Park, and across the canal which skirts the S. of the city and the Civil Station, the Martinière, and the Dilkusha Palace. From the W. side of the Park a broad thoroughfare (which is known in its central portion as Hazratganj, and has the Begam Kothi and the Imambarah of Amjad Ali Shah on its E. side) forms a chord to the arc of the river, and, passing the foot of the Kaisar Bagh, ends at the Residency. From the S.E. end of Hazratganj, just N.E. of Government House (once known as Banks House), Outram Road leads N.E. to the Sikandra Bagh, and Abbott Road (on which the four principal hotels are situated close together) leads S.W. to the railway station and the city. The hotels are about 1½ m. S.W. of the Sikandra Bagh, and nearly 2 m. S.E. of the Residency by the direct routes of Cantonment Road or Banks Road which unite in Cawnpore Road after passing the back of the Kaisar Bagh and the Roshan-ud-daulah Kothi, about ¾ m. from the Residency. The Alam Bagh lies 1½ m. S.W. of the Char Bagh. From the latter the new La Touche Road runs due N. past the Aminabad Park of 8 acres to the Residency.

History.

Lucknow is of recent origin, and owes its creation to the Nawabs of Oudh, generally known as the Kings of Oudh, a title accorded by the British in 1819. The first three of these, S'aadat Khan Burhan-ul-mulk (1732-39), Mansur Ali Khan, known as Safdar Jang (p. 207) (1739-1753), and Shuja-ud-daulah (1753-1775), who joined issue with the British at the battle of Buxar (1763), resided at Fyzabad, and the last of these is buried there. His son Asaf-ud-daulah removed the capital to Lucknow, which under him grew into a great city: the badge of the fish which appears on so many of the royal buildings is the mark of rank granted by the Emperor of Delhi to the Oudh Nawabs. It will be sufficient to note here the names of the rest of the Rulers of Oudh, and the buildings with which they adorned their capital. No reigning dynasty of India ever showed such a series of vicious and incompetent chiefs as the last of these. Any one who may have any doubts as to the condition of the province of Oudh under them has only to read the journals of Sir Wm. Sleeman to realise what their rule meant—a rule continued unchanged, in spite of threats and warnings, for a period of thirty years. The buildings at Lucknow are nearly all of a degraded and barbarous type, and apart from the two tombs in the Kaisar Bagh and the Jama Masjid, not one of them possesses any real architectural merits, though the large Hall of the great Imambarah is a very grand room.

Asaf-ud-daulah (1775-1797). Built the Daulat Khan Palace, Machhi Bhawan Palace, the great Imambarah and its mosque, the Rumi

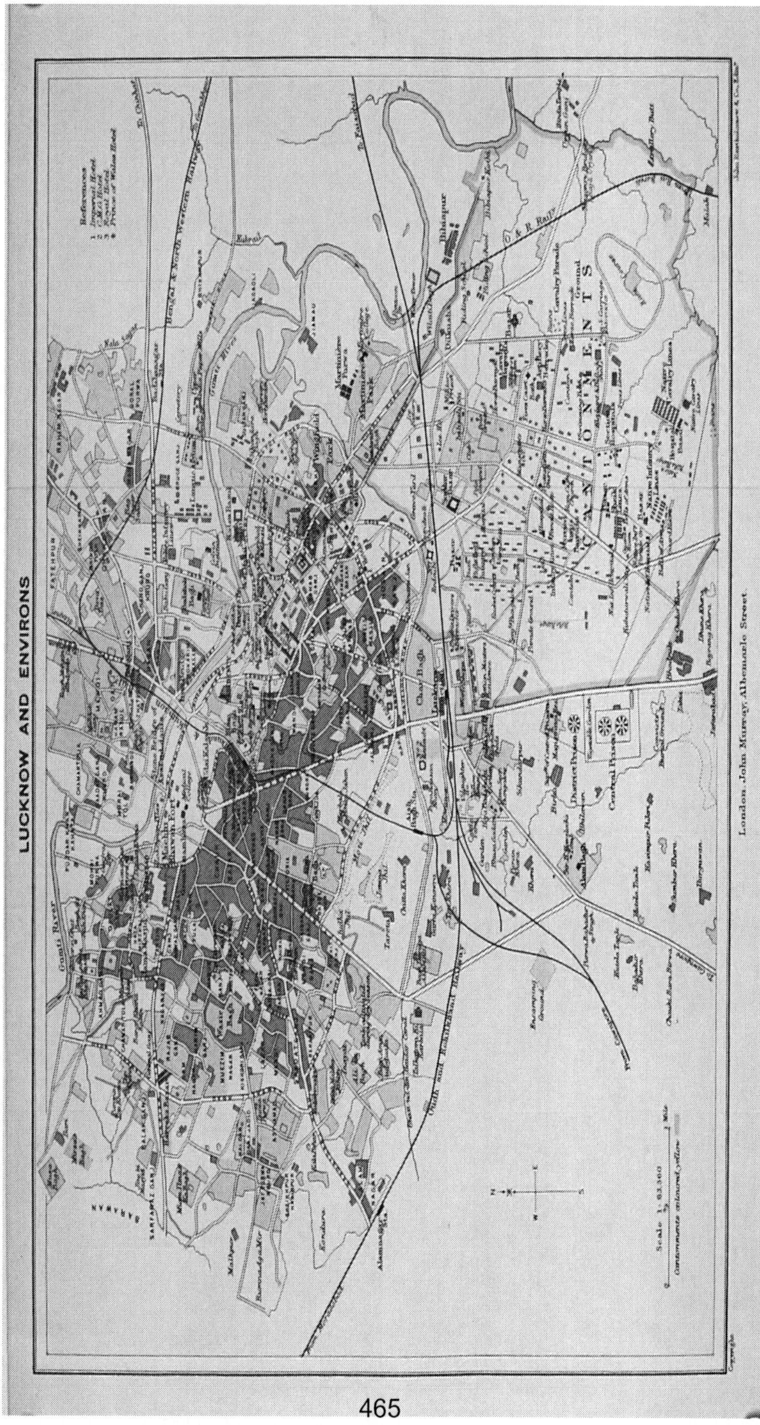
LUCKNOW AND ENVIRONS
London, John Murray, Albemarle Street.
CANTONMENTS

Darwazah, the Char Bagh and Musa Bagh, and bought the Farhat Bakhsh Palace off General Martin.

Saadat Ali Khan (1798-1814), the best of his line. Built the Moti Mahal and Dilkusha, the Throne Room (Lal Barahdarri), and the King's Stables—also the Residency.

Ghazi-ud-din Haidar, first king of Oudh (1814-1827). Built the Kaisar Bagh tombs, the Tomb at Shah Najaf and the Khurshaid Manzil, and constructed the canal on the S. side of the city.

Nasir-ud-din Haidar (1827-1837). Built the Chhatar Manzils.

Muhammad Ali Shah (1837-1842). Built the Husainabad Imambarah and Tank, the Sat Kanda, the Jama Masjid and the Badshah Bagh.

Amjad Ali Shah (1842-1847). Built the Hazratganj Imambarah.

Wajid Ali Shah (1847-1856). Built the Kaisar Bagh palaces, and Sikandra Bagh. In February 1856 Wajid Ali Shah was deposed, and on 13th March left for Calcutta. General Outram, who was Resident at the time, became First Chief Commissioner of Oudh. The ex-king lived 30 years in Calcutta, and there he died in 1887, aged 68. Portraits of most of the kings of Oudh will be found in the Talukdars Barahdarri at the Husainabad Tank.

The best books upon the siege of the Lucknow Residency are perhaps Mr M. Gubbins' *Mutinies in Oudh*, Lady Inglis' *Siege of Lucknow*, Lieutenant-General M'Leod Innes' *Lucknow and Oudh in the Mutiny*, and Sergeant Forbes Mitchell's *Reminiscences of the Great Mutiny* (Macmillan). The Lives of Sir Henry Lawrence, Sir Henry Havelock, Sir James Outram, and Sir Colin Campbell, Lord Clyde, will also be found full of interest, and most of all so will the volumes of Mutiny papers relating to Cawnpore and Lucknow, recently edited by Mr G. W. Forrest, which contain a number of photographs of the date of 1857-58.

An unusually good local guide has been published by Mr E. H. Hilton, who, as a Martinière boy, shared in the defence of the Residency.

The Mutiny of 1857.

That the annexation of Oudh—from which the great mass of the high caste[1] soldiers of the native army then came—justifiable and necessary as it was, became one of the principal causes of the Sepoy mutiny of 1857, is beyond doubt. As it happened, General Outram had been compelled to take leave in April 1856, and it was only after eleven months' interval that he was succeeded by Sir Henry Lawrence, a bare seven weeks before the outbreak of the mutiny at Meerut and Delhi.

At that time the garrison of Lucknow consisted of three Bengal Native Infantry regiments and one regiment of Light Cavalry, two regiments of Oudh Infantry, a regiment of Military Police, and three native batteries of Artillery, in all about 7000 men, the European force consisting of H.M. 32nd Regiment under Lieutenant-Colonel Inglis and one battery of Horse Artillery less than 1000 strong.

Already there had been a mutiny at Lucknow of the 7th Oudh Irregular Infantry at the Musa Bagh on 3rd May. Major Gall, commanding the 4th Irregular Cavalry, on being informed of the imminent danger of the European officers, galloped up to the vicinity with his troopers, and soon after Sir H. Lawrence arrived with a mixed force of Europeans and natives. The mutineers then broke and fled; some were made prisoners, and others gave up their arms. On 12th May, before the news of Meerut and Delhi had reached Lucknow, Sir H. Lawrence held a darbar in the Cantonment Residency, and harangued the troops and promoted two native officers who had given information of the intended outbreak; and this gave confidence for a short

[1] About 40,000 men. Nearly double this number had been discharged from the Oudh army.

time until the malcontents perceived that the Government was unable to take immediate steps to recover Delhi. Then it soon became apparent that nothing could prevent further serious trouble, and Sir H. Lawrence quietly set about collecting supplies in the Residency and the Machhi Bhawan to provide against all possible contingencies, and two companies of H.M.'s 32nd Regiment were placed in the former. On the 23rd May, two detachments of cavalry sent to Cawnpore, to clear the road between it and Agra, mutinied near Mainpuri, and killed one of their officers, the rest escaping by flight.

On the 30th May mutiny broke out in the Mariáon Cantonment, three miles N.E. of Lucknow across the Gumti, and quickly became general. Brigadier Handscombe was shot dead, and the mutineers attacked Sir Henry and his Staff at the artillery ground, but were driven off with some rounds of grape, which killed many of them. On the 31st of May a Mr Mendes was murdered in his own house in the city, and martial law was proclaimed; it was now decided that the supplies should be mainly placed in the Residency. The authorities maintained a bold front; but the news of mutiny came in from every side—Bareilly on 31st May, Sitapur on the 3rd of June, Cawnpore on the 4th, and Fyzabad on the 6th—and on the 11th of June the cavalry of the police mutinied and the infantry followed their example. Large bodies of mutineers now began to gather round Lucknow. These finally concentrated at Chinhat, a village lying 7 m. from Lucknow on the Sitapur road across the Kokrail nullah, and were attacked at Ismailganj, 1½ m. W. of this, by Sir Henry Lawrence on the 30th June with a small force of ten guns, 100 cavalry, and 550 infantry, of whom only 300 were British. Unfortunately the troops started later than had been intended, and, by some sad blundering, without having received any food, and in the end the overpowering heat prevented them from making a determined attack on the rebels, who were strongly posted and fought with great confidence; and finally the little force had to retreat with a loss of over 100 British soldiers. The enemy at once followed up their success and the siege of the Lucknow Residency, begun the next day, 1st July, was partially relieved by General Havelock on 25th September, and was finally relieved by Sir Colin Campbell on 17th November. At the commencement there were about 900 British troops and officers in the position, 150 volunteers and 700 native troops, 600 women and children and 700 non-combatant natives, in all about 3000 souls. At the time of the relief in September there were less than 1000. On the night of the 1st July the Machhi Bhawan garrison fell back to the Residency, blowing up the magazine and destroying the guns there as far as was possible. On 2nd July Sir H. Lawrence was mortally wounded by a shell fired from the howitzer captured from us at Chinhat, and died two days afterwards. Major Banks succeeded him in chief civil authority, and Colonel Inglis in command of the troops.

The defences of the Residency, which stood some 30 ft. above the level of the ground round it, will be understood from the accompanying plan and the following brief account. At the N.W. corner, running out above the depression in which the church and graveyard were situated, was Innes Garrison. In the centre of the N. face was the Redan, armed with two 18-pounders and a 9-pounder, which commanded the whole river side and the opposite bank; on its W. side was Evans' Battery with one 18-pounder and two 9-pounders. Just E. of the Redan was the Water Gate, beyond which a defence of fascines and sandbags ran to the Hospital, formerly the Banqueting Hall; the Water Gate had a battery of three guns with Alexander's Battery on its right, and the Hospital one of three mortars. The Residency lay in the centre of

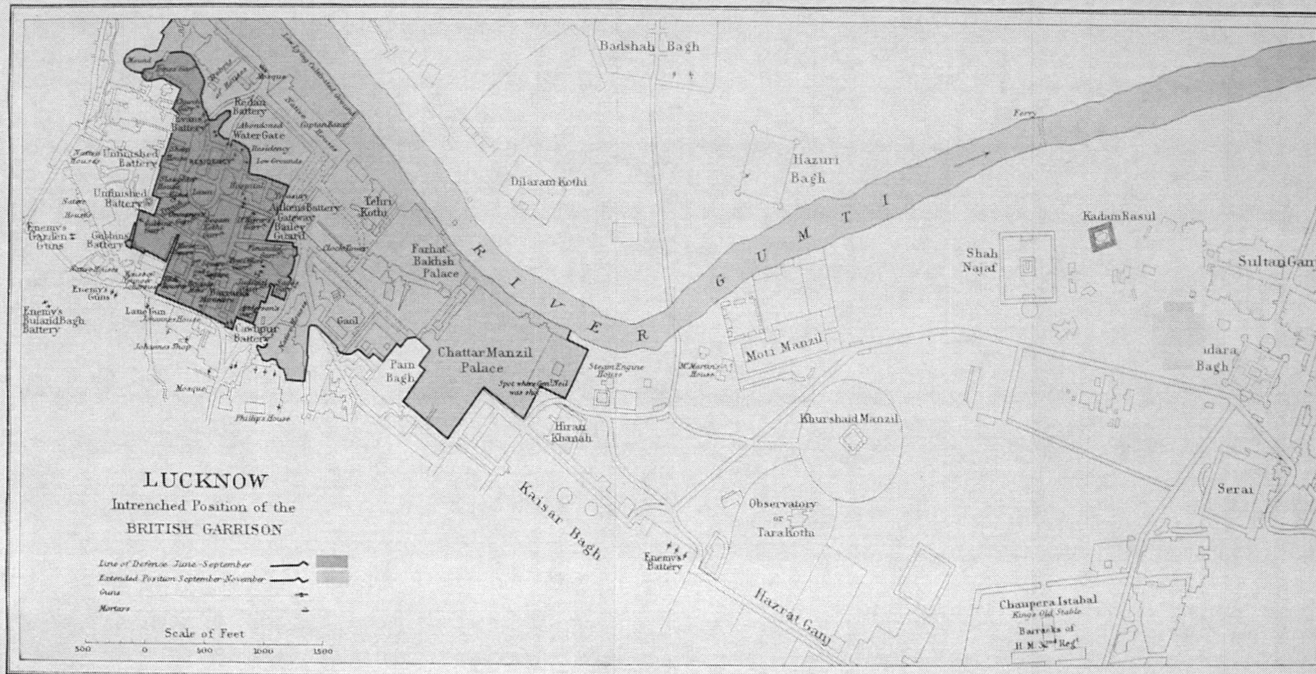
LUCKNOW
Intrenched Position of the
BRITISH GARRISON
Line of Defense June–September
Extended Position September–November
Guns
Mortars
Scale of Feet
500
0
500
1000
1500
RIVER GUMTI
Ferry
Badshah Bagh
Dilaram Kothi
Hazuri Bagh
Kadam Rasul
Shah Najaf
Sultan Ganj
Tehri Kothi
Farhat Bakhsh Palace
Chattar Manzil Palace
Pain Bagh
Gaol
Moti Manzil
Steam Engine House
Khurshaid Manzil
Hiran Khanah
Kaisar Bagh
Enemy's Battery
Observatory or Tara Kotha
Hazrat Ganj
Chupera Istabal
Kings Old Stable
Barracks of
Serai
Redan Battery
Water Gate
Residency
Low Grounds
Unfinished Battery
Aitkens Battery
Gateway
Bailey Guard
Clock Tower
Enemy's Garden Guns
Gubbins Battery
Enemy's Guns
Enemy's Bulaid Bagh Battery
Lane Gun
Johannes House
Cawnpur Battery
Mosque
Philip's House
Low Lying Cultivated Ground
Mound
London. John Murray, Albemarle Street.

the position S. of the Redan and W. of the Banqueting Hall. With its lofty rooms, fine verandahs, and large porticoes, its range of subterraneous apartments, its ground floor and two upper storeys, it afforded accommodation to nearly 1000 persons—men, women, and children. The Baillie Guard situated on the lower ground below the hospital, was partly used as a store-room, partly as the treasury and office, and partly as barracks for the Sepoys, who garrisoned it under Lieutenant Aitken. In the southern angle of the guard was a concave shaped guard-house, removed after 1857. On the S. side of the road leading up through the Baillie Gate to the centre of the Residency was the house of Dr Fayrer, with a garrison commanded by Captain Weston and Dr Fayrer. The Post Office was a very important position, commanding the jail and mosque to the right, and the Clock Tower and offices of the Tehri Kothi to the left outside the entrenchment, and was armed with three guns. It was also the headquarters of the Artillery and the Engineers. In front of it, on the part of the E. face projecting beyond the line of the Baillie Guard, were the Financial Garrison, Sago's Post (so-called from the owner of the house here being a schoolmistress of that name), and the Judicial or Germon's Garrison. The first was commanded by Captain Sanders of the 13th. It was a large two-storeyed house, and well barricaded. Between the Post Office and the Residency was the Begam Kothi nearly in the centre of all the defences, where a double range of out-offices formed a square within a square. At the S.E. corner of the defences were Anderson's Garrison and the Cawnpore Battery mounting an 18-pounder and two 9-pounders; these were the two most dangerous posts of all, being specially exposed to the fire of Phillips' Garden Battery. W. of these were Duprat's Post, held by a brave Frenchman, and behind it the Martinière Post; in front outside, at a distance of only 30 yds. was Johannes House. The Brigade Mess, the Sikh Square,[1] with a 24-pounder howitzer commanding the street, and the First and Second Squares filled up the rest of the S. side to the point where Grant's Post, Gubbins' Battery, with a 9-pounder, and Gubbins' Garrison defended the S.W. angle, which lay further N. than the first mentioned. Between Gubbins' Garrison and the Begam Kothi, and S. of the Residency lawn, was Ommanney's Garrison; while W. of the Residency were the Slaughter House and Sheep House Posts, the latter immediately S. of the church depression. All these posts are marked on the ground by memorial pillars, which enable the outline of the whole defences to be fully understood. As at present situated, the Residency appears a strong position to hold; but it will be seen from the model of it as it stood in 1857, contained in a room of the Taikhana (the original is in the Museum) that it was then commanded by so large a number of buildings close to it that it seems a marvel that any one in it should have escaped death from the bullets of the enemy.

On the 2nd of July, the day of Sir Henry's being wounded, the rebels attacked the Baillie Guard Gate. At first the deaths averaged from fifteen to twenty daily, many being killed by an African, who fired from Johannes's house without ever missing. On the 8th, Captain Mansfield and three other officers, and Maycock, a civilian, sallied out, spiked a gun, and killed about forty of the rebels without losing a man, though three were wounded. On the 9th another sortie was made, when a private named O'Keene spiked a gun. On the 10th, the ammunition of the rebels' cannon falling short, they began to fire pieces of wood, copper coin, iron, and even bullocks' horns. Fortunately the old State guns had been collected by the care of Sir Henry Lawrence on the low ground under the Redan, and luckily

[1] Four mines of the enemy were exploded between Duprat's Post and the S.W. corner of the Sikh Square.

for us there was no arsenal in Lucknow from which the mutineers could obtain unlimited quantities of gun ammunition. Had that been the case, the Residency would have been rendered untenable in a very short time. On the 14th the enemy made a general attack. On the 16th they made a night attack on Gubbins' Battery, but were beaten back. On the 20th of July they exploded a mine near the Redan, attempted to storm the Baillie Guard, and made their first general assault at every point, pouring in volleys of musketry, and sending shell after shell into the entrenchments. The mine did no harm to the Redan Battery, but the enemy, supposing a breach to have been made, rushed up the glacis at the double, with fixed bayonets.[1] Hundreds were shot down; but their leader, waving his sword, on which he placed his cap, shouted to them to come on. Again they advanced, but the grape made huge gaps in their ranks, a musket ball killed their leader, and they then retreated, leaving heaps of slain and wounded. At the same time a furious attack was made on Innes's outpost, where Lieutenant Loughnan, of the 13th Native Infantry, with 24 English soldiers, 12 civilians, and 25 Sepoys, beat back the whole host of rebels, who at last slowly retreated, carrying off 100 of their wounded comrades. At the Financial and Sago's Posts a column of rebels with a green standard was after some hours' hard fighting beaten off, with the loss of all their commanders and about 60 men. The fight ended at 4 P.M.

Though beaten at all points, on the 20th the enemy maintained a furious cannonade, and planted new batteries. On 21st July Major Banks was shot, and owing to their fire, the windows of the houses within the Residency had to be barricaded, and even then inmates were shot inside them. One great torment was the flies, which swarmed in incredible numbers, the ground being black with them. On the 25th July a letter was received from the Quartermaster-General of General Havelock's force, bidding the besieged to be of good cheer, as a large relieving force was coming. But days passed and the rebels were busy with their mines, and but for the countermining by Captain Fulton of the Engineers, the place must have fallen.

On the 10th of August there was a second general attack, but the enemy showed little courage, and they were easily beaten off. On the same day a mine was exploded at Sago's Garrison, which blew down some out-houses, and blew up two English soldiers into the air, who, however, were not killed. Another mine between the Brigade Mess and the Cawnpore Battery blew down a stockade, and the enemy attempted to enter, but were repulsed. The 8-in. howitzer which the rebels took at Chinhat played on Innes's Post with great effect, bringing down beam after beam, and making many breaches. On the 11th of August Major Anderson, the chief engineer, died. On the 14th, Captain Fulton exploded a mine under a house near Sago's Garrison, killing 50 to 60 of the enemy. On the 18th the second Sikh Square, garrisoned by 15 Christian drummers and musicians, and 15 Sikhs, was blown up by the rebels, and 7 Christians and 2 Sikhs were buried under its ruins. A large breach was made, and the enemy delivered their third home assault, which was the nearest of all to being successful, but their leader was killed and they retired.

[1] "What have they done? where is it? out yonder—guard the Redan!
Storm at the Water Gate! storm at the Baillie Gate! storm, and it ran
Surging and swaying all round us, as ocean on every side
Plunges and heaves at a bank that is daily drowned by the tide—
So many thousands that if they were bold enough who shall escape?
Kill or be killed, live or die, they shall know we are soldiers and men!
Ready, take aim at their leaders—their masses are gapped with our grape—
Backward they reel like the wave, like the wave flinging forward again.
Flying and foil'd at the last by the handful they could not subdue—
And ever upon the topmost roof the Banner of England blew."
—LORD TENNYSON.

Captain Fulton with a number of volunteers then sallied out, destroyed a number of houses, and blew up the shaft of another mine begun by the rebels.

On the 20th August the house called Johannes's was blown up by Captain Fulton, and 60 to 80 of the rebels were killed. Captain Fulton then headed a sally, and after driving out the insurgents from several buildings, blew them up. Lieutenant Macabe of the 32nd headed another party and spiked two guns. Previous to this Lieutenant Macabe had attacked Johannes's house, and bayoneted a number of the enemy, who were found asleep, and amongst them the African who had picked off so many of the English during the first days of the siege, and had been christened by the soldiers "Bob the Nailer." On the 29th of August Angad[1] the spy brought a letter from Cawnpore saying that the relief would take place in three weeks. On the 5th of September the rebels made their fourth and final attack, having previously exploded three mines. They advanced boldly to the Brigade Mess, but were driven back with the loss of 100 men. They then attacked the Baillie Guard and several other places, but were similarly repulsed. On the 14th Captain Fulton was killed at Gubbins's Battery by a 9-pound shot, which took his head completely off. On the 23rd of September a furious cannonade was heard outside the city, and confirmed the news received the day before that Generals Outram and Havelock were coming. On the 25th, smoke and the crack of musketry showed that street-fighting was going on. The fire advanced steadily towards the entrenchments, and the relievers finally entered them in the evening.

General Havelock, who had reached Cawnpore on the 17th July, and whose troops had destroyed the palace at Bithur on the 19th, crossed the Ganges, and advanced towards Lucknow on the 25th, with only 1200 men, and fought two actions with the enemy at Unao and Basiratganj on the 29th. In these actions he lost one-sixth of his force, and was compelled to fall back on Manglaur. Advancing once more from there, he defeated the enemy again severely at Basiratganj on 4th August, but thereafter had no option but to retreat to Cawnpore: before doing so he beat the enemy a third time at Basiratganj. Three days after his return there he drove a new force of rebels out of Bithur on 16th August; but it was not till the 18th September that sufficient reinforcements arrived to enable him and General Outram (who had joined the force meanwhile, but chivalrously waived his command in favour of General Havelock) to cross the Ganges again with 3000 men. On the 21st he defeated the enemy again at Manglaur, and on the 23rd at Alam Bagh, where the news of the capture of Delhi reached him. As the flooded state of the country across the Gumti made it impossible to move guns and so effect the relief of the Residency from the left bank, the forces moved forward for their final effort on 25th September by way of the Char Bagh, in front of which sharp fighting took place at the Yellow House.[1] Crossing the canal and leaving the 78th as a rear-guard on the bridge, the troops followed the line of the former to the old barracks of the 32nd, just to the N. of the E. end of Hazratganj and from there passed on to the Sikandra Bagh, and then followed the road past the Shah Najaf to the Moti Mahal, having encountered but little opposition up to the last point. Here they came under heavy fire from the Khurshaid Manzil and from

[1] He was still living in 1876, and was presented to King Edward.

[1] It was here that Captain William Olpherts, R.A., greatly distinguished himself and won the Victoria Cross. When a man of the dauntless courage of Sir James Outram records of the deed by which the reward for exceptional valour was won, "Bravery is a poor and insignificant epithet to apply to a valour such as yours," that deed ought not to be forgotten by Englishmen.

T

a battery at the corner of the Kaisar Bagh, and were checked for the moment. But the rear-guard, which had not followed the main column but had turned up the Hazratganj, now came up and took the battery in the rear; and the united column pushed on to the Chhatar Manzil Palace still under heavy fire. At the corner of this palace was a square enclosure, afterwards known as the Dhooly Square, in which a short pause took place while it was debated whether the troops should push on or not, and during this Brigadier-General Neill was shot through the head while seated on his charger in a gateway. The decision having been for an advance, the troops issued from the square and turned to their right towards the Residency. The Highlanders and Sikhs, who took the further road to the Khas Bazaar, suffered considerably; the rest of the force took the nearer road into the Pain Bagh, and passing E. of the Jail, took a battery of the enemy in the rear with but little loss; and both columns uniting once more by the Clock Tower, entered the Residency Gate and relieved the beleaguered garrison, though not without an unfortunate *contretemps*, which cost the lives of several brave Sikhs. The heavy guns and the wounded remained for the night at the Moti Mahal. When the latter were being brought in next day, the dhooly-bearers were by a terrible mistake led into the square above mentioned, instead of directly into the Chhatar Manzil, and were brought under a deadly fire of the enemy. Deserted by the bearers, the wounded were heroically defended by Surgeon A. C. Home and a few privates, who held one position after another with desperate resolution, and were finally rescued from the Residency after all hope of escape was lost: for this deed of valour the Surgeon and three privates received the Victoria Cross.

This relief was not, however, effected without most serious loss; for though 2000 soldiers had got into the Residency, 550 officers and men were killed and wounded. Among these Brigadier-General Neill and Major Couper were killed, and ten other officers fell, besides those who died of their wounds. At this time the houses in the Residency were all perforated with cannon-shot, and the Cawnpore Battery was a mass of ruins; the outpost at Innes's House was roofless, and out of the Brigade Mess alone 435 cannon-balls were taken. The besieged were not, however, free. Those who relieved them had possession of the Tehri Kothi and the Farhat Bakhsh Palace, as also the Chhatar Manzil Palace, from which and from the Clock Tower the enemy's fire had been most fatal. But though the garrison had extended their positions, the enemy were far from abandoning the city, and Generals Outram and Havelock with their troops were themselves blockaded. On the 26th of September a sortie was made, and the troops spiked two mortars and blew up a powder magazine. Captain Lowe brought in as trophies an 18-pounder, a 9-pounder, and five smaller guns. After this the garrison frequently took the offensive and captured several positions. Attempts were then made to open communications with the Alam Bagh, where the relieving force had left their baggage and ammunition with 4 guns and 300 men to defend these. The attempt failed, for an intervening mosque, filled with riflemen, was too strongly fortified to be taken without very great loss. The besieged now repaired their defences, and extended them near Innes's Post, by taking and fortifying a mound, which became one of their strongest positions. Desultory fighting went on incessantly, and the palaces which had been taken by our troops continued to be the object of severe attacks. Provisions also again became scarce. On the 10th of November Sir Colin Campbell[1]

[1] Sir Colin Campbell, then in his sixty-fifth year, left England on 11th July, and reached Calcutta on 13th August. There he was detained forwarding troops and making

reached the Alam Bagh, and relieved the garrison besieged there. His force consisted of 4500 men, with which he had to meet 30,000 to 40,000 trained rebels, and as many more irregular volunteers. It was at this time that James Kavanagh, an uncovenanted officer who had distinguished himself in several sorties, offered to carry despatches from Sir James Outram at Lucknow to Sir Colin Campbell at the Alam Bagh, and owing to his courage and address succeeded in conveying them through the lines of the enemy, a feat for which he received the Victoria Cross. After a reconnaissance towards the Char Bagh to deceive the enemy, Sir Colin left his baggage in the Alam Bagh and proceeded to the Dilkusha, in which movement his advanced guard encountered a heavy fire, and drove the rebels past the Martinière College. On the 12th an attack of the rebels was repulsed; on the 14th the rear-guard joined; and on the 16th the whole force, except the 8th Regiment, left to guard the Dilkusha, advanced against the Sikandra Bagh. After a fierce conflict, the 4th Panjab Rifles, the 93rd Highlanders, and the 52nd, broke into the enclosure, and next day 2000 dead bodies of the rebels told the result. While this fight was raging, the English suffered much from a murderous fire directed upon them from the Shah Najaf Tomb. This place was next attacked by Peel's Naval Brigade and the 93rd, and finally was fortunately taken, the enemy abandoning it at the last moment. The troops then rested for the night, throughout which they were fired on continually from the adjacent buildings. On the 17th the Khurshaid Manzil—which had been used by Her Majesty's 32nd as a Mess-house—a large, two-storeyed, flat-roofed house, flanked by two square turrets, was stormed. In the afternoon Generals Outram and Havelock, who had occupied the Hiran Khana outside the Chhatar Manzil, crossed by the Moti Mahal to the Mess-house, and met Sir Colin Campbell there, and the relief of Lucknow was finally effected. The British loss was 540 killed and wounded, of whom 10 officers were killed and 35 wounded. That evening, Sir Colin decided that the garrison, as well as the sick and wounded, women and children, should be withdrawn from the Residency to the Dilkusha, the enemy being deluded meanwhile by the capture of Banks House and a heavy bombardment of the Kaisar Bagh. This was carried out on the 22nd, the enemy continuing firing into the old positions long after they had been abandoned. On the 24th of November General Havelock died at Dilkusha and was buried next day in the Alam Bagh, to which the whole force fell back. On the 27th the convoy of the sick and women and children started for Cawnpore, General Outram being left at the Alam Bagh with a force finally made up to 3500 men and 25 guns.

Sir Colin returned in March 1858, before which time six attacks had been made on the British position (which lay across the road to Cawnpore slightly in the rear of the Alam Bagh), and had been beaten off. The forces under him for the recapture of Lucknow consisted of 17 regiments of infantry, 28 squadrons of cavalry, and 134 guns, in all 2000 men, and the supporting Nepal army under Sir Jung Bahadur and Genl. Franks of 6000 men, while the numbers of the enemy were 100,000, and the guns planted on their triple line of defence 100. On the 2nd of March the army moved from the Alam Bagh to the Dilkusha, and on the 6th a force under General Outram crossed the Gumti to operate against the enemy from the left bank. This completely turned the first line of defence along the canal of Ghazi-ud-din Haidar Khan, and it was abandoned by the mutineers without a struggle on the

arrangements till 27th October. On 1st November he reached Allahabad, and on 3rd November arrived at Cawnpore, and on 9th November left that place to join the force already well on the road to Lucknow.

10th. Captain Butler, who swam across the Gumti to inform the force on the right bank of its abandonment, received the Victoria Cross for this feat of daring. No opposition was offered either at the Sikandra Bagh or Shah Najaf, which were occupied next day. On the former date the advance on the enemy's right was also commenced by the seizure of Banks House, which was followed up on the 11th by the capture of the Begam-ki-Kothi, by the 93rd and 4th Panjab Rifles, where 800 of the enemy were killed, and where Major Hodson was shot. On the 14th the Hazratganj Imambarah, up to which a way had been sapped through the houses, was seized, and the right of the enemy's second line of defence, which ran from here past the Tarawali Kothi and Khurshaid Manzil to the river E. of the Moti Mahal, was thus turned. Nor was this all, for a party of the Highlanders and the 10th Regiment boldly pushing on established itself in a palace commanding the Kaisar Bagh enclosure, round which the last line of defence had been drawn, and being at once supported by Generals Franks and Napier, after desperate fighting inside and outside, the enemy abandoned this, and fell back into the city. On the 16th, General Outram, who had been kept back by the Commander-in-Chief, crossed the Gumti and occupied the Residency and the Machhi Bhawan, and on the next day the Husainabad Imambarah. Arrangements were then made to drive out and corner the enemy completely, the intention being to intercept the rebels at the Musa Bagh. This failed of execution, through the immobility of some of the commanding officers concerned, and the rebels streamed away to maintain the struggle in Oudh and Rohilkand for another year.

(*a*) **The Residency and the quarters E. and S.E. of it connected with the relief of Lucknow.**

The **Residency** is the spot which all Englishmen will wish to visit first in Lucknow. It is entered on the E. side by a road which runs under the Baillie Gate, and passes upwards between the Banqueting Hall on the right and Dr Fayrer's House on the left. The gate was banked up with earth inside during the siege, and Generals Havelock and Outram entered through an opening to the left of it. When the evacuation of the Residency on 22nd November 1857 was carried out, the doors of the gate were closed by Colonel Inglis as soon as Sir James Outram had passed through them. The gardens are beautifully arranged and perfectly kept, and the place is now one full of the peacefulness which properly belongs to sad scenes long since enacted, in the midst of which one can think, thankfully and proudly, of the events and deeds of that summer of 1857.

> "Ever the labour of fifty that had to be done by five,
> Ever the marvel among us that one should be left alive,
> Ever the day with its traitorous death from its loopholes around,
> Ever the night with its coffinless corpse to be laid in the ground,
> Heat like the mouth of a Hell, or a deluge of cataract skies,
> Stench of old offal decaying, and infinite torment of flies."

In front of the **Baillie Guard** is a memorial erected by Lord Northbrook to the faithful native soldiers who shared the defence with the British. The foundation-stone of it was laid by King Edward on 7th January 1876.

> "Praise to our Indian brothers, and let the dark face have his due,
> Thanks to the kindly dark faces who fought with us faithful and true,
> Fought with the bravest among us, and drove them and smote them and slew,
> That ever upon the topmost roof our banner in India blew."

On the lawn in the centre of the Residency is a fine marble runic cross inscribed :—

In memory of
MAJOR-GEN. SIR HENRY LAWRENCE,
K.C.B.,
And the brave men who fell
In defence of the Residency,
1857.

and near it is another memorial of the 32nd Regiment.

The 68-pounder guns in the Residency belong to the force which captured Lucknow in 1858, and not to the second relieving force in 1857.

The Residency Building is almost a complete ruin, though a very beautiful one; but it is still possible to ascend the staircase of one of the towers, where throughout the siege the Banner of England floated.

"Banner of England! not for a season, O Banner of Britain! hast thou
Floated in conquering battle or flapt to the battle-cry;
Never with mightier glory than when we raised thee on high,
Flying at top of the roofs in the ghastly siege of Lucknow—
Shot through the staff or the halyard, but ever we raised thee anew,
And ever upon the topmost roof our Banner of England blew!"

A tablet in Dr Fayrer's house indicates the room in which Sir Henry Lawrence died on 4th July.

"'Never surrender, I charge you, but every man die at his post!'
Voice of the dead whom we loved, our Lawrence, the best of the brave:
Cold were his brows when we kissed him —we laid him that night in his grave."

The house was occupied on the first relief by Sir James Outram and his Staff—as Mr Ommanney's house was occupied by Sir Henry Havelock. The subterranean rooms or "tai-khanas" here, and at the Residency and the Begam Kothi, in which most of the women and children were protected, will be found specially interesting. In a room of the Begam Kothi, so called for having been the residence of an European wife of a king of Oudh, and distinguished by its pretty mosque, is the model of the Residency in 1857, which should be viewed before the round is made of it as described on p. 286. In the Brigade Mess buildings were the rooms which Lady Inglis and Lady Cooper occupied. Every spot in the Residency is interesting, but the most interesting, if the saddest of all, is the cemetery round the ruined church in which Sir Henry Lawrence, Brigadier-General Neill, and so many brave men and women and hapless children, to the number of nearly 2000, sleep their last sleep. General Neill's grave is on the S. side of Sir Henry Lawrence's, which is enclosed by an iron railing, and bears the well-known inscription—

Here lies
HENRY LAWRENCE,
who tried to do his duty.
May the Lord have mercy on his soul!
Born 28th of June 1806.
Died 4th of July 1857.

Readers of Mr Bosworth Smith's *Life of Lord Lawrence* will be able to picture for themselves the scene of that Viceroy standing in deep thought over his brother's grave, after viewing the procession of the Talukdars of Oudh in front of the Residency.

Leaving the Residency enclosure most persons will probably wish to next visit the buildings and sites to the E. of it connected with the reliefs by Sir Henry Havelock and Sir Colin Campbell. 150 yards in front of the Baillie Gate, at the intersection of the roads, are still to be seen the foundations of the Clock Tower from which the enemy kept up a constant fire on the E. of the Residency. Farther on to the right of the road was the Jail, where the Court of the District Judge now is, while standing at a greater distance back on the left were the **Tehri Kothi**, now the residence of the Judicial Commissioner of Oudh, and the **Farhat Bakhsh** ("Delight-giving") Palace. The last designation originally included not only the above buildings but also those of the Chhatar Manzil Palace beyond, which constituted the ladies' apartments so long as the Farhat Bakhsh was the principal residence of the Oudh kings from S'aadat 'Ali Khan down to Wajid 'Ali Shah. S.E. of the Jail was the **Pain Bagh**, E. of which projected the S. portion of the Chhatar Manzil enclosure, containing the small Chhatar Manzil, the Kasr-i-Sultan, or the Lal Barahdarri, now the Museum, and the Darshan Vilas. It must be remembered that in 1857-58 these buildings did not stand separate and in the open, as they are now seen, but were all enclosed and divided off by high walls of great strength. Both the **Chhatar Manzils** are surmounted by an umbrella (*chhatar* or *chhatri*), whence their name. The larger, on the bank of the river, is used now as a club. After the relief of the 25th September 1857, the British position was extended from the Residency eastwards as far as the Chhatar Manzil. Near this, opposite the Kaisar Bagh, is the marble memorial statue of the Queen Empress under a canopy. The **Kasr-i-Sultan** was the throne-room in which the widow of Nasir-ud-din Haidar attempted to compel the Resident, Colonel Low, to place her son, born before the king married her, on the "masnad." **The Museum** is well arranged, and contains many objects of much interest, including some Buddhist remains from Muttra[1] and elsewhere. A little beyond these buildings is the Telegraph Office, and N. of it the **Sher Darwazah** gateway of the Dhooly Square, where General Neill was shot on 25th September 1857. E. again, and opposite the N.E. corner of the Kaisar Bagh, was the **Hiran Khana**, or Deer House, between which and the river and the road to the modern Bruce Bridge were the engine-house, stables, and sergeant's house, all of which played a part in the reliefs. Neill Road, which has been followed to the Sher Darwazah, now continues past the N. front of the Kaisar Bagh and the Memorial near the N.E. corner of this, and joins the Hazratganj, while Clyde Road, taking off from the Strand Road, which runs between the river and the Farhat Bakhsh and Chhatar Manzil, passes under the road to the river, and continues along the line of the buildings famous in connection with the reliefs. The fine stone mausolea in the **Kaisar Bagh** were constructed by S'aadat 'Ali Khan and his son; and the palace was built by Wajid 'Ali Shah with the utmost extravagance and in the vilest of taste. It was from the fire from the defences of the palace and the roofs of the tombs that our troops suffered so much in finally reaching the Residency, both in September and in November 1857. The palace originally had one great gate at the S.E. corner, and two others on the N. and S. sides, and its interior was divided into courts, and filled with confused masses of buildings, among which were the Chandiwali Barahdarri, paved with silver, and the Badshah Manzil. In the centre is a structure formerly used for the **Canning College**; the buildings round the enclosure, among which were the Chaulakhi and the Kaisar Pasand, have been made over to the Talukdars of Oudh. Much of the concealed jewellery of the ex-king was taken from the Kaisar Bagh to the Residency in May 1857, and was largely stolen there. The **Memorial** on the E. side marks the spot where two small parties of European refugees from Sitapur were shot on 24th September and 16th November.

Proceeding now by Clyde Road, the first building seen on the left is the **Moti Mahal**, with Martin's House between it and the bridge. It lies on the left side on the bank of the Gumti, and comprised, beside the structure once domed, and which gave its name to the whole, the Mubarik Manzil and the Shah Manzil, from which the king used to watch the fights of elephants and rhinoceros on the further side of the river. It was here that General Havelock's rear-guard remained on 25th September, and Sir Colin Campbell's force came into actual touch with the besieged on 17th November. To the right side

[1] See p. 165.

of the road, standing on a high site, the base of which is still surrounded by defensive works, is the **Khurshaid** (Sun) **Manzil**, used in 1857 as the Mess-house of the 32nd, and now occupied by the Girls' Martinière School. S. of it again is the **Tarawali Kothi**, or Observatory, now the Bank of Bengal. On the occasion of the relief of November 1857 the former was strongly held by the enemy, and barred the way of the relieving force for some time; but, after being subjected to a heavy bombardment by the Naval Brigade and Mortar Battery for three hours, was taken by the 53rd and 90th, and formed the place of meeting of Generals Outram and Havelock with Sir Colin Campbell. In March 1858 the enemy's second line of defence ran from the river at the Moti Mahal, past the Khurshaid Manzil and Tarawali Kothi, to the Hazratganj Imambarah. 500 yds. E. of the Moti Mahal and Khurshaid Manzil stand the Shah Najaf and Kadam Rasul, and nearly 1000 yds. on again lies the Sikandra Bagh, round which such desperate fighting took place in November 1857. **Shah Najaf** is the tomb of Ghazi-ud-din Haidar Khan, surmounted by a dome, and surrounded by walls of such immense thickness that neither the heavy guns of the Naval Brigade nor those of Captain Middleton's battery, brought quite close up, were able to make any impression on them, and the advance was severely checked here until some soldiers of the 93rd managed to scramble up a broken part of the wall at the back and found that the enemy had just fled, to avoid being caught like their comrades in the Sikandra Bagh. Some of the defenders made use of bows and arrows, for the last time probably in Indian warfare. Sergeant Paton received the Victoria Cross for the part he took in this escalade. An English middy, Martin Abbott Daniel, was killed serving his gun outside Shah Najaf. The decorations and contents of the interior, though tawdry, are curious; one picture represents a cock-fight at which the King of Oudh and General Claude Martin are present.

The **Kadam Rasul** is now a ruined building of red brick, the relic which it was built to cover in 1830 having disappeared in 1857: it is approached by a path through the garden to the E. of Shah Najaf, and has a fine view. The picturesque Horticultural Gardens now lie between these buildings and the **Sikandra Bagh**, through which the road to the bridge across the river near this point leads. The gateway of the garden, which is 120 yds. sq., still stands: in front of it was a sarai which was easily captured by the troops on 16th November 1857; but a breach[1] in the thick wall of the Sikandra Bagh was made only with great difficulty, and was carried by the 93rd, 53rd, and the Sikhs of the 4th P.I. "Never was a bolder feat of arms," wrote Sir Colin Campbell of it. The 93rd lost ninety killed and ninety-nine wounded: the dead were buried in a trench, still marked by a mound to the E. of the gate. None of these three posts were held by the enemy in September 1857, and all of them were abandoned with the first line of defence in March 1858. From this point the lines of the two reliefs and the capture diverge, Sir Colin Campbell's two advances having been made from the Martinière and Dilkusha to the S.E. of the Wingfield Park, while Generals Havelock and Outram pushed up to the Sikandra Bagh from the S., along what is now known as Outram Road, which passes N. of the Wingfield Park, and S. of the King's Chaupar or Cross Stables (now Lawrence Terrace), to close to Government House, formerly Banks House and originally the Hyat Bakhsh ("Life-giving") Kothi, where it joins Havelock Road, which marks up to the Char Bagh the route along the

[1] According to Sergeant Forbes Mitchell, the breach in the wall of the garden, which was wide enough to admit three men abreast, was made at the spot where the road to the river now passes through it, and the 53rd got into the enclosure through a window to the right of the gate. Private Dunlay of the 93rd received the Victoria Cross as the first man who penetrated into the garden and survived the desperate conflict in it.

canal followed by the troops in their advance from the latter place on 25th September 1857. The **King's Stables** had been used as barracks for the 32nd Regiment before the Mutiny.

At the N.W. corner outside Government House is *Christ Church.* It is a neat building with a tower. The church compound is prettily laid out with many flowers and creepers. There are a number of interesting tablets on the walls. Those in memory of Sir James Outram and Sir H. Lawrence deserve particular attention.

Wingfield Park is well laid out and is adorned with many white marble pavilions and statues, and has a large pavilion in the centre, surrounded by 80 acres of grounds and flower-gardens. It is named after Sir C. Wingfield, Chief Commissioner of Oudh.

Hazratganj, which leads to the N. from Government House, was the route of the rear-guard in September 1857, when, after holding the Char Bagh Bridge for several hours, it marched to join the main column in advance of it. A few hundred yards up it on the left side the Post-Office occupies the building of the **Begam ki Kothi**—once the residence of a queen of Amjad Ali Shah — taken with much slaughter of the enemy on 11th March 1858, and nearly ½ m. further is the **Hazratganj Imambarah,** as it is usually called, the tomb of Amjad Ali Shah, which was captured on 14th March, a feat which led to the occupation of the whole of the enemy's lines of defence at Lucknow. The interior, which once contained the most sumptuous fittings, is now neglected and dirty; but the garden court in front is rather pretty. Beyond the Imambarah is the high-standing **Nur Bakhsh**[1] **Kothi,** now the official residence of the Deputy Commissioner of Lucknow; and a little further N. the S.E. corner of the Kaisar Bagh and the Memorial in front of it are reached.

[1] Light-giving.

(*b*) The Quarters S. of the Railway connected with the Reliefs.

The scene of the operations of the relieving forces before Lucknow may now be completed by reference to the Martinière, the Dilkusha, and the Alam Bagh, the original base of each one of the reliefs. A pretty road, striking off to the left from the main road past the W. side of the Wingfield Park, leads through the Martinière Park to the buildings in it. Not very far from these will be seen two small grave enclosures, and in one of these will be found the grave of Major Hodson of Hodson's Horse, killed on 14th March 1858.

The **Martinière** is an irregular building, in a sort of debased Italian style. The basement storey is raised to a good height above the ground, and has extensive wings, but the superstructure is *bizarre,* and has been styled "a whimsical pile," though there is something striking in its great central tower. It was built by Major-General Claude Martin, whose tomb, restored in 1865, is in the E. crypt of the chapel; the plain sarcophagus was once guarded by a marble grenadier, with arms reversed, at each angle. To the E. of the college is a fine lake with a fluted masonry column in the centre.

General Martin was the son of a cooper, and served as a soldier under Lally in the regiment of Lorraine. He and some of his comrades formed a company of Chasseurs under Law, and garrisoned Chandernagore, till taken by Clive. He then entered the British army, and rose to the rank of captain. In 1776 he entered the service of the Nawabs of Oudh, but the British Government allowed him to retain his rank, and to enjoy promotion. In 1783 he formed the acquaintance of De Boigne, and took part with him in cultivating indigo and lending money to the Nawab, by which he acquired a large fortune. It is said that Asaf-ud-daulah offered him £1,000,000 sterling for the Martinière. But the Nawab died before the bargain was completed, and General Martin himself dying at the Farhat Bakhsh before the building was finished, directed it should be completed out of the funds left to endow a school in it. This school is now one of the best in all India for the education of children of European descent, whose parents are permanent residents in the country, or who hold subordinate positions in the Government service. The advance on the Martinière in November 1857 met with strong resistance by the rebels. It was held by them again in March 1858, and it was in the attack then made on it that Sir William Peel was wounded by a musket ball.

The **Dilkusha**, or "Heart-expanding," was a villa built by S'aadat 'Ali Khan, in the midst of an extensive deer-park. It stands about ¾ m. to the S. of the Martinière across the railway, and is now a ruin, but a very picturesque one. It was captured on the 12th of November 1857 by Sir Colin Campbell, and here twelve days later General Havelock expired, with the knowledge that the whole garrison of Lucknow had been safely rescued from the Residency. On the occasion of Sir Colin Campbell's second advance it was occupied on the 2nd March.

3½ m. to the S.W. from the Dilkusha, at the other side of the present cantonments, and about 1½ m. from the Char Bagh and railway station, is the **Alam Bagh**, with the grave and memorial of General Havelock. It was first taken by that General on 23rd September 1857, was occupied by a detachment left behind with the baggage and wounded till the arrival of Sir Colin Campbell on 12th November, and was guarded by Sir James Outram and his force of 4500 from 27th November 1857 till March 1858. It is a walled enclosure, 500 yds. square, and was built by Wajid 'Ali as an occasional residence for a favourite wife. General Havelock's tomb is surmounted by an obelisk 30 ft. high, with an inscription recording his death on the 24th of November 1857.

(c) Quarters N.W. of the Residency and across the Gumti.

Five hundred yds. to the N.W. of the Residency is the **Iron Bridge** across which our troops passed to the fight of Chinhat and again retreated from it, and over which General Outram passed on 16th March 1858. It was designed by Rennie and sent out from England at the end of the 18th century, but was not erected till 1840-1844. From it there is a beautiful view of the Farhat Bakhsh-Chhatar Manzil Palace.

Across the bridge to the right is the Badshah Bagh, from which the enemy kept up a severe fire on the Residency, and from which the shell which caused the death of Sir Henry Lawrence came. It was taken by Sir James Outram on 8th March 1858. It was given to the Raja of Kapurthalla in 1858, and was purchased from him for the new Canning College, built at a cost of 5½ lakhs, of which 1½ were given by the Maharaja of Balrampur. Further on at Hassanganj another road turns to the right and leads to the Kokrail Bridge and (3 m.) Ismailganj, 1½ m. in front of **Chinhat** (6½ m.), while the main road passes on to the old cantonment (2½ m.) of **Mariâon**, passing the Kerbela where Nasir-ud-din (died 1837) is buried: nothing is now left of the cantonment except the ruined walls of a few houses. Twelve hundred yards W. of the Residency is the great **Imambarah** which stood inside the **Machhi**[1] **Bhawan** enclosure. The Fort was dismantled in 1865, and nothing now remains of it except the high site to the E. of the Imambarah. It once extended 800 yds. along the road and 500 yds. to the S. of it, while the N.W. end reached almost to the river bank above the stone bridge which crossed the Gumti opposite the centre of it. At the back of it is the new Medical College and Hospital, the memorial of the Queen Empress, of which the foundation-stone was laid by King George on 26th December 1905. The cost of the whole building will be 33 lakhs, and

[1] See p. 176.

will include a hospital with 230 beds, a hostel for 200 students, a nurses' home, cottage wards, etc. Near the bridge is the so-called Mosque of Aurangzeb, built on the Lakhshman Tilla or Mound, which is believed to have been the centre of the original settlement of Lucknow, and to have given the present name of the city. Between the enclosure and the N. side of the city, with the Chauk Bazaar, is the new Victoria Park: it contains a bronze statue of the Queen Empress. The Imambarah court is entered by a fine gateway on the left of the road; though the details will not bear inspection, the great courtyard, with a lofty mosque and two minarets on the W. side, and the immense structure of the Imambarah at the head of steps on the S. side, is decidedly fine. It was built in 1784, partly to afford relief in the terrible famine of that time which swept over all N. India, by Asaf-ud-daulah, who is buried in it. The great hall is 163 ft. long, 53 ft. broad, and 49 ft. high, and is one of the largest vaulted galleries in the world.[1] It has a number of tawdry fittings in it, which have taken the place of the splendid articles described by Bishop Heber. European gentlemen are requested to remove their hats in the hall. At the end of the roadway passing in front of the Imambarah is the **Rumi Darwazah** or Turkish Gate, built probably on the analogy of the Sublime Porte, though not in the least resembling that; it is much disfigured by absurd decoration. One thousand yards again beyond this Gate is the **Husainabad Imambarah** and opposite it on the N. side of the road a beautiful garden with the Husainabad Clock Tower and tank and the **Satkanda** or seven-storeyed tower. The first was built by Muhammad 'Ali Shah, 1837 A.D., as a burial-place for himself, and consists of two large enclosures, one of which is at right angles to the other. It is small in comparison with that in the Machhi Bhawan, and stands in a large quadrangle, which has a marble reservoir of water in the centre. The Imambarah Hall is filled with mirrors and chandeliers, and contains the throne of the king, covered with beaten silver, and his wife's divan with solid silver supports. The seven-storeyed watch-tower, of which only four storeys were built, was commenced by Muhammad 'Ali Shah, but interrupted by his death.

[1] Fergusson's *Eastern Architecture*, ii. 239.

The tank is an extremely fine and picturesque work. On the N. side of it is a fine Barahdarri, now the **Talukdar's Hall**, with portraits of most of the Kings of Oudh; and behind that is the **Daulat Khana**, the original royal palace when Lucknow was first founded. The Clock Tower to the W. of the tank was built in 1881 and is 220 ft. high. Further again to the W. rises the **Jama Masjid**, begun by Muhammad 'Ali Shah, and perhaps the most satisfactory specimen of Oriental architecture in Lucknow. It has three domes and two minarets, and stands on a high platform approached by flights of steps. Rather more than 2 m. N.W. of the Husainabad and beyond the Water-works pumping station on the Gumti is the **Musa Bagh**, which is deserving of a visit, though the last ¾ of a mile to it must be accomplished on foot, on account of the magnificent brick walls which surround it. It was here that the first mutiny at Lucknow took place on 3rd May 1857, and it was here that our troops failed to intercept the mutineers when finally driven out of Lucknow on 19th March 1858.

ROUTE 22.

DELHI TO ALLAHABAD by **Ghaziabad**, **Aligarh**, **Hathras** Junction, **Tundla** Junction, **Etawah** and **Cawnpore**, and Cawnpore to Lucknow.

From Delhi 12 m. **Ghaziabad** junction station (see p. 220).

78 m. **ALIGARH** junction station (R.), D.B. between the civil station and the city. A line from here runs

N.E. to 53 m. Chandausi and to 97 m. Bareilly on the Oudh and Rohilkand main line.

Aligarh, "the high fort," is the name of the considerable fortress which adjoins and protects the town of Kol or Koil situated in the well-cultivated plain between the Jumna and Ganges. This town (70,000 inhabitants) is of undoubtedly great antiquity, and Buddhist remains have been found in excavating the eminence on which the citadel of Koil stood. Kutab-ud-din Aibak marched from Delhi to Koil, "one of the most celebrated fortresses of Hind," in 1194. In 1252 A.D. Ghiyas-ud-din Balban was governor of Koil. He set up a great minaret, which was inscribed with the name which he had before he ascended the throne—"Baha-ud-din Shamsi," and dated 1254 A.D. In 1862 this pillar, by an extraordinary act of vandalism, was pulled down.

Ibn Batuta mentions Koil in his account of his embassy from Delhi to China, 1342 A.D. He calls it a fine town surrounded by mango groves. In the 15th century it became the scene of many a battle between the armies of Jaunpur and Delhi. An inscription in the fort of Koil records its construction during the reign of Ibrahim Lodi, 1524 A.D. In 1759 A.D. the Afghans, under Ahmad Shah, expelled the Jats from Koil, and about 1776 A.D. Najaf Khan[1] repaired the fort of Ramgarh, and changed its name to Aligarh. In 1785 Maharaja Sindhia captured Aligarh, in which he found treasure in specie and jewels amounting to a crore of rupees. In 1788 it was taken by Ghulam Kadir Khan,[1] and retaken by Sindhia, and here, with the aid of De Boigne, that prince organised his battalions after the European fashion. In 1796 De Boigne was succeeded by Perron, who, when the British declared war against Sindhia in 1803, took refuge with the British. Aligarh was then taken by a brilliant *coup de main* by Lord Lake.

When the news of the mutiny at Meerut arrived, on the 12th of May, Aligarh was garrisoned by 300 Sepoys of the 9th Native Infantry, who mutinied on the 19th. Among those who were compelled to seek refuge in Agra was Lady Outram, who was living with her son, a recently-joined member of the Civil Service. On the 28th, Lieutenant Greathed reached Aligarh with 40 volunteer horsemen, who held their ground there up to the 21st of June; but were soon after obliged to retire to Agra. On the 5th of October Colonel Greathed's column from Delhi occupied Koil.

The **Civil Station** is admirably kept and well planted with fine trees. On one side of a large central space are private residences and the Post Office, and on the other, the Public Offices, Law Courts, District School, the cemetery, and the Aligarh *Institute*, founded in 1864 by the late well-known Sir Saiyad Ahmad Khan, K.C.S.I., LL.D. The *Lyall Library* was founded by the Hindus of Aligarh, and is built in the modern Saracenic style. The old cemetery of 1802 lies towards the Fort.

The object of chief interest is the Mohammedan **Anglo-Oriental College** for the education of Mohammedans of the upper class. The building is on the plan of an Oxford or Cambridge college, and is surrounded by grounds covering about 100 acres. It was opened in 1875, and has since made rapid progress; the Hyderabad State contributes Rs. 24,000 yearly to the funds. It consists of two departments, a college and a school; and its inmates, some 450 boys and 500 young men, come from all parts of India. The Principal and four Professors are English University men, and the Headmaster of the school is also an Englishman, and there are seven Indian Professors and four Assistant Professors. It is governed by a body of Mohammedan trustees, and as it is in no way connected with the State, careful instruction in the Mohammedan religion is given in it. Considerable prominence is given to

[1] See pp. 171, 198, and 212.

the encouragement of manly sports; and the institution marks a new and interesting departure in Indian education. The visit of King George to the College on 8th March 1906 gave unbounded satisfaction to the Muhammedan community of India.

The *Fort of Aligarh*, 2 m. N. of the town, was built in 1524, and reconstructed by French engineers in the 18th century. It is surrounded by a ditch 18 ft. deep and from 80 ft. to 100 ft. wide. The main entrance is on the N. There is no garrison now. General Perron's House is ½ m. to the S. of the Fort, between it and the College. It has a square gateway in front, with an arched entrance and a guard-room above it. In the garden is a well with a Persian inscription.

In the **City of Koil**, at the top of a long and rather steep slope, is the principal mosque, with three central domes, two side domes, and four minarets. It was built by Sabit Khan in 1728 during the reign of Muhammad Shah. The architecture is in the debased style of the 18th century, yet the mosque is by no means without beauty and even dignity. The eminence on which it stands is called the Bala Kila, and in it have been discovered remains of Buddhist and Hindu temples, some of which have been placed in the compound of the Institute.

S.E. of the great mosque is the *Moti Masjid*, or "Pearl Mosque." In the city is a fine *tank* surrounded by small Hindu temples and shrouded by magnificent trees swarming with monkeys.

The Aligarh annual **Fair** (held early in February) usually offers special opportunity for witnessing the inner life of an Indian district.

97 m. **Hathras** junction station. [The East Indian Railway is here crossed by the Cawnpore-Achnera line of the Bombay Baroda, and Central India Railway (Route 12). The branch to Cawnpore (187 m.) passes Fatehgarh (105 m.), Farukhabad (101 m.), and Kanauj (138 m.). The Europeans at Fatehgarh in 1857 defended themselves for some time after the outbreak of the mutiny on 18th June, but were finally compelled to leave the gun-carriage factory which they held and attempted to escape to Cawnpore in boats. Most of them were killed on the way, and the few who reached Bithur (p. 301), and were captured there, were murdered on the 10th and 15th July with the survivors of Cawnpore. **Kanauj**, the famous northern capital, first of the Tomar and then of the Rathor Rajputs, was taken by Mahmud of Ghazni in 1018, and by Shahab-ud-din Ghori and Kutab-ud-din Aibak in 1194, whereupon the Rathors removed to Rajputana and finally settled at Jodhpur. The ruins of this great city which now remain are very scanty. It was at Kanauj, too, that the Emperor Humayun was finally and totally defeated by Sher Shah in 1540 A.D.]

The thriving town of Hathras (population 43,000) is 6 m. from the station.

127 m. **Tundla** junction (R.). A line from here runs W. into *Agra*, distant 15 m. (see p. 170). Visitors to Agra book to the Fort Station. Some of the E.I.R. trains run to this, and some diverging at the Jumna Bridge junction to Agra City, reached by the new Strachey Bridge of 9 spans of 154 ft., clear. As the bridge over the Jumna is approached, a splendid view of the Taj and the Fort on the opposite bank is obtained.

150 m. **Shekohabad** junction for line to 66 m. Farukhabad.

184 m. **Etawah** station ✱ (R.), D.B., properly, *Itawah*, from *Int*, "a brick" (42,000 inhabitants), headquarters of the district of the same name, is said to have been founded about five centuries ago by Sangram Singh, a Chauhan chief, descended from the famous Prithvi Raja, King of Delhi (p. 208).

The *City* stands picturesquely amongst a network of ravines on the N. bank of the Jumna, at a point where it bends sharply backwards on

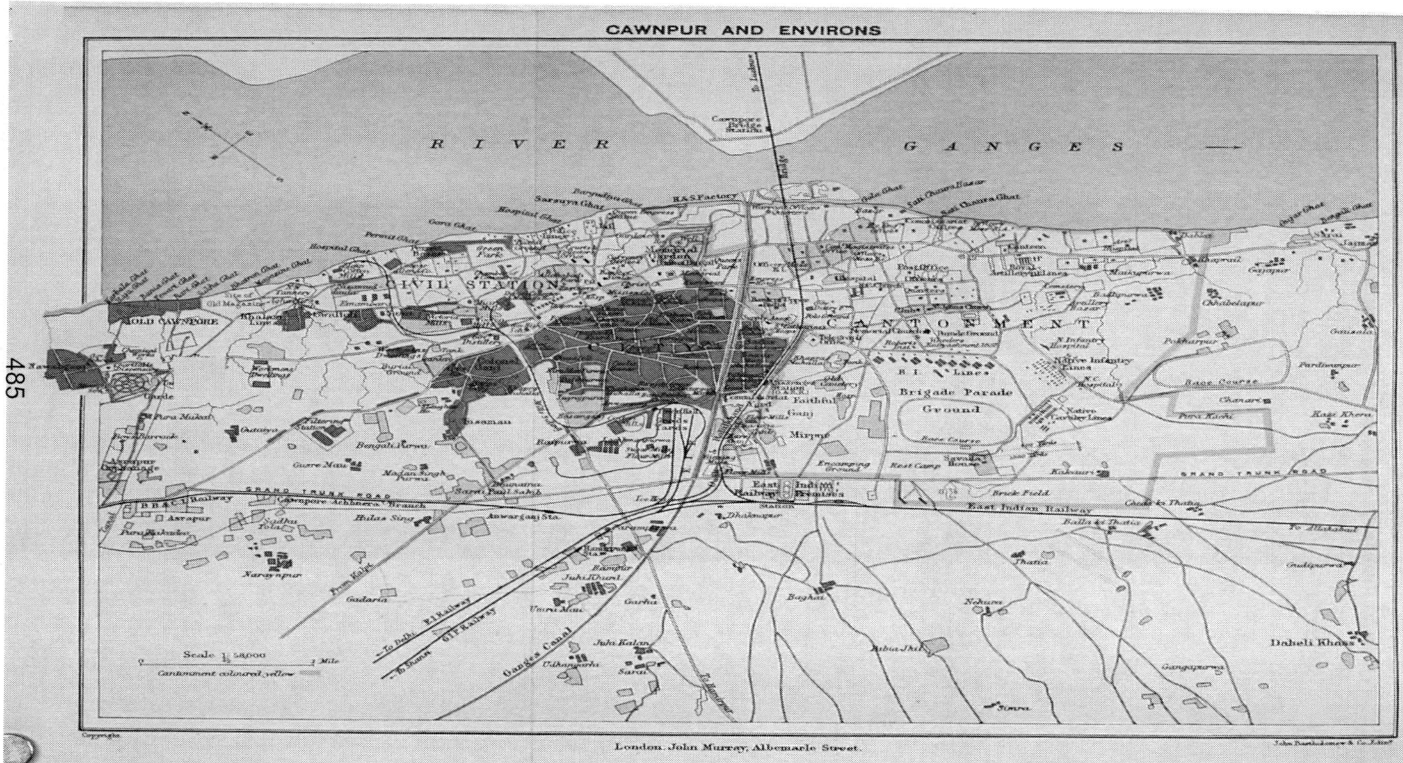
CAWNPUR AND ENVIRONS
RIVER GANGES
CIVIL STATION
CANTONMENT
OLD CAWNPORE
Brigade Parade Ground
Race Course
GRAND TRUNK ROAD
East Indian Railway
To Allahabad
Dabeli Khass
Ganges Canal
Scale 1/38,000
Cantonment coloured yellow
London, John Murray, Albemarle Street.

its own course. It is divided into two parts, a ravine from N.W. to S.E. separating the old city on the S. from the new. In the centre of the city is *Hume Ganj* Square; and adjoining it is a *Sarai* with a fine gateway. ½ m. to the N. lies the *Civil Station*. In a grove to the W. is the *Asthala*, an important Hindu temple of the 18th century.

The *Jama Masjid*, on high ground going toward the Jumna, is an old Buddhist temple, altered by the Mohammedans about 1430 A.D. The screen, 47 ft. high, before the dome is similar to that of the Atala Masjid of Jaunpur (p. 277). The façade is 130 ft. long, but only 20 ft. deep.

The *Bathing Ghats* on the Jumna are picturesque and worth a visit. From them is seen the white *spire* of a modern *Jain temple*.

271 m. **CAWNPORE** junction station. ✱ The junction of four railways—East Indian; Cawnpore - Achnera; Indian Midland; N.W. Bengal. Comfortable and convenient waiting-rooms.

The *City* (population, 174,000) is situated on the right bank of the Ganges in lat. 26° 28′, long. 80° 24′; old Cawnpore is 2 m. to the N.W. of the present city. The name means City of Kanh or Krishna. It is a great emporium for harness, shoes, and other leather-work, and the principal centre of the mill industry in N. India, and is likely to undergo many important improvements by an early date. Its importance dates from its cession to the East India Company by the Nawab Wazir of Oudh. The native city, which has some fine bazaars and markets always presenting a scene of bustle, lies to the left (N.W.) of the cantonment; while the Civil Station and most of the mills and factories lie N.W. again of the city and near the river.

On the Sirsaya Ghat there is a statue of the Queen Empress, the work of a local artist; it is intended to erect a public library and place of entertainment as a memorial of King Edward VII. The tail of the Ganges canal separates the S.E. side of the city from the Sadar Bazaar of the cantonment, and the railway to Lucknow runs to the Ganges bridge outside the latter.

The chief interest of the place for Englishmen lies in the sad events of the Mutiny in June 1857,[1] which ended in the cowardly massacre of a large number of women and children. The cantonment at the time straggled for 6 or 7 m., and though containing an unusually large non-combatant population, was imprudently garrisoned with about 3000 Indian soldiers and only 60 Europeans. Dhundu Pant, known as the Nana Sahib,[2] the adopted son of Baji Rao II. Peshwa, whose claims to succeed to the large pension enjoyed by the ex-Peshwa had been rejected by the British Government, was living near at Bithur, on friendly terms with the English at Cawnpore.

Sir Hugh Wheeler, a gallant veteran commanding the division, doubted the fidelity of the Sepoys, and resolved to store with provisions one spot which should be a rallying point for those under his charge. The natural position to select was the magazine in the N.W. corner of the civil lines, which rested on the river, and was surrounded by strong walls. But General Wheeler decided against this as he would have had to withdraw the Sepoy guard, and feared that by showing his mistrust he would hasten the rising. The spot he chose was the centre of a plain lying S. of the city where there were two barracks. Here he raised some earthworks about 4 ft. high, and barely 2 ft. thick at the crest, the soil being so hard that it was almost impossible to dig it, and so friable, that when dug, it did not cohere; but it was supposed at the

1 For a graphic account of the siege of Cawnpore, the traveller cannot do better than study T. R. E. Holmes's *History of the Indian Mutiny*, Allen & Co.

2 The third Peshwa Balwant Rao had been previously known as the Nana Sahib.

time that the mutineers would at once proceed to Delhi, and that only temporary protection was needed from the city mob. He applied to Sir H. Lawrence for reinforcements, which were generously sent under Lieutenant Ashe and Captain Fletcher Hayes. Much against the advice of others, the general and the Collector asked the Nana to send a body of his retainers for the defence of the Magazine and of the Treasury beyond it in Nawabganj. The same day (22nd May) all the non-combatants betook themselves to the entrenchment. On the 3rd June General Wheeler most unselfishly despatched reinforcements to Lucknow, though knowing that, in case of attack, his own position was not defensible.

On the night of the 4th of June the 2nd Cavalry rose and galloped off to Nawabganj, where the treasure was. The 1st Regiment Native Infantry followed them, and sacked the Treasury, threw open the Jail, burned the Public Offices and the Records, and captured the Magazine with all its ammunition and artillery, with which they prepared to march to Delhi. The 53rd and 56th eventually joined also, after being opened on by the guns in the entrenchment; but 80 men of them remained faithful to the end. The whole body of mutineers then started on the march to Delhi, but were persuaded by an emissary of the Nana to return. On 6th June General Wheeler was warned by the Nana to expect an attack; and by noon the siege of Cawnpore had begun.

Never had a besieged garrison been called upon to do greater things than this little body of about 200 British soldiers and 30 officers, hampered by every disadvantage and exposed to the continuous fire of 3000 trained foemen, well fed, lodged, and armed. The total number in the entrenchment is estimated at 900, of whom more than half were women and children. There were many heroes in this little band of whom any nation would be proud, and to Captain Moore of the 32nd has by common consent been assigned the first place among them.

The position which the doomed garrison had to defend will be understood from the accompanying plan, adapted from Captain Mowbray Thomson's *Story of Cawnpore.* All round it were buildings and cover from which the enemy could maintain a murderous fire with practical impunity—a mess-house on the E., a church and reading-room near the N.E. corner, a racket court and other buildings opposite the N.W. corner, a deep drain giving shelter to musketry men all along the W., and a row of incomplete barracks on the S., the nearest of which were only 250 yds. from the entrenchment. To prevent the enemy from absolutely enfilading our position it was necessary to occupy two of these, and Nos. 2 and 3 were accordingly held, the former by Captain Glanville first, and then by Captain Mowbray Thomson of the 53rd Native Infantry, and the latter by Captain Jenkins. By these barracks was a well which served as the general grave of all who were killed or died within the entrenchment. The lines of this were defended by the Redan under Major Vibart of the 2nd Bengal Cavalry on the N., by Ashe's Battery and by Ecford's on the E., by Totbury's Gun and Dempster's Battery in a projection on the W. side, and by brave hearts all round; but except for repelling assaults and keeping the enemy at a greater distance, the guns were of but little avail. The two barracks, one of them with a thatched roof, were entirely unprotected, and the only well in the entrenchment, 60 ft. deep, was exposed to the full fire of the enemy. And yet the dauntless British few held out for twenty days, and then only yielded because provisions were nearly exhausted. The proximity of the enemy's guns to the entrenchment would be incredible were it not that the distances were carefully recorded immediately after the recapture of

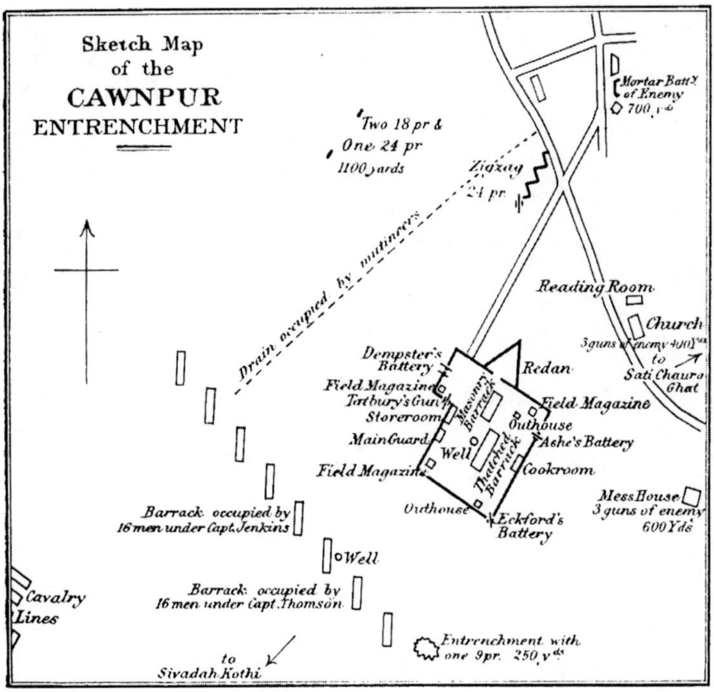
Sketch Map
of the
CAWNPUR
ENTRENCHMENT
Two 18 pr &
One 24 pr
1100 yards
Zigzag
24 pr
Mortar Batty
of Enemy
700 yds
Drain occupied by mutineers
Reading Room
Church
3 guns of enemy 400 yds
to
Sati Chaura
Ghat
Dempster's
Battery
Redan
Field Magazine
Tatbury's Gun
Storeroom
Masonry
Barrack
Field Magazine
Outhouse
Main Guard
Well
Thatched
Barrack
Ashe's Battery
Field Magazine
Cookroom
Mess House
3 guns of enemy
600 Yds
Outhouse
Eckford's
Battery
Barrack occupied by
16 men under Capt. Jenkins
Well
Cavalry
Lines
Barrack occupied by
16 men under Capt. Thomson
Entrenchment with
one 9pr. 250 yds
to
Sivadah Kothi

[To face p. 302.

the place in July. By the 11th June the enemy had three mortars, two 24-pounders, three 18-pounders, one or two 12- and 9-pounders, and one 6-pounder playing on the entrenchment; and on the 12th June the thatched barrack was set on fire, and thereafter over 200 of those within the entrenchment lived day and night in the open, in a temperature of 120-140 degrees of heat. On the 15th June Captain Moore led a successful sally which resulted in the spiking of five guns and the blowing up of a 24-pounder; but the supplies from the captured magazine were practically inexhaustible, and such bravery could produce no permanent results. No wonder that one-third of the numbers of the defenders were lost by the 21st June, that over 250 persons were buried in the outside well before the siege ended, that of fifty-nine artillery men only four survived at the end, and that when the British troops re-entered Cawnpore, they found that there was not a single square yard in the buildings in the entrenchment that was free of the scars of shot. On the 16th June the enemy received reinforcements from Lucknow, and on the 23rd, the anniversary of Plassey, they attempted a home assault which cost them over 200 of their numbers. On the 25th the Nana offered terms to the survivors, and these were accepted for the reason already given, though General Wheeler's voice was against surrender.

On the 26th there was an armistice, and it was arranged that the British should evacuate their fortified position and, leaving their guns and treasure, should march out with their arms and 60 rounds of ammunition for each man, the Nana promising safe conduct to the river-side, and a supply of boats to take them down the Ganges. The next morning, 27th June, the survivors, about 450 in number, marched down to the Sati Chaura Ghat, and went on board the boats. It was 9 A.M. before they were all embarked, Major Vibart entering last of all. Then on the order of Tantia Topi a bugle sounded, the native boatmen left the boats fixed in the mud, and a murderous fire of grape-shot and musketry opened on all sides. The thatch of the boats took fire, and while the sick and wounded were suffocated in them, the Sepoys jumped into the water and butchered others. Orders then came from the Nana to kill no more women, and about 125 women and children, wounded and half drowned, were carried back to Cawnpore.

One boat, which as it happened had been pushed off by the very bravest of the defenders, drifted down the river, and those on board propelled it as they could, with numbers rapidly diminished by the fire from the banks—Moore, Glanville, Ashe and Fagan all being shot on it. For thirty-six hours it floated down stream, pursued and attacked by the enemy on all sides. On the second morning the occupants woke to find themselves in a side stream with Sepoys on the banks ready to overwhelm them. Two officers and eleven soldiers gallantly leapt ashore and dispersed the astounded crowd. But meanwhile the boat had drifted out of sight and was lost to them, and they were compelled to take refuge in a small temple, in which they were surrounded. Breaking out, and once more scattering the armed mob, they took to the river, and four of them—Captains Mowbray Thomson and Delafosse, and Privates Murphy and Sullivan—being strong swimmers, reached the Oudh shore, and being succoured by the Talukdar of Murar Mau, afterwards Sir Digbijai Singh, lived to tell the story of Cawnpore. The boat was subsequently overtaken by the enemy and brought back with its eighty survivors. The men who survived in it were shot by order of the Nana, and the women and children sent to join the 125 who had been spared at the Massacre Ghat in the Savada Kothi,[1] where the Nana lived during the siege. They

[1] This lay to the W. of the row of incomplete barracks, and of the race-course W. of them, close to the Great Trunk Road.

were afterwards removed to a small house called the Bibi-garh, near which the Nana was residing in an hotel. This house contained two rooms, 20 ft. by 10 ft., and a number of dark closets, and had a courtyard 15 yds. square in front of it; and in it between the 7th and 14th of July twenty-eight of the captives died.

But retribution was not far off. On the 7th of July General Havelock marched from Allahabad with 1400 British and 600 Sikhs. On the 12th of July at 7 A.M. they halted at Balindah, 4 m. from Fatehpur. Here they were attacked by the Nana's army, and inflicted a crushing defeat on it. On the 15th of July Havelock again defeated the rebels at Aong, and drove them over the bridge across the Pandu Nadi, and the Nana, on learning that the British were advancing upon him, ordered the massacre of the captives in the Bibi-garh. The few men among them were brought out and killed in his presence. A party of Sepoys were then ordered to shoot the women and children, but they intentionally fired at the ceiling of the rooms, though they belonged to the regiment which had murdered the ten ensigns at Allahabad. Then a party of butchers were sent in to accomplish the foul deed, and all was quickly over. In the morning all the bodies were thrown into an adjoining well.

The Nana went out to oppose General Havelock with 5000 men and a formidable train of artillery, but the battle fought 2 m. S. of the cantonment on 16th of July ended in the confused flight of the rebels to Bithur, after they had blown up the magazine. On the 17th the British force marched on to occupy the cantonments, but ere it reached them learned the mournful story of the massacres.

Four months later Cawnpore—which had been the base of operations for General Havelock's advance on Lucknow, often begun and often suspended—was the scene, once more, of bloody engagements. Sir Colin Campbell marched thence on the 9th of November 1857 to relieve Lucknow, leaving behind him for the protection of Cawnpore, his base of operations, 500 British and 500 Madras troops, commanded by Major-General Windham, of Redan celebrity. On the 27th of November Sir Colin began his march back to Cawnpore, having with him 2000 women, children, sick, and wounded, and the treasure which had been rescued from Lucknow. On nearing the Bridge of Boats, on the 28th, he beheld a conflagration which showed him that the enemy had taken the city to which he was returning.

What had happened was that Tantia Topi, a follower of the Nana, at the head of 15,000 of the Gwalior insurgents, had marched on Cawnpore, and by well-concerted movements, completed on the 19th of November, had cut off the place from all communication with the W. and N.W., from which its supplies had been obtained. On the 26th General Windham moved out from Cawnpore, and attacked and repulsed Tantia's right wing; but on the two following days he was gradually driven back to his entrenchment on the river side, leaving the bridge—the link with Lucknow—dangerously exposed. Sir Colin arrived just in time to save the bridge, but the clothing and stores prepared for the refugees from Lucknow fell into the hands of the rebels. Having despatched his convoy of ladies and wounded to Allahabad, Sir Colin on December 6th took the initiative. The arrangements made for driving the enemy back from their line—which rested on the city and the brick kilns to the W. of it, and extended nearly as far as the Ganges Canal on that side—were completely successful; the Gwalior camp, with all its stores and magazines, was taken, and the enemy routed with great slaughter to beyond the canal. Owing to blundering, the pursuit of their right and centre was not properly pressed at the time; but it was taken up next day by

Brigadier-General Hope Grant, who finally scattered the enemy and captured fifteen guns.

There is one more sad memory connected with Cawnpore—the death there of Captain Sir Wm. Peel, the gallant leader of the Naval Brigade from the *Shannon*. He had been wounded on the taking of the Martinière on the 8th April, and unfortunately contracted smallpox from a dhooly in which he was taken to Cawnpore (having refused to occupy a stage-carriage, which his sailors had upholstered for him), and died there on 27th April. He is buried in the old cemetery ½ m. W. of the entrenchment. Among all the bravest men who fought to put down the Mutiny was none braver than he.

On the way to the Memorial Church, which is about 1¾ m. distant from the railway station, is the site of General Wheeler's *Entrenchment*. The line of defences and the principal buildings inside them are indicated by pillars, those of the former being connected by a low hedge. To the S. across the road and adjoining the barracks is a small garden enclosure surrounding the well in which 250 of the garrison were buried. The inscription on the cross runs:—*In a well under this Cross were laid, by the hands of their fellows in suffering, the bodies of men, women, and children, who died hard by during the heroic defence of Wheeler's Entrenchment when beleaguered by the rebel Nana.—June 6th to 27th*, A.D. MDCCCLVII.

The **Memorial Church** built on the N.E. edge of the entrenchment is in the Romanesque style; it cost over £20,000, and was consecrated in 1875. It contains a series of memorials to those who fell near here in the Mutiny. A fine view of Cawnpore is obtained from the belfry. Outside the Church on the S. side is a railed memorial slab with an inscription commemorating "those who were the first to meet their death, June 1857," and a few yards further E. is another enclosure with a cross recording

"Here lie the remains of
MAJOR EDWARD VIBART,
2nd Regt. Light Cavalry,
And about 70 officers and soldiers,
Who, after escaping from the
Massacre at Cawnpore,
On the 27th of June 1857,
Were captured by the rebels at Shivrajpur,
And murdered on the 1st of July."

The **Sati Chaura Ghat** is about ¾ m. N. by E. of the church. A grassy road between banks 10 ft. or 20 ft. high lined with trees, among which the murderers concealed themselves, leads down to the river. On the bank is a temple to Shiva, of hexagonal shape, old and going to ruin. Narrow flights of steps lead from this temple to a broad enclosed flight, which in the cold season descend some way to the water. It is only too easy to imagine the terrible scene which took place here on 27th June 1857. 1 m. up the stream near the fine bridge of the O.R. Ry. was the pontoon *Bridge*, over which the convoy, 3 m. long, of women and wounded, brought from Lucknow by Sir Colin Campbell, passed; and here was Windham's small entrenched camp, the site of which is now occupied by the Government Harness Factory. From the head of the Sati Chaura Ghat ravine the road runs N. over the railway and the Ganges canal and past the Queen's Park, with a statue of the Queen Empress, to the **Memorial Gardens**, situated at the E. corner of the city. These are beautifully laid out and well kept, and in the middle, upon a mound raised over the well in which the victims of the **Bibi-garh** massacre were buried, is the memorial in the form of an octagonal Gothic screen designed by Sir Henry Yule, R.E. In the centre of the enclosure, on the actual well, is the figure of the *Angel of the Resurrection* in white marble, by Marochetti, with arms crossed on her breast, as if resigned to the Almighty Will, each hand holding a palm, the emblem of peace. This figure was the gift of Lord and Lady Canning. Over the arch is inscribed, "These are they which came out of great tribulation." Around the screen wall which marks the circle of the well is the legend: "*Sacred to the perpetual Memory of a great company of Christian people, chiefly Women and Children, who near this spot were cruelly murdered by the followers of the rebel Nana Dhundu Pant, of Bithur, and cast, the dying with the dead, into the well below, on the xvth day of July, MDCCCLVII.*" Neither the screen nor the statue can be considered quite satisfactory. In front of the monument is a small enclosed cemetery. Two of the tombs in it are to the memory of the women and children of the 1st Company, 6th Battery, Bengal Artillery, and those of H.M.'s 32nd Regiment, who were slaughtered near this spot.

[Cawnpore to Lucknow 46 m. Both the broad gauge and the narrow gauge lines run over this length of country.

As far as Ajgain (22 m.) the railway closely follows the road along which Sir Henry Havelock and Sir Colin Campbell advanced to the relief of Lucknow. Beyond Unao (12 m.) and near Ajgain is Basiratganj, where the enemy was thrice defeated by the former. The line passes N. of the Alam Bagh, and the railway station at Lucknow is situated at the Char Bagh (p. 284) on the S. side of the old canal of Ghazi-ud-din Haidar.]

317 m. **Fatehpur**, the headquarters of a district, and once a place of some importance. On the outbreak of the Mutiny here on 7th June 1857 most of the Europeans escaped to Banda; but the Judge, Mr R. T. Tucker, who refused to quit his post, was killed fighting valiantly to the last. The Magistrate, Mr Sherer, afterwards accompanied General Havelock's force to Cawnpore.

354 m. Sirathu for **Korah.** This place was once of equal importance with Allahabad, which was known as the Province of Allahabad and Korah. There are still some interesting remains and ruins at it. It was here that Ala-ud-din Khilji basely murdered his uncle, the Emperor Jalal-ud-din, in 1296.

389 m. **Allahabad** junction (p. 31). The line passes the Khusru Bagh and affords glimpses of the mausolea in it.

ROUTE 23.

(*a*) CALCUTTA by the East India Railway loop line to **Lakhisarai** and **Mokamah** by **Nalhati Junction Azimganj, Tinpahar Junction (Rajmahal,** visit to **Malda** for **Gaur** and **Panduah), Bhagalpur,** and **Jamalpur** for **Monghyr.**

(*b*) MOKAMAH to **TIRHUT.**

(*c*) CALCUTTA to **Plassey** and **Murshidabad** by Eastern Bengal Railway and on to **Malda.**

(*d*) CALCUTTA by Eastern Bengal Railway to **Darjeeling** by **Damukdia, Silliguri** and **Kurseong.**

(*a*) **Lakhisarai** and **Mokamah,** by **Nalhati (Azimganj), Tin Pahar (Rajmahal), Bhagalpur** and **Jamalpur** for **Monghyr.**

Howrah (p. 67).

67 m. **Burdwan** (p. 39).

75 m. to **Khana** junction (see p. 39). Here the loop line branches off N. to

145 m. **Nalhati** junction station.

[Here it is necessary to change for the Nalhati State Railway branching E. to

27 m. **Azimganj** station on the right bank of the Bhagirathi river, opposite Murshidabad (joint population 28,000). The Bhagirathi is here 700 ft. broad, and rises in the rains 25 ft., when the current runs 7 m. an hour. A steamer runs at intervals from below the railway station to Murshidabad; if a conveyance has been arranged for, the river may be crossed to the E. bank, from where a metalled road leads in 5 m. to

Murshidabad. This place is reached direct from Calcutta now and is described under route (*c*),

195 m. **Tin Pahar** junction station.

[A branch line runs N.E. (7 m.) to 202 m. **Rajmahal** station, a subdistrict of the Santal Parganahs. The town stands on the W. or right bank of the Ganges. This place was once the capital of Bengal, and has many historical associations, and at it are opportunities of seeing some member of the remarkable tribe of Santals.

Up to 1592 A.D. it was known as Agmahal, but when Raja Man Singh (p. 142), Akbar's famous Rajput general, returned from the conquest of Orissa in 1592 A.D., he made it the seat of his government, and changed its name to Rajmahal. In 1607 Islam Khan transferred the seat of government to Dacca, but it was again brought to Rajmahal by Sultan Shuja in 1639. In the beginning of the next century Murshid Kuli Khan transferred the government to Murshidabad, and Rajmahal fell into decay. In 1863 the Ganges abandoned its channel, and Rajmahal was left 3 m. distant from the main stream, and this finally completed the fall of the place.

N. of the station are the Collector's Office and other public buildings. A little further on are remains of a building called the *Sangi Dalan*, "Hall of Stone." It is 100 ft. long from N. to S., and has three doors of black basalt in the centre. This is said to have been part of the palace of Sultan Shuja, son of Shah Jahan, and Governor of Behar.

The *Maina Tank* is ¾ m. due W. of the *Cutcherry*. At its S. end is a massive brick building, with an Arabic inscription; and 100 yds. to the S. is the Maina Mosque.

The *Hadaf* is 4 m. to the N.W. The road leads through a forest of tall trees, with ruined buildings at intervals. At 1½ m. it passes a solid brick building on the right hand, called the Tanksal, or Mint, with walls 5½ ft. thick. The Hadaf ruins are about 200 yds. off the road to the left, and are much hidden by the jungle. The entrance to the quadrangle is by the E. gateway, which is much injured. The mosque proper has a façade 200 ft. long, with seven arches, each 22 ft. high. In the centre of the quadrangle is a reservoir, with steps down to the water. The buildings are surrounded by dense jungle, but the actual structures have been cleared.

The journey from Rajmahal to English Bazaar, the headquarters of the Maldah district, 24 m. distant, used to be made from here. It can now be made by railway from Murshidabad or Katihar (p. 314) in 5 to 7 hours. There is a *steam ferry* across the Ganges at Rajmahal.

English Bazaar * (14,000 inhabitants) is situated on the right bank of the Mahananda about 4 m. below Old Maldah, from which the district takes its name. The place is not often visited by travellers, and arrangements for the present journey by road should be made by writing to the Collector at Maldah. The distance from English Bazaar to the N. edge of Gaur is about 4 m., and to the principal mosques 11 m., and to the Adina Mosque at Panduah is also about 11 m. The visit to each of these places will occupy a whole day.

Old Maldah lies at the confluence of the Kalindri with the Mahananda. It is an admirable position for river-traffic, and probably rose to prosperity as the port of the Mohammedan capital of Panduah. During the 18th century it was the seat of thriving cotton and silk manufactures, and the French and Dutch had factories at it. The English factory, established in 1656, however, was always at English Bazaar, lower down the Mahananda, and on the opposite bank of the river.

The ruins of Gaur and Panduah, successive capitals of Bengal, are very picturesque and interesting, but chiefly of course to the antiquarian. The sites of these old cities are being rapidly brought under the plough, and the dense jungles which thirty years ago sheltered tigers and leopards no longer exist.

Gaur was the metropolis of Bengal under its Hindu kings. Its most ancient name was Lakhnauti, a corruption of Lakshmanawati. But the name of Gaur also is of great antiquity, as is found in the *Gauriya Brahmana.* Its known history begins with its conquest about 1200 A.D.[1] by the Mohammedans, who made it the chief centre of their power in Bengal for more than three centuries. A son of the Emperor Altamsh was Governor here, and the eldest son of Balban, Nasir-ud-din Bugra, became King of Bengal and refused the throne of Delhi. He was succeeded by two sons and a grandson, and then about 1350 one Ilyas founded a kingdom which, with an interregnum, lasted till nearly 1500 A.D. When the Afghan kings of Bengal became independent, they made Panduah their capital (c. 1354 A.D.), and robbed Gaur of all the building material that could be removed. This accounts for the number of sculptured Hindu stones amongst the ruins of Panduah. When Panduah was in its turn deserted, Gaur again became the capital, and was called Jannatabad, "Terrestrial Paradise," a name which occurs in the *Ain-i-Akbari.* It was sacked by Sher Shah in 1537, and the last of the Afghan kings, Daud Khan, was absorbed into Akbar's empire in 1573 A.D. The city was entirely ruined by an outbreak of the plague in 1575.

The dimensions of the city proper, within the great continuous embankment, are 7½ m. from N. to S., and 1 to 2 m. broad. The W. side was washed by the Ganges, which flowed where the channel of the Little Bhagirathi now is. The E. side was protected by the Mahananda and by swamps. On the S. the Mahananda joined the Ganges, and left little space for an enemy to encamp. On the N. a fortification 6 m. long extends in an irregular curve from the old channel of the Bhagirathi at Sonatala to near the Mahananda and Bholahat. This rampart is 100 ft. wide at base.

In front of this rampart lay the most celebrated piece of artificial water in Bengal, the **Saugar Dighi,** 1600 yds. long by 800 broad, dating from 1126 A.D. On the bank is the tomb of Makhdum Shaikh Akhi Siraj-ud-din and a small mosque, and S. of these is a *ghat* called S'adullahpur leading down to the sacred river. S. of this rampart was the N. suburb, between which and the city was another strong rampart and ditch. Towards the Mahananda the city rampart was double, and in most parts there have been two immense ditches, and in places three.

1 m. inside the city to the S., on the Bhagirathi, was the *Citadel,* 1 m. long from N. to S., and from 600 to 800 yds. broad. The brick wall has been very strong, with many flanking angles, and round bastions at the corners. On the N. side is the fine Dakhil Gate, which can be reached from here only on elephant back. It is built of small red bricks and has been adorned with embossed bricks, which can still be seen on the towers at the four corners. The arch of the

[1] Blochmann says 1198 A.D.; Mr Thomas, 1202; Major Ràverty, 1194.

gateway is about 30 ft. high, and forms a corridor 112 ft. long. In the S.E. corner of the citadel was the palace, surrounded by a brick wall 66 ft. high and 8 ft. thick, with an ornamented cornice—hence called the *Báis Gaji*, "Twenty-two Yards Wall." At the S.E. corner of the citadel are two mosques; the smaller one, called the *Kadam Rasul*, built by Husain Shah, is kept in good repair by an endowment.[1] Mr Fergusson says of its style: "It is neither like that of Delhi, nor that of Jaunpur, nor any other style, but one purely local, and not without considerable merit in itself; its principal characteristic being heavy, short pillars of stone supporting pointed arches, and vaults in brick. The solidity of the supports goes far to redeem the inherent weakness of brick architecture. It also presents, though in a very subdued form, the curved linear form of the roof, which is so characteristic of the style. The Kadam Rasul was built by Nasrat Shah in 937 A.D. = 1530 A.D." Near it are the domed tomb of Fateh Khan and S.E. gateway of the citadel. Half a mile N. of this, outside the E. wall of the citadel, is a lofty brick tower, known as *Pir Asa Minar*, which had a chamber with four windows at the top, to which access was gained by a winding stair. Dr Hunter says: "One of the most interesting of the antiquities of the place is a *minar*. For two-thirds of the height it is a polygon of twelve sides; above that circular until it attains the height of 84 ft. The door is at some distance from the present level of the ground: and altogether it looks more like an Irish round tower than a *minar*." There is or was an inscription on this monument, which ascribed its erection to Firoz Shah (1490 A.D.).

Half a mile N.W. again of this, and above the N.E. corner of the citadel, is the finest ruin in Gaur, that of the *Golden Mosque* or *Barah Darwazah*. It measures 180 ft. from N. to S., 80 ft. from E. to W., and is 20 ft. high. The entrance is by an arched gateway of stone 26 ft. in height and 6 ft. in breadth. The mosque in plan is oblong, and originally consisted of four separate colonnades, arched and roofed over, and covered by handsome domes, in all 44 in number. Six minarets or columns of brown stone faced with black marble adorn the building; bands of blue marble about 12 in. in breadth embrace the column from the base to the capital, and are adorned with a profusion of flower-work carved in marble. The domes are built of brick. The whole appearance of this building is strikingly grand, exhibiting the taste and munificence of the prince who erected it.

Half a mile E. of the Kadam Rasul, on the side of the main road, is the *Tantipara Mosque*, remarkable for the specimens of embossed brickwork with which the front is adorned.

Half a mile S. again is the *Lattan Mosque*, also called the Painted Mosque, from the bricks being enamelled in green, yellow, blue, and white, and arranged in bands. When complete the effect of these must have been very striking.

Half a mile above it is the Piasbari Tank, with a small R.H.

In the S. wall of the city is a fine central gate, called the *Kotwali Darwazah*, and S. from it stretches an immense suburb called Firozpur. In it, 2 m. from the S. wall, is the *Lesser Golden Mosque*, which Mr Ravenshaw calls "the gem of Gaur."

Panduah is 7 m. N.E. from Maldah. It was called by the Mohammedans *Firozabad*. The first independent king of Bengal made it his capital. A road paved with brick, from 12 ft. to 15 ft. wide, passes through Panduah, and almost all the monuments are on the borders of it. Near the middle is a bridge of three arches, the materials of which have evidently been brought from the Hindu temples at Gaur, as figures of men

[1] The only detailed account of the ruins at Gaur and Panduah is contained in Mr Ravenshaw's *Gaur*. A brief description will be found in Mr Fergusson's *Indian Architecture*, ii. 253.

and animals are sculptured on them. On approaching the ruins from the S. the first objects that attract attention are the 17th-century shrines of *Makhdum Shah Jalal*, and his grandson, *Kutab 'Alam Shah*, called the Chhe Hazári and Báis Hazári, or 6000 and 22,000, from the area with which they were endowed. To the N. stands the small *Golden Mosque*, with granite walls and ten brick domes. An Arabic inscription says that it was built by Makhdum Shaikh, son of Muhammad Al-Khalidi, in 1585 A.D. N. of this is a high building, called *Eklakhi*, as having cost a lakh. It is perhaps one of the finest examples of the Bengali tomb. It is 80 ft. square, covered by one dome, and contains the remains of Ghiyas-ud-din, his wife, and his daughter-in-law. 2 m. beyond it is the tomb of Sikandar, father of Ghiyas-ud-din, and the greatest of the monarchs who made Panduah their capital. It forms part of the great mosque, called the **Adina Masjid**, the finest specimens of Mughal architecture in Lower Bengal. It was built about 1360 by Sikandar Shah, and shows traces of having been constructed out of Hindu and even Buddhistic remains. The "Buddhist railing" round the W. front is incapable of any other explanation. The Kiblah and Mimbar (pulpit) are gems of stone carving. According to Mr Fergusson, the ground-plan and dimensions are exactly similar to those of the Great Mosque at Damascus. It extends 500 ft. from N. to S., and 300 ft. from E. to W. This space is subdivided by transverse brick walls and stone pillars into 127 squares, each covered by a dome. On the outside are many small windows, highly decorated with carved tiles disposed in arches. The mosque proper is composed of a central apartment and two wings. The first is 62 ft. high in the centre from the floor to the middle of the dome. To the N. of it is a ruined gallery, as in the mosques at Ahmedabad, known as the Takht Badshashi.

The only other ruin of note in Panduah is the Satáisgarh, said to have been the king's palace It is situated opposite the Adina Mosque, in the midst of dense jungle.

There are still tigers and panthers in and near Gaur and Panduah, and in the Barindra tract and the jungles E. of them; but the English sportsman who desires to hunt them must be prepared to spend time and money, and must take advice from experienced Nimrods who know the locality.

From Tin Pahar Station the loop line continues N. to

219 m. **Sahibganj** junction for Manihari Ghat and Katihar, across the Ganges, on the Eastern Bengal Railway (p. 311).

265 m. **Bhagalpur**, D.B. (population 76,000), headquarters of a Division and District, picturesquely situated on rolling ground above the Ganges. There is a monument here to Mr Cleveland, who first reclaimed the Santals from savagery and robbery. Ferry and branch line to 23 m. Thana Bihpur on B.N.W. Railway.

298 m. **Jamalpur** junction, headquarters of the Locomotive Department of the East India Railway, and of the volunteer corps of that line, and consequently with an important European colony. The sacred Sita Kund hot springs are 3 m. from here.

Monghyr, 5½ m. from Jamalpur, is also the headquarters of a District, D.B., hotel (population 36,000). The Civil Station is most picturesquely situated inside an old Mughal fort, to which Mir Kasim fell back from Murshidabad in order to be further from the overwhelming influence of Calcutta. The place is still noted for the manufacture of arms. The N. side of the fort stands on a fine bluff over the Ganges, with temples below, and rocky islands in the stream; and there are but few bits of river scenery in India which are more pleasing than this. Ferry and branch line to Sahibpur Kamal on B.N.W. Railway.

336 m. **Lakhisarai** (p. 38).

346 m. **Mokamah** (p. 38).

(*b*) Tirhut.

Mokamah (p. 38) and Mokamah Ghat, through which the fast trains of the East India Railway run now, are the starting-points for the branches of the Bengal and North-Western Railway, all constructed within the last twenty-five years, and connecting the whole country between Oudh and the Teesta River with the south bank of the Ganges.

4 m. **Baraunl.** The main line of the Bengal and North-Western Railway runs E. from here to **Katihar** (112 m.), with branches to the river opposite Monghyr, Bhagalpur, and Sahibganj, and W. to Hajipur (54 m.), Sonepore (58 m.), and Chapra (87 m.). **Sonepore** is well known for its annual gathering of the Planters of Tirhut, and for its fair, which was once the principal fair in all India for the sale and purchase of elephants.

The main line to Tirhut proceeds N. to **Samastipur** (38 m.), from which the branch to **Darbhanga** (23 m.), and to Khanwa Ghat (99 m.), on the Teesta, and so to Katihar (96 m.), runs N.E. [Darbhanga is the residence of the Maharaja of that name, who is of Brahmin descent, and one of the largest landlords in Bengal. The title of Raja was granted to the family in 1700, and of Maharaja in 1839. The palace is a very fine building, and the city (population 66,000) contains a number of very large tanks], and then runs N.W. to **Muzaffarpur**, 70 m. from Mokamah Ghat (branch to Hajipur), Motihari (119 m.), Segowlie (132 m.), and **Bettiah** (146 m.). From Segowlie, a branch of 18 m. runs to Raxaul, the starting-point for **Khatmandu**, the capital of Nepal. 16 m. N. of Bettiah at **Lauriya** is a Buddhist stone Lat, crowned by a lion—the only isolated one in India which still bears a recognisable figure.

From **Sonepore**[1] the railway goes W. to Chapra (29 m.), where one branch (*a*) crosses the Gogra river, and runs W. to 101 m. Ghazipur (where the Governor-General Lord Cornwallis died on 5th October 1804) and Benares and Jaunpur (147 m.), a branch turning to **Azamgarh** (70 m.) and Shahganj (105 m.), on the Oudh-Rohilkand Railway, N. of Jaunpur, and another branch (*b*) runs to the N.W. up the left bank of the river to Gorakhpur (112 m. from Chapra) and Gonda (207 m.)—see p. 275.

From **Gorakhpur** a branch line runs N. to 40 m. Uska Bazaar, and goes on to Balrampur and Gonda (p. 275). This corner of the **Tarai** is of special interest as having been the undoubted seat of the birth of Buddha, and of many of the scenes connected with his life and death. Kusinagara, where the last event took place, was for a time considered to be identical with Kasia, 40 m. due E. of Gorakhpur, where colossal figures of Buddha as a teacher and reclining in death were found; but at present the sites of this place and of Kapilawasta, the city where the father of Buddha ruled, are unidentified. What has been identified beyond all doubt of late years are (1) a stupa raised over part of the relics of Buddha at **Piprâwá**, 6 m. N. of Birdpur, and (2) the Lambini Garden, now called the **Rummin Dei**, where Buddha was born, 9 m. E. of Piprâwá. At the former was found by Mr Peppé, owner of the estate, in January 1898, a relic casket inscribed, "This relic shrine of the Divine Buddha is that of the Sákyas" who received one-eighth of the relics and erected a stupa over them near Kapilawasta. At the latter was discovered a Lat of King Asoka, split down the middle, with an inscription that "here Buddha Sakyamuni was born." This column had been once surmounted by a horse; and Hiouen Thsang in his travels (*c.* 635 A.D.) recorded that he saw at the birthplace a pillar which had been split by lightning and which bore a horse. The bell-shaped capital of it has also been discovered, and

[1] A branch runs from here to Sonepore Ghat from which a steamer crosses the Ganges to Digha Ghat for Bankipur (p. 36).

in an adjoining temple a relief of the birth scene of Buddha, in which his mother Maya-devi stands erect holding the branch of a sal tree, and the child stands on the ground at her right, an unusual motive. Kapilawasta lay 10 to 15 m. west of this garden, and the site is possibly marked by extensive ruins at Tauliva Kot, 9 m. N.W. of Piprāwā. Kusinagra must lie some distance to the E. or S.E. The Lauriya Lat (p. 311) which some have supposed to mark its site, is about 90 m. to the S.E.

(c) Calcutta by E. Bengal Railway to Plassey and Murshidabad, 7-8 hrs.

Sealdah station (p. 64).

24 m. **Naihati.**

46 m. **Ranaghat** junction.

62 m. **Krishnagar.**

94 m. **Plassey,** so called from the Palás tree (*butea frondosa*), and famous for Clive's great victory in 1757. The position of the British forces is marked by a mound near the river bank and the old monument, and has now been more fully indicated on the ground at the instance of Lord Curzon, who has erected a second memorial.

The British force advanced from Chandernagore (p. 66) on 13th June, first to Katwa, and then across the Bhagirathi, between which and the Jalinghi channel of the Ganges Plassey was situated, and advanced against Suraj-ud-daulah's army at that place the same night. The battle opened the next day, 23rd June, at 8 A.M., the French in the service of the Nawab facing the left of the British line, which touched the river, and the huge native forces of the Nawab forming a semi-circle on the right front and right of that line. About midday a heavy downpour of rain occurred, and the British guns having been protected during it, overpowered the advance made by the enemy a little later. The native forces then fell back to the entrenched camp, the Nawab was counselled by traitors to flee, and Mir Jafir separated himself in accordance with his understanding with Clive, who thereupon advanced and drove the French from their position, and afterwards took the entrenched camp, the enemy then offering but little resistance. The British force amounted to 3000, of whom one-third were Europeans—800 of these being English—and the Nawab's force to over 60,000. Captain Coote, who had been a strong supporter of the counsel to fight which Clive ultimately adopted, distinguished himself greatly in the battle.

116 m. **Berhampur,** 5 m. below Murshidabad (D.B. — population 24,000), the civil headquarters of the Murshidabad district. After the battle of Plassey, as the factory-house at Kasim Bazar where Warren Hastings resided had been destroyed by Suraj-ud-daulah, Berhampur was chosen as a site for a cantonment, the *Barracks* of which cost £302,270. It will always be notorious as the scene of the first overt act of mutiny in 1857, which occurred on the 25th of February when the 19th Regiment of Native Infantry refused to receive their ammunition. Further than this the mutiny did not go, but the Regiment was marched down to Barrackpur and disbanded there.

118 m. **Kasim Bazar.** This was the British trading station previous to 1757, after which it was moved to Berhampur. In the old cemetery are buried the first wife of Warren Hastings and her daughter. She was the widow of Captain John Buchanan, a victim of the Black Hole. There is also an old *Dutch Cemetery* here.

123 m. **Murshidabad,** the chief city of the district of the same name. This was the residence of the Nawab Nazims of Bengal, and was called after

the great Nawab Murshid Kuli Khan,[1] the original name being Maksudabad, whence the Muxadabad of old records. It was a prosperous place in the last century, and owed much of its wealth to its being upon the line of trade from the interior of India to the European settlements on the Hoogly.

Though the population (87,000) is decreasing, a number of Jain merchants may yet be found here, who deal in carved ivory — a speciality of the place, embroideries, etc. An introduction to the Nawab of Murshidabad through the magistrate and collector, who resides at Berhampur, will greatly facilitate the sightseeing of the place.

The *Raft Festival* is still celebrated here, in honour of Khwaja Khizr (the prophet Elias) on certain nights.

The *Palace of the Nawab*, which with the surrounding buildings enclosed by a wall goes by the name of the *Nizamat Kila*, is situated on the river bank about the centre of the town, and is in the Italian style, somewhat resembling Government House at Calcutta. It was built in 1837 at a cost of £167,000, the architect being General Macleod of the Bengal Engineers. It contains a circular Darbar-room, and a Banqueting room 290 ft. long, with a picture of the burial of Sir John Moore, by Marshall, at the W. end, and many other handsome apartments. The Armoury is well worthy of a visit. In the Library are some very rare MSS.

In the same enclosure with the palace is the *Imambarah*, built in 1847.

Just outside the city is the *Katra*, containing the tomb of Murshid Kuli Khan. It was constructed on the model of the Great Mosque at Mecca, with two minarets 70 ft. high, but is now in ruins.

Near this, and 60 yds. from the road, is the *Great Gun*, the sister gun to that at Dacca. It is 17½ ft. long, with a girth of 5 ft. at the breech and a calibre of 6 in. This cannon, which had been left lying on the ground for many years, has been lifted up 5 ft. in the air by a pipal tree which has grown up from a seedling beneath it. The inscription is in Persian, with the date 1637. S.W. of it and 2 m. S. of the city is

The *Moti Jhil*, or "Pearl Lake," a beautiful spot. Little remains of the palaces at one corner of it, but what remains is very picturesque and is very interesting as containing the marble throne[1] of the Nawab Nazim, by taking his seat on which, as Diwan, Clive notified to the Indian world in 1766 the cession of the province of Bengal to the E.I. Company, under the farman of the Emperor of Delhi, Shah Alam, granted on 12th August 1765. The lake contains a good many alligators.

The *Khush Bagh*, or "Garden of Happiness," the old cemetery of the Nawabs, is opposite to the Moti Jhil on the right bank of the river. It consists of three walled enclosures. The entrance to the outer one, planted with flowers and shady trees, is from the E., close to where some ruined ghats stretch down to the deserted bed of the Bhagirathi, which now flows in another channel. In the central enclosure are the tombs of the good Nawab Ali Vardi Khan and his grandson Suraj-ud-daulah. They are almost level with the ground, and are covered with embroideries. The third enclosure contains a tank and Musafir Khana. (Rest-house.) Near this garden is the Hira (diamond) Jhil where the Mansurganj Palace stood.

The *Nizamat College* is exclusively for relatives of the Nawab.

The *Cemetery of J'afar Gunj*, about 1 m. to the N. of the palace of Murshidabad, is that of the Nawabs

[1] The well-known Subahdars and Nawab Nazims of Bengal were Murshid Kuli Khan (known also as Jafir Khan, a converted Brahman), died 1725; Shuja Khan, died 1728; Alivardi Khan, died 1756; Suraj-ud-daulah; Mir Jafir (p. 309), and Mir Kasim (pp. 35 and 312). The famous Jain Seth family of Murshidabad which bore the title of Jagat Seth, or World Trader, and played a prominent part in the affairs of Bengal in the 18th century, resided at Mahimapur, 2 m. N. of Murshidabad.

[1] This is to be removed to the Victoria Memorial Hall in Calcutta.

Nazim appointed by the English, and contains a number of interesting graves. Opposite the gate is a handsome mosque.

The Murshidabad district is noted for its *silk* industry. The villagers rear the silkworm at home, and sell the cocoons to the spinners, who export it. Silk-cloth and handkerchiefs are woven here on hand-looms.

From Murshidabad the railway runs on to

144 m. **Lal Gola Ghat** on the Ganges, whence there is occasional steamer service to Rajmahal (p. 307). A line from Godagari Ghat on the opposite side of the river runs to 195 m. Maldah (p. 307) and 251 m. Katihar (p. 311).

(*d*) From Calcutta by Eastern Bengal Railway to Darjeeling by Damukdia, Silliguri, and Kurseong.

Fares, Rs.49, Rs.25, and Rs.8. Mail train in 21 hours.

The train starts from the Sealdah station (p. 64).

23 m. Naihati junction for Hooghly junction bridge (p. 68).

45 m. **Ranaghat** junction, D.B. [Branch E. for Jessore and Khoolna, and W. to Murshidabad (77 m.).]

103 m. **Poradaha** junction station. [Branch line E. to 52 m. Goalundo Ghat on the Ganges, p. 318.]

122 m. **Damudkia** station on the right bank of the Ganges. — Steam ferry across the river to Sara Ghat.

The distance from the right bank station to **Sara Ghat** station, is about 13 m., crossed mostly on temporary rails in the dry season. The actual journey by steamer (R.) occupies about 20 minutes. The Lower Ganges Bridge, 3 m. below the Ghat, will be the longest in India, and is expected to cost £2,000,000. Its foundations are being sunk 150 ft. below the water, and the line will be 70 ft. above the stream. At Sara Ghat the Northern Bengal Railway, metre gauge, commences.

184 m. **Santahar** junction of line to Assam (p. 321).

244 m. **Parbatipur** junction (R.), from whence a line runs E. to Kaunia on the Assam mail route (p. 321), and W. to 88 m. Katihar (p. 311).

305 m. **Jalpaiguri** (R.), civil station of the E. Bengal district of the same name. In the district are nearly two hundred tea-gardens, producing 54,000,000 lbs. of tea yearly. Elephants are still found in considerable numbers in the district, and 198 were captured in 1901-02.

[From Jalpaiguri Ghat a boat leaves for *Teesta Ghat*; thence a train runs to *Dam Dim*.]

328 m. **Silliguri** station (R.), D.B.

From this place to Darjeeling the journey is made by the *Himalayan Railway* on a gauge of 2 ft. The distance is 50 m., and the time occupied 5½ hours.—Fares, Rs. 19, and Rs. 2 as. 10.

The line is constructed in the most substantial manner, with heavy steel rails (40 lbs. to the yd.). The locomotives, specially designed by Messrs Sharpe and Stewart of Manchester, weigh 10 tons. The running speed of the trains, both up and down, is about 12 to 13 m. per hour, and travellers ascend over 1000 ft. an hour. It is worthy of note that this is the first work of the kind for which the capital required was raised entirely in India.

Travellers are strongly advised to have extra warm clothing at hand, as the transition of temperature from the plains to the mountains is sometimes very great. Spectacles or veils should be used against the dust and blacks from the engine, especially on the front seats of the open carriages, from which the best views are obtained. Only hand luggage can be taken into the carriages.

[Silliguri was lately of special interest as the base of the expedition in Thibet, Lhassa being 359 m. distant by the most direct route. A road leads from Silliguri to the Teesta Bridge (p. 317), then rises steadily for two stages, and finally proceeds as a track to Gnathong (12,000 ft.), 83 m. from

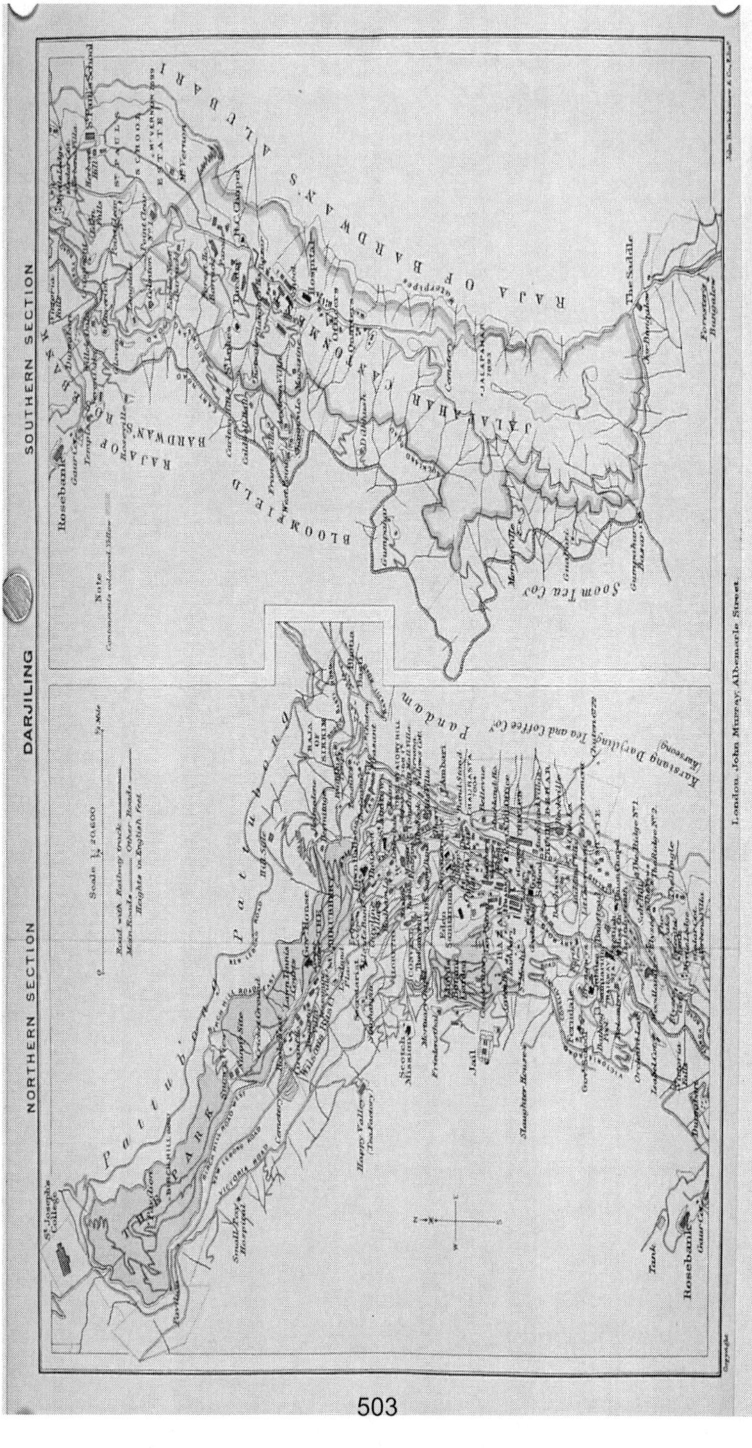
DARJILING
NORTHERN SECTION
SOUTHERN SECTION
London. John Murray, Albemarle Street.

the base. Between Gnathong and Chumbi, 20 m. N., the Jalap La Pass (14,400 ft.) is crossed, and 21 m. further Pari Jong is reached. From here the direct trade route turns N.E. to Lhassa, which is about 200 m. distant. The route to Gyangtse (13,200 ft.) crosses the Tang La Pass (16,200 ft.); 42 m. further on it crosses the Kharo La Pass (16,500 ft.), and then the Khamba La Pass (16,800 ft.), and finally reaches the Chaksam Ferry in 323 m. Crossing the Tsangpo here the route goes up the Kyi valley to Lhassa, 359 m., 12,300 ft. above sea-level.]

At **Sookna** station, 7 m. from Silliguri, the cars begin to ascend. The turns are very sharp, and at each a fresh landscape of surpassing beauty is opened out. The sides of the mountain are clothed with lofty trees and masses of jungle, with graceful tree-ferns in the ravines at the higher altitudes. At about 15 m. the cars pass round a spur which projects from the mountain, and the line runs on the edge of a precipice of 1000 ft. Further up the line threads an extraordinary loop. Breakfast can be taken at

19½ m. **Teendaria** (R.).

At 32 m. **Kurseong** station ✱ (R.), D.B., there are tea-gardens, with European managers and medical men residing on them. Kurseong is 5000 ft. above sea-level. Those who stray off the main paths in damp weather must take precautions against the leeches, which are numerous.

51 m. **Darjeeling**[1] (place of the thunderbolt). The beauty of its situation, upon a ridge high (about 7000 ft.) above the bed of the Great Ranjit River, the mountain-side scattered over with villas and bungalows, and the colossal background of Himalayan giants towering above it, together with its moderate temperature, which neither exceeds 80° in summer nor falls below 30° in winter, tend to make Darjeeling a most agreeable residence, and have rendered it the most important sanitorium of Bengal.

From Darjeeling the highest **Mountain Peaks** in the world can be seen. Of these the loftiest is *Mount Everest*, 29,002 ft. visible from *Tiger Hill* (a 6-m. ride from Darjeeling) or from *Jelapahar*, the military cantonment, though the distance is at least 120 m. The other peaks seen from Darjeeling or Jelapahar are: the magnificent array of the Kinchinjanga peaks (28,156 ft. high and 45 m. distant); to the W. of these, Kabru (24,015 ft.) and Jannu (25,304 ft.); to the E. of them Pandim (22,017 ft.), with Jubanu (19,450 ft.) in front of it and only 35 m. distant; and further E. again the fine snowy peak of Simolchun (22,270 ft.). Much of the surface of the highest peaks is too sheer for snow to lie upon it.

The view of unrivalled **Mountain Scenery**, is unspeakably grand, and there are many views, and particularly that of Kinchinjanga, which impress the mind more and more every time that they are seen. Too often, unfortunately, clouds veil the highest peaks for days together, and there is no certainty of an unclouded view of Kinchinjanga in the cold weather, though such views are often obtained, especially after rain. When the clouds roll away, and display the bare granite summits, one looks over the lofty hills and across a vast chasm to the line of perpetual snow, about 17,000 ft. high, on the side of the stupendous Kinchinjanga. Above that rises a glittering white wall, and then it seems as if the sky were rent and the view is closed by enormous masses of bare rock. There is one special feature in the summit of Kinchinjanga, and that is a lofty wall of granite of prodigious breadth, which appears to divide the summit into two portions. The effect is much more striking than if it were one great mass of snow. The extraordinary grandeur of this scene is heightened by the colouring given

[1] Every one visiting Darjeeling should read Mr Douglas Freshfield's delightful *Round Kinchinjanga*

to it by the rising and setting sun, or by the moon.

The **District of Darjeeling** (population over 155,000) is divided into two portions: the N. is from 4000 to 9000 ft. above the sea-level; the S., or *Morang*, consists of the spurs of the first range of the Himalayas and the plains thence to the District of Rungpur. Mountains which rise to between 12,000 and 13,000 ft. divide it from Nepal. When Dr. Campbell took charge in 1839, there were only twenty families in the whole district: he remained superintendent for twenty-two years, built the bazaar, the cutcherry, and church, made roads, and established a convalescent depôt at **Jelapahar**, the *Military Cantonment* S. of Darjeeling.

Darjeeling suffered severely from the earthquake of 1897 and the great storm of September 1899. On the *Mall* is the bandstand and a drinking fountain erected to the memory of Sir Ashley Eden. Near this are some pretty gardens, and the *Eden Sanatorium* or *Convalescent Hospital*, a most conspicuous building, in the charge of the Clewer Sisters.

Above the Secretariat is *St Andrew's Church*, the foundation-stone of which was laid by Bishop Milman in 1870.

The old church dates from 1843. There are tablets in it to George W. Aylmer Lloyd, C.B., Lieutenant-General H.M.'s Bengal Army, who died at Darjeeling 1865, aged 76. To his influence with the Raja of Sikkim, Bengal is indebted for this sanatorium. Another tablet runs

In Memoriam
CHARLOTTE, COUNTESS CANNING,
November 1862.

There is also a *Union Chapel*, in Auckland Road. About ½ m. beyond the church is *The Shrubbery*, the large and comfortable residence of the Lieutenant-Governor of Bengal, who spends May and June, September and October here. St Paul's and St Joseph's schools are large establishments.

The principal **Bazaar** is in the centre of the town; on Sundays it is so thronged by picturesque natives from all parts — Lepchas, Limbus, Bhutias, Tibetans, Nepalese, and Paharis, that it is difficult to make way through them.

On the top of the ridge above the church is a Buddhist stupa, round which tiny offerings and bits of rags will always be found. Some way below the ridge on the E. side is an interesting Buddhist temple of a distinctly Tibetan type in the picturesque village of **Bhutia Basti**. It is worthy of a visit not only on account of the temple, but also to see the hill-people who inhabit the small village.

The Botanical Gardens at **Rungarun** contain an interesting collection of trees and plants peculiar to the Himalayas.

The chief industry of Darjeeling is the cultivation and manufacture of *Tea*. The date of its commencement is 1856, when the first tea-garden was opened. There are now nearly 160, covering an area of some 51,000 acres, with an output of over 15,000,000 lbs.

There is not much game to be had in the immediate neighbourhood of Darjeeling, but to the able pedestrian, the botanist, the lover of the picturesque, there are endless excursions.

(1.) A good rider, or strong Alpine climber, may make an interesting expedition of four days by **Tonglu** to **Phallut**, in the heart of the snows. The distances are to

Jor Pokri (10,130 ft.);
Tonglu (10,070 ft.), 23 m.;
Sundukpho (11,975 ft.), 15 m.;
Phallut (11,811 ft.), 13 m.;
Suburkim (11,684 ft.).

The views are magnificent. There is a good D.B. at each of the above stations, except the last. Provisions and bedding must be taken.

(2.) Another very favourite and interesting excursion is to the **Bridge** *over the Great* **Ranjit River**, 6000 ft. below. An excellent road has been made, by which the whole descent can be easily performed on ponies, the distance by the road being 11 m. The zones of vegetation are clearly marked, first by the oak, chestnut, and magnolia, which grow from 10,000 ft. to 7000 ft.; secondly, below 6500 ft. by the *Alsophila gigantea* or tree-fern (to be seen from the Himalayas to the Malayan Peninsula, in Java and Ceylon); thirdly, by the Calamus and Plectocomia palms (6500 ft. is the upper limit of palms in Sikkim); fourthly, by the wild plantain, which in a lower elevation is replaced by a larger kind. At 1000 ft. below Darjeeling is a fine wooded spur called **Libong**, where English fruit trees flourish, and the tea-plant also succeeds admirably. Below is the village of Ging, surrounded by slopes cultivated principally with tea, also with rice, maize, and millet.

At 10 m. distance from Darjeeling is *the junction of the* **Ranjit** *with the* **Rangmo**. The Ranjit's foaming stream runs through a dense forest. From the opposite direction the Rangmo comes tearing down from the top of Senchal, 7000 ft. above. Its roar is heard and its course is visible, but its channel is so deep that the stream itself is nowhere seen.

Farther down is *the junction of the* **Ranjit** *with the* **Teesta**, which is sea-green and muddy, while the Great Ranjit is dark green and very clear. The Teesta is much the broader, deeper, and more rapid. This expedition will take two days.

If time permits and the weather is favourable, it is well worth following the Teesta valley down to Silliguri (see above) instead of returning by train from Darjeeling.

(3) **Senchal**, 8610 ft., is clearly seen from Jelapahar, and is about 6 m. off. It used to be a depôt for European troops. The water for Darjeeling is taken in pipes from the Senchal springs. An expedition may be made to it, starting early in the morning. It is comparatively easy of access, and from Jelapahar the path along the ridge of the mountains may be seen. This path abounds in rare and beautiful plants, and traverses magnificent forests of oak, magnolia, and rhododendron.

Nearly thirty ferns may be gathered on this excursion in the autumn. Grasses are very rare in these woods, except the dwarf bamboo.

ROUTE 23A.

Eastern Bengal and Assam.

The latest created Province of India was separated from Lower Bengal and combined with the charge of Assam on 16th October 1905. It lies between 20° 45′ and 28° 17′ N. lat., and 87° 48′ and 97° 15′ E. long., and contains an area of 111,569 sq. m., and a population of 31,000,000, of which 18,000,000 are Mohammedans. The headquarters of the Provincial Government are situated at Dacca in the cold weather, and at Shillong in the summer. The present Lieutenant-Governor is the Hon. Sir Lancelot Hare, K.C.S.I., C.I.E., and the Lieutenant-Governor Designate Sir C. S. Bayley, K.C.S.I. The southern portion of the Province comprises the deltas of the Ganges and Brahmaputra with the port of Chittagong. Assam Proper consists of the upper valley of the Brahmaputra, the Tsanpo of Thibet; and between these two main tracts lie the Sylhet and Cachar valleys drained by the Surma, with the Garo and Khasi hills N. of them, and the Manipur State and Naga country E. of them.

A combined visit to Eastern Bengal, the Sylhet and Cachar valleys and Assam is best made by the route by railway to Goalundo, and thence by (1) steamer to Narainganj, or (2) Chandpur routes below. A visit to Assam only, or a combined visit to Darjeeling and Assam, will be more comfortably accomplished by the Eastern Bengal Railway route by Santahar junction, Kaunia, Gitaldaha, and Golakganj—Route (3). The thro' river services, once the only means of approach to all ports of Assam, have now been superseded by the railways for the purposes of all ordinary travellers.

(1) Calcutta to Dacca *viâ* Goalundo and Naraingan j.

[For the journey from Calcutta to **Poradaha** junction station (103 m.) see p. 314.]

150 m. **Goalundo Ghat** station, the terminus of the Eastern Bengal Railway, is close to the junction of the Ganges and Brahmaputra rivers, which below this point are called first the Padma, and then the Meghna river, and form a body of water so wide across that in the centre the low shores are scarcely visible.

Goalundo has no permanent buildings, as the river banks at this point have for many years past changed constantly, and the river floods have destroyed everything that has been built.

"About £130,000 had been spent upon these protective works, and it was hoped that engineering skill had conquered the violence of the Gangetic floods. But in August 1875 the solid masonry spurs, the railway station, and the magistrates' court, were all swept away, and deep water covered their site. A new Goalundo terminus had to be erected 2 m. inland from the former river-bank" (Hunter).

There are plenty of native boats at Goalundo, and a regular daily service by steamer in 6 to 9 hours to Naraingan j (104 m. for Dacca); and to *Chandpur* for *Chittagong* and *Assam* by railway, in 7 hours.

259 m. **Naraingan j**, D.B. (population, 24,500), is the port of Dacca, and the terminus of the *Naraingan j-Dacca-Mymensing Railway.* There are several old forts in the neighbourhood, built by Mir Jumla in the 17th century; and almost opposite stands the *Kadam Rasul*, a small mosque held in great repute by the local Mohammedans.

10 m. **Dacca** (23° 43' N. and 90° 24' E.) The railway station lies N. of the city. The new D.B. is near it and beyond are the new buildings of the headquarters of the Government of Eastern Bengal and Assam.

The city, which was once a place of great importance, and is believed to have had 200,000 inhabitants as late as 1800, has now a population of 110,000 only. It fell on evil times from the middle of the 18th century, but is now likely to revive under its present new conditions and by the aid of railway communications with the west now under consideration. Much of the country round it is largely under water during the rainy season.

When Akbar's generals conquered Eastern Bengal in 1575 the capital was at Sunargaon 20 m. E. of Dacca. Early in the reign of Jahangir it was moved here by the Governor, Islam Khan, grandson of Shaikh Salem Chishti (p. 184). The old Mughal Fort has entirely disappeared; the Lal Bagh was built by Muhammad Azim, son of Aurangzeb, in 1677. The Court was removed to Murshidabad in 1704, and from that time the decay of the place set in. The English factors settled here first in 1666, and not long afterwards were subjected to great oppression by the Governor, Shaista Khan, nephew of the Empress Nur Jahan: a hundred years later their countrymen were masters of the whole country. Their factory was near the old Government College—the French factory was on the site of the Nawab's present palace, and the Dutch on that of the Mitford hospital. In 1857 the companies of N. Infantry in Dacca were disarmed by a body of sailors of the Indian Navy sent up from Calcutta.

The present city stretches for nearly 4 miles along the N. bank of the Buri Ganga, from beyond the Lal Bagh on the W. to beyond the suspension bridge over the Dholai creek on the E. Along the E. side the fine Buckland Band with grass slopes to the water's edge runs along the river, and behind this are the present palace of the Nawab of Dacca, Sir Salimullah Khan, K.C.S.I., grandson of the well-known Nawab Sir Abdul Ghani, and the residences of the Collector and Commissioner. From near the E. end of the Band a main route runs N. past the Club, the R.C. Cathedral, the old College, the Church, and the District Offices, and over the Dholai creek to the Railway Station. N.W. of the Station is the new Dacca College; N. of that is Govt. House, and W. are the Secretariat Offices. Near the Race-course, still further N., is an old Armenian and Protestant cemetery with some fine trees. The oldest English grave dates from 1724. The main street runs 1½ m. parallel to the river from the Dholai suspension bridge of 1830, past the Chauk, or central square, to the Lal Bagh. In the Chauk is a fine old gun said to be sister of that at Murshidabad (p. 313), and on the E. side of it is the mosque of Shaista Khan. From the Chauk another main thoroughfare leads N. to the new Quarter. Between it and the river are the Bara and Chota Katras, or market caravansarais built in 1645 by Sultan Muhammad Shuja, son of Shahjahan, and S.E. of them is the Mitford Hospital. The Lal Bagh contains the fine tomb of Pari Bibi, a daughter of Shaista Khan, and on the N. side the ruined mosque of Prince Azim.[1] Some distance to the N.W. of the Lal Bagh, and beyond the large mosque of Khan Muhammad Mirdha and the old elephant Kheddah, which used to be one of the sights of Dacca, is the Satgumbaz (seven-domed) mosque of Shaista Khan.

A considerable quantity of *gold* and *silver plate* of original design and excellent workmanship is still made at Dacca, chiefly for export to Calcutta; also gold and silver filigree work of great excellence. The manufacture of shell bracelets is a specialty.

The once celebrated Dacca *muslins* —*ábrawán*, or "running water," *baft-hawa*, or "woven air," *shabnam* or "evening dew"—are almost a thing of the past; and the demand in Europe for the old cotton flowered and sprigged muslin has almost entirely fallen off. But there is a brisk and increasing demand for *tussore* embroidered muslins (*kasidas*); and other kinds of muslin are still made here. When Burke prepared his impeachment of Warren Hastings, the output of the muslins and silks of Dacca was declared to have an annual value of £350,000.

[1] The S. bastions of the enclosure afford a fine view of the river and its city front.

Dacca is a good place for *Pig-sticking* and *Tiger-shooting*. There are extensive ruins at Sunargaon, but they can be visited only on an elephant.

The railway from Dacca proceeds N. to

86 m. **Mymensing** station (R.) and

139 m. **Jagganathganj**. The Assam steamer leaving Goalundo in the early morning, reaches Jagganathganj at 11 P.M. the same day.

(2) Calcutta by Goalundo and Chandpur to Chittagong, and to Gauhati in 41 hours, by Assam Bengal Railway.

Fares, Rs.74 and Rs.10.

There is a regular service of steamers from Goalundo, in connection with the mail train from Calcutta to **Chandpur**. There is also direct steamer communication from Dacca in 5½ hrs. From Chandpur the Assam Bengal Railway runs to

31 m. **Laksam Junction** station. Here the S. branch of the line runs to

81 m. **Chittagong** station the S. terminus (population 22,000; annual value of import trade £1,000,000, and of export trade £3,500,000). It is the chief town of the division and district of the same name, which came into British possession by cession in 1760. It was once part of the Hindu Kingdom of Tipperah—was burnt by the Portuguese in 1538—was recaptured by the Mughals from the Raja of Arrakan in 1668—and was the cause of the first Burmese War. The port, 12 m. from the sea up the Karnaphuli River, is a very good one, and its trade is rapidly increasing. The Port Trust income is £9000, the Pilotage Fund income £2200. It is proposed to construct a railway from Chittagong to Akyab, and on to Prome (p. 465).

From **Laksam** Junction the Bengal Assam Railway runs N. to 15 m. *Comilla*, 44 m. *Akhaura*, 124 m.

Kulaura, and 171 m. **Badarpur**, and from the last by a branch line 18 m. to

190 m. **Silchar** (D.B., population 9000), headquarters of the **Cachar** District, annexed in 1830. The wild tea-plant was discovered here in 1855. From Kulaura a branch line is being constructed to **Sylhet** (D.B., population 14,000), on the lower valley of the Surma river. At present this place is reached by road from Silchar to Fenchuganj 19 m., whence it is 15 m. on. There is also a steamer service to Fenchuganj from Naraingan. Both Sylhet and Silchar have suffered severely from earthquakes on various occasions.

From Akhaura a branch line runs S.W. to Bhadab Bazar, and will fork from that place to Dacca and Mymensingh.

From Badarpur the Bengal Assam Railway continues N. to

287 m. **Lumding Junction**, from which place the line runs 112 m. to Gauhati, and to 494 m. **Tinsukia Junction.**

Gauhati, D.B. The cold weather headquarters of Assam[1] were at Gauhati, once the capital of the Ahom (Shan) kings. The place was almost destroyed by the earthquake of 1897, but no signs of this catastrophe are now visible. The situation of it on the S. bank of the Brahmaputra, which here resembles a lake with mountains and wooded shores, is very pretty. In the middle of the river is Peacock Island, with a picturesque temple on it: and on the mainland is another temple on the top of a hill approached by winding flights of steps.

[There is a very good road (63 m.) from Gauhati S. to

Shillong,* D.B., the summer headquarters of the E. Bengal and Assam Government, and a military cantonment. Lat. 25° 33′, long. 91° 55′. The roadside vegetation makes this journey a delightful one. There is a motor and tonga-pony service to Shillong. The charge for each seat in the former is Rs. 18; only 20 seers of luggage are allowed. There is a motor lorry service for heavy luggage. There are small D.Bs. at Barni Hat (16 m.), at Naya Bungalow (45 m.), and Borpan (54m.); and at the half-way house, Nangpoh, there is a very comfortable bungalow, with servants, and the motor-car halts here for 45 m. After the last bungalow at Borpani the ascent becomes nearly continuous, and the pine forests (*Pinus Kasya*) give the landscape almost a European appearance. The height of Shillong is 4900 ft. above sea-level, the average rainfall 87·44 in. The temperature seldom reaches 80° F., and there is an almost total absence of mist, the great drawback of most Indian hill-stations.

32 m. S. of Shillong is **Cherrapunji** (4455 ft.), the road to which was badly damaged by the earthquake of 1897. The place is famous for the highest annual rainfall in the world, 450 inches: in 1861 an extraordinary record amounted to 905 inches, of which 366 inches fell in July alone. From Cherrapunji a steep road leads in 10 m. to Theria in the Surma Valley, and so to Sylhet.]

The railway from Lumding Junction continues N.E. past Manipur Road (Dimapur), Titabor and Moriani (from which two short branches run to Jorhat, and to Gosainganj on the Brahmaputra), and then 104 m. more to 494 m. **Tinsukia**, whence one branch of 27 m. leads to Dibrugarh, surrounded by tea-gardens, and another dividing at Makum runs N. to Talap, near the river, and S. to Margherita, called after the Queen of Italy, where the Assam coal-fields are situated: the output of coal is about 300,000 tons annually, paying a royalty of Rs. 72,000. Five m. farther S. the line ends at Ledo. It is under contemplation to construct a railway from here down the Hukong Valley to Mogaung (p. 461).

Dibrugarh (pop. 11,600) is the headquarters of the Lakhimpur District, and of the Assam Light Horse.

From Dimapur, the main road to Manipur (134 m.), runs S. through **Samaguting** and **Kohima** (46 m.). The road is tolerable except during the rains, but hilly; it is supplied

[1] Any one specially interested in Assam should consult Mr Rait's History of the country.

with Rest-Houses, but provisions must be taken: carts at a charge of R.1 as.8 to Rs.2 per diem can be hired for the journey.

Imphal, the capital of **Manipur**, was the scene of the lamentable disaster in 1891, when Mr Grimwood the Resident, Mr Quinton the Chief Commissioner of Assam, and several British officers and their men, were treacherously massacred by the natives. The game of hockey on horseback was formerly almost peculiar to Manipur, but has now become popular under the name of polo. The famous breed of Manipur ponies, which stand nearly 12 hands high, has suffered severely of late years. The valley is 2500 ft. above the sea.

Tea Industry.

Among all the Provinces of India that of Eastern Bengal and Assam is distinguished by its production of tea. The 934 gardens, with an area of 437,000 acres under tea, and an out-turn of 229,000,000 of lbs., are distributed as follows:—Assam, 439; Silchar, 159; Sylhet, 124; Julpaigari, 187. The industry shows a steady increase.

The wild tea was first discovered in Manipur, and from that State much tea seed was till lately imported to Cachar; but for 60-70 years little or no advantage was taken of the discovery. Any traveller wishing to visit tea-gardens will have no difficulty in obtaining an introduction to some planter from friends, or through friends from the London or Calcutta Agents of a tea estate, and thereupon will be sure of a hospitable reception. The tea districts are for the most part well furnished with driving roads and rest-houses.

(3) By E. Bengal Railway in 27 hours from Calcutta to 470 m. Gauhati, the centre of the Assam Valley proper.—Fares, Rs.44 and Rs.6.

The direct route to Gauhati from Calcutta (Sealdah) follows the same course as that to Darjeeling as far as

184 m. **Santahar** junction.

It then swings E. to

209 m. **Bogra**, and from that place runs N. parallel to the Brahmaputra to

277 m. **Kaunia**. [Here a branch line connecting N. Behar and Darjeeling with Assam runs W. to 33 m. Parbatipur.] From Kaunia the line proceeds to **Teesta** junction, crossing the Teesta by a bridge 2100 ft. long, to

287 m. **Lal Manir Hat**, and

295 m. **Gitaldaha** junction.

[From here a branch, 2′6″ gauge, line runs N. to **Cooch Behar**, of which the Koch Chief is Maharaja Colonel Nripendra Narayan, G.C.I.E., C.B., A.D.C. The State has an area of 1300 sq. m., a population of 600,000, and a revenue of 23 lakhs. The country has been famous for its large game shooting.]

The Assam line turns E. again round the elbow of the Brahmaputra, to

309 m. **Golakganj** junction.

[Branch to 332 m. **Dhubri**, once the usual starting-place of the short steamer route to Gauhati. Steamers still run between these two places by Goalpara, the journey of 330 m. occupying about 41 hours. Travellers can proceed by steamer to *Tezpore*, the next day to *Nigriting*, and about 24 hours later will reach *Dibrugarh*, but will probably prefer the railway route (*viâ* Lumding).

Travellers must remember that the cold wind caused by the movement of the vessel may be penetrating, and that warm clothes are therefore necessary. The scenery is moderately pretty only; on the right (left bank) are the Garo Hills, and away on the left, if the atmosphere is clear, may be seen the grand range of the Himalayas, and the wooded Bhutan Hills in the middle distance; the snowy range is seen all along the river, and showing to special advantage at sunrise. At **Goalpara**, D.B., situated at the foot of a conical hill (left bank), may be seen picturesque native merchants and wild hill tribesmen, who come down from the mountains to trade in skins, etc. Above this numbers of alligators will be noticed basking, on the sandbanks, in the sun.]

Hence the line runs at a distance from the river to 395 m. **Sorbhog** and

462 m. **Amingaon.** A ferry crosses the Brahmaputra between this and

464 m. **Panda,** from which a short line runs on to

470 m. **Gauhati** (p. 320).

ROUTE 24

CALCUTTA to MADRAS by **Balasore, Cuttack, Bhuvaneshwar** (visit to **Udyagiri Caves, Puri,** and the **Black Pagoda**), **Ganjam, Vizianagram, Waltair** for **Vizagapatam, Bezwada** and **Nellore**—Bengal Nagpur Railway from **Howrah** to **Waltair,** and Madras and S. Mahratta Railway, N.E. section, from **Waltair** to **Madras.**

(Distance 1032 m.; time occupied by mail train, 39½ hours; fares, Rs.91, Rs.44, Rs.13 as.7).

Howrah—Calcutta (see p. 67).

20 m. **Ulubaria** (see p. 70).

34 m. **Kola Ghat** (R.). Here the railway crosses the Rupnarain River, a large tidal river flowing into the Hooghly, near its junction with which are the famous James and Mary sands, the scene of so many wrecks in that river (p. 70). The bridge over this river, about ½ m. in length, is a very fine one, and from the engineering difficulties met with in construction it ranks as one of the most important bridges in India.

72 m. **Kharagpur** junction for line to Nagpur, Bhusawal, and Bombay (see Route 7).

[From Kharagpur there is also a branch to 8 m. **Midnapur,** an old station of the E.I. Company (population, 33,000). The spot in the Midnapur District originally famous was the Buddhist seaport of Tamluk (p. 70). Another branch to the N.W. runs through Bankurah to 103 m. Adra junction between Sini and Asansol (p. 87).

144 m. **Balasore** (R.), D.B. Headquarters of a Civil District and an Ordnance station for testing shells and guns. The open sea makes it a favourite resort, and it promises to become in the near future a large watering-place. The delicious pomfret fish is procurable, and is finding its way into the Calcutta market. There are large Roman Catholic and Baptist Missions in the town. The place, of which the correct name is Bhaleshwar, was once of great commercial importance, and both the Dutch and the Danes had factories here; Pipli in the district was the first spot at which in 1634 the English E.I. Company established a factory in Bengal, and from here the Balasore factory was founded in 1642 in accordance with the grant issued by the Delhi Emperor at the request of Mr Gabriel Broughton. There are two curious old Dutch tombs, dated 1683, built like three-sided pyramids about 20 ft. high in a small secluded enclosure near the native part of the town.

202 m. **Jajpur Road** for Jajpur, 7 m. to the W. (D.B.). The ruins[1] at Jajpur, once the capital of Orissa, are fine and interesting, but probably only an antiquarian will care to visit them. The chief object is a fine pillar 32 ft. high, standing on a base 5 ft. 5 in. high, square, and composed of large blocks of stone without any ornament. The shaft and capital are 26 ft. 7 in. high, and appear to be a monolith. The capital, of exquisite proportion, is carved to imitate lotus blossoms, and adorned below with lions' heads from whose mouths depend strings of roses or beads. The capital once was crowned with a figure of the Garuda or eagle-vehicle of Vishnu. The Garuda is said to have been hurled from the summit of the pillar by the Mohammedans, who attempted also to destroy the pillar itself; it is now in the temple of Narsingh, 1 m. S. of the temple of Jagannath. The finest temple was that of Trilochan, the Three-Eyed; on the Bingapur road is a well-built ancient bridge. In the compound of the District Magistrate adjoining

[1] There is an excellent little handbook of Cuttack, Jajpur, Bhuvaneshwar, Udyagiri, Puri, and Kanarak, by Mr Brown, Judge of Cuttack.

the D.B. are three monolithic statues of Indrani on her elephant, Varahani with the boar, and Chamundi (p. 77) represented as the Goddess of Famine; and in a dry bed of the river are seven other statues each 6 ft. high. Near the D.B. is also the fine mosque of Nawab Abu Nasir Khan, built in 1681 A.D.

254 m. **Cuttack,** ✱ D.B. (population, 51,000), is situated at the apex of the delta of the Mahanadi river, which rises in the Raipur district of the Central Provinces, and has a length of 529 m. It rushes down upon the delta through the narrow gorge of Naraj, 7 m. W. of the town of Cuttack, and, dividing into two streams, encircles the city on the N. and E., and on the W. by its branch, called the Katjuri. The river during the rains pour down a prodigious flood, and to prevent its sweeping away the city, an important stone embankment has been erected on the spit of land on which that stands.

Cuttack is the headquarters of **Orissa.** It was founded in the 10th century A.D. by one of the kings of the Kesari, or Lion, dynasty. Its position as the key of the Orissa hill territory, and the centre of the network of the Orissa canals, gives it both military and commercial importance. It is famed for its filigree work in gold and silver.

The **Fort**, called Fort Barabati, is in ruins, and all that remains of it now is a fine gateway. It was taken by the British in 1803. In the public gardens on the Taldanda Canal are a beautifully carved arch and some other carved stones.

Near Cuttack are important weirs for regulating the flow of the rivers. Two of these, the Birupa and Mahanadi, may be seen in quitting the place. A road a little to the N. of the Taldanda Canal leads to the Jobra Ghat, where are the Great D.P.W. workshops and the Mahanadi Weir, which is 6400 ft. long and 12½ ft. high, and cost in round numbers thirteen lakhs of rupees. It was begun in 1863 and completed in 1869-70. The Birupa river leaves the Mahanadi on its right bank, and the weir there is 1980 ft. long and 9 ft. high. Of the four canals which form the Orissa Irrigation System, two take off from the Birupa Wier, and one with its branch from the Mahanadi Weir.

Within 11 m. N. and S. of Cuttack the railway line is carried over no less than five big bridges, the whole section comprising the most difficult piece of riverain engineering to be seen anywhere in India.

271 m. **Bhuvaneshwar.** The Rest-House (supplies should be taken with one) is at Udyagiri, 4 m. to the N.W. of the station—permission to occupy it should be obtained from the Deputy Collector, Khurda Road, who will also accord leave to occupy a room in the police station at Bhuvaneshwar if this is desired. The best plan for sight-seeing is to proceed from the station to the Udyagiri Rest-House, spend a day in examining the Buddhist caves there, proceed early the second morning to the Asoka Rock at Dhauli, 5 m. S. of Bhuvaneshwar, and return to the latter to visit the temples there and pass the heat of the day at the police station. A palanquin is the only means of locomotion round Bhuvaneshwar, and should be ordered beforehand, with extra bearers if it is desired to move about with a moderate degree of speed.

The Udyagiri Rest-House is only a few yards from the Jain and Buddhist caves. The former are on the Khandagiri Hill at the back of it; the latter are on a projecting spur to the front of it, and date from between 250 B.C. to 100 A.D.

The *Udyagiri Hill*[1] is 110 ft. high, and the caves are excavated in the sides of it at various levels. The first reached from the Rest-House is the Swargapuri cave, from which a level path to the right (E.) leads

[1] See pp. 55-94 of *The Cave Temples of India*, and Fergusson's *Indian Architecture*, ii. 91.

round to the Rani ka Nur and Ganesh Gumpha caves, and winds upward and backwards to below the Hathi Gumpha, where it is joined by the path which runs up steeply to the left from the Swargapuri cave past the Jaya Vijaya and Vaikuntha caves to this point. The Rani ka Nur, or Queen's Palace, faces E. and consists of two rows of cells, one above the other, shaded by pillared verandahs, with a courtyard 49 by 43 ft. cut out of the hillside, and is probably intended to represent the side and two ends of a structural vihara. The upper storey, 63 ft. to the front, which stands back, has eight entrances giving access to four cells. At the N. end are two dwarpals, representing men in armour, with buskins and greaves, cut out of the solid rock in alto-relievo : these are probably figures of the Yavana warriors who conquered Orissa. At either end is a rock lion, executed with some spirit. The back wall of the verandah has an extensive series of tableaux, difficult to make out. First on the left are men carrying fruit, a group of elephants, and soldiers armed with swords—this is probably a scene from Ceylon. Then comes a scene, repeated at the Ganesh Gumpha, of a combat over a woman—and then one of the winged deer presenting itself to the king. The last scene which can be made out represents a love episode.

The lower storey also has eight entrances. The ground-floor front was formed of a colonnaded verandah 44 ft. long, having a raised seat or berm along its whole inner line. It was formerly supported by a row of eight square pillars, of which only the two end ones remain, and opened S. into an oblong chamber, and N. into three rooms. Here also there is an extensive frieze, much dilapidated, so that only four fragments admit of description. The first represents a house, and a female figure looks out of each of the three doors, and one from the balcony, which is protected by a Buddhist rail. A similar rail runs in front of the lower storey, with a large tree by its side. In the second fragment a saint or priest holds a piece of cloth in his left hand and extends the right as in the act of blessing; one servant holds an umbrella, and another carries a sword. Next a devotee on his knees, and beyond two kneeling women bring offerings, one dusting the feet of a boy, who has one hand on her head. In the third fragment is a saddle-horse with three attendants, and the holy man with an umbrella held over him, and two attendants with swords. In the fourth fragment there is a group of six women, three carrying pitchers on their heads, and one kneeling and offering her pitcher to a figure, which is lost. On the right wing are scenes of a man and woman making offerings, and of a woman dancing to the accompaniment of four musicians.

The *Ganesh Gumpha* is almost due N. of the Rani Nur Cave, and much higher in the hill. It has only one storey, and consists of two compartments with a verandah in front. There are three pillars in the front of the verandah, square and massive, and two others have fallen. The pillars have brackets, with female figures carved on them. The flight of steps leading to the verandah has a crouching elephant on either side, each holding a lotus in his trunk. The verandah wall is ornamented with a series of eight tableaux in alto-relievo. This frieze and that in the Rani Nur Cave represent the same story, the main difference being that in this cave the figures are more classical and better drawn, and, therefore, Mr Fergusson thinks, more modern. In the Rani's cave they are certainly more Hindu. The scenes include an escape on elephant back, dismounting from the elephant, and resting in the forest. The Buddhist trisula (trident) and shield are carved on this cave.

The *Swargapuri* has no carving or inscription except on some pilasters near the door, from the top of which runs a line of well-sculptured foliage with an elephant issuing from trees at the end of it.

The *Jaya Vijaya Cave*, a double storeyed one, has a frieze with three compartments, the base being formed of a line of Buddhist rails. In the central compartment is a Bo-tree (p. 37). Beside the tree are two male figures, that on the left with folded hands, and that on the right holding a bit of cloth tied to the tree and a small branch. Near the men are two females bringing trays of offerings. The semicircular bands of scroll-work over the doorways are different, and beyond them are two turbaned figures carrying trays of offerings.

The *Vaikuntha* is a small two-storeyed cave, with the upper storey set back, and a frieze of men and animals across the front. It was probably the prototype of the Rani ka Nur and Ganesh Gumpha.

75 yds. to the N.W. is the *Hathi Gumpha*, or "Elephant Cave," which Mr Fergusson describes as an extensive natural cave, unimproved by art. It is perfectly plain, but has an inscription above it of 117 lines, which is referred to 300 B.C., and is probably the oldest memorial here. To the left is a boulder which has been hollowed out into a cell 5 ft. sq. A few yds. N. of the Elephant Cave is the Pavana Gumpha, or "Cave of Purification"; and about 75 ft. to the S.W. of the Pavana Gumpha is the Sarpa Gumpha, or "Serpent Cave," having on the top of the entrance a rude carving of the hood of a three-headed cobra. Under this is the door, through which a man can just crawl; the interior is a cube of 4 ft. Beside the door is an inscription translated by James Prinsep.

50 feet to the N. is the very interesting *Bagh Gumpha* or Tiger Cave, cut externally into the shape of the upper part of a tiger's head, with the jaws at full gape. The eyes and nose of the monster are still well marked, but the teeth are now imperfectly discernible. The head at top, where it joins the hill, is 8 ft. 8 in. broad. The gape is 9 ft. wide, and the entrance to the cell occupies the place of the gullet. To the right of the entrance is an inseription in the Asoka character. At the beginning of the inscription is a Buddhist monogram, and at the end a Swastika cross.

The *Khandagiri Hill* is 133 ft. high, and faces E. It is thickly covered with trees. The path which leads to the top is steep, and at the height of about 50 ft. divides into two, one branch leading to the left, and to a range of Jain caves cut in the E. face of the hill (see below).

The path on the right leads to the *Ananta* cave, which is a narrow Buddhist excavation, with four doorways and a verandah with pillars and pilasters with decorated sides. Instead of a capital, these have a projecting bracket, shaped like a woman. The architrave is heavy, and over it is a parapet supported on corbels. In the centre of the back wall of the cave is a Buddha in bas-relief. The frieze is in five compartments, and represents figures running with trays of offerings, athletes fighting with bulls and lions, and two lines of geese running with spread wings, each with a flower in its bill. In the semicircular space under one of the arches is a nude female standing in a lotus-bush, and holding a lotus-stalk in either hand. Two elephants are throwing water over her with their trunks. This is a representation of Lakhshmi, the first of the Hindu Pantheon to be revered by the Buddhists. In the other tympanum is a scene of worshipping of a Bo-tree.

The left path leads to a modern gallery, and to the S. to a range of three openings. There is here a Sanscrit inscription of the 12th century recording that the cave belonged to Acharya Kalachandra, and his pupil Vellachandra. Next comes a range of caves facing the E., divided into two compartments by a partition in the middle. On the back wall is a row of seated Dhyani Buddhas, and some new images of Jaina Deva. At the E. end is an altar of masonry, on which are ranged a number of Jain images. The second compartment is very similar. On the back wall is a row of Dhyani Buddhas, 1 ft. high, and below, females seated on stools, some four-handed, others eight-handed, with one leg crossed and the other hanging. Under all are lions *couchant*.

From this to the top of the hill is a stiff climb, and the steps in one place are very steep. On the summit of the hill is a plateau and an 18th century temple to Parasnath. From it is a magnificent panoramic view 15 m. all round. The groves of mango and jack trees are most beautiful. In front of the temple is a fine terrace, 50 ft. sq., with a raised masonry seat all round. To the S.W. of the temple is a smooth terrace of 150 ft. diameter, gently sloping to the W., called the Deva Sabha. In the centre is a small square pillar, with a bas-relief of Buddha on each side, and round it four circles of Chaityas. Three small boulders, set in a triangle and covered by a dolmen of sandstone, stand in the inner circle. E. of the Deva Sabha, at 100 yds., is a tank cut in the solid rock, called the Akasha Ganga, or "heavenly Ganges." Immediately below the tank is a cave, where the remains of Rajah Lelat Indra Kesari are said to rest. These caves probably were originally Buddhist, and were afterwards converted by the Jains.

Bhuvaneshwar. The first mention of Bhuvaneshwar, in the Records of the Temple at Jagannath, dates from the reign of Yayati, 474-526 A.D., the first of the Kesaris, or Lion dynasty of Orissa. He expelled the Yavanas, thought by Stirling and Hunter to be the Buddhists who ruled Orissa for 150 years after a successful invasion about 300 A.D. His successors reigned in Bhuvaneshwar until Nripati Kesari in 940-50 A.D. founded Cuttack and made it his capital.

7000 shrines once encircled the sacred lake; now but 500 remain in various stages of decay, exhibiting every phase of Orissan art "from the rough conceptions of the 6th century, through the exquisite designs and ungrudging artistic toil of the 12th, to the hurried dishonest stucco imitations of the present day." It is easy to perceive that there are two styles of architecture which run side by side with one another. The first is represented by the temples of Parashurameshvara and Mukteshvara, the second by the Great Temple. They are not antagonistic but sister styles, and seem to have had different origins. "We can find affinities with the first two, but I know of nothing like the Great Temple anywhere else."

"The **Great Temple**[1] **is,**" says Mr Fergusson, "perhaps the finest example of a purely Hindu temple in India." Unfortunately none but Hindus may enter the enclosure, the high walls of which are 7 ft. thick and of large cut stones without mortar. From the top, however, of a platform outside the N. wall a view of the interior may be obtained. Besides the Great Temples and the halls of approach to it there are also many smaller temples in the enclosure, of which a plain one 20 ft. high is the oldest; at the N.E. corner is a pavilion perhaps built for a music hall, but now containing an image of Parvati.

The Great Temple was built by Lelat Indra Kesari (617-657) and consisted originally of only a vimanah and porch; the beautiful Nath and Bhog mandirs now in front of it were added between 1090 and 1104. The presiding deity is Tribhuvaneshvara, "Lord of the Three Worlds," generally called Bhuvaneshwar. He is represented in the sanctuary by a block of granite 8 ft. in diameter, and rising 8 in. above the floor, which is bathed with water, milk, and *bhang*. There are twenty-two *dhupas*, or ceremonies daily, consisting in washing the teeth of the divinity, moving a lamp in front, dressing, feeding, etc.

[1] *Indian Architecture*, ii. 92, where a plan and illustration of the Great Temple will be found.

"**The Great Tower** can be seen from outside the wall. It is 180 ft. high, and, though not so large, is decidedly finer in design than that at Tanjore. Every inch of the surface is covered with carving of the most elaborate kind; not only the divisions of the courses, the roll mouldings on the angles, or the breaks on the face of the tower, but every individual stone in the tower has a pattern carved upon it." Especially in the perpendicular parts seen from over the wall, "the sculpture is of a very high order and great beauty of design." The top of the spire is flat, and from the centre rises a cylindrical neck, supporting a ribbed dome, over which is placed the Kalasha or "pinnacle." Twelve statues of lions seated support the dome, and over all is a broken trident. The shrine itself is called the Bara Dewal, and the original Hall of approach to it, the Jagmohan. In front of the latter now is the Bhog Mandir, or Hall of Offerings, and E. of that the Nath Mandir or Dancing Hall. It is elegant, of course, but differs from the style of the porch, in that "all power of expression is gone which enabled the early architects to make small things look gigantic from the mere exuberance of labour bestowed on them."

Outside the enclosure are many small subterraneous temples. The jungle to the S. of the Great Tower, to the extent of 20 acres, is said to be the site of Lelat Indra Kesari's palace, and exhibits everywhere the remains of foundations and pavements. N. of the temple is the very fine tank called *Vindusaugar*, "ocean drop." In the centre is a Jal Mandir, or "Water Pavilion," consisting of several shrines, on which perch numerous cranes in motionless repose. In front of the central ghat of this tank there is a magnificent temple, with a porch, a more modern dancing-hall, and Bhog Mandir. All but the Bhog Mandir are lined with brick-red sandstone, elaborately sculptured. The temple is sacred to *Vasudev*, or Krishna, and *Ananta*, or Balaram, and no pilgrim is allowed to perform any religious ceremony in the town or to visit Bhuvaneshwar without praying for permission here. Along the E. side of the tank will be noticed several temples of the same shape as the Great Temple. About ¼ m. to the E.N.E. of the Ananta and Vasudev Temple is one about 40 ft. high, of *Kotitirtheshvara*, "The lord of ten millions of sacred pools." It is evidently built of stones from some other edifice. ½ m. to the E. of this is the *Temple of Brahmeshvara*, on a high mound, formed into a terrace. It is most sumptuously carved, inside as well as out, and was erected at the end of the 9th century A.D. Close to its terrace on the W. side is a tank called Brahma Kunda. N.E. is an old ruined temple of basalt, to *Bhaskareshvara*, "Sun-god," and said to belong to the close of the 5th or the beginning of the 6th century.

At the N.E. corner of the Great Temple is a very handsome tank surrounded by a row of 108 small temples, and ¾ m. E. of this beyond the Mukteshvara and Parashurameshvara temples is the once magnificent **Temple of Raj Rani.** Mr Fergusson says of it: "The plan is arranged so as to give great variety and play of light and shade, and as the details are of the most exquisite beauty, it is one of the gems of Orissan Art." It faces the E., and has a porch in front, both of dressed brick-red sandstone. The niches are filled with statues 3 ft. high, executed with great vigour and elegance. One pillar has three kneeling elephants and lions, with a Nagni or female Naga with her seven-headed snake hood. Over the doorways are represented the Navagraha or nine planets.

About 300 yds. to the W. of the Raj Rani is a grove of mango trees, called *Siddharanya*, "Grove of the perfect beings." Here many temples were built, of which more than twenty remain entire. Of these the most remarkable are Mukteshvara, Kedareshvara, Siddheshvara, and Parashurameshvara.

Mukteshvara is the handsomest, though the smallest. It is 35 ft. high, and the porch 25 ft. high. The floral bands are better executed than in most of the temples; the bas-reliefs sharp and impressive; the statuettes vigorous and full of action, with drapery well disposed, and the disposition of the whole elegant and most effective. Among the subjects are a lady mounted on a rearing elephant and attacking an armed giant; a figure of Annapurna presenting alms to Shiva; females, half-serpents, canopied under five or seven-headed cobras; lions mounted on elephants, or fighting with lions; damsels dancing or playing on the *mridang;* an emaciated hermit giving lessons. The scroll-work, bosses, and friezes are worthy of note. The chamber of the temple is 7 ft. sq., but outside measures 18 ft. In front of the porch is a Toran 15 ft. high. It is supported on two columns of elaborate workmanship, unlike anything of the kind at Bhuvaneshwar. Over it are two reclining female figures. It is said that it is used for swinging, in the Dol Festival.

Kedareshvara.—Close by a tank behind this temple is the Kedareshvara Temple, and near it against the outer wall of a small room is a figure of Hanuman, the monkey-god, 8 ft. high, and one of Durga, standing on a lion. Her statue is of chlorite, and has the finest female head to be seen in Bhuvaneshwar. The Kedareshvara Temple is 41 ft. high, and has an almost circular ground-plan: it is probably older than the Great Temple, and possibly dates from the middle of the 6th century.

N.W. of Mukteshvara is **Siddeshvara,** which is very ancient, and was once the most sacred spot on this side of Bhuvaneshwar. It is 47 ft. high, and has a well-proportioned porch.

The **Parashurameshvara,** 200 yds. to the W. of the *Mukteshvara,* is considered by Mr Fergusson the oldest temple at Bhuvaneshwar. "The sculptures are cut with a delicacy seldom surpassed." The ground-plan is a square, the porch is oblong and covered with bas-reliefs representing processions of horses and elephants in the upper linear bands under the cornice, and scenes from the life of Rama in the lower. The roof is a sloping terrace, in the middle of which is a clerestory with a slooping roof, flat in the middle. As the roof-stones project beyond the openings, neither direct rays of sun nor rain can penetrate.

The famous **Dhauli** or Aswatama rock, on which is inscribed the best preserved set of edicts of King Asoka, lies between 4 and 5 m. S.E. of Bhuvaneshwar. The rock, unlike that of Shahbazgarhi (p. 246), is an isolated one on the level of the plain in front of a low ridge: the face inscribed is 15 ft. by 10 ft., and above it are the remains of an elephant. The clearness of the inscription, which has been exposed to the sun and storms of twenty-two centuries, is wonderful.

283 m. **Khurda Road**—branch line to (28 m.) **Puri.** The great temple of Jagannath is seen soaring skywards long before Puri is reached. On the N. side of the line some miles W. of Puri may be seen an old Orissan bridge similar to that figured on p. 13, vol. ii. of Fergusson's *Indian Architecture.*

PURI, ✱ D.B. The railway station lies to the N. of the town, and the Civil Station runs along the seashore. Steamers occasionally call at Puri, but there is no shelter for them and no landing-place. The *Circuit House* is near the D.B.; it is roomy, and travellers with an introduction are sometimes allowed to stop there. The *Church* is about 80 yds. distant.

The town of Puri is about 1½ m. in breadth from E. to W., and 3½ m. long from N. to S. The population, which has greatly increased since the opening of the railway, is 49,000; but during the great festivals this number is increased by 100,000 pilgrims. The town covers an area of 1871 acres, including the *Kshetra*,[1] or sacred precincts. It is a city of lodging-houses, and the streets are mean and narrow, except the *Bara-dand*, or road for the Car of Jagannath, when he goes from his temple to his country-house. This road runs through the centre of the town N. and S., and is in places ⅛ furlong wide. The endowments of the temple provide a total annual income of £31,000; and the offerings of pilgrims amount to at least £50,000 a year, as no one comes empty-handed. The richer pilgrims heap gold and silver and jewels at the feet of the god; every one gives beyond his ability, and many cripple their fortunes for the rest of their lives. It may be remembered that when dying Maharaja Ranjit Singh of the Panjab bequeathed the Koh-i-Nur to Jagannath, but his successor did not give effect to his bequest. There are more than 6000 male adults as priests, warders of the temple, and pilgrim guides, and, including the monastic establishments, and the guides who roam through India to escort pilgrims, there are probably not less than 20,000 men, women, and children dependent on Jagannath. The immediate attendants on the god are divided into thirty-six orders and ninety-seven classes. At the head of all is the Raja of Khurda, who represents the royal house of Orissa, and who is the hereditary sweeper of the temple. There are distinct sets of servants to put the god to bed, to dress and bathe him, and a numerous band of nautch girls who sing before him.

The town is of great antiquity and was probably the Dantpura where the sacred relic of Buddha's tooth was preserved and was finally transferred to Ceylon.

[1] The whole country round is divided into kshetras, the Parvati round Jajpur, the Hara round Konarak, the Padma (or lotus) round Bhuvaneshwar, and the Parushottama round Puri. See the very interesting account of *Orissa* in the *Imperial Gazetteer*.

The title **Jagannath** (Juggurnath) (Sanscrit=" Lord of the Universe") is really a name of Krishna, worshipped as Vishnu: the immense popularity of the shrine was due to the doctrine artfully preached that before the god all castes were equal. The image so-called is an amorphous idol, a rudely carved log,[1] which some learned men believe to have been a Buddhist symbol, adopted as an object of Brahmanical worship. This idol is annually dragged in procession on a great car (Rath), and as crowds of fanatic pilgrims used to rush forward to draw it, fatal accidents used to occur occasionally, and in some instances also votaries were known to throw themselves beneath the advancing wheels. The number of such accidents and suicides, however, has been greatly exaggerated in the popular imagination, and since Orissa came under British rule the former have been reduced to a minimum. The annual mortality of the pilgrims used, however, to amount to many thousands, and a spread of cholera constantly followed their dispersion from Puri. Of late years much has been successfully done to improve the sanitation and water-supply of the place.

The **Temple** is situated in the centre of the town, nearly 1 m., as the crow flies, from the D.B. It stands upon rising ground, which is called Nilgiri, or the Blue Hill, and is surrounded by a square enclosing stone wall about 20 ft. high, with a gateway in the centre of each side. As the door stands open, it is possible to see the bands of pilgrims within, but not the temples, of which, besides the Great Pagoda, there are more than a hundred, thirteen of them being sacred to Shiva and one

[1] Strictly speaking, there are three of these idols, viz. Jagannath, his brother Balabhadra, and his sister Subhadra. Quaint representations of them in a wooden shrine may be bought in the Bazaar.

to the Sun. It is, of course, strictly closed to all non-Hindus, but the tower and front and the scene at the entrance can be comfortably viewed from the roof of a lodging-house on the opposite side of the street—fee to servants of the house. In front of the E. gate is an exquisite tional form, with one paw raised, which stand one at either side of the entrance. Within is a second enclosure surrounded by a double wall having an interval of 11 ft. between the walls, and within this again is the temple proper. The *Hall of Offerings*, or *Bhog Mandir* (D),[1] is

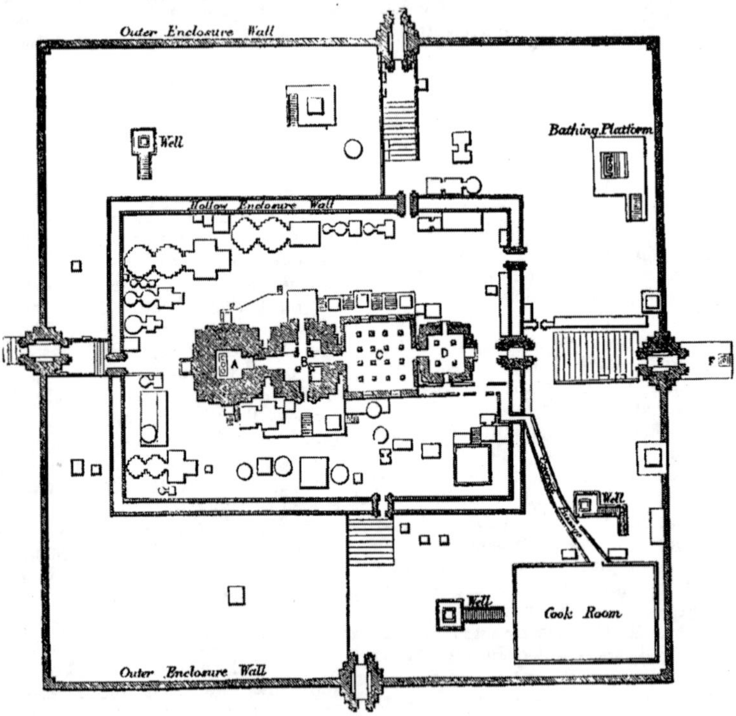

Scale 200 ft. to the Inch
Temple of Jagannath (from Fergusson's *Indian Arch.*).

Pillar brought from the Black Pagoda at Konarak. It stands on a platform of rough stones, and, reckoning to the top of the seated figure of the Garuda or eagle, which surmounts it, is 35 ft. high. The Lion Gate (E), on entering which the pilgrims are slightly struck with a wand by an official, has its name from two large lions of the conven-

said to have been built by the Mahrattas in the last century, at a cost of 40 lakhs of rupees. It was part of the Black Pagoda of Kanarak, and was brought thence by them. The *Nath Mandir* (C), or dancing-hall, also of late date, is a square hall measuring 69 ft. by 67 ft. inside.

[1] These letters refer to corresponding letters on the plan.

The walls are plain, with only two figures of dwarpals, called Jaya and Vijaya, and a marble figure of Garuda, 2 ft. high.

The *Jagmohan* (B), or Hall of Audience, where the pilgrims see the idols, is 80 ft. sq. and 120 ft. high. The *Baradewal* (A), or Sanctuary, where the idols are, is also 80 ft. sq., and is surmounted by a lofty conical tower or vimanah, 192 ft. high, black with time and surmounted by the Wheel and Flag of Vishnu.

The idols themselves, that is to say, Jagannath, with his brother Balabhadra and his sister Subhadra, are mere logs, without hands or feet, coarsely carved into a likeness of the human bust. The date of the erection of the temple is 1198, and it cost about half a million sterling; but it has since been repeatedly repaired greatly to "the ruin of it as a work of art." The building of 1198 was a reconstruction by Raja Anang Bhim Deo, in expiation of the offence of having killed a Brahman.

There is a street about 45 ft. broad all round the temple enclosure. Turning to the left, from the Lion Gate along this road, the visitor comes to the S. gate, where steps lead up to the entrance. The entrance itself is 15 ft. high, and is ornamented with many figures. Above are depicted scenes from the life of Krishna. The supports of the massive roof are of iron.

Rather more than a mile to the N. of the temple, and approached by the broad Baradand—a picturesque grassy route in the cold weather — is the famous **Garden House**, to which the Car of Jagannath is brought at the Car Festival, in June or July. The house is a temple within a garden enclosed with a wall 15 ft. high. The principal gateway faces the temple, and has a pointed roof, adorned with conventional lions. The gates to this temple are built upon the Hindu arch system, with a series of slabs supporting the roof, each a little longer than the other, and projecting beyond it. The temple is said to be very old, but it has not much pretension to architectural beauty exteriorly: the interior, however, which strangers are permitted to enter, is interesting as giving one an idea of the arrangement of the Great Temple. In one of the pillared halls kneels a Garuda on a column facing the shrine. On the side of the temple there is a plain raised seat, 4 ft. high and 19 ft. long, made of chlorite, and this is called the Ratnavedi, the throne on which the images are placed when brought to the temple. On the walls are some fine carvings of horsemen, etc. Outside, over the door, are various figures of women, 2 ft. high, supporting the roof; also carvings of Brahma with four heads, worshipping Narayan; of Krishna playing to the Gopis, etc.

The great Car in which the journey of the god is made is 45 ft. high and 35 ft. sq., and is supported on sixteen wheels of 7 ft. diameter. The brother and sister of Jagannath have separate cars a few feet smaller. The car is dragged by 4200 professionals, who come from the neighbouring districts, and during the festival live at Puri gratis. It is broken up at intervals, when the timbers are made into sacred relics, and another is made of exactly the same pattern. The idols of the Great Temple are also treated in this way.

The legend is that King Indradyumna, king of Malwa, pitched his camp here when he discovered Puri, and set up an image of Narsing. Here the Sacred Log from the White Island stranded, and here the Divine Carver made the images of Jagannath, etc., and here Indradyumna performed the horse sacrifice a hundred times over.

1 m. S.W., on the sea-shore S. of the Circuit House, is the *Swarga Dwara*, or "Door of Paradise," where, when all the ceremonies are finished, the pilgrims bathe in the surf and wash away their sins. There is a stump of a pillar 4 ft. high on the right hand, near a small temple. On this pillar offerings are placed, which are eaten by the crows. On the left

is the Lahore Math or Monastery. Within the enclosure is a well with excellent fresh water. Hundreds of men and women will be seen bathing, the surf rolling over them in its fury. Afterwards they make heaps of sand, and stick pieces of wood into them.

N.W. of the city, on the way to the Garden Temple, are the Chandan Tank and Temple, the Mitiani Tank, the Markhand Tank and Temple, and a *Bridge* built, according to Raja Rajendra Lal Mitra, in 1038-50. It is 278 ft. long by 38 ft. broad, and has nineteen arches.

[18 m. N.E. from Puri is **Konarak**, celebrated for its **Black Pagoda** (c. 1250-60), which every one should visit in spite of the discomforts of a night journey in a palanquin. A relay of bearers should be sent on half-way: provisions and drinking water must be taken. Cost—about Rs.15 to Rs.16.

Recent excavations at Konarak have led to a much higher appreciation of the great temple, which is figured at p. 323, vol. i. of Fergusson's *Indian Architecture*. The shrine at the W. end of it has been cleared of the mass of superincumbent ruins, and it is now possible to realise the splendid carvings on it, including the grand wheels and horses, which indicate the fact that the temple was the chariot of the Sun god, to whom it was dedicated. There are a number of very fine carved figures of green chlorite on the walls, but, unhappily, much of the decoration is of a licentious character; inside is a beautifully carved throne on which the idol once stood. In front of the shrine is the Jagmohan porch. It has a square base of 90 ft., is built of red laterite, and is called *black* on account of the shadow it casts. The roof is excessively beautiful, and covered with elaborate carvings free from all objectionable features, and Mr Fergusson says of it that there is no roof in India where the same play of light and shade is obtained, with an equal amount of richness and constructive propriety. Mr Fergusson adds of this building: "Internally the chamber is singularly plain, but presents some constructive peculiarities worthy of attention. On the floor it is about 40 ft. square, and the walls rise plain to about the same height. Here it begins to bracket inwards, till it contracts to about 20 ft., where it was ceiled with a flat stone roof, supported by wrought-*iron beams* . . . showing a knowledge of the properties and strength of the material that is remarkable in a people who are now so utterly incapable of forging such masses. . . . The employment of these beams here is a mystery. They were not needed for strength, as the building is still firm after they have fallen, and so expensive a false ceiling was not wanted architecturally to roof so plain a chamber. It seems to be only another instance of that profusion of labour which the Hindus loved to lavish on the temples of their gods" (*History of Architecture*, ii. 107). The entrance of the Jagmohan is on the E. side, guarded by two stone lions, with strongly marked manes, and one paw lifted up, resting on the backs of elephants, which are smaller in size. The height of the entrance is 16½ ft.; the roof was supported by two rafters of iron and four of stone. In front of the entrance, amongst the stones, lay a bar of iron 23 ft. long, and 11⅓ in. thick and broad.[1] The interior of the hall has now been completely filled up in order to save the outer walls. As the E. door is guarded by lions, the N. door is by elephants, and the S. by horses trampling down men, who from their tush-like teeth, crisped hair, knives and shields, are intended for aborigines. The spirit with which the horses are

[1] Other instances of the employment of large masses of iron occur at Dhar and at the Kutab Minar of Delhi (pp. 89 and 210). These iron beams have probably something to do with the fable that there was once a lodestone in the tower of the temple, which used to draw passing ships on to the shore.

carved, and also the device on one of the shields, of two climbing lizards, should be noticed. According to tradition the temple was dedicated by Sambhu, son of Krishna, on being cured here of leprosy.

Stirling fixes the date of the Black Pagoda in the year 1241, but Mr Fergusson attributes it to the latter half of the 9th century. When he visited Konarak in 1837 a portion of the Great Tower was still standing. He is of opinion that the destruction of it was owing, not to earthquakes, but to the nature of the soil, which was not solid enough to bear so enormous a structure. To the S. of the Jagmohan is a very large banyan tree, under which is a good place for the traveller to take his meal; and near the great tree is a grove of palms and smaller trees, and a garden with a *math*, or devotee's residence. Over the E. entrance used to be a chlorite slab, on which the emblems of the days of the week, with the ascending and descending nodes, were carved. Some English antiquaries attempted to remove this for the Museum at Calcutta, but after dragging it 200 yds., gave up the attempt, though the Indian builders, after excavating the block in the hills, and carving it, had carried it 80 m. across swamps and unbridged rivers to Konarak. It lies now about 200 yds. to the E. of the Temple, and is 20 ft. 2 in. long, 4 ft. deep, and 4 ft. 10 in. broad. It is sadly disfigured with oil and red paint, with which the Hindus have bedaubed it. The sea, about 2 m. off, is only visible from the *débris* of the Temple.]

327 m. **Balugan.** From here the railway line skirts the fine **Chilka Lake**, some of the scenery along which is of great beauty—in the background being the jungle-clad hills of the Eastern Ghats, while the lake itself is dotted with islands on which, as on the mainland, game of all kinds abound, and in the cold season has a surface crowded with wild-fowl. The lake is 45 m. long, averages 10 m. in width, is separated by a narrow stretch of sand from the sea, and is shallow, seldom exceeding 6 ft. in depth; the water is brackish, and there is a very slight tide at the southern end, the sea running into it at Manickpatnam. Trade is carried on in flat-bottomed boats of peculiar structure with lateen sails of bamboo-matting. At Rambha there is a large house on the margin of the lake built by Mr Snodgrass[1] in 1792—it is believed, from Famine Funds. It is now the property of the Raja of Kallicote.

345 m. Rambha.

352 m. **Humma** station for old **Ganjam**, situated on the Rushkuliya, and formerly chief port and town of the District; in the early part of the century it was ravaged by an epidemic of fever and abandoned in consequence. The Fort, which was commenced in 1768 by Mr Cotsford, the first Resident in Ganjam, still forms an interesting ruin, and recalls memories of former Residents and Chiefs in Council, who were engaged here partly in political, and partly in commercial, enterprises for the East India Company.

361 m. **Chatrapur station,** beautifully situated on high ground above the sea, headquarters of the District Magistrate and Collector. A canal runs parallel with the sea-shore to **Gopalpur**, the chief seaport of the Ganjam District.

375 m. **Berhampur.**—(Ganjam). Berhampur station (R.) chief town of the Ganjam District (population, 26,000). It is noted for its tussore silk cloths and gold-embroidered turbans.

437 m. **Naupada** junction, branch line to (25 m.) Parlakimedi.

1 This was the gentleman who extorted a pension from the E.I.C. by sweeping a crossing in front of the India House.

466 m. **Chicacole Road** station for **Chicacole,** a large town which contains a noble mosque built in 1641 by Sher Mahomed Khan, the first Governor of the Golkonda Dynasty. It was formerly celebrated for its very fine muslins.

509 m. **Vizianagram** (R.), the chief town of one of the most extensive Zemindari estates in India, and once included in the Kalinga kingdom. The town (population, 37,000), founded in 1712, adjoins the small station on rising ground. The Fort (1 m. distant) is almost entirely occupied by the *Palace Buildings*, etc., of the Maharaja. The place, which is 16 m. from the sea, is a rising one. Half-way between the Fort and station is a large tank with a constant supply of water. The *Market* was built to commemorate the visit of King Edward to India in 1875. It was a Vizianagram force which, with French assistance, attacked Bobbili ("the Royal Tiger") in 1756, when, after putting the women to death, the Raja Ranga Rao fell sword in hand in accordance with the old Rajput tradition. Not long after, four of his old retainers murdered the Raja of Vizianagram.

It is proposed to construct a railway from Vizianagram N. to Sointilla, and thence (1) N.W. to Raipur (p. 85), and (2) N. to Sambalpur and Jharsuguda (p. 86) on the Bengal Nagpur Railway.

547 m. **Waltair** junction station. [Short branch to

2 m. **Vizagapatam.**✱ Vizagapatam, the chief town (population, 41,000) of the District of that name, is a growing seaport, situated on a small estuary. The estuary forms the only naturally protected harbour on the Coromandel Coast; the bar is too shallow, however, to admit vessels of deep draught, which have to anchor outside. Colonel Forde landed here in 1759, and drove the French from the Northern Circars. Most of the European residents live in the suburb of Waltair, to the N. of the town, which stands on elevated ground composed of red laterite rocks. The manufacture of *panjam* cloth, and ornamental articles of ivory, buffalo-horn, and silver filigree work, are specialities of the District. In the neighbourhood are sources of manganese, of which 125,000 tons are exported yearly.

18 m. N.E. of **Vizagapatam** is **Bimlapatam** (population, 10,000), a thriving port where coasting steamers touch.]

641 m. **Samalkot** station junction for (8 m.) **Cocanada Town** (Kakinada = Crow Country) and (10 m.) **Cocanada Port**, connected with the Godavery River by navigable canals. Cocanada is the principal port, after Madras, on the Coromandel Coast. Ships lie in safety in the Roads (Coringa Bay), which, though shallow, are protected to the S. by a sandy promontory at the mouths of the Godavery. The jetties, wharves, and business houses are on the banks of a canal leading into the Roads. Trade of an annual value of 125 lakhs.

672 m. **Rajahmundry** (Rajamahendri) (R.) (population, 36,000) is the old seat of the Orissa kings in the S. and of the Vengi kings, and is regarded by the Telugus as their chief town. It contains a large jail, a museum, public gardens, and a provincial College. Historically it is chiefly interesting as the headquarters of M. Bussey from 1754-57, during which he held possession of the Northern Circars assigned to him by the Nizam. The Gorge, 20 to 30 m. to the W., where the Godavery issues from the hills, is well worth a visit, as it forms one of the most beautiful pieces of scenery in Southern India—a succession of Highland lochs in an Eastern setting. A few miles down the river from Rajahmundry are the head-works of the magnificent Godavery Delta Irrigation system, first designed by Sir Arthur Cotton; the *anikut*, or dam, is a huge piece of masonry, 4 m. in length from bank to bank, and is well worth a visit. In

the middle of it is a pretty well-wooded island.

676 m. **Godavery.** A spendid railway bridge of 56 spans of 150 ft. crosses the river here. This and the Kistna bridge are among the finest engineering works in all India.

727 m. **Ellore** station (R.). Formerly capital of the Northern Circars. Ellore is now famous only for its carpets. The Godavery and Kistna Canal systems join here.

764 m. **BEZWADA** Junction (R.), D.B., terminus of the Nizam's State Railway from Wadi, Hyderabad, and Warangal. Bezwada (population, 24,000) is an important trading-place on the most frequented crossing of the Kistna river. A fort was erected here in 1760, but has since been dismantled. In making excavations for canals many remains were exposed, which show that the place was, in the Buddhist period, a considerable religious centre; and as such it was visited by Hiouen Thsang in 637 A.D. It is shut in on the W. by a granite ridge 600 ft. high, running N. and S., and ending in a scarp at the river. At right angles to this ridge, and ½ m. from the stream, is a similar ridge sheltering the town on the N. Close to the E. end of N. ridge is a sharp-pointed detached mass of gneiss, on which are Buddhistic caves and cells. On the S. side of the river, opposite to Bezwada, is a hill similar to the W. ridge of which it is a continuation. It is 450 ft. high, and from Bezwada seems a perfect cone. On the S. side of the river, 1 m. to the W., is the Undavilli Cave-Temple.

In the town are some old shrines with inscriptions from the 7th century downwards. The caves of Bezwada—unimportant—are hollowed out of the E. side of the great hill at the foot of which the town stands. At the Library there is a colossal figure of Buddha in black granite, which came from the hill to the E. of Bezwada.

A branch **railway** 49 m. long connects Bezwada with **Masulipatam** (Machhli-patnam or Fish Town, population, 30,000), the head-quarters and the principal port of the Kistna District. It was taken by the Bahmani Kings in the 15th century, and was afterwards held by the Golkonda rulers. An English agency was established here in 1611, after the failure of that at Pulicat, and a factory eleven years later: the Dutch and French also had factories here. In 1690 a farman of the Delhi Emperor confirmed the English privileges; in 1750 the place was made over by the Nizam to the French, but was captured by Colonel Forde in 1759, 500 French and 2500 sepoys surrendering. The chintzes of Masulipatam were once famous. The C.M.S. has an important centre here, with a collegiate school.

Excursions from Bezwada.

(1) In order to reach **Undavilli** village, it is necessary to cross the Kistna from Bezwada by the railway or *anicut*, and go 1½ m. up the course of the river above and W. of Sitanagaram. There is a rock-temple of two storeys close to the village. Further round the hill in a recess to the S. and facing N. is the interesting five-storeyed Brahman excavation known as the Undavilli Cave. The upper storeys are all set back, one above the other, and there is no doubt the façade of the cave is meant to represent the exterior of some structural building. The lowest storey across the whole front has three rows of seven pillars partially hewn out. The second originally had four compartments; at the back of one of these is a shrine cell with an altar, and in another is a relief of Vishnu and his wives. The façade on the front here has a frieze of geese, and a cell at the left end one of elephants and lions. The third storey contains a hall 53 ft. by 36 ft., with a figure of Vishnu

seated on the serpent Ananta, and of Narayana, 17 ft. long, resting on the great snake Shesha. The top storey consists of circular domes of the shape used in all Dravidian Temples. The fifth storey, which was never completed across the whole front, is the lowest of all, to the right of the flight of steps up to the cave. The date of the excavation must be much the same as those of Mahabalipuram (Route 35) **viz.** 700 A.D.

(2) 17 m. W. of Bezwada by road is **Amaravati**, on the right or S. bank of the Kistna river, once the capital of the Andhra kingdom. It is a place of much book interest to antiquarians as an ancient centre of the Buddhist religion, and the site of a great Tope;[1] but scarcely anything remains *in situ* now, and what does is not worth a visit. The beauty of the tope can be judged of from the splendid remains of it in the British and Madras Museums.

N. and N.W. of Amaravati are the sites of former diamond-workings, all on the N. bank of the river.

Immediately S. of Bezwada is the Kistna Bridge, 1200 yards long outside abutments, with a depth of foundations 80 ft. below low water; it cost Rs.4,247,850.

810 m. **Bapatla** (R.)

850 m. **Ongole** (R.)

901 m. **Bitragunta** (R.)

923 m. **Nellore** (R.) Chief town of the district, stands on the right bank of the *River Pennar* 8 m. from its mouth (population, 32,000). In the ruins of a *Hindu Temple* was found a pot of *Roman gold coins* and *medals* of the 2nd century. There are here **Missions** of the Roman Catholics, Scotch Free Church, American Baptists, and Hermansburg Lutherans.

[1] See Fergusson's *History of Indian Architecture*, i. 80, 112, 119, 122, and *Tree and Serpent Worship*, and Mr J Burgess's *Amaravati and Jaggayapetta Stupas*, London, 1887.

946 m. **Gudur** (R.). Branch to 52 m. Renigunta (p. 350).

1010 m. **Ponneri** (R.).

1021 m. **Ennur**—once a popular retreat from Madras, on a large backwater.

1032 m. **Madras**—Central Station.

ROUTE 25.

BOMBAY TO MADRAS by Kalyan Junction, the **Bore Ghat, Karli, Hotgi** Junction, **Poona, Sholapur, Gulbarga, Wadi** Junction, **Raichur, Guntakal** Junction, **Renigunta** Junction, **Arkonam** Junction, with excursions by road to **Matheran,** the **Caves of Karli** and **Bhaja**, and by rail to **Ahmednagar** and **Tirupati.**

Rail 794 m. Mail train about 32 hours in transit. Fares, Rs.68, Rs.34, Rs.8½.

For the journey as far as 34 m. **Kalyan** junction station, see Route 2; from Kalyan the N.E. branch of the G.I.P. Railway goes up the Thal Ghat, whilst the S.E. branch ascends the Bore Ghat and passes through Poona to Madras. The

MATHERAN

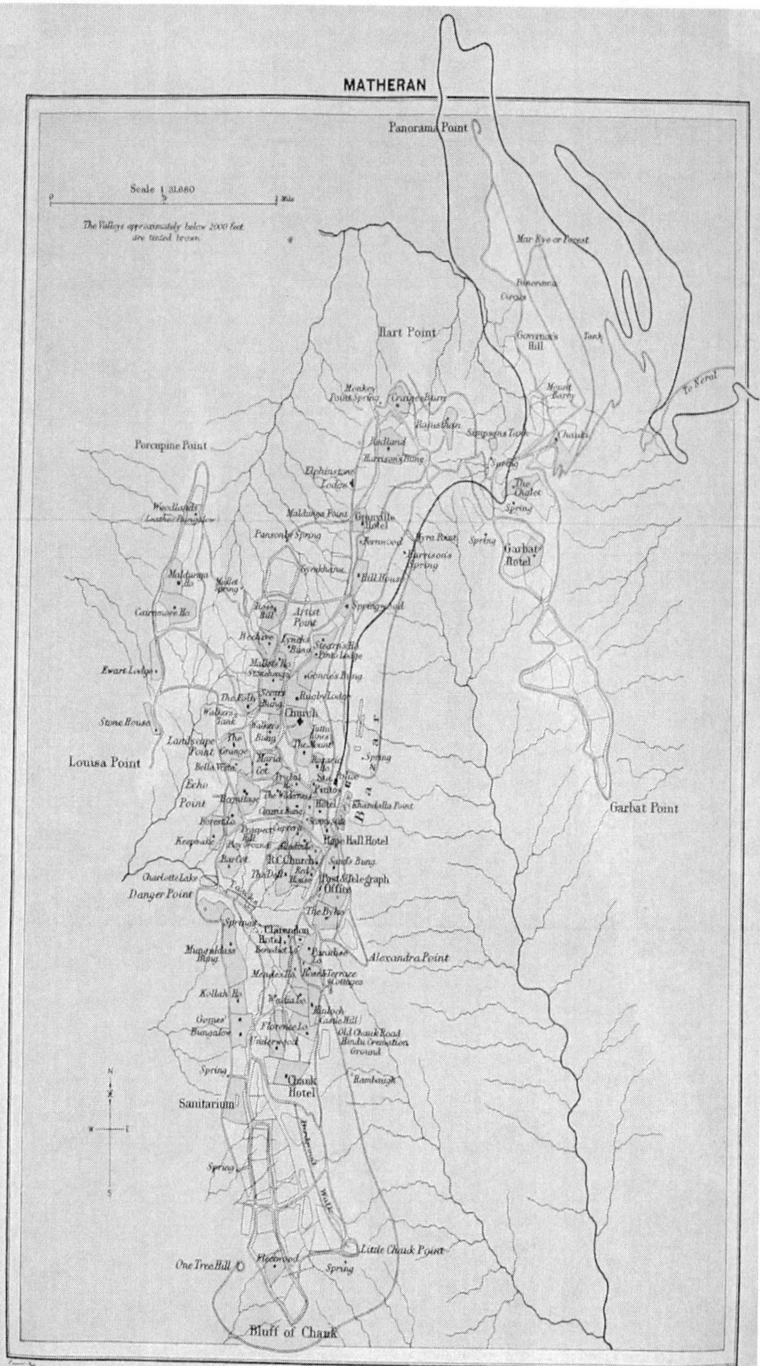

London. John Murray, Albemarle Street

country below the Ghats as far S. as N. Kanara is known as the Konkan—that above the Ghats from the Godavery (formerly from the Vindhya mountains) to the S. as the Deccan=right hand—*cf.* "dextra."

Proceeding by the latter branch the first station is

38 m. **Ambarnath,** "Immortal Lord," a village of 300 inhabitants which gives its name to the district in which the town of Kalyan is situated. 1 m. E. is the temple of Ambarnath in a pretty valley. It is an object of considerable interest as a specimen of genuine Hindu architecture, covered with beautiful designs, in which birds and the heads of the lion of the South are introduced. The roof of the hall is supported by four richly carved columns. The pediment of the doorway leading into the vimanah (shrine) is ornamented with elephants and lions, and in the centre with figures of Shiva. A curious belt of beautiful carving runs up each face of the vimanah. An inscription inside the lintel of the N. door gives the date of the building of the temple as=860 A.D.

54 m. **Neral** station (R.) [Passengers for **Matheran** leave the rail here, and proceed by steam tramway (2 ft. gauge) to that hill station, 14 m. distant.—Fares, Rs.4 as.8 and R.1 as.4.

Matheran "the wooded head" stands upon a spur of the Sahyadri range varying from 3100 ft. to 3400 ft. above the sea-level, and is an agreeable airy summer resort for the people of Bombay. The summit of the hill where the station is situated forms a narrow tableland running N. and S., with offshoots in many directions, limited on all sides by precipices sometimes 1500 ft. high, and terminating abruptly in bluffs called "Points." Among the finest of these are Porcupine Point 1 m. N.W. of the church, Louisa Point ⅞ m. W., Alexandra Point, about 1 m. to the S. —and Chauk Point lying 1 m. further to the S. of the main plateau. The finest of all is *Panorama Point*, to the N. of the bungalows. The distance is a little over 4 m. The road leads through a thick jungle of beautiful trees, and about ½ m. from Panorama Point comes to a point parallel with Porcupine Point, where a precipice descends abruptly 1000 ft. At 100 yds. from its termination the road goes quite round the brow of the peak, and affords an extremely beautiful panoramic view of the country from which the point gets its name. To the left are Hart Point and Porcupine Point, at the N. and N.W. extremities of the place. Far in the distance is Prabal Point, where there is a fort of the same name, which signifies "Mighty." Between Matheran and Prabal the mountain sinks down abruptly to the plain. Below and to the N. of Panorama Point is the Bawa Malang Range, 10 m. long, with strange cylindrical or bottle-shaped peaks. The huts of Neral village lie directly below, and beyond them is the curving line of the G.I.P. Railway. Bombay and its shipping may be seen from this point on a clear day under the evening light.

62 m. **Karjat** junction station. From here a short line runs S. 9 m. to **Campoli**, but it is only used in the dry season. At Karjat the engine is changed for one much more powerful to ascend the *Bore Ghat*, which begins 1 m. from Karjat. The gradient is 1 in 42, and even 1 in 37, and all the trains are furnished with powerful brakes. The line first rises up the slope of the long mountain arm which encloses the N. side of the Campoli valley, and at the height of 1000 ft. passes by a tunnel to another wooded valley on the N., which soon terminates in an extremely fine and beautifully wooded ravine. Along the S. side of this the line proceeds to the Reversing Station, 1350 ft. above the sea, affording grand views of the ravine all the way. In the rains as many as fifty waterfalls may be seen shooting and

streaming down the ravine sides, several near the head of it being very grand; and at all times of the year this part of the Ghat is extremely beautiful and should certainly be visited. From the Reversing Station the line winds round again to the E. side of the Campoli valley, and makes its way along the crest of the tableland to Khandala, which stands at the head of the ravine and is visible as the train ascends that. The length of the ascent is nearly 16 m., over which there are twenty-six tunnels with a length of 2500 yds., eight viaducts, and many smaller bridges: the actual height accomplished by the ascent is 1850 ft., and the cost of constructing the line was nearly £600,000.

78 m. **Khandala,** D.B.* This beautiful village has for long been a favourite retreat for the wealthy inhabitants of Bombay from the distressing heat of the summer months. The site is well chosen; it overlooks the great ravine, the sheer depth of which is in great part concealed by luxuriant trees. Above the head of the ravine to the N. is the magnificent hill called the Duke's Nose, whence is a fine view over the Konkan. The ascent is by the S. shoulder and is very steep. There is a *Convalescent Hospital* at Khandala in charge of the "All Saints'" Sisters from Margaret Street.

The *Waterfall* on the right side of the ravine near its head is very fine in the rains—the upper of the two falls into which it is divided having a clear leap of 300 ft.

80 m. **Lonauli** station* (R.). Here is the G.I.P. Railway Company's School and Church. Close to Lonauli are being constructed the storage and head works of the Tata Electro Hydraulic Scheme for Bombay (p. 18). A traveller desiring to see the great cave at *Karli* (7½ m.), and the caves of Bhaja (6½ m.), should, unless he is prepared to walk 8 to 10 m. (and even then the trains which stop at Karli station may not prove very convenient), arrange to make the expedition from Lonauli by tonga, which in fair weather can go off the Great Trunk Road S. to the Karli station, ¾ m. distant from the caves of Bhaja, and N. to the base of the rocky ridge of the Karli cave. At ordinary times, therefore, one can drive comfortably to the foot of the Karli cave and nearly to Bhaja. The ascent to the former is nearly 400 ft. by a good path with a fairly easy gradient; if a pony is desired for this, it must be sent out from Lonauli.

85 m. **Karli station** * D.B. The *celebrated cave* is on a hill about 4 m. from the station.

The following is from Mr Fergusson's description of it.[1] "The great cave of Karli is, without exception, the largest and finest chaitya cave in India, and was excavated at a time when the style was in its greatest purity, and is fortunately the best preserved. Its interior dimensions are 124 ft. 3 in. in total length, 81 ft. 3 in. length of nave. Its breadth from wall to wall is 45 ft. 6 in., while the width of the central aisle is 25 ft. 7 in. The height is only 46 ft. from the floor to the apex." The same writer says: "The building resembles an early Christian church in its arrangements, while all the dimensions are similar to those of the choir of Norwich Cathedral." The nave is separated from the side aisles by fifteen columns with octagonal shafts on each side, of good design and workmanship. On the abacus which crowns the capital of each of these are two kneeling elephants, and on each elephant are two seated figures, generally a male and female, with their arms over each other's shoulders, but sometimes two female figures in

[1] *Rock-cut Temples of India*, p. 27. See also *Indian Architecture*, i. 142.

the same attitude. The sculpture of these is very good, and the effect particularly rich and pleasing. Behind the altar are seven plain octagonal piers without sculpture, making thus thirty-seven pillars altogether, exclusive of the Lion-pillar in front, which is sixteen-sided, and is crowned with four lions with their hinder parts joined. The dagoba is plain and very similar to that in the large cave at Ajanta, but here, fortunately, a part of the wooden umbrella which surmounted it remains. The wooden ribs of the roof, too, remain nearly entire, proving beyond doubt that the roof is not a copy of a masonry arch; and the framed screen, filling up a portion of the great arch in front, like the centering of the arch of a bridge (which it much resembles), still retains the place in which it was originally placed. At some distance in advance of the arched front of this cave is placed a second screen, which exists only here and at the great cave at Kanhari, though it might have existed in front of the oldest chaitya caves at Ajanta. It consists of two plain octagonal columns with pilasters. Over these is a deep plain mass of wall, occupying the place of an entablature, and over this again a superstructure of four dwarf pillars. Except the lower piers, the whole of this has been covered with wooden ornaments; and, by a careful examination and measurement of the various mortices and footings, it might still be possible to make out the greater part of the design. It appears, however, to have consisted of a broad balcony in front of the plain wall, supported by bold wooden brackets from the two piers, and either roofed or having a second balcony above it. No part of the wood, however, exists now, either here or at Kanhari. It is more than probable, however, that this was the music gallery or Nakar Khana, which we still find existing in front of almost all Jain temples, down even to the present day. Whether the space between this outer and the inner screen was roofed over or not is extremely difficult to decide. To judge from the mortices at Kanhari, the space there would seem to have had a roof; but here the evidence is by no means so distinct, though there is certainly nothing to contradict the supposition. There are no traces of painting in this cave, though the inner wall has been plastered, and may have been painted; but the

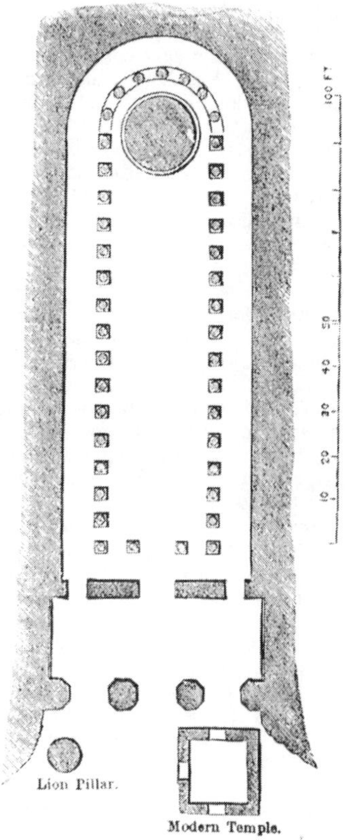

Cave at Karli.

cave has been inhabited, and the continued smoke of cooking-fires has so blackened its walls that it is impossible to decide the question. Its inhabitants were Shivites, and the cave was considered a temple dedicated to Shiva, the dagoba performing the part of a gigantic lingam, which it resembles a good deal. The outer porch is 52 ft. wide and 15 ft. deep. Here originally the fronts of three elephants in each end wall supported a frieze ornamented with a rail pattern, but at both ends this has been cut away to introduce figures. Above was a thick quadrantal moulding, and then a rail with small façades of temples, and pairs of figures.

"It would be of great importance if the age of this cave could be positively fixed; but though that cannot quite be done, it is probably antecedent to the Christian era; and at the same time it cannot possibly have been excavated more than 200 years before that era. From the Sinhasthamba (lion pillar) on the left of the entrance Colonel Sykes copied an inscription, which Mr Prinsep deciphered in vol. vi. of the *Journal of the Asiatic Society*. It merely says: 'This lion-pillar is the gift of Ajmitra Ukas, the son of Saha Ravisabhoti'; the character Mr Prinsep thinks is of the 1st or 2nd century B.C. From its position and import, the inscription appears to be integral, and the column is certainly a part of the original design. I am inclined to think the date, 160 B.C., is at least extremely probable.

"It would be a subject of curious inquiry to know whether the woodwork now existing in this cave is that originally put up or not. Accustomed as I had long been to the rapid destruction of everything wooden in India, I was half inclined to be angry when the idea first suggested itself to me; but a calmer survey of the matter has convinced me that it is. Certain it is that it is the original design, for we find it repeated in stone in all the niches of the front, and there is no appearance of change or alteration in any part of the roof. Every part of it is the same as is seen so often repeated in stone in other and more modern caves, and it must, therefore, have been put up by the Buddhists before they were expelled; and if we allow that it has existed 800 or 1000 years, which it certainly has, there is not much greater improbability in its having existed near 2000 years, as I believe to be the case. As far as I could ascertain the wood is teak. Though exposed to the atmosphere, it is protected from the rain, and has no strain upon it but its own weight, as it does not support the roof, though it appears to do so; and the rock seems to have defied the industry of the white ants."

The principal viharas at Karli to the right of the entrance to the Chaitya are three tiers in height. They are plain halls with cells, but without any internal colonnades, and the upper one alone possesses a verandah. The lower fronts have been swept away by great masses of rock which have rolled from above. To the left of the Chaitya are some smaller viharas and cisterns.

The **Caves of Bhaja and Bedsa.**[1]—Bhaja is a village ¾ m. S. of Karli Railway Station, and Bedsa is 5½ m. E. of the Bhaja. The caves of Bhaja date from 200 B.C. There are eighteen excavations of which the Chaitya No. 12 is one of the most interesting in India. It contains a dagoba, but no sculptures, and has its roof supported by twenty-seven sloping pillars. Outside there is a group executed in bas-relief, now much defaced, and marks show that a wooden front was once attached to the great arch. On both sides of the Chaitya the hill has been excavated into the usual halls of instruction, with cells. A little way to the S. is a curious collection of fourteen dagobas, five of which are inside and the others outside a cave. On the first of the latter there is an inscription. The last cave to the S. some way beyond the others is a vihara 16½ ft. by 17½ ft. decorated with excellent and interesting sculptures, including one of a

[1] A full account of these places will be found in *Cave Temples of India*, pp. 223, 228.

prince on an elephant and another of a prince in his chariot, and three armed figures. The caves at Bedsa lie about 4 m. S.E. from Kharkala, the station beyond Karli, and date a little later than Bhaja. The plan of the Chaitya resembles Karli, but is neither of so great extent, nor so well executed, and appears more modern. It contains a dagoba; and its roof, which is ribbed and supported by twenty-six octagonal pillars 10 ft. high, seems to have been covered with paintings, which are now, however, so indistinct that nothing can be made out of them. There are four pillars about 25 ft. high in front, surmounted by a group of horses, bulls, and elephants, with a male and female rider upon them. These groups resemble those found on the Indo-Mithraic coins of the N. The hall of instruction has an apsidal end and a vaulted roof, and is situated close to the left of the Chaitya. It contains eleven small cells, and over the door of one of them there is an indistinct and partly defaced inscription.

96 m. **Wargaon** station, a very large and flourishing village, celebrated for the defeat of a British force under Lieutenant-Colonel Cockburn, on the 12th and 13th of January 1779, and for a convention concluded there by Mr Carnac with the Mahrattas.

116 m. **Kirkee** station is only 3¾ m. from Poona, and may be considered part of the same place. It is interesting as being the scene of a splendid victory over Baji Rao II., the last Peshwa. On the 1st of November 1817, the dispositions of that prince had become so threatening, that Mr Elphinstone, then Resident at Poona, determined to remove the troops from the cantonment of that place to Kirkee, where, on the 5th, they took up a good position to the E. of an eminence, on which the village of Kirkee stands, and where the stores and ammunition were stationed. In the rear of the troops was the River Mula, and from the S. and W. advanced the masses of the Peshwa's army, amounting to 8000 foot, 18,000 horse, and 14 guns,[1] besides a reserve of 5000 horse and 2000 foot with the Peshwa, at the sacred hill of Parbati (see below). The cantonments at Poona and the Residency at the Sangam (or meeting of the rivers) had been plundered and burnt on the 1st, as soon as the British troops quitted them. One regiment, commanded by Major Ford, was at Dapuri, N. of Kirkee, and the total strength of the English, even when it joined, was, according to Grant Duff, but 2800 rank and file, of which 800 were Europeans.

Bapu Gokla, who had been a favourite of the Duke of Wellington, commanded the Peshwa's army. Its advance was compared by Grant Duff, an eye-witness, to the rushing tide called the Bore in the Gulf of Cambay. Colonel Burr, who commanded the British, was now informed that Major Ford was advancing with his regiment from Dapuri on the W. to join him; and in order to facilitate the junction, he moved the main force to a position about a mile in advance, and to the S.W. of the village of Kirkee. The Mahratta leaders had been tampering for some time with the regiment and they fully expected it would come over, as it was paid by the Peshwa. A strong body of horse, therefore, under Moro Dikshat, the prime minister of the Peshwa, advanced about 4 P.M. upon the Dapuri battalion, but Major Ford, throwing back his right wing, opened a heavy fire upon the Mahrattas, both of musketry and from three small guns commanded by Captain Thew. A good many Mahrattas fell, and among them Moro Dikshat. In the meantime, Gokla had organised an attack on the left flank of the British main force, and this was led by a regular battalion, commanded by a Portuguese named De Pento; and after his discomfiture,

[1] *Grant Duff*, vol. iii. p. 427.

a select body of 6000 horse, with the Jari Patka, or golden pennon, flying at their head, charged the 7th Native Infantry as they were pursuing De Pento's men. Gokla's horse was wounded in this charge, and his advance was stopped; but there were other gallant leaders, such as Naru Pant Apte and Mahadeo Rao Rastia, and it was well for the Sepoys that a swamp in their front checked the charge of the Mahrattas, whose horsemen rolled headlong over one another in the deep slough. As it was, some cut their way through the Sepoy battalion; but, instead of turning back, when they might have destroyed the regiment, they rode off to plunder the village of Kirkee, whence they were repulsed by a fire of grape. After this charge, the Mahrattas drew off with a total loss of about 500 men, while that of the British was but 86. On the 13th General Smith's army arrived from Sirur, and the Peshwa, after a slight resistance, retreated with his army. The most remarkable point in the battle of Kirkee was, perhaps, the extraordinary steadiness of Major Ford's regiment under great temptation. In it were upwards of seventy Mahrattas, yet not a man deserted on the day of battle, though promised vast sums to join their countrymen. After the action, the Mahrattas, but only the Mahrattas, joined the enemy.

Kirkee is the headquarters of a brigade of *Field Artillery*. ½ m. N.E. of the barracks is the *Small Arms Ammunition Factory*, and to the N. is the *Arsenal* (permission to enter either must be obtained from the Officer in charge).

Christ Church, Kirkee, in the Artillery Lines, was consecrated in 1841. There are two colours of the 23rd Regiment Bombay Native Infantry inside the W. door. Amongst the memorial tablets is one to thirty officers of the 14th King's Light Dragoons, who died or were killed between 1841 and 1859; and another to ninety non-commissioned officers of the same regiment.

N.E. of the Artillery Mess is *St Vincent De Paul's Roman Catholic Chapel.*

One of the most interesting spots at Kirkee, passed on the road to Poona, is *Holkar's Bridge*, over the Mula river, a stream which encircles Kirkee on the N., E., and S. The river is 200 yds. broad at this spot. On the right of the road is an old English cemetery, and, on the left, about 300 yds. to the N., is the New Burial Ground. After crossing the Mula, the road passes on the right the chhatri of Khande Rao Holkar, and on the left are the Sappers' and Miners' Lines, and after them the Deccan College and the lines of a Regiment of Pioneers, right. Beyond these are the *Jamsetjee Band*, the *Fitzgerald Bridge*, and the *Band Gardens*, for all of which see below under Poona.

Government House is at Ganesh Khind, 1½ m. S.W. of Kirkee Railway Station, and 3½ m. N.W. of the city of Poona. It derives its name from a small *khind* or pass between hills, about ¾ m. S.E. of the house, which resembles a modern French chateau, and has a tall slim tower, 80 ft. high, from the top of which there is a fine view including Kirkee, with its Arsenal, the Deccan College, and the Parbati Hill. The house contains the usual reception rooms, a ball-room, darbar-room, etc., and has a flower gallery or garden corridor, 90 ft. long.

119 m. **POONA** ✱ junction of the G.I.P. and Madras and S. Mahratta Railways. The railway station is situated at a corner of the city and cantonment, and close to the public offices. Poona (Lat. 18° 31′, Long. 73° 51′; altitude 1850; population, 157,000) is the residence of the Govt. of Bombay during the rains. It is the headquarters of the 6th Army Division, and the former

POONA AND KIRKEE

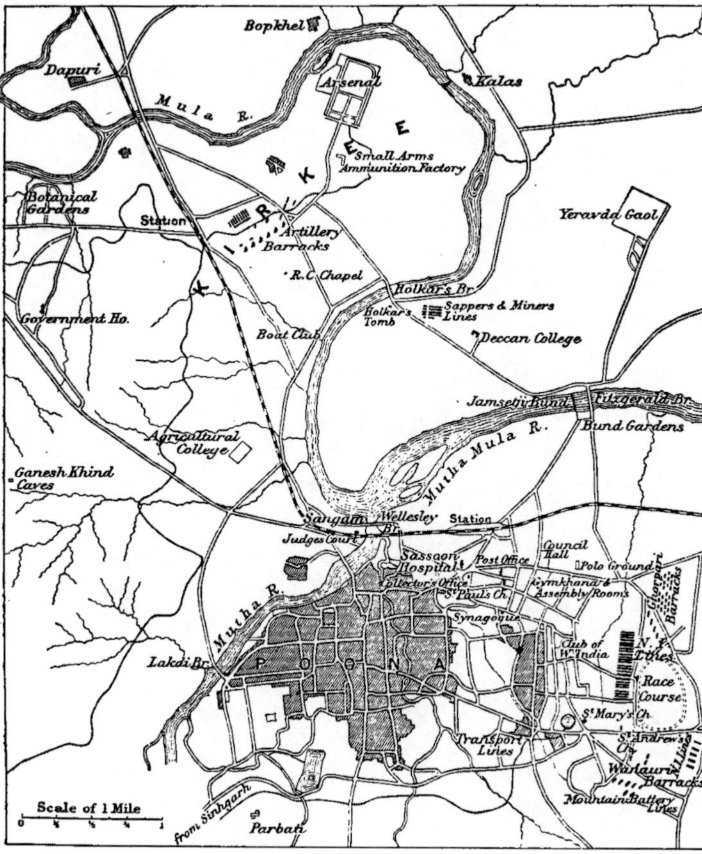

[To face p. 342.

capital of the Mahrattas. The first mention of Poona is in the Mahratta annals of 1599 A.D., when the parganahs of Poona and Supa were made over to Malaji Bhonsle (grandfather of Shivaji) by the Nizam Shahi Government. In 1750 it became the Mahratta capital under Balaji Baji Rao. In 1763 it was plundered and destroyed by Nizam 'Ali, and here, on the 25th of October, Jaswant Rao Holkar defeated the combined armies of the Peshwa and Sindhia, and captured all the guns, baggage, and stores of the latter. The city stands in a somewhat treeless plain on the right of the Mutha river, a little before it joins the Mula. At its extreme S. limit is the hill of Parbati, so called from a celebrated temple of the goddess Durga, or Parvati, on its summit (see p. 345). A few m. to the E. and S.E. are the hills which lead up to the still higher tableland in the direction of Satara. The station is healthy and the climate pleasant. The *Aqueduct* was built by one of the Rastias, a family of great distinction amongst the Mahrattas. There are also extensive waterworks, constructed by Sir Jamsetjee Jeejeebhoy, which cost upwards of £20,000. Of this sum the Parsi baronet contributed £17,500.

The **Gymkhana Assembly Rooms** in the middle of the station consist of a large building with a handsome ballroom, with a stage at one end for theatricals. In the grounds of the building are lawn-tennis courts, a covered Badminton court, and a fine cricket-ground.

Near the Assembly rooms, on the road to the Band Gardens, is the **Council Hall**, containing some pictures of interest, including those of Sir B. Frere, Lady Frere, Khan Bahadur Padamjee Pestanjee, Khan Bahadur Naushirwanjee, Lord Napier of Magdala, Khan Bahadur Pestanjee Sorabjee Framjee Patel, the Crown Prince of Travancore, Sir Mangaldas Nathubhai, Dr Bhau Daji, the Raja of Cochin, Sir Salar Jang, the Thakors of Bhaunagar and Morvi, and Khande Rao Gaekwar.

The *Sassoon Hospital* (nursed by the Wantage sisters), in the Gothic style, is at the end of the Arsenal Road. The accommodation for 150 patients of all classes is about to be doubled.

Opposite the hospital are the *Collector's Cutcherry* and the *Government Treasury*. About 250 yds. S. of St Paul's Church is the *Jews' Synagogue*, a red-brick building with a tower 90 ft. high, consecrated 29th September 1867. *Mr David Sassoon's tomb* adjoins the synagogue, which was built by him. The mausoleum is 16 ft. sq. and 28 ft. high.

1¼ m. to the S.E., passing the Arsenal, is *St Mary's Church*, consecrated by Bishop Heber in 1825. Here are buried many officers of distinction, and the tablets on the walls recall stirring incidents in the history of India. The Font in the S.W. corner of the church is surrounded by stained glass windows.

E. of the Church are the *General Parade Ground* and *Race-course*, the latter included in the former, and about 1 m. long. The Poona races are held from July to September. Close to it are the *Gymnasium*, *St Andrew's Church*, and the *Masonic Lodge*; to the N. are the *Ghorpari Barracks*, and to the S. the *Wanauri Barracks* for British troops.

Two Scottish Missions (Free and Established Church), the American Mahratta Mission and C.M. Zenana Mission, are conducted in the city and suburbs.

The *Society of St John the Evangelist* has a native Mission at Poona; the mission-house is at Panch Howds, Vetal Peit. There are boys' schools, an Industrial School, an Orphanage, a School for Catechists, and a Hospital.

The *Sisters of St Mary the Virgin* (Wantage) have also their mission-house at Panch Howds, and in the compound the Epiphany School for high class native girls, and St Michael's School for low-class girls.

The sisters have also under their charge St Mary's High School for European and Eurasian girls (self-supporting), a village school at Parbati, and another at Yerandaona 1 m. from Poona.

The **Sangam** is the name given to the tongue of land at the confluence of the Muta river flowing from the S., with the Mula river coming from the N.W., and is perhaps the most central spot of the combined city and cantonments. Upon it are several temples, and from it are pleasant views of the river.

The Wellesley Bridge, 482 ft. long and 28½ ft. broad, crosses the Mutha river to the Sangam promontory, close to its confluence with the Mula. It takes the place of a wooden bridge erected to commemorate the victories of the Duke of Wellington in India. The present bridge, designed by Col. A. U. H. Finch, R.E., cost Rs.110,932, and was opened in 1875.

On the left hand, after crossing the Wellesley Bridge, are the *Judges' Court*, the *Poona Engineering College*, and E. of it a long low building on the site of the Residency of the British Agent, Mountstuart Elphinstone, at the time of the rupture with the last Peshwa, Baji Rao II. Mr Elphinstone retired from it to Kirkee before the battle, and the Mahrattas plundered the building and pulled it down. At the E. end of Wellesley Bridge is a path to the left, which leads down to a pretty garden filled with fruit trees and containing several temples. The first has a tower 40 ft. high. In the middle of the garden is a second temple, nearly as broad but not so high. A third temple at the end of the garden was built by Holkar, who destroyed two other old temples to build it. All are dedicated to Mahadeo, and though small, are extremely handsome. At 300 yds. from the Engineering College is *Sir Edward Sassoon's House*, called Garden Reach. It was built between 1862 and 1864, and cost £80,000. Permission to view is usually granted on application when the family is not in residence. The gardens are beautiful, and extend along the banks of the river. The rooms in the principal house are floored with marble. The fine dining-room is connected with the house by a long, open gallery. Beside it is an open room, with sides of carved wood, where the family dine during the Feast of Tabernacles. The ceiling of the drawing-room is beautifully decorated by Poona artists. In it is a full-length portrait of Mr David Sassoon, Sir Edward's grandfather A fountain in the garden and the water-tower should be noticed.

From this it is a pleasant drive of 1¾ m. to the *Jamsetjee Band* and the *Fitzgerald Bridge*. The *Band* is of stone thrown across the Mula river, and on the S. side of it are the beautiful **Band Gardens** of six acres.

The view of the Fitzgerald Bridge from the *Band* is very pretty; above it is the broad stream, 350 yds. wide, on which regattas take place, chiefly in February. Farther along in the direction of Kirkee (see above), is the **Deccan College,** built of grey trap-stone, in the Gothic style, at a cost of Rs.245,963, of which half was contributed by Sir Jamsetjee Jeejeebhoy. It was designed by Captain H. C. Wilkins, R.E., and consists of the central block two storeys high, with two wings, forming three sides of a quadrangle, surmounted by a high-pitched iron rhef coloured red. At the N.W. corner of the main block is a tower 106 ft. high. The wings are occupied by students, and the main building contains class-rooms and laboratory, with a large College Hall 70 ft. long above, used for the Library.

For a native town the streets of the **City** of **Poona** are wide, and some of the older houses are substantial and picturesque buildings. It is divided into seven quarters, named after the days of the week on which the market was held. Amongst the industries of the town may be mentioned the making of gold and silver thread and wire for embroidery and for a simple kind of jewellery, the stringing of beads and berries for ornaments, and brass-work of all kinds. In the Shanwar, or Saturday division, are the remains of the *Peshwa's Castle*, called Junawada, or "old palace," a large enclosure about 180 yds. sq. It was built by the grandfather of the last Peshwa, and was a grand building, till burnt down in 1827. Only the massive walls remain. The doors are very large, and covered with iron spikes. Above the gateway is a small balcony supported on pillars. Here is the terrace from which, in 1795, the young Peshwa, Madhu Rao Narayan threw himself, and died two days afterwards of the injuries he received in the fall. Here, too, in 1773, Narayan Rao was savagely murdered by two of his guard, at the age of eighteen, after he had been but nine months Peshwa.

In front is an open space where a vegetable market is held. About 110 yds. to the N. is a stone bridge, over which a road leads to the village of Bamburda and the Sangam.

Not far from this castle is a street in which, under the Peshwas, offenders were executed by being trampled to death by elephants. One of the most memorable of these executions, on account of the princely rank of the sufferer, was that of Wittoji Holkar, brother of that Jaswant Rao Holkar who, the same year, won the battle of Poona. The last of the Peshwas, Baji Rao II., beheld the agonies of the victim from a window of his palace, where, on the morning of the 1st of April 1800, he took his seat with his favourite Balaji Kunjar in order to glut his eyes with the revolting sight.

In the Budhwar or "Wednesday" quarter of the city are some old Mahratta palaces, and the quondam residence of the well-known minister, Nana Farnavis, a shabby mansion with a small court-yard and fountain and many small dark rooms and dingy passages.

The **Parbati Hill**, with its temples, is situated at the extreme S.W. of the town; the road to Sinhgarh leads to it past the *Hira Bagh*, or "Diamond Garden." In a cemetery here, very well kept and shaded with trees, is interred the celebrated African traveller Sir William Cornwallis Harris, Major in the Bombay Engineers, who died in 1848.[1] The Hira Bagh, with its lake and island, and the villa of the Peshwas, mosque, and temples, is a charming place: Lord Valentia mentions it in his account of a visit to the Peshwa in 1804. The temple at Parbati was built by the Peshwa Balaji Baji Rao, who ruled from 1740 to 1761, but in honour, it is said, of the Raja of Satara. A long succession of steps and ramps leads up to the top of the hill and to the temples. At each corner of the first court are small shrines to Surya, "the Sun," Vishnu, Kartikkeya, the Hindu Mars, and Durga; and in the centre is the principal temple dedicated to the goddess Durga or Parvati, the wife of Shiva, so called from Parvat, "a mountain," as she is said to be the daughter of the Himalaya. In the temple is a silver image of Shiva, with images of Parvati and Ganesh, of gold, seated on his knees. The temple and its approaches are said to have cost £100,000. During the Diwali it is lighted up in a beautiful manner. On the N.W. side of the enclosing wall is a picturesque Moorish-looking window, whence it is said Baji Rao watched the defeat of his troops at Kirkee. From the top of this wall, reached by narrow steps, there is an extensive view over Poona, Kirkee, and surrounding country, including Parbati Tank to the E., and Parbati village S. of the tank, over the Hira Bagh to St Mary's Church and the Jews' Synagogue far to the N.E. To the S.W. is a ruined palace of the Peshwas which was struck by lightning in 1817, the year of Baji Rao's overthrow by the British. A donation of R.1 may

[1] He was the author of *Wild Sports in the West*, and the *Highlands of Ethiopia*.

be given to the Brahman who shows the place, for the benefit of the temple and the numerous blind persons who frequent the hill. At the foot of the hill is a square field, which in the time of the Peshwas was enclosed by high brick walls. Here at the end of the rains, about the time of the Dasahara, gifts in money were presented to all Brahmans. In order to prevent the holy men from receiving more than their share, they were passed into this enclosure, at the gate of which stood a vast cauldron filled with red pigment. Each as he entered was marked with this, and nothing was given till all had gone in. They were then let out one by one, and Rs. 3, 4, or 5 were given to each. On one occasion the Peshwa is said to have lavished £60,000 in this manner. There are several other temples and shrines at the top of the hill.

[15 m. S.W. from Poona is **Sinhgarh**, a place very famous in Mahratta annals, and very interesting on account of its scenery as well as its historic recollections. On the road to it is passed the Khandakwasla reservoir of the Poona Water-works. The Fort was taken by the renowned Tanaji Malusre, in February 1670.

"The loss of the assailants was estimated at one-third their number, or upwards of 300 killed or disabled. In the morning 500 gallant Rajputs, together with their commander, were found dead or wounded; a few had concealed themselves and submitted; but several hundreds had chosen the desperate alternative of venturing over the rock, and many were dashed to pieces in the attempt."

On the 1st of March 1818 Sinhgarh was taken by the English without loss. The garrison, 1100 men, of whom 400 were Arabs, capitulated, after being shelled for three days, in which time 1400 shells and upwards of 2000 shot were fired into the place. The ascent to Sinhgarh is in part almost perpendicular. Being 4162 ft. above the sea, it is delightfully cool, and the views are beautiful. There are several bungalows here usually occupied by Europeans in summer.

Purandhar is another hill-fort to the S.E., about 17 m. as the crow flies, and 24 m. by road from Poona. The upper and lower forts are situated more than 300 ft. below the summit, which is 4560 ft. above sea-level, and are protected by a perpendicular scarp. In March 1818 Purandhar was attacked and taken by the English column under General Pritzler (Blacker's *Mahratta War*, p. 241). It is still used as a convalescent depôt for troops. There is a D.B. there, and sportsmen may find panthers in the hills, and deer and other game in the neighbourhood.]

167 m. **Dhond** junction station (R.)

[From this place the Dhond Manmar State Railway runs N., joining the N.E. branch of the G.I.P. Railway at the latter place, 146 m. from Dhond. The only place of importance on this line is (51 m.) **Ahmednagar** station, usually called Nagar (R.), D.B., the third city of the Deccan (population, 42,000), covering 3 sq. m., and founded in 1494 by Ahmad Nizam Shah Bahri, son of a Brahman of Vijayanagar, the first of the Mohammedan dynasty which ruled Ahmednagar for 100 years. His territory was the only part of the W. coast to which the ravages of Portuguese piracy did not extend. They maintained a friendly intercourse for many years with Ahmednagar. The power of that State extended over the greater part of Berar and the province of Aurangabad and some districts in Khandesh, Kalyan, and from Bankot to Bassein in the Konkan. The Fort fell into Akbar's hands in 1605, after sustaining a celebrated siege under Chand Bibi, widow of 'Ali Adil Shah, of Bijapur, the "Noble Queen" of Meadows Taylor's novel. It was taken from the Nizam by the Mahrattas in 1760, after desperate fighting. In 1797 the fort was made over to Sindhia by the Peshwa, from whom it was taken by General Wellesley, afterwards Duke of Wellington, on the 12th of August 1803. A tamarind tree, under which the Duke of Wellington is said to have lunched, is pointed out on the S.W. side of the Fort.

The Fort is in the centre of the cantonment, 2½ m. N.E. of the railway station. Close to it are *Christ Church* and a R.C. Church. The European *Barracks* are 1 m. S.E. of it, and the N.I. Lines and D.B. are N.W. of it. The gate of the Fort towards the Poona road is called the Malle Darwazah; and just outside it are the graves of two British officers who fell here when the place was stormed in 1803. The town though flourishing and with good bazaars is now of no architectural interest. Ahmednagar is an important station of the S.P.G., the American Mission and Education Society, which have large schools and branch missions. 2 m. from the Fort is the Paria Bagh, or "fairy garden," an old palace of the Nagar kings, which has nothing attractive beyond historical associations.

The principal sight near Ahmednagar is the **Tomb of Salabat Khan**, commonly called that of **Chand Bibi**, 6 m. to E., on a hill 3080 ft. high. The building is octagonal and of three storeys, of which the lowest is now used as an hospital. Below is the crypt, in which are two tombs. There is no inscription.]

184 m. Diksal station, 3 m. beyond which the Bhima river is crossed.

234 m. **Barsi** Road station. From here a light railway leads N. to 44 m. Tadwale, and S. to

36 m. **Pandharpur** (population, 32,000), on the right bank of the Bhima river, with a very celebrated shrine to Witthoba, or Withthal. Immense crowds of pilgrims visit the temple at certain times, particularly in July and October, and suffer greatly from the crush and the want of ventilation. The scene on the Bhima river at the time of the pilgrimage is most animated and interesting. 28 m. E. is the beautiful unfinished temple said to have been built for the reception of this idol, which, however, refused to move there. The legend is, that a Brahman named Pandelli, who neglected his parents, going on a pilgrimage to Benares, stopped in a Brahman's house at Pandharpur, and saw Ganga, Yamuna, and Saraswati acting as handmaids to his host on account of his filial piety. Upon this he gave up his pilgrimage to Benares, stopped at Pandharpur, and treated his parents with great respect and honour, whereupon Vishnu became incarnate in him as Witthoba.]

283 m. **Sholapur** station, D.B. (population, 55,000), capital of a collectorate, and formerly protected by a small but strong fort, now in a ruined state, for many years the bone of contention between the Bijapur and Ahmednagar kingdoms.

In the city, which lies N. and E. of the fort, is a good **High School** for boys, and a school for girls. The cantonment lay S.E. of the railway station, and there was once a strong force here, but the troops have been withdrawn. In April 1818 General Munro marched against a body of Baji Rao's infantry, 4500 in number, with 13 guns, attacked them under the walls of Sholapur, and routed them with great slaughter. The fort, after a short siege, surrendered.

At about 3 m. N. of the city of Sholapur is the **Ekrukh Tank**, 6 m. in length, formed by a modern embankment of earth and rough stones, 1½ m. long, which has been carried across the Adhin river. Three canals from it irrigate the surrounding country.

292 m. **Hotgi** junction station (R.). From this point the Southern Mahratta Railway runs S. to *Bijapur* and Gadag junction (see Route 27).

353 m. **Gulbarga** station, D.B. Gulbarga was the first capital of the Bahmani Kingdom of the Deccan (1347-1500 A.D.), but was abandoned by the 9th of the dynasty in 1432 in favour of Bidar (p. 374). It stands in an undulating plain, a somewhat dreary expanse of black soil, relieved by outcrops of limestone and thriving young plantations of trees. It is included in the Hyderabad State, and houses for the Nizam's officers and public offices, have been erected on the *Maidan*, which stretches from the railway station to the city. The Old Fort in the background, black with age, and the numerous domes with which the plain is dotted, also help to relieve the generally monotonous aspect. The Bahmani Kingdom, which was founded at the close of the reign of the Emperor Muhammad Tughlak Shah of Delhi (1325-1351), dissolved gradually into the five kingdoms of Bijapur, Golkanda, Ahmednagar, Bidar, and Berar, of which the last three came to an end with the 16th century, and the first two struggled on against the Mughals till 1660 and 1672.

The outer walls and gateways and most of the old buildings of the **Fort** are in a very dilapidated condition. The *Citadel* or *Bala Hisar* has suffered least. On the top of it is a curious old gun, 26 ft. long, and having twenty pairs of iron rings attached to it, by which it used probably to be slung or lifted. Close by is an old Hindu temple, which has been converted into a mosque.

In the old fort is the **Jama Masjid**, one of the finest old Pathan mosques in India, built in the reign of Firoz Shah, and modelled after the great mosque of Cordova in Spain. Visitors entering it are expected to take off their boots. According to Mr Fergusson, it measures 216 ft. E. and W., and 176 ft. N. and S., and consequently covers an area of 38,016 sq. ft. Its great peculiarity is that alone of all the great mosques of India the whole area is completely covered over. There is therefore no court, and the solid roof affords protection from the sun to all worshippers, while the light is admitted through the side walls, which are pierced with great arches on all sides except the W. This arrangement is so good both for convenience and architectural effect that it is difficult to understand why it was never afterwards repeated. It stands in seemingly good repair after four centuries of neglect, and owes its greatness solely to its own original merit of design.

The *Talukdar's Court*, the *Judicial Offices*, and the *Treasury* of Gulbarga are located in the grand old **Tombs** in the eastern quarter of the town. These tombs are huge square buildings, surmounted by domes 100 ft. high, and are the burial-places of the kings who reigned here at the end of the 14th century. They are roughly yet strongly built, but, with the exception of some handsome stone tracery, which has unfortunately been whitewashed, none of them contain exterior ornaments of any kind. The interiors are more elaborately finished.

Some little distance from these tombs is the shrine or *Dargah of Banda Nawaz* or *Gisu Daraz* (accessible only to Mohammedans), a celebrated saint of the Chishti family (see p. 138) who came to Gulbarga during the reign of Firoz Shah in 1413. The present structure is said to have been erected in 1640 by one of his descendants during the reign of Mahmud 'Adil Shah. Shah Wali, Firoz Shah's brother, made many valuable presents to the Saint and gave him large *jagirs*, and built him a magnificent college close to the city. Some of his descendants still reside at his tomb. The shrine is much venerated by Mohammedans in this part of India, and none but true believers are admitted inside its portals. Close by are some buildings, consisting of a sarai, mosque, and college (*Madrassa*), said to have been erected by Aurangzeb, who visited Gulbarga on several occasions.

In the town is a bazaar 370 ft. by 60 ft., adorned by a row of sixty-one Hindu arches, with a very ornamental block of buildings at either end.

370 m. **Shahabad** station (R.). Known for its limestone quarries. Large quantities of the stone are exported.

376 m. **Wadi** junction station (R.). From here the Nizam's State Railway runs E. to Hyderabad, Secunderabad, Warangal, and Bezwada (Route 28). Passengers for it change carriages.

427 m. **Krishna** station. Here the railway crosses the Kistna river by a grand bridge 3854 ft long.

443 **Raichur** station (R.). At this point the G.I.P. Railway and the Madras and S. Mahratta Railway N.W. Branch Railway meet. Madras is distant 350 m.

Raichur formed part of the dominions of the Bahmani kings in 1357. It was included in the government of Bijapur, and was governed in 1478 by Khwajah Jahan Gawan. When Bijapur became an independent kingdom, Raichur was its first capital. The *Fort* is about 1½ m. from the railway station. The N. gate, flanked by towers, is best worth attention. There is a stone elephant not quite the natural size carved out of a boulder about 50 yds. outside the gate. At right angles to this gate is another called the Kasbah Darwazah. Outside the latter is the door of a tunnel out of which the garrison could come to close the gate, and then retire by the underground passage into the Fort. The W. gate is called the Sikandariah, and near it is the old palace, with immensely thick walls, now a jail.

The *Citadel* should be seen for the sake of the fine view, extending as far as the Tungabhadra river, 16 m. to the S., and the Kistna, 12 m. to the N. The ascent commences from near the N. gate. The hill on which it is built consists of immense boulders of rock, and is over 290 ft. high. The path up is broken and unsafe after dark. On the left is a row of cells belonging to the *dargah*, or shrine, and at the E. end, overhanging the precipice, is a stone pavilion. Near this on the E. is a mosque 18 ft. high; and on the S. side is a place for a bell or gong 7 ft. high, with stone supports and a stone roof. The whole surface of the top is 70 ft. square. The town is to the E. of the Fort.

486 m. **Adoni** station (Adwani—population, 30,500). This is one of the principal cotton-marts in the Deccan. The town is of some historical interest. According to tradition, it was founded 3000 years ago by Chandra Singh of Bidar. After the battle of Talikot in 1554, the Sultan of Bijapur appointed Malik Rahman Khan, an Abyssinian, to govern it, which he did for 39 years, and died there. His tomb on the Talibanda hill is still an object of religious veneration. He was succeeded by his adopted son Sidi Mas'aud Khan, who built the lower fort, and the fine Jama Masjid. In 1690 Adoni was taken, after a desperate resistance, by one of Aurangzeb's generals, and afterwards fell to the Nizam. Salabat Jang granted it in *jagir* to Basalat Jang, his younger brother, who made it his capital, and endeavoured to form an independent State. He died in 1782, and was buried at Adoni, and a fine mosque and tomb were erected over his grave and that of his mother. In 1786 the citadel was captured by Tipu Sultan after one month's siege. He demolished the fortifications, and removed the guns and stores to Gooty. In 1792 it was restored to the Nizam, and exchanged by him with the British in 1799 A.D. for other places. The citadel is built on five hills, two of which rise 800 ft. above the plain. Half-way up the rock is a fine tank containing good water, and never dry.

518 m. **Guntakal** junction station. (R.). From this junction the line runs S.E. to Madras, S. to Bangalore, N.E. to Bezwada, and W. to Bellary, Hospet (for Vijayanagar), and Goa. (See Route 29.)

536 m. **Gooty** station (R.). Nearly 2 m. S. of the railway station is an old hill-fort, the stronghold of Morari Rao, the ally of Clive at Arcot. It was taken by Hyder 'Ali in 1776 after a siege of nine months. The water failed, and the garrison were forced by thirst to surrender. The fort is 950 ft. above the plain, and 2000 ft. above the sea. Sir Thomas Munro died and was buried at Gooty in 1827, but his body was subsequently removed to Madras. There is a monument to him in the churchyard here.

566 m. **Tadpatri** station (R.). The town was founded during the time of the Vijayanagar kings about 1485, when the highly decorative temples were built. They are about 2 m. from the railway station. The one on the river-bank was never finished, but is the most imposing. (See Fergusson's *Indian Architecture*, i. 405. In the note there Tadpatri is confounded with Tirupati — see below).

632 m. **Cuddapah** station (R.). The Nawabs of Cuddapah, who played a part of no little importance in the latter half of the 18th century, established themselves early in that century. Situated between the Mahrattas, the Nizam and Mysore, they were gradually crushed, and finally were reabsorbed by the Hyderabad State. In 1799 the District, with Kurnool and Bellary, was ceded to the East India Company, and Sir Thomas Munro was appointed first Collector of all three.

710 m. **Renigunta** station (R.), junction of the Metre-gauge State Railway (1) N.E. to Gudur (p. 336), and (2) S. and S.E. to Tirupati, Vellore (p. 395) and Villupuram.

[8 m. **Tirupati** station, ✱ D.B. This town of 14,000 inhabitants, crowded at all times with pilgrims, is celebrated for one of the most sacred **Hill Pagodas** (Sri Venkateswara Perumal) in S. India; it stands at the top of the "holy hill" called *Tirumala*, and is about 8 m. from the railway station. Wooden and brass idols are a speciality of the lower town. A conveyance takes one to the foot of the hill, where there are two fine gates from which the ascent is made in a dhooly carried by bearers. It is well to obtain an introduction to the Mahant from the Collector of the District. There are several gopurams on the ascent visible from below. The antiquity of the temple is indisputable, but its origin is involved in obscurity. The idol is an erect stone figure 7 ft. high, with four arms, representing Vishnu. No European ascended the hill till 1870, when the Superintendent of Police, in spite of the remonstrances of the Mahant, went up in search of an escaped forger. It is 2500 ft. high and quite bare, and has seven peaks. On the seventh peak, Sri Venkataramanachellam, is the pagoda, surrounded by a broad belt of mango, tamarind, and sandal trees. In front of it is a Hall of 1000 Pillars, which cannot, however, compare with that at Madura, or those at Chidambaram or Conjeeveram. A picturesque stepped way leads from it to the temple gate, which is a fine one; admission to the temple is not granted. E. of the temple is a tank, and a bungalow, belonging to the Mahant, for the accommodation of European visitors.

14 m. **Chandragiri station.** After the defeat of Talikot in 1564 this was the residence of the Rajas of Vijayanagar. It was taken from them by the Golconda Ruler in 1646, and was occupied by the Nawab of Arcot in 1750, and by Hyder 'Ali in 1782. In the palace here one of these, Sri Ranga Raya, in 1639, made to the East India Company the original grant

of the land on which Fort St George (Madras) was built. The Government carefully preserve the palace, and it is used as a halting-place for officials. It is most picturesquely situated in the Fort, and at the back of it is a high rocky hill. The best way to visit it is to drive from Tirupati, and join the train at Chandragiri.

78 m. **Vellore** station (Route 31).

272 m. **Villupuram** station.]

From Renigunta station the line continues S.E. to

751 m. **Arkonam** junction station (R.). The N.W. and S.W. branches of the Madras and S. Mahratta Railway join at this point, and a branch of the South Indian Railway runs S. to Conjeeveram and Chingleput (Route 31 (*b*)).

765 m. **Trivalur** station. There is a large Vaishnava temple here; and 4 m. from the station is the site of the old fort of *Tripasore*, which was captured by Sir Eyre Coote in 1781. Tripasore Fort was at one time the station for the East India Company's cadets, and afterwards for pensioners.

794 m. **Madras** Central Station (p. 407).

ROUTE 26.

POONA to GOA by **Wathar Satara, Miraj, Belgaum, Londa,** the **Braganza Ghat** and **Mormugao,** with excursion by road to **Mahabaleshwar,** and rail to **Kolhapur.**

Poona (see p. 342). The Madras and Southern Mahratta Railway branches S. from the G.I.P. 2 m. E. of the station. Passing through three hill ranges it reaches

68 m. **Wathar** station ✱ (R.).

[Passengers leave the train here for **Mahabaleshwar,** the principal hill-station of the Bombay Presidency, about 40 m. distant by road to the W.

Motors, carriages, and tongas can be had at Wathar by giving notice to the mail contractor at Mahabaleshwar —charge for two last Rs. 30 as. 12, and Rs. 20 as. 12. Motors can be hired also direct from Poona. It is a charming drive of about five hours, the first part through rolling country to

18 m. **Wai,** D.B. (population, 12,000), one of the most beautiful rustic towns in the Deccan. It is situated on the left bank of the Kistna, which is lined with fine pipal and mango trees, and with

handsome flights of stone steps. Behind the city rise hills of all the shapes which are peculiar to the mountains in the Deccan. One hill near the city rises very abruptly, and has a hill-fort on the top: it is called Pandugarh, according to the tradition that Wai is the Vairatnagar visited by the Pandus (p. lviii.). The nearest temple to the D.B. — and the river is lined with beautiful temples — is dedicated to *Ganpati*; the next to *Mahadeo;* and one, at some distance, to *Lakhshmi.* They form the great beauty of this most picturesque spot. The *mandapam*, or canopy, in front of Mahadeo's temple is very light, and a fine specimen of carving in stone. Wai is a spot much famed in Hindu legend. Here, according to old tradition, the Pandus spent part of their banishment, and performed many great works (Introd. p. lviii.). On this account, as because of its proximity to the Kistna River so near its source, Wai is viewed as a place of great sanctity; and there is a college of Brahmans established at it, once in much repute.

The most curious thing to be seen near Wai is a gigantic *Banyan Tree*, at the foot of a mountain called Wairatgarh, about 8 m. distant. The exact area shaded by it is three-quarters of an acre. The space covered is a very symmetrical oval. There is no brushwood underneath, nor aught to impede the view save the stems of the shoots from the parent tree. (See p. 66.)

On leaving Wai the road begins a steep ascent to

29 m. **Panchganni**, a very large village, containing many bungalows belonging to Europeans, with nice plantations about them. In fact, many visitors who come to the hills prefer to stop at Panchganni rather than Mahabaleshwar, because the rainfall is less, and the place can be made a permanent residence. From Panchganni the road descends a little for one-third of a mile; the country round is covered with low jungle and patches of cultivation.

About 1 m. from Mahabaleshwar village, the small lake made by the Rajah of Satara is passed on the right; it winds picturesquely, and is about 810 yds. long, and not quite 200 yds. broad.

40 m. **Mahabaleshwar** * is a lofty tableland, 7 m. long by about 3 m. wide, bounded on the W. by abrupt precipices, covered with foliage except where bold rocks, called "points," break through. These stand about 4500 ft. above the sea, from which they are only 25 m. due E. The *Pteris aquilina*, or common brake, grows very plentifully on the hills, as do the willow, *Eugenia jambolana*, and *Gardenia montana*. There are a few oaks. There are thirty species of ferns, of which the principal are the *Acrostichum aureum*, the *Actiniopteris radiata*, the *Adiantum lunulatum*, the *Aspidium cochleatum*, the *Asplenium erectum* and *falcatum*, the *Pteris pellucida* and *quadriaurita*. The arrowroot lily, *Curcuma caulina*, also grows abundantly. Mahabaleshwar is a favourite resort from Bombay in the hot weather before the rains break. During the monsoon, from middle of June to end of September, it is uninhabitable on account of the rains.

The centre of the European quarter was called *Malcolm Peth* by the Raja of Satara in honour of Sir John Malcolm, who resided much on these hills when Governor; it contains a *Library*, *Club*, *Church* and Sir Sidney Beckwith's *Monument*, and a *Cemetery*. There is also a Government sanatorium with eight sets of quarters.

Amongst the sights near Mahabaleshwar are the **Falls of the Yena**, at the head of a wild mountain gorge of that name on the right of the road to the Tai Ghat, and reached by a bypath from a point on the Satara Road. The stream is here precipitated over the face of a steep cliff with a sheer descent of 500 ft., unbroken when the torrent is swollen by rain, but ordinarily divided by projecting rocks about one-third of the way down, and scattered below into thin white streaks and spray, which are often circled by rainbows from the oblique rays of the sun.

Lodwick Point lies to the N.E. of the village of Malcolm Peth. At about ½ m. before reaching the monument to General Lodwick the carriage stops, and the rest of the way must be done on foot. The column is about 25 ft. high. The spot commands a noble view over Pratabgarh to the W. and Makrangarh to the S.W.

Returning S.E. from Lodwick Point a series of pretty roads and paths lead to Government House, and from there S. to Bombay and Carnac points with beautiful views. From these a path leads E. along the south ravine which bounds Mahabaleshwar on the S., as the Elphinstone Point ravine does on the N.

To the N.W. of Lodwick Point is **Elphinstone Point**, the grandest of all the precipitous scarps which overhang the low country. This is about 3 m. from Malcolm Peth, W. of the good road to Mahabaleshwar Temple. There is a sheer descent of above 2000 ft., though not so steep at the summit but that wild bison have been seen to gallop down some parts. A rock rolled from the top thunders down and crashes into the forests below. The view extends to the mountains, among which is the hill-fort of Torna, over an apparently uninhabited jungle. To the N. of Elphinstone Point is **Arthur's Seat**, another fine point of view which should by no means be omitted. It has its name from Mr Arthur Malet, C.S., who first built a house here.

The ancient *village of Mahabaleshwar*, 3 m. from Malcolm Peth, is a small place, but of great sanctity in the eyes of the Hindus, as being the spot where the Kistna and four other rivers have their source. There are several temples, one very old, of black stone, said to have been built by a Gauli Raja. Another built by the same chief, and called Koteshwar, commands a grand view over the Wai valley. The principal temple is called Mahabaleshwar.

Pratabgarh is a picturesque hill-fort crowning a precipitous rock, remarkable as the stronghold of Shivaji, and as the scene of one of the most remarkable events in Indian history, the founding of the Mahratta empire. A charming drive of 6 m. leads to the foot of the hill, whence a steep and difficult path ascends to the gates of the fortress. Shivaji, the free-booter, having in 1656 provoked hostilities with Bijapur, whose army he could not meet in the open, determined to overcome its general, Afzal Khan, by stratagem, and pretending to be in a state of great alarm at the approach of the Bijapur army to besiege Pratabgarh, offered to make his submission to Afzal Khan at a personal interview, on condition that the two commanders should meet unarmed, in the midst, between the two armies with only one armed attendant. They accordingly approached from either side, attired, to all appearance, in white muslin robes, but Shivaji wore defensive mail under his robe and turban, and carried concealed in one hand a cruel weapon called a Wághnakh, "the tiger's claws," consisting of sharp steel hooks attached by rings to his fingers. In the very act of embracing the Khan in an attitude of humility Shivaji drove these claws into him and tore out his vitals, and despatched him with a hidden dagger. His head was struck off and buried under the old tower in the Fort, now fallen to ruin. Meanwhile the Mahratta army, which had been concealed in ambush in the jungle, rushed out upon the Bijapur forces and cut them to pieces.]

From Wathar station the railway line proceeds to

77 m. **Satara Road** station. From

here it is a 10 m. drive by tonga or carriage to Satara (3200 ft. high; D.B.; population, 26,000), situated in a hollow between two ranges of hills, which rise above it on the E. and W., and partly overlap it on the S. The hill on the W. is the termination of a spur from the Mahabaleshwar Hills. From this hill to the city there is an aqueduct 4 m. long, and there are also two fine tanks. The city has many historic recollections, and the station is one of the most salubrious and pleasant in the Deccan. The *Cantonment* is about 1½ m. from N. to S., and nearly the same from E. to W. In the S. end is the Residency compound. Outside the N. gate of the old Residency were the British lines, the native lines and Sadar bazaar lying N. of them.

The ruling family of Satara was descended from Shahu, the grandson of Shivaji, who was brought up at the Mughal Court. Direct descendents died out in 1848 with Raja Shahji, and the State then lapsed to the British Government.

The *New Palace*, built by Apa Sahib, near the centre of the city, adjoins the Old Palace. On the façade are a number of mythological pictures, much defaced by the weather. On the N. side of the court is a vast hall, one of the largest in India. In the front court are the offices of the Collector and his assistants, and W. of the hall are those of the Judge. The roof is supported by sixty-four teak pillars, with four more in front. About 200 yds. beyond this is a pretty garden and villa belonging to Raja Ram, who was adopted by the late Rani. He is in possession of the crown jewels of the Satara family, and of Jai Bhawani, the famous sword of Shivaji, and his other arms. The sword is 3 ft. 9 in. long in the blade, and the handle is 8 in. long, but so small that a European can hardly get his hand into it. Like most of the famous blades in India, it is of European make, and has the stamp of Genoa. The *Wághnakh*, or "tiger's claw," with which Shivaji wounded Afzal Khan, consists of four steel claws, with rings which pass over the first and fourth fingers, but are too small for a European hand. The shield is of rhinoceros hide, and has four stars or bosses of diamonds. The gold casket for holding Shivaji's seal is ornamented with diamonds, rubies, pearls, and emeralds, and there is an inkstand and penholder of gold similarly begemmed. The quilted coat which Shivaji wore when he murdered Afzal Khan may also be seen. It is lined with chain armour, which is hidden by thick masses of padding and silk, embroidered with gold, and is very heavy. The dagger is very handsome, and is 18 in. long. The diamonds, emeralds, and rubies in the handle are very fine.

The **Fort** rises finely on the S. side of the town, and may now be nearly reached by a driving road winding up from the cantonment. The gate of the Fort is on the N. side, is of stone, and is very strongly built, with buttresses 40 ft. high. The interior of the Fort is now nearly desolate. There are only a few bungalows, with one small temple, and a hospital. The Fort is said to have been built by a Raja of Panhala, who reigned in 1192.[1] By him, too, were erected the forts of Bairatgarh and Pandugarh, near Wai, and Chandan and Wandan, near Satara. Long before the time of the 'Adil Shahi dynasty at Bijapur, the Fort of Satara was used as a State prison, and Shivaji, who captured it in 1673, after a siege of several months, unwittingly furnished for his descendants a prison in which they were for years confined by the Peshwas. In 1698, at the suggestion of Ramchandra Pant, Satara was made the capital of the Mahratta Government. Next year Aurangzeb with a great army arrived before the city and pitched his tents on the N. side. His son, Prince Azim Shah, was on the W. side, at a village since called Shahpur: Shirzi Khan

[1] *Grant Duff*, vol. i. p. 260.

invested the S., and Tarbiyat Khan occupied the E. quarter. Chains of posts between the different camps effectually secured the blockade. The Fort was defended by Pryagji Prabhu, hawaldar, who had been reared in the service of Shivaji. As the Mughals advanced, he withdrew into the Fort, and rolled down huge stones from the rock above, which did great execution. The blockade, however, was complete, all communications were cut off, provisions were exhausted, and the besieged must have been compelled to surrender had not Parshuram Trimbak, who had thrown himself into the Fort of Prali, purchased the connivance of 'Azim Shah, and conveyed stores to the besieged. The grand attack was directed against the N.E. angle, which is one of the strongest points, the rock being 42 ft. high, with a bastion on the top of 25 ft. of masonry. Tarbiyat Khan undertook to mine this angle, and at the end of four and a half months had completed two mines. The storming party, confident of success, was formed under the brow of the hill. The Emperor moved out in grand procession to view the attack, and the garrison, and among them Pryagji, attracted by the splendour of the retinue, crowded to the rampart. The first mine burst several fissures in the rock, caused a great part of the masonry to fall inwards and crush many of the garrison to death; but the second and larger mine burst outwards with a terrible explosion, and destroyed upwards of 2000 of the besiegers. Pryagji was buried by the first explosion close to a temple to Bhavani, but was dug out alive. This was regarded by the Mahrattas as a happy omen, and, animated by it, the garrison would have made a prolonged and desperate defence, but provisions fell short, and 'Azim Shah would no longer connive at their introduction. Proposals of surrender were therefore made through him, and the honour of the capture, which he so ill merited, was not only assigned to him, but the very name of the place, in compliment to him, was changed by the Emperor to 'Azimgarh.

In 1705 the Fort was retaken by the Mahrattas, through the artifice of a Brahman named Anaji Pant. He ingratiated himself with the Mughals under the character of a mendicant devotee, amusing them with stories and songs, and, being allowed to reside in the Fort, introduced a body of Mawalis, and put every man of the garrison to the sword. Satara surrendered to the English in 1818, and Pratap Singh, eldest son of Shahu II., was installed as Raja. He held the principality twenty-one years, and was sent prisoner to Benares in 1839, being succeeded by his brother, Apa Sahib, on whose death, in 1848, the territory was annexed.

Mahuli.—This pretty place, at the confluence of the *Kistna* and *Yena* rivers, is about 3 m. E. of Satara, and thoroughly deserves a visit. It is considered a place of great sanctity, and the dead from Satara and the surrounding villages are brought there for cremation. Descending the river, the first temple is *Kshetra Mahuli*, built in 1825 and dedicated to Radha Shankar.

On the same side of the river is the temple of *Bholeshwar Mahadeo*, built in 1742. The next temple is on the same bank, dedicated to Rameshwar, and was built in 1700 A.D. Looking from the opposite bank, one is struck with the very fine flight of steps leading up to it from the river-bed. Close to the junction of the rivers, on the W. bank of the Kistna and the N. of the Yena, is the Temple of *Sangameshwar Mahadeo*, built in 1679. Below it and at the junction of the rivers is a triangular plot of ground, with the *tombs* of a Gusain named *Banshapuri*, and his disciples. That of the Gusain is an octagonal building of gray basalt, with open sides surmounted by a low dome. The largest of the temples is on the S. side of the Yena, at its confluence with the Kistna. It is sacred to

Vishveshwar Mahadeo, and was built in 1735 A.D.

---

160 m. **Miraj** junction station (R.), D.B.

[A branch line, constructed by the Kolhapur State, runs W. to

29 m. **Kolhapur** station, D.B. (population, 54,000), the capital of the native State with a total area of about 2816 sq. m., and a revenue of 44 lakhs. It is celebrated on account of the antiquity of its temples, and is now also distinguished for its fine modern buildings. The Raja Jaswant Rao traces his descent from the Mahratta chief Shivaji.

His *New Palace*, between the Residency and the city, was built at a cost of Rs.700,000, and is a very prominent object in the landscape.

The *Albert Edward Hospital* was built in commemoration of King Edward's visit to India, and contains a portrait of him.

Opposite is the *Town Hall*, situated in the *Public Gardens*. The *High School*, a handsome pile of buildings, is near the Old Palace in the centre of the town, and fronting it is the *Native General Library*. The *Political Agent's House* is a handsome building. 800 yds. W. of the D.B. is *All Saints' Church*, served by the S.P.G. clergy, whose *Mission-house* is 300 yds off, ½ m. S.W. of the Political Agent's house. The Ladies' Association of the S.P.G. has eight schools and a Mission-house in the town.

A *Nakkar Khana*, or "Music Gallery," forms the entrance to the *Palace Square*. To the right on entering is the *Rajwada*, or *Old Palace*, with a stone gateway in the centre and wooden pillars. On the second storey is a Darbar-room, with portraits of Aka Bai, mother of the late chief of Kagal, and of Ahalaya Bai, adoptive mother of the late Raja, Raja Ram. There is also a picture of the mausoleum at Florence erected over the spot where Raja Ram's body was burned; he died there returning from a visit to England. In the third storey is an Armoury, in which are many curious swords, one of which may have belonged to Aurangzeb, for it has in Persian the name 'Alamgir, and the date 1012 A.H. There is also a Persian sword given by Sir John Malcolm to the Raja of his time.

Adjoining the Treasury, in the S. face of the square, are other *Government Offices*, and behind them the shrine of *Amba Bai*, the tutelary deity of Kolhapur. The great bell of the temple is inscribed, "Ave Maria Gratiæ Plena Dominus Tecum," and must have been obtained from the Portuguese about the year 1739.

N. of the town is a sacred spot, the *Brahmapuri Hill*, where the Brahmans undergo cremation. About 100 yds. N. of this, close to the Panchganga river, is what is called the *Rani's Garden*, where the bodies of the ruling family are burned.

From this spot is seen a *bridge* over the river, with five arches, finished in 1878 at a cost of £14,000. Beyond Rani's Garden is a massive stone gateway, 20 ft. high, which leads to the *Cenotaphs* of Raja Sambhaji, just opposite the door, to that of Shivaji, and more to the left that of Tara-Bai.

Kolhapur was one of the few places in the Bombay Presidency which took part in the disastrous rebellion of 1857. The mutineers broke open the magazines, stole arms, and carried off public treasure to the amount of Rs.45,000.

[*Hill-forts of* **Panhala** *and* **Pawangadh.**—Before leaving Kolhapur, the traveller should pay a visit to Panhala, which lies 12 m. to the N.W. of the capital. There is an excellent road all the way right into the Fort. The last 5 m. are up a steep ascent.

The Fortress of **Panhala**, 2992 ft. above sea-level, is one of the most interesting in the W. of India. It stands up boldly at the top of a rocky height, and was the stronghold of a Raja in 1192 who reigned over the territory from Mahadeo Hills

N. of Satara to the river Hiranyakeshi. It was taken by the kings of Bijapur, who restored it in 1549; was captured in 1659 by Shivaji, who made some of his most successful expeditions from it; and surrendered to the Mughals in 1690; and in 1844 was stormed and taken by the English. At the *Char Darwazah*, or quadruple gate, is a temple of Maruti; passing on, there is a Mohammedan tomb of granite on the left, converted into a school; and a little farther on a temple of *Sambhaji* on the same side of the road. The Shivaji Tower (1600 A.D.) is a conspicuous building of two storeys, facing E. and standing at the brink of a precipice. About ¼ m. S.W. of the tower are the stone granaries which enabled Shivaji to stand a siege of five months. They are 30 ft. high, 57 ft. broad, and 130 ft. long. At the W. side of the Fort is the *Tin Darwazah*, a triple gate handsomely sculptured. To the right, at about 40 yds. distance, is the place were the English breached and stormed the Fort in 1844.]

Returning to Miraj junction, the line continues to

209 m. **Gokak Road** station (R.)—4 m. from here are the falls of the Ghatparba river, known as the **Gokak Falls.** In the rainy season they are very fine, but at other times of the year the volume of water is insignificant. The height of the falls is 176 ft. and the pool below is very deep. Near the falls, on both banks, are groups of old temples. There are the remains of many dolmens S.E. of the village of Konur, 1 m. from the falls. The Gokak Canal, an important irrigation work, starts from here.

245 m. **Belgaum** station (R.), D.B., a civil and military cantonment (population 37,000), is called by the natives Shahpur Belgaum, from the neighbouring *jagir* of Shahpur, which lies to the S. It is situated in a plain about 2500 ft. above the sea, with low hills in the distance. The Fort stands to the E. of the town, which contains nothing of especial interest, and to the W. of the cantonment. It is built of stone, is oval in shape, and has earthen ramparts and a ditch. It was taken by Brigadier-General, afterwards Sir, T. Munro, on the 10th of April 1818.

In the passage, through the gateway which curves to a second gate, is a row of arches with some good carving. At 120 yds. distant is the ruined Nakkar Khana, or music gallery, and on the left is the Fort *Church*, containing memorial tablets to C. J. Manson, C.S., who was murdered by a band of rebels in the night of the 29th May 1858, and to Lieutenant W. P. Shakespeare, A. P. Campbell, and Ensign W. Caldwell, who all fell in the insurrection of Kolhapur and Sawantwadi.

Beyond the Nakkar Khana to the E. is a neat plain mosque, and farther S. a *Jain Temple*, built of laterite. There is a low wall at the entrance, along which are carved figures of musicians. The façade has four pillars and two pilasters, all of a very complicated character. The inscription in the old Kanara language, beautifully cut on a slab of black porphyry, which once was here, and is now in Museum of the Bombay Asiatic Society, states that Malikarjuna, whose descent for three generations is given, built the temple.

The *second Jain Temple* is within the Commissariat Store Yard, and is very much finer than that outside. The roof is a most complicated piece of carving, rising in tiers, with eaves about 2 ft. broad, which rest on bar-like corbels from the pillars. The principal entrance faces the N.W., and has one elephant remaining at the side, much mutilated; there is a quadruple pendant in the centre. The niches are shell-shaped. There are four portals, 7 ft. sq. each, and each with four black basalt pillars. There is no image. Mr Burgess says: "The pillars of the temple are square and massive, but relieved by having all the principal facets, the triangles on the base and neck carved with floral ornamentations. The door leading from the mandapam to the temple has been carved with uncommon care. On the centre of the lintel is a Tirthankar, and above the cornice are four squat human figures. On the neat colonnettes of the jambs are five bands with human groups, in some of which the figures are little more than an inch high, yet in high relief; inside this is a band of rampant *Sinhas* (lions), with a sort of high frill round their necks. Outside the colonnettes is a band of *chakwas*, or sacred geese, another of *Sinhas*, and then one of human figures, mostly on bended knees."

To the S.E. of this temple is a mosque called the Masjid-i-Safa. Over the entrance a Persian inscription records its being built in 1519 A.D.

St Mary's Church stands in the cantonment N.W. of the town. It was consecrated 1869. There is a handsome Memorial Cross in the compound to twenty-three sergeants of H.M.'s 64th, who died during the Persian and Indian campaigns, 1856-1858.

[At **Sutgati**, 14 m. from Belgaum, there are two Indian fig-trees of very great size. The first is near the D.B. The stem forms a wall of timber extending 40 ft. and rises to a great height; the branches spread out 100 ft. round the trunk. The other tree is about 1 m. from the bungalow, and though not remarkable for height, covers a larger surface of ground.]

278 m. **Londa** junction station (R.) (Line to Hubli and thence E. to Bezwada at the head of the delta of the Kistna river, and S.E. to Bangalore, see p. 373.)

293 m. **Castle Rock** station (R.) Here, at the frontier of the **Portuguese territory of Goa**, the S. Mahratta line is joined by the West of India Portuguese Railway, which in 71 m. runs down the Braganza Ghat to Mormugão, the seaport of Goa. In the first 10 m. the line passes through a dozen tunnels, ranging from 150 to 838 ft. in length, which had to be cut almost entirely out of the solid rock. Apart from its commercial importance, the line possesses much interest for lovers of the picturesque, as it runs through magnificent scenery.

308 m. **Dudh Saugar** station, or the "sea of milk," where there is a very fine waterfall.

362 m. **Vasco da Gama.**

364 m. The terminus of the railway is on the quay at the **Port of Mormugão**, which, as well as the line, is the property of the West of India Portuguese Railway Company. Arrangements have been made that the trade there shall be as free as in British India.

The B.I.S.N. Co.'s and the Shepherd Co.'s vessels run to and from Bombay in twenty-six hours.

In approaching Goa from Bombay by sea the steamer enters a spacious harbour formed by two estuaries, with the Ilha de Goa in between them, and embraced by two rocky promontories. At the extremity of the S. arm Sakete is the landing-place and quay of *Mormugão*, where a steamer of 4000 tons can be berthed. Here at the foot of a sandy cliff is the *Terminus* of the railway. To reach New and Old Goa from it a small steamer crosses the estuary of Mormugão, rounds the *Cabo*, the W. point of the island, enters the estuary of Aguada, ascends the Mondavi, one of the two rivers falling into it, and passes, near its mouth, the fine *Fortress* and *Church* of *Reis Magos* on the N. promontory of Bardes. On the right is the island of Goa, and upon it, at about 4 m. from Mormugão, stands

New Goa,* otherwise *Panjim*, a town of no pretence. It contains 9500 inhabitants, and more than half the native population are Christian descendants of Hindus converted by the Jesuits.

A row of handsome buildings lines the quay, including the *Old Fort*, now the residence of the Viceroy, who removed hither from **Old Goa** about 1760, and in 1845 made this the seat of government and capital of the Portuguese territory in India. Here also is the *Palace of the Archbishop*, who is Primate of the Roman Catholic Church in India, and assessor of the Portuguese Viceroy in the Government.

Near it are the *Barracks*, which hold the standing army of 200 men. In front of them is a statue of Affonso de Albuquerque, the founder of Old Goa, brought from there.

The "*Goa Boys*," so well known in Bombay and in other parts of India as servants, come from Panjim.

A good road (conveyances available) leads from New to Old Goa about 5 m. higher up the valley, at first crossing a causeway thrown over the swamp to *Ribandar* village. From here cocoa-nut plantations and dwelling-houses line the way, which commands a fine view N. across the river to the hilly wooded country beyond, and includes a conspicuous round hill, crowned by a church and conventual buildings, upon the river-island of Divar. En route are passed the later Archiepiscopal Palace and the Fountain of Banguenim, which used to furnish water to old Goa.

Old Goa (Goa Velha, "Senhora Detodo o Oriente," Camoens, ii. 51), owes its origin to Affonso de Albuquerque, who at the head of 20 ships and 1200 troops carried by storm a small coast town of the Bijapur State in 1510 A.D. On this site he founded the Christian city. It rose rapidly into prosperity and importance, and by the middle of the 16th century became the wealthiest city in all India (Goa dourada) the capital and seat of government of the then vast Portuguese territory, with a population of 200,000—ilha illustrissima de Goa, Camoens. Moreover, it was the first Christian colony in the Indies, and the scene of the labours of St Francis Xavier in 1542-52. But decay followed rapidly, first owing to the attacks of the Dutch, whose fleets blockaded its harbour, and next because of its site proving pestilential, and it became deserted by its inhabitants, of whom in 1890 only eighty-six remained.[1] It is now literally a city of ruins, and is so hidden from view by the foliage of the jungle which has occupied it, that the stranger approaches it unawares, and drives into the midst unconscious that he is traversing streets of ruined empty dwellings, occupied by cocoa-nut and other tall trees instead of by human beings.

In the midst of all this ruin, Goa remains a city of magnificent churches, four or five ranking as first class and in perfect preservation, though the style of architecture betrays the degraded taste of the Jesuits.

The road from Panjim leads past the Arsenal on the left, and the hill of the Church of the Rosary on the right into a large central square named the Pelourinho from the stocks in it, and surrounded by churches and convents. The most important of these and the holiest, because it contains the body of St Francis Xavier, is the **Bom** (the Good) **Jesus**, on the right (S.) side, erected in 1594. Its handsome façade runs on into that of another great building with lofty halls and lengthy corridors, all empty, the *Convent of the Jesuits*, which, though not finished until 1590, thirty-eight years after the death of St Francis, had the merit of rearing and sending forth over the world an admirable and devoted band of missionaries, the children of that saintly man who worked so hard for the salvation of the heathen in India, China, Japan, Paraguay, and N. America. The Order was suppressed here in 1759, the other monastic orders in 1835, when their property was confiscated to the state. The endowments of the churches, however, have not been forfeited, and the Archbishop and the secular clergy of Goa still receive allowances from Government.

[1] Goa in its palmy state is admirably described by Captain Marryat in his *Phantom Ship;* in its present state by Graham Sandberg, *Murray's Magazine*, November 1890. J. N. Fonseca's *Sketch of the City of Goa* is full of interesting information.

The **Church of Bom Jesus** may be entered by a side door from the Jesuits' College, passing the Sacristy, a spacious hall, with wardrobes filled with rich priestly robes. Near it hangs a portrait of St Francis Xavier at the age of 44,—a dark face of sweet expression.

The Tomb and Shrine of St Francis Xavier (1696) occupy a side chapel, richly adorned; the walls are lined with pictures illustrating some of the acts of his life. The monument is a stately structure, consisting of three tiers of sarcophagi of costly jasper and marble, and was the gift of a Grand Duke of Tuscany. The upper tier is ornamented with panels curiously wrought in coloured marbles so as to represent scenes in the life of the saint; the whole is surmounted by the silver coffin containing the body, and adorned with reliefs also in silver, and with figures of angels in the same metal supporting a cross. The coffin, weighing 600 marks of silver, is unlocked by three keys, in the keeping of the Viceroy, the Archbishop, and another, and has been frequently opened, disclosing to public view the body, which was long in wonderful preservation, but has now shrunk to a mummy. The body of the Saint was translated here from St Paul's Church, where it was originally buried.

In the body of the church is a statue of the saint of solid silver, the gift of Donna Maria, wife of Pedro II. and Queen of Portugal; and behind the high altar one in marble of Ignatius Loyola.

250 yds. distant, on the opposite side (N.) of the square, stands the **Cathedral** of St Catherine,[1] built in 1562-1623, the church next in importance to the Bom Jesus, and known as the Se Primaçial. It is 250 ft. long, 180 wide, with façade 116 ft. high, and has a white-washed inside, with a high altar at the W. end. It alone of all the churches retains a staff of priests,—twenty-eight canons, who perform the service throughout the year. On looking from the terraced roof of the Cathedral one cannot but think of the solemn and terrible sights that have been seen in the square below, when the great bell of this church tolled to announce the celebration of an *Auto-da-Fé*.

N. of the Cathedral is the *Archbishop's Palace*, a magnificent residence still occupied occasionally. It contains some life-sized portraits of the Archbishops. In the adjoining monastery the Viceroy stops on his periodical visits to Old Goa. Here the archives of the city and some curiosities of the arsenal are preserved.

S. of the Cathedral is the once gorgeous *Church of* **San Francesco d'Assisi**, the oldest here, having been adapted from a mosque. It was, however, rebuilt 1521, except the porch, which is original, and is in fair repair.

In front of the Cathedral stood the *Palace of the Inquisition*, with its dungeons and prisons, established in 1560 and suppressed in 1814, now an overgrown heap of ruins an acre in extent.

S. of the Inquisition at the N.E. corner of the Square were the buildings of the **Misericordia** enclosing the Church of Nossa Senhora de Serra, built by Albuquerque in fulfilment of a vow at sea, and in which he was originally buried. From these the Rua Direita led to the river front and the Viceroy's Palace. **The Arch of the Viceroys**, which still bears the deer crest of Vasco da Gama, stands over the principal landing-place known as the Ribeira dos Vicereys, which extended W. to the Quai of the Galleys (Ribeira dos Galés) and E. to the customs house (Alfandanga) and the Great Bazar. **The Palace** is for the most part a ruin, but deserves a visit for its quaint windows with panes of oyster-shells and pictures of the Viceroys and Portuguese ships which came to India. E. of the Palace and the Bazar is the *Church of St Cajetan*, perhaps the best preserved, built 1665, and surmounted

[1] Goa was recaptured on St Catherine's day.

by a dome and by two low towers; the façade is of red laterite, whitewashed. Beyond lay the convent of the Dominicans, with that of the Carmelites on a hill, and the famous missionary **College of Saint Paul** or Santa Fé, which is about ½ m. E. from the Bom Jesus. The *autos-da-fé* used to take place in the Campo San Lazaro near this. At the W. end of the town, near the Arsenal, was the famous **Royal Hospital**, the first established by Europeans in the East.

The following facts concerning the Portuguese possessions in India will no doubt prove of interest. The total population is under 550,000, of which the Goa Territory contains 475,000. This territory has a coast-line of about 65 m. and includes the small island of Angediva near Carwar. It is divided into two tracts known as the Old and New Conquests (Velhas e Novas Conquistas), and these are subdivided into three and six district charges, at the head of each of which is an Administrator and a Municipal Council. Daman (p. 116) is divided into two such charges, while Diu, an island off the S.E. coast of Kathiawar, constitutes one only: these two are under separate Governors subordinate to the Viceroy, who is also Governor of Goa, as the Governor-General of India was once Governor of Bengal. There is a High Court (Tribunal de Relacão) of second instance at Goa consisting of five judges, which has jurisdiction over Macao and Timor as well as over the Portuguese possessions in India, and a subordinate judge in each district. The European military force is very small, consisting of only 200 men, and the European police force is less than 100: the native force amounts to 750. There are small engineering and health departments. Panjim has a High School, a normal school and a medical school, and some 125 primary schools exist in the Goa country. The Archbishop of Goa has among other titles that of S. Thome de Meliapor (Mylapur, p. 403). The annual revenue of the Portuguese possessions in India is about £115,000, of which customs yield about £25,000; this source of income is pledged for payment of interest on the Railway.

The following details regarding the conqueror and founder of Goa will be found interesting. Affonso de Albuquerque was born in 1453, and was therefore 50 years old when he visited Cochin and Quilon on his first journey to India in 1503. In 1506 he occupied Socotora on behalf of the Portuguese crown, and in November 1509 he became Governor of the eastern possessions of that crown. Panjim was taken and Goa surrendered early in the following year, and the latter was stormed and recovered from the Bijapur troops on 25th November following. During the next two years the Governor was occupied with the affairs of Malacca; in 1513 he attempted to capture Aden but failed, and in 1514 he caused a fort to be erected at Calicut after the Zamorin had been poisoned. In February 1515 he proceeded to Ormuz and obtained possession of the Fort there, and died on his way back from that place to Bombay on 18th December 1515. His body was finally transferred to Lisbon, and now rests there in the Church of Nossa Senhora da Graca.

ROUTE 27.

HOTGI JUNCTION TO BIJAPUR, Gadag, Hubli, Dharwar, and Londa, with excursion to **caves and temples** of Badami.

Hotgi junction station (R.) is 9 m. E. of **Sholapur**, on the line from Bombay to Madras (see Rte. 25). Between the 1st and 2nd stations from Hotgi the Bhima river is crossed, flowing in a deep rocky bed. From **Minchnal,** the station before Bijapur, the domes and minarets of the city are plainly seen to the S.

59 m. **BIJAPUR**[1] station ✱ (originally *Vijayapura,* city of victory) (R.), D.B. The railway station is E. of the city and close to the Gol Gumbaz, the great tomb of Muhammad 'Adil Shah.

Yusaf Khan, the first King of Bijapur on the decay of the Bahmani dynasty, was a son of Amurath II., of Anatolia, and a Turk of pure blood, whose mother was forced to fly with him from Constantinople while he was still an infant. After a varied career, he was purchased for the bodyguard at Bidar (p. 374), and raised himself to such pre-eminence, that in 1489 he was enabled to proclaim his independence, and establish himself as the founder of the 'Adil Shahi kings of Bijapur. The following is the order of their succession :—

		A.D.
Yusaf Khan,	'Adil Shah	1489
Ismail	,,	1510
Mallu	,,	1534
Ibrahim I.	,,	1534
'Ali I.	,,	1557
Ibrahim II.	,,	1580
Muhammad	,,	1627
'Ali II.	,,	1656
Sikandar	,,	1672 to 1686

in which year the city was taken by Aurangzeb. The great architectural outburst of the place followed on the capture and spoil of Vijayanagar (p. 380) after the battle of Talikot in 1565. The kingdom extended to the West Sea, and Goa was a portion of it.

The Kaladgi district was re-named Bijapur in 1883, when Government decided to reoccupy the old capital as administrative headquarters of the district. Great difficulty was experienced in clearing ground for roads and houses from the large areas of prickly pear that had to be removed, but this was gradually done, and the station is now well planted with trees. Those who object to the utilitarian uses to which a number of the buildings at Bijapur have been put, must also remember that by its action Government has saved these and the other buildings from the complete destruction which was threatening them.

Torwah about 1610 A.D. was a great suburb, a rival city, to the W. of Bijapur; but when Aurangzeb took the latter, the former was "quite depopulated, its ruined palaces only remaining, with a thick wall surrounding it, whose stately gateways were falling to decay." This suburb, then, whose walls extended 3 m. from the W. gate of the Fort, and probably other suburbs which have now utterly perished, must have been included in the 30 m. circuit which tradition ascribes to Bijapur. What is called the city now is the Fort, of which Grant Duff says it was 6 m. in circumference. Within the circuit of the Fort is the Citadel, with walls extending 1650 ft. from N. to S., and 1900 ft. from W. to E. An examination of the buildings will give proof of the former riches and magnificence of this old capital. Two days will not be too much to devote o the principal buildings alone.

The **Gates** of the Fort or city are—

The Fateh Gate (1),[1] in the centre of the S. wall of the city, by which Aurangzeb is said to have entered.

The Shahapur Gate (2), on the N.W. The gate itself is furnished with long iron spikes on the outside, to protect it from being battered in by the elephants of an enemy. This was a common device throughout India. S. of it, on the W. of the city, is the

Zohrapur Gate (3); and 600 ft. to the S. of that is the

Makka Gate (4), with representations on either side of lions trampling on an elephant. This gate is closed and converted into a school. A less imposing one (4a), a few hundred yds. farther N., serves its purpose. Almost exactly opposite to it, on the E. side of the City, is the

'Alipur Gate (5), or High Gate, wrongly called in maps and elsewhere the Allahpur Gate. N. of it is the

[1] An admirable guide by Mr H. Cousens C.I.E., giving details of all the buildings, and a valuable historical sketch of the 'Adil Shahi dynasty, can be bought at the principal booksellers in Bombay and Poona.

[1] The numbers refer to the corresponding numbers on the plan of Bijapur.

London. John Murray, Albemarle Street.

Padshahpur Gate (6), near the railway station.

In the centre of the N. wall is the Bahmani Gate (7).

On the E. side of the city, close to the railway station, is the *Mausoleum of Muhammad 'Adil Shah*, seventh king, a magnificent structure, generally called the **Gol Gumbaz**, or "Round Dome" (8). Mr Fergusson, in his *Hist. of Indian Arch.*, says of this building: "This tomb of Mahmud was in design as complete a contrast to that" of Ibrahim II., described below, "as can well be imagined, and is as remarkable for simple grandeur and constructive boldness as that of Ibrahim was for excessive richness and contempt of constructive properties. It is constructed on the same principle as that employed in the design of the dome of the great mosque, but on so much larger a scale as to convert into a wonder of constructive skill what, in that instance, was only an elegant architectural design." It is built on a platform 600 ft. square and 2 ft. high. In front is a great gateway, 94 by 88 ft., with a Nakkar Khana (music gallery), now a museum. The tomb is a square building, with sides measuring 196 ft. (exterior), and at each corner is a tower seven storeys high. In the centre is the great dome, 124 ft. in diameter, while that of St Peter's is 139 ft., and that of St Paul's 108 ft. Over the entrance are three inscriptions—"Sultan Muhammad, inhabitant of Paradise," "Muhammad, whose end was commendable," "Muhammad, became a particle of heaven (lit. House of Salvation), 1067." The date, thus three times repeated, is 1659 A.D. The surface of the building for the most part is covered with plaster. Each façade has a wide, lofty arch in its centre, pierced with small windows and a blind one on either side, and above it is a cornice of grey basalt and a row of small arches supporting a second line of plain work, surmounted by a balustrade 6 ft. high. The corner towers are entered from winding staircases in the thickness of the walls of the main building, and terminate in cupolas. Each storey has seven small arched windows opening into the court below. From the eighth storey there is an entrance to a broad gallery inside the dome, which is so wide that a carriage might pass round it. Here there is a most remarkable echo; a soft whisper at one point of the gallery can be heard most distinctly at the opposite point, and, as Mr Cousens says, "one pair of feet is enough to awaken the echoes of the tread of a regiment." The great hall, 135 ft. square, over which the dome is raised, is the largest domed space in the world. The internal area of the tomb is 18,225 sq. ft., while that of the Pantheon at Rome is only 15,833. "At the height of 57 ft. from the floor-line," says Mr Fergusson, "the hall begins to contract by a series of pendentives as ingenious as they are beautiful, to a circular opening 97 ft. in diameter. On the platform of the pendentives the dome is erected, 124 ft. in diameter. Internally, the dome is 175 ft. high; externally, 198 ft.; its general thickness being about 10 ft."[1] From the gallery outside there is a fine view over Bijapur. On the E. is 'Alipur; on the W. are seen the Ibrahim Roza, the Upari Burj, the Sherza, or Lion Bastion, and to the N.W. the unfinished tomb of 'Ali 'Adil Shah II., and about 1 m. towards the N. the ruins of the villages of the masons and painters employed on the Gol Gumbaz; and on the S.W. is the dome of the Jama Masjid. There is a small annexe to the mausoleum on the N., without a roof, built by Sultan Muhammad as a tomb, it is supposed, for his mother, Zohra Sahibah, from whom one of the suburbs was called Zohrapur. It was never finished or occupied.

Below the dome is the cenotaph of Sultan Muhammad in the centre.

[1] "The most ingenious and novel part of the construction is the mode in which its lateral and outward thrust is counteracted. This was accomplished by forming the pendentives so that they not only cut off the angles, but that, as shown in the plan, their arches intersect one another and form a very considerable mass of masonry perfectly

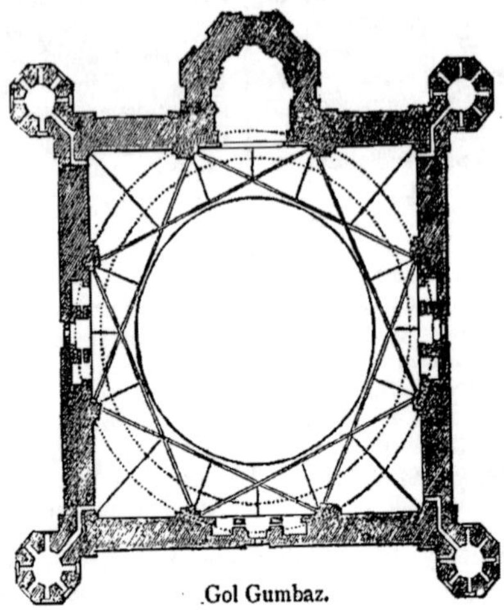

Gol Gumbaz.

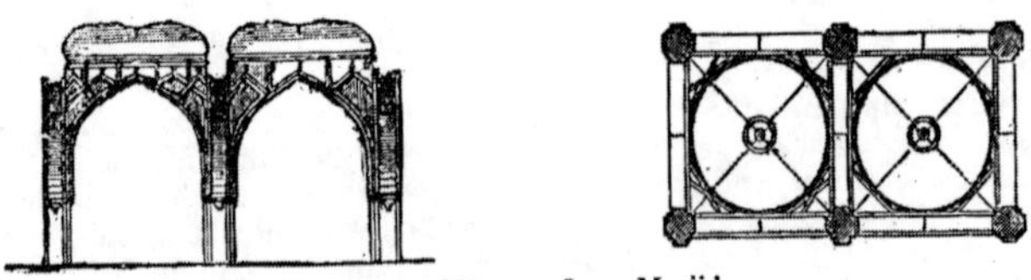

Section of Domes, Jama Masjid.

On the E. side are the graves of his youngest wife and of the son of 'Ali 'Adil Shah II.; on the W. are those of his favourite dancing-girl Rhumba, his daughter, and his eldest wife, mentioned by Bernier.

On the edge of the platform W. is the mosque attached to the mausoleum, a building of no mean size and of considerable beauty of design, but quite eclipsed by the size of the Gol Gumbaz.

The **Jama Masjid** (9), nearly ½ m. S.W. of the Gol Gumbaz, is entered by a gateway on the N. side. The surrounding wall was never completed on the E. The arcades on the N. and S. sides are 31 ft. broad. In the centre of the quadrangle is the hauz or tank for ablutions, now dry. Mr Fergusson says: "Even as it is, it is one of the finest mosques in India."

It was commenced by 'Ali 'Adil Shah I. (1557-79), and though continued by his successors, was never completely finished. The mosque proper has a façade of nine bays, and is five bays in depth. Each of the squares into which it is divided has a domed roof, beautiful, but so flat as to be concealed externally. The centre, a space 70 ft. square, corresponding to twelve of these squares, is roofed over by the great dome, which is 57 ft. in diameter. It is supported on pendentives in the same manner as the Gol Gumbaz. The pavement below the dome is of chunam, divided by black lines into numerous squares called *musallahs*, or compartments for persons to pray on, imitating the *musallah*, or prayer-carpet, which the faithful carry with them to the mosques. These were made by order of Aurangzeb when he carried away the velvet carpets, the large golden chain, and them valuables belonging to the mosque.

The mihrab, which marks the place on the W. to which the people turn in prayer, is gilded and ornamented with much Arabic writing. There is also a Persian quatrain. The date is 1636 A.D.

The **Mehtar Mahal** (10) is the name given to the entrance gateway to the Mehtar Mosque, a building of minor importance. It stands between the Jama Masjid and the citadel, on the S. of the road. It is a small but elegant structure, three storeys high, with minarets at the corners and ornamental carving in soft stone about its balconied and projecting windows. Mr Fergusson says of this structure: "Perhaps the most remarkable civil edifice is a little gateway, known as the Mehtar Mahal. It is in a mixed Hindu and Mohammedan style, every part and every detail covered with ornament, but always equally appropriate and elegant. Of its class it is perhaps the best example in the country, though this class may not be the highest."

The palace of the **Asár-i-Sharif** (11), "illustrious relics," which are hairs of the Prophet's beard, is a large heavy-looking building of brick and lime, standing outside the moat of the inner citadel and the centre of its E. rampart. The E. side is entirely open from the ground to the ceiling, which is supported by four massive teak pillars, 60 ft. high. This forms a deep portico 36 ft. broad, and looks upon a tank 250 ft. sq. The ceiling of the verandah or portico is panelled in wood and has been very handsomely painted. The whole of the W. side is occupied by rooms in two storeys. A flight of stairs ascends to a hall 81 ft. long and 27 ft. broad, where some of the fine old carpets of the palace are shown under glass. Opening right from this hall is an upper verandah or antechamber which looks down into the portico (already described) below. Its ceilings and walls have been gilded; the doors are inlaid with ivory; and in the palmy days of Bijapur the effect must have been very striking. The Asár-i-Sharif formerly communicated on its W. side with the citadel by means of a bridge, of which

stable in itself, and by its weight acting upwards, counteracting any thrust that can possibly be brought to bear upon it by the pressure of the dome."—*Fergusson.*

nothing now remains but the piers. Originally built as a court of justice by Muhammad Shah about 1646, it succeeded to the honour of holding the precious relics of the Prophet after a similar building within the citadel had been burned down.

The Arkilla or Citadel.—The only citadel gateway that remains is at the extreme S., facing E.; here the walls are full of ancient pillars and sculptured stones, taken from Jain temples which probably stood on this spot when the Mohammedans stormed the citadel. Other stones were utilised in the construction of the two "old mosques" within the citadel.

The **Old Mosque** (12), just N.W. of the gate, is a converted Jain temple. The central mandapam, or hall, two storeys high, serves as the porch. The inner doorway, with its perforated screens, is Mohammedan work. The mosque proper is made up of Hindu or Jain pillars of various patterns and heights. At the N. side, near the centre row, is a wonderfully handsome and elaborately carved black pillar, and to the N.E. of it an ancient Kanarese inscription. On several of the pillars around are inscriptions, some in Sanscrit and some in Kanarese. One bears the date 1320 A.D.

The **Anand Mahal** (13), or "palace of joy," where the ladies of the seraglio lived, is in the centre of the citadel. It was built by Ibrahim II. in 1589, and intended partly for his own use, but the façade was never finished. It contains a very fine hall, and is now the Assistant-Collector's residence.

The **Gagan Mahal** (14), or "heavenly palace," supposed to have been built by 'Ali 'Adil Shah I., is on the W. of the citadel close to the moat, and faces N. It has three magnificent arches. The span of the central one is 61 ft., and that of each of the side arches 18 ft. The height of all three is the same, about 50 ft. It was used as a Darbar Hall, and on the roof was a gallery from which the ladies could see what occurred on the open space in front. It is said that here the Emperor Aurangzeb received the submission of the king and the nobles on the fall of Bijapur.

A small building to the S.E. of the Gagan Mahal has been converted into the **Station Church** (15). In plan it is a square; the roof is supported by four pillars, and it is decorated with exquisite relief patterns in flat plaster-work. The beautifully wrought iron screen was found in the Chini Mahal.

About 150 yds. to the N.E. of the Gagan Mahal is another old mosque (16) built with the stones of a Jain temple. It has ten rows of pillars seven deep.

E. of this is the **Adalat Mahal**, now the Collector's residence, with a small mosque on the N. side, and an extremely pretty pavilion or pleasure house E. of it and in front of the Civil Surgeon's residence on a corner of the citadel wall. A little to the N. of this is *Yakut Dabuli's Tomb* and *Mosque*. The tomb is square, with stone lattice-work screens. It was Yakut Dabuli who decorated the mihrab of the Jama Masjid.

On the extreme W. of the citadel is the **Sat Manjli** (17), or "seven storeys," Rhumbha's pleasure-palace, from the top of which the whole city could be overlooked. Of this only five storeys now remain. A peculiarity of the building is the number of water-pipes and cisterns round about it. It formed the N.E. corner of a vast structure wrongly called the **Granary** (18), which was probably the public palace of the kings, where their public audiences were held.

At the S. end of this building is a palace which at one time must have been of considerable importance. It is called the **Chini Mahal** (19), from the quantity of broken china found there, and possesses a fine hall 128 ft. long.

In front of the Granary, in the centre of the road, stands a beautifully ornamented little pavilion (20), the purpose of which is unknown. From this the moat of the citadel is crossed by a causeway 140 ft. long, but the average breadth of the moat may be taken as 150 ft. Opposite the end of the causeway on the outside is the Malika Jahan or Jhanjhri Mosque, one of the most effective buildings in all Bijapur.

N.E. of the gateway and the Old Mosque is the **Makka Masjid** (21), a miniature mosque of beautiful proportions and great simplicity of design. The massive minarets at the corners of the high walls which surround it in all probability belonged to an earlier building. The façade of the mosque proper has five bays of arches about 8 ft. high, is two bays deep, and is surmounted by a dome.

Immediately to the W. is a huge walled space which is thought to have been an elephant stable (21a), and adjoining it S. is a tower which was probably used for the storage of grain. Close by on the E. wall of the citadel is the picturesquely situated high-standing Chinch Diddi Mosque.

The unfinished **Tomb of 'Ali 'Adil Shah II.** (22) lies outside the citadel to the N. It is a noble ruin, a square with seven large Gothic-looking arches on each side, constructed on a terrace 15 ft. high, and 215 ft. sq. Had not the death of the Sultan put a stop to its progress, and prevented its completion in conformity with the original design, it would have surpassed every other building at Bijapur, both in magnificence and size. The cenotaph is in the centre enclosure, which is 78 ft. sq., and if completed would have been crowned by a dome.

Close to this tomb on the S.W. is the pretty Bukhara Masjid, for a time used as the **Post Office** (23), and just N. of this is the beautiful mosque and tomb of Sandal Khan. To the W. again, half-way to the Haidar Burj, is the plain grave of the last ruler of Bijapur, who was compelled to surrender his kingdom to the Mughal Emperor.

To the W. of the city, and near the Makka Gate, are two domed tombs close together and very much alike, known as the Jor Gumbaz and to Europeans as "**The Two Sisters**" (24). The octagonal one (now the house of the Executive Engineer) contains the remains of *Khan Muhammad*, assassinated at the instigation of Sultan Muhammad for his treacherous dealings with Aurangzeb, and of his son *Khawas Khan*, Vazir to Sikandar. The dome is nearly complete, and springs from a band of lozenge-shaped leaves. The space within forms a beautiful room. The square building is the mausoleum of *Abdul Razak*, the religious tutor of Khawas Khan. It is a large building, now much decayed. Near it S. is the *Tomb*, with its unfinished brick dome, of *Kishwar Khan*, whose father, Asad Khan, is repeatedly mentioned by the Portuguese. He founded the fort of Dharur, in the time of 'Ali 'Adil Shah I., and was taken and put to death by one of the Nizam Shahi kings.

The **Andu Masjid** (25), 1608, stands on the E. side of the road which runs S. from the citadel. It is a two-storeyed building, the lower part forming a hall, and the upper part the mosque proper and its small court. The façade has three bays, it is surmounted by a fluted dome and four small minarets, and the masonry and workmanship are finer than those of any other building in Bijapur. A road running W. from here and S. of the Two Sisters leads to the tomb of the Begam Sahibah, a wife of the Emperor Aurangzeb, who died of plague, and to the Nau Bagh. Another road to the W. from opposite the house of the District Superintendent Police, 300 yds. S. of the Andu Mosque, leads to the Jama Masjid of Ibrahim I., and, according to tradition, the tomb of 'Ali I. It is a simple simple with a corridor all round it. In front of it, on a high platform, is a fine tombstone of dark green stone, both of which are richly and effectively carved.

700 ft. N. of the Jama Masjid is *Khawas Khan's Mahal*. *Nawab Mustafa Khan's Mosque*, 400 yds. N. of this and 500 yds. E. of the citadel, is a lofty building with a façade of three arches and a central dome supported on pendentives. Behind the mosque W. are the ruins of the Khan's **Palace**. Mustafa Khan Ardistani was a distinguished nobleman at the court of 'Ali 'Adil Shah I., and was murdered in 1581 A.D. by Kishwar Khan, who usurped the regency in the time of Ibrahim 'Adil Shah II.

Outside the W. wall of the city, 400 yds. from the Makka Gate, is

The **Ibrahim Roza** (pronounced *rauza*) (26), a group of buildings which includes the tombs of Ibrahim II. 'Adil Shah, his Queen Taj Sultana, and four other members of his family. It is said to have been erected by a Persian architect. It is enclosed by a strong wall with a lofty gateway. The courtyard within was once a garden; in the centre of it is raised an oblong platform upon which stands the tomb, and to the W. of it a mosque, with a fountain and reservoir between them. The five arches which form the E. façade of the *Mosque* are very graceful; above them, under the rich cornice, hang heavy chains cut out of stone. On each of the four sides of the *Tomb* is a colonnade of seven arches, forming a verandah 15 ft. broad round the whole edifice. The pavement of this colonnade is slightly elevated, and its ceiling is exquisitely carved with verses of the Koran, enclosed in compartments and interspersed with wreaths of flowers. The letters were originally gilded, and the ground is still a most brilliant azure. In some places the gilding also still remains. The border of every compartment is different from that of the one adjoining. The windows are formed of lattice-work of Arabic sentences, cut out of stone slabs, the space between each letter admitting the light. This work is admirably executed, and there is nothing to surpass it in all India. Above the double arcade outside the building is a magnificent cornice with a minaret four storeys high at each corner and eight smaller ones between them. From an inner cornice, with four minarets on each side, rises the dome. The plan of the building resembles that of the tombs at Golkonda. The principal apartment in the tomb is 40 ft. sq., with a stone-slab roof perfectly flat in the centre, and supported only by a cove projecting 10 ft. from the walls on every side. "How the roof is supported is a mystery which can only be understood by those who are familiar with the use the Indians make of masses of concrete, which, with good mortar, seems capable of infinite applications unknown in Europe. Above this apartment is another in the dome as ornamental as the one below it, though its only object is to obtain externally the height required for architectural effect, and access to its interior can only be obtained by a dark, narrow staircase in the thickness of the wall."[1] Over the N. door is an inscription in Persian, extolling the building in very exaggerated terms. The last line is a chronogram, which gives the date 1036 A.H. = 1626 A.D. Over the S. door is another inscription in praise of the monarch, with the date 1633. Over the same door is inscribed—

[*Translation.*]

The work of beautifying this Mausoleum was completed by Malik Sandal.[2]
Taj-i-Sultan issued orders for the construction of this Roza,
At the beauty of which Paradise stood amazed.
He expended over it 1½ lakhs of huns,
And 900 more.

---

[1] From Fergusson's *History of Indian Architecture*. The author also says that Ibrahim, commenced his tomb "on so small a plan, 116 ft. sq., that it was only by ornament that he could render it worthy of himself."

[2] The tomb of this personage is W. of the incomplete tomb of 'Ali 'Adil Shah II. See above.

The hun being Rs.3½, the total expense was about £50,000. When Aurangzeb besieged Bijapur in 1686 he took up his quarters in the Ibrahim Roza, which received some damage from the Bijapur guns. These injuries were partially repaired by the Raja of Satara, and the restoration was completed by the English.

Guns and Bastions.—The **Burj-i-Sherza**, or "Lion Bastion" (27), so called from being ornamented by two lions' heads in stone, is 300 yds. N. of the Zohrapur Gate. In the W. wall on the right-hand side on ascending the steps of the bastion is an inscription stating that it was built in five months, and giving the date 1671. On the top of this bastion is a huge gun, called the **Malik-i-Maidan**, "Lord of the Battle Plain." At the sides of the muzzle the representation of the mouth of a monster swallowing an elephant is wrought in relief. It was cast at Ahmednagar in a blue metal which takes a very high polish. It is 14 ft. long, the circumference is about 13 ft. 6 in., and the diameter of the bore is 2 ft. 4 in. Just above the touch-hole is the following inscription:—

The work of Muhammad Bin Husain Rumi.

At the muzzle is the following:—

The servant of the family of the Prophet of God, Abu'l Ghazi Nizam Shah, 956 A.H. = 1551 A.D.

At the muzzle is also—

In the 30th year of the exalted reign,
1097 A.H., Shah 'Alamgir, conqueror of infidels, King, Defender of the Faith,
Conquered Bijapur, and for the date of his triumph,
He fulfilled what justice required, and annexed the territory of the Shahs,
Success showed itself, and he took the Malik-i-Maidan.

About 150 yds E. of the Sherza Burj, and near the heavy Idgah, is a strange building, called the **Upari Burj**, or Upper Bastion, also called the *Haidar Burj* (28), after a general of 'Ali I. and Ibrahim II. It is a tower 61 ft. high, oval in plan, with an outside staircase. On the way up will be noticed a Persian inscription recording the building of the tower in 1583.

On the top are two guns made of longitudinal bars held together with iron bands. The larger, called the Lamcharri, "far flier," is 30 ft. 8 in. long, and has a diameter of 2 ft. 5 in. at the muzzle, and 3 ft. at the breech; the bore is 12 in. in diameter. The other gun is 19 ft. 10 in. long, with 1 ft. diameter at the muzzle, and 1 ft. 6 in. diameter at breech.

On the **Landa Kasab** bastion W. of the Fateh Gate, and near the road from the Andu Masjid leading through the S. wall, is also a fine gun measuring 21 ft. 7 in. long, with a diameter at the breech of 4 ft. 4 in., and at the muzzle of 4 ft. 5 in., which must weigh nearly 50 tons.

There are several **Tanks** in Bijapur. The principal one is the **Taj Bauri**, or "Crown Well" (29), 100 yds. inside the Makka Gate. The E. wing of the façade of the tank is partly ruined and partly used as a Kanarese school. The W. wing is occupied by the municipal offices. Two flights of steps lead down to the water beneath an arch of 34 ft. span, and about the same height, flanked by two octagonal towers. The tank at the water's edge is 231 ft. sq. The water comes partly from springs and partly from drainage, and is 30 ft. deep in the dry weather.

The **Chand Bauri** in the N.W. corner of the city was built in 1579 A.D., on the model of the Taj Bauri, and also has a fine arch over the steps leading down to it.

1½ m. to the S.W. of the Shahapur suburb situated to the N.W. of the city is the tomb and palace of Afzal Khan (p. 354). Adjoining the former is a mosque of two storeys, and on a platform to the S.W. are eleven rows of graves of women, which have given rise to the tale that they were the wives and slaves of Afzal Khan put to death by him. It will be remembered that the rise both of Shivaji and his father Shahji was intimately connected with the Bijapur kingdom, and it was only the contact of the Delhi Emperors with that which brought the Mahrattas into direct conflict with the Mughal power.

Water-works.—Bijapur was supplied with abundant water by underground ducts. One source of supply was a spring beyond the suburb of Torwah, 5 m. W. of the citadel; another was the Begam Tank, 3 m. to the S. Along the line of the supply water occur towers supposed to be for the purpose of relieving the pressure in the pipes. The people evidently appreciated the advantage of having plenty of cool water about them, and traces of innumerable baths and cisterns are found in every direction. The water from the reservoirs, for instance, in the ruined palace of Mustafa Khan, ran into a tank, from which it brimmed over into narrow stone channels, which passed in circuitous courses through the gardens, running over uneven surfaces to give it a sparkling and rippling effect.

From Bijapur the line continues to

115 m. **Bagalkot**, S. of the Kistna river. Some 25 m. E. from this on the river was fought the famous battle of Talikot on 23rd January 1565, which caused the downfall of the Vijayanagar kingdom (p. 380). The small town of Talikot lies 30 m. N. of the field of battle.

130 m. **Badami** station. The fort of Badami is to the N.E. of the town, 2 m. E. from the railway station, and on the heights above are some picturesque temples from which there is a fine view. To the S. is another rocky fort-crowned hill, in the face of which are four cave-temples. The two hills (about 400 ft. high) approach so close to each other as to leave only a gorge, into which the town extends. E. of this is a fine tank. Badami was once the capital of the Chalukyas.

Three of the **Cave Temples** are Brahman works, and date from 550 to 580 A.D.; the fourth is Jain, and probably dates from 650 A.D.

Mr Burgess writes of them: "They stand as to arrangement of parts between the Buddhist viharas and the later Brahmanical examples at Ellora, Elephanta, and Kanhari. The front wall of the Buddhist vihara, with its small windows and doors, admitted too little light; and so here, while retaining the verandah in front, and further protecting the cave from rain and sun by projecting eaves, the front of the Shala, or 'hall,' was made quite open, except the spaces between the walls and the first pillars from each end. In the sculptures, at least of the second and third caves, Vishnu occupies the most prominent place. In style they vary much in details, but can scarcely differ much in age; and as the third contains an inscription of Mangaleshvara, dated Shaka 500=578 A.D., we cannot be far wrong in attributing them all to the 6th century. The importance of this date can scarcely be overestimated, as it is the first of the kind yet discovered in a Brahmanical cave." In the verandah of the *First Cave*, excavated about 50 ft. up in the face of the rock, and consecrated to Shiva, are four pillars and two pilasters. The two pillars to the S. have been broken by lightning, and are now supported by wooden blocks. The pillars are slightly carved in relief, to about halfway from the top. The whole rests on a stylobate, along the front of which are Ganas (dwarf attendants of Shiva) in all sorts of attitudes. On the left of the verandah is a dwarpal with a Nandi over him. Opposite this dwarpal is a figure of Shiva, 5 ft. high, with eighteen arms, dancing the tandava.[1] Between it and the cave is a chapel, and beyond an antechamber leading to the hall. In it on the left is Vishnu or Harihara, with four hands, holding the usual

[1] See descriptions on pp. 19-20.

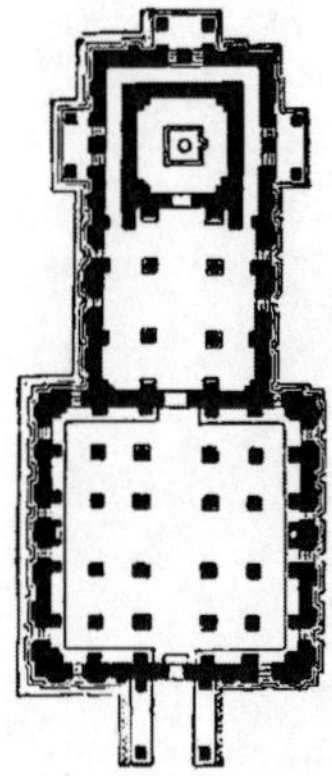

Temple at Pattadakal.

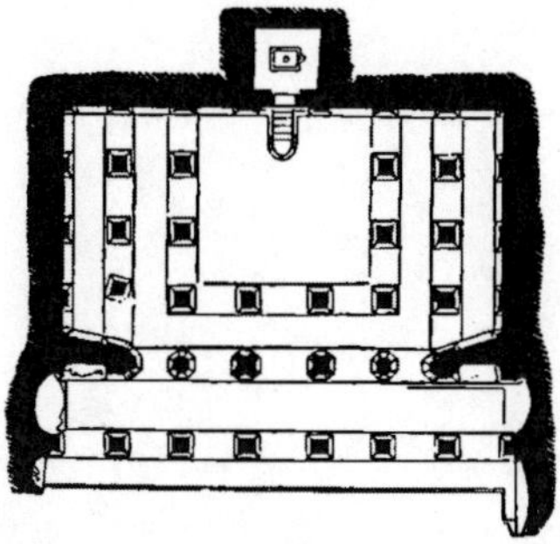

Cave at Badami, from a plan by Dr Burgess.

[*To face p.* 371].

symbols, and on the right the Arddhanarishwar, or combined male and female figure, attended by a Nandi bull and the skeleton Bringi. A figure of Maheshasuri or Durga destroying the buffalo-demon Maheshasur is on the back wall, on the right wall Ganpati, and on the left Skanda. Between the antechamber and the hall are two pillars only. The hall has eight columns of the Elephanta type and measures 42 ft. by 24½ ft. The ceiling and that of the antechamber are divided into compartments by carved beams. In the centre compartment of the former is a relief of the Great Snake's head. At the back of the hall is a small chapel with a lingam.

The *Second Cave Temple* is rather higher up the cliff and has a fine view. At the ends of the platform in front of it are two dwarpals with a female attendant. Four square columns, finely carved, separate the platform from the verandah, on the left of which is the Varaha Avatar, or Vishnu in the form of a boar, and on the right the Dwarf Avatar of Vishnu, dilated to an immense size, putting one foot on the earth and lifting the other over the heavens. On the ceiling in front of this is Vishnu with four arms, riding on Garuda, and in the central square of the ceiling is a lotus with sixteen fishes round it. On the top of the wall in a frieze are the figures of Vishnu as Krishna. The entrance to the inner chamber, 33 ft. by 23½ ft., is like that of the first cave; the roof of the chamber is supported by eight pillars; and the corbels are lions, human figures, vampires, elephants, etc. The adytum has only a square *Chavaranga*, or altar.

A sloping ascent and more flights of steps lead up to a platform, and a few steps beyond to a doorway; on the right of it is an inscription in old Kanarese. At the top of yet another flight of steps is the platform in front of the

Third Cave, below a scarp of 100 ft. of perpendicular rock. This cave, says Mr Burgess, is "by far the finest of the series, and, in some respects, one of the most interesting Brahmanical works in India." The façade is 70 ft. from N. to S., and has six square pillars and two pilasters 12½ ft. high. Eleven steps lead up to the cave, and on the stylobate Ganas are represented in relief. The brackets of the pillars represent male and female figures, Arddhanarishwar, Shiva, and Parvati, and on the columns themselves are carved elaborate festoons, and below medallions with groups of figures. Traces of painting are visible on the under-side of the eaves and the roof of the verandah. At the W. end of the verandah is a statue of Narsingh, the fourth incarnation of Vishnu, a very spirited figure, 11 ft. high. On the S. wall is Harihara, of the same height, and beyond the verandah at the side of the first is the Dwarf or Vamana Avatar. At the E. end is Narayan, seated under Sheshnag. On the outer side of this is Vishnu reclining on a great snake, and on the inner wall is the Varaha incarnation; to the right is an inscription in Kanarese. Between the verandah passage and the hall are four pillars. The hall measures 65 ft. by 37 ft. Eight pillars, four to the front, and two to the sides, form a space in front of the shrine; and on each side is a recess separated off by three pillars. The ceilings are divided into compartments throughout, with carved panels.

The *Fourth, or Jain Cave,* lies W. of the other three. The platform beyond the wall overlooks the lake or tank, and commands a fine view. A broad over-hanging eave has been cut out of the rock in front of this cave. The façade has four carved pillars and two pilasters. On the left of the verandah, 31 ft. by 6½ ft., is the Jain divinity Parasnath, with bands round his thighs, and cobras coming out below his feet. On the right of the verandah is a Gotama Swami attended by snakes. The hall behind is 25 ft. by 6 ft.; in the shrine is a seated statue of Mahavira.

At **Pattadakal**, 5 m. S.W. of Badami, on the left bank of the Malparba river, are several temples, both Brahmanical and Jain, dating from the 7th or 8th century. They "are very pure examples of the Dravidian style of architecture; they are all square pyramids divided into distinct storeys, and each storey ornamented with cells alternately oblong and square. Their style of ornamentation is also very much coarser than that of the Chalukyan style, and differs very much in character. The domical termination of the spires is also different, and much less graceful, and the overhanging cornices of double curvature are much more prominent and important" (Burgess). Besides these, the village possesses a group of temples, not remarkable for their size or architectural beauty, but interesting because they exhibit the two principal styles of Indian architecture, in absolute juxtaposition (see *Architecture of Dharwar and Mysore*, pp. 63, 64). The Temple of *Papnath* is of the N. style, and is probably rather older than that of *Virupaksha*, which dates from the early part of the 8th century. The Temple of Papnath is 90 ft. long, including the porch, and 40 ft. broad. There are sixteen pillars in the hall and four in the inner chamber, exclusive of those in the porches.

At **Aiwalli**, 5 m. to the N.E. of Badami, there are a *Jain Cave* and a *Brahmanical Cave*, both described by Mr Burgess. The latter is to the N.W. of the village. The *Durga Temple* has some very remarkable carving; and here, too, are many dolmens.

---

173 m. **Gadag** junction station (R.), D.B. (From Gadag the railway runs E. to Guntakal junction and W. to Hubli junction (for Bangalore and Mysore), Dharwar, and Londa junction.)

Gadag, anciently **Kratuka**, is a town of 30,000 inhabitants. In its N.W. corner is a *Vishnavite Temple*. The entrance is under a high gateway, or gopuram, with four storeys, and 50 ft. high. The door is handsomely carved with sixteen rows of figures in relief on either side. The Someshwara Temple, now a school, is richly decorated throughout.

In the Fort is a fine *Temple* dedicated to **Trimbakeshwar** or Trikuteshwar, "the Lord of the Three Peaks." The outside is one mass of most elaborate carving. Two rows of figures run along the entire front and back; those of the lower row are 2 ft. 9 in. high, including their canopy, and are 156 in number. In the upper row are 104 figures, 13 in. high, 52 in the front, and the same in the back. Between the four pillars on the E. is a colossal bull. Immediately behind the main portion of the temple, to the right of the enclosure, is a *Temple to Saraswati*. The porch is the finest part of it; it contains eighteen pillars, some of them exquisitely carved, and six pilasters. The three first of the two centre rows of pillars deserve particular notice for their elegance of design and exquisite carving.[1] There are numerous inscriptions at the temples, one of which has the date Shaka 790=868 A.D.

Lakkandi (anciently Lokkikandi) is about 8 m. S.E. of Gadag, and about half that distance from Harlapur station. The place is full of ancient temples.

[1] Colonel M. Taylor says: "It is impossible to describe the exquisite finish of the pillars of the interior of this temple, which are of black hornblende, or to estimate how they were completed in their present condition, unless they were turned in a lathe; yet there can be little doubt that they were set up originally as rough masses of rock, and afterwards carved into their present forms. The carving on some of the pillars and of the lintels and architraves of the doors is quite beyond description. No chased work in silver or gold could possibly be finer, and the patterns to this day are copied by goldsmiths, who take casts and moulds from them, but fail in representing the sharpness and finish of the original."

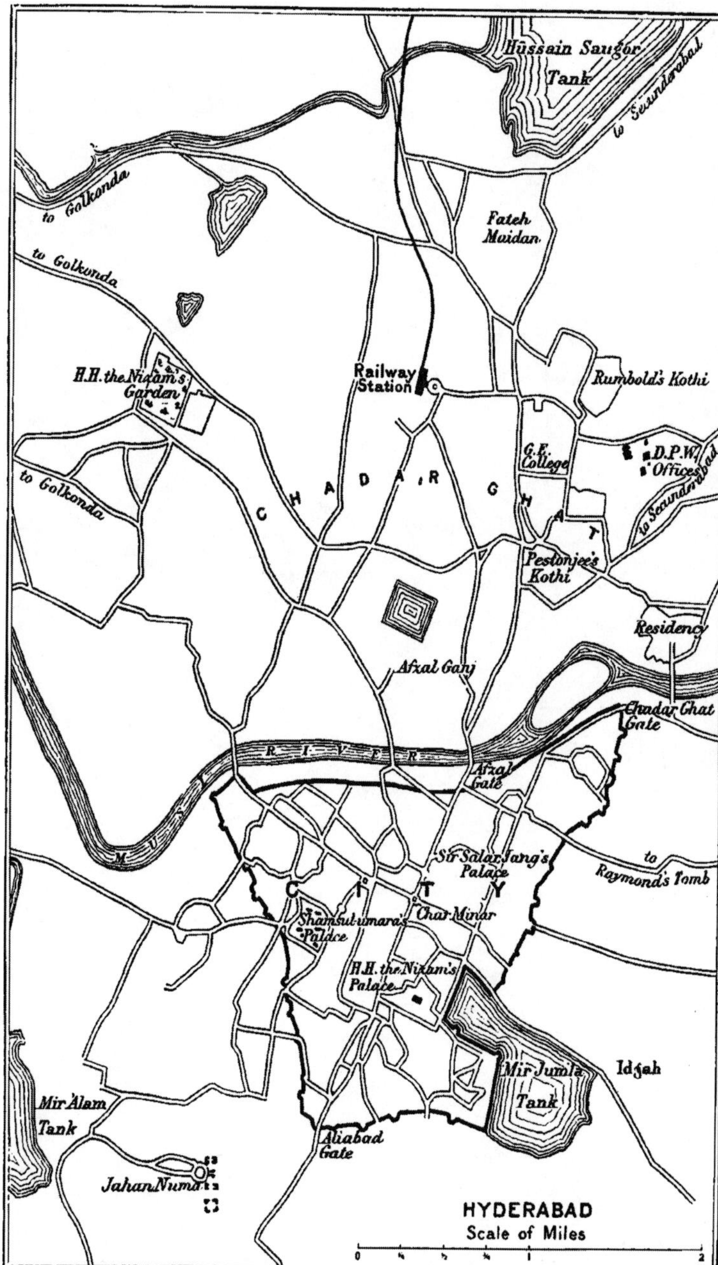
Hussain Saugor Tank
to Secunderabad
to Golkonda
Fateh Maidan
to Golkonda
Railway Station
H.H. the Nizam's Garden
Rumbold's Kothi
G.E. College
D.P.W. Offices
to Golkonda
C H A D A R G H A T
to Secunderabad
Pestonjee's Kothi
Residency
Afzal Ganj
Chadar Ghat Gate
M U S I R I V E R
Afzal Gate
Sir Salar Jang's Palace
to Raymond's Tomb
C I T Y
Shamsul-umara's Palace
Char Minar
H.H. the Nizam's Palace
Idgah
Mir Jumla Tank
Mir Alam Tank
Aliabad Gate
Jahan Numa
HYDERABAD
Scale of Miles
0
1
2

[To face p. 373.

The façade of the *Kashi Vishwanath Temple* has been supported by four pillars, of which that to the N. has gone. The doorways are elaborately carved, and though the roof is ruined, the temple is by far the handsomest in Lakkandi, and well worth seeing; but being built of coarse granite, the carving is not so clear and sharply defined as in the case of other famous temples.

To the W., on the opposite side of the road, is a *Temple to Nandeshwar*, or "Shiva, Lord of the Bull Nandi." There is a Kanarese inscription on the ledge of the W. division of the roof, between the four pillars. It stands on the N. side of a tank, which it overlooks.

The *Temple of Ishwara*, the roof of which has fallen in, is very old; the exterior is handsomely carved, and is said to be the work of Jakanacharya, the great sculptor (p. 390).

A narrow path, thickly shaded for about 100 yds., leads from it to a *Baoli*, or well, the sides of which are faced with stone. There are flights of steps to the water on three sides, and on either side of the first step is an elephant, so well carved, that the natives may be believed when they say that it is the work of Jakanacharya.

About 200 yds. from this, on the W. side of the tower, is a *Temple to Manikeshwar*, a name of Krishna, so called because every day he gave to Radha a ruby, which is called a manik. A very pretty small tank adjoins the temple. It is faced with stone, and has several buttresses projecting into the water, said to be carved by Jakanacharya. On either side of the entrance into the temple are four pillars of black basalt. This temple is surrounded by beautiful trees of great size.

From Gadag the line turns W. to

209 m. **Hubli** junction station (R.) (line S.E. to Harihar and Bangalore, Route 30).

222 m. **Dharwar** station (R.), D.B. This is a very important centre, being the old headquarters of the Southern Mahratta Railway. Dharwar is a large open town in a plain, with a population of 31,000.

On the N. is the *Fort*, which was taken from the Mahrattas by Haidar 'Ali in 1778, and stood a siege in 1789 from a British force co-operating with the Mahratta army under Parshuram Bhao. It next belonged to Tipu; and one of his ablest generals, Badr-ul-zaman, with 7000 regulars and 3000 irregulars, having thrown himself into it, defended it with great spirit. After a protracted siege of twenty-nine weeks, the brave Badr-ul-zaman surrendered on condition of being allowed to march out with all the honours of war. The allies took possession of the fort on 4th April, and the Mahrattas attacked Badr-ul-zaman as he was marching away, wounded him, made him prisoner, and dispersed the forces.

The *Church* is about 1 m. to the S. of the D.B. It belongs to the Basle German Evangelical Mission, and was built in 1844-45. The service by the missionaries is in Kanarese, and once on Sunday in English. The cantonments for the Native Infantry, lie 2 m. off to the N.W. of the Fort.

The line continues W. to

279 m. **Londa Junction** (p. 359).

ROUTE 28.

WADI JUNCTION TO HYDERABAD, Secunderabad, Warangal, and Bezwada, with expedition to **Bidar.**

H.H. the Nizam's State Railway.

376 m. from Bombay, **Wadi** junction station (R.) (see p. 349).

9 m. **Chittapur** station; extensive silk manufactures. About 1 m. to the S. is **Nagai**, a deserted town with ruined temples dating from 1050 A.D. In one of them is a life size bull cut out of a solid block of basalt.

24 m. **Seram** station. A richly carved temple, of 1200 A.D.

44 m. **Tandur** station (R.). Small and large game.

57 m. **Dharur** station for Bidar, 40 m. distant. Railway Bungalow which can be occupied by permission from Hyderabad.

[**Bidar**, Vidarba. This capital, first of the later Bahmani kings and then of the separate Barid dynasty, which maintained itself for only fifty years, is well deserving of a visit on account of the extremely picturesque walls and defences which still surround it, the fine, though partially ruined College of Khwaja Mahmud Gawán,[1] resembling those of Samarkand and Bukhara, and the tombs of the Bahmani and Barid kings, including that of Humayan the Cruel, known as the Khúni Sultan. Arrangements for the journey must be made from Hyderabad, and it will be desirable to obtain an introduction to the local State officials. Though Bidar is the headquarters of the fourth Subah of the State, the Subahdar usually resides in Hyderabad. Bidar *Bidri* work, so named from it, of silver inlaid on iron, was once famous, but is now inferior to that of Lucknow.]

[1] The date is 1471 A.D. This minister, who long upheld the dynasty, was unjustly put to death by Mohammed Shah II.

100 m. **Lingampalli** station. Soon after this the line is very picturesque, dotted with numerous granite peaks and isolated rocks. This stone belt extends to Bhunigaon, 28 m. E. of Hyderabad.

115 m. **HYDERABAD** station. ✱ $1\frac{3}{4}$ m. from the nearest city gate. The capital of H.H. the Nizam's territory. Lat. 17° 22′ N., long. 78° 30′ E. The city (population, with suburbs, 500,000) stands on the S. bank of the Musi river, with Golkonda to W., and the Residency and its bazaars, and the Cantonments of the British troops, and the Contingent to the N.

The State of which Hyderabad is the capital covers 82,000 sq. m., with a population of 11,141,142, and is by far the largest in India. The present ruler is His Highness Asaf Jah Nizam-ul-Mulk Nawab Mir Sir Mahbub Ali Khan, G.C.B., G.C.S.I.

There have been nine[1] Nizams since the dynasty was founded in 1740 A.D. by Asaf Jah Nizam-ul-Mulk (Subahdar or Viceroy of the Deccan from 1713 onwards), four in the 17th century, all sons of the first Nizam, and five in the 19th, including His Highness, who succeeded in 1869. The sons of Asaf Jah played a very prominent part in matters connected with the growth of the power of the East India Company in S. India. The city is famed for its warlike and varied population. Formerly the inhabitants always carried weapons. The practice is now confined to the old Arab mercenaries who may be seen disporting themselves in the streets with a perfect armoury of weapons stuck in their waistcloths.

[1] The principal **Nizams** have been Nasir Jang, Salabat Jang, Nizam Ali, d. 1803, Sikandar Jah, d. 1829, and Nasir-ud-daulah, d. 1857. Asaf Jah was the son of the first Ghazi-ud-din (p. 200), Subahdar of Berar, and the real conqueror of Bijapur: he died at the age of 104, and is buried at Roza (p. 73).

The place maintains a considerable manufacture of textile fabrics, carpets, velvets for horse-trappings, and a material composed of cotton and silk. Red earthenware is also extensively made here.

To the north of the railway station are the beautiful *Public Gardens* covering an extensive area and surrounded by a high wall castellated with two lofty gateways. In addition to rare plants and well-laid out beds of flowers the *Gardens* contain a large lake, a menagerie, lawn tennis courts, a bandstand and an iron pavilion. In the N. corner a Town Hall is under construction which will commemorate the Anniversary of the fortieth birthday of His Highness the Nizam.

Outside the gardens to the N. is a picturesque Black Rock — the *Naubat Pahar* or "Band Rock"—so called from the fact that in olden times all official communications of the Mogul Emperors with Nizams were proclaimed from this rock to the sound of music. N. of the gardens is the Saifabad Cantonment of the Nizam's regular troops, and S. are the lines of the Imperial Service Troops. S.E. lies the *Fateh Maidan*, a plain which is the Nizam's polo-ground.

The **Residency** stands about 1¾ m. S.W. of the railway station, and N.E. of the city in a suburb called Chadar Ghat, and is surrounded by a bazaar containing 12,000 inhabitants. The grounds are extensive and full of grand old trees, and are enclosed by a wall, which was strengthened by Colonel Davidson after the attack upon the Residency on the morning of 17th July 1857. That attack was made by a band of Rohillas and others, and was repulsed by the troops at the Residency under Major Briggs, Military Secretary. The bastions commanding the approaches were erected then.

On the site of the Residency there was formerly a villa belonging to a favourite of Nizam 'Ali, and in it Sir John Kennaway, who was appointed Resident in 1788, was received. The present Residency was built 1803-8. The N. front, with the Grand Entrance, looks away from the Musi river and the city. Among the trees are four enormous specimens of the *Ficus indica*, the trunk of one measuring 30 ft. round. There is also a very gigantic tamarind tree. The Park contains an obelisk raised to the memory of Lieutenant William John Darby, who was killed in 1815 within the city of Hyderabad, while gallantly leading the grenadiers in a charge against some rebels.

Within the Residency limits is the **Pestonji Kothi**, a large building erected on a high stone basement by the famous Parsi bankers, Postonji and Co., who farmed the revenues of Berar from 1839-45. Close to the **Kothi** is the St George's Church, adjoining which is the old burial ground now abandoned. The most remarkable tomb in it is that of William Palmer who was styled "King" Palmer, and was the head of the banking firm bearing his name. Further N. on the same side of the road is the Roman Catholic Chapel, a two-storied building standing on the summit of a hill and commanding an extensive view. Near the chapel is one of the old French gun foundries erected by M. Raymond.

The **City** is in shape a trapezoid. The total area is 2 m. sq.: it is modern and has but few remarkable buildings, but the *bazars* are extremely picturesque and thronged with natives from all parts of India. On the N.W. side are five *Gateways*, viz., on the extreme E. the Chadar Ghat Gate; next to the W. the Delhi or Afzal Ganj Gate; next in the same direction are the Champa, the Char Mahal, and the Old Bridge Gates in succession. In the S.W. side there is, first, the Dudhni Gate, then the Fateh, which is exactly in the centre, and then the 'Aliabad in the S.W. corner. In the S. side are the

Gaulipur and the Ghaziband; and on the E. side are the Mir Jumlah, the Y'akubpur, and the Daudpur Gates.

The Musi river on the N. side is crossed by four *Bridges*. Farthest to the E. is the Oliphant Bridge, which was erected in 1831 by Colonel Oliphant, of the Madras Engineers. The next bridge to the W. is the Afzal Ganj Bridge, and then comes the Old and the Musallam Bridge. N. of the second bridge are the *Residency School*, and the *City Hospital*. The *Afzal Ganj Masjid* (Mosque), which adjoins the hospital to the N., is a fine building with four lofty minarets. On the other side of the road is a *purdah* hospital for women; this establishment can be inspected by ladies only. The Musallam Bridge, built in 1898 A.D. by the late Nawab Laik-ud-Dowla and the Old Bridge were the only ones which withstood the terrible flood of 1908. This flood caused the loss of over 3000 lives, and the destruction of 24,000 houses.

Inside the Afzal Ganj Gate is a broad street, which runs right through the city. A few hundred yards on the left is the *Palace of the late Sir Salar Jang*, G.C.S.I., whose able administration of the State from 1853 to 1883 is a matter of history. The great drawing-room contains a number of portraits of former Residents and other distinguished personages. Close to it is the Chini Khana, about 14 ft. sq. and 12 ft. high, covered with china cemented to the walls. In the N.E. quarter behind it is a mosque which is well worth a visit. Further along the central street is a rectangular building with four minarets, hence called the *Char Minar*, 186 ft. high and 100 ft. wide on each side, built in 1591; it was formerly a college, and occupies the central position in the city where the four main roads meet. Just before reaching it, the road passes under an arch called the *Machhi Kaman*, or "Arch of the Fish," the fish being a badge of high rank. There are four arches 50 ft. high across the streets, one to each quarter of the compass. A little to the E. of the Char Minar is the *Mecca* (Makka) *Masjid*, the principal mosque in the city; the gateway was completed by Aurangzeb in 1692. It is a grand but sombre building, with four minars and five arches in front, occupying one side of the paved quadrangle 360 ft. sq.—date, 1614 A.D. In the quadrangle are the graves of all the Nizams since the first. Close to the *Char Minar* and to the left of the main road a narrow lane leads to the *Juma Masjid* erected in 1598 A.D. by Sultan Muhammad Kuli. The mosque is without architectural pretensions, but is the oldest in Hyderabad. Her Majesty Queen Mary laid the foundation-stone of the Victoria Zenana Hospital in the city on 9th February 1906.

The **Nizam's Chaumahalla Palace** lies to the S. of the Char Minar, 2½ m. from the Residency; from the Chauk, a fine gateway leads to a large quadrangle. At the S.W. corner of this a narrow road leads into a second quadrangle, in which are generally a great number of horsemen, etc.; a passage from the S.W. corner of this leads into a third quadrangle, where many attendants are also generally to be found. The buildings on each side are handsome, and resemble the Shah's palace at Teheran, but are finer.

During the Muharram, H.H.'s troops, to the number of 30,000, pass in procession in front of the palace, and the spectacle is altogether a very magnificent one. The procession takes place on the 5th of Muharram: it is called the *Langar*, and is said to be in honour of Mohammed Kuli Shah, the sovereign, who built the Char Minar and the Mecca Masjid. Various stories are told about this procession. It is said that *Langar* (a chain) means the chain with which an elephant is confined, and that Mohammed Kuli Shah was run away with by an elephant, which suddenly became furious and rushed about for three days, keeping the king without food and in peril of his life. On the third day it became tractable, and the *Langar* was fastened on it. In a side street 200 yds. beyond the palace is the house in which the well-known minister, Chandu Lal, died. It is a low but highly-ornamented Hindu house.

Near the W. wall of the city is the vast palace of the *Barahdarri*, which was built by the Shams-ul-umara. It covers a large space, is handsomely furnished, and contains a gigantic suit of armour and sword belonging to Tegh Jung, the founder of the family, whose statue is said to have been 6 ft. 6 in.

The *Jahan Numa*, also built by the Shams-ul-umara, in a suburb of the same name outside the 'Aliabad Gate, is reached by a causeway built across rice-fields. Adjoining it is a very long approach, consisting of neatly-built houses, forming two narrow ellipses.

To the S. of the city standing on a hill is the *Falaknuma Palace* of His Highness the Nizam, which is considered the finest in India. It was built as a private residence by the late minister, Sir Vikar ul Umara, but was afterwards purchased by the Nizam for the sum of 35 lacs. The approach to the palace is by a beautifully-constructed hill-road at the end of which is a fine gateway. The palace stands on a terrace, the front part of which is artistically laid out in flower beds in the English style. The façade is Grecian, the cornice resting on a double row of Corinthian columns. The handsome vestibule, the walls of which are beautifully painted, is fitted with marble seats surrounding a marble fountain. The vestibule leads into the waiting-room, adjoining which are the Library and Council Chamber. The staircase to the upper floor is of marble with beautifully-carved balustrades, supporting, at intervals, marble figures with candelabra. On the walls are oil paintings of His Highness the Nizam and the past Residents and other notable personages of the State. The Reception-Room is decorated and furnished in Louis XIV. style. The Ball-Room, the Dining-Room, the Smoking-Room and bedrooms are all artistically furnished. From the upper floor a fine view can be obtained of the city, the Mir 'Alam Tank, and the surrounding country. Since it came into the possession of His Highness the palace has been provided with electric installation, and a wing has been built, unfortunately, in a style out of harmony with the original design as a Museum of Indian Industries.

2 m. W. of the city palace is the *Mir 'Alam Tank*, a lake 8 m. round. The embankment is formed of twenty-one arches, side by side, presenting their convex surfaces to the pressure of the water. It is 1120 yds. long, and was built by French engineers at a cost of £80,000. It was commenced by *Mir 'Alam*, the great minister of the Nizam, who led his master's forces during the war with Tipu Sultan in 1799, the prize money which fell to his share after the fall of Seringapatam being used for the construction. The embankment was, however, completed in 1811 by his son-in-law, Munir ul Mulk (1809-32), the father of Sir Salar Jang I. The *Mir 'Alam* lake is now used as a reservoir for supplying a large portion of the city with water. Filter-beds have been constructed in proximity of the embankment from which water is led by gravitation. A number of steam launches are maintained on the lake, and water parties are given to distinguished visitors. At the extreme W. end of the lake, which has picturesque coves and windings, is a wooded hill about 80 ft. high, surmounted by a building which is the *Dargah*, or shrine, of *Mahbub Ali*. This is a beautiful structure and well placed, looking down on the waters of the lake that ripple at the foot of

the cliff on which it stands. It is small but symmetrical, and was once covered with blue tiles.

[EXCURSIONS FROM HYDERABAD.

(1) The **Tomb of M. Raymond.** This lies in Sarav Nagar (Cypress Town), 3 m. from the Oliphant Bridge to the S.E. of the city, and stands on very high ground. The tomb consists of an obelisk of grey stone, 25 ft. high, with simply the letters J. R. on each side, placed on a spacious platform. At the end of the platform is an edifice like a Grecian temple. No date is recorded; but the gallant Frenchman in whose honour this fine structure has been erected died in March 1798. At the time of his death he had 15,000 well-disciplined troops at his command, and possessed more power than the British Resident.

(2) **GOLKONDA.** 7 m. W. from the Char Minar are the ruins of the capital of the Kutab Shahi kingdom,[1] the third great Mohammedan dynasty of the Deccan, which lasted from 1512 to 1687, till overthrown by the Emperor Aurangzeb. Permission to visit the Fort must be obtained through the Resident of Hyderabad. The place is surrounded by a strongly-built crenellated stone wall or curtain, a little over 3 m. in circumference, with eighty-seven bastions of solid granite blocks at the angles, on which there are still some of the old Kutab Shahi guns. The moat which surrounds the outer wall is filled up in many places. The Fort originally had eight gates, but of these two only are now in use, namely, the Banjara and Fateh. It was besieged by Aurangzeb, while Viceroy of the Deccan, in treacherous concert with the Minister Mir Jumla, and was taken by him, as Emperor, after a desperate defence of eight months by the last king, Abul Hasan, Abdur Razzak Khan Lari being the hero of the siege. When the first of the Nizams took possession of the place, he added a new wall to the fortifications on the E., so as to include a small hill formerly situated outside the Fort. The large sheet of water in front of this portion of the Fort is styled the *Langar Talao.*

The *Fateh Gate* is a massive structure of granite, with chambers on either side for the guard, and a pair of high teak-wood gates studded with iron wrought into various fanciful devices and huge sharp-pointed iron spikes, which were intended to prevent elephants from battering them in. The road from here passes straight through the Fort to the gate on the N.W. side. The northern portion of the ground enclosed by the wall has very few ruins upon it, although it was at one time most thickly populated; indeed, the ground inside the walls is said to have been so valuable that it used to sell for one ashrafi (Rs. 20) per yard. The eastern and southern portions are strewn with the ruins of palaces, mosques, and the dwelling-houses of the nobles and retainers of the Kutab Shahi kings. Inside the Fateh Gate are two buildings constructed by the French as arsenals. Further on are the Kiladar's (commandant's) House and the Mubariz-ud-daulah palace, and to the S. of these two large enclosures with underground galleries, which probably served as magazines. In front of the citadel, which rises finely some 350 ft. above the rest of the Fort, is a triumphal arch. A paved path leads up through various gateways, past a well, and under many picturesque half-ruined defences, to the summit of the citadel, on which are the remains of a lofty palace, affording a splendid view of all the country round; on the roof is a stone throne.

The Kings' Tombs.—About 600 yds. to the N.W. of the fortress

[1] This kingdom included all the countr from Golkonda in the west to the east sea coast from Orissa to the Kistna. For a detailed account of it see Major Haig's *Historic Landmarks of the Deccan.*

stand the tombs of the Kutab Shahi kings, who reigned for upwards of 170 years in Golkonda. They are reached from the Fort and citadel by turning N. from the entrance to the latter and passing a fine stone tank to the Banjara Gate in the N.W. corner of the former. The tombs were much neglected until they were repaired at the instance of the late Sir Salar Jang, when the gardens which had formerly existed around some of them were also replanted, and the whole enclosed by a substantial stone wall. The tombs standing within the garden enclosure are those of Jamshid Kuli, the second king, who died in 1550; Haiyat Baksh Begam, the daughter of Ibrahim Kuli Kutab Shah, the wife of Sultan Muhammad, the fifth king, and the mother of Sultan Abdulla Kutab Shah, the sixth and last but one of the Kutab Shah line (the date of her death, as inscribed on the tomb, is 1027 A.H.=1617 A.D.). Outside the garden enclosure to the N. is the tomb of Muhammad Kuli Kutab Shah, who died in 1020 A.H. = 1612 A.D. This king founded the city of Hyderabad, and erected many public edifices and palaces, and his is the finest of the tombs, being 168 ft. high from the basement to the summit of the dome. Beyond this is the tomb of Ibrahim Kuli Kutab Shah, the fourth king, who died in 988 A.H.=1580 A.D. To the S. of it is the tomb of Sultan Muhammad Amin, King Ibrahim's youngest son, who died in 1004 A.H.=1595 A.D. A short distance from here in a N. direction is the tomb of Kulsum Begam, and close to it is that of the first of the Kutab Shahi kings, Sultan Kuli Kutab, who died in 950 A.H.=1543 A.D. Between the walled enclosure and the Fort walls is the tomb of the sixth king, Abdulla Kutab Shah, who died in 1083 A.H.= 1672 A.D., after a reign of forty-eight years. This is one of the finest tombs here, being enriched with very fine carvings and minarets at each corner of the platform.

The last of the Kutab Shahi kings, Abul Hasan, who was sent off by his imperial captor to end his days in the fortress of Daulatabad, and died there in 1701, is the only one not interred here.

The return to Hyderabad may be made by the N. road, passing at 1 m. to the N.W., the *Barahdarri* and *Masjid of Bhagmati* (after whom Hyderabad was first called Bhagnagar), a favourite mistress of the Kutab Shahi king, Muhammad Kuli. On all sides rise masses of granite, gneiss, and low hills, taking from weather wear the most fantastic shapes, and sometimes appearing like subsidiary forts erected by the hand of man. The popular legend as regards the peculiarity of their position and appearance is that the Creator after finishing the construction of the world threw away the surplus material here.

The *diamonds* of Golkonda, which have become proverbial, were cut and polished here, but came principally from *Purtial*, on the S.E. frontier of the Nizam's territory, and Kollur in the Kistna district.]

---

121 m. **Secunderabad** junction,* 5½ m. N. of the Hyderabad Residency, is the British military cantonment, and one of the largest in India, covering 19 sq. m. It is the Headquarters of the 9th Army Division. It stands 1830 ft. above sea-level. Two main roads lead from Hyderabad to Secunderabad. The old road runs along the bend of the *Husain Saugar*, 2 m. N. of the Railway Station, a fine lake about 11 m. in circumference constructed by Ibrahim Kutab Shah (16th century) at a cost of 2½ lacs. The principal feeder is a channel 36 m. long, which runs from the Musi river above Hyderabad. The lake forms the main water supply of Hyderabad, Chadarghat and Residency limits. The water is pumped into filter beds from which it is distributed by means of iron pipes. The scenery on both

sides of the bend is highly picturesque, and on a clear evening just before sunset a magnificent view may be obtained of Golkonda and the far country in the west. At the Secunderabad end of the lake is a *Boat Club* where pleasure boats, both rowing and sailing, may be obtained. A regatta is held annually by the Club.

On the southern bank of the tank stands a large and extensive modern building surrounded by high walls, and known as the *Saifabad Palace.* Built originally as a suburban residence of the Nizam, it is now used for certain public offices, the chief of which are the financial and the public works and railways. The palace opens on the Saifabad Road by an elaborate and imposing iron gateway.

The other road running along the western bank of the Husain Saugar lake is of recent construction. It passes through the new and growing suburb of Khairatabad, and leaving the Bidar Road just past the unfinished residence of the Nawab Fakhrul Mulk on a hill to the left, skirts the eastern bank of the lake rising to a height of over 20 ft. above the water. Some fine private residences dot the road on both sides. About a mile from Khairatabad the road crosses the Hyderabad Wadi line of railway just above the Husain Saugar junction. Here a new station called Begumpett has been recently built for the convenience of military officers stationed at Bolarum, Trimalgiri, and Begumpett. Passing over two Warren girder bridges, the road descends nearly to the level of the lake, rising again as it approaches Secunderabad. The Begumpett lines, where a native Infantry Regiment is stationed, lie to the left, and on the right a huge block of buildings, surrounded by a wall, marks the palace of the late minister, Sir Vikar ul Umara. Here the road joins the Secunderabad parade road.

The *Parade-ground* at Secunderabad is of immense extent, and admits of a large brigade manœuvring upon it. On the N. side are many officers' houses, the railway station, which is handsomely built of granite, and the church, which is large enough to hold a European regiment. On the S. side of the Parade-ground is the cemetery, in which a vast number of officers are buried. S. of the Parade-ground is the large two-storied building of the *United Service Club,* with its Bachelors' Quarters, Ladies' Rooms, and Library. Close to the Club is the *Mud Fort,* in which the staff offices are situated.

At **Trimalgiri,** 3 m. N.E. of Secunderabad, is an entrenched camp, which would serve as a place of refuge. The *Military Prison,* which stands due W. of the S.W. bastion of the entrenchment, is popularly called Windsor Castle, from its high tower and castellated look. The *European Hospital* is due S. of the S.E. bastion.

Bolaram, 6 m. N. of Secunderabad, and now incorporated with it, was the principal cantonment of the Hyderabad Contingent Force. Under the arrangement recently made with the Nizam (p. 83), this now ranks as part of the general Indian Army. There is also a Residency at Bolaram.

[From Secunderabad a line runs up the Godavery Valley to Aurangabad and Manmar, Route 6.]

149 m. **Bhangir (R.).**

202 m. **Kazipet** (R.). **Kazipet** is the station at which the headquarters of the Subah are situated, and where a visitor proposing to spend the night must stay by the courtesy of permission obtained at Hyderabad. It is 2 m. from **Hanamcondah,** and 6 m. from **Warangal**—the latter lies 2 m. N. of the famous Hindu Fort,

of which the great walls are very conspicuous from the railway. These defended the ancient capital of the Kakatiya or Ganpati dynasty which was attacked by Malik Kafur, in 1309, and captured by Muhammad Tughlak in 1323, after which the kingdom disappeared. The most interesting of the objects inside the Fort are the four gateways called Kirthi Stambhas, which were apparently openings to a Square, and which reproduce wooden forms in every detail, the side struts being specially remarkable. There is also a small half-ruined temple with some capital figures of bulls in front of it. The fine hall and other buildings belong to the Mohammedan period. The Hanamcondah temple (c. 1163) has been ruined by an earthquake, but is still well worthy of a visit as a fine specimen of the Chalukyan style of S. India. In front of the tri-apsidal temple was a splendid Hall of Columns; both of these are placed on high basements, and both contain numbers of elaborately decorated pillars of very hard dark stone with pierced screens between those in the outer rows. It is dedicated to Rudra, God of Thunder. (See Fergusson's *Indian Architecture*, i. 434).

208 m. **Warangal** station. A line will probably be constructed N. from here to join the G.I.P. Railway at Chanda (p. 83). The present line now turns sharply S.E. to

261 m. **Dornakal** junction station (R.) [Branch to **Yellanda** 14 m. Here are the Singareni coal-mines of the Deccan Mining Co., on which 8000 coolies are employed, with rich beds of iron ore.]

328 m. **Kondapalli** station. Ruins of a once celebrated fortress, built in 1360 A.D. It was taken by the Emperor Aurangzeb in 1687, and by the British, under General Caillaud, in 1766.

338 m. **Bezwada** or **Kistna station** (R.), D.B. (see p. 335).

ROUTE 29.

GADAG JUNCTION TO HOSPET (for **Hampi** and **Vijayanagar**), **Bellary** and **Guntakal** Junction, and from **Guntakal** Junction to
- (*a*) **Nandyal**, **Guntur**, and **Bezwada** (expedition by road to **Kurnool**) and
- (*b*) **Dharmavaram** and Bangalore.

Gadag junction station (R.) D.B. (p. 372).

53 m. **Hospet** station (R.), D.B. From this point *Hampi* (9 m.) and *Vijayanagar* can most conveniently be visited. The station-master will arrange for a country cart—the only local means of conveyance.

[Excursion to Vijayanagar (City of Victory) and Hampi.✱

Hampi is the site of the ancient capital of the Vijayanagar kings, who dominated S. India from 1336 to 1565 A.D. The ruins cover 6 sq. m., including *Kamalapur* on the S. and *Anagundi*, the latter seat of the dynasty, N. of the Tungabhadra. Mr R. Sewell's *A Forgotten Empire* deals fully with them.

The Kamalapur D.B. is 7 m. N.E. from Hospet; it is an old temple converted into a rough D.B. There is a good road from Kamalapur to Hampi, which winds round the rocky hills between which the old city was built. The site is watered by a channel from the river.

Hampi was founded on the fall of the Hoysala Ballala dynasty (p. 385), about 1336 A.D., by two brothers, Bukka and Harihara, who had been driven out of Warangal. Their descendants flourished here till the battle of Talikot (1565), and afterwards at Anagundi, Vellore, and Chandragiri for another century, until finally overwhelmed by the advancing Mohammedan powers of Bijapur and Golkonda. During the two and a quarter centuries that the Vijayanagar Rajas held the city of Hampi they extended it and beautified it with palaces and temples.

The traveller, Cæsar Frederick, who saw "Bezenagar" soon after its fall, describes it as being 24 m. round, enclosing several hills. The ordinary dwellings were mean buildings with earthen walls, but the three palaces and the pagodas were all built of fine marble.

The rout of the Hindu forces at Talikot was so complete, and the dismay caused by the death of the old King Rama Raja was so great, that no attempt was made to defend the city, which was completely gutted by the Mohammedan conquerors. Colonel Briggs states that for two centuries afterwards the head of the Hindu prince used to be annually exhibited at Ahmednagar.

The main portion of the city was enclosed by walls forming a semicircle on the S. bank of the river: in the middle of this was the inner walled citadel and palace, and on the N. bank of the river was another large fortified area by the suburbs of Anagundi; further outer lines of fortifications enclosed the city on the S. side.

Proceeding N. for ½ m. from the D.B., the first remarkable building is the **King's or Ladies' Bath**, forming a portion of the king's palace. It is a rectangular structure, with a *hauz*, or reservoir, in the centre, 50 ft. square and 6 ft. deep, in which fountains played; but there is no water now, and the whole has been a good deal injured. N.W. of the entrance are remains of the granite aqueduct which was carried from near the throne to the bath, The corridor of the bath, supported by twenty pillars, has an arched ceiling, richly carved with flowers. On either side is a projecting gallery ornamented with carving. Slightly to the W. of the bath and aqueduct is a fine tank, and N. of these is the structure called the Arena, or the **Sinhasan**, the King's Throne. It consists of a succession of granite platforms 31 ft. high, the outer walls of which are carved in relief with representations of elephants, dancing-girls, hunting-scenes from the Ramayana and camels, well executed. W. of the throne is an underground labyrinth, used, probably, as a cool retreat in the summer, and N. of the former are a remarkable stone trough and the ruins of a fine bazaar. The stones forming the trough measure about 11 ft. × 6 ft., and the supports are 5 ft. 8 in. high. N. of this again is the temple of Ramachendra-swami with pillars handsomely carved in relief with figures. The quadrangle, inside measurement, is 110 ft. from N. to S. and 200 ft. from E. to W. The temple has a vestibule carried on twelve pillars. The adytum is supported by black pillars most elaborately carved. On the plinth of the left gateway is a very long inscription in Old Kanarese.

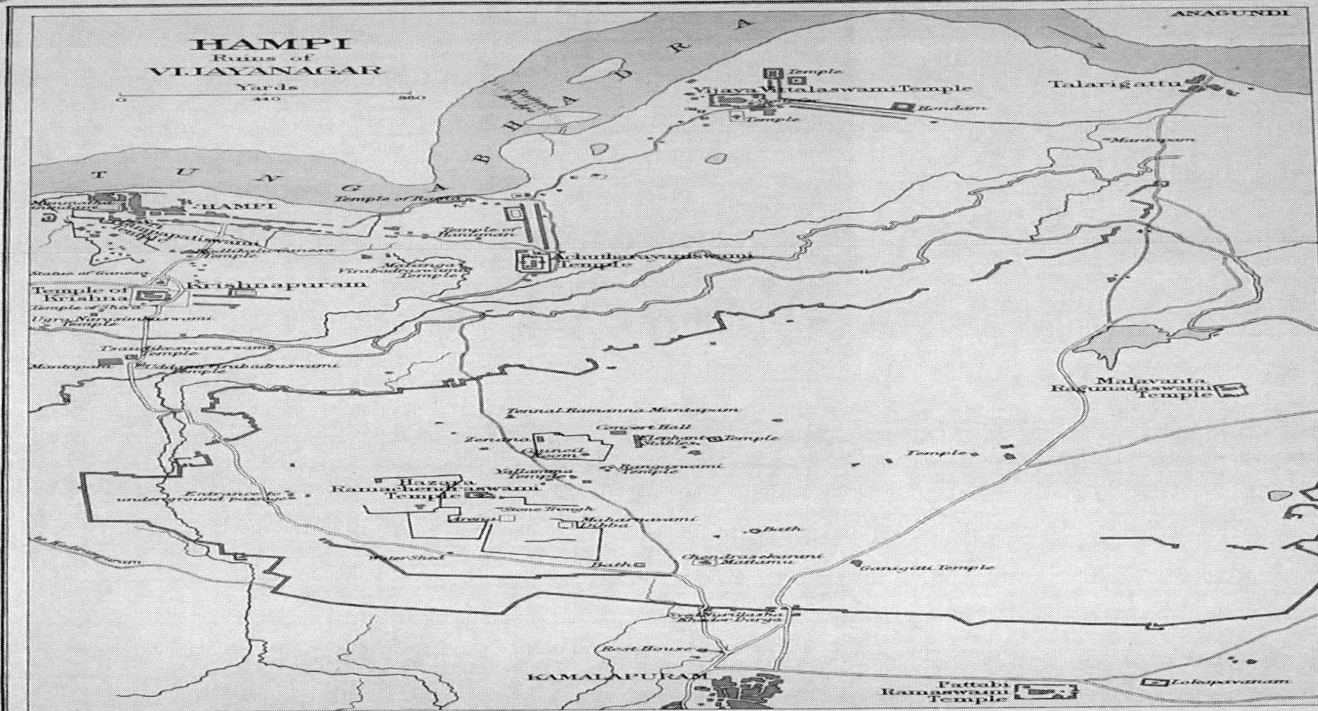

London. John Murray, Albemarle Street.

The stones of which this temple is built average 7 ft. 7 in. long and 2 ft. 6 in. deep.

To the E. of this group of buildings in the S.W. corner of the Citadel, and across the road leading through the Citadel to the N., are the ruins of three temples, one situated on the top of a small hill; while at a distance of ½ m. to the N.E. of it are situated the **Zananah**, the Elephant Stables and the Riding School. The first is an enclosure of walls 40 ft. high, with the building called the Zananah palace in the N.W. corner, and the pavilion, figured in Fergusson's *Indian Architecture*, and commonly called the Council Room, towards the S.E. corner. At various corners of the walls are similar small pavilions; in the N. wall is a large tower, and in the W. wall is a fine gateway closed over by projecting stones. The pavilions are too heavy to be really effective, but are picturesque in their present state of ruin; the painted decoration of the upper rooms of the main pavilion is still visible. To the E. of the enclosure is a smaller *sinhasan* or throne, and the fine range of **Elephant Stables** divided into eleven domed compartments, some of which were elaborately decorated inside. Along the front of the building is a broad dripstone carried by brackets. The so-called Riding School or Concert Hall stands at right angles to the stables on the N. side of the Zananah; the purpose which this building really served is uncertain. To the S.E. of the Zananah is another temple, and between it and the three temples above mentioned is an interesting rock excavation, one of the chambers of which has a dripstone carved on it.

Returning W. and passing outside the citadel on the N.W. side where the gateway figured in Fergusson's *Indian Architecture* stands, and crossing the remains of a fine bazaar, the next group of buildings of interest is reached on the S. side of the hill which dominates the village of Hampi. The first of these on the left of the road is a gigantic image of the **Narsingh Avatar**, carved out of a single block of granite, in an enclosure of ponderous granite blocks. The figure is that of a colossal lion-headed man with enormous projecting circular eyes and a huge mouth: it is seated, and has its legs and arms broken. A spirited carving of the Shesh Nag forms the canopy of the idol. The monolithic uprights at the door are 18 ft. 8 in. high out of the ground. Just outside the gate is an upright stone with a Kanarese inscription on both sides. A few yards N. of this enclosure is a small temple containing a huge Lingam and Yoni, the largest representation of these objects of worship existing.

N.E. is a vast **temple to Krisnaswami**, enclosed by a granite wall. The breadth of the chief court is 200 ft. from N. to S., and the length 320 ft. from E. to W. At the gopuram which forms the entrance is a stone 8 ft. high, with a Kanarese inscription on both sides. There is also on the columns of the gopuram an inscription in Nagri and Kanarese. The carving of the various portions of the temple is noticeable, and the whole enclosure is extremely picturesque. N. of this temple, about 50 yds. off the road, is a temple with a huge **Ganesh** 10 ft. high; and a few yards farther another, vastly solid, built of granite, dedicated to Ganesh, in which the idol is 18 ft. high. The size of the enormous granite slabs which form the roof is remarkable. After passing this temple, the precincts of what is now called *Hampi* are entered, and *Langur* monkeys may be seen in considerable numbers. Descending for 70 yds., a granite pavement cut into small steps, and passing on the left a square building, which may have been a *math*, and some gigantic trees, the portal of the **great temple of Hampi**, which is sacred to Shiva, under the name of Pampapati Swami is reached. The gopuram at the N. entrance is truly gigantic, and taken in all its dimensions is (being over 165 ft. high) perhaps the largest in India. The length of the first quadrangle from E. to W. is 208 ft., and its breadth from N. to S. 134 ft. The second quadrangle is smaller, and has arcades all round built of granite. The authorities of the temple do not allow a European, excepting officials, to go farther than a few steps beyond the second gopuram under which is the entrance to this second quadrangle.

At the E. end of the grassy avenue in front of the temple is another large temple, picturesquely situated on a ridge and approached by a long flight of steps with pavilions. The road turns N. from here and leads to the river, which makes a sudden bend at this point, and after passing a temple of Ramaswámi (Ramchandra) with a stone lamp-stand in front of it, and the ruins of the old bridge, reaches at a distance of ¾ m. the temple of **Witthoba** or Vijaya Vitalaswami, also figured in Fergusson. In front of this is a stone-weighing frame, and at the S. end of it is a stone rath (car) 26 ft. high, carved out of a monolith.

There are three temples in the enclosure, which has four Dravidian gopurams. The second temple, on the left of the entrance, is much the largest and finest. The ceiling was formed of slabs of granite 35 ft. long, but all the slabs have been thrown down except one in the centre. There are fourteen columns, which supported the roof. Most of them are carved into representations of horsemen mounted on *yali* lions. One represents the Narsingh Avatar. In some cases the yali is supported by elephants. Within is a court 100 ft. long from E. to W., and 62 ft. broad from N. to S. On the S. side are numerous Kanarese inscriptions. S. of the temple is a large dharmsala with sixty-two pillars, on which are curious reliefs of female monkeys and dwarfs. On the right of the entrance is a platform with thirty-nine shorter pillars. These are also carved with curious representations of monkeys, their heads crowned with two small figures of gods. The third temple is some 20 yds. N. of the car.

An hour or so may well be spent in the solitude of these beautiful ruins. Any one who may wish to ascend the hills above Anagundi on the left bank of the river, for the sake of a general view over Vijayanagar, can cross the Tungabhadra in a circular basket-boat, such as were used on the Tigris and Euphrates 2500 years ago, and are still so used. The Matanga Temple affords a fine general view of the ruins.

---

94 m. **Bellary** station (R.), D.B. A municipal town and large military station, headquarters of district of same name (population, 58,000). A spur from the Sandur range runs along the S. side of the Cantonment, and extends E. to Budihal, 8 m. distant, where it abruptly terminates. A high point in this range opposite the Fort is called the *Copper Mountain*, the height being 1600 ft. above the plain, and 2800 ft. above the sea. Excavations are still to be seen in it; these are said to be the remains of mines worked by order of Hyder 'Ali, but abandoned in consequence of the expense exceeding the profit. Besides copper, hæmatitic iron ore is found in large quantities, some possessing magnetic properties.

The *Fort*, built on a bare granite rock of semi-elliptical form, rises abruptly from the plain to the height of 450 ft. The rock is defended by two distinct lines of works, constituting the lower and upper Forts, both built of granite. In the upper one stands the citadel, which is reputed to be of great antiquity. Several tanks or cisterns have been hollowed out in the rock to hold rainwater. The lower Fort was built for Tipu Sultan in 1792 by a staff of French engineers, tradition adding that after the new citadel had been completed Tipu Sultan hanged them at the gate, as he found that his Fort was commanded by another rock. The place came into possession of the British in 1800.

123 m. **Guntakal** junction station (see p. 350).

(*a*) **Guntakal to Bezwada.**

167 m. **Kurnool Road** station (R.).

½ m. distant is **Dhone.** D.B. *

[From here **Kurnool** (pop. 25,000) is 33 m. N. by road: a railway is under construction. The town stands at the junction of the Hindri and Tungabhadra rivers. The old Fort was dismantled in 1862, but four bastions and three gates still stand, and it still contains the palace of the Nawabs. There are several mosques and a fine mausoleum of Abdul Wahab, the first Nawab, to whom the place was given in jagir by the Emperor Aurangzeb. These Pathan Nawabs and those of Cuddapah played a prominent part in the 18th century; like the former they were first absorbed by the Nizam and afterwards by Hyder 'Ali. The last Nawab was deposed in 1838.]

214 m. **Nandyal** station (R.). Called from Nandi, the bull of Shiva. There are several Shivite temples here. Before reaching it the line passes through the Gerramalai Hills by many picturesque curves.

277 m. **Cumbum** station (R.).

383 m. **Guntur** station (R.). This place, of some importance during the 18th century as the capital of one of the four Northern Circars (Sirkars), was held in jagir by Basalat Jang, brother of the Nizam Nizam 'Ali, long after the others had been ceded to the East India Company. In the Cemetery are a number of old French graves. Guntur is now an important centre of the American mission.

The railway crosses the Kistna river by a huge bridge (p. 336) just below the irrigation dam before entering.

402 m. **Bezwada** (R.) D.B.

(*b*) **Guntakal to Bangalore.**

42 m. **Anantapur,** headquarters of a district formed not long since.

63 m. **Dharmavaram** junction (R.). Branch of S. Indian Railway to Pakala (142 m.). 3½ m. from the Mulacalacheruva Station (65 m.) is the picturesque Sompalle Temple, with a stone car and beautiful monolithic flagstaff 50 ft. high.

102 m. **Hindupur** (R.). The temple here is the special object of pilgrimages.

142 m. **Dodbellapur.** 12 m. to the E. of this station rises

[**Nandidrug,** a strong hill-fort 4856 ft. above sea-level. It was thought impregnable by Tipu Sultan, being inaccessible except from the W., and there strongly fortified. It was taken, however, by General Meadows on the 19th October 1791, with the loss of only thirty killed and wounded, chiefly by the tremendous masses of granite rolled down the rock on the heads of the assailants. The rock called Tipu's Drop, protecting from the Fortress has a precipice of 1000 ft. clear below it.]

179 m. **Bangalore** junction (p. 388).

ROUTE 30.

HUBLI JUNCTION TO HARIHAR BIRUR (for **Shimoga** and the **Gairsoppa Falls**), **Banavar** (for expedition to the temples at **Hallabid** and **Belur,** also to the hill of **Indrabetta,** near **Shravana Belgola**), **Arsikere Tumkur,** and **Bangalore.**

Hubli junction station (R.) (p. 373).

81 m. **Harihar** station (R.) on the right bank of the Tungabhadra. In 1868 a very fine bridge was constructed over the river. An inscrip-

tion on copper has been found here of the 7th century, and there are several of the 12th. The fine temple was erected in 1223. In 1268 additions were made by Soma, the founder of Somnathpur in the Mysore district (p. 390).

124 m. **Holalkere.** From here the interesting fortified Hill of Chitaldrug D.B., lying 26 m. to the N.E., may be visited. From Hosdurga, 20 m. S. of Holalkere, may be visited the great Mari Kavane Lake, formed by a dam 1200 ft. long and 140 ft. high, across the Hagari Valley, and covering 35 sq. m. There is a penstock with a fall of 60 ft. by the dam. This work too was inaugurated by Sir K. Sheshadri Iyar (p. 391).

160 m. **Birur** junction, branch line to (38 m.) **Shimoga**, D.B., the headquarters of the N.W. district of the Mysore State. Just before Shimoga is reached the Bhadra river is crossed not very far from its sources.

This is now the most convenient starting-point for the **Gairsoppa** as they are usually called, or **Jog Falls** of the Sharavati, distant 65 m., the stages, each with a Rest-House, being Ayanur 15 m., Anantpur 15 m., Sagar 15 m., Talgappe 10 m., Gairsoppa Falls 10 m. A jatka mail cart now runs daily to Sagar (special Rs.8); if application is made beforehand to the Amaldar Sagar, he will be sure to lend courteous assistance to obtain a bullock tonga and arrange for relays of bullocks on to the Falls. The charge per pair of bullocks or buffaloes is 3 annas per mile. Supplies must be taken with one for the journey. The road is pretty and interesting, and passes through much fine bamboo and tree forest. The journey will occupy two full days, as the bullocks cannot go more than 4 m. an hour on an all-round average. Some miles above the Falls the road to the Mysore Bungalow on the left bank turns down to the Sharavati, which is here an extremely beautiful broad, deep stream, flowing between high finely-wooded banks, while the main Honawar road continues directly on to the Bombay bungalow at Kodkani, on the right bank close to the Raja Fall.

There are in all four falls, which have been called the Raja, the Roarer, the Rocket, and the Dame Blanche. In the first of these the water in considerable volume leaps sheer down a height of 829 ft., measured by line, and falls into a pool 132 ft. deep. The spectator can look right down into this abyss. Viewed from below and at some distance, this fall contrasts with magical effect with the next, the *Roarer*, in which the water rushes with less abruptness, foaming down a tortuous channel into a cavern or cup, which turns it into the rift of the Raja below. The name given to the third fall at a little distance to the S. the *Rocket*, is very appropriate. It continually shoots out in jets of foam, which burst like fire-rockets into showers of glittering drops. The *Dame Blanche* nearest the S. end of the cliff is exquisitely beautiful, and streams in a succession of lace-like cascades over the sloping surfaces of the rock-wall underneath it. The finest view is no doubt that from the Mysore side (though that from the front of the Rest-House on the N. bank is very beautiful also), as from it the black chasm into which the Raja and Roarer leap and pour is fully seen, as well as the curving face of the cliff down which the Rocket and Dame Blanche shoot and stream. A particularly fine view is that from Lady Curzon's seat and Watkin's platform to the W. of the Mysore Bungalow; and no one should fail to make the expedition to the foot of the falls, steep though the paths are for returning. A splendid surge of spray constantly rises from the pool into the chasm and the recess of the falls, and in the afternoon is touched with rainbow glories. The whole of the deep recess into which the waters are hurled is covered with fine trees and dense undergrowth (full of leeches !), and the river disappears to the W. between the dark walls of the gorge through which it hurries to the sea. In its full glory there are few more wonderful effects of nature to be seen anywhere in the world; but it must be remembered that in the dry season the amount of water in the falls becomes very small, and that in the rains the whole of the recess and the falls, or at least the chasm of the Raja, may be shrouded for hours, and perhaps even days, in thick impenetrable mist. The best time for a visit is probably early in the cold weather, as soon as the rains have ceased. The following account of the journey to the falls from Honawar is from the journal of an accomplished writer who visited the place in 1888. The trip from this side involves a journey by steamer to Carwar, a journey by sea-boat of 50 m. to Honawar (the steamers will, however, sometimes stop off this port), and a journey up the river for 18 to 20 m. in a small boat; and for the ordinary traveller the route by Shimoga is now much the more convenient one to take. "Arrangements had been made for our passage to the Gairsoppa Falls. We went on the same night 18 m. in boats up the moonlit river, grounded on a sandbank, and were pulled off only to find the rowers had landed to drink success to our future progress, to which this indulgence by no means conduced. Arrived at Gairsoppa, we slept in the D.B., awoke to the crowing of the jungle cock, and went on 20 m. by road to *Kodkani*. Here is another D.B., whence you look down into a boiling chaos of waters. The road from Gairsoppa to Kodkani is one long bower of evergreen trees, and at mid-day you scarcely see the sun. These jungles abound with tigers, bears, bison, and game of all kinds, large and small."

The Queen of Gairsoppa, called by the Portuguese the *Reinha da Pimento*, or Pepper Queen, was a great dignitary in the 17th century. Her subjects were chiefly Jains, by whom the nearest village to the falls is at present almost entirely inhabited. Among the ruins of the city are two ordinary Jain temples.

---

178 m. **Banavar** station.

[The renowned ruins of *Hallabid* lie 18 m. S.W. from this point by road, past *Jamgal* (12 m.). 10 m. beyond in the same direction is *Belur*. A pleasant round may be continued from Belur to Hasan (22 m.), Chennarayapatnam (18 m.), for Sravana Belgola (8 m.), and from Chennarayapatnam to Arsikere on the Railway (32 m.), the whole trip occupying four long days in favourable weather. The Mysore State authorities will arrange for relays of bullocks (see p. 384) on application being made beforehand. A railway between Hasan and Arsikere is under consideration.

At **Jamgal** there is a temple dedicated to Narsingh, and built entirely of *balapam*, or pot-stone. "It is highly ornamented after the Hindu fashion, and on the outside every part of its walls is covered with small images in full relievo."

Hallabid[1] (R.H.), named from the Kanarese words, *hale*, "old," *bidu*, "ruins," is a village on the site of Dorasamudra, the capital of the Hoysala Ballala kings. It was founded early in the 12th century, but was rebuilt in the middle of the 13th by Vira Someshwara, and some inscriptions represent him to be the founder. Attacked by leprosy, he withdrew to the neighbouring hill of Pushpagiri (Mountain of Flowers), where he was instructed to erect temples to Shiva to obtain a cure. The Mohammedan general Kafur took the city in 1310, and plundered it of immense wealth. In 1326 another army of Mohammedans carried off what remained and destroyed the city. The Raja then removed to Tonnur.

There are two most remarkable temples remaining. The northernmost of these, the **Ketaresvara**, is the smaller of the two, and was a

[1] See Fergusson's *Indian Architecture*, i. 442.

miracle of art. Unfortunately, a tree took root in the vimanah, or tower, over the sanctuary, and dislodging the stones, rendered much of the temple a heap of ruins. The temple was star-shaped, with sixteen points, and had a porch that from base to top "was covered with sculptures of the very best Indian art, and these so arranged as not materially to interfere with the outlines of the building." It was, when intact, the finest specimen of Indian art in existence.

The second temple, the **Hoysaleshwara**, "Lord of the Hoysalas," is much larger than the Ketaresvara. It stands on a terrace, 5 ft. 6 in. in height, paved with large slabs. The temple itself is 160 ft. from N. to S. by 122 ft. from E. to W., and beyond its walls there is a clear margin of platform all round of about 20 ft. The height from the terrace to the cornice is 25 ft. It is a double temple, one half being sacred to Shiva, and the other to his wife. Each half has a pavilion in front containing the *Basava*[1] *Nandi*, or bull. The larger of the two is 16 ft. long by 7 ft. broad and 10 ft. high, the animal being represented kneeling.

Some of the pillars in the inner part of the temple are of black hornblende, and have a dazzling polish. Mr Fergusson says: "Some of these friezes are carved with a minute elaboration of detail which can only be reproduced by photography, and may probably be considered as one of the most marvellous exhibitions of human labour to be found even in the patient East." He adds: "Here the artistic combination of horizontal with vertical lines, and the play of outline and of light and shade, far surpass auything in Gothic art. The effects are just what the mediæval architects were often aiming at, but which they never attained so perfectly as was done at Hallabid." In the friezes of sculptured animals which surround the building, the succession is always the same, the elephants being the lowest, next above them the *shardulas* (or conventional lions), then the horses, then the oxen, then birds. Mr Fergusson places Hallabid temple and the Parthenon as the two extremes of architectural art, and says: "It would be possible to arrange all the buildings of the world between these two extremes, as they tended toward the severe intellectual purity of the one, or the playful exuberant fancy of the other; but perfection, if it existed, would be somewhere near the mean." A whole day may well be devoted to the leisurely study of the wonderful work on these temples, but admiration for them should not cause neglect of the group of extremely beautiful **Jain Bastis** at the farther end of the village.

[1] Basava was founder in the 12th century of the Lingayat Saivite sect in S. and W. India. The members who are vegetarians, admit the equality of women with men, allow widow marriage, and disregard Brahman sanctity.

Belur (or Baillur) (R.H.) stands on the right bank of the Yagache (population about 3000). In the Puranas and old inscriptions it is called Velapura, and is styled the S. Benares. Here is the famous temple of Chenna Kesava, erected and endowed by the Hoysala king, Vishnu Vardhana, on exchanging the Jain faith for that of Vishnu in the beginning of the 12th century. The carving with which it is decorated rivals in design and finish that of Hallabid, and is the work of the same artist, Jakanacharya. The image of Chenna Kesava is said to have been brought from the Baba Budan hills, but that of his goddess was left behind, which obliges him to pay her a visit there at stated intervals. The *Great Temple* stands within a high wall which surrounds a court, 440 ft. by 360 ft. On the E. front are two fine gopurams. In this court are, besides the Great Temple, four or five smaller ones. "The first consists," says Mr Fergusson, "of a very solid vimanah, with an *anterala*, or porch; and in front of this a porch of the usual star-like form, measuring 90 ft. across. The arrangements of the pillars have much of that pleasing subordination and variety of spacing which is found in those of the Jains; but we miss here the octagonal dome, which gives such poetry and meaning to the arrangements they adopted. Instead of these we have only an exaggerated compartment in the centre, which fits nothing, and, though it does give dignity to the centre, it does it so clumsily as to be almost offensive in an architectural sense." The windows to the porch are twenty-eight, and all different. Some are pierced with star-shaped conventional patterns, and with foliaged patterns between. Others are interspersed with mythological figures, as the Varaha Avatar. The base is very richly carved, and is supported on carved elephants. Mr Fergusson says: "The amount of labour which each facet of this porch displays is such as never was bestowed on any surface of equal extent in any building in the world; and though the design is not of the highest order of art, it is elegant and appropriate, and never offends against good taste. The sculptures of the base of the vimanah are as elaborate as those of the porch, in some places more so; and the mode in which the under sides of the cornices have been elaborated and adorned is such as is only to be found in temples of this class." The carving at Belur is more graceful and finer than that at Hallabid, and many of the figures on the exterior are extremely beautiful.]

188 m. **Arsikere** station (R.) Gold-mining has been started here with but poor results as yet. It is under contemplation to construct a railway from here to Hasan and Mangalore.

[32 m. S. from this place is the ancient town of *Chennarayapatnam.*[1] The Fort was built subsequently, and Hyder 'Ali added the wet moat and traverse gateways.

[1] The temple was erected in 1600.

8 m. S.E. again is **Shravana Belgola.** Bhadra Bahu, a Jain sage who died here in the 4th century B.C., was a *Shruta kevala*, or immediate "hearer," of the six disciples of Mahavira, founder of the Jain sect. The chief attendant of this worthy is said to have been the famous Emperor Chandragupta, or Sandracottus, who abdicated to live the life of a recluse with him. These events are confirmed by inscriptions on the rock of very great antiquity. The grandson of Chandragupta is said to have visited the spot with an army, and from his camp arose the town of Shravana Belgola, or Belgola of the Shravans = Jains. Near the town, which has 1300 inhabitants, are two rocky hills —*Indrabetta* and *Chandragiri.* On Indrabetta, reached by a steep narrow flight of steps going straight up the steep slope of the rock, is a colossal statue of Gomata Raya,[1] 70 ft. 3 in. It is nude, and faces the N. The face has the calm look usual in Buddhist statues. The hair is curled in short spiral ringlets all over the head. From the knees downwards the legs are unnaturally short; the feet rest on a lotus. Ant-hills rise on either side, with a creeping plant springing from them which twines round the thighs and arms. These symbolise the deep abstraction of the sage, which allows ants to build and the plants to climb around him unnoticed. Though certainly 1000 years old, and probably 2000, the stone looks as fresh as if newly quarried: its preservation is due to its being profusely anointed at intervals of 25 years. Within the enclosure are 72 small statues, of like appearance, in compartments. An inscription on the front of the colossus states that it was erected by Chamunda Raya, who is said to have lived 60 B.C. The most interesting inscriptions are cut in the face of the rock at Indrabetta in ancient characters 1 ft. long.

[1] Another name of Gotama Swami. See p. lxii.

On Chandragiri there are fifteen Jain temples, making clusters of the kind known as Bastis, and a number of stone lamp shafts — see ii. 71 of Fergusson's *Indian Architecture.*]

248 m. **Tumkur** station (R.) (population, 10,000). Glass bangles, arms and cutlery are produced here.

219 m. **BANGALORE City** junction station (altitude 4000 ft., lat. 12° 57′, long. 77° 37′. ✱). The railway runs on S.W. to Mysore, N. to Guntakal, and E. to Jalarpat for Madras. The Cantonment station lies 2 m. N.E. of the city station. The name is literally "the town of bengalu," a kind of bean. The Cantonment area assigned to the British Government when the State of Mysore was restored to its native prince is 13½ sq. m. This State, which is the third largest in all India, comprises an area of 29,400 sq. m., and contains a population of 5½ millions. The present chief is H.H. Maharaja Sri Krishna Rajendra Wadiyar Bahadur, G.C.S.I. The ruling family was established as such early in the 15th century, was ousted by Hyder 'Ali, and was restored in the person of the grandson of the deposed prince, a child of five years of age, in 1799 A.D. The conduct of this chief, Krishna Raja Wadiyar, and the mismanagement of the State led to the assumption of the administration by the British Government in 1831, under treaty stipulation of 1799. Various applications of the Maharaja for the restoration of powers to him were rejected; but in 1866 it was decided to recognise his adoption as a son of Chama Rajendra, and that the State should be restored to this chief should he prove fit. Maharaja Krishna Raja Wadiyar died in 1868, and in 1881 the rendition of the State to Maharaja Chama Rajendra Wadiyar was carried out. The late Maharaja proved an excellent ruler, and died prematurely in 1894. During the minority of her son, till August 1902, Her Highness the Maharani Regent carried on the administration with a council of Regency, Sir K. Seshadri Iyar being Diwan. The late Diwan, Sir Krishna Murti, K.C.I.E., was descended from Diwan Purnaya, the famous Prime Minister of Mysore, a Mahratta Brahman who served alike Hyder 'Ali, Tipu Sultan, and the British Government. The present Diwan is Mr T. Ananda Rao, C.I.E.

The **Cantonment** (the largest in the S. of India—population, 100,000) and **City** of Bangalore (population, 88,000) stretch from the Maharaja's palace on the N., 6500 yds., to the Koramangala Tank on the S., and an equal distance from the Petta on the W., to the Sappers' Practice-ground on the E. Bangalore proper lies S. of the Lharmambudhi and Sampangi Tanks, which lie in the N.W. and E. corners of the *Petta* or town. Beginning with the Cantonment, and taking the noticeable things in order from N.W. to S.E., the first building is the handsome **Maharaja's Palace.** 2 m. north of the palace is the **Science Institute,** founded by the munificent liberality of the well-known **Tata** family of Parsi merchant princes, which bids fair to attain to a world-wide reputation. The gift to the Institute has been no less than 30 lakhs. S.E. of this 850 yds. is the Railway Station, and 300 yds. S. of that again is *Miller's Tank*, which communicates by a small stream with the much larger *Halsur Tank* on the E. edge of the Cantonment. Along the N. side of the Cantonment are the bazaars and the pleasant suburb of *Cleveland Town*, in which are some neat residences and Roman Catholic and Protestant *Churches*. The Sappers' quarters are at the E. corner of the Bazaar adjoining the village and large tank of *Halsur.*[1]

S. of the Sapper lines are the British Infantry Barracks, and then in order along the N. side of the great Parade-ground, St Andrew's kirk,

[1] Morris's Guide to Bangalore can be recommended.

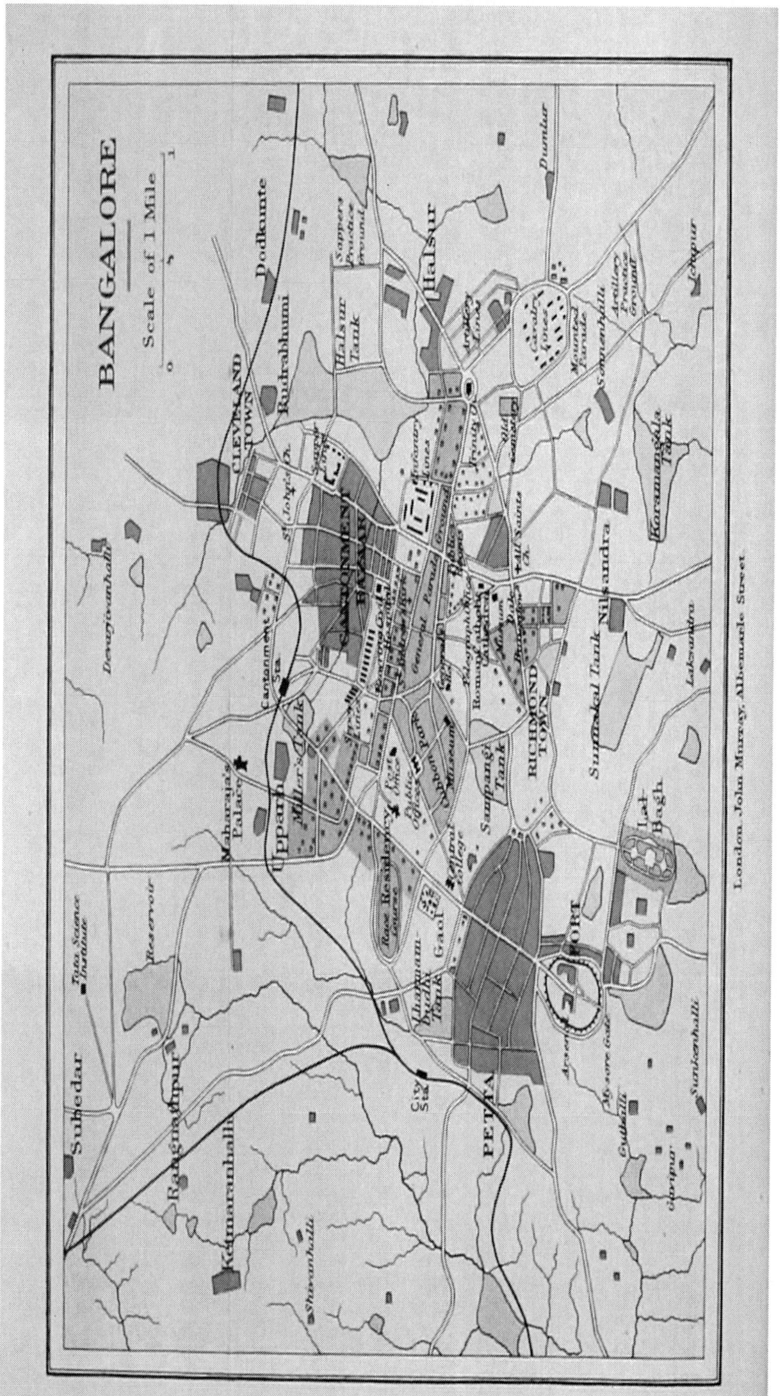
BANGALORE
Scale of 1 Mile
Suhedar
Tata Science Institute
Reservoir
Maharaja's Palace
Upparh
Miller's Tank
Cantonment Sta.
CANTONMENT BAZAAR
CLEVELAND TOWN
Rudrabhumi
Dodkunte
Halsur Tank
Halsur
Sappers Practice Ground
Domlur
General Parade Ground
Cavalry Lines
Artillery Practice Ground
Koramangala Tank
Nilsandra
Lakshandra
Sumpangi Tank
RICHMOND TOWN
Lal Bagh
FORT
Race Course
Residency
Cubbon Park
Museum
Central College
Gaol
Dharmambudhi Tank
City Sta.
PETTA
Rangnathpur
Ketmaranhalli
Shivanhalli
Guttalli
Sunkenhalli
London. John Murray, Albemarle Street

built 1864, the Main Guard, the London Mission Chapel, the Bowring Civil Hospital, and the Lady Curzon Women's Hospital. Directly S. of Halsur are the Artillery Barracks, and S. again of them the Cavalry Barracks, the old Cemetery, the Mounted Parade, and the Artillery Practice-ground.

N.W. of the Artillery Barracks is *Trinity Church*, which contains a half-length statue in white marble, by MacDowell, R.A., to General Clement Hill, who served through the Peninsular campaigns under his brother Lord Hill, and when commanding the Mysore Division died on the 20th of January 1845, while on a pleasure trip to the Falls of Gairsoppa. W. of Trinity Church are the *Wesleyan Chapel*, the *Public Rooms*, and the *Gymnasium*, standing in the General Parade-ground, which is more than 1 m. long from E. to W. A little S. of its centre is the Telegraph Office, and S.E. of that again the *Roman Catholic Cathedral* and *All Saints' Church*, and N.W. of these the Museum.

S. of the W. end of the Grand Parade-ground are the General's House, the Bandstand, and *St Mark's Church*, in which is a tablet to Lieut.-Col. Sir Walter Scott of Abbotsford, who died at sea in 1847, aged forty-six. W. of the General's House, and close to it, is the *Cubbon Park*, the fashionable afternoon resort. In this is the **Museum.** In the vestibule are a slab with twelve Persian distiches, brought from Tipu's Palace in the Fort, a figure of a Jain deity with very superb carving round it. In the large room adjoining there is a valuable collection of geological specimens. Upstairs are stuffed animals, butterflies, and native ornaments and dresses, and a most remarkable collection of fishes. N.E. of the Museum is the Memorial Statue of the Queen Empress, unveiled by King George on 5th February 1906, and W. is a fine building 525 ft. long from N.E. to S.W., which contains the *Public Offices*, and in front of them a good statue of General Mark Cubbon, Commissioner of Mysore. The **Residency** is about ¼ m. N. of the Public Offices.

The city of Bangalore proper has an area of only 2⅓ sq. m. The **Petta**, as it is called, was until recent times surrounded by a deep ditch and thorn hedge. There is an excellent market between the Fort and Mysore Gates. The Brahman quarter is called Siddi Katte. The streets are somewhat narrow and irregular, but scattered about there are well-built and imposing mansions belonging to wealthy inhabitants. The grain-market, *Taragu-petta*, and cotton market, *Arale-petta*, present busy scenes of traffic.

The **Fort** is due S. of the Petta. It is 2400 ft. from N. to S. and 1800 ft. from E. to W., and could never have been a strong place against European troops. It is of an oval shape, with two gateways, one the Delhi Gate on the N. face opposite the Petta, the other the Mysore on the S. face. The Delhi Gate is handsomely built of cut granite. When Lord Cornwallis on the 21st of March 1791 determined to storm the place, there were five powerful cavaliers (Wilks, *Historical Sketches of the S. of India*, vol. iii. p. 123), a fausse-braye, ditch, and covered way, but in no part was there a perfect flanking defence. The garrison, however, consisted of 8000 men under Bahadur Khan, and there were besides 2000 regular infantry in the Petta, and 5000 irregular. In addition to all, Tipu himself, with an army far superior in numbers to that of Lord Cornwallis, was prepared to take advantage of any error on the part of the besiegers. The Petta had been previously taken by the British on the 7th of March, with a loss on their part of 131 killed and wounded, and on the part of the Mysore garrison of upwards of 2000 men. The assault took place at eleven at night, and until the Kiladar fell a determined resistance was made. Tipu's camp that night was at Jigni, 6 m. to the S.W., and at nightfall he moved up within 1½ m. of the Fort, but the spirit of the assailants overcame all difficulties, and the Fort was captured, after a severe struggle, in a few hours.

In the centre of the Fort is the arsenal, and there are some remains of *Tipu's Palace*. There is a small temple near the Mysore Gate. The ramparts of the walls deserve a visit. Outside the N.W. corner of the Fort is a fine Hospital, maintained by the State.

1½ m. to the E. of the Petta and Fort is the **Lal Bagh**, a most beautiful garden, said to have been laid out in the time of Hyder 'Ali. There is a fine collection of tropical and subtropical plants, and a large collection of wild animals in cages.

In consequence of the prevalence of plague in Bangalore, several new extensions, with pretty isolated houses, small and large, have been built by Government encouragement to the S.W. and S.E. of the city and Fort, and are well worth a visit as constituting a new and enlightened departure in India.

ROUTE 31.

BANGALORE to

(*a*) **Falls of the Cauvery, Seringapatam** and **Mysore**, and

(*b*) **Bowringpet** (for **Kolar Gold Fields**), **Jalarpat** Junction, **Vellore, Arcot, Arkonam** Junction, **Conjeeveram**, and Chingleput.

(*a*) The Falls of the Cauvery, Seringapatam, and Mysore.

46 m. S.W. **Maddur** * station (R.) was formerly an important place, but suffered heavily during the wars with Tipu Sultan. There are two large Vaishnava temples here, sacred to Narasinh Swami, and Varada Raja, "The Man-Lion," and "The Boon-giving King." A fine brick bridge with seven arches, built in 1850, spans the Shimsha, on the right bank of which the town is built.

[By road 17 m. S. is **Malvalli**, D.B., headquarters of the Taluk of the same name, and a municipal town. The Mysore-Bangalore and Maddur-Sivasamudram roads cross at this place. On the 27th of March 1799 General Harris defeated the army of Tipu Sultan here, with a loss to the enemy of 1000 men. On this occasion the left wing of the British was commanded by Colonel Wellesley, afterwards Duke of Wellington.

[12 m. S.W. of Malvalli is the village of **Somnathpur**,[1] famous for the temple of Prasanna Channa Kesava. It is on the new direct road from Mysore to Sivasamudram, and may be visited *en route* from the old capital to the Falls, if arrangements can be made for that journey. The temple is an elaborately carved building, attributed to Jakanacharya, the famous sculptor and architect of the Ballala kings. Smaller than the temple at Hallabid, it is perhaps more pleasing, as the three pyramidal towers or vimanahs over the triple shrine are completely finished. The central shrine is that of Prasanna Channa Kesava, that on the S. is sacred to Gopala, and that on the N. to Janardhana. Round the outer base are carved with much spirit incidents from the Ramayana, the Mahabharata, and the Bhagavat Gita. The end of each scene is indicated by a closed door. Around lie seventy-four mutilated statues, which once stood on the basement. There is a fine inscription at the entrance, which declares that the building was completed in 1270 by Soma, a high officer of the Ballala State, and a member of the royal family. The vestibule is in ruins, and the images are more or

[1] See Fergusson's *Indian Architecture*, p. 394.

less damaged. There are also the ruins of a large Saiva temple, with inscriptions.]

From Malvalli the road leads S. 12½ m. to

30 m. **Sivasamudram.** 3 m. N. of the Cauvery the road turns off to the E., and conducts to the Cauvery Falls Electric Power Station, beyond the Gangan Chaki Fall. The Cauvery divides into two branches, embracing the Sivasamudram Island, about ¾ m. above the point where the main road reaches it. This island is connected with the left shore by an extremely picturesque bridge, built like that of Seringapatam, upon simple uprights of stone, at the further end of which is situated the little rest-house, near a small temple. The bridge was restored by a wealthy native a hundred years ago. On the up-stream side of the bridge has been constructed the curved regulator from which the channel leading to the penstock chamber takes off on the left. From the right bank the main road turns to the S. point of the island, where a similar bridge, known as the Kollegal Bridge, makes connection with the right shore in the Coimbatore district. At this point also is a regulator, by which the whole water of the stream can, if necessary, be diverted into the western channel.

The river, it should be noted, makes a sharp turn above the head of the island, and flows from S. to N. past it, turning sharp to the E. again at the junction below the Falls. These are known as the Bar Chaki Fall on the right arm, and the Gangan Chaki on the left arm; the former is 1¾ m. from the Rest-House, and the latter 2¼ m. The beds of both channels have fine trees on the banks, and some trees on the various rocky islands in the middle of them, which above the actual Falls are quite large. The sheer height of the Falls is 320 ft., but hardly any one of the many shoots into which they are divided has a clear leap of anything like this distance. They are spread over a considerable face of rock, and in the case of the Gangan Chaki (western branch) and its falls, curve round considerably to the left front. Both Falls are exceedingly beautiful when a large mass of water is going over them, and it is difficult to say which excels in picturesqueness. The foot of the Bar Chaki Fall can be reached by a long flight of slippery stone steps. The descent to the Gangan Chaki is possible on the W. bank only. On the E. bank, in front of it, are some Mohammedan shrines. A cloud of spray constantly rises from the pools below them, and at a distance may be observed overhanging the head of the Falls. The ordinary monsoon discharge is 18,000 cubic ft. per second, but the discharge of a high flood has been known to be 200,000 cubic ft. The power of the Falls is being utilised, as already explained, on the left bank, in front of the Gangan Chaki. The steel pipes, or penstocks, carry the water down a vertical height of 400 ft. to the six generators, which are now (1911) able to deliver no less than 9300 electric h.p. at the end of the receiving line, 93 m. distant, in the Kolar Gold Fields (p. 395). The whole cost of the scheme has been less than £350,000; it was initiated by Sir Seshadri Iyar, and was designed by Captain de Lotbiniere, R.E., and is one of the most remarkable of recent developments in India.]

75 m. **French Rocks** station, so called from being the place where the French soldiers in the service of Hyder 'Ali and Tipu Sultan were stationed. The name of the place is properly Hirode (population, 3000). The Fort, 2882 ft. above the sea, is 3 m. N. of the railway station.

77 m. **SERINGAPATAM** station, situated inside the Fort, which is built at the W. end of an island 3 m. long in the Cauvery river, 2412 ft. above sea-level (population, including the suburb of Ganjam, 10,000). The name is derived from a temple of Vishnu Sri Rangam, which is of

great celebrity, and of much higher antiquity than the city.

Seringapatam[1] has a bad reputation for fever, and the night should not be passed there. By permission of the Darbar the hot hours of the day can be spent at the Darya Daulat summer palace. If the train service is not convenient for going on to Mysore, 9 m. distant, a carriage can be ordered from there. In 1133 Ramanujachari, the Vaishnava reformer, took refuge in Mysore from the persecution of the Chola Raja, and converted from the Jain faith Vishnu Vardhana, a famous Raja of the Hoysala Ballala dynasty. The royal convert gave him the province of Ashtagrama, including Seringapatam, over which he appointed officers called Prabhurs and Hebbars. In 1454 the Hebbar Timmana obtained from the Raja of Vijayanagar the government of Seringapatam, with leave to build a fort there. His descendants governed till the Raja of Vijayanagar appointed a viceroy with the title of Shri-Ranga-Rayal. The last of these viceroys was Tirumala Raja, who in 1610 surrendered his power to Raja Wadiyar the rising ruler of Mysore; after which Seringapatam became the capital of the Mysore Rajas, and of Hyder and Tipu, till the Fort was stormed twice, viz. in 1792 and 1799, by British armies. After the 4th of May 1799 Mysore became the capital.

The **Fort** stands at the western extremity of the island, the northern, the longest, face being just a mile in extent. The breach by which it was stormed on 4th May 1799 lies only a short distance to the S.W. of the railway station, beyond a ruined mosque. Opposite it on the S. shore are two cannons buried in the ground which mark the spot from which the assaulting column advanced. From this point the route round the W. end of the defences should be followed, as it affords fine views of the defences and of the river. Just across the railway line on the N. side is the dungeon in which the captives from Polilore (see p. 400), including General Baird were imprisoned. S. of this is the Shri Rangam Temple, and considerably to the E. across the open space which was once the Parade-ground is the Gangadeshwar Temple, with the fragrant storehouse of State Sandal-wood to the S. of it occupying the site of Tipu Sultan's Palace. To the N.E. of this is the Water Gate, outside of which is a very picturesque enclosed space between walls with many stone idols and reliefs of serpents under Banyan trees. On the right of this space is the spot where Tipu Sultan fell, and outside it upon the river bank is a bridge over the Fort ditch and a fine ghat built in memory of the late Maharaja. S.E. of this point, and facing the Ganjam Gate, is the Ala (High) Masjid, with two lofty minarets, built in a style very different from any known in N. India. Outside to the N.E. of the Ganjam Gate is the Darya Daulat Palace, and E. of it, at a distance of nearly 2 m., is the Lal Bagh, with the mausoleum of Hyder 'Ali and Tipu Sultan.

The following brief account of the Sieges of Seringapatam will be found interesting. Lord Cornwallis had appeared before the place on 13th May 1791 after the capture of Bangalore, but was compelled by the weather and want of supplies to fall back from it. In February 1792 the attack was made from the N.W. side of the Fort from French Rocks, where an army of 19,000 European and 29,000 Native troops with 400 guns and a large force of Mahratta and Hyderabad Cavalry had been assembled under Lord Cornwallis. In a night attack on 6th February the town and camp on the N. side of the Fort were taken, and the British Force nearly penetrated into the Fort with the fugitives who took refuge in it. Trenches were then opened against the place, and General Abercrombie having arrived with 9000 additional

[1] An excellent account of the place, price one rupee, has been published by the station-master V. C. Subbaraya Moodeliar.

troops from Bombay, Tipu Sultan wisely decided to submit, and did so on 23rd April at the cost of surrendering a very considerable part of his territories.

The second siege commenced on 17th April and ended on the 4th of May, 1799, when Seringapatam was stormed. The forces under General Harris arrived before Seringapatam on 5th April, and were joined by the Bombay troops under General Stuart on the 14th. Outside the Fort on the N. and S. of the Cauvery a "bound hedge" enclosed a large space. That on the N. was 1 to 1½ m. deep by 3 m. long along the river, and was defended by six redoubts. Here Tipu had placed the camp of his army, consisting of 5000 cavalry and 40,000 to 50,000 infantry. The regular siege commenced on the 17th, and by the 27th the enemy had been driven out of the whole outer line of defence. By the 3rd May a practicable breach had been made in the walls, and this was attacked by a strong force of 4331 men (2494 British and 1887 native) under General Baird, at one o'clock noon on the 4th. For some reason the defenders were taken by surprise, and the troops having surmounted the outer wall within 7 m. of the commencement of the assault, turned right and left along the deep inner ditch, which some finally managed to pass. Tipu Sultan, who had hurriedly proceeded to the point of the breach, found that these troops were getting between him and the inner defences of the palace, and therefore fell back along the N. wall, seeking to regain the palace from that side. In front of the inner wicket gate there (see above) he was severely wounded and placed inside a palanquin, but meanwhile the wicket had been seized by the besiegers and it had become impossible to enter it. As he lay disabled outside it a European soldier attempted to snatch off his jewelled sword belt, and being wounded by the Sultan, shot him through the head. His two sons, who had been hostages with Lord Cornwallis, and his family then surrendered, and next day the eldest son, Fateh Haidar, who was commanding a force outside the Fort, surrendered also. The reserve on the occasion of the assault was commanded by Colonel Wellesley, who became commandant of the place and the troops left in it. The evening after the assault was ushered in by a storm of extraordinary violence. Tipu Sultan was buried next day in the Lal Bagh Mausoleum with military honours.

The island is connected with the N. bank of the Cauvery by the Wellesley Bridge, and with the S. bank by the Periapatam Bridge, both carried on stone uprights as at Sivasamudram. Just beyond the latter is a fine canal, and following the left bank of this to the W. one passes along the outer portion occupied by the defenders and taken from them by the British forces in the siege of 1799. Close to the bridge was Wallace's Post, captured on 26th April and held at first with some difficulty. Half a mile from it are the guns opposite the breach, and beyond these again is MacDonald's Post. Just S. of the canal is a very sacred Hindu Temple at a Sangam or junction of rivers. The island was evacuated on account of its unhealthiness in 1811. On it in the following year died the Diwan Purnaya, the famous Prime Minister, who served with equal loyalty Hyder 'Ali, Tipu Sultan, and the British.

The **Darya Daulat Bagh**, a summer palace of Tipu Sultan just outside the E. side of the Fort, is distinguished for its graceful proportions and the arabesque work in rich colours which covers it. The W. wall is painted with a representation of the victory of Hyder 'Ali over Colonel Baillie at Polilore near Conjeeveram (see p. 400). It had been defaced prior to the siege of 1799, but the Duke of Wellington, then Colonel Arthur Wellesley, who made this garden his residence, had it restored. It was afterwards whitewashed and almost obliterated, but Lord Dal housie, having visited the spot during his tour in Mysore, ordered it to be repainted by a native artist who remembered the original. The perspective is very bad, and the general effect grotesque, but the painter has succeeded in caricaturing the expression and attitude of the British soldiers, and the Frenchmen are very lifelike.

The **Lal Bagh** is a garden 2 m. E. of the Fort on the other side of the Ganjam suburb, which intervenes between it and the Darya Daulat. It contains the mausoleum of Hyder 'Ali and Tipu Sultan, a square building surmounted by a dome, with minarets at the angles, and surrounded by a corridor which is supported by pillars of black hornblende, a stone that is remarkable for its beautiful polish. The double doors, inlaid with ivory, were given by Lord Dalhousie. Each of the tombs is covered with a crimson pall. The whole is kept up by the Mysore State. The tablet on Tipu's tomb is in verse to this effect: The light of Islam and the faith left the world: Tipu became a martyr for the faith of Mohammed: The sword was lost and the son of Hyder fell a noble martyr. The inscription gives the date 1213 A.H. = 1799 A.D. In front of the Lal Bagh is a simple memorial to Colonel Baillie, who died in 1782, a prisoner of Tipu Sultan. On the way to the garden, on rising ground near the road, are interesting memorials of the officers and men of the 12th and 74th Regiments killed in action in 1799.

86 m. **MYSORE** station ✱ (D.B. on N. side of town), the old capital of the State (population, 68,000), situated at the N.W. base of Chamundi Hill, an isolated peak rising to 3489 ft. above the sea. The city is built in a valley formed by two ridges running N. and S. The streets are broad and regular, and there are many substantial houses two or three stories high, with terraced roofs. The town has a neat and thriving look, and the sanitation has been much attended to by the municipality. The Mary Holdsworth Hospital is a fine building. To the E. lie the Summer Palace and the Residency: to the W. are the public offices, the fine college with a statue of Sir James Gordon, and a new quarter similar to those at Bangalore. S. of the town is the Fort, a quadrangular, moated enclosure of some 450 yds.; in front of it is a statue of the late Maharaja in the Curzon Park. The foundation-stone of the Chhama Rajendra Institute was laid by King George on 30th January 1906.

The *Maharaja's Palace* in the Fort faces due E., and is built in the ultra-Hindu style. The front is supported by four fantastically carved wooden pillars. The Sajje or Dasahara hall is an open gallery where the Maharaja shows himself to the people, seated on his throne, on great occasions. The throne is very remarkable. According to one account it was presented to the ambassadors of Chikka Deva Raja in 1699 by the Emperor Aurangzeb (Wilks, vol. i. p. 106) for their prince. The palace legend at Mysore is that it was originally the throne of the Pandus, and was found buried at Penkonda by the founders of the Vijayanagar Empire, Hakka or Harihara and Bukka, who were told where it was by an ascetic. It is at all events certain that it was used by Chikka Deva and his successors up to the time of Tipu Sultan; that it was found in a lumber-room when Seringapatam was taken by the British, and that it was employed at the coronation of the Raja to whom they conceded the government. It was originally of fig-wood overlaid with ivory, but after the restoration of the Raja the ivory was plated with gold and silver carved with Hindu mythological figures. The palace is now undergoing a thorough renovation, in which wood-carving and stone-carving in local porphyry will form a prominent part, and when complete will be one of the finest native buildings in India.

Chamundi, the hill which overlooks Mysore, is 2 m. S.E. of the Fort. It is precipitous and rises to 3489 ft. above sea-level; a fine path 5½ m. long leads to the top, on which is a temple. Human sacrifices were offered here until the time of Hyder 'Ali. Two-thirds of the way up is a colossal figure of Nandi, the sacred bull of Shiva, 16 ft. high, hewn out of the solid rock—a well-executed work of the date of 1659 A.D. Chamundi is a title of the goddess Kali (see p. 77).

102 m. **Nanjangud**, 12 m. to the S. possesses a temple 385 ft. long by 160 ft. broad, supported by 147 columns. It is one of the most sacred in Mysore, and enjoys a Government grant of Rs. 20,197. There is a celebrated car-festival here in March, which lasts three days, and is resorted to by thousands.

[**Coorg**, of which the capital town, **Mercara**, lies 75 m. W. of Mysore, is reached by a tonga service in 15 hrs. At Hunsar (27 m., R.H.) are the headquarters of the breeding establishment of the famous Mysore bullocks; near Fraserpet, the N. branch of the Cauvery is crossed. Mercara has an old fort, which underwent a famous siege by the Raja of Coorg in 1791. The country, which had been overrun by Hyder 'Ali in 1773, was cruelly ravaged by Tipu Sultan in 1782 and 1785, and was resumed, in 1834, at the request of the people. A Commissioner now administers the country (of which the Resident of Mysore is Chief Commissioner), and has two assistants under him. As far as possible the administration is on the old native lines. The area under coffee in Coorg is 44,000 acres.]

(*b*) Bangalore City to Jalarpat Junction, Arkonum Junction, and Chingleput.

43 m. **Bowringpet** junction for the Kolar Gold Fields Railway (10 m.). The Gold Field (population 48,000) begins 8 m. from Bowringpet, and extends for several miles, presenting a very busy appearance with its numerous tall chimneys, mills, shaft-heads, buildings, and bungalows of all kinds. There are eight companies[1] at work on the Field, employing over 25,000 people, including 900 Anglo-Indians and Europeans. Since mining on modern principles was begun on the Field in 1883, the mines have yielded gold to the value of £33,000,000 sterling, and have paid dividends amounting to over £13,600,000. In June 1902 they were furnished with 4000 h.-p. for mining purposes, by the Cauvery Falls Power Works, and this power has since been increased to 9300 h.-p.

87 m. **Jalarpat** junction of Madras Railway (p. 409).

138 m. **Katpadi** station (R.)

From here a branch of the S. Indian Railway runs (1) S. past Vellore (6 m.) to (97 m.) Villupuram junction for Pondicherry (p. 420) and (2) N. to (21 m.) Chittoor, Pakala, Tirupati and Renigunta (p. 350). At Chittoor, now the headquarters of the N. Arcot District, Hyder 'Ali died in December 1788.

[**Vellore** is 4 m. S. of the railway station, on the opposite bank of the Palar river, which is spanned by a fine brick bridge. Jhatkas always meet the train.

The Fort of Vellore dates from the end of the 11th century. It was occupied by Narsingh Raja of Vijayanagar about 1500 A.D., and was the capital of Murtaza Ali.

The remarkable temple here is sacred to Jalagandar Ishwara "the god that dwells in water," *i.e.* Shiva. There are two dwarpals at the entrance of the gopuram of blue

[1] The principal mines are at present the Mysore, Champion Reef, Ooregum, Nandidrug, and Balaghat. Nearly £500,000 are paid away yearly in wages.

granite. The door is very handsome, of wood studded with bosses of iron like lotus flowers. The entrance under the gopuram is lined with pilasters ornamented with circular medallions containing groups of figures; the gopuram has seven storeys, and is 100 ft. high. On the left of the gopuram inside is a stone pavilion, called the *Kalyan Mandapam*, exquisitely carved. On either side of the steps ascending to the mandapam are pillars, which are monoliths, carved to represent various animals and monsters (including a Sinh, or Lion of the South, rearing up, with a round stone in its mouth), one above another, in a way which shows prodigious labour and great skill. In the portico or antechamber is a wonderfully carved ceiling, with a centre-piece representing a fruit, round which parrots are clustered in a circle, hanging by their claws with their heads down towards the fruit; the several richly carved pillars of the interior are all different from each other. Mr Fergusson says: "The great cornice here with its double flexures and its little trellis-work of supports is not only very elegant in form, but one of those marvels of patient industry such as are to be found hardly anywhere else. . . . The traditions of the place assign the erection of the Vellore porch to the year 1350, and though this is perhaps being too precise, it is not far from the truth." A corridor runs round the enclosure, supported by ninety-one pillars, all with carvings on them. There is a plain mandapam at each corner of the enclosure, corresponding to the Kalyan mandapam. The inner temple is a dark low building opposite the gopuram: it is entered from the N. side.

The Vellore **Mutiny** in 1806 (p. xcvi) was due partly to certain grievances of the native soldiers then stationed there, and partly to the intrigues of the members of the family of Tipu Sultan, then confined in the Fort. The garrison consisted of 380 British soldiers of the 69th Regt. and 1500 Sepoys. On the morning of 10th July the latter, led by the native officers, shot down the British officers as they issued from their residences, and penned the men of the 69th in their barracks, where 82 were killed and 91 wounded. Headed, however, by some officers who forced their way to them, they held their own until Colonel Gillespie galloped up from Arcot with a squadron of the 19th Dragoons and a troop of the 7th Native Cavalry. The mutineers were then attacked and 350 of them killed.[1] The numbers of the two regiments which mutined (the 1st battalion of the 1st Native Infantry and 2nd battalion of the 23rd Native Infantry) were removed from the Army list. Vazir Ali, the deposed Nawab Vazir of Oudh, who caused Mr Cherry to be murdered at Benares in 1799 (p. 45), died at Vellore in 1817, after eighteen years' captivity in that place and Fort-William.

In the old cemetery to the right of the entrance to the Fort is a walled-in enclosure with a low sarcophagus inscribed to the memory of Lieutenants Popham and Eley and 80 soldiers of the 69th Regiment, who fell during the mutiny of 1806.

¾ m. to the W. of the Fort are the *tombs of Tipu Sultan's family* in a well-kept enclosure. Right of the entrance is the tomb of Padshah Begam, wife of Tipu Sultan, who died in 1834 A.D. The second tomb on the right is that of Aftab Khan, who was second instructor to the ladies. Then comes a handsome tank, with stone embankment and steps. Next are two plain tombs of female attendants, and then a handsome granite pavilion with a massive roof supported by four pillars; inside is a black marble tomb to Mirza Raza, who married one of Tipu Sultan's daughters. At the end of these is the largest building of all, a domed mausoleum 20 ft. sq., to the memory of Bakhshi Begam, the widow of Hyder 'Ali, who died in 1806 A.D. Left of this is a

[1] Twenty more were formally executed in various ways.

mosque without any inscription, and beyond it scores of plain gravestones and other tombs of members of Tipu Sultan's family and retinue.]

154 m. **Walajah Road** junction for Ranipet (4 m.) and Arcot (5 m.). The Palar river flows between these two, and is crossed by a heavy road through the bed.

Near **Arcot** (Arkát) a small pagoda is reached and portions of the town-wall, which was a massive structure of red brick. It was blown up with gunpowder, but the foundations remain, and huge fragments are seen solid as rocks. ¼ m. further S.E., along the bank of the Palar, is the Delhi Gate, which is the only one that remains so far uninjured that it is possible to form an idea of what the fortification was. Above the gate is *Clive's room.* A road from here leads S. into the heart of the old town, and in ¼ m. to the *Taluk Cutcherry*, a pretty building erected in 1874. After passing this building and turning E., the broad moat, which surrounded the citadel, and is now dry, with trees growing in it, is passed. Here are two small tanks, which once had fountains in the centre, and near this is the *Makbarah*, or *Tomb of Sa'adatullah Khan.* In the same enclosure is the *Jama Masjid.* The tomb has a stone inserted over the door with an inscription, which says that the Nawab died in 1733 A.D.

W. of the Jama Masjid is the *ruined Palace of the Nawabs of the Carnatic*, on a mound overlooking the large lake called the Nawab's Tank. The walls of the darbar-room are still standing. Opposite is the *Kala Masjid*, or Black Mosque, and near the palace is the tomb of a Mohammedan ascetic, with a rather handsome dome. To the W. is the mosque of Fakir Muhammad. Near it is a tomb, apparently unfinished, in which was laid the body of the Nizam Nasir Jang, murdered by the Nawab of Cuddapah on 5th December 1750, till its removal to Hyderabad. Just across the road is the tomb of Tipu Auliya, of brick white-washed. In the W. wall is a stone with an inscription, which says that Sa'adatullah Khan erected this tomb for Tipu, who was a man of God. It was from this saint that Tipu Sultan got his name.

History.

When Zulfakar Khan, Aurangzeb's general, took Gingi in 1698 A.D., he made Daud Khan Governor of Arcot, under which district Gingi was included, and this officer colonised the place with Mohammedans. Until 1712 the Mohammedan governors resided at Gingee, when Sa'adatullah Khan, who first took the title of **Nawab of the Carnatic**, made Arcot his capital. Arcot, however, is chiefly known to us for the glorious capture and defence of it by Captain Clive, who here laid the foundation of his fame. When the French and Chanda Sahib[1] besieged Trichinopoly in 1751, Clive led an expedition against Arcot in order to divert a part of the enemy from the siege. Clive had with him only 200 British, with eight officers, six of whom had never before been in action, together with 300 Sepoys and three field-pieces. With this small force he left Madras, on the 26th of August, and arrived at Conjeeveram on the 29th. Here he learned that the garrison of Arcot amounted to 1100 men. On the 31st he arrived within 10 m. of Arcot, and marched on through a tremendous storm of thunder, lightning, and rain. The enemies' spies reported the *sang froid* with which the English advanced in these circumstances, and this made such an impression on the garrison that they abandoned the Fort. On the 4th of September Clive marched out against the garrison, which had taken up a position at

[1] Chanda Sahib was minister of Dost Ali nephew and successor of Sa'adatullah Khan. He set himself up against Muhammed Ali, son and successor of Anwar-ud-din, who was made Nawab of the Carnatic by the Nizam, and who was supported by the English, and subsequently received the title of Walajah (p. 403) from the Emperor of Delhi.

Timeri, a fort 6 m. S. of Arcot. The enemy retreated to the hills, and the English returned to the Fort, but marched out again a second time on the 6th, and drove the enemy from a tank near Timeri, where they had ensconced themselves. After ten days the enemy, who by reinforcements had grown to 3000 men, encamped within 3 m. of Arcot, where they were attacked at 2 A.M. on the 14th of September by Clive, and utterly routed. Two 18-pounders despatched from Madras had now nearly reached Clive, who sent out all the men he had, except thirty Europeans and fifty Sepoys, to bring them in. During this emergency the enemy attacked the Fort, but were signally repulsed. Chanda Sahib now sent 4000 men from Trichinopoly under his son Raja Sahib, who entered the town of Arcot on the 23rd of September. On the 24th Clive sallied from the citadel, and fought a desperate battle with Raja Sahib's force. On the 25th Murtaza 'Ali brought 2000 men more from Vellore to join Raja Sahib. Clive's situation now appeared desperate: "The fort was more than 1 m. in circumference" (*Orme*, book iii. p. 198); "the walls were in many places ruinous; the rampart too narrow to admit the firing of artillery; the parapet low and slightly built; several of the towers were decayed, and none of them capable of receiving more than one piece of cannon; the ditch was in most places fordable, in others dry, and in some choked up; there was between the foot of the walls and the ditch a space about 10 ft. broad, intended for a fausse-braye, but this had no parapet at the scarp of the ditch. The fort had two gates, one to the N.W., the other to the E., both of which were large piles of masonry projecting 40 ft. beyond the walls, and the passage from these gates was, instead of a drawbridge, a large causeway crossing the ditch. The garrison had from their arrival employed themselves indefatigably to remove and repair as many of these inconveniences and defects as the smallness of their numbers could attend to. They had endeavoured to burn down several of the nearest houses, but without success; for these having no woodwork in their construction, excepting the beams which supported the ceiling, resisted the flames. Of these houses the enemy's infantry took possession, and began to fire upon the ramparts, and wounded several of the garrison before night, when they retired. At midnight Ensign Glass was sent with ten men and some barrels of gunpowder to blow up two of the houses which most annoyed the fort. This party were let down by ropes over the walls, and entering the houses without being discovered, made the explosion, but with so little skill that it did not produce the intended effect; at their return the rope by which Ensign Glass was getting into the fort broke, and he was by the fall rendered incapable of further duty; so that, at the beginning of the siege, the garrison was deprived of the services of four of the eight officers who set out on the expedition, and the troops fit for duty were diminished to 120 Europeans and 200 Sepoys. These were besieged by 150 Europeans, 2000 Sepoys, 3000 cavalry, and 500 peons." Lord Macaulay writes of what followed: "During fifty days the siege went on. During fifty days the young captain maintained the defence with a firmness, vigilance, and ability which would have done honour to the oldest marshal in Europe. The breach, however, increased day by day. The garrison began to feel the pressure of hunger. Under such circumstances any troops, so scantily provided with officers, might have been expected to show signs of insubordination; and the danger was peculiarly great in a force composed of men differing widely from each other in extraction, colour, language, manners, and religion. But the devotion of the little band to its chief surpassed anything that is related of the Tenth Legion of Cæsar, or the Old Guard of Napoleon. The Sepoys came to Clive, not to complain of their scanty fare, but to propose that all the grain should be given to the Europeans, who required more nourishment than the natives of Asia. The thin gruel, they said, which was strained away from the rice, would suffice for themselves. History contains no more touching instance of military fidelity, or of the influence of a commanding mind."[1]

It was now that the gallantry of Clive's defence so impressed the Mahratta leader, Morari Rao, who was at the head of 6000 men, that he declared that he had till then never believed that Englishmen could fight, but seeing their spirit, was determined to help them, and he put his troops in motion. This alarmed Raja Sahib, and he determined to storm Arcot before succour could arrive. He chose the great day of the Muharram, and Clive, who was exhausted with fatigue, was roused by the shouts of the enemy rushing to the attack, and was instantly at his post. The struggle lasted about an hour; 400 of the assailants were killed, while the garrison lost four Europeans killed and two Sepoys wounded. At 2 A.M. next morning the enemy abandoned their camp, into which the garrison marched and brought off four guns, four mortars, and a large quantity of ammunition. Thus ended on the 15th November this famous siege, and Clive, being reinforced by Captain Kilpatrick, marched out on the 19th and took the Fort of Timeri, and a few days after defeated a force of 300 French, 2000 horse, and 2500 Sepoys, with four guns, and took Arni with Raja Sahib's treasure, and baggage.

In 1758 M. Lally got possession of the Fort of Arcot by bribing the native commandant; but in 1760 it was re-captured from the French by Colonel Coote. In 1780 Hyder 'Ali, after his victory at Conjeeveram over Colonel Baillie, made himself master of Arcot, and strengthened the fortifications, but Tipu Sultan abandoned it in 1783. Subsequently (1803) it passed into the hands of the British from the Nawabs of the Carnatic.

The line from Arcot to Madras was the first railway in the Presidency, and was opened in 1856.

176 m. **Arkonam** junction, 43 m. from Madras (p. 351).

194m. **Conjeeveram** (*Kanchipuram*, the Golden City), the Benares of Southern India, once the capital of the Pallavas, and then of the Cholas (population 46,000). The Saiva *Temple*, 2 m. from the railway station, is dedicated to Ekambarah Swami, the deity with the single garment. Just before reaching the great temple there is a mosque, which was formerly a Hindu temple. The *Great Gopuram*[1] is on the S. side of the outer enclosure, and has ten storeys, and an enormous top, without any window or means of ascent. The topmost five storeys have been repaired and somewhat altered. The total height is 188 ft. Outside the enclosure is a magnificently carved wooden car, very high, with massive wooden wheels. Passing through the Great Gopuram, an open space is entered, and at 60 yds. to the left is the Hall of a Thousand Pillars.[2] This hall stands to the W. of the Great Gopuram, and at its N. end has another fine gopuram, not so high as the first. In it are twenty rows of twenty-seven pillars each, making altogether 540. Most of the pillars have alto-relievo carvings. In the centre of the hall the pillars have been closed with wattle, so as to form a chamber, in which various figures carried in procession on high days are kept. Only Hindus are permitted to enter the adytum, where a lamp is kept burning.

The *Vishnu Temple* in Little Conjeeveram is about 2 m. off. The god is worshipped here under the name of Varada Raja, "Boon-giving King." The entrance is under a gopuram,

[1] As a matter of fact the history of the siege contains no such incident at all; the garrison had ample supplies up to the end.

[1] See Dr Burnell's note on p. 426.

[2] See Fergusson's *Indian Architecture*, i. 359.

which has seven storeys, and is about 100 ft. high. On both sides of the gateway are Sanscrit inscriptions in the Tamil character called Granthi. On the left, after passing through the gopuram, is a *hall of pillars*, which is the building best worth seeing in Conjeeveram. They are carved in most marvellous fashion, the bases representing riders on horses and on hippogriffs. At the S.E. corner is a remarkable carving of a chain with eight links, like a cable, terminating in the many heads of the Shesh Nag at one end, and at the other in a sort of tail. Visitors are not allowed to enter this hall. N. of the hall is a *Teppa Kulam* tank and a small man dapam, with a double row of pillars. E. of the tank is a small temple, dedicated to the Chakra, or discus, of Vishnu. At the Conjeeveram temples, and at nearly all the temples in the Madras Presidency, the jewels of the gods will be shown if desired, and a dance of the temple dancing-girls can be seen.[1] A present is, of course, expected in both instances—Rs. 5 - Rs. 15. 2 m. S. of Conjeeveram is a highly decorated Jain Temple of the Chola era.

In 1780 at Polilore, N.W. of Conjeeveram, Colonel Baillie's force was cut to pieces by Hyder 'Ali, and Sir Hector Munro, the victor of Buxar (p. 34), who had failed to support him, threw his guns and baggage into the temple tank on his retreat to Chingleput.

216 m. **Chingleput** (p. 419).

[1] Known as Devadasis, that is, consecrated to the God.

ROUTE 32.—MADRAS CITY AND ENVIRONS.

CONTENTS.

	PAGE
Agriculture, College of	408
Arsenal	405
Board of Revenue Offices	403
Cathedrals—	
Roman Catholic	405
St George's	408
San Thomé Roman Catholic	403
Central Railway Station	407
Chepauk Park and Buildings	403
Churches—	
Armenian	409
,, Great Mount	409
English Church (Great Mount)	409
St Andrew's	407
St Mary's	404
St Matthias' Vepery	407
San Thomé	408
Connemara Public Library	407
Fort St George	404
General Hospital	406
George Town	405
Governor's Country House, Guindy	409
Government House	402
Harbour Works	406
High Court Buildings	405
Horticultural Gardens	408
Hospitals—	
Caste and Gosha	403
General	406
Maternity	407
Ophthalmic	407
Institutions, Educational, etc.—	
Christian College	405
Civil Engineering College	403
Medical College	406
Law College	405
Old College	408
Institutions, Educational, etc.—*contd.*	
Pacheappah's College and Hall	405
Presidency College	403
School of Arts	407
Teachers' College	408
Veterinary Hospital	408
Island	403
Landing-place	406
Lighthouse	405
Little Mount	408
Marina Promenade	403
Marmalong Bridge	408
Memorial Hall	406
Mount Road	402
Museum Arsenal	405
,, Pantheon Road	407
Mylapur	403
Observatory	408
Old College	408
People's Park	407
Race-course, Guindy	409
Railway Stations—	
Central	407
Egmore (S. India R.)	407
Saidapet	408
St Thomas's Mount	409
Senate House	403
Statues—	
Queen Empress Victoria	403
King Emperor Edward VII.	402
Lord Cornwallis	404
Sir Thomas Munro	403
Brigadier-General Neill	402
Dr Miller	405
Sir Muthuswamy Iyer	405
Triplicane	403
Victoria Public Hall	407

Madras. * Capital of the South-East Presidency of India. Lat. 13° 4′, long. 80° 17′.

History.

Madras was the site of the earliest important settlement of the original East India Company, to which Queen Elizabeth granted a charter, and was founded from the station of Armagaum (which lay N. of Pulicat, itself 25 m. N. of Madras), in 1639 by Francis Day, on territory given by the deputy of the Raja of Chandragiri, the last representative of the Vijayanagar Royal family, and confirmed by the Raja six years later by a grant inscribed on a plate of gold. Little could the Mohammedan kings who drove out the dynasty of Vijayanagar in 1565 have supposed that within sixty-five years a scion of the exiled family would grant territory to another conquering race destined to acquire supremacy over all India. A small fort was at once erected in the settlement, which was known as Chennapatnam, and a town named the Black Town, now George Town, arose N. of it. In 1683 the settlement was made independent of that of Bantam (founded in 1602), and Mr Aaron

Baker was appointed its first President, and by 1667 the population had grown to nearly 30,000. The principal Governors in the 17th and 18th centuries were Sir William Langhorne (1670-78), Elihu Yale (1687-91), Pitt (1730-35), and Pigot—subsequently Lord Pigot (1755-63 and 1775), who was deposed by his Council and died in durance; and in the 19th century, Lord Clive, Lord William Bentinck, and Sir Thomas Munro. Warren Hastings was a member of the Madras Council from 1769 to 1772. Its subsequent history till the end of the 19th century has for the most part been part of that of the Fort (p. 404) and the Presidency. The Chamber of Commerce was constituted in 1836, and the municipality twenty years later, the Municipal Commission (which now consists of thirty-two commissioners, of whom twenty-four are elected, under a President appointed by Government) being created in 1884. The population of the city, 517,000 souls, comprises 411,000 Hindus, 57,000 Mohammedans, and 41,000 Christians. The income of the Municipal Commission is about 23 lakhs per annum. Over 1300 vessels, with a tonnage of 3½ million tons, enter the port yearly; the Port Trust has an income of £77,000. The value of the exports (chiefly hides, coffee, tea, oil seeds, cotton, and sugar) is 4¾ millions of pounds, and of the imports (cotton piece-goods and twist, grain, metals, and kerosene oil) 7 millions. A dozen mills employ 19,000 hands. The city has been one of the first in India to introduce electric tramways. The present Governor is the Honourable Sir Arthur Lawley, G.C.I.E., K.C.M.G.

The centre of Madras, for all purposes of a visitor, is **Mount Road,** on or near which most of the principal hotels and shops are situated. Half-way between Government House, situated on the Cooum river at the N.E. end of the road, and St George's Cathedral and the Horticultural Gardens lying at the S.W. end, is the Madras Club, and in front of it a statue of Brigadier-General Neill, C.B., Aide-de-Camp to the Queen, who "fell gloriously at the relief of Lucknow, 25th September 1857, aged 47" (p. 290). Opposite Government House is a statue of King Edward VII., by Mr G. E. Wade, presented to the city by Lod Krishnadas Balmukandas, and unveiled in 1903.

It is intended that the memorial of the late King Emperor shall take the form of a Sanatorium and Hospital for consumptive patients in the Nilgiris.

Government House (admission usually granted when the Governor is not in residence) has in the breakfast-room a picture of the installation of Nawab Ghulam Muhammad Ghaus Khan, under the Governorship of Lord Elphinstone, with the date 1842. In the drawing-room is a full-length portrait of Lady Munro, by Sir Thomas Lawrence—one of his finest pictures. There are also portraits of the Marchioness of Tweeddale, Lord Clive, Sir Arthur Wellesley by Hoppner, General Meadows by Home, and Lord Hobart by Mr Watts. The *Banqueting Hall*, in a detached building, is a noble room 80 ft. long and 60 ft. broad, and very lofty. The principal entrance is on the N., and is approached by a broad and lofty flight of stone steps. The hall was constructed during Lord Clive's government to commemorate the fall of Seringapatam. Round the walls are large pictures of the Queen - Empress Victoria; George III., taken at the beginning of his reign; a full-length of Sir Thomas Munro, by Shee; Robert, Lord Hobart, 1790-98; Lord Harris; Lord Mornington, afterwards Marquis Wellesley, seated on the terrace of the old Government House in the Fort, with two flags on his left, the British surmounting that of Tipu, and the steeple of old of Mary's Church; Sir C. Trevelyan; General Sir Eyre Coote; Lord Cornwallis; Lord Wm. Bentinck; Lord Napier and Ettrick, K.T., in the robes of a peer; the Marquis of

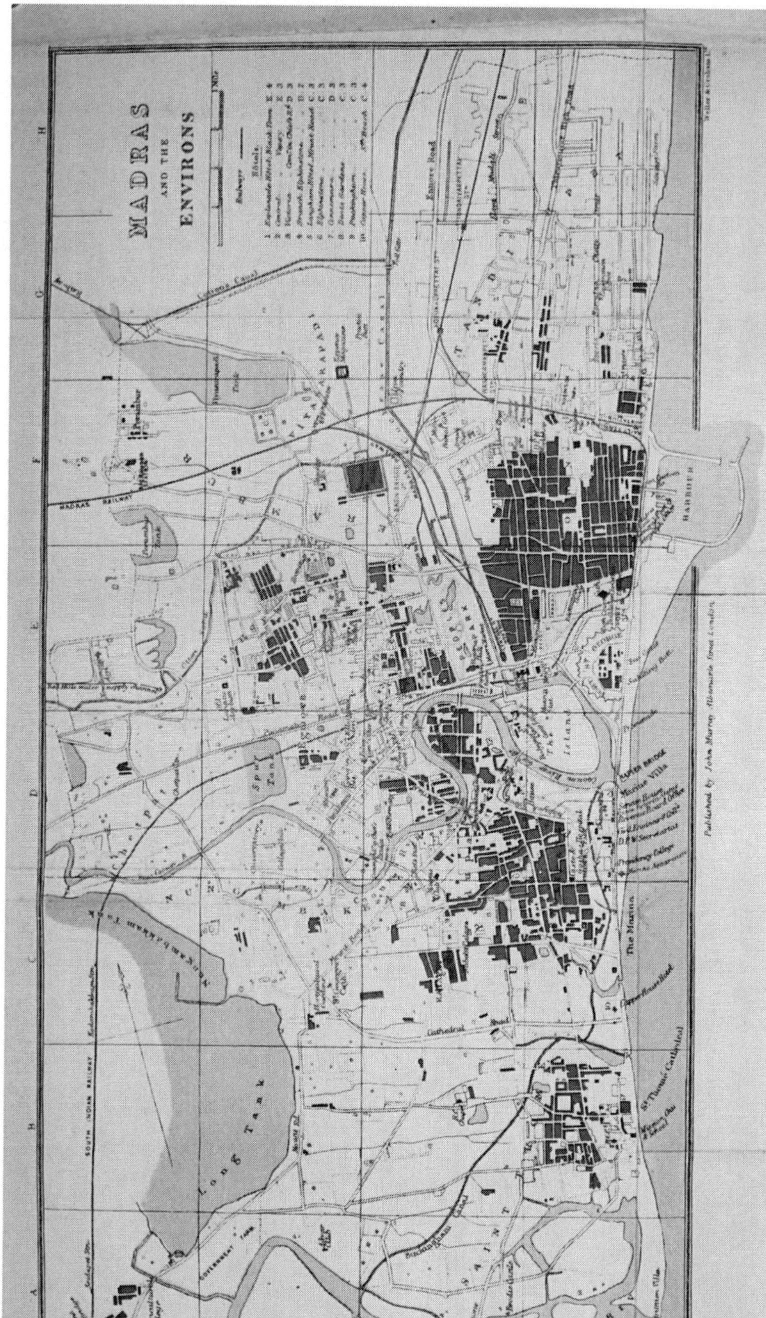
MADRAS
AND THE
ENVIRONS
MADRAS RAILWAY
SOUTH INDIAN RAILWAY
Long Tank
Spur Tank
Cathedral Road
Buckingham Canal
ADYAR R.
HARBOUR
The Marina
Island
Ennore Road
Published by John Murray, Albemarle Street, London.

Tweeddale; Sir M. S. Grant Duff; Lord Connemara, and others. In the Lower Hall is a portrait of Lord Elphinstone (also Governor of Bombay), and in the antechamber pictures of Colonel Stringer Lawrence and Nawab Muhammed Ali (p. 397). A detailed notice of the pictures has been lately published by the Military Secretary to the Governor.

Between Government House and the Fort is the *Island* embraced by two branches of the Cooum, and forming a large parade and recreation ground. The Gymkhana Club is a handsome structure in the S.W. corner. On the road to the Fort stands a bronze equestrian *Statue of Sir T. Munro*, by Chantrey, erected by public subscription in 1839 at a cost of £9000. The S. branch of the river is spanned by Govt. House Bridge, the N. branch by Walajah Bridge.

To the E. of Government House on the sea-front are the **Chepauk Park and Buildings.** Of this park, once the property of the Nawabs of the Carnatic, Burke gave a most vivid description in his report to the House of Commons upon the affairs of the East India Company. On the death of the last occupant of the *masnad*, the property escheated to the State. Government has since greatly improved the palace, and the whole building is now in the Moorish style. The entrance, by the Walajah Road, is through an ornamental gateway with representations in porcelain of the various incarnations of Vishnu, executed by the Madras School of Art. The building is now occupied by the *Board of Revenue Offices.* Attached to it on the S. is the *Civil Engineering College*, and beyond this the Public Works and Survey Offices, and the Presidency College, originally organised in 1855, a fine large building in the Italian style, with the students' Hostel behind it. E. of the last on the sea-shore is the interesting Marine Aquarium, or nated by Lord Ampthill and carried out by Mr Edgar Thurston in 1908. It is the only one in India. W. of the last is the Caste and Gosha Hospital (opened in 1886), hidden amongst trees, and beyond it is the fine ground and pavilion of the Madras Cricket Club. N. of the old palace is the *Senate House*, designed, like many other buildings in Madras, by Mr Chisholm. It was begun in 1874 and completed in 1879, at a cost of Rs.289,000. Close to the S. entrance, facing Chepauk Palace, is the *Jubilee Statue of the Queen Empress*, a replica of the Boehm statue at Windsor, presented to the city by Raja Gajapatee Rao of Vizagapatam, and unveiled on 20th June 1887. S.W. of the Chepauk Palace and S. of Government House is *Triplicane*, a crowded district containing the palace of the Prince of Arcot.

The fashionable drive and promenade of the **Marina**, which Madras owes to the Rt. Hon. M. E. Grant Duff, passes the statue on the E. It extends from the southern extremity of the Fort over the Napier Bridge, and past the above buildings as far as the Capper House Hotel, near the Roman Catholic Cathedral of St Thomé. Thence Cathedral Road runs nearly due W. about 2 m. to St George's Cathedral and the suburb of Adyar. A great part of these roads is overhung by mighty banyan trees, forming a tunnel of agreeable coolness even when the sun is hot.

The Roman Catholic Cathedral at San Thomé, founded by the Portuguese in 1504, has the reputation of standing over the earthly remains of St Thomas. His tomb is pointed out beneath a large trap-door on the S. side. On the E. side of the Cathedral is a pretty Anglican church situated on the top of a sand dune within a few yards of the sea. This tract and that stretching to the W. of it was once known as Mylapur (p. 409). To the S. of it and 1 m. below the Cathedral of San Thomé, the Adyar river finds its way into the sea. There is a picturesque Temple in Mylapur.

Fort St George, situated on the sea-front N. of the island, contains the European barracks, the Arsenal, St Mary's Church, the Military, and some Government Offices. The E. face of the Fort is separated from the sea only by a broad road, and a sandy beach accumulated during the present century. It is straight; but the W. face landward is in the form of a crescent, surrounded by a deep fosse, crossed by drawbridges. The Fort defences are supported by three detached batteries, one at the Marina, and one at each end of the sea-front of the Black Town.

The original Fort was founded in 1629—in which year Mr Francis Day obtained the concession of Chennapatnam—was remodelled by Mr Robins, once mathematical professor at Woolwich, and assumed its present shape after the siege by Lally. It had been unsuccessfully attacked by Daud Khan, General of Aurangzeb, in 1702, and by the Mahrattas in 1741; but in 1746 la Bourdonnais held the town to ransom for £400,000, and received in the name of the French king the surrendered keys, which were restored to the English by the Treaty of Aix-la-Chapelle. On 14th Dec. 1758 the French again arrived before the Fort,[1] under the command of M. Lally, but retreated on 16th February 1759 upon the arrival of a British fleet of six men-of-war, leaving behind them fifty-two cannon and many of their wounded. This time they made their approach on the N. side, and their principal battery, called Lally's, must have been near where the Christian College House now stands, as it was close to the beach, and about 580 yds. N. of the Fort. Another battery was at the native cemetery in George Town, and a third about 400 yds. to the S.W. The fleet arrived not a day too soon, as the enemy had pushed their trenches right up to the N.E. corner of the Fort, and 500 of the 1700 British soldiers had been killed, captured, or wounded. In April 1769, while the forces were far away, Hyder 'Ali made his appearance with his cavalry, and dictated to the Governor the terms on which he would spare the defenceless territory. Again, on 10th August 1780, and once more in January 1792, the garrison were alarmed by the appearance of the Mysore cavalry. Here in Writer's Buildings Clive twice snapped a pistol at his own head. From this Fort he marched to his first victories; and from it went the army which, on 4th May 1799, killed Tipu Sultan and captured Seringapatam.

[1] The defence was conducted by Governor Pigot and Colonel Stringer Lawrence.

On entering the Fort from the E. by the Sea Gate, the Secretariat buildings will be encountered in the middle of the side, with St Mary's Church to the S., and Cornwallis Square to the W. of them. In the square is a *statue of Lord Cornwallis* under a stone canopy, on the pedestal of which is sculptured the surrender of Tipu's two sons in 1792. This statue is by Banks, and was erected in 1800 at the joint expense of the principal inhabitants of Madras.

St Mary's Church,[1] built 1678-1680, was the first English church in India; but was entirely rebuilt in 1759. Lord Pigot, Sir Thomas Munro, Lord Hobart, and other distinguished persons are buried here, and Lord Clive was married here. One piece of the Church plate was presented by Governor Yale, afterwards the great benefactor of Yale College, U.S.A. The most remarkable monument is one reared by the E.I. Company (p. 426) to the famous missionary Schwartz, at one time the intermediary between the British and Hyder 'Ali. He is represented dying on his bed surrounded by a group of friends, with an angel

[1] *Fort St George, Madras*, by Mr S. E. Penny, and the *Vicissitudes of Fort St George*, by Mr D. Leighton, will be found to contain many interesting details regarding this church.

appearing above. In the church are hung the old colours of the Madras Fusiliers,[1] now the Royal Dublin Fusiliers, which were with the Regiment at Cawnpore and Lucknow. This was the first European regiment of the E.I. Company, and Lord Clive, Sir John Malcolm, and Sir Barry Close served in it. On the N. side of the church are a number of tombstones removed from the old cemetery of Madras near the site of the present High Court.

On the W. side of Charles Street leading to the gate of San Thomé (the S. gate of the Fort) are pointed out quarters which, according to tradition, were once occupied by Colonel Wellesley (the Duke of Wellington). The office of the Accountant-General, also in this quarter of the Fort, was formerly the Government House.

The Arsenal forms a long parallelogram. In the *Museum* on the first floor are four cornets, or flags, belonging to the 1st and 2nd Regiments of Madras Cavalry—old flags taken from the Dutch and French, sewn up in covers, to protect them from the squirrels; a very curious brass mortar from Kurnool, shaped like a tiger sitting with legs planted almost straight out: the colours taken at the capture of Sadras in 1780, and from the French at Pulicat in 1781; the Dutch colours taken at Amboyna in 1810; tiger-headed guns taken at Seringapatam in 1792; the six keys of Pondicherry, taken in 1778; and a projectile, which issuing from the cannon, opens out like a double-bladed sword.

N. of the Fort and at the S.E. corner of the city are the old **Lighthouse** on the Esplanade, which has been superseded by a tower on the **High Court**, furnished with the latest improved light apparatus, and the **New Buildings** of the latter forming a handsome pile, designed and erected in the Hindu-Saracenic style, by Messrs J. Brassington and H. Irwin, C.I.E. They cover an area of 100,000 sq. ft., and were commenced in 1888, and the Law Courts were formally opened in 1892. The arrangement of the interior is good, and the internal decoration of wood-carving and painted glass is well worthy of inspection. In the central vestibule is a fine statue of Sir Muthusawmy Iyer, a former Native Judge. The Lighthouse tower is 160 ft. high, and the light is visible 20 m. off at sea. Opposite the High Court is the fine Y.M.C.A. building of red sandstone, designed by Mr Harris, Government Architect, and presented by the Hon. W. Wanamaker, formerly Postmaster-General of the United States. W. of the Law Courts is the new Law College, a fine structure in similar style, designed by Mr Irwin, C.I.E.; and N. of this, across the Esplanade, are the **Pacheappah College** and Hall, which owe their erection to Pacheappah Mudelliar, a wealthy and benevolent Hindu gentleman, who, dying a hundred years ago when education was almost unknown in Madras, endowed various religious and scholastic institutions and private charities with no less than a lakh of pagodas. The former was opened in 1842. W. of these and occupying a long frontage on the Esplanade are the **Madras Christian College Buildings**, erected at a cost of £50,000, and forming one of the finest Colleges in India: it was originally founded in 1837. Opposite it is a statue of the Rev. Dr Miller, C.I.E., Principal of the College, erected by his pupils and admirers.

Along the sea-front stretching N. from the Esplanade are the Post Office, the new Bank of Madras, the **Port and Customs Offices**, and various houses of business. W. of these is the thickly inhabited native quarter once known as Black Town, but now as **George Town** in honour of the visit of King George. Armenian Street in this, running parallel to the sea-front, contains an old Armenian church and a Roman Catholic cathedral, dating from the

[1] Col. (Br.-Genl.) Neill, C.B., wrote a most interesting history of the Regiment in 1842.

beginning of the 18th century; further to the E. lie the Muncipal Offices and Popham's Broadway. N. of the city are the Monegar Choultry, a Poorhouse for destitute natives, and the Leper Asylum; and at the N.W. corner in Wall Tax Street are some remains of the old town walls. A new main drainage system for the city has been started, and will cost 16 lakhs.

The **Harbour** in front of the Black Town is formed of two breakwaters from the shore, originally curved round to an entrance on the E. side, and enclosing a pier. This arrangement failed to give proper protection in the N.E. monsoon, and the E. entrance has now been closed, and a new one has been substituted on the N. side secured by a further wall N.E. of it from the elbow of the old N.E. arm. The area protected is about 1000 yds. sq., and the pier is 1000 ft. long. The foundation-stone of the harbour works was laid by King Edward on 20th December 1875, but in October 1881 the works completed up to that time were almost wholly destroyed by a cyclone. These violent storms have visited Madras from time to time. On 3rd October 1746, there was a dreadful cyclone, in which the *Duc d'Orleans*, *Phœnix*, and *Lys* foundered with upwards of 1200 men. The *Mermaid* and *Advice*, prizes, also went down; and the flagship *Achille* was dismasted, and saved with difficulty. Out of twenty other vessels then in the Madras Roads, not one escaped. There have been other frightful hurricanes in 1782, 1807, and 1811. On the last occasion the *Dover*, frigate, and *Chichester*, store-ship, foundered, and ninety coasting vessels went down at their anchors, and the surf broke at 4 m. distance from the shore. On 2nd May 1872 there was another great storm, in which the *Hotspur* and eight European vessels and twenty native vessels of altogether 4133 tons were lost.

The coast is unusually flat seawards, reaching a depth of ten fathoms only at a distance of 1 m. from the shore, and to this may be partly attributed the peculiarity of the Madras surf. This prevails at all times of the year, and *masulah* boats, which are usually about 30 ft. long, 7 ft. wide, and 4 ft. deep, and of a special construction—the planks being sewn together by cocoanut fibre—and catamaran rafts made roughly of two or three planks may always be seen being beached through it. The rise and fall of the tide is between 3 to 4 ft. only. Passengers are now landed at the pier, but the number reaching Madras by sea is insignificant since the P. & O. steamers have ceased to call at the Port and the direct railway to Calcutta has been opened; the charge for ordinary boats is R.1 and for masulah boats Rs.2 8as. All the three lines of railway which serve Madras are connected with the harbour and the pier.

W. of the Fort, and between it and the People's Park, is a fine group of buildings, consisting of the Memorial Hall, the Medical College, the General Hospital, and the Madras Railway Station, while a little farther on, across the Cochrane Canal, are the Jail, the Moore Market, and Victoria Public Hall, at the entrance to the Park.

The **Memorial Hall** is a massive building of no great architectural beauty, erected by public subscription in commemoration of "the goodness and forbearance of Almighty God in sparing this Presidency from the Sepoy Mutiny which devastated the sister Presidency of Bengal in the year 1857." It is available for public meetings of a religious, educational, charitable, and scientific character. The Bible Society occupies the basement, and the Tract and Book Society an adjacent building somewhat in the same style of architecture.

The General Hospital opposite the

Central Railway Station is one of the largest and finest in India. The records go back to 1829. Dr Mortimer published an account of it in 1838. The hospital contains 500 beds, and is for both Europeans and natives. The Medical College is accommodated in a large detached building to the E. side. The **Central Railway Station** is one of the finest in India; the clock tower is 136 ft. high. Opposite it and adjoining the Jail is the Choultry or Rest-house of Sir Ramaswami Mudeliar. The Moore Market at the entrance to the People's Park well merits a visit in the morning. Alongside of it is the **Victoria Public Hall,** designed by Mr Chisholm, in keeping with the style of the Station; it was erected during 1883-1888, and is used chiefly for public social purposes. The principal hall in it measures 110 ft. by 40 ft. The **People's Park** originated with Sir Charles Trevelyan while Governor of Madras. It embraces 116 acres of land. It has eleven artificial lakes, an athletic ground, a fine zoological collection, tennis - courts, and a bandstand.

The Punamalli Road, skirting the S. of the quarter of Vepery and leading to the quarter of Egmore, passes the School of Arts and St Andrew's Church. The first quarter is largely occupied by Anglo-Indians, whose Association, founded in 1879, is the leading Society of its class in India. The Church of *St Matthias* was given by Admiral Boscawen in place of one destroyed during the war between the French and English, and W. of the Church is the Doveton Protestant College, founded in 1855.

In the **Egmore** quarter are the main **Station of the South Indian Railway,** the Maternity and Ophthalmic Hospitals, and the Museum.

The **School of Arts** was established as a private institution by Dr Alexander Hunter in 1850. Besides drawing, painting, engraving and modelling, the crafts of cabinet-making, and carpet weaving, pottery and lacquer, metal and jewellers' work, are taught to the 450 scholars.

St Andrew's Church was built in 1818-1820 at a cost of £20,000, the architect being Major de Havilland. The Madras stucco, or *chunam*, in the interior gives to the pillars all the whiteness and polish of the finest marble. The steeple rises to the height of 166 ft., and with the lighthouse tower of the High Court, is the principal landmark in Madras; the building is remarkable for the complete substitution of masonry for timber, which might be destroyed by white ants.

From St Andrew's Church, Pantheon Road leads S.W. to the **Museum,** which forms the centre of a fine group of buildings, including the Victoria Technical Institute, the Connemara Library, and the New Theatre, to which the Empress **Victoria Memorial Hall,** a graceful building, of which King George laid the foundation-stone on 26th January 1906, and which was opened in March 1909, has been added. The collection now in it was formed in 1846, and owes its present development to Dr Balfour. In the various Departments of Natural History, Botany, Geology and Industrial Arts are many objects of great interest; but the Department of Antiquities and Archæology, which contains some very beautiful remains of the Buddhist tope at Amaravati (p. 336), excavated by Mr R. Sewell, M.C.S., will probably be found most interesting of all. The sculptures originally discovered at this site are now exhibited on the great staircase of the British Museum. Other objects of interest formerly in the Arsenal and now in the Museum are: iron helmets captured at Manilla; a gun captured from Holkar in 1803; the cage in which Captain Anstruther, R.A., was confined in China, and some leathern petards.[1] The Library

[1] One object of special interest is a victim-post surmounted by an elephant's head, at which human sacrifices were made.

has a fine reading-room in which works relating to Madras and S. India can be consulted; the books of the Madras Branch of the Royal Asiatic Society have also been kept here of late. A number of archæological remains are arranged in the pretty grounds in front of the Museum.

From near the Museum the Commander-in-Chief's Road leads to the bridge so named, and so to Mount Road, opposite Club, and the road crossing the Cooum river by Anderson Bridge leads past the **Old College**, corresponding to the Writers' Buildings in Calcutta (p. 63), to the old **Observatory.** This originated in a small private observatory started in 1787 by Mr W. Petrie, a scientific member of Council. The present building was erected in 1793 by Michael Topping, under orders from the directors of the East India Company. It stands in N. latitude 13° 4′ 6″, E. longitude, 80° 14′ 19·5″, and used to give railway time for all India. It is now used as a meteorological station only, the actual observatory having been moved to Kodaikanal (p. 430).

From the Observatory a thoroughfare runs S. to the **Horticultural Gardens and St George's Cathedral** towards the S.W. end of Mount Road. The Gardens, which occupy an area of 22 acres, are laid out in a highly ornamental manner. Many rare trees, shrubs, and plants are to be seen there; one of the great attractions being the splendid *Victoria Regia*, in a couple of small ponds. The Society possesses a valuable Library containing many rare works. The Gardens were brought into existence mainly through the efforts of Dr Wright about the year 1836.

The **Cathedral** of St George stands in an enclosure on the E. side of the Gardens. The exterior is not handsome, but the dazzling white *chunam*, the decorated roof, the very numerous and remarkably handsome tablets and tombs, and the lofty and massive pillars in the interior, produce a very pleasing impression. At the E. end of the N. aisle is a fine monument to the Right Rev. Daniel Corrie, LL.D., first Bishop of Madras in 1835. The monument to Bishop Reginald Heber, of Calcutta, d. 1826, is on the N. wall of the N. aisle, and represents him confirming two natives. There is also a monument to Major George Broadfoot, C.B., who was one of the illustrious garrison of Jellalabad, and was killed at the battle of Ferozeshah (see p. 147). The church was consecrated in 1816, and became the cathedral church of the diocese when that was constituted in 1835.

From the cathedral the road to Guindy and the southern suburbs runs along the side of the great Long Tank, which should be viewed from the top of the embankment, for nearly 3 m. to the **Marmalong Bridge** (said to be *Mamillanna*, "Our Lady of the Mangoes") spanning the Adyar river. It has twenty-nine arches. Near the N. end is an inscription in English, Latin, and Persian, which says that the expenses of the bridge were defrayed from a legacy left for the purpose by Adrian Fourbeck, a merchant of Madras. To the right and left of the road before crossing the river will be observed the *College of Agriculture*, the *Saidapet Model Farm*, the *Teachers' College*, and the *Government Veterinary Hospital.* The Model Farm is no longer fully cultivated. Its situation turned out to be ill chosen on sandy unproductive soil, and it is now simply used for practical demonstrations to the students of the College of Agriculture. At Saidapet are the headquarters of the Chingleput district.

The **Little Mount.**—This curious spot is on a rocky eminence on the left after crossing Marmalong Bridge. A flight of steps leads to the church. On the left of the entrance is a portrait of St Thomas, with an old Portuguese inscription. Descending some steps on the left, a slope leads down to a cavern hewn out of the solid rock. It is necessary to stoop very low to enter the cave, and there is nothing to see but a narrow aperture which lets in the daylight, through which, it is said, St Thomas escaped the Indians who wished to slay him. In the vestry-room is a Missal with the date 1793. A dark cell full of bats is reputed to be the oldest part of the church, where St Thomas himself worshipped. To the W. is a hole in the rock in which is a little water, said to have been miraculously produced by him. This is called the Fountain. Outside are some rocks believed to be marked with the feet, knees, and hands of St Thomas. The general tradition that St Thomas was martyred[1] on the 21st of December 68 A.D. at Mylapur, which H. H. Wilson (*Transactions of Roy. As. Soc.* vol. i. p. 161) identifies with Mihilaropye, or Mihilapur, now San Thomé, is not accepted by modern criticism.

Beyond the Little Mount is Guindy Park, the **Governor's Country House**, standing in a large park with many deer. It has a very handsome appearance, being faced with the beautiful white *chunam* for which Madras is so famous; the centre room, which is used as a ball-room, contains a good bust of the Duke of Wellington. The flower-garden lies to the S., and is 8½ acres in extent, and there are detached bungalows for the Staff in the Park.

The **Race-course**, close to Government House, is 1½ m. long. On it is an obelisk to Major Donald Mackey, who died in 1783.

St Thomas's Mount, or the **Great Mount**, lies S. of Guindy Ry. Station and Palaveram, a double hill about 500 ft. high, with a long, low range extending from it (Station 1 m. distant) rises 3 m. further S. At the base of the Mount are the *Cantonment* and the building which used to be the headquarters of the Madras Artillery: the mess-rooms are among the finest in India.

[1] In Colonel Yule's *Marco Polo*, vol. ii., will be found references to other ancient notices of St Thomas's visit to India, and an illustration of the cross mentioned below.

The **English Church**, a few hundred yards from the mess-house, is a handsome building, with a well-proportioned steeple. There are monuments here to several distinguished officers.

The **Mount** is a knoll of greenstone and syenite about 300 ft. high, topped by an old **Armenian Church**. The ascent is by a succession of terraces and steps. Over an archway is the date 1726, and within are several slabs with epitaphs. The church is called "The Expectation of the Blessed Virgin," and was built by the Portuguese in 1547. Behind the altar and above it is a remarkable cross, discovered by the Dutch in 1547, with a Nestorian inscription in Sassanian Pahlavi of about 800 A.D. The inscription begins to the right of the top of the arch. Dr Burnell translates it; "Ever pure . . . is in favour with Him who bore the cross."

Palaveram is also a small Cantonment.

ROUTE 33.

MADRAS to **Salem**, **Erode**, **Podanur** for the **Nilgiris**, **Olavakkot**, **Shoranur** (for **Cochin**), **Calicut**, **Tellicherry**, **Cannannore**, and **Mangalore**, 552 m. by the S.W. Line of the Madras and S. Mahratta Railway, and the S. Indian Railway.

Madras to 43 m. Arkonam junction (Route 25).

Arkonam to 132 m. Jalarpat junction (Route 31 (*b*)). From here the line is that of the S. Indian Railway.

207 m. **Salem** station (R.). The railway station is at Suramungalam, 4 m. from the town. Salem (population, 59,000) is the headquarters of the district of the same name.

[**The Shevaroy Hills.*** A conveyance may be ordered beforehand from the Yercaud Hotel, for the journey from Suramungalam to the foot of the hills, a distance of about 7 m. This is made in a bullock-coach, or *jhatka*, and the ascent (5 m.) either by pony or in a chair carried by "bearers." Yercaud is not a town, but consists of a number of houses scattered about. There are churches, a club, and post and telegraph office.

On the hill-sides, for a third of the ascent, the common trees and shrubs of the plain are met with, the next third is overgrown with bamboo, and above this grow short coarse herbage, long rank grass and ferns. The coffee bush grows on these hills luxuriantly. The plants begin to bear in three years, are in full bearing at six years, and last thirty years.

The climate of the hills is peculiarly good for gardening operations and horticulture. A large number of imported trees and plants flourish. In an open room the thermometer seldom falls below 65° F. or rises above 78° in the hottest months.]

243 m. **Erode** junction station (R.). Here a branch of the South Indian Railway runs to 88 m. to **Trichinopoly** junction.

[On this branch at 19 m. **Unjalur** station is a very pretty village, with fine trees and a long cocoa-nut avenue. Close to the station, in an enclosure, several huge terra-cotta figures of horses and other animals can be seen from the train; similar ones may be seen at many places in the Madras Presidency.

40 m. **Karur** station. This was the capital of the ancient kingdom of Chera. The Fort was constantly besieged both in ancient times and during the wars with Tipu Sultan. In 1801 it was abandoned as a military station. The ruins of the Fort and old temple are both interesting.

88 m. **Trichinopoly** junction (Route 34).]

302m. **Podanur** junction station (R.).

From here the line for the Nilgiris turns N., and passes to

305 m. **Coimbatore** station 1480 ft. above sea-level (population, 53,000). There is a large central jail 1 m. N.W. of the railway station. All Souls' Church is ¾ m. to the N.E., and the club is near it. The great sight of Coimbatore, 3 m. distant, is the **Temple of Perur**. A view of a pillar in it is given at p. 399, vol. i. of the *Hist. of Indian Architecture.* Mr Fergusson says: "The date of the porch at Perur is ascertained within narrow limits by a figure of a Sepoy loading a musket being carved on the base of one of its pillars, and his costume and the shape of his arms are exactly those we find in contemporary pictures of the wars of Aurangzeb or the early Mahrattas in the beginning of the 18th century. The bracket shafts are attached to the piers, as in Tirumal Nayak's buildings, and though the general character of the architecture is the same, there is a coarseness in the details, and a marked inferiority in the figure sculpture, that betray the instance of date between these two examples." In front of the Temple, which is a small one, there is a **Dwaja Stambha** or stone flag-staff, 35 ft. high. The temple is sacred to Sabhapati, a name of Shiva, and there is a smaller one to Patteshwar. They were both built in Tirumal's time. There is only one goparum with five storeys, about 55 ft. high. In the corridor leading to the Yimanah there are eight very richly carved pillars on either side in the

front row, and behind them eight smaller and plainer. From the ceiling hang several chains, perhaps in imitation of the chains with bells which hang from the Dwaja Stambha in front of the building. The pillars represent Shiva dancing the Tandava; Shiva killing Gajasur, the elephant-headed demon, appropriate enough in a locality where wild elephants used to do such mischief; Vira Bhadra slaying his foes; and the Sinha, or lion of the S. Shiva is represented with a huge shell of a tortoise at his back, which forms his canopy.

327 m. **Mettupalaiyam** station ✱ (R.). This is the terminus of the broad gauge railway, and from here the narrow gauge Nilgiri railway runs to (17 m.) Coonoor, and has been extended to Ootacamund, 12 m. further on. This railway is the metre gauge, and on the mountain gradient is furnished with a central rack rail, enabling it to ascend one in twelve.[1] The scenery is fine, though not so fine as on the Darjeeling Railway, and the journey up, in the course of which the line ascends 4000 ft., occupies 5 hours, the journey down occupying 4 hours.

Coonoor ✱ is 6100 ft. above sea-level. The climate is about 6° warmer than that of Ootacamund, the mean annual temperature being 65°, and the rainfall 55 in.

In Coonoor itself there is not much to see, but there are pretty walks round the place, which will occupy the spare time of two days. A Pasteur Institute for S. India has been established here.

Sims's Park, a prettily laid-out public garden, contains an excellent collection of plants. One shady dell is full of splendid tree-ferns and other ferns of large size, and is overshadowed by large trees of scarlet rhododendron. Below the park is the *Wellington Race-course.* A ride of 4 m. as the crow flies, but of 7 m. following the windings of the path, brings the traveller to the *Kartairi Waterfall*, which is situated N.E. of Coonoor, and not quite half-way to Kotagiri. The road leads for 3 m. along the skirts of pretty woods, *sholas* as they are here called, and then turning off into a narrower valley not shaded by trees, reaches (4 m.) a rocky bluff called *Lady Canning's Seat.* Below to the S. lie extensive coffee plantations. The path then descends considerably, and turns S. to a high bluff with a path all round it, overlooking the chasm into which the stream that makes the Kartairi Fall descends 300 ft. into a very deep ravine. It has recently been harnessed to supply electric power for the Government Cordite Factory at Arvaghat, near Wellington—a huge enclosure with a high wall running round it for several miles.

An *Excursion* may be made to the **Hulikal drug**, or Tiger-rock Fort, which is on the summit of a hill that towers up to the left of the pass in ascending from Mettupalaiyam. It is one that requires the whole day from dawn to sunset, and is rather fatiguing. The road to it turns off at the first zigzag on the new ghat about 2 m. from Coonoor. A rough bridle-path along the ridge leads to it. The peak is about 7000 ft. high, and commands in clear weather a splendid view.

From the Post Office at Coonoor it is about 3 m. to the Barracks at **Wellington.** About ½ m. before reaching these a very pretty fountain at a cross-road is reached, and the road to the barracks turns off sharply to the left. The buildings, an unsightly pile, nearly 900 ft. long, but believed to be among the finest in India, lie half-way up a very steep hill, on which is the commandant's house with a pretty garden, the barracks, which were built in 1860, and were added to in 1875; the water supply is brought from the Brick Field Reservoir 3 m. away. A large piece of ground close to the barracks is cultivated by the soldiers, where both flowers and vege-

[1] It is under contemplation to work the whole line by electricity.

tables are very successfully grown. The mean annual range of the thermometer is 64°, of the barometer 24°. The rainfall is about 70 in.

Ootacamund. ✱ (Lat. 11° 24′, long. 76° 44′.) From Wellington to Ootacamund is 9 m. The old road is well planted with trees; in parts it skirts a precipice of some hundred feet in height. (Consult the History of Sir F. Price for Ootacamund.)

Ootacamund (*mund* = village of huts) is surrounded by lofty hills. Of these Dodabeta on the E. is the highest, being 8622 ft. above sea-level; but there are also other lofty hills, as Elk Hill, 8090 ft. high. The *Lake* is 1½ m. long from E. to W., but narrow. It is 7220 ft. above sea-level, and the road round it is one of the pleasantest drives in the place. The principal *Church, St Stephen's*, is near the Club, the Post Office, the Public Library, and the principal shops. The market is close to the E. end of the Lake, and the Jail is to its W. on the N. side. St Thomas's Church is on the S. side of the Lake and close to it W. of the Willow Band. The Railway crosses the Lake immediately to W. of the Band, and the Station lies N. of the Lake, between Lake Road and Hadfield Road.

The *Botanical Gardens*, through which Government House is approached, were established in 1840 by public subscription, and are beautifully laid out in broad terraces one above another at the foot of a hill, which gradually rises till it culminates in the peak of Dodabeta, 1206 ft. above the Gardens, and 8622 ft. above the sea. The Superintendent's house is charmingly situated, and has been used by the Governor before the new Government House was erected.

The Chinchona Plantations above the Gardens are not much in point of appearance, as the tree is low (25 ft.) and has but little foliage. The chief varieties cultivated are *cinchona Officinalis*, and *C. Succirubra* with resultant hybrids. Formerly the system pursued was, that after the tree had grown eight years it was barked, half of the bark being taken off in six months during the rains, and the other half the next year. The tree then rested one year, so that each yield took three years. The Dutch system, now followed, consists of shaving off the outer layers of bark, never completely stripping any portion of the tree. The bark is worked up into sulphate of quinine and cinchona febrifuge in the factory at Naduavattam.

From the top of the ridge a most superb panorama is seen. To the S.E. is Elk Hill, behind which, and not visible, is the *Lawrence Asylum*, 7330 ft. Farther to the S. of the Lake is *Chinna Dodabeta*, or Little Dodabeta, 7849 ft., and in the far W. *Cairn Hill*, 7583 ft., Ootacamund itself and its Lake and St Stephen's Church Hill, 7429 ft. Beyond, to the N. of the Lake, are still higher hills, as *Snowdon*, 8299 ft., and *Club Hill*, 8030 ft. The finest view, however, is to the E. Here is *Orange Valley*, where oranges grow wild. To the N. is the Moyar valley, ignobly termed "the Mysore Ditch," but really profound and gloomy with forests and the shadows of overhanging hills. To the E. are seen dimly the Gajalhatti Pass and N. Coimbatore, mountains covered with dense forests abounding with game.

The *Lawrence Asylum*, 5 m. from the Post office at Ootacamund, is a handsome structure, with a tower over 70 ft. high, situated in a lovely valley. The dining-room is large enough to accommodate 300 boys. In it are good portraits of Sir Hope and Lady Grant. The boys learn among other things telegraphy, and compete for appointments in the Government Telegraph Department; others are taught trades, and some are enlisted in regiments stationed in India. The return to Ootacamund may be made

OOTACAMUND
London: John Murray, Albemarle Street.

by another road, past a fine piece of water, and through tea-plantations.

In some of the compounds or grounds at Ooty are beautiful shrubs. Heliotrope has been known to grow to 10 ft. in height, and 30 ft. in circumference, and a verbena to 20 ft. in extent.

N.W. of the Lake are the Downs with the Golf Links. The Downs, which consist of grassy slopes and dales, with woods and streams interspersed (*sholas*) are the scene of the well-known hunting attractions of Ootacamund. Their presence and the absence of Alpine foliage, give Ootacamund a very different appearance from the Northern Hill Stations of India.

The **Murkurti Peak** (or *Taigannam*) is 16 m. due W. of Ootacamund, among the grand mountains of the Kundas, where the scenery is magnificent. 8 m. can be driven; the remaining 8 m. must be done on horseback. Refreshments must be taken. This peak is 8402 ft. high, while Avalanche Hill is 8502 ft., and Kunda Peak 8353 ft. "It is a spot held sacred by the Todas as the residence of a personage whom they believe to be the keeper of the gates of heaven." The religion of this singular tribe has not yet been definitely ascertained. The road to the peak follows the windings of the Pavak river to its confluence with the Paikara, and thence goes up the Paikara to its source, which is close to the Murkurti Peak. From the head of the Paikara an easy ascent of 1½ m. leads to the summit of the peak; and there, should the mist and clouds fortunately roll away, a grand scene will present itself to the view. The W. side of the mountain is a terrific and perfectly perpendicular precipice of at least 7000 ft. The mountain seems to have been cut sheer through the centre, leaving not the slightest shelf or ledge between the pinnacle on which the traveller stands and the level of the plains below. To add to the terror of this sublime view, the spot on which the gazer places his feet is as crumbling as precipitous, the ground being so insecure that with almost a touch large masses can be hurled down the prodigious height into the barrier forest at the foot of the hills, which at such a distance looks like moss.

Other sights on the Nilgiris are the *waterfalls at Kal-Hatti*, and those at the top of the Sigur Ghat, and the Paikara falls at the N.W. corner of the plateau; there is also another much finer fall, in the heart of the Kundas, formed by the Bhawani, 400 or 500 ft. high, and surrounded by scenery of the most savage grandeur, but it is difficult of access. The *Ranga Swami Temple*, and the fortress of Gangana Chaki, may also be visited. The native villages of the Todas (the aboriginal hill tribe) and other tribes may be seen in these expeditions.

The **stone-circles**, which the Todas call Phins, and which contain images, urns, relics, and some very prettily-wrought gold ornaments, are found in many parts of the hills; but the most convenient locality for a visit from Ootacamund is the hill of Karoni, 3 m. to the S. The circles are built of rough unhewn stones, some of them of a large size, which must have been brought from a considerable distance. The history of their construction is unknown.

It remains to say something of the sport to be obtained on the Nilgiris, and of the natural products. The woods in general are so ornamentally disposed as to remind one of the parks in a European country. They are easily beaten, and from the end of October to March woodcock are found in them. Jungle-fowl and spur-fowl are very numerous. Partridges and quails are common in the lower parts of the hills. Snipe come in in September, and are seldom found after April. The solitary snipe (*Scolopax major*) is occasionally shot. There are blackbirds, larks, thrushes, woodpeckers, imperial pigeons, blue wood-pigeons, doves, and green plovers in abundance. There is also an immense variety of hawks, and among them a milk-white species, with a large black mark between the wings, as also a cream-coloured species. Large black eagles are occasionally seen, and owls of various sorts, particularly an immense horned kind. Hares and porcupines abound, and do much damage to the gardens. Jungle sheep or *muntjak* can be found in nearly all the sholas around the station. In the most inaccessible parts of the Kundas the ibex may be seen, but are very shy and difficult to approach. Among the larger game wild hogs and sambar or elk afford good sport. Pole-cats, martins, jackals, wild dogs, and panthers are numerous. The black bear is occasionally met with. Bison and elephants are common to the west of the plateau; and among the tall grass, in the Wynaad, which is often as high as a man's head, and in the thicker and larger sholas the royal tiger is occasionally met with.

From Podanur (p. 410) the railway to the west coast runs through the extraordinary gap in the Ghats 20 m. broad, known as **Pal Ghat**. All this portion of the line is very picturesque, and the cliffs on the N. side of the great rift are very fine in some places. The rocky wall on the S. side of the pass is visible only here and there.

332 m. From **Olavakkot** junction there is a short line to (3 m.) **Pal Ghat** (population, 44,000). The Fort, built by Haider 'Ali, was taken in 1783, and again in 1790.

360 m. **Shoranur** junction (R.). From here a branch line runs to (21 m.) Trichur and (65 m.) Ernakulam (Cochin). At Trichur there is an ancient interesting temple, which was quite possibly a Buddhist shrine in the first instance; there is a Rest-House of the Cochin State here, and at Ernakulam is a beautiful Residency of the Resident of Travancore and Cochin. Between Trichur and Cochin is a most picturesque back-water, sometimes of the size of a lagoon, and sometimes of a broad river.

At **Ernakulam** on the mainland are the Residence of the Maharaja of **Cochin**, His Highness Raja Sir Sri Rama Varma, K.C.S.I., and the State offices. A mile from it, in the middle of the lagoon, is the Residency island, with a beautiful garden, and 3 m. across the lagoon, at the N. end of a long sandy spit, is the town of British Cochin, Kuchi Bandar (population, 18,000). The steamers which call at the port are obliged to lie out 1½ m. from the shore, and at times the shallow water on the bar makes it difficult even for country sailing craft. Trade is of a value of 210 lakhs yearly. The town runs along the western shore of the spit facing the lagoon; at the N.W. end are a grassy open space, round which the houses of the Europeans are built, and the remains of an old fort. The long main street is picturesque; at the S. end of it is the Jews' quarter, with their old synagogue in the middle. This contains some fine tile-work and wood-work. The Jews are divided into two sections, the Black, who are believed to have been settled in this country ever since the 3rd and 4th century A.D., and the White, who are believed to have arrived here at a much later date. Elephantiasis is unhappily common in Cochin.

There is also an interesting sect of Christians in Cochin State and elsewhere on the Malabar coast, especially at Kottayam—the **Nazarani**. They are often termed Nestorians, though they themselves do not accept the name. They ascribe their conversion to the preaching of St Thomas, and until the arrival of the Portuguese they were a united church, holding a simple faith. About 350 A.D. they were joined by a colony of Syrian Christians; and by more about 1000 A.D. from Bagdad, Nineveh, and Jerusalem. As early as the 9th century they were high in favour with the Raja of Travancore; subsequently they had to acknowledge the supremacy of the Cochin Raja.

About 1600 the Portuguese, under Cardinal Ximenes and the Goa Viceroys tried to extirpate the Jacobite heresy, which naturally took firm root in a community recruited from Persia and Turkish Arabia. The Dutch put an end to this persecution; but when the Portuguese rule ceased the Nazaranis were left a divided Church. From that date to the beginning of the present century the Church, by "schisms rent asunder," was administered partly by native bishops and partly by bishops from Syria; and to this day there are two bishops.

Cochin is of special interest as the scene of the first arrival of European conquerors in India.

In 1500 the Portuguese adventurer Cabral, after having cannonaded Calicut, landed at Cochin and met with a friendly reception from the Raja, a reluctant vassal of the Zamorin. Cabral returned to Portugal with a cargo of pepper, and was followed by Juan da Nova Castelho. In 1502 Vasco da Gama on his second voyage came to Cochin, and established a factory. In 1503 Albuquerque, the Portuguese admiral, arrived just in time to succour the Cochin Raja, who was besieged by the Zamorin in the island of Vypin. He built the Cochin Fort, called "Mannel Kolati," the first European fort in India, just five years after Da Gama had arrived on the Malabar coast. Albuquerque returned to Portugal, leaving Cochin guarded by only a few hundred men under Duarte Pacheco, when the Zamorin with a large host invaded the country by land and sea. Pacheco with his brave band of 400 men firmly resisted all the attacks of the Zamorin, and at last forced him to retreat to Calicut. In 1505 Francisco Almedya, the first Portuguese Viceroy of India, came to Cochin with a large fleet, and was in 1510 succeeded by Albuquerque. On Christmas Day 1524 Da Gama died here, and was buried in the principal chapel of the Franciscan monastery. His body was afterwards (1538) removed to Portugal, and rests in the Belem Church. In 1530 St Francis Xavier, the apostle of the Indies, preached in these parts and made many converts. In 1557 the church of Santa Cruz was consecrated as the cathedral of a bishop. In 1577 the Society of Jesus published at Cochin the first book printed in India. In 1585 Cochin appears to have been visited by the English traveller Ralph Fitch, with his band of adventurers. In 1616 the English, under Keeling, engaged to assist the Zamorin in attacking Cochin, on an understanding that an English factory was to be established there. In 1663 the town and fort were captured from the Portuguese by the Dutch, and the English retired to Ponani. The Dutch greatly improved the place and its trade, building substantial houses after the European fashion, and erecting quays, etc. In 1776 the State of Cochin was subjugated by Hyder 'Ali. In 1792 Tipu Sultan ceded the sovereignty to the British, and in 1796 it was taken by them from the Dutch.

Periyar. 80 m. E. of Cochin, *viâ* 35 m. Kottayam, and 70 m. W. of Kodaikanal is the notable Periyar (Great River) irrigation scheme. This river, which runs W. to the Arabian Sea, is blocked by a 60 ft. high dam, and from the lake of 8000 acres so formed the waters are led by a tunnel 30 ft. square and 5700 ft. long through the Eastern Ghats, with a discharge much larger than the Thames at Richmond, and pass into the Vaigai river, irrigating 200,000 acres in the Madura District. This great work was carried out under the control of Colonel Pennycuick, R.E., C.S.I.

---

388 m. **Tirur.**

404 m. **Kadalundi.** Station for Beypur, 10 m. S. of Calicut—a small port, for a long time the terminus of the S.W. line of the Madras Railway.

414 m. **Calicut** station.* Population 78,000. Good D.B., also an hotel. Anchorage 2 m. from shore. Boats Rs. 2½ each.

Buchanan (vol. ii. p. 474) says: "The proper name of this place is *Colicodu.* When Cheruman Perumal had divided Malabar among his nobles, and had no principality remaining to bestow on the ancestor of the *Tamuri*,[1] he gave that chief his sword, with all the territory in which a cock crowing at a small temple here could be heard. This formed the original dominions of the Tamuri, and was called Colicudu, or the cock-crowing." The native town consists of a long bazaar with numerous small cross streets leading from it. To the S. is the Mapilah[2] quarter, with a number of mosques. These turbulent people are descended from Arab settlers on the coast. At West Hill there are barracks for a small detachment of British troops kept there to overawe them. On the N.W. is the Portuguese quarter, with a R.C. Church and a large tank; the Collector's Cutcherry and the jail; and near this are the remains of the old palace and a new palace. To the N. of the jail is the old burial-ground, which is close to the pier. Here is interred Henry Valentine Conolly, collector and magistrate of Malabar, who was murdered by Mapilahs in September 1855. The oldest inscription that can now be read is to Richard Harrison, who died on the 14th April 1717. Facing the sea are the houses of the European residents and the custom house, and also the club. There is a great appearance of neatness and comfort in the houses even of the very poor in Calicut; and the whole place is rendered very picturesque by the fine trees and groves of cocoa-nut palms in which it is embowered. The French have still a *loge* at Calicut, in which one solitary watchman resides. Cotton cloth, originally imported from this town, derives from it its name of *calico.* The descendant of the Zamorin is now a British pensioner.

1 This title is a corruption of Zámúri, itself a corruption through Sámúri of Samundri, Sea Lord.

2 Commonly called Moplahs.

At Calicut, on the 11th of May 1498, arrived Vasco dá Gama, after a voyage of ten months and two days from Lisbon, of which the Os Lusiades of Camoens contain so interesting an account. It then contained many noble buildings, especially a Brahman temple. The native Raja,[1] the Tamurin, was called *Zamorin* by European writers. In 1509 the Marechal of Portugal, Don Fernando Coutinho, made an attack on Calicut with 3000 men, but was himself slain and his forces repulsed with great loss. In 1510 Albuquerque landed, burnt the town, and plundered the palace, but was eventually obliged to sail away with great loss. In 1513 the Raja concluded a peace with the Portuguese, and permitted them to build a fortified factory. In 1616 an English factory was established at Calicut. In 1695 Captain Kidd the pirate ravaged the port. In 1766 Hyder 'Ali invaded the country, and the Raja, finding that his offers of submission would be in vain, barricaded himself in his palace, and setting fire to it, perished in the flames. Hyder 'Ali was soon called off to the war in Arcot, and the territory of the Raja of Calicut revolted, but was re-conquered in 1773 by Mysore. In 1782 the victors were expelled by the English, and in 1789 Tipu Sultan overran the country, and laid it waste with fire and sword.

1 Calicut and the adjoining West Coast was under the suzerainty of Vijayanagar (p. 380).

Many women were hanged with their infants round their necks; others were trampled under the feet of elephants. The cocoa-nut and sandal trees were cut down, and the plantations of pepper were torn up by the roots. The town was almost entirely demolished, and the materials carried to *Nellore*, 6 m. to the S.E., to build a fort and town called *Farukhabad*, "Fortunate City." The next year Tipu Sultan's general was totally defeated and taken prisoner with 900 of his men by the British, who captured the so-called "Fortunate City"; and in 1792 the whole territory was ceded to the English Government. Since that time the country has gradually recovered itself, and the trade of the city is now about 100 lakhs. It is said that two pillars of the old palace in which Da Gama was received still remain. It is related that the Portuguese leader knelt down on his way to some Hindu idols, taking them for distorted images of Catholic saints. "Perhaps they may be devils," said one of the sailors. "No matter," said another, "I kneel before them and worship the true God."

451 m. **Mahé** (population, 8000; name derived from *Mahl*, "a fish"), is a dependent territory of 2 sq. m., belonging to the French—their only possession on the W. coast.

It is finely situated on high ground overlooking the river, the entrance of which is closed by rocks. None but small craft can pass the bar in safety, and that only in fair weather; but the river is navigable for boats to a considerable distance inland. On a high hill some way off is seen the German Mission House of the Basel Missionaries at Chombala. From this hill there is a beautiful view of the wooded mountains of *Wynaad*. The French settlement at Mahé dates from 1722. It was taken by the English under Major Hector Munro in 1761. The Peace of Paris, in 1763, gave it back to the French, but it was retaken by the English in 1779, and in 1793 the British establishment at Tellicherry moved to Mahé; but the place being restored to the French in 1815, the English officials returned to Tellicherry Mahé, in common with the other French Settlements in India, possesses all the institutions of a republic—manhood suffrage, vote by ballot, municipal and local councils, representation at the *Conseil-Général*, which sits at Pondicherry, and in the Chambers in France by a senator and a deputy, who in practice are always residents in France. The *Administrateur* is appointed from home. He represents the central, and the *Maire* the local Government. (See p. 421.)

457 m. **Tellicherry**. D.B. good (population, 28,000). Anchorage 1¼ m. from shore. Boat hire R. 1 per boat. The native town lies in a picturesque situation, backed by wooded hills, interspersed with valleys and watered by a fine river. There is a reef of rocks which forms a natural breakwater, within which is sufficient depth of water for a ship of 600 tons to ride at anchor. The value of the trade is about 65 lakhs per annum. In 1781 H.M. ship *Superb* of seventy-four guns was lost here. The Fort is built on a rising ground close to the sea, and is about 40 ft. above its level. The whole of the N.W. side of the citadel is occupied by an old lofty building.

The *Cardamoms and Coffee of Wynaad* are mostly exported from Tellicherry; the first are reckoned the best in the world. The seed ripens in September. Excellent sandal-wood is also exported. The **Wynaad** is a highland tract under the S.W. corner of the Nilgiris, which of late years has become notable for its coffee and anticipations of gold production. The latter occurs in the Devala tract which has been attached to the Nilgiri District. The area under coffee is 53,000 acres, and under tea 16,000, yielding 12,000,000 lbs. The English factory at Tellicherry, which was established chiefly for the purchase of pepper and cardamoms, was first opened in 1683, under orders from the Presidency of Surat. In 1708 the East India Company obtained from the Cherikal Raja a grant of the Fort. In 1782 Hyder 'Ali attacked the place, but was compelled by the vigorous sally of the garrison under Major Abington to raise the siege.

469 m. **Cannannore** has 28,000 inhabitants, and is a municipality and military station. D.B. good. Anchorage 2 m. from shore. Boat hire R.1 each passenger-boat. The cantonment is on a jutting portion of land, which forms the N.W. side of the bay. Near the end of this is a promontory, on which stands the Fort built by the Portuguese. This, since its acquisition by the English, has been improved and strengthened. The cliffs are from 30 ft. to 50 ft. high here, with piles of rocky boulders at their feet. The bungalows of the officials are most of them built on the edge of these cliffs, and enjoy a cool sea-breeze. Farther inland, and in the centre of the cantonment, are the *Church*, magazine, and English burial-ground, contiguous to one another. The Portuguese Church, once the Portuguese factory, is close to the sea. The climate of Cannannore is mild, equable, and remarkably healthy. The town is surrounded by small hills and narrow valleys. Clumps of cocoa-nut trees form one of the characteristic features of the place. The Portuguese had a fort here as early as 1505. They were expelled by the Dutch, who subsequently sold the place to a Mapilah family. The territory consists only of the town and the country for about 2 m. round, for which an annual rent of Rs.14,000 is paid; but the sovereignty of the Laccadive Islands also belongs to the Raja of Cannannore. In 1768 'Ali Raja, the then ruling chief, readily submitted to Hyder 'Ali, and joined him on his invading Malabar. In the war with Tipu Sultan, in 1783, it was occupied by the English; but on the conclusion of peace next year it was restored to the Mapilah chief. It soon, however, fell into the hands of Tipu Sultan, from whom it was wrested by General Abercromby.

552 m. **Mangalore**, the headquarters of the S. Kanara District (population, 44,000), 12° 52′ N.—74° 51′ E. The place is separated from the sea by a backwater formed by the junction of two streams. In the rains these rivers, which flow round two sides of a peninsula on which the town and cantonment of Mangalore stand, bring down a large quantity of water, and they are then navigable for boats of some burthen to a considerable distance inland. In the dry season there is but little current in either, except that caused by the influence of the tide, which flows to about 9 or 10 m. from their mouth. The banks of these rivers are high and steep, and are, where the soil permits, planted with cocoanut trees, or laid out in gardens and rice-fields. At the back of the present landing-place the great bazaar commences, and stretches N. on the edge of the backwater about ½ m. Of late years changes in the natural condition of the harbour have much injured it. These changes appear to have originated from an opening which was cut by the natives through a narrow part of the back sand to the N. of the present outlet, by which the sea entered and formed a permanent opening. The trade of the port has an annual value of 65 lakhs.

In ancient times Mangalore was a place of very great commerce. Ibn Batuta, in the middle of the 14th century, speaks of 4000 Mohammedan merchants as resident there. Forbes speaks of it, in 1772, as the principal seaport in the dominions of Hyder 'Ali, and well situated for commerce. Both Hyder 'Ali's and Tipu Sultan's ships of war were built at Mangalore of the fine teak produced on the slopes of the ghats.

Mangalore was most gallantly defended by Colonel Campbell of the 42nd from 6th May 1782 to 30th January 1783, with a garrison of 1850 men, of whom 412 were British soldiers, against Tipu Sultan's whole army (see *Wilks*, vol. ii. pp. 466-86), but in the end had to surrender.

The *German Mission* at Mangalore is worthy of a visit. Various industries and trades are taught—printing, book-binding, carpentry, tile manufacture, etc. There are two colleges, affiliated to the Madras University—the Government College and the *Jesuit College of St Aloysius.*

A recent traveller says: "We saw an exhibition of the products of this district. The description of Marco Polo will answer equally at the present day. He says: 'There is in this kingdom a great quantity of pepper, and ginger, and cinnamon, and of nuts of India. They also manufacture very delicate and beautiful buckrams. They also bring hither cloths of silk and gold, also gold and silver, cloves and spikenard, and other fine spices for which there is a demand here.'" Coffee is now the chief export from the place, the value being 48 lakhs annually.

There is an obelisk in the *Burial ground* to the memory of Brigadier-General Carnac, who died here, aged eighty-four, in 1806. He was second in command to Clive at the battle of Plassey.

ROUTE 34.

MADRAS by South Indian Railway to **Chingleput, Porto Novo Chidambaram, Kumbakonam, Tanjore, Trichinopoly, Dindigal, Madura, Tinnevelly** and **Quilon**, and **Tuticorin**, for **Colombo**, with excursions by road to **Gingee, Kodaikanal, Kuttallam, Cape Comorin** and **Trivandrum** and by rail to **Pondicherry, Negapatam** and **Rameswaram.**

Madras to **Tuticorin**, 443 m., in 21½ hrs. Fares, Rs.28, Rs.14, Rs.5.

Madras. Egmore Station (p. 407).

34 m. **Chingleput** junction station (R.). A line of 39 m. runs to Arkonam junction station (R.) on the Madras Railway (Route 31 (*b*)).

The Fort here, through part of which the railway passes, contains the Public Offices and Reformatory School, and was erected by the Rajas of Vijayanagar at the end of the 16th century. It played an important part during the contest between the English and French, and was once bombarded by Clive; it was afterwards a place of confinement for French prisoners, and during the siege of Madras by Lally (1758-59) it was of enormous use by enabling the garrison to annoy the French rear, and intercept their communications. This town is the centre of the Tamil Missions of the Free Church of Scotland.

75 m. **Tindivanam** station (R.) D. B.

[(1) 16 m. N.W. of this station, and 30 m. S.W. of Chingleput, is **Wandiwash** (Vandivasu), where Colonel Eyre Coote signally defeated Count Lally on 30th November 1759 and practically broke the French power in S. India.

(2) 18 m. W. of the station by road is **Gingee** (*Chenji*), the most famous fort in the Carnatic. The interest of the place is exclusively historical. The fortress comprises three strongly-fortified hills connected by long walls of circumvallation. The

highest and most important hill called Rajagiri, is about 500 or 600 ft. high, and consists of a ridge terminating in an overhanging bluff, facing the S., and falling with a precipitous sweep to the plain on the N. On the summit of this bluff stands the citadel. On the S.W., where the crest of the ridge meets the base of the bluff, a narrow and steep ravine probably gave a difficult means of access to the top, across which the Hindu engineer built three walls, each about 20 or 25 ft. high, rising one behind the other. On the N. side the fort is defended by a narrow chasm artificially prolonged and deepened, a wooden bridge over it being the only means of ingress into the citadel through a narrow stone gateway facing the bridge.

Several ruins of fine buildings are situated inside the Fort. Of these the most remarkable are the two pagodas and the Kaliyana Mahal, the latter consisting of a square court surrounded by rooms for the ladies of the Governor's household. In the middle is a square tower of eight storeys, with a pyramidical roof.

Other objects of interest are—the great gun on the top of Rajagiri, which has the figures 7560 stamped on it; the Raja's bathing-stone, a large smooth slab of granite, and the *prisoners' well*, a very singular boulder, about 15 to 20 ft. high, with a natural hollow passing through it, poised on a rock near the Chakrakulam, and surmounted by a low circular brick wall.

Gingee was a stronghold of the Vijayanagar power, overthrown by the allied Mohammedan kings of the Deccan in 1565 at Talikot. In 1677 the Fort fell to Shivaji by stratagem, and remained in Mahratta hands for twenty-one years. In 1690 the armies of the Delhi emperor, under Zulfikar Khan, were despatched against Gingee with a view to the final extirpation of the Mahratta power: the Fort ultimately fell in 1698, and became the headquarters of the standing army in Arcot. In 1750 the French, under M. Bussy, captured it by a daring night-surprise, and held it with an efficient garrison for eleven years, defeating one attack by the English in 1752.]

98 m. **Villupuram** junction station (R.) D.B.

[Branch N.W. to Vellore, Tirupati and Renigunta (p. 350), and E. to

24 m. **Pondicherry** (Puducheri) station ✱ (50,000 inhabitants, Long. 79° 53′, Lat. 11° 56′), capital of the French possessions in India, which have an extent of 178 sq. m., and a population of 280,385. The means of locomotion here is a *pousse-pousse*, which is like a bath-chair pushed by one or two men. The town, founded 1674 by François Martin, is divided by a canal into White[1] and Black Towns—the White Town next the sea. The *Government House*, a handsome building, is situated at the N. side of the *Place*, within 300 yds. of the sea. The *Cathedral*, built 1855, called *Notre Dame des Anges*, has two lofty square towers. The *Pier* is 150 metres long. In front of the entrance to it, ranged in a semicircle, are eight pillars, 38 ft. high, of a greyish blue stone, brought from Gingee (see above) which is 40 m. distant, said to have been given to M. Dupleix by the Governor of that place. On the third pillar on the left side, looking towards the sea, is an astronomical plan by some savants who were charged with fixing the longitude of Pondicherry. 50 yds. W. of the pier is the *Statue of Dupleix* (Governor 1741-54), on a pedestal formed of old fragments of temples brought from Gingee. At the S. end of the promenade is the *Hôtel de Ville*, a neat building, and E. of this on the beach is a battery of eight small guns. There is also a *Lighthouse*, which shows a light 89 ft. above the sea. The *High Court* (*La Cour d'Appel*) is a handsome square building. The Colonial College contains 200 students. The territory of Pondicherry comprises 4 communes and 141 villages.

In 1672 Pondicherry, then a small

[1] La Ville Blanche.

village, was purchased by the French from the king of Bijapur, seventy-one years after the first arrival of French ships in India. In 1693 the Dutch took Pondicherry, but restored it, in 1697, at the peace of Ryswick. Under Dupleix it increased wonderfully. On the 26th of August 1748 Admiral Boscawen laid siege to it with an army of 6000 men, but was compelled to raise the siege on the 6th of October, with the loss of 1065 Europeans. The French garrison consisted of 1800 Europeans and 2000 Sepoys. On the 29th of April 1758 M. Lally landed at Pondicherry, and commenced a war, which ended ruinously for the French. In the beginning of July 1760 Colonel Coote, with 2000 Europeans and 6000 natives, began to blockade Pondicherry. On the 9th of September the British army, having received reinforcements, carried the bound-hedge, and two of the four redoubts which defended it. On the 27th November M. Lally, finding the garrison hard pressed by famine, expelled all the native inhabitants from the town, 1400 in number. These being driven back by the English, attempted to re-enter the Fort, but were fired on by the French, and some of them killed. For eight days these unfortunates wandered between the lines of the two hostile armies, subsisting on the food which they had about them and the roots of grass. At last, finding Lally inexorable, the British suffered them to pass. The hopes of deliverance in the minds of the French were dispelled by the arrival of fresh British men-of-war from Ceylon and Madras raising the blockading fleet again to eleven sail of the line. On 16th December 1760 the town surrendered, as the garrison was reduced to 1100 men of the line fit for duty, and these enfeebled by famine and fatigue, and with but two days' provisions. In 1763 Pondicherry was restored to the French. On 9th August 1778 Sir Hector Munro, with an army of 10,500 men, of whom 1500 were Europeans, again laid siege to it. On the 10th Sir E. Vernon, with four ships, fought an indecisive battle in the roads with five French ships under M. Tronjolloy, who, some days after, sailed off at night, and left the town to its fate. Pondicherry, after an obstinate defence, was surrendered in the middle of October by M. Bellecombe, the Governor, and shortly after the fortifications were destroyed. In 1783 it was re-transferred to the French, and on the 23rd of August 1793 retaken by the British. The Treaty of Amiens, 1802, restored it to its original masters, whereupon Bonaparte sent thither General de Caen, with seven other generals, 1400 regulars, a bodyguard of eighty horse, and £100,000 in specie, with a view, doubtless, to extensive operations in India. His intentions, however, whatever they may have been, were defeated by the re-occupation of Pondicherry by the British in 1803. The place was then attached to S. Arcot, and yielded a yearly revenue of Rs. 45,000. When restored to the French in 1817, the population was only 25,000.

The principal French possessions in India are—

	Area.	Population.
Pondicherry	113 sq. m.	184,000
Karikal	43 ,,	56,600
Chandernagore	3 ,,	25,300
Mahé	5 ,,	10,600

Besides these are the small territory of Yanaon on the Godavery in S. Orissa, and the loges at Surat, Patna, Kasimbazar, Dacca, Balasore, Masulipatam, and Calicut. The supreme executive power rests with the Governor-General, who resides at Pondicherry, and is assisted by a Council, of whom the principal members are the Director of the Interior, the Treasurer, the *Procureur-Général*, and the chief of the Marine. There are Administrators under the Governor-General at Chandernagore, Karikal, Mahé, and Yanaon. The population includes about 1000 French and 2000 persons of mixed descent; by treaty engagement no French troops are maintained in the colonies, and no military works are erected in them. There are five local councils, ten municipal councils, and one *conseil-général* of 30, one-third chosen by the French voters, and two-thirds by the other residents of the colonies, the *renonçants*[1] and non-*renonçants:* the three lists include respectively 551, 2800, and 58,000 voters, and the seats are distributed as follows:—12 Pondicherry, 8 Karikal, 4 Chandernagore, 3 each Yanaon and Mahé. The *conseils locals* elect a representative member of the French Senate, while a member of the Chamber of Deputies is elected by general manhood suffrage. There is a High Appellate Court at Pondicherry, a court of first instance at that place and Karikal, and a *tribunal de pays* at both these places and at Chandernagore. The free Port of Pondicherry is visited by 500 vessels of a tonnage of 460,000 tons; the value of the sea trade amounts to 13,000,000 francs, and there is a chamber of commerce to look after the commercial interests of the colony. The number of schools in the whole of the colonies is about 300, with 16,000 pupils. The public expenditure is Rs. 1,000,000. For Chandernagore and Mahé, see pp. 68 and 417.

Karikal (Lat. 10° 55′, Long. 79° 52′) lies on a branch of the Cauvery 12 m. N. of Negapatam, and is reached by a line of railway from Peralam junction on the line from Mayaveram to Tiruvallur (p. 424). It contains three communes and 110 villages.

Tranquebar, 6 m. N. of Karikal, was a Danish settlement from 1616 to 1645, when it was acquired by the British Government with Chinsurah (p. 69). Owing to the railway advantages which its rival Nagapatam possesses, it is now a decaying place. The old Fortress and Citadel (Danneborg) are interesting. The first Protestant mission in India was founded at Tranquebar in 1706.]

[1] The *renonçants* are Indians who have given up their native status, and are subject to the general French Law somewhat modified.

125 m. **Cuddalore** New Town station. Population 56,000.

127 m. **Cuddalore** Old Town station (R.).

From the former station, Fort St David can most conveniently be visited; it is also nearest to the public offices in the civil station, and the D.B. At the Old Town station are the railway workshops, and the residences of a considerable number of Europeans, also the jail and church, which is interesting on account of the old tombs in and about it. A small church has recently been built in the New Town.

Fort St David,[1] 1½ m. from **New Town,** is interesting on account of its history. From 1691, when it was purchased by the East India Company, it remained in the hands of the British until 1758, Clive being Governor in 1756, when it was besieged and taken, after many unsuccessful attempts, by the French, only to fall back into British hands at the peace of 1783. All that now remains of the fort are the ditch, the foundations of the ramparts, and some masses of the fallen walls.

144 m. **Porto Novo** station. The town stands on the N. bank of the river Velar, close to the sea, and is called by the natives Mahmud Bandar and Firingipet. The Portuguese settled here during the latter part of the 16th century, being the first Europeans who landed on the Coromandel coast. In 1678 the Dutch abandoned their factory at Porto Novo and Devapatnam, and went to Pulicat.

The chief historical recollection which attaches to Porto Novo is that, within 3 m. of it to the N., close to the sea-shore, was fought one of the most important Indian battles of the last century. Sir Eyre Coote[2] had arrived

[1] Bernadotte, afterwards Marshal of France and King of Sweden, was captured in a sortie from the Fort during the siege of 1783.

[2] Sir Eyre Coote first distinguished himself at Plassey; won the great victory of Wandiwash on 30th November 1759; took Pondicherry in December 1760; was made K.C.B. in 1771; was Commander-in-Chief

at Porto Novo on the 19th of June 1781, after having been repulsed the day before in an attack on the fortified Pagoda of Chidambaram, which he conducted in person. Hyder 'Ali was encouraged by the success of his troops on that occasion to hazard a battle, and he took up and fortified an advantageous position on the only road by which the English could advance to Cuddalore. The British force consisted of 2000 Europeans and 6000 Sepoys, and Hyder 'Ali's forces of 40,000 natives. Of the victory won by the former, Sir J. Malcolm speaks in the following terms:—"If a moment was to be named when the existence of the British power depended upon its native troops, we should fix upon the battle of Porto Novo. Driven to the sea-shore, attacked by an enemy exulting in recent success, confident in his numbers, and strong in the terror of his name, every circumstance combined that could dishearten the small body of men on whom the fate of the war depended. Not a heart shrank from the trial. Of the European battalions it is, of course superfluous to speak, but all the native battalions appear from every account of the action to have been entitled to equal praise on this memorable occasion, and it is difficult to say whether they were most distinguished when suffering with a patient courage under a heavy cannonade, when receiving and repulsing the shock of the flower of Hyder's cavalry, or when attacking in their turn the troops of that monarch, who, baffled in all his efforts, retreated from this field of anticipated conquest with the loss of his most celebrated commander, and thousands of his bravest soldiers."

151 m. **Chidambaram** station, D.B., 1½ m. from station (population, 29,000). Once the capital of the Chola kingdom.

The *Temples* at Chidambaram are the oldest in the S. of India, and portions of them are gems of Dravidian art. The principal temple is sacred to Shiva, and is affirmed to have been erected, or at least embellished by Hiranya Varna Chakravarti, "the golden-coloured Emperor," who is said to have been a leper, and to have originally borne the name of Swetavarmah, "the white-coloured," on account of his leprosy, and to have come S. on a pilgrimage. He miraculously recovered at Chidambaram, after taking a bath in the tank in the centre of the temple, and thereupon rebuilt or enlarged the temples. He is said to have brought 3000 Brahmans from the N. According to tradition Vira Chola Raja (927-77 A.D.) saw the Sabhapati, *i.e.* Shiva, dancing on the sea-shore with his wife, Parvati, and erected the Kanak Sabha, or golden shrine in memory of the god, who is here called *Natesa* or *Nateshwar*, "god of dancing." The whole area is surrounded by two high walls, which contain thirty-two acres. The outer wall of all is 1800 ft. long from N. to S., and 1480 ft. from E. to W. Nearly in the centre of this vast space is a fine tank, 315 ft. by 180 ft. At the four points of the compass are four vast gopurams, those on the N. and S. being about 160 ft. high.

Near the Tank is the Hall of 1000 Pillars, which is 340 ft. long and 190 ft. broad. Mr Fergusson (*Hist. of Arch.* i. 376) makes the number of pillars in the hall 984. This is one of the very rare instances in S. India where the so-called Hall of 1000 Pillars is almost furnished with that number.

The *Temple of Parvati*, known as Shivagamiamman, the wife of Shiva, is principally remarkable for its porch, which is of singular elegance. The roof is supported by bracketing shafts tied with transverse purlins till a space of only 9 ft. is left to be spanned. The outer enclosure in which this temple stands is very elaborate, with two storeys of pillars.

Adjoining this Temple of Parvati is one to *Subrahmanya*, the enclosure of which is 250 ft. by 305 ft. The

in Bengal, 1779; was sent to Madras to check Hyder 'Ali in November 1780; and died, worn out by the campaign, on 26th April 1783.

images of a peacock and two elephants stand before it, then a portico with four pillars in front, with an inner court. Mr Fergusson assigns the end of the 17th or beginning of the 18th century as the date of this temple. There is another small one to Subrahmanya, and one to Ganesh in the corner of the great enclosure. There are also several small mandapams in other parts of the great enclosure and one to the S. of the court of Parvati's Temple.

The principal temple to Shiva is about 30 yards S. of the tank. In the S.W. corner of this enclosure is a temple to Parvati, and in the centre of the S. side an idol of Nateshwar. In the centre of all is the sanctuary, which consists of two parts. In this is the most sacred image of the dancing Shiva, which is that of a naked giant with four arms, his right leg planted on the ground, and his left lifted sideways. The roof of this building is covered with plates of gilt copper. There is also a tiny shrine of which Mr Fergusson says: "The oldest thing now existing here is a little shrine in the small enclosure with a little porch of two pillars about 6 ft. high, but resting on a stylobate ornamented with dancing figures, more graceful and more elegantly executed than any other of their class. At the sides are wheels and horses, the whole being intended to represent a car. Whitewash and modern alterations have sadly disfigured this gem, but enough remains to show how exquisite it was." This pagoda was surrendered to the British in 1760 without a shot; but in 1781 Hyder 'Ali garrisoned it with 3000 men, and Sir Eyre Coote was repulsed from it with the loss of one gun.

174 m. **Mayaveram** station. The town, 3 m. distant (24,000 inhabitants), is a place of pilgrimage in November. The Shiva Pagoda has one large gopuram and one small one. To the W. of the Great Gopuram is a *Teppa Kulam* Tank.

[From Mayaveram a line runs S. to (24 m.) Truvallur, on the line from **Tanjore to Negapatam (p. 427) (54 m.)**, Mutupet and **Pattukottai (71 m.)**, and Arantangi (93 m.)].

The richly endowed temple of Sri Tyagarajaswamiat **Trivalur** has a fine tank and car. It contrasts curiously with that at Tanjore in the principles on which it was designed, and serves to exemplify the mode in which, unfortunately, most Dravidian temples were aggregated. Mr Fergusson writes of it (*Indian Architecture*, i. 366):—

"The nucleus here was a small village temple. It is a double shrine, dedicated to Shiva and his consort, standing in a cloistered court which measures 192 ft. by 156 ft. over all, and has one gopuram in front. So far, there is nothing to distinguish it from the ordinary temples found in every village. It, however, at some subsequent period became sacred or rich, and a second or outer court was added, measuring 470 ft. each way, with two gopurams, higher than the original one, and containing within its walls numberless little shrines and porches. Additions were again made at some subsequent date, the whole being enclosed in a court 940 ft. by 701 ft.—this time with five gopurams, and several important shrines. When the last addition was made, it was intended to endow the temple with one of those great halls which were considered indispensable in temples of the first class. Generally they had, or were intended to have, 1000 columns; this one has only 688, and only about one half of these carry beams of any sort. There can, however, be very little doubt that, had time and money been available, it would have been completed to the typical extent. As it is, it is probably owing to our management of the revenues of the country that the requisite funds were not forthcoming, and the buildings stopped probably within the limits of the present century.

"The general effect of such a design as this may be gathered from the woodcut bird's-eye view. As an artistic design, nothing can be worse. The gateways irregularly spaced in a great blank wall lose half their dignity from their positions; and the bathos of their decreasing in size (see p. 426) and elaboration as they approach the sanctuary is a mistake which nothing can redeem." (See also p. lxxiv. of the Introd.)

193 m. **Kumbakonam** station (R.), D.B., in the Tanjore district (population, 64,000). The pagodas stand near the centre of the town, and about 1 m. from the station. The largest pagoda is dedicated to Vishnu, and the Great Gopuram here has eleven storeys.[1] The total height is 147 ft. A street arched over and 330 ft. long and 15 ft. broad, with shops on either side, leads to the Shiva Pagoda, or Temple of Kumbeshwara.

To the E. side of the road from the station to the temples is the *Mahamokam Tank*, a fine tank, into which it is said the Ganges flows once in twelve years, the last occasion having been in 1897. On these occasions so vast a concourse of people enter the water to bathe that the surface rises some inches. The tank has sixteen small but picturesque pagodas studding its banks. The principal one is on the N. side of the tank.

The *Government College* at Kumbakonam was formerly one of the leading educational institutions in India, and procured for the town the distinction of being called the Cambridge of Southern India.

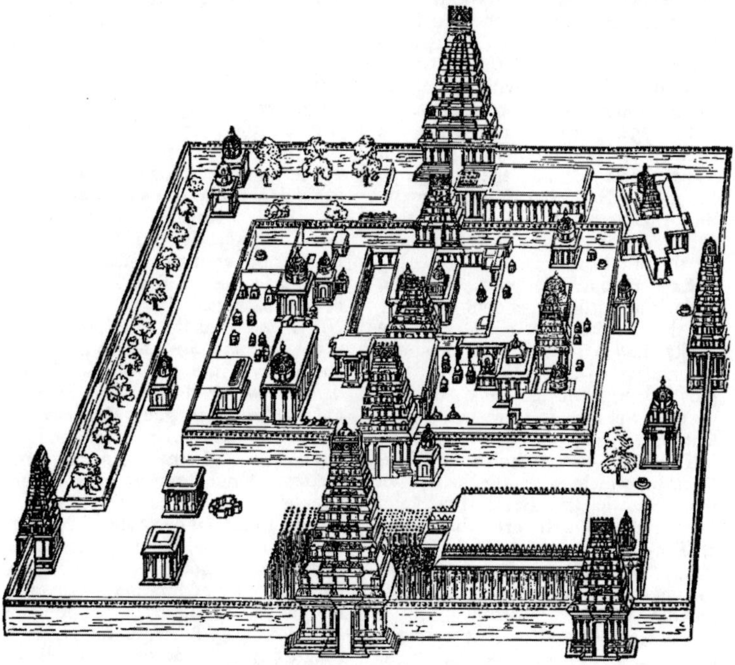

Bird's-eye View, Temple of Trivalur.

[1] See Fergusson's *Indian Architecture*, i. 394.

217 m. TANJORE junction station (R.), D.B. ✱ [Branch 48 m. E. to Negapatam, see below]. Lat. 10° 47′, Long. 79° 10′. Population, 60,000. The delta of the Cauvery river, near the head of which Tanjore stands, is considered the garden of Southern India. It carries a dense population, and is highly irrigated.

The Tanjore country was under the Cholas during the whole of their supremacy. Venkaji, the brother of Shivaji, the Great Mahratta, reduced Tanjore, proclaimed himself independent, and established a Mahratta dynasty, which lasted till 1799. The British first came into contact with the place, by their expedition in 1749, with a view to the restoration of a deposed Raja.

In 1758 it was attacked by the French under Lally, who extorted large sums from the reigning Mahratta Raja. Colonel Joseph Smith captured the Fort in 1773, and again in 1776 it was occupied by the English.

Raja Sharabhoji, by a treaty in 1779, ceded the dependent territory to the British, retaining only the capital and a small tract of country around, which also at last lapsed to the Government in 1855, on the death of the then ruler without legitimate male issue.

The *Little Fort* contains the *Great Temple*, which with the palace of the Raja in the Great Fort and Schwartz's Church are the sights of Tanjore. The *two Forts* of Tanjore, which are much dismantled, are so connected that they may be almost regarded as one.

The **Great Pagoda.**—The entrance is under a gopuram 90 ft. high. Then follow a passage 170 ft. long, and a second gopuram of smaller dimensions. There is a long inscription in Tamil characters of the 4th century on either side of the passage through the second gopuram. From this the outer enclosure of the temple is entered. It is 415 ft. by 800 ft., and is surrounded by cloister chapels, each containing a large lingam. Visitors may walk everywhere in the enclosure, but cannot enter the Great Temple or the Halls of approach to it, though the sanctity of the temple was destroyed by its occupation on one occasion by the French. On the right is the *Yajasala*, a place where sacrifices are offered, and the Sabhapati Kovil, or Shrine of Shiva as the presiding god of an assembly. There are two *Balipirams*, or altars, close to the E. wall, one inside and one outside; and at about 40 ft. from the E. wall is a gigantic *Nandi* in black granite, a monolith 12 ft. 10 in. high. W. of this again is the *Kodi Maram* or great temple, the most beautiful and effective of all Dravidian temples. A portico supported by three rows of pillars leads to two halls 75 ft. by 70 ft. each; beyond these is the adytum, 56 ft. by 54 ft., over which rises the vast tower of the vimanah, 200 ft. high, including the great monolithic dome-shaped top and the *Sikra*, or spiked ornament. N.E. of the Great Tower is the Chandikasan Kovil, or shrine of the god who reports to the chief god the arrival of worshippers. W. of this at the N.W. corner of the outer enclosure, is the *Subrahmanya Kovil*, Shrine of Kartikkeya, the son of Shiva and deity of war, who is called Subrahmanya (from *su*, good, *brahman*, a Brahman) because he is so good to Brahmans and their especial protector. Mr Fergusson says of this wonderful shrine that it "is as exquisite a piece of decorative architecture as is to be found in the S. of India, and though small, almost divides our admiration with the temple itself" (i. 365). It consists of a tower 55 ft. high, raised on a base 45 ft. sq., adorned with pillars and pilasters, which ornament is continued along a corridor 50 ft. long, communicating with a second building 50 ft. sq. to the E. Dr Burnell considers the Subrahmanya Temple to be not older than the commencement of the 16th century. Its beautiful carving seems to be in imitation of wood.

The base of the grand temple, *i.e.* the vimanah and halls leading to it, is covered with inscriptions in the old Tamil of the 11th century, which Dr. Burnell deciphered. The pyramidal tower over the vimanah has evidently often been repaired in its upper part, where the images of gods and demons with which it is covered are now only of cement. This tower is only 38 ft. lower than the Kutab Minar at Delhi. Many picturesque views of it are obtained across the moat and walls of the Fort; and it is well worth while making the whole circuit of these.

Dr. Burnell says in his pamphlet, *The Great Temple of Tanjore:* "This temple is really the most remarkable of all the temples in the extreme S. of India; is one of the oldest; and as it has been preserved with little alteration, if not, perhaps, the largest, it is the best specimen of the style of architecture peculiar to India S. of Madras.

"This style arose under the Chola (or Tanjore) kings in the 11th century A.D., when nearly all the great temples to Shiva in S. India were built, and it continued in use in the 12th and 13th centuries, during which the great temples to Vishnu were erected. Up to the beginning of the 16th century these temples remained almost unchanged, but at that time all S. India became subject to the kings of Vijayanagar, and one of these, named Krishnaraya (1509-30), rebuilt or added to most of the great temples of the S. The chief feature of the architecture of this later period is the construction of the enormous gopurams which are so conspicuous at Conjeeveram, Chidambaram, and Sri Rangam. All these were built by Krishnaraya; they do not form part of the original style, but were intended as fortifications to protect the shrines from foreign invaders, and certain plunder and desecration, as the Hindus first discovered on the Mohammedan invasion of 1310 A.D."

The Palace of the Princess of Tanjore.—This building is in the Great Fort, lying E. of the Little Fort. The palace is a vast building of masonry, and stands on the left of the street, which runs northward through the Fort; it was built about 1550 A.D. After passing through two quadrangles a third is entered, on the S. side of which is a building like a gopuram, 190 ft. high, with eight storeys. It was once an armoury. Mr Fergusson writes of this tower: "As you approach Tanjore, you see two great vimanahs not unlike each other in dimensions or outline, and at a distance can hardly distinguish which belongs to the great temple. On close inspection, however, that of the palace turns out to be made up of dumpy pilasters and fat balusters, and ill-designed mouldings of Italian architecture, mixed up with a few details of Indian art! a more curious and tasteless jumble could hardly be found in Calcutta or Lucknow." On the E. of the quadrangle is the *Telugu Darbar-room.*[1] On the sides of a platform of black granite are sculptured in alto-relievo Surs and Asurs fighting. On this platform stands a white marble statue, by Flaxman, of Sharfoji, the pupil of Schwartz, and the last Raja but one. He is standing with the palms of his hands joined as if in prayer, and he wears the curious triangular pointed cap used by the Tanjore princes in the last half-century of their rule. On the wall are a picture of Lord Pigot, and numerous pictures of the Rajas, and a fine bust of Nelson, presented to the Raja by the Hon. Anne Seymour Damer, whose work it is. On the opposite side of the quadrangle is the *Library*, in which is a remarkable collection of 18,000 Sanscrit MSS., of which 8000 are written on palm leaves. This library is unique in India, and dates from the end of the 16th or beginning of the 17th century. In the *Mahratta Darbar*, which is in another quadrangle, is a large picture of Shivaji, the last Raja, with his chief secretary and his Diwan.

E. again lies *Schwartz's Church*

[1] See p. 383 of Fergusson's *Indian Architecture.*

close to the Shivaganga Tank. Over the gate is the date 1777, and over the façade of the church is 1779 A.D. In the centre, opposite the communion-table, is a very fine group of figures in white marble, by Flaxman, representing the death of Schwartz. The aged missionary is extended on his bed, and on his left stands the Raja Sharfoji, his pupil, with two attendants, while on his right is the missionary Kohlmer, and near the bottom of the bed are four boys. The inscription contains a summary of his career. The small house N.W. of the church, and close to it, is said to have been Schwartz's habitation.

Next to the Shivaganga Tank is the *People's Park*. On a high bastion not far from this is a monster gun called the Raja Gopala, 24½ ft. long, and with a bore of 2½ ft.

The Tanjore district was the scene of the earliest labours of Protestant missionaries in India. In 1706 the German missionaries Ziegenbalg and Plütschau established a Lutheran mission in the Danish settlement of Tranquebar, under the patronage of King Frederick IV. of Denmark; and in 1841 their establishments were taken over by the Leipzig Evangelical Lutheran Mission, which subsequently extended its operations into the district. The mission at Tanjore was founded in 1778 by the Rev. C. F. Schwartz of the Tranquebar Mission, who some time previously had transferred his services to the Society for Promoting Christian Knowledge. The mission establishments at Tanjore were taken over in 1826 by the Society for the Propagation of the Gospel, which subsequently founded new stations in several parts of the district.

Roman Catholic missions in Tanjore date from the first half of the 17th century. Their churches and chapels are scattered over the whole district, but their principal seats are Negapatam, Velanganni (on the coast, 6 m. S. of Negapatam), Tanjore, Vallam, and Kumbakonam. The St Joseph's College, founded by French Jesuits at Negapatam in 1846, was removed to Trichinopoly in 1883.

Tanjore is famous for its silk carpets, jewellery *repoussé* work, copper ware, and models in pith. The *repoussé* work, and the copper work inlaid with brass and silver *swámi* (or god) figures, are among the best in all India.

[**Negapatam** (R.) (population, 87,000), 48 m. E. from **Tanjore**, and 14 m. E. of Trivalur Junction (p. 424), is a flourishing port doing a brisk trade (Exports, £600,000; Imports, £200,000) with the Straits Settlements and Coast Ports, and contains the large workshops of the S.I. Railway. It was one of the earliest settlements of the Portuguese, was taken by the Dutch in 1660 and by the British in 1781. The Dutch Church and the old graves in the cemetery are interesting. Steamers belonging to the B.I.S.N. Company run once a week to Colombo *viâ* Pamban. Ramesvaram is now more conveniently reached by railway from Madura, as Colombo itself will probably be shortly (see p. 433). The line runs on from Negapatam to

53 m. **Nagore.**]

248 m. **Trichinopoly** junction station (R.) ✱ (branch W. to Erode, p. 410), D.B. (population, 122,000). The name is properly Tirusirapalli, or the City of the Three-headed Demon. St John's Church, in which Bishop Reginald Heber is buried, is close to the station: the grave in the chancel is marked by a fine brass. The bath in which he accidentally met with his death in 1826 is in the compound of the house and court of the Judge of Trichinopoly. The two historic masses of granite, the Golden Rock and the Fakir's Rock, are in the plain to the S. Close to the former is the Central Jail. Near it the French were defeated in two engagements in the second siege, which followed at once on the first, and the demand of the Mysore

General that the town should be made over to him.

3 m. S.W. of Trichinopoly is the fortified pagoda which was occupied by the French in 1753, and recaptured by the British under Colonel Stringer Lawrence.

251 m. **Trichinopoly Fort** station on the *Erode Branch.* The Fort has been dismantled, but this part of the town is still known as "the Fort."

It will be remembered that it was to relieve the siege of Trichinopoly—in which the English candidate for the Nawabship of Arcot, Muhammad 'Ali, was beleaguered by Chanda Sahib—that Clive seized the Fort of Arcot in 1751. (See p. 397.)

In November 1753 the French made a night attack on the Fort, and succeeded in entering the outer line of fortifications at *Dalton's Battery* at the N.W. angle. Here there was a pit 30 ft. deep, into which many of the assailants fell. Their screams alarmed the garrison, who repelled them, and made 360 of the French prisoners. This portion of the Old Fort is all that has been left standing. The moat that surrounded it has been filled in and planted as a boulevard.

On the N. side of the town, with a temple on it, is the *Rock.* At the foot of the W. side is a handsome *Teppa Kulam* tank with stone steps and a mandapam, or pavilion, in the centre. At the S.E. corner of this tank are a square corner-house, and adjoining it a house with a porch. In one of these Clive lived, but it is not certain in which. The ascent of the Rock is by a covered passage which leads up to the top from the South; and on the sides of the passage are stone elephants and pillars about 18 ft. high, which bear the stamp of Jain architecture. The pillars have carved capitals representing the lion of the S., and various figures of men and women. The frieze above is ornamented with carvings of animals. Flights of very steep steps, 290 in number, coloured white with red stripes, lead through this passage to the vestibule of a Saiva temple on the left, whence on certain days the images of the gods—viz. of Shiva, Parvati, Ganesh, and Subrahmanya or Skanda—are carried in procession. In front of the temple is a huge Nandi Bull covered with silver plates, which must be very valuable. The temple and the original Fort were built by a Madura prince in 1660-70. The steps of the ascent were the scene of a terrible disaster in 1849. A vast crowd had assembled to worship Ganesh, here called Pilliar, or "The Son." A panic arose, and in the crush which ensued 500 people were killed. From the temple the stairs turn E. and lead out on to the surface of the Rock, up which a rough approach has been cut to the mandapam, or pavilion, crowning the top, from which there is one of the finest panoramic views to be seen in the plains of India. On all sides the eye traverses the plain for 20 or 30 m. The height of the Rock is only 236 ft., but the plain is so flat that this height is sufficient to dominate a vast expanse of country. On the S. the most conspicuous object is the *Golden Rock,* about 100 ft. high. Carrying the eye to the S.E. of this rock, a patch of low rocky ground is seen about 40 ft. high. This is *French Rocks,* about 2 m. from the Fort. Within the town, distant only a few hundred yards, is the *Nawab's Palace,* which has been restored by Government, and is used for courts and public offices. To the N. of the Fort Rock is the broad shallow bed of the Cauvery, in which, except in the rains, there is but a narrow streak of water. Beyond is the *Island of Sri Rangam,* which the French occupied for several years, taking up their quarters in the two great temples, that of *Sri Rangam* to the W., and that of Jambukeshwar to the E. Owing to dense groves the temples are not very distinctly seen. Beyond to the N. in the far distance rises a long line of hills. To the N.W. is the Tale Malai range, the greatest height of which is 1800 ft.; while due N. of the Fort Rock are the Kale Malai Hills, which attain 4000 ft.; and E. of these are the Pachaï Malais (Green-Hills), which in some parts rise to 2300 ft. Turning to the W. the old Chola capital of *Wariur* is seen, where there was once a cantonment.

The most important local *Industries* are weaving, and tobacco and cigar making. The cigars are well known, though the so-called Trichinopoly cheroots come for the most part from Dindigal. The silver and gold manufactures are famous, the local gold and silver smiths being very successful in their filigree-work.

About 2 m. N. from the Rock, on an island, 17 m. long and 1½ broad, formed by a bifurcation of the river **Cauvery**, is the town of *Sri Rangam* (23,000 inhabitants). A bridge of thirty-two arches joins the mainland to the island on the South.

The **Great Temple of Sri Rangam** is about 1 m. N.W. of the bridge. The entrance is on the S. side of the temple, by a grand gateway, 48 ft. high, which appears to have been built as the base of a great gopuram. The sides of the passage are lined with pilasters, and ornamented. The passage is about 100 ft. long, and the inner height, exclusive of the roof, is 43 ft. Vast monoliths have been used as uprights in the construction, some of them over 40 ft. high. The stones on the roof, laid horizontally, are also huge. The stone on the inside of the arch is 29 ft. 7 in. long, 4 ft. 5 in. broad, and about 8 ft. thick. From the terrace at the top of the gateway is seen the vast outer wall which encloses the gardens as well as the buildings of this the largest temple in India. The outer enclosure, 2475 ft. by 2880 ft., contains a bazaar. Within this is a second wall 20 ft. high, enclosing the dwellings of the Brahmans in the service of the temple. The general design is marred by the fact that the buildings diminish in size and importance from the exterior to the innermost enclosure; and Mr Fergusson says: "If its principle of design could be reversed, it would be one of the finest temples in the S. of India."[1] There are two great gopurams on the E. side, two smaller on the W., and three of a medium height on the S. Beyond the incomplete gopuram the road passes under a small mandapam, and then through a gopuram about 60 ft. high. The decoration of the gopurams is all painted, and the ceiling of this one represents the Varaha, or Boar Incarnation, of Vishnu, as well as other Avataras with multitudes of human beings adoring them. A second mandapam is then passed, and a second and third gopuram. Hard by is another enclosing wall, which surrounds the more sacred part, or real temple, beyond which is the vimanah, or adytum, which none but Hindus are allowed to enter. At a third mandapam the jewels of the temple may be examined.

In the court round the central enclosure is the so-called *Hall of 1000 Pillars*. (Mr Fergusson counted 960, but the number is now much reduced.) They are granite monoliths 18 ft. high, with pediments, slightly carved to the height of 3 ft., and they all have the plantain bracket at the top. The pillars of the front row looking N. represent men on rearing horses spearing tigers, the horses' feet being supported by the shields of men on foot beside them. The great gopuram on the N. is 152 ft. high. In the floor of the passage under this gopuram is a stone with a Kanarese inscription. Mr Fergusson is of opinion that the building was commenced about 1600 A.D.[2]

Temple of Jambukeshwar.—In the S. of India temples are often found in pairs. If there is one dedicated to Vishnu, there will be one dedicated to Shiva. So here, at about 1½ m. E. of the Great Temple

1 See i. 368 of his *Indian Architecture*, where an illustration and a description of the temples will be found.

2 See p. 372.

of Sri Rangam, is a smaller one sacred to Jambukeshwar, or Shiva, from *jambuka*, "rose-apple," and *ishwar*, "lord," or Lord of India, Jambu being a division of the world= "India."

The Jambukeshwar temple has three courts, and is very much smaller than Sri Rangam: it has been lately restored by Ramasami Chettiar. The plan, however, of the building is more artistic, and the main corridor and proportions are fine. On the right of the entrance is an upright stone 4 ft. high, with a long Tamil inscription. The first gopuram is also the gateway of entrance. The ceiling is painted with flowers of the lotus. Within the inner court is a remarkable *Teppa Kulam*, or tank, of spring water, with a pavilion in the centre. Round the S., the E., and the N. sides, runs a corridor of two storeys supported by pillars. Beyond this is a second gopuram, and a third which forms part of the wall enclosing the adytum. Thence a broad corridor leads to the vimanah. On the whole, this is a very fine temple, and well worth a visit. It is, no doubt, older than that of Sri Rangam, probably about 1600 A.D.

The **Anikuts**, or **dams**.—About 9 m. to the W. of Trichinopoly the Cauvery separates into two branches which enclose the island, the N. branch being called the *Coleroon* or *Kolidun*, and the S. the Cauvery. A dam was constructed across the Coleroon in 1836 to prevent the river deserting the S. arm, from which a number of branches irrigate Tanjore, the chief one being called the Vennar, which falls into the sea 20 m. S. of the spot where the Coleroon disembogues. The dam or Anikut, which was designed by Sir Arthur Cotton, R.E., consists of three parts, being broken by two islands: it is a brick wall 7 ft. high and 6 ft. thick, capped with stone, and is based on two rows of wells sunk 9 ft. below the river's bed. It is defended by an apron of cut stone from 21 to 40 ft. broad, and has twenty-four sluices, which help to scour the bed. It controls the irrigation of about 600,000 acres. About 9 m. E. of Trichinopoly is the Grand Anikut, an ancient work, and below that is the Lower Anikut, also built in 1836.

306 m. **Dindigal** station (R.), a municipal town (25,000 inhabitants) in the Madura Collectorate. It also has a considerable tobacco manufacture. The great rock on which the Fort is built forms a conspicuous object; its summit is 1223 ft. above sea-level, 280 ft. above the plain. Its inaccessible sides were strongly fortified under the first Nayakkan kings of Madura, and for a long time it was the W. key of the province of Madura. Dindigal was taken by the British from Tipu Sultan in 1781, restored to him in 1784, and finally ceded in 1792.

319 m. **Ammayanayakkanur** station, or Kodaikanal Road.✱ The distance to **Kodaikanal** is 48 m. by road. A motor service runs in the season to 33 m. Krishnamanaikam, whence a siding path ascends 6000 ft. to Kodaikanal in 11 m. This station, which enjoys a growing popularity, is 7209 ft. above sea-level, and its climate is more even than that of Ootacamund. The scenery round it is not very picturesque, but there are places where the views of the low country and the Animalei Hills to the W. are beautiful past description. The sportsman may find bison, tigers, panthers, bears, wild dogs, which hunt in packs, and sambar. There are also woodcock. Nutmeg, cinnamon, and pepper-vine grow wild. Coffee, orange-trees, lime-trees, citron, and sago are cultivated. The Observatory, moved from Madras in 1889, stands 7700 ft. above sea-level.

344 m. **Madura** station (R.), D.B. ✱ (population, 133,000), upon

the *Vaigai* river, the capital of the Pandya kings, one of whom sacked Anuradhapura c. 155 A.D. (p. 494). A Jesuit mission settled here in 1606.

The **Great Temple**[1] (about ½ m. E. of railway station) forms a parallelogram about 847 ft. by 729 ft., surrounded by nine gopurams, of which the largest is 152 ft. high. All the most beautiful portions of the temple as it now stands were built by Tirumala Nayak, who succeeded in 1623, and reigned gloriously thirty-six years. It consists of two parts—on the E. a temple to *Minakshi*, "the fish-eyed goddess," the consort of Shiva; and on the W. one to Shiva, here called *Sundareshwar*, the legend being that the god under this form married the daughter of the local Pandya Chief, an event celebrated by the annual car Festival. Owing to the facilities accorded for visiting all the outer courts and corridors up to the doors of the two adyta, this temple is perhaps the most interesting to visit of all the Hindu shrines of India, and gives one the most complete idea of Hindu ritual. It should be visited at night as well as in the daytime, the dark corridors with a lamp gleaming here and there being peculiarly weird then. The entrance is by the gate of Minakshi's Temple, through a painted corridor about 30 ft. long, which is called the Hall of the Eight Saktis, from eight statues of that goddess which form the supports of the roof on either side; in it various dealers ply their trade. On the right of the gate at the end of the hall is an image of Subrahmanya, or Kartikkeya, the Hindu Mars. On the left is an image of Ganesh. This gateway leads to a second stone corridor with rows of pillars on either side, called the *Minakshi Nayakka Mandapam*, built by Minakshi Nayak, Diwan of the predecessor of Tirumala, where the elephants are kept. Some of the pillars have for capitals the curved plantain-flower bracket, but much of the detail is hidden by the stall shops. At the end of the second corridor, 166 ft. long, is a large door of brass, which has stands to hold many lamps that are lighted at night. A third dark corridor, under a small gopuram, ends in one broader, with more light, which has three figures on either side carved with spirit, and leads to a quadrangle with a *Teppa Kulam*. This tank is called *Swarnapushpakarini* or *Pattamarai*, "Tank of the Golden Lilies." All round it runs an arcade. On the N. and E. sides the walls of this are painted with the representations of the most famous pagodas in India: from the S. side a very good view is obtained of the different towers of the gopurams. On the N.W. side is the belfry, with an American bell of fine tone. The corridor in front of the entrance to the temple is adorned with twelve very spirited figures, which form pillars on either side, six of them being the Yali, a name given to a strange monster which is the conventional lion of the S., sometimes represented with a long snout or proboscis. Between every two of them is a figure of one of the five Pandu brothers (see p. lviii. of the *Introduction*). First on the right is Yudhishthara, and opposite to him on the left is Arjan with his famous bow. Then come Sahadeva on the right, and Nakula on the left. Then follows Bhima on the right with his club, and opposite to him, on the left, is the shrine of the goddess, and the figure of a Dwarpal. From here a gopuram leads from the Minakshi Temple into that of Sundareshwar, surrounded by a fine corridor. On the S. side of it is a Nandi bull, and eight steps lead into the *Aruvatti Murar, the Temple of the Rishis*, in which are a very large number of statues of Hindu saints and gods. The jewel house adjoining is opened for a fee of Rs. 15. S.E. of the groups of statues are the chambers where the Vahanas, or vehicles, of Minakshi and Sundareshwar are kept. There are two golden

[1] See Fergusson's *Indian Architecture*, i. 390.

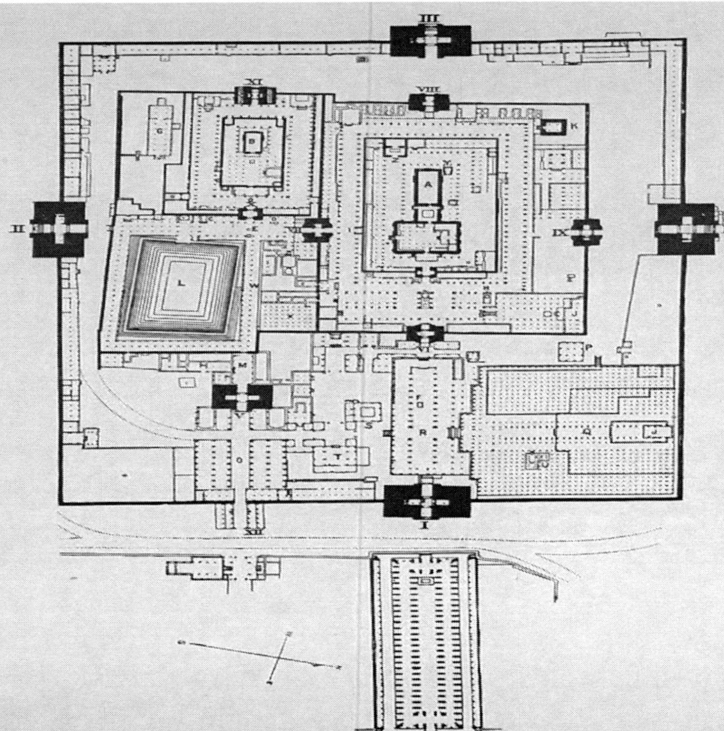

PLAN OF THE MADURA TEMPLE.

KEY TO THE PLAN.

A Shrine of God Sundareshwar.
AA Pudu mandapam (Tirumala's Choultry).
B Shrine of Goddess Minâkshi-devi.
C Small shrine of Ganesa.
D Small shrine of Subrahmanya.
E Vedi or Altar.
F Nandi Pavilion.
G Javandisvara mandapam.
H Navagraha or nine planets.
I Large Ganesa.
JJ Shrines of Natesvar.
K Poet's College.
L Tank of Golden Lilies.
M Mudali Pillai mandapam.
O Ashta Sakti hall.
P 16 pillar mandapam.
Q Thousand pillar mandapam.
R Viravasantarâya mandapam.
S Katyâna Sundara mandapam.
T Servaikaran mandapam.
U Lingam.
W Chitra mandapam.
Y Ellamvatta-siddha.
Z Madura Nâyaka temple.
I-IV Four outer Gopurams.
V Tiruvachi Gopuram.
VI, VIII, IX Three Gopurams of the second Prâkarâ.
X, XI, Gates to the Minâkshi prakârâm.
VII, Gate between the temples.
XII, Ashta-Sakti mandapam.

Plan of the Temple, Madura.

[To face p. 433.

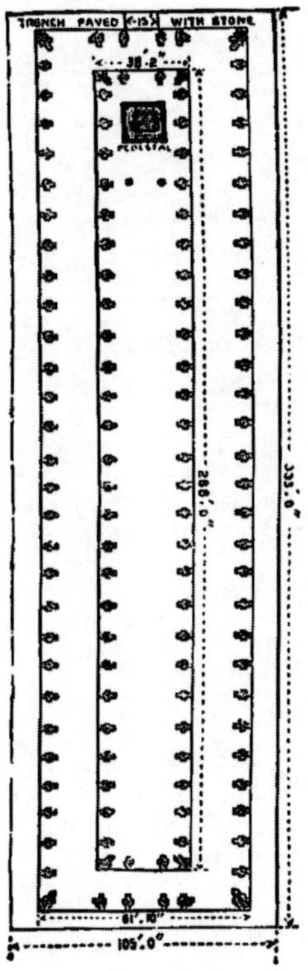

Plan of Tirumala's Choultry.

[*To face p.* 433.

palkis, or litters, plated with gold, and two with rods to support canopies. There are also vehicles plated with silver, such as a *Hansa*, or "goose," a *Nandi*, or "bull."

In the N.E. corner is the most striking feature of the temple, the *Sahasrastambha Mandapam*, or **Hall of 1000 Pillars**. There are in fact 997, but many are hid from view, as the intervals between them have been bricked up to form granaries for the temple. "There is a small shrine dedicated to the god Nateshwar, the tutelary deity of the place, which occupies the space of fifteen columns, so the real number is only 985; but it is not their number but their marvellous elaboration that makes it the wonder of the place, and makes it in some respects more remarkable than the choultry (see below) about which so much has been said and written" (Fergusson). This hall, whose sculptures surpass those of any other hall of its class, was built c. 1560 A.D. by Arianayakkam Mudali, Minister of the Founder of the dynasty of the Nayakkans. He is represented on the left of the entrance sitting gracefully on a rearing horse. In the row behind him are some spirited figures of men and women, or male and female deities dancing.

Opposite the great Gopuram is the *Pudu*[1] *Mandapam*, or New Gallery, known as **Tirumala's Choultry**, and built by him for the presiding deity of the place, Sundareshwar, who paid him a visit of ten days annually. This, had it been finished, would have surpassed in magnificence all the other buildings of this monarch; and as the date of its construction is known (1623-45), it forms a fixed point in the chronology of the style. The hall is 333 ft. long and 105 ft. broad, and has four rows of pillars supporting a flat roof, and on either side of the centre corridor five pillars represent ten of the Nayakkan dynasty. Tirumala is distinguished by having a canopy over him and two figures at his back; the figure on the left is his wife, the Princess of Tanjore. On the left of the doorway is a singular group, representing one of the Nayaks shooting a wild boar and sows, according to the legend, which says that Shiva commiserated the litter of little pigs, took them up in his arms, and assuming the shape of the sow suckled them. A portly figure either that of Shiva or the Nayak, is seen holding up the dozen little pigs. The Hall is said to have cost a million sterling.

1 Also called the Vasanta Mantapam, as the god's visit was to it in the spring.

The *Great Raya Gopuram* is on the E. side of the hall; had it been completed in accordance with its foundations, it would have been by far the loftiest Gopuram in all S. India.

¾ m. from the temple to the N.E. is the **Palace of Tirumala Nayak**. The building which looks modern, and has pillars of rough granite cased with beautiful chunam or cement supporting scalloped arches, has been restored and is utilised for public offices. The entrance to it is on the E. side, by a granite portico built in honour of Lord Napier and Ettrick, who first ordered the restoration. At each corner of the E. face of the palace is a low tower. The Napier Gateway gives access to a quadrangle 252 ft. by 151 ft. On the E., N., and S. sides is a corridor, the roof supported by arches resting on granite pillars. "On one side of the court stands the Swarga Vilas, or Celestial Pavilion, formerly the throne-room of the palace, now used as the Judge's Court. It is an arcaded octagon, covered by a dome 60 ft. in diameter and 73 ft. high. On another side of the court is the splendid Hall corresponding with the Diwan-i-Khas and Diwan-i-'Am of Mohammedan palaces. The Hall is 126 ft. long by 67 ft. wide, and its height to the centre of the roof is 70 ft.; but what is more important than its dimensions, it possesses all the structural propriety and character of a Gothic building." Fergusson's *Indian*

Architecture, i. 412. Fine as the hall is, the illustration in Fergusson's *Indian Architecture* taken from Daniell's drawing utterly exaggerates the proportions and beauty of it. This old palace now forms one of the finest public buildings in India.

The *English Church*, designed by Mr Chisholm, C.E., and built at the expense of Mr Fischer, a former well-known resident at Madura, stands in an open space in the middle of the town S.W. of the Great Temple.

On the N. side of the river Vaigai, N. of the city, and about 1 m. from the bridge (recently completed), is a curious building called the *Tamkam*, built by Tirumala for exhibiting fights between wild beasts and gladiators. It is now the Collector's residence. North again is the Civil Station. 3 m. E. of the station is the fine Vandiyen *Teppa Kulam*, enclosed by a granite parapet (1000 ft. square), and with a pretty temple in the middle. On the way is passed a garden with a very fine specimen of the *Ficus indica*. The main stem has been much mutilated, but is still 70 ft. in circumference. The ground shaded by this tree has a diameter of 180 ft. in every direction.

The branch railway from Madura to (67 m.) Ramnad and (90 m.) Mandapam is connected with Pamban, on the island of Ramesvaram, by a steam launch, but a railway embankment and bridge are being constructed across the channel. The line runs on from Pamban to (105 m.) Ramesvaram, and 11 m. further to Dhanuskodi. From here a steamer will connect this route with Talai Mannaar, 25 m. distant, from which Colombo is 207 m. (p. 496). This route from India to Ceylon, with its short sea passage, is no doubt destined to supersede that *viâ* Tuticorin.

The temple of **Ramesvaram**, about 7 m. distant from Pamban, is one of the most venerated Hindu shrines in India, having been founded, according to tradition, by Rama himself, and therefore being associated with Rama's journey to Ceylon in search of Sita, and the *Ramayana* (p. lviii. *Introduction*). For centuries it has been the object of pilgrimages from all parts of India. It is to their control of the passage from the mainland that the Chiefs of Ramnad owe their hereditary title of Setupati, "Lord of the Causeway."

The island is to a great extent covered with *babûl* (*Acacia arabica*) trees and by quaint umbrella trees. It is inhabited principally by Brahmans supported by the profits derived from the temples.

The great **Temple** stands on rising ground above a fresh-water lake, about three miles in circumference, in the northern part of the island. It is built in a quadrangular enclosure 657 ft. broad by about 1000 ft. long, and is entered by a gateway 100 ft. high. With its majestic towers, its vast colonnades, and its walls encrusted with carved work and statuary, it is a grand example of the Dravidian style. The best and oldest portion is built of a dark, hard limestone, to which there is nothing similar in the rest of the building. Local tradition asserts that this part was erected by the Vara Raja Sekkarar, of Kandy, with stone cut and polished in Ceylon, and that its cost was defrayed by the seaport dues of all the coast towns during the year it was building. The massiveness of the workmanship (slabs 40 ft. long being used in the doorways and ceilings), and the wonderful pillared halls which surround the inner shrine are noticeable.

Mr Fergusson[1] says: "If it were proposed to select one temple which should exhibit all the beauties of the Dravidian style in their greatest perfection, and at the same time exemplify all its characteristic defects of design, the choice would almost inevitably fall upon that of Ramesvaram. In no other temple has the same amount of patient industry been exhibited as here; and in none, unfortunately, has that labour been so

[1] *Indian Architecture*, i. 380.

thrown away for want of a design appropriate to its display. While the temple at Tanjore produces an effect greater than is due to its mass or detail, this one, with double its dimensions and ten times its elaboration, produces no effect externally, and internally can only be seen in detail, so that the parts hardly in any instance aid one another in producing the effect aimed at.

"The glory of the temple is in its corridors. These extend to a total length of nearly 4000 ft. Their breadth varies from 20 ft. to 30 ft. of free floor space, and their height is apparently about 30 ft. from the floor to the centre of the roof. Each pillar or pier is compound, and richer and more elaborate in design than those of the Parvati porch at Chidambaram (p. 423), and more modern in date."

As the corridors run for the most part round open spaces, and have light admitted to them through the back walls, they have none of the mysterious half-light of those of Madura, and will perhaps strike some visitors as less impressive.

The temple, its ceremonies, and its attendant Brahmans, are maintained from the revenue of fifty-seven villages, yielding an annual income of about £4500, granted by former Rajas of the Ramnad *Zamîndârî*. The *lingam*, which is supposed to have been placed here by Rama, is daily washed with Ganges water, which is afterwards sold.]

425 m. **Maniyachi** junction (line to Tinnevelly and Quilon — see below).

443 m. **Tuticorin** station (Tuttukudi), ✱ D.B., terminus of S. Indian Railway. Lat. 8° 48′, long. 78° 11′. A municipal and commercial town, exporting quantities of cotton, coffee, chillies, tea, cattle; value of exports, £3,300,000, and of imports, £550,000 annually (population, 28,000). The anchorage is 5 m. from the shore. Passengers are conveyed to and from the steamers of the B.I.S.N. Company in their steam-launch. Fare, Rs.2 each. The daily steamer to and from Colombo, in connection with the S.I. express from Madras, leaves Tuticorin at 5 P.M., and reaches Colombo (185 m.) at 8 A.M. The Ceylon boat leaves at 6 P.M., and reaches Tuticorin at 7 A.M. This sea route will be superseded by that *viâ* Madura, Ramesvaram and Mannaar (see pp. 434 and 496). There is an enormous passenger traffic of coolies by the present route.

The place was famous for its pearl-fishery, which extended from Cape Comorin to the Pambam Channel. This was accurately described by Marco Polo, who noted that the fishermen paid Brahmans to charm away the sharks. Cæsar Frederick, who visited India 1563-1581, recorded that the fishing began in March or April, and lasted fifty days. "It is never in the same spot during two consecutive years; but when the season approaches, good divers are sent to examine where the greatest number of oysters are to be found, and when they have settled that point, a village is built of stone opposite to it." The fishers and divers are mostly native Christians. Owing to the deepening of the Pambam Channel, these banks no longer produce the pearl-oysters in such remunerative quantities, but shank shells are still found and exported to Bengal. The fisheries are carried on at intervals under Government supervision.

The **S.P.G.** have a Mission-house here, and a Training School.

Tuticorin was originally a Portuguese settlement, founded about 1540. In 1658 it was captured by the Dutch, and in 1782 by the British. It was restored to the Dutch in 1785 and again taken by the British in 1795. During the Poligar war of 1801, it was held for a short time by the

Poligar of Panchalamkurichi, and was ceded to the Dutch in 1818. It was finally handed over to the English in 1825.

The old Dutch cemetery, containing several tombstones on which are carved armorial bearings and raised inscriptions, is worthy of a visit.

20 m. S. of Tuticorin on the sea lies the village of **Trichendur**, which contains a large and important temple dedicated to Subrahmanya, the god of war, and second son of Shiva. The temple contains some excellent sculpture and several inscriptions.

---

19 m. from Maniyachi is **Tinnevelly** (Tirunelveli—population, 40,000), on the left bank of the Tambrapurni river, and $1\frac{1}{2}$ m. from it. It is $2\frac{1}{2}$ m. from Palamcotta (population, 39,000). A bridge of eleven arches of 60 ft. span each, erected by Sulochenam Mudelier, connects the two places.

Tinnevelly is the most Christian district in India. The S.P.G. and the C.M.S., established 1820, have important stations at the headquarters and at Palamcottah, as have also the Jesuits. It was here that St Francis Xavier began his preaching in India.

The *Temple* at Tinnevelly, though, as Mr Fergusson says (i. 392), "neither among the largest nor the most splendid of S. India, has the advantage of having been built on one plan and at one time, without subsequent alteration or change." It is, like the temple at Madura, divided into two parts, of which the S. half is dedicated to Parvati, the consort of Shiva, and the N. to Shiva himself. There are three gateways, or gopurams, to either half, those on the E. being the principal, and having porches outside them. In front, on entering, is an internal porch of large dimensions, on the right of which is a *Teppa Kulam*, and on the left a thousand-pillared hall, which runs nearly the whole breadth of the enclosure, and is 63 ft. broad. There are a hundred rows of pillars ten deep. The temple is deserving of a visit, and can easily be reached, as Tinnevelly is but little out of the way of a traveller going to Tuticorin.

Palamcottah, $3\frac{1}{2}$ m. E. of Tinnevelly, is a municipal town, with a population of 39,000, of whom 2000 are Christians. The old Fort has been demolished.

Between the bridge over the Tambrapurni and the Fort stands the church of the C.M.S., the spire of which is 110 ft. high. The C.M.S. have several schools here.

(1) The railway turns N.W. from Tinnevelly, and runs past 50 m. **Shencottah**, and through a dip in the Ghats to Punalur, 79 m., and so to

107 m. **Quilon**—the Koilum of Marco Polo—on the W. coast of the Travancore State, the ancient Kerala, which has an area of nearly 7000 sq. m., and a population of 3,000,000. **Trivandrum**,*population 58,000, D.B., the capital of the State lying 30 m. S.E. of Quilon, is the headquarters of the Resident. No less than 20 per cent. of the population of the State is Christian, 238,000 being members of the old Syrian Church. The present chief of the State is H.H. Maharaja Sir Rama Varna, G.C.S.I. The ancient custom of descent through the female line still prevails, both in the royal family and in the State generally. The Fort at Trivandrum (Tiruvananantapuram) contains, besides the fine palace of the Maharaja, an old temple of Vishnu, known as the Padmanabha. The palace may generally be visited on application to the Private Secretary to the Maharaja. There is an observatory at the capital, and a good museum, and a fine public garden. The attack on the lines of Travancore by Tipu Sultan led to the great Mysore war in 1780-81.

(2) 38 m. N.W. of Tinnevelly is **Kuttallam**, much resorted to by European residents. It is not very elevated, but the S.W. winds pass

over it through a chasm in the W. ghats, and bring with them coolness and moisture, so that the temperature of this favoured spot is from 10° to 15° lower than that of the plains beyond, and it is particularly enjoyable in June, July, and August. Close to the bungalows there are three falls in the channel of the Sylar river, the lowest cataract having a plunge of 200 ft., but being broken midway. The average temperature of the water is from 72° to 75° F., and invalids derive great benefit from bathing in it. The bathing-place is under a fine shelving rock, which affords the most delightful shower-bath possible. The scenery is strikingly picturesque, being a happy mixture of bold rocks and umbrageous woods.

(3) From Palamcottah to **Papanasham** (*Papa*, "sin," *nasham*, "effacing") is 29 m. Here, near a pagoda, the Tambrapurni river takes its last fall from the hills to the level country. The height is only 80 ft., but the body of water is greater than at Kuttallam.

(4) From Palamcottah to Cape Comorin is a distance of about 50 m. along a fair unmetalled road. If arrangements are made beforehand the journey can be easily done in less than 15 hours, the night being spent in the bullock coach, which is the only means of conveyance procurable.

Cape Comorin (Lat. 8° 4′ Long. 77° 35′)—the "κομαρια ακρον" of Ptolemy and "Comori" of Marco Polo—is named from the temple of Kumari (the Virgin, an attribute of Durga) built at the southernmost point of the Indian peninsula. The temple and village, standing on rocks, and the long sandy promontory, backed by groves of palms, are very picturesque; and there are considerable remains of fortifications a few miles N. of the temple. The Rest-House on the promontory, which is in the Travancore State, may be occupied by permission of the Resident.

ROUTE 35.

MADRAS TO **MAHABALIPURAM**, or the **Seven Pagodas**, by canal, or by rail and road.

A highly interesting expedition from Madras is to **Mahabalipuram**, D.B. (*the city of gre it Bali*, see note, p. 439), or **the Seven Pagodas**, one of the most remarkable places in India.[1]

It is about 35 m. S., six of which can be done in a carriage to Guindy Bridge, where the Buckingham Canal is reached. A boat must be engaged beforehand through one of the Hotels or Agents; the cost is about Rs.7. If more than one person is going, another boat must be engaged for the servants. The boatmen tow the boat and the journey is done in from twelve to fourteen hours. Another route is by Jhatka (fare Rs. 2½) from Chingleput through Tirukalikundram to the canal, and on by boat, Rs. 2.

3 m. N. of Balipitham, the landing-place for the modern village of Mahabalipuram, is Saluvan Kuppan with two cave temples. One of these is usually filled with drift sand. The other is quaintly carved with nine lions' heads round the cells, and has two elephants' heads under miniature cells to the right of it. Running S. from Balipitham and between the canal and the sea, distant nearly 1½ m., is a low granite ridge rising about 120 ft. above the plain in its highest part. Upon this ridge are various excavations and carvings; on the E. face of it is a famous relief of the so-called Penance of Arjan, and 700 yds. beyond the southern extremity of it are the five monolithic temples called the *Raths*, all works, it is believed, of the Pallavas (p. 399), and dating from 600-25 A.D. The

1 A full description of the excavations and carvings at Mahabalipuram will be found in the *Cave Temples of India*, by Mr Fergusson and Mr Burgess, and in the collection of papers published by Captain M. W. Carr in 1869. See also Fergusson's *Indian Architecture*, i. 171, 327, 341.

modern village lies E. of the great relief, and the old temple lies beyond it again on the sea-shore. The traveller can either proceed in his boat to opposite the Raths, or by foot from Balipitham along the top of the ridge, or below its eastern side as he may feel disposed. Every one will probably prefer to visit the Raths first, as they are absolutely unique in the whole of India.

The most northerly of the Raths is called after Draupadi, the wife of the five Pandavas (see p. lviii. *Introduction*). It is the smallest of all, measuring only 11 ft. sq., and has a pointed roof, like that of a thatched hut, rising 18 ft. from the ground, and once crowned by a stone finial: the interior has a statue of Lakhshmi. W. of this Rath are an elephant and a lion carved out of single blocks of stone, and E. of it is a Nandi Bull. The second Rath is that of Arjan, which, like the fourth named after Dharma Raja, is a copy of a terraced Buddhist Vihara. The first, which is three storeyed, measures 11 ft. sq. and is 20 ft. high: the cell in the interior is only partly excavated. The second measures nearly 27 ft. by 29 ft., and is 35 ft. high; it has four storeys, three with simulated cells round them, and the fourth of a dome-shape, reminding one of the crowning cupola of the Great Temple at Tanjore. In each round window decorating the cells, is a head as of a monk looking out of it. The basement storey has round it columns of the Elephanta type (p. 19), with lions at their base; the excavation of the other two storeys has been commenced only. Between these two Raths is that of Bhima, and W. of this, and outside the line of the other four, the Rath of Sahadeva and Nakula. The former is the largest of all, measuring 48 ft. by 25 ft., and rising 26 ft. from the ground, and represents a Dharmsala or Hall of Assembly. Only part of the hall has been excavated, the pillars having cushion capitals and lion bases (see above). The carved roof of the upper storey closely simulates the wooden form of a free structure of the kind. The fifth Rath is smaller again, 18 ft. by 11 ft. by 16 ft. high; it has an apsidal end on the S. side, and is intended to represent a Chaitya (p. lxxii.). At the N. end is a porch with two pillars in front of a cell, beyond which excavation of the Chaitya never proceeded. Simulated cells are represented on the terraces of this Rath also. Each of these works is carved out of a single mass of stone, and probably these masses once formed a detached continuous outcrop of the rocky ridge.

Proceeding N. from the Raths to the southern extremity of the ridge, there will be found on the isolated rocks near the E. corner, a representation of a penance of Arjan, and on the W. side the Varáhaswami Temple, used for Hindu worship and not accessible. Between these, rather further to the N., is the Yamapuri or Maheshamarddani mantapam, a cave 33 ft. long and 15 ft. deep, with representations of the combat between Durga, wife of Shiva, and the buffalo-headed demon, and of Vishnu reclining on the Shesh Snake; at the back of the cave are three cells. Farther N. again beyond various incomplete excavations and the Ramanujya mantapam, a cave 18 ft. by 10 ft., with two pillars resting on lions' heads, are the excavations known locally as the throne or couch of the Dharmaraja, and the bath or vat of Draupadi, nearly opposite the fine gateway of the Vishnu temple, known as the Rayula Gopuram, which was begun about the 12th century, on the E. side of the ridge above the great bas-relief, but was left only begun. To the N. of the gopuram is a very graceful monolithic temple, called after Ganesha, measuring 19 ft. by 11 ft., and rising 28 ft. from the rock. It has three storeys, the two lower with simulated cells and the carved roof of the topmost carrying a row of finials; the pillars of the base are of very slender and wooden form. N.W. of this and facing W. is a cave, 19½ ft. by 9½ ft., with bold representations of the Varaha or Boar incarnation[1] of (1) Vishnu; (2) elephants pouring water over Lakhshmi; (3) Durga; (4) Maha Bali and the Dwarf (Vamánah) incarnation. Farther N. again is one cave on the W. side and another on the E. side known as the Isvara mantapam, containing three shrines with statues of the Hindu Triad; there is a large stone bowl in front of the cave, and at the back of it a relief of elephants, and a monkey, and a peacock. Just beyond the N. end of the ridge, and near the hamlet of Pillaiyan Kovil, is a life-like sculpture of three monkeys in the round.

Turning S. again from this point, below the E. face of the ridge the great bas-relief 90 ft. long and 30 ft. high will be found at the back of the village temple, also probably dating from the 12th century. The N. half of the relief is occupied below by two life-size full-grown elephants and four small ones, and above by a crowd of figures hurrying to the centre. In the rift between this and the southern face is a statue of the Nag Raja, overshadowed by a seven-hooded serpent, and of his wife below him, with other serpent-crowned figures and animals. On the southern face is Shiva with an ascetic, from whom the relief is named the Penance of Arjan, on his left, and a large number of dwarfs, flying figures, human beings, and animals, including lions, monkeys, hares, deer, and birds, round him. The relief is very picturesque and interesting, and is unique in all India. S. of this is a large unfinished cave known as the mantapam of the Páncha Pandavas with two rows of pillars and models of cells on the façade; and farther again and not far above the S.E. corner of the ridge, is the Krishna mantapam, of later date than any of the other excavations, supported by twelve columns in four rows, and containing at the back a sculptured relief of Krishna holding up the mountain of Govardhan (p. 167). The central figure of a cow being milked is very natural.

A path leads from the bas-relief past a fine tank to the sea-shore temple, dating from the 8th century, and being one of the oldest Dravidian temples extant. It is in the form of a five-storeyed Vihara about 50 ft. high, and 60 ft. at the base (*Indian Architecture*, i. 362). Inside the temple is a fallen lingam, and inside a vestibule on the W. of it is a recumbent figure of Vishnu, 11 ft. long: 75 ft. distant in the sea are the remains of a *dipa stambha* or lamp pillar. S. of the temple are two rocks with recesses surrounded by lions' heads excavated on their W. side. In front of these is a stone lion, and at the back an elephant's head and a horse.

Sadras, an old Dutch settlement lies on the canal 3 m. S. of Mahabalipuram, but hardly merits a visit. The place, like Masulipatam, was once famous for its printed cottons.

[1] The representation of the *Varaha* incarnation is fairly well done, but unfinished. The central figure is Vishnu with a huge boar's head. He has his right leg bent up, and resting on a figure issuing apparently from waves. The Shesh Nag, or six-headed serpent, over-canopies the figure, which has the face of a handsome youth, whose hands are joined in prayer. In front of him are two male figures, the nearest of which is praying with joined hands to Vishnu. Vishnu supports on his right thigh his wife Lakhshmi. The time is supposed to be that when Vishnu slew the giant Hiranyakah, "golden eye," who had carried off the earth into the infinite abyss. Vishnu, with the head of a boar, pursued and slew him, and brought back the earth. The representation of the *Vamanah Avatara*, or dwarf incarnation, is very spirited. Vishnu, dilated to an immense size, places one foot on the earth, and lifts another to the sky. The god has eight arms, with which he holds a sword, a quoit, a shield, a bow, and a lotus, and with one he points. The other two are indistinct. Worshippers or attendants are at his feet, and other figures appear in the skies. One to the W. has the head of a dog. The legend is that when Bali became Ruler over the whole earth, Vishnu approached him in the shape of a dwarf, and asked for so much space as he could plant his foot upon. Bali granted this modest request, whereupon Vishnu dilated to immense proportions and planted one foot on earth, one on the sky, and with a third thrust Bali down to Hell.

BURMA AND CEYLON

BURMA

INTRODUCTION

(The portion of the Handbook relating to Burma was originally written by Mr C. S. Symes, C.I.E.)

General Description.—The province of Burma lies to the E. of the Bay of Bengal, and covers a range of country stretching from the 10th to, roughly speaking, the 27th parallel of latitude. It is bounded on the N. and N.E. by China; on the N.W. by Bengal, Assam, and the feudatory State of Manipur, and on the W. and S.W. by the sea. To the S.E. lies the kingdom of Siam. The total area, including the Shan States, is about 238,000 sq. m., and the population, according to the census of 1911, was 12,570,000. It is formed of three separate tracts, Arakan, the Irrawaddy Valley, and Tenasserim, and is watered by five great streams, viz. the *Irrawaddy*, the *Chindwin*, the *Sittang*, the *Salween*, and the *Myitnge*. The first two rivers have their sources somewhere in the northern chain of mountains in the interior, one head-stream of the Irrawaddy probably coming from Tibet, where are also the sources of the Salween; the Sittang rises in the hills S.E. of Mandalay, and the Myitnge drains the Shan States to the E. of that city. The Irrawaddy and the Salween are great rivers which, in the lower part of their course, overflow the flat country below their banks during the rainy season, and, higher up, find their way through magnificent defiles. The Irrawaddy is navigable for over 900 m., but the Salween is practically useless as a means of communication, owing to the frequent obstacles in its channel.

The northern portion of the province is in the main an upland territory containing much rolling country intersected by occasional hill ranges, and with a few isolated tracts of alluvial plain. The country throughout the delta is flat and uninteresting. Towards Prome the valley of the Irrawaddy contracts, and the monotony of the plain is diversified by a wooded range of hills, which cling to the western bank nearly all the way to the frontier. The Salween valley contains occasional harmonies of forest, crag, and mountain stream. On the other hand, the scenery in Tavoy and Mergui, and among the myriad islets which fringe the Tenasserim coast, is almost English in its verdure and repose. The forests of Burma abound in fine trees. Among these teak holds a conspicuous place. Almost every description of timber known in India is produced in the forests, from which also an abundant supply is obtained of the varnish used by the Burmese in the manufacture of lacquered ware. Sticklac of an excellent quality is obtained in the woods, and rubber has of late years been largely exported. A marked feature in all the forests, and indeed all over Burma are the beautiful flowering trees. Although there is plenty of large game in the country, it is not easy to get at owing to the dense forests and the difficulty of obtaining experienced *shikaris* and baggage-animals ; but good bags of snipe are made all over the country from August to December, and partridge, hare, jungle fowl, and duck shooting is to be had without difficulty in many parts of the province.

Burma is fairly rich in minerals. Gold, silver, and other valuable metals have been found in small quantities in various parts : fine marble is worked near Mandalay ; coal of fair quality has recently been discovered in several parts of Upper Burma. Mogok supplies the world with rubies ; and sapphires are found there, and in the Shan States. Petroleum is obtained in large quantities at Yenangyoung in Upper Burma, and in smaller quantities in Arakan and elsewhere. Jade and amber are extracted in considerable quantities in the northern part of the Bhamo district. In Lower Burma agriculture is the main employment of the people. Cotton, sesamum, and tobacco are extensively grown, and orchards are found near every village, but rice covers about five-sixths of the total area under cultivation. The soil is lavish in its yield, requires little labour and no artificial stimulus beyond the ash of the past year's stubble, which is burned down and worked into the land. Upper Burma, though inferior in point of fertility to the low-lying tracts of Lower Burma, is far from unproductive. The chief crops are rice, maize, millet, wheat, pulses, tobacco, cotton, and sesamum.

The commercial prosperity of Lower Burma has more than kept pace with its rapidly increasing population. The chief articles exported are rice, timber, cutch, hides, petroleum, and precious stones. The chief imports are piece-goods, silk, cotton, and wool, liquors, tobacco, iron, and sugar.

The main commercial industries are those connected with the rice and timber trade. The indigenous manufactures of the country produce little beyond what is required for home consumption. Silk, lacquered ware, gold and silver work, wood and ivory carving, are among the most justly admired of Burmese handicrafts. The best silks are woven at Mandalay ; the principal lacquer-workers are at Nyaungu, near Pagan ; gold and silver work is carried on at Rangoon, Moulmein, Thayetmyo, Mandalay, and to a greater or less extent in all the larger towns ; the best wood-carvers are in Rangoon, Tharrawaddy and Mandalay, and the best ivory-carver at Moulmein. The characteristics of Burmese art are vigour and novelty in design, but there is also a want of delicacy and finish in execution.

Should Burma be visited after a tour in India, the traveller cannot fail to be struck with the great difference in the people and the scenery of the two countries. The merry, indolent, brightly-clothed Burmese have no counterpart in Hindustan, and the richness of the soil and exuberance of the vegetation will be at once remarked. The life of the natives is free from the deadening effects of caste and seclusion of the women—two customs which stereotype the existence of so large a part of the inhabitants of India.

The Burmese, as a race, are of short stature and thick-set. The men wear long hair on their heads, but have little or none on their faces: flat in feature, they show unmistakably their near relationship to the Chinese. The women are well treated and attractive-looking; they go to market, keep shops, and take their full share in social and domestic affairs. Men and women alike are well clad, and delight in gay colours and silk attire.

In religion the Burmese are Buddhists, 88 per cent. of the population professing that religion. But the great majority of Burmans everywhere, and practically all village Burmans, retain the primitive reverence, born of fear, for the *Nats*, the spirits of the forests, mountains, etc. This, Sir George Scott observes, "is the heritage of an immemorial past; it is the core of the popular faith." The Burman has learnt certain formulas; he is scrupulous in giving alms to the monks, and he worships on set days at the pagoda: "but he governs his life and actions by a consideration of what the spirits of the air, the forest, the stream, the village or the house may do if they are not propitiated." To these *Nats*, who have their appropriate shrines, he makes offerings to avert misfortune, and of them he seeks favour for any undertaking, such as building a house or a boat, or making a journey. Every Burman is supposed to spend a certain part of his life as a novice, wearing the yellow robe, in the *pongyi kyaung* (monastery). This is now frequently only a ceremonial observance for a single week; but some stay longer, and some remain to become *pongyis* or monks. The monks are the schoolmasters of the country, and perform this duty in return for the support they receive from the people. The shaven head and yellow robe of the monk are a common sight in all Burmese villages and towns.

History.—The earliest European connection with Burma was in 1519, when the Portuguese concluded a treaty with the King of Pegu, and established factories at Martaban and Syriam. Before 1600 the Dutch settled on the island of Negrais, at the mouth of the Bassein river, and soon after the English East India Company had factories at Syriam, Prome, Ava, and perhaps Bhamo. About the middle of the 17th century all European merchants were expelled from the country, owing to a dispute between the Burmese Governor of Pegu and the Dutch. The Dutch never returned. In 1688 the Burmese Governor of Syriam wrote to the English Governor of Madras inviting British merchants to settle in Pegu, and in 1698 a commercial Resident was sent to Syriam, and a factory was built there, and others at Negrais and Bassein. The French also had a settlement at Syriam. Meanwhile the Burmese dynasty of Ava was destroyed by the rebellion of the Talaing kingdom of Pegu, and the Talaings held sway in Burma till the middle of the 18th century, when Alaung-paya, known as Alompra, whose dynasty till recently reigned in Upper Burma, succeeded in uniting his countrymen, and crushing the Talaings. In 1755 Alompra founded Rangoon to celebrate his conquest of the Talaings, and destroyed Syriam. After Alompra's success he found that the French merchants had been supplying warlike stores to the Talaings, and he put all Frenchmen to death. The English, who had generally supported the Burmese, were granted the island of Negrais and a factory at Bassein. In 1759, however, they were suspected of assisting rebels, so their factories were destroyed, and 10 Englishmen and 100 natives of India were murdered. In the following year Alompra died while laying siege to Ayuthia, the capital of Siam, and the English obtained permission from his successor, Naungdawgyi, to re-establish the Bassein factory. Sinbyushin, who succeeded Naungdawgyi, took Manipur and Siam, and defeated two inroads from China. He died in 1776, and was succeeded by Bodawpaya, who conquered Arakan in 1784. This brought Burma into collision with the British in Chittagong. The Arakanese outlaws took refuge over the border, and harassed the Burmese rulers by inroads from British territory. This gave rise to friction, and in order to assist in the adjustment of matters in dispute, an envoy was sent to Burma in 1795 by the Governor-General of India. In 1819 Bodawpaya died, and was succeeded by Bagyidaw. Matters had not improved on the border, and in 1824 the Burmese invaded Manipur and Assam, and Maha Bandula, the great Burmese general, started with an army from Ava to take command in Arakan and invade Bengal.

The British Government formally declared war against Burma on 5th March 1824. The Burmese were driven out of Assam, Cachar, and Manipur; and Rangoon, Mergui, Tavoy, and Martaban were occupied by British troops. These, however, suffered much from sickness as soon as the rains began; all movements by land became impracticable, and by December the force occupying Rangoon had been reduced by sickness and otherwise to about 1300 Europeans and 2500 natives fit for duty. The Burmese, under Maha Bandula, made a determined effort to drive the invaders into the sea; but their attack, in which 60,000 men are said to have taken part, was repulsed with great slaughter, and the Burmese army dwindled away, a portion of it retiring to Donabyu, which Maha Bandula fortified with some skill for a further effort. The British troops, having been reinforced, marched up the Irrawaddy valley, and on 2nd April 1825, took Donabyu. Maha Bandula was killed in the cannonade, and with him all serious resistance came to an end. Prome was occupied, and the troops went into cantonment for the rains. In September 1825 the Burmese endeavoured to treat, but as they would not agree to the terms offered, hostilities recommenced; and in December the British advanced, and, after several actions with the Burmese troops, reached Yandaboo, 16th February 1826. Here the envoys of the king signed a treaty ceding to the British Assam, Arakan, and the coast of Tenasserim, and agreeing to pay a million sterling towards the cost of the war. In November 1825 a commercial treaty was signed at Ava, and in 1830 the first British Resident was appointed under the treaty to the Burmese capital. In 1837 Bagyidaw was deposed by his brother Tharrawaddy, who in 1846 was succeeded by his brother Pagan Min.

In 1852, owing to a succession of outrages committed on British subjects by the Burmese Governor of Rangoon, for which all reparation was refused, the British again declared war against the King of Burma; and towards the close of the same year Lord Dalhousie proclaimed that the whole of the province of Pegu, as far N. as the parallel of latitude 6 m. N. of the fort at Myede, was annexed to the British Empire. Almost immediately after this Pagan Min was deposed by his brother Mindon Min, who ruled his curtailed kingdom with wisdom and success.

The pacification of Pegu and its reduction to order occupied about ten years of constant work. In 1862 the British possessions in Burma—namely, the provinces of Arakan, Pegu, Martaban, and Tenasserim—were amalgamated and formed into the province of British Burma, under the administration of a Chief-Commissioner, Lieutenant-Colonel (afterwards Sir Arthur) Phayre being appointed to that office.

In Oct. 1878 King Mindon died, and was succeeded by his son, King Thebaw, ninth in descent from Alompra. Early in 1879 the execution of a number of the Royal family excited much horror in Lower Burma, and relations became much strained owing to the indignation of Englishmen at the barbarities of the Burmese Court, and the resentment of the king and his ministers at the attitude of the British Resident. In October 1879, owing to the unsatisfactory position of the British Resident in Mandalay, the Government of India withdrew their representative from the Burmese Court. Meanwhile, under the lax rule of Thebaw the condition of Upper Burma had been gradually drifting from bad to worse. The Central Government lost control of many of the outlying districts, and the elements of disorder on the British frontier were a standing menace to the peace at Lower Burma. The king, in contravention of treaty obligations, created monopolies to the detriment of the trade of both England and Burma, and, while the Indian Government was unrepresented at Mandalay, representatives of France and Italy were welcomed, and two separate embassies were sent to Europe for the purpose of contracting alliances with sundry Continental powers. Matters were brought to a crisis in 1885, when the Burmese Court imposed a fine of £23,000 upon the Bombay Burma Trading Corporation, and refused the proposal of the Indian Government to submit the matter to arbitration. In view of the long series of unsatisfactory episodes in the British relations with Burma during Thebaw's reign, the Government of India decided once for all to adjust the relations between the two countries. An ultimatum was sent to King Thebaw, requiring him to suspend action against the Corporation; to receive at Mandalay an envoy from the Viceroy, who should be treated with the respect due to the Government which he represented; and to regulate the external relations of the country in accordance with the advice of the Government of India. This ultimatum was despatched on 22nd October 1885. On 9th November a reply was received in Rangoon, amounting to an unconditional refusal of the terms laid down. On 7th November King Thebaw issued a proclamation calling on his subjects to drive the British heretics into the sea. On 14th November 1885 the British expedition crossed the frontier, and advanced to Mandalay without encountering any serious resistance. On 28th the British occupied Mandalay, and next day the King and his evil genius, the Queen Supaya Lat, were sent down to Rangoon and afterwards to India. He is still living, under surveillance, at Ratnagiri, S. of Bombay.

Upper Burma was formally annexed on 1st January 1886, and the work of restoring the country to order and introducing settled government commenced. For some years the country was disturbed by the lawless spirits who had been multiplying under the late régime, but by the close of 1889 all the larger bands of marauders had been broken up, and since 1890 the country has enjoyed greater freedom from crimes of violence than the province formerly known as British Burma. In the time of Burmese rule China claimed a certain shadowy suzerainty over the Burmese empire. In July 1886 a convention was signed at Pekin, whereby China recognised British rule in Burma, and agreed to the demarcation of the frontier and the encouragement of international trade. By a further treaty, signed in 1894, the frontier has been defined, and new arrangements made for the encouragement of trade, and the linking of the telegraph systems of Burma and China. In 1897 the province was constituted a Lieutenant-Governorship under Sir Frederick Fryer. The present Lieutenant-Governor is the Hon. Sir Harvey Adamson, Kt., K.C.S.I. The Army in Burma is now under the command of a separate Lieutenant-General, and forms the 10th Army Division.

The census of 1911 showed that the population had increased during the past decade by 15 per cent. The trade of the province has greatly developed under British rule. The standard of living among the agricultural classes has improved, and large areas of cultivable land still exist, and in most districts may be had for the asking.

Climate, etc.—The climate of the province, for some distance from the coast, consists of a wet season from 15th May to 15th November, and a dry season for the rest of the year. Farther inland the rain becomes less: but, as Burma must at present be reached from the sea, the best time for visiting the province is from November until February. During the wet season the rainfall at Rangoon is heavy—amounting to upwards of 90 in., and after February the heat is considerable till the first refreshing showers fall in May.

Means of Access.—The quickest route to Burma is by Brindisi to Bombay, rail to Calcutta or Madras, and thence steamer to Rangoon. A favourite route is by the Bibby line, which despatches steamers to Rangoon from Liverpool and London every fortnight. The steamers are large and well found in every respect, and perform the journey from Liverpool to Rangoon in about twenty-five days (see p. 503). They call at Marseilles and Colombo, and if the traveller proceeds to Marseilles by train he can complete the journey to Rangoon in seventeen days. Messrs Henderson also run steamers from Liverpool (15 Vincent Street) to Rangoon. Rangoon can also be reached from Calcutta, Madras, or Colombo, by the steamers of the British India Steam Navigation Co. The voyages from Calcutta and Madras occupy three and four days; that from Colombo takes six to seven days. The steamers from Calcutta to Rangoon start twice a week; those from Madras (90 hours' sea voyage) once a week, and from Colombo once a fortnight. Charge for electric fans (on notice given beforehand) £1. The days of starting vary at different seasons of the year.

General Hints.—Burma has hitherto been little visited by tourists, and travelling arrangements, except on the railway and by a few main lines of steamer communication, are primitive. Letters of introduction will be useful. Except at a few places (Rangoon, Moulmein and Mandalay) there are no hotels, and the traveller, when he quits line of railway or Irrawaddy steamer, must get leave from the Deputy Commissioner of the district to put up at Government bungalows and must take bedding and a few cooking utensils with him. He will do well also to provide himself with some books about Burma. *Bird's Wanderings in Burma* is a useful guide-book, and the illustrations in *Burma* by Max and Bertha Ferrars will be found charming. Of recent books the best is undoubtedly *The Burman: His Life and Notions*, by Shway Yoe (Sir J. G. Scott), lately republished by Macmillan. (See also p. xxviii. of *General Introduction*) and for general reference *Burmese Handbook of Practical Information*, by Sir G. Scott. Captain Forbes' *Burma* (Murray) is also a useful book, and Bishop Bigandet's *Legend of Gaudama* (Trübner) is invaluable for students of Burmese Buddhism. *Under the Shadow of the Pagoda*, by Mr Cumming, contains some capital sketches of Burma and the Burmese,[1] and Mr R. Talbot Kelly's *Burma* some beautiful illustrations. For more detailed information reference may be made to the *Gazetteer of British Burma*, which has been recently republished, and to the *Administration Report of the Province for* 1901-2, and the *Burma Census Report*, issued in 1902. *Notes of a Tour in Burma*, by Dr Oertel (Government Press, Rangoon, 1893), will be of interest, especially to the archæologist, and contains a number of photographs of various parts of Burma. *The Silken East* and *Mandalay and Other Cities of Burma*, by Mr V. Scott O'Conner, may also be recommended, and for historical information *Phayre's History* (Trübner). Free use is made of the above works, and especially of Shway Yoe, in the following pages. Marlborough's *Burmese Self-Taught* is a useful little work.

Pagodas and Monasteries.—The pagodas and monasteries form the chief objects of interest throughout Burma, and as they are mostly built on very similar plans a general description of these two classes of religious buildings will be useful. The following description is taken in the main from Shway Yoe. The *Pagodas*, while differing in various minor details, consist almost invariably of a masonry terrace, a high plinth, a bell-shaped body, and a *ti* or "umbrella" spire, a construction formed of concentric rings of beaten iron lessening to a rod with a small vane on the top. From the rings hang little bells with flat elongated clappers, which are caught by the wind and maintain day and night a melodious ringing. They are usually built upon elevated platforms, and are erected over relics of Gautama or Buddha. In almost all the larger pagodas there are arched wings on each face serving, as it were, as antechapels, and each containing a figure of Gautama, while the surrounding platform is frequently studded with minor temples, image houses, altars for the deposit of offerings, large bells, flag-posts, images of strange monsters, and other curious objects. These pagodas are to be found in every village in Burma, capping the hills frequently in out-of-the-way places, and contributing everywhere to the picturesqueness of the country. There is a special reason for this multiplication of fanes. No work is so highly regarded as the

[1] Messrs Thos. Cook's *Guide to Burma* contains some nice illustrations.

building of a pagoda. The builder is looked upon as a saint on earth, and when he dies he attains the holy rest. It avails little to repair a previous dedication, unless it be one of the great world shrines at Rangoon, Pegu, Prome, or Mandalay. Hence old pagodas are seldom repaired, but new ones are constantly springing up. Outside most villages in Burma, however small, there stands also a *monastery* or *pongyi kyaung*, where the monks pass their tranquil lives and supply a simple education to the children of the village. Ordinarily the monastery is built of teak, but in many places brick buildings are now being erected. The shape is always oblong, and the inhabited portion is raised on posts or pillars some 8 or 10 ft. above the ground. They are never more than one storey high, for it would be an indignity to a holy monk to have any one over his head. A flight of steps leads up to the verandah, which extends all along the N. and S. sides and frequently all round the building. The steps are usually adorned with carvings or plaster figures of nats or ogres. From the raised floor rises the building with tier upon tier of dark massive roofs capped at intervals with tapering spires or *pyathats.* The buildings are in many cases ornamented with the most elaborate carving. The interior accommodation is very simple. It consists, in the main, of a great central hall divided into two portions, one level with the verandah where the scholars are taught, and the other a raised daïs 2 ft. or so above the level of the building. Seated upon this the priests are accustomed to receive visitors, and at the back, against the wall, are arranged images of Gautama interspersed with manuscript chests, small shrines, fans, and other religious implements, and miscellaneous gifts of the pious, heaped together ordinarily in very careless fashion. There are occasionally dormitories for the monks, but, as a rule, they sleep in the central hall, where the mats which form their beds may be seen rolled up round the pillows against the wall. In many monasteries there is a special room for the palm-leaf scribes, often detached from the main building, as are the cook-room and the bathing-houses. In one corner is usually a *thein*, a building for the performance of various rites and ceremonies, and more particularly for the examination and ordination of priests. The traveller will find it perfectly easy to visit and closely inspect as many pagodas and monasteries as he pleases. The pagodas are open to all, and at the monasteries he may be generally certain of a friendly welcome from the priests, provided he can speak Burmese or is accompanied by any one acquainted with that language. The priests are treated with great respect by the people of the country, and are invariably addressed as *paya* or lord; and any one who visits a monastery should therefore bear in mind that the monks are accustomed to be treated with deference.

Pwes.—The traveller should make a point, before leaving Burma, of seeing something of the *Pwe*, the national amusement of the people. Pwes are of three kinds, the *Zat pwe*, which consists of acting, singing, dancing and clowning; the *Yokthe pwe*, in which a similar performance is gone through by marionettes; and the *Yein pwe*, a kind of ballet, with music and song, performed by a considerable company of young men or maidens, as the case may be. Yein pwes are usually performed only on special occasions, in honour of some high official, or at a great pagoda feast, but zat pwes and yokthwe pwes are of constant occurrence on nearly all moonlight nights in every large town, and the traveller should have no difficulty in seeing both forms of entertainment, either in Rangoon or Mandalay. The performances take place in the open air, last all night, and usually for several nights in succession, and are free and open to all, the actors being paid by the giver of the entertainment. The majority of the audience stay the whole night, say from 8 P.M. till sunrise, but an hour or two of the performance will probably satisfy the English traveller. A full description of the different kinds of pwe is given by Shway Yoe in chapter xxix. of *The Burman.*

The Irrawaddy Flotilla Company deserves special notice as one of the most successful steamer enterprises of modern days. The various vessels of the Company's fleet are nearly 300 in number, representing a tonnage of 92,000 tons; and regular services by express and cargo-boats are maintained between Rangoon and Mandalay, Bassein, and Henzadah, between Mandalay and Katha and Bhamo, up the Chindwin, and for a short way up the Salween river. For sailings to Mandalay and Bhamo, see Index under these places.

RANGOON.

Arrival.—It may be taken for granted that the traveller, either from England or from India, will land at Rangoon, and it will therefore be convenient first to describe the principal objects of interest in that city, and then to mention a few of the principal tours which can be made thence to other parts of the province.

RANGOON ✱ (Lat. 16° 47′, Long. 96° 13′) is the capital of the province, and the seat of the local government. It is situated on the Rangoon river, which is connected by water-way with the Irrawaddy. In 1852 it was a mere fishing village. In 1911 it is a city of over 289,000 inhabitants, having a trade larger than that of any Indian port save only Calcutta and Bombay. The value of the private sea-borne trade is now £28,000,000. Thirty years ago it was under £3,000,000. The trade is divided into £11,000,000 of import, and £17,000,000 of export. The imports are principally cotton goods, metals, provisions, silk, machinery, and sugar; the exports, rice (two-thirds of the whole), wood, raw cotton, oils and hides. The number of steamers entering and clearing from the port is about 1000, with a tonnage of 1,000,000 tons; and the receipts of the Port Trust amount to £192,000 yearly. The number of sailing vessels is 2400, with a tonnage of 3½ million tons. During the same period the population has increased from about 90,000 to nearly 290,000 souls, of whom 80,000 are Burmese, 77,000 Hindus, 40,000 Mohammedans, 9000 Christians, and 12,000 Chinese. An electric tramway runs E. and W. through the business quarters and to the Shwe Dagon Pagoda. The municipality has an income of 38½ lakhs.

The principal objects of interest in and around Rangoon may be classified as follows:—

1. The pagodas and monasteries.
2. The bazaars and native shops.
3. The rice, timber, and oil-works.
4. The public buildings.
5. The cantonments and lakes.
6. The remains at Syriam.

A new chief court and general hospital and a new museum are under construction at Rangoon.

(1) **PAGODAS AND MONASTERIES.**—There are numerous pagodas in and about Rangoon. The *Shwe Dagon* and the *Sule* deserve special mention. The great **Shwe Dagon Pagoda** is the most venerable, the finest, and the most universally visited of all places of worship in Indo China. Its peculiar sanctity is due to the fact that it is the only pagoda known to Buddhists which is credited with containing actual relics, not only of Gautama, but of the three Buddhas who preceded him in this world. Hence it attracts countless pilgrims, not only from all parts of Burma, but also from Cambodia, Siam, Corea, and Ceylon. It is situated about 2 m. from the Strand, and may be reached either by steam tramway (chiefly used by natives) or by ticca gharry. The stately pile stands upon a mound, partly natural and partly artificial, which has been cut into two rectangular terraces one above the other, each side, as in the case of all pagodas, facing one of the cardinal points of the compass. The upper terrace, which has been carefully levelled and paved and repaved by the pious, rises 166 ft. from the level of the ground, and is 900 ft. long by 685 wide. The ascent was by four flights of brick steps, one opposite the centre of each face—but the western face has been closed by the fortifications built by the British conqueror to dominate the town and secure the pagoda, where there was so much desperate fighting in the Burmese wars. The southern ascent is that most frequently used. At the foot are two gigantic leogryphs, built of brick and covered with plaster. The effect is rather spoilt by an external porch recently added. From them up to the platform the long stairs are covered by a rising series of handsomely-carved teak roofs, supported on huge wood and masonry pillars. The heavy cross-beams and the panelling are in many places embellished with frescoes, representing scenes in the life of Gautama and his disciples, and with hideously curious representations of the tortures of the wicked. The steps themselves are exceedingly primitive and dilapidated, consisting in some parts of broad stone flags, and in others of simple sun-dried bricks, worn by the feet of myriads of worshippers. On either side are beggars and numerous stalls, at which gold-leaf, flowers, and other offerings may be bought, and many other articles. The stairs debouch on a broad, open, flagged space which runs all round the pagoda, and is left free for worshippers. In the centre of this springs, from an octagonal plinth, the pagoda itself (see Fergusson's *Eastern Architecture*, ii. 146). It has a circumference of 1355 ft., and rises to a height of about 370 ft., or a little higher than St Paul's Cathedral. It is profusely gilt from base to summit, and is surmounted by the usual gilt iron-work *ti* or "umbrella," on each of whose many rings hang multitudes of gold and silver jewelled bells. This *ti* was presented by Mindon Min, the late king of Burma, and was placed on the summit at a cost of about £50,000. It was constructed by voluntary labour, and subscriptions in money and jewels, with which the vane and uppermost band are richly studded, flowed in from all parts of Burma. A few years ago the whole pagoda was regilt, and the *ti* was then lowered to the platform, and replaced, renovated, and with many costly jewels added. At the corners of the basement are somewhat Assyrian-like figures of *Manotthiha*—creatures with two bodies and one head, half lion, half man, with huge ears and ruffled crest—and all round about are figures of lions displaying an ample show of teeth between their grinning lips. The tale is that long years ago a king's son, who had been abandoned in the forest, was found by a lioness and suckled by her. When the prince grew to man's estate he left his foster-mother, and swam a broad river to escape from her. The tender mother's heart burst when he reached the other side, and she died; and, in

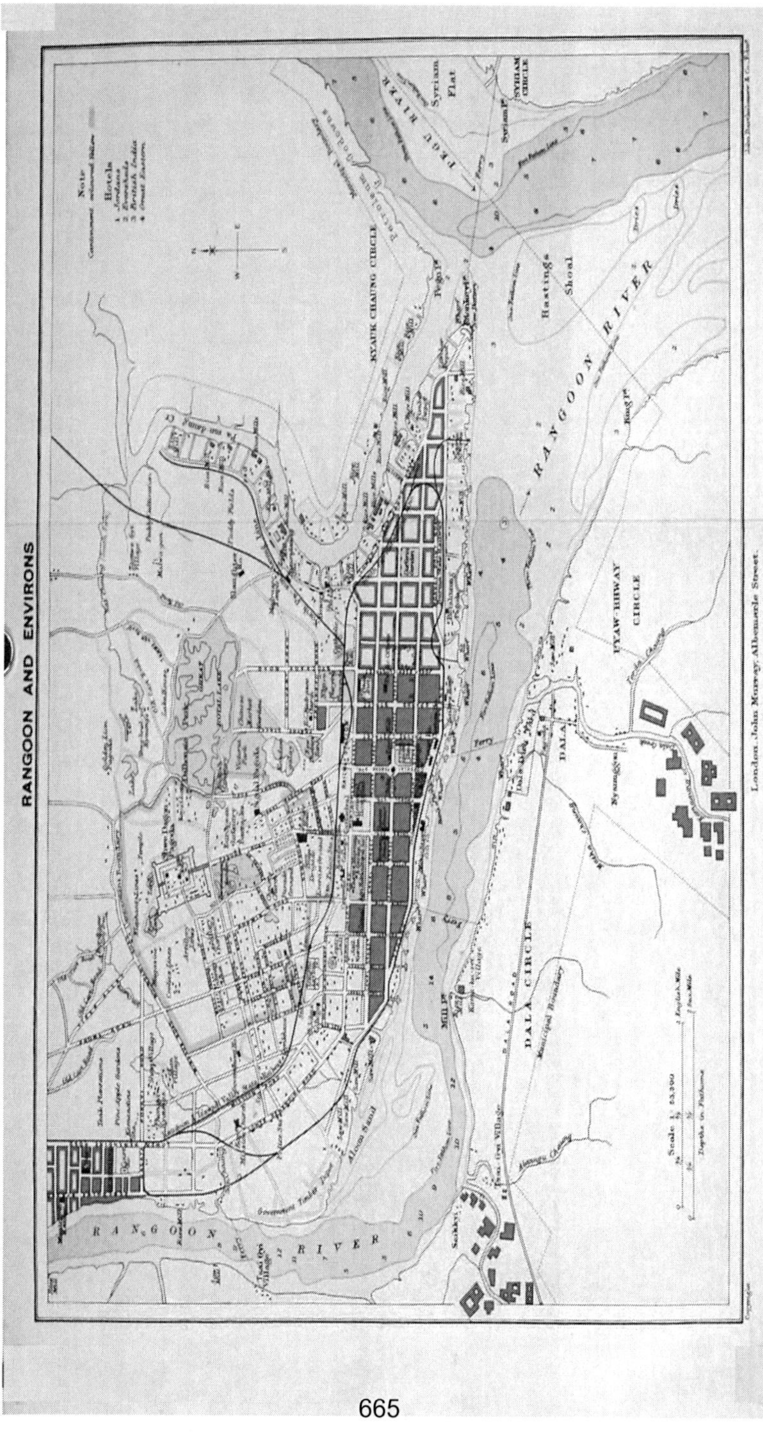
RANGOON AND ENVIRONS
RANGOON RIVER
PEGU RIVER
Syriam Flat
SYRIAM CIRCLE
Hastings Shoal
KYAUK CHAUNG CIRCLE
DALA CIRCLE
DALA
London. John Murray, Albemarle Street.

remembrance of her love, lions' figures are placed at the foot of all pagoda steps, and round the building itself.

The four chapels at the foot of the pagoda are adorned by colossal figures of the sitting Buddha, and in the farthest recess, in a niche of its own, is a still more goodly figure, the thick gilding darkened in many places by the fumes of thousands of burning tapers and candles. Hundreds of Gautamas, large and small, sitting, standing, and reclining, white and black, of alabaster, sun-dried clay, or wood, surround and are propped up on the larger images. High stone altars for the offering of rice and flowers stand before the lions, interspersed with niche altars for burnt-offerings. On the outer edge of the platform are a host of small pagodas, each with its *ti; tazaungs*, image-houses overflowing with the gifts of generations of pilgrims; figures of Buddha in single low stone chapels; tall posts (called *tagundaing*), flaunting from which are long cylindrical streamers of bamboo framework, pasted over with paper depicting scenes from the sacred history, and often inscribed with pious invocations from the offerer, or surmounted by the sacred *hintha* (Brahminy goose), the emblem of the Talaings, or the *kalaweik*, the crane of the Burmese. Interspersed among these are multitudes of bells of all sizes. The bells are hung on stout crossbeams, and beside them lie deers' antlers and wooden stakes with which the worshipper strikes them as he passes, and so calls the attention of nats and men to his acts of piety. In the N. E. corner, covered by a gaily decorated wooden shed, hangs a bell of enormous size, inside which half a dozen men can stand. It was presented by King Tharrawaddy in 1840, and is said to weigh 42¼ tons, and to be the third largest bell in the world. It bears a long inscription recounting the merits gained by the monarch who presented it. The bell has a curious history. After the second Burmese war the British made an attempt to carry it off to Calcutta as a trophy, but by some mishap it was sunk to the bottom of the river. The European engineers failed to raise it. The Burmans after some years begged that the sacred bell might be restored to them, if they could recover it. The petition was granted with a sneer; but they set to work, got it out, and carried it in triumph to the place where it now hangs. It would be impossible to describe in any detail the myriad objects of interest which are gathered on the pagoda platform; but the traveller should not fail to examine the magnificent carving at the head of the eastern ascent, nor that on the canopy of the colossal recumbent figure of Gautama on the western face of the platform. The carving and inlaid glass-work on all four of the chapels attached to the pagoda itself deserve notice, the carving over the eastern chapel being particularly curious, inasmuch as it appears to be illustrative of the capture of the pagoda by the British. The British soldiers with their rifles, and their officers each holding a telescope to his eye, are clearly recognisable on the highest tier, while on a lower tier the defeated Burmese show little sign of despondency. In the N.E. corner of the platform will be found the graves of certain officers killed in the second Burmese war. To the W. of the platform is the Government Arsenal. At the base of the pagoda hill are many monasteries embowered in groves of palmyra palms and shady trees, and to the S. is a small convent of nuns, not far from the Rest-House built by the King of Siam for pilgrims from his dominions.

The platform is never deserted. Even long after midnight the voice of the worshipper may be heard in the night air chanting his pious aspirations, while on feast days the laughing, joyous crowd of men and maidens in their gay national dress makes the platform of the Shwe Dagon one of the finest sights in the world. The visitor should, if possible, take an interpreter with him, and should provide himself with a few rupees. He can then, if he pleases, have his fortune told by one of the numerous *sayas*, who are always to be found on the platform; or he can buy for a rupee or two one of the quaint triangular gongs used by the religious mendicants to attract the attention of the pious, or supply himself with gold-leaf, prayer flags, flowers, or specimens of the curious marionettes and other toys which are offered for sale on the steps and on the platform.

Buddhists fix the date of the erection of the Shwe Dagon pagoda at 588 B.C.; but state that the site was sacred for cycles before, since the relics of the three preceding Buddhas were found interred when the two Talaing brothers, *Pu* and *Ta Paw*, came with their precious eight hairs of Gautama to the sacred hill. The original pagoda is said to have been only 27 ft. high, and to have attained its present height by being repeatedly cased with an outer covering of bricks several feet in thickness. The shrine has remained unaltered in size and shape since 1564, and probably will never be altered again. At all times and at all distances it appears imposing and sublime, like the religion whose followers have built it. It looks best, perhaps, on a bright moonlight night, and the traveller is advised, if practicable, to pay a visit to the platform by night as well as by day. The above description comes mainly from Shway Yoe. A useful little local guide can be purchased in Rangoon. The ashes of Buddha discovered at Peshawar (p. 247) are now in the Treasure House of the pagoda.

The **Sule Pagoda**, close to the Strand, is well worth a visit, and the traveller will be much interested if he ascends the platform and examines the many curious shrines and figures with which it is adorned. Among others will be found a representation of the *Sule Nat*, the spirit after whom the pagoda is named, and the legendary guardian of the hill upon which the Shwe Dagon pagoda is erected.

The Rangoon **Monasteries** are very numerous. They are none of them of any special interest, and the traveller will probably be satisfied by paying a brief visit to two or three of them. Some of the most picturesque are at Kemmendine, near the railway station, and a visit to them may be combined with an inspection of the images of Gautama in process of manufacture hard by, and of the shops of the *kalaga* makers, which are also at Kemmendine. The *kalaga* is a kind of blanket, usually red, covered with strange figures in appliqué work. *Kalagas* can sometimes be purchased ready-made, but must usually be ordered beforehand. They make quaint and handsome *portières* or hangings. There are other large monasteries in Godwin Road, and at Pazundaung.

(2) **The Bazaars and Native Shops.**—The bazaars are a great institution throughout Burma. They are large markets, usually the property of the State or of the Municipality, in which much of the retail trade of the country is carried on. They are also the great centres of gossip among the Burmese. A visit should be made to the *Municipal bazaars* on the Strand Road and at Kemmendine. and to the *Suratee Bazaar* in China Street. At the bazaar in Strand Road specimens of the silks and lacquer work for which Burma is famous can be purchased. Apart from the bazaars, the native shops are not of special interest. The best shops for the traveller who wishes to buy without waiting while Burmese craftsmen make to his order are *Hirst*, in Barr Street, for Burmese curios; *Tejmal*, in Phayre Street, for Burmese, Chinese, and Japanese curios and for oriental silks, etc.; *Klier*, in Merchant Street, for curios and photographs: *Goonamal*, in Merchant Street, for Burmese and Indian goods. In the above shops

he will find fair specimens of oriental art at reasonable prices; but if he desires the best or wishes to see the articles in process of manufacture, and to buy rather more cheaply, he should go to Godwin Road for silver- or wood-work carving. He will find several shops on the W. side of the road. For silver-work *Maung Shwe Yon* and *Maung Po Thet* are about the best. But these men maintain little or no stock of articles for sale. The traveller must order what he wants and wait till he gets it. The usual charge for embossed silver bowls is double the weight of the bowl in rupees; but for the finest work prices are higher.

(3) **The Rice, Timber, and Oil Works.**—It will be worth while to visit one of the great rice mills. Those of *Messrs Mohr Bros.*, at Kemmendine, and of *Messrs Bulloch Bros.*, at Pazundaung, are two of the largest, and permission to visit them can generally be obtained. There are over 150 rice mills in Burma, and nearly 100 saw mills, employing 43,000 hands. *Messrs Macgregor's Timber-yard* at Aloon should also be visited. Elephants are employed there to stack the timber, and it is interesting to observe the intelligence with which they perform the task. The oil-works of *Messrs Finlay, Fleming, and Co.*, at Pazundaung, are also worth seeing.

(4) **The Public Buildings.**—Rangoon cannot at present boast of many fine public buildings. The **Court Houses** and **Post** and **Telegraph Offices** and the **Sailors' Home** are on the Strand, and a fine pile of buildings has recently been erected, at a cost of seven lakhs of rupees, in Dalhousie Street, for the accommodation of the **Secretariat** and other public offices. This is at present, undoubtedly, the finest building in Rangoon and deserves a visit. In front of it will be noticed the "**Services Memorial**," a drinking fountain erected by members of the various civil services of the Province in memory of their comrades who were killed or died during the 3rd Burmese war. The names of the officers commemorated are inscribed on the shields surrounding the fountain. In China Street is the new **Cathedral**, and in the Kemmendine Road the new **Government House**, a handsome three-storeyed building, erected at a cost of six lakhs of rupees. The architect of these three buildings was Mr Hoyne Fox, an engineer of the Public Works Department. The **Rangoon College** and the **General Hospital**, situated on either side of China Street, are spacious buildings. Travellers interested in the progress of education in the East would do well to pay a visit to the College, and also to **St John's** (S.P.G.), Kemmendine (behind the Gymkhana), **St Paul's** (Roman Cath.) near the new public buildings, and the **Baptist Institutions** at Aloon. The **Bernard Free Library** attached to the Rangoon College contains an interesting collection of ancient Pali and Burmese palm-leaf manuscripts, and the **Phayre Museum** close by may be considered worth a visit. In the N.E. corner of the Parade Ground the "**Jubilee Hall**" is now in process of erection. It is intended to erect a statue as a memorial of King Edward. Lastly among public buildings may be mentioned the **Dufferin Hospital** in Mission Road, and the **Jail** in Jail Road, one of the largest in the British Empire, having accommodation for over 3000 prisoners. Many different industries are conducted by the prisoners, and in the jail salesroom specimens of their handicraft may be purchased, including excellent carvings and furniture.

(5) **The Cantonments and Lakes.**—These afford pretty rides and drives, but the traveller who can obtain no better means of conveyance than a hackney carriage will probably not care to drive far. He should, however, take at least one drive

in **Cantonments**, say along Godwin Road, past the Parade Ground and Race Course, then to the left past the Pegu Club to the Prome Road, then along Prome Road to Halpin Road (the "ladies' mile"), along Halpin Road to the Gymkhana, thence past Government House along Kemmendine Road to the Great Pagoda, and thence through the Cantonment gardens and back by Voyles Road to the town.

Another drive which should on no account be omitted starts from behind Phayre Street Station, passing northward through the Victoria Memorial Park, opened by King George on 13th January 1906. On the way are enclosures for wild beasts, which form a great attraction to the Burmese. Thence the drive circles round the Royal Lakes, the banks of which are planted with flowering shrubs. There is a favourite promenade with a bandstand on a spot of land jutting out from the north. The view of the Shwe Dagon Pagoda across the water is very striking, the effect being particularly fine when the sun is setting behind that. The Boat Club (private) is just opposite on the southern shore. The drive continues to the cantonments or more directly back to the town; but those who prepared to go further afield can obtain a very pretty drive by going along the Prome Road to the **Victoria Lake**, which supplies Rangoon with water, skirting the lake and returning by the Kokine Road. By this road (total distance about 15 m.) they will pass through miles of pineapple gardens, among which various picturesque and shady rides can be had.

(6) **Syriam**.—The traveller who has an afternoon to spare, and who can obtain the use of one of the numerous steam launches belonging to the Government or to any of the local firms, may well pay a visit to Syriam. This is now a mere village of some 2000 inhabitants, but was formerly a place of some importance, and is of special interest as being the site of the earliest European settlements of any importance in Burma. The town is said to have been established in A.D. 787, but little is known of its history up to the 16th century, when it was presented by the king of Arakan to Philip de Brito, who, with his Portuguese, had assisted the king in the conquest of Pegu. In 1613 Syriam was besieged and captured by the king of Ava, all the Portuguese being either slain or sent to Upper Burma, where a few of their descendants exist to this day. From 1631 to 1677 the Dutch maintained a factory at Syriam. The English also had a factory, which was re-established in 1698, and destroyed by the Burmese in 1743. Nothing now remains of these once flourishing depôts except the substantial ruins of an old church, some tombs, and the foundations of a few masonry houses. The **Church** was built by Monseigneur Nerini, the second vicar apostolic of Ava and Pegu, in the early part of the 18th century. In 1756 the Bishop was murdered by Alompra. From that year until 1760 the mission remained deserted, and was then removed to Rangoon. The ruined church is now buried in the jungle, about ½ m. from the landing stage. If the traveller is accompanied by an interpreter he will have no difficulty in finding some one in the village to show him the way to the ruins. 6 m. from Syriam is a large **Pagoda** standing on a hill, which affords a fine view. This is a prominent landmark as one approaches Rangoon from the sea.

ROUTE 1

To Mandalay, Bhamo, and the first defile returning to Rangoon *viâ* **Prome.**

The arrangements for this tour will depend entirely upon the amount of time which the traveller is prepared to devote to it. If he has only a few days at his disposal he will not be able to do more than proceed to *Mandalay* by rail, spend two or three days there, and return by the same route to Rangoon. If he has a week at his disposal he may proceed to Mandalay by rail, stopping an afternoon at *Pegu*, and may return by steamer to *Prome*, and thence by rail to Rangoon. To the leisurely traveller the whole voyage (a week) in the comfortable Irrawaddy steamers from Rangoon to Mandalay may be recommended. There is much beauty of a quiet kind in the river below. Three weeks will enable him to extend his tour to *Bhamo;* and a longer period to go on to the first defile and to break the return journey at the *Ruby Mines*, at *Pagan*, and at *Yenangyaung*. A visit to the Ruby Mines, 50 m. from the river bank, can now be made by motor service. Pagan and Yenangyaung can be more easily managed as they are near the river bank, but a visit to either place will involve small special arrangements. In the following paragraphs a few brief particulars will be given of the principal places which may be visited on a somewhat prolonged tour. The traveller must decide for himself what to see and what to omit.

An express train leaves Rangoon daily at 11 A.M., reaches Pegu at 1 P.M., and Mandalay at 6.30 A.M. The mail train to Mandalay leaves Rangoon at 4.30 P.M., and reaches Pegu at 6.30, and Mandalay at about 3 o'clock on the following afternoon. The traveller who wishes to see Pegu can thus allow himself a few hours of daylight there, after which he can dine at the railway refreshment rooms and go on by the night mail to Mandalay.

46 m. **PEGU**, station (R.) (hackney carriages procurable), a town of 14,000 inhabitants, the headquarters of the district of that name, is said to have been founded in 573 A.D. by emigrants from Thaton, and was once the capital of the Talaing kingdom. It is described by European travellers of the 16th century as of great size, strength, and magnificence. It was destroyed by Alompra, but rebuilt under Bodawpaya. Of late years the population has very greatly increased. It is interesting chiefly on account of its pagodas and a colossal figure of Gautama.

The **Shwemawdaw Pagoda**, lying E. of the Railway Station and said to contain two hairs of Buddha, is a shrine of great sanctity. Successive kings of Burma and Pegu lavished their treasures on it in repairing and enlarging it. When originally built it was only 75 ft. high, but as it now stands it is about 288 ft. high and about 1350 ft. in circumference at the base. It was last repaired by Bodawpaya about 100 years ago, and has recently been regilt under the supervision of the local elders. (See Fergusson, ii. 343-4.)

A good panoramic view of Pegu and its suburbs is obtained from the **Shweaunggyo** pagoda which is situated at the south-east corner of the city walls. At about 700 yards from the southern face is **Jetuvati**, the encampment of Alompra when he beleaguered the town in 1757 A.D. Within the walls are visible the sites of the palaces of the kings of Hanthawaddy. Traces of a double wall and moat may also be seen.

The enormous recumbent figure of Gautama, known as the **Shwethayaung**, is close to the railway station to the W. It is 181 ft. long, and 46 ft. high at the shoulder. Its history is unknown. Pegu was taken by Alompra in 1757 A.D., and utterly destroyed for a generation. In the meanwhile all remembrance of this gigantic image was lost. The place on which it was situated had become dense jungle, and the image itself turned into what appeared to be a jungle-covered hillock. In 1881 the railway was being constructed, and laterite was required for the permanent way. A local contractor, in searching for laterite, came across a quantity in the jungle, and on clearing the place uncovered the image which has become an object of deep veneration. It has been completely restored, and a lofty pavilion has been erected over it.

Not far from this is the **Kyaikpun** pagoda with four colossal figures of Buddha, each about 90 ft. high, seated back to back. Near it is the **Kalyanisima** or ancient Hall of Ordination in the Zainganaing quarter, founded by King Damacheti in 1476 A.D., with ten large stones covered with Pali and Talaing inscriptions. 1 m. further W. is the **Shweguzale** pagoda with its sixty-four images of Buddha constructed by Siamese architects.

[From Pegu a line 121 m. in length running through Sitang and Thaton has recently been opened to Martaban opposite Moulmein] (p. 457).

Joining the mail train at about 7 o'clock the traveller will pass through the *Shwegyin* and **Toungoo** districts of Lower Burma during the night, and will in the early morning cross the old British frontier into the Upper Burma district of *Pyinmana*. [From Toungoo a motor service leads in 6 hours to the hill station of **Thandaung**, 4500 feet above the sea. It is a growing place, has a comfortable boarding-house, and is a good introduction to jungle scenery.] He will obtain *chhota hâzri* at *Yamethin* (R.), the head-quarters of the district of that name, and breakfast at Thazi Junction. From here a branch line to the W. runs to Meiktila (14 m.), the headquarters of a Division and Myingyan (7 m.). Between Pyinmana and Yamethin, and thence on to Kyaukse, is seen to the E. the range of hills which divides Burma from the Shan States. In this hill-country, approached by road from Thazi, are **Taung-gyi**, the headquarters of the Southern Shan states, and, at a higher level still, **Kalaw**. Both are increasingly used as hill stations. Kalaw especially is likely to become popular. The Kyaukse district is the most fertile in Upper Burma, an ingenious system of irrigation works enabling the cultivator to obtain three or four crops of rice annually from the same ground. Here the hills approach much nearer to the railway, and Kyaukse itself (R.) is picturesquely situated. The train now crosses a stream running to *Ava*, and passing through *Amarapura*, reaches *Mandalay* at about 2 o'clock.

386 m. **MANDALAY.** ✱ station. (Lat. 21° 59′, Long. 96° 8′; altitude, 950 ft.). Several days can be spent very pleasantly at Mandalay. The city contains about 184,000 inhabitants, mostly Burmese, and was from 1860 up till 1885 the capital of the Burmese kingdom and the residence of the king. The growth of the city has been more rapid even than that of Rangoon, but it was in great part due to temporary causes. The city proper was in Burmese times within the walled enclosure, which is now used as a Cantonment and called '*Fort Dufferin*.

A traveller bent on studying the capital should commence by ascending **Mandalay Hill**, Yankintaung, an isolated mound rising abruptly near the N.E. corner of the Fort. From this point of vantage he can see spread out like a great map the town of 138,000 inhabitants, the Fort with the palace in the centre, the temples and monuments worthy of a royal city, and the system of irrigation built by King Mindon, with its great artificial

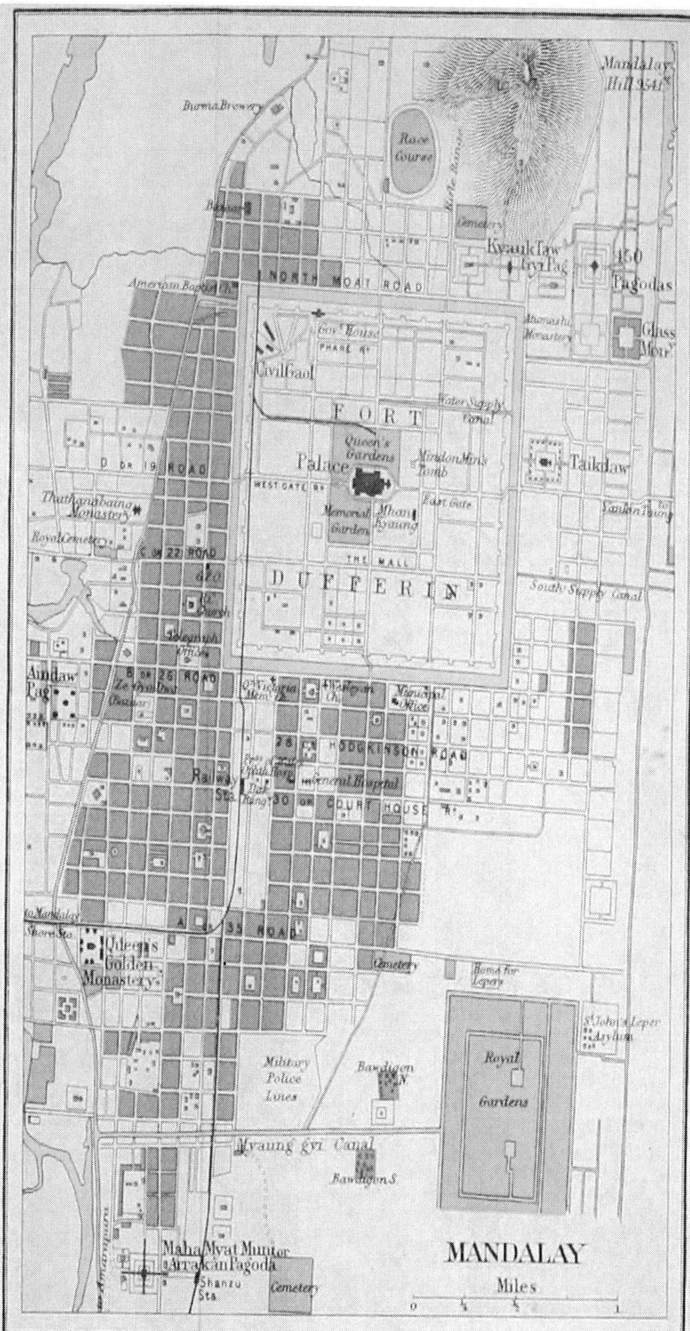

London. John Murray, Albemarle Street.

THE PALACE, MANDALAY.

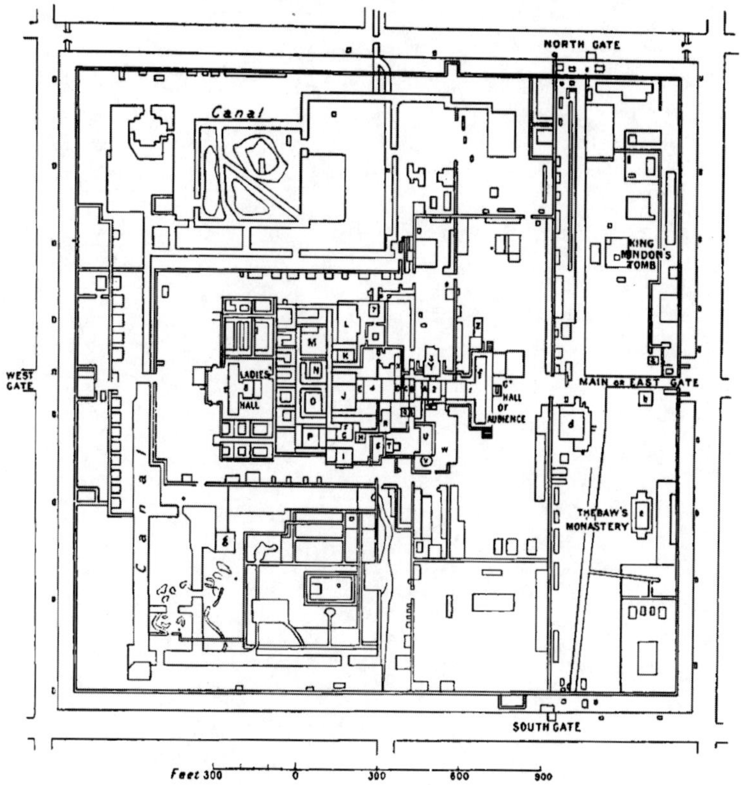

Reproduced, by kind permission of the Secretary of State for India, from the Annual Report for 1902-3 of the Archæological Survey of India.

lake and numerous canals. At the summit of the hill was formerly a wooden temple containing a huge standing figure pointing with his finger at the palace beneath. This temple and the figure were destroyed after 1885 by fire. The new temple built lately has a covered way to it with a terrible roof of corrugated iron. An electric tramway has recently been constructed in Mandalay.

Fort Dufferin next claims attention. This great square, built to guard the inner city and palace, with sides 1¼ m. long, is enclosed by walls of red brick 26 ft. high, machicolated at the top to serve the purpose of loopholes. They are backed by a mound of earth, so that defenders can look over them. On each of the four sides stand, at equal distances, thirteen peculiar and elegant watch-towers of Burman design, built of teak and freely ornamented with gold. One on the N. side, enclosed and enlarged, forms the nucleus of **Government House,** the residence of the Lieutenant-Governor when at Mandalay. Outside the walls, and surrounding the Fort, is a broad **Moat** full of water, 100 yards wide. It is crossed by five wooden bridges, one in the middle of each side, and an extra one on the W. face which was formerly reserved for funeral processions. It abounds with fish, and at certain seasons of the year large patches of the surface of the water are covered with the broad circular leaves and beautiful pink and white flowers of the lotus plants, which have their roots at the bottom. On this moat, in the King's time, were several state barges, gilt from stem to stern, some of them propelled by as many as sixty rowers.

There are twelve **gates** through the wall wall, three on each side equally spaced. In front of each gate stands the wooden image of a guardian *nat*, and a massive teak post bearing the name and sign of the gate. The old Burmese custom of burying alive human victims at the gates of a new city was not, as is sometimes stated, followed here. By King Mindon's order jars of oil were buried instead, and images of guardian spirits were set up in shrines.

Exactly in the centre of the Fort stands the royal **Palace** or *Nandaw*, brought here in the main from Amarapura. A plan showing the disposition of the palace buildings at the time of the annexation will be found in Dr. Oertel's *Notes on a Tour in Burma* (Government Press, Rangoon, 1893). The plan given here is reproduced, by permission from the Archæological Survey, Report for 1902-3. The palace was formerly a square fortified enclosure, defended by an outer palisade of teak posts 20 ft. high and an inner brick wall, with an open esplanade of about 60 ft. width between them. This walled square was cut up into numerous courts surrounded by high walls, and in the very centre, to make it as secure as possible, was an inner enclosure containing the palace. To the N. and S. of the inner palace enclosure are two walled-in gardens, containing royal pavilions, and laid out with canals, artificial lakes, and grottoes. The outer stockade and all the brick walls have now been removed, as also many of the minor structures; the chief palace buildings are, however, still standing.

Four strongly guarded gates led through the outer defences. The large gates were only opened for the king; all other people had to squeeze through the red postern at the side, which obliged them to bow lowly as they drew near the royal precincts. Entering the eastern gate, which is still standing, one crossed a wide enclosure which contained a number of subsidiary buildings, such as the armoury, printing press, mint, quarters for servants and guard, the royal monastery, King Mindon's mausoleum, and the houses of a few of the highest officials. Beyond this was another spacious court in front of the palace, at the northern end of which races and sports used to take place before the king. In the centre of this court stands the great

Hall of Audience,[1] with the lion throne, projecting out boldly from the face of the palace, with which it is connected at the back. The private part of the palace is behind this, on an elevated oblong platform in an inner enclosure, which was entered through two jealously-guarded gates on each side of the Hall of Audience. At the western end of the palace platform is a private Audience Hall, with the lily throne, where ladies were received, and between the two Halls of Audience are numerous wooden pavilions, formerly occupied by the various queens and princesses. Over the lion throne rises the high seven-storeyed gilded spire or *shwepyathat*, the external emblem of royalty. The Burmans used to call this spire the "Centre of the Universe." It has been lately taken down and restored at great expense.

In the S. garden is a small pavilion, on the verandah of which King Thebaw surrendered himself to General Prendergast and Colonel Sladen on 29th November 1885. A brass tablet records the fact. Near it is the lofty wooden tower from which the king used to view the city. The richly-carved Pongyi Kyaung to the E. of the palace, where King Thebaw passed the period of priesthood, is worthy of notice. It is now used as a chapel. Hard by is King Mindon's mausoleum, a brick and plaster structure, consisting of a square chamber surmounted by a seven-storeyed spire. Mindon Min was buried here in 1878. The palace buildings were for a time used for barracks and offices, but they were found unhealthy, and the troops have been removed to the new barracks outside. The great Hall of Audience was used by the military as a church. The private Audience Hall and surrounding buildings for some years afforded accommodation to the Upper Burma Club; but this was discontinued in the viceroyalty of Lord Curzon, who feared the risk from fire, to this absolutely unique example of the old Burmese palace built according to the traditional pattern. The necessity of protection is all the greater as experience in Ava shows that Burmese buildings perish in 50 to 60 years when at all neglected.

PAGODAS AND MONASTERIES.—The whole neighbourhood of Mandalay, Amarapura, and Ava is rich with splendid fanes. Some of the finest, including the *Atumashi*, or "incomparable" monastery, have been burnt down within the past few years; but the "**450 pagodas**" S.E. of the Mandalay hill, and the **Glass Monastery** hard by, remain, and should be visited, as also the **Queen's Golden Monastery** in B. Road and the **Arakan Pagoda.**

Facing the E. gate of the Palace is the Taik Taw monastery of the Buddhist Archbishop, decorated with wonderful dragons. N. of it at the S.E. corner of Mandalay hill is the Kuthodaw or **450 Pagodas**, a remarkable work. King Thebaw's uncle, anxious that the holy books of Buddhism should be recorded in an enduring form, called together the most learned of the priests to transcribe the purest version of the commandments; this he caused to be engraved on 450 large stones of the same pattern. These stones were set up in an enclosed square, and over each was erected a small domed building to preserve it from the weather. The enclosure is about ½ m. square, surrounded by a high wall with ornamental gates; in the centre stands a temple of the usual form. S. of this stood the Atumashi. W. of this on the road to Mandalay hill is the Kyauk Taw Gyi Pagoda, built over a huge monolithic image of Buddha.

The **Glass Monastery**, so called from the profusion of inlaid glass-work with which the interior and exterior are decorated, is close by.

[1] The Hall is 250 ft. across from wing to wing, but only 45 ft. deep. N. of it at the back was the stable of the White Elephant. The King's throne has now been transferred to the Calcutta Museum — a most absurd proceeding.

The Queen's Golden Monastery built by Supaya Lat, in Road 36 city, across the railway to Mandalay shore, is the handsomest building of the kind in Burma. It is built of teak in the ordinary form, but is profusely decorated with elaborate carving, and is heavily gilded within and without. The traveller should ask permission from one of the yellow-robed fraternity, of whom he will be sure to find some in the courtyard, to inspect the interior of this monastery. On the road to it the gilded Aindaw Yah Pagoda is passed; and not far from this is the picturesque structure known as the Serpent Pagoda. To the S.E. of the city is *Maha Myat Muni*, or "**Arakan Pagoda**," rendered especially sacred by the great sitting image of Gautama there preserved, and is on this account regarded by Upper Burmans as not inferior in sanctity to the Shwe Dagon itself. The huge brass image, 12 ft. in height, was brought over the hills from Akyab in 1784. The image was originally set up, so says Shway Yoe, quoting the ancient legend, during the lifetime of the great master. The utmost skill and most persistent energy had failed in fitting the parts together, till the Buddha, perceiving from afar what was going on, and ever full of pity, came himself to the spot, and embracing the image seven times, so joined together the fragments that the most sceptical eye cannot detect the points of junction. So like was the image, and so sublime the effulgence which shone around during the manifestation, that the reverently-gazing crowd could not determine which was the model and which was the master. The resemblance has no doubt faded away with the wickedness of later times, for, unlike most Burmese images, this *paya* has most gross and repulsive features. The shrine in which it stands is one of the most splendid in the country. The image itself is covered by a great seven-roofed *pyathat* with goodly pillars, the ceiling gorgeous with mosaics. Long colonnades, supported on 252 massive pillars, all richly gilt and carved with frescoed roof and sides, lead up to it. All day long circles of constantly-renewed worshippers chant aloud the praises of the Buddha, and the air is thick with the effluvia of candles and the odours from thousands of smouldering incense sticks. Within the precincts of the pagoda is a large tank tenanted by sacred turtle, who wax huge on the rice and cakes thrown to them by multitudes of pilgrims. Probably not even at the Shwe Dagon pagoda is more enthusiastic devotion shown than here.

The **great Zagyo Bazaar** lies near the centre of the city. Grain and vegetable vendors, silversmiths, toy, umbrella, and lacquer makers, silk merchants, and numerous other traders, occupy streets of stalls. Burmese ladies in the usual tight-fitting petticoat of gay silk and white jacket, attended by a maid, may be seen making their daily household purchases; groups of girls, with flowers in their hair and huge cigars in their mouths, price the silks of which all Burmans are so fond. Many strangers to the city, come on business or pleasure, wander about deeply interested in the display on the stalls. Nowhere else can be seen gathered together so many widely-separated tribes,—Chins from the western mountains, Shans from the E., Kachins from the N., Chinese from the little-known inland borders, Sikhs, Goorkhas, Madrassis, and other Indians, and the scene is as lively as it is uncommon. The bazaar deserves several visits, and is, indeed, the best place in Burma for purchasing silks. Curious old specimens of silver-work may also sometimes be picked up there. N. of the bazaar is the Diamond Jubilee Clock Tower, and the principal shops of Mandalay are in Street No. 22 on this side.

[After exploring Mandalay proper, short excursions may be made to **Yankintaung**, to **Amarapura**, to **Sagaing** and **Ava**, and to **Mingun**.

The hills called **Yankintaung** are about 5 m. due E. from Mandalay, and as the road is not practicable for carriages, the traveller should ride. There are a number of pagodas and monasteries, and a deep fissure in the ground containing an image of Gautama. The foundations of the colossal pagoda which Mindon Min commenced here may also be examined.

Amarapura, the Immortal city, founded in 1783, the capital till 1860, with an interval of 1822-1837, lies 6½ m. S. of Mandalay, and can be reached by rail. It is fully described in Yule's *Mission to Ava* and Mr Scott O'Connor's *Mandalay*. Only ruins now remain, but they are well worth a visit. The principal sights are a monster gun near the Tower of the Palace, and the Shinbinkugyi and Patawdawgyi Pagodas, and a colossal image of Buddha on the shore of the S. lake.[1] The station-master will provide a local guide. Near the station is a fine Chinese Temple.

Sagaing and **Ava** (7 m. S.E. of Amarapura, the capital of Burma from 1822 to 1837) can also be visited by rail. Little trace now remains of the city itself, but on both sides of the river are hundreds of pagodas of every variety and degree of decoration. There are the *Nagayon paya*, the whole building wrought into the form of a dragon; the huge round-domed *Kaunghmudaw*, built in 1636, and with "glistening white pinnacles or flashing gold spires on the Sagaing hills, and on the Amarapura side, great massy temples frowning over the river with all the stern solidity of a knightly hold, each with its legend—some tale of bloodshed or piety, some event in Burmese history, or birth story of the Buddha."

Sagaing is now the headquarters of the Commissioner of the division and of the Deputy-Commissioner of the Sagaing district. The traveller who wishes to explore the pagodas of Sagaing and Ava should endeavour to obtain an introduction to one of these officers.

The last of the excursions near Mandalay deserving special mention is that to **Mingun**, about 9 m. above Mandalay. The up-steamers of the Irrawaddy Flotilla Company call there, but the down-steamers do not, unless by special arrangement. Mingun is picturesquely situated, and is interesting for its great unfinished pagoda and for its huge bell recently reswung. The groundwork of the great misshapen Mingun Pagoda covers a square of 450 ft., and its height is 155 ft., about one-third of the elevation intended; but Mintayagyi, the crack-brained monarch who founded it, ran short of funds, and the building was stopped. In 1839 an earthquake rent the gigantic cube, the largest mass of brickwork in the world, with fantastic fissures from top to bottom, and cast down great masses of masonry, tons in weight. Overlooking the river, in front of the eastern face of the temple, stood two gigantic leogryphs in brick. These figures were originally 95 ft. high, and each of the white marble eyeballs intended for the monsters measured 13 ft. in circumference. The leogryphs are now in ruins. N. of the temple, on a low circular terrace, stands the biggest bell in Burma—the biggest in the world, probably, after the one at Moscow. It is slung on a triple beam of great size, resting on two tiers of brickwork, enclosing massive frames of teak. The supports were so much shaken by the earthquake that it was found necessary to put props under the bell; in consequence it no longer swings free, and of course, no tone can now be got out of it. The diameter of the bell at the lip is 18 ft., and its height to the top of the shackle 31 ft. Its weight is about 80 tons. There are other curious pagodas in the neigbourhood.

The new railway line from Mandalay

[1] Mr Bird's book contains many details of these.

to Lashio (180 m.) makes it possible to visit **Maymyo** and the **Gokteik Viaduct.** The former (42 m. D.B.), which is 3300 ft. above the sea, is the hill station of Burma. It lies in a trough between low wooded hills, pretty, but without wide views. There is a large English society, many excellent houses and gardens, a good club with polo-ground, a golf course, excellent rides in the jungle; and there is a pack of hounds. The hot weather temperature is fully 20° below that at Mandalay. At Gokteik (23 m.) is a wonderful steel trestle bridge, 320 ft. high and 2260 ft. long, built on a natural bridge of rock 500 ft. high with a great cavern under it. The bridge was prepared in America and was put up on the spot by American workmen. There is a Rest-House belonging to the railway near the station with beautiful views, and the manager of the refreshment room at Maymyo Railway Station arranges, at a day's notice, to send up provisions and a cook. The scenery on the way and at Gokteik is fine. It is worth while descending the 900 ft. by a good path to the cavern through which the river flows under the two bridges.

The traveller who has time to proceed farther N. may either take one of the Irrawaddy Flotilla steamers which leave Mandalay every Monday and Thursday for *Bhamo*, or he may take the train. In the latter case he will be able to reach **Myitkyina**, 724 m. from Rangoon, passing through Sagaing (393 m.), Shwebo (446 m.), Naba Junction (592 m.), for Katha (14 m.), and Mogaung (688 m.), the probable point of junction of the railway from Assam to Burma. The steamer route to Bhamo and back (2½ days up and 1½ days down) is recommended. The steamers are well fitted, and the scenery is fine. Passing Sheinmaga on the right, and Singu and Kyaukmyaung on the left, the steamer passes through the third defile to Thabeikkyin and Kyanhnyat. Tigyaing on the left bank is prettily situated on a hill. Katha is next passed on the left. It is the head-quarters of the district of that name, and a daily steamer to and from Bhamo (70 m.) may be joined or left there by the railway. The pagodas of Shwegu next come into sight on the right, and on Royal Island in the river, and the steamer then passes through the second defile to Bhamo.

The **defiles** of the river, as Bhamo is approached, are very fine. The wide stream narrows to 1000 yds. and flows for 30 m. through a chain of hills covered with splendid foliage. The successive reaches of the river resemble lakes, being apparently shut in all round. Beyond the first hills is a plain, and then another defile through a second chain of hills, which is even finer than the last. The river narrows to 200 or 300 yds. and rushes through the gap with great velocity. This defile extends for 5 m., and in one place a rock rises straight out of the water to a height of 600 ft.

There is not much to be seen at **BHAMO** (population 11,000 and some 3,000 Chinese), but the place is of interest as being the highest station on the Irrawaddy held by British troops, and the nearest point on the Irrawaddy to the Chinese frontier. The Theindawgyi Pagoda resembles those of Siam in shape, and a fine Chinese Joss-House will be interesting to those who have not seen the farther East. Several trade routes from Yunnan converge on Bhamo, and the importance of the place may be expected to increase. At present the value of that trade, of which the major portion passes through Bhamo, varies from Rs.60-80 lakhs per annum. The Bhamo district is chiefly inhabited by Kachins, wild hill-men, who, in Burmese times, were practically independent, and were a constant source of terror to the caravans passing between Bhamo and China. The Kachins are now being reduced to order, and the trade routes are at present comparatively safe.

At certain seasons the Irrawaddy Flotilla Company run a small steamer from Bhamo to **Myitkyina.** By taking this steamer, the first defile, which is perhaps the finest of the three, can be seen. W. of Myitkyina are the jade and amber mines, but these are not at present accessible to travellers. It is intended to construct a railway 124 m. long from Bhamo to Tengyüeh or Moumein.

In order to visit the **Ruby Mines** it will be necessary to break the journey between Mandalay and Bhamo at Thabeikkyin. A good road connects Thabeikkyin with Mogok (50 m.), and the journey is worth undertaking. There is a daily motor service now running through in 6 hrs. The road passes through fine mountain scenery, and the traveller cannot fail to be interested in observing the primitive methods of mining followed by the Burmese, as well as the more civilised operations of the English Company. The mines are all situated in the Mogok valley, which is 2 m. long and 1 m. broad. The system is one of open workings from which the ruby earth (byon) is hauled up to the washers—some fifty Europeans and Anglo-Indians, and a large number of Burmese and Shans are employed on the works. The mines are lighted and the machinery is worked by electricity. By a recent arrangement with the Indian Government, the Ruby Mines Company has secured a lease for twenty-eight years on payment of a minimum rent of Rs.200,000, and a royalty of 30 per cent. of the net profits. The annual out-turn of rubies varies from 266,000 to 325,000 carats.

Having returned to Mandalay, the traveller should proceed by Flotilla steamer to *Prome* (Express steamer twice a week—three days), stopping *en route* at Nyaungu for *Pagan*, and at Yenangyaung for a visit to the *oil-wells*. After passing Sagaing, the headquarters of the Sagaing division, the steamer calls at **Myingyan** and **Pakokku**, both large towns and headquarters of British districts. The latter is the base for the Chin Hills (see Route 5), and is a thriving and rapidly-growing city.

Nyaungu is situated about 120 m. below Mandalay, on the eastern bank of the river, and is interesting both as being the principal place for the manufacture of the celebrated Burmese lacquer work,[1] and as being the nearest halting-place to old Pagan, the capital of Burma from the 9th to the 13th century. There is a Government Rest-House at Nyaungu, permission to occupy which should be obtained from the Deputy-Commissioner of Myingyan, and the traveller, who wishes to make anything like a detailed examination of the extensive and very interesting remains in the immediate neighbourhood, should arrange to remain at least two days there. A pretty full description of the pagodas at Pagan will be found in Yule's *Embassy to Ava*, in Bird's *Wanderings in Burma*, and in Scott O'Connor's *Mandalay and other Cities of Burma*. A very brief account (taken chiefly from Yule) of some of the principal monuments is all that can be given here.

The **PAGAN** ruins[2] extend over a space about 8 m. in length along the river, and averaging about 2 m. in breadth. The brick rampart and fragments of an ancient gateway, showing almost obliterated traces of a highly architectural character, are the only remains which are not of a religious description. The total number of temples was roughly estimated by Yule at from 800 to 1000. All kinds and forms are to be found among them; the bell-shaped pyramid of brickwork in all its varieties; the same raised over a square or octagonal cell containing an image of Buddha; the bluff knob-like dome of the Ceylon dagobas; the fantastic *Bopaya*, or Pumpkin pagoda,

[1] A full description of the process of manufacture will be found in chapter xxvii. of *The Burman*, by Shway Yoe.

[2] A museum of remains discovered at Pagan has recently been established there.

and many variations on these types. But the predominant form is that of the cruciform, vaulted temple. Three of the great temples, and a few of the smaller ones, have been repaired, and are still more or less frequented by worshippers; but by far the greater number have been abandoned to the owls and bats, and some have been desecrated into cow-houses by the villagers. The three principal temples are the Ananda, the Thapinyu, and the Gaudapalin, all close together near the S. side of the city and nearly 5 m. distant from Nyaungu. The **Ananda**, as will be seen from the annexed plan, is a square of nearly 200 ft. on each side, with projecting portions on each face, so that it measures 280 ft. across each way. It is seven storeys in height; six of these are square and flat, each diminishing in extent, so as to give the whole a pyramidal form; the seventh, which is, or simulates, the cell of the temple, takes the form of a Hindu or Jain temple, the whole in this instance rising to the height of 183 ft. Internally the building is extremely solid, being intersected only by two narrow concentric corridors; but in rear of each projecting transept is a niche, artificially lighted from above, in which stands a statue of Buddha, more than 30 ft. in height. These four great statues represent the four Buddhas who have appeared in the present world period, viz.—E., Kankathan; W., Kathaba; N., Gautama; and S., Ganugun. They are all richly gilt. The Ananda was built in the 11th century, in the reign of Kyanyittha. The name is derived from *Ananda*, the favourite pupil of Buddha. (See Fergusson's *Eastern Architecture*, ii. 360.)

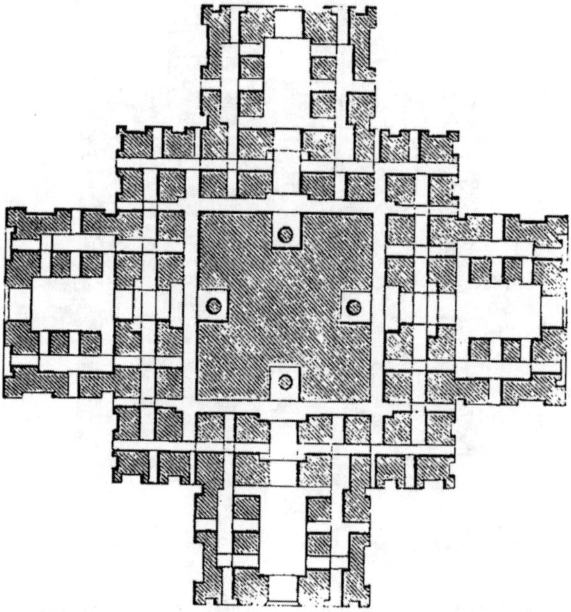

Plan of the Ananda Temple (from Yule). Scale 100 ft. to 1 in.

Next in importance is the **Thapinyu** (the Omniscient), erected about the year 1100 by the grandson of Kyanyittha, and third is the **Gaudapalin** (Mound of the Dragon), built in

1200. These two temples are of very similar form, but the Thapinyu is considerably larger. The height of the Thapinyu is 201 ft., that of the Gaudapalin 180 ft. They differ from the Ananda in having each only one porch instead of four, and consequently only one great statue in its cell instead of four standing back to back. A plan of the Thapinyu is given below.

mentioned the ***Dhamayangyi*** and the ***Sinbyoku***. The former resembles the Ananda. The latter is in its details perhaps the most beautiful of all. The *Seinnyet* with cells at the corners of its terraces, the *Sapada* with circular terraces, and the *Bidayat Library* are also noticeable. Recent excavations round the *Pet leak paya* have brought to light a series of Buddhist terra-cotta reliefs.

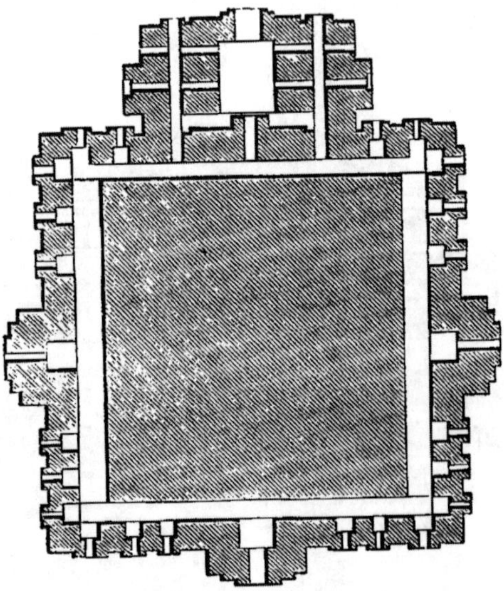

Plan of Thapinyu (from Yule). Scale 100 ft. to 1 in.

One other important temple within the city walls has been kept in repair. It is known as the *Maha Bodhi*, and was erected about 1200 by King Nandaungmya. It is different in style from the other temples. The basement is a quadrangular block of no great height, supporting a tall spire, strongly resembling the original temple of Buddh Gaya (p. 37). Both base and spire are covered with niches, bearing seated Gautamas and interspersed with ornamental panels and mouldings.

Among other temples may be There is a local museum of these and other remains. Between Pagan and Nyaungu on the road which follows the river is the fine Shwe-zi-gon Pagoda, near which the principal workers in lacquer reside: the surroundings are extremely picturesque. 1½ m. N. of Nyaungu is the **Kyaukku** temple. This is built in three terraces; the hall in the centre of it contains a huge statue of Buddha, which, like the decoration of the temple, is of Indian type. The gorge in which it stands contains a number of small caves. Pagan ceased to be a capital in 1284 A.D. The Emperor of China had sent a vast army to avenge the murder of an ambassador. The Burmese king pulled down 1000 arched temples, 1000 smaller ones, and 4000 square temples, to strengthen the fortifications. But a prophecy found under one of the desecrated shrines robbed him of his courage and he fled to the S., and ever since Pagan has remained in its present practically deserted state.

The Irrawaddy just below Pagan widens out like a gigantic lake to over 2 m. in breadth, and the view of the sacred city obtained from the steamer is particularly fine.

Continuing his course down stream past Salemyo, the traveller will shortly reach **Yenangyaung**, on the E. bank, and, here again, if time allows, and the necessary arrangements have been made, a halt is desirable. The oil wells are situated about 3 m. from the river bank, and well deserve a visit. A number of wells are being successfully worked by steam power on the American system by the Burma Oil Company, while, in the neighbourhood, the Burmese continue to extract oil in smaller quantities by primitive methods. The output of oil is over 230,000,000 gallons, and the duty royalty payable over 135 lakhs. Dr Noetling's exhaustive report on the oil wells of Yenangyaung (Government Press, Rangoon) contains full details.

The principal places of call below Yenangyaung are **Magwe** and **Minbu**, both headquarters of British districts; and the former headquarters of the division of that name. *Minhla*, where there is an old Burmese fort, which was the scene of a brief fight in the last Burmese war, and **Thayetmyo**, a military station, was formerly of some importance as the frontier station of British Burma. At Thayetmyo and thence to Prome the river scenery is pleasing. At Prome, unless he prefers to complete the journey to Rangoon by river, which he can do in three days, the traveller will leave his steamer, and return to Rangoon by train (9 hours).

PROME, now a town of about 27,000 inhabitants, and the headquarters of the district of that name, is a very ancient city, and is mentioned as the capital of a great kingdom before the Christian era. The town extends N. from the foot of the Prome hills to the bank of the Nawin, with a suburb on the other side of that stream, and E. for some distance up the Nawin valley. On the bank of the river, on the high ground, opposite the centre of the town, are the Government Offices, the Public Gardens, the Anglican Church, and the Jubilee Clock Tower. The Strand Road extends from one end of the town to the other, and from it well-laid-out streets run E., and are intersected at right-angles by others. N. of the high laterite ground, on which are the Law Courts, and under the high bank, a sand-bank stretches up to the mouth of the Nawin, under water in the rains, but covered with brokers' huts in the dry weather, when a fleet of merchant boats is moored along it, of which many are laden with Ngapi, or fish paste, the odour of which pervades the whole Nawin quarter. Here, on the high bank, a little inland, and on the inner side of the Strand, are the Markets.

The **Shwesandaw Pagoda** is on a hill ½ m. from the left bank of the Irrawaddy, and covers an area of 11,925 sq. ft., rising from a nearly square platform to a height of 180 ft. It is surrounded by 83 small gilded temples. These unite at their bases, and form a wall round the pagoda, leaving a narrow passage between it and them. There are four approaches to the platform on which the pagoda stands. The N. and W. are covered in with ornamented roofs, supported on massive teak posts, some partly gilded and partly painted vermilion. The platform on the top of the hill is paved with stone slabs, and round its outer edge are carved wooden houses, facing inwards, interspersed with small pagodas, in which are figures of Gautama, standing, sitting, or lying. Between these and the main pagoda are many Tagundaing posts with streamers, and many large bells. The pagoda has two gigantic lions of the usual conventional form at the N. entrance. In 1753 A.D. this pagoda was re-gilt by Alompra; in 1841, King Tharrawaddy had it repaired and re-gilt, and surmounted with a new Ti, or crown of iron, gilt and studded with jewels; in 1842 the carved roofs over the N. and W. approaches were put up by the Governor. In 1858 the pagoda was again put in repair at a cost of Rs.76,800, raised by public subscription, and subsequently it was re-gilt at a cost of Rs.25,000. The annual festival, when the pagoda is visited by thousands of pious Buddhists, is held in March.

The **Shwenattaung Pagoda.**—This pagoda, 16 m. S. of Prome, richly gilt, and glittering in the sun, stands out conspicuously on the first hill of a low range, overhanging the Shwenattaung plain, and has, in a line behind it, several other pagodas, all of which may be visited by the traveller, if not already tired with buildings of the kind. The Shwenattaung is said to have been built during the reign of the founder of Prome by his Queen. It was repaired and raised by Thihathu, King of Prome, and again in the 16th century by Tabinshweti, King of Toungoo, who had conquered Prome.

Prome is celebrated for its gold lacquer work, small specimens of which may be purchased for a few rupees.

The mail train leaves Prome at 9.30 o'clock at night, and reaches Rangoon (161 m.) at about 6 o'clock on the following morning.

From Letpadan (84 m.) a branch runs (132 m.) to Henzada ferry, and (82 m.) to Bassein (Route 4); 9 m. S. of Letpadan, on the main line, is **Tharawaddy,** headquarters of the district of that name, and noted for its wood-carving.

ROUTE 2.

From RANGOON to MOULMEIN, with possible extension to Tavoy and Mergui.

MOULMEIN, ✱ the third largest city of Burma, is one of the prettiest spots in the Province, and deserves a visit. It is reached by the new railway line branching off at Pegu in 8 hrs., or in about 10 hrs. from Rangoon, by the steamers of the B.I.S.N. Co. It is the headquarters of the Amherst district, and of the Tenasserim division. It is situated on the left bank of the Salween, at its junction with the Gyaing and the Ataran. Immediately to the W. is Bilugyun, an island 107 sq. m. in extent. To the N., on the opposite bank of the Salween, is Martaban, once the capital of a kingdom, but now a moderate-sized village. Low hills, forming the N. end of the Taungmyo range, run N. and S. through Moulmein, dividing it into two distinct portions, which touch each other at the N. base of the hills on the bank of the Gyaing. These are crowned at intervals with pagodas in various stages of preservation, from the dark brick grass-covered and decaying relic with its rusty and falling *ti*, to the white and gold restored edifice gleaming in the sunlight, and with monasteries richly ornamented with gilding, colour, and carved work.

On the W. are four out of the five divisions of the town, which extends N. between the Salween and the hills from Mopun, with its steam mills for husking rice, and timber and ship-building yards, to the military cantonment on the point formed by the junction of the Gyaing and the Salween opposite Martaban, a distance of 6 m. The breadth nowhere exceeds 1200 yds. The view from the hills in the centre of the town is of great beauty, probably unsurpassed in all Burma. W. the foreground is occupied by trees of every shade of foliage, from the dark olive of the mango to the light green of the pagoda tree, varied by the, graceful plumes of the bamboo with buildings showing here and there, and the magnificent sheet of water beyond, studded with green islands, among which stands out conspicuously the little rocky Gaungsekwin completely occupied by white and glittering pagodas, and a monastery sheltered by trees, and in the distance are the forest-clad hills of Bilugyun and Martaban. E. at the foot of the hills is a large and regularly laid out town, on the edge of a rice plain, from which, beyond the Attaran, rise isolated, fantastically shaped ridges of limestone, in part bare, and elsewhere with jagged peaks, partially concealed by straggling clumps of vegetation, and in the extreme distance a faint blue outline of the frowning Dawna hills. To the N. are the Zwekabin rocks of limestone, 13 m. long, while to the S. rise the dark Taungwaing hills, their sombre colour relieved by a glistening white pagoda and monasteries on their side; while winding through the plain like silver bands are the Gyaing and Attaran.

The population of Moulmein is about 58,000. It formerly rivalled Rangoon in population and trade, but has now fallen far behind. Moulmein is largely dependent on the timber trade, and obtains its teak mainly from Karenni and Chiengmai. The forests have been overworked, and the supply of timber is falling off. Moulmein is noted for carving on wood, ivory, and cocoa-nut shells. The show-room of the jail is worth a visit. The traveller will no doubt visit some of the pagodas and monasteries which abound here as elsewhere in Burma, and if he visits the **Kyaikthanlan** Pagoda, should notice the big bell with its quaint English inscription, "This bell is made by Koonalenga, the priest, and weight 600 viss. No one body design to destroy this Bell. Moulmein, March 30, 1855. He who destroyed to this Bell, they must be in the great Heell, and unable to coming out." This is probably the only bell in Burma bearing an English inscription. The pagoda is the largest in Moulmein, and is 152 ft. high and 377 ft. in circumference. It is said to have been originally erected about 1000 years ago.

The only other pagoda deserving special mention is the **Uzina**, or south pagoda, in the precincts of which are some remarkably well carved figures of life-size, representing the four objects, the sight of which determined Gautama to become a hermit (p. lxii.), a decrepit old man leaning on a staff, a man suffering from a loathsome disease, a putrid corpse, and a recluse in yellow garments, with features expressive of contentment and absence of worldly care. There are also figures of an old man and woman. The figures are startlingly life-like.

The traveller should not leave Moulmein without paying a visit to some at least of the **Caves** in the neighbourhood. The principal caves are—

1. *The Farm caves*, about 10 m. from Moulmein on the Attaran river.
2. *The Dammathat caves*, 18 m. from Moulmein on the Gyaing river.
3. *The Pagat caves* on the Salween river, 26 m. from Moulmein.
4. *The Kogun caves* on the Kogun creek near Pagat, 28 m. from Moulmein.
5. *The Bingyi caves* on the Dondami, 51 m. from Moulmein.

All of these, except the last named, are within an easy day's journey of Moulmein, there and back by steam launch; but none of them are much visited except the Farm caves, of which an account, condensed from an article by Major (now Sir R.) Temple in the *Indian Antiquary* for December 1893 is given below. For a description of the remaining caves, reference should be made to the above article.

The best way of visiting the Farm

caves is to take a hackney carriage to the Nyaungbinzeik ferry on the Attaran river, about 4 m., then to cross the ferry, and thence proceed the remaining 4 m. by bullock-cart. The caves are a favourite resort for picnic parties, both of the European and of the native population, and there is no difficulty about the journey. The Burmese name is *Kayun*. The caves are situated in isolated hills of limestone, which rise picturesquely and abruptly out of the surrounding alluvial plain. They were evidently excavated by the sea, and are full of stalactites and stalagmites. The principal cave consists of an entrance-hall running parallel with the face of the rock, a long hall running into the rock at the S. end, and a subsidiary entrance and hall at the N. end. Along these halls run brick and plaster platforms erected for images of Gautama and his worshippers. Near the S. entrance, and in the entrance-hall, are small pagodas, and near the N. entrance is a *ti* of interesting construction. The whole of the caves were clearly at one time crammed with images of all sizes, materials, and ages, as are to-day some of the caves further from Moulmein. Many of these have been destroyed. There remain, however, several huge recumbent figures of Gautama, one measuring 45 ft. in length, and others not much less, sitting figures of various sizes, and small figures, mostly mutilated. Some of the stalactites have been ornamented, and all over the sides of the cave and its roof are signs of former ornamentation with small images of plaster, painted white and red, and made of terra-cotta. The best preserved of them are high up on the S. wall at the deep end of the principal hall, where a number of worshippers are represented kneeling opposite one of the huge recumbent Gautamas, and in the roof near the entrance.

From Moulmein the traveller may, if he pleases, extend his journey to *Tavoy* and *Mergui*, to which places the B.I.S.N. Co. run a weekly steamer. Unless, however, he is proceeding to the Straits he will probably find that this journey will occupy more time than he can devote to it. **Tavoy**, the headquarters of the district of that name, is a town of 22,400 inhabitants, on the Tavoy river, about 30 m. from its mouth. The town lies low, and parts of it are flooded at high tide, and swampy during the rains. It is laid out in straight streets, and the houses are, for the most part, built of timber or bamboo. To the E. and W. ranges of hills run nearly due N. and S., and the surrounding land is under rice cultivation. Tavoy contains court-houses, a custom-house, and the usual public offices, besides numerous pagodas and monasteries of no special interest. Its trade is of little importance, and is carried on chiefly with ports in Burma and the Straits Settlements.

The trip from Tavoy to Mergui is interesting, inasmuch as it passes through the **Mergui archipelago**—a large group of islands which, commencing in the N. with Tavoy island, stretches southwards beyond the limits of British territory in Burma. They have been described as "a cluster of islands and islets with bays and coves, headlands and highlands, capes and promontories, high bluffs and low shores, rocks and sands, fountain streams and cascades, mountain, plain, and precipice, unsurpassed for their wild fantastic and picturesque beauty." They are but sparsely inhabited, and are the resort of a peculiar race, the Selungs, who rarely leave them to visit the mainland. The principal products are edible birds' nests and *bêches de mer*. The islands are infested by snakes and wild animals. **Mergui** itself, the chief town of the district of that name, stands on an island in the principal mouth of the Tenasserim river, which falls into the Bay of Bengal about 2 m. N. of the town. It has a population of

10,000, consisting of many races. It promises to acquire additional importance from the recent discovery of valuable pearl-beds in its immediate vicinity. Tin mining is also carried on in the southern part of the district. The traveller who can spare the time should inspect the pearl-diving and the mining operations. The town itself contains little of special interest.

ROUTE 3.

RANGOON TO **KYAUKPYU** and **AKYAB**.

The traveller who desires to see something of the Arakan division, or who is proceeding from Rangoon to Calcutta, and has a week to spare, may proceed by B.I.S.N. Co.'s steamer (weekly) to **Kyaukpyu** and **Akyab**, calling (except in the monsoons) at the mouth of the beautiful Sandoway river.

Kyaukpyu is the headquarters of the district of that name. It was formerly a British cantonment, but the troops have been withdrawn, and it is now a place of little interest or importance. It is situated in the N. of Ramri island, and the town lies close to the seashore, upon a sandy plain, bounded on the S.W. by a low range of sandstone hills, which breaks the severity of the monsoon. The whole tract is lined with mangrove jungles, and the place is very unhealthy. The town contains the usual public buildings, but nothing of special interest.

Akyab is a place of more importance, and is the headquarters of the Arakan division, and the third seaport of Burma. Originally a Magh fishing village, Akyab dates its prosperity from the time when it was chosen as the chief station of the Arakan province at the close of the first Burmese war (1826). It has now a population of 36,000. It contains the usual public buildings and several large rice mills. A pleasant excursion may be made to **Myohaung**, the ancient capital of Arakan, 50 miles up the Kaladan river, where the remains of the old town are still to be seen. For a description of them reference may be made to the reports of the late Dr Forchhammer, which were issued by the Burma Government Press in 1891. The ruins of the ancient Fort, with traces of the massive city wall and the platform on which the old palace stood, and the **Andaw Shitthaung** and **Dukhanthein** pagodas, with their dark passages, images, and inscriptions, and the **Pittekataik** or ancient depository of the Buddhist scriptures, are among the most interesting sights of the place.

The antiquarian will thus find that Myohaung is full of interest, as also, if he has time to visit it, the **Mahamuni Pagoda**, some 48 m. farther N. A trip may also be made by river steamer to **Paletwa**, the headquarters of the Arakan hill tracts district, which is inhabited by Chaungthas, Shandus, Kwemis, Chins Mros, and other strange hill tribes.

ROUTE 4.

From RANGOON to BASSEIN and back.

Bassein can now be reached by railway from Rangoon (see Route 1, end), but the trip can be made with ease and comfort in one of the steamers of the Irrawaddy Flotilla Company, which leave for Bassein three times a week, and may be of interest to those who wish to see something of the lower reaches of the Irrawaddy, and of the mode of life of the thriving people of the delta. It may be extended to **Henzada** (steamer twice a week) and other river stations, according to the time which the traveller has at his disposal. All necessary information about times of starting, places of call, etc., will be readily obtainable at the office of the Irrawaddy Flotilla Company on the Strand Road, Rangoon.

Bassein is a town of about 32,000 inhabitants and the headquarters of the Irrawaddy division. On the left bank of the river on a slight eminence stands the *Shwemakdaw Pagoda*, now in the centre of a fort constructed by the English, within the walls of which are the court houses and a public garden. To the E. is the Myothit quarter, with two principal streets running through it E. and W. about a mile in length, terminating in a plain covered with pagodas, rest-houses, monasteries, and massive images in all stages of decay, where the inhabitants assemble for their religious festivals. Across the river is the Thinbawgyin suburb, containing the rice mills and store yards of the principal merchants. There are two fine markets and a large jail besides the usual public buildings. The *Shwemakdaw* pagoda is said to have been originally erected by Asoka a few years after the death of Gautama ; the other principal pagodas are the *Tagaung* Pagoda, the *Thayaungyaung* Pagoda, and the *Mahabawdi* Pagoda.

ROUTE 5.

Up the CHINDWIN to KINDAT.

This trip will take up a good deal of time, and as it contains little of special interest it is not likely to be undertaken by the ordinary traveller. It may be performed by a weekly Irrawaddy Flotilla steamer from Pakokku, or from Aloon, 73 m. by railway from Sagaing (p. 460). The river scenery is good but not specially remarkable. Kindat is the headquarters of the upper Chindwin district, but is not otherwise a place of any importance.

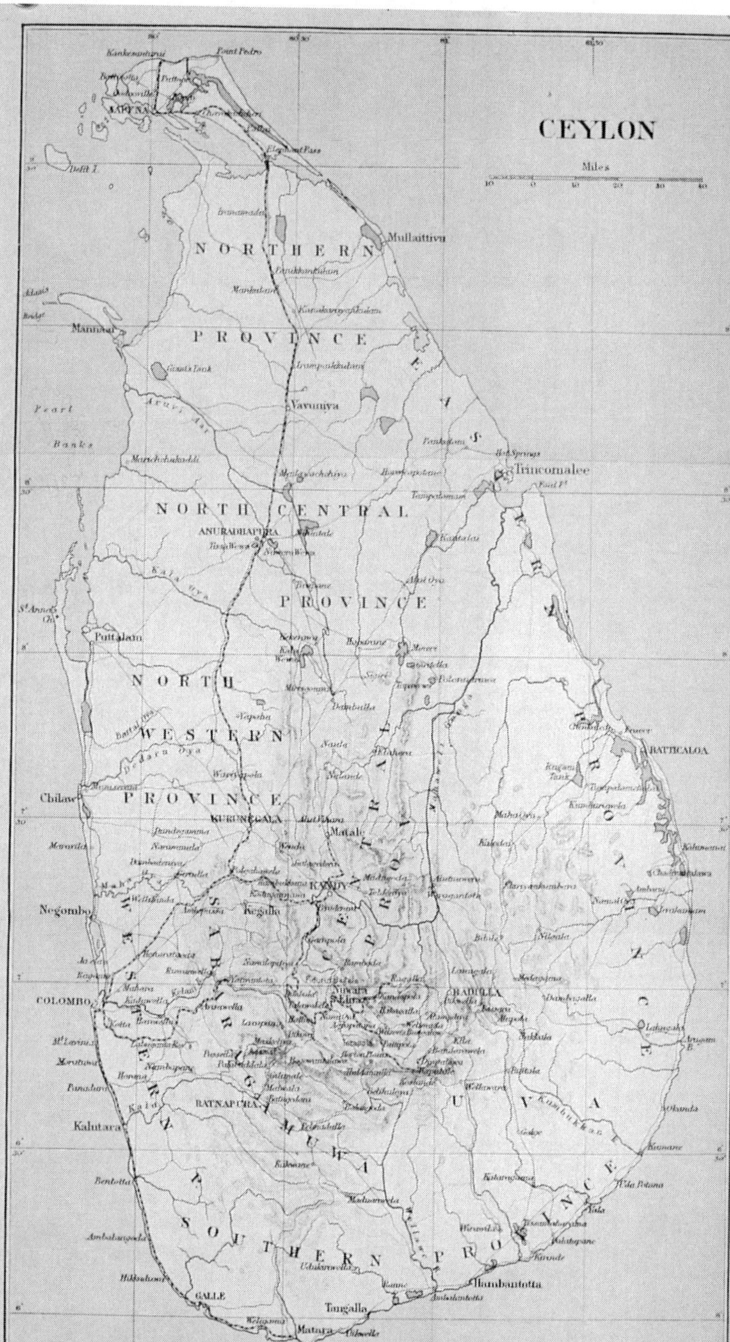

London. John Murray.

CEYLON

"The traveller who can choose his own time for visiting Ceylon and make sure of fine weather in Colombo, as well as for travelling in the interior, should choose February to May inclusive, when Nuwara Eliya also is climatically quite delightful, while often enjoyable in August, September, December, and January."—*Ferguson.*

The area of the Island is 25,481 sq. m., and the total population (including coolies) for 1911, 4,092,000. Details in 1907 were:—6559 Europeans, 24,946 Burghers, 2,565,095 Sinhalese, 1,128,006 Tamils (including coolies), 238,757 Moors, 12,035 Malays, and 12,666 others. The exports from Ceylon have averaged during the last three years:—Tea (black), 180,000,000 lbs.; (green), 5,800,000 lbs.; coffee (Plantation), 1,500 cwts.; (Liberian), 108 cwts.; cardamoms, 7,760 cwts.; cinnamon (quills), 29,111 cwts.; (chips), 28,160 cwts.; plumbago, 594,360 cwts.; cocoa, 78,614 cwts.; coco-nut oil, 576,009 cwts. Total quantity of Ceylon rubber exported in 1910 was 1,492,000 lbs., value 1¼ millions, as compared with 556,000 lbs. in 1907. The value of the exports during 1909 was 13 millions; that of the imports 15 millions. The public debt amounts to £5,200,334; it has been incurred for the construction of harbour works, railways, and irrigation projects. The revenue is, in round figures, 4 millions. The shipping of Colombo amounts to 4,000,000 tons, and the Harbour dues to Rs.1,582,000.

The **Currency** of the Island is rupees, divided, not into annas as in India, but into cents. The sovereign is now legal tender, £1 = Rs.15. The rupee is therefore equal to 1s. 4d., from which rate it varies only fractionally, according to the exchange operations of the Banks.

History.—"Ceylon has been continuously, but not entirely, ruled by European races since 1507, when the Portuguese settled on the west and south coasts. The Dutch dispossessed the Portuguese in 1656, but gave way in turn to the British, who have held the Maritime Provinces since 1796, and the whole Island, including the interior and Kandyan kingdom, which neither the Portuguese nor the Dutch ever occupied, since 1815."—*White.*

Administration.—"Ceylon belongs to the class of what are known as Crown Colonies. . . . It is administered direct from the Crown by the Secretary of State for the Colonies, with whom, at the Colonial Office in Downing Street, the Governor communicates on all matters of State. Locally the executive and administrative power is in the hands of the Governor, who is assisted by an Executive Council of five official members.

"The Executive Council consists of the Lieutenant-Governor and Colonial Secretary, the Officer commanding the troops, the Attorney-General, the Auditor-General, and the Treasurer.

"The Legislative Council consists of the Governor, the above five Executive Councillors, the Government Agents of the Western and Central Provinces, two other official and eight unofficial members appointed by the Governor.

"For purposes of general administration the Island is divided into nine Provinces, presided over by Government Agents."—*White.*

The Governor is appointed for a term of six years, at a salary of Rs.80,000 per annum, with residences in Colombo, Kandy, and Nuwara Eliya. The present Governor is Sir Henry E. McCallum, R.E., G.C.M.G., A.D.C.

Travelling[1] in Ceylon is, for the most part, comparatively easy. The **Railways** are constructed on a broad gauge (5 ft. 6 in.) with exception of the Kelani Valley Railway and the Nuwara Eliya section (2 ft. 6 in. gauge). On the main lines, the chief trains are provided with refreshment cars and good sleeping accommodation (Rs. 2. 50 c. above 1st class fare). The **Roads** are in most places excellent, and the Rest-Houses are far more comfortable places of abode than the corresponding institutions in India. In the larger towns, such as Badulla, Ratnapura, Matara, and at some of the stations on the great north road, they are, in all but name, hotels; but the traveller is not allowed to remain in them more than three days without permission, which, however, is easily procured. On all the principal roads, they are usually provided with bed and table-linen, baths, tea and dinner-services, etc. This is not, however, the case at those on the less-frequented roads, where the Rest-Houses often furnish only shelter. The **Coaches** are not very comfortable or well horsed, but are still in some places the only vehicles available. Seats should be engaged as long beforehand as possible. Carriages for long journeys can be hired in the larger towns. The rate for two horses is generally R. 1 per mile, the hirer paying all tolls. In remote places the **Bullock** cart or the **Hackery** (a light cart with a trotting bull) is the only conveyance possible. **Bicycles** (with *strong* brakes) are most useful. The **Motor-car**, however, is now commonly used and affords the most perfect means of touring the Island. Cost may be calculated roughly at R. 1, 25 c. per mile. Cars may be hired at Colombo or Kandy. Motorists are warned to be careful of the sharp elbows and **S** turns on the roads. The gradients in some places are severe. Messrs H. W. Cave & Co. publish a Motor Map of the island, price Rs. 2. 50. A coasting steamer makes a circuit of the island twice weekly, once north and once south.

[1] *The Pocket Time and Fare Table* (10 c.), published by the Ceylon Government Railway, is a most useful compilation.

Books. — Among the innumerable books written about the Island, Sir J. Emerson Tennent's *Account*, published in 1859, retains its pre-eminence. Other works are Ferguson's *Ceylon in 1903*, H. W. Cave's *Book of Ceylon* (Cassell), *Ruined Cities*, *Golden Tips*, and *Picturesque Ceylon*; John Still's *A Guide to the Ancient Capitals of Ceylon*, price Rs. 2. 50 (Cave); and Burrow's *Buried Cities of Ceylon*, and Farrer's *In Old Ceylon.* White's *Ceylon Manual* contains a wealth of detail concerning the Island, while Ferguson's *Directory* is a mine of information, statistical and otherwise.[1] Skeen's Guides to Colombo and Kandy should be consulted locally. The best books on sport are Sir Samuel Baker's *Rifle and Hound in Ceylon*, and the section, by Hon J. Ferguson, on the subject in the St Louis Exhibition Handbook. Good maps may be procured at the Surveyor-General's Office.

Travellers generally enter Ceylon by the **PORT OF COLOMBO.** ✱ Population, 163,000. Lat. 6.55 N., long. 79.50 E. The flashing light is visible 18 m. at sea. It is situated at the S. end of the harbour, on the top of the *Clock Tower.*

The **Landing-place and Custom House** lie at the S. end of the harbour, which receives the full pro-

[1] Ferguson's *Ceylon Handbook and Directory* contains all the usual detailed information in such works.

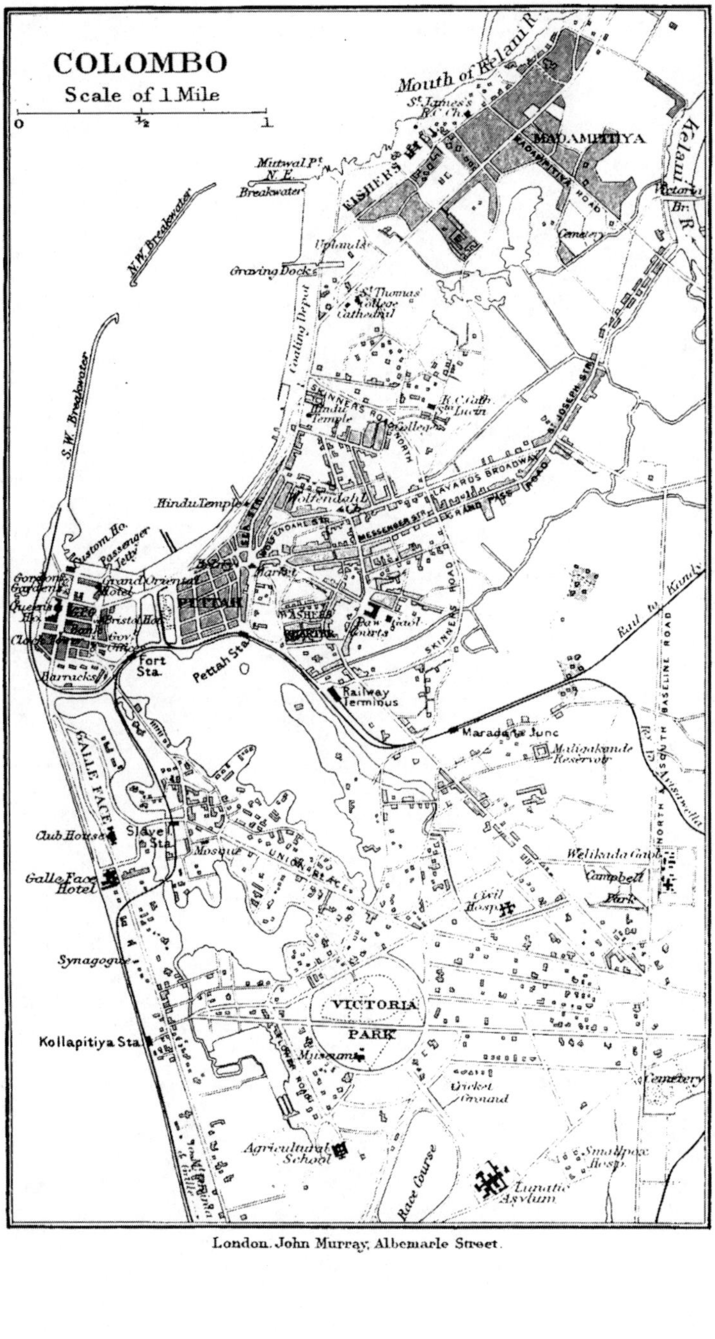

London. John Murray, Albemarle Street.

tection of a magnificent breakwater. This structure, the first stone of which was laid by King Edward on 8th December 1875, was completed in 1885 at a cost of about £700,000. It is 4210 feet long, and is formed of concrete blocks of from 16 to 32 tons each, capped by a solid concrete mass which rises to a height of 12 ft. above low-water level. It terminates in a circular space 62 ft. in diameter, with a second and smaller lighthouse in the centre, showing a red light. The area protected by the breakwater is 500 acres, one-half of which has water more than 25 feet deep. It is now proposed to extend it 2000 ft. further N. so as to protect the entrance between it and the N.W. breakwater. The cost up to date has been $2\frac{3}{4}$ millions. A graving dock capable of taking the largest vessels ever likely to sail the Eastern seas, a slip for the repair of small vessels, and a coaling depôt have been constructed.

The charge for conveying each person between the jetty and any vessel in the harbour, or between vessel and vessel in the harbour, is 25 cents., from 6 A.M. to 7 P.M., and 40 cents. from 7 P.M. to 6 A.M.[1]

Close to the landing-jetty and the Custom House are the Grand Oriental, and the Bristol Hotels (see Index), "Queen's House," the Barracks, and some remains of the old Dutch Fort.

The traveller who intends to stop a day or two may prefer to drive on, a little more than a mile, to the Galle Face Hotel. He will pass by the *Government Offices*, looking out on the *Gordon Gardens*, and proceeding between Queen's House on his right (the Governor's residence, a large but ugly mass of buildings), and the new General Post Office on the left, he will after passing the *Clock Tower* (good view of the city from the top, see p. 475), and the *Barracks*, consisting of several blocks, built *en échelon*, at a great cost to the Colony, find himself on the fine open space called the **Galle Face**, intersected by the direct road to Galle.

1 Licensed money-changers are to be found on the jetty.

Nearly in the centre of the Galle Face Esplanade is a small fort, and a little further to the S. is the *Colombo Club*, a fine oval building looking on the sea. About the middle of the Promenade, near the sea, is a stone like a mile-stone, with an inscription in which Sir Henry Ward, who made it, recommends the walk to the care of his successors for the use of ladies and children.

The city of Colombo extends to the 4th m. on the Galle Road, and has a breadth of $3\frac{1}{2}$ m. from the sea to the E. outskirts.

Drives.—Colombo and its neighbourhood afford scope for a multitude of charming and picturesque drives. Two especially may be mentioned, one of which might be taken in the morning and the other in the evening of the same day. The first is recommended to those who have not yet seen anything of the East, and to whom the native town of Colombo will afford a pleasing introduction to the distinguishing characteristics of Oriental life and scenery; but, excepting the latter part of it, which is pretty, there is little in this drive to interest one already familiar with India.

(1) Commence at the Galle Face Hotel, and take the road along the sea past the Barracks, until the statue of Sir E. Barnes is reached. He was Governor between 1824 and 1831. Then turn to the right into the Pettah, or Native Town, past an old Dutch belfry, beyond which are the *Town Hall* and *Public Market-place.* Here two streets diverge—the one to the left, Sea Street, where dwell the dealers in rice and cotton, and where are two *Hindu temples*, quaint and picturesque, but of no great size or importance; the other, Wolfendahl Street, to the right, conducts to **Wolfendahl Church**, a massive cruciform building on high ground, built

by the Dutch in 1749, on the site of an old Portuguese church called *Aqua de Lupo*, and commanding a fine view of the city and harbour. Here are monuments and hatchments recording the decease of Dutch officials. It is the most interesting as well as the most complete of the few remaining relics of the Dutch occupation. Thence the drive may be continued in a N.E. direction to the R.C. *Cathedral of Santa Lucia*, adjoining which is a college for Roman Catholic boys, and a convent with school and orphanage attached. Then N. and a little W. the Anglican *Cathedral and College of St Thomas* are reached. They stand in a park, given by Dr Chapman, the first Bishop. About 1 m. to the N. is *St James's Roman Catholic Church*. The drive through the suburb of **Mutwal** is extremely picturesque. It is chiefly inhabited by fishers, who are mostly Roman Catholics, as the numerous large and imposing R.C. churches testify. In Mutwal are the new **Graving Dock**, and a reservoir in connection with the town water supply. On reaching the **Kelani River** at the end of the long street of Mutwal, turn to the right, and crossing a tongue of land till the river is again reached, follow its bank to the **Victoria Bridge**, which carries the great road to Kandy, and supersedes a most picturesque **Bridge of Boats**, long one of the most attractive spots in Colombo to an artist. This part of the drive shows to perfection the way in which the tiny houses and small churches are so nestled under the shelter of the trees as to be altogether invisible from above. Turning to the right at the bridge, follow the dusty and ever-crowded "St Joseph" or "Grand Pass" Road till Skinner's Road is reached. Turn left along it under a fine avenue of Madras thorn, till the **Railway Station** at Maradana is reached, and thence follow the side of the fresh-water lake, across which good views may be obtained, till Galle Face is once more reached.

(2) The second drive commences by crossing the bridge from Galle Face, almost immediately behind the hotel, to Slave Island, and then driving along the edge of a beautiful fresh-water lake past the pretty residence of the General commanding the troops in Ceylon, to the **Victoria Park**. The traveller should not omit to notice a picturesque little Buddhist temple on the other side of the lake nearly opposite the General's house. The Park occupies the site of the old **Cinnamon Gardens**, and is well laid out with ornamental grounds, in the midst of which a **Museum** was built in 1877. It is exclusively devoted to the exhibition of Ceylon products, antiquities, and natural history, and is on that account of the very greatest interest to the visitor. The famous tortoise, said to have been over two hundred years old at his death, is preserved here. On the basement are some interesting stone fragments, and particularly a colossal lion, brought from Polonnaruwa, on which the King sat to administer justice, one of the unique windows from the ruins of Yapahu (p. 492), the cast of a colossal portrait statue of King Prakrama Bahu, A.D. 1153, and some fine bronze statues from Anuradhapura. The copies of the frescoes at Sigiri (p. 493) on the walls of the staircase should be noticed. The entrance-hall is handsome, and to the right of it is a library, to which the public have access from 6.30 to 10 A.M., and from 3 to 5 P.M. In front of the Museum is a statue of the Rt. Hon. Sir W. Gregory, Governor from 1872 to 1877.

(3) A tram car (1st class seats in front) may be taken at the Bristol Hotel to **Borella** and back. The interest of this drive is the bright picture it gives of the life of the people, the town, and its characteristic features.

(4) If time and opportunity permit, the traveller should mount to the summit of the **Great Reservoir** at Maligakande, part of the fine engineering work which furnishes Colombo with an abundant supply of good water carried in pipes from Labugama, about 25 m. distant. (See

p. 484.) A city of over 150,000 people lies at the spectator's feet, but, except for a few towers and domes, it is invisible, the whole being concealed by the mass of vegetation which overshadows it. Another good view of Colombo is to be had from the Clock Tower. The attendant expects a small fee (see p. 473).

Excursions.—One of the pleasantest in the neighbourhood of Colombo is that to a Buddhist temple at the village of **Kelani**, 2 m. up the river of the same name. Pass through the hot and dusty **Pettah**, or native town, for about 4 m., as far as the river, which is crossed by the massive iron **Victoria Bridge** (see above). After crossing the bridge the road passes through cocoa-nut groves and among the houses of the dense population for another 2 m., when the temple itself is reached. The *Mahawanso* refers to it as contemporary with Buddha. The original dagaba was built at a very early period, but the one that is now standing was constructed between the years 1240-67 A.D., and re-built about 1301 A.D. It stands on the river-bank, and is handsomely, though gaudily, decorated. According to the *Colombo Guide*, it stands on the site of a shrine erected by Prince Yatalatissa, 306 B.C. A great festival takes place here at the full moon of May, and lasts four days.

None of the exclusiveness which distinguishes Hindu and Mohammedan shrines is to be found in the Buddhist temples, to every part of which a stranger is freely welcomed by the yellow-robed monks. This, however, does not apply to the dewalas, which are, strictly speaking, Hindu shrines.

The **Kelani Valley Railway**, opened in 1902, was the first line constructed on a narrow gauge in Ceylon.

A favourite excursion by train is to **Mount Lavinia**, 7 m. from Colombo. (See p. 487.)

Trips to **Kaduwella** (see p. 484) and to **Kotta**, where there is a College of the Church Missionary Society, prettily situated, may also be taken.

Also 23 m. N. to **Negombo**, going by steamer along the canal and returning by coach. (See Rte. 6.)

Excursions round the Island may be made by the boats of the Ceylon S.S. Co., which sail alternate Wednesdays S., and alternate Fridays N., and make the circuit in about 8 days.

ROUTE 1.

COLOMBO TO KANDY.

(By rail 75 m.) Opened 1867.

The line on leaving Colombo passes first through portions of the Cinnamon Gardens, and then crosses the river Kelani by a very fine girder bridge. To those who have never before visited the tropics this journey will be full of interest. They will see for the first time vast stretches of paddy land of the most vivid green, the unfamiliar but soon recognised forms of the cashew, the bread-fruit, the jack, the frangipani, and the various forms of palm—cocoa-nut, areca, kitool, and above all the talipot, a specimen of the gigantic white flower of which is generally visible at some point on the journey.

From ½ m. **Maradana Junction** a branch line runs to Avisawella and Yatiyantota (p. 484).

At 9 m. **Ragama** Station. Here the Boer mercenaries taken prisoner during the war were interned. The buildings are now used as a Camp for the Cooly Immigrants. A branch line is in construction from Ragama to Negombo (see p. 490).

At 10½ m. **Mahara** there is a Convict establishment. The Convicts quarry the stone for the breakwater. The stone is conveyed in vast quantities by rail direct from the quarry to the Harbour.

16 m. **Henaratgoda** station. ¾ m. from this station are the Government Tropical Gardens, planted for experiments in trees and plants which could not be expected to thrive in the higher elevation of Kandy. Amongst the species that may be studied in them are many varieties of the tropical caoutchouc, or rubber-giving trees, and plants from West Africa, South America, and Panama, gutta-percha trees from the Malay Peninsula, Trinidad cacao, and Liberian coffee. From this place onward for some 15 m. the country is covered with cocoa-nut trees to an extent not to be seen in many other localities.

34 m. **Ambepussa** station (R. H.). The line here enters the lower hills, and is considered to pass through some of the most unhealthy country in the island. The mortality was terrible when the original cart-road was made from Colombo to Kandy; but in constructing the railway this was to some degree avoided by taking the labourers back to Colombo every night.

45 m. **Polgahawela Junction** station, 244 ft. above sea-level. This is the junction for the direct line to **Kurunegala**, **Anuradhapura**, **Jaffna**, and **Kankesanturai** (257 m. from Colombo) in the extreme north of the Island (Rte. 7).

Ultimately, it is hoped to link Ceylon with India across the Island of Ramesvaram (p. 433).

[Coach to Kegalla 8 m.

8 m. S. of Polgahawela is **Kegalla** (R.H.✱), a small town in a most lovely situation, and encompassed by the most delightful scenery. It is the headquarters of the Assistant Government Agent of the Sabaragamuwa Province.]

52 m. **Rambukkana** station (R. H.). Here the ascent of the "Incline" commences at an elevation of 313 ft., and continues 12 m. with a gradient of 1 in 45 to an elevation of 1698 ft. The vegetation is here of great richness and beauty.

65 m. **Kadugannawa** station is at the top of the pass. On the way up three telegraph stations are passed, and the beautiful scenery and increasing coolness of the air make the journey most enjoyable. Two new tunnels (one of them a very long one) have been constructed to secure immunity from rock falls, which, during the monsoons have hitherto interrupted through-communication for prolonged periods. Near the top of the incline, the road made by Sir Edward Barnes is seen on the right, winding up the hill. The two roads reach the summit of the pass at the same spot, and there a column (a model of the Duke of York's column in London) has been erected to the memory of Captain Dawson, the engineer of the first road. Just over the station is the Hill of Belungala (the Watcher's Rock), 2543 ft. above sea-level, from which, in the troubled days of old, a watch was kept to report an enemy advancing from the plains.

71 m. **Peradeniya Junction** station. This place is 136 ft. lower than the top of the pass. The main line continues S., whilst the branch line to Kandy and Matale strikes N. Half a mile from the Junction is New Peradeniya Station, where, if the visitor is pressed for time, he should arrange to have a carriage waiting for him, drive round the Gardens and on to Kandy. The beautiful **Satinwood Bridge** at Peradeniya, which spanned the *Mahaweli-ganga* by a single bold and graceful arch (a model is in the South Kensington Museum), has been replaced by an iron structure of three spans. At this place a loop of the river nearly surrounds the beautiful **Royal Botanic Gardens**, (less than 4 m. from Kandy by road, through a suburb in which every house is surrounded by a garden of cocoa-nut palms, bread-fruit and cacao trees and coffee-bushes, and bright tropical shrubs). Near the entrance to the Gardens on the left is a grove of Assam rubber-trees (*Ficus elastica*), whose enormous roots sprawl over the ground like some antediluvian reptile.

The trees are suffering from senile decay, being over seventy years of age. On entering the Gardens is seen a group of palms unsurpassed in beauty and grandeur. Further on amongst the exotic species of palms is a "Double Coconut Palm," the wonderful Coco-de-Mer of the Seychelles (*Lodoicea Sechellarum*), "the large and singular fruits of which were found for a century, washed up on the shores of the Indian Ocean, before the palm itself was discovered. This specimen being a male, produces no fruit; it is now fifty-five years old, and has flowered freely for the past fifteen years. The 'Double Coconut' is noted for its slow rate of growth, producing but one leaf a year; the nut takes ten years to ripen."[1] Formerly, medicinal virtues were ascribed to it, and the Emperor Rudolph II. offered 4000 florins for a single specimen. The Gardens cover nearly 150 acres, and overlook the noble river the Mahaweli-ganga that bounds them on three sides. An extensive tract of land on the opposite side of the river has recently been added for the experimental cultivation of tropical products. There is a monument in the grounds to Dr Gardner, and another to Dr Thwaites, two able Directors of the institution. It is not possible to describe even a tenth of the sights of these singularly beautiful Gardens, whether in respect of flower, fruit, or foliage. Year by year they increase in interest and attractiveness, owing to the unremitting care lavished upon them by the devoted and highly-trained staff.—"The vegetation is purely tropical, being characterised by an abundance of climbing plants or lianas, palms, bamboos, pandanus or screw-pines, epiphytes (orchids, ferns, etc.), and lofty trees, the latter often having buttressed roots. The leaves are generally large, thick, and leathery; the flowers usually brilliant, and considerable in size; and the fruits often of immense proportions, and borne on the trunks of trees or older branches. Other striking tropical features are the great variety of bird, insect, and reptile life."[1]

"All the main roads are open to carriages, ... and visitors are usually content, through want of time or other causes, with what they can see from their carriages. But it should be remembered that, really to see the Garden, and properly appreciate its beauty and treasures, it should be explored on foot."[1]

A visit should be paid to the Pará Rubber Trees, which show the most up-to-date methods of extracting the latex. A very successful Rubber Exhibition took place in the Gardens in September 1906, the first of its kind. The new rubber industry is one in which much capital is invested, and of which large hopes are entertained. The amount of rubber exported in 1908 was 912,125 lbs. value Rs. 2,864,072.50.

At the gates of the Gardens, and 10 minutes' walk from New Peradeniya Station, is a comfortable R.H.

A tea-estate and factory opposite the railway station may be visited by arrangement.

75 m. **KANDY** station.* (Junction for Matale, p. 492.) The capital of the former kingdom of Kandy, 1680 ft. above sea-level; population, 26,000.

History.—The first mention of Kandy as a city is at the beginning of the 14th century, when a temple was built there to contain Buddha's tooth and other relics. From possessing these, it became an important seat of the Buddhist hierarchy, and eventually the residence of branches of the royal family; but it was not till the close of the 16th century that it was adopted as the capital of the island, after the destruction of Kotta, and the defeat of Raja Singha II. by Wimala Dharma in

[1] These paragraphs are quoted from the *Official Guide*, by H. F. MacMillan, F.L.S., F.R.H.S.—a useful and well illustrated booklet, furnished with a map Price Rs. 2. The visitor should provide himself with a copy *before* visiting the Gardens.

1592. During the wars with the Portuguese and Dutch, Kandy was so often burned that scarcely any of the ancient buildings except the temples and the royal residence were remaining when the English took it in 1815. The *Palace*, a wing of which is still occupied by the Government Agent of the Province, was built by Wimala Dharma about 1600 A.D., and the Portuguese prisoners were employed in erecting it. This gave a European character to the architecture of some portions, such as the octagon tower adjoining the Maligawa Temple. That temple, in which the sacred tooth is deposited, well deserves a visit.

Description. — Kandy is picturesquely situated on the banks of a small artificial lake, overhung on all sides by hills. A road called Lady Horton's Walk winds round one of those hills, and on the E. side, which is almost precipitous, looks down on the valley of Dumbera, through which the Mahaweli-ganga rolls over a channel of rocks, "presenting a scene that in majestic beauty can scarcely be surpassed. In a park at the foot of this acclivity is The Pavilion of the Governor. Serpents are numerous here, especially the cobra and carawilla. The large black scorpion, as big as a crayfish, is also found here.

The **Maligawa Temple** or "Temple of the Tooth," though not grand or imposing, is one of the most picturesque buildings in Ceylon. It stands with its back against a wooded hill; at its feet lies the long moat or tank, alive with tortoises, and crossed by a small bridge, flanked by two carved stone elephants. Above an enclosing battlemented wall looks over a flat expanse of the greenest grass dotted over with trees.

In the centre of the courtyard, and occupying the greater part of it, is the sacred building. On a lotus flower of pure gold, hidden under seven concentric bell-shaped metal shrines, increasing in richness as they diminish in size and containing jewels of much beauty, now reposes the sacred relic.

The "sacred tooth," was brought to Ceylon some time before Fa Hian's arrival in 411 A.D., in charge of a princess of Kalinga, who concealed it in the folds of her hair. It was taken by the Malabars about 1315 A.D., and again carried to India, but was recovered by Prakrama Bahu III. It was then hidden, but in 1560 was discovered by the Portuguese, taken to Goa by Don Constantine de Braganza, and burned by the archbishop in the presence of the Viceroy and his court. Vikrama Bahu manufactured a new tooth, which is a piece of discoloured ivory 2 in. long and less than 1 in. in diameter, resembling the tooth of a crocodile rather than that of a man. There are many other jewels and ornaments of interest in the shrine, the brazen doors of which merit observation. The eaves of the projecting roof, the massive supporting pillars, corbels, and ceilings are profusely decorated in bright colours with painted figures, grotesque monsters, and floral patterns. The octagon tower contains a fine Oriental library.

The **Kacheri**, the District Court, and the Supreme Court form three sides of a triangle. The Supreme Court is the audience hall of the kings; the carving of the wooden pillars is notable. If the Court is sitting, the English visitor will be struck by the system of interpreting evidence.

Near the Kacheri is the Museum of the Kandyan Art School, where articles in silver and brass are for sale.

No one should leave Kandy without seeing the Peradeniya Gardens (see p. 476).

An interesting excursion may be made to three Buddhist temples situated near each other at a little distance from Kandy—**Gadaladenya**, **Galangolla**, and **Lanka Telika**. Each is curious in a different way. One is a modern temple, very well kept up, and situated most romantically among huge boulders of rock: the second is very ancient, but in the last stage of neglect, decay, and dilapidation; the third, Lanka Telika, is remarkable alike for its situation on the top of a rock and for the character of its architecture, which is very unlike that of any other temple in Ceylon. The best mode of performing this expedition is to drive 5 m. out on the road to Kadugannawa, and thence send the carriage back to a point 9 m. on the road to Gampola, riding across from one of these points to the other by the bridle-path on which the temples are situated.

There are many other pleasant drives and rides to be taken in the neighbourhood of Kandy.

With a motor many delightful and more extensive excursions can be made. The extensive plantations of cacao on the banks of the Mahaweli-ganga, a few miles below Kandy, deserve a visit.

(1) To **Kurunegala**, *viâ* the (16 m.) **Galagedera** (R.H.) **Pass** and **Weuda** (R.H.) (where there is good snipe-shooting in season).

(2) To (15 m.) **Teldeniya** * (R.H.). 6 m. from here is the **Medahamahanuwara Peak**, on which is an old Sinhalese Fort and City of Refuge. The road leads on

(3) To **Madugoda** (R.H.) thence by bridle-path to **Weragantota** (R.H.) in the Central Province. The Mahaweli-ganga is crossed by a ferry to **Alutnuwera** (see p. 482) in the Uva Province. The traveller is now in the Bintenna Country. The straight course due north taken by the river is remarkable.

Burrows' *Visitors' Guide to Kandy and Nuwara Eliya* may be consulted with advantage.

ROUTE 2.

COLOMBO TO **NUWARA ELIYA, BANDARAWELLA, BADULLA, and BATTICALOA.**

(Rail to Nuwara Eliya; carriage to Badulla; or *alternatively* rail to Bandarawella; coach to Badulla and on to Batticaloa —total distance 274 m.)

This route so far as Peradeniya junction is the same as Route 1.

The line then continues to 78 m. **Gampola*** (R.H.). From here a road strikes off to Nuwara Eliya. (See p. 480.)

87 m. **Nawalapitiya**, whence a road leads to (22 m.) Talawakele. (See below.)

From that point the stations are on a constantly rising level to

108 m. **Hatton** station,* 4141 ft. above the sea.

At Hatton roads from Navalapitiya Dickoya (including Maskeliya and Bogowantalawa) and Talawakelle meet.

[The drive to **Talawakele*** (12 m.) (see below) is very pleasant. The traveller gets good views of the very pretty *Devon Falls* and the magnificent *St Clair Falls*. A two-horse carriage may be hired of Pate & Co. Fare, Rs. 12.]

[From Hatton the **ascent of Adam's Peak** (7420 ft.), the most celebrated though not the highest mountain in Ceylon, is most easily made. It is an expedition of much interest and the wonderful shadow cast by the peak at sunrise is a sight which will repay the trouble and fatigue. Camoens refers to the Peak in his *Lusiads*. The manager of the Hatton Hotel makes all arrangements for the visitor. A moonlight night is generally chosen. It is a very beautiful drive of 12 m. to Maskeliya (4200 ft.), and 14 m. to **Laxapana.** * From here it is 8 m. to the top, the first 5 fairly easy going, and the last 3 rough, and possibly likely to be trying to any persons easily made giddy, though the worst places are protected and chains of very old date facilitate the scramble to the actual summit. Stout boots and warm clothing are needed for the trip, and blankets should be taken up from the hotel—also means of making tea on the summit, which is only 150 ft. square, and where a few Buddhist monks live. Under a wooden canopy is the sacred object of the pilgrimage—an impression of the foot of Buddha on the natural rock. It is about 5½ ft. long and 2¾ ft. broad, and varies from 3 ins. to 5 ins. in depth.]

Hatton is also the point from which the great tea districts of **Dikoya** and **Dimbula** may be most conveniently visited. These valleys, formerly celebrated for their production of coffee, are now entirely devoted to tea cultivation. About the year 1870 the coffee plantations were attacked by a new fungus, *Hemileia vastatrix*, which choked the breathing pores of the leaves and gradually exhausted the energies of the plant. It was at first little regarded, but in ten years' time it had well-nigh destroyed the production of coffee, and reduced the planting community to a state of ruin. The revenue of the island fell from over Rs.17,000,000 in 1877 to Rs.12,161,570 in 1882, and large numbers of the wealthiest proprietors lost their estates, or remained on them merely as managers for their creditors. With indomitable energy the planting community set itself to work to remedy the disaster, and by the substitution of tea for coffee, they may be said to have thoroughly succeeded in doing so, though of course not without great individual loss and suffering. In 1875 but 282 lbs. of tea were exported from Ceylon. The export of 1906 amounted to 180,000,000 lbs., while the revenue of the colony now largely exceeds the amount received in 1877.

The valley of **Maskeliya,** a more newly-planted district, is separated by a ridge from that of Dickoya, to which it is parallel. The Dimbula valley is traversed by a road from Nawalapitiya to Nuwara Eliya, into which a branch road from Hatton leads.

On leaving Hatton the train passes through the longest tunnel on the railway. Just after the 114th mile the very fine *St Clair Falls* are seen on the left (see p. 479).

116 m. **Talawakelle** station (R.H.)*

[The Horton Plains (see p. 481), may be reached by this route, by coach to **Agrapatanas** (14 m.), thence on foot or horse-back (about 6 m.).

From Talawakelle the line again rises steadily to

128 m. **Nanuoya** station,[1] 5291 ft. This is the junction for the narrow gauge railway to **Nuwara Eliya** and **Ragalla.** For persons who prefer to drive to Nuwara Eliya, from Nanuoya there is (4½ m.) a good road, with an ascent of 1000 ft. A carriage should be arranged for.

4½ m. The town of **Nuwara Eliya** * is 6210 ft. above the sea-level. The summer residence of the Governor, the Club, and Hotels are to the N.W. of the lake. Much of the ground about Nuwara Eliya is open and moor-like, and is thickly dotted with bushes of crimson rhododendron. The eucalyptus and the wattle have been largely planted about Nuwara Eliya, and give the landscape a peculiar character, which has also a somewhat Italian air imparted to it by the numerous *keena* trees (*Calophyllum tomentosum*), which, though not a conifer, has a great general resemblance in its habit of growth to a stone-pine. In the beautiful climate of this station ex-

[1] Travellers are recommended to have warm wraps with them, as the temperature here is very much lower than that of the plains, or even of Kandy.

peditions of all sorts may be enjoyed.[1] The finest are:—

(1) Round the *Moon Plains*, 8 m. (2) To the top of *Ramboda Pass* and back, 6 m. (3) Round the *Lake*, 6 m. To Hakagalla (see below) 6 m. *Pidurutalagala*, the highest mountain in Ceylon (8280 ft.), may be easily ascended from Nuwara Eliya. There is a bridle-path to the top, whence the view is extensive, but not specially striking.

(4) A longer excursion is that to the **Horton Plains**, 28 m. from Nuwara Eliya. (See also under Talawakelle, p. 480.)

This excursion will take at least two days, one to go and one to return, and must be made on horseback. A bridle-path through wild and beautiful scenery terminates at a large R.H.,* in the neighbourhood of which are tremendous precipices, which descend to the great plain of the Kalu Ganga. Enquiries should be made beforehand if the bridges are standing, as they are frequently washed away by the monsoon rains. At the "World's End," ¾ m. easy walk from the R.H. along a charming jungle path, there is a very striking view. The mountains, **Totapella and Kirigalpota** (the highest peaks in the island after *Pidurutalagala*), may be ascended from here. The path to the summit of the latter (about 2 hrs. from R.H.) is somewhat difficult; a guide should be taken. The view is magnificent. The Horton Plains can also be reached, and more conveniently, from Pattipola (see p. 482).

(5) A drive out to **Kandapolla** (8 m.) is very agreeable on a fine day.

(6) The **Botanic Gardens** at **Hakagalla**, 6 m. (See below on Road to Badulla.)

From Nuwara Eliya the traveller may return to (20 m.) Gampola, (p. 479) by the Ramboda Pass. The Pass is negotiated by a series of zigzags on a very severe gradient, with dangerous corners. A number of very pretty waterfalls are seen at (12 m.) **Ramboda** (R.H.).

Just before entering Gampola, the Mahaweli-ganga is crossed by a fine suspension bridge, erected in 1859.

The drive from Nuwara Eliya to Badulla is extremely picturesque, but is seldom taken since the railway has been opened to the latter place.

On leaving Nuwara Eliya, the road rises slightly after quitting the lake, and then commences a continuous and for the most part very steep descent of several thousand feet. At 6 m. from Nuwara Eliya we reach the *Botanic Gardens* at **Hakagalla**, a visit to which ought on no account to be omitted by any one making a stay, however short, at Nuwara Eliya. The visitor is equally repaid by the beauty of the views from the Gardens, and by the beauty of the Gardens themselves, in which all the flowers and plants of temperate climates flourish freely, combined with much beautiful natural vegetation. Behind the Gardens rises the precipitous wall of bare rock which forms the face of the Hakagalla mountain, whilst in front the ground sinks abruptly to valleys and low hills far below, and backed in the distance by the mountains of Uva. A distant view of the camp where the Boer prisoners were confined is to be had from the Gardens. The road continues to descend very rapidly to 13 m. *Wilson's Bungalow* and to **Welimada** (R.H.), a picturesque village, from which a bridle-path branches off to the right to Bandarawella (10 m.).

26 m. **Atampitiya** where we are again on the same level as Wilson's Bungalow. The traveller cannot fail to be struck by the extent of terrace-cultivation in the valleys traversed, the steepest hillsides being fashioned into an endless series of narrow terraces, carefully irrigated, on which abundant crops of paddy are grown. From Atampitiya the road again falls continuously, until, after passing **Dikwella**, where it is joined by the road from Bandarawella, it reaches (37 m.) Badulla (see p. 482.)

[1] Burrows' *Visitor's Guide to Kandy and Nuwara Eliya* is a useful handbook.

The main railway from Nanuoya continues to

138 m. **Pattipola** station. A bridle-path (6 m.) leads to the Horton Plains (see p. 481). Shortly after the train reaches the summit level (6219 ft.). It then enters a tunnel, and emerging, a most magnificent view of the Uva country is disclosed with dramatic suddenness to the left.

153 m. **Haputale** station (R.H.) (see p. 486).

156 m. **Diyatalawa** station. Below to the left is seen the **Boer Camp,** where about 5000 prisoners were confined during the war. It is now used as a military training camp and sanitorium for the sailors of the East India Station.

161 m. **Bandarawella** sta. (R.H.✱) the terminus of the main railway.

About 10 m. from Bandarawella are the headquarters of the Errebodde Hunt Club, where the jackal is hunted from Oct. to Jan. Particulars may be obtained at the Hill Club in Nuwara Eliya.

[Six miles out of Bandarawella, on the way to Badulla, a road breaks off to the right to (10 m.) **Ella**, where there is a R.H. most beautifully situated. This may be made the object of an excursion from Bandarawella, or the traveller may continue by this road to (18 m.) Passara (see below), through very fine scenery.]

A coach takes the traveller on to 18 m. **BADULLA** (R.H.✱), the capital of the Province of Uva, one of the oldest, most cheerful, and most attractive towns in Ceylon. It is situated on a slight eminence, entirely surrounded by green paddy-fields, and in the immediate vicinity of a fine river, while on all sides the background is formed by mountains of very beautiful outline.

Fine avenues of *Inga saman* and other trees adorn the town, which, besides the usual Government buildings — Kacheri, Government Agent's residence, etc. — contains a handsome Market and a fine Hospital. There is also an exceedingly pretty race-course, surrounding a small lake. It is in the centre of a very flourishing group of tea-estates. The Church and old Churchyard merit a visit. The fine **Dunhinde Waterfall** is only 6 miles away, but is rather difficult of access.

Of the ancient city few traces remain. Not a vestige is to be seen of the palace of the kings, and scarcely any indication of any buildings of considerable antiquity. There are, however, two large and wealthy Buddhist temples, the *Maha Vihara* and the *Maha Dewale*, which, though the present edifices are of no very great age, are picturesque and worth a visit. They occupy ancient sites, and the dagaba at the Maha Vihara is undoubtedly of very early origin.

A very interesting excursion may be made from Badulla to **Alutnuwera,** 25 m. N., on the Mahaweli-ganga, where there is an ancient dagaba in the midst of fine scenery. Alutnuwera may also be reached from Kandy, and one of the views on that route at the head of the sudden descent to the great eastern plain is among the finest in Ceylon (p. 479).

Leaving Badulla, the road, which passes chiefly through fine tea-estates, rises rapidly to

27 m. **Passara** (R.H.). [From here the traveller may return to Bandarawella by a short road by Ella through beautiful scenery (see above).]

Proceeding, the road continues through some of the finest scenery in Ceylon to

36 m. **Lunugala** (R.H. ✱). Here the road descends. Nothing can exceed the beauty of the drive between this place and

48 m. **Bibile** (R.H.), a good starting-point for excursions into the wild and beautiful country to the E. and S. (see p. 500). There are some springs of warm water near here. We are now in the Veddah country, and either here or at the next following Rest-Houses,

58 m. **Ekiriyankumbara** (R.H.) or

66 m. **Kalodai** (R.H.) the traveller is likely to meet with some of these singular specimens of humanity. They are a remnant of the aboriginal inhabitants of Ceylon, and are divided into two classes, the Rock and the Village Veddahs. The Rock Veddahs are absolute savages, who remain concealed in the forests, and are rarely seen by a European eye—indeed few now exist. The Village Veddahs, though often indulging their migratory instincts, live in collections of mud and bark huts, in the vicinity of which they carry on some rude cultivation. Their skill in handling the bow and arrow, of which they still habitually make use, is remarkable.

76 m. **Maha Oya** (R.H.). A very pretty R.H. on the borders of a low country tank with excellent shooting in season. Here, at some distance off in the jungle, is a spring of *hot* water.

83 m. **Kumburuwella** (R.H.). About 5 miles beyond Kumburuwella is the great tank of Rugam, restored by Sir H. Ward, and now irrigating a large tract of country. From Bibile to Kumburuwella the traveller passes through what is known as the Bintenna country, where very good shooting may be had in season.

About 89 m. **Chumpalam Solum** (R.H.), near the Rugam Tank.

98 m. **Chenkaledi** or **Eraoor** (R.H.). We have now entered a country almost wholly inhabited by Tamils and "Moors," as the Sinhalese Mohammedans are called. The familiar dagaba is no longer seen in the villages, and its place is taken by the Hindu pagoda or the mosque. From Rugam onwards the country is highly cultivated and populous. After crossing the bridge at Eraoor, the road turns sharply at right-angles S.E. to

110 m. **Batticaloa** (R.H., ✱ the capital of the Eastern Province. Batticaloa is situated on an island in a remarkable salt-water lake, which communicates with the sea only by one long and narrow channel, but which extends for over 30 m. in length by from 5 to 2 m. in breadth, and is separated from the sea by a broad sandy belt now rich with cocoa-nut groves, and swarming with Tamil and Moorish villages from one end to the other. The approach to the town by a causeway across the lake is picturesque. The walls of the small old Dutch fort, now converted into a prison, are well preserved. Batticaloa is famous as the abode of that singular natural curiosity the "singing-fish." On calm nights, especially about the time of the full moon, musical sounds are to be heard proceeding from the bottom of the lagoon. They resemble those which are produced by rubbing the rim of a glass vessel with a wet finger. The writer has never heard more than two distinct musical notes, one much higher than the other, but credible witnesses, such as Sir E. Tennent, assert that they have heard a multitude of sounds, "each clear and distinct in itself, the sweetest treble mingling with the lowest bass." The natives attribute the production of the sound to the shell-fish *Cerithium palustre*. This may be doubtful, but it is unquestionable that the sounds come from the bottom of the lagoon, and may be distinctly heard rising to the surface on all sides of a boat floating on the lake. If a pole be inserted in the water, and its upper end applied to the ear, much louder and stronger sounds are heard than without such aid.

The edible oyster is good and plentiful.

The Tamils call Batticaloa "Tamarind Island," from the graceful tamarind tree which is frequently seen.

A steamer N. or S. about the Island leaves Batticaloa on advertised dates.

[From Batticaloa there is a good road for some 60 m. to Arugam Bay, thence by track to **Palutupane** (p. 490), through the *Yala Sanctuary*. Good shooting in season.]

ROUTE 3.

COLOMBO TO RATNAPURA and BANDARAWELLA.

(Rail to Avisawella, Coach to Ratnapura, and on by special conveyance to Haputale (p. 482); and rail to Bandarawella, *or alternatively* by special conveyance the whole way. As the drive is a beautiful one, the road to Avisawella is described in place of the railway.)

For convenience of arrangement this route has been described from Colombo to Bandarawella. The long ascent, however, takes time, and the traveller who has not much leisure is recommended to go to Bandarawella by railway (Route 2), and to return to Colombo by this route.

No excursion could show more of the characteristic features of Sinhalese scenery and Sinhalese life than this. It is one strongly recommended to those having time to perform it. The journey to Bandarawella will occupy about three days. Those who have less time to spare are strongly recommended to go as far as Ratnapura, returning to Colombo by the alternative route (No. 4) mentioned on p. 486. At **Maradana Junction** the narrow gauge Kelani Valley Railway begins.

Leaving Colombo by special conveyance through the narrow and crowded streets of the "Pettah," we follow either a very pretty road along the S. bank of the Kelani river, or a more direct but less picturesque road across the plain, to

10 m. **Kaduwella**, a R.H. charmingly situated on a bluff of red rocks above the river at a point where it makes a sharp turn. The R.H. verandah all but overhangs the river, and commands a delightful view, enlivened by the constant passage of leaf-thatched barges and sailing boats, and by the picturesque groups all day crossing the river at the ferry close by. A short distance off is an ancient Buddhist temple of some size. The road continues near the river, through a rapid succession of villages and groves, to

21 m. **Hanwella** (R.H.), a large village with a R.H., commanding a beautiful view up and down the river. [9 m. S. of Hanwella is the tank of Labugama, which supplies Colombo with water. It is picturesquely situated among wooded hills, and well repays a visit.] The road now leaves the river and passes over country in which tea-cultivation is conspicuous and clearings for the growing of Pará Rubber are numerous, to

30 m. **Avisawella** station (R.H.✱), surrounded by country of very great natural beauty. [The railway from Colombo to Avisawella proceeds to 11 m. **Yatiyantota** (R.H.), the present terminus. A road leading N. from Avisawella crosses the Sitiwaka and Kelani rivers by fine iron bridges, both commanding lovely views, and passes, by **Ruwanveli** (where there is an old Dutch Fort converted into a very charming R.H.), through a lovely wooded and undulating country to *Kegalla* (p. 476).]

At Avisawella the traveller leaves the railway and proceeds by coach. The scenery assumes a bolder character. After passing

44 m. **Pussella** (R.H.), we cross the Kuriweti river near the village of Ekneligoda, in which is situated the picturesque *walawa* of Ekneligoda Dissawe, a great Sinhalese chief and landholder, and we reach

56 m. **Ratnapura** (R.H.✱), a considerable town, the capital of the Province of Sabaragamuwa, with a rainfall of fully 150 ins. Ratnapura is situated in the midst of the most exquisite scenery, and the views from the summit of the Fort, the Suspension Bridge, and the Circular Road are especially recommended. A ride of a few miles up the bridle-path leading from the Suspension Bridge to Gilimale will amply repay the trouble, revealing as it does the magnificent

mountain-wall which rises all but perpendicularly to the N. to the height of many thousand feet. It is from Ratnapura that the finest views of Adam's Peak are to be obtained. There is a specially good one within a few minutes' walk of the R.H. Ratnapura is the headquarters of the gemming industry, and the whole country is dotted with pits from which gems have been removed. Sapphires, topazes, and cat's-eyes are those most commonly found. The *modus operandi* is simple. A pit is dug, and when the *illan*, a peculiar clay in which the gems are usually found, is reached, all that is dug up is carefully washed and sifted, and the good stones set aside. *Genuine* stones are certain to be found in large quantities, but stones of any marketable value are more rare, the greater part having only a faint shade of colour and being disfigured by flaws. Plumbago also is mined for.

A mile or two W. from Ratnapura is the *Maha Saman Dewale*, one of the richest Buddhist temples in Ceylon, and possessed of considerable estates. Some interesting relics are preserved there, but the building itself, though picturesque, has no architectural interest. In the outer court, built into the wall, stands one of the very few monuments of the Portuguese domination remaining in Ceylon —a slab representing the full-length figure of a Portuguese knight in armour killing and trampling upon a prostrate Sinhalese.

[Ascent of **Adam's Peak** (23 m.); see also Route 2.

5 m. from Ratnapura is **Malwala** on the river *Kalu Ganga*.

2 m. farther up the river is **Gilimale**, a large village (horses as a rule cannot proceed farther).

5 m. **Palabaddala**, 1200 ft., halting-station of pilgrims. Here the path becomes very steep and rugged.

8 m. **Heramitipana**, 4400 ft., ✱ halting-station at the base of the Peak.

3 m. farther is the summit of the mountain (7420 ft.), where is a small permanent room built for the accommodation of the resident monks.]

Leaving Ratnapura by the Suspension Bridge, and not forgetting to notice the beautiful views obtainable from it, we pass through paddy-fields fertilised by the Batugedara irrigation works, and after a drive of 13 m. reach

69 m. **Pelmadulla** (R.H.), whence a road to the S. leads to **Rakwane**, the chief village of a rising tea-district. The views on this road are some of the most beautiful in Ceylon.

[From Rakwane an interesting trip may be made southwards to Hambantotta in the southern province. It is a riding road only, though practicable for bullock-carts in most places. As far as Maduanwela the scenery is very pretty. At Maduanwela is a very interesting specimen, the only one with which the writer is acquainted, of the ancient *walawes* of the Kandyan chiefs. It consists of several small courts built on a sort of Pompeiian plan, the small rooms looking into the court which, as at Pompeii, is in every case furnished with an impluvium. There is a small private chapel (Buddhist), and the massive outer door, made of one huge piece of wood, is marked by bullets and other traces of resistance to assailants in olden times. Within is displayed the silver staff shaped like a crozier, the badge of office of one of the ancestors of the family, who was chief Adigar or Prime Minister of the King of Kandy. Afterwards the track leads chiefly through thick forest and jungle, attractive to the sportsman as being a great resort for elephants and deer. After passing the irrigation works on the Wellawe River, the main road between Galle and Hambantotta is joined at Ambalantotta (see p. 489).]

The woods about Pelmadulla, at the proper season, are bright with the splendid blooms of the *Dendrobium Maccarthii*.

85 m. **Balangoda** (R.H.). Nothing can exceed the beauty and variety of

the scenery along the whole road from Ratnapura to this place. It is entirely free from that monotony which sometimes renders the most luxuriant tropical scenery oppressive and wearisome.

97 m. **Belihuloya.** There is a good R.H. here, romantically situated on the edge of a rushing mountain stream. From this spot an ascent can be made to the Horton Plains (see Route 2). We now get into coffee and tea-estates, whence the whole of the wood has been cleared, and the bare hillsides now lack all trace of their original beauty. But the crops are fine, and coffee has not in this part of Ceylon been so wholly exterminated as elsewhere by leaf disease. Ever since leaving Pelmadulla the road, though varied by occasional descents, has been rising, and by the time we have reached

105 m. **Haldamulla** (R.H.), we are at a very considerable elevation, from which a truly magnificent view is obtained over all that part of the island lying between Haldamulla and the sea to the S. With few exceptions, the eye seems to range over an unbroken extent of forest; the rivers, villages, and tracts of cultivation being for the most part concealed by the trees surrounding them.

[From Haldamulla the traveller may proceed to **Koslande** (R.H.) thence, passing the very fine **Naula Waterfall** *en route*, to **Wellawaya** (R.H.), headquarters for excellent shooting.]

A very steep ascent of about 8 m. brings us to the top of the pass at **Haputale** (R.H.), on the railway line, at an elevation of 4765 ft. The view hence is even grander than that from Haldamulla, but from partaking of a greater extent of the nature of a bird's-eye view it is less picturesque. By road or rail the traveller proceeds to

120 m. **Bandarawella** (R.H.✱) (p. 482), which is said to enjoy the best and most equable climate in Ceylon.

ROUTE 4.

COLOMBO TO **RATNAPURA** *via* **Panadura and Nambapane.**

(Rail and road.)

This is an alternative route to Ratnapura, but somewhat longer. It passes through very pretty country, and those who go no farther than Ratnapura are strongly recommended to go by one and return by the other of these routes.

The traveller proceeds as far as *Panadura* by the Southern Railway from Colombo (see Route 5), and thence proceeds by coach or private conveyance.

A few miles after quitting Panadura he crosses the Bolgoda Lake by a bridge, and at

10 m. reaches **Horana.** The R.H. here is built among the remains of an ancient Buddhist monastery, and on the opposite side of the road is the large and handsome Buddhist temple. It contains a bronze candlestick worthy of notice. It is about 8 ft. high and of remarkably fine workmanship.

28 m. **Nambapane** (R.H.), prettily situated. The road here approaches the Kalu Ganga river, along the bank of which it passes as far as the Kuruwitti river which it crosses. The road now keeps at a greater distance from the river, though it follows its general course till it reaches

42 m. **Ratnapura** (R.H.✱) (see p. 484). Shortly before arriving at Ratnapura the Maha Saman Dewale is passed (see p. 485). The whole road is extremely beautiful and cannot fail, if the day be fine, to give pleasure to those passing along it. Fine views of Adam's Peak and the other principal points of the Central Mountains are to be obtained on this route.

ROUTE 5.

COLOMBO TO **GALLE, MATARA, Hambantotta, and Tissamaharama.**

(Rail to Matara; thence special conveyance. Beyond Kirinde ride.)

The journey is worth making, at all events so far as Galle or Matara, for the sake of the coast scenery. As far as Matara it can be performed by rail, but it is unnecessary to say that much is lost by adopting this mode of travelling. The first six stations—namely, the Pettah, the Fort, Slave Island (the drive from Galle Face Hotel to this station is about ¼ m.), Kollupitiya, Bambalapitya, and Wellawatta, are all in the suburbs of Colombo.

At 7 m. **Mount Lavinia** station is the Grand Hotel, which was built by Sir E. Barnes, when Governor, as his Marine Villa. It stands on a rocky eminence close to the station. It is a very favourite place to stay at, and has first-rate accommodation.

17½ m. **Moratuwa** station is a very flourishing place. It is justly celebrated for its wood-carving.

21 m. **Panadura** station (R.H.), a flourishing village prettily situated on a narrow inlet of the sea (see Route 4).

26 m. **Kalutara** station (R.H.✱) is approached by a fine iron bridge over the Kalu Ganga. It is over 1200 ft. long, being composed of twelve spans of 100 ft. each. Kalutara is a large place, with a great air of cheerfulness and comfort. The R.H. is a good starting-point for the excursions which may be made over excellent roads into the very pretty country to the E. of the town. There is an interesting Buddhist temple on the N. side of the river. Snipe and whistling teal are plentiful from November to February. The hog-deer (*Cervus porcinus*) not found anywhere else in Ceylon, is said to have been introduced into the Kalutara District by the Dutch from its home in the Ganges Delta.

The Mangosteen grows well in Kalutara. Its fruit, at once pleasing to the eye and delicious to the palate, is recommended to the attention of the traveller. The neighbourhood is now most celebrated as the locality where Pará Rubber is most successfully grown in Ceylon.

Plumbago or graphite is largely mined for in the Kalutara District.

41 m. **Bentotta** station (R.H. very good) was at one time the railway terminus, and from thence the journey to Galle had to be made by road. The drive is charming, always near and generally within sight of the sea, and passing under an uninterrupted grove of cocoa-nut and other trees. The district is extremely populous, and the traveller is rarely, if ever, out of sight of a house or two, while villages of greater or less size are of constant occurrence. Bentotta is celebrated for its edible oysters.

54 m. **Ambalangoda** station is a large and rapidly increasing village. The R.H. (very good) is close to the sea, and has a good bathing-place among the rocks below it.

61 m. **Hikkaduwa** station (R.H.). There is a fine Buddhist temple here in a somewhat unusual position, approached by a long, narrow, and steep flight of stone stairs.

74 m. **GALLE** station ✱ was the principal port of call for vessels between Aden and the far East, before the completion of the breakwater at Colombo. The harbour at Galle is very small, and not very safe in rough weather. The entrance is so narrow as to be hardly visible until very near. *The lighthouse* is about 60 ft. high. To the E. there is a hill 2170 ft. high called the Haycock, and in the distance to the E.N.E. Adam's Peak, 7420 ft. high, is often seen. The landing-place at Galle is on the N. side of the harbour. The deep water comes close into the shore. *All Saints' Church* is about ½ m. from the

landing-place. It is a handsome stone building of pointed architecture, and can seat 500 persons. The ramparts of the old *fort* form a charming promenade towards the sea. The population of the town according to the last census is 37,000. The harbour is entered yearly by some 150 steamers with a tonnage of 300,000 tons.

The place is hardly mentioned in the native chronicles before 1267. Ibn Batuta, in the middle of the 14th century, calls it a small town. It was not till the Portuguese occupation that it rose to importance. When the Dutch succeeded the Portuguese, they greatly strengthened the fortifications, which had been vigorously defended against their admiral, Kosten. In the marriage treaty of the Infanta of Portugal with Charles II. of England, it was agreed that if the Portuguese recovered Ceylon they were to hand over Galle to the English, but they never did recover it.

The name of Galle is from the Sinhalese, *galla*, a rock; but the Portuguese and Dutch settlers derived it from the Latin, *gallus*, a cock, and carved an image of a cock on the front of the old Government House, which dated from 1687. The environs of Galle are charming, and a number of pleasant and interesting excursions may be made among them. The scenery is always delightful, and there are many old and curious Buddhist monasteries to be explored. Buddhism is here seen in its best aspect. The monks are far more austere and more intelligent than in the Kandyan provinces, and the religion seems to exercise a greater influence over the lives of the people.

91 m. **Weligama** station (R.H.), a populous and thriving village, beautifully situated on the lovely little bay of the same name. Half a mile before entering the village on the right-hand side of the high road from Galle is a remarkable rock-cut colossal statue of a Sinhalese king in perfect preservation. The statue is popularly styled that of the "Leper King," but the legends attached to it are obscure and contradictory.

The road continues along the seashore, through an almost uninterrupted grove of cocoa-nut trees which overshadow a constant succession of picturesque fishing-villages. The whole district is densely populated, and the drive one of the most charming character.

101 m. **Matara** station, ✱ the birthplace of Sir Henry Lawrence, 1806, a large and flourishing town of about 9000 inhabitants. The Nilawa Ganga is here crossed by a fine bridge. Matara itself is a particularly pretty and pleasing town, and is the residence of many of the oldest and richest Sinhalese lowland families. In the fort there is a R.H. and a handsome clock tower.

At Matara there is a Buddhist Hermitage called Chula Lauka. It is an islet connected with the mainland by a causeway, and founded as a Buddhist Seminary by a Siamese Prince Priest.

Matara is the railway terminus. The traveller proceeds by carriage to

104 m. **Dondra**, a fishing-village situated on the southernmost point of Ceylon. There was here a stately temple, destroyed by the Portuguese, of which few fragments now remain. There is, however, in the modern vihara a fine gateway elaborately sculptured, and about half a mile to the N. is a stone cell in perfect preservation. On the point itself, about a mile to the S. of the road, is a magnificent lighthouse, erected at great cost in 1889.

The villages, though still frequent, now become fewer in number.

114 m. **Dikwella** (R.H. good).

125 m. **Tangalla,** a pretty little village with a remarkably good R.H. close to the sea.

N. of Tangalla are the extensive irrigation works of the Kirima valley, and the large tank of Udukiriwella; a few miles to the S. of which is situated one of the oldest and most remarkable Buddhist monasteries in Ceylon—**Mukirigala,** an isolated rock rising abruptly from the plain, and honeycombed with caves and temples.

130 m. **Ranne** (R.H. poor). About a mile before reaching it we see on the S. a picturesque Buddhist temple on the summit of a high wooded rock.

The country now becomes bleaker and barer and the population far more sparse.

140 m. **Ambalantotta** (R.H. fair), a small village on the banks of the Welawe river, a noble stream here shrouded in dense forest, and crossed by a long and picturesque wooden bridge.

Ten miles N. of Ambalantotta are the head works of the Welawa irrigation scheme. A massive stone dam, constructed by Government, diverts part of the stream into a system of canals and channels which convey water for agricultural purposes for many miles on the W. bank of the river.

The road now passes through a desolate country to

149 m. **Hambantotta** (R.H.), the chief place of an Assistant Agency, a large town on a small bad harbour. Here are the headquarters of the district, a large gaol, the Assistant Agent's and District Judge's residences, the Kacheri, Court-house, etc. Here too is one of the two chief salt manufactories in Ceylon. A great part of the population are Malays. In the immediate vicinity of the town are sand-hills, which long threatened to overwhelm the town, and have in fact buried several streets, the old post-office, and some other buildings. Their onward progress is now checked by the growth of a peculiar grass, and by plantations of the palmyra palm. Hambantotta is a great place for catching turtles.

About 20 m. N.E. of Hambantotta is **Tissamaharama**, the oldest of the abandoned royal cities of Ceylon. Except as a place of pilgrimage, the site had been wholly abandoned till the restoration of the tank by the Ceylon Government. From this tank more than three thousand acres are now cultivated in paddy, and both population and the area under cultivation are annually increasing. The ruins are of great antiquity and interest. One of the oldest and largest of the dagabas, over 150 ft. high, which was in a very ruinous condition, has been entirely restored by the unassisted labour of the Buddhist population. There are several other very large dagabas, mostly in ruins, and some smaller ones in fair condition. The remains of large buildings are numerous, and the ruins of what is styled the King's palace, but is more probably the lower storey of a many-storeyed monastery like the *Brazen Palace* at Anuradhapura (p. 495), are worthy of notice. They consist of rows of huge monolithic columns, much larger than any at Anuradhapura or Polonnaruwa. Ruins are everywhere scattered through the dense forest, and excavations here would probably be better repaid than at any other spot in Ceylon.

There are two ways of reaching Tissamaharama from Hambantotta—

(1) The easiest route is that by the high road to Badulla. On leaving Hambantotta, the great *lewayas*, or natural salt-pans, whence great amounts of salt, a Government monopoly, are annually taken, are passed. When the salt has formed in them they present the appearance of frozen lakes covered with snow of dazzling whiteness.

15 m. **Wirawila** (R.H.). The high road is here left, and about four miles of bad country road conducts the traveller to the Government bungalow above the tank, which does duty as a Rest-House.

(2) A more interesting route is along the coast 21 m. to **Kirinde** (R.H.), a small port of picturesque appearance. There is a road thence to Tissamaharama, about 8 m. in length, which passes many remains of antiquity.

8 m. beyond Kirinde, along the coast, is **Palutupane**, an excellent centre for shooting excursions, as elephants, wild buffaloes, bears, leopards, deer, and peacocks abound in the wild and unpeopled forests and plains around it. There are also antiquarian remains of considerable interest scattered through the jungle.

From Palutupane there is a track, good for horses, and generally passable for a rough bullock-cart, to Batticaloa (130 m.) (see p. 483). The forest scenery on the *Yala* river is very beautiful, and the whole route presents great attractions to the sportsman.

ROUTE 6.

COLOMBO TO **TRINCOMALEE by Negombo, Puttalam, and Anuradhapura.**

(Coach to Chilaw; thence by special conveyance.)

A steamboat goes daily, or almost daily, from Colombo to Negombo, and from Negombo to Colombo, by the canal, but it is usually both crowded and uncomfortable, and very slow.

The coach-road leaves Colombo by the *Victoria Bridge* (see p. 474), and turning to the left, proceeds by

13 m. **Jaela** (R.H.)

23 m. **Negombo** (R.H. *), a thriving town, population 20,000, picturesquely and singularly situated among lagoons and canals,—a true Dutch settlement. There is a picturesque Dutch gateway, which "improvers" have, happily, as yet failed to remove, and a banyan tree of magnificent dimensions. The brass work of Negombo is celebrated; also its prawns. The whole district between Colombo and Negombo is densely inhabited. The innumerable villages are scattered through cocoa-nut groves, cinnamon gardens, and groves of jack fruit. The artist and the photographer can find at every corner of the countless roads and lanes an inexhaustible variety of vignettes of striking beauty. Leaving Negombo, the road crosses the Maha Oya by a fine bridge, about 400 ft. in length, and proceeds through luxuriant cocoa-nut groves and tobacco plantations to

36 m. **Maravila** (R.H. *), a village rapidly increasing in size and importance. Near it is an enormous and very costly Roman Catholic church. One of the most striking features on this route is the number and size of the Roman Catholic churches, erected for the most part by the people of the fishing-villages along the coast, who almost all profess that religion.

41 m. **Tinnipitiyawewa** tank, one of the most successful irrigation restorations of the Ceylon Government, is passed (right).

48 m. **Chilaw** (R.H. good), another large town, seat of an Assistant Government Agency and of the District Court. Here again is another huge Roman Catholic church. A large Hindu temple at Muniseram, in the neighbourhood, is worth a visit. There is a road from Chilaw to Kurunegala (p. 491) passing Dundegamma, where there is a picturesque temple. 4 m. beyond Chilaw the great river Dedaru Oya is passed by an iron bridge. A bad road, through a sandy and uninteresting country, which, however, is being rapidly covered with thriving cocoa-nut plantations, leads to

59 m. **Battul Oya**, another large river, crossed by a ferry, and then continues its way through country of a similar character to

80 m. **Puttalam** (R.H. poor), a considerable place, the headquarters

of an Assistant Government Agent. What gives Puttalam its importance is the existence of the largest salt-pans in Ceylon. The whole island is supplied with salt from this place or Hambantotta. The process of manufacture, and the salt-pans, are well worth seeing, if the visit to Puttalam is made at the right season. Salt is a Government monopoly. It is manufactured here, and at Hambantotta, and thence retailed throughout the island. On the tongue of land which lies between Puttalam Lake and the sea is St Anna's Roman Catholic Church. On the Saints' festival, about 29th July, enormous crowds go thither on pilgrimage—all sorts and conditions of people—Buddhists, Mohammedans, Hindus, as well as Roman Catholics and other Christian sects; a regular town of palm huts is formed for their accommodation.

A canal connects Puttalam with Negombo, but except between Chilaw and Negombo it is little used. It is, however, kept up for the transport of salt.

The road after leaving Puttalam strikes inland, and proceeds through a sandy and thinly-peopled country to

103 m. **Kala Oya** (R.H.). The *Kala Oya river* is here crossed by a bridge 55 feet above the ordinary level of the stream, which was nevertheless carried away by a flood in 1885.

127 m. **Anuradhapura** (R.H.✱) (see p. 494). (Here the Railway is joined, see Route 6a and 7.) The road from Anuradhapura to Trincomalee passes through

135 m. **Mihintale** (R.H.) (see p. 496). After leaving Mihintale, the road (constructed 1886) passes through a thinly-inhabited country, the villages, with their tanks and cultivation, being sparsely scattered through the forest.

160 m. **Horowapotane** (R.H.). A large tank and village.

177 m. **Pankulam** (R.H.). A few miles beyond Pankulam, on the right of the road, and half a mile from it, are the remarkable hot springs of Chimpiddi (Kanhiya). They are nine in number, but though of different temperatures, rise close together in one ancient stone basin. They are considered equally sacred by Buddhists, Hindus, and Mohammedans, and the ruins of a dagaba, a temple of Vishnu, and a mosque stand together in the immediate vicinity.

192 m. **Trincomalee** (see p. 499).

ROUTE 6a.

COLOMBO TO KANKESANTURAI *viâ* Polgahawela, Kurunegala, Anuradhapura and Jaffna.

(Rail 256½ m, opened 1904-5. This is the best route for reaching Anuradhapura.)

The route from Colombo to

45 m. **Polgahawela Junction** is described in Route. 1.

58½ m. **Kurunegala** (R.H.), the chief town of the North Western Province, is situated at the foot of a remarkable rock which starts up alone in the plain—an enormous black boulder, over 1000 feet in height. Similar isolated rocks are not uncommon in different parts of the Province. From the top of the "Rock of Kurunegala" a noble view is to be obtained. At its foot is an artificial lake which is used for irrigation purposes.

From Kurunegala there are good roads S.W. to Negombo, and N.W. to Puttalam (see Route 6). 13 m. from Kurunegala on the latter road is **Wariyapola** (R.H.) (near here in 1902, 102 elephants were driven into a kraal, but only forty-five of these were finally noosed), 10 m. N. of which, a few miles off a cross-road to Anuradhapura, is **Yapahu**, one of the most picturesque and curious of the remains of antiquity in Ceylon. It was at one time the abode of the sacred tooth: the ruins of the *Maligawa*, standing at the head of a great flight of steps, are quite unique. Its traceried windows, one of which is in the Museum at Colombo, are especially curious. A few miles N.E. of Kurunegala is the **Ridi** (or silver) **Vihare**, a very ancient Buddhist monastery, most picturesquely situated at a considerable elevation.

The road from Kurunegala to Negombo, passing through **Narammula**, Dambadeniya, Giriulla, and Wellihinda, is very pleasing from its varying character and constant succession of woodlands, paddy-fields, and cocoa-nut groves. At Dambadeniya is a large and famous temple, close to which is a high apparently inaccessible isolated rock, on which, according to tradition, prisoners were confined.

92½ m. **Ambanpola.**

126½ m. **Anuradhapura** station (R.H.)* (see Route 7). The country onwards to Kankesanturai is described in Route 7.

142½ m. **Madawachchiya** station (R.H.) * See p. 496.

157½ m. **Vavuniya - vilankulam** station (R.H.)* See p. 496.

185½ m. **Mankulam** station (R.H.).

222 m. **Pallai** station (R.H.).

245½ m. **Jaffna** (R.H.). See p. 497.

256½ m. **Kankesanturai** station (R.H.).*

ROUTE 7.

KANDY TO **JAFFNA by Anuradhapura.**

(To Matale by rail, thence by road as far as Anuradhapura, where the main railway line from Colombo to Jaffna is joined, or by private conveyance all the way from Kandy to Anuradhapura.)

The railway, which crosses the *Mahaweli - ganga* by a fine bridge on leaving Kandy, takes us to

16 m. **Matale** terminus station (R.H. good), a large and flourishing village beautifully situated. Tea and cacao plantations, together with cocoa-nut and other palm trees, and paddy-fields, mixed with indigenous scrub and patches of jungle, form a pleasing panorama. The ground is well broken and beautifully varied with wood and cultivation. About a couple of miles out of Matale, only a few hundred yards from the road-side, is the remarkable Buddhist temple of **Alut Vihara**, which it is well worth stopping for a few minutes to visit. Huge masses of granite rock have, at some remote period, fallen from the mountains overhanging the valley. In the fissures of these boulders, at a considerable height above the road, the monastery has been constructed. It is difficult to imagine a site more picturesque, or more theatrical.

30 m. **Nalande**. The R.H. * is prettily situated under fine trees, A steep descent leads to a bridge; a path from which, of about ½ m. to the E., conducts the traveller to the ruins of a *Hindu temple* beautifully situated. The road for the first 5 m. after leaving Nalande is very pleasing, passing through fine open woods, among the trees of which peeps of bare rocky mountains and a rushing stream are obtained. At **Naula** a road to the W. leads to *Elahera*, the head works of an ancient irrigation system of colossal dimensions.

45 m. **Dambool** (Dambulla) (R.H. *), a large village immediately under the huge black rock in which is situated the **Cave Temple** that makes this place famous, but which presents no great attraction to those who have seen the cave temples of India. At the same time, Sir Emerson Tennent says of it, "from its antiquity, its magnitude, and the richness of its decoration, it is by far the most renowned in Ceylon." There is a fine view from the top of the rock. The temple has large landed possessions in the neighbourhood.

[15 m. from Dambool is **Sigiri** (R.H.), which is well worth a visit. The Rest-House keeper at Dambool will afford all information and make the necessary arrangements. It is best to go overnight to Sigiri and ascend the rock early in the morning, returning the same morning or that afternoon to Dambool. Sigiri is a rock fortress to which the parricide King Kasyapa retired in the 5th century after obtaining the throne of Ceylon by the murder of his father, Dhatu Sena. This extraordinary natural stronghold is situated in the heart of the great central forest, above which it rises abruptly, like the Bass Rock out of the sea. There are but few traces of the hand of man remaining upon the rock, except some galleries on the N.W. side and some frescoes high up in a cavity near its summit—accessible by the aid of some iron ladders and steps cut in the rock. Copies may be seen in the Museum at Colombo (see p. 474). The palace, the site of which is just traceable on the N.W. side, and the rock itself, are supposed to have been surrounded by a fosse; a tank still exists on the S.W. side. Cave's *Ruined Cities of Ceylon*, Burrows' *Buried Cities of Ceylon*, and Bell's *Administration Reports* should be studied.]

3 m. after leaving Dambool the *Mirisgoni Oya* is crossed by a very high bridge. Immediately after passing it the road divides. The road straight on leads N.E. to Trincomalee (see Route 8); 4 m. along this road on the right, just opposite to a Public Works barracks or "lines," is the turn off to Sigiri; the branch turning to the left, N., is that for Anuradhapura and Jaffna, and passes over an undulating park-like country and past many newly restored irrigation works to

58 m. **Kekerawa** (R.H. ✚).

[From Kekerawa an expedition should be made, 8 m. by good carriage-road, to the **Great Tank** of **KALAWEWA.*** This magnificent sheet of water was originally formed by King Dhatu Sena about 460 A.D., who built a bund 6 m. long, 60 ft. high, and 20 ft. broad on the top. This bund retains the waters of two rivers, and forms a lake which even now, when the spill only reaches a height of 25 ft., has a contour of nearly 40 m. A great canal from one of the sluices of this tank carries water to Anuradhapura, a distance of 52 m., and supplies over 100 village tanks in its course. A few miles of the canal at the end nearest Anuradhapura were restored by Sir William Gregory nearly 40 years ago, but the tank itself and the remainder of the canal remained in ruin, as they had been for many centuries, till 1884, when the Ceylon Government decided to restore them. The work was completed at the end of 1887. The bungalow of the engineer in charge commands a fine view over the lake. The ancient spill, 260 ft. long, 200 ft. wide, and 40 ft. high, is still in perfect preservation; the tank having been destroyed, not by any failure of the spill, but by an enormous breach on one side of it, — now covered by the new spill wall, a fine structure nearly 1000 ft. in length, which reflects much credit on its designer and builder, Mr W. Wrightson, of the Ceylon Public Works Department. 2 m. W. of Kalawewa is the **Aukuna Vihara**, an ancient monastery in a wild and secluded situation, where is an enormous rock-cut standing statue of Buddha, 40 ft. high. The statue stands almost entirely free of the rock from which it is carved, and the right arm is raised and free from the body of the statue. At the foot of the bund are ruins of the very ancient city of **Vigitipura.**]

The road from Kekerawa passes for the most part through monotonous and uninteresting forest to

70 m. **Tirapane** (R.H.). 4 m. farther there is a division in the road. The branch leading due N. is the direct road to Jaffna through Mihintale; that to the N.W. proceeds in nearly a straight line to

84 m. **ANURADHAPURA** (R.H. ✚). Owing to the number of visitors since the direct Northern Railway from Colombo *viâ* Polgahawella and Anuradhapura to Jaffna and Kankesanturai (see p. 476), has been opened, the Government Agent requests travellers to advise the R.H. keeper well beforehand of their coming, as the accommodation is limited. A carriage to visit the ruins should also be arranged for beforehand. A bicycle is most useful. The traveller who contemplates a thorough examination of the ruins will obtain all necessary information and assistance at the **Kacheri.** For such an examination the companionship of Cave's *Ruined Cities of Ceylon*, Burrows' *Buried Cities of Ceylon*, Still's *Guide to the Ancient Capitals of Ceylon*, and Bell's *Archæological Reports* will be useful, though the ordinary traveller will perhaps find the chapter on Ceylon in Fergusson's *Eastern Architecture* sufficient for him. A certain number of the ruins lie within 1 m. distance of either side of the Rest-House, the so-called Brazen Palace and the Bo-Tree being nearest to it on the S. side, and the Thuparama and Ruanwelli dagabas on the N. The larger Jetawanarama and Abhayagiriya dagabas lie respectively 1½ m. and ½ m. N. and N.E. of the Rest-House. The accompanying map shows the general disposition of the ruins: they cannot be thoroughly seen in less than two days' time, if a visit to Mihintale is included. Anuradhapura became the capital of Ceylon in the 4th century B.C., and attained its highest magnificence about the commencement of the Christian era. It suffered much during the earlier Tamil invasions, and was finally deserted as a royal residence in the 9th century. A small village has always remained on the site, but it is only since the constitution of the North Central Province, in 1872, by Sir W. Gregory, that any revival has taken place in this much neglected district. Since that date, hundreds of village tanks have been restored; famine and the dreadful disease called *parangi* (produced by the use of bad water and food) have been driven away, and the population, now 3700, is yearly becoming more prosperous and healthy. The newly constructed railway is expected to re-vivify this moribund part of the Island. Steps are being taken to encourage the growth of cotton.

The main objects of interest at Anuradhapura may be divided into *Dagabas*, *Monastic buildings*, and *Pokunas or Tanks*. (See Fergusson's *Eastern Architecture*, i. 228-242.)

I. **Dagabas.**—A dagaba is a bell-shaped construction erected over some relic of Buddha or a disciple (see p. lxxi.). It is always solid, and is surmounted by a cubical structure called the *ti*, which again is surmounted by a lofty spire. The number of dagabas in Anuradhapura is countless, and they vary in size from the enormous masses of the four great dagabas to tiny objects barely two or three feet in diameter. The four chief dagabas are—

1. The *Ruanwelli Dagaba*, completed about 90 B.C. Its diameter is 252 ft., but it does not retain its original altitude, having been much injured by the Tamils in different invasions. It is now only 180 ft. in height. The

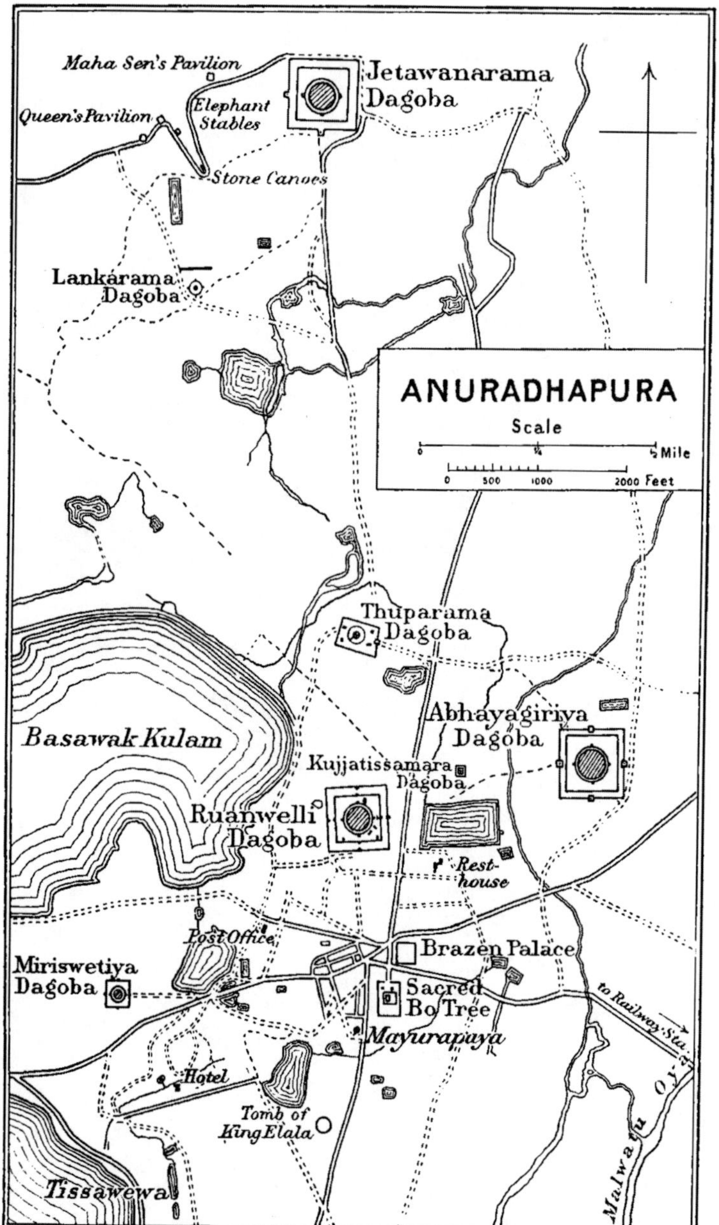
Maha Sen's Pavilion
Jetawanarama Dagoba
Queen's Pavilion
Elephant Stables
Stone Canoes
Lankarama Dagoba
ANURADHAPURA
Scale
0
¼
½ Mile
0
500
1000
2000 Feet
Thuparama Dagoba
Basawak Kulam
Abhayagiriya Dagoba
Kujjatissamara Dagoba
Ruanwelli Dagoba
Rest-house
Post Office
Brazen Palace
Miriswetiya Dagoba
Sacred Bo Tree
to Railway Sta.
Mayurapaya
Hotel
Tomb of King Elala
Malwatu Oya
Tissawewa

[To face p. 494

lower part of the structure and the platform on which it stands were cleared about the year 1873, and the various fragments of the so-called four "chapels" facing the cardinal points were put together and restored.

2. The *Abhayagiriya* (Mount of Safety) is the largest dagaba of all. Its diameter is 327 ft., and its height when perfect was about 270 ft. It has now lost great part of the pinnacle, and its present height is only about 260 ft. It stands on a grand paved platform, eight acres in extent, raised some feet above the surrounding enclosure. The enormous mass of bricks in this structure baffles conception. Sir Emerson Tennent calculates that they are sufficient to construct a town of the size of Ipswich or Coventry, or to build a wall 10 ft. high from London to Edinburgh. The *ti* on the summit having shown symptoms of falling, it and what remained of the stump of the spire above it have been put into a thoroughly safe condition by the Ceylon Government, but the lower part remains untouched. It was erected in the 1st century B.C. The summit can now be easily reached, and commands a magnificent view.

3. The *Jetawanarama*, built in the 4th century A.D., was of about the same dimensions as the Abhayagiriya. No restoration has been attempted here, but the trees which grew all over it have been cleared off its surface.

4. The *Mirisweliya*, though smaller than the foregoing, is remarkable for the unusually fine sculpture of its "chapels" or shrines of the Dhyani Buddhas. It has been partly restored, at the expense of a Siamese prince.

Among the minor dagabas, the Thuparama and Lankarama, the latter surrounded by three and the first by four circles of carved columns, are among the most remarkable and most elegant. These columns are a special feature of Ceylon dagabas.

II. The remains of **Monastic Buildings** are to be found in every direction, in the shape of raised stone platforms, foundations, and stone pillars. The walls themselves between the pillars—being of brick—have disappeared. One of the most remarkable of these remains, to the S. of the R.H., consists of 1600 stone pillars about 12 ft. high and only a few feet distant from each other, arranged in 40 parallel rows. These formed the lowest storey of the famous nine-storeyed "**Brazen Palace**," or monastery, erected by King Dutthagamani about 100 B.C.: the upper storeys were no doubt of wood. The clusters of pillars and of platforms of pavilions in every direction for 10 m. are innumerable. Among the most remarkable is one called the Queen's Palace, the semicircular door-step of which is carved with a double procession of animals and studies of flowers.

III. The **Pokunas** are bathing-tanks, or tanks for the supply of drinking water. They differ from irrigation tanks in being wholly constructed of masonry or of cement. These too are countless in number, and are to be found everywhere through the jungle. The finest is the double (Kuttum) tank in the outer circular road, into which elaborately carved staircases descend.

But there is one object of interest in Anuradhapura which does not come under these heads — **the sacred Pipal or Bo-Tree**—originally brought from Buddh-Gaya (p. 37), and though only a fragment now remains, probably the oldest historical tree existing. It was planted about 240 B.C., and from that time to this has been watched over by an uninterrupted succession of guardians. It stands on a small terraced mound, and is surrounded by a number of descendants. The adjacent buildings are all modern, but the entrance to the enclosure possesses a fine semicircular door-step or "moon-stone."

Some fine bronze statues found at Anuradhapura in 1908 are now in the Colombo Museum.

Another object of interest not to be omitted is the **Rock Temple** at **Isurumuniya**, carved in the solid rock with a large seated Buddha inside, and sculptures in low relief on the terraces.

The large tanks of Nuwarawewa, Tissawewa, and Basawakulam, the two latter of which are filled from Kalawewa, have restored to the neighbourhood of Anuradhapura some of its former fertility.

[8 m. E. of Anuradhapura is **Mihintale** (R.H.), a rocky hill crowned with a large dagaba, and literally covered with the remains of temples and hermitages. Ancient and picturesque stairs of many hundred steps lead to the summit, whence there is a very fine view over the forest plain, from which the great dagabas of Anuradhapura stand up like the pyramids or natural hills. The centre of attraction at Mihintale is *Mahindo's Bed*, the undoubted cell occupied by Mahindo, the apostle of Buddhism in Ceylon, and containing the stone couch on which he lay. Beside it is the Ambasthala dagaba erected on the traditional spot where King Devanampiya Tissa met the missionary Mahindo. On the summit is the Mahaseya dagaba. An idea prevails that it is difficult of access. This is not so. The view, in itself fine, is rendered more so by the position from which it is obtained between the rocks which overhang the "bed."]

On leaving Anuradhapura, travellers for the North can either go direct by rail to Jaffna and Kankesanturai or by road as below. The road is uninteresting all the way to *Elephant Pass*. The stages are as follows:—

95 m. from Kandy (by direct road through Mihintale), **Madawachchiya**, R.H. (see p. 492) ✦.

[From here a road leads N.W. to (47 m.) **Mannaar**, R.H., passing the *Giant's Tank* and the magnificent masonry dam which was to divert the *Aruvi Aru* to fill it. This will be superseded in 1912, it is hoped, by a line of railway, 65 m. long, to Talai Mannaar at the N.W. point of that Island, forming the Ceylon connection of the through route with India, *viâ* Ramesvaram and Pambam (p. 434). Passengers will be conveyed from Talai to (25 m.) Dhanuskodi by a steamer of the S.I. Railway. Mannaar is a dreary spot, commanded by an old Dutch fort, and only remarkable for the number of the African *Baobabs* which grow freely there, having probably been imported by Arabs in the Middle Ages.]

Due S. of Mannaar, and half way between it and Puttalam is *Marichchukaddi* the scene of the camp for the last **Pearl Fishery** in 1905, when the enormous number of 50 millions of oysters were fished, and the Government netted the sum of Rs. 2,626,175—a record. The "Banks" lie mostly in the Gulf of Mannaar at a depth of about 7 fathoms. The pearl Banks of Ceylon have excited the cupidity of the nations of all ages from the Phoenicians onwards. There is a large literature on the subject. The enquirer is referred to the recent monograph on the subject by Mr James Hornell, the Marine biologist, who has discovered the true causation of the Orient pearl in the body of the oyster. The Pearl Banks have now been leased by the Government to a London Company for 20 years at a rental of Rs. 310,000 per annum.

111 m. **Vavuniya-vilankulam**, R.H. ✦ a small town, the headquarters of the district, on the edge of a newly-restored tank.

120 m. **Irampaikkulam** R.H.

[Road branches off here to **Mullaittivu** on N.E. coast.]

132 m. **Kanakarayankulam** R.H. to **Mankulam** R.H.

[Here the road branches off to Mullaittivu on N.E. coast.]

142 m. **Panikkankulam** R.H.

154 m. **Iranamadu** R.H.

All these are small R.Hs., with a certain amount of rough furniture, but without linen or any stock of provisions.

The scrub gets lower and smaller, and the soil poorer and sandier, as we pursue the tedious straight road to

166 m. **Elephant Pass**, so named because here the herds of elephants were in the habit of coming from the mainland through the shallow water to the peninsula of Jaffna, which is now entered by a long causeway crossing the arm of the sea which all but divides the district of Jaffna from the remainder of Ceylon.

The R.H. is the old Dutch fort at the edge of the water—quaint and picturesque.

174 m. **Pallai** (R.H.). The railway line from here to Jaffna was opened in 1902. We are now in a totally different region from that between Anuradhapura and Elephant Pass. The peninsula of Jaffna is the home of a busy, noisy, and closely-packed population. Every acre is cultivated and the garden-culture is of beautiful neatness. Great quantities of tobacco of a very coarse description are grown, most of which is exported to S. India. The fine road passes through a succession of large villages as it proceeds.

187 m. **Chavakachcheri** (R.H. good), a large village surrounded by immense groves of the palmyra palm, which in this Province takes the place occupied by the cocoa-nut palm in the south.

201 m. **Jaffna** or Jaffnapatam (R.H.), a large and flourishing town of 34,000 inhabitants, See of a Roman Catholic bishop, and seat of the Government Agent of the Northern Province.

The old *Dutch Fort*, of considerable size, is in perfect preservation, and is a good specimen of a 17th century fortification. Within it are the *Queen's House* (the Governor's residence when he visits Jaffna), an old *Dutch Church* containing curious tombstones, the residences of certain officials, and the prison. On the esplanade between the fort and the city stands a graceful *Clock Tower*, built in 1882. The Dutch expelled the Portuguese from Jaffna, their last station in Ceylon, in 1633. The following interesting excursions may be made from Jaffna :—

1. To the American Mission Stations at Oodooville, Batticotta, and Kopay, where thousands of children are educated.
2. To Puttoor, where is a very remarkable well of great depth, which is apparently inexhaustible and ebbs and flows slightly daily.
3. To Point Pedro, the northern port of Jaffna.

There are some interesting Hindu temples at Jaffna and in its vicinity.

Jaffna is celebrated for its Mangoes, esteemed by some as superior to the far-famed Bombay variety. Grapes are also grown. *Turtles* are caught, and *bêche-de-mer* or *trepang*, a species of sea slug is fished for, and exported to China, where it is considered a great delicacy. *Shankhs* (the shells of a Mollusc) are also fished for and exported to India, where they are highly esteemed. In the little Island of Delft, W. of the Jaffna Peninsula, ponies used to be bred.

Kankesanturai (R.H.) + (12 m. from Jaffna). The terminus of the Northern Railway and a port of call for the round-the-island steamers (see Route 6A). A very pretty seaside village.

ROUTE 8

KANDY TO **TRINCOMALEE (with excursion to Polonnaruwa).**

Since the construction of the Northern Railway through Anuradhapura and the practical abandonment of Trincomalee, no horse or bullock coach runs on this road. The traveller must make his own arrangements for transport to Polonnaruwa. To Trincomalee a motor (Rs.20 per seat) runs (64 m.) from Anuradhapura.

As far as *Dambool* this route is the same as Route 7.

On crossing the bridge over the *Mirisgoni Oya*, instead of turning left to Anuradhapura and Jaffna (Route 7), the road proceeds straight on and passing right the road to Sigiri (p. 493), continues chiefly through dense but poor forest, varied by one or two villages in the midst of small clearings, to

60 m. (from Kandy) **Habarane** (R.H.). The village, though small, is increasing since the restoration of its tank. There is a picturesque *Buddhist Temple* of considerable antiquity, in which are paintings of better design and execution than are usually found in such places. From the lofty rock by the tank a singular view is obtained over the great sea of forest to the N. and E., out of which rises with startling abruptness the rock pillar of Sigiri (see Route 7).

[From Habarane an extremely interesting excursion may be made to **Polonnaruwa** (32 m.), one of the ancient and deserted capitals of Ceylon. This expedition must be made on horseback, or by country bullock-cart, which can be arranged for at Dambool (p. 493), as the road is merely a rough country one through the forest. After passing for about 18 m. through wood so dense that it is seldom the eye can penetrate more than a few yards on either side of the path, **Mineri** is reached. The journey varies in length according to the state of the lake, which has to be skirted, and which varies con-considerably in size according to the season. This lake is all that remains of a huge tank, the bund of which still exists, but the sluices, of which though not destroyed, are now permanently kept open by fallen masses of masonry. The scenery of this lake is enchanting, and nothing can exceed the beauty both in form and colour of the mountain ranges to the S. Half-way between Mineri and Polonnaruwa is the small lake of **Giritella**, also an abandoned tank, and also highly picturesque. The approach to **Polonnaruwa**[1] (R.H.), like that to Mineri, varies considerably in length according to the height of water in the lake. On the bund is a rough R.H. overlooking the lake. The view is very similar to that from Mineri, and is of great beauty.

Polonnaruwa first became a royal residence in 368 A.D., when the lake of *Topawewa* was formed, but it did not take rank as the capital till the middle of the 8th century. The principal ruins, however, are of a later date, being chiefly of the time of Prakrama Bahu, 1164-1197 A.D. It is now wholly deserted, and the masses of ruin, which are strewed for miles around, have to be sought in the dense jungle. It seems to have been abandoned about the end of the 13th century. The following are the principal objects of interest.

About 1 m. S. of the R.H. is the colossal rock-cut statue of **Prakrama Bahu**, a cast of which is to be seen in the Colombo Museum. To the W. lie the ruins of what appears to have been a strong tower, the probably wooden interior of which is wholly gone; and a little farther in the same direction are the royal pavilions and bathing-tank, ornamented by much elegant sculpture.

About 1 m. to the N. is a remarkable group of buildings: The misnamed **Dalada**, or tooth-shrine—really a Hindu temple of about 1200 A.D. —a fine granite building having much elegant ornament of quasi-Hindu design; the **Thuparama**, a large massive brick building, of

[1] See Cave; Burrows; and Fergusson's *Indian Architecture*, i. 245-9.

which the front and eastern roof have fallen, while the inner chamber preserves its vault, and a tower; the **Wata Dage**, a curious circular edifice, 58 ft. in diameter, on a raised mound, with four carved staircases, and a low stone terrace with an ornamental parapet, once 14 ft. high, of unique design; and the **Ata Dage**, a large ruined temple. In the same vicinity are the **Satmahal Prasada**,—a tower of seven storeys of diminishing size; a **Buddhist "post and rail" enclosure** (see p. lxxii.); and a little farther to the E. the **Vishnu Dewale**, a very ornamental structure of Hindu design, in good preservation.

1 m. further N. is the **Rankot Dagaba**, built in the 12th century. It is 200 ft. in height, with a diameter of 180 ft. The spire is very perfect; even the statues surrounding the drum being clearly discernible. Near it, but to the N., is the **Jetawanarama**, a temple 170 ft. long, 70 ft. wide, and 70 ft. high, at the end of which is a statue of Buddha over 60 ft. in height. The **Kiri dagaba**, about 100 ft. high, the chunam coating of which is still very perfect, adjoins this building.

Another 1 m. of jungle has to be traversed to reach the **Gal Vihara**, a spot where are a rock-cut figure of Buddha sitting, a colossal statue, now named after Ananda, Buddha's favourite disciple, and a reclining figure of the dying Buddha, 46 ft. long, cut out of the solid rock.

1 m. farther N. again is the **Demala Maha Seya**, a very large building, highly ornamented, of which the roof and upper part of the walls have fallen in. The *débris* was partially cleared away in 1886, when many interesting frescoes were found on the walls, but these have since to a great extent perished from exposure.

The dagabas of Polonnaruwa will not compare with those of Anuradhapura, but the buildings of the temples and other structures are in far better preservation. A huge red *lotus* grows in great profusion in the lake, probably the descendant of those cultivated for use in the temples and palaces of the city.]

75 m. **Alutoya** (R.H.), in the midst of the thick forest; not a bad station for sportsmen. The country is flat, and the jungle of such uniform character as to become very monotonous. Monkeys are certain to be seen crossing the road in large troops, during this portion of the journey.

92 m. **Kantalai** (R.H.), on the bund of the great tank of Kantalai, restored by Sir W. Gregory in 1875.

106 m. **Palampoddaru** (R.H.), on the edge of a stream in a very wild country.

116 m. **Trincomalee** (R.H.), a town with a magnificent natural harbour, on the N.E. coast of the island. It is built on the N. side of the bay, on the neck of a bold peninsula, separating the inner from the outer harbour. The latter is about 4 sq. m. in extent, with very deep water. The place is well laid out, but the houses are poor. Population, 12,000.

The town was one of the earliest settlements of the Malabar race in Ceylon. They built a great temple on the spot where Fort Frederick now stands. The building was destroyed by the Portuguese when they took the place in 1622, and the materials were employed to build the fort; but the site is still held in great veneration, and every week a Brahman priest, in the presence of a large crowd, throws offerings into the sea from a ledge near the summit of a huge precipice of black rock,—a most picturesque scene. A monument on the summit of the rocky eminence bears an inscription in Dutch commemorating the death of a young Dutch lady, who in 1687, being disappointed in a love affair, committed suicide at the spot. Since the expulsion of the Portuguese, European nations have held the place in the following order: Dutch, 1639 A.D.; French, 1673 A.D.; Dutch, 1674 A.D.; French, 1782 A.D.; Dutch, 1783 A.D.; English, 1795. It was taken by the English fleet after a siege of three weeks, and was formally ceded to Great Britain by the Treaty of Amiens in 1801.

About 8 miles out of the town, at a place called Kanhiya, there are some *hot* springs (see p. 491).

Trincomalee, for many years the headquarters of the East India Squadron, has quite recently been entirely abandoned by the Military and almost entirely by the Navy.

The entrance to the Bay is marked out by a fine Lighthouse at Foul Point and another light is placed further in on Round Island. The Mahaweli-ganga, the largest river in the Island, taking its rise in the Nuwara Eliya Lake, disembogues here.

Good shooting is to be had in season in the neighbourhood of Trincomalee, which is a port of call for the round-the-island steamers.

In *Tampalakam Bay*, a few miles to the S.E. of Trincomalee, the *window-pane* oyster (*Placuna placenta*) is found—so called from the use to which the Chinese sometimes put the flat translucent shells. The Placuna pearls, valueless as gems, are used by the wealthy classes in India, to chew with "betel."

ROUTE 9.

Sporting Tours.

The attention of sportsmen is called to the work of the Game Preservation Society (headquarters Nuwara Eliya) whose main object is to enforce "the close seasons." Visitors who profit by the work of the Society are invited to contribute to its funds, the meagreness of which restricts its operations.

Such tours as the following, of course, requires some degree of preparation. Though there are Rest-Houses on the routes indicated, they are but few. They contain probably no furniture save a table and a bench or two, and are quite destitute of supplies. The traveller or sportsman will have to carry his own food, cooking utensils, bedding and tent; and this will necessitate the employment of numerous porters, whose pace must regulate his own, though, if on horseback, he can get over the ground more rapidly than they do. If expense is not an object, it would be well to get temporary shelters of bamboo and leaf thatch put up at those places where there is no Rest-House, for the tent is but an indifferent protection against either fierce sun or heavy rain, and health may seriously suffer in consequence.

1. The **Yala Sanctuary**. Of course it is not supposed to be likely that any sportsman would make the *whole* of this tour, but it indicates a line of country any part of which would make a good centre for sport. The animals to be found are elephants,[1] bears, leopards, deer, and in some places wild buffaloes; wild peacocks abound in the forests, and the tanks and marshes are full of wild fowl; they also swarm with crocodiles.

Starting from **Badulla** (R.H. ✱), by carriage the road to **Bibile** (R.H.) is described in Route 2.

Here wheel conveyance must be abandoned, and the distance must be counted not by miles but in hours, the hour being calculated on the ordinary pace of a loaded porter.

6 hrs. **Nilgala**. A small village with a little patch of paddy cultivation, situated most picturesquely on a river at the entrance to a wild and narrow pass.

4 hrs. **Dambagalla** (R.H.). A small village, in the vicinity of which irrigation works have recently been constructed.

3 hrs. **Medagama** (R.H.). In a very pretty jungle country abounding with elephants.

5 hrs. **Nakkala** (R.H.). There is a picturesque Buddhist temple on the side of a mountain in the neighbourhood.

3 hrs. **Buttala** (R.H. ✚ good). An oasis of cultivation in the jungle, due to the restoration of its ancient

[1] A licence to shoot an elephant costs Rs.100, a buffalo Rs.20, and a general game licence Rs.3 cts.50 per annum.

irrigation works. Everywhere through the forests the ruins of ancient systems of irrigation and other vestiges of civilisation are to be found. Excellent snipe-shooting in season.

4 hrs. **Galge.** A mass of bare rocks rising from the jungle. There is no Rest-House here, and though some shelter may be obtained in caves, tents or a temporary house would be needed.

3 hrs. **Kataragama** (R.H.). A famous palace of Hindu pilgrimage, to which worshippers were wont to resort from all parts of India, as, indeed, they occasionally still do. The pilgrimage was found to produce such mischievous effects in the spread of disease that the Ceylon Government has for many years endeavoured to check it, and it is now reduced to comparatively small numbers. Still, at the time of the annual pilgrimage, the temple and its vicinity form a picturesque and interesting sight. The temple itself is but an insignificant building, and a single gilt-metal tile forms the only relic of the golden roof for which it was once celebrated.

6 hrs. **Palutupane** (see p. 490). In the Southern Province.

4 hrs. **Yala River** (R.H. a mere hut). Here begins the district in which wild buffaloes are still found. Near the Yala River a large tract of country has been "proclaimed" by Government, and is known as the "Yala Sanctuary," in which *no shooting or hunting of any sort* is allowed. The Sanctuary lies between the rivers Yala and Kumbukkan, the other limits being the Sea on one side and the boundary of the Province on the other. The area is computed at 150 sq. miles. Good forest scenery on river.

3 hrs. **Uda Potana.** No R.H. About two hours from Uda Potana we reach the ford crossing the Kumbakan Aar, the boundary between the Southern and Eastern Provinces, and about an hour farther is **Kumane**, near a small village.

4 hrs. **Okanda** at the foot of a bare rock rising out of the sea of jungle. Peacocks are to be found in great abundance in the neighbourhood of Okanda.

6 hrs. **Lahugalawewa.** A restored tank, the haunt of many wild-fowl. There is a Public Works Bungalow at the tank. Its accommodation is limited. Many elephants in the neighbourhood.

From this point an excursion of some days may be made through the wild country on the border of Uva and the Eastern Province. There are next to no villages, and the only accommodation, not specially provided for, would have to be found in the meagre hospitality of some secluded Buddhist monastery of which a few are scattered through the forests. It is useless to indicate any particular route, as that would certainly be made to depend upon the reports received as to the haunts of wild animals at the time.

It may, however, be assumed that a return to comparative civilisation will be made at **Irrakamam**, a restored tank, where there is a Public Works Bungalow. In its vicinity are the scanty ruins of what was once an enormous dagaba, and a good road leads hence to **Kalmunai** (R.H. ✦) on the coast, and thence to (22 m.) **Batticaloa** (see Route 2). The sportsman, however, will probably prefer to proceed through the jungles to **Ambarai** and **Chadiyantalawa** tanks, both of which are swarming with crocodiles; and from the latter to

6 hrs. the river **Namal Aar**, the boundary of the Eastern Province, on crossing which the traveller finds himself again in Uva.

5 hrs. riding along a good track will bring him back to **Nilgala**, from whence he may either return to Badulla the way he came, or by six hrs. **Medagama** (R.H.) and four hrs. Alupota in a lovely position, rejoining the main road to Badulla at (two hrs.) **Passara** (R.H.) see Route 2.

The foregoing tour, under the title of "The Park Country and the Batticaloa Tanks," is more fully described in Sir Samuel Baker's *Rifle and Hound in Ceylon.*

2. **The Horton Plains** (see Rte 2). Here deer are hunted on foot and knifed; there is also excellent trout fishing in season. Full particulars may be obtained at *The Hill Club* or from the Assistant Government Agent at Nuwara Eliya

3. **The Trincomalee District** (see Rte 8).

4. **The Puttalam District** (see Rte 6).

The Wil Pattu Sanctuary. This sanctuary was formed in 1903 on the lines of that of Yala. Its area is 150 sq. m. and its limits are well defined; the eastern boundary being the sea coast at Portugal Bay.

5. **The Hambantotta District** (some parts of this district are referred to in Rte. 1).

6. **Minneri and Polonnaruwa** Rte 8).

Comparative Table of Steamship Services to India.

Line and Date of Sailings.	Tonnage of Steamers.	Length of Voyage.	Fares. 1st Class.	Fares. 2nd Class.	Extra Charges, etc.
To Bombay and Karachi.					
P. & O.—	7—11,000				
From London every Friday		21	£46—52	£32—38	Surtax of 10 p.c
,, Marseilles do.		14	£42—48	£30—35	Charge of £1 for electric fan.
,, Brindisi, Sunday night		11¼	£48	...	Passengers proceed by B.I. steamer from Bombay to Karachi.
From London *viâ* Brindisi, Friday evening.		14	{ 51, 10/- 57, 10/	...	
Anchor, from Liverpool about 3rd and 16th of each month.	5—6,700	23	£35	£26	
Ellerman's City and Hall Lines, from Liverpool twice monthly.	7—9,000	23	£35	£26	10 p.c. surtax. Usual stay at Bombay 6 days.
Messageries Maritimes, monthly from Marseilles.	6—7,000	16	£44—45	£35—42	Charge of 12/ for electric fan. Table claret free.
Societa Nationale di Servizi Maritimi, from Genoa 17th of each month.	4,500	17	£33—37	£23—27	Wine and beer free.
Austrian Lloyd, from Trieste 1st and 16th of each month.	5,500	15	£30—33	£	Through from London £41, 10
To Calcutta.					
P. & O.—Every second Saturday from London.		32	£42	£32	Plus 10 p.c. surtax, and £1 charge for fans.
Ellerman's City Line, from London.		27—30	£37	£27, 10/	Plus 10 p.c. surtax.
Messageries Maritimes, from Marseilles.		23	£44—57	£35—42	
To Colombo.					
Orient S.S. Line—	7—12,000				
From London, every second Friday.		22	£36—52	£32—34	Plus 10 p.c. surtax.
From Marseilles, every second Thursday.		16	£34—43	£30—32	
P. & O.—					
From London, every second Friday.		25	£42—52	£32—38	As above.
From Marseilles, every second Friday.		17	£40—48	£30—36	
Norddeutscher Lloyd—	9—10,000				
From Southampton, every second Tuesday.		25	£57	£37, 10/	
From Genoa, every second Thursday.		16	£53	£35	
Bibby Line—					
From Liverpool, alternate Thursdays.	{ 5,500— 8,000	25	£42	...	One class only.
From Marseilles, alternate Fridays.		17	£40	...	
Messageries Maritimes—					
Alternate Sundays from Marseilles.		18	£44—52	£33—39	12s. charge for fans.
To Rangoon.					
Bibby Line—					
From London.		30	£50	...	
From Marseilles.		23	£45	...	

INDEX AND DIRECTORY FOR 1911-12

(Reference to persons are given in small capital type.)

Mr Murray will feel greatly obliged to travellers who are kind enough to send him notes of any mistakes or omissions that they may notice in this Directory, giving at the same time a permanent address to refer to in case of necessity.

(R.)=Refreshment Room ; **D.B.** = Dak or Travellers' Bungalow ; **R.H.** = Rest House ; **H.** = Hotel.

A

ABBOTABAD, **D.B.**, 245.

ABUL FAZL, 101, 109, 178, 182, 185.

ABU ROAD (R.), 131.
D.B. close to rly. sta. Conveyances to Mt. Abu (17 m.): Phaeton, 20 rs. ; tonga, 10 rs., per seat, 4 rs.; ekka, 4½ rs.

ABU, MOUNT, 132.

ACHILGHAR, 132.

ACHNERA **(R.)**, 163.

ADAM'S PEAK, 479, 485.

ADAMWAHAN BRIDGE, 261.

ADONI, **D.B.**, 349.

ADRA, 87.

AFRIDIS, 249.

AGRA (R)., **D.B.** good, 113, 163, 169, 170. Railway from Bombay, Routes 8(2), 10 and 12; from Delhi and Allahabad, Route 22.
Hotels: *Cecil H.* (Mrs Holtz), excellent, 8 rs. ; *H. Métropole*, newly organised, well spoken of, and *Savoy H.*, 5 rs. ; *Laurie's Great Northern H.*, all about 1 m. from Fort rly. sta. ; *Empress H.* opposite Club.
Banks: *Bank of Bengal*; *Alliance Bank of Simla.*
Churches: *St. George's*, Cantonment, *St Paul's*, Civil Lines, 8 A.M., *St Mathias's*, Agra Fort, *R.C. Cathedral* in Civil Lines.
Club: *Agra C.*, near Post Office.
Missions: *C.M.S.*, St John's College, Baptist Mission.
Shops: *Shawl Merchants, Gold and Silver Embroidery*, Ganeshi Lall and Sons, Drummond Rd., Gulab Chand & Lakhmi Chand Kiniri Bazaar; *Soap-stone, and Inlaid Marble Work*, Nathoo Ram, opposite Agra College; *Miniature Painter*, Badri Pershad; *Photographers*, Priya Lal; *Carpet Factory*, Otto Weylandt & Co., near Itimad ud daulah; *Motors*, Pestonji cantonments and Nathu Mal Mahadeo, Beliganj.
Hackney Carriages:
By distance—

	Class I.	II.
Per mile .	1 r.	8 as.

By time—

	Class I.	II.
Day of 9 hrs.	3 rs.	2 rs.
Half-day .	2 rs.	1¼ rs.
2 hrs. . . .	1 r.	10 as.
1 hr. . . .	12 as.	8 as.

AHALAYA BAI, 26, 28, 49, 90, 160.

AHMAD SHAH DURANI, liii., 188, 198, 215, 225, 230, 299.

AHMEDABAD (R.), 123.
Hotel: *Grand H.*, 6 rs. ; *Empire H.*, 2 m. from rly. sta., near the Church; **Bedrooms**, noisy, attached to the rly. sta. Refreshment Rooms.
Bank: *Bank of Bombay.*
Mission: *Irish Presbyterian Mission, R.C. Church.*
Hackney Carriages

	Class I.	II.
1st hr. . . .	1 r. 12 as.	
Each subs. hr.	12 as.	6 as.
Day . . .	8 rs.	4½ rs.
To city or camp . .	1 r. 12 as.	

AHMEDNAGAR (R.), **D.B.** 346.
Club, good.
Golf Club.
Mission: *S.P.G.*

AIWALLI, 371.

AJANTA, 28, 39.

AJMER (R.), 97, 136.
Sleeping Rooms at the rly. sta. excellent. **D.B.** *Railway H.*, mediocre.
Club: *Kaiser Bagh.*
Mission: *Medical* of U.F. Church of Scotland.
Bank: *Alliance Bank of Simla.*
Hackney Carriages:
By time—

	Class I.	II.
Day of 9 hrs.	5 rs.	3 rs.
Half-day . .	3 rs.	2 rs.
1 hr. . . .	1½ rs.	12 as.

AJODHYA, 275.

AKBAR, EMPEROR, lii., 32, 85, 89, 91, 93, 101, 105, 122, 136, 137, 171, 177, 178, 179, 180, 181, 185, 204, 211, 215, 232, 234, 241, 246, 254, 276, 346.

AKOLA, 83.

AKYAB, D.B., 469.
Club: *Akyab Gymkhana Club*, Main Road.
General Stores: *Woodward & Co., Jacob & Co.*

ALAUDDIN, EMPEROR, 44, 72, 91, 92, 131, 158, 187, 208, 211, 379*b*.

ALBUQUERQUE, ALFONSO DA, 2, 361, 416.

ALEXANDER THE GREAT, 242, 259, 268.

ALIABAD SARAI, 257.

ALIGARH, 298.
D.B. Kellner's Refreshment and Sleeping Rooms.
Mission: *American Methodist Episcopal, R.C. Church.*

ALI MASJID, 249.

ALIPUR, 61.

ALIWAL, 224.

ALLAHABAD (R.), 31, 306.
Railway: From Bombay and to Calcutta, Route 2; from Delhi and Agra, Route 22; to Benares, 23 (*b*); to Lucknow, Route 2, p. 31.
Hotels: *Laurie's Great Northern H.; Grand H.*, Canning Rd.; *Raja H.*
Club: *N.W.P. Club.*
Banks: *Bengal, Upper India, Allahabad.*
Shops: *Jewellers*, Betchler, Hanhart; *Chemists*, Buncombe, Robbie; *Photographer*, Dagg; *Drapers*, Hathaway; Trevellon & Clarke.
Churches: *Cathedral, R.C. Cathedral.*
Missions: *C.M.S.*, St Paul's Church; Divinity College; Presbyterian, American Methodist Episcopal.
Newspapers: *The Pioneer*, a daily paper, one of the most important in India; *The Pioneer Mail*, for readers in Europe.
Tailor: Hathaway.
Bookseller: Sen & Co.
Motors: H. Clerke.
Hackney Carriages:
By time—

	Class I.	II.
1st. hr. . . .	1 r.	12 as.
Subs. hr. .	8 as.	6 as.
½ day . .	2¾ rs.	2 rs.
Day,	4 rs. 8 as.	3 rs. 8 as.

By distance—
(By agreement) . 8 as. per mile.

ALMORA, 283.
D.B., but no hotels.

ALOR, 262.

ALTAMSH, EMPEROR, 104, 110, 165, 200, 208, 210, 212.

ALUTNUWERA, 482.

ALUTOYA, **R.H.** small, well situated for sportsmen, 499.

ALWAR (Ulwar), 143.
D.B. close to rly. sta. Application should be made beforehand to the Senior member of Council for the use of a carriage, which is kindly put at the disposal of visitors (there is a small charge); also for permission to visit the Palace, Library, Treasury, and Armoury.
Mission: U.F. Ch. of Scotland.

AMALNER, 118.

AMARAPURA, 460.

AMARAVATI, 336.

AMARKANTAK, 86.

AMARNATH CAVE, 256.

AMBALANGODA, **R.H.** good; good bathing-place, 487.

AMBALANTOTTA, **R.H.** fair, 489.

AMBARNATH, 337.

AMBEPUSSA, **R.H.** ½ m. from rly. sta., 476.

AMBER, (R.), 142.

AMGAON, 85.

AMIR KHUSRAU, POET, 206, 208.

AMMAYANAYAKKANUR, 432.
D.B. comfortable, close to rly. sta., convenient for travellers to and from Kodaikanal, Palny Hills.

AMRAOTI, 83.
Waiting and Refreshment Rooms. Good **D.B.**

AMRITSAR (R.), 225.
D.B. poor.
Hotels: *Grand, Amritsar, Cambridge*, poor. Amritsar can be conveniently visited from Lahore.
Banks: *Panjab Banking Co.; Commercial Bank of India.*
Missions: *C.M.S.*, St Paul's Church; Schools and Hospital.
Devi Sahai Chambamal, *Carpet and Shawl Manufacturers.* Dealers in Oriental goods; Karamchand Poplai near Golden Temple, Lachman Des Bharani.

ANAGUNDI, 382.

ANAND, 122.

ANANDALE, 219.

ANANTAPUR, 384.

ANDHER, 100.

ANURADHAPURA (R.),
Hotel good, 491-2, 494.
Carriages:

Whole day .	4 rs.
6 hrs. . . .	2 rs.
1 hr. . . .	1 r.
Each subs. hr. . . .	25 cents.

Rickshas:

1st hour . . .	35 cents.
each further ½ hr.	10 cents.

ARCOT, 398.

ARKONAM **(R.)**, 351, 400, 410.
Excellent sleeping accommodation at rly. sta.

ARRAH, **D.B.**, 34.

ARSIKERE **(R.)**, 388.

ASAF KHAN, 129, 172, 238.

ASANSOL **(R.)**, 38, 87, 320.

ASIRGARH HILL-FORT, 29.

ASOKA, EMPEROR, 33, 36, 45, 52, 91, 100, 153, 155, 157, 203, 204, 246, 276, 328, 470.

ASOKA'S PILLARS, 32, 45, 52, 203-4.

ASOKA'S ROCK INSCRIPTIONS, 155, 246, 328.

ASSAM VALLEY, 320.
Mail Communication with Calcutta by Dhubri and by Chandpur. See pp. 320-321*a*.

ASSAYE, 82.

ATCHIBAL, 255.

ATGAON, 23, 25.

ATTOCK, R.H., 245.

AUCKLAND, LORD, 55, 57, 146, 218.

AURANGABAD, D.B. good, but small, 79.

AURANGZEB, EMPEROR, lxii., 49, 50, 73, 79, 80, 91, 92, 97, 108, 113, 117, 133, 159, 165, 171, 173, 197, 198, 199, 203, 206, 212, 233, 239, 265, 349, 355, 363, 367, 369, 376, 379, 383.

AVA, 460.

AVANTIPORE, 255.

AVISAWELLA, **R.H.** excellent, 484.

AWATKOOLA, 253.

AZAMGARH, 311.

AZIMGANJ, 307.

B

BABAR, EMPEROR, 104, 109, 179, 185, 214, 246.

BADAMI, 369.
Rly. **R.H.** Permission to occupy granted by District Traffic Superintendent S. Madras Rly. Bijapur.
BADARPUR, 214.
BADLI, 203, 214.
BADNERA (**R.** and **Waiting Room**) **D.B.,** 83.
BADULLA, R.H. good, 482.
Bank: B. of Uva.
BAGALKOT, 370.
BAGDEHI, 86.
BAHAWALPUR, D.B., 261.
BAHMANI DYNASTY, 348, 349, 373.
BAIZA BAI OF INDORE, lxx., 48, 50.
BALANGODA, **R.H.,** 485.
BALASORE, **D.B.,** 322.
BALBAN EMPEROR, 211, 299, 308.
BALIPITHAM, 436.
BALLYGUNGE (BALLIGANJ), 60.
BALRAMPUR, 275.
BALSAR, 116.
BALTAL, 256.
BALUGAN, 333.
BAMBURA, 266.
BANAVAR, 385.
BANDA (**R.**), **D.B.,** 114.
Club: *Banda C.*
BANDARAWELLA, 482, 486.
R.H. excellent, conducted as an hotel. Coach to Badulla, 18 m.
BANDEL, 69.
BANDIKUI (**R.**), 143, 162.
BANDRA, 115.
BANGALORE (**R.** at City Sta. Tea and Coffee Room at Cantonment Sta.), 384, 389. Railway from Bombay and Poona, Routes 25 and 30; from Madras Route 31(*a*).
Hotels: *Bronson's West End H.*, *Cubbon H.* (accommodation at these 2 hotels is above the average), from 6 rs.; *Grand H.*; *Central H.*; *King's H.*
Missions: *Wesleyan Methodist; Methodist Episcopal; R.C. Cathedral.*
Banks: *Bank of Madras.*
Chemists: Forster, W. E. Smith & Co., Captain & Co.
Jewellers: Barton & Son.
Motors: Indian Cycle & General Engineering Co.
Bookseller: Higginbotham.
Photographers: Wiele, Barton & Son.
Club: *United Service C.*, Residency Road.
Hackney Carriages:
By time—

	Class I.	II.
1st hr. . .	1 r.	12 as.
Each subs. hr.	6 as.	4 as.

By distance—

	Class I.	II.
3 m. . .	1 r.	12 as.
Each subs. m.	4 as.	3 as.

BANKIPUR (R.), 35.
D.B. good, near rly. sta.
Bank: *Bank of Bengal.*
Churches: *St Mark's* and *St Thomas's.*
BANYAN TREES, 33, 66, 119, 352, 358, 404, 434.
BAPATLA, 336.
BARABANKI, 275.
BARA, **D.B.,** 249.
BARAKAR, 38.
BARAMGALLA., **D.B.,** 257.
BARAMULA, 252.
D.B., good.
BARAN, 100.
BARAUNI, 311.
BAREILLY, D.B., 273.
Refreshment Rooms at the rly. sta. with sleeping-rooms.
Club: *Bareilly C.*
Hotel: *Coronation, Civil and Military.*
Banks: *Upper India, Allahabad.*
BARODA, 120.
Good Refreshment and Waiting Rooms and sleeping accommodation.
D.B. in camp. 1½ m. from rly. sta.
Churches: ANGLICAN consecrated by Bp. Heber, 1824; restored 1838. There are also *R.C.* and *Methodist Churches.*
BARRACKPUR, 66.
BARSI ROAD (**R.**), **R.H.** 347.
BARWARI, 203.
BARWA-SAUGAR, **D.B.,** 113.
BASSEIN (*Burma*), 466, 470.
BASSEIN ROAD, 115.
Waiting Room at rly. station.
D.B. near ruins. Write to station-master for conveyance.
BATALA, 228.
BATTICALOA, R.H. new and good, 483.
BATTUL OYA, 490.
BATWA, 129.
BAWAN, 255.
BAYANA BIANA, 122, 185.
BEAWAR, **D.B.,** 136.
BEDSA CAVES, 341.
BEGUMPUR (Delhi), 207.
BELGAUM (R.), 357.
D.B. ½ m. from sta. Hotel near sta.
Mission: *Methodist Episcopal; R.C. Church.*
BELIHULOYA. **R.H.** good, 486.
BELLARY (R.), D.B., Royal Hotel, 383.
London Missionary Society.
BELLS, 451, 460, 467.
BELPAHAR, 86.
BELUR, R.H., 387.
BENARES. Railway from Bombay and Calcutta, Route 2; from Lucknow, 20 (*a*): from Allahabad, 23 (*b*). **D.B.,** 34, 43, 279.
Hotels: *Clarke's H.*, *H. de Paris*, 5 rs., both good.
Bank: *Bank of Bengal.*
Missions: *C.M.S.* (at Sigra), St Paul's Church, College and Normal Schools, London Mission, Wesleyan, Baptist Zanana, R.C. Church.
Hackney Carriages.

1 hr. . .	10 as.
Each subs. hr.	5 as.
To Sarnat and back . .	2½ rs.

BENTINCK, LOR WM., cvii., 55, 57, 224, 403.
BENTOTTA, **R.H.** very good, 487.
BERAR, 82.
BERARLI, 258.
BERHAMPORE (Bengal), **D.B.,** 312.
BERHAMPUR (Ganjam), 333.
BERNIER, 197, 254.
BESNAGAR, 100.
BET, 161.
BETTIAH, 311.
BEYPUR, 416.
BEZWADA (R.)
D.B., 335, 380-383.
BHAGALPUR, **D.B.,** 310.
BHAJA CAVES, 340.
BHAKKUR (R.), D.B., 267.

BHAMO, 461.
Express steamboats from Mandalay every Wednesday, and Katha, due at Bhamo Friday. Return from Bhamo every Saturday. Rly. open to Myitkyina.
BHANDARA ROAD, **D.B.**, 85.
BHANDUP, 21.
BHANGIR, 379*a*.
BHARATPUR, 162.
D.B. outside the Muttra Gate.
BHATINDA, 146.
BHAUNAGAR, 151.
D.B. Horse and bullock shigrams to be had.
BHAYANDAR, 115.
BHILSA, 98.
BHIMBER, **D.B.**, 256.
BHIM TAL, 282.
BHIWANI, 145.
BHOJEEPURA, 281.
BHOJPUR, 100.
BHOPAL (R.), 97.
D.B. near rly. sta.
BHUSAWAL **(R.)**, 28, 82.
BHUTIA BASTI, 316.
BHUVANESHWAR, 323, 326.
BIBILE, **R.H.**, 482.
BIDAR, 373.
BIDERRA, 69.
BIJAPUR (R.), 363.
D.B. in the town. Tongas are to be had at the rly. sta. Fares whole day, 2 rs.; from station to any residence, 8 as.
BIKANER, **D.B.**, 135.
BIKRAMPUR, 29.
BILASPUR (R.), 86.
BILESHWAR, 161.
BIMLAPATAM, 334.
BINA **(R.)**, 100.
BIRUR, 385.
BLACK PAGODA, 332.
BOBBILE, 334.
BOGRA, 321.
BOLAN PASS, 270.
BOLARAM, 379.
BOMBAY, 1-18, *see* Special Index, p. 1.
Railways: To Calcutta by G.I.P. and E.I. Rlys. Routes 2 and 7; to Poona, Madras, and Bangalore, by G.I.P. and Madras Rlys., Routes 25 and 31; to Ahmadabad by B.B. and C.L. Rlys., Route 10; to Allahabad, Route 2; to Agra, Routes 9 and 12*a*; to Delhi, Routes 10*a* and 12*c*.
Hotels: *Taj Mahal Palace H.* (Tata's), near the Apollo Bandar, one of the best in India; *Watson's Esplanade H.*, close to Secretariat: this hotel has an *Annexe*, where travellers will probably be more comfortable; *Great Western H.* in Apollo Street; *Apollo H.*; *Camballa H.*, on Khamballa Hill (good for a lengthened stay).
Restaurants: *Victoria Station Restaurant*; *The Apollo*, Apollo Bandar; *Cornaglia*, late *Peliti* (confectioner), 83 Meadow St.
Agents: *Messrs King, King & Co.*, Standard Buildings, Hornby Row (branch of *Henry S. King & Co.*, 65 Cornhill); *Grindlay, Groom & Co.*, Hornby Road; *Latham & Co.*, Apollo Street. These firms undertake all business in connection with travelling and financial arrangements, forwarding of goods, engaging of native servants, etc., in India.
Thos. Cook & Son, Esplanade Road, supply all kinds of information about excursions and tours in India, and provide circular tickets, etc.
Bands: On certain days of the week at the *Yacht Club* and on the *Esplanade*, a favourite promenade; also at *Victoria Gardens*, Byculla.
Bankers: *Bank of Bombay*, *Bank of Bengal*, and *Chartered Bank of India*, Elphinstone Circle; *Hong-Kong and Shanghai Bank*, 40 Church Gate Street; *National Bank of India*, Rampart Row; *Mercantile Bank of India*, Esplanade Road; *Bank of Australia and China*, Esplanade Road; *Comptoir National d'Escompte*, Esplanade Road.
Baths: Salt-water *Swimming Baths* on *Back Bay*, and at *Breach Candy*.
Booksellers: *Thacker & Co., Ltd.*, Esplanade Rd.; *A. J. Combridge & Co.*, Hummam Street.
Chemists: *Kemp & Co.*, corner of Church Gate St. and Elphinstone Circle; *Treacher & Co.*, Esplanade Road; *Phillips & Co.*, Esplanade Road.
Churches, etc., *see* Special Index, p. 1.
Clubs: *Byculla Club*, Bellasis Road, Byculla, with sleeping accommodation attached.
Bombay Club, 26 Esplanade.
Yacht Club, on the Apollo Bandar, overlooking the bay. Subscriptions for Strangers admitted as members, 16 rs. a month. Ladies are admitted when accompanied by a member or hon. member.
The Bombay Gymkhana and *Golf Club*, Queen's Road.
Ladies' Gymkhana, The Ridge, Malabar Hill, with lawn tennis and badminton grounds. A favourite resort in the evenings.
Consuls: *Austro-Hungary*, Count Von Thurmond Valsasina.
France, M. Charles Barret, Roosevelt House, Apollo Bandar.
Germany, Herr E. Hever.
Italy, Sr. Giovanni Gorio, Marsaban Row.
U.S.A., Mr E. Haldeman, Dennison.
There are representatives of most other nations, including Japan, Turkey, and Persia.
Conveyances: Carriages with a single horse, 5 rs. a day, with 2 horses, 10 rs. There are plenty of victorias in the streets to be hired by the trip or for the hour at very moderate fixed fares—only 8 as. inside the Fort limits.
Taxis: Inside 5 m. radius. First mile, 8 as. and 6 as.; each subsequent ½ m., 2 as.; halts, 1 anna for every 2 and 3 minutes; 1 r. 14 as. per hour.
Motors: For morning 15 rs. for afternoon 20 rs. for afternoon and evening 20 rs., for day of 12 hrs. 60 rs.

Dentists: *Campbell and Barr*, Esplanade Road. *Dr Gheesta.*

General Stores: *Treacher & Co., Army and Navy Stores, Phillips & Co.*, all on the Esplanade.

Hairdressers: *Fucile*, under Bombay Club.

House Agent: *E. Flower*, Hummam St.

Libraries: *Asiatic Society Library* in the Town Hall; the *Sassoon Institute*, Esplanade, adjoining Watson's Hotel (strangers can join the lending library for a week).

Markets: *Crawford*, for fruit, vegetables, flowers, poultry, meat, etc.

Cloth, in Native Quarter, Shaikh Memon Street.

Copper, close to Mombadevi Tank, Native Quarter.

Medical Practitioners *Dr Sidney Smith*, Mazagon Road; *Lt. Col. Barry*, Apollo Bandar; *Major S. H. Burnett, Lt. Col. J. Crimmin, V.C., C.I.E.*, Pres. Surgeons, *Miss Eliz. Walker*, Carnac Road.

Milliner, Dressmaker, etc., *Laidlaw & Whiteway*, Esplanade; *Badham & Co.*

Missions, etc., see p. 18.

Newspapers: There are two leading English papers in Bombay, the *Times of India* and the *Bombay Gazette*, besides a number of native papers. The *Advocate of India* is an English evening paper.

Oculist: *Dr Herbert.*

Opticians: *Lawrence & Mayo; Marcks & Co.*—both in Esplanade Road.

Outfitters: *Badham & Pile, Limited; Asquith & Co.; Laidlaw & Whiteway; Hoar & Co.*—all in Esplanade Road.

Photographers: *Raja Dindiyal, Bourne & Shepherd*, 18 Esplanade Road.

Steamship Agencies: *P. & O. S.S. Co.*, 19 Rampart Row. Steamers every week to Aden, Ismailia, Port Said, Brindisi, Marseilles, Gibraltar, Plymouth, and London; and every fortnight to Malta, Colombo, Madras, Calcutta, Straits Settlements, China, Japan, and Australia.

British India S.N. Co., Mackinnon, Mackenzie & Co., Ballard Road, for Calcutta, and coast ports, Karachi, Persian Gulf, Burma, and E. Coast of Africa.

Hall and *Ellerman's City Lines*, Killick Nixon, Home Street.

Messageries Maritimes, Albert Buildings, Hornby Road.

Societa Nationale di Servizi Marittimi (*Rubattino*), Elphinstone Circle.

Austro-Hungarian Lloyd's S.N. Co., to Trieste, H. von Hoffer, 50 Church Gate St.

Wilson Line of Steamers, Finlay, Muir & Co., Esplanade. To Karachi, Middlesbro or Hull every fortnight.

Anchor Line of Steamers, W. & A. Graham & Co., Graham's Buildings; Nord Deutscher Lloyd, Glade & Co.

Bombay Steam Navigation Co. (Shepherd & Co.), Frere Road—for neighbourhood of Bombay, Ratnaghiri, Goa, Mangalore.

Nippon Yusen Kaisha, to China and Japan, Hornby Road.

Theatres: The *Gaiety* and the *Novelty*, near the Victoria sta. at the S. end of Esplanade Market Road, and the *Native Theatre* in Grant Road.

Tourist Office: *Messrs T. Cook & Son*, opposite Esplanade H., are also agents for rly. tickets and all kinds of information in connection with excursions and tours (*e.g.* to Elephanta and Kanbari). "Cook's Indian Tours," a pamphlet (1s.), containing full information about tours, price of tickets, etc., will be found very useful.

Tramways run from end to end of Bombay, and extend from *Colaba* and the *Fort* to *Grant Road*, to *Parell*, and to the *Docks*. They are not much used by higher classes of Europeans.

Wine Merchants: *Phipson & Co.* and *Treacher & Co.*, in Esplanade Road.

BOONDI, 97.

BORE GHAT, 23.

BORIVLI, 21, 115.

BOSTAN (R.), 272.

BOWRINGPET, 396.
See Kolar Gold Fields.

BOTAD, 149.

BRAHMAPUTRA RIVER, 321.

BRINDABAN, 168.

BROACH, 119.
D.B. in town. Waiting Room at sta.

BUDDH GAYA, 36.

BUDDHA (Gautama or Gaudama in Burma), lxii., 36, 37, 41, 43, 52, 58, 76, 231, 243, 247-8, 276, 294, 312, 452, 456, 459, 466, 467, 495, 499.

BUDDHIST TEMPLES, 36, 463, 478, 490, 495.

BUDDHIST TOPES, *see* Stupas.

BUDGE BUDGE, 70.

BUNDELKUND PROVINCE, 101.

BURDWAN (R.), D.B., 39.

BURHANPUR, D.B. 28.

BUTTALA, R.H. (good), 500.

BUXAR (R.), 34.
D.B. near Fort.

C

CACHAR, D.B., 320.

CALCUTTA, 53. *See* special Index there.

Railways: From Bombay by Allahabad and by Nagpur, Routes 2 and 7; from Madras, Route 24; from Darjeeling, Route 23(*d*); from Dacca Route 23(*a*); from Lucknow and Benares, Routes 20(*a*) and 2.

Hotels: The *Grand H.*, *H. Continental*, 8 rs., both in Chowringhee; *The Great Eastern H.*, Old Court House Street, good; *Spence's H.*, Wellesley Place, moderate; *H. de Paris* (*Bonsard's*), Dharamtolla; *Hotel Métropole.* For a great capital all the hotels of Calcutta are disappointing. Electric fans usually 1 r. per diem.

Boarding Houses are numerous, and are often preferred to hotels, especially for a lengthened stay in Calcutta. The approximate charges are 175 rs. a month, or 7 rs. a day, for board and lodging (wine not included). In the height of the season, about Christmas time, charges sometimes run up to 9 rs. and 10 rs. a day, and accommodation must be secured weeks beforehand. Meals are taken together as a rule, but in some houses suites or single rooms may be engaged, with meals served in private.

Mrs Walter's, 6-9 Russell Street, *Mrs Pell's*, 1 Camac Street, 9 Middleton Row; *Mrs Monk's*, 11 Middleton Row, Camac Street, Harrington Street, and Park Street; *Mrs Baily*, 10 Middleton Row.

Restaurant and Confectioners: *Peliti*, 11 Govt. Place; *Gt. Eastern H.*

Bankers and Agents: *Grindlay & Co.*, 11 Hastings Street.

King, Hamilton and Co. (Branch of Henry S. King & Co., 65 Cornhill), 4, 5 Koila Ghat Street, undertake all business in connection with travelling and financial arrangements for travellers in India.

T. Cook & Son, 9 Old Court House Street, supply all kinds of information about excursions and tours in India, and provide circular tickets, etc.

Banks: *Bank of Bengal*, 3 Strand; *Ch. Bank of India, Australia, and China*, 5 Clive St.; *Merc. Bank of India, Ltd.*, 28 Dalhousie Sq.,; *Delhi and London Bank.*, 4 Council House St.; *Hong - Kong and Shanghai Banking Corpor.*, 31 Dalhousie Sq., *National Bk. of India*, 104 Clive St.; *Alliance Bk. of Simla*, 5 Council House St., *Deutsch Asiatische Bk.*, 32 Dalhousie Sq.

Bath: An excellent *Swimming Bath* on the Esplanade, admission through members.

Booksellers and Stationers: *Thacker, Spink, & Co.*, Government Place; *W. Newman & Co.*, Dalhousie Sq.

Chemists: *R. Scott Thomson & Co.*, 15 Chowringhee Road, E.; *Bathgate & Co.*, Old Court House St.; *Smith Stanistreet*, Dalhousie Sq.

Churches: (ANGLICAN) —*St Paul's Cathedral*; *St John's Church*, formerly the cathedral; *The Old Church* (C.M.S.); *St Peter's*, in the Fort; *St Thomas's* (the Free School Church).

(CHURCH OF SCOTLAND) —*St Andrew's*, Dalhousie Sq.; *U.F. Church of Scotland*, Wellesley Sq. Manse, Park St.

OTHERS: The *Wesleyan Church*; the *Baptist Chapel*, Lal Bazar and Circular Road; Congregational *Union Chapel*, Dharamtolla & Hastings: *American Meth. Episcopal*, Dharamtolla; *R.C.*, Middleton Row; Portuguese Church Street; Dharamtolla Rd.

Clubs (Residential): *Bengal Club*, 33 Chowringhee Road, S. side of Esplanade. The houses, 1 Park St., and 1 and 5 Russell St., are fitted as chambers for residents; 33 Chowringhee Road, contains bedrooms for members. Members of this Club, are hon. members of the *Madras*, *Byculla*, *Hong-Kong*, and *Shanghai Clubs*, and *vice versa*.

The United Service Club, 31 Chowringhee Road. Attached to it are the houses 1, 2, and 3 Kyd St. and 56 Park St.

German Club, 40 Free School St.

Consuls: *Austro-Hungary*, Dr Ferdinand Freyesleben, C.G., 36 Theatre Rd.

France, Mons. A. E. Roussin, Office, 28 Pollock Street.

Germany, Prinz Heinrich XXXI., Reuss, C.G.

Italy, Cavaliere A Pittaluga Office, 1 Rawdon Street.

Russia, R. C. Arsenieff.

U.S.A., Mr W. H. Michael, C.G., Office, 3 Esplanade Row, E.

All leading countries are represented at Calcutta by Consuls.

Conveyances: Motors can be hired at about 10 rs. per hr., or 60 rs. per day of 8 hrs., of the French Motor Car Co., 55 Bentinck St., and of the British Engineering Co., 47 Bentinck Street. Taxi-cabs can be hired at rates of 8 as. per m. 1st class, and 5 as. per m. 2nd class. Carriages can be hired at from 6 to 15 rs. a day. Cabs (commonly called *ticca gharries*) are plentiful; charges are:

By time—

	Class I.	II.
1st hr. .	1 r.	12 as.
Subs. hr. .	8 as.	6 as.
Half-day	3 rs.	2 rs.
Day . .	5 rs.	3 rs. 8 as.

By distance—

	Class I.	II.
1st mile . .	8 as.	6 as.
Subs. miles	6 as.	4 as.

Dentists: *H. Pedler*, 35 Chowringhee Road; *Smith Bros.*, 9 Chowringhee Rd.

Drapers: *Clark & Co.*, Old Court House Street; *Francis, Harrison, Hathaway & Co.*, Government Place; *Whiteway & Laidlaw*, Chowringhee.

Hairdressers: *Watson & Summers*, Old Court House St.; *Youd & Co.*, 6 Hare Street.

Jewellers, Silversmiths, and Watchmakers: *Hamilton & Co.*, Old Court House St.; *Cooke & Kelvey*, Old Court House St.; *Boseck & Co.*, Wellesley Place.

Lady Doctors: *Miss Baumler*, 7 Chowringhee Place.

Medical Men: *Lt. Col. Green*, 6 Harrington Street; *Lt. Col. Bird*, 2 Middleton Row; *Major Rogers*, 3 Loudon Street; *Major Stevens*, 8 Middleton Street

Missions: *Oxford Mission*, 42 Cornwallis Street. The clergy have charge of a Boys' High School, an Industrial School for Natives, and St James's School for Eurasians—a in the city; and of village schools in the Sunderbans 3 m. off. The Superior is Principal of Bishop's College, Circular Road.

S.P.G. 224 Lower Circular Road.

The *Clewer Sisters*, working since 1881, nurse the General Hospital, Medical Staff Hospital, and Eden Hospital, and have charge of the Canning Home for Nurses, European Girl's Orphanage, and Pratt Memorial School. In 1890 they took over from the *Ladies' Assocn.* (*S.P.G.*) their work.

C.M.S., 10 Mission Row, Divinity School, Old Church, Trinity Church, and Christ's Church, Boys' and Girls' Schools.

Church of Scotland, Cornwallis Square.

U.F. Church of Scotland, 2 Cornwallis Square.

Baptist Mission Society, 42 Lower Circular Road.

Native Booksellers: *S. K. Lahiri & Co.* 54 College Street.

Newspapers: *The Englishman*, 9 Hare St., the leading paper in Bengal; *Indian Daily News*, 19 British India St.; *Statesman*, 8 Chowringhee Road; *The Asian* devoted to sport and planting interests. The leading Native papers in English are—*The Hindu Patriot*, *Indian Mirror*, *Amrita Bazar*, *Patrika*.

Opticians: *Lawrence & Mayo*; *Solomons & Co.*; *N. Lazarus.*

Outfitters: *Gt. Eastern Hotel Co.*; *Ramsay, Wakefield & Co.*; *Whiteway, Laidlaw & Co.*; 7 Esplanade, East; *Army & Navy Stores*, Chowringhee and Middleton Streets; *Francis Harrison Hathaway*, 13 Government Place.

Photographers: *Johnston & Hoffmann*, 22 Chowringhee Road; *Bourne & Shepherd*, 9 Chowringhee Road.

Photographic Apparatus: *W. Newman & Co.* Dalhousie Sq.; *John Blees*, 2 Hare St.

Societies: CHARITABLE AND RELIGIOUS.—Besides the Societies mentioned above the following have their Indian headquarters in Calcutta—*The Additional Clergy Society*; *The Methodist Episcopal Mission*; *The London Missionary Society*; *The Wesleyan Missions*; several special *Zanana Missions.*

SCIENTIFIC, ETC. — *The Asiatic Society*, Park Street, founded by Sir William Jones; *The Microscopical Society and the Photographic Society* have rooms in the same building.

Steamship Agencies (General).

P. & O. S.N. Co., (*Best & Co.*), 10 Strand. Steamers every fortnight for Colombo, Aden, Ismailia, Port Said, Marseilles, Plymouth, and London; also for Bombay, China, Japan, Australia, etc.

British India S.N. Co., *Mackinnon, Mackenzie & Co.*, 16 Strand, for London, Colombo, Coast ports, Karachi, Persian Gulf, Burma, Straits Settlements, and Australia *via* Torres Straits.

Ellerman's, Hall & City Lines of S.S., *Gladstone, Wyllie & Co.*, 101 Clive St.

Clan Line Steamers, *Finlay, Muir & Co.*, 1 Clive St.

Messageries Maritimes, 5-6 Hare St.

Austro - Hungarian Lloyd's S.N. Co., 30 Dalhousie Sq.

Anchor Line, *Graham & Co.*, 9 Clive St.

Nord Deutscher Lloyd, *Schröder, Smidt & Co.*

Steamship Agencies (Local): *River S.N. Co.*, *Macneill & Co.*, 2 Clive Ghat St.

Orissa Carrying Company's Steamers, *Macneill & Co.*, plying between Calcutta and Chandbally.

Calcutta S.N. Co., *Hoare, Miller & Co.* 38 Strand Road.

Tailors: *Ranken & Co.*, 4 Old Court House St.; *Harry Clark*, 5 do. do.; *W. H. Phelps & Co.*, 15 do. do.; *Harman & Co.*, 12 Govt. Place, E.

Theatres: *The Corinthian*, Dharamtolla; *The Royal*, Chowringhee Road; *The Opera House*, Lindsay St. *Native Theatres* are chiefly in Beadon St.

CALICUT, 417.

Hotel: *Mr P. Canaren's Esplanade H.* near the Beach. Good **D.B.**

Steamship Agents: *B.I.S.N. Co.*

CAMBAY, 122.

CAMPBELL, SIR COLIN, LORD CLYDE, cii., 286, 290-92, 295, 297, 304, 306.

CAMPOLI, 337.

CANNANORE, 419.

D.B. good.

Hotel: Esplanade.

CANNING, LADY, 60, 66, 316.

CANNING, LORD, xcix., ciii., 56, 57, 305.

CAPE COMORIN, 437.

CARNATIC, NAWABS OF, 397, 403.

CASTLE ROCK (**R.**), 358.

CAUVERY FALLS, **D.B.**, 392. Tonga from Maddur (not always available—order beforehand).

CAVES, BUDDHIST, 22, 27, 36, 40, 74, 81, 153, 324, 338, 340, 438, 467, 493.

— BRAHMAN, 19, 23, 76, 335, 370, 438.

— JAIN, 79, 326, 370.

CAWNPORE, ci., 103, 301 (**R.** good).

Railways: From Delhi and Agra and to Allahabad, Route 22. From Lucknow, Route 22, p. 306.

Hotels: *Civil and Military*, the best, 5 rs.; *Empress H.*, *Victoria H.*—all poor.

Club: *Cawnpore C.*, Mall.

Banks: Bengal, Allahabad, National Bank of India, Alliance Bank of Simla.

Hackney Carriages:

By distance—

	Class I.	II.
Per mile .	8 as.	6 as.

By time—

	Class I.	II.
Full day .	4 rs.	3 rs.
Half-day .	2½ rs.	2 rs.
1 hr. . .	12 as.	8 as.

Missions: the *S.P.G.* (Mission House, Christ-Church) have charge of Christ Church School, Generalganj School, and a Girl's Boarding School.

The *Ladies' Association* (*S.P.G.*) have six schools and work in the zananas.

Woman's Union Missionary Society of America.

Methodist Epis. Mission.

R.C. Church.

CHAGOTI, **D.B.**, 252.

CHAIBASA, 87.

CHAKARDARPUR, 87.

CHAKRATA, **D.B.**, 281.

CHALISGAON, 28.

CHAMAN, 272.
CHAMBA, D.B., 228.
CHAMPA, 86.
CHAMPANIR, 120.
CHANDA, D.B., 83.
CHANDAUSI (R), 273, 299.
CHANDERNAGORE, 39, 68.
Two Hotels in Fort.
CHANDIL, 87.
CHANDNI, 29.
CHANDOD, 120.
CHANDPUR, 319.
CHANDRAGIRI, 350.
CHANGAS SARAI, D.B., 257.
CHAPPAR RIFT, 272.
CHARNOCK, JOB, 53, 63, 66.
CHATRAPUR, 333.
CHATTISGARH, 85.
CHAUMUKH, 257.
CHAVAKACHCHERI, R.H., good, 497.
CHAYA, 161.
CHENNARAYAPATNAM, 387.
CHERAT, D.B., 246.
CHERRA-POONJI, 320.
D.B. commodious, with servants.
CHICACOLE, 334.
CHIDAMBARAM, 424.
D.B. 1½ m. from rly. sta.
CHILAW, R.H., good, 490.
CHILIANWALA, 242.
CHILKA LAKE, 333.
CHINDWIN, 470.
CHINGLEPUT, (R), D.B. good, 401, 419.
CHINHAT, 286, 297.
CHINSURAH, 69.
CHISHTI SAINTS, 72, 138, 184, 206, 222, 259, 348.
CHITALDRUG, 385.
CHITORGARH, 92.
D.B. 1 m. from rly. sta., belonging to Udaipur State, good.
For permission to see the fort, and for the use of the elephant, which is kept at the place by the Darbar for the use of visitors, application must be made to the Hákim (chief official) on the spot.
CHITTAGONG, D.B. 319.
Club: *Chittagong C.*
Bank: *Bank of Bengal.*
Mission: *Baptist*, *R.C. Church.*
CHITTAPUR, 373.
CHORAL, 89.
CHOTA-NAGPUR, 34, 87.
Mission: Headquarters of *Trinity College Dublin Mission.*
CHUNAR, 33.
CLIVE, LORD, 2, 54, 61, 67, 70, 312-13, 398-9, 405, 430.
COAL, 29, 39, 83, 321.
COCANADA, 334.
Hotel: *Victoria H.*
Bank: *Madras.*
COCHIN, 415.
Hotel: *Family H.*; D.B. fair.
Church: *R.C. Cathedral.*
Steamers: *B.I.S.N. Co.*
COIMBATORE, D.B., 411.
COLOMBO, 472.
Hotels: *Grand Oriental H.* (usually known as the G.O.H.), very good; excellent cuisine.
Bristol H., good.
Galle Face H., quieter and in a pleasanter situation than the G.O.H., close to the sea. 1½ m. from the landing-place. There is a swimming bath attached to the hotel.
The *Grand H.* at *Mount Lavinia*, 7 miles distant by rail from Colombo, is much frequented by visitors. It is delightfully situated on a promontory overlooking the sea. Excellent fish tiffins on Sundays.
Agents: *H. W. Cave & Co.*, for Henry S. King & Co.; *Thos. Cook & Son*, 1 Victoria Arcade, opposite G.O.H.; *George Steuart & Co.*, 14 Queen St., for Coutts & Co., Cox & Co., Grindlay & Co., London County Bank, etc.
Banks: *National Bank of India Ltd.; Bank of Madras; Hongkong and Shanghai Bank; Chartered Bank of India, Australia, and China; Mercantile Bank of India, Ltd.*
Chemists: *Colombo Apothecaries Co. Ltd.*
Churches: *St Thomas's Cathedral*, Mutwal; *S. Peter's*, The Fort; *Christ Church* (*C.M.S.*); *Trinity Church*, Maradana; *S. Michael's*, Polwatte; and others.
St Lucia (R.C. CATHEDRAL), *St Philip Neri* (most convenient for visitors), and many others.
(CHURCH OF SCOTLAND)—*St Andrew's*, near the Galle Face Hotel.
(NONCONFORMIST)—*Wesleyan*, Pettah; *Baptist*, Cinnamon Gardens; *Dutch Church*, Wolfendahl; and others.
Clubs: the *Colombo C.* on the Galle Face.
Golf C. 2 m. from The Fort. Also the *Garden Club* and *Princes Club.*
Consuls: *Austro-Hungary*, Sr. C. O. Pöhn.
France, Mon. A. Philippe.
Germany, Herr Ph. Freudenberg.
Italy, Sr. Clemente O. Pöhn.
U.S.A., Mr W. C. Magalssen.
Dentists: *Dr H. W. Atkins Smith*, at the G.O.H.; *Dr Sidney Garne*, Bristol Hotel.
Doctors: *J. Llewellyn Thomas; D. Rockwood; A. Castellani.*
Booksellers, Stationers, etc.: *H. W. Cave & Co.*, Queen St., and the *Colombo Apothecaries' Co. Ltd.*
General Outfitters: *Cargills Ltd.* (also at Kandy and Nuwara Eliya); *Whiteaway, Laidlaw & Co.*
General Stores: *Cargills Ltd.* (also Kandy and Nuwara Eliya); *Miller & Co.* (also Kandy); *Whiteaway, Laidlaw & Co.; Colombo Apothecaries Co. Ltd.* (also Kandy).
Hackney Carriages: 1 r. 50 c. per hr., 4½ rs. per diem.
Hospitals: *General Civil Hospital*, with three wards for Europeans; *Eye Hospital; Stirling Nursing Home.*
Ivories, Tortoiseshell Jewellery, Moon-stones, etc.: *P. G. Silva*, Chatham St.; *O. L. M. Macan Marcar*, at the G.O.H.
Missions: *S.P.G.*, St Thomas's College; *C.M.S.*, Galle Face; Christ Church; St. Luke's and several schools.
E. Grinstead Sisters Schools and Orphanage (at Polwatte).
Motors: *Walker & Son.*
Photographers: F. Skeen & Co., 41 Chatham St., Fort.

Railway and Coaching Rates and Carriage and Rickshaw Fares: See *The Pocket Time and Fare Table*, 10 cents; published by Government.

Steamship Agencies:

The P. & O. S.N. Co. office is in the Victoria Arcade, opposite the G.O.H. and the Messageries at No. 5 Prince Street.

Messageries Maritimes. Agent, De Bure.

Orient. Agent, Whittall & Co.

Norddeutscher Lloyd. Agents, Freudenberg & Co.

Bibby Line. Agents, Carson & Co.

British India S.N. Co. Agents, Madura & Co.

Ellerman's Hall and City Lines. Agents, Aitken, Spence & Co.

Anchor Line. Agents, Delmege, Forsyth & Co.

Clan Line. Agents, Jas. Finlay & Co.

Note.—Over sixty different "lines" of steamers call at Colombo.

CONJEEVERAM, 399.
No **D.B.** here, but good waiting room at station. Conjeeveram can be visited from Chingleput or Arkonam.

COOCH BEHAR, 321.

COONOOR (R.), 412.
Hotels: *Glenview H.*, *Gray's H.*, *Hill Grove H.* (all good).
Coonoor Club.
Pasteur Institute.

COORG, 396.

COOTE, SIR EYRE, 54, 403, 420, 422, 423, 424.

CORNWALLIS, MARQUIS OF, 8, 56, 57, 390, 393, 405.

CORRYAT, T., 118, 137.

CUDDALORE, D.B., 423.
Steamship Agents: *B.I.S.N. Co.*, Parry & Co.

CUDDAPAH, **D.B.**, 350.

CUMBUM, 384.

CURZON, LORD, lxxvii., cx.-xi., 32, 60-1, 137, 173, 197-8, 236.

CUTCH, 148.

CUTTACK (R.), D.B., 323.
Club: within the Fort enclosure.
Missions: *Orissa Baptist*, *R.C. Church.*

D

DABHEJI, 265.

DABHOI, 120.

DACCA, 318.
D.B. near rly. sta.
Club: *Dacca C.*
Bank: *Bank of Bengal.*
Hackney Carriages: 1st hr., 12 as.; subsequent hrs., 6 as. Half-days, 2 rs.; day, 3 rs. 8 as.
Missions: *Baptist*, *R.C. Cathedral.*

DAGSHAI, 218.

DAKOR, 122.

DALHOUSIE, 228.
Hotels: *Strawberry Bank H.* (best); *Springfield H.*; *Bull's Head H.*; *Grandview H.*
Between Pathankot and Dalhousie it is most convenient to sleep at the **D.B.**, Danera.
Tonga from Pathankot to Danera, rs. 15. Seat in do., rs. 7.
Dhooli Danera to Dalhousie, rs. 9.
Pony or Rickshaw, rs. 5.

DALHOUSIE, MARQUIS OF xcvi., cviii., 56, 62, 395, 445.

DAL LAKE, 254.

DALTONGANJ, 34.

DAMAN ROAD, 116.
D.B. beyond town at mouth of river, good.

DAMBOOL or **DAMBULLA, R.H.** excellent, 493.

DAM DIM, 314.

DAMODAR RIVER, 70.

DAMOH, 66, 100.

DAMUKDIA, 314.

DANERA, **D.B.**, 228.

DARBHANGA, 311.

DARJEELING, 315.
Hotels: *Woodlands H.*, good, with fine views; *Grand H.* (Mrs Monk), open all the year, good; *Richardson's H.*; *Drum Druid H.*; *Rockville H.*
Boarding Houses: *Ada Villa*; *Bellevue*; *Himalaya Cottage.*
Club: *Darjeeling C.*, Auckland Road.
Bank: *Alliance Bank of Simla.*
Chemists: Partridge, Roberts.
Outfitters: Whiteaway, Laidlaw & Co.
Churches: *Scotch Church*, *R.C. Church.*

DATIA, 103.

DAULATABAD (R.) D.B., 71.
Station for Ellora; see Ellora in Index.

DEESA, **D.B.**, 131.

DEHRA DUN, D.B., 280.
Hotel: *Alexandra H.*
Club: *Dehra Dun C.*
Bank: *Bank of Upper India.*

DELHI (R.), c., 147 186.
Hotels: *Maidens H.* (electric light and fans). *Cecil H.* (Mrs Holtz), both in the Civil Lines, near Ludlow Castle, and very good, 7-8 rs. per diem; *Woodlands H.*, by St James's Church, *Civil and Military H.*, Kashmir Gate, 5-6 rs.
Railways: From Bombay, Routes 10, 11(*a*) and 12(*c*); to Lahore, Route 15; to Agra, Cawnpur, and Allahabad, Route 22; to Lucknow, Routes 15(*b*) and 20.
Club: *Delhi Club* in Ludlow Castle.
Banks: *Bank of Bengal*, *Delhi Bank*, *Bank of Upper India*, and others.
Motor cars on hire at *Maidens H.*
Hackney Carriages:

	Class I.	II.
Per day[1]	5 rs.	$3\frac{1}{4}$ rs.
1st. hr.[1]	1 rs.	12 as.
Subs. hr.[1]	8 as.	6 as.
To the Kutab	12 rs.	8 rs.

Newspaper: The *Morning Post.*
Churches: *St James's*, *St Stephen's* of Cambridge Mission, *R.C. Church.*
Mission: *S.P.G.* and *Cambridge Mission*; *Baptist Mission*; *Baptist Zanana Mission.*
Photographer: *Sultan Ahmad Khan*, inside Delhi Gate.
Merchants: Many well-known shops in the Chandni Chauk of jewellers and sellers of embroideries and all kinds of ornamented ware. *Imre Schwaiger*, Kashmir Gate, has been highly recommended.

DEOLALI, 25.

DEOLI, 97.

[1] These rates apply to trips to Humayuns Tomb, Nizam-ud-din and Safdar Jang.

DERA GHAZI KHAN, D.B., 242.
DERA ISMAIL KHAN, D.B., 242.
DEWAL, **D.B.**, good, 252.
DHANUSHKODI, Indian Terminus of direct rly. route to Ceylon and Colombo, p. 434, 496.
DHAR, 89.
D.B., Tonga from Mhow (33 m.), rs. 12-15.
Tonga on to Mandu (22 m.), rs. 10-12.
DHARMAVARAM, 384.
DHARMSALA, D.B., *Switzer's H.*, 228.
DHARMPUR, 218.
D.B. good.
DHARUR, 374.
DHARWAR (R.), D.B. $1\frac{1}{2}$ m. from station, 372.
DHAULI, 328.
DHOLA **(R.)**, 149.
DHOLPUR **(R.), D.B.**, 113.
DHOND **(R.), D.B.**, 346.
DHONE or **KURNOOL ROAD (R.), D.B.**, 383.
Starting point for Kurnool, 33 m. distant. Carts, bullock, and pony transits, procurable.
DHORAJI, 161.
DHUBRI, D.B., 321.
Hotel: *Dhubri H.*
DIAMOND HARBOUR, 71.
DIBRUGARH, D.B., 320.
Club: *Dibrugarh C.*
DIKOYA, 480.
DIG or **DEEG, D.B.**, 167.
DIKSAL, 347.
DIKWELLA, 481, 488.
DILWARRA TEMPLES, Mount Abu, 132.
DIMBULA, 480.
DINAPUR, D.B., 34, 35.
Kellner's Refreshment and Retiring Rooms.
DINDIGAL (R.), 432.
DIYATALAWA, 482.
DODBELLAPUR, 384.
DOHAD, 121.
DOMEL, **D.B.**, good, 252.
DONDRA, 488.
DONGARGARH (R.), 85
DORNAKAL, 380.
DRAS, 256.
DUDH SAUGAR, 358.
DULAI, **D.B.**, good, 252.
DUM DUM, D.B., 67.
DUNCAN, JON., 4, 7.
DWARKA, 161.

E

EISHMAKAM, 255.
EKIRIYANKUMBARA, 482.
EKLINJI LAKE, 96.
EKNELIGODA, 484.
ELEPHANT PASS, **R.H.** in old Dutch Fort, 497.
ELEPHANTA CAVES, 18.
ELLA, **R.H.**, 482.
ELLENBOROUGH, EARL, 56, 61, 147.
ELLORA CAVES, 74.
The caves are now most easily reached from Daulatabad station. Write beforehand to Nusserwanji, Aurangabad, asking him to send a tonga (10 rs. + 2 rs. per diem for detention) to meet train.
Daulatabad station is 10 m. from Ellora. **D.B.**, small, at Roza, and state **R.Hs.** at Ellora, but permission to occupy them must be obtained from the P. Sec. to H. E. the Minister, Hydrabad.
ELLORE **(R.)**, 335.
ELPHINSTONE, HON. M., 3, 4, 8, 10, 341, 344.
ELPHINSTONE, LORD, 4, 8, 402.
ENGLISH BAZAR, Maldah Dt. starting-place for Gaur, 307.
Accommodation: The magistrate's permission should be obtained beforehand to occupy the Maldah **Circuit-house**. A servant who can cook should be taken. A carriage can be obtained only by the kind services of the magistrate.
ENNUR, 336.
ERAOOR, **R.H.**, 483.
ERINPURA Rd. 133.
ERNAKULAM, 415.
ERODE Junction (for Trichinopoly), **(R.)**, 411.
Excellent sleeping accommodation at the rly. sta.
ETAWAH (R.), 300.
D.B., $\frac{1}{4}$ m. from rly. sta.
EVEREST MOUNT, 315.

F

FAGU, **D.B.**: grand view, 219.
FALTA, 70
FARDAPUR, **D.B.**, 39.
Permission to occupy the **D.B.** is no longer required; but it is desirable to send notice in the vernacular of a proposed visit.
FARIDKOT, 146.
FARUKHABAD, 163, 300.
FATEHABAD **(R.)**, 91.
FATEHPUR, 304, 306.
FATEHPUR-SIKRI, 180.
New **D.B.**
FAZILKA, 146.
FENCHUGANJ, 320.
FERGUSSON, JAS., *passim.*
FIROZABAD, 204.
FEROZEPORE (R.), 140.
D.B. 100 yds. E. of N. end of Mall (good).
American Presbyterian Mission, R.C. Church.
FEROZESHAH, 147.
FIROZ SHAH, EMPEROR, 146, 187, 200, 201, 203, 204, 207, 210, 213, 265.
FORT DUFFERIN, 457.
FORT ST DAVID, 423.
FRENCH IN INDIA, cv., cvi., 68, 220, 296, 299, 334, 335, 377, 392, 398, 400, 405, 417, 418, 421, 423, 426, 428, 429, 444.
FRENCH POSSESSIONS, 421.
FRENCH ROCKS, 392.
FRERE, SIR BARTLE, 4, 8, 266, 343.
FYZABAD (R.), 275.
D.B., close to rly. sta.
Graham's H.
Ajodhya, an ancient centre of Hinduism, is 4 m. distant.

G

GADAG (R.), 371.
D.B. $\frac{1}{4}$ m. from rly. sta.
GADARWARA, 29.
GAECKWARS OF BARODA, lxix., 7, 9, 25, 121, 216.
GAGANGAIR, 256.
GAIRSOPPA FALLS, D.B., 385.
GALLE, 487.
(R.) Hotel: *Oriental H.*, fairly comfortable.
Steamship Agencies: *Clan Line*, Clark, Spence & Co.; *British India S.N. Co.* and *Anchor Line*, Delmege, Forsyth & Co.
Banks: *Mercantile Bank of India, Ltd.*; *National Bank of India, Ltd.*: *Clark, Spence & Co., Agents.*
Store: *A. R. Ephraim & Co.*

GALLIES (Hill Stations near Murree), 244.

GAMA, VASCO DA, 415, 416.

GANDARBAL, 256.

GANESH KHIND, 342.

GANJAM, 333.

GARHI, D.B., good, 252.

GARHI HABIBULLA, D.B. 258.

GARPOS, 86.

GAUHATI, D.B., 320, 322.
Daily Motor Service to Shillong. *See* under latter.

GAUR, 308.
(See English Bazar.)

GAYA, D.B., 36.

GHAZIABAD, 220, 298.
Waiting and Refreshment Rooms at rly. sta. with sleeping accommodation, poor.

GHAZIPUR, 313.

GHUMLI, 161.

GHULAM KADIR, 198, 212, 299.

GINGI FORT, 420.

GIRIDIH, 38.

GIRNAR MOUNTAIN, 155.

GITALDAHA, 321.

GOA, 358.
Hotels: *Gomes' H.*, *Crescent H.*, poor. Carriages available for drive to Old Goa.
In the cold season steamers leave Bombay daily at noon, arriving at Goa the following afternoon, and proceeding twice a week to Mangalore.
Steamship Agents: *B.I.S.N. Co.*, L. S. Ribeiro.

GOALPARA, D.B., 321.

GOALUNDO GHAT, 318.
Steamers (comfortable), daily mail service to Narainganj.

GODAVERY, 335.

GODHRA, 121.

GOKAK ROAD (R.), 357.

GOKTEIK, 461.

GOKUL, 166.

GOLAKGANJ, 321.

GOLKONDA, 377.

GOLRA, 244.

GONDA, 275.

GONDAL, 161.
There are a good **Guest House** and D.B.

GONDIA, 85.

GOOTY (R.), 350.

GOPALPUR, 333.

GORAKHPUR, 275, 311.

GOREGAON, 23, 115.
Sta. for Jogeshwar Caves.

GOUGH, LORD, 56, 147, 241, 242.

GOVARDHAN, 167.

GUDUR, 336.

GUJRANWALA (R.), D.B., 239.
D.B. close to sta., poor.

GUJRAT, D.B., 241.

GULISTAN, 272.

GULBARGA, D.B., 348.

GULMARG, 256.
Hotel: *Nedou's* is the only *H.*, good. Visitors, as a rule, take up their quarters in wooden huts procurable at a small rent from the State, and generally engaged in advance, or in tents.

GUND, 256.

GUNTAKAL (R.), 350, 383, 384.
Junc. of Madras and S. Mahratta Rlys.

GUNTUR, 383.

GURDASPUR, D.B., 228.

GURGAON, 147

GWALIOR (R.), ciii. 103.
Gwalior H. (Old Musafir Khana).
The New **Musafir Khana**, ½ m. from the rly. sta., is a handsome, well-furnished guest house. It is necessary to write beforehand to the "Officer in Charge" to obtain permission to occupy rooms there, and also to insure accommodation, as it is frequently full. Persons staying there are charged for accommodation at the usual hotel rates. No permission is now necessary to visit the Fort. Visitors merely sign their names in a book kept there.
Bank: *Bank of Bengal.*
Missions: *Methodist Episcopal; Do. Zanana Mission; R.C. Church.*
Hackney Carriages, poor. Fares to Gwalior, 12 as. and 8 as.; to Morar, 1 r. and 12 as.; per hour of detention, 4 as.; double fare for return journey.
Gaol Carpets, etc., made to order, reasonable price, good work.

H

HABARANE, R.H., 498.

HAKGALLA, 481.

HALDAMULLA, R.H. 486.

HALLABID, 386.

HAMBANTOTTA, R.H., 489.

HAMPI (Vijayanagar), 380.
(The rly. sta. for Hampi is Hospet.)
D.B. at Kamalapur (8 m. from Hospet, and within ½ m. of Ruins), poor. The fee for its use is 1 r. per diem (1 r. 8 as. for a married couple), and the visitor must make his own arrangements about food, procurable at Hospet Sta. Mosquito curtains should be brought. There is a Peon in charge of the rooms, who will act as guide for a small fee.

HANAMCONDAH, 379*b*.

HANSI, R.H., 145.

HANWELLA, R.H. 484.

HAPUTALE, R.H., 486.

HARAPA, 259.

HARDA, 29.
D.B. 3 minutes' walk from rly. sta., good.

HARDINGE, LORD, 56, 57, 147.

HARDOI, 274.

HARDWAR, D.B. good, 279.
Rly. to Dehra Dun.

HARIHAR (R.), 384.

HARIPUR, D.B., 245, 258.

HARNAI, D.B., 272.
Bullock dhumni or tonga available.

HARPALPUR, 113.

HASAN ABDAL, D.B., 245.

HASTINGS, WARREN, cvi., 34, 45, 46, 54, 56, 59, 274, 275, 312, 403.

HATHRAS (R.), D.B., 169, 300.

HATTI, 251.

HATTON (R.), 479.
Hotel: *Hatton Hotel* for Adam's Peak (p. 479-485).
Physician: *Dr Thomas* at Norwood (4½ m.).
Store and Chemist: *Brown & Co. Ltd.*
Bank: *Hatton Bank.*
Livery Stables: *Pate & Co.* Carriage to Talawakelle, 12 rs.; to Laxapana, for Adam's Peak 18 rs.

HAUZ KHAS, 208.

HAVELOCK, GENERAL SIR H., xcix., ci., cii., 32, 62, 289, 290, 294-95, 297, 304, 306.
HAZARIBAGH, 34.
Hotel: *Hampton Court H.*
HEBER, BISHOP REGINALD, 24, 54, 60, 120, 123, 409, 430.
HENARATGODA, R.H., 476.
HENZADA, 466, 470.
HERAMITIPANA, 485.
Lodgings to be had at large Pilgrim Bungalow.
HIKKADUWA, R.H., 487.
HINDAUN, 122.
HINDUPUR, 384.
HINGANGHAT, D.B., 83.
HINGOLI, 83.
HIRPUR, R.H., 257.
HISSAR (R.), D.B., 146.
HODSON, MAJOR, 191, 194, 205, 292, 296.
HOLALKERE, 385.
HOLKAR, MAHARAJAS OF INDORE, lxx., 90, 91, 167, 188, 201, 216, 344.
HOLWELL, MR J. Z., 63.
HONAWAR, 385.
HOOGHLY, 39, 68.
Hotel: *Chinsurah H.*
HORANA, R.H., 486.
HOROWAPOTANE, 491.
HORTON PLAINS, R.H. excellent, write beforehand, 481.
HOSHANGABAD, D.B., 97.
HOSPET (R.), D.B., 380.
Rly. sta. for Hampi. Stationmaster will order conveyance.
HOTGI (R.), 347, 361.
HOTI MARDAN, 246.
HOWRAH (see also *Calcutta*), 39, 67, 87, 322.
HOYSALA BALLALA DYNASTY, 381, 386-7, 391, 393.
HUBLI (R.), 372, 384.
HULLABID, R.H., 385.
HUMAYUN, EMPEROR, 104, 120, 185, 194, 205, 206, 232, 300.
HUMMA, 333.
HYDERABAD (Kashmir), D.B., 258.
HYDERABAD (Deccan), (R.), 373.
Hotels: *Montgomery H.*; *Parade H.*
Bank: *Bank of Bengal.*
Chemists: *Leister & Co.*; *N. Cusetjir & Co.*
Dentist to H.H. the Nizam: *J. Morris.*
Hackney Carriages:
By time—

	Class I.	II.
Per day	9 rs.	4½ rs.
Per hour	1 r.	12 as.

Distances more than 5 m. from the Residency by agreement.
HYDERABAD (Sindh), 263.
D.B. good in Cantonment.
Missions: *C.M.S.*, Church and Schools.
HYDER ALI, 383, 391, 393, 395, 401, 405, 415, 416, 417, 424.

I

IDAR, 130.
IGATPURI (R.), 25.
D.B. ½ m. from sta.
Church: (Anglican).
Railway Institute.
IMPEY, SIR ELIJAH, 55, 56.
INDORE (R.), D.B., 90.
INDRA-BETTA HILL, 387.
IRAMPAIKKULAM, 496.
IRANAMADU, 497.
IRRAKAMAM, 501.
ISLAMABAD, D.B., 255.
ITARSI, 29, 97.
D.B. (R.), and waiting room at rly. sta.

J

JACOBABAD, 270.
D.B. at Wan Radharam, ¼ m. from rly. sta.
JAELA, R.H., 490.
JAFFNA (*Jaffnapatam*), R.H., 497.
JAGGANATHGANJ, 319.
JAHANGIR, EMPEROR, 31, 32, 50, 89, 96, 98, 101, 119, 171, 175-7, 183, 232, 235, 238, 254-5.
JAIN CAVES, 79, 326, 370.
JAIN STATUES, 109, 111, 388.
JAIN TEMPLES, lxiv., 38, 71, 103, 114, 118, 119, 128, 132-3, 138, 150, 156, 200, 208, 279, 357, 388.
JAINA, 82.
JAIPUR (R.), 139.
Hotels: *Jaipur H.* good and well managed, formerly *Rustom Family H.*; *Kaiser-i-Hind H.*, also fair. The proprietors of either of the hotels have carriages for hire, and will, if necessary, make arrangements for elephants for visitors (if they are to be obtained), or for tongas, bullock carts, or ponies, for the ascent to Amber.
Hackney Carriages:
By time—

	Class I.	II.
Per day.	4½ rs.	2¼ rs.
Per ½ day	2½ rs.	1 r. 6 as.
Per hr.	1½ rs.	8 as.

By distance—

	Class I.	II.
1st mile	8 as.	3 as.
Subs. mile	4 as.	1½ as.

Open carriages, 8 rs. per diem.
Dealer in Silks, Indian Curiosities, etc., *Zoroaster and Co.*, good showrooms.
Enamel Work: *Sabhag Chard Gulab Chand.*
School of Art has also good display, work to order.
Scottish Mission.
JAISAMAND LAKE, 97.
JAI SINGH II., RAJA OF JAIPUR, 47, 91, 140, 207.
JAITPUR, 114.
Dharmsala comfortable.
JAJPUR, 322.
JAKKO HILL (Simla), 218.
JALAMB, 83.
JALARPET Junction (for Bangalore) (R.), 396, 409.
JALGAON, 28, 39, 119.
JALNA, 82.
JALPAIGURI (R.), B.D., 314.
JAMALPUR, 310.
Kellner's Refreshment and Retiring Rooms at sta.
JAMGAL, 386.
JAMMU, 240.
State D.B.
Travellers recommended by the Resident may be accommodated at the State R.H.
JAMRUD, 249.
JAMSETJEE JEEJEEBHOY, SIR, 8, 11, 12, 15, 344.
JANAM STHAN, 276.
JAUNPUR (R.), 276.
D.B. close to police Lines.
Hackney Carriages

	Class I.	II.
1st hr.	10 as.	6 as.
Subs. hr.	5 as.	3 as.
Ry station to city	6 as.	4 as.
Ry station to civil station	12 as.	8 as.

JELAPAHAR, 316.
JETALSAR (R.), 152.

JHANSI (R.), 101.
Hotel: *H. de Paris.* D.B. good.
Club: *Jhansi Club.*
JHANSI, RANI OF, xcvii., ciii., 102, 105, 106.
JHARSUGUDA, 86.
JHELUM (**R.**), 242.
D.B., in cantonment..
JODHPUR, D.B., 133.
For permission to see the palace application must be made to the Resident or the senior member of the Mahkamah Khas.
JOGESHWAR CAVE, 23.
JOHAR (Immolation), 92, 110, 334.
JUBBULPORE (**R.**), **D.B.** 29.
Hotels: *Smith's H.; Cowdeary's H.; Nerbuddah Club.* This is the station for the expedition to the Marble Rocks (p. 30).
Missions: *C.M.S.; Ch. of England Zanana; R.C. Church.*
Motors: *Messrs Dinshaw & Co.*
Hackney Carriages:
By time—

	Class I.	II.
By day . . .	4 rs.	3 rs.
By ½ day . .	2½ rs.	2 rs.

By distance—

	Class I.	II.
First mile . .	8 as.	6 as.
Subs. mile . .	4 as.	3 as.

JULLUNDUR, 225.
Hotel: *Cheltenham H.*, on the Mall, opposite the church in Cantonment suburb. **D.B.** 5 minutes' drive from cantonment rly. sta.
JUNAGARH, 152.
Accommodation and **conveyances** on application to the Prime Minister of the State. There is a fine **Guest House** for natives and officials of rank. **D.B.** close to rly. sta.
JUNGSHAHI (**R**.), 265.
Rooms at the rly. sta. Camels or carriages for Tatta should be ordered beforeband through the station-master.
JUTOGH, 218.

K

KABUL, cvii., cix., 247.
KACH for Ziarat, **D.B.** open May to October. Tonga fare 15 rs.
KADALUNDI, 417.
KADUGANNAWA, 476.
KADUWELLA, **R.H.**, 484.
KAHOOTA, 258.
KAIRA, 122.
KALA KISARAI, **D.B.** 245.
KALA OYA, **R.H.**, 491.
KALA POKRI, 316.
KALAW, 456.
KALAWEWA, 493.
Travellers will find accommodation at the Govt. Bungalow on the Bund by arrangement beforehand.
KALINJAR, 114.
KALKA, 217.
Hotels: *Lowrie's H.*, next door to P.O. and T.O. (open throughout the year). Railway to Simla now open.
KALMUNAI, R.H., good, 501.
KALPI, Bengal, 71.
KALPI, D.B., 103.
KALUNGA, 87.
KALUTARA, **R.H.**, new and excellent, 487.
KALYAN, 24, 336.
R. and Waiting Rooms. Bullock-carts for hire.
KAMALAPUR, 380.
D.B. See *Hampi.*
KAMPTI, D.B., 85.
KANAKARAYANKULAM, 496.
KANAUJ, 300.
KANBAL, **D.B.**, 255.
KANDAHAR, cix., 272.
KANDAPOLLA, 481.
KANKESANTURAI, **R.H.** excellent, 497.
KANDY, 477.
Hotels: *Queen's H.*, excellent; *Florence Villas H.*, small but comfortable.
Club: near Queen's H.
Hackney Carriages: 2½ rs. per ½ day; 1st hr., 1 r. 20 c.; subsequent hrs., 30 c.
Chemist: *Miller & Co.*
Banks: *Mercantile Bank of India Ltd.; National Bank of India Ltd.*
Shops: *Cargills Ltd.; Miller & Co.: Skeen & Co.* (for photographs).
Doctor: *G. Powell Hay.*
Missions: *C.M.S.* sta. Trincomalee St.; Christ Church; Trinity Church, College, and Schools.
KANGAN, 256.
KANGRA VALLEY, 228.
KANHARI, 22.
KANKARIYA LAKE, 128.
KANKESANTURAI, 497.
KANKHAL, 279.
KANKROLI LAKE, 96.
KANTALAI, **R.H.**, 499.
KAPADVANJ, **D.B.**, good 122.
KARACHI (**R.**), **D.B.**, close to arsenal, 265.
Railways: From Lahore, Route 18; from Bombay and Rajputana, Route 10, p. 133.
Hotels: *Paul's H.*, good: close to Frere St. sta. *The Devon Villa H.*, good; *Reynold's H.; Killarney H.; Grand Central H.; Victoria H.*
Banks: *National Bank of India; Bank of Bombay; Panjab Bank; Commercial Bank of India*, Forbes Forbes & Co.
Agents: *Latham & Co.*, Bandar Rd.
Newspaper: *Sindh Gazette.*
Bazaar: *Sadar Bazaar*, good.
Club: *Sindh Club*, adjoining the Frere Hall Compound. A handsome building containing considerable sleeping accommodation. Members can introduce friends as honorary members for three days.
Gymkhana and *Ladies' Club* within five minutes' walk from Sindh Club.
Golf Club.
Hackney Carriages:
By time—

	Class I.	II.
Per day	5 rs.	4 rs. 2 as.
½ day	3 rs.	2 rs. 10 as.
per hr.	1 r.	12 as.

By distance—

	Class I.	II.
Per mile . .	8 as.	6 as.

Missions: *C.M.S.; Methodist Episcopal.*
Churches: *R.C.; Scotch.*
Steamship Agencies: *P. & O. British India S.N. Co., Mackinnon, Mackenzie & Co.* Direct weekly S.S. meet in-coming and outgoing P. & O. steamers to and from Europe at Bombay. Weekly steamer to Persian Gulf; coast steamer biweekly to Bombay.
Austrian Lloyd's, Anderson & Co.
Messageries Maritimes. H. Curjel, Bombay Co.

Monthly to and from Marseilles.
Clan Line, James Finlay & Co.
Ellerman's Hall and City Lines, Forbes, Forbes, Campbell & Co. Ltd.
Wilson Line, Finlay, Muir & Co. To Bombay, Middlesboro', or Hull every fortnight.
Anchor Line; Hansa Line; Wilson (Hull) *Line, D. Graham and Co.*
Forwarding Agents: *Latham & Co.*
Stores: *Army and Navy* (branch of London establishment), Bandar Road.
Consuls: *France*, M. T. L. Beaumont.
Germany, Mr A. Thole.
Austria-Hungary, Mr W. Nicholas.
U.S.A., Mr S. K. Lupton.
KARIKAL, 422.
KARJAT, 337.
KARLI, 23, 338.
The best way to visit the **Caves** is to alight at Lanauli (G.I.P. Rly.), and drive to and from Karli.
KARNAL, **D.B.**, 216.
KARUR, 411.
KARWI, 115.
KASARA (**R.**), 25.
KASAULI, 217.
Hotels: *Norton's H.*, *Hotelde France.*
(*Pasteur Institute.*)
KASHMIR, 250. See *Srinagar.*
KASIM BAZAR, 312.
KATAS, 242.
KATARAGAMA, 501.
KATHA, 461.
KATHGODAM (**R.**), 282.
Hotel: *Railway H.*
Tongas, *ponies*, *dandies*, *bearers* and *porters*, await the trains. Tongas to Naini Tal Brewery should be secured beforehand by letter or telegram to station-master. Fare 11 rs.; one seat 4½ rs. *Ekkas* at moderate rate are available for native servants.
KATHIAWAR PROVINCE. 149.
KATIHAR, 311, 314.
KATNI, 30, 86.
KATPADI (**R.**), 396. Junc. for Vellore.
KAUNIA, **D.B.**, 321.
KAURAVAS, lviii., 216.
KAZIPET, 379.
KEGALLA, **R.H.**, good, 476.
KEKERAWA, **R.H.**, small but good, 493.
KELANI, 475.
KHAIBAR PASS, 248.
KHAIRABAD, (**R.**), 246.
KHAIRI GHAT (**D.B.**), 218.
KHAIRPUR, 263.
KHAJURAHU, 114.
Country cart from Mahoba, 3-4 rs.
KHANA, 39, 307.
KHANDAGIRI CAVES, 325.
KHANDALA, 338.
D.B. on the edge of the Ghat ravine.
Hotel: *Glendale H.*, good.
KHANDWA, 29, 87.
R. and Waiting Rooms. Conveyances procurable **D.B.**
KHARAGHODA, 148.
KHARAGPUR, 87, 322.
KHARIAN, 242.
KHATMANDU, 311.
KHERALU, 131.
KIRKI (Delhi), 212.
KHURDA ROAD, 328.
KHWAJAH KHIZR ISLAND, 267.
KHYRNA, 283.
KIAMARI, 266.
KILLA ABDULLA (**R.**), 272.
KINCHINJANGA MOUNTAIN, 315.
KINDAT, 470.
KING EDWARD VII., EMPEROR OF INDIA, 9, 10, 15, 32, 56, 90, 198, 199, 203, 218, 231, 236, 240, 292, 356, 403, 407, 473.
KING GEORGE V., EMPEROR OF INDIA, 9, 45, 90, 107, 178, 266, 297, 300, 390, 408.
KIRI ELA, 486.
KIRINDE (**R.H.**), 489.
KIRKEE, 341.
H. de Paris.
KODAIKANAL (Palny Hills). See *Ammayanayakkanur*, 432.
In the season a motor bus service (3 days notice of intended journey desirable; 25 seers of luggage allowed) runs in 3 hrs. to 33 m. Krishnamanaikan — charge per seat 6 rs. Pony and chair on to Kodaikanal, 2½rs. and 6½-8½ rs.
KODKANI. Two **D.Bs.**, 385.
KOHALA, **D.B.**, good, 252.
KOHAT, **D.B.**, 245, 250.
KOHIMA, 321.
KOIL (ALIGARH), 299.
KOJAK PASS, 272.
KOLA GHAT, 322.
KOLAR GOLD FIELDS, 396.
A short branch railway runs from Bowringpet to the Gold-fields, where there is a good **D.B.** in the Mysore Company's Camp.
KOLHAPUR, 356.
D.B. at S. end of Cantonment.
KONARAK, 332.
KONDAPALLI, 380.
KORAH, 306.
KORBA, 86.
KOSI, 169.
KOSLANDE, **R.H.**, 486.
KOTAH, 100, 122.
KOTAGIRI, 411.
Hotels: *Spencer's H.*, good; *Blue Mountain H.*
KOTAWARA, 273.
KOTGARH, **D.B.**, 219.
KOT-KAPURA (**R.**), 146.
KOTLI, 258.
KOTRI (**R.**), 264.
D.B. (provisions must be taken), not far from Bandar rly. sta.
KOTTA, 475.
KRISHNA, 349
KRISHNA, lv., 160, 166, 167, 168, 301, 372, 439.
KUCHAMAN ROAD, 136.
KULLU VALLEY, 219.
KUMANE, 501.
KUMBAKONAM (**R.**), **D.B.**, 424.
KUMBURUWELLA, **R.H.**, 486.
KUPURTHALLA, 225.
KURLA, 24.
KURNOOL (Madras), 384. **D.B.**
KURSEONG (**R.**), **D.B.**, 315.
Hotel: *Grand H.* (Mrs Monk's), late *Clarendon H.*, good, pleasant place for breaking journey. Some people prefer this place to Darjeeling.

KURUNEGALA, R.H., 491.

KUTAB-UD-DIN, KING OF DELHI, liii., 44, 137, 208, 210, 299, 300.

KUTTALLAM, 436.

KUTAB (*Delhi*), 208.
Small **D.B.** close to the great mosque.
Police Rest House in the tomb of Adham Khan. Comfortable quarters. Application must be made beforehand to the Deputy-Commissioner, Delhi, for permission to stop there.

KYAUKPYU, 469.

KYAUKSE, 456.

L

LAHORE (R.), 229.
Railway: From Bombay, Routes 10, 12*c*, 15*b*; Delhi, Route 15*b*; Calcutta to Peshawar, Route 16; to Karachi and Quettah, Routes 18 and 19.
Hotels: *Nedou's (New) H.*, 8 rs.; *Faletti's Hotel*, Cecil.
Club: *Panjab Club*, Lahore and Meean Meer Institute.
Missions: *C.M.S.* St. John's Divinity School; Zanana Mission, and Trinity Church. *American Presbyterian*: Forman College and Church; *R.C. Cathedral*; Scotch Church
Banks: *Bank of Bengal; Panjab Banking Co; Alliance Bank of Simla; Commercial Bank of India.*
Photographers: *Craddock; Jadukishan.*
Chemist: *Plomer.*
Tailors: *Phelps; Ranken.*
Bootmaker: *Watts.*
Drapers: *Whiteaway Laidlaw; Lawrence; Ball Moody; Trevilion.*
Hackney Carriages:

	Class I.	II.
Per day . . .	4 rs.	3 rs.
1st. hr. . . .	1 rs.	8 as.
subs. hr. . . .	8 as.	4 as.
To Meean Meer, Shalimar or Shahdara and back . .	2 rs.	1 r.
For each hr. of detention . .	8 as.	4 as.

Newspapers: *Civil and Military Gazette; Tribune.*
Churches: *Cathedral; Railway Church; R.C. Cathedral: Presbyterian.*

LAHORE CANTONMENT, D.B., 229, 237.

LAHUGALAWEWA, 501.

LAKE, LORD, 56, 145, 163, 171. 178, 188, 198, 216, 220, 299.

LAKHI SARAI, 38, 310.

LAKI (R.), 269.
No D.B. but good rooms at the rly. sta.

LAKKANDI, 371.

LAKSAM, 319.

LALA MUSA (R.), 241.

LAL GOLA GHAT, 314.

LALITPUR, D.B., 101.

LALLY, COUNT, 405, 422 427.

LANDI KOTAL, 249.

LANDOUR, 281.
Hotel: *Woodville H.*

LANSDOWNE, 273.

LARKANA, D.B., 268.

LASALGAON, 28.

LASHKAR GWALIOR, 107.

LASSUNDRA, 122.

LASWARI, 145.

LATS OF STONE, 33, 45, 203, 204, 311.

LAURIYA, 311.

LAWRENCE ASYLUMS:
Mount Abu, 132.
Murree, 244.
Ootacamund, 412.
Sanawar, 218.

LAWRENCE, SIR HENRY, 146, 167, 218, 230, 285, 286, 293, 488.

LAWRENCE, SIR JOHN, LORD, C., 56, 57, 219, 230, 231, 293.

LAWRENCE, COL., STRINGER, 404, 405, 430.

LAXAPANA, 480.
Hotel good.

LEH, 256.

LETPADAN, 466.

LHAKSAR, 273, 279.

LIDDAR VALLEY, 255.

LIMBDI, 149.

LINGAMPALLI, 373.

LODHRAN, 147, 261.

LOLAB VALLEY, 253.

LONAULI (R.), 338.
Lonauli H.; Woodland's H.; Taj Mahal H. ¼ m. from rly. sta.
Best starting-place for drive to the Karli Cave.

LONDA (R.), 358, 372.

LORALAI, 272.

LUCKNOW (R.), cii., 283.
Railway: From Saharanpur and Benares, Route 20(*a*); from Cawnpur, Route 22; from Allahabad, Route 2, p. 31.
Hotels: *Wutzler's Royal H.*, good; *Savoy & Imperial H.* (good and clean), *Civil and Military H.: Prince of Wales's H.*—all in Abbott Road.
Clubs: *United Service*, in the Chatar Manzil Palace; *Mohammed Bagh C.*, Cantonments.
Banks: *Bengal; Upper India; Delhi & London; Allahabad.*
Chemist: *Peake Allen.*
General Merchants: *Murray & Co.*
Photographer: *Lawrie.*
Drapers: *Whiteaway Laidlaw; Trevellion.*
Hackney Carriages
By time.—

	Class I.	II.
Day	3½ rs.	2 rs.
½ day	2¼ rs.	1 r. 8 as.
per hr.	12 as.	8 as.

Motors: 50 rs. per diem.
Missions: *C.M.S.* (at Zahur Bakhsh), Church of Epiphany and Schools; *Methodist Episcopal of U.S.A.; R.C. Churches.*
The **Museum** (Ajaib Ghar) is closed at 3.30 and on Fridays.

LUDHIANA, 224.
D.B. at rly. sta.
Missions: *American Presbyterian; Medical and Zanana.*

LUNI, 133.

LUNUGALA, R.H., good, 482.

LUMDING, 320.

M.

MADAWACHCHIYA, R.H., good, 496.

MADDUR (R.), 391.
For the Cauvery Falls. Tonga (24 hrs. notice needed), 10 rs.; jatka, 5 rs.

MADHAVAPUR, 161.

MADHUBAN, 38.

MADHUPUR (R.), D.B. 38.

MADRAS, 336, 351, 402.

Railways: From Calcutta, Route 24; from Bombay, Route 25; from Bangalore, Routes 25 and 31; from Ootacamund, Route 33; from Tuticorin and Ceylon, Route 34.

Hotels: *Connemara, H.* best; *Castle H., D'Angelis H.; Spencer's H.*—all in good positions close to Mount Road; *Elphinstone H., Balmoral H., Victoria H.,* and *Branch Elphinstone H.*—all in central position on or near Mount Road, not far from the Madras Club, and 1 m. from rly. sta.; *Prince of Wales's H.*, Westcott Road. *See* 6-7 rs. and upwards; *Capper House H.*, on the Beach, 3 m. from rly. sta. There are also several hotels in *GEORGE TOWN* near the harbour.

Agents: *Binny & Co.*, Armenian St. (agents for Grindlay & Co., Parliament St.), undertake all business in connection with travelling, banking, and financial arrangements for travellers in India.

Banks: *Bank of Madras*, Beach; *Chartered Bank of India, Australia and China*, Esplanade; *Chartered Mercantile Bank of India, London, and China*, First Line Beach; *Commercial Bank of India, Ltd.*, N. Beach; *National Bank of India, Ltd.*, First Line Beach.

Booksellers: *Higginbotham & Co., Combridge & Co., Addison & Co., Vest & Co.*—all in Mount Road; *Kalyanarum Iyer*, George Town.

Chemists: *W. E. Smith & Co.*, Mount Road and Esplanade; and *Maclure & Co.*, Mount Road.

Clubs: The *Madras C.* Central situation at 1 m. from the rly. sta. on Mount Road.

The *Adyar Club* admits ladies as well as gentlemen; it is 3 m. S. of Madras Club, and in its grounds the *Madras Boat Club* has its sheds. *Gymkhana Club* (Island); *Madras Cricket Club* and grounds, Chepank.

Restaurants and Confectioners: *D'Angelis* and *Doraswamy*, both in Mount Road.

Consuls: Most countries are represented by Consuls or Consular Agents.

America, N. B. Stuart, Popham's Broadway.

Austro-Hungary, Herr A. Scholl.

Germany, Fritz T. Simon.

Italy, G. Fraser.

Taxi-Cabs and Motors for hire have not yet made their appearance in Madras.

Hackney Carriages:

By time—

Per day . . .	7 rs.
½ day . . .	3 rs.
1 hr.	1 r.
subs. hr. . . .	8 as.

By distance—

Not exceeding 2 m.	12 as.
Each subs. mile .	8 as.

Dentists: *M. C. Badcock*, Egmore; *Dr Eaton*, Mount Road.

Drapers: *Oakes & Co.; Smith & André; Whiteaway, Laidlaw & Co.*, Mount Road.

General Merchants: *Orr & Sons; Oakes & Co.; Spencer & Co.*

Jewellers: *P. Orr and Sons*, Mount Road; *Framjee Pestonjee Bhumgara*, Mount Road; *Ranganadha Tawker*, Mount Road.

Library: *Connemara Public Library*, Egmore.

Market: *Moore Central Market*, near Central Rly. Sta.

Medical Men: *Captain Falconer*, Egmore; *Dr Clarence Smith*, Egmore and George Town.

Missions: The *S.P.G.* (Mission House in Rundall's Road, Vepery), serve the following churches:—St Thome, St Paul's, Vepery, and St John's, Egmore, and have charge of a Theological College in Sullivan's Gardens; also of schools and orphanages. *C.M.S.* (at Egmore), Holy Trinity Church; Divinity School, and Harris High School; R.C. Church, Armenian St.

There are also other Missions: *U.F. Church of Scotland, Lutheran, Wesleyan,* and *American Baptist.*

Newspapers: Daily Papers, *The Madras Mail, The Madras Times, The Hindu, The Madras Standard.*

Opticians: *P. Orr and Sons; W. E. Smith & Co.*, and *Lawrence & Mayo*, all in Mount Road.

Photographers: *Nicholas & Co., Del Tufo,* and *Wiele & Klein*—all in Mount Road.

Railways: There are two Railway systems terminating at Madras:—

(1) Madras and S. Mahratta Railway; (*a*) S.W. line for Bangalore, Nilgiris, West Coast and South-West Districts; (*b*) N.W. line for Guntakal, Wadi, the Deccan Districts and Bombay, and for Bezvada, Vizagapatam, Cuttack, and Calcutta.

(2) South Indian Railway for Tanjore, Madura, Trichinopoly, Tinnevelly, Quilon, and Tuticorin and Colombo.

Steamship Agencies: *British India S. N. Co.; Binny & Co.,* Frequent sailings for Coast Ports, Calcutta, Burma, Straits Settlements, Colombo for London.

Messageries Maritimes. Volkart Bros. Once a month between Calcutta and Colombo and back, calling at Madras and Pondicherry.

P. & O. S. N. Co., Best & Co. The Company's ships do not call at Madras, but the Agents effect bookings *via* Bombay, Calcutta, and Colombo.

Asiatic S. N. Co., Wilson and Co. For Coast Ports, Calcutta, Burma, Andamans, etc.

Clan Line, Gordon, Woodroffe & Co.

Austrian Lloyd's, Volkart Bros.

Bibby Line and Orient Pacific Line, Leighton & Co.

Ellerman's City and Hall Lines, Best & Co.

Norddeutscher Lloyd, Carl Simon Sohne.

Norddeutscher Lloyd's, Carl Simon & Sons.

Tailors: *Smith & Andre, Moses & Co; Oakes & Co*—all in Mount Road.

MADUGODA, R.H., 479.

MADURA (R). 432.
D.B. close to rly. sta. Sleeping accommodation at the rly. sta.
Bank: *Bank of Madras.*
Club: *Madura Club*, 2½ m. from the rly. sta.
Conveyances: poor.
Guides: 2 rs. per diem.

MAGAR PIR, 267.

MAGWE, 465.

MAHA OYA, **R.H.**, 483.

MAHABALESHWAR, 352.
Hotels: *Race-View H. Fountain H.*—both good, fine views; *Mahabaleshwar H.*; *Ripon H.*
Club with bedrooms attached.
Mail Contractor, *Ardeshir Framjee*, Civil Lines, Poona.
Motor Cars from Poona, in 4½ hrs.
For 3 persons 75 rs.
" 6 " 110 "
From Wathar—3 to 7 persons 50 rs.
Mail Motor Car: (15 Oct. to 15 Dec., 15 March to 15 June), 8 rs. per seat.

MAHABALIPURAM, D.B., good, 437.

MAHABAN, 165.

MAHABHARATA, lvii., 216, 217, 391.

MAHANADI RIVER, 86.

MAHARA, 475.

MAHASU, 219.

MAHÉ, 418.

MAHIM, 115.
Scottish Orphanage, established 1859, the only institution of its kind in the Bombay Presidency.

MAHMUD, EMPEROR OF GHAZNI, l., 131, 136, 160, 163, 165, 223, 228.

MAHMUD KOT (**R.**), 242.

MAHOBA, D.B., 114.

MAHRATTAS, lxviii., 24, 25, 31, 65, 84, 101, 116, 117, 135, 202, 215, 220, 341-2, 353-4, 427.

MAHRAULI (Delhi), 212.

MAHULI, 355.

MAKKALLI HILLS, 263.
D.B. (necessary to bring food), 1½ m. from Tatta; the building was originally a mosque.

MALCOLM, SIR JOHN, 4, 8, 16, 90, 406.

MALCOLM PETH, 353.

MALDAH, 307.

MALVALLI, D.B., good, 391.

MANASBAL LAKE, 253.

MANCHHAR LAKE, 269.
Any one making a shooting expedition on this lake will do well to engage rooms at the rly. sta., which are best for a night or two, as the **D.B.** at Sehwan is 1½ m. from the rly. sta. A telegram to the station-master a day or two beforehand will generally ensure a shikari and camels being in readiness.

MANDALAY, 456.
Hotels: *Gale's H.*; *Salween House H.*; *De Villa H.* All hotels in Mandalay are poor.
Irrawaddy Flotilla Express Steamers from Rangoon every Wednesday and Saturday, from Mandalay every Friday and Tuesday.
Club: *The Upper Burma Club.*
Bankers: *National Bank of India.*
Missions: *American Baptist*; *Wesleyan*; *R.C. Church.*
Chemists: *Burma Medical Hall*; *Mandalay Pharmacy.*
Drapers: *Whiteaway Laidlaw*; *Rowe & Co.*
Conveyances: Ticca gharries (or cabs) of an inferior description can be hired at fixed rates by time or distance.
General Stores: *E. Solomon & Co.*; *Rowe & Co.*
Medical Men: The Civil Surgeons.
Newspapers: *The Mandalay Herald* and *The Mandalay Times.*
Photographer: *Samuels.*

MANDAPAM, 433.

MANDOR, 135.

MANDSAUR, 92.

MANDU, 89.

MANDVI, 162.

MANGALORE. D.B., 419.
Steamship Agency: *British India S.N. Co.* Shepherd's steamer twice weekly in the cold weather.
Bank: *Bank of Madras.*
R.C. Cathedral.

MANGI, 272.

MANHARPUR, 87.

MANIKPUR (**R.**), 30, 115.

MANIKYALA, 243.

MANIPUR, 321.

MANIYACHI, 435. Junc. for Tinnevelly and Quilon.

MANMAR (**R.**), **D.B.**, 28, 71.

MANNAAR, **R.H.**, 496.

MAN SINGH, RAJA OF GWALIOR, 104, 109.

MAN SINGH, RAJA OF JAIPUR 47, 142, 243, 307.

MANSERAH, **D.B.**, 258.

MARADANA, 475.

MARAVILA, **R.H.** good, 490.

MARBLE ROCKS, 2 small **D.Bs.**, 30. Tonga from Jubbulpore, 4 rs.

MARCO POLO, 24, 419, 434, 435.

MARDAN, 246.

MARGALA, 244.

MARGAN, 256.

MARIAM UZ ZAMANI, 179, 183, 235.

MARIAON, 281, 297.

MARTABAN, 466.

MARTAND, 255.

MARWAR, Junc., 133.

MASHOBRA, 219.

MASKELIYA, 480.

MASULIPATAM, **D.B.**, 335.

MATALE, 492.
R.H. good, practically an hotel.

MATARA, 488.
R.H. very comfortable Hotel.

MATHERAN, 337.
Much frequented from Sat. till Mon. in the season.
Hotels: *Granville H.*; *Rugby, H.*; *Gymkhana H.*

MATTIANA, **D.B.**, 219.

MAU, 113.
D.B. ¼ m. from rly. sta.

MAYAVERAM (R.) D.B., 425.

MAYMYO, 461.

MAYO, EARL, cix., 32, 57, 139, 141, 236.

MEDAHAMAHANUWARA, 479.

MEERUT, D.B., 220.
Hotels: The *Empress H.*, best; *Meerut H.*; *N.W. H.*
Club: *Wheleer C.*
Bank: *B. of Upper India.*
Motors: *Messrs Graduate, Bros.*

Missions: *C.M.S.; do., Zanana; Methodist Episcopal; R.C. Church; Scotch Church.*

MEHMADABAD, 122.
Good Waiting Room at rly. sta.

MEHSANA, 130.

MEIKTILA, 456.

MEKAR, 83.

MERCARA, 396.

MERGUI, 468.

MERTA ROAD, 135.

METTUPALAIYAM (R.), 412.
Junction of Madras and Nilgiri Mountain Railway to Coonoor and Ootacamund.
Warm wraps should be kept handy.

MHOW, 89.
D.B.; Refreshment and Waiting Room at rly. sta.

MIANI, 264.

MIDNAPUR: 322.
B.D close to rly. sta.
Mission: *American Baptist.*

MIHINTALE, R.H., 491, 496.

MINBU, 465.

MINERI, 498.

MINGUN, 460.

MINHLA, 465.

MIRAJ (**R.**), 356.
D.B. near sta.

MIRZAPUR, **D.B.**, 33.
Club: *Mirzapur C.*

MIYAGAM, 120.

MOGOK, **D.B.**, 462.

MOHPANI COAL-MINES, 29.

MOKAMAH (**R.**), 38, 310.

MONGHYR, D.B., Hotel, 310.

MONTGOMERY (**R.**), **D.B.**, 259.

MONTPEZIR CAVES, 21.

MOOLTAN, 259.
Refreshment and Waiting Rooms; **D.B.** exactly opposite the Cantonment sta.
Hackney Carriages:

	Class I.	II.
Day	4 rs.	3 rs.
1 hr.	1 r.	10 as.
Subs. hr.	8 as.	6 as.

MORADABAD, 273.
D.B. $1\frac{1}{2}$ m. N. of rly. sta.; accommodation at rly. sta. on application to station-master.
Hotel: *Imperial H.*

MORAR, 104.

MORATUWA, 487.

MORMUGÃO, 359.
Old Palace H. good.

MORTAKKA, **R.H.**, 87.
Starting-place for Unkarji.

MORVI, 162.

MOULMEIN, 456, 466.
Hotels: *Criterion* and *British India*—poor.
Club: *The Moulmein Gymkhana.* No sleeping accommodation.
Bankers: *Bank of Bengal.*
Chemists: *Surgical Hall; Town Dispensary.*
Conveyances: Cabs (ticca gharries) of an inferior description can be hired at fixed rates by time or distance.
Medical Man: The Civil Surgeon.
Newspaper: *The Moulmein Advertiser.*

MOUNT ABU, 132.
Good Refreshment and Waiting Rooms at Abu Road Sta. 17 m. from Mt. Abu.
Conveyances. *See* Abu Road.
D.B. on the hill.
Hotel: *Rajputana H.* good; lately enlarged.
Bazaar for English stores.
Club: *Rajputana C.*
Missions: *C.M.S.; do. Zanana; R.C. Cathedral.*

MOUNT LAVINIA, 487.
Hotel: *Grand H.*, first-rate accommodation.

MUDKI, 147.

Mughal Emperors, liv.

MUGHAL SARAI (**R.**), 34, 279.

MUKAND-DARRAH, 121.

MUHAMMAD SHAH, KING OF DELHI, 188, 206, 216.

MUMTAZ MAHAL, 29, 173.

MUNRO, SIR HECTOR, xcvi., 34, 401, 418, 422.

MUNRO, SIR T., 347, 350, 403, 404, 405.

MURREE, 244.
Hotels: *Powell's H.; Rowbury's H.*
Club: *Murree C.*
Banks: *Alliance; Commercial; Panjab Banking Co.*
Schools: *Lawrence Asylum; St Denys' School; St Thomas's R.C. College.*

MURSHIDABAD, D.B. at Berhampore, 312.

MUSEUMS, 15, 57, 141, 197, 201, 231, 294, 408, 436, 451-3, 474.

MUSHKAF, 270.

MUSSOOREE, 281.
Hotels: *Charleville H.* (Wutzler's) very good; *Savoy H.*, good; (both on Mall); *Woodville H.; Zephyr Hall H.; Kenilworth Hall H.*
Club: *Himalaya.*
Banks: *Delhi; Alliance Bank of Simla.*
Churches: *Scotch; R.C.*
Newspaper: *Mussouree Times.*
Chemists: *Fitch; Keogh.*
Dentist: *C. Batten.*
Photographers: *Hamer; Dagg.*
Drapers: *Clark; Moore; Trevellion, Hall & Anderson; Whiteaway Laidlaw.*
Schools: *Philander Smith; St George's College; E. I. R. Schools; Diocesan School; Woodstock Girls' School; Hampton Court.*

MUTTRA, D.B., 163.
Missions: *C.M.S.; Methodist Episcopal; Wesleyan; R.C. Church.*

MUZAFFARPUR, D.B., 311.

MYMENSING (**R.**), 319.

MYINGYAN, 462.

MYITKYINA, 461.
Rly. from Mandalay now open.

MYOHAUNG, 469.

MYSORE (R.), D.B. near Jail, 395.
Hotels: *Gordon H.* fair; *Royal H.*

N

NABHA, 223.

NADIR SHAH, KING OF PERSIA, li., 188, 198, 201, 216.

NAGA RAJAS, 42, 43, 327, 439.

NAGAI, 374.

NAGAR, 220.

NAGAUR, 135.

NAGDA, 121.

NAGINA (**R.**), 273.

NAGORE, 427.

NAGPUR, D.B., 83.
Empress H. close to sta. Waiting rooms at sta.
Club: *Nagpur.*

Bank: *Bank of Bengal.*
Missions: *United Free Church of Scotland; R.C. Church.*
Chemist: Nicholas.
Hackney Carriages:

	Class I.	II.
Day . . .	3 rs.	2½ rs.
Half-day	2 rs.	1½ rs.
1st hr. . .	12 as.	8 as.
Subs. hr. .	6 as.	4 as.

NAIHATI, 68, 314.
NAINI (R.), 30.
NAINI TAL, 282.
Hotels: *Metropole H.; Grand Hotel* (formerly *Albion*); *Waverley H.*, S. Mall; *Lake House H.; Royal H.; Grand Central H.*, all from 6-7 rs.
Club: *Naini Tal C.*, near St John's Church.
Banks: *Allahabad; Upper India; Delhi and London Alliance; Bank of Simla.*
Newspapers: *Naini Tal Gazette.*
Chemists: *Morrison; Bird; Peake Allen.*
Photographer: *Lawrie.*
General Merchants: *Murray & Co.*
Drapers: *Whiteaway Laidlaw; Trevellion.*
From Kathgodam to Naini Tal Brewery by tonga, see *Kathgodam.*
NAJIBABAD, 273.
NAKKALA, 500.
NALANDE, R.H. good, 492.
NALHATI, 307.
NANDIDRUG, 384.
Hotel, managed by proprietor of *Cubbon H.*, Bangalore.
NANDYAL, 384.
NANJANGUD, 396.
NANUOYA (R.), 480.
NARAINA, 139.
NARAINGANJ, D.B., 318.
NARI, 272.
NARKANDA, 219.
D.B. Six rooms, splendid view of snowy range.
NARNAUL, 145.
NASIK ROAD, 25.
Waiting Rooms. Capital **Tongas** on hire.

By time—

	Class I.	II.
For day (inside Station limits)	3½ rs.	2½ rs.
Per hr. . . .	8 as.	6 as.
Rly. Station to City or Dak Bungalows . .	1 r.	12 as.

Tramway to City 5 m. distant.
NASIK, **D.B.**, good, 25.
Mission: *C.M.S.* sta. at Sharanpur, see p. 26.
Headquarters of *Royal Western India Golf Club*; good links.
NASIRABAD, 97.
D.B., 1 m. from rly. sta.
NAULA, 486, 492.
NAUPADA, 333.
NAVSARI, 116.
NAWAB VIZIRS, KINGS OF OUDH, lii., 34, 45, 61, 207, 275, 284, 301, 397.
NAWANAGAR, 162.
NAZARANI CHRISTIANS, 414.
NEEMUCH (R.), 92.
D.B. Good **Club**, with cricket ground, etc., attached.
NEGAPATAM (R.), 429.
Steamship Agents: *B.I.S.N. Co.*, weekly service to coast ports. Rooms at railway station.
NEGOMBO, 475, 490.
R.H. excellent.
NEIL, BRIG.-GENL., ci., 44, 62, 294, 403.
NELLORE, 336.
D.B. good.
NELSON, LORD, 3, 427.
NERAL (R.), 337.
Very good **Waiting Room**, with *Baths*, etc., at rly. sta.
NERBUDDA RIVER, 29, 30, 32, 119.
NICHOLSON, BRIG.-GENL. JOHN, c., 62, 191, 193-4, 201, 202, 228, 230, 244, 248.
NILGIRI HILLS, 411.
NIZAM-UD-DIN (Delhi), 206.
NIZAMS OF HYDERABAD, 73, 82, 200, 373, 398.
NOWGONG, **D.B.**, p. 113.
18 m. from Harpalpur. Tonga, 10 rs.; seat in mail tonga, 3 rs.
NOWSHERA, 246.
D.B. near Post Office.

NOWSHERA (Kashmir), 257.
NUR JAHAN OR NUR MAHAL, EMPRESS, 172, 179, 221, 238, 254, 255.
NUWARA ELIYA, 480.
Hotels: *Grand H.*, good; *New Keena House* (annexe to *Grand H.*); *St Andrew's H.; Grand Central H.* There are also Boarding Houses.
Clubs: *Hill Club; United Club; Golf Club.*
Store and Chemist: *Cargills, Ltd.*
The Golf Links are excellent.
NYAUNGU, 462.

O

OCHTERLONY, GENL. SIR D., 57, 97, 182.
OIL, 465.
OKANDA, 501.
OKHAMANDAL, 161.
OLAVAKKOT, 415.
ONGOLE, 336.
OOTACAMUND, 413.
Hotels: *Sylk's H.; Central H.; Rosemount H.; Shoreham H.; Longwood H.*
Boarding House: *Longwood; Alta Villas.*
Clubs: *Ootacamund C.* and *Gymkhana C.*
Bank: *Bank of Madras.*
Schools: *Lawrence Asylum; Breaks Memorial High School.*
Chemists: *E. W. Smith & Co.*
Photographers: *Wiele & Kleine.*
Drapers: *Wren & Bennett.*
General Merchants: *Oakes; Spencer; Wrenn, Bennett & Co.; Whiteaway, Laidlaw & Co.*
Jewellers: *Barton & Sons.*
OPIUM, xciv., 35, 90.
ORAI (R), **D.B.**, 103.
ORCHHA, 113.
ORISSA, 323.
OUTRAM, GENL. SIR JAS., cii., 59, 62, 289, 290-2, 295, 297.

P

PABBI, 246.
PACHBADRA, 133.

PACHMARHI, 29.
Hotel: *Hill H.*
Tonga from Piparia, 16 rs. Seat 4 rs.

PAGAN, R.H., 462.

PAILGAM, 255.

PAKOKKU, 462.

PAK PATTAN, 259.

PALAMCOTTAH, 436.
Missions: *C.M.S.* Training Institution; Schools; Sarah Tucker Institution; Tamil Mission Church.

PALANPUR (R.), D.B., 131.

PALAVERAM, 410.

PALETWA, 469.

PAL GHAT, 415.

PALHALLAN, 256.

PALITANA, 149. See *Songad.*
D.B. Doolies can be obtained either privately or through the officers of the Palitana Darbar.

PALLAI, R.H., 497.

PALNI HILLS, 430.
See *Ammayanayakkanur.*

PALUTUPANE, R.H., 490.

PAMBAN, 433.

PANCHGANNI, 352.

PANDAVAS, lviii., 216, 280, 433, 437-8.

PANDHARPUR, 347.

PANDUAH, 309.

PANHALA, 356.

PANIPAT, R.H., lii., 214.

PANJIM, see *Goa.*

PANKULAM, R.H., 491.

PAPANASHAM, 437.

PARASNATH MOUNTAIN, 38.

PARBATI, 345.

PARBATIPUR (R), 314, 318.

PARSIS, lxx., 12, 16, 117.

PARULIA, 87.

PASTEUR INSTITUTE, KASAULI, 217; and COONOOR, 411.

PATAL PANI, 89.

PATAN (Anhilvara), 131.

PATAN (Kashmir), 253.

PATAN SOMNATH, 158.
R.H. of Junagarh State.

PATHANKOT (R.), D.B., 228.

PATIALA, 223.

PATNA, D.B., 35.
Missions: *Baptist; R.C. Church.*

PATTADAKAL, 371.

PATTIPOLA, R.H., 482.

PAWANGARH, Champanir, 120.

PAWANGARH, Kolhapur, 357.

PAYECH, 255.

PEARL FISHERY, 496.

PEEL, SIR WM., CAPTAIN R.H., 55, 291, 297, 305.

PEGU (R.), 455.
Railway: From Bombay and Madras; Dhond and Manmar; Mahabhaleshwar and Bangalore.

PENDRA, 86.

PERADENIYA, R.H. good, 476.

PERIYAR, 416.

PESHAWAR, D.B., 247.
Hotel: *Flashman's H.*, on the Mall, 7 rs.
Club, near the Church.
Bank: *Panjab Banking Co.*
Dealers in C. Asian goods in city: *Safdar Ali; Haji Rahman.*
Missions: see p. 247. *R.C. Church.*

Hackney Carriages:

	Class I.	II.
Per day . .	4 rs.	3 rs.
Per 1st hr. .	1 r.	12 as.
Subs. hr. .	8 as.	6 as.

Tonga with 2 horses: To Ali Masjid, 7 rs.; to Landi Kotal, 14 rs. Permission to visit either place must be obtained from the Political Officer, Khyber. The visit to the latter is not now so readily allowed, as it was some years back.

PESHWAS (HEAD OF THE MAHRATTAS), lxviii.-ix. xcvii., 8, 24, 26, 30, 50, 101, 113, 215, 301, 341, 345.

PERSIAN GULF, p. 267.

PETLAD, 122.

PHALERA (R.), 136, 139.

PHALLUT, 316.

PHILLAUR, 224.

PILIBHIT, D.B., 273, 281.

PIND DADAN KHAN, 242.

PIPARIA, 29.
D.B. Notice should be sent to ensure meals being provided. Country carts available for luggage, **Tongas** available by writing to Mail Contractor. Charge, 16 rs.; seat in mail tonga, 8 rs.

PIPRAWA, 311.

PIR PANJAL, 257.

PIRTHI RAJA (RAI PITHORA), 187, 208, 216, 223, 300.

PISHIN, 272.

PLASSEY, 312.

PODANUR (R.) 411.
Excellent sleeping accommodation at the rly. sta.

POLGAHAWELA (R.), 476, 491.

POLONNARUWA, R. H. poor, 498.
The Government Bungalow on the Bund does duty as the R.H.—poor.

PONDICHERRY, D.B., 421.
Hotels: *Grand Hotel de l'Europe; Hotel de Paris et Londres; Cecil H.*
English Consul: *Lieut.-Col. A. de C. Rennick.*
Steamship Agents: *B.I.S.N. Co.: Messageries Maritimes*, Virieux, Agent.

PONNERI, 336.

POONA (R.), 342, 352.
Hotels: *Connaught H.*, best; *Napier H.; Royal Family H.; Poona H.*
Bank: *Bombay Bank.*
Clubs: *Western India C.*
The *Boat Club* forms an important feature in the amusements of the place. *Gymkhana Club and Library.* A visitor, introduced by a member, can join the Club. On the cricket-ground, attached, are played the principal matches during the monsoon months.
Golf Club, fair links.
Mail Contractor: *Ardeshir Framjee*, Civil Lines.
Motors can be hired of Mehta & Co. and Mody's Cycle and Motor mart. Hire 7 rs per hr., 50 rs. per diem. Outside limits of place, 8 as. per mile. To Mahabaleshwar (in 4 hrs., 3 passengers), 75 rs.
Hackney Carriages:
By time—

Per day . .	6 rs.
Half-day . .	4 rs.
Per hr. . . .	1 r.

Large number of fares by distance.
Newspaper: *Deccan Herald.*

Dentist: *E. H. Hamilton.*

Chemists: *Philips: Treacher; Beynon.*

Photographers: *Stewart; Metzker.*

Drapers: *Badham & Pile; Whiteaway Laidlaw.*

General Merchants: *Ladha Ibrahim*; *Treacher & Co.*

Missions: see p. 343. *R.C. Cathedral; Scotch Church.*

Cowley Wantage Mission, Panch Howds, Poona City.

C.M.S. station (Mission House at Cyprus Lodge), Divinity School.

PORADAHA, 314, 318.

PORBANDAR, D.B., 161.

PORTO NOVO, 422.

PORTUGUESE IN INDIA, civ., cv., 2, 9, 21, 24, 64, 68, 116, 117, 319, 359, 386, 410, 416-19, 443, 454, 471, 497.

POSHIANA, D.B., 257.

PRATABGARH HILL-FORT, 353.

PRINCE CONSORT, 15, 56.

PRINSEP, JAS., lxiii., 33, 59, 61.

PROME, 465.

PUNCH, D.B., 258.

PURANDHAR, 346.

PURI (Jagannath), 328.

D.B., ½ m. from rly. sta.

Hotels: *Seaside H.; Sanitorium H.; Beach H.*

PURULIA, D.B., 87.

PUSHKAR LAKE, D.B., 139.

PUTTALAM, R.H. indifferent, 490.

PYINMANA, 456.

Q

QUEEN EMPRESS VICTORIA, 7, 32, 33, 51, 56, 60, 129, 178, 199, 201, 203, 226, 231, 403, 407, 454.

QUEEN MARY, 13, 236, 375.

QUETTA (R.), D.B., *Lansdowne H.*, 271.

Club: *Quetta C.*

Banks: *Panjab Banking Co.*

Missions: *C.M.S., R.C. Church; Scotch Church.*

Chemists: *Milne; Bliss.*

Outfitters: *Ball. Moody & Co.*

Hackney Carriages:

By time—

	Class I.	II.
Per day . .	6½ rs.	4 rs.
1st hr. . . .	1½ rs.	1 r.
Subs. hr. .	12 as.	8 as.

Special rates by distance.

QUILON, 436.

R

RAE BAREILLY, 275.

RAEWIND (R.), 259.

RAGALLA, 480.

RAICHUR (R.), D.B., 349.

RAIDANI, 258.

RAIGARH, 86.

RAIPUR, D.B., 85.

RAJAHMUNDRY (R.), 334.

RAJAORI, D.B., 257.

RAJKOT, 161.

D.B. near the Jn. Rly. Sta.

RAJMAHAL, 307.

RAJPUR, D.B., 280.

Hotels: *Royal H.; Ellenborough H.* Hurst's Agency for jhampans, ponies, and dandies available. Forwarding Agencies, Lawson, Lindsay & Co.

RAJPURA, 223.

RAKWANE, 485.

RAMAYANA, lviii.

RAMBHA, 333.

RAMBODA, R.H., 481.

RAMBUKKANA, R.H., 476.

RAMESVARAM, 433.

RAMNAD, 433.

RAMNAGAR, 51.

RAMPUR, Simla, 219.

RAMPUR, Kashmir, 252.

RAN OF CUTCH, 148.

RANAGHAT, 314.

RANCHI, 87.

RANDER, 119.

RANGMO RIVER, 317.

RANGOON, 449.

Hotels: *Sarkie's Strand H.; Royal*, 4 Merchant St., 10 rs.; *Minto Mansions H.*; *Grand H.*, Strand Road; *Central H.*, Dalhousie St. None equal to good Indian Hotels. *Criterion H.*, Dalhousie St.

English Boarding Houses: *Mrs Sedgfield*, 3 Ahlone Road, next to Government Lodge, 15 min. drive from the Wharf: *Mrs Smith*, "Allendale," in cantonments 2 m. from Post Office, well spoken of — rooms should be engaged beforehand; *Oriental Boarding Establishment*, Phayre Street; *Aberdeen House.*

Restaurants at the above hotels; also at Chiesa's, Italian Confectioner, Warwick House, Fytche Sq.

Clubs: *Pegu Club*, Prome Road Cantonments.

Burma Club, Merchant Street.

German Club, Commissioners Road.

Gymkhana Club, Halpin Road. A favourite resort in the evenings. Lady members. Tennis courts, billiard tables, reading-room, bar, etc. Military band most evenings.

Boat Club, Royal Lakes.

Agent: *Thos. Cook & Son*, 5 Phayre Street.

Bankers: *Bank of Bengal*, Strand Road; *Chartered Bank of India, Australia, and China*, Strand Road; *Hongkong and Shanghai Banking Corporation*, *National Bank of India*, Phayre St.; *Bank of Burma.*

Booksellers: *Myles Standish & Co.*, 75 Merchant Street.

Chemists: *E. M. de Souza & Co.*, 271 Dalhousie Street; *Rangoon Medical Hall*, 68 Merchant Street.

Consuls: Most countries are represented by Consuls or Vice-Consuls.

Austro-Hungary, M. Sevastopulo.

France, M. Montplanque.

Germany, Herr K. Kauffield.

Italy, Cavaliere Fred. Storck.

U.S.A., M. K. Moorhead.

Conveyances: Cabs (ticca gharries) of a somewhat inferior kind, drawn by single ponies, can be hired at moderate charges, viz., 1st class, per hour, 1½ rs. and 1 r.; 2nd class, 1 hour, 12 as.; each subs. hour 8 as.; not exceeding 2 miles 8 as.; each additional mile. 4 as. The drivers are usually Madrassis, who understand neither English, Burmese, nor Hindustani, and know neither the names of the streets nor the situation of the principal offices or houses.

Craftsmen: The principal Burmese silversmiths, goldsmiths, and wood carvers, are to be found in Godwin Road; specimens of Burmese wood carving can also be obtained at the Central Jail; images of Gaudama in brass and alabaster, and kalagas (applique work) in Kemmendine. Dealers in these and Oriental goods, Hirst, 6 Barr St., Goona Mal Parasram, 71 Merchant St., Khemchand Tejamal, 82 Dalhousie, St.

Dentists: *R. W. Ransford; W. M. Cameron.*

General Stores: *Scott & Co.*, Merchant Street; *Rowe & Co.*, Sule Pagoda Road.

Hairdressers: *Watson & Allen*, 73 Merchant Street.

Medical Men: The Senior and Junior Civil Surgeons at the General Hospital.

Outfitters: *Whiteaway Laidlaw; Rowe.*

Missions: *American Baptist; Scotch Church; R.C. Church.*

Newspapers: The two leading English newspapers are the *Rangoon Gazette* and the *Rangoon Times*, and the leading vernacular newspaper is the *Burma Herald.*

Photographers: *P. Klier*, Merchant Street.

Railways: There are two lines out of Rangoon—

(1) The *Irrawaddy Line* running to Prome, and connecting with Henzadah and Bassein.

(2) The *Sittang Line* running to Pegu (branch to Moulmein), Toungoo and Mandalay, and thence to Myitkyina.

The terminus for both lines is at the junction of Phayre Street and Montgomery Street. The Irrawaddy line has pick-up stations at Godwin Road, Prome Road, and Alon, and a large station at Kemmendine.

Steamship Agencies: *Bibby Line*, 74 Phayre St.; *P. & O.* Thos. Cook & Son, Gillanders, Arbuthnot; *Norddeutsche Lloyd*, Krüger & Co.

British India S.N. Co., Messrs Bulloch Bros., Strand Road.

Irrawaddy Flotilla Co., 4 Phayre Street.

Tramways: A steam tramway, which is being converted into an electric line, runs from the Strand Road to the Great Pagoda along China Street and Pagoda Road, and another along Dalhousie Street from Alon to Pazundaung.

RANIGANJ, 3 **D.Bs.**, 38.
Hotel: *William's H.*

RANIKHET, D.B., 283.

RANIPET, 397.

RANJIT RIVER, 316, 317.

RANJIT SINGH, MAHARAJA, lxvi., 49, 146, 224, 227, 228, 230, 232-4, 238-9, 246, 329.

RANNE, **R.H.** small and poor, 489.

RATANPUR, 86.

RATNAPURA, R.H. good, 484, 486.

RATTAN PIR, 257.

RAWAL PINDI (R.), 244.
Cantonment **D.B.** close to Post Office.

Hotels: *Flashman's H.*, best, opposite the club; *Cantonment H.*, near sta.; *Rawal Pindi H.; Mellor's H.; Mrs Bryant's H.; Mrs Stewart's H.; Imperial H.*

Club: *Rawal Pindi C.*

Banks: *Alliance Bank*; *Commercial Bank of India.*

Missions: *American Presbyterian; Scotch Church; R.C. Church.*

Chemist: *Wilson.*

Drapers: *Whiteaway Laidlaw.*

General Merchants: *Jamasji & Sons.*

Imperial Carrying Co.: *Dhanjibhoy & Sons.*

Saddler: Clarence.

Tailors: *Ranken; Shaw.*

Hackney Carriages:

	Class I.	II.
1st hr.	1 r. 12 as.	
Sub. hr.	8 as.	6 as.

Tonga, 1 hr. 8 as.; subs. hr. 4 as.

READYMONEY, SIR C. J., 6, 8, 15, 18.

RENIGUNTA **(R.)**, 350.
Junction for Tirupati and S.I.R., and for Nellore.
Rooms at rly. sta.

RETI **(R.)**, 262.

REWAH, 30.

REWARI **(R.)**, 145.
R.H. not far from rly. sta.

RINDLI, 270.

RITRAGANTA, 336.

ROE, SIR T., 29, 89, 119, 123, 137.

ROHRI, D.B., 262.

ROHTAS, **D.B.**, 243.

ROORKEE, D.B., 273.

ROSE, SIR HUGH, LORD STRATHNAIRN, ciii., 103, 105, 106.

ROZA, 72.
See Ellora.

RUWANVELI, **R.H.**, 484.

RUBY MINES, BURMA, 462. **Motor Service** from Thabeikkyin in 6 hrs.

RUK **(R.)**, **D.B.**, 269.

RUNGARUN, 316.

RUNGPUR, **D.B.**, 321.

RUPAR, 224.

RUPNARAIN RIVER, 70.

RUTLAM, D.B. (R.), 91, 122.

S

SABARMATI, 130.

SABATHU, 218.

SADHARA, 100.

SADRAS, 439.

SAGAING, 460.

SAHARANPUR (R.), D.B., 222.

SAHIBGANJ **(R.)**, 310-11.

SAHRI, 258.

SAIDABAD, **D.B.**, 256.

SAINT THOMAS MOUNT, 410.

SALEM (R.), 411.

Starting point for Yercaud and Shevaroy Hills. The native town of Salem is 4 m. distant from the rly.

Comfortable sleeping accommodation at rly. sta. 7 m. to foot of Shevaroys (pony carts available, 1 r.). 7 m. further up the Ghaut to Yercaud (chairs, each coolie 6 as., and ponies).

SALT, lxxxvi., 136, 242.
SALUVAN KUPPAN, 436.
SAMAGUTING, 321.
SAMALKOT, 334.
SAMASATA, 262.
SAMASTIPUR, 311.
SAMBAL, 253.
SAMBALPUR, D.B., 86.
SAMBHAR LAKE, 136.
SAMRU, BEGAM, 201, 221.
SAMRU, W. REINHARDT, 35, 178, 221.
SANAWAR, 218.
SANCHI (Gt. Tope), 98.
D.B. good, but provisions should be taken.
SANGAM (Poona), 344.
SANGANER, 143.
SANTAHAR JUNCTION, 314, 321.
SARA GHAT, 314.
SARDHANA, D.B., 221.
SARKHEJ, 129.
SARNATH, 51.
SASSERAM, D.B., 37.
SATARA, 354.
Good Waiting Room at station. D.B. at Satara.
SATGAON, 70.
SATNA (R.), D.B., 30. Tonga dak to Rewah, 31 m., 10 rs.
SATRUNJAYA HILL, 150.
SAUGAR ISLAND, 70.
SAUGOR, D.B., 100.
SECUNDERABAD, 82, 378.
Hotels: *The Parade H.*; *Montgomery H.*
Club: *United Service C.*, *Gymkhana*.
Photographer: *Raja Dindayal*.
SEHWAN, 268.
D.B. It is necessary for the traveller to bring provisions with him.
SENCHAL, 317.
SERAM, 373.
SERAMPORE, 39, 67.
Missions: *Baptist College* and *Schools*; *Zanana*.
SERINGAPATAM, 392.
R.H. at Darya Daulat Bagh may be used by permission of the Darbar.
SEVEN PAGODAS, 436. See *Mahabalipuram*.
The journey is best made from Madras *via* the Buckingham Canal in a house-boat—a comfortable night journey.
SHADIPORE, 253.
SHAHAB-UD-DIN GHORI, l., lii., 210, 216, 223, 300.
SHAHABAD, 349.
SHAH DARA (Delhi), 220.
SHAH DARA (Lahore), 238.
SHAH JAHAN, EMPEROR, li., lxxvi., 39, 68, 96, 137, 139, 166, 171, 175, 177, 179, 189, 195, 199, 201, 204, 237, 265, 273, 322.
SHAHJAHANPUR (R.), 274.
Club: *Sahjahanpur C.*
SHAHPURA, 29.
SHAKAHABAD, 300.
SHALIMAR, 236.
SHALIMAR GARDENS, 203, 236, 254.
SHARANPUR, 26.
SHARKI DYNASTY OF JAUNPUR, 276.
SHEKHUPURA, 239.
SHENCOTTAH, 436.
SHELA BAGH, 272.
SHERSHAH, D.B., 259, 261.
SHER SHAH, EMPEROR, liv., 33, 37, 114, 187, 204, 205, 241, 243, 300.
SHEVAROY HILLS (Yercaud), 411. See *Salem*.
Two small **Hotels**.
Boarding House kept by *Miss Norfor*, *Miss White*, and several others.
SHIKARPUR, Kashmir, D.B., 257.
SHIKARPUR, Sindh, 270.
SHILLONG, D.B., 320.
Hotels: *Ferndale H.*; *Grand H. de l'Europe*. Motor service (6-9 seats), and pony tonga (3 seats) service daily to Gauhati. Motor fares 18 rs. per seat. 20 seers of luggage allowed. Luggage by bullock carts, in 48 hours, 2 rs. per maund. *R.C. Cathedral*.
SHIMOGA, 385.
Shivaji, lxviii., 353-6, 369.
SHOLAPUR, D.B., 347.
SHORANUR (R.), 415.
Junc. of branch line to Cochin.
SHRAVAN BELGOLA, 388.
SHRINAGAR, 161.
SHUKALTIRTH, 119.
SHUPIYAN, D.B., 257.
SHWEGYIN, 456.
SIALKOT, 240.
Good D.B.
SIBI (R.), D., 270.
SIDHPUR, 131.
SIGIRI, R.H., 493.
SIHORE, D.B., 151.
SIKANDARAH, 179.
SIKHS, lxvi., c., 147, 223, 224, 226, 241, 242, 249, 260.
SILCHAR, 320.
SILLIGURI (R.), D.B., 314.
SIMLA, 218.
Hotels: *Cecil H.*, excellent; *Grand* (*Peliti's*) *H.*, good; *Lowrie's H.*, on the Mall, close to the Church, Library, and Club (open throughout the year; it is also an **Agency** for Coolies, and general forwarding purposes). *Longwood H.*; *C. M. H.*; *Elysium*; *Metropole*.
Churches: *Scotch*; *R.C.*
Banks: *Alliance Bank*; *Bank of Upper India*; *Delhi and London Bank*; *Panjab Banking Co.*
Newspapers: *Simla News*.
Chemists: *Plomer*; *Symes*.
Photographers: *Bourne & Shepherds*; *Hots*.
Drapers: *Whiteaway Laidlaw*; *Clarke*; *Cowmeadow*.
Tailors: *Coutts*; *Ranken*; *Phelps*; *Fillingham*; *Harman*.
General Merchants: *Cotton & Morris*.
Clubs: *United Service*, above Combermere Bridge.
SINDHIA, MAHARAJAS OF GWALIOR, lxix., 29, 82, 91, 101, 103, 105, 107, 137, 145, 171, 188, 216, 299, 346.
SINDH VALLEY, 256.
SINHGARH, 346.
SINI, 87.
SIRATHU, 306.
SIRHIND, 223.
SIRI, 207.
SIRSA (R.), 146.
SITABALDI, 84.
SITANG, 456.
SITAPUR, 281.
SITARAMPUR, 38.

SIVASAMUDRAM, D.B., 392.

SIWÁI MADHOPUR, 122.

Slave Dynasty, li., 137, 208.

SOBRAON, 147.

SOLON, 218.
D.B. excellent, and *Khansamah's H.*

SOMNATHPUR, 391.

SOMPALLE, 383.

SONAGIR, 103.

SONAMARG, 256.

SONARI, 100.

SONEPAT, 214.

SONEPORE, 311.

SONGAD, 149.
This is the station for Palitana. Write to Dep. Ass. Pol. Agent at Songad for a conveyance.

SONAGIR, 103.

SOOKNA, 315.

SOPOR, 253.

SRINAGAR (Kashmir), **B.D.**, 253.
Nedou's Hotel, very good. 6 rs. per diem.
Visitors to Srinagar generally live in their houseboats, or in tents pitched in the various lovely groves which surround the city.
The best camping grounds are the Munshi Bagh, the Ram Bagh, and the Nasim Bagh (on the Dal Lake).
The **Native Agent** of the Maharaja for visitors will give any information as to quarters, prices, coolies, etc.
Bank: *Panjab Bank.*
Cockburn's Agency, undertakes the hire of boats, tents, furniture, and all camp requisites, which should be ordered to be ready on arrival. They also advise visitors as to purchases, and give every kind of information.
English Church Service every Sunday in the new English Church in the Munshi Bagh.
Missions: The *C.M.S.* has a station and doctors here, and a fine hospital.
Official Rules for Travellers: Copies are obtainable from the above Agent.
There are fair **Gunsmiths** and **Tacklemakers** in the town. There is a **Library** from which travellers are allowed to take books out.
Residency Surgeon attends visitors during the season.
Photographers: *Mr Millais; Jadu Kishan.*

SRI RANGAM, 429.

STUPAS, PAGODAHS (dagabas) IN BURMA, lxxi., 22, 30, 40, 43, 51-2, 58, 76, 98, 100, 243, 247, 336, 339, 340, 407, 448, 451, 453, 455, 456, 466, 468, 494-6.

SUBURKIM, 316.

SUKKUR (R.), 268.
D.B. ½ m. from the station, the best in Sindh.

SULTANPUR, KULLU, 219.
D.B. bad.

SUNDUKPHO, 316.

SURAMUNGALAM (**R.**), 410. See *Salem.*
Railway station for the town of Salem, and starting point for Yercaud and the Shevaroy Hills.

SURAT, 117.
R. Some sleeping accommodation and Waiting Room at railway station.
D.B. on river bank.
Inlaid Work and Carved Sandal Wood are specialities of Surat.

SUTGATI, 358.

SYLHET VALLEY, 4 **D.Bs.**, 320.

SYRIAM, 454.

T.

TADPATRI, **D.B.** in the town, 350.

TALAI MANNAAR, Ceylon terminus of rly. route to India—steamer to Dhanushkodi, 25 m., 434, 496.

TALAWAKELLE, **R.H.**, 480.
Chemist and Store: *Jordan & Co.* (2½ m.).

TALBAHAT, **D.B.**, 101.

TALIKOT, li., 370.

TAMLUK, 70.

TANDUR, 373.

TANGALLA, 488.
R.H. remarkably good and pleasantly situated close to the sea.

TANGROT, **D.B.**, 257.

TANJORE (R.), 427.
Rooms for five persons at the rly. sta.
D.B., not very comfortable, close to station, to the E. of the Little Fort, where pony and bullock-carts are available.
Mission: *S.P.G. Wesleyan.*

TANSA WATER SUPPLY, 23.

TANTIA TOPI, cii., ciii., 105, 112, 303, 304.

TAPTI BRIDGE, 28.

TARAGARH, 138.

TARN TARAN, D.B., 228.

TAVERNIER, 165, 172, 197.

TAVOY, 468.

TEA, 228, 316, 320, 321.

TEENDARIA (**R.**), 315.

TEESTA, **D.B.**, 317, 321.

TEESTA GHAT, 321.

TEHRI, 113.

TELLICHERRY, 418.
D.B. good. There is also an excellent little **Club.**

TEZPUR, **D.B.**, 321*a*.

THABEIKKYIN, 462.

THAL GHAT, 23, 25.

THANA, **D.B.**, 24.
Diamond Jubilee H.

THANDAUNG, 456.

THANESAR, 216.

THANNA MANDI, **D.B.**, 257.

THARAWADDY, 466.

THATON, 456.

THATTA, 265.
There is only a native R.H. here, but there is a **D.B.** (food must be taken) on the *Makkalli Hills.*

THAYETMYO, 465.

THEOG, 219.

THERIA GHAT, **D.B.**, 320.

TIGYAING, 461.

TIMUR, lii., 203, 207, 260, 279.

TINDIVANAM, 420.
D.B. good.

TINNEVELLY, D.B., 436.
Missions: *S.P.G.* station (at Nazareth); *C.M.S.* College; *Baptist Mission.*

TINSUKIA, 320.

TIN PAHAR, **R.H.**, 307.

TIPU, SULTAN, 57, 69, 382, 383, 389, 391-4, 396, 415, 416, 419.

TIRHUT, 311.

TIRUPATI, 350.

Refreshment and sleeping rooms at Renigunta Junction Station. Write beforehand to station-master for conveyance.

TIRUR, 416.

TISSAMAHARAMA, 489.

TONGLU, 316.

TOSHAM, 145.

TOUNGOO, 456.

TOWERS OF SILENCE, 16, 119.

TRANQUEBAR, 423.

TRAVANCORE, 435.

TRICHENDUR, 435.

TRICHINOPOLY (R.), 411, 429.

Club: *Trichinopoly C.*

Sleeping accommodation at rly. sta. (rather noisy); *Robert's H.* in Cantonments; **D.B.** 1 m. from sta.

Missions: *S.P.G., Wesleyan. Lutheran Evangelist, R.C. Cathedral.*

TRICHUR, 414.

TRIMALGIRI, 379.

TRIMBAK, 28.

TRIMURTI (Triad), 19, 78.

TRINCOMALEE, R.H., 491, 499.

Motor Service from Anuradhapura, 20 rs. per seat.

Steamship Agents: *Ceylon Steamship Co. Ltd.*

TRIVALUR, 351.

TRIVALUR (Tanjore Dt.), **D.B.**, 425.

TRIVANDRUM, 436.

D.B. close to Residency. Boats from Quilon, 2 rs. per diem; each rower 1 a. per mile.

TUGHLAKABAD, 169, 212.

TUMKUR, 389.

TUMLUK, 70, 322.

TUNDLA (**R.**), 300.

TUTICORIN (R.) D.B, 435.

Hotel: *Roberts' H.*, good.

Railway Facilities: First and second class carriages are run to and from the pier in connection with the departure and arrival of the Mail steamers to and from Colombo. Waiting accommodation is provided at the station for ladies and gentlemen, and there is also a Refreshment Room under the management of Messrs Spencer & Co.

Shipping Arrangements: A British India Steam Navigation Company's steamer leaves daily at 5 P.M. for Colombo, and one arrives from Ceylon (daily Mondays excepted) at about 8 A.M., the passage occupying about 16 hours. The journey between the pier and steamer is made in a steam launch belonging to the British India Steamer Agents at Tuticorin, and occupies about three-quarters of an hour.

Bank: *Bank of Madras. National Bank of India.*

Missions, Churches, &c.: The Society for the Propagation of the Gospel maintains a Training School, and a College named after the late Bishop Caldwell.

Club: A Club for Europeans is situated on the sea front.

U.

UDAIPUR, 94.

Hotel, fair, visitors should write beforehand to manager, as the accommodation is rather limited. Tongas can be hired.

Mission: *U.F. Church of Scotland*, medical.

UDVADA, 116.

UDYAGIRI CAVES, R.H., 323.

UJJAIN, D.B., 91, 122.

ULUBARIA, 70.

UMARIA, 30.

UMBALLA (R.), D.B., 217.

Hotels: *Lumley's H.*, near the rly. sta.; *Robson's H.*

Agents: *R. Norton & Co.* undertake the clearing and forwarding of goods between Umballa, Kasauli, Sabathu, etc.

Club: *Sirhind C.*

Bank: *Alliance Bank of Simla.*

Mission: *American Presbyterian.*

Chemists: *Ball, Hobson.*

General Merchant: *Norton.*

Tailor: *Coutts.*

Hackney Carriages:

	Class I.	II.
Per. day .	4 rs.	3 rs.
1st. hr. . .	.	1 r. 12 as.
subs. hr. .	8 as.	6 as.

UNDAVILLI, 335.

UNJALUR, 411.

UNJHA, 131.

UNKARJI, D.B., 88.

URI, **D.B.**, good, 252.

V

VADNAGAR, 131.

VALABHIPUR, 151.

VANKANER, 162.

VASCO DA GAMA, 358.

VEHAR LAKE, 21.

VELLORE, 351, 396.

VERAWAL, 157.

Travellers may find it convenient to get permission from the station-master to retain their first-class rly. carriage at the sta., and to sleep in it at night. There is a good R.H. of the Junagarh State.

VERNAG, 255.

VICTORIA, QUEEN EMPRESS. *See* Queen Empress.

VIGITIPURA, 494.

VIJAYANAGAR (Hampi), 381; 346, 350, 363, 370, 384, 394, 401, 419, 420, 426.

D.B. at Kamalapur. See *Hampi.*

VILLUPURAM (**R**), 351, 421, **D.B.** 1 m. from rly. sta.

VIRAMGAM, 131, 148.

Waiting Room at rly. sta.

Dharmsala near Great Tank, well furnished.

VISNAGAR, 131.

VIZAGAPATAM, D.B., 334.

Missions: *L.M. Soc. R.C. Cathedral.*

VIZIANAGRAM (R.), 334.

W

WADHWAN (R.), 148.
D.B. close to rly. sta.

WADI, 349, 373.
R. and beds.

WAI, 351.
D.B. good.
On side nearest Mahabaleshwar Hill.

WALAH, 151.

WALAJAH ROAD, 398.

WALTAIR (R.), 334.

WANDIWASH, 420.

WANGAT, 256.

WARANGAL, 6, 380.

WARDHA, D.B., 83.
Waiting and Refreshment Rooms at rly. sta.

WARGAON, 341.

WARIYAPOLA, R.H., 491.

WARORA, D.B., 83.

WATHAR (R.), and Waiting Room at rly. sta., 351.
Meals are provided for passengers bound for Mahabaleshwar, if previous notice be given. **Tongas** can be ordered by writing to the Mail Contractor; **Motors** to Mahabaleshwar 3 to 7 persons, 50 rs.; **Mail Motor** per seat 8 rs., in season only.

WATSON, ADMIRAL, 2, 63, 68.

WAZIRABAD (R.), D.B., 240.

WELIGAMA, R.H., 488.

WELIMADA, R.H., 481.

WELLAWAYA, R.H., 486.

WELLESLEY, MARQUIS, xcvi., 8, 56, 57, 403.

WELLESLEY, SIR ARTHUR, DUKE OF WELLINGTON, cvii., 3, 10, 29, 56, 57, 82, 341, 344, 347, 391, 394, 403, 406.

WELLINGTON, 412. See *Mettupalaiyam* and *Coonoor.*

WULAR LAKE, 253.

WYNAAD, 418.

X

XAVIER, ST FRANCIS, 12, 359, 360, 416.

Y

YALA SANCTUARY, R.H., 501.

YAMETHIN, 456.

YANKINTAUNG, 460.

YAPAHU, 492.

YARU KAREZ, 272.

YATIYANTOTA, R.H., 484.

YENA FALLS, 352.

YENANGYAUNG, 465.

YERCAUD (Shevaroy Hills), 410. See *Salem.*
Hotels: *Fair Lawn H.*; *Silver Oaks H.*

Z

ZAFARABAD, 279.

ZIARAT, D.B. open May to Oct. Tonga from Kach, 15 rs., 272.